S0-BWY-768

HANDBOOK
of
PSYCHOLOGY

HANDBOOK
of
PSYCHOLOGY

VOLUME 2
RESEARCH METHODS IN PSYCHOLOGY

John A. Schinka
Wayne F. Velicer

Volume Editors

Irving B. Weiner

Editor-in-Chief

WILEY

John Wiley & Sons, Inc.

This book is printed on acid-free paper. ∞

Copyright © 2003 by John Wiley & Sons, Inc. All rights reserved.

Published by John Wiley & Sons, Inc., Hoboken, New Jersey.
Published simultaneously in Canada.

No part of this publication may be reproduced, stored in a retrieval system or transmitted in any form or by any means, electronic, mechanical, photocopying, recording, scanning or otherwise, except as permitted under Sections 107 or 108 of the 1976 United States Copyright Act, without either the prior written permission of the Publisher, or authorization through payment of the appropriate per-copy fee to the Copyright Clearance Center, 222 Rosewood Drive, Danvers, MA 01923, (978) 750-8400, fax (978) 646-8600, or on the web at www.copyright.com. Requests to the Publisher for permission should be addressed to the Permissions Department, John Wiley & Sons, Inc., 111 River Street, Hoboken, NJ 07030, (201) 748-6011, fax (201) 748-6008.

Limit of Liability/Disclaimer of Warranty: While the publisher and author have used their best efforts in preparing this book, they make no representations or warranties with respect to the accuracy or completeness of the contents of this book and specifically disclaim any implied warranties of merchantability or fitness for a particular purpose. No warranty may be created or extended by sales representatives or written sales materials. The advice and strategies contained herein may not be suitable for your situation. The publisher is not engaged in rendering professional services, and you should consult a professional where appropriate. Neither the publisher nor author shall be liable for any loss of profit or any other commercial damages, including but not limited to special, incidental, consequential, or other damages.

This publication is designed to provide accurate and authoritative information in regard to the subject matter covered. It is sold with the understanding that the publisher is not engaged in rendering professional services. If legal, accounting, medical, psychological or any other expert assistance is required, the services of a competent professional person should be sought.

Designations used by companies to distinguish their products are often claimed as trademarks. In all instances where John Wiley & Sons, Inc. is aware of a claim, the product names appear in initial capital or all capital letters. Readers, however, should contact the appropriate companies for more complete information regarding trademarks and registration.

For general information on our other products and services please contact our Customer Care Department within the United States at (800) 762-2974, outside the United States at (317) 572-3993, or fax (317) 572-4002.

Wiley also publishes its books in a variety of electronic formats. Some content that appears in print may not be available in electronic books. For more information about Wiley products, visit our web site at www.wiley.com.

Library of Congress Cataloging-in-Publication Data:

Handbook of psychology / Irving B. Weiner, editor-in-chief.
     p.   cm.
    Includes bibliographical references and indexes.
    Contents: v. 1. History of psychology / edited by Donald K. Freedheim — v. 2. Research methods in psychology / edited by John A. Schinka, Wayne F. Velicer — v. 3. Biological psychology / edited by Michela Gallagher, Randy J. Nelson — v. 4. Experimental psychology / edited by Alice F. Healy, Robert W. Proctor — v. 5. Personality and social psychology / edited by Theodore Millon, Melvin J. Lerner — v. 6. Developmental psychology / edited by Richard M. Lerner, M. Ann Easterbrooks, Jayanthi Mistry — v. 7. Educational psychology / edited by William M. Reynolds, Gloria E. Miller — v. 8. Clinical psychology / edited by George Stricker, Thomas A. Widiger — v. 9. Health psychology / edited by Arthur M. Nezu, Christine Maguth Nezu, Pamela A. Geller — v. 10. Assessment psychology / edited by John R. Graham, Jack A. Naglieri — v. 11. Forensic psychology / edited by Alan M. Goldstein — v. 12. Industrial and organizational psychology / edited by Walter C. Borman, Daniel R. Ilgen, Richard J. Klimoski.
    ISBN 0-471-38513-1 (cloth : alk. paper : v. 2); ISBN 0-471-66665-3 (pbk.) —
ISBN 0-471-66675-0 (set : pbk.)
    1. Psychology. I. Weiner, Irving B.

BF121.H1955 2003
150—dc21

                                      2002066380

Printed in the United States of America.

10 9 8 7 6 5 4 3 2 1

Editorial Board

Volume 1
History of Psychology

Donald K. Freedheim, PhD
Case Western Reserve University
Cleveland, Ohio

Volume 2
Research Methods in Psychology

John A. Schinka, PhD
University of South Florida
Tampa, Florida

Wayne F. Velicer, PhD
University of Rhode Island
Kingston, Rhode Island

Volume 3
Biological Psychology

Michela Gallagher, PhD
Johns Hopkins University
Baltimore, Maryland

Randy J. Nelson, PhD
Ohio State University
Columbus, Ohio

Volume 4
Experimental Psychology

Alice F. Healy, PhD
University of Colorado
Boulder, Colorado

Robert W. Proctor, PhD
Purdue University
West Lafayette, Indiana

Volume 5
Personality and Social Psychology

Theodore Millon, PhD
Institute for Advanced Studies in
        Personology and Psychopathology
Coral Gables, Florida

Melvin J. Lerner, PhD
Florida Atlantic University
Boca Raton, Florida

Volume 6
Developmental Psychology

Richard M. Lerner, PhD
M. Ann Easterbrooks, PhD
Jayanthi Mistry, PhD

Tufts University
Medford, Massachusetts

Volume 7
Educational Psychology

William M. Reynolds, PhD
Humboldt State University
Arcata, California

Gloria E. Miller, PhD
University of Denver
Denver, Colorado

Volume 8
Clinical Psychology

George Stricker, PhD
Adelphi University
Garden City, New York

Thomas A. Widiger, PhD
University of Kentucky
Lexington, Kentucky

Volume 9
Health Psychology

Arthur M. Nezu, PhD
Christine Maguth Nezu, PhD
Pamela A. Geller, PhD

Drexel University
Philadelphia, Pennsylvania

Volume 10
Assessment Psychology

John R. Graham, PhD
Kent State University
Kent, Ohio

Jack A. Naglieri, PhD
George Mason University
Fairfax, Virginia

Volume 11
Forensic Psychology

Alan M. Goldstein, PhD
John Jay College of Criminal
        Justice–CUNY
New York, New York

Volume 12
**Industrial and Organizational
Psychology**

Walter C. Borman, PhD
University of South Florida
Tampa, Florida

Daniel R. Ilgen, PhD
Michigan State University
East Lansing, Michigan

Richard J. Klimoski, PhD
George Mason University
Fairfax, Virginia

Editorial Board

My efforts in this work are proudly dedicated to Katherine, Christy, and John C. Schinka.

J. A. S.

This work is dedicated to Sue, the perfect companion for life's many journeys and the center of my personal universe.

W. F. V.

Handbook of Psychology **Preface**

Psychology at the beginning of the twenty-first century has become a highly diverse field of scientific study and applied technology. Psychologists commonly regard their discipline as the science of behavior, and the American Psychological Association has formally designated 2000 to 2010 as the "Decade of Behavior." The pursuits of behavioral scientists range from the natural sciences to the social sciences and embrace a wide variety of objects of investigation. Some psychologists have more in common with biologists than with most other psychologists, and some have more in common with sociologists than with most of their psychological colleagues. Some psychologists are interested primarily in the behavior of animals, some in the behavior of people, and others in the behavior of organizations. These and other dimensions of difference among psychological scientists are matched by equal if not greater heterogeneity among psychological practitioners, who currently apply a vast array of methods in many different settings to achieve highly varied purposes.

Psychology has been rich in comprehensive encyclopedias and in handbooks devoted to specific topics in the field. However, there has not previously been any single handbook designed to cover the broad scope of psychological science and practice. The present 12-volume *Handbook of Psychology* was conceived to occupy this place in the literature. Leading national and international scholars and practitioners have collaborated to produce 297 authoritative and detailed chapters covering all fundamental facets of the discipline, and the *Handbook* has been organized to capture the breadth and diversity of psychology and to encompass interests and concerns shared by psychologists in all branches of the field.

Two unifying threads run through the science of behavior. The first is a common history rooted in conceptual and empirical approaches to understanding the nature of behavior. The specific histories of all specialty areas in psychology trace their origins to the formulations of the classical philosophers and the methodology of the early experimentalists, and appreciation for the historical evolution of psychology in all of its variations transcends individual identities as being one kind of psychologist or another. Accordingly, Volume 1 in the *Handbook* is devoted to the history of psychology as it emerged in many areas of scientific study and applied technology.

A second unifying thread in psychology is a commitment to the development and utilization of research methods suitable for collecting and analyzing behavioral data. With attention both to specific procedures and their application in particular settings, Volume 2 addresses research methods in psychology.

Volumes 3 through 7 of the *Handbook* present the substantive content of psychological knowledge in five broad areas of study: biological psychology (Volume 3), experimental psychology (Volume 4), personality and social psychology (Volume 5), developmental psychology (Volume 6), and educational psychology (Volume 7). Volumes 8 through 12 address the application of psychological knowledge in five broad areas of professional practice: clinical psychology (Volume 8), health psychology (Volume 9), assessment psychology (Volume 10), forensic psychology (Volume 11), and industrial and organizational psychology (Volume 12). Each of these volumes reviews what is currently known in these areas of study and application and identifies pertinent sources of information in the literature. Each discusses unresolved issues and unanswered questions and proposes future directions in conceptualization, research, and practice. Each of the volumes also reflects the investment of scientific psychologists in practical applications of their findings and the attention of applied psychologists to the scientific basis of their methods.

The *Handbook of Psychology* was prepared for the purpose of educating and informing readers about the present state of psychological knowledge and about anticipated advances in behavioral science research and practice. With this purpose in mind, the individual *Handbook* volumes address the needs and interests of three groups. First, for graduate students in behavioral science, the volumes provide advanced instruction in the basic concepts and methods that define the fields they cover, together with a review of current knowledge, core literature, and likely future developments. Second, in addition to serving as graduate textbooks, the volumes offer professional psychologists an opportunity to read and contemplate the views of distinguished colleagues concerning the central thrusts of research and leading edges of practice in their respective fields. Third, for psychologists seeking to become conversant with fields outside their own specialty and for persons outside of psychology seeking information about psychological matters, the *Handbook* volumes serve as a reference source for expanding their knowledge and directing them to additional sources in the literature.

The preparation of this *Handbook* was made possible by the diligence and scholarly sophistication of the 25 volume editors and co-editors who constituted the Editorial Board. As Editor-in-Chief, I want to thank each of them for the pleasure of their collaboration in this project. I compliment them for having recruited an outstanding cast of contributors to their volumes and then working closely with these authors to achieve chapters that will stand each in their own right as

valuable contributions to the literature. I would like finally to express my appreciation to the editorial staff of John Wiley and Sons for the opportunity to share in the development of this project and its pursuit to fruition, most particularly to Jennifer Simon, Senior Editor, and her two assistants, Mary Porterfield and Isabel Pratt. Without Jennifer's vision of the *Handbook* and her keen judgment and unflagging support in producing it, the occasion to write this preface would not have arrived.

IRVING B. WEINER
Tampa, Florida

Volume Preface

A scientific discipline is defined in many ways by the research methods it employs. These methods can be said to represent the common language of the discipline's researchers. Consistent with the evolution of a lexicon, new research methods frequently arise from the development of new content areas. By every available measure—number of researchers, number of publications, number of journals, number of new subdisciplines—psychology has undergone a tremendous growth over the last half-century. This growth is reflected in a parallel increase in the number of new research methods available.

As we were planning and editing this volume, we discussed on many occasions the extent to which psychology and the available research methods have become increasing complex over the course of our careers. When our generation of researchers began their careers in the late 1960s and early 1970s, experimental design was largely limited to simple between-group designs, and data analysis was dominated by a single method, the analysis of variance. A few other approaches were employed, but by a limited number of researchers. Multivariate statistics had been developed, but multiple regression analysis was the only method that was applied with any frequency. Factor analysis was used almost exclusively as a method in scale development. Classical test theory was the basis of most psychological and educational measures. Analysis of data from studies that did not meet either the design or measurement assumptions required for an analysis of variance was covered for most researchers by a single book on nonparametric statistics by Siegel (1956). As a review of the contents of this volume illustrates, the choice of experimental and analytic methods available to the present-day researcher is much broader. It would be fair to say that the researcher in the 1960s had to formulate research questions to fit the available methods. Currently, there are research methods available to address most research questions.

In the history of science, an explosion of knowledge is usually the result of an advance in technology, new theoretical models, or unexpected empirical findings. Advances in research methods have occurred as the result of all three factors, typically in an interactive manner. Some of the specific factors include advances in instrumentation and measurement technology, the availability of inexpensive desktop computers to perform complex methods of data analysis, increased computer capacity allowing for more intense analysis of larger datasets, computer simulations that permit the evaluation of procedures across a wide variety of situations, new approaches to data analysis and statistical control, and advances in companion sciences that opened pathways to the exploration of behavior and created new areas of research specialization and collaboration.

Consider the advances since the publication of the first edition of Kirk's (1968) text on experimental design. At that time most studies were relatively small N experiments that were conducted in psychology laboratories. Research activity has subsequently exploded in applied and clinical areas, with a proliferation of new journals largely dedicated to quasi-experimental studies and studies in the natural environment (e.g., in neuropsychology and health psychology). Techniques such as polymerase chain reaction allow psychologists to test specific genes as risk candidates for behavioral disorders. These studies rely on statistical procedures that are still largely ignored by many researchers (e.g., logistic regression, structural equation modeling). Brain imaging procedures such as magnetic resonance imaging, magnetoencephalography, and positron-emission tomography provide cognitive psychologists and neuropsychologists the opportunity to study cortical activity on-line. Clinical trials involving behavioral interventions applied to large, representative samples are commonplace in health psychology. Research employing each of these procedures requires not only highly specific and rigorous research methods, but also special methods for handling and analyzing extremely large volumes of data. Even in more traditional areas of research that continue to rely on group experimental designs, issues of measuring practical significance, determination of sample size and power, and procedures for handling nuisance variables are now important concerns. Not surprisingly, the third edition of Kirk's (1995) text has grown in page length by 60%.

Our review of these trends leads to several conclusions, which are reflected in the selection of topics covered by the chapters in this volume. Six features appear to characterize the evolution in research methodology in psychology.

First, there has been a focus on the development of procedures that employ statistical control rather than experimental control. Because most of the recent growth involves research in areas that preclude direct control of independent variables, multivariate statistics and the development of methods such as path analysis and structural equation modeling have been critical developments. The use of statistical control has allowed psychology to move from the carefully controlled confines of the laboratory to the natural environment.

Second, there has been an increasing focus on construct-driven, or latent-variable, research. A construct is defined by multiple observed variables. Constructs can be viewed as more reliable and more generalizable than a single observed variable. Constructs serve to organize a large set of observed variables, resulting in parsimony. Constructs are also theoretically based. This theory-based approach serves to guide study design, the choice of variables, the data analysis, and the data interpretation.

Third, there has been an increasing emphasis on the development of new measures and new measurement models. This is not a new trend but an acceleration of an old trend. The behavioral sciences have always placed the most emphasis on the issue of measurement. With the movement of the field out of the laboratory combined with advances in technology, the repertoire of measures, the quality of the measures, and the sophistication of the measurement models have all increased dramatically.

Fourth, there is increasing recognition of the importance of the temporal dimension in understanding a broad range of psychological phenomena. We have become a more intervention-oriented science, recognizing not only the complexity of treatment effects but also the importance of the change in patterns of the effects over time. The effects of an intervention may be very different at different points in time. New statistical models for modeling temporal data have resulted.

Fifth, new methods of analysis have been developed that no longer require the assumption of a continuous, equal-interval, normally distributed variable. Previously, researchers had the choice between very simple but limited methods of data analysis that corresponded to the properties of the measure or more complex sophisticated methods of analysis that assumed, often inappropriately, that the measure met very rigid assumptions. New methods have been developed for categorical, ordinal, or simply nonnormal variables that can perform an equally sophisticated analysis.

Sixth, the importance of individual differences is increasingly emphasized in intervention studies. Psychology has always been interested in individual differences, but methods of data analysis have focused almost entirely on the relationships between variables. Individuals were studied as members of groups, and individual differences served only to inflate the error variance. New techniques permit researchers

to focus on the individual and model individual differences. This becomes increasingly important as we recognize that interventions do not affect everyone in exactly the same ways and that interventions become more and more tailored to the individual.

The text is organized into four parts. The first part, titled "Foundations of Research," addresses issues that are fundamental to all behavioral science research. The focus is on study design, data management, data reduction, and data synthesis. The first chapter, "Experimental Design" by Roger E. Kirk, provides an overview of the basic considerations that go into the design of a study. Once, a chapter on this topic would have had to devote a great deal of attention to computational procedures. The availability of computers permits a shift in focus to the conceptual rather than the computational issues. The second chapter, "Exploratory Data Analysis" by John T. Behrens and Chong-ho Yu, reminds us of the fundamental importance of looking at data in the most basic ways as a first step in any data analysis. In some ways this represents a "back to the future" chapter. Advances in computer-based graphical methods have brought a great deal of sophistication to this very basic first step.

The third chapter, "Power: Basics, Practical Problems, and Possible Solutions" by Rand R. Wilcox, reflects the critical change in focus for psychological research. Originally, the central focus of a test of significance was on controlling Type I error rates. The late Jacob Cohen emphasized that researchers should be equally concerned by Type II errors. This resulted in an emphasis on the careful planning of a study and a concern with effect size and selecting the appropriate sample size. Wilcox updates and extends these concepts. Chapter 4, "Methods for Handling Missing Data" by John W. Graham, Patricio E. Cumsille, and Elvira Elek-Fisk, describes the impressive statistical advances in addressing the common practical problem of missing observations. Previously, researchers had relied on a series of ad hoc procedures, often resulting in very inaccurate estimates. The new statistical procedures allow the researcher to articulate the assumptions about the reason the data is missing and make very sophisticated estimates of the missing value based on all the available information. This topic has taken on even more importance with the increasing emphasis on longitudinal studies and the inevitable problem of attrition.

The fifth chapter, "Preparatory Data Analysis" by Linda S. Fidell and Barbara G. Tabachnick, describes methods of pre-processing data before the application of other methods of statistical analysis. Extreme values can distort the results of the data analysis if not addressed. Diagnostic methods can preprocess the data so that complex procedures are not unduly affected by a limited number of cases that often are the result of some type of error. The last two chapters in this part, "Factor Analysis" by Richard L. Gorsuch and "Clustering and Classification Methods" by Glenn W. Milligan and Stephen C. Hirtle, describe two widely employed parsimony methods. Factor analysis operates in the variable domain and attempts to reduce a set of p observed variables to a smaller set of m factors. These factors, or latent variables, are more easily interpreted and thus facilitate interpretation. Cluster analysis operates in the person domain and attempts to reduce a set of N individuals to a set of k clusters. Cluster analysis serves to explore the relationships among individuals and organize the set of individuals into a limited number of subtypes that share essential features. These methods are basic to the development of construct-driven methods and the focus on individual differences.

The second part, "Research Methods in Specific Content Areas," addresses research methods and issues as they apply to specific content areas. Content areas were chosen in part to parallel the other volumes of the Handbook. More important, however, we attempted to sample content areas from a broad spectrum of specialization with the hope that these chapters would provide insights into methodological concerns and solutions that would generalize to other areas. Chapter 8, "Clinical Forensic Psychology" by Kevin S. Douglas, Randy K. Otto, and Randy Borum, addresses research methods and issues that occur in assessment and treatment contexts. For each task that is unique to clinical forensic psychology research, they provide examples of the clinical challenges confronting the psychologist, identify problems faced when researching the issues or constructs, and describe not only research strategies that have been employed but also their strengths and limitations. In Chapter 9, "Psychotherapy Outcome Research," Evelyn S. Behar and Thomas D. Borkovec address the methodological issues that need to be considered for investigators to draw the strongest and most specific cause-and-effect conclusions about the active components of treatments, human behavior, and the effectiveness of therapeutic interventions.

The field of health psychology is largely defined by three topics: the role of behavior (e.g., smoking) in the development and prevention of disease, the role of stress and emotion as psychobiological influences on disease, and psychological aspects of acute and chronic illness and medical care. Insight into the methodological issues and solutions for research in each of these topical areas is provided by Timothy W. Smith in Chapter 10, "Health Psychology."

At one time, most behavioral experimentation was conducted by individuals whose training focused heavily on animal research. Now many neuroscientists, trained in various fields, conduct research in animal learning and publish findings that are of interest to psychologists in many fields. The major goal of Chapter 11, "Animal Learning" by Russell M. Church, is to transfer what is fairly common knowledge in experimental animal psychology to investigators with limited exposure to this area of research. In Chapter 12, "Neuropsychology," Russell M. Bauer, Elizabeth C. Leritz, and Dawn Bowers provide a discussion of neuropsychological inference, an overview of major approaches to neuropsychological research, and a review of newer techniques, including functional neuroimaging, electrophysiology, magnetoencephalography, and reversible lesion methods. In each section, they describe the conceptual basis of the technique, outline its strengths and weaknesses, and cite examples of how it has been used in addressing conceptual problems in neuropsychology.

Whatever their specialty area, when psychologists evaluate a program or policy, the question of impact is often at center stage. The last chapter in this part, "Program Evaluation" by Melvin M. Mark, focuses on key methods for estimating the effects of policies and programs in the context of evaluation. Additionally, Mark addresses several noncausal forms of program evaluation research that are infrequently addressed in methodological treatises.

The third part is titled "Measurement Issues." Advances in measurement typically combine innovation in technology and progress in theory. As our measures become more sophisticated, the areas of application also increase.

Mood emerged as a seminal concept within psychology during the 1980s, and its prominence has continued unabated ever since. In Chapter 14, "Mood Measurement: Current Status and Future Directions," David Watson and Jatin Vaidya examine current research regarding the underlying structure of mood, describe and evaluate many of the most important mood measures, and discuss several issues related to the reliability and construct validity of mood measurement. In Chapter 15, "Measuring Personality and Psychopathology," Leslie C. Morey uses objective self-report methods of measurement to illustrate contemporary procedures for scale development and validation, addressing issues critical to all measurement methods such as theoretical articulation, situational context, and the need for discriminant validity.

The appeal of circular models lies in the combination of a circle's aesthetic (organizational) simplicity and its powerful potential to describe data in uniquely compelling substantive and geometric ways, as has been demonstrated in describing interpersonal behavior and occupational interests. In Chapter 16, "The Circumplex Model: Methods and Research Applications," Michael B. Gurtman and Aaron L. Pincus discuss the application of the circumplex model to the descriptions of individuals, comparisons of groups, and evaluations of constructs and their measures.

Chapter 17, "Item Response Theory and Measuring Abilities" by Karen M. Schmidt and Susan E. Embretson, describes the types of formal models that have been designed to guide measure development. For many years, most tests of ability and achievement have relied on classical test theory as a framework to guide both measure development and measure evaluation. Item response theory updates this model in many important ways, permitting the development of a new generation of measures of abilities and achievement that are particularly appropriate for a more interactive model of assessment. The last chapter of this part, "Growth Curve Analysis in Contemporary Psychological Research" by John J. McArdle and John R. Nesselroade, describes new quantitative methods for the study of change in development psychology. The methods permit the researcher to model a wide variety of different patterns of developmental change over time.

The final part, "Data Analysis Methods," addresses statistical procedures that have been developed recently and are still not widely employed by many researchers. They are typically dependent on the availability of high-speed computers and permit researchers to investigate novel and complex research questions. Chapter 19, "Multiple Linear Regression" by Leona Aiken, Stephen G. West, and Steven C. Pitts, describes the advances in multiple linear regression that permit applications of this very basic method to the analysis of complex data sets and the incorporation of conceptual models to guide the analysis. The testing of theoretical predictions and the identification of implementation problems are the two major foci of this chapter. Chapter 20, "Logistic Regression" by Alfred DeMaris, describes a parallel method to multiple regression analysis for categorical variables. The procedure has been developed primarily outside of psychology and is now being used much more frequently to address psychological questions. Chapter 21, "Meta-Analysis" by Frank L. Schmidt and John E. Hunter, describes procedures that have been developed for the quantitative integration of research findings across multiple studies. Previously, research findings were integrated in narrative form and were subject to the biases of the reviewer. The method also focuses attention on the importance of effect size estimation.

Chapter 22, "Survival Analysis" by Judith D. Singer and John B. Willett, describes a recently developed method for analyzing longitudinal data. One approach is to code whether an event has occurred at a given occasion. By switching the focus on the time to the occurrence of the event, a much more powerful and sophisticated analysis can be performed. Again, the development of this procedure has occurred largely outside psychology but is being employed much more frequently. In Chapter 23, "Time Series Analysis," Wayne

Velicer and Joseph L. Fava describe a method for studying the change in a single individual over time. Instead of a single observation on many subjects, this method relies on many observations on a single subject. In many ways, this method is the prime exemplar of longitudinal research methods.

Chapter 24, "Structural Equation Modeling" by Jodie B. Ullman and Peter M. Bentler, describes a very general method that combines three key themes: constructs or latent variables, statistical control, and theory to guide data analysis. First employed as an analytic method little more than 20 years ago, the method is now widely disseminated in the behavioral sciences. Chapter 25, "Ordinal Analysis of Behavioral Data" by Jeffrey D. Long, Du Feng, and Norman Cliff, discusses the assumptions that underlie many of the widely used statistical methods and describes a parallel series of methods of analysis that only assume that the measure provides ordinal information. The last chapter, "Latent Class and Latent Transition Analysis" by Stephanie L. Lanza, Brian P. Flaherty, and Linda M. Collins, describes a new method for analyzing change over time. It is particularly appropriate when the change process can be conceptualized as a series of discrete states.

In completing this project, we realized that we were very fortunate in several ways. Irving Weiner's performance as editor-in-chief was simply wonderful. He applied just the right mix of obsessive concern and responsive support to keep things on schedule. His comments on issues of emphasis, perspective, and quality were insightful and inevitably on target.

We continue to be impressed with the professionalism of the authors that we were able to recruit into this effort. Consistent with their reputations, these individuals delivered chapters of exceptional quality, making our burden pale in comparison to other editorial experiences. Because of the length of the project, we shared many contributors' experiences-marriages, births, illnesses, family crises. A definite plus for us has been the formation of new friendships and professional liaisons.

Our editorial tasks were also aided greatly by the generous assistance of our reviewers, most of whom will be quickly recognized by our readers for their own expertise in research methodology. We are pleased to thank James Algina, Phipps Arabie, Patti Barrows, Betsy Jane Becker, Lisa M. Brown, Barbara M. Byrne, William F. Chaplin, Pat Cohen, Patrick J. Curren, Glenn Curtiss, Richard B. Darlington, Susan Duncan, Brian Everitt, Kerry Evers, Ron Gironda, Lisa Harlow, Michael R. Harwell, Don Hedeker, David Charles Howell, Lawrence J. Hubert, Bradley E. Huitema, Beth Jenkins, Herbert W. Marsh, Rosemarie A. Martin, Scott E. Maxwell, Kevin R. Murphy, Gregory Norman, Daniel J. Ozer, Melanie Page, Mark D. Reckase, Charles S. Reichardt,

Steven Reise, Joseph L. Rogers, Joseph Rossi, James Rounds, Shlomo S. Sawilowsky, Ian Spence, James H. Steiger, Xiaowu Sun, Randall C. Swaim, David Thissen, Bruce Thompson, Terence J. G. Tracey, Rod Vanderploeg, Paul F. Velleman, Howard Wainer, Douglas Williams, and several anonymous reviewers for their thorough work and good counsel.

We finish this preface with a caveat. Readers will inevitably discover several contradictions or disagreements across the chapter offerings. Inevitably, researchers in different areas solve similar methodological problems in different ways. These differences are reflected in the offerings of this text, and we have not attempted to mediate these differing viewpoints. Rather, we believe that the serious researcher will welcome the opportunity to review solutions suggested or supported by differing approaches. For flaws in the text, however, the usual rule applies: We assume all responsibility.

JOHN A. SCHINKA
WAYNE F. VELICER

REFERENCES

Kirk, Roger E. (1968). *Experimental design: Procedures for the behavioral sciences.* Pacific Grove, CA: Brooks/Cole.

Kirk, Roger E. (1995). *Experimental design: Procedures for the behavioral sciences* (3rd ed.). Pacific Grove, CA: Brooks/Cole.

Siegel, S. (1956). *Nonparametric statistics for the behavioral sciences.* New York: McGraw-Hill.

Contents

PART ONE
FOUNDATIONS OF RESEARCH ISSUES: STUDY DESIGN, DATA MANAGEMENT, DATA REDUCTION, AND DATA SYNTHESIS

PART TWO
RESEARCH METHODS IN SPECIFIC CONTENT AREAS

PART THREE
MEASUREMENT ISSUES

PART FOUR
DATA ANALYSIS METHODS

Contributors

Leona S. Aiken, PhD
Department of Psychology
Arizona State University
Tempe, Arizona

Russell M. Bauer, PhD
Department of Clinical and Health Psychology
University of Florida
Gainesville, Florida

Evelyn S. Behar, MS
Department of Psychology
Pennsylvania State University
University Park, Pennsylvania

John T. Behrens, PhD
Cisco Networking Academy Program
Cisco Systems, Inc.
Phoenix, Arizona

Peter M. Bentler, PhD
Department of Psychology
University of California
Los Angeles, California

Thomas D. Borkovec, PhD
Department of Psychology
Pennsylvania State University
University Park, Pennsylvania

Randy Borum, PsyD
Department of Mental Health Law & Policy
Florida Mental Health Institute
University of South Florida
Tampa, Florida

Dawn Bowers, PhD
Department of Clinical and Health Psychology
University of Florida
Gainesville, Florida

Russell M. Church, PhD
Department of Psychology
Brown University
Providence, Rhode Island

Norman Cliff, PhD
Professor of Psychology Emeritus
University of Southern California
Los Angeles, California

Linda M. Collins, PhD
The Methodology Center
Pennsylvania State University
University Park, Pennsylvania

Patricio E. Cumsille, PhD
Escuela de Psicologia
Universidad Católica de Chile
Santiago, Chile

Alfred DeMaris, PhD
Department of Sociology
Bowling Green State University
Bowling Green, Ohio

Kevin S. Douglas, PhD, LLB
Department of Mental Health Law & Policy
Florida Mental Health Institute
University of South Florida
Tampa, Florida

Du Feng, PhD
Human Development and Family Studies
Texas Tech University
Lubbock, Texas

Elvira Elek-Fisk, PhD
The Methodology Center
Pennsylvania State University
University Park, Pennsylvania

Susan E. Embretson, PhD
Department of Psychology
University of Kansas
Lawrence, Kansas

Joseph L. Fava, PhD
Cancer Prevention Research Center
University of Rhode Island
Kingston, Rhode Island

Linda S. Fidell, PhD
Department of Psychology
California State University
Northridge, California

Brian P. Flaherty, MS
The Methodology Center
Pennsylvania State University
University Park, Pennsylvania

Richard L. Gorsuch, PhD
Graduate School of Psychology
Fuller Theological Seminary
Pasadena, California

John W. Graham, PhD
Department of Biobehavioral Health
Pennsylvania State University
University Park, Pennsylvania

Michael B. Gurtman, PhD
Department of Psychology
University of Wisconsin-Parkside
Kenosha, Wisconsin

Stephen C. Hirtle, PhD
School of Information Sciences
University of Pittsburgh
Pittsburgh, Pennsylvania

John E. Hunter, PhD
Department of Psychology
Michigan State University
East Lansing, Michigan

Roger E. Kirk, PhD
Department of Psychology and Neuroscience
Baylor University
Waco, Texas

Stephanie T. Lanza, MS
The Methodology Center
Pennsylvania State University
University Park, Pennsylvania

Elizabeth C. Leritz, MS
Department of Clinical and Health Psychology
University of Florida
Gainesville, Florida

Jeffrey D. Long, PhD
Department of Educational Psychology
University of Minnesota
Minneapolis, Minnesota

Melvin M. Mark, PhD
Department of Psychology
Pennsylvania State University
University Park, Pennsylvania

John J. McArdle, PhD
Department of Psychology
University of Virginia
Charlottesville, Virginia

Glenn W. Milligan, PhD
Department of Management Sciences
Ohio State University
Columbus, Ohio

Leslie C. Morey, PhD
Department of Psychology
Texas A&M University
College Station, Texas

John R. Nesselroade, PhD
Department of Psychology
University of Virginia
Charlottesville, Virginia

Randy K. Otto, PhD
Department of Mental Health Law & Policy
Florida Mental Health Institute
University of South Florida
Tampa, Florida

Aaron L. Pincus, PhD
Department of Psychology
Pennsylvania State University
University Park, Pennsylvania

Steven C. Pitts, PhD
Department of Psychology
University of Maryland, Baltimore County
Baltimore, Maryland

Karen M. Schmidt, PhD
Department of Psychology
University of Virginia
Charlottesville, Virginia

Frank L. Schmidt, PhD
Department of Management and Organization
University of Iowa
Iowa City, Iowa

Judith D. Singer, PhD
Graduate School of Education
Harvard University
Cambridge, Massachusetts

Timothy W. Smith, PhD
Department of Psychology
University of Utah
Salt Lake City, Utah

Barbara G. Tabachnick, PhD
Department of Psychology
California State University
Northridge, California

Jodie B. Ullman, PhD
Department of Psychology
California State University
San Bernadino, California

Jatin Vaidya
Department of Psychology
University of Iowa
Iowa City, Iowa

Wayne F. Velicer, PhD
Cancer Prevention Research Center
University of Rhode Island
Kingston, Rhode Island

David Watson, PhD
Department of Psychology
University of Iowa
Iowa City, Iowa

Stephen G. West, PhD
Department of Psychology
Arizona State University
Tempe, Arizona

Rand R. Wilcox, PhD
Department of Psychology
University of Southern California
Los Angeles, California

John B. Willett, PhD
Graduate School of Education
Harvard University
Cambridge, Massachusetts

Chong-ho Yu, PhD
Cisco Networking Academy Program
Cisco Systems, Inc.
Chandler, Arizona

FOUNDATIONS OF RESEARCH ISSUES: STUDY DESIGN, DATA MANAGEMENT, DATA REDUCTION, AND DATA SYNTHESIS

CHAPTER 1

Experimental Design

ROGER E. KIRK

SOME BASIC EXPERIMENTAL DESIGN CONCEPTS

Experimental design is concerned with the skillful interrogation of nature. Unfortunately, nature is reluctant to reveal her secrets. Joan Fisher Box (1978) observed in her autobiography of her father, Ronald A. Fisher, "Far from behaving consistently, however, Nature appears vacillating, coy, and ambiguous in her answers" (p. 140). Her most effective tool for confusing researchers is variability—in particular, variability among participants or experimental units. But two can play the variability game. By comparing the variability among participants treated differently to the variability among participants treated alike, researchers can make informed choices between competing hypotheses in science and technology.

We must never underestimate nature—she is a formidable foe. Carefully designed and executed experiments are required to learn her secrets. An *experimental design* is a plan for assigning participants to experimental conditions and the statistical analysis associated with the plan (Kirk, 1995, p. 1). The design of an experiment involves a number of interrelated activities:

1. Formulation of statistical hypotheses that are germane to the scientific hypothesis. A statistical hypothesis is a statement about (a) one or more parameters of a population or (b) the functional form of a population. Statistical hypotheses are rarely identical to scientific hypotheses—they are testable formulations of scientific hypotheses.

2. Determination of the experimental conditions (independent variable) to be manipulated, the measurement (dependent variable) to be recorded, and the extraneous conditions (nuisance variables) that must be controlled.

3. Specification of the number of participants required and the population from which they will be sampled.

4. Specification of the procedure for assigning the participants to the experimental conditions.

5. Determination of the statistical analysis that will be performed.

In short, an experimental design identifies the independent, dependent, and nuisance variables and indicates the way in which the randomization and statistical aspects of an experiment are to be carried out.

Analysis of Variance

Analysis of variance (ANOVA) is a useful tool for understanding the variability in designed experiments. The seminal ideas for both ANOVA and experimental design can be traced

3

to Ronald A. Fisher, a statistician who worked at the Rothamsted Experimental Station. According to Box (1978, p. 100), Fisher developed the basic ideas of ANOVA between 1919 and 1925. The first hint of what was to come appeared in a 1918 paper in which Fisher partitioned the total variance of a human attribute into portions attributed to heredity, environment, and other factors. The analysis of variance table for a two-treatment factorial design appeared in a 1923 paper published with M. A. Mackenzie (Fisher & Mackenzie, 1923). Fisher referred to the table as a convenient way of arranging the arithmetic. In 1924 Fisher (1925) introduced the Latin square design in connection with a forest nursery experiment. The publication in 1925 of his classic textbook *Statistical Methods for Research Workers* and a short paper the following year (Fisher, 1926) presented all the essential ideas of analysis of variance. The textbook (Fisher, 1925, pp. 244–249) included a table of the critical values of the ANOVA test statistic in terms of a function called z, where $z = \frac{1}{2}(\ln \hat{\sigma}^2_{\text{Treatment}} - \ln \hat{\sigma}^2_{\text{Error}})$. The statistics $\hat{\sigma}^2_{\text{Treatment}}$ and $\hat{\sigma}^2_{\text{Error}}$ denote, respectively, treatment and error variance. A more convenient form of Fisher's z table that did not require looking up log values was developed by George Snedecor (1934). His critical values are expressed in terms of the function $F = \hat{\sigma}^2_{\text{Treatment}}/\hat{\sigma}^2_{\text{Error}}$ that is obtained directly from the ANOVA calculations. He named it F in honor of Fisher. Fisher's field of experimentation—agriculture— was a fortunate choice because results had immediate application with assessable economic value, because simplifying assumptions such as normality and independence of errors were usually tenable, and because the cost of conducting experiments was modest.

Three Principles of Good Experimental Design

The publication of Fisher's *Statistical Methods for Research Workers* and his 1935 *The Design of Experiments* gradually led to the acceptance of what today is considered to be the cornerstone of good experimental design: randomization. It is hard to imagine the hostility that greeted the suggestion that participants or experimental units should be randomly assigned to treatment levels. Before Fisher's work, most researchers used systematic schemes, not subject to the laws of chance, to assign participants. According to Fisher, random assignment has several purposes. It helps to distribute the idiosyncratic characteristics of participants over the treatment levels so that they do not selectively bias the outcome of the experiment. Also, random assignment permits the computation of an unbiased estimate of error effects—those effects not attributable to the manipulation of the independent variable—and it helps to ensure that the error effects are statistically independent.

Fisher popularized two other principles of good experimentation: replication and local control or blocking. *Replication* is the observation of two or more participants under identical experimental conditions. Fisher observed that replication enables a researcher to estimate error effects and obtain a more precise estimate of treatment effects. *Blocking*, on the other hand, is an experimental procedure for isolating variation attributable to a nuisance variable. As the name suggests, *nuisance variables* are undesired sources of variation that can affect the dependent variable. There are many sources of nuisance variation. Differences among participants comprise one source. Other sources include variation in the presentation of instructions to participants, changes in environmental conditions, and the effects of fatigue and learning when participants are observed several times. Three experimental approaches are used to deal with nuisance variables:

1. Holding the variable constant.
2. Assigning participants randomly to the treatment levels so that known and unsuspected sources of variation among the participants are distributed over the entire experiment and do not affect just one or a limited number of treatment levels.
3. Including the nuisance variable as one of the factors in the experiment.

The last experimental approach uses local control or blocking to isolate variation attributable to the nuisance variable so that it does not appear in estimates of treatment and error effects. A statistical approach also can be used to deal with nuisance variables. The approach is called analysis of covariance and is described in the last section of this chapter. The three principles that Fisher vigorously championed— randomization, replication, and local control—remain the cornerstones of good experimental design.

THREE BUILDING BLOCK DESIGNS

Completely Randomized Design

One of the simplest experimental designs is the randomization and analysis plan that is used with a t statistic for independent samples. Consider an experiment to compare the effectiveness of two diets for obese teenagers. The independent variable is the two kinds of diets; the dependent variable is the amount of weight loss two months after going on a diet. For notational convenience, the two diets are called treatment A. The levels of treatment A corresponding to the specific diets are denoted by the lowercase letter a and a subscript: a_1 denotes one diet and a_2 denotes the other. A particular but unspecified level of treatment A is denoted by a_j, where j ranges over the values 1 and 2. The amount of weight loss in pounds 2 months after participant i went on diet j is denoted by Y_{ij}.

The null and alternative hypotheses for the weight-loss experiment are, respectively,

$$H_0: \mu_1 - \mu_2 = 0$$
$$H_1: \mu_1 - \mu_2 \neq 0,$$

where μ_1 and μ_2 denote the mean weight loss of the respective populations. Assume that 30 girls who want to lose weight are available to participate in the experiment. The researcher assigns $n = 15$ girls to each of the $p = 2$ diets so that each of the $(np)!/(n!)^p = 155{,}117{,}520$ possible assignments has the same probability. This is accomplished by numbering the girls from 1 to 30 and drawing numbers from a random numbers table. The first 15 numbers drawn between 1 and 30 are assigned to treatment level a_1; the remaining 15 numbers are assigned to a_2. The layout for this experiment is shown in Figure 1.1. The girls who were assigned to treatment level a_1 are called Group$_1$; those assigned to treatment level a_2 are called Group$_2$. The mean weight losses of the two groups of girls are denoted by $\overline{Y}_{.1}$ and $\overline{Y}_{.2}$.

The t independent-samples design involves randomly assigning participants to two levels of a treatment. A completely randomized design, which is described next, extends this design strategy to two or more treatment levels. The *completely randomized design* is denoted by the letters CR-p, where CR stands for "completely randomized" and p is the number of levels of the treatment.

Again, consider the weight-loss experiment and suppose that the researcher wants to evaluate the effectiveness of

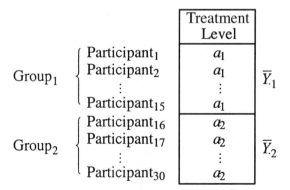

Figure 1.1 Layout for a t independent-samples design. Thirty girls are randomly assigned to two levels of treatment A with the restriction that 15 girls are assigned to each level. The mean weight loss in pounds for the girls in treatment levels a_1 and a_2 is denoted by $\overline{Y}_{.1}$ and $\overline{Y}_{.2}$, respectively.

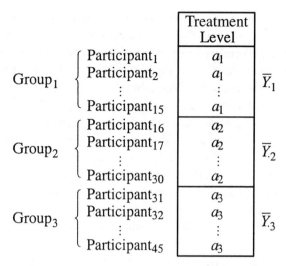

Figure 1.2 Layout for a completely randomized design (CR-3 design). Forty-five girls are randomly assigned to three levels of treatment A with the restriction that 15 girls are assigned to each level. The mean weight loss in pounds for the girls in treatment levels a_1, a_2, and a_3 is denoted by $\overline{Y}_{.1}$, $\overline{Y}_{.2}$, and $\overline{Y}_{.3}$, respectively.

three diets. The null and alternative hypotheses for the experiment are, respectively,

$$H_0: \mu_1 = \mu_2 = \mu_3$$
$$H_1: \mu_j \neq \mu_{j'} \quad \text{for some } j \text{ and } j'.$$

Assume that 45 girls who want to lose weight are available to participate in the experiment. The girls are randomly assigned to the three diets with the restriction that 15 girls are assigned to each diet. The layout for the experiment is shown in Figure 1.2. A comparison of the layout in this figure with that in Figure 1.1 for a t independent-samples design reveals that they are the same except that the completely randomized design has three treatment levels. The t independent-samples design can be thought of as a special case of a completely randomized design. When p is equal to two, the layouts and randomization plans for the designs are identical.

Thus far I have identified the null hypothesis that the researcher wants to test, $\mu_1 = \mu_2 = \mu_3$, and described the manner in which the participants are assigned to the three treatment levels. In the following paragraphs I discuss the composite nature of an observation, describe the classical model equation for a CR-p design, and examine the meaning of the terms *treatment effect* and *error effect*.

An observation, which is a measure of the dependent variable, can be thought of as a composite that reflects the effects of the (a) independent variable, (b) individual characteristics of the participant or experimental unit, (c) chance fluctuations in the participant's performance, (d) measurement and recording errors that occur during data collection, and (e) any other nuisance variables such as environmental conditions that have not been controlled. Consider the weight loss of the fifth participant in treatment level a_2. Suppose that two months after beginning the diet this participant has lost 13 pounds ($Y_{52} = 13$). What factors have affected the value of Y_{52}? One factor is the effectiveness of the diet. Other factors are her weight prior to starting the diet, the degree to which she stayed on the diet, and the amount she exercised during the two-month trial, to mention only a few. In summary, Y_{52} is a composite that reflects (a) the effects of treatment level a_2, (b) effects unique to the participant, (c) effects attributable to chance fluctuations in the participant's behavior, (d) errors in measuring and recording the participant's weight loss, and (e) any other effects that have not been controlled. Our conjectures about Y_{52} or any of the other 44 observations can be expressed more formally by a model equation. The classical model equation for the weight-loss experiment is

$$Y_{ij} = \mu + \alpha_j + \varepsilon_{i(j)} \quad (i = 1, \ldots, n; j = 1, \ldots, p),$$

where

Y_{ij} is the weight loss for participant i in treatment level a_j.

μ is the grand mean of the three weight-loss population means.

α_j is the treatment effect for population j and is equal to $\mu_j - \mu$. It reflects the effects of diet a_j.

$\varepsilon_{i(j)}$ is the within-groups error effect associated with Y_{ij} and is equal to $Y_{ij} - \mu - \alpha_j$. It reflects all effects not attributable to treatment level a_j. The notation $i(j)$ indicates that the ith participant appears only in treatment level j. Participant i is said to be nested within the jth treatment level. Nesting is discussed in the section titled "Hierarchical Designs."

According to the equation for this completely randomized design, each observation is the sum of three parameters μ, α_j, and $\varepsilon_{i(j)}$. The values of the parameters in the equation are unknown but can be estimated from sample data.

The meanings of the terms grand mean, μ, and treatment effect, α_j, in the model equation seem fairly clear; the meaning of error effect, $\varepsilon_{i(j)}$, requires a bit more explanation. Why do observations, Y_{ij}s, in the same treatment level vary from one participant to the next? This variation must be due to differences among the participants and to other uncontrolled variables because the parameters μ and α_j in the model equation are constants for all participants in the same treatment level. To put it another way, observations in the same treatment

level are different because the error effects, $\varepsilon_{i(j)}$s, for the observations are different. Recall that error effects reflect idiosyncratic characteristics of the participants—those characteristics that differ from one participant to another—and any other variables that have not been controlled. Researchers attempt to minimize the size of error effects by holding sources of variation that might contribute to the error effects constant and by the judicial choice of an experimental design. Designs that are described next permit a researcher to isolate and remove some sources of variation that would ordinarily be included in the error effects.

Randomized Block Design

The two designs just described use independent samples. Two samples are independent if, for example, a researcher randomly samples from two populations or randomly assigns participants to p groups. Dependent samples, on the other hand, can be obtained by any of the following procedures.

1. Observe each participant under each treatment level in the experiment—that is, obtain repeated measures on the participants.
2. Form sets of participants who are similar with respect to a variable that is correlated with the dependent variable. This procedure is called *participant matching*.
3. Obtain sets of identical twins or littermates in which case the participants have similar genetic characteristics.
4. Obtain participants who are matched by mutual selection, for example, husband and wife pairs or business partners.

In the behavioral and social sciences, the participants are often people whose aptitudes and experiences differ markedly. Individual differences are inevitable, but it is often possible to isolate or partition out a portion of these effects so that they do not appear in estimates of the error effects. One design for accomplishing this is the design used with a t statistic for dependent samples. As the name suggests, the design uses dependent samples. A t dependent-samples design also uses a more complex randomization and analysis plan than does a t independent-samples design. However, the added complexity is often accompanied by greater power—a point that I will develop later in connection with a randomized block design.

Let's reconsider the weight-loss experiment. It is reasonable to assume that ease of losing weight is related to the amount by which a girl is overweight. The design of the experiment can be improved by isolating this nuisance variable. Suppose that instead of randomly assigning 30 participants to the treatment levels, the researcher formed pairs of participants

	Treatment Level	Treatment Level
Block$_1$	a_1	a_2
Block$_2$	a_1	a_2
Block$_3$	a_1	a_2
$\vdots$	$\vdots$	$\vdots$
Block$_{15}$	a_1	a_2
	$\overline{Y}_{\cdot 1}$	$\overline{Y}_{\cdot 2}$

Figure 1.3 Layout for a t dependent-samples design. Each block contains two girls who are overweight by about the same amount. The two girls in a block are randomly assigned to the treatment levels. The mean weight loss in pounds for the girls in treatment levels a_1 and a_2 is denoted by $\overline{Y}_{\cdot 1}$ and $\overline{Y}_{\cdot 2}$, respectively.

so that prior to going on a diet the participants in each pair are overweight by about the same amount. The participants in each pair constitute a block or set of matched participants. A simple way to form blocks of matched participants is to rank them from least to most overweight. The participants ranked 1 and 2 are assigned to block one, those ranked 3 and 4 are assigned to block two, and so on. In this example, 15 blocks of dependent samples can be formed from the 30 participants. After all of the blocks have been formed, the two participants in each block are randomly assigned to the two diets. The layout for this experiment is shown in Figure 1.3. If the researcher's hunch is correct that ease in losing weight is related to the amount by which a girl is overweight, this design should result in a more powerful test of the null hypothesis, $\mu_{\cdot 1} - \mu_{\cdot 2} = 0$, than would a t test for independent samples. As we will see, the increased power results from isolating the nuisance variable (the amount by which the girls are overweight) so that it does not appear in the estimate of the error effects.

Earlier we saw that the layout and randomization procedures for a t independent-samples design and a completely randomized design are the same except that a completely randomized design can have more than two treatment levels. The same comparison can be drawn between a t dependent-samples design and a randomized block design. A *randomized block design* is denoted by the letters RB-p, where RB stands for "randomized block" and p is the number of levels of the treatment. The four procedures for obtaining dependent samples that were described earlier can be used to form the blocks in a randomized block design. The procedure that is used does not affect the computation of significance tests, but the procedure does affect the interpretation of the results. The results of an experiment with repeated measures generalize to a population of participants who have been exposed to all of the treatment levels. However, the results of an experiment with matched participants generalize to a population of

participants who have been exposed to only one treatment level. Some writers reserve the designation *randomized block design* for this latter case. They refer to a design with repeated measurements in which the order of administration of the treatment levels is randomized independently for each participant as a *subjects-by-treatments design*. A design with repeated measurements in which the order of administration of the treatment levels is the same for all participants is referred to as a *subject-by-trials design*. I use the designation *randomized block design* for all three cases.

Of the four ways of obtaining dependent samples, the use of repeated measures on the participants typically results in the greatest homogeneity within the blocks. However, if repeated measures are used, the effects of one treatment level should dissipate before the participant is observed under another treatment level. Otherwise the subsequent observations will reflect the cumulative effects of the preceding treatment levels. There is no such restriction, of course, if carryover effects such as learning or fatigue are the researcher's principal interest. If blocks are composed of identical twins or littermates, it is assumed that the performance of participants having identical or similar heredities will be more homogeneous than the performance of participants having dissimilar heredities. If blocks are composed of participants who are matched by mutual selection (e.g., husband and wife pairs or business partners), a researcher should ascertain that the participants in a block are in fact more homogeneous with respect to the dependent variable than are unmatched participants. A husband and wife often have similar political attitudes; the couple is less likely to have similar mechanical aptitudes.

Suppose that in the weight-loss experiment the researcher wants to evaluate the effectiveness of three diets, denoted by a_1, a_2, and a_3. The researcher suspects that ease of losing weight is related to the amount by which a girl is overweight. If a sample of 45 girls is available, the blocking procedure described in connection with a t dependent-samples design can be used to form 15 blocks of participants. The three participants in a block are matched with respect to the nuisance variable, the amount by which a girl is overweight. The layout for this experiment is shown in Figure 1.4. A comparison of the layout in this figure with that in Figure 1.3 for a t dependent-samples design reveals that they are the same except that the randomized block design has $p = 3$ treatment levels. When $p = 2$, the layouts and randomization plans for the designs are identical. In this and later examples, I assume that all of the treatment levels and blocks of interest are represented in the experiment. In other words, the treatment levels and blocks represent fixed effects. A discussion of the case in which either the treatment levels or blocks or both are randomly sampled from a population of levels, the mixed and

	Treatment Level	Treatment Level	Treatment Level	
Block$_1$	a_1	a_2	a_3	$\overline{Y}_1.$
Block$_2$	a_1	a_2	a_3	$\overline{Y}_2.$
Block$_3$	a_1	a_2	a_3	$\overline{Y}_3.$
⋮	⋮	⋮	⋮	⋮
Block$_{15}$	a_1	a_2	a_3	$\overline{Y}_{15}.$
	$\overline{Y}._1$	$\overline{Y}._2$	$\overline{Y}._3$	

Figure 1.4 Layout for a randomized block design (RB-3 design). Each block contains three girls who are overweight by about the same amount. The three girls in a block are randomly assigned to the treatment levels. The mean weight loss in pounds for the girls in treatment levels a_1, a_2, and a_3 is denoted by $\overline{Y}._1$, $\overline{Y}._2$, and $\overline{Y}._3$, respectively. The mean weight loss for the girls in Block$_1$, Block$_2$, ..., Block$_{15}$ is denoted by $\overline{Y}_1.$, $\overline{Y}_2.$, ..., $\overline{Y}_{15}.$, respectively.

random effects cases, is beyond the scope of this chapter. The reader is referred to Kirk (1995, pp. 256–257, 265–268).

A randomized block design enables a researcher to test two null hypotheses.

H_0: $\mu._1 = \mu._2 = \mu._3$
(Treatment population means are equal.)

H_0: $\mu_1. = \mu_2. = \cdots = \mu_{15}.$
(Block population means are equal.)

The second hypothesis, which is usually of little interest, states that the population weight-loss means for the 15 levels of the nuisance variable are equal. The researcher expects a test of this null hypothesis to be significant. If the nuisance variable represented by the blocks does not account for an appreciable proportion of the total variation in the experiment, little has been gained by isolating the effects of the variable. Before exploring this point, I describe the model equation for an RB-p design.

The classical model equation for the weight-loss experiment is

$$Y_{ij} = \mu + \alpha_j + \pi_i + \varepsilon_{ij} \quad (i = 1, \ldots, n; j = 1, \ldots, p),$$

where

Y_{ij} is the weight loss for the participant in Block$_i$ and treatment level a_j.

μ is the grand mean of the three weight-loss population means.

α_j is the treatment effect for population j and is equal to $\mu._j - \mu$. It reflects the effect of diet a_j.

π_i is the block effect for population i and is equal to $\mu_i. - \mu$. It reflects the effect of the nuisance variable in Block$_i$.

ε_{ij} is the residual error effect associated with Y_{ij} and is equal to $Y_{ij} - \mu - \alpha_j - \pi_i$. It reflects all effects not attributable to treatment level a_j and Block$_i$.

According to the model equation for this randomized block design, each observation is the sum of four parameters: $\mu, \alpha_j, \pi_i,$ and ε_{ij}. A residual error effect is that portion of an observation that remains after the grand mean, treatment effect, and block effect have been subtracted from it; that is, $\varepsilon_{ij} = Y_{ij} - \mu - \alpha_j - \pi_i$. The sum of the squared error effects for this randomized block design,

$$\sum\sum \varepsilon_{ij}^2 = \sum\sum (Y_{ij} - \mu - \alpha_j - \pi_i)^2,$$

will be smaller than the sum for the completely randomized design,

$$\sum\sum \varepsilon_{i(j)}^2 = \sum\sum (Y_{ij} - \mu - \alpha_j)^2,$$

if π_i^2 is not equal to zero for one or more blocks. This idea is illustrated in Figure 1.5, where the total sum of squares and degrees of freedom for the two designs are partitioned. The F statistic that is used to test the null hypothesis can be thought of as a ratio of error and treatment effects,

$$F = \frac{f(\text{error effects}) + f(\text{treatment effects})}{f(\text{error effects})}$$

where $f( )$ denotes a function of the effects in parentheses. It is apparent from an examination of this ratio that the smaller the sum of the squared error effects, the larger the F statistic and, hence, the greater the probability of rejecting a false null

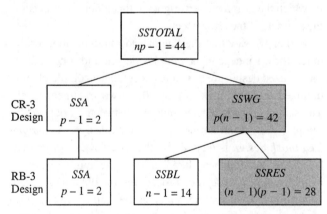

Figure 1.5 Partition of the total sum of squares (SSTOTAL) and degrees of freedom ($np - 1 = 44$) for CR-3 and RB-3 designs. The treatment and within-groups sums of squares are denoted by, respectively, SSA and SSWG. The block and residual sums of squares are denoted by, respectively, SSBL and SSRES. The shaded rectangles indicate the sums of squares that are used to compute the error variance for each design: $MSWG = SSWG/p(n-1)$ and $MSRES = SSRES/(n-1)(p-1)$. If the nuisance variable (SSBL) in the randomized block design accounts for an appreciable portion of the total sum of squares, the design will have a smaller error variance and, hence, greater power than the completely randomized design.

hypothesis. Thus, by isolating a nuisance variable that accounts for an appreciable portion of the total variation in a randomized block design, a researcher is rewarded with a more powerful test of a false null hypothesis.

As we have seen, blocking with respect to the nuisance variable (the amount by which the girls are overweight) enables the researcher to isolate this variable and remove it from the error effects. But what if the nuisance variable doesn't account for any of the variation in the experiment? In other words, what if all of the block effects in the experiment are equal to zero? In this unlikely case, the sum of the squared error effects for the randomized block and completely randomized designs will be equal. In this case, the randomized block design will be less powerful than the completely randomized design because its error variance, the denominator of the F statistic, has $n - 1$ fewer degrees of freedom than the error variance for the completely randomized design. It should be obvious that the nuisance variable should be selected with care. The larger the correlation between the nuisance variable and the dependent variable, the more likely it is that the block effects will account for an appreciable proportion of the total variation in the experiment.

Latin Square Design

The Latin square design described in this section derives its name from an ancient puzzle that was concerned with the number of different ways that Latin letters can be arranged in a square matrix so that each letter appears once in each row and once in each column. An example of a 3×3 Latin square is shown in Figure 1.6. In this figure I have used the letter a with subscripts in place of Latin letters. The Latin square design is denoted by the letters LS-p, where LS stands for "Latin square" and p is the number of levels of the treatment. A Latin square design enables a researcher to isolate the effects of not one but two nuisance variables. The levels of one nuisance variable are assigned to the rows of the square; the levels of the other nuisance variable are assigned to the columns. The levels of the treatment are assigned to the cells of the square.

Let's return to the weight-loss experiment. With a Latin square design the researcher can isolate the effects of the amount by which girls are overweight and the effects of a second nuisance variable, for example, genetic predisposition to be overweight. A rough measure of the second nuisance variable can be obtained by asking a girl's parents whether they were overweight as teenagers: c_1 denotes neither parent overweight, c_2 denotes one parent overweight, and c_3 denotes both parents overweight. This nuisance variable can be assigned to the columns of the Latin square. Three levels of the amount by which girls are overweight can be assigned to the rows of the

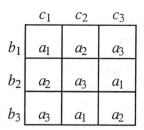

Figure 1.6 Three-by-three Latin square, where a_j denotes one of the $j = 1, \ldots, p$ levels of treatment A; b_k denotes one of the $k = 1, \ldots, p$ levels of nuisance variable B; and c_l denotes one of the $l = 1, \ldots, p$ levels of nuisance variable C. Each level of treatment A appears once in each row and once in each column as required for a Latin square.

Latin square: b_1 is less than 15 pounds, b_2 is 15 to 25 pounds, and b_3 is more than 25 pounds. The advantage of being able to isolate two nuisance variables comes at a price. The randomization procedures for a Latin square design are more complex than those for a randomized block design. Also, the number of rows and columns of a Latin square must each equal the number of treatment levels, which is three in the example. This requirement can be very restrictive. For example, it was necessary to restrict the continuous variable of the amount by which girls are overweight to only three levels. The layout of the LS-3 design is shown in Figure 1.7.

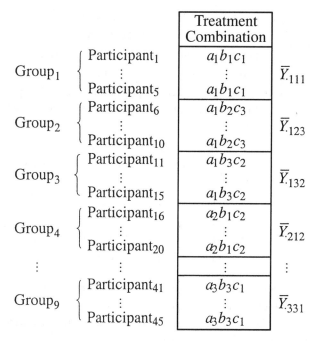

Figure 1.7 Layout for a Latin square design (LS-3 design) that is based on the Latin square in Figure 1.6. Treatment A represents three kinds of diets; nuisance variable B represents amount by which the girls are overweight; and nuisance variable C represents genetic predisposition to be overweight. The girls in Group$_1$, for example, received diet a_1, were less than fifteen pounds overweight (b_1), and neither parent had been overweight as a teenager (c_1). The mean weight loss in pounds for the girls in the nine groups is denoted by $\overline{Y}_{.111}, \overline{Y}_{.123}, \ldots, \overline{Y}_{.331}$.

The design in Figure 1.7 enables the researcher to test three null hypotheses:

H_0: $\mu_{1..} = \mu_{2..} = \mu_{3..}$
(Treatment population means are equal.)

H_0: $\mu_{.1.} = \mu_{.2.} = \mu_{.3.}$
(Row population means are equal.)

H_0: $\mu_{..1} = \mu_{..2} = \mu_{..3}$
(Column population means are equal.)

The first hypothesis states that the population means for the three diets are equal. The second and third hypotheses make similar assertions about the population means for the two nuisance variables. Tests of these nuisance variables are expected to be significant. As discussed earlier, if the nuisance variables do not account for an appreciable proportion of the total variation in the experiment, little has been gained by isolating the effects of the variables.

The classical model equation for this version of the weight-loss experiment is

$$Y_{ijkl} = \mu + \alpha_j + \beta_k + \gamma_l + \varepsilon_{jkl} + \varepsilon_{i(jkl)}$$
$$(i = 1, \ldots, n; j = 1, \ldots, p; k = 1, \ldots, p; l = 1, \ldots, p),$$

where

Y_{ijkl}	is the weight loss for the ith participant in treatment level a_j, row b_k, and column c_l.
α_j	is the treatment effect for population j and is equal to $\mu_{j..} - \mu$. It reflects the effect of diet a_j.
β_k	is the row effect for population k and is equal to $\mu_{.k.} - \mu$. It reflects the effect of nuisance variable b_k.
γ_l	is the column effect for population l and is equal to $\mu_{..l} - \mu$. It reflects the effects of nuisance variable c_l.
ε_{jkl}	is the residual effect that is equal to $\mu_{jkl} - \mu_{j..} - \mu_{.k.} - \mu_{..l} + 2\mu$.
$\varepsilon_{i(jkl)}$	is the within-cell error effect associated with Y_{ijkl} and is equal to $Y_{ijkl} - \mu - \alpha_j - \beta_k - \gamma_l - \varepsilon_{jkl}$.

According to the model equation for this Latin square design, each observation is the sum of six parameters: $\mu, \alpha_j, \beta_k, \gamma_l, \varepsilon_{jkl},$ and $\varepsilon_{i(jkl)}$. The sum of the squared within-cell error effects for the Latin square design,

$$\sum\sum \varepsilon_{i(jkl)}^2 = \sum\sum (Y_{ijkl} - \mu - \alpha_j - \beta_k - \gamma_l - \varepsilon_{jkl})^2,$$

will be smaller than the sum for the randomized block design,

$$\sum\sum \varepsilon_{ij}^2 = \sum\sum (Y_{ij} - \mu - \alpha_j - \pi_i)^2,$$

if the combined effects of $\sum\beta_k^2, \sum\gamma_l^2,$ and $\sum\varepsilon_{jkl}^2$ are greater than $\sum\pi_i^2$. The benefits of isolating two nuisance variables are a smaller error variance and increased power.

Thus far I have described three of the simplest experimental designs: the completely randomized design, randomized block design, and Latin square design. The three designs are called *building block designs* because complex experimental designs can be constructed by combining two or more of these simple designs (Kirk, 1995, p. 40). Furthermore, the randomization procedures, data analysis, and model assumptions for complex designs represent extensions of those for the three building block designs. The three designs provide the organizational structure for the design nomenclature and classification scheme that is described next.

CLASSIFICATION OF EXPERIMENTAL DESIGNS

A classification scheme for experimental designs is given in Table 1.1. The designs in the category *systematic designs* do not use random assignment of participants or experimental units and are of historical interest only. According to Leonard and Clark (1939), agricultural field research employing systematic designs on a practical scale dates back to 1834. Over the last 80 years systematic designs have fallen into disuse because designs employing random assignment are more likely to provide valid estimates of treatment and error effects and can be analyzed using the powerful tools of statistical inference such as analysis of variance. Experimental designs using random assignment are called *randomized designs*. The randomized designs in Table 1.1 are subdivided into categories based on (a) the number of treatments, (b) whether participants are assigned to relatively homogeneous blocks prior to random assignment, (c) presence or absence of confounding, (d) use of crossed or nested treatments, and (e) use of a covariate.

The letters p and q in the abbreviated designations denote the number of levels of treatments A and B, respectively. If a design includes a third and fourth treatment, say treatments C and D, the number of their levels is denoted by r and t, respectively. In general, the designation for designs with two or more treatments includes the letters CR, RB, or LS to indicate the building block design. The letter F or H is added to the designation to indicate that the design is, respectively, a factorial design or a hierarchical design. For example, the F in the designation CRF-pq indicates that it is a factorial design; the CR and pq indicate that the design was constructed by combining two completely randomized designs with p and q treatment levels. The letters CF, PF, FF, and AC are added to the designation if the design is, respectively, a confounded factorial design, partially confounded factorial design, fractional factorial design, or analysis of covariance design.

TABLE 1.1   Classification of Experimental Designs

Experimental Design	Abbreviated Designation[a]	Experimental Design	Abbreviated Designation[a]
I. Systematic Designs (selected examples).		b. Randomized block completely confounded factorial design.	RBCF-p^k
1. Beavan's chessboard design.		c. Randomized block partially confounded factorial design.	RBPF-p^k
2. Beavan's half-drill strip design.		4. Designs with treatment-interaction confounding.	
3. Diagonal square design.		a. Completely randomized fractional factorial design.	CRFF-p^{k-i}
4. Knut Vik square design.			
II. Randomized Designs With One Treatment.		b. Graeco-Latin square fractional factorial design.	GLSFF-p^k
A. Experimental units randomly assigned to treatment levels.		c. Latin square fractional factorial design.	LSFF-p^k
1. Completely randomized design.	CR-p	d. Randomized block fractional factorial design.	RBFF-p^{k-i}
B. Experimental units assigned to relatively homogeneous blocks or groups prior to random assignment.		B. Hierarchical designs: designs in which one or more treatments are nested.	
1. Balanced incomplete block design.	BIB-p	1. Designs with complete nesting.	
2. Cross-over design.	CO-p	a. Completely randomized hierarchical design.	CRH-$pq(A)$
3. Generalized randomized block design.	GRB-p	b. Randomized block hierarchical design.	RBH-$pq(A)$
4. Graeco-Latin square design.	GLS-p	2. Designs with partial nesting.	
5. Hyper-Graeco-Latin square design.	HGLS-p	a. Completely randomized partial hierarchical design.	CRPH-$pq(A)r$
6. Latin square design.	LS-p		
7. Lattice balanced incomplete block design.	LBIB-p	b. Randomized block partial hierarchical design.	RBPH-$pq(A)r$
8. Lattice partially balanced incomplete block design.	LPBIB-p	c. Split-plot partial hierarchical design.	SPH-$p \cdot qr(B)$
9. Lattice unbalanced incomplete block design.	LUBIB-p	IV. Randomized Designs With One or More Covariates.	
10. Partially balanced incomplete block design.	PBIB-p	A. Designs that include a covariate have the letters AC added to the abbreviated designation as in the following examples.	
11. Randomized block design.	RB-p		
12. Youden square design.	YBIB-p	1. Completely randomized analysis of covariance design.	CRAC-p
III. Randomized Designs With Two or More Treatments.			
A. Factorial designs: designs in which all treatments are crossed.		2. Completely randomized factorial analysis of covariance design.	CRFAC-pq
1. Designs without confounding.		3. Latin square analysis of covariance design.	LSAC-p
a. Completely randomized factorial design.	CRF-pq	4. Randomized block analysis of covariance design.	RBAC-p
b. Generalized randomized block factorial design.	GRBF-pq	5. Split-plot factorial analysis of covariance design.	SPFAC-$p \cdot q$
c. Randomized block factorial design.	RBF-pq	V. Miscellaneous Designs (select examples).	
2. Design with group-treatment confounding.		1. Solomon four-group design.	
a. Split-plot factorial design.	SPF-$p \cdot q$	2. Interrupted time-series design.	
3. Designs with group-interaction confounding.			
a. Latin square confounded factorial design.	LSCF-p^k		

[a]The abbreviated designations are discussed later.

Three of these designs are described later. Because of space limitations, I cannot describe all of the designs in Table 1.1. I will focus on those designs that are potentially the most useful in the behavioral and social sciences.

It is apparent from Table 1.1 that a wide array of designs is available to researchers. Unfortunately, there is no universally accepted designation for the various designs—some designs have as many as five different names. For example, the completely randomized design has been called a one-way classification design, single-factor design, randomized group design, simple randomized design, and single variable experiment. Also, a variety of design classification schemes have been proposed. The classification scheme in Table 1.1 owes much to Cochran and Cox (1957, chaps. 4–13) and Federer (1955, pp. 11–12).

A quick perusal of Table 1.1 reveals why researchers sometimes have difficulty selecting an appropriate experimental design—there are a lot of designs from which to choose. Because of the wide variety of designs available, it is important to identify them clearly in research reports. One often sees statements such as "a two-treatment factorial design was used." It should be evident that a more precise description is required. This description could refer to 10 of the 11 factorial designs in Table 1.1.

Thus far, the discussion has been limited to designs with one treatment and one or two nuisance variables. In the following sections I describe designs with two or more treatments that are constructed by combining several building block designs.

FACTORIAL DESIGNS

Completely Randomized Factorial Design

Factorial designs differ from those described previously in that two or more treatments can be evaluated simultaneously in an experiment. The simplest factorial design from the standpoint of randomization, data analysis, and model assumptions is based on a completely randomized design and, hence, is called a *completely randomized factorial design*. A two-treatment completely randomized factorial design is denoted by the letters CRF-*pq*, where *p* and *q* denote the number of levels, respectively, of treatments *A* and *B*.

In the weight-loss experiment, a researcher might be interested in knowing also whether walking on a treadmill for 20 minutes a day would contribute to losing weight, as well as whether the difference between the effects of walking or not walking on the treadmill would be the same for each of the three diets. To answer these additional questions, a researcher can use a two-treatment completely randomized factorial design. Let treatment *A* consist of the three diets (a_1, a_2, and a_3) and treatment *B* consist of no exercise on the treadmill (b_1) and exercise for 20 minutes a day on the treadmill (b_2). This design is a CRF-32 design, where 3 is the number of levels of treatment *A* and 2 is the number of levels of treatment *B*. The layout for the design is obtained by combining the treatment levels of a CR-3 design with those of a CR-2 design so that each treatment level of the CR-3 design appears once with each level of the CR-2 design and vice versa. The resulting design has $3 \times 2 = 6$ treatment combinations as follows: a_1b_1, a_1b_2, a_2b_1, a_2b_2, a_3b_1, a_3b_2. When treatment levels are combined in this way, the treatments are said to be *crossed*. The use of crossed treatments is a characteristic of all factorial designs. The layout of the design with 30 girls randomly assigned to the six treatment combinations is shown in Figure 1.8.

The classical model equation for the weight-loss experiment is

$$Y_{ijk} = \mu + \alpha_j + \beta_k + (\alpha\beta)_{jk} + \varepsilon_{i(jk)}$$
$$(i = 1, \ldots, n; \; j = 1, \ldots, p; \; k = 1, \ldots, q),$$

where

Y_{ijk} is the weight loss for participant i in treatment combination a_jb_k.

μ is the grand mean of the six weight-loss population means.

α_j is the treatment effect for population a_j and is equal to $\mu_{j.} - \mu$. It reflects the effect of diet a_j.

β_k is the treatment effect for population b_k and is equal to $\mu_{.k} - \mu$. It reflects the effects of exercise condition b_k.

$(\alpha\beta)_{jk}$ is the interaction effect for populations a_j and b_k and is equal to $\mu_{jk} - \mu_{j.} - \mu_{.k} - \mu$. Interaction effects are discussed later.

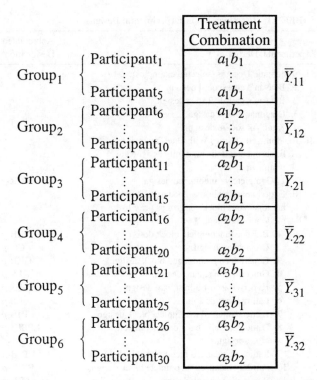

Figure 1.8   Layout for a two-treatment completely randomized factorial design (CRF-32 design). Thirty girls are randomly assigned to six combinations of treatments *A* and *B* with the restriction that five girls are assigned to each combination. The mean weight loss in pounds for girls in the six groups is denoted by $\overline{Y}_{.11}, \overline{Y}_{.12}, \ldots, \overline{Y}_{.32}$.

$\varepsilon_{i(jk)}$ is the within-cell error effect associated with Y_{ijk} and is equal to $Y_{ijk} - \mu - \alpha_j - \beta_k - (\alpha\beta)_{jk}$. It reflects all effects not attributable to treatment level a_j, treatment level b_k, and the interaction of a_j and b_k.

The CRF-32 design enables a researcher to test three null hypotheses:

H_0: $\mu_{1.} = \mu_{2.} = \mu_{3.}$
       (Treatment *A* population means are equal.)

H_0: $\mu_{.1} = \mu_{.2}$
       (Treatment *B* population means are equal.)

H_0: $\mu_{jk} - \mu_{jk'} - \mu_{j'k} + \mu_{j'k'} = 0$ for all j and k
       (All $A \times B$ interaction effects equal zero.)

The last hypothesis is unique to factorial designs. It states that the joint effects (interaction) of treatments *A* and *B* are equal to zero for all combinations of the two treatments. Two treatments are said to interact if any difference in the dependent variable for one treatment is different at two or more levels of the other treatment.

Thirty girls are available to participate in the weight-loss experiment and have been randomly assigned to the six treatment combinations with the restriction that five girls are assigned to

TABLE 1.2   Weight-Loss Data for the Diet (a_j) and Exercise Conditions (b_k)

a_1b_1	a_1b_2	a_2b_1	a_2b_2	a_3b_1	a_3b_2
7	7	9	10	15	13
13	14	4	5	10	16
9	11	7	7	12	20
5	4	14	15	5	19
1	9	11	13	8	12

TABLE 1.4   Analysis of Variance for the Weight-Loss Data

Source	SS	df	MS	F	p
Treatment A (Diet)	131.6667	2	65.8334	4.25	.026
Treatment B (Exercise)	67.5000	1	67.5000	4.35	.048
$A \times B$	35.0000	2	17.5000	1.13	.340
Within cell	372.0000	24	15.5000		
Total	606.1667	29			

each combination. The data, weight loss for each girl, are given in Table 1.2. A descriptive summary of the data—sample means and standard deviations—is given in Table 1.3.

An examination of Table 1.3 suggests that diet a_3 resulted in more weight loss than did the other diets and 20 minutes a day on the treadmill was beneficial. The analysis of variance for the weight-loss data is summarized in Table 1.4, which shows that the null hypotheses for treatments A and B can be rejected. We know that at least one contrast or difference among the diet population means is not equal to zero. Also, from Tables 1.3 and 1.4 we know that 20 minutes a day on the treadmill resulted in greater weight loss than did the no-exercise condition. The $A \times B$ interaction test is not significant. When two treatments interact, a graph in which treatment-combination population means are connected by lines will always reveal at least two nonparallel lines for one or more segments of the lines. The nonsignificant interaction test in Table 1.4 tells us that there is no reason for believing that the population difference in weight loss between the treadmill and no-treadmill conditions is different for the three diets. If the interaction had been significant, our interest would have shifted from interpreting the tests of treatments A and B to understanding the nature of the interaction. Procedures for interpreting interactions are described by Kirk (1995, pp. 370–372, 377–389).

Statistical Significance Versus Practical Significance

The rejection of the null hypotheses for the diet and exercise treatments is not very informative. We know in advance that

TABLE 1.3   Descriptive Summary of the Weight-Loss Data: Means ($\overline{Y}$) and Standard Deviations (S)

	Diet a_1	Diet a_2	Diet a_3	Mean Standard Deviation
No treadmill exercise (b_1)	$\overline{Y}_{.11} = 7.0$ $S_{.11} = 4.0$	$\overline{Y}_{.21} = 9.0$ $S_{.21} = 3.4$	$\overline{Y}_{.31} = 10.0$ $S_{.31} = 3.4$	$\overline{Y}_{..1} = 8.7$ $S_{..1} = 3.8$
Treadmill exercise (b_2)	$\overline{Y}_{.12} = 9.0$ $S_{.12} = 3.4$	$\overline{Y}_{.22} = 10.0$ $S_{.22} = 3.7$	$\overline{Y}_{.32} = 16.0$ $S_{.32} = 3.2$	$\overline{Y}_{..2} = 11.7$ $S_{..2} = 4.6$
	$\overline{Y}_{.1.} = 8.0$ $S_{.1.} = 3.8$	$\overline{Y}_{.2.} = 9.5$ $S_{.2.} = 3.6$	$\overline{Y}_{.3.} = 13.0$ $S_{.3.} = 4.4$	

the hypotheses are false. As John Tukey (1991) wrote, "the effects of A and B are always different—in some decimal place—for any A and B. Thus asking 'Are the effects different?' is foolish" (p. 100). Furthermore, rejection of a null hypothesis tells us nothing about the size of the treatment effects or whether they are important or large enough to be useful—that is, their practical significance. In spite of numerous criticisms of null hypothesis significance testing, researchers continue to focus on null hypotheses and p values. The focus should be on the data and on what the data tell the researcher about the scientific hypothesis. This is not a new idea. It was originally touched on by Karl Pearson in 1901 and more explicitly by Fisher in 1925. Fisher (1925) proposed that researchers supplement null hypothesis significance tests with measures of strength of association. Since then over 40 supplementary measures of effect magnitude have been proposed (Kirk, 1996). The majority of the measures fall into one of two categories: measures of strength of association and measures of effect size (typically, standardized mean differences). Hays (1963) introduced a measure of strength of association that can assist a researcher in assessing the importance or usefulness of a treatment: omega squared, $\hat{\omega}^2$. Omega squared estimates the proportion of the population variance in the dependent variable accounted for by a treatment. For experiments with several treatments, as in the weight-loss experiment, partial omega squared is computed. For example, the proportion of variance in the dependent variable, Y, accounted for by treatment A eliminating treatment B and the $A \times B$ interaction is denoted by $\hat{\omega}^2_{Y|A \cdot B, AB}$. Similarly, $\hat{\omega}^2_{Y|B \cdot A, AB}$ denotes the proportion of the variance accounted for by treatment B eliminating treatment A and the $A \times B$ interaction. For the weight-loss experiment, the partial omega squareds for treatments A and B are, respectively,

$$\hat{\omega}^2_{Y|A \cdot B, AB} = \frac{(p-1)(F_A - 1)}{(p-1)(F_A - 1) + npq}$$

$$= \frac{(3-1)(4.247-1)}{(3-1)(4.247-1) + (5)(3)(2)} = 0.18$$

$$\hat{\omega}^2_{Y|B\cdot A, AB} = \frac{(q-1)(F_B - 1)}{(q-1)(F_B - 1) + npq}$$

$$= \frac{(2-1)(4.376 - 1)}{(2-1)(4.376 - 1) + (5)(3)(2)} = 0.10.$$

Following Cohen's (1988, pp. 284–288) guidelines for interpreting omega squared,

.010 is a small association

.059 is a medium association

.138 is a large association,

we conclude that the diets accounted for a large proportion of the population variance in weight loss. This is consistent with our perception of the differences between the weight-loss means for the three diets: girls on diet a_3 lost five more pounds than did those on a_1. Certainly, any girl who is anxious to lose weight would want to be on diet a_3. Likewise, the medium association between the exercise conditions and weight loss is practically significant: Walking on the treadmill resulted in a mean weight loss of 3 pounds. Based on Tukey's HSD statistic, 95% confidence intervals for the three pairwise contrasts among the diet means are

$$-5.9 < \mu_{.1} - \mu_{.2} < 2.9$$
$$-9.4 < \mu_{.1} - \mu_{.3} < -0.6$$
$$-7.9 < \mu_{.2} - \mu_{.3} < 0.9.$$

Because the confidence interval for $\mu_{.1} - \mu_{.3}$ does not contain 0, we can be confident that diet a_3 is superior to diet a_1. Hedges's (1981) effect size for the difference between diets a_1 and a_3 is

$$g = \frac{|\overline{Y}_{..1} - \overline{Y}_{..2}|}{\hat{\sigma}_{\text{Pooled}}} = \frac{|8.0 - 13.0|}{3.937} = 1.27,$$

a large effect.

Unfortunately, there is no statistic that measures practical significance. The determination of whether results are important or useful must be made by the researcher. However, confidence intervals and measures of effect magnitude can help the researcher make this decision. If our discipline is to progress as it should, researchers must look beyond significance tests and p values and focus on what their data tell them about the phenomenon under investigation. For a fuller discussion of this point, see Kirk (2001).

Alternative Models

Thus far, I have described the classical model equation for several experimental designs. This model and associated procedures for computing sums of squares assume that all cell ns in multitreatment experiments are equal. If the cell ns are not equal, some researchers use one of the following procedures to obtain approximate tests of null hypotheses: (a) estimate the missing observations under the assumption that the treatments do not interact, (b) randomly set aside data to reduce all cell ns to the same size, and (c) use an unweighted-means analysis. The latter approach consists of performing an ANOVA on the cell means and then multiplying the sums of squares by the harmonic mean of the cell ns. None of these procedures is entirely satisfactory. Fortunately, exact solutions to the unequal cell n problem exist. Two solutions that are described next are based on a regression model and a cell means model. Unlike the classical model approach, the regression and cell means model approaches require a computer and software for manipulating matrices.

Suppose that halfway through the weight-loss experiment the third participant in treatment combination a_2b_2 ($Y_{322} = 7$) moved to another area of the country and dropped out of the experiment. The loss of this participant resulted in unequal cell ns. Cell a_2b_2 has four participants; the other cells have five participants. The analysis of the weight-loss data using the regression model is described next.

Regression Model

A qualitative regression model equation with $h - 1 = (p-1) + (q-1) + (p-1)(q-1) = 5$ independent variables ($X_{i1}, X_{i2}, \ldots, X_{i2}X_{i3}$) and $h = 6$ parameters ($\beta_0, \beta_1, \ldots, \beta_5$),

$$Y_i = \beta_0 + \overbrace{\beta_1 X_{i1} + \beta_2 X_{i2}}^{A \text{ effects}} + \overbrace{\beta_3 X_{i3}}^{B \text{ effects}} + \overbrace{\beta_4 X_{i1} X_{i3} + \beta_5 X_{i2} X_{i3}}^{A \times B \text{ effects}} + e_i,$$

can be formulated so that tests of selected parameters of the regression model provide tests of null hypotheses for A, B, and $A \times B$ in the weight-loss experiment. Tests of the following null hypotheses for this regression model are of particular interest:

$$H_0: \beta_1 = \beta_2 = 0$$
$$H_0: \beta_3 = 0$$
$$H_0: \beta_4 = \beta_5 = 0$$

In order for tests of these null hypotheses to provide tests of ANOVA null hypotheses, it is necessary to establish a correspondence between the five independent variables of the regression model equation and $(p-1) + (q-1) + (p-1)(q-1) = 5$ treatment and interaction effects of the CRF-32 design. One way to establish this correspondence is to code the independent variables of the regression model as follows:

$$X_{i1} = \begin{cases} 1, & \text{if an observation is in } a_1 \\ -1, & \text{if an observation is in } a_3 \\ 0, & \text{otherwise} \end{cases}$$

$$X_{i2} = \begin{cases} 1, & \text{if an observation is in } a_2 \\ -1, & \text{if an observation is in } a_3 \\ 0, & \text{otherwise} \end{cases}$$

$$X_{i3} = \begin{cases} 1, & \text{if an observation is in } b_1 \\ -1, & \text{if an observation is in } b_2 \end{cases}$$

$$X_{i1}X_{i3} = \begin{cases} \text{product of coded values} \\ \text{associated with } a_1 \text{ and } b_1 \end{cases}$$

$$X_{i2}X_{i3} = \begin{cases} \text{product of coded values} \\ \text{associated with } a_2 \text{ and } b_1 \end{cases}$$

This coding scheme, which is called *effect coding,* produced the **X** matrix in Table 1.5. The **y** vector in Table 1.5 contains weight-loss observations for the six treatment combinations. The first column vector, $\mathbf{x}_0$, in the **X** matrix contains ones; the second through the sixth column vectors contain coded values for $X_{i1}, X_{i2}, \ldots, X_{i2}X_{i3}$. To save space, only a portion of the 29 rows of **X** and **y** are shown. As mentioned earlier, observation Y_{322} is missing. Hence, each of the treatment combinations contains five observations except for a_2b_2, which contains four.

TABLE 1.5 Data Vector, y, and X Matrix for the Regression Model

	$\begin{matrix}\mathbf{y}\\29\times1\end{matrix}$	$\mathbf{x}_0$	A $\mathbf{x}_1$	A $\mathbf{x}_2$	B $\mathbf{x}_3$	$A\times B$ $\mathbf{x}_1\mathbf{x}_3$	$A\times B$ $\mathbf{x}_2\mathbf{x}_3$
a_1b_1	7 $\vdots$ 1	1 $\vdots$ 1	1 $\vdots$ 1	0 $\vdots$ 0	1 $\vdots$ 1	1 $\vdots$ 1	0 $\vdots$ 0
a_1b_2	7 $\vdots$ 9	1 $\vdots$ 1	1 $\vdots$ 1	0 $\vdots$ 0	-1 $\vdots$ -1	-1 $\vdots$ -1	0 $\vdots$ 0
a_2b_1	9 $\vdots$ 11	1 $\vdots$ 1	0 $\vdots$ 0	1 $\vdots$ 1	1 $\vdots$ 1	0 $\vdots$ 0	1 $\vdots$ 1
a_2b_2	10 $\vdots$ 13	1 $\vdots$ 1	0 $\vdots$ 0	1 $\vdots$ 1	-1 $\vdots$ -1	0 $\vdots$ 0	-1 $\vdots$ -1
a_3b_1	15 $\vdots$ 8	1 $\vdots$ 1	-1 $\vdots$ -1	-1 $\vdots$ -1	1 $\vdots$ 1	-1 $\vdots$ -1	-1 $\vdots$ -1
a_3b_2	13 $\vdots$ 12	1 $\vdots$ 1	-1 $\vdots$ -1	-1 $\vdots$ -1	-1 $\vdots$ -1	1 $\vdots$ 1	1 $\vdots$ 1

F statistics for testing hypotheses for selected regression parameters are obtained by dividing a regression mean square, MSR, by an error mean square, MSE, where $MSR = SSR/df_{\text{reg}}$ and $MSE = SSE/df_{\text{error}}$. The regression sum of squares, SSR, that reflects the contribution of independent variables X_1 and X_2 over and above the contribution of X_3, X_1X_3, and X_2X_3 is given by the difference between two error sums of squares, SSE, as follows:

$$SSR(\overbrace{X_1\ X_2}^{A} \mid \overbrace{X_3}^{B}\ \overbrace{X_1X_3\ X_2X_3}^{A\times B})$$

$$= SSE(\overbrace{X_3}^{B}\ \overbrace{X_1X_3\ X_2X_3}^{A\times B}) - SSE(\overbrace{X_1\ X_2}^{A}\ \overbrace{X_3}^{B}\ \overbrace{X_1X_3\ X_2X_3}^{A\times B})$$

An error sum of squares is given by

$$SSE(\ ) = \mathbf{y}'\mathbf{y} - [(\mathbf{X}_i'\mathbf{X}_i)^{-1}(\mathbf{X}_i'\mathbf{y})]'(\mathbf{X}_i'\mathbf{y}),$$

where the $\mathbf{X}_i$ matrix contains the first column, $\mathbf{x}_0$, of **X** and the columns corresponding the independent variables contained in $SSE(\ )$. For example, the **X** matrix used in computing $SSE(X_3\ X_1X_3\ X_2X_3)$ contains four columns: $\mathbf{x}_0$, $\mathbf{x}_3$, $\mathbf{x}_1\mathbf{x}_3$, and $\mathbf{x}_2\mathbf{x}_3$. The regression sum of squares corresponding to SSA in ANOVA is

$$SSR(\overbrace{X_1\ X_2}^{A} \mid \overbrace{X_3}^{B}\ \overbrace{X_1X_3\ X_2X_3}^{A\times B})$$

$$= SSE(\overbrace{X_3}^{B}\ \overbrace{X_1X_3\ X_2X_3}^{A\times B}) - SSE(\overbrace{X_1\ X_2}^{A}\ \overbrace{X_3}^{B}\ \overbrace{X_1X_3\ X_2X_3}^{A\times B})$$

$$= 488.1538 - 360.7500 = 127.4038$$

with $p - 1 = 2$ degrees of freedom. This sum of squares is used in testing the regression null hypothesis $H_0\colon \beta_1 = \beta_2 = 0$. Because of the correspondence between the regression and ANOVA parameters, a test of this regression null hypothesis is equivalent to testing the ANOVA null hypothesis for treatment A.

The regression sum of squares corresponding to SSB in ANOVA is

$$SSR(\overbrace{X_3}^{B} \mid \overbrace{X_1\ X_2}^{A}\ \overbrace{X_1X_3\ X_2X_3}^{A\times B})$$

$$= SSE(\overbrace{X_1\ X_2}^{A}\ \overbrace{X_1X_3\ X_2X_3}^{A\times B}) - SSE(\overbrace{X_1\ X_2}^{A}\ \overbrace{X_3}^{B}\ \overbrace{X_1X_3\ X_2X_3}^{A\times B})$$

$$= 436.8000 - 360.7500 = 76.0500$$

with $q - 1 = 1$ degree of freedom.

The regression sum of squares corresponding to $SSA \times B$ in ANOVA is

$$SSR(\overbrace{X_1 X_3 \; X_2 X_3}^{A \times B} \mid \overbrace{X_1 \; X_2}^{A} \; \overbrace{X_3}^{B})$$

$$= SSE(\overbrace{X_1}^{A} \; \overbrace{X_2}^{B} \; \overbrace{X_3}^{}) - SSE(\overbrace{X_1}^{A} \; \overbrace{X_2}^{B} \; \overbrace{X_3}^{} \; \overbrace{X_1 X_3 \; X_2 X_3}^{A \times B})$$

$$= 388.5385 - 360.7500 = 27.7885$$

with $(p-1)(q-1) = 2$ degrees of freedom.

The regression error sum of squares corresponding to $SSWCELL$ in ANOVA is

$$SSE(\overbrace{X_1}^{A} \; \overbrace{X_2}^{B} \; \overbrace{X_3}^{} \; \overbrace{X_1 X_3 \; X_2 X_3}^{A \times B}) = 360.7500$$

with $N - h = 29 - 6 = 23$ degrees of freedom.

The total sum of squares is

$$SSTO = \mathbf{y}'\mathbf{y} - \mathbf{y}'\mathbf{J}\mathbf{y}N^{-1} = 595.7931,$$

where $\mathbf{J}$ is a 29×29 matrix of ones and $N = 29$, the number of weight-loss observations. The total sum of squares has $N - 1 = 28$ degrees of freedom. The analysis of the weight-loss data is summarized in Table 1.6. The null hypotheses $\beta_1 = \beta_2 = 0$ and $\beta_3 = 0$ can be rejected. Hence, independent variables X_1 or X_2 as well as X_3 contribute to predicting the dependent variable. As we see in the next section, the F statistics in Table 1.6 are identical to the ANOVA F statistics for the cell means model.

Cell Means Model

The classical model equation for a CRF-pq design,

$$Y_{ijk} = \mu + \alpha_j + \beta_k + (\alpha\beta)_{jk} + \varepsilon_{i(jk)}$$
$$(i = 1, \ldots, n; \, j = 1, \ldots, p; \, k = 1, \ldots, q),$$

focuses on the grand mean, treatment effects, and interaction effects. The cell means model equation for the CRF-pq design,

$$Y_{ijk} = \mu_{jk} + \varepsilon_{i(jk)}$$
$$(i = 1, \ldots, n; \, j = 1, \ldots, p; \, k = 1, \ldots, q),$$

focuses on cell means, where μ_{jk} denotes the mean in cell a_j and b_k. Although I described the classical model first, this is not the order in which the models evolved historically. According to Urquhart, Weeks, and Henderson (1973), Fisher's early development of ANOVA was conceptualized by his colleagues in terms of cell means. It was not until later that cell means were given a linear structure in terms of the grand mean and model effects, that is, $\mu_{jk} = \mu + \alpha_j + \beta_k + (\alpha\beta)_{jk}$. The classical model equation for a CRF-pq design uses four parameters, $\mu + \alpha_j + \beta_k + (\alpha\beta)_{jk}$, to represent one parameter, μ_{jk}. Because of this structure, the classical model is overparameterized. For example, the expectation of the classical model equation for the weight-loss experiment contains 12 parameters: μ, α_1, α_2, α_3, β_1, β_2, $(\alpha\beta)_{11}$, $(\alpha\beta)_{12}$, $(\alpha\beta)_{21}$, $(\alpha\beta)_{22}$, $(\alpha\beta)_{31}$, $(\alpha\beta)_{32}$. However, there are only six cells means from which to estimate the 12 parameters. When there are missing cells in multitreatment designs, a researcher is faced with the question of which parameters or parametric functions are estimable. For a discussion of this and other problems, see Hocking (1985), Hocking and Speed (1975), Searle (1987), and Timm (1975).

The cell means model avoids the problems associated with overparameterization. A population mean can be estimated for each cell that contains one or more observations. Thus, the model is fully parameterized. Unlike the classical model, the cell means model does not impose a structure on the analysis of data. Consequently, the model can be used to test hypotheses about any linear combination of population cell means. It is up to the researcher to decide which tests are meaningful or useful based on the original research hypotheses, the way the experiment was conducted, and the data that are available.

I will use the weight-loss data in Table 1.2 to illustrate the computational procedures for the cell means model. Again,

TABLE 1.6   Analysis of Variance for the Weight-Loss Data (Observation Y_{322} is missing)

Source	SS	df	MS	F	p
$X_1 \; X_2 \mid X_3 \; X_1X_3 \; X_2X_3$	127.4038	$p - 1 = 2$	63.7019	4.06	.031
$X_3 \mid X_1 \; X_2 \; X_1X_3 \; X_2X_3$	76.0500	$q - 1 = 1$	76.0500	4.85	.038
$X_1X_3 \; X_2X_3 \mid X_1 \; X_2 \; X_3$	27.7885	$(p-1)(q-1) = 2$	13.8943	0.89	.426
Error	360.7500	$N - h = 23$	15.6848		
Total	595.7931	$N - 1 = 28$			

we will assume that observation Y_{322} is missing. The null hypothesis for treatment A is

$$H_0: \mu_{1.} = \mu_{2.} = \mu_{3.}.$$

An equivalent null hypothesis that is used with the cell means model is

$$H_0: \mu_{1.} - \mu_{2.} = 0 \tag{1.1}$$
$$\mu_{2.} - \mu_{3.} = 0.$$

In terms of cell means, this hypothesis can be expressed as

$$H_0: \frac{\mu_{11} + \mu_{12}}{2} - \frac{\mu_{21} + \mu_{22}}{2} = 0 \tag{1.2}$$
$$\frac{\mu_{21} + \mu_{22}}{2} - \frac{\mu_{31} + \mu_{32}}{2} = 0,$$

where $\mu_{1.} = (\mu_{11} + \mu_{12})/2$, $\mu_{2.} = (\mu_{21} + \mu_{22})/2$, and so on. In matrix notation, the null hypothesis is

$$H_0: \frac{1}{2} \underset{(p-1) \times h}{\begin{bmatrix} 1 & 1 & -1 & -1 & 0 & 0 \\ 0 & 0 & 1 & 1 & -1 & -1 \end{bmatrix}}^{\mathbf{C}_A'} \underset{h \times 1}{\begin{bmatrix} \mu_{11} \\ \mu_{12} \\ \mu_{21} \\ \mu_{22} \\ \mu_{31} \\ \mu_{32} \end{bmatrix}}^{\boldsymbol{\mu}} = \underset{(p-1) \times 1}{\begin{bmatrix} 0 \\ 0 \end{bmatrix}}^{\mathbf{0}},$$

where p is the number of levels of treatment A and h is the number of cell means. In order for the null hypothesis $\mathbf{C}_A'\boldsymbol{\mu} = \mathbf{0}$ to be testable, the $\mathbf{C}_A'$ matrix must be of full row rank. This means that each row of $\mathbf{C}_A'$ must be linearly independent of every other row. The maximum number of such rows is $p - 1$, which is why it is necessary to express the null hypothesis as Equation 1.1 or 1.2. An estimator of the null hypothesis, $\mathbf{C}_A'\boldsymbol{\mu} - \mathbf{0}$, is incorporated in the formula for computing a sum of squares. For example, the estimator appears as $\mathbf{C}_A'\hat{\boldsymbol{\mu}} - \mathbf{0}$ in the formula for the treatment A sum of squares

$$SSA = (\mathbf{C}_A'\hat{\boldsymbol{\mu}} - \mathbf{0})'[\mathbf{C}_A'(\mathbf{X}'\mathbf{X})^{-1}\mathbf{C}_A]^{-1}(\mathbf{C}_A'\hat{\boldsymbol{\mu}} - \mathbf{0}), \tag{1.3}$$

where $\hat{\boldsymbol{\mu}}$ is a vector of sample cell means. Equation 1.3 simplifies to

$$SSA = (\mathbf{C}_A'\hat{\boldsymbol{\mu}})'[\mathbf{C}_A'(\mathbf{X}'\mathbf{X})^{-1}\mathbf{C}_A]^{-1}(\mathbf{C}_A'\hat{\boldsymbol{\mu}})$$

because $\mathbf{0}$ is a vector of zeros. In the formula, $\mathbf{C}_A'$ is a coefficient matrix that defines the null hypothesis, $\hat{\boldsymbol{\mu}} = [(\mathbf{X}'\mathbf{X})^{-1}(\mathbf{X}'\mathbf{y})] = [\overline{Y}_{.11}, \overline{Y}_{.12} \cdots \overline{Y}_{.23}]'$, and $\mathbf{X}$ is a structural matrix. The structural matrix for the weight-loss

TABLE 1.7   Data Vector, y, and X Matrix for the Cell Means Model

	y 29×1	$\mathbf{x}_1$	$\mathbf{x}_2$	$\mathbf{x}_3$	$\mathbf{x}_4$	$\mathbf{x}_5$	$\mathbf{x}_6$
a_1b_1	7 ⋮ 1	1 ⋮ 1	0 ⋮ 0	0 ⋮ 0	0 ⋮ 0	0 ⋮ 0	0 ⋮ 0
a_1b_2	7 ⋮ 9	0 ⋮ 0	1 ⋮ 1	0 ⋮ 0	0 ⋮ 0	0 ⋮ 0	0 ⋮ 0
a_2b_1	9 ⋮ 11	0 ⋮ 0	0 ⋮ 0	1 ⋮ 1	0 ⋮ 0	0 ⋮ 0	0 ⋮ 0
a_2b_2	10 ⋮ 13	0 ⋮ 0	0 ⋮ 0	0 ⋮ 0	1 ⋮ 1	0 ⋮ 0	0 ⋮ 0
a_3b_1	15 ⋮ 8	0 ⋮ 0	0 ⋮ 0	0 ⋮ 0	0 ⋮ 0	1 ⋮ 1	0 ⋮ 0
a_3b_2	13 ⋮ 12	0 ⋮ 0	0 ⋮ 0	0 ⋮ 0	0 ⋮ 0	0 ⋮ 0	1 ⋮ 1

experiment is given in Table 1.7. The structural matrix is coded as follows:

$$\mathbf{x}_1 = \begin{cases} 1, & \text{if an observation is in } a_1b_1 \\ 0, & \text{otherwise} \end{cases}$$

$$\mathbf{x}_2 = \begin{cases} 1, & \text{if an observation is in } a_1b_2 \\ 0, & \text{otherwise} \end{cases}$$

$$\mathbf{x}_3 = \begin{cases} 1, & \text{if an observation is in } a_2b_1 \\ 0, & \text{otherwise} \end{cases}$$

$$\vdots$$

$$\mathbf{x}_6 = \begin{cases} 1, & \text{if an observation is in } a_3b_2 \\ 0, & \text{otherwise} \end{cases}$$

For the weight-loss data, the sum of squares for treatment A is

$$SSA = (\mathbf{C}_A'\hat{\boldsymbol{\mu}})'[\mathbf{C}_A'(\mathbf{X}'\mathbf{X})^{-1}\mathbf{C}_A]^{-1}(\mathbf{C}_A'\hat{\boldsymbol{\mu}}) = 127.4038$$

with $p - 1 = 2$ degrees of freedom.

The null hypothesis for treatment B is

$$H_0: \mu_{.1} = \mu_{.2}.$$

An equivalent null hypothesis that is used with the cell means model is

$$H_0: \mu_{\cdot 1} - \mu_{\cdot 2} = 0.$$

In terms of cell means, this hypothesis is expressed as

$$H_0: \frac{\mu_{11} + \mu_{21} + \mu_{31}}{3} - \frac{\mu_{12} + \mu_{22} + \mu_{32}}{3} = 0.$$

In matrix notation, the null hypothesis is

$$H_0: \frac{1}{3} \underset{(q-1) \times h}{\mathbf{C}'_B} \begin{bmatrix} 1 & -1 & 1 & -1 & 1 & -1 \end{bmatrix} \underset{h \times 1}{\boldsymbol{\mu}} \begin{bmatrix} \mu_{11} \\ \mu_{12} \\ \mu_{21} \\ \mu_{22} \\ \mu_{31} \\ \mu_{32} \end{bmatrix} = \underset{(q-1) \times 1}{\mathbf{0}} [0],$$

where q is the number of levels of treatment B and h is the number of cell means. The sum of squares for treatment B is

$$SSB = (\mathbf{C}'_B \hat{\boldsymbol{\mu}})'[\mathbf{C}'_B(\mathbf{X}'\mathbf{X})^{-1}\mathbf{C}_B]^{-1}(\mathbf{C}'_B \hat{\boldsymbol{\mu}}) = 76.0500$$

with $q - 1 = 1$ degree of freedom.

The null hypothesis for the $A \times B$ interaction is

$$H_0: \mu_{jk} - \mu_{jk'} - \mu_{j'k} + \mu_{j'k'} = 0 \text{ for all } j \text{ and } k.$$

For the weight-loss data, the interaction null hypothesis is

$$H_0: \mu_{11} - \mu_{12} - \mu_{21} + \mu_{22} = 0$$
$$\mu_{21} - \mu_{22} - \mu_{31} + \mu_{32} = 0$$

The two rows of the null hypothesis correspond to the two sets of means connected by crossed lines in Figure 1.9. In matrix notation, the null hypothesis is

$$H_0: \underset{(p-1)(q-1) \times h}{\mathbf{C}'_{A \times B}} \begin{bmatrix} 1 & -1 & -1 & 1 & 0 & 0 \\ 0 & 0 & 1 & -1 & -1 & 1 \end{bmatrix} \underset{h \times 1}{\boldsymbol{\mu}} \begin{bmatrix} \mu_{11} \\ \mu_{12} \\ \mu_{21} \\ \mu_{22} \\ \mu_{31} \\ \mu_{32} \end{bmatrix} = \underset{(p-1)(q-1) \times 1}{\mathbf{0}} \begin{bmatrix} 0 \\ 0 \end{bmatrix}.$$

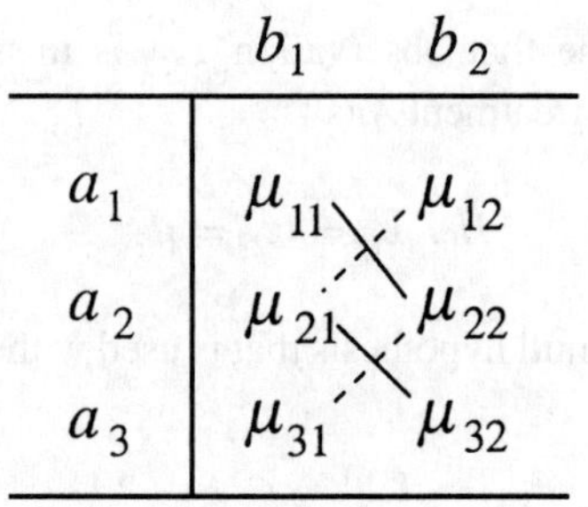

Figure 1.9   Two interaction terms of the form $\mu_{jk} - \mu_{jk'} - \mu_{j'k} + \mu_{j'k'}$ are obtained from the crossed lines by subtracting the two μ_{ij}s connected by a dashed line from the two μ_{ij}s connected by a solid line.

The sum of squares for the $A \times B$ interaction is

$$SSA \times B = (\mathbf{C}'_{A \times B} \hat{\boldsymbol{\mu}})'[\mathbf{C}'_{A \times B}(\mathbf{X}'\mathbf{X})^{-1}\mathbf{C}_{A \times B}]^{-1}(\mathbf{C}'_{A \times B} \hat{\boldsymbol{\mu}})$$
$$= 27.7885$$

with $(p - 1)(q - 1) = 2$ degrees of freedom.

The within-cell sum of squares is

$$SSWCELL = \mathbf{y}'\mathbf{y} - \hat{\boldsymbol{\mu}}'(\mathbf{X}'\mathbf{y}) = 360.7500,$$

where $\mathbf{y}'$ is the vector of weight-loss observations: $[7 \; 13 \; 9 \ldots 12]$. The within-cell sum of squares has $N - h = 29 - 6 = 23$ degrees of freedom.

The total sum of squares is

$$SSTO = \mathbf{y}'\mathbf{y} - \mathbf{y}'\mathbf{J}\mathbf{y}N^{-1} = 595.7931,$$

where $\mathbf{J}$ is a 29×29 matrix of ones and $N = 29$, the number of weight-loss observations. The total sum of squares has $N - 1 = 28$ degrees of freedom.

The analysis of the weight-loss data is summarized in Table 1.8. The F statistics in Table 1.8 are identical to those in Table 1.6, where the regression model was used.

The cell means model is extremely versatile. It can be used when observations are missing and when entire cells are missing. It allows a researcher to test hypotheses about any linear combination of population cell means. It has an important advantage over the regression model. With the cell means model, there is never any ambiguity about the hypothesis that is tested because an estimator of the null hypothesis, $\mathbf{C}'\hat{\boldsymbol{\mu}} - \mathbf{0}$, appears in the formula for a sum of squares. Lack of space prevents a discussion of the many other advantages of the model; the reader is referred to Kirk (1995, pp. 289–301, 413–431). However, before leaving the subject, the model will be used to test a null hypothesis for weighted means.

Occasionally, researchers collect data in which the sample sizes are proportional to the population sizes. This might

TABLE 1.8 Analysis of Variance for the Weight-Loss Data (Observation Y_{322} is missing)

Source	SS	df	MS	F	p
Treatment A (Diet)	127.4038	$p - 1 = 2$	63.7019	4.06	.031
Treatment B (Exercise)	76.0500	$q - 1 = 1$	76.0500	4.85	.038
$A \times B$	27.7885	$(p - 1)(q - 1) = 2$	13.8943	0.89	.426
Within cell	360.7500	$N - h = 23$	15.6848		
Total	595.7931	$N - 1 = 28$			

occur, for example, in survey research. When cell ns are unequal, a researcher has a choice between computing unweighted means or weighted means. *Unweighted means* are simple averages of cell means. These are the means that were used in the previous analyses. *Weighted means* are weighted averages of cell means in which the weights are the sample cell sizes, n_{jk}. Consider again the weight-loss data in which observation Y_{322} is missing. Unweighted and weighted sample means for treatment level a_2 where observation Y_{322} is missing are, respectively,

$$\hat{\mu}_{2.} = \frac{\hat{\mu}_{21} + \hat{\mu}_{22}}{q} = \frac{9.00 + 10.75}{2} = 9.88$$

$$\hat{\bar{\mu}}_{2.} = \frac{n_{21}\hat{\mu}_{21} + n_{22}\hat{\mu}_{22}}{n_{j.}} = \frac{5(9.00) + 4(10.75)}{9} = 9.78;$$

$n_{j.}$ is the number of observations in the jth level of treatment A. The null hypothesis using weighted cell means for treatment A is

$$H_0: \frac{n_{11}\mu_{11} + n_{12}\mu_{12}}{n_{1.}} - \frac{n_{21}\mu_{21} + n_{22}\mu_{22}}{n_{2.}} = 0$$

$$\frac{n_{21}\mu_{21} + n_{22}\mu_{22}}{n_{2.}} - \frac{n_{31}\mu_{31} + n_{32}\mu_{32}}{n_{3.}} = 0.$$

The coefficient matrix for computing SSA is

$$\mathbf{C}_A' = \begin{bmatrix} \frac{5}{10} & \frac{5}{10} & -\frac{5}{9} & -\frac{4}{9} & 0 & 0 \\ 0 & 0 & \frac{5}{9} & \frac{4}{9} & -\frac{5}{10} & -\frac{5}{10} \end{bmatrix},$$

where the entries in $\mathbf{C}_A'$ are $\pm n_{jk}/n_{j.}$ and zero. The sum of squares and mean square for treatment A are, respectively,

$$SSA = (\mathbf{C}_A'\hat{\boldsymbol{\mu}})'[\mathbf{C}_A'(\mathbf{X}'\mathbf{X})^{-1}\mathbf{C}_A]^{-1}(\mathbf{C}_A'\hat{\boldsymbol{\mu}}) = 128.2375$$

$$MSA = SSA/(p - 1) = 146.3556/(3 - 1) = 64.1188.$$

The F statistic and p value for treatment A are

$$F = \frac{MSA}{MSWCELL} = \frac{64.1188}{15.6848} = 4.09 \quad p = .030,$$

where *MSWCELL* is obtained from Table 1.8. The null hypothesis is rejected. This is another example of the versatility of the cell means model. A researcher can test hypotheses about any linear combination of population cell means.

In most research situations, sample sizes are not proportional to population sizes. Unless a researcher has a compelling reason to weight the sample means proportional to the sample sizes, unweighted means should be used.

Randomized Block Factorial Design

Next I describe a factorial design that is constructed from two randomized block designs. The design is called a *randomized block factorial design* and is denoted by RBF-pq. The RBF-pq design is obtained by combining the levels of an RB-p design with those of an RB-q design so that each level of the RB-p design appears once with each level of the RB-q design and vice versa. The design uses the blocking technique described in connection with an RB-p design to isolate variation attributable to a nuisance variable while simultaneously evaluating two or more treatments and associated interactions.

In discussing the weight-loss experiment, I hypothesized that ease of losing weight is related to the amount by which a girl is overweight. If the hypothesis is correct, a researcher can improve on the CRF-32 design by isolating this nuisance variable. Suppose that instead of randomly assigning 30 girls to the six treatment combinations in the diet experiment, the researcher formed blocks of six girls such that the girls in a block are overweight by about the same amount. One way to form the blocks is to rank the girls from the least to the most overweight. The six least overweight girls are assigned to block 1. The next six girls are assigned to block 2 and so on. In this example, five blocks of dependent samples can be formed from the 30 participants. Once the girls have been assigned to the blocks, the girls in each block are randomly assigned to the six treatment combinations. The layout for this experiment is shown in Figure 1.10.

The classical model equation for the experiment is

$$Y_{ijk} = \mu + \pi_i + \alpha_j + \beta_k + (\alpha\beta)_{jk} + (\alpha\beta\pi)_{jki}$$
$$(i = 1, \ldots, n; j = 1, \ldots, p; k = 1, \ldots, q),$$

	Treatment Combination	Treatment Combination	Treatment Combination	Treatment Combination	Treatment Combination	Treatment Combination	
Block$_1$	a_1b_1	a_1b_2	a_2b_1	a_2b_2	a_3b_1	a_3b_2	$\overline{Y}_{1..}$
Block$_2$	a_1b_1	a_1b_2	a_2b_1	a_2b_2	a_3b_1	a_3b_2	$\overline{Y}_{2..}$
Block$_3$	a_1b_1	a_1b_2	a_2b_1	a_2b_2	a_3b_1	a_3b_2	$\overline{Y}_{3..}$
Block$_4$	a_1b_1	a_1b_2	a_2b_1	a_2b_2	a_3b_1	a_3b_2	$\overline{Y}_{4..}$
Block$_5$	a_1b_1	a_1b_2	a_2b_1	a_2b_2	a_3b_1	a_3b_2	$\overline{Y}_{5..}$
	$\overline{Y}_{.11}$	$\overline{Y}_{.12}$	$\overline{Y}_{.21}$	$\overline{Y}_{.22}$	$\overline{Y}_{.31}$	$\overline{Y}_{.32}$	

Figure 1.10   Layout for a two-treatment randomized block factorial design (RBF-32 design). Each block contains six girls who are overweight by about the same amount. The girls in a block are randomly assigned to the six treatment combinations.

where

Y_{ijk} is the weight loss for the participant in Block$_i$ and treatment combination a_jb_k.

μ is the grand mean of the six weight-loss population means.

π_i is the block effect for population i and is equal to $\mu_{i..} - \mu$. It reflects the effect of the nuisance variable in Block$_i$.

α_j is the treatment effect for population a_j and is equal to $\mu_{.j.} - \mu$. It reflects the effect of diet a_j.

β_k is the treatment effect for population b_k and is equal to $\mu_{..k} - \mu$. It reflects the effects of exercise condition b_k.

$(\alpha\beta)_{jk}$ is the interaction effect for populations a_j and b_k and is equal to $\mu_{.jk} - \mu_{.j.} - \mu_{..k} - \mu$.

$(\alpha\beta\pi)_{jki}$ is the residual error effect for treatment combination a_jb_k and Block$_i$.

The design enables a researcher to test four null hypotheses:

H_0: $\mu_{1..} = \mu_{2..} = \cdots = \mu_{5..}$
(Block population means are equal.)

H_0: $\mu_{.1.} = \mu_{.2.} = \mu_{.3.}$
(Treatment A population means are equal.)

H_0: $\mu_{..1} = \mu_{..2}$
(Treatment B population means are equal.)

H_0: $\mu_{.jk} - \mu_{.jk'} - \mu_{.j'k} + \mu_{.j'k'} = 0$ for all j and k
(All $A \times B$ interaction effects equal zero.)

The hypothesis that the block population means are equal is of little interest because the blocks represent different amounts by which the girls are overweight.

The data for the RBF-32 design are shown in Table 1.9. The same data were analyzed earlier using a CRF-32 design. Each block in Table 1.9 contains six girls who at the beginning of the experiment were overweight by about the same amount. The ANOVA for these data is given in Table 1.10. A comparison of Table 1.10 with Table 1.4 reveals that the RBF-32 design is more powerful than the CRF-32 design. Consider, for example, treatment A. The F statistic for the randomized block factorial design is $F(2, 20) = 8.09$, $p = .003$; the F for the completely randomized factorial design is $F(2, 24) = 4.25$, $p = .026$. The randomized block factorial design is more powerful because the nuisance variable—the amount by which participants are overweight— has been removed from the residual error variance. A schematic partition of the total sum of squares and degrees of freedom for the two designs is shown in Figure 1.11. It is apparent from Figure 1.11 that the *SSRESIDUAL* will always be smaller than the *SSWCELL* if

TABLE 1.9   **Weight-Loss Data for the Diet (a_j) and Exercise Conditions (b_k)**

	a_1b_1	a_1b_2	a_2b_1	a_2b_2	a_3b_1	a_3b_2
Block$_1$	5	4	7	5	8	13
Block$_2$	7	7	4	7	5	16
Block$_3$	1	14	9	13	10	12
Block$_4$	9	9	11	15	12	20
Block$_5$	13	11	14	10	15	19

TABLE 1.10   **Analysis of Variance for the Weight-Loss Data**

Source	SS	df	MS	F	p
Blocks	209.3333	4	52.3333	6.43	.002
Treatments	234.1667	5			
Treatment A (Diet)	131.6667	2	65.8334	8.09	.003
Treatment B (Exercise)	67.5000	1	67.5000	8.30	.009
$A \times B$	35.0000	2	17.5000	2.15	.142
Residual	162.6667	20	8.1333		
Total	606.1667	29			

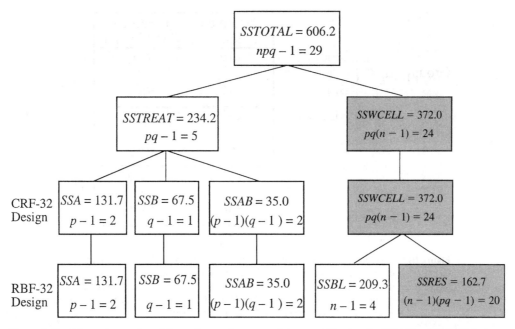

Figure 1.11 Schematic partition of the total sum of squares and degrees of freedom for CRF-32 and RBF-32 designs. The shaded rectangles indicate the sums of squares that are used to compute the error variance for each design: $MSWCELL = SSWCELL/pq(n-1)$ and $MSRES = SSRES/(n-1)(pq-1)$. If the nuisance variable ($SSBL$) in the RBF-32 design accounts for an appreciable portion of the total sum of squares, the design will have a smaller error variance and, hence, greater power than the CRF-32 design.

the *SSBLOCKS* is greater than zero. The larger the *SSBLOCKS* in a randomized block factorial design are, the greater the reduction in the *SSRESIDUAL*.

FACTORIAL DESIGNS WITH CONFOUNDING

Split-Plot Factorial Design

As we have just seen, an important advantage of a randomized block factorial design relative to a completely randomized factorial design is greater power. However, if either p or q in a two-treatment randomized block factorial design is moderately large, the number of treatment combinations in each block can be prohibitively large. For example, an RBF-45 design has blocks of size $4 \times 5 = 20$. Obtaining blocks with 20 matched participants or observing each participant 20 times is generally not feasible. In the late 1920s Ronald A. Fisher and Frank Yates addressed the problem of prohibitively large block sizes by developing confounding schemes in which only a portion of the treatment combinations in an experiment are assigned to each block. Their work was extended in the 1940s by David J. Finney (1945, 1946) and Oscar Kempthorne (1947). One design that achieves a reduction in block size is the two-treatment split-plot factorial design. The term *split-plot* comes from agricultural experimentation in which the levels of, say, treatment A are applied to relatively large plots of land—the whole plots. The whole plots are then split or subdivided, and the levels of treatment B are applied to the subplots within each whole plot.

A two-treatment split-plot factorial design is constructed by combining two building block designs: a completely randomized design having p levels of treatment A and a randomized block design having q levels of treatment B. The assignment of participants to the treatment combinations is carried out in two stages. Consider the weight-loss experiment again. Suppose that we ranked the 30 participants from least to most overweight. The participants ranked 1 and 2 are assigned to block 1, those ranked 3 and 4 are assigned to block 2, and so on. This procedure produces 15 blocks each containing two girls who are similar with respect to being overweight. In the first stage of randomization the 15 blocks of girls are randomly assigned to the three levels of treatment A with five blocks in each level. In the second stage of randomization the two girls in each block are randomly assigned to the two levels of treatment B. An exception to this randomization procedure must be made when treatment B is a temporal variable such as successive learning trials or periods of time. Trial 2, for example, cannot occur before Trial 1.

The layout for a split-plot factorial design with three levels of treatment A and two levels of treatment B is

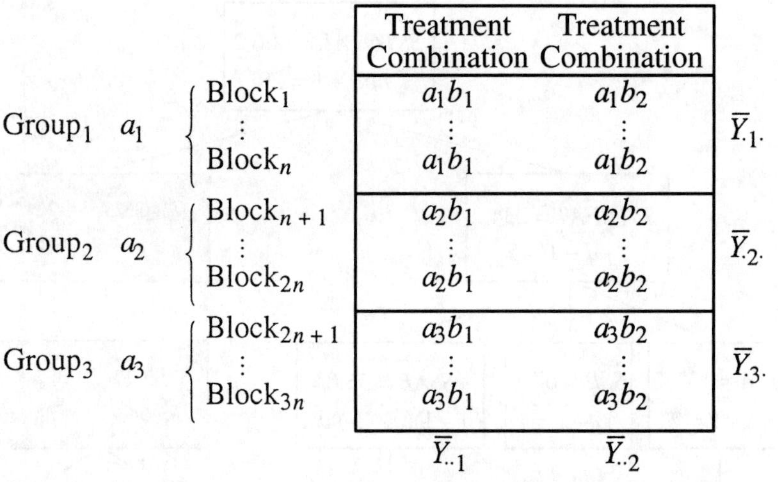

Figure 1.12 Layout for a two-treatment split-plot factorial design (SPF-3·2 design). The $3n$ blocks are randomly assigned to the $p = 3$ levels of treatment A with the restriction that n blocks are assigned to each level of A. The n blocks assigned to each level of treatment A constitute a group of blocks. In the second stage of randomization, the two matched participants in a block are randomly assigned to the $q = 2$ levels of treatment B.

shown in Figure 1.12. Treatment A is called a *between-blocks treatment;* B is a *within-blocks treatment.* The designation for a two-treatment split-plot factorial design is SPF-$p·q$. The p preceding the dot denotes the number of levels of the between-blocks treatment; the q after the dot denotes the number of levels of the within-blocks treatment. Hence, the design in Figure 1.12 is an SPF-3·2 design.

An RBF-32 design contains $3 \times 2 = 6$ treatment combinations and has blocks of size six. The SPF-3·2 design in Figure 1.12 contains the same six treatment combinations, but the block size is only two. The advantage of the split-plot factorial—smaller block size—is achieved by confounding groups of blocks with treatment A. Consider the sample means $\overline{Y}_{.1.}$, $\overline{Y}_{.2.}$, and $\overline{Y}_{.3.}$ in Figure 1.12. The differences among the means reflect the differences among the three groups as well as the differences among the three levels of treatment A. To put it another way, we cannot tell how much of the differences among the three sample means is attributable to the differences among Group$_1$, Group$_2$, and Group$_3$ and how much is attributable to the differences among treatments levels a_1, a_2, and a_3. For this reason, the three groups and treatment A are said to be *completely confounded.*

The use of confounding to reduce the block size in an SPF-$p·q$ design involves a tradeoff that needs to be made explicit. The RBF-32 design uses the same error variance, *MSRESIDUAL*, to test hypotheses for treatments A and B and the $A \times B$ interaction. The two-treatment split-plot factorial design, however, uses two error variances. *MSBLOCKS* within A, denoted by *MSBL(A)*, is used to test

treatment A; a different and usually much smaller error variance, *MSRESIDUAL*, is used to test treatment B and the $A \times B$ interaction. As a result, the power of the tests for B and the $A \times B$ interaction is greater than that for A. Hence, a split-plot factorial design is a good design choice if a researcher is more interested in treatment B and the $A \times B$ interaction than in treatment A. When both treatments and the $A \times B$ interaction are of equal interest, a randomized block factorial design is a better choice if the larger block size is acceptable. If a large block size is not acceptable and the researcher is primarily interested in treatments A and B, an alternative design choice is the confounded factorial design. This design, which is described later, achieves a reduction in block size by confounding groups of blocks with the $A \times B$ interaction. As a result, tests of treatments A and B are more powerful than the test of the $A \times B$ interaction.

Earlier, an RBF-32 design was used for the weight-loss experiment because the researcher was interested in tests of treatments A and B and the $A \times B$ interaction. For purposes of comparison, I analyze the same weight-loss data as if an SPF-3·2 design had been used even though, as we will see, this is not a good design choice. But first I describe the classical model equation for a two-treatment split-plot factorial design.

The classical model equation for the weight-loss experiment is

$$Y_{ijk} = \mu + \alpha_j + \pi_{i(j)} + \beta_k + (\alpha\beta)_{jk} + (\beta\pi)_{ki(j)}$$
$$(i = 1, \ldots, n; j = 1, \ldots, p; k = 1, \ldots, q),$$

where

Y_{ijk} is the weight loss for the participant in $\text{Block}_{i(j)}$ and treatment combination $a_j b_k$.

μ is the grand mean of the six weight-loss population means.

α_j is the treatment effect for population a_j and is equal to $\mu_{\cdot j \cdot} - \mu$. It reflects the effect of diet a_j.

$\pi_{i(j)}$ is the block effect for population i and is equal to $\mu_{ij\cdot} - \mu_{\cdot j\cdot}$. The block effect is nested within a_j.

β_k is the treatment effect for population b_k and is equal to $\mu_{\cdot\cdot k} - \mu$. It reflects the effects of exercise condition b_k.

$(\alpha\beta)_{jk}$ is the interaction effect for populations a_j and b_k and is equal to $\mu_{\cdot jk} - \mu_{\cdot j\cdot} - \mu_{\cdot\cdot k} + \mu$.

$(\beta\pi)_{ki(j)}$ is the residual error effect for treatment level b_k and $\text{Block}_{i(j)}$ and is equal to $Y_{ijk} - \mu - \alpha_j - \pi_{i(j)} - \beta_k - (\alpha\beta)_{jk}$.

The design enables a researcher to test three null hypotheses:

H_0: $\mu_{\cdot 1\cdot} = \mu_{\cdot 2\cdot} = \mu_{\cdot 3\cdot}$

(Treatment A population means are equal.)

H_0: $\mu_{\cdot\cdot 1} = \mu_{\cdot\cdot 2}$

(Treatment B population means are equal.)

H_0: $\mu_{\cdot jk} - \mu_{\cdot jk'} - \mu_{\cdot j'k} + \mu_{\cdot j'k'} = 0$ for all j and k

(All $A \times B$ interaction effects equal zero.)

The weight-loss data from Tables 1.2 and 1.9 are recasts in the form of an SPF-3·2 design in Table 1.11. The ANOVA for these data is given in Table 1.12. The null hypothesis for treatment B can be rejected. However, the null hypothesis for treatment A and the $A \times B$ interaction cannot be rejected. The denominator of the F statistic for treatment A [$MSBL(A) = 20.1667$] is almost twice as large as the denominator for the tests of B and $A \times B$ ($MSRES = 10.8333$). A feeling for the relative power of the test of treatment A for the SPF-3·2, CRF-32, and RBF-32 designs can be obtained by comparing their F statistics and p values:

Treatment A			
SPF-3·2 design	$F = \dfrac{131.6667/2}{242.0000/12} = \dfrac{65.8334}{20.1667} = 3.26$		$p = .074$
CRF-32 design	$F = \dfrac{131.6667/2}{372.0000/24} = \dfrac{65.8334}{15.5000} = 4.25$		$p = .026$
RBF-32 design	$F = \dfrac{131.6667/2}{162.6667/20} = \dfrac{65.8334}{8.1333} = 8.09$		$p = .003$

For testing treatment A, the SPF-3·2 design is the least powerful. Clearly, if one's primary interest is in the

TABLE 1.11 Weight-Loss Data for the Diet (a_j) and Exercise Conditions (b_k)

		Treatment Level b_1	Treatment Level b_2
Group$_1$ a_1	Block$_1$	5	4
	Block$_2$	7	7
	Block$_3$	1	14
	Block$_4$	9	9
	Block$_5$	13	11
Group$_2$ a_2	Block$_6$	7	5
	Block$_7$	4	7
	Block$_8$	9	13
	Block$_9$	11	15
	Block$_{10}$	14	10
Group$_3$ a_3	Block$_{11}$	8	13
	Block$_{12}$	5	16
	Block$_{13}$	10	12
	Block$_{14}$	12	20
	Block$_{15}$	15	19

effectiveness of the three diets, the SPF-3·2 design is a poor choice. However, the SPF-3·2 design fares somewhat better if one's primary interests are in treatment B and the $A \times B$ interaction:

Treatment B			
SPF-3·2 design	$F = \dfrac{67.5000/1}{130.0000/12} = \dfrac{67.5000}{10.8333} = 6.23$		$p = .028$
CRF-32 design	$F = \dfrac{67.5000/1}{372.0000/24} = \dfrac{67.5000}{15.5000} = 4.35$		$p = .048$
RBF-32 design	$F = \dfrac{67.5000/1}{162.6667/20} = \dfrac{67.5000}{8.1333} = 8.30$		$p = .009$

$A \times B$ interaction			
SPF-3·2 design	$F = \dfrac{35.0000/2}{130.0000/12} = \dfrac{17.5000}{10.8333} = 1.62$		$p = .239$
CRF-32 design	$F = \dfrac{35.0000/2}{372.0000/24} = \dfrac{17.5000}{15.5000} = 1.13$		$p = .340$
RBF-32 design	$F = \dfrac{35.0000/2}{162.6667/20} = \dfrac{17.5000}{8.1333} = 2.15$		$p = .142$

TABLE 1.12 Analysis of Variance for the Weight-Loss Data

Source	SS	df	MS	F	p
1. Between blocks	373.6667	14			
2. Treatment A (Diet)	131.6667	2	65.8334	[2/3]^a 3.26	.074
3. Blocks within A	242.0000	12	20.1667		
4. Within blocks	232.5000	15			
5. Treatment B (Exercise)	67.5000	1	67.5000	[5/7] 6.23	.028
6. $A \times B$	35.0000	2	17.5000	[6/7] 1.62	.239
7. Residual	130.0000	12	10.8333		
8. Total	606.1667	29			

^{a}The fraction [2/3] indicates that the F statistic was obtained by dividing the mean square in row two by the mean square in row three.

The SPF-3·2 design is the first design I have described that involves two different building block designs: a CR-p design and an RB-q design. Also, it is the first design that has two error variances: one for testing the between-blocks effects and another for testing the within-blocks effects. A weighted average of the two error variances is equal to *MSWCELL* in a CRF-pq design, where the weights are the degrees of freedom of the two error variances. This can be shown using the mean squares from Tables 1.4 and 1.12:

$$\frac{p(n-1)MSBL(A) + p(n-1)(q-1)MSRESIDUAL}{p(n-1) + p(n-1)(q-1)}$$

$$= MSWCELL$$

$$\frac{3(5-1)20.1667 + 3(5-1)(2-1)10.8333}{3(5-1) + 3(5-1)(2-1)} = 15.5000$$

A schematic partition of the total sum of squares and degrees of freedom for the CRF-32 and SPF-3·2 designs is shown in Figure 1.13.

Confounded Factorial Designs

As we have seen, an SPF-p·q design is not the best design choice if a researcher's primary interest is in testing treatments A and B. The RBF-pq design is a better choice if blocks of size $p \times q$ are acceptable. If this block size is too large, an alternative choice is a two-treatment confounded factorial design. This design confounds an interaction with groups of blocks. As a result, the test of the interaction is less powerful than tests of treatments A and B. Confounded factorial designs are constructed from either a randomized block design or a Latin square design. The designs are denoted by, respectively, RBCF-p^k and LSCF-p^k, where RB and LS identify the building block design, C indicates that the interaction is completely confounded with groups of blocks, F indicates a factorial design, and p^k indicates that the design has k treatments each having p levels. The simplest randomized block confounded factorial design has two treatments with two levels each. Consider the RBCF-2^2 design in Figure 1.14. The $A \times B$ interaction is completely confounded with Group$_1$ and Group$_2$, as I will now show. An interaction effect for treatments A and B has the general form $\mu_{jk} - \mu_{jk'} - \mu_{j'k} + \mu_{j'k'}$. Let μ_{ijkz} denote the population mean for the ith block, jth level of A, kth level of B, and zth group. For the design in Figure 1.14, the $A \times B$ interaction effect is

$$\mu_{.111} - \mu_{.122} - \mu_{.212} + \mu_{.221}$$

or

$$(\mu_{.111} + \mu_{.221}) - (\mu_{.122} + \mu_{.212}).$$

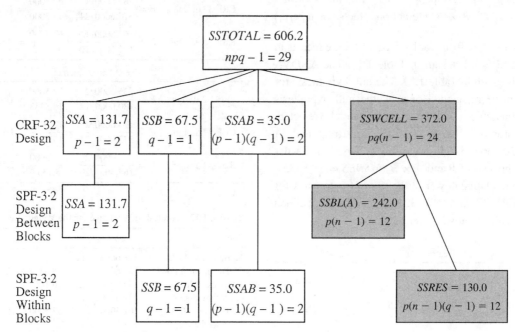

Figure 1.13   Schematic partition of the total sum of squares and degrees of freedom for CRF-32 and SPF-3·2 designs. The shaded rectangles indicate the sums of squares that are used to compute the error variance for each design. The SPF-3·2 design has two error variances: $MSBL(A) = SSBL(A)/p(n-1)$ is used to test treatment A; $MSRES = SSRES/p(n-1)(q-1)$ is used to test treatment B and the $A \times B$ interaction. The within-blocks error variance, $MSRES$, is usually much smaller than the between-blocks error variance, $MSBL(A)$. As a result, tests of treatment B and the $A \times B$ interaction are more powerful than the test of treatment A.

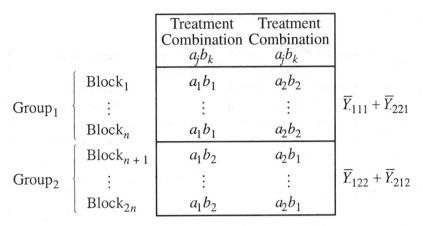

Figure 1.14 Layout for a two-treatment randomized block confounded factorial design (RBCF-2^2 design). A score in the ith block, jth level of treatment A, kth level of treatment B, and zth group is denoted by Y_{ijkz}.

The difference between the effects of Group$_1$ and Group$_2$,

$$(\mu_{.111} - \mu_{.221}) - (\mu_{.122} + \mu_{.212}),$$

involves the same contrast among means as the $A \times B$ interaction effect. Hence, the two sets of effects are completely confounded because we cannot determine how much of the difference $(\mu_{.111} + \mu_{.221}) - (\mu_{.122} + \mu_{.212})$ is attributable to the $A \times B$ interaction and how much is attributable to the difference between Group$_1$ and Group$_2$.

The RBCF-p^k design, like the SPF-$p \cdot q$ design, has two error variances: one for testing the between-blocks effects and a different and usually much smaller error variance for testing the within-blocks effects. In the RBCF-p^k design, treatments A and B are within-block treatments and are evaluated with greater power than the $A \times B$ interaction that is a between-block component. Researchers need to understand the tradeoff that is required when a treatment or interaction is confounded with groups to reduce the size of blocks. The power of the test of the confounded effects is generally less than the power of tests of the unconfounded effects. Hence, if possible, researchers should avoid confounding effects that are the major focus of an experiment. Sometimes, however, confounding is necessary to obtain a reasonable block size. If the power of the confounded effects is not acceptable, the power always can be increased by using a larger number of blocks.

One of the characteristics of the designs that have been described so far is that all of the treatment combinations appear in the experiment. The fractional factorial design that is described next does not share this characteristic. As the name suggests, a fractional factorial design includes only a fraction of the treatment combinations of a complete factorial design.

Fractional Factorial Designs

Two kinds of confounding have been described thus far: group-treatment confounding in an SPF-$p \cdot q$ design and group-interaction confounding in an RBCF-p^k design. A third form of confounding, treatment-interaction confounding, is used in a fractional factorial design. This kind of confounding reduces the number of treatment combinations that must be included in a multitreatment experiment to some fraction— $\frac{1}{2}, \frac{1}{3}, \frac{1}{4}, \frac{1}{8}, \frac{1}{9}$, and so on—of the total number of treatment combinations. A CRF-22222 design has 32 treatment combinations. By using a $\frac{1}{2}$ or $\frac{1}{4}$ fractional factorial design, the number of treatment combinations that must be included in the experiment can be reduced to, respectively, $\frac{1}{2}(32) = 16$ or $\frac{1}{4}(32) = 8$.

The theory of fractional factorial designs was developed for 2^k and 3^k designs by Finney (1945, 1946) and extended by Kempthorne (1947) to designs of the type p^k, where p is a prime number that denotes the number of levels of each treatment and k denotes the number of treatments. Fractional factorial designs are most useful for pilot experiments and exploratory research situations that permit follow-up experiments to be performed. Thus, a large number of treatments, typically six or more, can be investigated efficiently in an initial experiment, with subsequent experiments designed to focus on the most promising independent variables.

Fractional factorial designs have much in common with confounded factorial designs. The latter designs achieve a reduction in the number of treatment combinations that must be included in a block. Fractional factorial designs achieve a reduction in the number of treatment combinations in the experiment. The reduction in the size of an experiment comes at a price, however. Considerable ambiguity may exist in interpreting the results of an experiment when the design includes only one half or one third of the treatment combinations. Ambiguity occurs because two or more names can be given to each sum of squares. For example, a sum of squares might be attributed to the effects of treatment A and the $BCDE$ interaction. The two or more names given to the same sum of squares are called *aliases*. In a one-half fractional factorial design, all sums of squares have two aliases. In a one-third fractional factorial design, all sums of squares have three aliases, and so on. Treatments are customarily aliased with higher-order interactions that are assumed to equal zero. This helps to minimize but does not eliminate ambiguity in interpreting the outcome of an experiment.

Fractional factorial designs are constructed from completely randomized, randomized block, and Latin square designs and denoted by, respectively, CRFF-p^{k-1}, RBFF-p^{k-1}, and LSFF-p^k. Let's examine the designation CRFF-2^{5-1}. The letters CR indicate that the building block design is a completely randomized design; FF indicates that it is a fractional factorial design; and 2^5 indicates that each of the five treatments has two levels. The -1 in 2^{5-1} indicates that the design is a one-half fraction of a complete 2^5 factorial design. This follows because the designation for a one-half fraction of a 2^5 factorial design can be written as $\frac{1}{2}2^5 = 2^{-1}2^5 = 2^{5-1}$. A one-fourth fraction of a 2^5 factorial design is denoted by CRFF-p^{5-2} because $\frac{1}{4}2^5 = \frac{1}{2^2}2^5 = 2^{-2}2^5 = 2^{5-2}$.

To conserve space, I describe a small CRFF-2^{3-1} design. A fractional factorial design with only three treatments is unrealistic, but the small size simplifies the presentation. The layout for the design is shown in Figure 1.15. On close inspection of Figure 1.15, it is apparent that the CRFF-2^{3-1} design contains the four treatment combinations of a CRF-22 design. For example, if we ignore treatment C, the design in Figure 1.15 has the following combinations of treatments A and B: a_1b_1, a_1b_2, a_2b_1, and a_2b_2. The correspondence between the treatment combinations of the CRF-22 and CRFF-2^{3-1} designs suggests a way to compute sums of squares for the latter design—ignore treatment C and analyze the data as if they came from a CRF-22 design.

Earlier, I observed that all sums of squares in a one-half fractional factorial design have two aliases. It can be shown (see Kirk, 1995, pp. 667–670) that the alias pattern for the design in Figure 1.15 is as follows:

Alias (Name)	Alias (Alternative name)
A	$B \times C$
B	$A \times C$
$A \times B$	C

The labels—treatment A and the $B \times C$ interaction—are two names for the same source of variation. Similarly, B and the

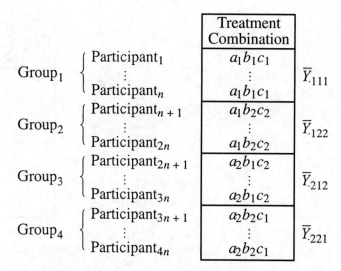

Figure 1.15 Layout for a three-treatment completely randomized fractional factorial design (CRFF-2^{3-1} design). A score for the ith participant in treatment combination $a_jb_kc_l$ is denoted by Y_{ijkl}. The $4n$ participants are randomly assigned to the treatment combinations with the restriction that n participants are assigned to each combination. The mean for the participants in the four groups is denoted by $\overline{Y}_{\cdot 111}$, $\overline{Y}_{\cdot 122}$, $\overline{Y}_{\cdot 212}$, and $\overline{Y}_{\cdot 221}$.

$A \times C$ interaction are two names for another source of variation, as are $A \times B$ and C. Hence, the F statistics

$$F = \frac{MSA}{MSWCELL} \quad \text{and} \quad F = \frac{MSB \times C}{MSWCELL}$$

test the same sources of variation. If $F = MSA/MSWCELL$ is significant, a researcher does not know whether it is because treatment A is significant, the $B \times C$ interaction is significant, or both.

At this point you are probably wondering why anyone would use such a design—after all, experiments are supposed to help us resolve ambiguity, not create it. In defense of fractional factorial designs, recall that they are typically used in exploratory research situations where a researcher is interested in six or more treatments. In addition, it is customary to limit all treatments to either two or three levels, thereby increasing the likelihood that higher order interactions are small relative to treatments and lower order interactions. Under these conditions, if a source of variation labeled treatment A and its alias, the $BCDEF$ interaction, is significant, it is reasonable to assume that the significance is probably due to the treatment rather than the interaction.

Continuing the defense, a fractional factorial design can dramatically decrease the number of treatment combinations that must be run in an experiment. Consider a researcher who is interested in determining whether any of six treatments having two levels each is significant. An experiment with six treatments and two participants assigned to each treatment combination would have 64 combinations and require $2 \times 64 = 128$ participants. By using a one-fourth fractional factorial design, CRFF-2^{6-2} design, the researcher can reduce the number of treatment combinations in the experiment from 64 to 16 and the number of participants from 128 to 32. Suppose that the researcher ran the 16 treatment combinations and found that none of the F statistics in the fractional factorial design is significant. The researcher has answered the research questions with one fourth of the effort. On the other hand, suppose that F statistics for treatments C and E and associated aliases are significant. The researcher has eliminated four treatments (A, B, D, F), their aliases, and certain other interactions from further consideration. The researcher can then follow up with a small experiment to determine which aliases are responsible for the significant F statistics.

In summary, the main advantage of a fractional factorial design is that it enables a researcher to investigate efficiently a large number of treatments in an initial experiment, with subsequent experiments designed to focus on the most promising lines of investigation or to clarify the interpretation of the original analysis. Many researchers would consider ambiguity in interpreting the outcome of the initial experiment a small price to pay for the reduction in experimental effort.

The description of confounding in a fractional factorial design completes a cycle. I began the cycle by describing group-treatment confounding in a split-plot factorial design. I then described group-interaction confounding in a confounded factorial design, and, finally, treatment-interaction confounding in a fractional factorial design. The three forms of confounding achieve either a reduction in the size of a block or the size of an experiment. As we have seen, confounding always involves a tradeoff. The price we pay for reducing the size of a block or an experiment is lower power in testing a treatment or interaction or ambiguity in interpreting the outcome of an experiment. In the next section I describe hierarchical designs in which one or more treatments are nested.

HIERARCHICAL DESIGNS

All of the multitreatment designs that have been discussed so far have had crossed treatments. Treatments A and B are crossed, for example, if each level of treatment B appears once with each level of treatment A and vice versa. Treatment B is *nested* in treatment A if each level of treatment B appears with only one level of treatment A. The nesting of treatment B within treatment A is denoted by $B(A)$ and is read "B within

A." A *hierarchical design* has at least one nested treatment; the remaining treatments are either nested or crossed.

Hierarchical Designs With One or Two Nested Treatments

Hierarchical designs are constructed from completely randomized or randomized block designs. A two-treatment hierarchical design that is constructed from CR-p and CR-q designs is denoted by CRH-$pq(A)$, where $pq(A)$ indicates that the design has p levels of treatment A and q levels of treatment B that are nested in treatment A. A comparison of nested and crossed treatments for a CRH-24(A) design and a CRF 22 design is shown in Figure 1.16. Experiments with one or more nested treatments are well suited to research in education, industry, and the behavioral and medical sciences. Consider an example from education in which two approaches to introducing long division (treatments levels a_1 and a_2) are to be evaluated. Four schools (treatments levels $b_1, \ldots, b_4$) are randomly assigned to the two levels of treatment A, and eight teachers (treatment levels $c_1, \ldots, c_8$) are randomly assigned to the four schools. Hence, this is a three-treatment CRH-24(A)8(AB) design: schools, treatment $B(A)$, are nested in treatment A and teachers, treatment $C(AB)$, are nested in both A and B. A diagram of the nesting of treatments for this design is shown in Figure 1.17.

A second example is from medical science. A researcher wants to compare the efficacy of a new drug denoted by a_1 with the currently used drug denoted by a_2. Four hospitals, treatment $B(A)$, are available to participate in the experiment. Because expensive equipment is needed to monitor the side effects of the new drug, it was decided to use the new drug in two of the four hospitals and the current drug in the other two hospitals. The hospitals are randomly assigned to the drug conditions with the restriction that two hospitals are assigned to each drug. Patients are randomly assigned to the hospitals. Panel A of Figure 1.16 illustrates the nesting of treatment B within treatment A.

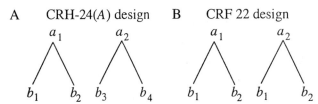

Figure 1.16 Comparison of designs with nested and crossed treatments. In panel A, treatment $B(A)$ is nested in treatment A because b_1 and b_2 appear only with a_1 while b_3 and b_4 appear only with a_2. In panel B, treatments A and B are crossed because each level of treatment B appears once and only once with each level of treatment A and vice versa.

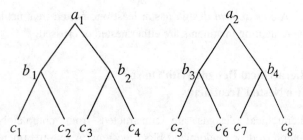

Figure 1.17   Diagram of a three-treatment completely randomized hierarchical design (CRH-24(A)8(AB) design). The four schools, $b_1, \ldots, b_4$, are nested in the two approaches to introducing long division, treatment A. The eight teachers, $c_1, \ldots, c_8$, are nested in the schools and teaching approaches. Students are randomly assigned to the $pq_{(j)}r_{(jk)} = (2)(2)(2) = 8$ treatment combinations with the restriction that n students are assigned to each combination.

As is often the case, the nested treatments in the drug and educational examples resemble nuisance variables. The researcher in the drug example probably would not conduct the experiment just to find out whether the dependent variable is different for the two hospitals assigned to drug a_1 or the hospitals assigned to a_2. The important question for the researcher is whether the new drug is more effective than the currently used drug. Similarly, the educational researcher wants to know whether one approach to teaching long division is better than the other. The researcher might be interested in knowing whether some schools or teachers perform better than others, but this is not the primary focus of the research. The distinction between a treatment and a nuisance variable is in the mind of the researcher—one researcher's nuisance variable can be another researcher's treatment.

The classical model equation for the drug experiment is

$$Y_{ijk} = \mu + \alpha_j + \beta_{k(j)} + \varepsilon_{i(jk)}$$
$$(i = 1, \ldots, n; \ j = 1, \ldots, p; \ k = 1, \ldots, q),$$

where

Y_{ijk} — is an observation for participant i in treatment levels a_j and $b_{k(j)}$.

μ — is the grand mean of the population means.

α_j — is the treatment effect for population a_j and is equal to $\mu_{j.} - \mu$. It reflects the effect of drug a_j.

$\beta_{k(j)}$ — is the treatment effect for population $b_{k(j)}$ and is equal to $\mu_{jk} - \mu_{j.}$. It reflects the effects of hospital $b_{k(j)}$ that is nested in a_j.

$\varepsilon_{i(jk)}$ — is the within-cell error effect associated with Y_{ijk} and is equal to $Y_{ijk} - \mu - \alpha_j - \beta_{k(j)}$. It reflects all effects not attributable to treatment levels a_j and $b_{k(j)}$.

Notice that because treatment $B(A)$ is nested in treatment A, the model equation does not contain an $A \times B$ interaction term.

This design enables a researcher to test two null hypotheses:

H_0: $\mu_{1.} = \mu_{2.}$
(Treatment A population means are equal.)

H_0: $\mu_{11} = \mu_{12}$ or $\mu_{23} = \mu_{24}$
(Treatment B(A) population means are equal.)

If the second null hypothesis is rejected, the researcher can conclude that the dependent variable is not the same for the populations represented by hospitals b_1 and b_2, that the dependent variable is not the same for the populations represented by hospitals b_3 and b_4, or both. However, the test of treatment $B(A)$ does not address the question of whether, for example, $\mu_{11} = \mu_{23}$ because hospitals b_1 and b_3 were assigned to different levels of treatment A.

Hierarchical Design With Crossed and Nested Treatments

In the educational example, treatments $B(A)$ and $C(AB)$ were both nested treatments. Hierarchical designs with three or more treatments can have both nested and crossed treatments. Consider the partial hierarchical design shown in Figure 1.18. The classical model equation for this design is

$$Y_{ijkl} = \mu + \alpha_j + \beta_k + \gamma_{l(k)} + (\alpha\beta)_{jk} + (\alpha\gamma)_{jl(k)} + \varepsilon_{i(jkl)}$$
$$(i = 1, \ldots, n; \ j = 1, \ldots, p; \ k = 1, \ldots, q; \ l = 1, \ldots, r),$$

where

Y_{ijkl} — is an observation for participant i in treatment levels a_j, b_k, and $c_{l(k)}$.

μ — is the grand mean of the population means.

α_j — is the treatment effect for population a_j and is equal to $\mu_{j..} - \mu$.

β_k — is the treatment effect for population b_k and is equal to $\mu_{.k.} - \mu$.

$\gamma_{l(k)}$ — is the treatment effect for population $c_{l(k)}$ and is equal to $\mu_{.kl} - \mu_{.k.}$.

$(\alpha\beta)_{jk}$ — is the interaction effect for populations a_j and b_k and is equal to $\mu_{jk.} - \mu_{jkl} - \mu_{j'k.} + \mu_{j'kl}$.

$(\alpha\gamma)_{jl(k)}$ — is the interaction effect for populations a_j and $c_{l(k)}$ and is equal to $\mu_{jkl} - \mu_{jkl'} - \mu_{j'kl} + \mu_{j'kl'}$.

$\varepsilon_{i(jkl)}$ — is the within-cell error effect associated with Y_{ijkl} and is equal to $Y_{ijkl} - \mu - \alpha_j - \beta_k - \gamma_{l(k)} - (\alpha\beta)_{jk} - (\alpha\gamma)_{jl(k)}$.

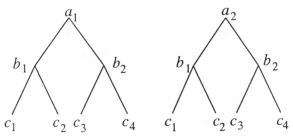

Figure 1.18 Diagram of a three-treatment completely randomized partial hierarchical design (CRPH-$pqr(B)$ design). The letter P in the designation stands for "partial" and indicates that not all of the treatments are nested. In this example, treatments A and B are crossed; treatment $C(B)$ is nested in treatment B because c_1 and c_2 appear only with b_1 while c_3 and c_4 appear only with b_2. Treatment $C(B)$ is crossed with treatment A because each level of treatment $C(B)$ appears once and only once with each level of treatment A and vice versa.

Notice that because treatment $C(B)$ is nested in treatment B, the model equation does not contain $B \times C$ and $A \times B \times C$ interaction terms.

This design enables a researcher to test five null hypotheses:

H_0: $\mu_{1..} = \mu_{2..}$
> (Treatment A population means are equal.)

H_0: $\mu_{.1.} = \mu_{.2.}$
> (Treatment B population means are equal.)

H_0: $\mu_{.11} = \mu_{.12}$ or $\mu_{.23} = \mu_{.24}$
> (Treatment $C(B)$ population means are equal.)

H_0: $\mu_{jk} - \mu_{jk'} - \mu_{j'k} + \mu_{j'k'} = 0$ for all j and k
> (All $A \times B$ interaction effects equal zero.)

H_0: $\mu_{jkl} - \mu_{jkl'} - \mu_{j'kl} + \mu_{j'kl'} = 0$ for all j, k, and l
> (All $A \times C(B)$ interaction effects equal zero.)

If the last null hypothesis is rejected, the researcher knows that treatments A and C interact at one or more levels of treatment B.

Lack of space prevents me from describing other partial hierarchical designs with different combinations of crossed and nested treatments. The interested reader is referred to the extensive treatment of these designs in Kirk (1995, chap. 11).

EXPERIMENTAL DESIGNS WITH A COVARIATE

The emphasis so far has been on designs that use *experimental control* to reduce error variance and minimize the effects of nuisance variables. Experimental control can take various forms such as random assignment of participants to treatment levels, stratification of participants into homogeneous

blocks, and refinement of techniques for measuring a dependent variable. In this section, I describe an alternative approach to reducing error variance and minimizing the effects of nuisance variables. The approach is called *analysis of covariance* (ANCOVA) and combines regression analysis and analysis of variance.

Analysis of covariance involves measuring one or more *concomitant variables* (also called *covariates*) in addition to the dependent variable. The concomitant variable represents a source of variation that was not controlled in the experiment and one that is believed to affect the dependent variable. Analysis of covariance enables a researcher to (a) remove that portion of the dependent-variable error variance that is predictable from a knowledge of the concomitant variable, thereby increasing power, and (b) adjust the dependent variable so that it is free of the linear effects attributable to the concomitant variable, thereby reducing bias.

Consider an experiment with two treatment levels a_1 and a_2. The dependent variable is denoted by Y_{ij}, the concomitant variable by X_{ij}. The relationship between X and Y for a_1 and a_2 might look like that shown in Figure 1.19. Each participant in the experiment contributes one data point to the figure as determined by his or her X_{ij} and Y_{ij} scores. The points form two scatter plots—one for each treatment level. These scatter plots are represented in Figure 1.19 by ellipses. Through each ellipsis a line has been drawn representing the regression of Y on X. In the typical ANCOVA model it is assumed that each regression line is a straight line and that the lines have the same slope. The size of the error variance in ANOVA is determined by the dispersion of the marginal distributions (see Figure 1.19). The size of the error variance in ANCOVA is determined by the

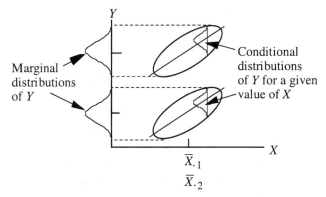

Figure 1.19 Scatter plots showing the relationship between the dependent variable, Y, and concomitant variable, X, for the two treatment levels. The size of the error variance in ANOVA is determined by the dispersion of the marginal distributions. The size of the error variance in ANCOVA is determined by the dispersion of the conditional distributions. The higher the correlation between X and Y is, the greater the reduction in the error variance due to using analysis of covariance.

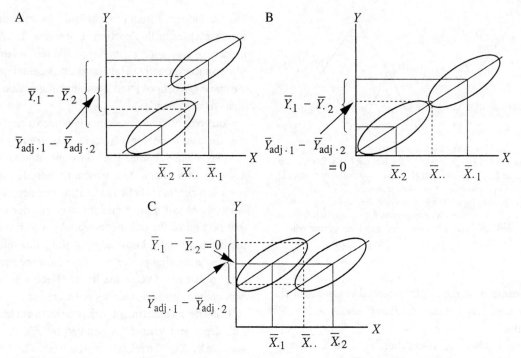

Figure 1.20 Analysis of covariance adjusts the concomitant-variable means, $\overline{X}_{\cdot 1}$ and $\overline{X}_{\cdot 2}$, so that they equal the concomitant-variable grand mean, $\overline{X}_{\cdot\cdot}$. When the concomitant-variable means differ, the absolute difference between adjusted means for the dependent variable, $|\overline{Y}_{\text{adj}\cdot 1} - \overline{Y}_{\text{adj}\cdot 2}|$, can be less than that between unadjusted means, $|\overline{Y}_{\cdot 1} - \overline{Y}_{\cdot 2}|$, as in panels A and B, or larger, as in panel C.

dispersion of the *conditional distributions* (see Figure 1.19). The higher the correlation between X and Y, in general, the narrower are the ellipses and the greater is the reduction in the error variance due to using analysis of covariance.

Figure 1.19 depicts the case in which the concomitant-variable means, $\overline{X}_{\cdot 1}$ and $\overline{X}_{\cdot 2}$, are equal. If participants are randomly assigned to treatment levels, in the long run the concomitant-variable means should be equal. However, if random assignment is not used, differences among the means can be sizable, as in Figure 1.20. This figure illustrates what happens to the dependent variable means when they are adjusted for differences in the concomitant-variable means. In panels A and B the absolute difference between adjusted dependent-variable means $|\overline{Y}_{\text{adj}\cdot 1} - \overline{Y}_{\text{adj}\cdot 2}|$ is smaller than that between unadjusted means $|\overline{Y}_{\cdot 1} - \overline{Y}_{\cdot 2}|$. In panel C the absolute difference between adjusted means is larger than that between unadjusted means.

Analysis of covariance is often used in three kinds of research situations. One situation involves the use of intact groups with unequal concomitant-variable means and is common in educational and industrial research. Analysis of covariance statistically equates the intact groups so that their concomitant variable means are equal. Unfortunately, a researcher can never be sure that the concomitant variable used for the adjustment represents the only nuisance variable or the most important nuisance variable on which the intact

groups differ. Random assignment is the best safeguard against unanticipated nuisance variables. In the long run, over many replications of an experiment, random assignment will result in groups that are, at the time of assignment, similar on all nuisance variables.

A second situation in which analysis of covariance is often used is when it becomes apparent that even though random assignment was used, the participants were not equivalent on some relevant variable at the beginning of the experiment. For example, in an experiment designed to evaluate the effects of different drugs on stimulus generalization in rats, the researcher might discover that the amount of stimulus generalization is related to the number of trials required to establish a stable bar-pressing response. Analysis of covariance can be used to adjust the generalization scores for differences among the groups in learning ability.

Analysis of covariance is useful in yet another research situation in which differences in a relevant nuisance variable occur during the course of an experiment. Consider the experiment to evaluate two approaches toward introducing long division that was described earlier. It is likely that the daily schedules of the eight classrooms provided more study periods for students in some classes than in others. It would be difficult to control experimentally the amount of time available for studying long division. However, each student could record the amount of time spent studying long division. If test scores on long division were related to amount of study time, analysis of covariance could be used to adjust the scores for differences in this nuisance variable.

Statistical control and experimental control are not mutually exclusive approaches for reducing error variance and minimizing the effects of nuisance variables. It may be convenient to control some variables by experimental control and others by statistical control. In general, experimental control involves fewer assumptions than does statistical control. However, experimental control requires more information about the participants before beginning an experiment. Once data collection has begun, it is too late to assign participants randomly to treatment levels or form blocks of dependent participants. The advantage of statistical control is that it can be used after data collection has begun. Its disadvantage is that it involves a number of assumptions such as a linear relationship between the dependent and concomitant variables and equal within-groups regression coefficients that may prove untenable in a particular experiment.

In this chapter I have given a short introduction to those experimental designs that are potentially the most useful in the behavioral and social sciences. For a full discussion of the designs, the reader is referred to the many excellent books on experimental design: Bogartz (1994), Cobb (1998), Harris (1994), Keppel (1991), Kirk (1995), Maxwell and Delaney (1990), and Winer, Brown, and Michels (1991). Experimental designs differ in a number of ways: (a) randomization procedures, (b) number of treatments, (c) use of independent samples or dependent samples with blocking, (d) use of crossed and nested treatments, (e) presence of confounding, and (f) use of covariates. Researchers have many design decisions to make. I have tried to make the researcher's task easier by emphasizing two related themes throughout the chapter. First, complex designs are constructed from three simple building block designs. Second, complex designs share similar layouts, randomization procedures, and assumptions with their building block designs.

REFERENCES

Bogartz, R. S. (1994). *An introduction to the analysis of variance.* Westport, CT: Praeger.

Box, J. F. (1978). *R. A. Fisher: The life of a scientist.* New York: Wiley.

Cobb, G. W. (1998). *Introduction to design and analysis of experiments.* New York: Springer-Verlag.

Cochran, W. G., & Cox, G. M. (1957). *Experimental designs* (2nd ed.). New York: Wiley.

Cohen, J. (1988). *Statistical power analysis for the behavioral sciences* (2nd ed.). Hillsdale, NJ: Erlbaum.

Federer, W. T. (1955). *Experimental design: Theory and application.* New York: Macmillan.

Finney, D. J. (1945). The fractional replication of factorial arrangements. *Annals of Eugenics, 12,* 291–301.

Finney, D. J. (1946). Recent developments in the design of field experiments. III. Fractional replication. *Journal of Agricultural Science, 36,* 184–191.

Fisher, R. A. (1918). The correlation between relatives on the supposition of Mendelian inheritance. *Transactions of the Royal Society of Edinburgh, 52,* 399–433.

Fisher, R. A. (1925). *Statistical methods for research workers.* Edinburgh: Oliver & Boyd.

Fisher, R. A. (1926). The arrangement of field experiments. *Journal of the Ministry of Agriculture, 33,* 503–513.

Fisher, R. A. (1935). *The design of experiments.* Edinburgh: Oliver & Boyd.

Fisher, R. A., & Mackenzie, W. A. (1923). Studies in crop variation. II. The manurial response of different potato varieties. *Journal of Agricultural Science, 13,* 311–320.

Harris, R. J. (1994). *ANOVA: An analysis of variance primer.* Itasca, IL: Peacock.

Hays, W. L. (1963). *Statistics.* Fort Worth, TX: Holt, Rinehart and Winston.

Hedges, L. V. (1981). Distributional theory for Glass's estimator of effect size and related estimators. *Journal of Educational Statistics, 6,* 107–128.

Hocking, R. R. (1985). *The analysis of linear models.* Pacific Grove, CA: Brooks/Cole.

Hocking, R. R., & Speed, F. M. (1975). A full rank analysis of some linear model problems. *Journal of the American Statistical Association, 70,* 706–712.

Kempthorne, O. (1947). A simple approach to confounding and fractional replication in factorial experiments. *Biometrika, 34,* 255–272.

Keppel, G. (1991). *Design and analysis: A researcher's handbook* (3rd ed.). Englewood Cliffs, NJ: Prentice-Hall.

Kirk, R. E. (1995). *Experimental design: Procedures for the behavioral sciences* (3rd ed.). Pacific Grove, CA: Brooks/Cole.

Kirk, R. E. (1996). Practical significance: A concept whose time has come. *Educational and Psychological Measurement, 56,* 746–759.

Kirk, R. E. (2001). Promoting good statistical practices: Some suggestions. *Educational and Psychological Measurement, 61,* 213–218.

Leonard, W. H., & Clark, A. G. (1939). *Field plot techniques.* Minneapolis, MN: Burgess.

Maxwell, S. E., & Delaney, H. D. (1990). *Designing experiments and analyzing data.* Belmont, CA: Wadsworth.

Pearson, K. (1901). On the correlation of characters not quantitatively measurable. *Philosophical Transactions of the Royal Society of London, 195,* 1–47.

Searle, S. R. (1987). *Linear models for unbalanced data.* New York: Wiley.

Snedecor, G. W. (1934). *Analysis of variance and covariance.* Ames, IA: Iowa State University.

Timm, N. H. (1975). *Multivariate analysis with applications in education and psychology.* Pacific Grove, CA: Brooks/Cole.

Tukey, J. W. (1991). The philosophy of multiple comparisons. *Statistical Science, 6,* 100–116.

Urquhart, N. S., Weeks, D. L., & Henderson, C. R. (1973). Estimation associated with linear models: A revisitation. *Communications in Statistics, 1,* 303–330.

Winer, B. J., Brown, D. R., & Michels, K. M. (1991). *Statistical principles in experimental design* (3rd ed.). New York: McGraw-Hill.

CHAPTER 2

Exploratory Data Analysis

JOHN T. BEHRENS AND CHONG-HO YU

Quantitative research methods in the twentieth century were marked by the explosive growth of small-sample statistics and the expansion of breadth and complexity of models for statistical hypothesis testing. The close of the century, however, was marked primarily with a frustration over the limitations of common statistical methods and frustration with their inappropriate or ineffective use (Cohen, 1994). Responding to the confusion that emerged in the psychological community, the American Psychological Association convened a task force on statistical inference that published a report (Wilkinson & Task Force, 1999) recommending best practices in the area of method, results, and discussion. Among the recommendations in the area of conducting and reporting results, the task force suggested researchers undertake a cluster of activities to supplement common statistical test procedures with the aim of developing a detailed knowledge of the data, an intimacy with the many layers of patterns that occur, and a knowledge of the implications of these patterns for subsequent testing.

Unbeknownst to many psychological researchers, the general goals recommended by the task force, as well as specific graphical techniques and conceptual frameworks mentioned in the report, are rooted in the quantitative tradition of exploratory data analysis (EDA). Exploratory data analysis is a well-established tradition based primarily on the philosophical and methodological work of John Tukey. Although Tukey is clearly recognized as the father of EDA in statistical circles, most psychologists are familiar only with small aspects of his work, such as that in the area of multiple-comparison procedures. Although Tukey worked in mathematical statistics throughout his life, the middle of his career brought dissatisfaction with the value of many statistical tools for understanding the complexities of real-world data. Moreover, Tukey fought what he perceived as an imbalance in efforts aimed at understanding data from a hypothesis-testing or confirmatory data analysis (CDA) mode while neglecting techniques that would aid in understanding of data more broadly. To fill this gap and promote service to the scientific community, as well as balance to the statistical community, Tukey developed and implemented the processes and philosophy of exploratory data analysis to be discussed shortly. To introduce the reader to this tradition, the chapter is divided into four parts. First, the background, rationale, and philosophy of EDA are presented. Second, a brief tour of the EDA toolbox is presented. The third section discusses computer software and future directions for EDA. The chapter ends with a summary and conclusion.

This work was completed while Dr. Behrens was on leave from Arizona State University, Division of Psychology in Education. He would like to thank the staff and administration of the department for their support.

HISTORY, RATIONALE, AND PHILOSOPHY OF EDA

John Tukey and the Origins of EDA

The tradition of EDA was begun and nurtured by John Tukey and his students through his many years at Princeton University and Bell Laboratories. As a young academic, Tukey was a prodigious author and formidable mathematical statistician. He received his PhD in mathematics from Princeton at the age of 25 and at 35 reached the rank of full professor at the same institution (Brillinger, Fernholz, & Morgenthaler, 1997). A sense of Tukey's breadth and impact can be gleaned from examination of the eight volumes of his collected works. Volumes 1 and 2 (Brillinger, 1984, 1985) highlight his contributions to time-series analysis (especially through spectral decomposition). Volumes 3 (Jones, 1986a) and 4 (Jones, 1986b) address *Philosophy and Principles of Data Analysis,* and volume 5 is devoted to graphics (Cleveland, 1988). Volume 6 (Mallows, 1990) covers miscellaneous mathematical statistics, whereas volumes 7 (Cox, 1992) and 8 (Braun, 1994) cover factorial and analysis of variance (ANOVA) and multiple comparisons, respectively. More may appear at a future date because Tukey remained an active researcher and writer until his death in July of 2000.

In addition to the many papers in his collected works, Tukey authored and coauthored numerous books. In the EDA literature his central work is *Exploratory Data Analysis* (Tukey, 1977), whereas *Data Analysis and Regression: A Second Course* (Mosteller & Tukey, 1977) is equally compelling. Three volumes edited by Hoaglin, Mosteller, and Tukey (1983, 1985, 1991) complete the foundational corpus of EDA. Brillinger, Fernholz, and Morgenthaler (1997) provide a Festschrift for Tukey based on writings of his students at the time of his 80th birthday in 1995.

As Tukey became increasingly involved in the application of statistics to solve real-world problems, he developed his own tradition of values and themes that emphasized flexibility, exploration, and a deep connection to scientific goals and methods. He referred to his work as *data analysis* rather than statistics because he believed the appropriate scientific work associated with data was often much broader than the work that was followed by the traditional statistical community. Tukey did not seek to supplant statistics; rather, he sought to supplement traditional statistics by restoring balance to what he considered an extreme emphasis on hypothesis testing at the expense of the use of a broader set of tools and conceptualizations.

Although most psychologists are unaware of the specific proposals Tukey made for EDA (but see Tukey, 1969;

Behrens, 1997a, 2000), the work of EDA is slowly filtering into daily practice through software packages and through the impact of a generation of statisticians who have been trained under the influence of Tukey and his students. For example, although highly graphical data analysis was rare in the 1970s, the current reliance on computer display screens has led statistical graphics to hold a central role in data analysis as recommended in common software packages (e.g., Norusis, 2000; Wilkinson, 2001). Tukey's work inspired entire paradigms of statistical methods, including *regression graphics* (Cook & Weisberg, 1994), *robustness studies* (e.g. Wilcox, 1997, 2001), and computer graphics for statistical use (Scott, 1992; Wilkinson, 1999).

Despite these advances in the application of EDA-like technique, statistical training remains largely focused on specific techniques with less than optimal emphasis on philosophical and heuristic foundations (cf. Aiken, West, Sechrest, & Reno, 1990). To prepare the reader for appropriate application of the techniques discussed later, we first turn to a treatment of the logical and philosophical foundations of EDA.

Rationale and General Tenets

It's all about the World

Exploratory data analysis is an approach to learning from data (Tukey & Wilk, 1966/1986) aimed at understanding the world and aiding the scientific process. Although these may not be "fighting words" among psychologists and psychological methodologists, they were for Tukey as he first raised his concerns with the statistical community.

Tukey's emphasis on the scientific context of data analysis leads to a view of data analysis as a scientific endeavor using the tools of mathematics, rather than a mathematical endeavor that may have value for some real-world applications. A number of changes to standard statistical practice are implied in this view. First, the statistician cannot serve as an aloof high priest who swoops down to sanctify a set of procedures and decisions (Salsburg, 1985). Data analysts and scientists (not mutually exclusive categories) must work interactively in a cyclical process of *pattern extraction* (mathematics) and *pattern interpretation* (science). Neither can function without the other. This view has implications for the organization of academic departments and organization of graduate training.

Second, because the effort of data analysis is to understand data in all circumstances, the role of probability models relates primarily to confirmatory aspects of the scientific process. This leaves a wide swath of the scientific processes for which researchers are left to use nonprobabilistic methods such as statistical graphics. This emphasis is based on the fact that in many stages of research the working questions are not probabilistic. When probabilistic methods are applied, there are layers of assumptions which themselves need to be assessed in nonprobabilistic ways to avoid an unending loop of assumptions. Contrasting classical statistics with data analysis, Tukey (1972/1986a) wrote, "I shall stick to 'data analysis' in part to indicate that we can take probability seriously, or leave it alone, as may from time to time be appropriate or necessary" (p. 755).

The probabilistic approaches taken in most confirmatory work may lead to different practices than the nonprobabilistic approaches that are more common to working in the exploratory mode. For example, a number of researchers have looked at the issue of *deleting outliers* from reaction time data. From a probabilistic view this problem is addressed by simulating distributions of numbers that approximate the shape commonly found in reaction time data. Next, extreme values are omitted using various rules, and observation is made of the impact of such adjustments on long-run decision making in the Monte Carlo setting. As one would expect in such simulations, estimates are often biased, leading the researcher to conclude that deleting outliers is inappropriate.

Working from the exploratory point of view, the data analyst would bring to bear the scientific knowledge he or she has about the empirical generating process of the data—for example, the psychological process of comparison. Using this as the primary guideline, outliers are considered observations whose value is such that it is likely they are the result of nonexperimental attributes. If common sense and previous data and theory suggest the reaction times should be less than 3 s, extreme values such as 6 or 10 s are most likely the result of other generating processes such as distraction or lack of compliance. If this is the case, then a failure to exclude extreme values is itself a form of biasing and is deemed inappropriate.

These divergent conclusions arise from approaching the problem with different assumptions. From a probabilistic view, the question is likely to be formulated as *If the underlying process has a distribution of X and I exclude data from it, is the result biased in the long run?* On the other hand, the exploratory question addressed is *Given that I do not know the underlying distribution is X, what do I know about the processes that may help me decide if extreme values are from the same process as the rest of the data?* In this way EDA emphasizes the importance of bringing relevant scientific knowledge to bear in the data-analytic situation rather than depending solely on probabilistic conceptualizations of the phenomenon under study. As with all techniques, EDA does

not reject probabilistic approaches, but rather considers them within a larger context of the many tools and ideas that bear on scientific work.

A central idea in the EDA corpus is the goal of developing a detailed and accurate mental model that provides a sense of intimacy with the nuances of the data. Such an experience assists both in constructing scientific hypotheses and building mathematical representations that allow more formal confirmatory methods to be used later. All of these issues argue against the routine use of statistical procedures and the lockstep application of decision rules. Tukey (1969) saw the commonplace use of statistical tests to prove "truth" as a social process of "sanctification." In this approach, the codifying of specific actions to be undertaken on all data obscures the individual nature of the data, removes the analyst from the details of the world held in the data, and impedes the development of intimacy and the construction of a detailed mental model of the world.

Consider the story of the researcher who sought to analyze the ratings of university faculty of various ethnicities according to the ethnicities of the students providing the ratings. To make sure the job was done properly, the researcher contacted the statistical consulting center and spoke with the director. After a brief description of the problem, it was clear to the consultant that this situation required a series of two-way ANOVAs of rating value across levels of teacher ethnicity and student ethnicity. A graduate student was assigned to compute the ANOVAs using commonly available statistical software, and both the researcher and consultant were quite pleased with the resulting list of p values and binary significance decisions.

In this true story, as in many, it was unfortunate that the discussion focused primarily on choosing a statistical model (ANOVA) to fit the design, rather than being a balanced discussion of the need for a broader understanding of the data. When the researcher later sought help in answering a reviewer's question, a simple calculation of cell frequencies revealed that the scarcity of students and faculty in many minority groups led to a situation in which almost half of the cells in the analysis were empty. In addition, many cells that were not empty had remarkably few data points to estimate their means. In many ways the original conclusions from the analysis were more incorrect than correct.

The error in this situation occurred because a series of unspoken assumptions propagated throughout the data analysis processes. Both the researcher and the director were concerned primarily with the testing of hypotheses rather than with developing a rich understanding of the data. Because of this, the statistician failed to consider some basic assumptions (such as the availability of data) and focused too much on an abstract conceptualization of the design. It was such lockstep application of general rules (factorial means between groups implies ANOVA) that Tukey sought to discourage.

Unfortunately, it is not unusual that authors of papers published in refereed journals neglect detailed examination of data. This leads to inferior mental models of the phenomenon and impedes the necessary assessment of whether the data conform to parametric test assumptions. For example, after reviewing more than 400 large data sets, Micceri (1989) found that the great majority of data collected in behavioral sciences do not follow univariate normal distributions. Breckler (1990) reviewed 72 articles in personality and social psychology journals and found that only 19% acknowledged the assumption of multivariate normality, and fewer than 10% considered whether this assumption had been met. Reviewing articles in 17 journals, Keselman et al. (1998) found that researchers rarely verified that statistical assumptions were satisfied and typically used analyses that were nonrobust to assumption violations. These authors noted that many of these types of problems could be detected by the application of techniques from the EDA tradition.

Detective Work and the Continuum of Method

In working to learn about the world, EDA holds several complementary goals: to find the unexpected, to avoid being fooled, and to develop rich descriptions. The primary analogy used by Tukey to communicate these goals is that of the data analyst as detective. Detective work is held up as a valuable analogy because the process is essentially exploratory and interactive; it involves an iterative process of generating hypotheses and looking for fit between the facts and the tentative theory or theories; and the process is messy and replicable only at the heuristic level. Detective work also provides a solid analogy for EDA because it is essentially a bottom-up process of hypothesis formulation and data collection.

Tukey (e.g., 1972/1986a, 1973/1986b) did not consider methodology as a bifurcation between EDA and CDA, but considered quantitative methods to be applied in stages of exploratory, rough confirmatory, and confirmatory data analyses. In this view EDA was aimed at the initial goals of hypothesis generation and pattern detection, following the detective analogy. Rough CDA is sometimes equated with null-hypothesis significance testing or the use of estimation procedures such as confidence intervals with the aim to answer the question, "With what accuracy are the appearances already found to be believed?" (Tukey, 1973/1986b, p. 794). With regard to strict confirmatory analysis Tukey notes, "When the results of the second stage is marginal, we need a third stage. . . . It is at this stage . . . that we require our best statistical techniques" (Tukey, 1973/1986b, p. 795). As a researcher moves through these stages, he or she moves from hypothesis generation to hypothesis testing and from pattern identification to pattern confirmation.

Whereas CDA is more ambitious in developing probabilistic assessments of theoretical claims, the flexibility and bottom-up nature of EDA allows for broader application. In many cases an appropriate model of parametric statistics may be unavailable for full CDA, while the simpler techniques of EDA may be of use. Under such a circumstance the maxim should be followed that "[f]ar better an approximate answer to the *right* question, which is often vague, than an *exact* answer to the wrong question, which can always be made precise" (Tukey, 1962/1986c, p. 407).

Summarization and the Loss of Information

Behrens and Smith (1996) characterize the nature of data analysis as being oriented toward generating summary and extracting gist. When faced with numerous pieces of data, the goal of the analyst is to construct a terse yet rich mathematical description of the data. This is analogous to the summarization process that occurs in natural language processing. After reading a long book, one does not recall every individual word, but rather remembers major themes and prototypical events. In a similar way, the data analyst and research consumer want to come away with a useable and parsimonious description rather than a long list of data. An essential concept associated with summarization is that every summary represents a loss of information. When some aspects of data are brought to the foreground, other aspects are sent to the background.

Algebra Lies, So You Need Graphics

Anscombe (1973) described a data set of numbers, each measured on the scales of x and y. He described the data as having a mean of 9 and standard deviation of 3.3 in x and a mean of 7.5 and standard deviation of 2.03 in y. The data were fit by ordinary least squares (OLS) criteria to have a slope of .5, an intercept of 3, and a correlation of .83. This allows the terse and easily interpretable summary for the data in the form $y = 3 + .5(x) +$ error. As a thought experiment, we encourage the reader to try to visualize a scatter plot that depicts such data.

If you imagined a scatter plot similar to that shown in Figure 2.1, then you are quite correct, because this represents the data Anscombe provided that met the descriptive statistics we described previously. This, however, is only a small

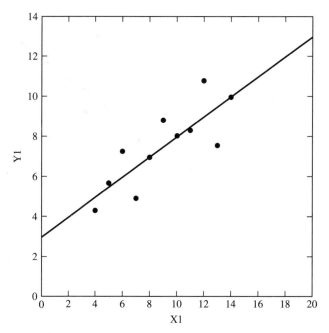

Figure 2.1 Plot of bivariate normal version of Anscombe data.

part of the story, for if you imagined the data to have the shape shown in panel A of Figure 2.2 then you are also correct. If you imagined the pattern in panels B or C of Figure 2.2, you are also correct because all the patterns shown in Figures 2.1 and 2.2 conform to the same algebraic summary statistics given by Anscombe. Although this example speaks to the weakness of overdependence on algebraic representations alone, it points to the larger issue that all summarization leads to a loss of information.

Graphics Lie, So You Need Algebra

Although graphics are a mainstay of EDA, graphics are not immune from this general principle. Consider the following data set: 1,1,2,2,3,3,4,4,5,5,5,5,6,6,6,6,6,6,7,7,7,7,8,8, 9,9,10,10,11,11. Entering this data into a standard statistics package produces the display presented in Figure 2.3. As the reader can see, a slight skew is evident that may not be detected in the listing of numbers themselves. It is important to consider the computational model that underlies this graphic. It consists of a mapping of bar height to frequency and bar width to bin width in the frequency table. *Bin width* refers to the size of the interval in which numbers are aggregated when determining frequencies. (The term *bandwidth* is similarly used in many domains, including nonparametric smoothing; cf. Härdle, 1991). Different bin widths and starting points for bins will lead to different tables, and hence, different graphics. Using the same data with different combinations of bin

starting point and bin widths produces the displays seen in Figure 2.4.

In sum, all data analysis is a process of summarization. This process leads to a focus on some aspects of data while taking focus off of other aspects. Conscious of these issues, the exploratory analyst always seeks multiple representations of the data and always holds a position of skepticism toward any single characterization of data.

The Importance of Models

Apart from the cognitive aspects of statistical information just discussed, there is an additional epistemic layer of meaning that must be dealt with. As George Box (1979) wrote: "All models are wrong but some are useful" (p. 202). An important aspect of EDA is the process of model specification and testing with a focus on the value and pattern of misfit or residuals. Although some psychologists are familiar with this view from their experience with regression graphics or diagnostics, many individuals fail to see their statistical work as model building. In the EDA view, all statistical work can be considered model building. The simple t test is a model of mean difference as a function of group membership considered in terms of sampling fluctuation. Regression analyses attempt to model criteria values as a function of predictor variables, whereas analysis of variance (ANOVA) models means and variances of dependent variables as a function of categorical variables.

Unaware of the options, many individuals fail to consider the wide range of model variants that are available. In regression, for example, the "continuous" dependent variable may be highly continuous or marginally continuous. If the dependent variable is binary, then a logistic regression is appropriate and a multilevel categorical dependent variable can likewise be fit (Hosmer & Lemeshow, 2000). The closely related variant of Poisson regression exists for counts, and probit and Tobit variants also can be used.

The application of models in these instances is central to EDA. Different models will have different assumptions and often describe the data well in one way, but fail in others. For example, in the world of item response theory, there is often great consternation regarding the choice of models to use. One-parameter models may misfit the data in some way, but have the desirable properties of sufficiency and consistent ordering of individuals. Two- and three-parameter models generally fit the data more tightly but without the conceptual advantages of the one-parameter model. From an EDA point of view, each model is "correct" in some respect insofar as each brings some value and loses others. Depending on the exact scientific or practical need, the decision maker may choose to emphasize one set of values or another.

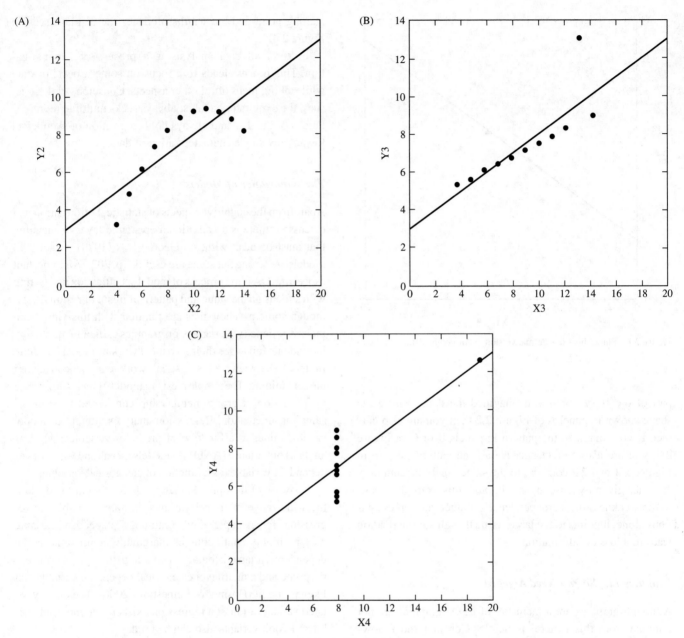

Figure 2.2   Additional data sets with same algebraic summaries as the data in Figure 2.1, with varying patterns and model fit.

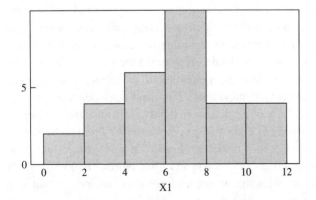

Figure 2.3   Histogram of small data set revealing slight skew.

Regardless of individual decisions about models, the most important issues are that one realizes (a) that there is always model being used (even if implicitly), (b) that for real-world data, there is no such thing as the perfect model, and (c) that the way in which the model is wrong tells us something about the phenomenon.

Abduction as the Logic of EDA

Because of the rich mathematical foundation of CDA, many researchers assume that the complete philosophical basis for inferences from CDA have been worked out. Interestingly, this is not the case. Fisher (1935, 1955) considered his

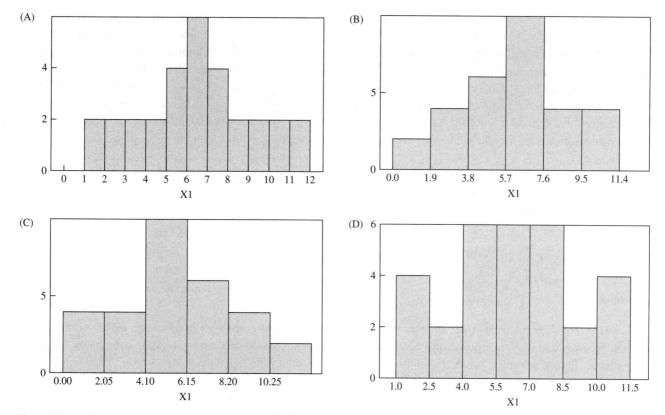

Figure 2.4   Additional histograms of the same data depicted in Figure 2.3 with varying appearances as a function of bin width and bin starting value.

approach to significance testing an as implementation of "inductive inference" and argued that all knowledge is gained in this way. Neyman and Pearson (1928, 1933a, 1933b), on the other hand, developed the concepts of power, type II error, and confidence intervals, to which Fisher objected (Gigerenzer, 1987, 1993; Lehmann, 1993). Neyman argued that only deductive inference was possible in statistics, as shown in the hypothesis testing tradition he developed. Others argue that classical statistics involves both logical modes, given that the hypothesis is generated deductively and data are compared against the hypothesis inductively (Lindsey, 1996).

Where, then, does this leave EDA? Because Tukey was primarily a mathematician and statistician, there has been little explicit work on the logical foundations of EDA from a formal philosophical viewpoint. A firm basis for understanding EDA, however, can be found in the concept of *abduction* proposed by the American philosopher Charles Sanders Peirce. Peirce, whose name is pronounced "pers," was a tour de force in American philosophy as the originator of modern semiotics, an accomplished logician in logic of probability, and the originator of pragmatism that was popularized by James and Dewey. Peirce (1934/1960) explained the three logical processes by arguing, "Deduction proves something must be. Induction shows that something actually is

operative; abduction merely suggests that something may be" (vol. 5, p. 171). Put another way: *Abduction* plays the role of generating new ideas or hypotheses; *deduction* functions as evaluating the hypotheses; and *induction* justifies the hypotheses with empirical data (Staat, 1993).

Deduction involves drawing logical consequences from premises. The conclusion is true given that the premises are true also (Peirce, 1868). For instance,

First premise: All As are Bs (True).
Second premise: C is A (True).
Conclusion: Therefore, C is B (True).

Deductive logic confines the conclusion to a dichotomous answer (true-false). A typical example is the rejection or failure of rejection of the null hypothesis. To be specific, the formulated hypothesis is regarded as the first premise. When the data (the second premise) conform to the hypothesis, the conclusion must assert that the first premise is true.

Some have argued that deduction is incomplete because we cannot logically prove all the premises are true. Russell and Whitehead (1910) attempted to develop a self-sufficient logical-mathematical system. In their view, not only can mathematics be reduced to logic, but also logic is the foundation of mathematics. However, Gödel (1947/1986) found that it is impossible to have such a self-contained system. Any lower order theorem or premise needs a higher order theorem or premise for substantiation, and it goes on and on; no system can be complete and consistent at the same time. Building on this argument, Kline (1980) held that mathematics had developed illogically with false proof and slips in reasoning. Thus, he argued that deductive proof from self-evident principles in mathematics is an "intellectual tragedy" (p. 3) and a "grand illusion" (p. 4).

For Peirce, inductive logic is based upon the notion that probability is the relative frequency in the long run and that a general law can be concluded based on numerous cases. For example,

> A1, A2, A3 . . . A100 are B.
> A1, A2, A3 . . . A100 are C.
> Therefore, B is C.

Hume (1777/1912) argued that things are inconclusive by induction because in infinity there are always new cases and new evidence. Induction can be justified if and only if instances of which we have no experience resemble those of which we have experience. Thus, the problem of induction is also known as "the skeptical problem about the future" (Hacking, 1975). Take the previous argument as an example. If A101 is not B, the statement "B is C" will be refuted. We never know when a line predicting future events will turn flat, go down, or go up. Even inductive reasoning using numerous accurate data and high-power computing can go wrong, because predictions are made only under certain specified conditions (Samuelson, 1967).

Induction suggests the possible outcome in relation to events in the long run. This is not definable for an individual event. To make a judgment for a single event based on probability, such as saying that someone's chance of surviving surgery is 75%, is nonsensical. In actuality, the patient will either live or die. In a single event, not only is the probability indefinable, but also the explanatory power is absent. Induction yields a general statement that explains the event of observing, but not the facts observed. Josephson and Josephson (1994) gave this example:

> Suppose I choose a ball at random (arbitrarily) from a large hat containing colored balls. The ball I choose is red. Does the fact that all of the balls in the hat are red explain why this particular ball is red? No. . . "All A's are B's" cannot explain why "this A is a B" because it does not say anything about how its being an A is connected with its being a B. (p. 20)

The function of abduction is to look for a pattern in a surprising phenomenon and suggest a plausible hypothesis (Peirce, 1878). Despite the long history of abduction, it remains overlooked among many texts of logic and research methodology, while gaining ground in the areas of artificial intelligence and probabilistic computing (e.g., Josephson & Josephson, 1994; Schum, 1994). However, as logic is divided into formal types of reasoning (*symbolic logic*) and informal types (*critical thinking*), abduction is represented as informal logic. Therefore, unlike deduction and induction, abduction is a type of critical thinking rather than a formalism captured by symbolic logic. The following example illustrates the function of abduction, though illustrated with symbols for simplification:

> The surprising phenomenon, X, is observed.
> Among hypotheses A, B, and C, A is capable of explaining X.
> Hence, there is a reason to pursue A.

At first glance, abduction may appear as no more than an educated guess among existing hypotheses. Thagard and Shelley (1997) addressed this concern. They argued that unifying conceptions are an important part of abduction, and it would be unfortunate if our understanding of abduction were limited to more mundane cases where hypotheses are simply assembled. Abduction does not occur in the context of a fixed language, since the formation of new hypotheses often goes hand in hand with the development of new theoretical terms such as *quark* and *gene*. Indeed, Peirce (1934/1960) emphasized that abduction is the only logical operation that introduces new ideas.

Although abduction is viewed as a kind of "creative intuition" for idea generation and fact explanation (Hoffmann, 1997), it is dangerous to look at abduction as impulsive thinking and hasty judgment. In *The Fixation of Belief*, Peirce explicitly disregarded the tenacity of intuition as the source of knowledge. Peirce strongly criticized his contemporaries' confusion of propositions and assertions. Propositions can be affirmed or denied while assertions are final judgments (Hilpinen, 1992). The objective of abduction is to determine which hypothesis or proposition to test, not which one to adopt or assert (Sullivan, 1991).

In EDA, after observing some surprising facts, we exploit them and check the predicted values against the observed values and residuals (Behrens, 1997a). Although there may be more than one convincing pattern, we "abduct" only those that are more plausible for subsequent confirmatory experimentation. Since experimentation is hypothesis driven and EDA is data driven, the logic behind each of them is quite different. The abductive reasoning of EDA goes from data to hypotheses, whereas inductive reasoning of experimentation goes from hypothesis to expected data. In fact, closely (and unknowingly) following Tukey (1969), Shank (1991), Josephson and Josephson (1994), and Ottens and Shank (1995) related abductive reasoning to detective work. Detectives collect related "facts" about people and circumstances. These facts are actually shrewd guesses or hypotheses based on their keen powers of observation.

In short, abduction can be interpreted as observing the world with appropriate categories, which arise from the internal structure of meanings. Abduction in EDA means that the analyst neither exhausts all possibilities nor makes hasty decisions. Researchers must be well equipped with proper categories in order to sort out the invariant features and patterns of phenomena. Quantitative research, in this sense, is not number crunching, but a thoughtful way of peeling back layers of meaning in data.

Exploration, Discovery, and Hypothesis Testing

Many researchers steeped in confirmatory procedures have appropriately learned that true hypothesis tests require true hypotheses and that unexpected results should not be treated with the same deference as hypothesized results. A corollary is that one should keep clear what has been hypothesized in a research study and not modify a hypothesis to match data. This is certainly true and is an essential aspect of confirmatory inference. In some researchers, however, a neurosis develops that extends the avoidance of hypothesis-modification based on knowledge of the data to an avoidance of intimacy with the data altogether. Sometimes this neurosis is exacerbated by the fear that every piece of knowledge has an amount of Type I error associated with it and, therefore, the more we know about the data the higher our Type I error. The key to appropriately balancing exploratory and confirmatory work is to keep clear what has been hypothesized in advance and what is being "discovered" for the first time. Discoveries are important, but do not count as confirmations.

After years of extensive fieldwork an entomologist develops a prediction that butterflies with a certain pattern of spotting should exist on top of a particular mountain, and sets off for the mountaintop. Clearly, if the entomologist finds such butterflies there will be evidence in support of her theory; otherwise, there is an absence of evidence. On her way to the mountain she traverses a jungle in which she encounters a previously unknown species of butterflies with quite unanticipated spottings. How does she handle this? Should she ignore the butterfly because she has not hypothesized it? Should she ignore it because it may simply be a misleading Type I error? Should she ignore it because she may change her original hypothesis to say she has really hypothesized this jungle butterfly?

For most individuals it is clear that a new discovery is valuable and should be well documented and collected. The entomologist's failure to have hypothesized it does not impugn its uniqueness, and indeed many great scientific conclusions have started with unanticipated findings (Beveridge, 1950). Should the entomologist worry about Type I error? Since Type I error concerns long-run error in decision making based on levels of specific cutoff values in specific distributions, that precise interpretation does not seem to matter much here. If she makes an inference about this finding then she should consider the probabilistic basis for such an inference, but nevertheless the butterfly should be collected. Finally, should she be concerned that this finding will contaminate her original hypothesis? Clearly she should continue her travel and look for the evidence concerning her initial hypothesis on the mountaintop. If the new butterfly contradicts the existing hypothesis, then the entomologist has more data to deal with and additional complexity that should not be ignored. If she is concerned about changing her hypothesis in midstream to match the new data, then she has confused hypothesis *generation* and hypothesis *testing*. With regard to any new theories, she must create additional predictions to be tested in a different location.

EDA and Exploratory Statistics

EDA and exploratory statistics (ES) have the same exploratory goals; thus, the question sometimes arises as to whether ES is simply a subset of EDA or EDA is a subset of ES. Because EDA is primarily an epistemological lens and ES is generally presented in terms of a collection of techniques, a more appropriate question is *Can ES be conducted from an EDA point of view?* To this question we can answer *yes*. Furthermore, EDA is a conceptual lens, and most research procedures can be undertaken with an EDA slant. For example, if one is conducting an "exploratory" factor analysis without graphing of data, examination of residuals, or attention to specific patterns of raw data underlying the correlations that are central to the analysis, then little seems to be consistent with the EDA approach. On the other hand, a clearly probabilistic analysis can be well augmented by plots of data on a number of dimensions (Härdle, Klinke, & Turlach, 1995; Scott, 1992), attention to residual patterns in a number of dimensions, and the use of detailed diagnostics that point to patterns of fits and misfits. Regardless of the software or specific statistical procedures used, such activity would clearly be considered EDA and ES. ES does not necessarily imply EDA, but ES can be conducted as EDA if the conceptual and procedural hallmarks of EDA are employed.

Summary

Exploratory data analysis is a rich data-analytic tradition developed to aid practical issues of data analysis. It recommends a data-driven approach to gaining intimacy with one's data and the phenomenon under study. This approach follows the analogy of the detective looking for clues to develop hunches and perhaps seek a grand jury. This counters the more formal and ambitious goals of confirmatory data analysis, which seeks to obtain and present formal evidence in order to gain a conviction. EDA is recommended as a complement to confirmatory methods, and in no way seeks to replace or eliminate them. Indeed, effective researchers should incorporate the best aspects of all approaches as needed.

HALLMARKS OF EDA

In this section, the techniques and attitudes that are standard aspects of EDA are discussed. The tools described here are only recommendations that have worked to allow researchers to reach the underlying goals of EDA. However, it is the underlying goals that should be sought, not the particular techniques. Following Hoaglin, Mosteller, and Tukey (1983), we discuss these tools under the *four Rs* of EDA: *revelation, residuals, reexpression,* and *resistance*.

Revelation

Graphics are the primary tool for the exploratory data analyst. The most widely cited reason for this is Tukey's (1977) statement that "The greatest value of a picture is when it forces us to notice what we never expected to see" (p. vi). In many ways, the graphics in Figures 2.1 and 2.2 illustrate all the rationale of graphics in EDA. First, even though the algebraic summaries are "sufficient statistics," they are sufficient for only the very limited purpose of summarizing particular aspects of the data. For specifying the exact form of the data without additional assumptions regarding distributional shapes, the summary statistics are not only "insufficient" but are downright dangerous. Second, the indeterminacy of the algebra calls us to fill in the details with possibly untenable assumptions. In the Anscombe data-thought experiment, participants almost universally imagine the data to be of the canonical form shown in Figure 2.1. In the absence of a skeptical mind and in the light of the history of statistics textbooks that are focused on mathematical idealizations at the expense of real-world patterns, many psychologists have developed schemas and mental models (Johnson-Laird, 1983) that lead to erroneous inferences.

Another psychological advantage of graphics is that it allows for a parsimonious representation of the data. The facts that are easily derivable from the image include all the individual values, the relative position of each data point to every other, shape-based characterizations of the bivariate distribution, and the relationship between the data and the proposed regression line. After some practice, the trained eye can easily discern and describe the marginal distributions as well as the distribution of residuals. The construction of a text-based representation of all of this information would require an extensive set of text-based descriptors. In short, visual images of the type shown here exploit the visual-spatial memory system to support efficient pattern recognition (Garner, 1974), problem solving (Larkin & Simon, 1987), and the construction of appropriate mental models (Bauer & Johnson-Laird, 1993).

Tukey's early work and concomitant advances in computing have led to an explosion in graphical methods over the last three decades. Numerous authors, including Tufte (1990, 1997, 1983/2001) and Wainer (1997; Wainer & Velleman, 2001) have worked to popularize data-based graphics. William Cleveland has had a large impact on the statistical community with his empirical studies of the use of graphics (Cleveland & McGill, 1984), the initiation of cognitive models of graph perception (Cleveland, 1985), and his application of these principles to statistical graphics (especially Cleveland, 1993). Wilkinson (1993, 1994, 1999) made substantial contributions to the study of proper use of statistical graphics, and has recently provided a comprehensive volume regarding graphics in software and statistical analysis (Wilkinson, 1999) that is required reading for anyone interested in the field. Kosslyn (1994) provided a discussion of numerous potential rules for graph construction from a psychological perspective, and Lewandowsky and Behrens (1999) provide a recent review of cognitive aspects of statistical graphs and maps.

Graphics Made for EDA

During the emergence of the EDA tradition, Tukey developed a large number of graphical tools, some of which have become commonplace, others of which have had little visibility outside specialized applications. It is important to remember that at the time of their original construction, much of what Tukey sought to do was to support quick summarization and analysis when data were available, and the analysis was to occur by hand.

Perhaps the best known of Tukey's graphical devices for EDA is the *box-and-whisker plot,* otherwise called the *box-plot.* The box-plot is a graph based on a five-number summary of a distribution of data; these numbers are the median, the first and second hinges, and either the lowest and highest number or a similar measure of range number arrived at by separating very extreme values. The median is equal to the 50th percentile of the distribution. The hinges are either equal to or very close to the 25th and 75th percentiles—although they are found using a simpler rank-based formula for computation. To construct a box-plot, a scale is drawn, and a box is placed on the scale with one end of the box indicating the scale value of the lower hinge (25th percentile) and the other end of the box occurring at the scale position of the upper hinge (75th percentile). An additional line is drawn in the middle to indicate the scale value of the median. The scale-value difference between the two hinges is called either the *hinge spread* or the *interquartile range* (often abbreviated IQR), and in a normal distribution corresponds to approximately 0.67 standard deviations on each side of the mean.

Rules for the construction of the "whisker" portion of the display vary. In the most common version, lines are extended along the scale from the hinges to the farthest data value in each direction up to 1.5 hinge spreads. If there are data past that point, the whiskers extend to the farthest data point prior to the 1.5 hinge-spread cutoff. Data points beyond the whiskers are usually identified individually to bring attention to their extremeness and potential characterization as outliers.

An example of multiple box-plots is presented in Figure 2.5, panel A, with individual raw data values presented in panel B for comparison. These graphics depict the distributions of effect sizes from the meta-analysis of social memory conducted by Stangor and McMillan (1992). The categorical variable on the horizontal axis is the length of stimulus presentation in seconds. The continuous variable on the vertical axis is the size of the effect for each study included in the meta-analysis. As the reader may see, the box-plots provide a compact description of each distribution and allow relatively easy comparison of both the level and spread of each distribution. The distribution farthest to the left represents all the studies for which no presentation speed is reported. The range is approximately from −2 to +2, with a median slightly below zero. The second box-plot depicts the distribution of effect sizes from studies that used a 2-s presentation speed. It is the highest distribution of all, with some positive skew. The median of this distribution is higher than the 75th percentile of the remaining distributions, indicating a clear trend toward larger values. The median is also higher than the 75th percentile of the 6- and 10-s studies. The studies with presentation times of 6 s show very little variance with the exception of two outliers, which are indicated separately.

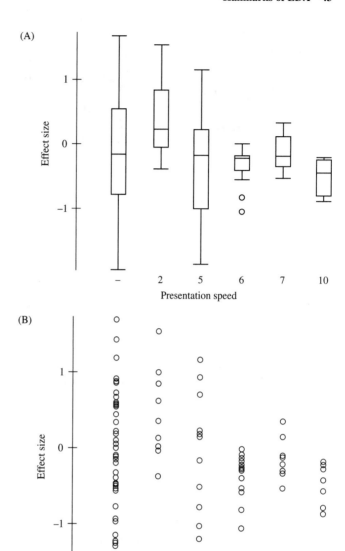

Figure 2.5 Panel A consists of multiple box-plots of effect sizes in social memory meta-analysis, organized by presentation speed (from Stangor & McMillan, 1992). Panel B depicts the same data by plotting individual values in a dot-plot.

When two box-plots are compared, the analyst is undertaking the graphical analog of the *t test*. Displays with additional boxes, as shown here, are analogous to the analysis of variance: Group-level measures of central tendency are displayed relative to the amount of within-group variability in the data.

Although the box-plots are very useful and informative in their current state, working in the exploratory mode raises additional issues. First, how might we be fooled by these displays? The answer to this is that there are times when the

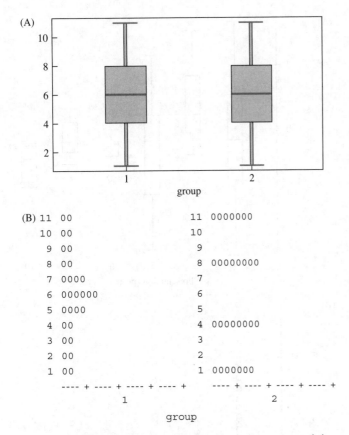

Figure 2.6 Panel A is two box-plots with identical summary statistics. Panel B depicts the underlying data used to make panel A, illustrating the possibility that different data may produce identical graphs.

five-number summaries are the same for different distributions. This leads to a case in which the box-plots look identical yet the data differ in structure. Consider the top panel of Figure 2.6, in which each of two box-plots is identical, indicating identical values of the five-number summary. The lower panel of Figure 2.6 depicts the underlying raw data values that vary in form. Distortions can also occur if there are very few levels of the variable being measured, because it will cause many data points to have the same value. In some cases the appearance of a plot may be distorted if the hinges are equal to the minimum or maximum, because no whiskers appear.

A second point of interest concerns how we can learn more from the data by enhancing the box-plot. Toward this end, recommendations abound. Tufte (1983/2001) recommended the omission of the box (an idea not well supported by empirical data; Stock & Behrens, 1991). Other suggested improvements include indicating the sample size of the subset below the box (e.g., Becker, Chambers, & Wilks, 1988), adding confidence intervals around the median in the box, or distorting the box shape to account both for sample size and the confidence intervals (McGill, Tukey, & Larsen, 1978).

Berk (1994) recommended the overplotting of a dot-plot (as seen in the lower panel of Figure 2.6) on top of the box-plot so that two levels of detail can be seen simultaneously. Regardless of the exact implementation used, users must be wary that software packages vary on the algorithms used to calculate their five-number summaries, and they may not be looking at the summaries one expects (Frigge, Hoaglin, & Iglewicz, 1989).

Interactive Graphics

Although much can be gained by modifying the static appearance of plots such as the box-plot, substantial gains in data analysis can be made in computerized environments by using interactive graphics with brushing and linking (Cleveland & McGill, 1988). *Interactive graphics* are graphic displays that respond to the *brushing* (selection) action of a pointing device (such as a mouse) by modifying the graphics in real time. *Linking* is the connection of values on the same observation through brushing or selecting across different graphics. Highlighting an observation in one display (say, a scatter plot) causes the value of the same observation to appear highlighted in another display (say, a histogram) as well. In this way, an analyst working to analyze one graphic can quickly see how information in that graphic relates to information in another graphic. For example, in Figure 2.5 the conditional level of each distribution varies greatly. An analyst may wonder if this is primarily from the categorical variables listed on the horizontal axis, or if there are other variables that may also covary with these medians. One possibility is that different research laboratories tend to use different speeds and therefore, that laboratory covaries with speed.

Prior to the advent of interactive graphics, one would stop the analysis in order to look in a table to determine which data came from which laboratory. Such a process could easily become tedious and distracting from the main task. Using a program that has high graphical interactivity, in this case Data Desk (Data Description, 1997), highlighting the data of interest in one graphical display highlights the same data in other graphical displays or in the variable listings. To accomplish this in Data Desk we simply turn off the box-plots using the pull-down menu at the top of the graph window (thereby changing panel A of Figure 2.5 to panel B), indicate "Show identifying text" from a menu at the top of the screen, click on the identifying variable of interest (study name), and highlight observations to be linked. The final outcome of these few quick hand movements is presented in Figure 2.7. Here the graphics reveal some unexpected results. Eight of the nine effect sizes in this group come from only two studies

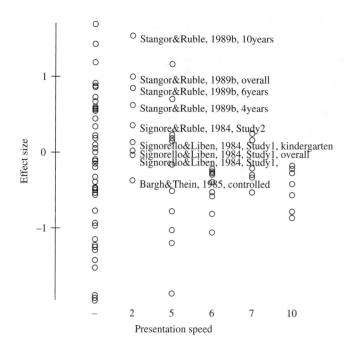

Figure 2.7 Dot-plot with identifying text obtained by selecting and linking.

and the studies are highly stratified by effect size. When the eight data points of the 7-s effects are circled, the study names indicate that all these effects come from a single study.

Moving Up the Path of Dimensionality

Whereas box-plots are often considered univariate graphics because they are often used to display a single variable, our simple example has demonstrated that the box-plot can easily function in three variables. In this case the variables are presentation speed, effect size, and study origin. In highly interactive environments, however, additional variables are easily added. For example, in Data Desk, palettes available on the desktop allow one to choose the shape or color of symbols for individual data points. This is accomplished through selecting the data points of interest by circling the points on the graphic and clicking on the desired shape or color. Symbol coloring can also be accomplished automatically by using a pull-down menu that indicates a desire to color symbols by the value of a specific variable. In our meta-analysis data, coloring the data points by sample size and varying the shape to indicate the value of another categorical variable of interest may aid in finding unanticipated patterns. In this way, we would have created a rather usable yet complex five-dimensional graphic representation of the data.

For combinations of categorical and measured data, the box-plot and corresponding dot-plot provide an excellent starting point. For analyses that focus more heavily on

measured (continuous or nearly continuous) data, the scatter plot is the common fundamental graphic. Here variations abound, as well. Whereas the scatter plot is often used to understand two dimensions of data, when faced with high-dimensional data, one often uses a matrix of scatter plots to see the multidimensionality from multiple bivariate views. An example of a scatter plot matrix is presented in Figure 2.8. The data portrayed here are a subset of the data that Stangor and McMillan (1992) used in a weighted least-squares regression analysis of the effect sizes. The plot can be thought of as a graphical correlation matrix. Where we would have placed the value of the correlation, we instead put the graphical bivariate display. For each individual scatter plot, one can identify the variable on the vertical axis by looking at the variable named at the far left of the row. The horizontal axis is identified by looking down the column of the matrix to the variable identified at the bottom of the scatter plot. For example, the plot in the upper right corner has "*N*" (sample size) on the vertical axis and "con / incon" on the horizontal axis, indicating the ratio of congruent to incongruent stimuli. The top of the "con / incon" label is hidden due to plot size in the plot in the lower right corner. The plots in the diagonal cells are normal-probability plots whose interpretation is discussed below.

In this situation, as is often the case, the scatter plot matrix does an excellent job of revealing unexpected structure. For many of the bivariate relationships there is great departure from bivariate normality. Of particular concern is the combination of high skew in the congruent-incongruent ratio and the floor effect in the targets and traits variables. These issues lead to L-shaped distributions that will present a clear challenge to any continuous linear model. Outliers and combinations of missing data should also be considered carefully. Of particular note in these data is that the higher level of the dummy-coded delay variable exists in only two observations, but one of those observations has no matching data on many variables and thus functions as a single point. In a multivariate situation such as regression analysis, this is quite problematic because the estimation of the relationship of this variable with all others rests precariously on the value of the single point. Error at this point will thereby be propagated through the system of partial correlations used to estimate regression effects.

Plots with multiple straight lines indicate the 0 and 1 levels of dummy coding. A number of additional dummy-coded variables subjected to simultaneous regression by Stangor and McMillan (1992) were omitted because the number of plots became too large to present here clearly. Earlier versions of this matrix revealed additional unusual values that were traced back to the present authors' transcription process

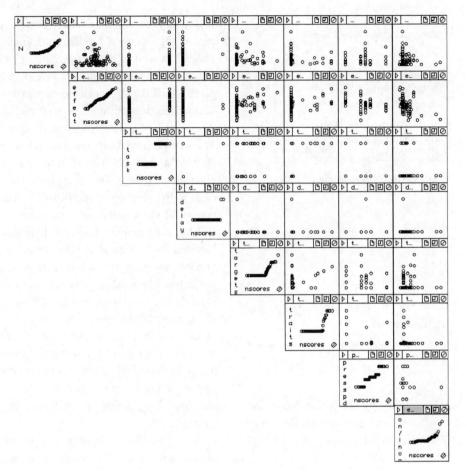

Figure 2.8   Scatter plot matrix of meta-analysis data from Stangor and McMillan (1992).

and have been since corrected. In this case, the graphics revealed structure and avoided error.

Going Deeper

Although the scatter plot matrix is valuable and informative, it is important that the reader recognize that a series of two-dimensional views is not as informative as a three-dimensional view. For example, when Stangor and McMillan computed a simultaneous regression model, the variables indicating the number of targets and traits used in each study reversed the direction of their slope, compared with their simple correlations. Although a classical "suppressor" interpretation was given, the exploratory analyst may wonder whether the simple constant and linear functions used to model these data were appropriate. One possibility is that the targets variable mediates other relationships. For example, it may be the case that some variables are highly related to effect size for certain levels of target, but have different relationships with effect size at other levels of targets.

To provide a quick and provisional evaluation of this possibility, we created a histogram of the target variables, selected those bins in the graphic that represent low levels of targets, and chose a unique color and symbol for the observations that had just been selected. From here, one can simply click on the pull-down menu on any scatter plot and choose "Add color regression lines." Because the observations have been colored by low and high levels of the target variable, the plots will be supplemented with regression lines between independent variables and the effect size–dependent variable separately for low and high levels of targets, as displayed in Figure 2.9.

Moving across the second row of Figure 2.9 (which corresponds to the response variable), first we see two regression lines with low identical slopes indicating little relationship between task and effect, which is constant across levels of target. The delay variable in the next column shows a similar pattern, whereas the next three variables show small indications of interaction. The interaction effect is very clear in the relationship between effect size and the congruent-incongruent ratio in the rightmost column. This relationship is positive for

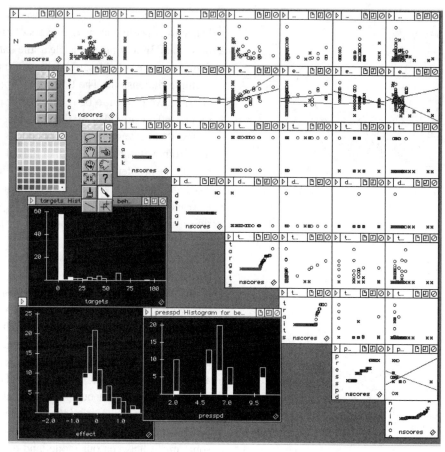

Figure 2.9 View of computer screen using Data Desk software for selecting, brushing, and linking across multiple plots. Several plots have been enhanced with multiple regression lines that vary by subsets of selected data.

observations with high numbers of targets, but negative for low numbers of targets. Unfortunately, in failing to recognize this pattern, one may use a model with no interactions. In such a case the positive slope observations are averaged with the negative slope observations to create an estimate of 0 slope. This would typically lead the data analyst to conclude that no relationship exists at all, when in fact a clear story exists just below the surface (one variable down!).

Although the graphics employed so far have been helpful, we have essentially used numerous low-dimensional views of the data to try to develop a multidimensional conceptualization. This is analogous to the way many researchers develop regression models as a list of variables that are "related" or "not related" to the dependent variable, and then consider them altogether. Our brushing and coding of the scatter plot matrix has shown that this is a dangerous approach because "related" is usually operationalized as "linearly related"—an assumption that is often unwarranted. Moreover, in multidimensional space, variables may be related in one part of the space but not in the other.

Working in an exploratory mode, these experiences suggest we step back and ask a more general question about the meta-analytic data: In what way does the size and availability of effects vary across the variety of study characteristics? To begin to get such a view of the data, one may find three-dimensional plots to be useful. A graphic created using a nonlinear smoother for the effect size of each study as a function of the number of targets and presentation speed is presented in panel A of Figure 2.10. The general shape is similar to the "saddle" shape that characterizes a two-way interaction in continuous regression models (Aiken & West, 1991). The graphic also reveals that little empirical work has been undertaken with high presentation speed and a low number of targets, so it is difficult to assess the veracity of the smoothing function given the lack of data in that area. At a minimum, it suggests that future research should be conducted to assess those combinations of study characteristics. Panel B of Figure 2.10 shows an alternate representation of the data with a traditional linear surface function that is designed to provide a single additive prediction across all the data.

(A)

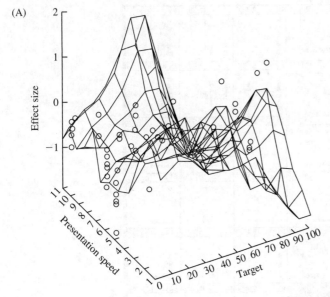

(B)

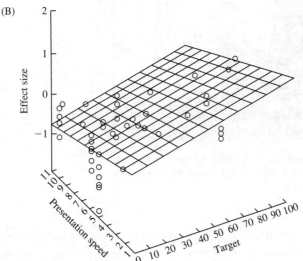

Figure 2.10 Panel A is a nonlinear surface estimate of the interaction of presentation speed, number of targets, and effect size in the Stangor and McMillan (1992) meta-analysis data. Panel B is a completely linear prediction surface as would be obtained using common least squares regression.

For another impression of the data, we can take a series of slices of the three-dimensional data cube and lay the slices out side by side. Such an arrangement is possible using a general framework called a *trellis plot* (Becker, Cleveland, & Shyu, 1996; Clark, Cleveland, Denby, & Liu, 1999) as implemented in Splus (Insightful, 2001) and shown in Figure 2.11. The three panels show progressive slices of the data with linear regression lines overlaid. As the reader can see, the plots correspond to three slices of the three-dimensional cube shown in Figure 2.10, panel A, with changes in the regression line matching different portions of the "hills" in the data.

The simple graphics we have used here provide an excellent start at peeling away the layers of meaning that reside in these data. If nothing else is clear, the data are more complex than can be easily described by a simple linear model in multiple dimensions. The theoretical concerns of Anscombe (1973) have proven to be realistic after all. Despite the interocular effect provided by these graphics, some readers will assure themselves that such difficulties appear primarily in data from meta-analyses and that the data they work with will not be so problematic. Unfortunately this is not often the case, and there is a cottage industry among EDA proponents of reanalyzing published data with simple graphics to show rich structure that was overlooked in original work.

Residuals and Models

In the EDA tradition, the second *R* stands for *residual,* yet this word signifies not simply a mathematical definition, but a foundational philosophy about the nature of data analysis. Throughout Tukey's writings, the theme of DATA = FIT + RESIDUALS is repeated over and over, often in graphical analog: DATA = SMOOTH + ROUGH. This simple formula reminds us that our primary focus is on the development of compact descriptions of the world and that these descriptions will never be perfect; thus there will always be some misfit between our model and the data, and this misfit occurs with every observation having a residual.

This view counters implicit assumptions that often arise in statistical training. First, many students acquire an unfortunate belief that "error" has an ontological status equivalent to "noise that can be ignored" and consequently believe the results of a model-fitting procedure (such as least squares regression) is the "true" model that should be followed. Such a view fails to emphasize the fact that the residuals are simply a byproduct of the model used, and that different models will lead to different patterns of residuals. As we saw in the previous section, different three-dimensional models provide different degrees of hugging the data, and hence, different amounts of residual. Second, in EDA the analyst focuses on the size and pattern of individual residuals and subsets of residuals. A curve that remains in a residual plot indicates the model has failed to describe the curve. Multiple modes remaining in the residuals likewise suggest that a pattern has been missed. On the other hand, if students are taught to focus on only the gross summary of the sums of squares, they will also miss much of the detail in the pattern that is afforded by a careful look at residuals. For example, as indicated by the common *r* among the Anscombe (1973) data sets, all four data sets have the same sums-of-squares residual, but dramatically different patterns of residuals.

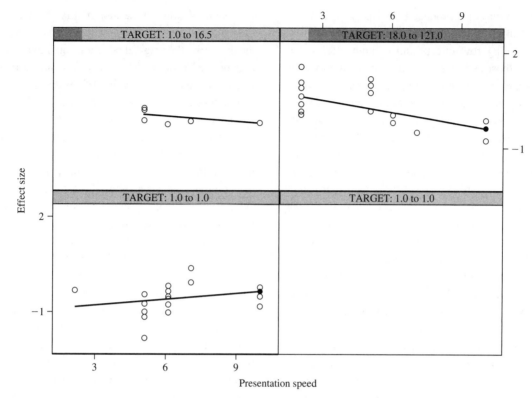

Figure 2.11   Plot of presentation speed by effect size at different ranges of number of targets using a trellis display. Data are identical with those presented in Figure 2.10.

This emphasis on residuals leads to an emphasis on an iterative process of model building: A tentative model is tried based on a best guess (or cursory summary statistics), residuals are examined, the model is modified, and residuals are reexamined over and over again. This process has some resemblance to forward variable selection in multiple regression; however, the trained analyst examines the data in great detail at each step and is thereby careful to avoid the errors that are easily made by automated procedures (cf. Henderson & Velleman, 1981). Tukey (1977) wrote, "Recognition of the iterative character of the relationship of exposing and summarizing makes it clear that there is usually much value in fitting, even if what is fitted is neither believed nor satisfactorily close" (p. 7).

The emphasis on examining the size and pattern of residuals is a fundamental aspect of scientific work. Before this notion was firmly established, the history of science was replete with stories of individuals that failed to consider misfit carefully. For example, Gregor Mendel (1822–1884), who is considered the founder of modern genetics, established the notion that physical properties of species are subject to heredity. In accumulating evidence for his views, Mendel conducted a fertilization experiment in which he followed several generations of axial and terminal flowers to observe how specific genes carried from one generation to another. On

subsequent examination of the data, R. A. Fisher (1936) questioned the validity of Mendel's reported results, arguing that Mendel's data seemed "too good to be true." Using chi-square tests of association, Fisher found that Mendel's results were so close to the predicted model that residuals of the size reported would be expected by chance less than once in 10,000 times if the model were true.

Reviewing this and similar historical anomalies, Press and Tanur (2001) argue that the problem is caused by the unchecked subjectivity of scientists who had the confirmation of specific models in mind. This can be thought of as having a weak sense of residuals and an overemphasis on working for dichotomous answers. Even when residuals existed, some researchers tended to embrace the model for fear that by admitting any inconsistency, the entire model would be rejected. Stated bluntly, those scientists had too much focus on the notion of DATA = MODEL. Gould (1996) provides a detailed history of how such model-confirmation biases and overlooked residuals led to centuries of unfortunate categorization of humans.

The Two-Way Fit

To illustrate the generality of the model-residual view of EDA, we will consider the extremely useful and flexible model of the two-way fit introduced by Tukey (1977) and Mosteller and Tukey (1977). The *two-way fit* is obtained by iteratively estimating row effects and column effects and using the sum of those estimates to create predicted (model or fit) cell values and their corresponding residuals. The cycles are repeated with effects adjusted on each cycle to improve the model and reduce residuals until additional adjustments provide no improvement. This procedure can be applied directly to data with two-way structures. More complicated structures can be modeled by multiple two-way structures. In this way, the general approach can subsume such approaches as the measures of central tendency in the ANOVA model, the ratios in the log-linear model, and person and item parameter estimates of the one-parameter item response theory model.

Consider the data presented in Table 2.1. It represents average effect sizes for each of a series of univariate analyses conducted by Stangor and McMillan (1992). Such a display is a common way to communicate summary statistics. From an exploratory point of view, however, we would like to see if some underlying structure or pattern can be discerned. Reviewing the table, it is easy to notice that some values are negative and some positive, and that the large number of -2.6 is a good bit larger than most of the other numbers which are between 0 and $+/- 1.0$.

To suggest an initial structure with a two-way fit we calculate column effects by calculating the median of each column. The median of each column then becomes the model for that column, and we subtract that initial model estimate from the raw data value to obtain a residual that replaces the

original data value in the data matrix. After this simple first pass, we have a new table in which each cell is a residual and the data from the original table are equal to the column effect plus the cell residual. The row effects are estimated next by calculating the median value of residuals in each row and subtracting the cell values (first-stage residuals) from these medians. The row effects are generally placed in the margin of the table and the new residuals replace the residuals from the previous stage. A similar calculation occurs on the row of medians that represents the column effects; the median of the column effects becomes the estimate of the overall or "grand" effect and the estimates of the column effects are likewise adjusted through subtraction.

This process is repeated iteratively until continued calculation of effects and residuals provides no improvement. The result of such a summary is provided in Table 2.2. Here we see an overall effect of $-.02$ as well as a characterization of each row and column. It is clear which columns are low, medium, and high, and likewise which rows stand out. Each cell in the original table can be reconstructed using the formula Data = grand effect + row effect + column effect + residual. For example, the memorization task for the bias condition can be recreated using the model of $1.01 = -0.02 + 0.69 + 0.14 - 0.02$.

To form a visual impression of these values, Tukey (e.g., Mosteller & Tukey, 1977) recommended a two-way fit plot such as that shown in Figure 2.12, panel A. In this figure,

TABLE 2.1   Average Effect Sizes by Dependent Variable and Study Characteristic. From Stangor and McMillan (1992).

Variable	Recall	Recognition	Bias
Strength of expectations			
a. Experimental session	−0.37	−0.47	0.32
b. Existing	0.32	−0.8	0.93
Content of the stimuli			
c. Behaviors	−0.21	−0.1	0.66
d. Traits	0.71	−2.16	1.98
Type of behavioral inconsistency			
e. Evaluative and descriptive	−0.27	0.1	0.29
f. Descriptive only	0.36	−0.54	0.85
Type of target			
g. Individual	−0.32	−1.14	1.04
h. Group	0.22	−0.38	0.33
Processing goal			
i. From impressions	−0.46	0.19	0.57
j. Memorize	0.12	−0.71	1.01
Interpolated task			
k. No	−0.44	−0.30	0.62
l. Yes	0.06	−1.26	0.75
Type of delay			
m. Within single session	−0.19	−0.65	0.82
n. Separate session	−0.02	−0.03	0.66

TABLE 2.2   Two-Way Decomposition of Average Effect Sizes by Dependent Variable and Study Characteristic. From Stangor and McMillan (1992).

Variable	Recall	Recognition	Bias	Row Effect
Strength of expectations				
a. Experimental session	0.00	0.43	0.00	−0.35
b. Existing	0.08	−0.51	0.00	0.26
Content of the stimuli				
c. Behaviors	−0.18	0.46	0.00	−0.00
d. Traits	0.00	−2.34	0.58	0.73
Type of behavioral inconsistency				
e. Evaluative and descriptive	0.00	0.90	−0.13	−0.25
f. Descriptive only	0.20	−0.17	0.00	0.19
Type of target				
g. Individual	0.00	−0.29	0.67	−0.30
h. Group	0.07	0.00	−0.51	0.17
Processing goal				
i. From impressions	−0.34	0.84	0.00	−0.10
j. Memorize	0.00	−0.30	0.20	0.14
Interpolated task				
k. No	−0.37	0.30	0.00	−0.05
l. Yes	0.00	−0.79	0.00	0.08
Type of delay				
m. Within single session	−0.07	0.00	0.25	−0.10
n. Separate session	0.00	0.52	−0.01	0.00
Column effects	0.00	−0.53	0.69	−0.02

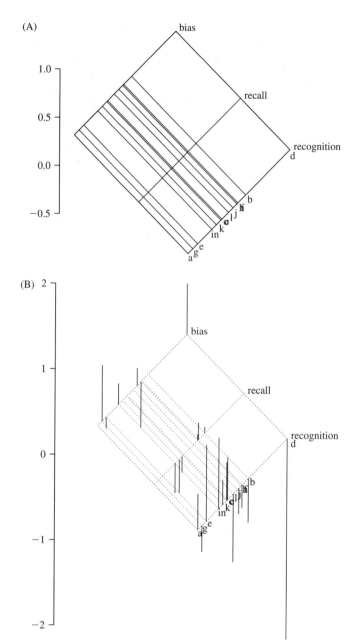

Figure 2.12 Panel A is a plot of main effects of a two-way fit. The height of the intersection of lines represents the sum of row, column, and grand effects and the corresponding predicted value for that cell. Panel B shows main effects of two-way fit with additional lines extending from predicted to actual values to highlight the location and size of residuals.

there is a line for each row and column effect in the model. For each row and column effect, the height of the intersection of the two lines is equal to the value of the predicted value in the model (overall effect + column effect + row effect). This plot clearly portrays the separation of the bias, recall, and recognition conditions, shows the clear separation of row d (trait levels), and displays a cluster of common small effects for rows a, g, and e. For us, this view was surprising because

when we first characterized row d, it was with a focus on the large −2.16 value, which is the largest (negative) value in the table. This graphic, however, suggests more needs to be considered. Reexamining the data for that row we see that not only does that row have the largest negative value, but also two of the largest positive values. All together, we end up with a strong positive row effect. For individual cells, however, the effect may be low or high, depending on the column.

Because the grand, row, and column effects represent the model, an assessment of that model requires an examination of where the model fits and does not fit. The residuals for these models are presented in the center of Table 2.2. Examination of these values reveals that the extreme value observed in the raw data remains extreme in this model, and that this value is not simply the result of combining row and column effects. A graphical analog to the residuals can also be provided, as shown in Figure 2.12, panel B. In this diagram, lines are drawn from the value of the predicted values (the intersection of row and column lines), downward or upward to the actual data value. The length of each line thereby indicates the size of the residual. Clearly, the size of the trait residual for recognition tasks dwarfs the size of all other effects and residuals in the data. Other patterns of residuals may provide additional information about the data because they tell us what departs from a standard description.

In this example we used simple raw residuals. In other applications, the actual value of residuals may be modified in a number of ways. One common method is to report residuals reexpressed as *normal-deviates* in the distribution of residuals. This approach, often used in structural equation analysis, can help identify the locations of the extremes, but hides the scale values of the error. In the highly developed area of regression diagnostics, residuals may be adjusted for the size of the leverage associated with the value of the criterion variable (*studentized residuals*) or calculated using a model that obtained predicted values without the presence of the observation in the model (externally studentized). This prevents extreme values from distorting the model to the point that an aberrant value leads to a small residual, as displayed in panel C of Figure 2.2.

As illustrated previously, complementary to the notion of patterns of residuals and meaning in individual residuals is the emphasis on mathematical models of effects that provide rich and parsimonious description. This view is very much in line with the recently emerging view of the importance of effect sizes suggested by Glass (1976) and renewed by Cohen (1994) and the APA Task Force on Statistical Inference (Wilkinson, 1999). EDA reminds us that at the same time we focus on effects as a description of the data, we must also focus on the size and pattern of misfits between effects and the data.

Reexpression

The data examined previously remind us that data often come to the exploratory data analyst in messy and nonstandard ways. This should not be unexpected, given the common assumption that the data distributions are either always well behaved, or that statistical techniques are sufficiently robust that we can ignore any deviations that might arise, and therefore skip detailed examination. In fact, it is quite often the case that insufficient attention has been paid to scaling issues in advance, and it is not until the failure of confirmatory methods that a careful examination of scaling is undertaken (if at all). In the exploratory mode, however, appropriate scaling is considered one of the fundamental activities and is called *reexpression*. Although mathematically equivalent to what is called *transformation* in other traditions, reexpression is so named to reflect the idea that the numerical changes are aimed at appropriate scaling rather than radical change.

Because reexpression requires an understanding of the underlying meaning of the data that are being reexpressed, the EDA approach avoids using the common categorizations of data as nominal, ordinal, interval, and ratio that follow Stevens (e.g., 1951). Rather, Mosteller and Tukey (1977) discussed broad classes of data as (a) amounts and counts; (b) balances (numbers that can be positive or negative with no bound); (c) counted fractions (ratios of counts); (d) ranks; and (e) grades (nominal categories).

When dealing with common amounts and counts, Tukey suggested heuristics that hold that (a) data should often be reexpressed toward a Gaussian shape, and (b) an appropriate reexpression can often be found by moving up or down "the ladder of reexpression." A Gaussian shape is sought because this will generally move the data toward more equal-interval measurement through symmetry, will often stabilize variance, and can quite often help linearize trend (Behrens, 1997a). In EDA, the term *normal* is avoided in favor of *Gaussian* to avoid the connotation of prototypicality or social desirability.

The ladder of reexpression is a series of exponents one may apply to original data that show considerable skew. Recognizing that the raw data exists in the form of X^1, moving up the ladder would consist of raising the data to X^2 or X^3. Moving down the ladder suggests changing the data to the scale of $X^{1/2}$, $-X^{-1/2}$, $-X^{-1}$, $-X^{-2}$, and so on. Because X^0 is equal to 1, this position on the ladder is generally replaced with the reexpression of $\log_{10}(X)$. To choose an appropriate transformation, one moves up or down the ladder toward the bulk of the data. This means moving down the ladder for distributions with positive skew and up the ladder for distributions with negative skew. By far the most common re-expression for positively skewed data is the logarithmic transformation. For ratios of counts, the most common recommendation is to "fold" the counts around a midpoint (usually .5) so that equal fractions equal 0. This generally means using $P/1 - P$, where P is the proportion of the total that the count comprises. A second step is to take the log of this folded fraction to create a "flog" equal to $\log(P/1 - P)$. In more common parlance, this is a logit that serves as the basis for logistic regression, survival, or event-history analysis, and measurement via item response theory. Additional techniques recommend that balances should generally be left alone whereas grades and ranks should be treated much like counted fractions (see, e.g., Mosteller & Tukey, 1977).

Although reexpression is a long-standing practice in the statistical community, going back at least to Fisher's (1921) construction of the r to z transformation, only recently has its use become more widespread in psychological literature. In fact, it often continues to arise more out of historic tradition than as the result of careful and comprehensive analysis. Consider, for example, the subset of data from a word-recognition experiment recently reported by Paap, Johansen, Chun, and Vonnahme (2000) and depicted in Figure 2.13. The experiment reported in this paper concerns the percentage of times participants correctly identify word pairs (%C) from a memory task as a function of the word pair's correct-incorrect confusability (CIC), percentage correct-letter distinctiveness (CD), number of neighbors (N), percentage of friends in the lexical neighborhood (%F), number of higher frequency neighbors (H), log of frequency of the test word (LTF), and log of frequency formed by incorrect alternative (LAF).

As the reader may see, although the distributions associated with the logarithmic reexpression are quite Gaussian, the variables that are not reexpressed differ quite a bit in this respect and lead to quite non-Gaussian bivariate distributions. The CIC variable is the most skewed. This leads to quite distorted correlations that would suffer from variance compression. Distributional outliers in CIC are indicated with X symbols, and regression lines on the %C against CIC scatter plot are present both for all data (lower line) and for the data with the outliers removed (sloped line).

Because these authors have already reexpressed the two frequency (count) variables, it will be useful to reverse the reexpression to see the original data, which are presented in Figure 2.14. The top panels show the histograms of the original raw data along with the *quantile-quantile (QQ) plot*, which is often called the *normal-probability plot* in cases like these because the ranks of the data are plotted against the z scores of corresponding ranks in a unit-normal distribution. When the points of the QQ plot are straight, this reflects the

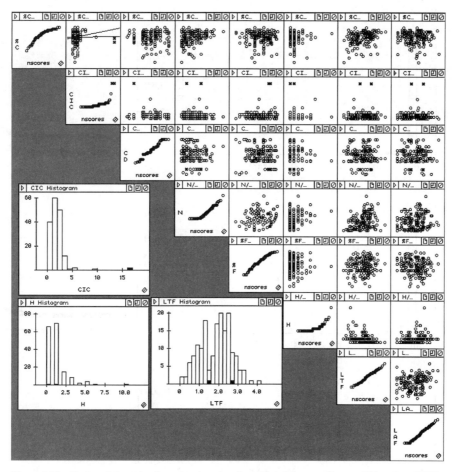

Figure 2.13   Scatter plot matrix of reaction time data from Paap, Johansen, Chun, and Vonnahme (2000). Patterns in the matrix reflect skew and outliers in some marginal distributions as well as nonlinearity in bivariate distributions. Outliers are highlighted in all graphics simultaneously through brushing and linking.

match between the empirical and theoretical distributions, which in this case is Gaussian. The data running along the bottom of these displays reflect the numerous data values at the bottom of the scales for the original frequency data. Panels E and F show the scatter plot of the raw data before reexpression and the corresponding simple regression residuals, which indicate that the spread of the error is approximately equal to the spread of the data. Although this logarithmic transformation is quite appropriate, it was chosen based upon historical precedent with data of this type rather than on empirical examination. Accordingly, in the view of EDA, the outcome is correct while the justification is lacking.

Turning to how remaining variables may be improved, we consider the four percentage variables, especially the highly distorted CIC variable. Working directly with percentages can be quite misleading because differences in values are not equally spaced across the underlying continuum. For example, it is generally easier to move from an approval rating of 50 to 55% than it is to move from 90 to 95%. All content

aside, the variance for the underlying binomial distribution is largest around .5 and smallest near 0 and 1. As noted above, this mathematical situation leads to a general rule for substituting logits (a.k.a., flogs) for raw percentages. Accordingly, we move forward by converting each percentage into a proportion (using the sophisticated process of dividing by 100) and constructing the logit for each proportion. The effect of this reexpression on the %C and CIC variables is portrayed in Figure 2.15. As the reader can see, the distributions are greatly moved toward Gaussian, and the appearance of the scatter plot changes dramatically.

The impact of this reexpression is considerable. Using the correlation coefficient in the original highly skewed and variance-unstable scale of percentages resulted in a measure of association of $r = .014$, suggesting no relationship between these two values. However, when the scale value and corresponding variance are adjusted using the logistic reexpression, the measure of relationship is $r = .775$—a dramatic difference in impression and likely a dramatic effect on

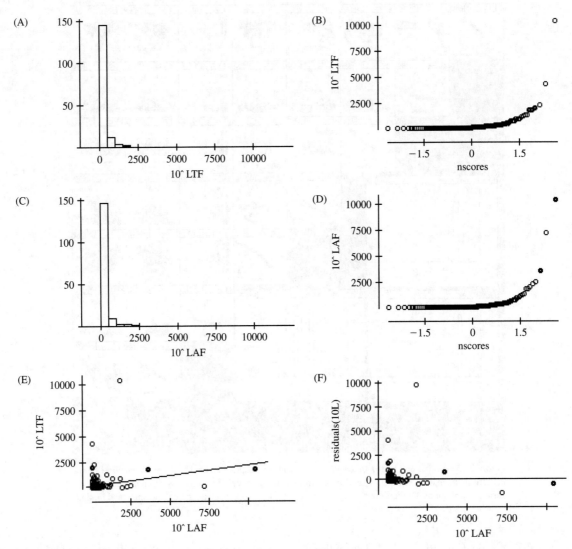

Figure 2.14   Histograms, normal-probability plots, and scatter plots for reaction time data as they would appear without the logarithmic reexpression used by the original authors.

theory development and testing. In a similar vein, Behrens (1997a) demonstrated how failure to appropriately reexpress similar data led Paap and Johansen (1994) to misinterpret the results of a multiple regression analysis. As in this case, a simple plotting of the data reveals gross violations of distributional assumptions that can lead to wildly compressed correlations or related measures.

The H variable is likewise of interest. Because it is a count, general heuristics suggest a square-root or logarithmic reexpression. Such reexpressions, however, fail to improve the situation substantially, so another course of action is required. Because the H variable is a count of high-frequency neighbors, and this number is bounded by the number of neighbors that exist, a logical alternative is to consider H as the proportion of neighbors that are high frequency rather

than the simple count. When such a proportion is computed and converted to a logit, the logit-H variable becomes very well behaved and leads to much clearer patterns of data and residuals. The revised scatter plot matrix for these variables is presented in Figure 2.16. As the reader may see, a dramatic improvement in the distributional characteristics has been obtained.

Although some researchers may reject the notion of reexpression as "tinkering" with the data, our experience has been that this view is primarily a result of lack of experience with the new scales. In fact, in many instances individuals often use scale reexpressions with little thought. For example, the common practice of using a proportion is seldom questioned, nor is the more common reexpression to z scores. In daily language many people have begun to use the $\log_{10}$

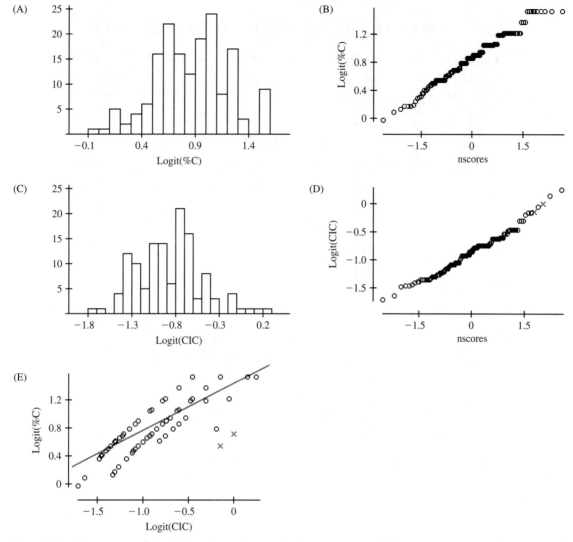

Figure 2.15 Histograms, normal-probability plots, and scatter plot for percent correct (%C) and percent congruent-incongruent ratio (CIC) following logistic reexpression.

reexpression of dollar amounts as "five-figure," "six-figure," or "seven-figure." Wainer (1977) demonstrated that the often recommended reexpression of $1/X$ for reaction-time tasks simply changes the scale from seconds per decision (time) to decisions per second (speed). Surely such tinkering can have great value when dramatic distributional improvements are made and sufficient meaning is retained.

Resistance

Because a primary goal of using EDA is to avoid being fooled, resistance is an important aspect of using EDA tools. *Resistant methods* are methods that are not easily affected by extreme or unusual data. This value is the basis for the general preference for the median rather than the mean. The

mean has a smaller standard error than the median, and so is an appropriate estimator for many confirmatory tests. On the other hand, the median is less affected by extreme scores or other types of perturbations that may be unexpected or unknown in the exploratory stages of research.

In general, there are three primary strategies for improving resistance. The first is to use rank-based measures and absolute values, rather than measures based on sums (such as the mean) or sums of squares (such as the variance). Instead, practitioners of EDA may use the tri-mean, which is the average of Q1, Q3, and the median counted twice. For measures of spread, the interquartile range is the most common, although the median absolute deviation (MAD) from the median is available as well. The second general resistance-building strategy is to use a procedure that emphasizes more

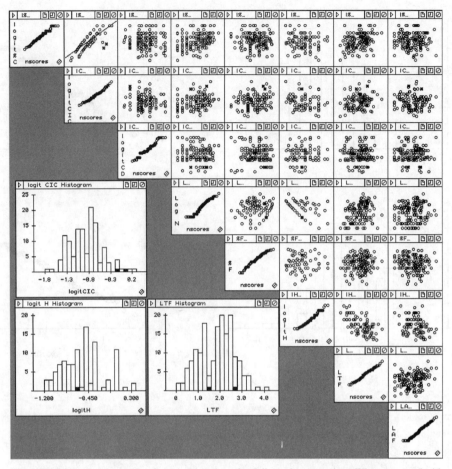

Figure 2.16   Scatter plot matrix of reaction time data after full set of reexpressions. When compared with the original data shown in Figure 2.13, this matrix reflects the improved ability to model the data using linear models.

centrally located scores and that uses less weight for more extreme values. This category includes trimmed statistics in which values past a certain point are weighted to 0 and thereby dropped from any estimation procedures. Less drastic approaches include the use of the biweight, in which values are weighted as an exponential function of their distance from the median. A third approach is to reduce the scope of the data one chooses to model on the basis of knowledge about extreme scores and the processes they represent.

Dealing with Outliers

The goal of EDA is to develop understandings and descriptions of data. This work is always set in some context and always presents itself with some assumptions about the scope of the work, even when these assumptions are unrecognized. Consider, for example, the task described in Behrens and Smith (1996) of developing a model of state-level economic aspects of education in the United States. In this analysis,

simple use of a scatter plot matrix revealed three consistent outliers in distributions of variables measured in dollars. The first outlier was the observation associated with the District of Columbia. How should this extreme value be approached? If the original intention was state-level analysis, the outlier in the data simply calls attention to the fact that the data were not prescreened for non-states. Here the decision is easy: Reestablish the scope of the project to focus on state-level data.

The remaining two outliers were observations associated with the states of Hawaii and Alaska. These two states had values that were up to four times higher than the next highest values from the set of all states. In many cases, the mean of the data when all 50 states were included was markedly different from the mean computed using values from only the contiguous 48 states. What should the data analyst do about this problem? Here again, the appropriate role of the exploratory work has led to a scope-clarification process that many data analysts encounter in the basic question *Do I model all the data poorly, or do I model a specific subset that I can describe well?* Although this question needs to be answered on a case-by-case basis, in the situation described here there is little doubt. Alaska and Hawaii should be set aside and the researcher should be content to construct a good model for the 48 contiguous states. Furthermore, the researcher should note that he or she has empirical evidence that Alaska and Hawaii follow different processes. This is a process of setting aside data and focusing scope. Clearly this process of examination and scope revision would need to be reported.

In this case, the rationale is clear and the data have semantic clarity. In other cases, however, quite extreme values may be found in data that are not simply victims of poor measurement models (e.g., the end of a long tail awaiting logarithmic reexpression). Under these circumstances the fundamental question to ask is *Do we know something about these observations that suggest they come from a different process than the process we are seeking to understand?* In experimentally oriented psychology, rogue values could be caused by numerous unintended processes: failure to understand instructions (especially during opening trials), failure to follow the instructions, failure to pay attention to the task (especially during closing trials), or equipment or data transcription failures. Under such circumstances, it is clear the data are not in the domain of the phenomenon to be studied, and the data should be set aside and the situation noted.

In other cases, extreme values present themselves with little auxiliary information to explain the reason for the extremeness. In such a situation we may first assess how much damage the values create in the model by constructing the model with all the data involved as well as with the questionable data set aside. For example, Behrens (1997b) conducted a meta-analysis of correlations between subscales of the White Racial Identity Attitude Scale (Helms, 1997). Initial review of the data suggested the distributions were not homogeneous and that some study results differed dramatically from the average. To assess the effect of these extreme values, Behrens calculated the average correlations, first, using all the data, and second, using a 20% trimmed mean. Results were consistent across approaches, suggesting the data could remain or be set aside with little impact on the inferences he was to make. What would have happened if, on the other hand, the trimmed results deviated from the full-data results? In such a case both sets of analysis should be conducted and reported and the difference between the two results considered as a measure of the effect of the rogue values. The most important aspect in either case is that a careful and detailed description of the full data, the reduced data, and the impact of the rogue data be reported. Unfortunately, the extremely terse and data-avoidant descriptions of much research reporting is inconsistent with this highly descriptive approach.

Summary

The tools described in this section are computational and conceptual tools intended to guide the skilled and skeptical data analyst. These tools center on the four *R*s of revelation, residuals, reexpression, and resistance. The discussion provided here provides only a glimpse into the range of techniques and conceptualizations in the EDA tradition. In practice, the essential elements of EDA center on the attitudes of flexibility, skepticism, and ingenuity, all employed with the goals of discovering patterns, avoiding errors, and developing descriptions.

CURRENT COMPUTING AND FUTURE DIRECTIONS

Computing for EDA

While EDA has benefited greatly from advances in statistical computing, users are left to find the necessary tools and appropriate interfaces spread across a variety of statistical packages. To date, the software most clearly designed for EDA is Data Desk (Data Description, 1997). Data Desk is highly interactive and completely graphical. Graphical windows in Data Desk do not act like "static" pieces of paper with graphic images, but rather consist of "live" objects that respond to brushing, selecting, and linking. The philosophy is so thoroughly graphical and interactive that additional variables can be added to regression models by dragging icons of the variables onto the regression sums-of-squares table. When this occurs, the model is updated along with all graphics associated with it (e.g., residual plots). Data Desk has a full range of EDA-oriented tools as well as many standards including multivariate analysis of variance (MANOVA) and cluster analysis—all with graphical aids. Because of its outstanding emphasis on EDA, Data Desk has been slower to develop more comprehensive data management tools, as has been the case with more popular tools like those offered by SAS, SPSS, and SYSTAT.

Both SAS (SAS Institute, 2001) and SPSS (SPSS, Inc., 2001) have improved their graphical interactivity in recent years. The SAS Insight module allows numerous interactive graphics, but linking and other forms of interaction are less comprehensive than those found in Data Desk. SYSTAT serves as a leader in graphical and exploratory tools, placing itself between the complete interactivity of Data Desk and the more standard approach of SAS and SPSS.

The *S* language and its recent incarnation as S-PLUS (Insightful, 2001) has long been a standard for research in statistical graphics, although it appears also to be emerging as a more general standard for statistical research. Venables and Ripley's 1999 book titled *Modern Applied Statistics with S-PLUS* (often called MASS) provides an outstanding introduction to both the Splus language and many areas of modern statistical computing of which psychologists are often unaware, including projection pursuit, spline-based regression, classification and regression trees (CART), *k*-means clustering, the application of neural networks for pattern classification, and spatial statistics.

High-quality free software is also available on the Internet in a number of forms. One consortium of statisticians has created a shareware language, called *R*, that follows the same syntax rules as S-PLUS and can therefore be used interchangeably. A number of computing endeavors have been based on Luke Tierney's XLISP-STAT system (Tierney, 1990), which is highly extensible and has a large object-oriented feature set. Most notable among the extensions is Forrest Young's (1996) ViSta (visual statistics) program, which is also free on the Internet.

Despite the features of many of these tools, each comes with weaknesses as well as strengths. Therefore, the end user must have continuing facility in several computing environments and languages. The day of highly exchangeable data and exchangeable interfaces is still far off.

Future Directions

The future of EDA is tightly bound to the technologies of computing, statistics, and psychology that have supported its growth to date. Chief among these influences is the rise of network computing. Network computing will bring a number of changes to data analysis in the years ahead because a network allows data to be collected from throughout the world, allows the data to have extensive central or distributed storage, allows computing power a distributed or centralized location, and allows distribution of results quickly around the world (Behrens, Bauer, & Mislevy, 2001). With regard to the increase in data acquisition, storage, and processing power, these changes will lead to increasing availability and need for techniques to deal with large-scale data. With increasingly large data sets, data analysts will have difficulty gaining detailed familiarity with the data and uncovering unusual patterns. Hopefully, the capacity for ingenuity and processing power will keep up with the increase in data availability.

Data Projections

Currently, most existing visualization tools are based upon *variable space,* in which data points are depicted within the Cartesian coordinates. With the advent of high-powered computing, more and more statistical software packages incorporate graphical tools that utilize other spatial systems. For example, several statistical packages implement the *biplot* (Gabriel, 1981; Gower & Hand, 1996), which combines variable space and subject space (also known as *vector space*). In *subject space* each subject becomes a dimension, and vectors are displayed according to the location of variables mapping into this subject space. In addition, SYSTAT implements additional projections, including triangular displays, in which both the Cartesian space and the barycentric space are used to display four-dimensional data.

Interactive methods for traversing multivariate data have been developed as well. Swayne, Cook, and Buja (1998) developed the X-GOBI system, which combines the high-dimensional search techniques of projection pursuit (Friedman & Tukey, 1974) and grand tour (Asimov, 1985). The *grand tour* strategy randomly manipulates projections for high-dimensional data using a biplot or similar plotting system, so that the user has an experience of touring "around" three- (or higher) dimensional rotating displays. *Projection pursuit* is a computing-intensive method that calculates an "interestingness function" (usually based on nonnormality) and develops search strategies over the multidimensional gradient of this function. Grand tour can provide interesting views but may randomly generate noninteresting views for quite some time. Projection pursuit actively seeks interesting views but may get caught in local minima. By combining these two high-dimensional search strategies and building them into a highly interactive and visual system, these authors leveraged the best aspects of several advanced exploratory technologies.

Data Immersion

To deal with the increasing ability to collect large data sets, applications of EDA are likely to follow the leads developed in high-dimensional data visualization used for physical systems. For example, orbiting satellites send large quantities of data that are impossible to comprehend in an integrated way without special rendering. To address these issues, researchers at the National Aeronautics and Space Administration (NASA) have developed tools that generate images of planetary surface features that are rendered in three-dimensional virtual reality engines. This software creates an imaginary topology from the data and allows users to "fly" through the scenes.

Although most psychologists are unlikely to see such huge (literally astronomical!) quantities of data, desktop computers can provide multimedia assistance for the creation of interactive, three-dimensional scatter plots and allow the animation of multidimensional data (e.g., Yu & Behrens, 1995).

Distributed Collaboration

Because data analysis is a social process and groups of researchers often work together, EDA will also be aided by the development of computer–desktop sharing technologies. Internetworking technologies currently exist that allow individuals to share their views of their computer screens so that real-time collaboration can occur. As statistical packages become more oriented toward serving the entire data-analytic process, developers will consider the social aspects of data analysis and build in remote data-, analysis-, image-, and report-sharing facilities. Such tools will help highly trained data analysts interact with subject-matter experts in schools, clinics, and businesses.

Hypermedia Networks for Scientific Reporting

While the natures of scientific inquiry, scientific philosophy, and scientific data analysis have changed dramatically in the last 300 years, it is notable that the reporting of scientific results differs little from the largely text-based and tabular presentations used in the eighteenth century. Modern print journals, under tight restrictions for graphics and space, have largely omitted the reporting of exploratory results or detailed graphics. Although a textual emphasis on reporting was necessary for economic reasons in previous centuries, the rise of network-based computing, interactive electronic information display, and hypertext documents supports the expansion of the values of EDA in scientific reporting. In a paper-based medium, narrative development generally needs to follow a linear development. On the other hand, in a hypertext environment the textual narrative can appear as traditionally implemented along with auxiliary graphics, detailed computer output, the raw data, and interactive computing—all at a second level of detail easily accessed (or ignored) through hypertext links. In this way, the rich media associated with EDA can complement the terse reporting format of the American Psychological Association and other authoring styles (Behrens, Dugan, & Franz, 1997).

To illustrate the possibility of such a document structuring, Dugan and Behrens (1998) applied exploratory techniques to reanalyze published data reported in hypertext on the World Wide Web. Figure 2.17 is an image of the interface

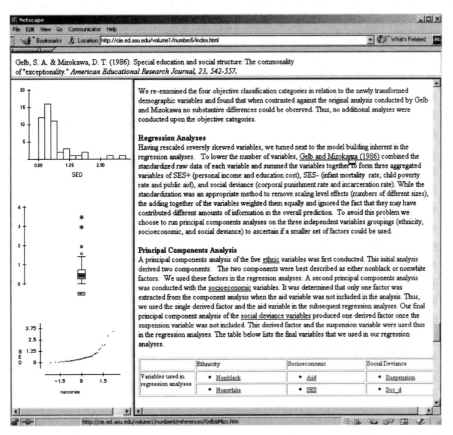

Figure 2.17   Screen appearance of electronic document created from EDA perspective by Dugan and Behrens (1998).

used by these authors. The pages were formatted so that the names of variables were hyperlinked to graphics that appeared on a side frame, and the names of references were hyperlinked to the references that appeared on the top frame of the page. References to *F* tests or regression-results linked to large and well-formatted result listings, and the data were hyperlinked to the paper as well.

While we wait for arrival of widespread hypertext in scientific journals, personal Web sites for improving the reporting of results can be used. For example, Helms (1997) criticized the analysis of Behrens (1997b), which questioned the psychometric properties of a commonly used scale in the counseling psychology racial-identity literature. Part of the concern raised by Helms was that she expected large amounts of skew in the data, and hence, likely violations of the statistical assumptions of the meta-analyses and confirmatory factor analyses that Behrens (1997b) reported. In reply, Behrens and Rowe (1997) noted that the underlying distributions had been closely examined (following the EDA tradition) and that the relevant histograms, normal-probability plots, scatter plot matrices (with hyperlinks to close-up views), and the original data were all on the World Wide Web (Behrens & Dugan, 1996). This supplemental graphical archive included a three-dimensional view of the data that could be navigated by users with Web browsers equipped with commonly available virtual-reality viewers. Such archiving quickly moves the discussion from impressions about possibilities regarding the data (which can be quite contentious) to a simple display and archiving of the data.

Summary

Emerging tools for EDA will continue to build on developments in integration of statistical graphics and multivariate statistics, as well as developments in computer interface design and emerging architectures for collecting, storing, and moving large quantities of data. As computing power continues to increase and computing costs decrease, researchers will be exposed to increasingly user-friendly interfaces and will be offered tools for increasingly interactive analysis and reporting. In the same way that creating histograms and scatter plots is common practice with researchers now, the construction of animated visualizations, high-dimensional plots, and hypertext reports is expected to be commonplace in the years ahead. To offset the common tendency to use new tools for their own sake, the emergence of new technologies creates an increased demand for researchers to be trained in the conceptual foundations of EDA. At the same time, the emergence of new tools will open doors for answering new scientific questions, thereby helping EDA evolve as well.

CONCLUSION

Despite the need for a wide range of analytic tools, training in psychological research has focused primarily on statistical methods that focus on confirmatory data analysis. Exploratory data analysis (EDA) is a largely untaught and overlooked tradition that has great potential to guard psychologists against error and consequent embarrassment. In the early stages of research, EDA is valuable to help find the unexpected, refine hypotheses, and appropriately plan future work. In the later confirmatory stages, EDA is valuable to ensure that the researcher is not fooled by misleading aspects of the confirmatory models or unexpected and anomalous data patterns.

There are a number of missteps the reader can make when faced with introductory materials about EDA. First, some readers may focus on certain aspects of tradition and see their own activity in that area as compelling evidence that they are already conducting EDA. Chief among these aspects is the use of graphics. By showing a broad range of graphics, we sought to demonstrate to the reader that statistical graphics has become a specialization unto itself in the statistics literature, and that there is much to learn beyond what is commonly taught in many introductory courses. Whereas the exploratory data analyst may use graphics, the use of graphics alone does not make an exploratory data analyst.

A second pitfall the reader should be careful to avoid is rejecting the relevance of the examples used in this chapter. Some might argue that the pathological patterns seen herein exist only in data from meta-analyses or reaction time experiments, or in educational data. Our own work with many types of data sets, and in conversations with psychologists in numerous specializations, suggests that these are not isolated or bizarre data sets but are quite common patterns. The reader is encouraged to reanalyze his or her own data using some of the techniques provided here before making judgments about the prevalence of messy data.

A third pitfall to avoid is overlooking the fact that embracing EDA may imply some confrontation with traditional values and behaviors. If EDA is added to the methodology curriculum then other aspects may need to be deemphasized. If new software is desired, changes in budgets may need to occur, with their associated social conflicts. Additionally, conflict may arise within the researcher as he or she works to balance the value of EDA for scientific advancement while finding little explicit value for EDA in manuscript preparation.

Psychological researchers address complex and difficult problems that require the best set of methodological tools available. We recommend EDA as a set of conceptual and computational tools to supplement confirmatory statistics, and expect psychological research will increase in efficiency and precision by its wider applications.

REFERENCES

Aiken, L. S., & West, S. G. (1991). *Multiple regression: Testing and interpreting interactions.* Newbury Park, CA: Sage.

Aiken, L. S., West, S. G., Sechrest, L., & Reno, R. R. (1990). Graduate training in statistics, methodology, and measurement in psychology: A review of Ph.D. programs in North America. *American Psychologist, 45,* 721–734.

Anscombe, F. J. (1973). Graphs in statistical analysis. *The American Statistician, 27,* 17–21.

Asimov, D. (1985). The grand tour: A tool for viewing multidimensional data. *SIAM Journal of Statistical Computing, 6,* 138–143.

Bauer, M. I., & Johnson-Laird, P. N. (1993). How diagrams can improve reasoning. *Psychological Science, 4*(6), pp. 372–378.

Becker, R. A., Chambers, J. M., & Wilks, A. (1988). *The new S language: A programming environment for data analysis and graphics.* New York: CRC Press.

Becker, R. A., Cleveland, W. S., & Shyu, M. J. (1996). The visual design and control of Trellis Display. *Journal of Computational and Statistical Graphics, 5,* 123–155.

Behrens, J. T. (1997a). Principles and procedures of exploratory data analysis. *Psychological Methods, 2,* 131–160.

Behrens, J. T. (1997b). Does the white racial identity attitude scale measure racial identity? *Journal of Counseling Psychology, 44,* 3–12.

Behrens, J. T. (2000). Exploratory data analysis. In A. E. Kazdin (Ed.), *Encyclopedia of psychology* (Vol. 3, pp. 303–305). New York: Oxford University Press.

Behrens, J. T., Bauer, M., & Mislevy, R. (2001, April). *Future prospects for assessment in the on-line world.* Paper presented at the Annual Meeting of the American Educational Research Association, Seattle, WA.

Behrens, J. T., & Dugan, J. G. (1996). *A graphical tour of the White Racial Identity Attitude Scale data in hypertext and VRML.* Retrieved from http://research.ed.asu.edu/reports/wrias.graphical.tour/graphtour.html.

Behrens, J. T., Dugan, J. T., & Franz, S. (1997, August). *Improving the reporting of research results using the World Wide Web.* Paper presented at the 106th Annual Convention of the American Psychological Association, Chicago, IL.

Behrens, J. T., & Rowe, W. (1997). Measuring White racial identity: A reply to Helms (1997). *Journal of Counseling Psychology, 44,* 17–19.

Behrens, J. T., & Smith, M. L. (1996). Data and data analysis. In D. C. Berliner & R. C. Calfee (Eds.), *Handbook of educational psychology* (pp. 949–989). New York: Macmillan.

Berk, K. N. (1994). *Data analysis with Student SYSTAT.* Cambridge, MA: Course Technology.

Beveridge, W. I. B. (1950). *The art of scientific investigation.* New York: Vintage Books.

Box, G. E. P. (1979). Robustness in scientific model building. In R. L. Launer & G. N. Wilkinson (Eds.), *Robustness in Statistics* (pp. 201–236). New York: Academic Press.

Braun, H. I. (Ed.). (1994). *The collected works of John W. Tukey: Vol 8. Multiple comparisons, 1948–1983.* New York: Chapman & Hall.

Breckler, S. J. (1990). Application of covariance structure modeling in psychology: Cause for concern? *Psychological Bulletin, 107,* 260–273.

Brillinger, D. R. (Ed.). (1984). *The collected works of John W. Tukey: Vol 1. Time series: 1949–1964.* Monterey, CA: Wadsworth.

Brillinger, D. R. (Ed.). (1985). *The collected works of John W. Tukey: Vol 2. Time series: 1965–1984.* Monterey, CA: Wadsworth.

Brillinger, D. R., Fernholz, L. T., & Morgenthaler, S. (1997). *The practice of data analysis: Essays in honor of John W. Tukey.* Princeton, NJ: Princeton University Press.

Clark, L. A., Cleveland, W. S., Denby, L., & Liu, C. (1999). Competitive profiling displays: Multivariate graphs for customer satisfaction survey data. *Marketing Research, 11,* 25–33.

Cleveland, W. S. (1985). *The elements of graphing data.* Monterey, CA: Wadsworth.

Cleveland, W. S. (Ed.). (1988). *The collected works of John W. Tukey: Vol. 5. Graphics.* Belmont, CA: Wadsworth.

Cleveland, W. S. (1993). *Visualizing data.* Summit, NJ: Hobart Press.

Cleveland, W. S., & McGill, R. (1984). Graphical perception: Theory, experimentation, and application to the development of graphical methods. *Journal of the American Statistical Association, 79,* 531–554.

Cleveland, W. S., & McGill, R. (1988). *Dynamic graphics for statistics.* Monterey, CA: Wadsworth.

Cohen, J. (1994). The earth is round ($p < .05$). *American Psychologist, 49,* 997–1003.

Cook, R. D., & Weisberg, S. (1994). *An introduction to regression graphics.* New York: Wiley.

Cox, D. R. (Ed.). (1992). *The collected works of John W. Tukey: Vol. 7. Factorial and ANOVA, 1949–1962.* Monterey, CA: Wadsworth.

Data Description, Inc. (1997). Data Desk (version 6.1) [computer software]. Ithaca, NY: Data Description.

Dugan, J. G., & Behrens, J. T. (1998, November 18). A Hypermedia exploration of the classification problem in special education. *Current Issues in Education, 1,* (6). Retrieved from http://cie.ed.asu.edu/volume1/number6/.

Fisher, R. A. (1921). On the "probable error" of a coefficient of correlation deduced from a small sample. *Metron, 1,* 3–32.

Fisher, R. A. (1935). The logic of inductive inference. *Journal of the Royal Statistical Society, 98,* 39–82.

Fisher, R. A. (1936). Has Mendel's work been rediscovered? *Annals of Science, 1,* 115–117.

Fisher, R. A. (1955). Statistical methods and scientific induction. *Journal of the Royal Statistical Society B, 17,* 69–78.

Friedman, J. H., & Tukey, J. W. (1974). A projection pursuit algorithm for Exploratory Data Analysis. *IEEE Transactions on Computers, 23,* 881–889.

Frigge, M., Hoaglin, D. C., & Iglewicz, B. (1989). Some implementations of the boxplot. *The American Statistician, 43,* 50–54.

Gabriel, K. R. (1971). The biplot graphical display of matrices with application to principal component analysis. *Biometrics, 58,* 453–467.

Garner, W. R. (1974). *The processing of information and structure.* Potomac, MD: Erlbaum.

Gigerenzer, G. (1987). Probabilistic thinking and the fight against subjectivity. In L. Kroger, G. Gigerenzer, & M. S. Morgan (Eds.), *The probabilistic revolution: Vol. 2. Ideas in the sciences* (pp. 11–33). Cambridge, MA: MIT Press.

Gigerenzer, G. (1993). The superego, the ego, and the id in statistical reasoning. In G. Keren & C. Lewis (Eds.), *A handbook for data analysis in the behavioral sciences: Methodological issues* (pp. 311–339). Hillsdale, NJ: Erlbaum.

Glass, G. V (1976). Primary, secondary, and meta-analysis of research. *Educational Researcher, 5,* 3–8.

Gödel, C. (1986). *Collected works.* New York: Oxford University Press. (Original work published 1947)

Gould, S. J. (1996). *The mismeasure of man* (2nd ed.). New York: Norton.

Gower, J. C., & Hand, D. J. (1996). *Biplots.* London: Chapman & Hall.

Hacking, I. (1975). *The emergence of probability: A philosophical study of early ideas about probability, induction and statistical inference.* New York: Cambridge University Press.

Härdle, W. (1991). *Smoothing techniques with implementation in S.* New York: Springer-Verlag.

Härdle, W., Klinke, S., & Turlach, B. A. (1995). *XploRe: An interactive statistical computing environment.* New York: Springer-Verlag.

Helms, J. E. (1997). Implications of Behrens for the validity of the White Racial Identity Attitude Scale. *Journal of Counseling Psychology, 44,* 13–16.

Henderson, H. V., & Velleman, P. F. (1981). Building multiple regression models interactively. *Biometrics, 37,* 391–411.

Hilpinen, R. (1992). On Peirce's philosophical logic: Propositions and their objects. *Transaction of the Charles S. Peirce Society, 28,* 467–488.

Hoaglin, D. C., Mosteller, F., & Tukey, J. W. (Eds.). (1983). *Understanding robust and exploratory data analysis.* Reading, MA: Addison-Wesley.

Hoaglin, D. C., Mosteller, F., & Tukey, J. W. (Eds.). (1985). *Exploring data tables, trends, and shapes.* Reading, MA: Addison-Wesley.

Hoaglin, D. C., Mosteller, F., & Tukey, J. W. (Eds.). (1991). *Fundamentals of exploratory analysis of variance.* Reading, MA: Addison-Wesley.

Hoffmann, M. (1997). *Is there a logic of abduction?* Paper presented at the 6th congress of the International Association for Semiotic Studies, Guadalajara, Mexico.

Hosmer, D. W., & Lemeshow, S. (2000). *Applied logistic regression.* New York: Wiley.

Hume, D. (1912). *An enquiry concerning human understanding, and selections from a treatise of human nature.* Chicago: Open Court. (Original work published 1777)

Insightful. (2001). Splus 6 [Computer software]. Available at http://www.insightful.com/.

Johnson-Laird, P. N. (1983). *Mental models: Towards a cognitive science of language, inference, and consciousness.* Cambridge, MA: Harvard University Press.

Jones, L. V. (Ed.). (1986a). *The collected works of John W. Tukey: Vol. 3. Philosophy and principles of data analysis: 1949–1964.* Belmont, CA: Wadsworth.

Jones, L. V. (Ed.). (1986b). *The collected works of John W. Tukey: Vol. 4. Philosophy and principles of data analysis (1965–1986).* Belmont, CA: Wadsworth.

Josephson, J. R., & Josephson, S. G. (1994). (Ed.). *Abductive inference: Computation, philosophy, technology.* Cambridge, England: Cambridge University Press.

Keselman, H. J., Huberty, C., Lix, L. M., Olejnik, S., Cribbie, R. A., Donahue, B., Kowalchuk, R. K., Lowman, L. L., Petoskey, M. D., & Keselman, J. C. (1998). Statistical practices of educational researchers: An analysis of their ANOVA, MANOVA, and ANCOVA analyses. *Review of Educational Research, 68,* 350–386.

Kline, M. (1980). *Mathematics: The loss of certainty.* New York: Oxford University Press.

Kosslyn, S. (1994). *Elements of graph design.* New York: W. H. Freeman.

Larkin, J., & Simon, H. (1987). Why a diagram is (sometimes) worth a thousand words. *Cognitive Science, 11,* 65–99.

Lehmann, E. L. (1993). The Fisher, Neyman-Pearson theories of testing hypotheses: One theory or two? *Journal of the American Statistical Association, 88,* 1242–1249.

Lewandowsky, S., & Behrens, J. T. (1999). Statistical graphs and maps. In F. T. Durso, R. S. Nickerson, R. W. Schvaneveldt, S. T. Dumais, D. S. Lindsay, & M. T. H. Chi (Eds.), *The handbook of applied cognition* (pp. 514–549). New York: Wiley.

Lindsey, J. K. (1996). *Parametric statistical inference.* Oxford, England: Clarendon Press.

Mallows, C. L. (Ed.). (1990). *The collected works of John W. Tukey: Vol. 6. More mathematical: 1938–1984.* Monterey, CA: Wadsworth.

McGill, R., Tukey, J. W., & Larsen, W. A. (1978). Variations of box plots. *American Statistican, 32,* 12–16.

Micceri, T. (1989). The unicorn, the normal curve, and other improbable creatures. *Psychological Bulletin, 105,* 156–166.

Mosteller, F., & Tukey, J. W. (1977). *Data analysis and regression: A second course in statistics.* Reading, MA: Addison-Wesley.

Neyman, J., & Pearson, E. S. (1928). On the use and interpretation of certain test criteria for purposes of statistical inference. Part I and II. *Biometrika, 20,* 174–240, 263–294.

Neyman, J., & Pearson, E. S. (1933a). The testing of statistical hypotheses in relation to probabilities a priori. *Proceedings of Cambridge Philosophical Society, 20,* 492–510.

Neyman, J., & Pearson, E. S. (1933b). On the problem of the most efficient tests of statistical hypotheses. *Philosophical Transactions of Royal Society; Series A, 231,* 289–337.

Norusis, M. J. (2000). *SPSS 10.0 Guide to data analysis.* New York: Prentice Hall.

Ottens, J., & Shank, G. (1995). The role of abductive logic in understanding and using advanced empathy. *Counselor Education & Supervision, 34,* 199–213.

Paap, K. R., & Johansen, L. S. (1994). The case of the vanishing frequency effect: A retest of the verification model. *Journal of Experimental Psychology: Human Perception and Performance, 20,* 1129–1157.

Paap, K. R., Johansen, L. S., Chun, E., & Vonnahme, P. (2000). Neighborhood frequency does affect performance in the Reicher task: Encoding or decision? *Journal of Experimental Psychology: Human, Perception, and Performance, 26,* 1691–1720.

Peirce, C. S. (1868). Some consequences of four incapacities. *Journal of Speculative Philosophy, 2,* 140–157.

Peirce, C. S. (1878). How to make our ideas clear. *Popular Science Monthly, 12,* 286–302.

Peirce, C. S. (1960). *Collected papers of Charles Sanders Peirce.* Cambridge, MA: Harvard University Press. (Original work published 1934)

Press, S. J., & Tanur, J. M. (2001). *The subjectivity of scientists and the Bayesian approach.* New York: Wiley.

Russell, B., & Whitehead, A. N. (1910). *Principia mathematica.* Cambridge, MA: Cambridge University Press.

Salsburg, D. S. (1985). The religion of statistics as practiced in medical journals. *American Statistician, 39,* 220–223.

Samuelson, P. (1967). Economic forecast and science. In P. A. Samuelson, J. R. Coleman, & F. Skidmore (Eds.), *Reading in economics* (pp. 124–129). New York: McGraw-Hill.

SAS Institute (2001). SAS/Insight [Computer software]. Retrieved from http://www.sas.com.

Schum, D. A. (1994). *The evidential foundations of probabilistic reasoning.* New York: Wiley.

Scott, D. W. (1992). *Multivariate density estimation: Theory, practice, and visualization.* New York: Wiley.

Shank, G. (1991, October). *Abduction: Teaching to the ground state of cognition.* Paper presented at the Bergamo Conference on Curriculum Theory and Classroom Practice, Dayton, OH.

SPSS, Inc. (2001). SYSTAT [Computer software]. Retrieved from http://www.spss.com.

Staat, W. (1993). On abduction, deduction, induction and the categories. *Transactions of the Charles S. Peirce Society, 29,* 225–237.

Stangor, C., & McMillan, D. (1992). Memory for expectancy-congruent and expectancy-incongruent information: A review of the social and social development literatures. *Psychological Bulletin, 111,* 42–61.

Stevens, S. S. (1951). Mathematics, measurement, and psychophysics. In S. S. Stevens (Ed.), *Handbook of experimental psychology* (pp. 1–49). New York: Wiley.

Stock, W. A., & Behrens, J. T. (1991). Box, line, and mid-gap plots: Effects of display characteristics on the accuracy and bias of estimates of whisker length. *Journal of Educational Statistics, 16,* 1–20.

Sullivan, P. F. (1991). On falsification interpretation of Peirce. *Transactions of the Charles S. Peirce Society, 27,* 197–219.

Swayne, D. F., Cook, D., & Buja, A. (1998). XGobi: Interactive dynamic data visualization in the X Window System. *Journal of Computational and Graphical Statistics, 7*(1), 113–130.

Thagard, P., & Shelley, C. (1997). *Abductive reasoning: Logic, visual thinking, and coherence.* Retrieved from http://cogsci.uwaterloo.ca/Articles/Pages/%7FAbductive.html.

Tierney, L. (1990). *Lisp-Stat: An object-oriented environment for statistical computing and dynamic graphics.* New York: Wiley.

Tufte, E. R. (1990). *Envisioning information.* Cheshire, CT: Graphics Press.

Tufte, E. R. (1997). *Visual explanations: Images and quantities, evidence and narrative.* Cheshire, CT: Graphics Press.

Tufte, E. R. (2001). *The visual display of quantitative information* (2nd ed.). Cheshire, CT: Graphics Press. (Original work published 1983)

Tukey, J. W. (1969). Analyzing data: Sanctification or detective work? *American Psychologist, 24,* 83–91.

Tukey, J. W. (1977). *Exploratory data analysis.* Reading, MA: Addison-Wesley.

Tukey, J. W. (1986a). Data analysis, computation and mathematics. In L. V. Jones (Ed.), *The collected works of John W. Tukey: Vol. 4. Philosophy and principles of data analysis: 1965–1986* (pp. 753–775). Pacific Grove, CA: Wadsworth. (Original work published 1972)

Tukey, J. W. (1986b). Exploratory data analysis as part of a larger whole. In L. V. Jones (Ed.), *The collected works of John W. Tukey: Vol. 4. Philosophy and principles of data analysis: 1965–1986* (pp. 793–803). Pacific Grove, CA: Wadsworth. (Original work published 1973)

Tukey, J. W. (1986c). The future of data analysis. In L. V. Jones (Ed.), *The collected works of John W. Tukey: Vol. 3. Philosophy and principles of data analysis: 1949–1964* (pp. 391–484). Pacific Grove, CA: Wadsworth. (Original work published 1962)

Tukey, J. W., & Wilk, M. B. (1986). Data analysis and statistics: An expository overview. In L. V. Jones (Ed.), *The collected works of John W. Tukey: Vol. 4. Philosophy and principles of data analysis: 1965–1986* (pp. 549–578). Pacific Grove, CA: Wadsworth. (Original work published 1966)

Venables, W. N., & Ripley, B. D. (1999). *Modern Applied Statistics with S-PLUS*. (3rd ed.). New York: Springer-Verlag.

Wainer, H. (1977). Speed vs. reaction time as a measure of cognitive performance. *Memory and Cognition, 5,* 278–280.

Wainer, H. (1997). *Visual Revelations: Graphical tales of fate and deception from Napoleon Bonaparte to Ross Perot*. Mahwah, NJ: Erlbaum.

Wainer, J., & Velleman, P. (2001). Statistical graphs: Mapping the pathways of science. *Annual Review of Psychology, 52,* 305–335.

Wilcox, R. (1997). *Introduction to robust estimation and hypothesis testing*. San Diego, CA: Academic Press.

Wilcox, R. (2001). *Fundamentals of modern statistical methods: Substantially improving power and accuracy*. New York: Springer.

Wilkinson, L. (1993). Comments on W. S. Cleveland, a model for studying display methods of statistical graphs, *Journal of Computational and Graphical Statistics, 2,* 355–360.

Wilkinson, L. (1994). Less is more: Two- and three-dimensional graphs for data display. *Behavior Research Methods, Instruments, & Computers, 26,* 172–176.

Wilkinson, L. (1999). *The grammar of graphics*. New York: Springer.

Wilkinson, L. (2001). Graphics. In *Systat User's Guide*. Chicago: SPSS Inc.

Wilkinson, L., & Task Force on Statistical Inference, APA Board of Scientific Affairs. (1999). Statistical methods in psychology journals: Guidelines and explanations. *American Psychologist, 54,* 594–604.

Young, F. W. (1996). *ViSta: The Visual Statistics System*. Chapel Hill, NC: UNC L.L. Thurstone Psychometric Laboratory Research Memorandum.

Yu, C. H., & Behrens, J. T. (1995). Applications of scientific multivariate visualization to behavioral sciences. *Behavior Research Methods, Instruments, and Computers, 27,* 264–271.

CHAPTER 3

Power: Basics, Practical Problems, and Possible Solutions

RAND R. WILCOX

There are, of course, two major types of errors one might commit when testing any hypothesis. The first, called a *Type I error,* is rejecting when in fact the null hypothesis is true, and the second is failing to reject when the null hypothesis is false. Certainly it is undesirable to claim that groups differ or that there is an association between two variables when this is false. But simultaneously, it is undesirable to fail to detect a difference or to detect an association that is real, particularly if the difference has important practical implications. This latter error, failing to reject when the null hypothesis is false, is called a *Type II error,* and the probability of rejecting when the null hypothesis is false is called *power.* The roots of modern approaches to power date back two centuries to Laplace, who derived the frequentist approach to computing confidence intervals used today. And even before Laplace, the basic idea can be gleaned from the work of de Moivre, who derived the equation for the normal curve.

Consider, for example, the usual one-way analysis of variance (ANOVA) design where the goal is to test the hypothesis of equal means among J independent groups. That is, the goal is to test

$$H_0: \mu_1 = \cdots = \mu_J,$$

where $\mu_1, \ldots, \mu_J$ are the corresponding population means. Power analyses are used to plan studies with the goal that the power of the statistical tests used will be adequate for the smallest effect deemed to be important. Under normality and homoscedasticity (meaning that all J groups have a common variance), exact control over the probability of a Type I error can be achieved with the classic ANOVA F test, as is well known. Moreover, there is a standard method for assessing power as well, which is described and illustrated later in this chapter. In essence, based on a certain measure of the difference among the population means, it is possible to determine power exactly given the sample sizes and a choice for the probability of a Type I error. In particular, the adequacy of proposed sample sizes can be assessed by determining how much power they provide. Today, the term *power analysis* brings to mind this technique, so it is important to cover it here.

However, a goal in this chapter is to take a broader look at power, paying particular attention to modern insights and advances. A half century ago, the method for assessing power mentioned in the previous paragraph was certainly reasonable, but little was known about its properties when violating the assumptions of normality and homoscedasticity. Indeed, there were some indications that assumptions could be violated with impunity, but during the ensuing years there have been many insights regarding the consequences of violating these assumptions that have serious practical implications.

So one of the goals here is to summarize why there are practical concerns and how they might be addressed. The theme in this paper is that conventional methods have proven to be useful but that they are far from perfect and sometimes disastrous. Moreover, our understanding of factors that are relevant to power continues to grow, as does the collection of statistical tools for dealing with problems that have been discovered. In addition, there is more to power than determining adequate sample sizes. Generally, it is a complex problem that requires a plethora of tools, and one goal is to describe some of the tools that might be used.

A related issue is power when dealing with associations among two or more variables. Again, relatively simple methods are available under normality and homoscedasticity. For example, when testing the hypothesis that Pearson's correlation is zero, if in reality it is equal to .3, say, the sample size can be determined so that the probability of rejecting is equal to .8, say, or any value deemed important. But when these assumptions are violated, practical problems are even worse relative to ANOVA. Of course, one could simply ignore these problems, so a goal in this chapter is to explain why this strategy can be highly unsatisfactory and summarize some of the modern methods that might be used instead. Substantial progress has been made, but it will be argued that even more needs to be done.

Generally, achieving high power, and even judging whether power will be high in a given situation, is an extremely complex problem that has seen many major advances in recent years. These advances include a better understanding of what affects power and how power might be maximized. Consider, for example, the problem of comparing two groups in terms of some measure of location such as the mean or median. A variety of factors affects power, and some are well known whereas others are being found to be more important than was previously thought. A basic factor is the smallest difference between the groups deemed important, which is reflected by some type of effect size, examples of which will be given. Certainly the variance associated with some outcome variable is well known to influence power when making inferences based on sample means, and additional factors influencing power are skewness, heavy tailedness (roughly referring to situations where outliers are common), and heteroscedasticity (unequal variances). Achieving relatively high power, as well as understanding the limitations of standard approaches to power, requires an understanding of how these factors influence power, so another goal here is to address this issue.

Note that at best, there is a limited amount of control one can exert over these factors. In some situations, the outcome variable of interest can be constructed in a way that influences its variance, but once a population of individuals has been selected for study, and once the outcome (dependent) variable has been settled upon, the variance becomes an unknown state of nature that is now beyond our control. Other factors over which we have partial control are α (the probability of a Type I error), the reliability of the measures being used, and the sample sizes. Steps can be taken to improve reliability; nevertheless, it remains an issue when dealing with power. As is well known, the choice for α influences power, but typically there are limits on how large α can be. And of course there are limits on how many observations one can obtain.

At this stage, factors that remain within our control include the estimator used (such as the mean vs. the median) and the hypothesis-testing technique employed. It has long been known that under normality and homoscedasticity, Student's T test achieves relatively high power. However, a practical concern is that arbitrarily small departures from a normal curve toward a heavy-tailed distribution can destroy power when working with any method based on means. Also, skewness can contribute to this problem in a substantial way, and even under normality heteroscedasticity is yet another factor that can lower power. Increasing sample sizes is one way of dealing with these concerns, but as will be explained, restricting attention to this one approach can be relatively unsatisfactory.

A CONVENTIONAL POWER ANALYSIS

Although the goal in this paper is to provide a broad perspective on power, a description of a conventional power analysis is first presented for readers unfamiliar with it. Consider two independent groups, assume normality and homoscedasticity, and assume that the population means are to be compared with Student's T test. If the means differ, we should reject, so the issue is the probability of rejecting as a function of the sample sizes. For example, if the sample sizes are $n_1 = n_2 = 20$, what is the power, and if the power is judged to be too low, how large must the sample sizes be to correct this problem? Typically, a researcher specifies a desired amount of power and consults specially designed tables or software that indicates the required sample size. Doing this requires first specifying some difference between the means that is judged to be important. A natural way of doing this is with the difference between the means, $\mu_1 - \mu_2$, but it is impossible to determine the required sample size based on this approach (Dantzig, 1940). (Switching to a two-stage procedure, power can be addressed based on the difference between the means, as will be explained later.) If a standardized difference is used instead, namely,

$$\Delta = \frac{\mu_1 - \mu_2}{\sigma},$$

where σ^2 is the assumed common variance, this technical difficulty is avoided. Cohen (1977) defined a large effect as something that is visible to the naked eye and concluded that for two normal distributions having a common variance, small, medium, and large effect sizes correspond to $\Delta = .2$, $\Delta = .5$, and $\Delta = .8$, respectively. Given that the probability of a Type I error is α, Cohen provides tables for determining the required sample sizes (also see Kraemer & Thiemann, 1987). For example, with $n_1 = n_2 = 20$, $\Delta = .8$, and $\alpha = .05$, power is .68. Rather than specify a value for Δ, one can plot a so-called power curve where power is plotted versus Δ, given the sample sizes and α. An advantage of this approach is that it provides a more global sense of how power is related to Δ based on the sample sizes used. (For software, see Bornstein, 2000; Elashoff, 2000; O'Brien, 1998.)

An extension of this standard power analysis to more than two groups, still assuming normality and homoscedasticity, has been derived. That is, given α, the sample sizes corresponding to J groups, and a difference among the means deemed to be important, power can be computed. Assuming equal sample sizes, now the difference among the means is typically measured with

$$\frac{1}{\sigma} \sqrt{\frac{\sum (\mu_j - \overline{\mu})^2}{J}},$$

where again σ^2 is the assumed common variance. There are fundamental problems with this standard approach, not the least of which is the interpretation of this last equation when dealing with nonnormal distributions. Some of these problems arise under arbitrarily small departures from normality, as will be illustrated.

FACTORS OVER WHICH WE HAVE LIMITED CONTROL

Achieving relatively high power requires, among other things, a more detailed understanding about how factors over which we have limited control are related to power so that the relative merits of factors within our control can be understood. Consider some population of individuals and suppose that some outcome measure, X, has been chosen for study. When working with means, it is well known that the variance of a distribution, σ^2, has a direct effect on power: The larger σ^2 happens to be, the lower power will be with α and the

sample sizes fixed. More generally, power is related to the squared standard error of the measure of location being used. For the sample mean, $\overline{X}$, the squared standard error is the variance of the sample mean (if a study could be repeated infinitely many times), which is

$$\text{VAR}(\overline{X}) = \frac{\sigma^2}{n}, \tag{3.1}$$

where n is the sample size. It is this connection with the variance that wreaks havoc when using any method based on means.

A classic illustration of why is based on a particular mixed (or contaminated) normal distribution where with probability .9 an observation is sampled from a standard normal distribution and otherwise sampling is from a normal distribution having a standard deviation of 10. Figure 3.1 shows the standard and mixed normal distributions. The mixed normal is said to have thick or heavy tails because its tails lie above the normal curve, which implies that unusually small or large values, called outliers, are more common when sampling from the mixed normal versus the normal. As is evident, the two distributions are very similar in a certain sense, but there is a crucial difference: The standard normal has variance 1, but the mixed normal has variance 10.9. This illustrates the well-known result that an arbitrarily small change in any distribution, including normal distributions as a special case, can cause the variance to become arbitrarily large. That is, σ^2 is extremely sensitive to the tails of a distribution. One implication is that arbitrarily small departures from normality can result in low power (relative to other methods we might use) when comparing means.

To begin to appreciate that alternative estimators can make a practical difference in applied work, consider the median versus the mean. Figure 3.2 shows a plot of 5,000 medians and means, each based on 20 observations randomly sampled from the mixed normal shown in Figure 3.1. Note that the medians are more tightly clustered around zero, the value being estimated, than are the means. That is, the median has a much smaller standard error than the mean, which can translate into more power. However, if observations are sampled from a standard normal distribution instead, the plot of the medians versus the means now appears as shown in Figure 3.3. That is, using medians can result in low power relative to using the mean (as well as other estimators described later in this chapter).

To provide an explicit illustration regarding the effect of nonnormality on power when using means, suppose that 25 observations are randomly sampled from each of two normal distributions both having variance 1, the first having mean 0 and the second having mean 1. Applying Student's T test with

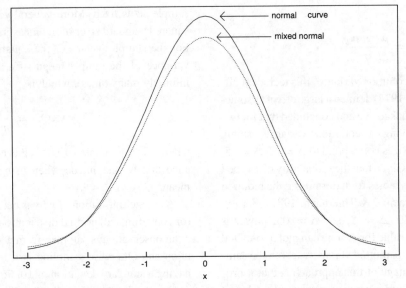

Figure 3.1 A mixed normal and standard normal distribution. Despite the similarity, the mixed normal has variance 10.9, whereas the standard normal which has variance 1.

$\alpha = .05$, the probability of rejecting (power) is .96. But if sampling is from mixed normals instead, with the difference between means again 1, power is only .28. (A complication when discussing means vs. medians is that for skewed distributions, each generally estimates different quantities, so it is possible for means to have more power regardless of their standard errors, and the reverse is true as well.)

For the situation just described, if medians are compared with the method derived by McKean and Schrader (1984), power is approximately .8 when sampling from the normal distributions. So a practical issue is whether a method can be found that improves upon the power of the McKean-Schrader method for medians when sampling from normal distributions and continues to have relatively high power when sampling from a heavy-tailed distribution such as the mixed normal. Such methods are available and are described later in this chapter.

Student's *T* Can Be Biased

To illustrate the effects of skewness on power when using Student's *T*, suppose that 20 observations are sampled from

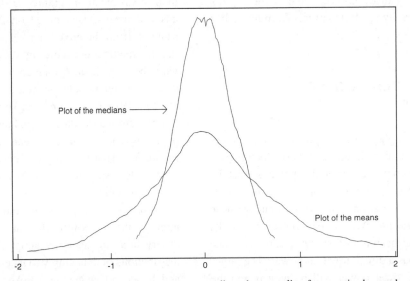

Figure 3.2 Distribution of the mean versus median when sampling from a mixed normal distribution.

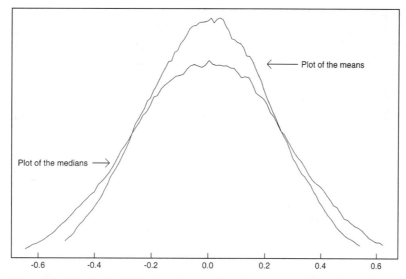

Figure 3.3   Distribution of the mean versus median when sampling from a standard normal distribution.

the (lognormal) distribution shown in Figure 3.4, which has a mean of .4658. From basic principles, inferences about the mean are based on

$$T = \frac{\overline{X} - \mu}{s/\sqrt{n}}, \qquad (3.2)$$

assuming T has a Student's T distribution with $n - 1$ degrees of freedom, where s is the sample standard deviation and μ is the population mean. In particular, the distribution of T is assumed to be symmetric about zero, but when sampling from an asymmetric distribution, this is not the case. For the situation at hand, the distribution of T is given, approximately, by the asymmetric curve shown in Figure 3.5, which is based on

values for T generated on a computer. The symmetric curve is the distribution of T under normality. The main point here is that the mean (or expected value) of T is not 0—it is approximately $-.5$. This might appear to be impossible because under random sampling the expected value of the numerator of T, $\overline{X} - \mu$, is 0, which might seem to suggest that T must have a mean of 0 as well. However, for nonnormal distributions, $\overline{X}$ and s are dependent, and this dependence makes it possible for the mean of T to differ from zero. (Gosset, who derived Student's T distribution, was aware of this issue.) This property is important because it has practical implications about power: Power can actually decrease as we move away from the null hypothesis. That is, situations arise where

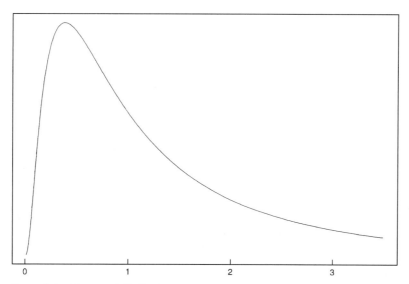

Figure 3.4   A lognormal distribution.

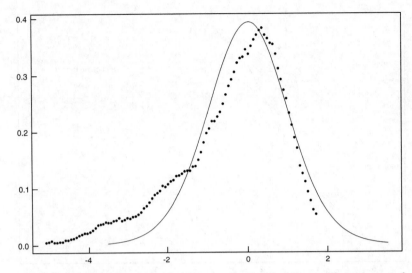

Figure 3.5   The ragged line is the plot of *T* values based on data generated from a lognormal distribution. The smooth symmetric curve is the distribution of *T* under normality.

there is a higher probability of rejecting when the null hypothesis is true versus situations where the the null hypothesis is false. In technical terms, Student's *T* test is *biased*.

To provide perspective, Figure 3.6 shows the power curve of Student's *T* with $n = 20$ and when δ is added to every observation. That is, when $\delta = 0$, the null hypothesis is true; otherwise, the null hypothesis is false, and the difference between the true mean and the hypothesized value is δ. In this case, power initially decreases as we move away from the null hypothesis, but eventually it goes up (cf. Sawilowsky, Kelley, Blair, & Markham, 1994). The value $\delta = .6$ represents a departure from the null value of slightly more than one fourth of a standard deviation. That is, moving a quarter

standard deviation from the null, power is approximately the same as when the null hypothesis is true.

The central limit theorem implies that with a sufficiently large sample size, the distribution of *T* will converge to a normal distribution. It is known that for a lognormal distribution (which is a skewed relatively light-tailed distribution among the class of g-and-h distribution derived by Hoaglin, 1985), even with 160 observations, there are practical problems with obtaining accurate probability coverage and control over the probability of a Type I error. (Westfall & Young, 1993, note that for a one-sided test, the actual probability of a Type I error is .11 when testing at the .05 level.) With about 200 observations, these problems become negligible. But when

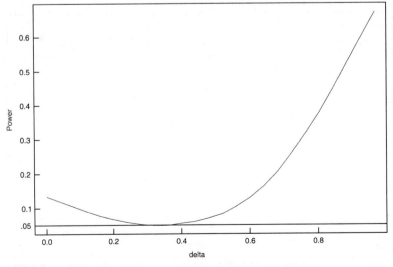

Figure 3.6   Power curve of *T* when sampling from a lognormal distribution.

sampling from a skewed, heavy-tailed distribution, a sample size greater than 300 might be required. It remains unclear, however, how quickly practical problems with bias disappear as the sample size increases.

The properties of the one-sample T test, when sampling from a skewed distribution, have implications about comparing two independent groups. To get a rough indication as to why, consider the sample mean from two independent groups, $\overline{X}_1$ and $\overline{X}_2$. If the two groups have identical distributions and equal sample sizes are used, the difference between the means has a symmetric distribution, and problems with bias and Type I errors substantially higher than the nominal level are minimal. But when distributions differ in skewness, practical problems arise because the distribution of $\overline{X}_1 - \overline{X}_2$ will be skewed as well. This is not to suggest, however, that bias is not an issue when sampling from symmetric distributions. For example, even when sampling from normal distributions, if groups have unequal variances, the ANOVA F test can be biased (e.g., Wilcox, Charlin, & Thompson, 1986).

A possible criticism of the problems with Student's T illustrated by Figures 3.5 and 3.6 is that in theory the actual distribution of T can be substantially asymmetric, but can this problem occur in practice? Using data from various studies, Wilcox (2001, in press) illustrated that the answer is yes. Consider, for example, data from a study conducted by Pedersen, Miller, Putcha, and Yang (in press) where $n = 104$. Figure 3.7 shows an approximation of the distribution of T based on resampling with replacement 104 values from the original data, computing T, and repeating this process 1,000 times. (That is, a bootstrap-t method was used, which is described in more detail later.) In fact, all indications are that problems with T are underestimated here for at least two reasons. First, an extreme outlier was removed. If this outlier is included, the approximation of the distribution of T departs in an even more dramatic manner from the assumption that it is symmetric about zero. Second, studies of the small-sample properties of the bootstrap-t suggest that Figure 3.7 underestimates the degree to which the actual distribution of T is skewed.

SAMPLE SIZE AND POWER

Perhaps the most obvious method for controlling power is simply to adjust the sample size. This is relatively easy to do when working with means and when sampling is from normal distributions, but such methods are fraught with peril.

Choosing Sample Sizes Before Sampling Observations

First, consider how the sample sizes might be chosen prior to collecting data when comparing the means of two independent normal distributions. A commonly used approach is to characterize the difference between the groups in terms of a standardized effect size:

$$\Delta = \frac{\mu_1 - \mu_2}{\sigma},$$

where by assumption the two groups have a common variance, σ^2. As mentioned, Cohen (1977) defined a large effect as something that is visible to the naked eye and concluded that for two normal distributions having a common variance, small, medium, and large effect sizes correspond to $\Delta = .2$, $\Delta = .5$, and $\Delta = .8$, respectively. Given α, the sample sizes

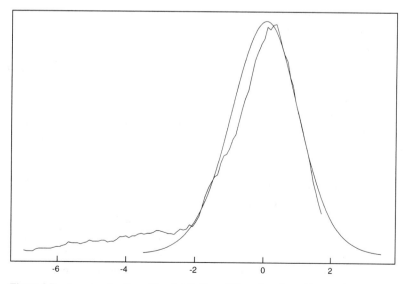

Figure 3.7   An approximation of the distribution of T based on data with $n = 104$.

can be chosen so that for a given value of Δ, power will be equal to some specified value—assuming normality (e.g., Cohen, 1977; Kraemer & Thiemann, 1987).

For example, with $\Delta = 1$, and $\alpha = .05$, and sample sizes of 25, power will be equal to .96 when using Student's T, as previously indicated. What this reflects is a solution to choosing sample sizes under the most optimistic circumstances possible. In reality, when comparing means, power will be at most .96, and a realistic possibility is that power is substantially lower than intended if Student's T is used. As already noted, an arbitrarily small departure from normality can mean that power will be close to zero. Yet another concern is that this approach ignores the effects of skewness and heteroscedasticity.

Despite its negative properties, this approach to determining sample sizes may have practical value. The reason is that when comparing groups with a robust measure of location (described later) by design power will be approximately equal to methods based on means and when sampling from a normal distribution. Unlike means, however, power remains relatively high when sampling from a heavy-tailed or asymmetric distribution. So a crude approximation of the required sample size when using a modern robust method might be based on standard methods for choosing samples sizes when comparing means.

Stein-Type Methods for Means

When some hypothesis is rejected, power is not an issue—the probability of a Type II error is zero. But when we fail to reject, the issue becomes *why*. One possibility is that the null hypothesis is true, but another possibility is that the null hypothesis is false and we failed to detect this. How might we decide which of these two possibilities is more reasonable? When working with means, one possibility is to employ what is called a Stein-type two-stage procedure. Given some data, these methods are aimed at determining how large the sample sizes should have been in order to achieve power equal to some specified value. If few or no additional observations are required to achieve high power, this naturally provides some assurance that power is reasonably high based on the number of observations available. Otherwise, the indication is that power is relatively low due to using a sample size that is too small. Moreover, if the additional observations needed to achieve high power are acquired, there are methods for testing hypotheses that typically are different from the standard methods covered in an introductory statistics course.

To describe Stein's (1945) original method, consider a single variable X that is assumed to have a normal distribution and suppose that the goal is to test $H_0: \mu = \mu_0$, where μ_0 is

some specified constant. Further assume that the Type I error probability is to be α and that the goal is to have power at least $1 - \beta$ when $\mu - \mu_0 = \delta$. For example, if the goal is to test $H_0: \mu = 6$, it might be desired to have power equal to .8 when in reality $\mu = 8$. Here, $1 - \beta = .8$ and $\delta = 8 - 6 = 2$. The issue is, given n randomly sampled observations, how many additional observations, if any, are required to achieve the desired amount of power. If no additional observations are required, power is sufficiently high based on the sample size used; otherwise, the sample size was too small. Stein's method proceeds as follows. Let $t_{1-\beta}$ and t_{α} be the $1 - \beta$ and α quantiles of Student's T distribution with $\nu = n - 1$ degrees of freedom. (So if T has a Student's T distribution with $\nu = n - 1$ degrees, $P[T \leq t_{1-\beta}] = 1 - \beta$.) Let

$$d = \left(\frac{\delta}{t_{1-\beta} - t_{\alpha}} \right)^2.$$

Then the required sample size is

$$N = \max\left(n, \left[\frac{s^2}{d} \right] + 1 \right),$$

where the notation $[s^2/d]$ means that s^2/d is computed and rounded down to the nearest integer. For example, if $s = 21.4$, $\delta = 20$, $1 - \beta = .9$, $\alpha = .01$, and $\nu = 9$, then

$$d = \left(\frac{20}{1.383 - (-2.82)} \right)^2 = 22.6,$$

so

$$N = \max(10, [21.4^2/22.6] + 1) = \max(10, 21) = 21.$$

If $N = n$, the sample size is adequate; but in the illustration, $N - n = 21 - 10 = 11$. That is, 11 additional observations are needed to achieve the desired amount of power. With $\delta = 29$, $N = 10$, and no additional observations are required.

If the additional $N - n$ observations can be obtained, $H_0: \mu = \mu_0$ can be tested, but for technical reasons the obvious approach of applying Student's T is not used. Rather, a slight modification is applied that is based on the test statistic

$$T_A = \frac{\sqrt{n}(\hat{\mu} - \mu_0)}{s},$$

where $\hat{\mu}$ is the mean of all N observations. You test hypotheses by treating T_s as having a Student's T distribution with $\nu = n - 1$ degrees of freedom. What is peculiar about Stein's method is that the sample variance based on all N observations is not used. Instead, s, which is based on the original

n observations, is used. For a survey of related methods, including techniques for controlling power when using the Wilcoxon signed rank test or the Wilcoxon-Mann-Whitney test, see Hewett and Spurrier (1983).

Stein's method has been extended to the problem of comparing two or more groups. Included are both ANOVA and multiple comparison procedures. The extension to ANOVA, when comparing the means of J independent groups, was derived by Bishop and Dudewicz (1978) and is applied as follows. Imagine that power is to be $1 - \beta$ for some given value of α and

$$\delta = \sum (\mu_j - \bar{\mu})^2,$$

where $\bar{\mu} = \sum \mu_j / J$. Further assume that n_j observations have been randomly sampled from the jth group, $j = 1, \ldots, J$. One goal is to determine how many additional observations are required for the jth group to achieve the desired amount of power.

Let z be the $1 - \beta$ quantile of the standard normal random distribution. For the jth group, let $v_j = n_j - 1$. Compute

$$v = \frac{J}{\sum \frac{1}{v_j - 2}} + 2,$$

$$A = \frac{(J - 1)v}{v - 2},$$

$$B = \frac{v^2}{J} \times \frac{J - 1}{v - 2},$$

$$C = \frac{3(J - 1)}{v - 4},$$

$$D = \frac{J^2 - 2J + 3}{v - 2},$$

$$E = B(C + D),$$

$$M = \frac{4E - 2A^2}{E - A^2 - 2A},$$

$$L = \frac{A(M - 2)}{M},$$

$$C = Lf,$$

where f is the $1 - \alpha$ quantile of an F distribution with L and M degrees of freedom. The quantity c is the critical value used in the event that the additional observations needed

to achieve power equal to $1 - \beta$ can be obtained. Next, compute

$$b = \frac{(v - 2)c}{v},$$

$$A_1 = \frac{1}{2} \{ \sqrt{2}z + \sqrt{2z^2 + A(2b - J + 2)} \},$$

$$B_1 = A_1^2 - b,$$

$$d = \frac{v - 2}{v} \times \frac{\delta}{B_1}.$$

Then the required number of observations for the jth group is

$$N_j = \max \left\{ n_j + 1, \left[\frac{s_j^2}{d} \right] + 1 \right\}. \tag{3.3}$$

For technical reasons, the number of observations needed for the jth group, N_j, cannot be smaller than $n_j + 1$. (The notation $[s_j^2/d]$ means that s_j^2/d is computed and then rounded down to the nearest integer.) Software for applying this method can be found in Wilcox (in press).

In the event the additional $N_j - n_j$ observations can be obtained from the jth group, exact control over both the Type I error probability and power can be achieved even when the groups have unequal variances—still assuming normality. In particular, for the jth group compute

$$T_j = \sum_{i=1}^{n_j} X_{ij},$$

$$U_j = \sum_{i=n_j+1}^{N_j} X_{ij},$$

$$b_j = \frac{1}{N_j} \left(1 + \sqrt{\frac{n_j(N_j d - s_j^2)}{(N_j - n_j)s_j^2}} \right),$$

$$\tilde{X}_j = \frac{T_j \{ 1 - (N_j - n_j)b_j \}}{n_j} + b_j U_j.$$

The test statistic is

$$\tilde{F} = \frac{1}{d} \sum (\tilde{X}_j - \tilde{X})^2,$$

where

$$\tilde{X} = \frac{1}{J} \sum \tilde{X}_j.$$

The hypothesis of equal means is rejected if $\tilde{F} \geq c$ and power will be at least $1 - \beta$.

Multiple Comparisons

Stein-type multiple comparisons procedures were derived by Hochberg (1975) and Tamhane (1977). One crucial difference from the Bishop-Dudewicz ANOVA is that direct control over power is no longer possible. Rather, these methods control the length of the confidence intervals, which of course is related to power. When sample sizes are small, both methods require critical values based on the quantiles of what is called a Studentized range statistic. Tables of these critical values can be found in Wilcox (in press). For the details of how to use these methods, plus easy-to-use software, see Wilcox (in press).

DEALING WITH SKEWNESS, HETEROSCEDASTICITY, AND OUTLIERS

Although Stein-type methods are derived assuming normality, they deal with at least one problem that arises under nonnormality. In particular, they have the ability of alerting us to low power due to outliers. When sampling from a heavy-tailed distribution, the sample variance will tend to be relatively large, which in turn will yield a large N when using Equation 3.3. This is because the sample variance can be greatly inflated by even a single outlier. In modern terminology, the sample variance has a finite sample breakdown point of only $1/n$, meaning that a single observation can make it arbitrarily large. As a simple example, consider the values 8, 8, 8, 8, 8, 8, 8, 8, 8, 8. There is no variation among these values, so $s^2 = 0$. If we increase the last value to 10, the sample variance is $s^2 = .36$. Increasing the last observation to 12, $s^2 = 1.45$, and increasing it to 14, $s^2 = 3.3$. The point is that even though there is no variation among the bulk of the observations, a single value can make the sample variance arbitrarily large. In particular, outliers can substantially inflate s^2, but what can be done about improving power based on the observations available, and how might problems due to skewness, heteroscedasticity, and outliers be approached?

Heteroscedasticity

Today, virtually all standard hypothesis-testing methods taught in an introductory course have heteroscedastic analogs, summaries of which are given in Wilcox (in press). This is true for methods based on measures of location as well as for rank-based techniques such as the Wilcoxon-Mann-Whitney

test, and even for inferential methods used in regression and when dealing with correlations. When comparing groups having *identical* distributions, homoscedastic methods perform well in terms of Type I errors, but when comparing groups that differ in some manner, there are general conditions under which these techniques are using the wrong standard error, which in turn can result in relatively lower power. For example, when using the two-sample Student's T test, the assumption is that the distribution of the test statistic T approaches a standard normal distribution as the sample sizes increase. In particular, the variance of the test statistic is assumed to converge to one, but Cressie and Whitford (1986) described general conditions under which this is not true. In a similar manner, the Wilcoxon-Mann-Whitney test is derived under the assumption that distributions are identical. When distributions differ, the wrong standard error is being used, which causes practical problems. Methods for dealing with heteroscedasticity have been derived by Fligner and Policello (1981), Mee (1990), and Cliff (1994), as well as by Brunner and Munzel (1999). The techniques derived by Cliff and Brunner and Munzel are particularly interesting because they include methods for dealing with tied values.

Skewness and the Bootstrap

The central limit theorem says that under random sampling and with a sufficiently large sample size, it can be assumed that the distribution of the sample mean is normal. Moreover, Student's T approaches a normal distribution as well, but a practical concern is that it approaches a normal distribution more slowly than $\overline{X}$ does when sampling from a skewed distribution (e.g., Wilcox, 2001). The problem is serious enough that power is affected, as previously demonstrated.

One approach is to replace Student's T and its heteroscedastic analogs with a bootstrap-t method. This approach is motivated by two general results. First, the theory indicates that problems with nonnormality will diminish more rapidly than with more conventional methods. To provide a rough idea of what this means, note that under nonnormality there will be some discrepancy between the actual and nominal level value for α, the probability of a Type I error. When sample sizes are large, the rate at which conventional (heteroscedastic) methods converge to the correct nominal level is $1/\sqrt{n}$. In contrast, methods based on the bootstrap-t converge at the rate of $1/n$—namely, faster. This does not necessarily imply, however, that with small to moderate sample sizes, problems with low power due to skewness will be negligible with a bootstrap technique. In terms of Type I errors, for example, problems are often reduced considerably, but for skewed heavy-tailed distributions, problems can persist even with $n = 300$ when attention is restricted to means. Nevertheless, the bootstrap-t offers a practical advantage because when making inferences based on means, it generally performs about as well as conventional techniques and in some cases offers a distinct advantage. As for power, the bootstrap-t reduces problems due to bias, but just how large the sample sizes must be to eliminate all practical concerns remains unclear.

In the one-sample case, the bootstrap-t is applied as follows. Resample with replacement n observations from the observed values $X_1, \ldots, X_n$ yielding a bootstrap sample: $X_1^*, \ldots, X_n^*$. Compute

$$T^* = \frac{\sqrt{n}(X^* - \overline{X})}{s^*},$$

where $\overline{X}^*$ and s^* are the mean and sample standard deviation based on the bootstrap sample. Repeat this process B times yielding $T_1^*, \ldots, T_B^*$. The middle 95% of these B values provides an approximation of the .025 and .975 quantiles of the distribution of T, which can be used to test hypotheses or compute confidence intervals. That is, rather than approximate the distribution of T by assuming normality, approximate its distribution based on the data available.

Dealing With Low Power Using Robust Estimators

Robust estimators provide another method for dealing with low power due to skewness, and they can provide a substantial advantage in power when sampling from heavy-tailed distributions such as the mixed normal. Moreover, some robust estimators have been designed to provide relatively high power under normality and simultaneously provide high power when sampling from a heavy-tailed distribution.

It is noted that three criteria are used to judge the robustness of any measure of location (e.g., Huber, 1981). Roughly, these criteria reflect how small changes in *any* distribution (including normal distributions as a special case) can affect their values. The population mean (μ) and population variance (σ^2) are not robust because arbitrarily small changes in a distribution can alter their values by an arbitrarily large amount. One practical consequence is that arbitrarily small departures from normality can result in very poor power compared to others methods that might be used.

As previously noted, outliers inflate the sample variance, which can result in low power when comparing groups based on means. So dealing with this problem might seem trivial: Check for outliers, discard any that are found, and apply some method for means to the data that remain. In symbols, if we begin with N observations, discard those that are declared outliers, leaving n observations, and then estimate

$\text{VAR}(\overline{X})$, the squared standard error of the sample mean, with s^2/n, where s^2 is the sample variance based on the n observations left after outliers are discarded. However, there are two concerns with this approach. First, it results in using the wrong standard error; second, discarding outliers in some manner is often met with incredulity because it seems counterintuitive based on what has become traditional training in statistics. In particular, it might seem that this must result in less accurate results and less power.

First consider the issue of accuracy and power when some of the smallest and largest observations are discarded. To take an extreme case, consider the usual sample median, which discards all but the middle one or two values. As illustrated in Figure 3.2, it can be more accurate on average versus the mean, as was first noted by Laplace in 1775. By 1818 Laplace was aware of more general conditions under which the median beats the mean in accuracy. To provide some sense of why this occurs, imagine that 20 observations are randomly sampled from a standard normal distribution. Now put these values in ascending order and label the results $X_{(1)} \leq \cdots \leq X_{(20)}$. It can be shown that with probability .983, the smallest value will be less than -0.9. That is, $P(X_{(1)} \leq -0.9) = .983$. Similarly, $P(X_{(20)} \geq 0.9) = .983$. That is, there is a high probability that the smallest and largest observations will be relatively far from the population mean, the value we are trying to estimate. Of course, averaging these values gives a reasonable estimate of the population mean, but the point is that in general we would expect them to add a relatively large amount of variation versus the two middle values, which have a much higher probability of being close to the population mean. But as is well known, despite this property, the sample mean performs much better than does the median under normality. The concern, however, is that for nonnormal distributions there are situations where the opposite is true.

Why does the mean beat the median in accuracy under normality? The answer is that when we put the observations in order, they are no longer independent, and the correlation among the ordered observations is such that under normality the mean beats the median. To elaborate a bit, consider three observations randomly sampled from a normal distribution: X_1, X_2, and X_3. Then each has probability .05 of being less than or equal to -1.645. But suppose we put the observations in ascending order, yielding $X_{(1)} \leq X_{(2)} \leq X_{(3)}$. Thus, $X_{(1)}$ is the smallest of the three observations, and $X_{(3)}$ is the largest. To see why these three variables are no longer independent, first note that there is some positive probability that $X_{(2)}$ is less than -1.645. If $X_{(1)}$ is independent of $X_{(2)}$, then knowing the value of $X_{(1)}$ should not alter the probabilities associated with $X_{(2)}$. But given that $X_{(1)}$ is greater than -1.645, for example, then $P(X_{(2)} < -1.645) = 0$, because by definition, $X_{(2)} \geq X_{(1)}$. That is, $X_{(1)}$ and $X_{(2)}$ are dependent. More generally, if independent observations are put in order and some extreme values are removed, the remaining observations are no longer independent.

When sampling from a normal distribution, or from any light-tailed distribution, methods based on medians can have substantially less power than do methods based on means. Is there some alternative measure of location that performs about as well as the mean under normality but that guards against low power when sampling from a heavy-tailed distribution? There are in fact three such measures of location that seem to have considerable practical value: trimmed means, M-estimators, and a modified one-step M-estimator called MOM. Not only do they enhance power, but also excellent methods for controlling the probability of a Type I error have been devised that continue to perform well in situations where methods based on means are highly unsatisfactory.

Trimmed Means

Trimmed means are characterized by trimming a fixed (pre-determined) proportion of observations. Typically, the same amount of trimming is done from both tails. That is, a trimmed mean removes a specified proportion of the largest observations and repeats this for the smallest observations; then the remaining observations are averaged. Note that the mean and median represent two extremes: no trimming and the maximum amount of trimming that can be done.

Trimming 20% from both tails maintains relatively high power under normality, but power remains fairly high when sampling, for example, from the mixed normal. As previously mentioned, removing extreme values creates a technical problem: The remaining observations are dependent, so there is the practical issue of how to estimate its standard error. Tukey and McLaughlin (1963) were the first to deal with this issue. A description of their method is given in the next section.

Another strategy is to check empirically for outliers, remove any that are found, and average the values that remain. This includes the class of skipped estimators that was originally suggested by Tukey. Recently, the particular variation of this method called MOM has been found to be especially useful (Wilcox, in press). In the past, technical problems precluded the routine use of these estimators when testing hypotheses, but recent advances make them a viable option.

To explain part of the motivation behind MOM requires some preliminary remarks about detecting outliers. There are some well known and fairly obvious ways of detecting outliers based on the mean and variance. A commonly used

strategy is to declare the value X an outlier if it lies more than 2 standard deviations from the sample mean. That is, declare X to be an outlier if

$$\frac{|X - \overline{X}|}{s} > 2. \tag{3.4}$$

However, it has long been known that this approach is highly unsatisfactory (e.g., Rousseeuw & Leroy, 1987) because it suffers from what is called *masking*. That is, outliers can greatly influence the sample mean, and particularly the sample standard deviation, which in turn can mask outliers. For example, consider the values

$$2, 2, 3, 3, 3, 4, 4, 4, 100,000, 100,000.$$

Surely, 100,000 is unusual compared with the other values, but it is readily verified that 100,000 is not declared an outlier when using Equation 3.4. Methods for dealing with this problem are available (e.g., Barnett & Lewis, 1994), and some variation of these methods is recommended when dealing with power. One method that stands out is based on the median, M, and a measure of scale called the median absolute deviation (MAD) statistic, which is just

$$\text{median}(|X_1 - M|, \ldots, |X_n - M|).$$

That is, MAD is the median of $|X_1 - M|, \ldots, |X_n - M|$. A rule for detecting outliers that is a special case of a general approach proposed by Rousseeuw and van Zomeren (1990) is to declare X an outlier if

$$\frac{|X - M|}{\text{MAD}/.6745} > 2.24. \tag{3.5}$$

(The constant .6745 stems from the fact that under normality, MAD/.6745 estimates the population standard deviation, σ.)

Now consider using as a measure of location the mean of the observations left after outliers identified with Equation 3.5 are removed. Called MOM, the only difference between it and Tukey's skipped estimators is that Tukey's estimator identifies outliers using a box-plot rule rather than Equation 3.5. An appealing feature of MOM is that it introduces more flexibility than does the trimmed mean. In particular, MOM allows the possibility of no trimming and different amounts of trimming from each tail, and it can handle more outliers than can the 20% trimmed mean. An inconvenience of MOM is that an explicit expression for its standard error has not been derived, so the more obvious approaches to testing hypotheses are not readily applied. However, a percentile bootstrap method has been found to provide excellent control over the probability of a Type I error. Moreover, good results are obtained in situations where methods based on M-estimators are unsatisfactory, and all indications are that using MOM with a percentile bootstrap method competes well with the best methods for comparing 20% trimmed means. By design, methods based on MOM will have about as much power as methods based on means when sampling from normal distributions, but power can be vastly higher when using MOM because its standard error is relatively unaffected by outliers. Moreover, ANOVA methods have been developed, including methods where the goal is to compare dependent groups; multiple comparison procedures are available also (Wilcox, in press).

The third strategy is to alter how we measure the distance between an observation and some constant, say c, which is to be used as a measure of location. To elaborate, suppose we measure the typical distance between the observations we make and c with the sum of squared differences: $\sum(X_i - c)^2$. The least squares principle is to choose as a measure of location the value c that minimizes this sum and leads to $c = \overline{X}$, the sample mean. But if the typical distance is measured with $\sum|X_i - c|$ instead, minimizing this sum results in $c = M$, the sample median. That is, different measures of location are obtained depending on how distance is measured. Rather than use squared error or absolute error, M-estimators use other measures of error that result in measures of location with good properties under normality as well as when sampling from skewed or heavy-tailed distributions. The idea appears to have been first proposed by Ellis in 1844, and a modern treatment of this approach was first developed by Huber (1964). Among the measures of distance that have been proposed, one due to Huber currently stands out and leads to the so-called one-step M-estimator. (For theoretical details, see Huber, 1981; Hampel, Ronchetti, Rousseeuw, & Stahel, 1986.) To compute it, let L be the number of observation such that

$$\frac{X_i - M}{\text{MAD}/.6745} < 1.28, \qquad (3.6)$$

and let U be the number of observation such that

$$\frac{X_i - M}{\text{MAD}/.6745} > 1.28. \qquad (3.7)$$

That is, these last two equations are used to determine whether an observation is an outlier. L is the number of outliers less than the median, and the number of outliers greater than the median is U. The constant 1.28 arises because it provides relatively high power under normality. Let B be the sum of the observations not declared outliers. Then the one-step

M-estimator (based on Huber's measure of distance) is

$$\frac{1.28(\text{MADN})(U - L) + B}{n - L - U}, \qquad (3.8)$$

where $\text{MADN} = \text{MAD}/.6745$. Note that if 1.28 is changed to 2.24 in Equation 3.7 and we calculate $B/(n - L - U)$ in place of Equation 3.8, we get MOM.

Inferences Based on a Trimmed Mean

This section illustrates that the choice of method can make a substantial difference in the conclusions reached. Here, for convenience, a nonbootstrap method based on 20% trimmed means is described, the only point being that in some situations it can have a substantially lower significance level than can a method based on means. (The choice of 20% trimming is made because it provides relatively high power under normality, but power remains relatively high when sampling from heavier tailed distributions.)

First we need an estimate of the standard error of the trimmed mean. Recall that when computing a 20% trimmed mean, the smallest and largest 20% of the observations are removed. Winsorizing the observations by 20% simply means that rather than remove the smallest 20%, their values are set equal to the smallest value not trimmed when computing the 20% trimmed mean. Simultaneously, the largest 20% are reset to the largest value not trimmed. The 20% Winsorized variance is the usual sample variance based on the Winsorized values, which will be labeled s_w^2. It can be shown that $s_w^2/.36n$ estimates the squared standard error of $\overline{X}_t$, the sample trimmed mean.

Yuen (1974) proposed testing the hypothesis of equal population trimmed means for two independent groups with

$$T_y = \frac{\overline{X}_{t1} - \overline{X}_{t2}}{\sqrt{d_1 + d_2}},$$

where

$$d_j = \frac{(n_j - 1)s_{wj}^2}{h_j(h_j - 1)},$$

h_j is the number of observations left in the jth group after trimming, and for the jth group, s_{wj}^2 is the Winsorized variance. The (estimated) degrees of freedom are

$$\hat{v}_y = \frac{(d_1 + d_2)^2}{\frac{d_1^2}{h_1 - 1} + \frac{d_2^2}{h_2 - 1}},$$

and the hypothesis of equal population trimmed means is rejected if

$$|T_y| > t,$$

where t is the $1 - \alpha/2$ quantile of Student's t distribution with $\hat{\nu}_y$ degrees of freedom. (With zero trimming, Yuen's method reduces to Welch's test for means.)

Consider the following data, which are from a study dealing with self-awareness:

Group 1:	77 87 88 114 151 210 219 246 253
	262 296 299 306 376 428 515 666 1310 2611
Group 2:	59 106 174 207 219 237 313 365 458 497 515
	529 557 615 625 645 973 1065 3215

(These data were generously supplied by E. Dana and reflect the time participants could keep a portion of an apparatus in contact with a specified target.) Comparing means with Welch's heteroscedastic test, the significance level is .475. With Yuen's test, the significance level is .053.

Judging Sample Sizes When Using Robust Estimators

Stein-type methods provide a way of judging the adequacy of a sample size based on data available. If a nonsignificant result is obtained, again there is the issue of whether this is due to low power based on the available sample size. Under normality, and when working with means, this issue can be addressed with Stein-type methods, but how might such techniques be extended to other measures of location? Coming up with reasonable methods for estimating power, based on estimated standard errors, is a fairly trivial matter thanks to modern technology, and in fact there are many methods one might use with robust measures of location. For example, theoretical results suggest how to extend Stein-type methods to trimmed means, but finding a method that performs reasonably well with small or even moderately large sample sizes is quite another matter. One practical difficulty is that the resulting methods tend to be biased and that they can be relatively inaccurate. For example, suppose that based on n observations from each group being compared, the standard error for each group is estimated, yielding an estimate of how much power there is based on the observations available. For convenience, let $\hat{\gamma}$ be some estimate of γ, the true amount of power. Of course there will be some discrepancy between γ and $\hat{\gamma}$, and typically it seems that this discrepancy can be quite high. The problem is that estimated standard errors are

themselves inaccurate. That is, if the true standard errors were known, methods for estimating power can be devised, but because they are estimated, $\hat{\gamma}$ can be rather unsatisfactory. Moreover, methods for deriving an appropriate estimate of γ usually are biased. Even when a reasonably unbiased estimator has been found, what is needed is some method for assessing the accuracy of $\hat{\gamma}$. That is, how might a confidence interval for γ be computed based on the data available? Again, solutions are available, but the challenge is finding methods for which the precision of $\hat{\gamma}$ can be assessed in an adequate manner with small to moderate sample sizes.

A method that performs relatively well when working with 20% trimmed means is described by Wilcox and Keselman (in press). It is limited, however, to the one- and two-sample case. A comparable method when comparing more than two groups remains to be developed. The method, along with easy-to-use software, is described in Wilcox (in press) as well.

The method just mentioned could be extended to MOM and M-estimators, but nothing is known about its small-sample properties. This area is in need of further research.

Rank-Based Methods and Outliers

Yet another approach to low power due to outliers is to switch to some rank-based method, but as already noted, modern heteroscedastic methods are recommended over more traditional homoscedastic techniques. Ranks are assigned to observations by putting the observations in ascending order, assigning a rank of 1 to the smallest value, a rank of 2 to the next smallest, and so on. So regardless of how extreme an outlier might be, its rank depends only on its relative position among the ordered values. Consider, for example, the values 198, 199, 245, 250, 301, and 320. The value 198 has a rank of one. But if this smallest value were 2 instead, 2 is an outlier, but its rank is still one, so when using a rank-based method to compare groups, power is not affected. A summary of modern rank-based methods, developed after 1980, can be found in Wilcox (in press).

REGRESSION

When dealing with regression, issues related to power become more complex. To explain the basic issues, it helps to begin with simple regression, where two variables are observed, X and Y, and it is assumed that

$$Y = \beta_1 X + \beta_0 + \epsilon, \tag{3.9}$$

where β_1 and β_0 are the unknown population slope and intercept, respectively; X and ϵ are independent; and ϵ has variance σ^2. This model is homoscedastic, meaning that the conditional variance of Y, given X, does not change with X. If it is further assumed that ϵ has a normal distribution, methods for assessing power, given n, are available when the goal is to test hypotheses about the slope and intercept based on the randomly sampled pairs of observations $(X_1, Y_1), \ldots,$ (X_n, Y_n) (e.g., Kraemer & Thiemann, 1987). But even under normality, if the error term is heteroscedastic, meaning that the conditional variance of Y varies with X, serious practical problems with power can result. And under nonnormality, the situation deteriorates even further. In fact, two fundamental problems associated with heteroscedasticity affect power. The first is that poor probability coverage can result when using conventional methods for computing a confidence interval for the slope or intercept. In terms of Type I errors, if the goal is to test H_0: $\beta_1 = 0$ with $\alpha = .05$, there are situations where the actual Type I error probability exceeds .5! That is, when computing a .95 confidence interval for β_1, the actual probability coverage can be less than .5. Perhaps in some situations this inadequacy unintentionally increases power when in fact H_0 is false, but it could decrease it as well. Generally, if there is an association between two variables, there is no reason to expect homoscedasticity; under heteroscedasticity standard hypothesis testing methods are using the wrong standard error, and this can result in relatively low power. A reasonable suggestion is to test the hypothesis that the error term is homoscedastic and, if not significant, to use a homoscedastic method when testing the hypothesis of a zero slope. A practical problem, however, is that researchers do not know how to determine whether a test of homoscedasticity has enough power to detect situations where heteroscedasticity creates practical problems. The second fundamental problem is that there are situations where the least squares estimator has a standard error thousands of times larger than some competing method!

Heteroscedasticity and Probability Coverage

A variety of methods have been proposed for dealing with poor probability coverage due to heteroscedasticity, several of which were compared by Wilcox (1996) when making inferences about the slope. The only method that performed reasonably well among those that were considered is based on a modified percentile bootstrap method. Derivation of the method is based in part on Gosset's approach, which led to Student's T distribution: When the sample size is small, make adjustments to the critical value assuming normality and homoscedasticity, and then hope that good probability coverage (and accurate control over the probability of a Type I error) is achieved when these assumptions are violated. Although Student's T does not perform well when these assumptions are violated, it currently seems that a similar approach is relatively effective for the problem at hand.

To provide some detail, let $(X_1, Y_1), \ldots, (X_n, Y_n)$ be n randomly sampled pairs of points. A bootstrap sample is obtained by resampling with replacement n pairs of points from $(X_1, Y_1), \ldots, (X_n, Y_n)$. Let b_1^* be the least squares estimate of the slope based on this bootstrap sample. Next, repeat this process 599 times, yielding $b_{11}^*, \ldots, b_{1,599}^*$. The standard percentile bootstrap method uses the middle 95% of these 599 bootstrap estimates as a .95 confidence interval for β_1. But when using least squares, a modification is needed. In particular, put the 599 bootstrap estimates of the slope in ascending order yielding $b_{1(1)}^* \leq \cdots \leq b_{1(599)}^*$. The .95 confidence interval is

$$\left(b_{1(a)}^*, b_{1(c)}^*\right) \tag{3.10}$$

where for $n < 40$, $a = 7$ and $c = 593$; for $40 \leq n < 80$, $a = 8$ and $c = 592$; for $80 \leq n < 180$, $a = 11$ and $c = 588$; for $180 \leq n < 250$, $a = 14$ and $c = 585$; while for $n \geq 250$, $a = 15$ and $c = 584$. More recently, an alternative heteroscedastic method was studied and recommended by Long and Ervin (2000). However, there are situations where it is rather unsatisfactory, in terms of probability coverage (or Type I error probabilities), when the bootstrap performs fairly well, and so far no situations have been found where the reverse is true.

In some instances, simply restricting the range of the X values to eliminate obvious outliers can make least squares competitive with other estimators. And the derivation of the standard error of the least squares estimator, assuming homoscedasticity, remains valid because the X values are treated as constants (i.e., the variance of the least squares estimator is derived by conditioning on X). However, this strategy does not necessarily address problems due to heteroscedasticity among the points that remain, and eliminating points for which the Y values are outliers leads to technical problems because the derivation of the standard error of the least squares estimator is no longer valid (for reasons similar to why the derivation of $\text{VAR}[\overline{X}]$ is invalid when outliers among the X values are discarded).

Another facet to the relative merits of restricting the range of the X values is related to good and bad leverage points. A leverage point is an outlier among the X values. A bad leverage point is an outlier that is relatively far from the regression

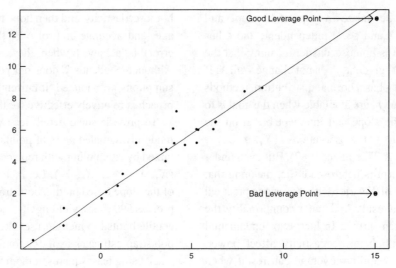

Figure 3.8 An example of good and bad leverage points.

line for the bulk of the points. That is, it has a relatively large residual. A good leverage point is a leverage point that is reasonably close to the regression line. Figure 3.8 shows both a good and bad leverage point. An advantage of a good leverage point is that it lowers the standard error of the least squares estimator, which helps increase power. But a bad leverage point can result in a poor fit to the bulk of the points, resulting in a misleading summary of the data.

ROBUST REGRESSION ESTIMATORS AND POWER

Although it has been clearly established that in terms of power, simply applying the least squares estimator to data can be highly unsatisfactory, no single alternative estimator has been found that can be recommended for general use to the exclusion of all estimators that have been proposed. All indications are that several estimators should be considered, particularly in the exploratory phases of a study. Indeed, once some familiarity with the issues that affect power has been obtained, it seems to be an almost trivial matter to find fault with any single strategy that might be used. That is, situations can be found where many estimators offer substantial gains in power versus least squares, but among these estimators, situations can be found where method A beats method B, and situations can be found where the reverse is true as well. Moreover, at least for the moment, certain strategies present computational problems and inconveniences that need to be addressed. Nevertheless, least squares can result in relatively low power (and a poor reflection of the association among the majority of points). Some simple and effective methods are available for addressing this problem, so knowing some

alternative estimators is important and can make a substantial difference in the conclusions reached.

The Theil-Sen Estimator

There are many alternatives to least squares regression that offer important advantages, including the possibility of relatively high power. The immediate goal is to illustrate the potential advantages of just one of these methods with the understanding that arguments for other estimators can be made. The estimator discussed here was proposed by Theil (1950) and Sen (1968). For comments on the relative merits of some competing estimators, see Wilcox (in press).

The Theil-Sen estimate of the slope is the value b that makes Kendall's τ statistic, between $Y_i - bX_i$ and X_i, (approximately) equal to zero. Alternatively, for any $X_i > X_j$, let $S_{ij} = (Y_i - Y_j)/(X_i - X_j)$. That is, S_{ij} is the slope of the line connecting the ith and jth points. Then b, the median of the S_{ij} values, is the Theil-Sen estimate of the slope. The usual estimate of the intercept is $M_y - bM_x$, where M_y and M_x are the sample medians corresponding to the Y and X values, respectively. (For results on extending this estimator to more than one predictor, see Hussain & Sprent, 1983; Wilcox, 1998.)

Because power is related to the standard error of an estimator, an indirect comparison of the power associated with least squares, versus the Theil-Sen estimator, can be obtained by comparing their standard errors. Here, consideration is given to $n = 20$ with X and ϵ having one of four distributions: normal, symmetric with heavy tails, asymmetric with relatively light tails, and asymmetric with relatively heavy tails. The specific distributions used are from the family of g-and-h distributions derived by Hoaglin (1985). The parameter g controls skewness, and h controls heavy-tailedness. Here, both g and h were taken to have one of two values: 0 and .5. Setting $g = h = 0$ yields a standard normal distribution. (For more details about these distributions, see Hoaglin, 1985.) Tables 3.1 and 3.2 provide an estimate (labeled R) of the standard error of the least squares estimator divided by the standard error of the Theil-Sen estimator. So $R < 1$ indicates that least squares is more accurate on average, and $R > 1$ indicates the opposite. Included are values for R when there is heteroscedasticity. Specifically, observations were generated from the model $Y = X + \lambda(X)\epsilon$ with three choices for $\lambda(X) : \lambda(X) = 1$ (homoscedasticity), $\lambda(X) = X^2$, and $\lambda(X) = 1 + 2/(|X| + 1)$. For convenience, these three function are called variance patterns (VP) 1, 2, and 3. (The values of R in Tables 3.1 and 3.2 are based on simulations with 5,000 replications.)

Note that under normality and homoscedasticity, Table 3.1 indicates that least squares is slightly more accurate, the value of R being 0.91. However, even when the error term is normal but heteroscedastic, least squares performs rather poorly—the Theil-Sen estimator can be hundreds of times more

TABLE 3.1   Estimates of R, the Ratio of the Standard Errors for Least Squares, versus Theil-Sen When the X Distribution is Symmetric, $n = 20$

X		ϵ			
g	h	g	h	VP	R
0.0	0.0	0.0	0.0	1	0.91
				2	2.64
				3	202.22
0.0	0.0	0.0	0.5	1	4.28
				2	10.67
				3	220.81
0.0	0.0	0.5	0.0	1	1.13
				2	3.21
				3	183.74
0.0	0.0	0.5	0.5	1	8.89
				2	26.66
				3	210.37
0.0	0.5	0.0	0.0	1	0.81
				2	40.57
				3	41.70
0.0	0.5	0.0	0.5	1	3.09
				2	78.43
				3	38.70
0.0	0.5	0.5	0.0	1	0.99
				2	46.77
				3	39.32
0.0	0.5	0.5	0.5	1	6.34
				2	138.53
				3	43.63

Note. $g = h = 0$ is standard normal; $(g, h) = (0, .5)$ is symmetric heavy tailed; $(g, h) = (.5, 0)$ is skewed light tailed; $g = h = .5$ is skewed heavy tailed.

TABLE 3.2   Estimates of R, the Ratio of the Standard Errors for Least Squares, versus Theil-Sen When the X Distribution is Asymmetric, $n = 20$

X		ϵ			
g	h	g	h	VP	R
0.5	0.0	0.0	0.0	1	0.88
				2	6.83
				3	207.35
0.5	0.0	0.0	0.5	1	4.27
				2	30.57
				3	404.35
0.5	0.0	0.5	0.0	1	1.08
				2	8.44
				3	151.99
0.5	0.0	0.5	0.5	1	8.62
				2	79.52
				3	267.09
0.5	0.5	0.0	0.0	1	0.78
				2	87.64
				3	55.71
0.5	0.5	0.0	0.5	1	3.09
				2	182.12
				3	78.91
0.5	0.5	0.5	0.0	1	0.95
				2	112.18
				3	66.51
0.5	0.5	0.5	0.5	1	5.71
				2	394.67
				3	96.49

accurate. Among the situations considered, there are many instances where the Theil-Sen estimator provides a striking advantage, and there are none where the reverse is true, the lowest value for R being 0.76. It should be remarked that direct comparisons in terms of power are hampered by the fact that for many of the situations considered in Tables 3.1 and 3.2, conventional hypothesis testing methods based on least squares perform very poorly. Perhaps there are situations where the very inadequacies of conventional techniques result in relatively high power. That is, probability coverage might be extremely poor, but in a manner that increases power. Experience suggests, however, that it is common to find situations where the hypothesis of a zero slope is rejected when using Theil-Sen, but not when using least squares.

A technical issue when using the Theil-Sen estimator is that when there is heteroscedasticity, an explicit expression for its standard error is not available. However, a percentile bootstrap method has been found to provide fairly accurate probability coverage and good control over the probability of a Type I error for a very wide range of situations, including situations where the conventional method based on least squares is highly inaccurate. But rather than use the modified percentile bootstrap method previously described, now it suffices to use the standard percentile bootstrap method instead.

In particular, again let $(X_1, Y_1), \ldots, (X_n, Y_n)$ be n randomly sampled pairs of points and generate a bootstrap sample by resampling with replacement n pairs of points from $(X_1, Y_1), \ldots, (X_n, Y_n)$. Let b_1^* be the Theil-Sen estimate of the slope based on this bootstrap sample. Next, repeat this process B times yielding $b_{11}^*, \ldots, b_{1B}^*$. The standard percentile bootstrap method uses the middle 95% of these B bootstrap estimates as a .95 confidence interval for slope. That is, put the B bootstrap samples in ascending order, label the results $b_{1(1)}^* \leq \cdots \leq b_{1(B)}^*$, in which case a $1 - \alpha$ confidence interval for the population slope is $(b_{1(L+1)}, b_{1(U)})$, where $L = \alpha B / 2$, rounded to the nearest integer, and $U = B - L$. ($B = 600$ seems to suffice, in terms of accurate probability coverage, when using Theil-Sen.) Obviously this approach requires a computer, but even with a moderately large sample size, execution time is fairly low.

CORRELATION

Certainly one of the most common goals is to test

$$H_0: \rho = 0, \tag{3.11}$$

the hypothesis that Pearson's correlation is zero. One approach is to use what is called Fisher's Z transformation, which is also called the r-to-z transformation. It provides a simple method for determining sample size when dealing with power, but the method assumes normality. When sampling from a nonnormal distribution, there are general conditions under which Fisher's Z does not converge to the correct answer even as the sample size gets large (e.g., Duncan & Layard, 1973).

A more general and perhaps a more serious problem is that at least six features of data affect the magnitude of ρ (e.g., Wilcox, 2001), which in turn makes it very difficult to find a satisfactory method for dealing with power. These six features are (a) the slope of the line around which the points are clustered, (b) the magnitude of the residuals, (c) outliers, (d) curvature, (e) a restriction of range, and (f) reliability. So if a sample size for achieving high power is determined under normality, the extent to which power will indeed be high in reality is far from clear.

Figure 3.9 illustrates the effect of outliers on r, the standard estimate of ρ. Shown are the surface temperature and light intensity of 47 stars plus the least squares regression line. As is evident, the bulk of the points appear to have a positive association, but $r = -.21$, and Student's T test of Equation 3.10 has a significance level of .16. The points in the upper left corner of Figure 3.9 have a tremendous influence on r. A box plot indicates that X values less than or equal to 3.84 are outliers. If these points are eliminated, $r = .68$ with a significance level less than .001. In this case, simply restricting the range of X seems to correct problems with detecting a positive association among the majority of the points, but it is well known that restricting the range of X values can lower r as well.

Robust Correlations

Another way of dealing with low power due to outliers is to replace Pearson's correlation with some type of so-called robust estimator. Such methods include Kendall's tau, Spearman's

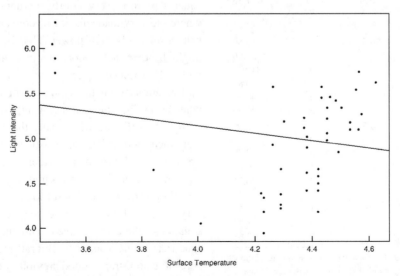

Figure 3.9   Surface temperature and light intensity of 47 stars.

rho, a Winsorized correlation, and what is called the *percentage bend correlation*. The first two are well known, so further details are not given. Details about the Winsorized correlation coefficient can be found in Wilcox (1997).

The percentage bend correlation is based in part on an empirical check for outliers and is computed as follows: For the observations $X_1, \ldots, X_n$, let M_x be the sample median. Choose a value for ξ between 0 and 1 and compute

$$W_i = |X_i - M_x|,$$
$$m = [(1 - \xi)n],$$

where the notation $[(1 - \xi)n]$ is $(1 - \xi)n$ rounded down to the nearest integer. Using $\xi = .2$ appears to be a good choice in most situations. Let $W_{(1)} \leq \cdots \leq W_{(n)}$ be the W_i values written in ascending order and let

$$\hat{\omega}_x = W_{(m)}.$$

Let i_1 be the number of X_i values such that $(X_i - \hat{\theta})/\hat{\omega}_x < -1$, and let i_2 be the number of X_i values such that $(X_i - \hat{\theta})/\hat{\omega}_x > 1$. Compute

$$S_x = \sum_{i=i_1+1}^{n-i_2} X_{(i)}$$

$$\hat{\phi}_x = \frac{\hat{\omega}_x(i_2 - i_1) + S_x}{n - i_1 - i_2}.$$

Set $U_i = (X_i - \hat{\phi}_x)/\hat{\omega}_x$. Repeat these computations for the

Y_i values yielding $V_i = (Y_i - \hat{\phi}_y)/\hat{\omega}_y$. Let

$$\Psi(x) = \max[-1, \min(1, x)].$$

Set $A_i = \Psi(U_i)$ and $B_i = \Psi(V_i)$. The percentage bend correlation is estimated to be

$$r_{pb} = \frac{\sum A_i B_i}{\sqrt{\left(\sum A_i^2\right)\left(\sum B_i^2\right)}}.$$

Under independence, the population percentage bend correlation is zero. To test the hypothesis that the population percentage bend correlation is zero, compute

$$T_{pb} = r_{pb}\sqrt{\frac{n - 2}{1 - r_{pb}^2}} \qquad (3.12)$$

and reject if $|T_{pb}| > t_{1-\alpha/2}$, where $t_{1-\alpha/2}$ is the $1 - \alpha/2$ quantile of Student's T distribution with $n - 2$ degrees of freedom.

For the star data in Figure 3.9, $r_{pb} = .31$, and the significance level based on the method just described is .03. That is, without restricting the range of the X values, a significant result is obtained, and the percentage bend correlation indicates a positive association among the bulk of the observations. Spearman's rho and Kendall's tau are also positive with significance levels of .044 and .013, respectively.

There are, however, situations where outliers can affect all three of these correlation coefficients, which in turn can affect power. Consider, for example, the 20 pairs of observations shown in Figure 3.10 (ignoring the point in the lower right corner) which were generated from the standard regression

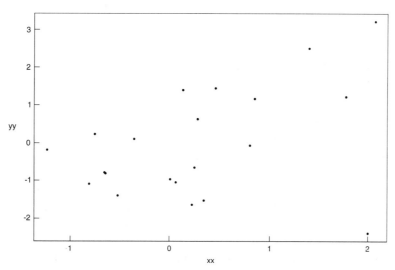

Figure 3.10 Robust measures of correlation reduce the effects of outliers, but depending on where they are located, outliers can still have an undue influence.

model $Y = X + \epsilon$ where both X and ϵ have standard normal distributions. All three of these correlation coefficients yield significance levels less than .05.

Now suppose that two points are added, both at $(X, Y) = (2, -2.4)$, which correspond to the point in the lower right corner of Figure 3.10. These two points are unusual compared to how the original 20 observations were generated because they lie more than 4.5 standard deviations away from the regression line. Note that in order to eliminate these points by restricting the range of the X values, a point that is not an outlier would be removed as well. Now the significance levels based on Kendall's tau, Spearman's rho, and the percentage bend correlation are .34, .36, and .26, respectively. If these two aberrant points are moved to the left to $(X, Y) = (1, -2.4)$, the significance levels are now .23, .20, and .165. All three of these correlation coefficients offer protection against outliers among X values; they do the same for the Y values, but none of them take into account the overall structure of the data. That is, the power of all three methods can be affected by unusual points that are not outliers among the X values (ignoring the Y values), nor outliers among the Y values (ignoring X), yet they are outliers among the scatter plot of points. There are methods for detecting outliers that take into account the overall structure of the data, but the better known methods (e.g., Rousseeuw & van Zomeren, 1990) can eliminate too many points, resulting in a poor reflection of how the bulk of the observations are associated (Wilcox, in press). It seems that no method is perfect in all situations, but a technique (called the MGV regression estimator) that addresses this issue and that seems to have practical value can be found in Wilcox (in press).

CONCLUDING REMARKS

It would be convenient if a single method could be identified that has the highest power relative to all other statistical methods one might use. It is evident, however, that no such method exists. The optimal method, in terms of maximizing power, will depend on how groups differ or how variables are related, which of course is unknown. However, the choice of statistical method is far from academic. A general rule is that methods based on least squares perform well under normality, but other methods have nearly the same amount of power for this special case yet maintain relatively high power under arbitrarily small departures from normality—in contrast to methods based on means or least squares regression. At a minimum, use a heteroscedastic rather than a homoscedastic method. Robust measures of location and rank-based methods represent the two main alternatives to least squares, but in terms of power

there is no clear choice between them. Each gives a different and useful perspective on how groups differ. There is weak evidence that in practice, methods based on robust measures of location are a bit more likely to reject, but we can be fairly certain that in some situations the reverse is true.

One of the many remaining problems is finding ways of assessing power, based on available data, when using a robust measure of location. If a nonsignificant result is obtained, why? If power is low, it is unreasonable to accept the null hypothesis. Relevant methods have been developed when using conventional (homoscedastic) rank-based methods, but how should power be assessed when using more modern techniques? Progress has been made when comparing two groups with 20% trimmed means, but extensions to other measures of location are needed, as well as extensions to more complex designs. Of course, similar issues arise when dealing with correlation and regression.

REFERENCES

Barnett, V., & Lewis, T. (1994). *Outliers in statistical data*. New York: Wiley.

Bishop, T., & Dudewicz, E. J. (1978). Exact analysis of variance with unequal variances: Test procedures and tables. *Technometrics, 20,* 419–430.

Bornstein, M. (2000). *Power and precision* (Version 2.0) [Computer software]. Englewood, NJ: Biostat.

Brunner, E., & Munzel, U. (1999). Rank-score tests in factorial designs with repeated measures. *Journal of Multivariate Analysis, 70,* 286–317.

Cliff, N. (1994). Predicting ordinal relations. *British Journal of Mathematical and Statistical Psychology, 47,* 127–150.

Cohen, J. (1977). *Statistical power analysis for the behavioral sciences*. New York: Academic Press.

Cressie, N. A. C., & Whitford, H. J. (1986). How to use the two-sample *t* test. *Biometrical Journal, 28,* 131–148.

Duncan, G. T., & Layard, M. W. (1973). A Monte-Carlo study of asymptotically robust tests for correlation. *Biometrika, 60,* 551–558.

Elashoff, J. D. (2000). *nQuery Advisor* (Version 4.0) [Computer software]. Saugus, MA: Statistical Solutions.

Fligner, M. A., & Policello, G. E., II. (1981). Robust rank procedures for the Behrens-Fisher problem. *Journal of the American Statistical Association, 76,* 162–168.

Hampel, F. R., Ronchetti, E. M., Rousseeuw, P. J., & Stahel, W. A. (1986). *Robust statistics: The approach based on influence functions*. New York: Wiley.

Hewett, J. E., & Spurrier, J. D. (1983). A survey of two stage tests of hypotheses: Theory and application. *Communications in Statistics: Theory and Methods, 12,* 2307–2425.

Hoaglin, D. C. (1985). Summarizing shape numerically: The *g*-and-*h* distributions. In D. Hoaglin, F. Mosteller, & J. Tukey (Eds.), *Exploring data tables, trends, and shapes* (pp. 461–515). New York: Wiley.

Hochberg, Y. (1975). Simultaneous inference under Behrens-Fisher conditions: A two sample approach. *Communications in Statistics, 4,* 1109–1119.

Huber, P. (1964). Robust estimation of location. *Annals of Statistics, 35,* 73–101.

Huber, P. (1981). *Robust statistics.* New York: Wiley.

Hussain, S. S., & Sprent, P. (1983). Non-parametric regression. *Journal of the Royal Statistical Society, 146,* 182–191.

Kraemer, H. C., & Thiemann, S. (1987). *How many subjects?* Newbury Park: Sage.

Long, J. S., & Ervin, L. H. (2000). Using heteroscedasticity-consistent standard errors in the linear regression model. *American Statistician, 54,* 217–224.

McKean, J. W., & Schrader, R. M. (1984). A comparison of methods for Studentizing the sample median. *Communications in Statistics: Simulation and Computation, 13,* 751–773.

Mee, R. W. (1990). Confidence intervals for probabilities and tolerance regions based on a generalization of the Mann-Whitney statistic. *American Statistical Association, 85,* 793–800.

O'Brien, R. G. (1998). *UnifyPow* [Computer software]. Cleveland, OH: Author.

Pedersen, W. C., Miller, L. C., Putcha, A. D., & Yang, Y. (in press). Evolved sex differences in sexual strategies: The long and the short of it. *Psychological Science.*

Rousseeuw, P. J., & Leroy, A. M. (1987). *Robust regression and outlier detection.* New York: Wiley.

Rousseeuw, P. J., & van Zomeren, B. C. (1990). Unmasking multivariate outliers and leverage points (with discussion). *Journal of the American Statistical Association, 85,* 633–639.

Sawilowsky, S., Kelley, D. L., Blair, R. C., & Markman, B. S. (1994). Meta-analysis and the Solomon four-group design. *Journal of Experimental Education, 62,* 361–376.

Sen, P. K. (1968). Estimate of the regression coefficient based on Kendall's tau. *Journal of the American Statistical Association, 63,* 1379–1389.

Stein, C. (1945). A two-sample test for a linear hypothesis whose power is independent of the variance. *Annals of Statistics, 16,* 243–258.

Tamhane, A. (1977). Multiple comparisons in model I one-way ANOVA with unequal variances. *Communications in Statistics: Theory and Methods, A6,* 15–32.

Theil, H. (1950). A rank-invariant method of linear and polynomial regression analysis. *Indagationes Mathematicae, 12,* 85–91.

Tukey, J. W., & McLaughlin, D. H. (1963). Less vulnerable confidence and significance procedures for location based on a single sample: Trimming/Winsorization 1. *Sankhya A, 25,* 331–352.

Westfall, P. H., & Young, S. S. (1993). *Resampling-based multiple testing.* New York: Wiley.

Wilcox, R. R. (1996). Confidence intervals for the slope of a regression line when the error term has non-constant variance. *Computational Statistics and Data Analysis.*

Wilcox, R. R. (1997). *Introduction to robust estimation and hypothesis testing.* San Diego, CA: Academic Press.

Wilcox, R. R. (1998). Simulation results on extensions of the Theil-Sen regression estimator. *Communications in Statistics: Simulation and Computation, 27,* 1117–1126.

Wilcox, R. R. (2001). *Fundamentals of modern statistical methods.* New York: Springer.

Wilcox, R. R. (in press). *Applying contemporary statistical methods.* San Diego, CA: Academic Press.

Wilcox, R. R., Charlin, V. L., & Thompson, K. (1986). New Monte Carlo results on the robustness of the ANOVA *F*, *W*, and *F** statistics. *Communications in Statistics: Simulation and Computation, 15,* 933–944.

Yuen, K. K. (1974). The two-sample trimmed *t* for unequal population variances. *Biometrika, 61,* 165–170.

CHAPTER 4

Methods for Handling Missing Data

JOHN W. GRAHAM, PATRICIO E. CUMSILLE, AND ELVIRA ELEK-FISK

A LITTLE HISTORY

In the past, when data were missing from our data sets, any number of reactions were common. Positive emotions, such as happiness and contentment, never occurred. Rather, the emotions we felt (often in this order) were frustration, anger, guilt, fear, and sadness.

When we wanted to do a particular analysis but some data were missing, the number of cases available for the analysis was reduced to the point that the result was often not

significant. It was particularly frustrating when data were missing from one part of a model we might be testing, but not from other parts, but we had to test the model using only those cases with no missing data. Alternatively, we could test something simpler than the preferred model. All of the choices we seemed to face were bad. We could accept the nonsignificant result. We could employ some procedure of questionable validity. We could just lie. We could try again to wade through one of the highly technical journal articles that supposedly dealt with the issue of handling missing data. After going around in circles, we always found ourselves back again at the starting place, and angry.

If we tried one of the procedures that has questionable validity, we would immediately feel guilty. Questions would

This research was supported in part by grants from the Hanley Family Foundation and The JM Foundation, and by NIDA Grants P50-DA-10075 and R01-DA-05629.

bedevil us: Do the results represent reality? Or are they just a figment of our imagination? Will we be able to defend our procedure to the reviewers? If by some miracle our article is published, will we find out later that the results were not valid? Not everyone in psychology faces the problem of missing data, but we do. We knew that every time we embarked on an analysis, we could look forward to the sequence of frustrating setbacks, and this knowledge always made us sad.

Four separate pieces were published in 1987 that would forever change the way researchers looked at data analysis with missing data. Two papers were published describing a procedure for analyzing missing data using standard structural equation modeling (SEM) software (Allison, 1987; Muthén, Kaplan, & Hollis, 1987). Although somewhat unwieldy, and extremely error prone for most real-life applications, this procedure provided researchers with the first truly accessible and statistically sound tool for dealing with missing data. Of course, this procedure assumed that one knew how to use the SEM programs to begin with.

Little and Rubin's (1987) highly influential book on analysis with missing data also appeared in 1987. In this book, Little and Rubin, following Dempster, Laird, and Rubin (1977), laid the groundwork for development of the expectation maximization (EM) algorithm for numerous missing data applications. In addition, Rubin (1987) published the first book on multiple imputation in 1987. Although practical applications of multiple imputation would not appear for another 10 years, this was the beginning of what would be the most general approach to handling missing data.

Since 1987, numerous software products have become available that address the issue of missing data. Many of the best of these are free. For the ones that are not free, the cost is more than offset by their usefulness. Although we need to continue to move forward in this area, we have made tremendous progress in making missing data analysis accessible to researchers all over the world. In fact, we stand at the beginning of an era in which useful and accessible missing data procedures are an integral part of mainstream statistical packages.

A LITTLE PHILOSOPHY

One of the concerns most frequently heard in the early days of missing data procedures was something like, "Aren't you helping yourself unfairly when you use this procedure?" The short answer to this questions is "no!" In general, use of the prescribed missing data procedures does not give something for nothing. These procedures simply allow one to minimize losses. In particular, these procedures allow one to make full use of any partial data one may have. As we shall see in the following pages, making use of partial data often proves to be a tremendous advantage.

A similar concern in the early days, especially with respect to data imputation, was something along these lines: "How can you say that this imputed value is what the person would have given if he or she had given us data? It sounds like magic." Well, it would be magic if it were true. That is why we always tell people not to focus on the imputed values themselves. We do not impute a value because we are trying to fathom what an individual would have said if he or she had given us data. That would typically be impossible. Rather, we impute in order to preserve important characteristics of the whole data set. That is, we impute to get better estimates of population parameters (e.g., variances, covariances, means, regression coefficients, etc.) and distributions. As it turns out, this is a very possible goal.

Any good procedure will yield *unbiased* and *efficient* parameter estimates. By *unbiased,* we mean that the expected value of the parameter estimate (e.g., a *b* weight) is the same as the true population value. By *efficient,* we mean that the variability around the estimated value is small. A second characteristic of a good missing data procedure is that it provides a reasonable estimate of the variability around the parameter estimate (i.e., standard errors or confidence intervals).

MISSING DATA PATTERNS AND MECHANISMS

There are two general patterns of missing data. With the first pattern, the respondent does take part in a measurement session, but for whatever reason does not respond to some questions. This type of missingness might be referred to as *item nonresponse.* With one manifestation of this pattern, the person omits the last *k* items of a long survey, for example, due to slow reading. Second, the respondent may fail to answer individual items in the middle of a survey that is otherwise complete. Third, the respondent may omit blocks of questions, but not necessarily at the end of the survey.

A second general missing data pattern occurs when the respondent is missing from a whole wave of measurement in a longitudinal study. This is sometimes referred to as *attrition* and sometimes as *wave nonresponse.* With this sort of missingness, the person may be absent from one or more waves of measurement and then reappear at a later wave. Alternatively, the person may fail to appear at one wave of measurement and all subsequent waves. A third version of this pattern occurs when the person is not present at the first wave of measurement but drops in to the study at a subsequent wave.

Numerous explanations are possible for each of these patterns of missing data. These explanations, or missing data mechanisms, fall into three general categories (e.g., see Little & Rubin, 1987). First, the data may be *missing completely at random* (MCAR). Data are MCAR if the mechanism for the missingness is a completely random process, such as a coin flip. Data are also MCAR if the cause of missingness is not correlated with the variable containing missingness. An important consequence of MCAR missingness is that there is no estimation bias if the cause of missingness is omitted from the missing data model.

A second missing data mechanism has been referred to as *missing at random* (MAR; e.g., Little & Rubin, 1987). With this mechanism, the cause of missingness is correlated with the variable(s) containing the missing data, but variables representing this cause have been measured and are thus available for inclusion in the missing data model. Inclusion of MAR causes of missingness in the missing data model corrects for all biases associated with them.

Unfortunately, the term MAR (which is sometimes referred to as *ignorable missingness*) has produced considerable confusion among psychologists and other social scientists. First, this mechanism is neither random (at least, not in the sense that most of us think of when we see the word *random*), nor is it ignorable (at least, not in the sense in which the word *ignorable* is typically used). In fact, one of the very characteristics of this missing data mechanism is that one must not ignore it. Rather, one must include the cause of missingness in the model, or there will be estimation bias.

Technically, MAR missingness occurs when the missingness is not due to the missing data themselves. Because of this definition, it turns out that MCAR is a special case of MAR missingness. The term *missing at random* does make sense if we realize that the missingness is *conditionally* random. That is, once one has conditioned on the cause of missingness (which is available), the missingness is random.

The term *accessible missingness* (Graham & Donaldson, 1993) was coined in an attempt to define the mechanism in a less confusing way. However, because the term MAR is so well established in the statistical literature, it would be a disservice to psychologists not to use this term. Thus, we endorse the term MAR and will use it exclusively in the future to refer to this sort of missingness.

A third missing data mechanism has been referred to as *missing not at random* (MNAR; Collins, Schafer, & Kam, 2001; Schafer & Graham, in press). In this case, the cause of missingness is correlated with the variable(s) containing missing data, but the cause has not been measured, or it is otherwise unavailable for inclusion in the missing data model. This type of missingness is related to the missing data, even after conditioning on all available data. Thus, it is not missing at random.

Each of the two general kinds of missing data (item nonresponse, wave nonresponse) can be caused by any of the three missing data mechanisms (MCAR, MAR, MNAR). Each of the six combinations may be represented in any given data set. As we suggested above, missing data may be due to (a) processes that are essentially random, (b) processes that are represented by variables in the data set, or (c) processes that have not been measured. In addition, MCAR missingness within a wave, or even across waves, can be part of a planned missing data design (Graham, Hofer, & MacKinnon, 1996; Graham, Hofer, & Piccinin, 1994; Graham, Taylor, & Cumsille, 2001; McArdle, 1994). Given the increasing usefulness of missing data analysis procedures, such as those described in this chapter, Graham, Taylor et al. (2001) have argued that it may be time to begin considering such designs in most research endeavors.

OLD (UNACCEPTABLE) PROCEDURES FOR ANALYSIS WITH MISSING DATA

Complete Cases Analysis (Listwise Deletion)

Over the years, the most common approach to dealing with missing data has been to pretend there are no missing data. That is, researchers (including the present authors, of course), have simply omitted any cases that are missing data on the relevant variables. There are two possible problems with this approach. At an intuitive level, it is easy to see that this approach could introduce estimation biases. The people who provide complete data in a study are very likely going to be different from those who do not provide complete data. There has been ample evidence in the prevention literature, for example, that people who drop out of a prevention study are generally very different from those who remain in the study. For example, adolescents who drop out of a longitudinal study are much more likely to be drug users at the last wave of measurement for which they did provide data.

Although bias with complete cases analysis is certainly a possibility (e.g., see Schafer & Graham, in press; Wothke, 2000), we argue that for many kinds of analysis, for example, for multiple-regression analysis, the amount of bias produced by complete cases analysis will generally be small, even trivial. For example, suppose we plan a multiple-regression analysis with several predictors (with no missing data) and a dependent variable that is sometimes missing, for example, due to attrition. If the dependent variable is missing due to an MCAR mechanism, then complete cases analysis is known to yield unbiased estimates. If the missing data mechanism is MAR, that is, if the missingness on the dependent variable is due to some combination of the predictor variables, then the biases are completely controlled by the complete cases analysis (e.g., see Heckman, 1979; also see Graham & Donaldson, 1993). If the cause of missingness on the dependent variable is an MNAR process, then the degree of bias due to complete cases will be the same as the bias that will occur with the *acceptable* analysis procedures described below (e.g., Graham & Donaldson, 1993). Of course, this is true only under somewhat limited conditions. In more complex analysis situations, complete cases analysis could introduce bias to the parameter estimates.

In short, we do not side with those who argue that complete cases analysis should not be used because of the potential for bias. Rather, we argue that complete cases analysis should not be used because of loss of statistical power. In virtually all research situations, using complete cases analysis means that the researcher must discard at least some information. In fact, it is becoming more and more common that a large proportion of cases is lost if listwise deletion is used.

In order to illustrate this issue, consider two proportions: the proportion of complete cases, and the proportion of nonmissing data points. The latter figure is calculated easily by considering the total number of data points in a data set, $N \times k$, where N is the number of cases and k is the number of variables. One can simply divide the number of nonmissing data points by $N \times k$ to determine the proportion of nonmissing data points. Of course, if most of the data points are missing, the results may be suspect regardless of the analysis used. However, there are many situations in which the proportion of nonmissing data points is actually quite high but the proportion of complete cases is disturbingly low. Three common research situations can produce this pattern: (a) missing data on different variables in different cases; (b) a substantial amount of missing data in one part of a model, with very little missing data in other parts of the model; and (c) planned missing data designs such as the three-form design (Graham et al., 1994, 1996, Graham, Taylor, et al., 2001).

In sum, we argue that complete cases should not be used as the general analysis strategy. Although bias may be minimal in many research situations, the loss of power could be tremendous. However, we explicitly stop short of saying that complete cases analysis should never be used. First, we have argued previously (Graham & Hofer, 2000; Graham, Taylor, et al., 2001) that if the number of cases lost to missing data is small, for example if 5% or fewer cases are lost, then the amount of bias would very likely be trivial, and even the loss of power would be minimal. Second, the standard errors (and confidence intervals) based on complete cases are quite reasonable (Schafer & Graham, in press).

Pairwise Deletion

Pairwise deletion (sometimes referred to as *pairwise inclusion*) involves calculating each element of a covariance matrix using cases that have data for both variables. Using this procedure, one would then analyze the covariance matrix using some analytic procedure that can analyze the covariance matrix directly. Conceptually, this procedure makes sense in that one appears to be making use of all available data. However, statistically, this is not a desirable procedure. Parameter estimates based on pairwise deletion can be biased. More of a problem, however, is the fact that the resulting covariance matrix is not guaranteed to be positive definite; that is, there may be less information in the matrix than would be expected based on the number of variables involved.

A third problem with analysis based on pairwise deletion is that one is limited to analyses that can be performed directly from the covariance matrix. Finally, there is no basis for estimating standard errors of the parameters based on the pairwise covariance matrix. Although all of these problems could be overcome—for example, standard errors might be obtained with bootstrapping—the work required to patch up the procedure will very likely turn out to be more than what is involved in the preferred analyses to be described later.

Even for quick and dirty analyses, we recommend other procedures (see the section "A Few Loose Ends," near the end of this chapter).

Mean Substitution

With this procedure, whenever a value is missing for one case on a particular variable, the mean for that variable, based on all nonmissing cases, is used in place of the missing value. (The term *mean substitution,* as it is used here, applies to substituting the mean for the variable. It is also possible to substitute the mean, for that particular case, of other highly correlated variables. As described in a later section, we do recommend this latter procedure under some circumstances.)

Mean substitution has been shown in several simulation studies to yield highly biased parameter estimates (e.g., Graham et al., 1994, 1996; Graham, Hofer, Donaldson,

MacKinnon, & Schafer, 1997). We argue that it should never be used. Even for quick and dirty analyses, and even with small rates of missingness, we recommend the procedures described in the following sections.

Regression-Based Single Imputation

The idea of imputation is to substitute a plausible value for the one that is missing. One of the most plausible values, at least in theory, is the value that is predicted by a regression equation involving a number of other predictor variables. In brief, suppose a variable, Y, is sometimes missing, and another set of variables, $X_1 - X_k$, is never missing. We can calculate the predicted value for Y (i.e., Y-hat), based on the cases for which we have data on Y. For cases with Y missing, we can substitute Y-hat instead.

In theory, this is an excellent approach to doing imputation. The problem, however, is that regression-based single imputation produces substantial bias, especially in the estimates of variance (and therefore in correlations as well). Also, it has been shown that this procedure is valid only under certain, rather limited, patterns of missing data (i.e., monotone missing data patterns). In addition, there is no reasonable basis for calculating standard errors. Regression-based single imputation does form the statistical basis for many of the acceptable procedures described below, but as a stand-alone procedure it is not recommended. We argue that it should never be used. Even for quick and dirty analyses, and even with small rates of missingness, we also recommend the procedures described in the acceptable methods section.

Summary of Unacceptable Procedures

In summary, we argue that pairwise deletion, mean substitution, and regression-based single imputation should never be used. Even for quick and dirty analyses, and even with small rates of missingness, we recommend other procedures (see section "A Few Loose Ends"). We do, however, conditionally endorse the use of complete cases analysis. In particular, when one loses only a small proportion of cases (e.g., 5% or less), use of complete cases analysis seems reasonable. Please note that we always prefer other methods (e.g., multiple imputation), even with small amounts of missing data. From our perspective, further along on the learning curve, it costs us very little to use the better procedures, and the payoff, however small, is worth it. However, for many researchers (nearer the start of the learning curve), the payoff may not be worth it under these circumstances. Still, in the very near future, these better procedures, or at least rudimentary versions of them, will be available in ways that are more or less transparent to the end user. We look forward to those days.

ACCEPTABLE MODEL-BASED MISSING DATA PROCEDURES

Before embarking on a description of acceptable procedures, we should note that our description of acceptable procedures is neither highly technical nor exhaustive. For more technical and more general treatments on these topics, other publications are available (e.g., Little & Schenker, 1995; Schafer & Graham, in press).

Model-based missing data procedures deal with the missing data at the same time that they deal with parameter estimation. That is, missing data and data analysis are handled in a single step. As we see below, most of these procedures have been built around latent variable procedures and are thus somewhat less accessible for the average data analyst than are the data-based procedures described next. Still, some of these procedures are extremely easy to use and, when used properly, can be enormously valuable as a general tool for dealing with missing data.

Multiple Group Structural Equation Modeling

At the outset of this chapter we mentioned this method as being one of the first accessible approaches to analysis with missing data. We cannot go into great detail here in describing this procedure (greater detail about this procedure may be found in Allison, 1987; Duncan & Duncan, 1994; Graham et al., 1994). In brief, the procedure divides up the sample into groups containing cases with the same pattern of missing and nonmissing values. A system of equality constraints is then placed on the parameter estimates across groups, such that parameters are estimated based only on those cases having data that bear on that parameter estimate. This procedure has some serious limitations and has thus been supplanted by the other procedures to be described below. However, this procedure continues to be valuable for particular applications.

The main limitation of this procedure is that it can be extremely unwieldy and error prone, especially when there are many distinct missing data patterns. Because the SEM code must be changed in subtle ways from group to group in the multiple group design, it is very easy to introduce errors into the code. In addition, one requirement of this procedure is that there must be more cases than variables for every group. With a typical longitudinal data set, this means that some data must be discarded in order to produce groups (of missing data patterns) with sufficiently large sample sizes.

Beyond these limitations, however, this procedure can be quite good. The parameter estimates are good (i.e., unbiased and efficient), and the standard errors are reasonable. This procedure can be especially good for certain specialty models. For example, Duncan, Duncan, and Li (1998; also see McArdle & Hamagami, 1991) have shown how this procedure can be useful with cohort sequential designs in which not all combinations of measures are available. In addition, Graham, Taylor, et al. (2001) have shown how this procedure can be extremely useful in simulation work involving missing data.

Full-Information Maximum Likelihood for SEM

Full-information maximum likelihood (FIML) procedures for SEM, like other model-based procedures, solve the missing data problem and the parameter estimation problem in a single step. With all of these FIML procedures for SEM, the program yields excellent parameter estimates and reasonable standard errors, all in a single analysis (however, see the discussion in the later section "A Comparison of Model-Based and Data-Based Procedures" for some limitations to these statements).

Amos

Amos (Arbuckle & Wothke, 1999) has become one of the more commonly used SEM programs available today. Amos provides good, quick parameter estimation, along with reasonable standard errors, in the missing data case. Two of the most desirable features of Amos are (a) that it has an excellent and extremely flexible graphical interface and (b) that it is now part of the SPSS package. This latter fact means that one can create one's SPSS data set, making any desired data modifications, and then click on *Amos* as one of the available analyses within the SPSS package. Despite the drawbacks described in the next paragraph, the array of nifty features makes Amos a highly desirable option for researchers in the social sciences. Amos is not free, but it is available at a reasonable price, especially if one can obtain it at the same time one obtains the latest version of SPSS.

Unfortunately, Amos is not without limitations. Perhaps the most important limitation is that one of its most desirable features, the graphical interface, becomes quickly loaded down with squares, circles, and arrows when more than a few latent variables are included in the model. For example, a model with five independent latent variables, three latent mediating variables, and three latent outcomes variables, would be a jumble of wires (regression and correlation paths) and extremely difficult to read. This problem is further exacerbated if one makes use of one of the models recommended for enhancing the missing data estimation (described later).

Fortunately, Amos provides two solutions to these problems. First, Amos warns the user whenever two variables are not connected by correlation or regression paths. Although we cannot guarantee that this warning catches all possible problems, we have found it to be very useful. Second, the text version of Amos offers a clear solution for estimation of larger models. Although the text version is a bit clunky in comparison to the graphical version, it is a completely serviceable alternative.

A second drawback to the use of Amos is that it is not quite up to the state of the art regarding the SEM analysis itself. First, the goodness of fit indices are a bit nonstandard in the missing data case. The *independence* or *null* model, on which many goodness of fit indices are based, assumes that all means are zero. This assumption is so far wrong (unless the input variables are standardized) that almost any model looks very good in comparison. The solution is to estimate one's own independence model, which estimates all item variances and means, but no item covariances. This corresponds to the independence model in use by the other major SEM programs.

A second way in which Amos is not quite up to existing SEM standards relates to its modification indices. They are not available at all in the missing data case and are sometimes quite misleading even in the complete data case. Also not available in Amos 4.0 is the Satorra and Bentler (1994) correction to standard errors when data are not normally distributed. Note that some or all of these limitations may be resolved in newer versions of Amos.

To finish on an up note, one of the key advantages of the Amos program is that it provides a reasonable estimate of the chi-square in the missing data case. This is something that is not yet available with the data-based procedures described next. In short, where possible, we highly recommend having Amos as one of your missing data analysis tools.

Other FIML Programs for SEM

Three other options for FIML programs for SEM are LISREL (Jöreskog & Sörbom, 1996), Mx (Neale, Boker, Xie, & Maes, 1999), and Mplus (Muthén, 2001; Muthén & Muthén, 1998). LISREL (Jöreskog & Sörbom, 1996) has been the most often used of the SEM programs since its introduction in the late 1970s. The recently released version 8.50 has both FIML and multiple-imputation capabilities. A single statement converts the standard, complete-cases version of LISREL to its FIML counterpart. The new missing data features of this program are very good news for the regular LISREL users.

Mx is a free program that takes the same analysis approach as Amos. Although Mx's interface is not as fancy as Amos, it is an extremely useful program. The fact that it is available for free makes it especially appealing for some researchers. In addition, Mx has features that were especially designed to facilitate analysis of behavioral genetics data.

Mplus is a flexible SEM program developed with the intention of presenting the data analyst with a simple and nontechnical language to model data (Muthén & Muthén, 1998). Mplus includes many of the features offered by other SEM programs and a few that are not offered by other programs. For example, the ability to work with categorical variables is not easily implemented in other SEM programs. A major innovation of Mplus is its ability to use mixture models to model categorical and continuous data simultaneously. For example, Mplus allows one to model different latent classes of trajectories in latent growth curve modeling, a kind of model referred to as second-generation structural equation modeling by Muthén (2001).

Mplus includes missing data analysis for continuous outcomes under the assumption of MAR or MCAR. Parameters are estimated using maximum likelihood. Mplus also allows for missing data in categorical variables in mixture models.

FIML for Latent Class Analysis

In addition to Mplus, which has latent class features, LTA (Latent Transition Analysis; Collins, Hyatt, & Graham, 2000; Hyatt & Collins, 2000) also offers missing data capabilities in conjunction with latent class analysis. Although a full description of the capabilities of these programs is beyond the scope of this chapter, both programs share with other FIML procedures the feature of dealing with missing data and parameter estimation in a single step.

ACCEPTABLE DATA-BASED MISSING DATA PROCEDURES

With data-based missing data procedures, the missing data issues are handled in a preliminary step, and the main data analysis (parameter estimation) is handled in a second, separate step. The two procedures discussed here are the EM algorithm for covariance matrices, and multiple imputation.

EM Algorithm

The EM algorithm for covariance matrices reads in the data matrix, with missing and nonmissing values, and reads out a maximum-likelihood variance-covariance matrix and vector of means. This variance-covariance matrix and vector of means may then be used by other programs for further analyses of substantive interest. Analyses that may be performed with the output from the EM algorithm include SEM (e.g., with LISREL or EQS), multiple regression (e.g., with SAS), exploratory factor analysis (e.g., with SAS), and coefficient alpha analysis (e.g., with the utility ALPHNORM).

EM Algorithm in Brief

Details of the EM algorithm for covariance matrices are given in Little and Rubin (1987; also see Graham & Donaldson, 1993; Schafer, 1997). In brief, EM is an iterative procedure. In the E-step, one reads in the data, one case at a time. As each case is read in, one adds to the calculation of the sufficient statistics (sums, sums of squares, sums of cross products). If nonmissing values are available for the case, they contribute to these sums directly. If a variable is missing for the case, then the best guess is used in place of the missing value. The best guess is the predicted score based on a regression equation with all other variables as predictors. For sums of squares and sums of cross products, if neither element is missing, or if just one element is missing, the best guess is used as is. If both elements are missing, a correction term is added. This correction term amounts to added variability.

In the *m* step, once all the sums have been collected, the variance-covariance matrix (and vector of means) can simply be calculated. Based on this covariance matrix, the regression equation can also be calculated for each variable as a dependent variable. The regression equation from iteration 1 is then used in the next *e* step for iteration 2. Another (better) covariance matrix is produced in the *m* step of iteration 2. That covariance matrix and regression equations are used for the next *e* step, and so on. This two-step process continues until the change in the covariance matrix from one iteration to the next becomes trivially small.

EM provides maximum-likelihood estimates of the variance-covariance matrix elements. Some analyses that are based on this covariance matrix are also maximum likelihood. For example, if the EM covariance matrix is used to perform a multiple-regression analysis, the resulting regression weights are also maximum-likelihood estimates. With this type of analysis, EM and FIML procedures (e.g., Amos) yield identical results.

However, for other analyses—for example, SEM with latent variables—parameter estimates based on the EM covariance matrix are technically not maximum likelihood. Nevertheless, even these parameter estimates based on the

EM covariance matrix are excellent in that they are unbiased and efficient.

The biggest drawback with EM is that it typically does not provide standard errors (and confidence intervals) as a by-product of the parameter estimation. Thus, although the parameter estimation itself is excellent with EM, it is not possible to do hypothesis testing with the EM-based estimates unless one does a separate step specifically for that purpose, such as the bootstrap (Efron, 1982). The more common approach to obtaining standard errors for general analysis is a procedure related to EM: multiple imputation (described in a later section).

However, for special purposes, using the excellent parameter estimation of EM serves an extremely useful function. If hypothesis testing is not important, for example, with exploratory factor analysis, or coefficient alpha analysis, analyzing the EM covariance matrix is an excellent option. We present an illustration of this type of analysis later in this chapter. In a later section ("A Few Loose Ends"), we also discuss briefly the use of the EM covariance matrix for taking a quick and dirty look at one's data, even when hypothesis testing is required. Use of the EM matrix is also good for establishing goodness of fit in SEM when data are missing (Graham & Hofer, 2000).

EM Algorithm Programs

There are many programs available for the EM algorithm for covariance matrices. Perhaps the best option is Schafer's (1997) NORM program. The program is designed to perform multiple imputation, but one of the intermediate steps is to calculate the EM covariance matrix. Utility programs (e.g., ALPHNORM) are easily written that allow the use of NORM's EM covariance matrix for performing analysis with SAS (and other programs) and for doing coefficient alpha analysis.

Other programs for performing EM include EMCOV (Graham et al., 1994), SPSS, and SAS. EMCOV is a DOS-based program that was developed in the early 1990s. Nearly all of its functions are better handled by Schafer's (1997) NORM program, except that, as a stand-alone program, EMCOV is sometimes easier to use with simulation studies. The current implementation of the EM algorithm within SPSS (version 10) is disappointing. First, the program is painfully slow, and it often crashes with problems of any size. Second, the EM routine is not integrated into the other SPSS procedures. An excellent, but nonexistent option, for example, would be to use the EM covariance matrix (automatically) as input into the factor analysis and reliability procedures. In fact, this should be the default for handling missing data in these two procedures. Watch for substantial improvements in future releases of SPSS. SAS 8.2 offers all these functions in PROC MI. (Please check our web site, http://methodology.psu.edu, for updated information relating to the software described in this chapter.)

Multiple Imputation

The problem with regression-based single imputation is that there is too little variability in the variables containing missing values. This lack of variability comes from two sources. First, the singly imputed values lack error variance. Every imputed value lies right on the regression line. In real (i.e., nonmissing) data, the data points are above or below the regression line but seldom right on it. This sort of variability can be restored simply by adding a random error term to each imputed value (EM adds a similar kind of error to the sums of squares and sums of cross products). This random error could come from a distribution of the known error terms for the variable in question, or it could simply be a value from a normal distribution. Schafer's (1997) NORM program takes this latter approach.

The second reason that single imputation lacks variability is that the regression equation used for imputing values is just one estimate of the regression equation. That is, this regression equation is based on the data at hand, and the data at hand represent just a single (random) draw from the population. Another random draw from the population would yield a slightly different regression equation. This variability translates into slightly different imputed values. Restoring this kind of variability could be done easily if a person could simply make multiple random draws from the population. Unfortunately, this is almost never possible; we typically have just one data set to work with. However, it may be possible to simulate multiple random draws from the population.

One approach to this simulation is to use bootstrap methods. Creating multiple bootstrap data sets would (to an extent) be like taking multiple random draws from the population. Another approach is to simulate these random draws with data augmentation (Tanner & Wong, 1987). Data augmentation, which is used in Schafer's (1997) NORM program, bears some similarity to EM. Like EM, data augmentation is a two-step, iterative procedure. For each step of data augmentation, one has an i (imputation) step and a p (posterior) step (the accepted jargon is *steps* of data augmentation and *iterations* of EM). In each i step, data augmentation simulates the data based on the current set of parameters. In each p step, data augmentation simulates the parameters given the current data.

With this process, which is one in a family of Markov Chain Monte Carlo procedures, the parameters from one step of data augmentation are dependent upon the parameters from the immediately preceding step. However, as one moves more and more steps away from the original step, the parameter estimates become less and less dependent upon the initial estimates, until the two sets of parameter estimates, and the imputed data sets that are generated from them, are as independent of one another as one might find with two random draws from the same population. It is important to discover how many steps apart two imputed data sets must be in order for them to simulate two random draws from the population. We will elaborate on this point during the practical example.

Doing Multiple Imputation

The multiple-imputation process requires three steps. First, one creates m imputed data sets, such that each data set contains a different imputed value for every missing value. The value of m can be anything greater than 1, but it typically ranges from 5 to 20. Second, one analyzes the m data sets, saving the parameter estimates and standard errors from each. Third, one combines the parameter estimates and standard errors to arrive at a single set of parameter estimates and corresponding standard errors.

Implementation of Multiple Imputation

There are many implementations of multiple imputation. An excellent option is Schafer's (1997) set of programs, headed by the NORM program for multiple imputation under the normal model. This program works with continuous data, but it has been shown to perform well with categorical data (3+ categories with no missing data, 2− category data with missing data). NORM performs well with nonnormal data and with small sample sizes (Graham & Schafer, 1999). NORM can also be used with longitudinal panel data and with cluster data, as long as the number of clusters is relatively small (cluster membership in k clusters is modeled as $k − 1$ dummy codes, which are included in the multiple-imputation model).

Schafer's (1997) NORM program (or any normal-based imputation procedure) is an excellent choice with most longitudinal data sets. Many longitudinal models—for example, standard growth models—are fully captured by the NORM model. Nothing is gained in this context by using specialized, general linear mixed model programs, such as Schafer's PAN program. It is only under special longitudinal circumstances (e.g., when all cases are missing for one variable at one point in time, or when some pair of variables is missing for all subjects, as with cohort-sequential designs) that these specialized programs are better.

Schafer (1997) also has three other multiple-imputation programs. PAN is available for special longitudinal panel data situations and cluster data when there are many clusters (Schafer, 2001; also see Verbeke & Molenberghs, 2000 for another treatment of mixed models for longitudinal data). CAT is available for strictly categorical data and is especially suited for missing data when the categorical variable has three or more levels. MIX is available for mixed categorical and continuous data.

All four of the programs are available as Splus routines. NORM is also available as a stand-alone Windows (95/98/NT/2000) program, and the current implementation is version 2.03. All of Schafer's (1997, 2001) programs are available at no cost at http://methodology.psu.edu.

We have already mentioned that LISREL 8.50 (Jöreskog & Sörbom, 1996) has a multiple-imputation feature. In addition, PROC MI and PROC MIANALYZE have been implemented in SAS version 8.2. Both of these implementations of multiple imputation are based on Schafer (1997) and promise to increase greatly the usefulness of these procedures.

A COMPARISON OF MODEL-BASED AND DATA-BASED PROCEDURES

The conventional wisdom regarding missing data procedures holds that the model-based procedures and data-based procedures, especially multiple imputation, are essentially equivalent in the quality with which they deal with missing data and differ only in the preferences researchers may have regarding the use of one or the other. However, recent evidence has shown that, although the conventional wisdom remains true in theory, there may be important differences in the quality of these two approaches as they are typically practiced (Collins et al., 2001). The main difference relates to the use of model-irrelevant variables.

Model-based procedures—for example, FIML procedures for SEM—deal with the missing data and parameter estimation at the same time. Thus, by their very nature, these models tend to be limited to the variables that are deemed to be of substantive relevance. The idea of including substantively irrelevant variables into the model, although quite possible with many model-based procedures, is not typical. With multiple imputation, it is quite common, and also quite easy, to include substantively irrelevant variables into the model. Without understanding fully the reasons behind this, researchers have been adding such variables for some time under the belief that it is valuable to do so in order to help with the missing data aspect of the model. It is not so much the number of variables that is important, but which variables are or are not included.

Recent research (Collins et al., 2001) has shown that there is good reason for including such substantively irrelevant variables into all missing data models. Collins et al. have shown several points relevant to this discussion. All of these points relate to the inclusion of variables, which, although outside the model of substantive interest, are highly correlated with variables containing missing data. First, including such variables when the missing data mechanism is MCAR can reduce the standard errors of estimated parameters. Second, with MAR missingness, although there is bias when the causes of missingness are not included in the model, the bias is much less of a problem than previously thought. Also, including highly correlated variables into the model under these circumstances reduces the standard errors of estimated parameters.

Finally, Collins et al. (2001) have shown that with MNAR missing data mechanisms, where the cause of missingness cannot be included in the missing data model, bias can be substantial. However, including highly correlated, substantively irrelevant variables into the model can reduce this bias, often substantially and, as with the other missing data mechanisms, can reduce the standard errors of estimated parameters, without affecting the important parameter estimates. In short, it is essential to include variables that, although substantively irrelevant, are highly correlated with the variables containing missing data.

Because of these recent findings, users of model-based missing data procedures must make every attempt to include these model-irrelevant variables. With some model-based procedures, such as LTA (Collins et al., 2000), this is simply not possible (at least at present). Thus, for many analysis problems, the use of multiple imputation is clearly preferred. However, for FIML-based SEM programs such as Amos, Mx, LISREL 8.50, and Mplus, it is quite possible to introduce these substantively irrelevant variables into the model in a way that helps deal with the missing data and does not alter the substantive aspects of the original model. Models of this sort have been described recently by Graham (in press).

The preliminary evidence is that the practice of adding substantively irrelevant variables has no real drawback, other than increased model complexity. One of the problems with multiple imputation is that as the number of variables increases, EM and data augmentation require more iterations and more time for each iteration. Thus, one practical drawback to adding many extra variables to the model will be that it may take longer to run. In extreme cases, it may even be necessary to break the problem apart in reasoned fashion (e.g., see Graham & Taylor, 2001) and impute the parts separately.

ILLUSTRATIONS OF MISSING DATA PROCEDURES: EMPIRICAL EXAMPLES

In this section, we illustrate the use of two basic missing data procedures: multiple imputation with NORM (Schafer, 1997) and FIML with Amos (Arbuckle & Wothke, 1999). We illustrate these procedures with two types of data analysis. First, we illustrate the use of NORM, along with the utility ALPHNORM, to perform basic data quality analyses (coefficient alpha). We illustrate this by analyzing the EM covariance matrix directly and also by imputing a single data set from EM parameters. Second, we illustrate a straightforward multiple-regression analysis with multiple imputation. We illustrate this with both SAS and SPSS. For comparison, we perform this same multiple-regression analysis using the Amos program. Although we do not illustrate latent-variable regression analysis, we do discuss SEM analysis with multiple imputation and Amos.

Participants and Missing Data Patterns

The empirical data for these examples are drawn from the Alcohol-Related Harm Prevention (AHP) project (Graham, Roberts, Tatterson, & Johnston, in press; Graham, Tatterson, Roberts, & Johnston, 2001). The participants for the AHP study were undergraduate college students, the majority of whom were sophomores in fall 1999. Longitudinal data are included from five waves of data collected from September 1999 to November 2000 from the same students.

Describing the sample size in a study with missing data is not a straightforward thing. We recommend describing the sample size as follows. First, the population was defined as the 1,702 students enrolled in one large college course in fall 1999. Of this number, $N = 1,024$ took part in at least one of the five waves of measurement. A subset of these students (634, 489, 707, 714, 628, respectively) participated in waves 1 through 5 of measurement. Table 4.1 summarizes the student participation over the course of the study.

The "0" values in Table 4.1 represent wave nonresponse or attrition. In addition to the wave nonresponse, students may not have completed all items within the questionnaire. For example, due to slow reading, they may have left questions blank at the end of the survey. To minimize this problem, the AHP questionnaire used a version of the "3-form design" (Graham et al., 1994, 1996, 1997; Graham, Taylor, et al., 2001). With this measurement design, the order of

TABLE 4.1 Participation Patterns for the Five Waves of the AHP Study

Wave						
1	2	3	4	5	Frequency	Percent
0	0	0	0	1	56	5.5
0	0	0	1	0	44	4.3
0	0	0	1	1	47	4.6
0	0	1	0	0	38	3.7
0	0	1	1	0	44	4.3
0	0	1	1	1	64	6.3
0	1	1	1	1	33	3.2
1	0	0	0	0	58	5.7
1	0	1	0	0	23	2.2
1	0	1	1	0	32	3.1
1	0	1	1	1	64	6.3
1	1	0	0	0	24	2.3
1	1	1	0	1	21	2.1
1	1	1	1	0	69	6.7
1	1	1	1	1	253	24.7
					870	85.0

Note. 1 = participated; 0 = did not participate. The 15 patterns shown are those involving the largest numbers of participants. Sixteen additional patterns, each containing fewer than 20 students, are not shown.

presentation of the main item sets was rotated across the three forms so that slow readers would leave different questions blank depending upon which form they received.

Measures

Because the focus of this chapter is the methods more than the substantive analyses, we describe the measures only briefly. The main analysis to be described was multiple regression.

Dependent Variable

For the main substantive analyses, we treated heavy alcohol use at the last wave of measurement (November 2000) as the dependent variable. This measure was made up of three questionnaire items. One question asked for the number of times in the previous two weeks the person had consumed five or more drinks in a row. A second asked how many times in the previous two weeks the person had consumed four or more drinks in a row. The third question asked how many times in the previous 30 days the person had consumed enough alcohol to get drunk. For the regression analyses, these items were summed to form a composite scale for heavy alcohol use.

Predictors

There were six predictor variables in the multiple-regression models. Three of these were considered background variables: gender, religiosity, and the personality variable,

introversion. Gender was coded 1 for women and 0 for men. The gender variable was the average of the gender question over the five waves of measurement. For 1,021 students, this average was exactly 1 or exactly 0, implying complete consistency. For two students, the average was 0.8, meaning that these students were most likely women but responded male on one of the five questionnaires. For this chapter, these were assumed to be women. For only one student was this variable missing altogether.

The religion question was a single item asking how important it was for the student to participate in religion at college. Because the answer to this question was so highly intercorrelated from wave to wave, the religion variable used in this chapter was a simple average of this variable over the five waves of measurement.

The introversion variable was a composite of 10 items from a 50-item version of the Big-5 (Saucier, 1994). The items were scored such that higher values implied greater introversion.

Also included as predictors were three other variables from the September 1999 survey: negative attitudes about authority (DefyAuthority), perceptions of alcohol consumption by students in general at this university (PeerUse), and intentions to intervene in possible harm situations (IntentIntervene). The number of items and coefficient alpha for each scale are presented in Table 4.2.

The patterns of missing data for the variables included in the main regression analyses (described later) are shown in Table 4.3. Two of the predictor variables (gender and religiosity), which were formed by combining data from all five waves of measurement, had so few missing values (12 cases were missing for religiosity and 1 case was missing for gender) that they were omitted from Table 4.3. A third predictor variable (introversion) was measured at only one time (at whichever time was the first measurement for any given individual) but had slightly more missing data and appears in Table 4.3.

TABLE 4.2 Summary of Questionnaire Items and Coefficient Alpha

		Coefficient Alpha	
AHP Predictors	Number of Items	Impute from EM	Analyze EM Directly
gender (men = 0, women = 1)	1	—	—
religion (higher value = religion more important)	1	—	—
introversion	10	.89	.89
Defy Authority (Sep 1999)	3	.60	.60
Perceptions of Peer alcohol use (Sep 1999)	3	.84	.85
Intent to Intervene (Sep 1999)	4	.74	.74
Main DV: Heavy alcohol use (Nov 2000)	3	.94	.94

TABLE 4.3   Missing Data Patterns for Variables Included in Main Analyses

DV	Predictors					
Heavy Drinking Nov 2000	Intro-version	Defy Auth	Peer Use	Intent Intervene	Freq	Percent
0	0	1	1	1	23	2.2
0	1	0	0	0	147	14.4
0	1	1	1	1	193	18.8
1	1	0	0	0	227	22.2
1	1	0	1	1	26	2.5
1	1	1	1	1	357	34.9
Totals					**973**	**95.0**

Note. "1" means student provided data; "0" means student did not provide data. These six patterns are those involving the largest numbers of participants. Ten additional patterns, each involving fewer than 20 students, are not shown. The predictor variables *gender* and *religiosity,* which were formed by combining data from all five waves, had so little missing data that they are not shown here.

Other Variables

As we noted previously, there is value in including other variables in the missing data model, whether or not they are related to missingness, if they are highly correlated with the variables containing missing data. In any study involving longitudinal data, it is always possible to include measures from all waves of measurement, even if all waves are not involved in the analysis of substantive interest. Because it is often the case that measures from one wave are rather highly correlated with the same measures from an adjacent wave, it is generally an excellent idea, from a missing data standpoint, to include such variables where possible.

For our analysis of substantive interest, the dependent variable was from the November 2000 measure (wave 5), and the predictors of interest were mainly from the September 1999 measure (wave 1). In our case, we also included 21 relevant variables from all five waves of measurement. We included measures of alcohol use (i.e., three items measuring alcohol consumption without focusing on heavier drinking) from all five waves, heavy drinking (same as main dependent variable) from waves 1–4, and defiance of authority (same as predictor variable), perceptions of peer alcohol use (same as predictor), and intent to intervene (same as predictor) from waves 2–5.

Data Quality Analysis with NORM

With most analyses, the researcher wishes to test hypotheses. For these analyses, it is important to have good parameter estimation and good estimation of standard errors (and confidence intervals). However, with data quality analysis, it is

generally sufficient to have good parameter estimation. Thus, for data quality analysis, there are two good options that are not available for hypothesis testing. These two options are (a) to analyze the EM covariance matrix directly and (b) to analyze a single data set imputed from the EM parameters (with error).

EM produces maximum-likelihood estimates of the covariance matrix. From this, one may perform exploratory factor analysis and may get excellent estimation of coefficient alpha in the missing data case. The main drawback to analyzing the EM covariance matrix has been the logistics of producing a matrix that is readable by existing software. We will describe a solution to this logistical problem.

Producing a single imputed data set from EM parameters is not normally a good solution to hypothesis-testing problems. Although the data set itself is a plausible one, the fact that there is just one data set means that it is not possible to estimate standard errors accurately for the parameters estimated from this data set. Nevertheless, if one must produce a single imputed data set, using EM parameters is the best option in that EM parameters are, in a sense, in the center of parameter space. Another way of thinking about this is to note that the EM parameters are very similar to the average parameters obtained from a large number of imputed data sets.

The key advantage of using a single data set imputed from EM parameters is that one is dealing with a data set with no missing data. Thus, standard statistical software (e.g., SAS or SPSS) can be used. The only caveat is that in analyzing this single data set, one should NOT rely on the t values and p values generated by the analysis.

Multiple Imputation with NORM

In this section, we describe in some detail the use of the NORM software (version 2.03; Schafer, 1997). NORM will very likely be modified and improved in the future. In order to maximize the value of the information provided in the present chapter, step-by-step instructions for the operation of the current version of NORM will be maintained at our web site, http://methodology.psu.edu.

Although the step-by-step instructions described here apply specifically to the NORM program, most of the issues covered will, or should, have counterparts in any multiple-imputation program. Thus, the instructions provided in the following pages should be seen as being applicable in a quite general way to other multiple-imputation software as well.

In order to perform item analysis (coefficient alpha) or exploratory factor analysis, we must first perform the first part of multiple imputation with NORM (Schafer, 1997). For more detail about the operation of NORM, please see Schafer and Olsen (1998; also see Graham & Hofer, 2000).

Running NORM, Step 1: Getting NORM

If you do not have NORM already, it can be downloaded for free from our web site. Please note that all software illustrated in this chapter (except Amos) can be downloaded for free from this web site. Click on *Software* and follow the links for NORM. Once you have it downloaded, install the program. The defaults usually work well.

Running NORM, Step 2: Preparing the Data Set

First, one must prepare the data set. Do this by converting all missing values in the data set to the same numeric value (e.g., −9). Whatever value it is, this missing value indicator should be well out of the legal range for all variables in the data set. Next, write the data out as an ASCII, or text data set. We find that using the suffix *.dat* tends to work best, but *.txt* will also work. Each value in the output data set should be separated by a space (i.e., it should be space delimited). Be careful to write out the data for each case in one long line.

It really helps if you have a separate file containing just the variable labels (in order) as one long column vector (i.e., one variable name per line). This should also be an ASCII, or text file, and it should have the same name as your data file, except that it should have *.nam* as the suffix, rather than *.dat* or *.txt*.

Many of these data preparation steps, which are required with NORM 2.03, may not be required in other programs. For example, one clear advantage of working with PROC MI in SAS is that the data sets are already prepared, and this step is, to a large extent, unnecessary.

Running NORM, Step 3: Variables

For the most part, NORM is a rather user-friendly program. It works like most Windows programs, and very often one can simply accept the default options at each step. With NORM 2.03, begin by starting a new session. Locate your recently created data file, and read it into NORM.

Once your data have been read into NORM, you are ready to go. If you want to name your variables (e.g., if you have not created a separate *.nam* file), look at their distributions, perform any temporary transformations, request rounding for imputed values, or select variables for inclusion in the model. You can do so by clicking on the *Variables* tab.

We have two points to make here. First, if you have a very large data set (e.g., 100 variables and 3,000 cases), you will want to consider applying appropriate transformations (e.g.,

log transformation if skew is to the right or square transformation if skew is to the left) before running NORM. It will speed up EM and data augmentation to a substantial degree. Please note that if you choose to transform variables in NORM, NORM uses these transformations during calculations but always writes out its imputed data sets using the original, untransformed scales.

Second, NORM 2.03 has *Not recommended* for the *No rounding* option. We take exactly the opposite view. Except for special cases (e.g., needing a dichotomous dependent variable for logistic regression), we argue that less rounding is better. We argue that rounding is rather like adding more random variability to a variable once it has been imputed. This is typically not desirable. In any case, the difference between rounding and not rounding is generally small. For our example, we changed all *integer* rounding (the default for integer variables), to *hundredths* rounding.

Running NORM, Step 4: Summarize

Click on the *Summarize* tab, and click on *Run* (accepting the defaults). The results of this summary will be much more meaningful if you have included a *.nam* file with the variable names or if you have explicitly named your variables in the *Variables* tab. Otherwise, you have to know which variable is which.

This summary is an extremely valuable troubleshooting tool. Look at the number and percent missing for each variable. Do the numbers make sense, given what you know about the data set? If any variable is missing for 100% of the cases, it may mean that you have made a coding error somewhere. If it is not an error, the variable should be omitted from the analysis.

The matrix of missingness patterns is also very useful. If the number of patterns is small, this could be reported, as is, in your article where you would normally talk about the sample size. If the number of patterns is large, it might be useful to present in table form only the patterns with the largest numbers of cases. If there is a very large number of missingness patterns, it will be necessary to summarize the patterns, as we have done in this chapter.

Please note that the pattern representing complete data (if it exists) always appears at the top and that the pattern with the least data appears at the bottom. It is not good if the pattern at the bottom shows all zeros (no data). If the number of cases with no data is large or puzzling, it could be due to a coding error somewhere. Whether or not it is an error, you should delete such cases before continuing.

Our first example involved the 25 individual variables described above and in Table 4.2, as well as the 21 variables included to help with imputation. In this first example, there were 205 patterns of missing and nonmissing data. Most of these patterns involved just a single individual. The largest pattern ($N = 106$) was the pattern for which the cases had complete data for all 46 variables included in the missing data analysis.

Running NORM, Step 5: EM Algorithm

Next, click on the *EM algorithm* tab. It is often possible to accept all the defaults here and simply click on *Run* (this worked in our example). However, there are some options you should consider before doing this. For some of these options, click on the *Computing* button. The options here are maximum iterations, convergence criterion, and ML or posterior mode.

Maximum Iterations. The default here (1,000 iterations) will usually be enough. However, if this is a large job (e.g., anywhere near 100 variables), you might want to bump this up to something larger (e.g., 2,000). Please note that you can always stop the iterations at any point and use the interim results as a new starting place. Also, if EM stops after 1,000 iterations and has still not converged, you can always use that (interim) result as the new starting place.

Convergence Criterion. The default in NORM is .0001. We have always used this default. NORM automatically standardizes all variables prior to running EM. All variables are back-transformed to the original scales for imputation. Standardizing all variables to variance = 1 gives the convergence criterion clear meaning. Bear in mind that other missing data programs may not routinely standardize the variables prior to running EM. Thus, the convergence criterion for other programs may have different meaning if the variables involved have variances that are substantially smaller or larger than 1. Also, note that for other programs the meaning of the convergence criterion may be something different from the criterion in NORM. With EMCOV and SAS, for example, convergence is achieved when the largest covariance matrix element change is smaller than the convergence criterion. However, with NORM, convergence is achieved when the largest change, divided by the parameter value, is smaller than the convergence criterion. Thus, the convergence criterion in version 2.03 of NORM is generally more conservative than the corresponding criterion in SAS PROC MI.

ML or Posterior Mode. If you have a relatively large number of complete cases, you should use the ML estimate or at least try that first. Use of the ridge prior is not well described in the substantive literature, but it is defensible if you have relatively few complete cases. Adding a hyperparameter has an effect similar to adding that number of new (complete) cases to your data set, such that all the variables are uncorrelated. The benefit of adding complete cases is that it adds stability to the EM and data augmentation models. The drawback of adding a hyperparameter is that all covariances will be suppressed toward zero. For this latter reason, it is critical that this hyperparameter be kept small. In fact, Schafer (1997) talks about the possible benefit of a hyperparameter of less than 1. Think like a critic when selecting this value. How would you, as a critic, react to someone's adding 100 new (bogus) cases to a data set if the original sample was only 200? On the other hand, how would you react to someone's adding 10 new (bogus) cases to a data set when the original sample size was 1,000? We argue that the second example is much easier to accept.

Other Options. The EM part of NORM produces two files, *em.out* and *em.prm. Em.out* is a nicely formatted output file that is meant to be viewed. The EM means, variances, and covariances shown in this file are the best available single estimates of these values. We recommend that it is these values that should be reported in your article. If you are interested in seeing the EM correlations (rather than variances and covariances), you can select *Correlation matrix* before you run EM. The file *em.prm* is the parameter file and is meant to be used in analysis, but not to be viewed. Be careful when you are starting EM that you are not overwriting another file with the same name. You could be throwing away hours of work! You can rename these output files if you like.

It is also possible to specify one of these *.prm* files from a previous job. For example, if you have previously allowed EM to run for 1,000 iterations, and it did not converge, you can rename the old *em.prm* file to be, say, *em_old.prm,* and then specify that as your starting values for the new analysis.

Speed of EM. The speed of convergence of EM depends on many factors. The most important factor is the number of variables. The number of cases does not matter as much. Another factor that affects the speed of EM is the amount of missing information. This is not the same as the amount of missing data, per se, but it is certainly related to that. If you have much missing data, EM (and data augmentation) will take longer.

Our Example. In our initial example, we had 46 variables and 1,024 cases. EM converged normally in 146 iterations. By *normal* convergence we mean that there were no error messages and that the fit function changed monotonically throughout the iteration history.

Pause to Perform Data Quality Analyses with Interim Results from NORM

Coefficient Alpha Analysis: Analysis of EM Covariance Matrix With the ALPHNORM Utility

The ALPHNORM utility can be downloaded for free from our web site (note that the current version of ALPHNORM works only if you have made no data transformations with NORM). This utility makes use of the EM output from NORM. The current version of the program is a bit clunky and works only from the DOS prompt. However, it is useful for calculating standardized coefficient alpha and alpha-if-item-deleted from the EM covariance matrix produced by NORM. If you have previously used a *.nam* file with NORM, then ALPHNORM reads these names. Each variable is also identified by number. You select the number of variables to be analyzed and the corresponding variable numbers. ALPHNORM provides the standardized coefficient alpha, along with information about alpha-if-item-deleted.

We do not actually describe the coefficient alpha analysis here, but the results of these analyses appear in the rightmost column of Table 4.2.

Exploratory Factor Analysis: Using ALPHNORM to Create SAS-Ready Data Sets

The ALPHNORM utility can also be used simply to write out SAS-ready data sets. Specifying 1 when prompted results in the utility's writing out a SAS-ready version of the EM covariance matrix, along with the actual SAS code needed to read that matrix. This SAS code (see Appendix A) includes the variable names, if available. The SAS data step should run as is. The utility also sets up the syntax for PROC FACTOR, leaving out only the variable names. The utility also provides syntax for PROC REG, but this should be used with caution, because there is no basis for the T and *p* values. The ALPHNORM utility sets the sample size arbitrarily to 500. If there is a good rationale, you can change this number manually to something more reasonable.

We do not actually perform an exploratory factor analysis here, but the code provided in Appendix A will facilitate this analysis. With version 8.2 of SAS it is very convenient to do exploratory factor analysis based on the EM covariance matrix all within SAS. First, specify *PROC MI nimpute = 0;* and *EM emout = sasdatasetname.* Then specify *PROC FACTOR data = sasdatasetname (type = cov)....* Unfortunately, this shortcut is not available in earlier versions of SAS, and a similar shortcut is not available for performing coefficient alpha analysis.

Multiple Imputation: Running NORM, Continued

Running NORM, Step 6: Impute From EM Parameters

To impute from EM parameters in NORM, simply click on the *Impute from parameters* tab, and click on the *Run* button. Be sure that the window *Use parameters from parameter (*.prm) file* has been selected and that *em.prm* is indicated. By default, NORM writes out a data set with the root of the data set name, followed by *_0.imp.* This data set may then be analyzed using SAS, SPSS, or any program of your choosing.

Coefficient Alpha Analysis: Using NORM to Impute From EM Parameters (Analysis With SAS or SPSS)

We have argued above that using one imputed data set based on EM parameter estimates is a reasonable way to proceed for analyses that require raw data but not hypothesis testing. Because this approach is so much like analyzing a complete cases data set, many users will find this to be a desirable alternative to analyzing the EM covariance matrix for performing coefficient alpha analysis or exploratory factor analysis.

We do not actually show these analyses here, but the results of the coefficient alpha analyses (using SAS) for these data appear in Table 4.2. Note how similar these results were in comparison with direct analysis of the EM covariance matrix. Of the five scales analyzed, coefficient alpha was the same (to two decimal places) for four and differed by only one one-hundredth for the remaining scale.

Many programs have the capability of imputing a single data set from EM parameters (e.g., SPSS and EMCOV). If programs other than NORM are used for this purpose, be certain that error is added to each imputed value. In SPSS (version 10.1), for example, the values are imputed, but error is not added. This will produce important biases in exploratory analyses.

Running NORM, Step 7: Data Augmentation and Imputation

Please note that the following analyses were based on a slightly different data set from what we just described. The remainder of our empirical example involves imputation of the seven intact scales described above and in Table 4.2, along with the 21 other variables added to help with imputation. EM analysis of the individual items was required for the coefficient alpha analysis. However, multiple imputation of the intact scales, which was all that was required for performing the multiple regression, was much more efficient. For example, note the difference in number of iterations required for EM to converge (42 versus 146).

We summarize briefly the preliminary NORM analyses with this new data set. For these analyses, there were 28 variables in total. There were 105 patterns of missing and nonmissing values, 56 of which involved just a single individual. The largest pattern ($N = 218$) was the pattern of complete data. For this data set, EM converged normally in 42 iterations.

Once you have run EM within NORM, the next step for multiple imputation is data augmentation. Click on the *Data augmentation* tab.

The *Series* Button. The information here is for setting up the diagnostics for data augmentation. In order to run the diagnostics, you should click one of the *Save* options. Click on *Save all parameters* to save information about all of the parameters (variances, covariances, and means). If the number of variables is small, or if you have little experience with a particular data set, this may be a good option. However, with this option, the program saves all parameter estimates at every step of data augmentation. Thus, with a large number of variables and a large number of steps, the file containing this information could be huge (e.g., 50 to 100 MB or larger).

Thus, a good compromise is to click on *Save only worst linear function*. If the results for the worst linear function are acceptable, then the results for all other parameter estimates will be no worse than this. This file is generally very small.

The *Imputation* Button. Usually you will want to click on *Impute at every kth iteration*. However, what value should be used for k? We noted earlier that one of the key questions when doing data augmentation is how many steps are required before two imputed data sets are like two random draws from a population. There are two approaches to be taken here: (a) One can select a conservative number of steps between imputed data sets, or (b) one can perform the diagnostics to see how many steps between imputed data sets are suggested by the data. We recommend a combination of these two approaches.

With other implementations of multiple imputation, the entire process may be more automated than the process described for NORM. For example, in SAS 8.2 one runs EM, MCMC, and imputation all in a single step without user input. This reduction of steps, however, is only apparent. Regardless of what software one uses, the user must, as we describe below, make decisions along the way.

First, determine how many iterations it took EM to converge. We recommend that you begin with this number for k. For example, it took EM 42 iterations to converge in our example. Thus, to be somewhat conservative, we began by setting k to 50. That means that NORM will produce an imputed data set every 50 steps of data augmentation. If, after viewing the diagnostics, you believe that k should have been larger, you can (a) redo data augmentation using the larger value for k, or (b) simply use every imputed data set with an even number, discarding those with odd numbers. This effectively doubles k. Then create as many new imputed data sets as needed using the larger number of k between imputed data sets.

The *Computing* Button. The number of iterations is the total number of iterations. For example, if k is set to 50 and you wish to produce 20 imputed data sets, this value should be $20 \times 50 = 1,000$. If you have used the ridge prior for EM, you should use the same thing here (this will be the default).

How many imputed data sets? Schafer and Olsen (1998) provide a table for assisting with this decision. The larger the fraction of missing information, the greater m should be. Unfortunately, one obtains the estimate of the fraction of missing information only after one imputes the data. Further, the fraction of missing information provided by NORM is itself just an estimate. Thus, for small values of m, this estimate is rather unstable (unreliable). Thus, our somewhat nonstatistical recommendation is to set m to at least 10 (20 is better). You can always decide to analyze only the first $m = 5$ imputed data sets if it turns out that is all you need.

Running Data Augmentation. Once all the information has been given, click on *run*. With smaller problems (relatively few variables), this process will be rather quick. With larger problems (many variables), this may take some time. You will notice that every time the number of steps passes a multiple of k, NORM pauses to write out an imputed data set.

Multiple-Imputation Data Sets. The result of all your efforts will be m imputed data sets. Each data set will be like a complete data set. For every nonmissing value, that nonmissing value will appear in each of the data sets. For every value initially missing, an imputed value will appear. That value will be different, sometimes quite different, across the m different data sets.

Our Example. In our example, we created 20 imputed data sets. We set $k = 50$, and the total number of data augmentation steps was 1,000. The imputation process took just under three minutes on a 366 MHz Pentium II laptop.

Running NORM, Step 8: Data Augmentation Diagnostics

To check the diagnostics, click on the word *Series* at the top of the screen. Click on *Open* to see a menu of the available

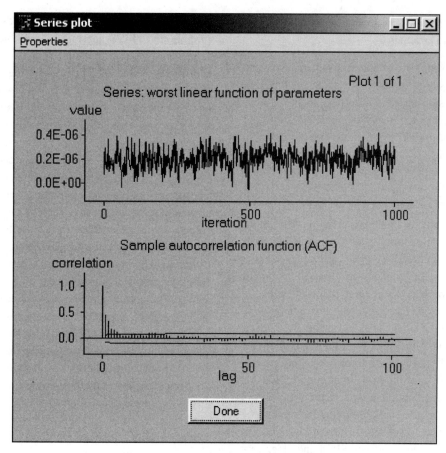

Figure 4.1   Multiple Imputation Diagnostic Plots

series. The default name is *da.prs*. Once the data set is open, click on *Series* again and on *Plot*. If you asked for the worst linear function, that is all that will appear. Figure 4.1 shows the diagnostic plots for the worst linear function from 1,000 steps of data augmentation for the sample data used in this chapter. The upper plot is simply a plot of the value of the worst linear function at each step of data augmentation. Ideally, you will see a pattern in this upper plot that looks something like a rectangle. The plot shown in Figure 4.1 is reasonably close to the ideal. Schafer & Olsen (1998) show figures of two additional NORM plots, including plots of solutions that are problematic. Additional figures are presented in the Help documentation for NORM. If the plot snakes gradually up and down, you may have a problem. If you do notice this sort of problem (please see Schafer & Olsen for a particular kind of problem), you may be able to solve it adequately by using the ridge prior with a small hyperparameter.

The lower plot (see Figure 4.1) is the plot of the autocorrelation. It is the correlation of a parameter estimate (in this case the worst linear combination) at one step with the same estimate 1, 2, 50, or 100 steps removed. When the autocorrelation dips below the red line (and stays there), you have evidence

that this value of k (the number of steps of data augmentation between imputed data sets) is sufficient to produce a nonsignificant autocorrelation between estimates. That is, setting k to this value will be sufficient for multiple imputation. In our experience, this value is typically much smaller than the number of iterations it took EM to converge. In this context, we caution that our experience is based on the use of NORM, for which the convergence criterion is "the maximum relative change in the value of any parameter from one cycle to the next" (according to the NORM help documentation). That is, the change in a parameter estimate from one iteration to the next is scaled according to the magnitude of each parameter estimate in question. Other software may use different convergence criteria, in which case the relationship between the convergence properties of EM and MCMC will be different.

In our example, it appeared that the autocorrelation plot became nonsignificant around $k = 10$. That is, we would have been justified in using $k = 10$ for imputing our data sets. Thus, our original decision to use $k = 50$ was fully justified and, in fact, proved to be quite conservative. Based on the diagnostics, we retained the 20 imputed data sets without further work.

Multiple-Regression Analysis With the Multiple-Imputation Data Sets

The main analysis used here is one researchers use very often. Thus, we will say only that this was a simultaneous linear multiple-regression analysis. The dependent variable was the composite scale for heavy alcohol use from the November 2000 measure. The six independent variables were described previously.

In theory, analysis with multiple imputation is extremely easy to do. One simply runs the analysis of choice—for example, SAS PROC REG—with one data set and then repeats the process, changing only the input data set name. The whole process takes only a few minutes. Because one is dealing with raw data, it is very easy to recode the data (e.g., log transformations, reverse coding, or standardization) and to compute new variables (e.g., averages of standardized variables).

The biggest problem one faces with multiple imputation is saving parameter estimates and standard errors from each analysis and combining them into a form that is usable with NORM for hypothesis testing (MI Inference). Fortunately, with SAS 8.2, even if one imputes the data with NORM, analysis and MI Inference with SAS is extremely easy. This process is outlined in the next section. With older versions of SAS, with SPSS, and with other statistical programs, the process is more complicated. However, SPSS and older versions of SAS do provide users with a macro language that facilitates the process. The process of analysis and MI Inference with SPSS is described in a later section.

The SAS code we used to perform multiple imputation on the 20 imputed data sets appears in Appendix B. SAS code for other variations of PROC REG and for other procedures can be found on our web site and on the SAS web site. SAS code for the more complicated macro version (for use with older versions of SAS) may be found on our web site.

Preparation of NORM-Imputed Data Sets

With NORM, one creates 20 separate imputed data sets. With SAS PROC MI, the 20 imputed data sets are stacked into a single large data set. The special variable _imputation_ keeps track of the 20 different data sets. In order to prepare NORM-imputed data sets for use with SAS 8.2, one simply needs to stack them into one large data set. A utility for this is available at our web site. Alternatively, one could simply read in the data sets, create the _imputation_ variable, and use the SET statement in SAS to stack the imputed data sets. For the example given below (statements shown in Appendix B), we used the utility that created a stacked version of the NORM-imputed data sets.

The SAS code (see Appendix B) reads in the _imputation_ variable and all 28 substantive variables, standardizes the variables to be used in the analysis (to facilitate comparison with Amos results), and performs the regression analysis. The regression parameter estimates are written out to a data set (named c), and the option Covout also writes out a covariance matrix of estimates, the diagonal of which is the square of the standard errors. The BY statement in PROC REG allows the analysis to be repeated for each imputed data set.

PROC MIANALYZE reads the data set containing parameter estimates and standard errors. Except for specifying which parameter estimates are of interest (in the VAR statement), this procedure is automatic to the user. In the output from PROC MIANALYZE, look for the Multiple Imputation Parameter Estimates. The usual information is all there: parameter (predictor) name, b weight, standard error, t value, degrees of freedom (see below), p value, and confidence intervals. These are the values to be reported in the formal write-up of the results.

The Fraction of Missing Information (which appears under the output section Multiple Imputation Variance Information) is also quite useful. This fraction (presented as a percentage) is related to the proportion of variability that is due to missing data. Schafer and Olsen (1998) present a table showing the percent efficiency of multiple-imputation (MI) estimation based on the number of imputed data sets and the fraction of missing information. From this table one can justify choosing a particular number of imputed data sets (m). For example, if the fraction of missing information is .5, multiple-imputation parameter estimates are 86% efficient with only $m = 3$ imputed data sets. With 5, 10, and 20 imputed data sets, the same estimates are 91, 95, and 98% efficient, respectively. Thus, when the fraction of missing information is .5, one might decide that 10 imputed data sets are sufficient, because the parameter estimates are 95% efficient.

Alternative Approach With SAS PROC MI

Although an SAS user could certainly impute with NORM (as we have done here) and analyze the data with the procedure of choice, summarizing with PROC MIANALYZE, a second option is to impute in the first place using PROC MI. This is indeed a desirable option for SAS users. However, SAS users should be sure that for each decision made along the way (described here using NORM), corresponding decisions are all made with PROC MI.

Analysis of Multiple Data Sets With SPSS Regression

The SPSS version of this process was much like that just described with SAS. However, there were some important differences, which we will point out here. First, the SPSS macro language does a nice job of standardizing variables, computing the new composite scales, and performing the regression analysis (the SPSS macro syntax for performing all this appears in Appendix C). However, the regression results themselves were in a form that was a bit difficult for NORM to read directly, so a utility program, NORMSPSS.EXE, was created to facilitate the process. This utility is available free from our web site. The user executes NORMSPSS from the DOS command line and is asked for a few pieces of information along the way. In the middle of the largely automatic process, SPSS is invoked, and the analyses are performed on the m (e.g., 20) imputed data sets. After one (manually) closes SPSS, the NORMSPSS utility asks how many imputations were performed and then automatically performs the MI Inference for hypothesis testing. In addition, a data set is saved that can be used with NORM to perform a somewhat more complete version of MI inference.

Regression Results

The summary regression results based on multiple imputation appear in Table 4.4. These are the results (after rounding) from the output of PROC MIANALYZE, based on the SAS PROC REG analysis. The results shown are also identical to those obtained with the NORMSPSS utility based on the SPSS regression results.

Meaning of Multiple Imputation Degrees of Freedom. Degrees of freedom (DF) in the multiple-imputation analysis are a little different from what typically appears in this sort of analysis. It does not relate to the number of predictors, nor does it relate to sample size. Rather, DF in the multiple-imputation analysis relates much more closely to the fraction of missing information in estimating a particular parameter. If the amount of missing information is large, the DF will be small ($m - 1$ is the minimum, where m is the number of imputed data sets). If the amount of missing information

is small, the DF will be large. If the amount of missing information is very small (e.g., if there are no missing data), the DF will approach infinity, and the t value becomes a Z value. Key DF values very close to the minimum ($m - 1$) usually imply that the estimates are still somewhat unstable and that m should be larger.

These results show that all six predictors had a significant, unique effect on the dependent variable, heavy drinking at the November 2000 measure. The results are not particularly surprising. Students for whom religion is important drink less. Women students drink less. Introverts drink less. Those who dislike authority tend to drink more. Students who perceive their college student peers to drink more also drink more. Finally, students who would intervene to prevent harm from coming to a friend who was drinking tend to drink less themselves.

Multiple Regression With Amos

Because Amos 4.0 is distributed with SPSS, a good option is to obtain the two products as a package through your organization. For information directly from the Amos distributor, please see http://www.smallwaters.com.

Running Amos

Running Amos is exceptionally easy. Once you have a data set in SPSS, you can simply click on *Analyze* and on *Amos*. When Amos comes up, you draw your model by selecting model components from the icon list and creating the component in the drawing area. For the regression model in our example, we selected the box from the icon list and drew one box. We then selected the copy machine icon to make several copies of the box. In total, we had six boxes on the left for the predictors and one box on the right for the dependent variable. Then select the single-headed arrow icon. First, click on a left box and drag the arrow to the right box. When all the regression arrows are drawn, click on the double-headed arrow icon. This is the part of the process during which errors are possible with larger models. However, if you are systematic, the risk is not substantial. Click on each box for the predictor variables and drag the double-headed arrow to each of the other boxes. This models the correlations among the predictors. Finally, select the icon with a little box with a circle coming out of it. Then click on the box for the dependent variable. This models the residual variance. The final model (without labels) is now complete, and it should look like the model shown in Figure 4.2.

With Amos, all enclosed objects (boxes and circles) must have labels. A nice feature when working within SPSS is that

TABLE 4.4   Regression Results Based on Multiple Imputation

Predictor	b	SE	t	df	p	Fraction of Missing Information
religion	−.160	.032	5.01	447	<.0001	21.0%
gender	−.207	.034	6.00	271	<.0001	27.0%
introvert	−.199	.035	5.64	158	<.0001	35.5%
defyauth	.146	.036	4.07	183	.0001	32.9%
peeruse	.161	.040	4.05	78	.0001	50.5%
intent	−.122	.039	3.15	116	.0021	41.3%

Note. Sample size for multiple imputation was $N = 1024$. DV = Heavy Alcohol Use at time 5.

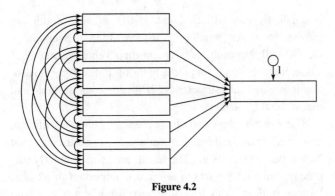

Figure 4.2

all of the variables in the SPSS data set are available for inclusion in the model. Select the *Variables in the data set* icon. It is not easy to describe, so as an alternative, click on *View/Set* and on *Variables in the data set*. Find the variable names corresponding to the predictors and dependent variable, and simply click and drag the variable names to the proper boxes in the model. We had previously standardized the seven variables to be included in order that the results of Amos and multiple regression would be more comparable. This would not normally be a necessary step. Finally, double-click on the small circle connected with the dependent variable box. In the *Object properties* dialog box that pops up, look for the *Variable name* box. Enter some label. It could be something as simple as *r* for *residual*.

Before running the job, click on the *Analysis properties* icon, or find it after clicking on *View/set*. Click on the *Estimation* tab, and click in the box for *Estimate means and intercepts*. Close the box, and you are ready. Click on the abacus icon, and the job will run. If it is a small job like our example, it will run in just a few seconds. If it is a larger job, with many parameters, it may take some time.

When the job is finished, click on the *View spreadsheets* icon (or find it under *View/set* under *Table output*). The key

information for our problem will be under *Regression weights*. The results for the Amos analysis are summarized below.

Comparison of Results for MI, Amos, and Other Procedures

For comparison, Table 4.5 presents multiple-regression results (*b* weights and *t* values) for the same data using five different missing data approaches. For convenience, the key results from Table 4.4 are repeated in the leftmost column under the *MI+* heading. Also presented are results based on mean substitution, complete cases, multiple imputation on just the seven variables included in the regression analysis (under *MI*), and Amos (analysis just described).

Time after time, simulation results involving known parameter estimates show multiple-imputation parameter estimates to be unbiased, that is, very close to the population parameter values (e.g., Collins et al., 2001; Graham et al., 1994, 1996; Graham & Schafer, 1999). In addition, in multiple imputation, standard errors are known to perform as well as the same analysis when there are no missing data. Finally, including additional variables is known to improve estimation under some circumstances. With the addition of even 20 or 30 variables, there is no known statistical down side (Collins et al., 2001).

For these reasons, we take the multiple-imputation results (MI+) to be the standard in Table 4.5, and any differences from the MI+ values shown in Table 4.5 should be interpreted as estimation bias or as statistical conclusion bias. In order to provide a summary of the results for each method, we have included two statistics at the bottom of each column in Table 4.5. The first is the simple mean of the absolute values of the elements in the column. The second is the sum of the squared differences between the elements

TABLE 4.5   Comparison of Standardized *b* Weights and *t* Values

| Predictor | *b* weights | | | | | *t* values | | | | |
	MI+	Mean Subst	CC	MI	Amos	MI+	Mean Subst	CC	MI	Amos
relig	−.160	−.154	−.216	−.174	−.187	5.01	5.10	4.34	4.64	4.93
female	−.207	−.162	−.156	−.220	−.206	6.00	5.24	2.92	5.71	5.14
introvrt	−.199	−.148	−.142	−.181	−.177	5.64	4.89	2.79	4.97	4.64
defysep	.146	.073	.114	.118	.116	4.07	2.38	2.26	2.43	2.36
pusesep	.161	.089	.153	.143	.161	4.05	2.95	3.05	3.08	3.52
iintvsep	−.122	−.068	−.131	−.065	−.077	3.15	2.19	2.41	1.47	1.56
mean	.166	.116	.152	.150	.154	4.65	3.79	2.96	3.72	3.69
SumSq		.018	.010	.005	.004		6.14	22.9	7.12	7.48

Note. MI+ = multiple imputation with 21 additional variables. Mean Subst = mean substitution. CC = complete cases (*N* = 357). MI = multiple imputation with seven relevant variables only. Amos = Analysis with Amos (seven relevant variables only). Sample size for all analyses except complete cases was *N* = 1,024. Means shown at bottom of table are a simple average of the absolute value of the elements in that column. SumSq is the sum of squared differences between the elements in that column with those in the MI+ column. In Amos, the figure corresponding to *t* value is listed as CR (critical ratio).

in that column and the corresponding elements in the MI+ column.

The results appearing in Table 4.5 show the kinds of results that are obtained with the four other procedures. For the most part, parameter estimates based on complete cases are similar to those obtained with multiple imputation. However, the standard errors were consistently larger (and *t* values consistently smaller) because the estimation is based on fewer cases, so that the power to detect significant effects is reduced.

Table 4.5 also illustrates the kind of result that is obtained with mean substitution. Note that, for all six of the predictors, the *b* weight based on mean substitution was smaller than that obtained with multiple imputation, sometimes substantially so. The sum of squared differences between the mean substitution *b* weights and MI+ *b* weights was the largest of the other four methods.

Interestingly, the standard errors for the mean substitution *b* weights (not shown) were smaller than what was estimated with multiple imputation. The result was that the smallness of the *b* weights was partially compensated for. However, we view this as an example of two wrongs not making a right. The clear bias in parameter estimates based on mean substitution will be a big problem in many settings, and one cannot count on the *t* values to be reasonable (although they appear to be in this case). Thus, we continue to reject mean substitution as a reasonable alternative for dealing with missing data.

Table 4.5 also illustrates the effects of failing to include additional variables that may be relevant to the missing data model, even if they are not relevant to the analysis model. Both the MI and Amos models, although having reasonably unbiased estimates of the *b* weights, had noticeably lower *t* values compared to the MI+ analysis.

It should be noted that it is possible to include additional variables in the Amos model (and other FIML/SEM models) in a way that does not affect the model of substantive interest. Graham (in press) has outlined two such models. The slightly better of the two models, described as the "saturated correlates model," includes the additional variables as follows. The additional variables are all specified to be correlated with one another and are specified to be correlated with all other manifest variables in the model (or with their residuals, if they have them). This model has been shown in simulations to perform as well as MI+ and to have no effect on the model of substantive interest when there are no missing data. This latter fact means that any differences observed by estimating the saturated correlates model are due to missing data correction, and not to some sort of interference of the added variables. Unfortunately, in the current version of Amos (4.0), this saturated correlates model in our example with 21 extra variables would be virtually impossible to draw with the Amos graphical interface. However, it would be relatively straightforward with the

text version of Amos, an example of which is included in Graham (in press). It is also straightforward in LISREL and other text-based FIML procedures.

Latent-Variable Regression With Amos or With LISREL/EQS and Multiple Imputation

A latent-variable example is beyond the scope of this chapter. However, we would like to make a few points in this regard. First, the extension to latent-variable analysis is trivial in Amos (assuming prior knowledge of SEM). One simply performs the analysis with individual variables as indicators of latent variables rather than with the composite indices. Amos handles the rest. The model for including additional variables is the same as previously described.

With LISREL 8.50 (Mx, and the FIML aspect of Mplus), latent-variable models with incomplete data are a trivial extension of latent variable models with complete data. With LISREL, one simply adds the statement "MI = −9" (assuming the missing value indicator is −9) to the Data Parameters statement. As previously mentioned, the addition of missing-data relevant variables to the model is straightforward.

For using multiple imputation with EQS 5.x (Bentler, 1986) and Mplus (Muthén, 2001), the situation is a little more complicated, but no more so than the analysis with SPSS previously described in this chapter. Utility programs have been written to use these two programs with NORM (Schafer, 1997). The two utilities, NORMEQS and NORMplus, make use of a single EQS 5.x or Mplus 2 input file to read and analyze the multiple imputed data sets, combine the results, and provide MI inference. These utilities, along with user guides, can be obtained free at our web site.

A FEW LOOSE ENDS

Recommendations for Quick and Dirty Analyses

In this chapter, we have said that we do not recommend pairwise deletion or mean substitution, even for quick and dirty analyses. So what is the option? As we said earlier, if you do not lose too many cases to missing data, complete cases analysis is a quite reasonable basis for quick and dirty analyses. However, what does one do if complete cases analysis is not an option?

Perhaps the best of the quick and dirty analyses is to run EM in NORM (or SAS) and to perform the analysis directly from the EM covariance matrix. With NORM, this can be done by making use of the ALPHNORM utility previously described. With SAS, the EM covariance matrix may be used directly by certain other procedures (PROC REG,

PROC FACTOR). The sample size can be set manually (with NORM, this is done in the EM covariance matrix itself; with SAS, one must add a sample size line to the output EM matrix). If one is wise in choosing this sample size, reasonable quick and dirty analyses can be done this way. It is important to realize, however, that a different sample size may be appropriate for different parameter estimates.

It is also possible to impute a single data set from EM parameters in NORM. This does not take long in most cases and gives reasonable parameter estimates. Of course, it is more difficult to adjust the sample size in this case. Still, if one is judicious in interpreting the results, it is a reasonable option for quick and dirty analyses.

Rubin (1987) argues that analysis based on even two imputations provides much better inference than analysis based on just one. Using one of the macro language procedures described previously for SAS or SPSS, analyzing a small number of imputed data sets (say, 2–5) would often constitute a quite reasonable quick and dirty approach.

Some Practicalities

One of the problems that arises with missing data analysis is the following dilemma. One would prefer to include as many variables as possible in the missing data model, but one cannot overload the model with estimation of massive numbers parameters. One solution to the problem is to impute intact scales rather than individual variables and then to create scales. The problem is that the individual items that make up the scale are sometimes missing. The potentially reasonable solution is to estimate the scale score based on the variables that are nonmissing. For example, if a scale has 10 variables but the participant has given data for only 6, it may be reasonable to estimate the scale score based on the 6 variables for which you have data. This makes most sense when the items are rather highly correlated, that is, when the scale has high alpha. It also makes sense only when the variables have equal variances and means. If the latter requirement is not met, then the scale will have a different expected value depending upon which items are missing. Sometimes this procedure is used only when a certain proportion (e.g., more than half) of scale items have data.

This procedure may be thought of as a kind of mean substitution, but it is the mean of nonmissing variables, not the mean of nonmissing cases. This makes all the difference. In one sense, this is a kind of regression-based single imputation, wherein the *b* weights are all equal. However, this approach does not appear to present the problem of the usual kind of single imputation (i.e., too little variability), because in this case we are talking about the sum of items. In this

case, a scale based on the sum of 6 items will, quite appropriately, have more error variability than the corresponding scale based on the sum of 10 items.

One possible solution to the problem of having a large number of variables is to break up the problem into two or more subsets of variables. The general problem of excluding a variable (say, *X*) from the imputation model is that the imputation proceeds under assumption that *X* has a zero correlation with all other variables in the data set. This has the effect of biasing all correlations toward zero. Thus, if you must divide up a large set of variables, it makes most sense to do so only if you can find two subsets that are relatively uncorrelated anyway. One approach to this might be to perform a principal-components analysis on the overall set and examine the two factor solution. Multiple imputation could then be performed separately on the two sets (which are maximally uncorrelated). There are other versions of this approach that could be even more acceptable. For example, it might be possible to include a small number of linear composites to represent the excluded set of items (see Graham & Taylor, 2001). More work is certainly needed in this area.

Recommendations

It should be obvious from even a cursory reading of this chapter that we are partial to multiple imputation with Schafer's (1997) suite of programs. However, please do not get the wrong idea. The best general solution to one's missing data problems is to have several tools available. There are many things that multiple imputation (i.e., with NORM or SAS) handles best. However, there are some things that EM does best, and some things that FIML SEM procedures do best. In fact, there are some things that the old multiple-group SEM procedure handles best. Our general advice is to be ready to use whichever tool is best for the particular situation.

One big reason that using one of the prescribed missing data procedures is advisable has to do with the ability of all of these procedures to include additional variables. Given the recent evidence (Collins et al., 2001) and the empirical results shown in this chapter, it is obvious that you can help yourself, in a completely acceptable way, by adding variables to the missing data model that are highly correlated with variables containing missingness. One of the reasons that multiple imputation has such appeal is that the process of adding these variables is relatively easy.

Other Methods

One question that often arises when we discuss multiple imputation and FIML methods has to do with the assumptions underlying them. In particular, these methods assume that the missing data mechanism is MAR but not MNAR. Pattern-mixture methods have been developed for dealing with such situations (e.g., see Little, 1994, 1995), but these are beyond the scope of this chapter.

A Look at the (Near) Future

We now have several programs that help us deal with missing data. In the future, these programs will be imbedded into mainstream software in ways that allow the researcher to perform the correct analysis (or one that is very nearly correct) without having to jump through hoops. The unveiling of PROC MI (multiple imputation) in SAS version 8.2 is very good news. LISREL has also unveiled multiple imputation and FIML features in version 8.50. EQS has also added a (non-FIML) missing data feature in its long-awaited version 6 and is rumored to be preparing further missing data enhancements for future release.

We have no knowledge of plans by SPSS to update its current, very clunky missing data procedure. However, our guess is that they will be making important updates in the near future. SPSS has always been at the forefront of usability, and this is a feature they simply must have to remain competitive. They will have it.

Researchers around the world will continue to stay at the forefront of research in analysis with missing data, and it is very likely that the very latest techniques will not be available in the mainstream packages. Schafer and his colleagues will continue to make improvements to NORM (Schafer, 1997) and its siblings CAT, MIX, and PAN. The latter three programs will all be released as stand-alone Windows programs in the near future. The wide availability of PAN will greatly improve the usefulness of MAR multiple-imputation programs.

Some Final Thoughts

It is important not to draw too many generalizations from the empirical example given in this chapter. Different analysis situations pose different problems and potentially different solutions. The empirical example in this chapter poses a particular challenge. Very clearly, complete cases analysis would just not do here. Also, because of the particular nature of the analyses described, the 21 additional variables were extremely helpful. This was a sample of college students, and the measures were taken at relatively close (2- to 3-month) intervals. For both of these reasons, a variable at one wave was very highly correlated (often with $r > .90$) with the same variable measured at another wave. Under these circumstances, the inclusion of the additional variables was very valuable. However, if this were a sample of adolescents, and the measures were taken at 1-year intervals, or if this were a cross-sectional sample, we would expect the correlations to be much lower. Under such circumstances, including the additional variables might be of much less value.

The missing data patterns in the empirical example presented here were such that the value of the missing data procedures was rather obvious. In other contexts, that value will be less clear. If one has just two waves of data—for example, a pretest and a single posttest—and if one has essentially complete data at the pretest, then complete cases analysis might be nearly as good as it gets, regardless of how much data are missing at the posttest.

We simply cannot describe all possible missing data scenarios here. Suffice it to say that in some instances, the statistical advantage of the prescribed procedures will be small in comparison to more traditional approaches (e.g., complete cases analysis). However, the prescribed procedures will always be at least as good as other approaches, and in most circumstances, there will be a clear advantage of the prescribed procedures, in terms of estimation bias, statistical power, or both. In many circumstances, the advantage will be huge.

Under these circumstances, the only reason for not employing these procedures is that they are not easy to use. As the software developers erase this objection, and make the best analysis more and more accessible, we end users will begin to have the best of both worlds.

APPENDIX A: SAS PROC FACTOR CODE PRODUCED BY THE ALPHNORM UTILITY

```
options nocenter ls=80;
data a(type=cov);infile 'alphnorm.cov' lrecl=5000;input
_type_ $ 1-4 _name_ $ 6-13
relig female wa242 wa222 ra215 ra246 wa186
ra243 ra195 wa192 wa202 wa225 we15 we16
we17 wa127 ra128 wa129 wa23 wa24 wa27
```

```
wa67 wa100 wa103 wa182 defynov defyfeb defyapr
defynv0 pusenov pusefeb puseapr pusenv0 iintvnov iintvfeb
iintvapr iintvnv0 drunksep drunknov drunkfeb drunkapr alcsep
alcnov alcfeb alcapr alcnv0 ;
run;

proc factor data=a(type=cov) method=prin rotate=promax reorder round;var

*** Use of PROC REG with this EM covariance matrix should be done with extreme
    caution, because sample size has been set arbitrarily at N=500 ***;
/*
proc reg data=a(type=cov);
model . . .
*/
```

APPENDIX B: SAS DATA STEP AND PROC REG CODE FOR MULTIPLE IMPUTATION

```
data a;infile 'jan06all.imp' lrecl=5000;
 input
  _imputation_
  relig female introvrt
  alcsep alcnov alcfeb alcapr alcnv0
  drunksep drunknov drunkfeb drunkapr drunknv0
  defysep defynov defyfeb defyapr defynv0
  pusesep pusenov pusefeb puseapr pusenv0
  iintvsep iintvnov iintvfeb iintvapr iintvnv0;
run;

*** The following statements standardize the variables for more
direct comparison with Amos results. ***

proc standard data=a out=b mean=0 std=1;var
 drunknv0 relig female introvrt defysep pusesep iintvsep;
run;

***=================================================================;

*** This analysis is a simple regression analysis with several
    predictor variables of interest, but only a single DV.
        The 'by _imputation_' statement repeats the analysis with all 20 imputed data sets.
***=================================================================;

proc reg data=b outest=c covout noprint;model
 drunknv0 = relig female introvrt defysep pusesep iintvsep;
 by _imputation_;
run;

***=================================================================;
```

*** PROC MIANALYZE performs the MI Inference Analysis similar to what is done with NORM.
The variables listed in the VAR statement below are the predictors in the regression analysis.

```
***=====================================================================;

proc mianalyze;var intercept relig female introvrt defysep
pusesep
                iintvsep;
run;
```

APPENDIX C: SPSS MACRO AND REGRESSION CODE FOR MULTIPLE IMPUTATION

Note: This code automates the process of standardizing items, computing new scales, and
performing the regression analysis for the 20 imputed data sets. However, the immediate results
of this macro are not readable by NORM.

For these analyses, we used the utility NORMSPSS to read the SPSS Regression output, create
the NORM-readable data set, and create a partial MI Inference data set (NORMSPSS.OUT)
automatically.

The NORMSPSS utility and related files can be obtained at our web site: http://methcenter.psu.edu.

```
DEFINE !NORMIMP() .

*** modify the following statement (number of imputed datasets)
as needed *** .

!DO !I = 1 !TO 20 .

*** modify the /FILE = line (shown as 'jan06') as needed *** .
*** modify the /VARIABLES = statements as needed *** .
*** NOTE that the format given behind each variables appears to
be necessary, but arbitrary *** .
***  That is, it appears that F2.2 may be used for all numeric variables *** .

GET DATA /TYPE = TXT
 /FILE = !CONCAT ('jan06_' , !I , '.IMP' )
 /DELCASE = LINE
 /DELIMITERS = " "
 /ARRANGEMENT = DELIMITED
 /FIRSTCASE = 1
 /IMPORTCASE = ALL
 /VARIABLES =
relig F2.2
female F2.2
introvrt F2.2
alcsep F2.2
alcnov F2.2
```

```
alcfeb   F2.2
alcapr   F2.2
alcnv0   F2.2
drunksep F2.2
drunknov F2.2
drunkfeb F2.2
drunkapr F2.2
drunknv0 F2.2
defysep  F2.2
defynov  F2.2
defyfeb  F2.2
defyapr  F2.2
defynv0  F2.2
pusesep  F2.2
pusenov  F2.2
pusefeb  F2.2
puseapr  F2.2
pusenv0  F2.2
iintvsep F2.2
iintvnov F2.2
iintvfeb F2.2
iintvapr F2.2
iintvnv0 F2.2
  .


*** Modify the data manipulations as needed *** .
*** The following standardizes variables for better comparison
with Amos *** .

DESCRIPTIVES
 VARIABLES=
drunknv0 relig female introvrt defysep pusesep iintvsep /SAVE
 /STATISTICS=MEAN STDDEV MIN MAX .

*** No computations are needed for this analysis, but if needed,
they could go here, for example *** .

*** COMPUTE fuse7=mean(zwa1,zwa3,zwa5,zwa7) .
*** EXECUTE .

*** Modify the Regression analysis as needed *** .
*** As is, the output dataset names are all1.out, all2.out, etc.
***  Keep them like this, or modify them as needed *** .

REGRESSION
 /MISSING LISTWISE
 /STATISTICS COEFF OUTS R ANOVA
 /CRITERIA=PIN(.05) POUT(.10)
 /NOORIGIN
 /DEPENDENT zdrunknv0
```

```
/METHOD=ENTER zrelig zfemale zintrovrt zdefysep zpusesep
ziintvsep
 /outfile=model(!CONCAT('nrmreg' , !I, '.out')) .

!DOEND .

!ENDDEFINE .

!NORMIMP .
```

REFERENCES

Allison, P. D. (1987). Estimation of linear models with incomplete data. In C. Clogg (Ed.), *Sociological Methodology 1987* (pp. 71–103). San Francisco: Jossey Bass.

Arbuckle, J. L., & Wothke, W. (1999). *Amos 4.0 User's Guide.* Chicago: Smallwaters.

Bentler, P. M. (1986). *Theory and implementation of EQS: A structural equations program.* Los Angeles: BMDP Statistical Software.

Collins, L. M., Hyatt, S. L., & Graham, J. W. (2000). LTA as a way of testing models of stage-sequential change. In T. D. Little, K. U. Schnabel, & J. Baumert (Eds.), *Modeling longitudinal and multiple-group data: Practical issues, applied approaches, and specific examples* (pp. 147–161). Hillsdale, NJ: Erlbaum.

Collins, L. M., Schafer, J. L., & Kam, C. M. (2001). A comparison of inclusive and restrictive strategies in modern missing data procedures. *Psychological Methods, 6,* 330–351.

Dempster, A. P., Laird, N. M., & Rubin, D. B. (1977). Maximum likelihood from incomplete data via the EM algorithm (with discussion), *Journal of the Royal Statistical Society, B39,* 1–38.

Duncan, S. C., & Duncan, T. E. (1994). Modeling incomplete longitudinal substance use data using latent variable growth curve methodology. *Multivariate Behavioral Research, 29,* 313–338.

Duncan, T. E., Duncan, S. C., and Li, F. (1998). A comparison of model- and multiple imputation-based approaches to longitudinal analysis with partial missingness. *Structural Equation Modeling, 5,* 1–21.

Efron, B. (1982). *The jackknife, the bootstrap, and other resampling plans.* Philadelphia: Society for Industrial and Applied Mathematics.

Graham, J. W. (in press). *Adding missing-data relevant variables to FIML-based structural equation models. Structural Equation Modeling.*

Graham, J. W., & Donaldson, S. I. (1993). Evaluating interventions with differential attrition: The importance of nonresponse mechanisms and use of followup data. *Journal of Applied Psychology, 78,* 119–128.

Graham, J. W., & Hofer, S. M. (2000). Multiple imputation in multivariate research. In T. D. Little, K. U. Schnabel, & J. Baumert (Eds.), *Modeling longitudinal and multiple-group data: Practical issues, applied approaches, and specific examples* (pp. 201–218). Hillsdale, NJ: Erlbaum.

Graham, J. W., Hofer, S. M., Donaldson, S. I., MacKinnon, D. P., & Schafer, J. L. (1997). Analysis with missing data in prevention research. In K. Bryant, M. Windle, & S. West (Eds.), *The science of prevention: Methodological advances from alcohol and substance abuse research* (pp. 325–366). Washington, DC: American Psychological Association.

Graham, J. W., Hofer, S. M., & MacKinnon, D. P. (1996). Maximizing the usefulness of data obtained with planned missing value patterns: An application of maximum likelihood procedures. *Multivariate Behavioral Research, 31,* 197–218.

Graham, J. W., Hofer, S. M., & Piccinin, A. M. (1994). Analysis with missing data in drug prevention research. In L. M. Collins & L. Seitz (Eds.), *Advances in data analysis for prevention intervention research.* National Institute on Drug Abuse Research Monograph Series 142, pp. 13–63, Washington DC: National Institute on Drug Abuse.

Graham, J. W., Roberts, M. M., Tatterson, J. W., & Johnston, S. E. (2002). Data quality in evaluation of an alcohol-related harm prevention program. *Evaluation Review, 26,* 147–189.

Graham, J. W., & Schafer, J. L. (1999). On the performance of multiple imputation for multivariate data with small sample size. In R. Hoyle (Ed.), *Statistical strategies for small sample research* (pp. 1–29). Thousand Oaks, CA: Sage.

Graham, J. W., Tatterson, J. W., Roberts, M. M., & Johnston, S. E. (2001). *Preventing alcohol-related harm in college students: Program effects on proximal outcomes.* Manuscript submitted for publication.

Graham, J. W., & Taylor, B. J. (2001). Splitting variables for multiple-pass multiple imputation. Unpublished manuscript, Pennsylvania State University.

Graham, J. W., Taylor, B. J., & Cumsille, P. E. (2001). Planned missing data designs in analysis of change. In L. Collins & A. Sayer (Eds.), *New methods for the analysis of change* (pp. 335–353). Washington, DC: American Psychological Association.

Heckman, J. J. (1979). Sample selection bias as a specification error. *Econometrica, 47,* 153–161.

Hyatt, S. L., & Collins, L. M. (2000). Using Latent Transition Analysis to examine the relationship between parental permissiveness and the onset of substance use. In J. Rose, L. Chassin, C. Presson, & S. Sherman (Eds.), *Multivariate applications in substance use research* (pp. 259–288). Hillsdale, NJ: Erlbaum.

Jöreskog, K. G., & Sörbom, D. (1996). *LISREL 8 user's reference guide.* Moorseville, IN: Scientific Software.

Little, R. J. A. (1994). A class of pattern-mixture models for normal incomplete data. *Biometrika, 81,* 471–483.

Little, R. J. A. (1995). Modeling the drop-out mechanism in repeated-measures studies. *Journal of the American Statistical Association, 90,* 1112–1121.

Little, R. J. A., & Rubin, D. B. (1987). *Statistical analysis with missing data.* New York: Wiley.

Little, R. J. A., & Schenker, N. (1995). Missing Data. In: G. Arminger, C. C. Clogg, & M. E. Sobel (Eds.), *Handbook of statistical modeling for the social and behavioral sciences* (pp. 39–75). New York: Plenum Press.

McArdle, J. J. (1994). Structural factor analysis experiments with incomplete data. *Multivariate Behavioral Research, 29*(4), 409–454.

McArdle, J. J., & Hamagami, F. (1991). Modeling incomplete longitudinal and cross-sectional data using latent growth structural models. In L. M. Collins & J. C. Horn (Eds.), *Best methods for the analysis of change* (pp. 276–304). Washington, DC: American Psychological Association.

Muthén, B. (2001). Second-generation structural equation modeling with a combination of categorical and continuous latent variables. In L. M. Collins & A. Sayer (Eds.), *New methods for the analysis of change* (pp. 291–322). Washington, DC: American Psychological Association.

Muthén, B., Kaplan, D., & Hollis, M. (1987). On structural equation modeling with data that are not missing completely at random. *Psychometrika, 52,* 431–462.

Muthén, L. K., & Muthén, B. O. (1998). *Mplus user's guide.* Los Angeles, CA: Author.

Neale, M. C., Boker, S. M., Xie, G., & Maes, H. H. (1999). *Mx: Statistical modeling* (5th ed.). Richmond, VA: Department of Psychiatry, Virginia Commonwealth University.

Rubin, D. B. (1987). *Multiple imputation for nonresponse in surveys.* New York: Wiley.

Satorra, A., & Bentler, P. M. (1994). Corrections to test statistics and standard errors in covariance structure analysis. In A. von Eye & C. C. Clogg (Eds.), *Latent variables analysis: Applications for developmental research* (pp. 399–419). Thousand Oaks, CA: Sage.

Saucier, G. (1994). Mini-markers: A brief version of Goldberg's unipolar Big-Five markers. *Journal of Personality Assessment, 63,* 506–516.

Schafer, J. L. (1997). *Analysis of incomplete multivariate data.* New York: Chapman and Hall.

Schafer, J. L. (in press). Multiple imputation with PAN. In L. Collins & A. Sayer (Eds.), *New methods for the analysis of change* (pp. 357–377). Washington, DC: American Psychological Association.

Schafer, J. L., & Graham, J. W. (2002). Missing data: Our view of the state of the art. *Psychological Methods.*

Schafer, J. L., & Olsen, M. K. (1998). Multiple imputation for multivariate missing data problems: A data analyst's perspective. *Multivariate Behavioral Research, 33,* 545–571.

Tanner, M. A., & Wong, W. H. (1987). The calculation of posterior distributions by data augmentation (with discussion). *Journal of the American Statistical Association, 82,* 528–550.

Verbeke, G., & Molenberghs, G. (2000). *Linear mixed models for longitudinal data.* New York: Springer.

Wothke, W. (2000). Longitudinal and multigroup modeling with missing data. In T. D. Little, K. U. Schnabel, & J. Baumert (Eds.), *Modeling longitudinal and multiple-group data: Practical issues, applied approaches, and specific examples* (pp. 219–240). Hillsdale, NJ: Erlbaum.

CHAPTER 5

Preparatory Data Analysis

LINDA S. FIDELL AND BARBARA G. TABACHNICK

RATIONALE FOR PREPARATORY DATA ANALYSIS

Preparatory data analyses are conducted to locate and correct problems in a data set prior to a main analysis. Missing data are located and dealt with (see chapter by Graham, Cumsille, & Elek-Fisk in this volume), and various assumptions of the planned analyses are tested. Much of the material in this chapter is adapted from Chapters 2 and 3 in Tabachnick and Fidell (2001a) and Chapter 4 in Tabachnick and Fidell (2001b), where more extended discussions are available.

Previous cavalier attitudes toward violation of the assumptions of an analysis have given way to a growing concern that the integrity of the inferential test depends on meeting those assumptions (Wilkinson & the Task Force on Statistical Inference, 1999). Inferential tests are based on estimating probability levels for the null hypothesis from a sampling distribution such as F, Wilks's lambda, or chi-square. The distribution of a statistic (e.g., the distribution of all possible ratios of two variances drawn from the same population of scores) is tested against known sampling distributions (e.g., the F ratio) to see which it most closely resembles. If the distribution of the statistic is the same as that of a known sampling distribution, probabilities associated with various statistical values along the sampling distribution are used to assess the Type I error rate. However, when the fit is assessed, it is with assumptions about the nature of the data that are to be processed.

For an example, it may be assumed, among other things, that the analyzed variable has a normal distribution. When the analyzed variable is normally distributed, the probability value associated with the statistical test is an accurate estimate of the probability under the null hypothesis. But when the analyzed variable is not normal, the estimated probability value may be either too conservative or too liberal. The issue, in this example and others, is how much the distribution of the variable can deviate from the assumption of normality without throwing the estimated Type I probability level into disarray.

Preparatory data analysis is usually a time-consuming and frustrating business. It is time-consuming because numerous features of the data need to be examined and frustrating because the main analysis that provides the answer to your main research question is often just a few menu selections away. Further, violation of some assumptions is more serious than violation of others because sometimes violation leads to the wrong inferential conclusion and other times the analysis is correct as far as it goes but misses certain additional relationships in the data. However, a believable (and replicable) inferential result depends on assessing the fit between the assumptions of the analysis used and the data analyzed, with correction for violations applied as necessary or an alternative analytic strategy employed.

SOME CONSIDERATIONS

Screening for violation of assumptions can be conducted in several different ways. Relevant issues in the choice of when and how to screen depend on the level of measurement of the variables, whether the design produces grouped or ungrouped data, whether cases provide a single response or more than one response, and whether the variables themselves or the residuals of analysis are screened.

Level of Measurement: Continuous, Ordinal, and Discrete Variables

One consideration in preparatory data analysis is whether the variables are continuous, ordinal, or discrete. Continuous variables are also referred to as interval or ratio; discrete variables are also called categorical or nominal; discrete variables with only two levels are often called dichotomous. Continuous variables assess the *amount* of something along a continuum of possible values where the size of the observed value depends on the sensitivity of the measuring device. As the measuring device becomes more sensitive, so does the precision with which the variable is assessed. Examples of continuous variables are time to complete a task, amount of fabric used in various manufacturing processes, or numerical score on an essay exam. Most of the assumptions of analysis apply to continuous variables.

Rank-order/ordinal data are obtained when the researcher assesses the relative positions of cases in a distribution of cases (e.g., most talented, least efficient), when the researcher has others rank order several items (e.g., most important to me), or when the researcher has assessed numerical scores for cases but does not trust them. In the last instance, the researcher believes that the case with the highest score has the most (or least) of something but is not comfortable analyzing the numerical scores themselves, so the data are treated as ordinal. Numbers reveal which case is in what position, but there is no assurance that the distance between the first and second cases is the same as, for instance, the distance between the second and third cases, or any other adjacent pair. Only a few statistical methods are available for analysis of ordinal variables, and they tend to have few or no assumptions (Siegel & Castellan, 1988).

Discrete variables are classified into categories. There are usually only a few categories, chosen so that every case can be classified into only one of them. For instance, employees are classified as properly trained or not; eggs are divided into medium, large, and extra large; respondents answer either "yes" or "no"; manufactured parts either pass or do not pass quality control; or dessert choice is sorbet, tiramisu, chocolate mousse, or apple tart. In many analyses, discrete variables are the grouping variables (treatment group vs. control) for a main analysis such as analysis of variance (ANOVA) or logistic regression. Assumptions for discrete variables relate to the frequency of cases in the various categories. Problems arise when there are too few cases in some of the categories, as discussed later.

Grouped and Ungrouped Research Designs

Assumptions are assessed differently depending on whether the data are to be grouped or ungrouped during analysis. The most common goal in grouped analyses is to compare the central tendency in two or more groups; the most common goal in ungrouped analyses is to study relationships among variables. Grouped data are appropriately analyzed using univariate or multivariate analysis of variance (ANOVA and MANOVA, including profile analysis of repeated measures), logistic regression, or discriminant analysis. Ungrouped data are analyzed through bivariate or multiple regression, canonical correlation, cluster analysis, or factor analysis. Some techniques apply to either grouped or ungrouped data. For example, time-series analysis and survival analysis can be used to track behavior over time for a single group of cases or to compare behavior over time for different groups. Chi-square and multiway frequency analysis can be used to compare contingencies in responses among categorical variables for a single group or to look for differences in responses among different groups. Similarly, structural equations can be used to model responses of a single group or compare models among groups.

Tests of assumptions are performed differently depending on whether data are to be grouped or ungrouped during analysis. Basically, ungrouped data are examined as a single set, while grouped data are examined separately within each group or have entirely different criteria for assessing fit to some assumptions, as discussed later.

Single Versus Multiple Responses

Participants provide a single response in the classical between-subjects ANOVA or chi-square designs. In other designs participants may provide several responses, and those responses may be measured either on the same or on different scales. Multivariate statistical techniques deal with multiple responses on different scales and are analyzed using such methods as MANOVA, canonical correlation, discriminant analysis, factor analysis, and structural equation modeling.

Multiple responses on the same scale (e.g., pretest, posttest, and follow-up scores on a measure of depression) are generally considered to produce univariate statistical designs (e.g., within-subjects ANOVA), although they are sometimes treated multivariately. Having multiple responses complicates data screening because there are also relationships among those responses to consider.

Examining the Variables or the Residuals of Analysis

Another issue is whether the examination of assumptions is performed on the raw variables prior to analysis or whether the main analysis is performed and its residuals examined. Both procedures are likely to uncover the same problems. For example, a peculiar score (an outlier) can be identified initially as a deviant score in its own distribution or as a score with a large residual that is not fit well by the solution.

Temptation is a major difference between these two alternatives. When residuals are examined after the main analysis is performed, the results of the main analysis are also available for inspection. If the results are the desired ones, it is tempting to see no problems with the residuals. If the results are not the desired ones, it is tempting to begin to play with the variables to see what happens to the results. On the other hand, when the assumptions are assessed and decisions are made about how to handle violations prior to the main analysis, there is less opportunity for temptation to influence the results that are accepted and reported.

Even if raw variables are screened before analysis, it is usually worthwhile to examine residuals of the main analysis for insights into the degree to which the final model has captured the nuances of the data. In what ways does the model fail to fit or "explain" the data? Are there types of cases to which the model does not generalize? Is further research necessary to find out why the model fails to fit these cases? Did the preparatory tests of assumptions fail to uncover violations that are only evident in direct examination of residuals (Wilkinson et al., 1999)?

SCREENING CONTINUOUS VARIABLES

Univariate Assumptions

These assumptions apply to a single variable for which a confidence interval is desired or, more commonly, to a single continuous dependent variable (DV) measured for each participant in the two or more groups that constitute the independent variable (IV). We illustrate both statistical and graphical methods of assessing the various assumptions.

Normality of Individual Variables (or the Residuals)

Several statistical and graphical methods are available to assess the normality of raw scores in ungrouped data or the normality of residuals of analysis. The next section contains guidelines for normality in grouped data.

Recall that normal distributions are symmetrical about the mean with a well-defined shape and height. Mean, median, and mode are the same, and the percentages of cases between the mean and various standard deviation units from the mean are known. For this reason, you can rescale a normally distributed continuous variable to a z score (with mean 0 and standard deviation 1) and look up the probability that corresponds to a particular range of raw scores in a table with a title such as "standard normal deviates" or "areas under the normal curve." The legitimacy of using the z-score transformation and its associated probabilities depends on the normality of the distribution of the continuous variable.

Although it is tempting to conclude that most inferential statistics are robust to violations of normality, that conclusion is not warranted. Bradley (1982) reported that statistical inference becomes less robust as distributions depart from normality—and rapidly so under many conditions. And even with a purely descriptive study, normality of variables (as well as pair-wise linearity and homoscedasticity, discussed in the section titled "Multivariate Assumptions") enhances the analysis, particularly when individual variables are nonnormal to varying degrees and in varying directions.

Skewness and kurtosis are statistics for assessing the symmetry (skewness) and peakedness (kurtosis) of a distribution. A distribution with positive skewness has a few cases with large values that lengthen the right tail; a distribution with negative skewness has a few cases with small values that lengthen the left tail. A distribution with positive kurtosis is too peaked (*leptokurtic*); a distribution with negative kurtosis is too flat (*platykurtic*—think "flatty"). A normal distribution is called *mesokurtic*. Nonnormal distributions have different percentages of cases between various standard deviation units than does the normal distribution, so z-score transformations and inferential tests applied to variables with nonnormal distributions are often misleading. Figure 5.1 shows a normal curve and several that depart from normality.

In a normal distribution, skewness and kurtosis are zero. The standard error of skewness is

$$s_{\text{skewness}} = \sqrt{\frac{6}{N}} \tag{5.1}$$

The standard error of kurtosis is

$$s_{\text{kurtosis}} = \sqrt{\frac{24}{N}} \tag{5.2}$$

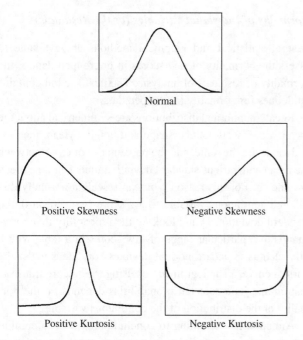

Figure 5.1   Normal distribution, distributions with skewness, and distributions with kurtosis. Reprinted with permission of Tabachnick and Fidell (2001b), *Using multivariate statistics* (Boston: Allyn and Bacon).

For the fictitious data of DESCRPT.* (downloaded from www.abacon.com/tabachnick) where $N = 50$ for all variables, the standard errors of skewness and kurtosis are

$$s_{\text{skewness}} = \sqrt{\frac{6}{50}} = 0.346$$

$$s_{\text{kurtosis}} = \sqrt{\frac{24}{50}} = 0.693$$

These standard errors are used to test whether a distribution departs from normal by dividing the skewness or kurtosis values for the distribution by their respective standard errors and looking up the result as a z score from a standard normal table of values. For skewness,

$$z_{\text{skewness}} = \frac{\text{skewness} - 0}{s_{\text{skewness}}} \qquad (5.3)$$

and for kurtosis,

$$z_{\text{kurtosis}} = \frac{\text{kurtosis} - 0}{s_{\text{kurtosis}}} \qquad (5.4)$$

The output in Figure 5.2 shows, among other descriptive statistics produced by SAS INTERACTIVE, skewness and kurtosis values for the continuous variables in the data set.

After calculating the standard errors using Equations 5.1 and 5.2, the z score for Var_A for skewness is [0.220/0.346 =] 0.64, and the z score for kurtosis is −0.94. For Var_C (which was generated with skewness) the z score for skewness is 3.92, and the z score for kurtosis is 2.65. (Var_D also has a z score indicative of skewness, but it is due to the presence of an outlier, as becomes clear in a later section.) Two-tailed alpha levels of .01 or .001 and visual inspection of the shape of the distribution are used to evaluate the significance of skewness and kurtosis with small to moderate samples. There also are formal statistical tests for the significance of the departure of a distribution from normality such as Shapiro, Wilks's W statistic, and the Anderson-Darling test available in MINITAB, but they are very sensitive and often signal departures from normality that are not important for the analysis.

By these criteria, Var_A is normal, but Var_C has statistically significant positive skewness. However, if the sample is much larger, normality is assessed through inspection of the shape of the distribution instead of formal inference because the equations for standard error of both skewness and kurtosis contain N and normality is likely to be rejected with large samples (e.g., around 300 or larger) even when the deviation is slight.

Graphical methods for assessing normality include frequency histograms and normal probability plots. SPSS FREQUENCIES produced the frequency histograms in Figure 5.3 for Var_A, which is relatively normally distributed, and Var_C, which is not. The normal curve overlay is selected along with the frequency histogram to assist the judgment of normality. The positive skewness of Var_C is readily apparent.

Normal probability plots (sometimes called normal quantile-quantile, or QQ, plots) require some explanation. In these plots, the scores are first sorted and ranked. Then an expected normal value is computed and plotted against the actual normal value for each case. The expected normal value is the z score that a case with that rank holds in a normal distribution; the actual normal value is the z score it has in the actual distribution. If the actual distribution is normal, the two z scores are similar, and the points fall along the diagonal, running from lower left to upper right. Deviations from normality shift the points away from the diagonal.

When normal probability plots are inspected side by side, the equivalence of the standard deviations is also assessed by looking at the slope of the pattern of points for each distribution; when the slopes for several distributions are relatively equal, so are the standard deviations (Cleveland, 1993). This can be useful for evaluating homogeneity of variance in grouped data.

1. Open SAS Interactive Data Analysis with appropriate data set (here SASUSER.DESCRPT).
2. Choose Analyze and then Distribution(Y).
3. Select Y variables: VARA, VARB, VARC, and VARD.
4. In Output dialog box, select Moments and Basic Confidence Intervals.

▶ VARA

Moments			
N	50.0000	Sum Wgts	50.0000
Mean	51.1600	Sum	2558.0000
Std Dev	9.4747	Variance	89.7698
Skewness	0.2202	Kurtosis	-0.6498
USS	135266.000	CSS	4398.7200
CV	18.5197	Std Mean	1.3399

95% Confidence Intervals			
Parameter	Estimate	LCL	UCL
Mean	51.1600	48.4673	53.8527
Std Dev	9.4747	7.9145	11.8067
Variance	89.7698	62.6398	139.3989

▶ VARB

Moments			
N	50.0000	Sum Wgts	50.0000
Mean	49.7200	Sum	2486.0000
Std Dev	1.9171	Variance	3.6751
Skewness	0.0373	Kurtosis	-0.6842
USS	123784.000	CSS	180.0800
CV	3.8557	Std Mean	0.2711

95% Confidence Intervals			
Parameter	Estimate	LCL	UCL
Mean	49.7200	49.1752	50.2648
Std Dev	1.9171	1.6014	2.3889
Variance	3.6751	2.5644	5.7069

▶ VARC

Moments			
N	50.0000	Sum Wgts	50.0000
Mean	49.8000	Sum	2490.0000
Std Dev	11.6759	Variance	136.3265
Skewness	1.3582	Kurtosis	1.8361
USS	130682.000	CSS	6680.0000
CV	23.4456	Std Mean	1.6512

95% Confidence Intervals			
Parameter	Estimate	LCL	UCL
Mean	49.8000	46.4817	53.1183
Std Dev	11.6759	9.7533	14.5497
Variance	136.3265	95.1263	211.6944

▶ VARD

Moments			
N	50.0000	Sum Wgts	50.0000
Mean	51.1200	Sum	2556.0000
Std Dev	8.1407	Variance	66.2710
Skewness	-0.2307	Kurtosis	-0.0263
USS	133910.000	CSS	3247.2800
CV	15.9247	Std Mean	1.1513

95% Confidence Intervals			
Parameter	Estimate	LCL	UCL
Mean	51.1200	48.8064	53.4336
Std Dev	8.1407	6.8002	10.1444
Variance	66.2710	46.2428	102.9088

Figure 5.2 Syntax and descriptive statistics for VAR_A to VAR_D; produced by SAS Interactive.

Figure 5.4 contains normal probability plots (requested as **NPPLOT**) for Var_A and Var_C produced by SPSS EXPLORE.

As shown in Figure 5.4, the data points fall very close to the diagonal for Var_A but some distance from it for Var_C. The low values and the high values of Var_C have z scores that are too low, whereas the z scores for the middle values are too high. (The data point far from the others in the upper right-hand part of the plot for Var_C also looks suspiciously like an outlier.) If a distribution is acceptably normal, the mean is interpreted instead of the median.

```
FREQUENCIES
 VARIABLES=var_a var_c
 /FORMAT NOTABLE
 /HISTOGRAM NORMAL
 /ORDER ANALYSIS .
```

Histogram

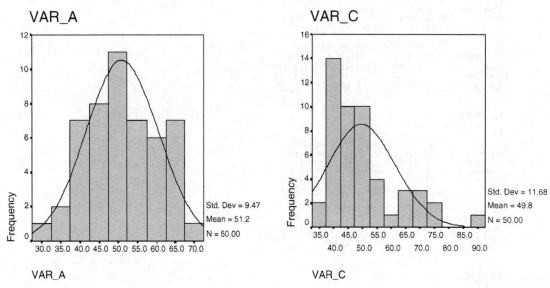

VAR_A

VAR_C

Figure 5.3 Syntax and frequency histograms with normal curve overlay for VAR_A and VAR_C; produced by SPSS FREQUENCIES for the DESCRPT.SAV data set.

Normality in Grouped Data

Less stringent guidelines are used when assessing grouped data because tests of differences in means among groups use sampling distributions rather than raw-score distributions. If you have several DV scores at each level of the IV, you can estimate the mean and standard error of the sampling distribution of all possible mean differences in the population under the null hypothesis. The central limit theorem tells us that the shape of this sampling distribution approaches normal as sample size increases.

The reason that the advantages of sampling distributions (i.e., their known shapes and corresponding probabilities) are available for grouped but not ungrouped data can be seen in Figure 5.5. Panel A shows a potential relationship between the IV (plotted on the x-axis) and DV scores (plotted on the y-axis) for grouped data. Notice that although each group may have a different distribution of scores (with size of circle indicating size of sample), there are numerous scores for each group from which to estimate the sampling distribution. When data are not grouped, as in panel B, some values of X (e.g., 70) have a single associated Y score;

some have no associated Y score (e.g., $X = 110$); and some have two or more associated Y scores (e.g., $X = 80$). Thus, it is not possible to estimate central tendency or dispersion of a sampling distribution of scores for each value of X unless data are grouped.

Because the assumption of normality for grouped data applies to the sampling distribution, and because that distribution approaches normal as sample size increases, the assumption is acceptably met with large enough sample sizes. A useful guideline for both univariate and multivariate analyses is at least 20 deg of freedom (*df*) for error. No such convenient guideline is available for ungrouped data.

Although normality is not at issue when there are sufficient *df* for error, it is still worthwhile to examine distributions of scores within each group for possible anomalies. Frequency histograms may be especially interesting when presented separately for each group on the same scale, as in Figure 5.6, which uses the MANOVA.sas7bdat data set (from www.abacon.com/tabachnick). The grouping (class) variable, MASC, has two levels (high and low masculinity on the Bem Sex Role Scale), and the continuous variable ESTEEM (self-esteem) is shown for each group of

```
EXAMINE
  VARIABLES=var_a var_c
  /PLOT NPPLOT
  /COMPARE GROUP
  /STATISTICS NONE
  /CINTERVAL 95
  /MISSING LISTWISE
  /NOTOTAL.
```

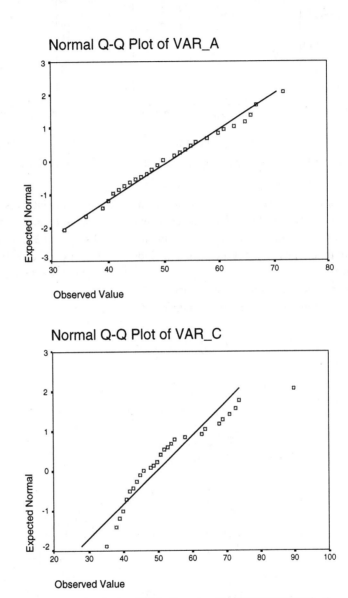

Figure 5.4   Syntax and normal probability plots of VAR_*A* and VAR_*C*; produced by SPSS EXPLORE for the DESCRPT.SAV data set.

women. A normal curve is superimposed over the histograms by request, and the midpoints and scale intervals (by) are defined. Remaining syntax defines the inset requested for basic descriptive statistics. (This syntax also produces a great deal of statistical output that is not shown here.)

The histograms show the lower self-esteem values for women in group 2 (low masculinity) as well as a suggestion of positive skewness for them, to be discussed in a later section.

Absence of Outliers (in Variables or the Residuals)

Outliers are deviant cases with undue impact on the results of analysis. They can either raise or lower means and, by doing so, create artificial significance or cover up real significance.

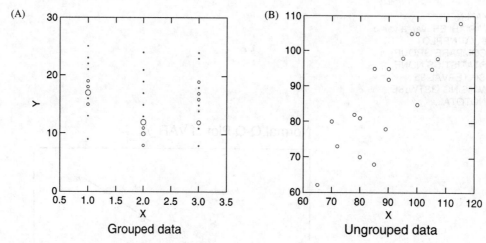

Figure 5.5 Grouped and ungrouped data, sampling distributions, and the central limit theorem.

They almost always increase dispersion, thereby increasing Type II errors and distorting correlations. Their inclusion in a data set makes the outcome of analysis unpredictable and not generalizable except to a population that happens to include the same sort of outlier.

An outlier is a score that is far from the grand mean in ungrouped data or from the mean of its group in grouped data, and apparently disconnected from the rest of the scores. The z-score (standard normal) distribution is used to assess the distance of a raw score from its mean. In Equation 5.5, Y is the raw score, $\overline{Y}$ is the mean, and s_{N-1} is the unbiased estimate of the standard deviation:

$$z = \frac{Y - \overline{Y}}{s_{N-1}} \qquad (5.5)$$

```
proc univariate data=SASUSER.MANOVA;
  class MASC;
    var ESTEEM;
  histogram ESTEEM /
    normal href=16.9
    midpoints=6 to 32 by 2 vscale=count;
        inset n="N" (5.0)
              mean="Mean" (5.1)
                std="Std Dev" (5.1)/
              pos = ne height=3;
run;
```

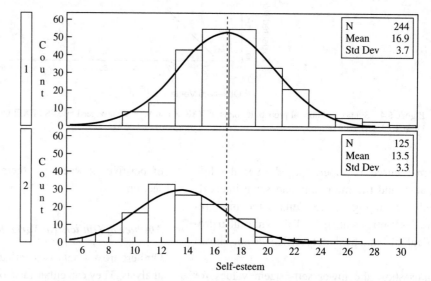

Figure 5.6 Syntax and frequency histograms for ESTEEM on the same scale for two groups; produced by SAS MANOVA.

If the sample is fairly large (e.g., 100 or more), a case with an absolute *z* value of 3.3 or greater is probably an outlier because the two-tailed probability of sampling a score of this size in random sampling from the population of interest is .001 or less. If the sample is smaller, an absolute value of *z* of 2.58 ($p < .01$, two-tailed) is appropriate. Visual inspection of the distribution is also needed to conclude that a case is an outlier.

In DESCRIPT.*, Var_D was created with an outlying score. Features of SPSS EXPLORE appropriate for identifying outliers are shown in Figure 5.7. The PLOT instruction requests a BOXPLOT; the STATISTICS instruction requests EXTREME values (to identify outliers) as well as DESCRIPTIVES. Box plots from two or more groups side by side are available through box and whisker plots under graphing or quality control menus. The remaining instructions are default values generated by the SPSS menu system.

The output segment labeled DESCRIPTIVES contains most of the important descriptive statistics for a continuous variable, and that labeled EXTREME values shows information relevant for identifying outliers. The case numbers with the highest and lowest five scores are listed along with the scores themselves. For Var_A the highest and

Extreme Values

			Case Number	Value
VAR_A	Highest	1	20	72.00
		2	16	67.00
		3	2	67.00
		4	39	66.00
		5	36	66.00
	Lowest	1	45	32.00
		2	8	36.00
		3	22	36.00
		4	1	39.00
		5	30	.a
VAR_D	Highest	1	48	69.00
		2	40	64.00
		3	5	63.00
		4	41	62.00
		5	38	.b
	Lowest	1	12	13.00
		2	34	32.00
		3	2	33.00
		4	46	35.00
		5	32	38.00

a. Only a partial list of cases with the value 40 are shown in the table of lower extremes.

b. Only a partial list of cases with the value 62 are shown in the table of upper extremes.

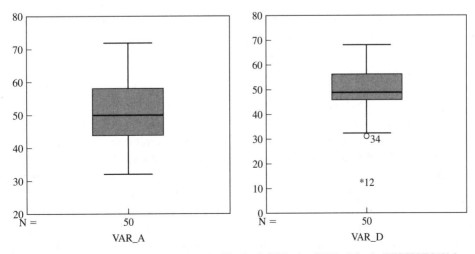

Figure 5.7   Descriptive statistics and outlier identification in VAR_A and VAR_D for the DESCRPT.SAV data set through SPSS EXPLORE.

lowest scores do not differ much from the scores near them, but for Var_D the lowest score of 13 (case 12) appears disconnected from the next higher score of 32, which does not differ much from the next higher score of 34. The z score associated with the raw score of 13 is extreme [$z = (13 - 50.52)/9.71 = -3.86$].

Further evidence comes from the box plot in Figure 5.7 for Var_D where case 12 is identified as below the interval containing the rest of the scores. In the box plot for Var_A no case has a score outside the interval. The box itself is based on the interquartile range—the range between the 75th and 25th percentile that contains 50% of the cases. The upper and lower borders of the box are called *hinges*. The median is the line through the box. If the median is off center, there is some skewness to the data. The lines outside the box are 1.5 times the interquartile range from their own hinges. That is, the top line is $1.5 \times$ (75th percentile − 25th percentile) above the 75th percentile, and the lower line is $1.5 \times$ (75th percentile − 25th percentile) below the 25th percentile. These two lines are called the *upper* and *lower inner fences,* respectively. (There can be outer fences, as well, which are three times the interquartile range from their respective hinges, but only if there are very extreme data points.) Any score that is above or below the inner fences, such as that for case 12, is likely to be an outlier.

Researchers often are reluctant to deal with outliers because they feel that the sample should be analyzed as is. However, not dealing with outliers is, in a way, letting them deal with you because outliers potentially limit the population to which one can generalize and distort inferential conclusions. Once outliers are identified and dealt with, the researcher reports the method used to reduce their impact together with the rationale for the choices in the results section to reassure readers concerning the generalizability and validity of the findings.

The first steps in dealing with a univariate outlier are to check the accuracy with which the score was entered into the data file and then to ensure that the missing value codes have been correctly specified. If neither of these simple alternatives corrects the score, you need to decide whether the case is properly part of the population from which you intended to sample. If the case is not part of the population, it is deleted with no loss of generalizability of results to your intended population (although problems with the analysis—such as unequal sample sizes in treatment groups—may be created). The description of outliers is a description of the kinds of cases to which your results do not apply. Sometimes investigation of the conditions associated with production of outlying scores is even more substantive because it reveals unintended changes in your research program (i.e., shifts in delivery of treatment). If the case is properly part of the sample, it may be retained for analysis by transforming the distribution or by changing the outlying score.

When transformation of the entire distribution is undertaken, the outlying case is considered to have come from a nonnormal distribution with too many cases falling at extreme values. After transformation, the case is still on the tail of the distribution, but it has been pulled toward the center. The other option for univariate outliers is to change the score for just the outlying case so that it is one unit larger (or smaller) than the next most extreme score in the distribution. This is an attractive alternative to reduce the impact of an outlier if measurement is rather arbitrary anyway. In the example, the score of 12 for case 13 might be changed to a score of 30, for instance. Such changes are, of course, reported.

Homogeneity of Variance and Unequal Sample Sizes in Grouped Data

The ANOVA model assumes that population variances in different levels of the IV are equal—that the variance of DV scores within each level of the design is a separate estimate of the same population variance. In fact, the error term in ANOVA is an average of the variances within each level. If those variances are separate estimates of the same population variance, averaging them is sensible. If the variances are not separate estimates of the same population variance, averaging them to produce a single error term is not sensible.

ANOVA is robust to violation of this assumption as long as there are no outliers, sample sizes in different groups are large and fairly equal (say, ratio of largest to smallest n is not more than about 4 to 1), a two-tailed hypothesis is tested, and the ratio of largest to smallest sample variance between levels is not more than 10 to 1. The ratio can be evaluated by calculating the F_{max} statistic, whose value should not exceed 10. If these conditions are met, there is adequate homogeneity of variance:

$$F_{max} = \frac{s^2_{largest}}{s^2_{smallest}} \qquad (5.6)$$

As the discrepancy between cell sizes increases (say, goes to 9 to 1 or so), an F_{max} as small as 3 is associated with an inflated Type I error if the larger variance is associated with the smaller cell size (Milligan, Wong, & Thompson, 1987). If sample sizes are discrepant, a more formal test of homogeneity of variance is useful; some tests are described in Winer, Brown, and Michels (1991) and in Keppel (1991). However, all of these tests tend to be too sensitive, leading to overly conservative rejection of ANOVA. Except for Levene's (1960) test, most also are sensitive to nonnormality of the

DV. Levene's test performs ANOVA on the absolute values of the residuals (differences between each score and its group mean) derived from a standard ANOVA and is available in SPSS ONEWAY and GLM. Significance indicates possible violation of homogeneity of variance.

Violations of homogeneity can often be corrected by transformation of the DV scores, with interpretation, then, of the transformed scores. Another option is to test untransformed DV scores with a more stringent alpha level (e.g., for nominal $\alpha = .05$, use .025 with moderate violation and .01 with severe violation of homogeneity).

Heterogeneity of variance should always be reported and, in any event, is usually of interest in itself. *Why* is spread of scores in groups related to level of treatment? Do some levels of treatment affect all the cases about the same, while other levels of treatment affect only some cases or affect some cases much more strongly? This finding may turn out to be one of the most interesting in the study and should be dealt with as an issue in itself, not just as an annoyance in applying ANOVA.

Homogeneity of variance is also an assumption of planned and post hoc comparisons where groups are often pooled and contrasted with other groups. Details of adjustment for unequal sample sizes and failure of the assumption in various types of comparisons are discussed in (gory) detail in Tabachnick and Fidell (2001a, Sections 4.5.5, 5.6.4, 5.6.5).

Independence of Errors and Additivity in Between-Subjects Designs

Two other assumptions of between-subjects ANOVA are independence of errors and additivity. The first assumption is that errors of measurement are independent of one another—that the size of the error for one case is unrelated to the size of the error for cases near in time, space, or whatever. This assumption is easily violated if, for instance, equipment drifts during the course of the study and cases measured near each other in time have more similar errors of measurement than do cases measured farther apart in time. Care is needed to control such factors because violation of the assumption can lead to both larger error terms (by inclusion of additional factors not accounted for in the analysis) and potentially misleading results if nuisance variables are confounded with levels of treatment.

Nonindependence of errors is possible also if an experiment is not properly controlled. For experimental IVs, unless all cases from all groups are tested simultaneously, errors within groups may be related if all cases within a group are tested together because cases tested together are subject to the same nuisance variables. Thus, a mean difference found between groups could be due to the nuisance variables unique

to the group rather than to the treatment unique to the group. If there are potentially important nuisance variables, cases should be tested individually or simultaneously for all levels, not in groups defined by levels. This assumption rarely is applicable for nonexperimental IVs because in the absence of random assignment to levels of treatment, there is no justification for causal inference to the treatments and the assumption of independence loses relevance.

If cases are entered into the data set in sequential order and the problem is analyzed through regression, the Durbin-Watson statistic is a formal test of contingencies of errors among scores close together in the sequence. This statistic assesses autocorrelation among residuals. If the errors (residuals) are independent, autocorrelation is zero. If you suspect violation of this assumption due to contingencies in the sequence of the cases, use of this analysis is appropriate. If violation is found, addition of another IV representing the source of the nonindependence (e.g., time: early, middle, and late in the study) might account for this source of variability in the data set.

For between-subjects designs, the assumption of additivity is that all the factors that contribute to variability in scores are identified and their effects are properly included in the model by summing those factors. Part of the assumption is that there are no other cross products or powers of factors present beyond the ones that are explicitly entered into the general linear model (GLM) as sources of variability. The GLM for a two-factor design (where, e.g., A is type of treatment and B is type of participant) is written as follows:

$$Y = \mu + \alpha + \beta + \alpha\beta + e \qquad (5.7)$$

The sources of variability in the DV (Y) identified in this equation are the grand mean (μ), type of treatment (α), type of participant (β), the interaction of type of treatment with type of participant ($\alpha\beta$), and error (e). Here the interaction term is explicitly part of the GLM and is automatically developed during the analysis. The assumption of additivity is violated if scores are not simple sums of their components, factors are not additive, or if cross products or powers of factors are present but not included in the analysis. In between-subjects designs, assessment of this assumption is mostly the logical problem of including all of the potential factors and their interactions in an analysis.

Independence of Errors, Additivity, Homogeneity of Covariance, and Sphericity in Within-Subjects Designs

In within-subjects ANOVA with more than two levels of the repeated measures, independence of errors and additivity are often untenable assumptions. In these designs, scores measured more than once for each participant are almost always correlated because of consistency in individual differences among cases. Although some kinds of individual differences are removed by calculating variance due to subjects in the analysis, there are likely still correlations among the repeated measures. When such correlations are present, the F test for the effect of treatment is too liberal, and the probability of Type I error is greater than the nominal value.

The relevant assumption of sphericity is violated when the variances of difference scores among pairs of levels of a repeated-measure IV are unequal. That is, the variance in difference scores between two adjacent levels (e.g., a_1 and a_2) is likely to differ from the variance in difference scores between, say, a_1 and a_5 when the IV is something like time because scores taken at adjacent periods in time are apt to be more like each other (lower difference scores) than are scores taken farther apart in time.

There is some confusion in the literature regarding assumptions of sphericity, additivity, and compound symmetry (the combination of the assumption of homogeneity of variance and the assumption of homogeneity of covariance). Often these are discussed as if they are more or less interchangeable. Table 5.1 describes differences among them in greater detail (and a yet more extended discussion is available in Tabachnick & Fidell, 2001a).

Additivity is the absence of a true treatment (A) by participant (S) interaction (i.e., AS); this serves as the error term in standard repeated-measures ANOVA and is supposed to represent only error. However, if treatment and participants truly interact (i.e., if some participants react differently than other participants to the different levels of treatment), this is a distorted error term because it includes a true source of variance (the interaction) as well as random error. Because the interaction means that different cases have different patterns of response to treatment, a better, more powerful, and generalizable design takes the interaction into account by blocking on cases that have similar patterns of response to the levels of IV. For example, if younger participants show one consistent pattern of response over the levels of the repeated measures IV and older participants show a different consistent pattern of response, age should be included as an additional between-subjects IV. This provides an explicit test of the former nonadditivity (treatment by age) and removes it from the error term.

The relevant assumption is of sphericity—that the variances of *difference* scores between *pairs* of levels of A are equal. This explains why the assumption does not apply when there are only two levels of A: There is only one variance of difference scores. With complete additivity, there is zero variance in difference scores, and because all zeros are equal, there is also sphericity. Thus, additivity is the most restrictive form of the assumption.

The next most restrictive assumption is compound symmetry: that both the variances in levels of A and correlations between pairs of levels of A are equal. In this situation the variances in difference scores are not zero (as they are with additivity), but they are equal. With either additivity or compound symmetry, then, the assumption of sphericity is met. However, it is possible to have sphericity without having either additivity or compound symmetry, as demonstrated in Myers and Well (1991).

If your data meet requirements for either additivity or compound symmetry, you can be confident about sphericity. However, if requirements for additivity or compound symmetry are not met, you may still have sphericity and have a noninflated F test of treatment. In practice, researchers rely on the results of a combination of tests for homogeneity of variance and the Mauchly (1940) test for sphericity.

SYSTAT ANOVA and GLM as well as SPSS GLM offer the Mauchly test of sphericity by default; SAS GLM and ANOVA produce it by request. In addition, all programs in the three packages that do within-subjects ANOVA display epsilon factors that are used to adjust degrees of freedom should the assumption of sphericity be violated. (MINITAB does not recognize within-subjects designs and thus offers no information about sphericity or correction for its violation.) If the Mauchly test is nonsignificant, if the adjustment based on epsilon (described below) does not alter the nominal probability of rejecting the null hypothesis, and if conditions for homogeneity of variance are met, the F test for routine within-subjects ANOVA is appropriate.

The Mauchly test, however, is sensitive to nonnormality of the DV as well as to heterogeneity of covariance. Therefore, it is sometimes significant when there is nonnormality rather than failure of sphericity. If the Mauchly test is

TABLE 5.1   Definitions of Sphericity, Compound Symmetry, and Additivity

Assumption	Definition
Sphericity	Variances of difference scores between all pairs of levels of A are equal.
Compound symmetry	
Homogeneity of variance	Variances in different levels of A are equal.
Homogeneity of covariance	Correlations between pairs of levels of A are equal, and variances of difference scores between all pairs of levels of A are equal.
Additivity	There is no true AS interaction; difference scores are equivalent for all cases. Variances of difference scores are zero.

significant, then, closer examination of the distribution of the DV is in order. If it is markedly skewed, the sphericity test should be repeated after a normalizing transformation of the DV. If the test is now nonsignificant, the problem with the data set is probably nonnormality rather than failure of sphericity. If the test is still significant, there is probably nonsphericity. The Mauchly test also has low power for small samples and is overly sensitive with very large samples. Thus, with large samples it is sometimes significant when departure from sphericity is slight. It is always worthwhile, then, to consider the magnitude of the epsilon factor, even when the test of sphericity is explicitly provided.

There are five options when the assumption of sphericity is not tenable: (a) use comparisons on the IV in question (usually trend analysis) instead of the omnibus test; (b) use an adjusted F test; (c) use a multivariate test of the within-subjects effects; (d) use a maximum likelihood procedure that lets you specify that the structure of the variance-covariance matrix is other than compound symmetry; or (e) use a multilevel modeling approach in which the multiple responses over time are the lowest level of analyses and are nested with subjects, the next higher level of analysis.

The first option—comparisons—takes advantage of the fact that sphericity is not required when there is only one df for the within-subjects IV. This option, in the form of trend analysis, is often a good one because questions about trends in the DV over time are usually the ones that researchers want answered anyway, and the assumption of sphericity is most likely to be violated when the IV is time related. Trend analysis asks, "Does the DV increase (or decrease) steadily over time?" "Does the DV first increase and then decrease (or the reverse)?" "Are both patterns present, superimposed on each other?" and "Are there other, more complicated, patterns in the data?" Before the sophisticated software was available for other options, trend analysis (or other comparisons) was preferred on strictly computational grounds. It is still preferred if the researcher has questions about the shape of the patterns in the DV over time. However, a disadvantage of trend analysis (or any set of comparisons) in within-subjects design is that each comparison develops its own error term. This reduces the number of df for error—and consequently the power—available for the test of the comparison.

The second option is to use a more stringent F test of the IV in question. Both Greenhouse-Geisser (1959) and Huynh-Feldt (1976) adjustments are offered by all three software packages that recognize within-subjects designs. Both compute an adjustment factor, epsilon (ε), that is used to reduce df associated with both numerator and denominator of the F test. Reducing df makes the F test more conservative. Both Greenhouse-Geisser and Huynh-Feldt compute an epsilon value, but Greenhouse-Geisser usually produces a stronger adjustment (larger value) than Huynh-Feldt. The more liberal Huynh-Feldt adjustment is usually preferred because it seems to produce results closer to nominal alpha levels.

The third option is to use the multivariate approach to repeated measures (a form of MANOVA called profile analysis of repeated measures) that does not require sphericity. Description of multivariate tests is available in Harris (2001), Stevens (2001), and Tabachnick and Fidell (2001b, chaps. 9 and 10), among others.

A fourth option is to use a maximum likelihood strategy instead of ANOVA, in which the variance-covariance matrix is user-specified or left unspecified. SAS MIXED, SYSTAT MIXED REGRESSION, and SPSS MIXED MODEL produce this type of analysis. The appropriate variance-covariance matrix structure for a time-related within-subjects IV, for example, is first-order autoregressive—AR(1)—in which correlations among pairs of levels decrease the farther apart they are in time.

The fifth option, multilevel modeling (MLM), circumvents the assumption of sphericity by viewing individuals as levels of an IV, with repeated measurements nested (and modeled) separately within each subject. An advantage of MLM over repeated-measures ANOVA is that there is no requirement for complete data over occasions (although it is assumed that data are missing completely at random); nor need there be equal intervals between measurement occasions for any units. That is, there is no need for equal numbers or intervals of measurements for each case. Another important advantage of MLM for repeated-measures data is the opportunity to test individual differences in growth curves (or any other pattern of responses over the repeated measure). Are the regression coefficients the same for all cases? Each case gets its own regression equation, and it is possible to evaluate whether individuals do indeed differ in pattern of responses over the repeated measure or in their mean response.

ANOVA programs in all three packages that recognize within-subjects designs give trend analyses, multivariate tests, and Huynh-Feldt adjustment by default, so the researcher can easily choose any of those three options. The fourth and fifth options, maximum likelihood analysis and multilevel, are included in special "mixed" programs.

Multivariate Assumptions

Multivariate analyses differ from univariate analyses by simultaneously considering two or more variables. For example, MANOVA is the multivariate extension of ANOVA where all participants provide scores for two or more DVs (e.g., speed and accuracy of response). Multiple regression is the extension of bivariate regression to predicting the DV from several (potentially correlated) IVs instead of from a single IV. Most multivariate analyses have all the assumptions of the univariate analysis plus others due to the relationships between multiple DVs or multiple IVs. For the most part, these assumptions are a logical extension of their univariate counterparts.

Multivariate Normality

Multivariate normality is the assumption that all variables and all linear combinations of those variables are normally distributed. When the assumption is met, the residuals of analysis are normally distributed and independent. The assumption of multivariate normality is not readily tested because it is impossible to test all linear combinations of variables for normality. Those tests that are available are overly sensitive.

The assumption of multivariate normality is partially checked by examining the normality of individual variables and the linearity and homoscedasticity of pairs of variables (discussed later) or by examining the residuals of analysis. The assumption is certainly violated, at least to some extent, if the individual variables are not normally distributed (or lack pair-wise linearity and homoscedasticity) or the residuals are not normally distributed. Figure 5.8 shows scatter plots of some idealized residuals from a regression analysis in which residuals for a group of IVs are plotted against predicted scores on a DV (Y'). When there is multivariate normality, the envelope of residuals is roughly the same width over the range of the predicted DV, and the relationship is linear. Similar residuals plots are available in many programs of all major statistical packages.

Transformations that improve univariate normality also facilitate multivariate normality. The analysis is likely to be enhanced when variables are transformed to more nearly normal, especially if the variables have different amounts and directions of skewness and kurtosis.

Linearity and Homoscedasticity Between Pairs of Variables

The assumption of multivariate linearity is that there are straight-line relationships between all pairs of variables. Multivariate analyses based on correlation capture only the linear relationships among variables, so nonlinear relationships among variables are ignored unless specifically added into the analysis by the researcher.

The assumption of homoscedasticity for ungrouped data is that the variability in scores for one continuous variable is

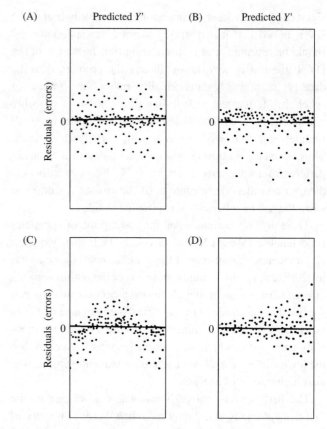

Figure 5.8 Plots of predicted values of the DV (Y') against residuals, showing (A) assumptions met, (B) failure of normality, (C) nonlinearity, and (D) heteroscedasticity. Reprinted with permission of Tabachnick and Fidell (2001b), *Using multivariate statistics* (Boston: Allyn and Bacon).

roughly the same at all values of another continuous variable. Failures of linearity and homoscedasticity of residuals are illustrated in Figure 5.8 (panels C and D).

Heteroscedasticity, the failure of homoscedasticity, occurs because one of the variables is not normally distributed (i.e., one variable is linearly related to some transformation of the other), because there is greater error of measurement of one variable at some levels, or because one of the variables is spread apart at some levels by its relationship to a third variable (measured in the design or not), as seen in Figure 5.9. An example of true heteroscedasticity is the relationship between age (X_1) and income (X_2), as depicted in Figure 5.9, panel B. People start out making about the same salaries, but with increasing age, people spread farther apart on income. In this example, income is positively skewed, and transformation of income is likely to improve the homoscedasticity of its relationship with age. An example of heteroscedasticity caused by greater error of measurement at some levels of an IV might be weight. People in the age range of 25 to 45 are probably more concerned about their weight than are people who are younger or older. Older

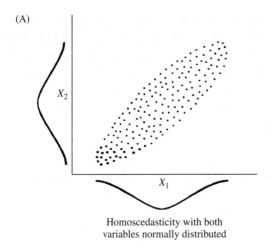

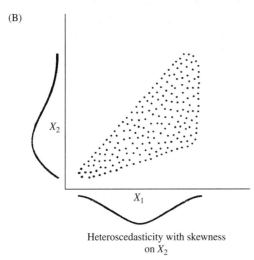

Figure 5.9 Bivariate scatter plots under conditions of homoscedasticity and heteroscedasticity. Reprinted with permission of Tabachnick and Fidell (2001b), *Using multivariate statistics* (Boston: Allyn and Bacon).

and younger people, then, are likely to give less reliable estimates of their weight, increasing the variance of weight scores at those ages.

Nonlinearity and heteroscedasticity are not fatal to an analysis of ungrouped data because at least the linear component of the relationship between the two variables is captured by the analysis. However, the analysis misses the other components of the relationship unless entered by the researcher.

Nonlinearity and heteroscedasticity are diagnosed either from residuals plots or from bivariate scatter plots. As seen in Figure 5.8 (for residuals) and Figure 5.9 (for bivariate scatter plots), when linearity and homoscedasticity are present, the envelope of points is roughly the same width over the range of values of both variables and the relationship is adequately represented by a straight line. Departures from linearity and homoscedasticity distort the envelope over certain ranges of one or both variables. Normalizing transformations improve

linearity and homoscedasticity of the relationship and, usually, the results of the overall analysis.

Sometimes, however, skewness is not just a statistical problem; rather, there is a true nonlinear relationship between two variables, as seen in Figure 5.10, panel A. Consider, for example, the number of symptoms and the dosage of drug. There are numerous symptoms when the dosage is low, only a few symptoms when the dosage is moderate, and lots of symptoms again when the dosage is high, reflecting a quadratic relationship. One alternative to capture this relationship is to use the square of the number of symptoms instead of the number of symptoms in the analysis. Another alternative is to recode dosage into two dummy variables (using linear and then quadratic trend coefficients) and then use the dummy variables in place of dosage in analysis. Alternatively, a nonlinear analytic strategy could be used, such as that available through SYSTAT NONLIN.

In panel B of Figure 5.10 two variables have both linear and quadratic relationships. One variable generally gets smaller (or larger) as the other gets larger (or smaller), but there is also a quadratic relationship. For instance, symptoms might drop off with increasing dosage, but only to a point; increasing dosage beyond the point does not result in further change of symptoms. In this case, the analysis improves if both the linear and quadratic relationships are included in the analysis.

Assessing linearity and homoscedasticity through bivariate scatter plots is difficult and tedious, especially with small samples and numerous variables, and more especially when

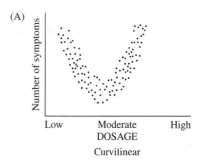

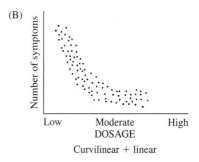

Figure 5.10 Curvilinear and curvilinear plus linear relationships. Reprinted with permission of Tabachnick and Fidell (2001b), *Using multivariate statistics* (Boston: Allyn and Bacon).

subjects are grouped and the search is conducted separately within each group. If there are only a few variables, screening all possible pairs is possible; but if there are numerous variables, you may want to use statistics on skewness to screen for only pairs that are likely to depart from linearity. Think, also, about pairs of variables that might have true nonlinearity and heteroscedasticity and examine them through bivariate scatter plots. Bivariate scatter plots are produced by PLOT procedures in SPSS, SYSTAT, MINITAB, and SAS, among other programs. You could also detect nonlinearity and heteroscedasticity through residuals (cf. Figure 5.8).

Absence of Multivariate Outliers in Variables and the Solution

A multivariate outlier is a case with a peculiar combination of scores on two or more variables. For example, a person who is 5 feet 2 inches tall is within normal range, as is a person who weighs 230 pounds, but a short person who is that heavy has an unusual combination of values. A multivariate outlier such as this may have more impact on the results of analysis than other cases in the sample. Consider, for example, the bivariate scatter plot of Figure 5.11, in which several regression lines, all with slightly different slopes, provide a good fit to the data points inside the swarm. But when the data point labeled A in the upper right-hand portion of the scatter plot is also considered, the regression coefficient that is computed is the one from among the several good alternatives that provides the best fit to the extreme case. The case is an outlier because it has much more impact on the value of the regression coefficient than do any of those inside the swarm.

One statistic used to identify multivariate outliers is *Mahalanobis distance,* the distance of a case from the centroid of the remaining cases where the centroid is the intersection of the means of all the variables in multidimensional space. In most data sets the cases form a swarm around the centroid in multivariate space. Each case is represented in the swarm by a

single point at its own peculiar combination of scores on all of the variables. A case that is a multivariate outlier lies outside the swarm, some distance from the other cases. Mahalanobis distance is one measure of that multivariate distance, and it can be evaluated for each case using the chi-square distribution with a very conservative probability estimate for a case being an outlier (e.g., $p < .001$).

Other statistical measures used to identify multivariate outliers are leverage, discrepancy, and influence. Although developed in the context of multiple regression, these measures are now available for some other analyses. Leverage is related to Mahalanobis distance (or variations of it in the hat matrix) and is variously called HATDIAG, RHAT, or h_{ii}. Although leverage is related to Mahalanobis distance, it is measured on a different scale so that significance tests based on a chi-square distribution do not apply. Lunneborg (1944) suggested that outliers be defined as cases with leverage greater than 2 (k/N), where k is the number of variables. Equation 5.8 shows the relationship between leverage B(h_{ii})B and Mahalanobis distance:

$$\text{Mahalanobis distance} = (N - 1)(h_{ii} - 1/N) \quad (5.8)$$

Or, as is sometimes more useful if you want to find a critical value for leverage at $\alpha = .001$ by translating the critical chi-square value for Mahalanobis distance:

$$h_{ii} = \frac{\text{Mahalanobis distance}}{N - 1} + \frac{1}{N} \quad (5.9)$$

Cases with high leverage are far from the others, but they can be far out along the same line as the other cases, or far away and off the line. *Discrepancy* measures the extent to which a case is in line with the others. Panel A of Figure 5.12 shows a case with high leverage and low discrepancy; panel B shows a case with high leverage and high discrepancy. Panel C is a case with low leverage and high discrepancy. In all of these figures, the outlier appears disconnected from the remaining scores.

Influence is a product of leverage and discrepancy (Fox, 1991). It assesses the change in regression coefficients when a case is deleted; cases with influence scores larger than 1.00 are suspected of being outliers. Measures of influence are variations of Cook's distance and are identified in output as Cook's distance, modified Cook's distance, DFFITS, and DBETAS. Fox (1991, pp. 29–30) described these statistics in more detail.

Leverage or Mahalanobis distance values are available as statistical methods of outlier detection in several statistical packages. However, some studies (e.g., Egan & Morgan, 1998; Hadi & Simonoff, 1993; Rousseeuw & van Zomeren, 1990) indicate that these methods are not perfectly reliable.

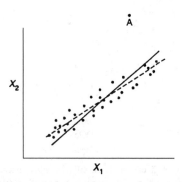

Figure 5.11 Bivariate scatter plot for showing impact of an outlier. Reprinted with permission of Tabachnick and Fidell (2001b), *Using multivariate statistics* (Boston: Allyn and Bacon).

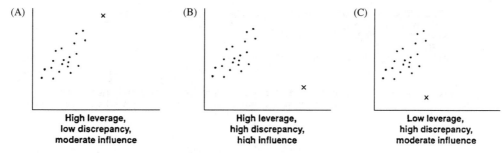

Figure 5.12   The relationships among leverage, discrepancy, and influence. Reprinted with permission of Tabachnick and Fidell (2001b), *Using multivariate statistics* (Boston: Allyn and Bacon).

Unfortunately, methods with greater reliability are currently unavailable in popular statistical packages. Therefore, multivariate outliers are detected through Mahalanobis distance, or one of its cousins, but cautiously.

Statistics assessing the distance for each case, in turn, from all other cases are available through SPSS REGRESSION (among others) when you specify some arbitrary variable (e.g., the case number) as DV and the set of variables of interest as IVs. Outliers are detected by evoking Mahalanobis, Cook's, or Leverage values through the Save command in the Regression menu (where these values are saved as separate columns in the data file and examined using

standard descriptive procedures) or by examining the 10 cases with largest Mahalanobis distance printed out by SPSS REGRESSION through the **RESIDUALS** subcommand. A number of other regression programs, including those in SAS and SYSTAT, provide a leverage value, h_{ii}, for each case that converts easily to Mahalanobis distance (Equation 5.8). These values are also saved to the data file and examined using standard statistical and graphical techniques.

Figure 5.13 shows syntax and output for identifying multivariate outliers for ungrouped data using the downloaded SCREEN.SAV data set (available from www.abacon.com/tabachnick). In this data set (described more fully in

```
REGRESSION
 /STATISTICS COLLIN
 /DEPENDENT subno
 /METHOD=ENTER ltimedrs attdrug atthouse income emplmnt mstatus race
 /RESIDUALS=OUTLIERS(MAHAL)  .
```

Outlier Statistics[a]

		Case Number	Statistic
Mahal. Distance	1	117	21.837
	2	193	20.650
	3	435	19.968
	4	99	18.499
	5	335	18.469
	6	292	17.518
	7	58	17.373
	8	71	17.172
	9	102	16.942
	10	196	16.723

a. Dependent Variable: Subject number

Figure 5.13 Syntax and Mahalanobis distance for ungrouped data produced by SPSS REGRESSION for the SCREEN.SAV data set.

```
MODEL EMPLMNT = TIMEDRS ATTDRUG ATTHOUSE MSTATUS RACE
DISCRIM
PRINT NONE / MAHAL
ESTIMATE
PRINT SHORT
```

```
                   Mahalanobis distance-square from group means and
                     Posterior probabilities for group membership
          Priors =          .500          .500
                         0             1

0
            2   -->    1.7   .45     1.3   .55
            3   -->    1.3   .44      .8   .56
            6   -->    1.1   .44      .6   .56
           10         5.4   .74     7.4   .26
           16        11.7   .55    12.1   .45
           18         5.9   .76     8.2   .24
           20   -->   5.4   .36     4.3   .64
           21   -->   3.7   .48     3.5   .52
           22         8.9   .58     9.6   .42
           23   -->   1.2   .44      .7   .56
           25   -->   2.7   .38     1.7   .62
           26   -->   7.0   .43     6.5   .57
           29         6.0   .78     8.5   .22
           30   -->   4.6   .42     3.9   .58
           31         4.1   .51     4.2   .49
           32         2.7   .50     2.7   .50
           33   -->   3.3   .41     2.6   .59
           36         4.9   .50     4.9   .50
           38        12.5   .60    13.3   .40
           39   -->   4.2   .39     3.3   .61
           40   -->  25.7   .30    23.9   .70
           41   -->   2.1   .40     1.3   .60
           42   -->   2.5   .39     1.6   .61
           44   -->   4.1   .47     3.9   .53
```

Figure 5.14 Syntax and Mahalanobis distance for grouped data produced by SYSTAT DISCRIM for the SCREEN.SAV data set.

Tabachnick & Fidell, 2001b), the TIMEDRS variable has been logarithmically transformed to become LTIMEDRS. SUBNO (case label) and is used as a dummy DV, convenient because multivariate outliers among IVs are unaffected by the DV. (The COLLIN instruction requests collinearity diagnostics, described in a later section.) Mahalanobis distance is evaluated as χ^2 at $p < .001$ with degrees of freedom equal to the number of variables, in this case five: LTIMEDRS, ATTDRUG, ATTHOUSE, MSTATUS, and RACE. Any case (such as cases 117 and 193) with a Mahalanobis distance greater than 20.515 (χ^2 value at $\alpha = .001$ with 5 df), then, is a probable multivariate outlier.

In grouped data, multivariate outliers are sought separately within each group. SYSTAT DISCRIM can be used to print out Mahalanobis distance for each case with grouped data. Use of other programs, including SPSS and SAS REGRESSION, requires separate runs for each group. However, different error terms are developed, and different cases may be identified as outliers when separate runs for each group are used instead of a single run for within-group outliers.

Figure 5.14 shows syntax and output using SYSTAT DISCRIM with the SCREEN.SAV data set. Mahalanobis distance may be shown either in output or added to the data file. Figure 5.14 shows part of the section that provides Mahalanobis distance for each case from the centroid of each group. The grouping variable, EMPLMNT, has two levels, 0 (paid workers) and 1 (housewives).

Mahalanobis distance is shown first for the paid workers (group 0) with case sequence number in the first column. The next two columns show Mahalanobis distance (and posterior probability) for those cases from their own group. The last two columns show Mahalanobis distance (and posterior probability) for those cases from the other group (group 1). Using $\chi^2 = 20.515$ ($\alpha = .001$ with 5 df) as the criterion, Figure 5.14 shows that case 40 (identified as SUBNO = 48 in the data set) is a multivariate outlier among paid workers.

Sometimes multivariate outliers hide behind other multivariate outliers (Rousseeuw & von Zomren, 1990). When the first few cases identified as outliers are deleted, the data set becomes more consistent so that other cases become extreme.

Robust approaches to this problem have been proposed (e.g., Egan & Morgan, 1998; Hadi & Simonoff, 1993; Rousseeuw & von Zomren, 1990), but these are not yet implemented in popular software packages. These methods can be approximated by screening for multivariate outliers two or more times, each time dealing with cases identified as outliers on the previous run, until finally no new outliers are identified. But if there seem to be too many outliers, do a trial analysis with and without later-identified outliers to see if they are truly changing results. If not, retain them in the analysis. (This is also a worthwhile strategy to apply for early-identified outliers if there seem to be too many of them.)

Once multivariate outliers are identified, you need to discover why the cases are extreme. (You already know why univariate outliers are extreme.) It is important to identify the variables on which the cases are deviant to help you decide whether the case is properly part of your sample and to provide an indication of the kinds of cases to which your results do not generalize. If there are only a few multivariate outliers, it is reasonable to examine them one at a time through multiple regression in which a dichotomous DV is formed on the basis of the outlying case. If there are several outliers, you may want to examine them as a group to see if there are any variables that consistently separate the group of outliers from the rest of the cases. These procedures are illustrated in Tabachnick and Fidell (2001b).

First, identify potential univariate outliers and then begin the search for multivariate outliers. The solutions that eliminate univariate outliers also tend to reduce the number of multivariate outliers, but sometimes not completely because the problem with a true multivariate outlier is the combination of scores on two or more variables, not the score on any one variable. To deal with multivariate outliers, first consider the possibility that one variable is implicated for many of them. If so, and the variable is highly correlated with others in a multivariate design or is not critical to the analysis, deletion of it is a good alternative. Otherwise, multivariate outliers are usually deleted.

After the analysis is complete, look for outliers in the solution as a hint to the kinds of cases for which the solution does not work very well. Outliers in the solution for ungrouped data are found through examination of residuals. Outliers in the solution for grouped data are available as Mahalanobis distance through SPSS DISCRIMINANT. This program produces Mahalanobis distance based on discriminant function scores (with df = number of discriminant functions) rather than raw scores and so provides information about outliers in the solution. The lists of outliers produced by SYSTAT DISCRIM are not the same because the program identifies outliers among the original variables. Or you can visually examine residuals produced by running each group separately through any multiple regression program.

Absence of Collinearity and Singularity

Problems with collinearity and singularity occur when two or more variables are too highly or perfectly correlated. With collinearity, the variables are very highly correlated—for example, scores on the Wechsler Adult Intelligence Scale (WAIS) and scores on the Stanford-Binet Intelligence Scale. With singularity, the variables are redundant because one variable is a combination of two or more other variables (e.g., total WAIS score is a combination of subscale scores). In statistical terms, a singular correlation matrix is not of full rank because there are not as many variables as columns.

Collinearity and singularity cause both logical and statistical problems. The logical problem is that redundant variables are not needed in the same analysis unless you are analyzing structure (through factor analysis, principal components analysis, or structural equation modeling), dealing with repeated measures of the same variable, or dealing with interactions or powers of variables along with the original variables in the same analysis (Aiken & West, 1991). Before including two variables with a bivariate correlation of, say, .70 or more in the same analysis, consider omitting one of the variables or creating a composite score from the correlated variables.

Statistical problems with a singular correlation matrix occur because matrix inversion (the equivalent of division in scalar algebra) is impossible and the determinant is zero. Therefore, runs for an analysis requiring matrix inversion are aborted until the redundant variable is eliminated. With collinearity, the determinant is not exactly zero, but it is zero to several decimal places. Division by a near-zero determinant produces very large and unstable numbers in the inverted matrix that fluctuate considerably with only minor changes (e.g., in the second or third decimal place) in the sizes of correlations. The portions of a multivariate solution that follow this matrix inversion are unstable. In regression, for instance, standard error terms for the regression coefficients get so large that none of the coefficients is significant (Berry, 1993). When r is .9 or above, the precision of estimation of weighting coefficients is halved (Fox, 1991).

Statistical problems are also present when there is collinearity caused by interactions among continuous variables or variables taken to powers. The remedy is to center those continuous variables by replacing raw scores for those variables with scores that are deviations from their means (see Aiken & West, 1991, for further discussion of centering).

Collinearity Diagnostics[a]

Model	Dimension	Eigenvalue	Condition Index	(Constant)	Attitudes toward medication	Attitudes toward housework	Whether currently married	RACE	TIMEDRS
					Variance Proportions				
1	1	5.656	1.000	.00	.00	.00	.00	.00	.01
	2	.210	5.193	.00	.00	.00	.01	.02	.92
	3	.026E-02	9.688	.00	.00	.01	.29	.66	.01
	4	.271E-02	11.508	.00	.03	.29	.46	.16	.06
	5	.476E-02	15.113	.00	.53	.41	.06	.04	.00
	6	.785E-03	28.872	.99	.43	.29	.18	.12	.00

a. Dependent Variable: Subject number

Figure 5.15   Collinearity diagnostics produced by SPSS REGRESSION for the SCREEN.SAV data set. Syntax in Figure 5.13.

Both bivariate and multiple correlations can be collinear or singular. A bivariate collinear relationship has a correlation of .90 or above and is resolved by deletion of one of the two variables. With a multivariate collinear relationship, diagnosis is more difficult because the collinearity is not necessarily apparent through examination of bivariate correlations. Instead, multivariate statistics are needed, such as squared multiple correlations (SMCs, in which each variable, in turn, serves as the DV with the others as IVs), tolerances (1 − SMC), or collinearity diagnostics. SMCs are available through factor analysis and regression programs in statistical software packages. However, SMCs are *not* evaluated separately for each group if you are analyzing grouped data. PRELIS provides SMCs for structural equation modeling.

Most modern programs automatically protect against singularity. Screening for collinearity that causes statistical instability is also routine with most programs because they have tolerance criteria for inclusion of variables. If the tolerance is too low, the variable does not enter the analysis. Default tolerance levels range between .01 and .0001, so SMCs are .99 to .9999 before variables are excluded. You may wish to take control of this process, however, by adjusting the tolerance level (an option with many programs) or deciding yourself which variables to delete instead of letting the program make the decision on purely statistical grounds.

SAS, SYSTAT, and SPSS have recently incorporated *collinearity diagnostics* proposed by Belsley, Kuh, and Welsch (1980) in which both a condition index and variance proportions associated with each standardized variable are produced for each root (dimension, factor, principal component). Variables with large variance proportions are those with problems.

Condition index is a measure of tightness or dependency of one variable on the others. The condition index is monotonic with SMC, but not linear with it. A high condition index is associated with variance inflation in the standard error of a parameter estimate for a variable. As the standard error increases, parameter estimation becomes more and more uncertain. Each root (dimension) accounts for some proportion of the variance of each parameter estimated. There is a collinearity problem when a root with a high condition index contributes strongly (has a high variance proportion) to the variance of two or more variables. Criteria for collinearity suggested by Belsely et al. (1980) are a condition index greater than 30 for a given root coupled with at least two variance proportions for individual variables greater than 0.50.

Figure 5.15 shows output of SPSS REGRESSION for assessing collinearity for the SCREEN.SAV data set. Although the last dimension (root) has a Condition Index that approaches 30, no variable (column) has more than one Variance Proportion greater than .50. Therefore, no collinearity is evident.

Homogeneity of Variance, Homoscedasticity, and Homogeneity of Variance/Covariance Matrices in Grouped Designs

The assumption of homoscedasticity for ungrouped data becomes the assumption of homogeneity of variance for grouped data where the variability in a DV is expected to be about the same at all levels of an IV. As previously discussed, heterogeneity of variance affects the robustness of ANOVA and ANOVA-like analyses.

In multivariate ANOVA-like analyses, homogeneity of variance becomes homogeneity of variance-covariance matrices because more than one DV is measured each time. Within each cell of the design, there is a matrix of variances and covariances for the several DVs. Homogeneity of variance is present if each of the DVs has an F_{max} value

(Equation 5.6) of less than 10 across the cells of the design (when there is nearly equal *n*). Further, within each cell, the DVs covary (are correlated with each other) to varying extents, and the pattern of those correlations should be about the same across the cells. There is homogeneity of the variance/covariance matrices, then, when the DVs have about the same variability and are related to each other to similar extents in all cells.

Box's *M* is a formal test of homogeneity of variance/ covariance matrices, but it is too strict with the large sample sizes and the roughly equal *n* often associated with multivariate analyses. The researcher can, with confidence, assume homogeneity of variance/covariance matrices if Box's *M* is not significant, if sample sizes are equal, or if larger sample sizes are associated with larger variances. But Monte Carlo studies by Hakstian, Roed, and Lind (1979) show that robustness is not guaranteed if Box's *M* is significant, if there is substantial unequal *n*, and if the larger variances are associated with smaller samples. The greater the discrepancy in cell sample sizes is, the greater the potential Type I error rate. One remedy is to use an alternative criterion for testing the multivariate significance of differences among group means such as Pillai's criterion instead of the more common Wilk's lambda (Olson, 1979). Another is to equalize sample sizes by random deletion of cases if power can be maintained at reasonable levels.

Normalizing Transformations for Minimizing Violation of Assumptions

Transformations are often undertaken because a variable violates normality, has outliers, has heterogeneity of variance, or has heteroscedasticity and nonlinearity in its relationship with other variables. Transformation is a sensible practice when variables are assessed on scales that are more or less arbitrary anyway, as are many scales in psychology. However, interpretation is of the transformed variable and may be bothersome for scores measured on well-known scales or scales with carefully developed psychometric properties.

If you decide to transform, check that the distribution is improved by transformation. If a variable is only moderately positively skewed, for instance, a square root transformation may make the variable moderately negatively skewed so nothing is gained. Often, you need to try first one transformation and then another until you find the transformation that reduces skewness and kurtosis values to near zero, has the fewest outliers, or produces homogeneity of variance and linearity.

The type of transformation necessary to improve the fit to assumptions also conveys substantive information. For ex-

ample, a transformation that makes an IV-DV relationship linear also conveys information about how much the DV is changing with the same-sized changes in the IV. That is, the DV may grow exponentially with linear changes in the IV, the DV may grow linearly with exponential changes in the IV, or there may be a linear relationship between the IV-DV exponents. If the IV-DV relationship is linear, DV scores go from 1 to 2 to 3 as the IV goes from 1 to 2 to 3; if the relationship is a square root, the DV scores go from 1 to 4 to 9 as the IV goes from 1 to 3; and if the relationship is $\log_{10}$, the DV scores go from 10 to 100 to 1,000.

The log is probably the easiest transformation to understand because in the simplest, most familiar situation ($\log_{10}$ and, e.g., a DV score of 10 associated with a score of 1 on the IV), a change in the IV from 1 to 2 changes the DV from 10 to 100, whereas a change in the IV from 2 to 3 changes the DV from 100 to 1,000. Two therapy sessions are 10 times more effective than one, and three therapy sessions are 100 times more effective than one (and three therapy sessions are 10 times more effective than two). That is, each change of one unit in the IV increases the DV by a factor of 10. If $\log_2$ is used instead, a one-unit change on the IV changes the DV by a factor of 2 (i.e., doubles it).

With square root transformations, the change is not as rapid as with logs. For example, a change in the IV from 1 to 2 changes the DV from 3.16 (square root of 10) to 10 (square root of 100) while a change from 2 to 3 changes the DV from 10 to 31.6 (square root of 1,000). That is, three therapy sessions are 10 times more effective than one (instead of 100 times more effective than one), and two sessions are about 3 times as effective as one.

Figure 5.16 presents distributions of single variables that diverge from normality to different degrees, together with the transformations that are likely to render them normal. If the distribution differs moderately from normal, a square root transformation is tried first. If the distribution differs substantially, a log transformation is tried. If the distribution differs severely, the inverse is tried; or if preserving order is desired, the negative of the inverse is used (Tukey, 1977). According to Bradley (1982), the inverse is the best of several alternatives for J-shaped distributions, but even it may not render the distribution acceptably normal. Finally, if the departure from normality is severe and no transformation seems to help, you may want to try dichotomizing the variable.

The direction of the deviation is also considered. When distributions have negative skewness, the best strategy is to reflect the variable and then apply the appropriate transformation for positive skewness. To reflect a variable, find the largest score in the distribution and add 1 to it to form a

```
EXAMINE
VARIABLES=var_a var_d
/PLOT BOXPLOT
/COMPARE GROUP
/STATISTICS DESCRIPTIVES EXTREME
/CINTERVAL 95
/MISSING LISTWISE
/NOTOTAL.
```

Explore

Descriptives

			Statistic	Std. Error
VAR_A	Mean		51.1600	1.3399
	95% Confidence Interval for Mean	Lower Bound	48.4673	
		Upper Bound	53.8527	
	5% Trimmed Mean		51.1000	
	Median		50.0000	
	Variance		89.770	
	Std. Deviation		9.4747	
	Minimum		32.00	
	Maximum		72.00	
	Range		40.00	
	Interquartile Range		14.2500	
	Skewness		.220	.337
	Kurtosis		-.650	.662
VAR_D	Mean		50.5200	1.3727
	95% Confidence Interval for Mean	Lower Bound	47.7615	
		Upper Bound	53.2785	
	5% Trimmed Mean		51.1111	
	Median		50.0000	
	Variance		94.214	
	Std. Deviation		9.7064	
	Minimum		13.00	
	Maximum		69.00	
	Range		56.00	
	Interquartile Range		10.5000	
	Skewness		-1.218	.337
	Kurtosis		3.498	.662

Figure 5.16   Shape of distributions and common transformations to produce normality. Reprinted with permission of Tabachnick and Fidell (2001b), *Using multivariate statistics* (Boston: Allyn and Bacon).

constant that is larger than any score in the distribution. Then create a new variable by subtracting each score from the constant. In this way, a variable with negative skewness is converted to one with positive skewness prior to transformation. When you interpret a reflected variable, be sure to reverse the direction of the interpretation as well. For instance, if big numbers meant good things prior to reflecting the variable, big numbers mean bad things afterward.

Instructions for transforming variables in four software packages are given in Table 5.2. Notice that a constant is added if the distribution contains zero or negative numbers. The constant (to bring the smallest value to at least 1) is added to each score to avoid taking the log, square root, or inverse of zero.

This section on transformations merely scratches the surface of the topic about which a great deal more is known. The

TABLE 5.2   Original Distributions and Common Transformations to Produce Normality

	MINITAB LET[a]	SPSS COMPUTE	SAS DATA	SYSTAT DATA TRANSFORM
Moderate positive skewness	LET NEWX = SQRT(X).	NEWX = SQRT(X)	NEWX = SQRT(X);	LET NEWX = SQR(X)
Substantial positive skewness	LET NEWX = LOGTEN(X).	NEWX = LG10(X)	NEWX = LOG10(X);	LET NEWX = L10(X)
with zero	LET NEWX = LOGTEN($X + C$).	NEWX = LG10($X + C$)	NEWX = LOG10($X + C$);	LET NEWX = L10($X + C$)
Severe positive skewness, L-shaped	LET NEWX = 1/X.	NEWX = 1/X	NEWX = 1/X ;	LET NEWX = 1/X
with zero	LET NEWX = 1/($X + C$).	NEWX = 1/($X + C$)	NEWX = 1/($X + C$);	LET NEWX = 1/($X + C$)
Moderate negative skewness	LET NEWX = SQRT($K - X$).	NEWX = SQRT($K - X$)	NEWX = SQRT($K - X$);	LET NEWX = SQR($K - X$)
Substantial negative skewness	LET NEWX = LOG($K - X$).	NEWX = LG10($K - X$)	NEWX = LOG10($K - X$);	LET NEWX = L10($K - X$)
Severe negative skewness, J-shaped	LET NEWX = 1/($K - X$).	NEWX = 1/($K - X$)	NEWX = 1/($K - X$);	LET NEWX = 1/($K - X$)

[a] *Calc* provides transforms in the MINITAB Windows menu system.

Note. C = a constant added to each score so that the smallest score is 1. K = a constant from which each score is subtracted to that the smallest score is 1; usually equal to the largest score +1.

Source: Reprinted with permission of Tabachnick and Fidell (2001b), *Using multivariate statistics* (Boston: Allyn and Bacon).

interested reader is referred to Emerson (1991) or the classic Box and Cox (1964) for a more flexible and challenging approach to the problem of transformation.

DISCRETE DATA AND LOG-LINEAR ANALYSES

Several analytic techniques are available for discrete variables, or data sets with a combination of discrete and continuous variables. The most familiar example is chi-square, an inferential test of the relationship between two discrete variables (where one of them may be considered a DV). An extension is multiway frequency analysis, which provides a test of relationships in a data set with several discrete variables; sometimes the researcher is simply interested in which of them are related to which others, and sometimes the researcher seeks to examine whether a discrete DV is related to several other discrete IVs. Logistic regression is available to examine whether a discrete (or ordinal) DV is related to several other IVs, both discrete and continuous.

Multiway frequency analysis and logistic regression develop a linear equation that weights the IVs according to their relationship with the discrete DV and with each other, similar to the general linear model of Equation 5.7. In Equation 5.10, Y_i^1 is the predicted value on the DV for the ith case, A is the intercept (the value of Y when all the X values are zero), the Xs represent the various IVs (of which there are k), and the Bs are the coefficients assigned to each of the IVs during regression:

$$Y_i^1 N = A + B_1 X_1 + B_2 X_2 + \cdots + B_k X_k \quad (5.10)$$

Equation 5.10 is the familiar equation for multiple regression, but in analyses for discrete variables the equation is called the *logit* and is found in the exponents of the equation

for predicting the DV ($\hat{Y}_i$). In Equation 5.11, $\hat{Y}_i$ is the estimated probability that the ith case is in one of the cells. That is, there is a linear relationship among the IVs but it is in the logit of the DV, and the goal of the equation is to predict the frequencies (or probabilities) of cases falling into various combinations of levels of variables rather than predicting the DV score itself for each case.

$$\hat{Y}_i = \frac{e^{A+B_1 X_1+B_2 X_2+\cdots+B_k X_k}}{1 + e^{A+B_1 X_1+B_2 X_2+\cdots+B_k X_k}} \quad (5.11)$$

These analyses have many fewer assumptions than the corresponding analyses for continuous variables and are therefore sometimes preferred. In this context, recall that you always have the option of rescaling a poorly behaved continuous variable into a discrete one.

Adequacy of Expected Frequencies

The fit between observed and expected frequencies is an empirical question in tests of association among discrete variables. Sample cell sizes are observed frequencies; statistical tests compare them with expected frequencies derived from some hypothesis, such as independence between variables. The requirement in chi-square and multiway frequency analysis and for discrete variables in logistic regression is that expected frequencies are large enough. Two conditions produce expected frequencies that are too small: a small sample in conjunction with too many variables with too many levels, and rare events.

When events are rare, the marginal frequencies are not evenly distributed among the various levels of the variables. A cell from a low-probability row or a low-probability column will have a very low expected frequency. One way to avoid low expected frequencies is to attempt to determine the levels that are likely to be rare in advance of data collection and then sample until obtained frequencies on the margins are adequate.

For chi-square and multiway frequency analysis, examine expected cell frequencies for all two-way relationships to ensure that all are greater than 1 and that no more than 20% are less than 5. Except in some applications of chi-square, inadequate expected frequencies do not lead to increased Type I error but rather to reduction in power, which can become notable as expected frequencies for two-way associations drop below 5 in some cells (Milligan, 1980).

If low expected frequencies are encountered, several choices are available. First, you can simply choose to accept reduced power. Second, you can collapse categories for variables with more than two levels. For example, you could collapse the categories "three" and "four or more" into one category of "three or more." The categories you collapse should be carefully considered because it is quite possible that associations will disappear as a result. Because this is equivalent to a complete reduction in power for testing those associations, nothing has been gained.

Finally, you can delete variables to reduce the number of cells as long as care is taken to delete only variables that are not associated with the remaining variables. For example, in a table with three discrete variables you might consider deleting a variable if there is no three-way association and if at least one of the two-way associations with the variable is nonsignificant (Milligan, 1980). The common practice of adding a constant to each cell is not recommended because it has the effect of further reducing power. Its purpose is to stabilize Type I error rate, but as noted earlier, that is generally not the problem, and other remedies are available when it is. Some of the programs for multiway frequency analysis, such as SPSS LOGLINEAR and HILOGLINEAR, add the constant by default anyway under circumstances that do not affect the outcome of the analysis.

In logistic regression, when a goodness-of-fit inferential test is planned to compare observed with expected frequencies in cells formed by combinations of discrete variables, the analysis also has little power if expected frequencies are too small. When inference is desired, the guidelines for chi-square and multiway frequency analysis are applicable together with the remedies for low expected frequencies. An additional remedy in logistic regression is use of a goodness-of-fit criterion that is not based on observed versus expected frequencies, as discussed in Hosmer and Lemeshow (1989) and Tabachnick and Fidell (2001b, Sections 7.3.2.2, 12.6.1.1).

Absence of Collinearity

Like their counterparts for continuous variables, these analyses are degraded by inclusion of collinear variables. Signals of the presence of collinearity include failure of the analysis to converge or extremely large estimates of standard error for one or more parameters. The solution is to identify and eliminate one or more redundant variables from the analysis.

Independence of Errors

In most circumstances, these analyses are used only for between-subjects designs in which the frequency of cases in each cell is independent of the frequencies in all other cells. If the same case contributes a hash mark to more than one cell, those cells are not independent. Verify that the total N for the analysis is equal to the number of cases before proceeding.

McNemar's test provides chi-square analysis for some types of repeated measures when each case is in a particular combination of "yes-no" cells. For example, in a 2×2 design, a person attends karate classes but does not take piano lessons (yes on karate, no on piano), does neither (no on both), does both (yes on both), or takes piano lessons but not karate (no on karate, yes on piano). Independence of errors is preserved because each case is in only one of four cells, despite having "scores" on both karate and piano.

Absence of Outliers in the Solution

Multiway frequency analysis and logistic regression often proceed by developing a model that provides the tightest fit between the observed frequencies and the frequencies expected from the model in the many cells of the design. Along the way, some variables are deleted because they do not contribute to the fit. After the best model is chosen, there are sometimes still substantial differences between observed frequencies and the expected frequencies for some cells. If the differences are large enough, there may be no model that adequately fits the data until levels of some variables are redefined or new variables are added. Examination of the residuals of the analysis reveals the adequacy of the analysis, as discussed in Hosmer and Lemeshow (1989) and Tabachnick and Fidell (2001b, Sections 7.4.3.1, 7.7.2.3, 12.4.4).

SPECIAL ASSUMPTIONS FOR SPECIAL ANALYSES

ANCOVA: Homogeneity of Regression

Analysis of covariance (ANCOVA) and multivariate analysis of covariance (MANCOVA) are ANOVA-like analyses that include covariates as well as the usual IVs and DVs. Covariates (CVs) are variables known to be related to the DV that increase the variability in DV scores. When CVs are assessed and their effects on the DV accounted for in the analysis, the error term for the test of the effect of the IV is usually smaller because there is less spread in the DV; this increases the power of the analysis. In some disciplines (and software programs), *all* continuous predictors are called covariates. That is, continuous IVs are labeled covariates.

Covariates are usually continuous variables. One or several of them may be in an analysis, and they may be measured once or more than once during the course of a study. Use of CVs is not controversial in experimental research when care is taken to keep assessment of the CV uncontaminated by the effects of the IV, but their use is problematic in other research settings. These issues and others are discussed in Myers and Well (1991), Tabachnick and Fidell (2001a, 2001b), and elsewhere.

The special assumption of homogeneity of regression is that the slope of the relationship between the DV and the CVs is the same for all cells of a design. Put another way, the assumption is that the DV and the CV have the same relationship in all levels of the IV—that there is no CV by IV interaction. Both homogeneity and heterogeneity of regression are illustrated in Figure 5.17. During analysis, slope is computed for every cell of the design and then averaged to provide the value used for overall adjustment of DV scores. It is assumed that the slopes in different cells will differ slightly due to chance, but they are really all estimates of the same population value. If the null hypothesis of equality among slopes is rejected, the analysis of covariance is inappropriate, and an alternative strategy, such as blocking on the CV to turn it into an additional IV, is required.

The most straightforward programs for testing homogeneity of regression in between-subjects designs are SYSTAT GLM or ANOVA and SPSS MANOVA. The general strategy involves inclusion of the IV by CV interaction in a preliminary ANCOVA run; homogeneity of regression is signaled by a nonsignificant interaction. Syntax for accomplishing this test is available in the SYSTAT manual (SPSS Inc., 2000, p. I-463) and in the SPSS Base manual (SPSS Inc., 1999, pp. 159–160); syntax for the test through SAS GLM and SPSS MANOVA is available in Tabachnick and Fidell (2001a). Tabachnick and Fidell also illustrated syntax for simultaneously testing homogeneity of regression for multiple, pooled CVs and syntax for testing homogeneity of regression for covariates measured repeatedly, both through the SPSS MANOVA program.

Logistic Regression: Linearity in the Logit

Logistic regression investigates the predictability of group membership from a set of both discrete and continuous predictors. Although there is no assumption that the continuous predictors themselves have pair-wise linear relationships, there is the assumption that each of the continuous predictors has a linear relationship with the logit. (Recall that the logit is the GLM prediction of Equation 5.10 in the exponent of the solution.) Using the Box-Tidell approach (Hosmer & Lemeshow, 1989), the assumption is tested by forming interactions between each continuous variable and its own natural logarithm and adding the interaction terms to the equation. There is linearity in the logit when these interaction terms are not significant.

Significance for one or more of the interaction terms leads to transformation of the continuous variable. A test of this assumption through SYSTAT DATA and LOGIT is provided in Tabachnick and Fidell (2001b).

Survival Analysis

Survival analysis is a set of techniques for analyzing the length of time until something happens and for determining if that time differs for different groups or for groups offered different treatments. An approach similar to logistic regression is used when assessing group differences. In medical settings survival analysis is used to determine the time course of

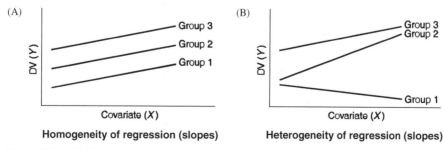

Figure 5.17   DV-CV regression lines for three groups plotted on the same coordinates for conditions of (A) homogeneity and (B) heterogeneity of regression. Reprinted with permission of Tabachnick and Fidell (2001b), *Using multivariate statistics* (Boston: Allyn and Bacon).

various medical conditions and whether different modes of treatment produce changes in that time course. In industry the same analysis is called failure analysis and is used to determine time until failure of a specific part and whether parts manufactured differently have different rates of failure.

An advantage of survival analysis over traditional logistic regression is that the analysis can handle censored cases. These are cases for which the time is not known at the conclusion of the study either because the case is still apparently well (or the part is still functioning) or the case has been lost to follow-up. However, there are special assumptions related to such cases, as well as other assumptions particular to the analysis.

Differences Between Withdrawn and Remaining Cases

The first assumption is that the cases that have been lost to follow-up do not differ from the cases with complete data at the conclusion of the study. If there are systematic differences between the two types of cases, you have a missing data problem with nonrandom loss of cases. If the study was initially an experiment with random assignment to treatment conditions, the advantages of random assignment have been lost due to nonrandom loss of cases.

Change in Survival Conditions Over Time

Because these data are collected over time, it is assumed that the factors that influence survival at the beginning of the study are the same as the factors that influence survival at the end of the study. Put another way, it is the assumption that the conditions have not changed from the beginning to the end of the study. If, for example, a new medical treatment is offered to patients during the course of the study and that treatment influences survival, the assumption is violated.

Proportionality of Hazards

If the Cox proportional-hazards model, one of the more popular models, is used to evaluate the effects of various predictors on survival, there is the assumption that the shape of the survival function over time is the same for all cases and for all groups. That is, the time until failures begin to appear may differ from one group to another, but once failures begin to appear, they proceed at the same rate for all groups. This assumption is violated when there is interaction between time and group. To test the assumption, a time variable is constructed and its interaction with groups tested. A test of the assumption through SAS PHREG is demonstrated in Tabachnick and Fidell (2001b).

Time Series: Analysis of Residuals

Time series analysis is used when numerous observations (50 or more) are made of the same event over time. The event can be the behavior of a single case or aggregated behavior of numerous cases. One goal is to find patterns, if any, in the behavior of the cases over time. A second goal is to determine if an intervention (naturally occurring or an experimental treatment) changes the pattern over time. A third goal may be to forecast the future pattern of events.

The overall pattern of scores over time is decomposed into several different elements. One element is random shocks, conceptually similar to the random errors in other analyses. A second element is overall trends (linear, quadratic) in the scores over time; is the average generally increasing (or decreasing) over time? A third element is potential lingering effects of earlier scores. A fourth element is potential lingering effects of earlier shocks. One popular time series model is ARIMA (auto-regressive, integrated, moving-average). The auto-regressive part represents the lingering effects of previous scores. The integrated part represents trends in the data; the moving-average part represents lingering effects of previous shocks.

Patterns in the data (which may be completely random or any combination of auto-regressive, integrated, or moving-average) produce different patterns of autocorrelations (and partial autocorrelations) among the scores. That is, scores at adjacent time periods correlate differently with each other depending on the types of contingencies present. The goal is to provide an equation that mimics the patterns in the data and reduces the residuals to random error. When the assumptions are met, the residuals have a normal distribution, with homogeneous variance and zero mean over time, and no outliers. There are also no lingering autocorrelations (or partial autocorrelations) among the residuals remaining to be analyzed. Tests of the assumptions and other issues in time series analysis are discussed in McCleary and Hay (1980) and Tabachnick and Fidell (2001b).

REFERENCES

Aiken, L. S., & West, S. G. (1991). *Multiple regression: Testing and interpreting interactions.* Newbury Park, CA: Sage.

Belsley, D. A., Kuh, E., & Welsch, R. E. (1980). *Regression diagnostics: Identifying influential data and sources of collinearity.* New York: Wiley.

Berry, W. D. (1993). *Understanding regression assumptions.* Newbury Park, CA: Sage.

Box, G. E. P., & Cox, D. R. (1964). An analysis of transformations. *Journal of the Royal Statistical Society, Series B, 26,* 211–243.

Bradley, J. V. (1982). The insidious L-shaped distribution. *Bulletin of the Psychonomic Society, 20*(2), 85–88.

Cleveland, W. S. (1993). *The elements of graphing data* (2nd ed.). Murray Hill, NJ: AT&T Bell Laboratories.

Egan, W. J., & Morgan, S. L. (1998). Outlier detection in multivariate analytical chemical data. *Analytical Chemistry, 70,* 2372–2379.

Emerson, J. D. (1991). Introduction to transformation. In D. C. Hoaglin, F. Mosteller, & J. W. Tukey (Eds.), *Fundamentals of exploratory analysis of variance* (pp. 365–400). New York: Wiley.

Fox, J. (1991). *Regression diagnostics.* Newbury Park, CA: Sage.

Greenhouse, S. W., & Geisser, W. (1959). On methods in the analysis of profile data. *Psychometrika, 24,* 95–112.

Hadi, A. S., & Simonoff, J. W. (1993). Procedures for the identification of multiple outliers in linear models. *Journal of the American Statistical Association, 88,* 1264–1272.

Hakstian, A. R., Roed, J. C., & Lind, J. C. (1979). Two-sample *T*5 procedure and the assumption of homogeneous covariance matrices. *Psychological Bulletin, 86,* 1255–1263.

Harris, R. J. (2001). *A primer of multivariate statistics* (3rd ed.). Mahwah, NJ: Erlbaum.

Hosmer, D. W., & Lemeshow, S. (1989). *Applied logistic regression.* New York: Wiley.

Huynh, H., & Feldt, L. S. (1976). Estimation of the Box correction for degrees of freedom from sample data in the randomized block and split-plot designs. *Journal of Educational Statistics, 1,* 69–82.

Keppel, G. (1991). *Design and analysis: A researcher's handbook* (3rd ed.). Englewood Cliffs, NJ: Prentice-Hall.

Levene, H. (1960). Robust tests for equality of variance. In I. Olkin (Ed.), *Contributions to probability and statistics.* Palo Alto, CA: Stanford University Press.

Lunneborg, C. E. (1944). *Modeling Experimental and Observational Data.* Belmont, CA: Durbury Press.

Mauchly, J. W. (1940). Significance test for sphericity of a normal *n*-variate distribution. *Annals of Mathematical Statistics, 11,* 204–209.

McCleary, R., & Hay, R. A. (1980). Applied time series analysis for the social sciences. Beverly Hills, CA: Sage.

Milligan, G. W. (1980). Factors that affect Type I and Type II error rates in the analysis of multidimensional contingency tables. *Psychological Bulletin, 87,* 238–244.

Milligan, G. W., Wong, D. S., & Thompson, P. A. (1987). Robustness properties of nonorthogonal analysis of variance. *Psychological Bulletin, 101*(3), 464–470.

Myers, J. L., & Well, A. D. (1991). *Research design and statistical analysis.* New York: HarperCollins.

Olson, C. L. (1979). Practical considerations in choosing a MANOVA test statistic: A rejoinder to Stevens. *Psychological Bulletin, 86,* 1350–1352.

Rousseeuw, P. J., & van Zomeren, B. C. (1990). Unmasking multivariate outliers and leverage points. *Journal of the American Statistical Association, 85,* 633–639.

Siegel, S., & Castellan, N. J. (1988). *Nonparametric statistics for the behavioral sciences* (2nd ed.). New York: McGraw-Hill.

SPSS, Inc. (1999). SPSS base 10.0 applications guide [Computer program manual]. Chicago: SPSS, Inc.

SPSS, Inc. (2000). SYSTAT 10 [Computer program]. Chicago: SPSS, Inc.

Stevens, J. P. (2001). *Applied multivariate statistics for the social sciences* (4th ed.). Mahwah, NJ: Erlbaum.

Tabachnick, B. G., & Fidell, L. S. (2001a). *Computer-assisted research design and analysis.* Boston: Allyn & Bacon.

Tabachnick, B. G., & Fidell, L. S. (2001b). *Using multivariate statistics* (4th ed.). Boston: Allyn & Bacon.

Tukey, J. W. (1977). *Exploratory data analysis.* Reading, MA: Addison-Wesley.

Wilkinson, L., & the Task Force on Statistical Inference. (1999). *American Psychologist, 54,* 594–602.

Winer, B. J., Brown, D. R., & Michels, K. M. (1991). *Statistical principles in experimental design* (3rd ed.). New York: McGraw-Hill.

CHAPTER 6

Factor Analysis

RICHARD L. GORSUCH

A major task of science is to develop theoretical constructs that bring together many observed phenomena. Historical examples of doing this include both ability and personality research. In the former, the moderate to high correlations observed among ability measures have led to the theoretical construct of general intelligence. In the latter, the moderate to high correlations among personality variables such as emotionality and frustration have led to the theoretical construct of anxiety (also called neuroticism). The construct validity of these theoretical constructs has been examined by factor analyses. Factor analysis is a statistical technique that reproduces the data by as few factors (potential theoretical constructs or latent variables) as possible.

A popular current use for factor analysis is scale development. When selecting a subset of the items for a scale, one needs to know how many constructs might be measured from the item pool and which items could measure each construct. This information is provided by a factor analysis. The items are factor analyzed to find the fewest number of factors that can represent the areas covered by the items. The relationship of each item to the factors indicates how it might be used in measuring one of the factors.

Whereas a factor analysis might result in a scale to measure a theoretical construct in a future study, confirmatory factor analysis and extension analysis in exploratory factor analysis allow another option. Factor analysis can be used in a new study to confirm or disconfirm the relationships between factors themselves or with other variables not in the factor analysis. No sales or factor scores are needed.

Although no factor analysis is ever completely exploratory—there is always an underlying theoretical model by which the data are collected—some factor analyses are primarily exploratory with no hypotheses, and others are primarily confirmatory, specifically testing hypotheses. Both types of factor analysis are examined in this chapter.

The purpose of this chapter is to provide a basic but comprehensive treatment of factor analysis. The intention is to give the reader the background to read, appreciate, and critique research from a factor analytic perspective, whether it be an article using factor analysis, an article using factor analysis inappropriately, or an article that could be strengthened if factor analysis were used. While no particular statistical package is assumed, this chapter also provides material needed to select the options for a factor analysis that are most appropriate to the purpose of the study.

The chapter starts with the basic equations and definitions of factor analysis. This section introduces the terms needed to understand factor analytic models and variations in the models. The second section of the chapter presents factor models, including component analysis (CA) and common factor analysis (CFA). CFA includes both exploratory (ECFA) and confirmatory (CCFA) factor analysis. In addition, all of these variants can be used with correlated or uncorrelated factor models. Presented with each model is the essential theoretical information to understand the model and the essential practical information to use the model.

Rather than reviewing all the possible procedures that could apply to each model, each section includes the procedures that now have sufficient empirical and theoretical support to be the generally desired procedures for that model. In some cases, however, there are still minor variations in what procedure is used, and these are discussed with the model to which the variations apply.

Although the last decades have led to clear choices of some procedures over others for one or more models, several areas in factor analysis still present major unsolved problems. Three such problems are addressed after the models have been presented. The first is the continuing debate between advocates of two types of exploratory analysis: components and common factor. Second is the issue of how many factors to extract from a particular data set. Third is the question of how the factors in one data set can be related to other variables that were in the data set but were not included in the factor analysis, and how factors may be related across studies.

The concluding section points to elements of all good research designs that need to be remembered in designing a factor analytic study. Included in this section are discussions of the need for high-quality variables and how many cases are needed.

Three examples are used to illustrate factor analysis. The first example is of six psychological tests for which the structure is easily seen in the correlation matrix (Gorsuch, 1983). Three of the variables are related to verbal ability and three to anxiety. The second example is a case in which we know what the factors should be: boxes (Gorsuch, 1983). Graduate students took 10 measures from ordinary boxes they found in their homes. Because these are all measures within three-dimensional space, we expect the factors to be those three dimensions: length, height, and width.

The third example uses the Canadian normative sample for the Wechsler Adult Intelligence Scale–III (WAIS-III; Gorsuch, 2000). The published correlation matrix among the scaled scores form the basis of analysis. The factor structure of the WAIS, and its children's version, the WISC (Wechsler Intelligence Scale for Children), have been extensively analyzed. (Detailed discussions of factor analytic topics are in Gorsuch, 1983; when no other references are provided, please consult that reference.)

BASICS OF FACTOR ANALYSIS

The purpose of factor analysis is to parsimoniously summarize the relationships among that which is being factored, referred to here as variables, with a set of fewer constructs, the factors. The analysis serves as an aid to theory development and scale construction. The term *variables* is used because most factor analyses are of scales and measures to which that term is immediately applicable; however, other types of data,

such as people, can be used (see Gorsuch, 1983; Thompson, 2000).

Understanding is aided when several variables are found to correlate sufficiently so that they are measuring the same construct (i.e., factor). In the area of intelligence, for example, scales with labels of *vocabulary* and *similarities* correlate highly together and can be considered manifestations of verbal ability. Because vocabulary and similarities have been found to relate to the same factor, theoretical development may account for vocabulary and similarities simultaneously by accounting for the factor.

Scale construction is aided when the correlations among items show the items to fall into a certain number of clusters or groups. In psychology of religion, motivation items, for example, fall into groups of items representing an intrinsic motivation (e.g., *the main reason I go to church is to worship God*) and extrinsic motivations (e.g., *the only reason to go to church is to meet friends*). The items fall into several groups so that within a group the items correlate with one factor and not with the other factors. Items can then be picked by their correlations with the factors to form scales.

Note that there is little generalization across factors (because the variables of one factor do not correlate with the variables of another factor) and so factor analysis identifies qualitatively different dimensions. Within a factor there is generalization identified with quantitative differences (i.e., how each variable correlates with the factor).

In addition to the classical factor analysis of scales, there are other uses of factor analysis. It can be used to reduce several problems encountered in data analysis.

One problem in data analysis is the *multiple collinearity* problem. This occurs when several scales that are designed to measure the same construct are used in the same study. Such scales correlate so well that it affects the statistics, such as multiple correlation. First, with multiple collinearity, multiple regression beta weights are unstable, and therefore are difficult to replicate. Second, another degree of freedom is used for each additional scale that measures what one of the other scales also measures. Yet having the additional measures is desirable because they increase the overall accuracy of the study. Multiple collinearity can be among either the independent or dependent variables.

A solution to the multiple collinearity problem is to factor the variables; then the factors are used instead of the variables. The same domains are covered with the factor analysis as the ones covered by the variables, and the factor analysis also shows the overlap among the scales. The multiple collinearity among the factors will be low.

Another problem with statistics such as multiple correlation is that the regression weights have all the covariation among the variables eliminated. It does this by partialing out the other variables from the weights. The common—that is, predictive variance that two or more variables have in common—may not be seen at all in the beta weights. Hence, a multiple regression can be significant even though none of the weights are significant; it is the variance that the variables have in common that predicts the dependent variable. The solution is to extract as many factors as there are variables and restrict the solution so that the factors are uncorrelated. These are then orthogonalized versions of the original variables. When these are used as the predictors in a multiple regression, all of the covariation is distributed among the variables and appears in the weights.

Development of factor analysis as a statistical procedure proceeds from the generalized least squares (GLS) model used in regression and other least squares analyses. Assuming all variables to be in Z score form for convenience, the model is based on this set of equations:

$$X_{i1} = w_{1A}A_i + w_{1B}B_i + w_{1C}C_i + w_{1D}D_i + \cdots + u_{i1}$$
$$X_{i2} = w_{2A}A_i + w_{2B}B_i + w_{2C}C_i + w_{2D}D_2 + \cdots + u_{i2}$$
$$X_{i3} = w_{3A}A_i + w_{3B}B_i + w_{3C}C_i + w_{3D}D_i + \cdots + u_{i3}$$
$$\cdots$$
$$X_{iv} = w_{vA}A_i + w_{vB}B_i + w_{vC}C_i + w_{vD}D_i + \cdots + u_{iv}$$

$$(6.1)$$

where, for the first line, X is the score for person i on variable 1, w is the weight for variable 1 for factor A, and A is the score for person i on factor A. The equation shows factors A through D and indicates that there may be more. Additional variables are indicated, for a total of v variables in the analysis.

The last element of each equation, u, is that which is unique to that particular variable, often called *error* or *residual*. Each u is in a separate column to indicate that each is distinct from any other u. There are as many distinct us as there are variables. It is important to note that each variable's uniqueness (us) includes two sources of variance. First is random error due to unreliability and second is that variance in the variable that is not estimable from the factors.

When the preceding equation is solved for each dependent variable, the multiple correlation of the factors with that variable can be computed. In factor analysis, the square of that multiple correlation is called the *communality* (h^2) because it is an index of how much that variable has in common with the factors.

How high can the communality be? The absolute maximum is 1.0, because then all the variation of the variable would be reproduced by the factor. But the psychometric maximum is the variable's reliability coefficient, which by definition is the maximum proportion of the variable that can be reproduced from a perfect parallel form, although occasional capitalization on chance may produce a sample communality slightly above the reliability. (Note: The reliability referred to in this chapter is always the reliability in the sample for the factor analytic study.) Of course, the reliability gives the communality only if all the nonerror variance is reproduced by the factors. The more likely result is that the factors reproduce only part of the reliable variance, and so the communalities are expected to be less than the reliabilities.

While Equation 6.1 gives the mathematical definition of factor analysis in terms of the data matrix (X), the analysis itself can, as in regression analyses, proceed mathematically from the Pearson correlations among the variables. Factor analysis can be presented as an analysis of correlations without reference to actual scores, but that can be misleading. Some techniques that proceed from the correlation matrix (e.g., cluster analysis) have no direct mathematical relationship to the observed variables. Factor analysis does; it is an analysis of the observed data using correlations only as a convenient intermediate step. (Note that phi, Spearman rank, and point-biserial correlations are all special cases of the Pearson correlation coefficient and so are appropriate for factor analysis. Although other coefficients, such as biserial correlations, have been tried, they do not proceed directly from Equation 6.1 and can produce matrices that cannot be factored.)

Factor analysis could proceed from covariances instead of correlations. If covariances are used, then the variable with the largest variance is given more weight in the solution. For example, if income were measured in dollars per year and education measured in number of years spent in schooling, the former's variance would, being in the tens of thousands, influence the results much more than would the latter, whose variance would be less than 10. With social science data in which the variances are arbitrary, weighting the solution towards variables with higher variances is seldom useful. However, do note that correlations are affected by restriction of range. When the range is less than is normally found with a variable, the correlations are lower. When such restriction does occur, the factor loadings will be lower than when the range is larger. In such a situation, it is appropriate to either correct the correlations for the restriction of range or use covariances. Factoring covariances produces factor weights that are the same despite restrictions of range. However, they may, in addition to the inconvenient weighting, be more difficult to interpret because they are not in the range of -1 to 1 as are correlations. The discussion here assumes that correlations are being factored unless stated otherwise.

Table 6.1 gives a simple example of six variables (Gorsuch, 1983). The left part of the table gives the observed correlation matrix, and the second part gives the factors' correlations with

TABLE 6.1   Factor Analysis of 6 Variables

Variable	r with Variables						r with Factors		
	1.	2.	3.	4.	5.	6.	I.	II.	h^2
1. Information	—						.76	−.09	.59
2. Verbal ability	.67	—					.81	−.07	.66
3. Verbal analogies	.43	.49	—				.58	−.07	.34
4. Ego strength	.11	.12	.03	—			.06	−.67	.45
5. Guilt proneness	−.07	−.05	−.14	−.41	—		−.05	.59	.35
6. Tension	−.17	−.14	−.10	−.48	.40	—	−.12	.66	.45

Note. Correlation between factors = −.14.

the variables. They show that the first three variables form one factor and the second three form another. The reason the communalities are small is because these are all brief forms with low to moderate reliabilities in this sample.

The results of a factor analysis includes the degree to which each factor relates to each variable. When a factor relates to a variable, the common usage is to say that the factor *loads* the variable. Loading refers to the relationship of a factor to a variable in general but not to one particular numeric values. It is appropriate to use the term *loading* when one wishes to refer to whether the factor contributes to a variable. However, whenever a number is referred to, the type of factor loading must be reported. Thus it is appropriate to ask *Does factor A load variable 3?* and appropriate to respond *Yes, it correlates .58 with the variable.* There are three types of factor loadings. First are the weights for each factor's *z* scores to estimate the variable *z* scores. Second are the correlations of each factor with each variable. The last, and least used, is the partial correlation of each factor with each variable with the other factors partialled out. (These are discussed more in this chapter's section on correlated factor solutions.)

There is an assumption in least squares analyses of Equation 6.1, including factor analysis. Use of the model assumes that each equation applies equally to each person. It is difficult for these analyses to work well if the *X* is a function of Factors A and B for half the sample but a function of Factors C and D for the other half. Such may occur, for example, when there are multiple ways in which the variable can be changed. Consider a hypothetical situation in which children in poor communities only receive high exam scores if they are innately bright (because poor communities, we shall assume, cannot contribute much to their scores). Then those in rich communities would receive high exam scores less related to innate brightness because of the resources that led to a strong learning environment. Because different influences are at work in different parts of the sample, the factor analysis will be an averaged one and not represent either community well.

In factor analysis, the desire is to find a limited number of factors that will best reproduce the observed scores. These factors, when weighted, will then reproduce the observed scores in the original sample and, in new samples, will

estimate what the observed scores would be if measured. Of course, the reverse may also be of interest: using the observed scores to measure the factor. But in the latter case, the factor is measured not to estimate the observed scores, but rather to generalize to other variables that also are correlated with the factor. These two approaches are seen in the examples. The boxes are analyzed to identify the factors: length, height, and width. Knowing the factors, we can in the future just measure length, height, and width directly and compute other variables such as a diagonal. The reverse is of interest in intelligence testing; scales such as Similarities and Vocabulary are used to measure verbal capability. Psychologists then examine, for example, a person's college grades in courses demanding high verbal capability to see whether they are as expected, given the person's verbal ability.

Note that in factor analysis, only the observed scores, the *X*s in Equation 6.1, are known; the factor scores (*A*, *B*, etc.), the weights (the *w*s), and the uniquenesses (*u*s) are unknown. With one known and three unknowns, it is mathematically impossible to solve for them without further restrictions. The restrictions adopted to allow solving for both factors and weights are a function of the factor model.

FACTOR ANALYTIC MODELS AND THEIR ANALYSES

To solve Equation 6.1 for both the factors and the weights, restrictions must be made. The restrictions can be minimal or extensive. The former—minimal restrictions—includes the class of models known as exploratory factor analysis (EFA). Mathematical principles are selected for the restrictions but there are no restrictions that take into account any theory that the investigator might have. The results are based solely on the observed data. The latter—extensive restrictions—includes the models known as confirmatory factor analysis (CFA). Based on theory or past research, a set of weights is proposed and tested as to whether the weights adequately reproduce the observed variables. Note that restrictions are not necessarily a dichotomy between minimal and extensive. Some forms of EFA are more restricted than others and some forms of CFA are less restricted than others. These variations arise out of what the investigator is willing to or needs to specify.

Component Analysis

Component analysis (CA) restricts Equation 6.1 by dropping the uniqueness term, u. Thus the interest is in factors (also called components when using CA) that reproduce all of each and every variable, and so have expected communalities of 1.0. Of course, CA users would never argue their variables have reliabilities of 1.0 and so the actual maximum communality is generally much lower than 1.0. And CA users know the variables will not have multiple correlations of almost 1.0 with the other variables (needed for the factors to have a multiple correlation of 1.0 with each variable). Therefore no variable can, except by capitalization on chance, actually have a communality of 1.0. But proponents feel CA gives, with solid variables that correlate well, a reasonable approximation, with negligible distortion from the ignored unreliability and ignored multiple correlations less than 1.0.

Derivations easily show that the first step in all exploratory factor analyses is to compute the correlations among the observed variables. It is important to note that technically it is a covariance matrix among Z scores that is being factored. The main diagonal contains the variances—which are 1.0 by the definition of Z scores. The off-diagonal elements are technically the covariances among the Z scores which, because Z scores have variances of 1.0, are also the correlations among the variables. Procedures mentioned below are then applied to the correlation matrix to extract the components.

To extract factors from the data matrix, more restrictions need to be made than just assuming the us are zero. The restrictions are mathematical and use one of two procedures. The first, principal components, has the restriction that the first factor is the largest possible one, the second is the largest one after the first has been extracted, and so forth for all the factors. The second, maximum likelihood, adds the restriction that each should have the maximum likelihood of that found in the population. The latter is more difficult to compute, but both are quite similar—and both become more similar as the N increases. It would be surprising if there were any interpretable difference between these two procedures with a reasonable N.

The factors as extracted are seldom directly interpretable. Hence the factors are rotated (a term which comes from a geometric development of factor analysis; see Gorsuch, 1983, particularly chapter 4)—that is, are transformed to meet some criterion while keeping the same communalities. The usual criterion for rotation is simple structure, which can be briefly defined as the maximum number of variables loading only one factor with a side condition that these loadings be spread among as many factors as possible. Table 6.1

shows excellent simple structure. Each variable is loaded by only one factor and each factor loads a distinct set of variables. Because rotation applies to all EFA methods but has correlated and uncorrelated models in terms of how the factors are restricted, it is discussed further in the section of this chapter entitled "Restricting to Uncorrelated Factors" after the other EFA methods are noted.

CA is more parsimonious than are other models based on Equation 6.1 in that the equations are simpler when the unique term is dropped from Equation 6.1. One of the effects is that factor scores can be directly calculated (which, as noted below, is not true for the other major exploratory model, common factor analysis). These factors are linear combinations of the observed variables that can serve as summaries of the function represented by the factor. Such factors appeal to those who wish to stay close to the data and who philosophically hold that all constructs are just convenient summaries of data. (This is a discussion to which we return later.)

CA has been considered to be only an EFA procedure, with no CFA version. That is true within the narrower definition of factor analysis generally employed. But in terms of the model of Equation 6.1 and the logic of CA, a confirmatory components analysis is technically possible. The problem is that no significance tests are possible because the CA model has no place for errors.

Common Factor Analysis

Common factor (CFA) models use Equation 6.1, including the uniqueness term. Each uniqueness is the sum of several types of variance not in the factor analysis. These include random error (from unreliability and sampling error) and residual error in the sense that part of the variable is unrelated to the factors. The term *uniqueness* is used for all error because the random error, sampling error, and that which cannot be estimated from the factors can be considered unique to each variable. In CFA models, the focus is on the commonly shared variance of the variables and factors, hence the name common factor analysis.

Having the uniquenesses in the equations requires assumptions to restrict the analysis sufficiently for there to be a solution. These assumptions parallel those of residual-error-uniqueness in regression analysis. The uniquenesses are assumed to be both

- Uncorrelated with each other.
- Uncorrelated with the common factors.

Because nontrivial uniqueness may exist for each variable, the variance associated with the factors is reduced for each variable. The variables' Z scores have an original variance of 1.0, but the part of each variable's Z scores that can be accounted for by the common factors is 1.0 minus u^2, and so will be less than 1.0. The importance of this for CFA is that the correlation matrix of the observed scores needs to be altered to take this into account. This is done by estimating the expected communality of each variable (because that is the squared multiple correlation of the factors with that variable and so is the variance of the reproduced variable) and replacing the 1.0 in the main diagonal of the correlation matrix with the communality. This is appropriate because the matrix is technically a covariance matrix, with the main diagonal elements being the variances of the variables.

Common factor analysis generally attracts those who wish to acknowledge the fact that all psychological variables have error and who prefer a model that is consistent with other methods of analysis, such as regression analysis and structural equations modeling. Factor scores, they originally felt, were not an issue because the factor score estimates correlate so high with the factors that the problem of factor scores' being only close approximations is minor; now proponents of common factor analysis suggest that factor scores are seldom needed because extension analysis can be used instead, and so the factor score issue is a moot question. (We return to the issue of CA vs. CFA later in this chapter.)

Common factor analysis has both an exploratory and a confirmatory model. An exploratory common factor analysis (ECFA) is one in which the restrictions are minimal both in number and in regard to the investigator's theories. It is an inductive analysis, with the results coming from the data as undisturbed by the investigator's thinking as possible. The advantage of not specifying an expectation is that the analysis is a multitailed test of any theory or expectation the investigator might have. If the investigator's expectations are found by ECFA, then they would certainly be found by a confirmatory analysis. However, due to the lack of restrictions and the complexities of the analyses, significance tests are not available for ECFA, so large Ns are to be used to reduce the need for significance tests.

Communalities could be calculated exactly if the factors were known and vice versa: The factors could be calculated exactly if the communalities were known. To cut this Gordian knot, the communality can be estimated and then the factors extracted. The observed communalities should differ only slightly from the estimated communalities.

Communality estimation is readily done by several methods. The following are four:

- *SMC:* Use the squared multiple correlation (SMC) of all other variables with that variable. This generally works well and is independent of the number of factors.

- *Pseudoiteration:* Use anything as the initial estimate, solve for the number of factors (see the following discussion for how to estimate the number of factors), and calculate the communalities from these factors. Then use the observed communalities as new estimates of the communalities, extract factors again, and calculate the communalities from these factors. Continue the process until little change is noted from one pass to the next or a maximum number of passes has made. Note that this is *not* true iteration. True iteration occurs when it has been proven both that the iterated values necessarily converge and that they necessarily converge to the right values. But neither necessarily happens with pseudoiteration. Gorsuch (1974, 1983) has noted a case in which the process would not converge, so the requirement for true iteration that the values converge is not met. The condition that they converge to the right values is not met because they sometimes converge to an impossibly large value. For example, in practice, communalities computed by this process often exceed 1.0. (Values greater than 1.0 are referred to as Heywood cases after the author of the first published discussion of the situation. Actually, those using the criterion of 1.0 to conclude the estimates are incorrect are optimists; the actual upper limit for communalities are the reliabilities of the variables, which are almost always less than 1.0. Thus, more violations of the upper limit occur than just the Heywood cases.) The fact that the process need not converge to values that are possible means this process is not an iterative process in the mathematical sense. In mathematics a procedure is iterative if and only if it is found to converge on the population value. Therefore the so-called iteration for communalities is only pseudoiteration. Why is pseudoiteration widely used? I suspect that there are two reasons. First, mathematical iteration is an excellent procedure, so iteration was certainly worth a try even though there is no mathematical proof it meets mathematical criteria for iteration. Second, when starting from 1.0 as the initial communality estimate, we see that the first few pseudoiterations obviously lower the communality estimates from the too-high value of 1.0 to a more reasonable estimate.

- *SMCs with two to three iterations:* This procedure starts with the SMC noted previously. Then the solution is iterated two or three times and stopped. Although it is still a pseudoiteration, it has never in my usage produced an estimate over 1.0. Snook and Gorsuch (1989) found the resulting communalities to not differ significantly from the communalities designed into the study. This is a good procedure.

- *Minres analysis:* This procedure minimizes the off-diagonal elements while using no communality estimates. Communalities result from the analysis. It is an excellent procedure if exact communalities are desired.

Some of the concern with communality estimates has been found to be an overconcern. Any reasonable estimate (plus several other similar ones, including special adaptations of b. in CFA) produces a final solution that is indistinguishable from the others. This is probably the reason that Minres is seldom used.

Note that the number of elements of the main diagonal of the correlation matrix—which are replaced with the communality estimates—increases linearly with the number of variables, while the number of nondiagonal elements increases much faster. For example, with six variables the communality estimates form 29% of the values being analyzed. With 30 variables, the communalities form only 7%. With 60 variables, the percentage is down to 4%. The impact of the communality estimates becomes increasingly unimportant as the number of variables increases.

In addition to the number of variables, a second parameter that is important in evaluating the importance of the communality estimates is how high the communalities are. The higher they are, the narrower the range of estimates for the communalities. With higher communalities, it is less likely that using a different communality estimation procedure would result in an interpretable difference.

Table 6.2 contains communalities for the box, WAIS, and psychological variable examples. They were computed from three initial estimates, 1.0, SMC, and SMC plus two iterations. The resulting communalities from the factors based on each estimation procedure are given. (The 1.0 column contains the actual communities from component analysis even though they were assumed to be 1.0.)

For the psychological variables—where the communality estimates are low to moderate and form 29% of the coefficients being analyzed—using 1.0 as the initial communality estimate makes a difference, but there is little difference between the other two initial estimates. In both the box and the WAIS examples, the communalities are high, so the estimates give quite similar results. Table 6.2 contains the factor loadings for the SMR plus the two-iterations solution for the six psychological variables data set.

Any of the parameters of Equation 6.1 can be zero. Now note what happens if the variables have high multiple correlations with the other variables. As the multiple correlations increase, the uniquenesses, *us*, approach zero. If they were zero, then the *us* would drop out and it would be a CA. Hence, CA is a special case of ECFA. An unrestricted ECFA

TABLE 6.2 EFA Communalities Using Different Initial Values

Estimation:	1.0	SMR	SMR + 2 Iterations
	Psychological Variables (2 Factors)		
1.	.73	.55	.59
2.	.77	.61	.66
3.	.56	.34	.34
4.	.65	.41	.45
5.	.57	.33	.35
6.	.64	.41	.45
	Boxes (3 Factors)		
1.	.95	.93`	.91
2.	.96	.93	.93
3.	.93	.97	.98
4.	.96	.98	.98
5.	.97	.99	.99
6.	.98	.98	.99
7.	.91	.90	.88
8.	.87	.84	.82
9.	.98	.97	.97
10.	.90	.73	.68
	WAIS-III (4 Factors)		
1.	.65	.59	.60
2.	.70	.51	.54
3.	.76	.42	.46
4.	.81	.44	.49
5.	.79	.65	.66
6.	.65	.52	.55
7.	.69	.40	.43
8.	.63	.34	.35
9.	.77	.68	.69
10.	.76	.51	.56
11.	.84	.74	.77

will give CA if the variables have high multiple correlations with each other. (It is for this reason that CA and ECFA are part of the same statistical model even though it they may be used for different purposes.)

As is the case with CA, ECFA proceeds by extracting factors by principal or maximal likelihood methods. The restrictions are then changed in the rotation of the factors (mentioned in the discussion of CA and discussed further later in this chapter). For example, the rotation reduces the number of factors loading each variable so that the relationships will be simpler than if most factors loaded most variables.

Confirmatory Common Factor Analysis

Confirmatory common factor analysis (CCFA) has been developed and used within the common factor model. It proceeds directly from equation 6.1 and includes the uniquenesses. But unlike ECFA, which uses mathematical restrictions to gain a solution, confirmatory methods use theory to develop appropriate restrictions.

The restrictions can be placed on any or all of the following of Equation 6.1:

- The number of factors.
- The weights of a factor to reproduce a variable.
- The uniqueness for each variable.
- The means and standard deviations of the factor scores. These are generally set to either Z scores (mean = 0, SD = 1) or the mean and SD of a particular variable.

It is possible also to place restrictions in addition to the elements of equation 6.1. The prime such restrictions are on the following:

- The correlations (or covariances, if covariances are being analyzed) among the factors.
- The correlations (or covariances) among the uniquenesses. These are generally restricted to 0, but they can be placed at other values. If non-zero, they can represent correlated method or errors.

The restrictions vary in the values that can be used. The more useful variations are to restrict a parameter to 1 or 0. When the means and standard deviations of the factors are set to 0 and 1, respectively, the factors are then Z scores. The correlations among the factors are set to 0 to restrict the factors to being uncorrelated.

The weights can be restricted in multiple ways. Here are the usual weight restrictions:

- The most widely used weight restriction is to set some weights to 0. This means that the variable is defined without regard to that factor.
- A predefined weight may be used; this is useful in evaluating whether the weights from another study are cross-validated in the current study.
- Several weights can be restricted to being the same value, with the value not predefined; for example, this is used if one has two parallel forms of the same measure.

If the weight is unrestricted, then the factor extracted is expected to have a nonzero weight on that variable, and the investigator wishes to know if that is so. The number of restrictions must be sufficient to identify a unique solution. Identification can be a problem in that no one has yet developed a formula to say when a unique solution is identified. It has been impossible to give a specific answer because the value depends on not just the number of restrictions but also their location. However, a correlation-based CCFA is generally sufficiently restricted if each variable is only allowed to be loaded by one factor and each factor has at least three

TABLE 6.3 Confirmatory Common Factor Analysis of 6 Psychological Variable Problem

	Hypothesized Weights		ECFA Principal Factor Weights		CCFA Weights (maximum likelihood)	
1.	?	0	.77	0	.77*	0
2.	?	0	.87	0	.86*	0
3.	?	0	.57	0	.57*	0
4.	0	?	0	−.70	0	−.70*
5.	0	?	0	.58	0	.58*
6.	0	?	0	.69	0	.70*
	r = ?		r = −.12		r = −.21*	

Note. *p < .05. ? means the value is left free to vary.

such variables. Usually the computer program reports any problems occurring that could be caused by insufficient restricting, referred to as *underidentification*.

For a CFA example, consider the six psychological variable example. From general psychological knowledge, we would expect that any factor of the verbal ability measures would not load the psychological distress variables, and vice versa. Hence, the hypothesized pattern would have six values set to zero. The other three values for each factor would be allowed to vary (i.e., would be set by the program). The correlation between the factors is unrestricted (see Table 6.3).

Consider just the first factor in Table 6.3. What the restrictions in the hypothesized weights say is that the last three variables are not to be considered in the solution of that factor. But it does not say how the weights for the first three variables are to be found. What is needed is the factor that best reproduces the scores of these three variables. Note that this is the same question asked in ECFA, and the same restriction is used so that a solution can be found: *principal factoring* (maximizing the variance that is reproduced) or *maximum likelihood factoring* (maximizing the variance with the further restriction of maximizing the generalization to the population). To illustrate this connection with ECFA, one principal factor was extracted from the first three variables; then, separately, one factor was extracted from the last three using an ECFA program (communalities were started at reliabilities and then iterated nine times). That is the second part of Table 6.3. It gives the weights for each of the factors to reproduce each of the variables. Using extension analysis (discussed later in this chapter), the correlation between these two so-called exploratory factors was found to be −.12.

And what if a real CCFA is computed from these data? Using the original maximum likelihood program for CCFA gives the final two columns of Table 6.3. The very slight differences may be a function of the differences between principal and maximum likelihood factors or the number of iterations for communalities. (It does illustrate how few differences there can be between principal and maximum likelihood factors.)

There is a warning in the use of CCFA: Changing the parameters of the model after looking at the data may well lead to a nonreplicable solution. The model needs to be set before the analysis begins. If more than one model needs to be tested, then all models need to be completely specified in advance.

If a hypothesized CCFA model gives a less-than-desired fit to the data, investigators occasionally make some adjustments to produce a better fitting model. This is a dangerous practice because it capitalizes on chance. The literature suggests such changes often lead the model away from the population model, not towards it. None of the significance tests nor the goodness-of-fit measures take this capitalization into account. If any changes are made to improve the fit, the report needs to explicitly state the original model, give the basis for all changes, and warn that some capitalization on chance will have occurred. It is recommended that a cross-validation sample be used to test any model containing data-based changes.

What is the advantage of a real CCFA over just extracting factors from subsets of the variables? The answer is *significance tests*. In Table 6.3, the CCFA found all the loadings to be statistically significant. These significance tests are possible because the solution is sufficiently restricted to be mathematically tractable.

Restricting to Uncorrelated Model Factors

The previous discussion of component and common factor models fits the general case in which there are no restrictions on the correlations among the factors. This is appropriate in most cases because either the variables are all drawn from the same domain, or how the domains relate is of interest. But allowing for correlations among the factors adds some complexity.

The simplicity introduced by uncorrelated factors is the same as with uncorrelated predictors in multiple regression. Multiple regression analysis simplifies if the predictors are uncorrelated with each other. With uncorrelated predictors,

- The correlation of the independent variable with the dependent variable is also its Z score weight, and its correlation when all the other predictors are partialed out (the partial correlation).
- There is no overlapping variance among the independent variables, so the correlation is unchanged if one of the other independent variables is partialed out or is not in the equation.
- The multiple correlation is the square root of the sum of the squared correlations of the independent variables with the dependent variable.

In factor analysis, the factors are the predictors or independent variables, the observed variables are the dependent variables, and the communalities are the squared multiple correlations of the factors with the observed variables. Thus, with uncorrelated factors,

- The correlation of the factor with an observed variable is also its Z score weight, and its correlation when all the other factors are partialled out (the partial correlation).
- There is no overlapping variance among the factors, so the correlation is unchanged if one of the other factors is partialled out or is not in the equation. However, because the uncorrelated restriction is applied to this specific set of factors, dropping a factor from the solution can change the weights.
- The communality is the square root of the sum of the squared correlations of the factors with the variable.

Because the correlation is equal to the weight and is equal to the partial correlation, there is only one interpretation for the term *loading* when the factors are uncorrelated. With correlated predictors or factors, the three conditions previously noted do not hold. Instead the beta weight (in regression analysis; factor weight in factor analysis) differs from the correlation, and those differ from the partial correlation (when the other predictors/factors are held constant). The multiple correlation/communality is computed by a more complex formula that takes the correlations among the variables/factors into account.

In factor analysis with correlated factors, each type of loading is put into a separate matrix. These have been named

- The factor pattern that contains the beta weights given to the factor Z scores to reproduce the variable Z scores.
- The factor structure that contains the correlations of the factors with the variables.
- The reference vector structure that contains the correlations of each factor with the variables with all other factors partialled out.

The factor pattern is generally considered to be the one to interpret, but the other matrices can be of interest also. Often the reference vector structure is clearer than that of the others because the correlations of factors with variables solely due to how the factors intercorrelate have been removed.

Because uncorrelated factors are easier to work with, why not restrict all factor solutions to being uncorrelated? The answer is that it may lead to a misleading representation of the data. For example, ability scales are all generally correlated together. This is true of the WAIS-III data; the lowest correlation is .22 (Digit Span with Digit Symbol) but correlations in the .50s and .60s are common. This is true not only among the scales, but also among the IQ and Index scores. Restricting to uncorrelated factors fails to inform us that the abilities are highly related.

Solutions restricted to uncorrelated factors are also referred to as orthogonal, a term from the geometric representation of factors. In the same manner, unrestricted solutions are also referred to as oblique. However, that term can be misleading. It implies that the solution is restricted to having correlated factors, which is not the case. Unrestricted rotation is just that: unrestricted. Factors can and often are uncorrelated when unrestricted factor rotation is used.

Many procedures exist for rotating factors, but the decision usually is just whether the factors will, on an a priori basis, be restricted to being orthogonal or will be unrestricted. If restricted, the program of everyone's choice is Varimax. For unrestricted rotation, there are several options, with most giving reasonable solutions. Some such as Oblimax have a parameter to set that influences the degree to which the solution is forced towards orthogonality. The most elegant unrestricted rotation is to start with Varimax, and then use Promax to provide an unrestricted version of the Varimax solution. Like other unrestricted solutions, there is a parameter to be set, referred to as k. Part of Promax's advantage is that the value of k is no longer a choice to be made because it makes little difference . It can always set to 4. With this setting, uncorrelated factors will result if appropriate, because orthogonal rotation is a special case of unrestricted rotation.

Note that Promax may produce factors with correlations so trivial that they can be treated as uncorrelated factors, as in Table 6.1 in which the correlation was a trivial $-.14$. Milliron (1996) found in a simulation study that Promax was good not only for correlated factors, but also replicated the known factor pattern better than Varimax did for factors uncorrelated in the population. In the samples, Varimax had to slightly distort the loadings to keep the factors correlating exactly zero, whereas Promax allowed for chance correlations among the factors.

Occasionally there are unexpected results with Varimax. Not only is an obvious general factor completely missed, but also the zero correlations among the factors can disappear at the next calculation. Several studies have used Varimax and then estimated factor scores. The factor scores were obviously correlated, indicating that the restriction could not be applied through all the calculations because the restricted rotation fit the data so poorly. Other studies have used the orthogonal factors of a prior study in a new sample, only to find the factors correlating .6 to .8. Highly correlated data will not be denied. It is best to be forewarned about this situation by leaving the rotation unrestricted.

If the factors are correlated, then those correlations can be factored (just as the original variable correlations were factored). The factors from the variables themselves are called the primary factors, whereas those extracted from the primary factors are called secondary factors; third-order factors would be factors from the second-order factors, and so forth. All factors after the primary factors are referred to as *higher-order factors*. Conceptually, the primary factors are more specific than are the secondary factors and so should predict more specific variables better than do the secondary factors. With more general variables, the secondary factors should predict better. Using the results of a higher-order factor analysis and the desired dependent variables, it is possible to show (Gorsuch, 1984) and even test (Mershon & Gorsuch, 1988) when the primary or second-order factors are more useful.

An example of higher order factoring is the WAIS-III. The primary factors are in Table 6.4. The four primary factors were correlated, and a general second-order factor was extracted. This factor, the last column of Table 6.4, represents the classical g, or general ability factor (IQ). The correlations of the individual scales with g were computed by extension analysis (discussed later in this chapter). It is g that has a long history of relating to many areas of achievement.

TABLE 6.4 Higher-Order Analysis of the WAIS-III (Canadian) First-Order Factors and Correlations of the Primary Factors

Variables	1. Verbal Comprehension	2. Processing Speed	3. Working Memory	4. Perceptual Organization	g
Arithmetic	.25	.02	.38	.26	.69
Block design	$-.08$	.11	.03	.70	.63
Digit span	$-.01$	$-.02$	.70	$-.01$	.47
Digit symbol	.05	.69	.00	$-.03$	.46
Information	.75	$-.05$	.09	.04	.63
Matrix reasoning	.07	$-.03$	.05	.68	.64
Letter number cancellation	$-.03$	.07	.61	.03	.48
Picture completion	.10	.01	.01	.51	.41
Similarities	.69	.05	$-.08$	.22	.46
Symbol search	$-.01$	.68	.04	.09	.54
Vocabulary	.85	.06	.03	$-.03$	.66
Correlations of the primary factors					
1.	1.00	.44	.51	.67	.73
2.	.44	1.00	.50	.56	.65
3.	.51	.50	1.00	.60	.71
4.	.67	.56	.60	1.00	.85

Note. The first-order and second-order factors used SMRs plus 2 iterations as communality estimates for the ECFA using principal factors extraction and Promax rotation. The correlations of g (i.e., the general factor) with the scales was by extension analysis (Gorsuch, 1997).

If one suspects that there is a general factor and CA or ECFA is used, that general factor will usually be found if and only if a higher-order analysis is computed from unrestricted rotation.

Item analysis is probably the most common situation in which a rotation restricted to orthogonality is misleading. The author of a scale includes items that each measure the underlying characteristic; then a total score is computed by adding the items together. So the author is assuming that there is a general factor—that is, one that loads all of the items. What happens when the scale is factored? Because factor analysis is a sensitive tool, it will take into account the almost universal fact that some items will correlate more highly with each other than with the rest of the items. There are generally several subsets of items that correlate slightly higher among themselves than with the other items because they have the same distributions or use similar words. Then several factors will be found. These factors may, for example, be one for the easy items, one for the medium-difficulty items, and one for the hard items. None of these factors will be a general factor because, as in Table 6.4, the general factor is found in the correlations among the factors. Varimax, however, never allows such correlations to occur. The decision to restrict item analysis rotation to orthogonality is a decision with major implications. It is far better to use Promax, an unrestricted rotation, and see whether a general factor happens to occur among the factors.

An instructive example can be drawn from the factor analyses of the Beck Depression Inventory (BDI). Chan (Gorsuch & Chan, 1991) ran analyses in Chinese and U.S. samples, and computed the relationships of previous U.S. and Canadian factor analyses to her factors. The table clearly showed that (a) primary factors did not replicate, whether within or across countries; (b) all primary factors correlated highly; and (c) the second-order depression factor replicated both within and across countries. That general factor is the same as the total score. The prior studies missed this fact because they only provided first-order analyses, and the erroneous conclusion from those would have been that there were no replicable factors. Chan showed the correct conclusion to be that there is one factor in the BDI, just as the author designed it.

MAJOR UNRESOLVED ISSUES

In the previous discussion, suggestions have been made for computing a factor analysis using reasonable and generally accepted solutions. These include using Promax unrestricted rotation. Also widely acceptable are squared multiple correlations with two iterations for community estimation (although pseudoiteration is most widely used, and is alright until it gives communalities higher than the observed reliabilities). But some major issues are currently being debated with little common agreement on their resolution, although there is evidence to evaluate the usefulness of different methods.

Two methods are used to evaluate the usefulness of a factor analytic technique. These are simulation studies and plasmodes (Cattell, 1978). Simulation studies start with a population factor pattern and factor correlations as givens (they are selected by the investigator to be sensitive to the parameter being investigated). The pattern and correlations may be systematically varied. Then hundreds to thousands of samples are derived using the population parameters, but allowing chance variations due to sampling. These multiple samples are analyzed, and the conditions under which the selected parameters are best recovered are noted.

Plasmodes are data sets in which it can be reasonably assumed that we know what the results should be. The examples used in this chapter fit that category. The history of psychology suggests that verbal ability and emotional distress are separate factors (the six psychological variables), and who would question the need for factors of length, height, and width to underlie boxes? The WAIS family of ability measures, of which the WAIS-III Canadian data set is one example, has a long history of factor analysis; the four-factor solution presented previously was replicated with multiple samples across both the WISC and WAIS. Which of several competing factor analytic techniques most ably find the expected results?

Although it is easy to vary parameters in simulation studies, there is always the question of generalization to the type of data commonly analyzed. And although plasmodes are data like those commonly analyzed, it is difficult to systematically vary parameters. Hence, our discussion of the problem areas relies heavily on both simulation studies and the plasmodes already presented as examples in this chapter.

What is the final arbitrator of factor analytic methodology? The ultimate arbitrator in science is well established: replication. Any procedure that produces replicable results is worthy of consideration. If several procedures lead to replicable results, then the choice is based on fit to the investigator's theory and situation. If there is still a choice, then parsimony and elegance are the deciding factors.

Component Versus Common Factor Models for Exploratory Factor Analysis

Both CA and CFA are used for EFA. Although the existence of two models is not surprising, the level of debate has been extensive. For detailed discussions of the pros and cons of these two models, see the special issue of *Multivariate Behavioral Research,* 1990, Volume 25, Issue 1 (also see 1996, Volume 31, Issue 4 for discussion of indeterminacy per se).

In understanding this debate, it is important to note that all procedures for CA and ECFA are the same except for one: CA starts with 1.0 in the main diagonal of the correlation matrix and CFA starts with a communality estimate (thus taking into account the existence of variance unique to the single variable). This is the only mathematical difference between the two. Everything else is the same (which is why they are both special cases of the general factor analytic model).

The Case for Common Factor Analysis

The rationale for CFA comes from Equation 6.1 and assumptions about data. Including the uniqueness term in the equation makes it a CFA. The uniqueness term includes all of the variable's variance not associated with the factors, part of which is random error. So, the CFA rationale goes, CFA should be used whenever at least some reliabilities are less than 1.0—that is, whenever some variables contain any random error. Of course, this argument runs, who can show, or *assume,* that all their variables are without random error? Where is the evidence for such variables in the social sciences? And if we know the variables have error, is it not rational to build that into our mathematical models?

Dropping the uniqueness term also means that the factors and only the factors underlie the scores for each variable. Hence in the population, the communality is to be 1.0. This is the justification for using 1.0 in the main diagonal of the correlation matrix. This means that the multiple correlation of the factors with each of the variables is also 1.0. Unfortunately, the derivative is that the variables, being sets of linear combinations of a fewer number of factors, will form a non-Gramian correlation matrix. Such a matrix has an infinite number of solutions and so cannot be factored at all. Therefore, CA is a self-contradictory model. (The only reason that CA works is that the model is wrong for the data—no two of the variables being analyzed have a multiple correlation of 1.0 with the same factors, so none truly fit the model.)

Although component advocates raise the problem of estimating communalities and factor scores, such estimates are consistent and easily made. The variations on factor scores are variations among scores that generally correlate .9 or better in simulation and plasmode studies. This is much better than in other areas. For example, major ability tests often correlate .7 to .8, yet are seen as interchangeable. Also the correlation between CA factor scores from one study to the next is much less than 1.0 and is probably no greater then that from one CFA to another, so where is the added precision

TABLE 6.5   Component Analysis of 10 Variables: Promax Factor Pattern

Variable	Factors		
	1	2	3
1. Length squared	.34	−.72	.09
2. Height squared	.57	−.26	−.14
3. Width squared	.13	.51	.16
4. Length + width	.49	−.12	.26
5. Length + height	.07	.61	−.06
6. Width + height	.40	.18	.14
Inner diagonals			
7. Longest	−.24	−.12	.44
8. Shortest	.59	.08	−.07
9. Space	.10	−.04	−.48
10. Edge thickness	.26	−.02	.80

Note. $N = 100$.

from CA? And with extension analysis (discussed later in this chapter), there is no need to compute factor scores because the correlations of variables not in the factor analysis with the factors can be mathematically computed.

The ECFA versus CA is a real question because the results vary dramatically in a few special situations. Table 6.5 presents the results of a CA. Factor 1 has two to four good markers, Factor 2 has two excellent and one good loading, and Factor 3 has one excellent and two moderate loadings. The loadings are clear and both the author and the reader would interpret them.

Unfortunately the matrix from which Table 6.5 was computed has not a single significant correlation. Each and every multiple correlation of one variable with the rest is, when shrunken for capitalization on chance, zero. The high loadings come from the assumption that all the variance of each variable is to be reproduced by the factors. Although this may be an unusual case, ECFA is better at protecting the discipline from such data than is CA.

There is also the principle of parsimony and elegance. That mathematical model is more elegant when it accounts for a wider range of situations. Equation 6.1 with the uniqueness term is using the same model as regression analysis, CCFA, structural equations modeling, and all other least squares techniques. To introduce a new model is to reduce parsimony and elegance among our statistical models.

The Case for Component Analysis

CA is more parsimonious because its equation is simpler. That makes it easier to teach and easier to program.

But the major arguments for CA go beyond having a simpler equation. One such rationale is a philosophical one. Factors are abstractions from data that we make for our convenience, not to be reified into realities. Factors are just

TABLE 6.6   Component Analysis of WAIS-III Canadian Data

Variables	Components			
	1	2	3	4
Arithmetic	.39	.04	.36	.21
Block design	−.09	.13	.02	.81
Digit span	.00	−.06	.91	−.04
Digit symbol	.06	.93	−.04	−.08
Information	.91	−.05	.04	−.03
Matrix reasoning	.14	−.03	.04	.71
Letter-number cancellation	−.06	.06	.83	.01
Picture completion	−.01	−.09	−.07	.86
Similarities	.80	.04	−.10	.16
Symbol search	−.04	.82	.03	.12
Vocabulary	.93	.04	−.01	−.04

that—convenient constructs that help our generation relate to the data consistencies we find in our discipline. And because they are *our* constructs, we choose to define them by the CA model.

Another rationale for CA is a set of pragmatics. One such pragmatic is that using CA instead of CFA seldom makes much difference. Many factor analyses are of 25 or more variables with, if the study is designed well, reasonably high communalities. In such cases, the results of CA and CFA lead to the same conclusions. Compare the CA in Table 6.6 against the CFA of Table 6.4. Is there really an interpretable difference? And in fact do not the high loadings stand out better from the low ones in the CA?

Other rationales for CA arise as much from classical limitations of CFA as from the CA model. A major limitation arises from the communality problem. Because we never know the communalities but only estimate them, there are a set of solutions that fit the data equally well. And iterating for communalities can produce Heywood cases.

As the communalities can only be estimated, the further mathematical conclusion is that there are an infinite number of factor scores that could be computed that would fulfill the ECFA model equally well for any given data set (a result of what is called the indeterminacy problem). With CA, the factor scores are a linear combination of the variables of which there is only one set.

The Ongoing Debate

While the existence and use of two models is not surprising, the level of debate is surprising. The results from both are, except in special cases, quite similar. Table 6.7 gives the correlations between the factors of CA and ECFA for the three examples. Particularly instructive is the psychological variables example. It has the fewest variables and the lowest

TABLE 6.7   Correlations Between Component Analysis and Exploratory Common Factor Analysis Solutions

	CA Solution								
	Psychological Variables		Boxes			WAIS-III			
	1.	2.	1.	2.	3.	1.	2.	3.	4.
ECFA Solution Psychological Variables									
1.	.88	−.20							
2.	−.18	.82							
Boxes									
1.			.99	.67	.65				
2.			.60	.95	.62				
3.			.70	.74	.96				
WAIS-III									
1.						.93	.45	.54	.68
2.						.38	.81	.44	.49
3.						.42	.43	.81	.52
4.						.59	.51	.55	.85

Note. ECFA was with SMRs plus 2 iterations for communities. Correlations computed by extension analysis (Gorsuch, 1997).

communalities, which are the conditions under which the CA and CFA might be expected to differ. It seems that the replication of factors between CA and ECFA are good for the six psychological variables and excellent for the other two data sets. These are so high that we would be delighted to get them if testing for replication from one sample to another within either CA or CFA.

Personally, I had the good fortune both to study with a major exponent of CFA (Cattell, 1978) and to work with a major exponent of CA (Nunnally, 1967), both scholars I respect highly. The former was my mentor in graduate school; I was employed by the latter to calculate all the examples for his book and gave paragraph-by-paragraph feedback on it. (Nunnally returned the favor by providing paragraph-by-paragraph feedback on the first edition of my *Factor Analysis;* Gorsuch, 1974.) So I heard both arguments multiple times. And in following the dialogue for the past 30 years, the only major change seems to be that the heat of the debate has increased.

Professional debates are good, but the search is (should be?) for procedures that address the critiques of both sides. I proposed such in the *Multivariate Behavioral Research* special issue (Vol. 25(1); Gorsuch, 1990): image analysis. Image analysis is a special case of common factor analysis, which factors the part of the variable that correlates with the other variables. Thus, it is oriented toward the common factors (i.e., factors that load at least two variables). The part that does not relate to another variable is dropped from the model. Thus, image analysis includes all that the supporters of ECFA want. This should satisfy the proponents of ECFA. For the proponents of CA, image analysis answers their critiques of ECFA because there is no communality problem and factor scores can be calculated, not estimated. Thus image analysis should satisfy both the common factor and component advocates. Except for Velicer and Jackson (1990), this suggestion was ignored.

Personally, I opt for CFA for two reasons. First, including the uniqueness term means that the same equation is used for factor analysis as is used for regression and SEM (structural equations modeling). Second, a procedure should be as fail-safe as possible, which means that loadings based on random correlations (Table 6.5) should look low to reduce the chance of believing there are significant loadings when there are no significant correlations. The issues of estimating communalities and estimating factor scores are, with contemporary procedures, trivial issues; the results correlate so highly that these are not problems. I do find it interesting that CFA was the original mode of factor analysis. Little if any consideration of CA is found before 1960. Instead common factor analysis was assumed and that was the only model presented. Insomuch as component analysis appeared at this point, it was just a special case of common factor analysis.

In 1960 computers entered psychology, but they were simple and slow. In illustration, the 1960 computer was slower and had less memory than the first Apple personal computer. Hence all programs had to be kept simple—very simple. It was then Henry Kaiser at the University of Illinois introduced the simplest complete computer package, called "Little Jiffy." It was doable in those computers because it was CA and had no communality estimation procedure (pseudo-iterated communalities would have literally taken too long for students to run). In his later discussions of this, he indicated that it was an oversimplified model. In 1970 (Kaiser, 1970) he introduced "A Second Generation Little Jiffy" but then it was too late. The computer packages had already picked up the runable "Little Jiffy" and that is still often the default in major statistical packages. My personal opinion is that the rationales for CA developed as a post hoc explanation because so many used a computer package which had "Little Jiffy" as the default. BUT NOTE: the origin of any construct in science is not judged by its history but only by its merits.

An important point to me is that CA versus CFA is a minor point with a reasonable number of variables and reasonable communalities. They give the same conclusions regardless of the philosophical or theoretical model the investigator wishes to assume. Only with a limited number of variables is there a difference, and then the best solution seems to be CFA because CA can make insignificant correlations into loadings that appear major. Much more important are issues such as variable selection, sample of cases, the number of factors to

extract, whether there is warrant to restrict the solution to uncorrelated factors, and whether to run confirmatory or exploratory analyses. Particularly important is underestimating the number of factors (see the next section) and any decision to restrict the rotation to uncorrelated factors.

Number of Factors Issue

In the proceeding discussions, the number of factors has been assumed. That was to enable the major points of the models to be presented. Unfortunately, there is no adequate way of determining the number of factors in either exploratory or confirmatory factor analysis. It is not for want of trying, for numerous proposals have been made and numerous simulations studies have been run (Velicer, Eaton, & Fava, 2000, summarizes the results of the simulation studies for CA and EFA). Generally, it is recommended that the user examine several of the following procedures in setting the number of factors.

The following tests are only a sample of the total available and include the most widespread and those with the best simulation results.

Eigenvalue/Characteristic Root Criteria. From a correlation matrix eigenvalues can be extracted (formerly the common name for eigenvalues was *characteristic roots,* which is why the criteria in this section use the term *roots* so often). These have many characteristics, with the important one (for the present purposes) being that they are the sum of squared correlations of the variables with a principal or maximum likelihood factor. Each of these factors accounts for the maximum amount of the variance of the correlation matrix. They are extracted in order of size. Hence, the set of roots for a problem gives the sizes of the extracted factors from the largest to the smallest. (Note: Rotated factors have no roots; the term and theory apply only to factors extracted from the correlation matrix with 1.0 in the main diagonal because the estimated communalities depend on the number of factors. All were originally developed for the CF model.)

The roots for each of our examples are in Table 6.8. They are ranked in order of size, and show the pattern typical of roots of correlation matrices.

To put the roots into perspective, consider what the roots would be if there were no factors at all. In that case, the correlation matrix would have the variable correlations (off-diagonal elements) all equal to zero while the diagonal elements would be 1.0. A legitimate solution would be with the first extracted factor loading the first variable 1.0, with all other loadings being zero. This root, the sum of the squared loadings, would be 1.0. The second factor would be the

TABLE 6.8   Roots for Example Problems

Extracted Factor	Psychological Variables	Boxes	WAIS-III
1	2.30	8.22	5.36
2	1.63	.78	1.06
3	.71	.39	.86
4	.53	.31	.80
5	.51	.18	.64
6	.32	.05	.60
7	—	.03	.43
8	—	.02	.40
9	—	.02	.35
10	—	.01	.26
11	—	—	.23

second variable, with a loading of 1.0 and a root of 1.0. The rest of the factors would follow the same pattern, and all roots would be 1.0.

Roots Greater Than 1.0

Because all roots would be 1.0 in a matrix with no factors, one suggestion is that any root greater than 1.0 will reflect a value greater than zero in the off-diagonal elements and so will be variance that can be attributed to a common factor. In actuality, smaller roots may also reflect correlations, so technically roots greater than 1 is the minimum number of factors to extract, but common usage treats it as the number of factors to extract. This has been the most widely programmed, and so the most widely used, of all the criteria. Unfortunately, the simulation studies have found it to be the prime candidate for the worst criterion ever tried (Gorsuch, 1983; Velicer et al., 2000). In our examples, it is only correct with the psychological variables.

Parallel Analysis

The rationale of roots greater than 1 is for the population matrix, not for a sample matrix. All sample matrices will have random correlations that will produce roots greater than 1. Parallel analysis consists of doing parallel analyses of random data. They are parallel in that the same number of cases and variables are used as in the factor analytic study, but they consist of random data only. Fifty to 100 of these are run, and the roots are averaged to show what the roots would be if the data were only random. The roots always start over 1.0 and then drop fairly sharply. The larger the N, the flatter the slope of the roots.

Tables (Lauhenschlagen, Lance, & Flaherty, 1989) have been provided so that each person does not need to compute multiple analyses of random data. Equations can also be used (Velicer et al., 2000). In each of these cases, the parallelism is established by having the same number of variables and

cases. It may be more appropriate to base the parallel analyses on matrices that also match the observed data in skew and kurtosis as well.

All roots from the factors of the study that are larger than the same numbered averaged random root are considered valid roots. For example, for the psychological problem with six variables and $N = 147$, the closest tabled values give the first parallel roots as 1.2, 1.1, and 1.0. The first observed root of Table 6.8 is larger than 1.2 and the second is larger than 1.1, but the third is less than 1.0. Therefore, parallel analysis indicates that two factors should be extracted because there are only two roots that exceed their randomly based equivalent. For the box problem, it gives one factor instead of three. The number of WAIS factors is also underestimated, giving two instead of four. It has serious problems with small but replicable factors.

Simulation studies have found parallel analysis to be a prime candidate for the best procedure for estimating the number of exploratory factors.

Scree Test

The scree test has a somewhat different logic for use of the roots. It is assumed that the variables cover a domain of interest and have at least moderately strong correlations. That means the factors of interest should be noticeably stronger than the factors of little interest, including random correlations. So when the roots are plotted in order of size, the factors of interest will appear first and be obviously larger than the trivial and error roots. The number of factors is that point at which the line formed by plotting the roots from largest to smallest stops dropping and levels out.

The name is from an analogy. *Scree* refers to the rubble at the bottom of a cliff. The cliff itself is identified because it drops sharply. The last part of the cliff that can be seen is where it disappears into the scree, which has a much more gradual slope. Note that the cliff is still seen at the top of the rubble; in the same way the number of factors includes the last factor associated with the drop.

Following the suggested use of the scree test gives three factors for the psychological variables and four for the boxes. That is one more than are assumed to exist in these two data sets. For the WAIS, the scree gives three factors, a number that does not lead to replicable factors (Gorsuch, 2000).

The suggestion to define the number of factors as the first factor among the trivial roots is what gives three factors for the psychological variables instead of two. This has been controversial in what some would see as extracting one too many factors. That leads to the question of whether extracting too many or too few factors would be more harmful. The simulation studies have found that extraction of one too many factors seldom does any harm, but extracting one too few distorts the factors that are extracted.

The extraction of an extra factor in the psychological variables leaves the first two with only minor changes and the third factor has two small loadings in the .20s. The box problem is more interesting. The fourth factor brings in a variable not loaded highly by the previous length, height, and width factors: thickness of the edge of the box. The fourth factor loads thickness highly, and also width to some degree. (There is still a factor with width as its major variable.) It seems that boxes in our culture are likely to be stronger if they are wider, a finding that extends the understanding of this example. Even so, the so-called extra factor does not seem to be a handicap in that the first three factors are essentially unchanged.

Simulation studies have generally found the scree test to be one of the better tests. We assume that the scree plots were by someone with training who knew nothing about how many factors were designed into the study, but this information is missing from most articles. (If the scree rater or raters were not blind as to the number of factors, that would invalidate the ratings.) Do note that it is often a choice between several possible screes, and several investigators may come to a different conclusion from the same roots. This suggests that training may be usefully investigated in future simulation studies.

Evaluation Via Plasmodes of Roots-Based Criteria

The three examples being used are plasmodes in the sense that the actual number and nature of the factors are established. The correct number of factors is two, three, and four for the three examples.

Given the correct number of factors and the roots in Table 6.8, it is apparent that both the criteria of roots greater than 1 and the parallel analysis criteria are incorrect two out of three times. The former always treat all roots less than 1 as nonfactors and the latter usually suggests even fewer factors, and yet two of the examples have clear and replicable factors with roots less than 1. And the scree test suggests three factors for the first example, three or four for the second, and three for the third, meaning it is correct for the first two examples but misses the third.

With the different results for the simulation studies compared to the three plasmodes here, what is to be concluded? The most likely conclusion is that the simulations used factors stronger than those found in the last two examples. This suggests that an assumption for the use of parallel analysis is that the factors of interest are assumed to have loadings of .8

or so by at least two or three variables. That may be doable in areas with well-established factors, but that is seldom the case in exploratory factor analyses of little-researched areas.

Two conclusions can be reached. The first is that simulation studies should contain more small factors. The second is that root-based criteria may be a dead end for procedures for establishing the number of factors in EFA. (These conclusions apply to both CA and CFA.)

Residual Based Criteria

The purpose of all models of factor analysis is to reproduce the variables. The better that is done, the better the correlations among the variables and the better the variable scores are reproduced. When the reproduced correlation matrix is subtracted from the observed correlation matrix, the result is referred to as the residual matrix. In the perfect data set with the perfect analysis, all of the residual correlations would be zero. To the degree that the residuals are nonzero, then either another factor is needed or these are the chance variations in the correlations due to sampling error. A number of proposals have been made for basing an index for the number of factors on functions of the residuals.

Although the root tests have been for EFA number of factors, residual-based indices of the adequacy of the factors extracted have also been developed for CCFA. In the case of CCFA, an index is evaluating not only the number of factors (as in EFA), but also the adequacy of the specified factors. Two different hypothesized patterns may produce sufficiently different residuals so that one of the hypothesized patterns is obviously better than the other. Hence, for CCFA the criteria evaluate the total solution.

Statistical Significance

The residual matrix can be tested for significance. If the test is significant, there is more nonrandom variance that can be extracted. If it is nonsignificant, then the extracted factors as a set account for all the correlations among the variables. As with all significance tests, a larger N allows detection of smaller differences.

The psychological variables whose CCFA is presented in Table 6.3 also had a chi-square of 5.53 with df of 8. That has a $p > .10$, so the residual matrix after the hypothesized two factors had been extracted has no covariance that could be considered nonchance. Hence, the conclusion is that these two factors account for all the correlations among these six variables. Note an unusual characteristic of testing the residuals for significant: A nonsignificant result is desirable.

So the problems of predicting a null hypothesis occur, primarily that there are many ways of getting nonsignificant results. These include having variables of low reliability and too small an N.

The significance test of the residuals tests whether the extracted factors do account for *everything*. There is no other commonly used test of significance that operates in this manner; all others test whether the hypothesis accounts for some of the variance, not all of it.

The significance test used gives a chi-square. Chi-squares are additive, and two approaches to analyzing the goodness of fit are based on this additivity. First, a suggestion has been to divide the chi-square by the degrees of freedom, giving the average chi-square (which is also F because $df = 1$). The advantage of the average chi-square is that it allows a comparison across models that have used a different number of parameters. The averaged chi-square for the six-variable example is .69, because any chi-square/F this small shows no chance of anything significant. It further reinforces the conclusion that these two factors are sufficient to account for all the correlations among the six variables.

The second use of chi-square, using the knowledge that chi-squares are additive, notes that the chi-square can be broken down to give a direct comparison between two models when one of the two models is a subset of the other. This is useful because it changes the test from one that tests whether we know everything to one that tests whether adding the hypothesized factor helps. For example, the WAIS began with two factors, Verbal and Performance. And three factors is a solution suggested by the Scree test. Does adding a third and fourth factor account for significantly more of the correlations? That can be tested by running two CCFAs, one for the two factors and one for the four factors (which includes the same parameters for the first two factors as the two-factor model). Each will give a chi-square; the four-factor chi-square is subtracted from the two-factor chi-square to give the chi-square of the two additional factors (the df of the difference is computed by subtracting the larger df from the smaller). The chi-squares and difference for the WAIS are in Table 6.9. Using the difference chi-square and the difference degrees of freedom allows a sig-

nificance test of adding the further specification. It does not have the problems of the significance test of residuals, wherein the test is of a null hypothesis. The difference in Table 6.9 is highly significant, showing the four-factor solution to be better significantly than the two-factor solution. But also note that, with the N of 1,105, even the four-factor model does not account for all the significant variance. No one has proposed more than four factors because they would be so small that they could not be interpreted. Although a chi-square test has been proposed for EFA, it has seldom been found to be useful.

Size of the Residuals

Because both EFA and CFA are to reduce the residuals to zero, measuring the size of the residuals is another method of evaluating the adequacy of the factor solution. There are two major approaches, one based on the residuals themselves and another based on the results when they are converted to partial correlations. The former is used with CCFA and the later with EFA.

Two residual-based tests are given in Table 6.9 for the WAIS-III analyses. *RMS* can be interpreted as *root mean square* because it is, roughly, the square root of the mean of the squared residuals. Two varieties of this criterion are in the table (Steiger & Lind, 1980); as can be seen, they generally proceed in the same direction because both are related to the same residuals. By these, it can be seen that the two additional factors do reduce the residuals. (Bentler & Bonett, 1980 give another set of useful indices for CCFA; for overviews of the many indices available for CCFA, see Bentler, 1989.)

An index of the residuals in EFA is Velicer's MAP (minimum averaged partial). Instead of using the residuals, MAP standardizes the residuals by converting them to partial correlations by dividing by the variances of the two variables involved (the residuals are the variances and covariances with the factors partialled out). These are then, in the original MAP, squared and averaged. The logic is that each factor that accounts for covariation among the variables will reduce the residual covariances. As long as the main diagonal elements remain relatively stable, then each factor extracted will lower the averaged partial. But when a factor is extracted that is based less on the covariances, then it will be more specific to one variable and lower the variance (in the main diagonal) of that variable. Because this is divided into the residual covariance, dropping the variance without dropping the covariance increases the partial correlations for that variable. So the minimum averaged partial is used for the number of factors. Minor shifts in MAP suggest that two

TABLE 6.9   Tests for the Adequacy of Fit in CCFA: WAIS-III

| Model | Chi-square | | | RMS | |
	df	Value	Chi/df	Residual	Square
Two factors	43	324.4	7.52	.051	.088
Four factors	38	232.1	6.11	.041	.075
Chi-square difference	5	92.3			

solutions are about the same. The principle noted previously that one too many factors is better than one too few suggests that the minimum with the greater number of factors be chosen. MAP is still evolving in that a version that raises the partial to the fourth power (instead of the original second power) is being tried. Evaluative studies suggest it is often helpful (Velicer, Eaton, & Fava, 2000).

The MAPs for the three examples were computed (using the fourth power). For the six psychological variable data, the first three MAPs were .03, .03, and .11, thus giving two factors. For the box data, the five MAPs were .07, .08, .11, .07, and .11, thus suggesting four factors. For the WAIS-III, they were .002, .002, .008, .027, and .061, suggesting two or three factors.

Simulation studies are supportive of MAP in its fourth-power form, but it misses the WAIS factors by suggesting one too few.

How to Select the Number of Factors

The procedures noted previously are typical of the possibilities for establishing the number of factors. Dozens of others have been suggested. As yet, they provide no clear solution to deciding the number of factors. For example, parallel analysis has been one of the best in the simulation studies and yet was clearly inadequate in the plasmode examples used in this chapter. What, then, shall be done?

There are two principles that can guide in establishing the number of factors. First, the prime criterion is the *replication* of the factors. The fact that the WAIS-III four-factor solution has been often replicated in children and adults and in the United States and in Canada is the convincing rationale for the number of factors. What the criteria for the number of factors suggest is much less important than whether the factors can be replicated. The replication of EFA results can

occur through a CCFA in a new sample as long as it is accepted that the CCFA will not help in the development of the model, only in its confirmation. More impressive is the confirmation of the EFA factors in new EFA analyses. EFA presents the best possible solution regardless of past results, whereas CCFA analyzes whether the hypothesized solution is one appropriate solution (there could be others, some even better). Both types of confirmation are useful.

The second principle for establishing the number of factors is the interest of the investigator. In the WAIS data, one factor gives *g*, general intelligence, which has been historically of considerable usefulness. Two factors gives the classical Verbal and Performance IQs. And four factors adds two smaller factors that may be of special interest to some investigators, but without rejecting the other two factors.

Consider the three solutions for the box data in Table 6.10. The one-factor solution is technically good. The factor, Volume, accounts for a surprising amount of the variance. It seems that the prime difference among boxes graduate students had available to measure was overall size. The three-factor solution is as expected: length, weight, and height. That also is a good solution. With the four-factor solution, the factors are length, thickness of edge, height, and width. This also could be a useful solution. It depends on the context of the study and the investigator's intent as to which solution is preferable.

In the two examples that can have different numbers of factors extracted, nothing is lost by going to the solution with the greater number of factors. The four-factor box solution still contains length, height, and width factors, and the volume factor occurs at the second-order level. The four-factor WAIS solution still contains verbal and performance types of factors, with *g* occurring at the second-order level.

It appears that taking out more factors and doing a higher-order analysis is the best answer to the number of factors.

TABLE 6.10   Alternate Solutions for the Box Data

Variable	Factor Solutions							
	1 Factor	3 Factor			4 Factor			
1. Length squared	.84	1.02	−.08	−.02	1.07	.01	−.03	−.07
2. Height squared	.85	.05	.17	.81	.05	.15	.83	.03
3. Width squared	.85	.02	.98	.01	−.03	.67	.03	.51
4. Length + width	.96	.73	.46	−.13	.64	.27	−.12	.38
5. Length + height	.96	.69	−.04	.43	.66	−.01	.45	.00
6. Width + height	.96	.18	.58	.41	.11	.77	.12	−.01
Inner diagonals								
7. Longest	.92	.74	.18	.11	.68	.11	.12	.17
8. Shortest	.91	.49	.27	.26	.36	.05	.29	.41
9. Space	.97	.76	.15	.16	.66	.03	.18	.26
10. Edge thickness	.74	.03	.71	.14	.11	.77	.12	−.01

Note. The values greater than 1.0 are because the loadings are weights, not correlations, and the factors have high intercorrelations.

Rotate several different numbers of factors with only casual use of the criteria suggested for the number of factors. Replication will ultimately decide which factors are useful.

My current conclusion is that the appropriate number of factors is, and will be for the immediate future, a semisubjective decision—partially because our attempts to create a universal rule for the number of factors has failed so far. Investigators may well rotate several different numbers of factors and pick the one that they feel is most interpretable, just so long as it has a greater, rather than lesser, number of factors. Indeed, it may be desirable to report the several solutions that replicate. However, this position means that one can never say that one number of factors is the only number that can be, just that it is one of the possible replicable solutions. In the WAIS-III data, one factor gives *g*, two factors give the classical verbal and performance, three factors are not replicable, and four factors give verbal, perceptual organization, working memory, and processing speed. Which solution is best depends on the work at hand, but only the solution with the greater number of factors and a higher-order analysis gives the total story.

Relating Factors

Relating Factors to Other Available Variables

Not all variables that may be available from the sample should be included in a factor analysis. Nonfactored variables may be from another domain or have correlated error with variables being factored (as when scoring the same responses two different ways). How do the factors relate to other data available from the sample but that have not been included in the factor analysis?

There are several major reasons for relating factors to variables not in the factor analysis: Some variables cannot be included in a factor analysis. First, variables that are a linear combination of other variables cannot be included (principal factor and maximum likelihood extraction methods give an infinite number of solutions if a linear combination is included). An example is the total score from a set of items. The total score is a linear combination of the items and so must be excluded. Second, any variable that has correlated error with another variable would adversely affect a factor analysis. One example is scoring the same items for several scales. Another example is including the power of a variable to test for curvilinear relationships, which has correlated error with the original variable. The correlated error can be modeled in a CCFA but not in an exploratory factor analysis. The relationship of factors to total scores, scores that have one or more items in common, and powers of variables can only be analyzed using extension analysis.

Nominal variables cannot be included in a factor analysis, but how the factors relate to such variables may be of interest. Whether the nominal variable be gender, ethnicity, experimental versus control groups, or some other variable, the relationship of nominal variables can be statistically analyzed by extension analysis.

What is the relationship of the factors to ordinal or better variables excluded from the factor analysis? Is a factor related to age or education? Assuming that one is not interested in an age or education factor, it is more appropriate to use extension analysis than to include such variables in the factor analysis.

The need to relate to other variables also occurs when a factor analysis is computed to reduce multiple colinearity or to orthogonalize a set of variables. If the factors are of the independent variables, then those factors need to be entered into the appropriate statistical analysis to relate them to the dependent variables, which were not in the factor analysis. If the dependent variables were factored, then these factors need to be related to the independent variables. If both independent and dependent variables were factored, then the independent variable factors would be tested to see how they correlate with the dependent variable factors.

Another need for extension analysis is in evaluating proposed scales from factor analysis. The factor analysis identifies the dimensions or constructs that can be measured. It also provides the correlations of each item with each factor. Items are then selected for a proposed scale for Factor A from those items that correlate highly with Factor A but not with the other factors. The item set for the scale would contain those that show the highest correlation with the factor— that is, have the highest factor validity. In practice, the first several items for a proposed scale are obvious due to their high correlations. But does adding a moderately correlated item increase or decrease the factor validity of the proposed scale? That question is answered by scoring the items to measure the factor both without and with the moderate item to determine which version of the proposed scale gives the highest factor validity. The set of items with the best factor validity with Factor A is then recommended to be the scale to measure Factor A. (Note that this cut-and-fit item selection method requires a large *N* to avoid capitalizing on chance, and the observed factor validities will shrink when computed in a new sample. A cross-validation sample is recommended for reporting factor validity correlations.) Relating factors to variables not in the factor analysis is called *extension analysis* because it extends the factors to new variables. The older procedure for extension analysis has been based on computing factor scores (formulas can be used so the actual scores need not be computed), and then analyzing these factor scores with the extension variables. There are several methods for computing factor scores, but the choice is usually between only two variations. The first is multiple regression analysis. The variables loaded by a factor are the predictors and the factor is the dependent variable. The regression analysis provides the beta weights, which are then used to calculate the factor scores. However, regression weights have the *bouncing beta* problem: Unless the sample is over 400, they bounce around when a new sample is collected or when the variable mix is changed slightly.

The instability of beta weights has led to the other recommended procedure for computing factor scores: unit weighting. Unit weighing is defined as adding together the scores of the variables that have high weights in the multiple regression from the variables to the factors, after the variables have been converted to the same metric, e.g., Z scores. Each of the variables clearly related to the factor is weighted +1 if the weight is positive or −1 if the weight is negative. With samples less than 400, unit weights have higher factor validities when cross-validated than do multiple regression weights (due to the latter's capitalization on chance).

Factor scores have problems. In addition to indeterminacy of CFA scores, each variable weighted in the scoring equation has its unique part added to the score as well as the part loaded by the factor. This is the same problem that occurs when the items are correlated with the total score from the items. The item-total correlations are inflated because that part of the item not measuring the construct is included both in the total score and in the item. To avoid correlations inflated by correlated error, item-remainder correlations have been suggested. Correlating the item with a total score from the remaining items eliminates the inflated correlation. However, it also ignores the valid part of the item that should be part of the total score, and so gives an underestimate of the correlation. The same is true with factor scores: Items or variables contributing to that factor score will have higher correlations due to the shared error.

In the past, extension analysis has been by factor scoring, even when called extension analysis. For that reason it has the problems previously noted for variable–factor score (or item-total and item-remainder) correlations.

However, a new extension analysis procedure has been developed without these problems (Gorsuch, 1997). The new extension analysis can find the effect size and significance levels between factors and any variable collected from the same sample but not in the factor analysis. These may be variables such as gender or age and age squared to check for curvilinear relationships with age. For item development, it gives the factor validity of any proposed scale (without inflation from correlated error).

Extension analysis allows factor analysis to be used as a scoring procedure. The dependent variables (or the independent variables, or both) can be factored and then the other variables of interest related directly to the factors.

Extension analysis is only available at this time in one statistical package (Gorsuch, 1994). However, a detailed example in the original article (Gorsuch, 1997) shows how it can, with patience, be computed even with a hand calculator.

Relating Factors to Prior Studies

Do the factors of Study B replicate those of Study A? This question is addressed by CCFA, which applies when the variables are the same in the two studies. The test is of the overall solution.

But not all situations can be solved by CCFA. What if only part of the factors are included in the new study? Or what if the population sampled is so different that new factors could occur and that would be important information? In these types of situations, some prefer another EFA as a multitailed test that allows unexpected factors to occur. Then it is appropriate to use a factor score procedure. The factor score weights from the first sample are used in the new sample to produce first study factor scores. They are correlated with the new study factors through the Gorsuch extension analysis (not by new study factor scores because they would have correlated error with the first study factor scores and so have inflated correlations). This extension analysis extends the factor analysis of the second study to the factor scores created with the weights from the first study.

The only appropriate measure of how factors relate is how they correlate. (Coefficients of congruence remain a poor choice and cannot be recommended except in rare cases when no estimate of the factor correlations is possible.)

RELEVANT RESEARCH DESIGN PRINCIPLES

The preceding discussion has dealt with the general models and proceedings for factor analysis, whether it be by components or maximum likelihood, exploratory or confirmatory methods. There are, however, some aspects of crucial importance that have not been directly germane to the specifics of the discussion to this point. These are mostly the same issues as in any research study and can be summarized briefly.

The variable and case sampling are crucial to a quality solution. Here is a remainder of aspects to be noted for a factor analysis that hold true of all good research studies:

- Each variable should be interpretable so that a factor's loading or not loading is meaningful.

- The higher the reliability of the variables, the higher the correlations and the communality.
- The higher the validity of the variables, the more meaningful the results.
- For significance testing, uniqueness scores should be normally distributed.

Variables should have similar distributions in the sample for maximum correlations. They need not be normally distributed, but a variable with a skew incompatible with the majority of the other variables should be avoided.

All variables need to have some cases that score high and some that score low. Normal distribution is fine, but it is not desired if it obscures true highs and true lows. This avoids restriction of range, which lowers observed correlations and so weakens the factor structure. The sample size needs to be large enough for stable correlations. Before the plasmode and simulation studies, the best guess was that the N needed would be a function of the number of variables being analyzed. Unlike multiple regression analysis and many previous discussions (e.g., Nunnally, 1967; Gorsuch, 1974, 1983), factor analytic accuracy appears to be relatively independent of the number of variables (with the exception that, for mathematical reasons, the total N must always be larger than the total number of variables). However, both plasmode and simulation studies suggest that the N and the purpose of the study are crucial. The N gives the stability of a correlation, and stability increases as the square root of the N decreases. A zero correlation with an N of 100 has a standard error of .10, 150 is .08, 200 is .07, 300 is .06, and 400 is .05. This is a reasonable guide to sample size. Because the purpose of a study is generally to distinguish between observed correlations of .30 and .40, for example, the safe sample size is 400. If one just wishes to determine which correlations are different from zero and is only interested in correlations .30 and higher, an N of 150 is reasonable. A larger sample is needed for item factor analysis because one needs to differentiate between correlations differing by only .10 ($N = 400$) and to reduce capitalization on chance in item selection.

The number of variables that each factor is expected to load should be in the range of three to six. Fewer than three variables makes a factor difficult to define, so using four to six is better. Simulation studies have suggested more variables be used, but these are only when there are available new variables that are truly different from the original ones, except for being loaded by the same factors. Experience suggests that such a situation seldom occurs, and the variables added after the first six lead to minor factors.

More than six variables can lead to problems due to the sensitivity of factor analysis. In EFA, a factor with more than six variables often gives two subfactors. Unless the factors are restricted to being uncorrelated (in which case there is no recovery), the factor of interest tends to be recovered as a higher-order factor. That higher-order factor may relate well to another analysis which, using fewer variables, finds the factor among the primary factors. In CCFA, more than six variables per factor often leads to statistically significant residuals—even when they are not relevant—due to minor factors found within the six variables.

REFERENCES

Bentler, P. M. (1989). *EQS Structural equations program manual.* Los Angeles: BMDP Statistical Software.

Bentler, P. M., & Bonett, D. G. (1980). Significance tests and goodness of fit in the analysis of covariance structures. *Psychological Bulletin, 88,* 588–606.

Cattell, R. B. (1978). *The scientific use of factor analysis in behavioral and life sciences.* New York: Plenum Press.

Gorsuch, R. L. (1974). *Factor analysis.* Philadelphia: W. B. Saunders Co.

Gorsuch, R. L. (1983). *Factor analysis* (2nd ed.). Hillsdale, NJ: Erlbaum.

Gorsuch, R. L. (1984). Measurement: The boon and bane of investigating religion. *American Psychologist, 39,* 228–236. (Reprinted in *Psychology of religion: Personalities, problems, possibilities,* 1991, pp. 267–283, by H. N. Malony, Ed., Grand Rapids, MI: Baker Book House.)

Gorsuch, R. L. (1990). Common factor analysis versus component analysis: Some well and little known facts. *Multivariate Behavioral Research, 25,* 33–39.

Gorsuch, R. L. (1994). UniMult: For univariate and multivariate data analysis [Computer program and manual]. Pasadena, CA: UniMult.

Gorsuch, R. L. (1997). Exploratory factor analysis: Its role in item analysis. *Journal of Personality Assessment, 68,* 532–560.

Gorsuch, R. L. (1997). New procedure for extension analysis in exploratory factor analysis. *Educational and Psychological Measurement, 57,* 725–740.

Gorsuch, R. L. (2000). Results of the WAIS-III Canadian Study. In D. Wechsler (Ed.), *WAIS-III: Wechsler Intelligence Scale for Adults: Canadian Manual* (3rd ed.). Toronto, Canada: The Psychological Corporation, Harcourt Brace.

Gorsuch, R. L., & Chan, M. Y. A. (1991). *Development and evaluation of a Chinese translation of the State Trait Anxiety Inventory and the Beck Depression Inventory.* Paper presented at the annual meeting of the International Congress of Psychology, San Francisco, CA.

Kaiser, H. F. (1970). A second generation Little Jiffy. *Psychometrika, 35,* 401–415.

Lauhenschlagen, G. J., Lance, C. E., & Flaherty, V. L. (1989). Parallel analysis criteria: Revised equations for estimating the latent roots of random data correlation matrices. *Educational and Psychological Measurement, 49,* 339–345.

Mershon, B., & Gorsuch, R. L. (1988). Number of factors in the personality sphere: Does increase in factors increase predictability of real life criteria? *Journal of Personality and Social Psychology, 55,* 675–680.

Nunnally, J. (1967). *Psychometric theory.* New York: McGraw-Hill.

Snook, S. C., & Gorsuch, R. L. (1989). Component analysis vs. common factor analysis: A Monte Carlo study. *Psychological Bulletin, 106,* 148–154.

Steiger, J. H., & Lind, J. C. (1980, May). *Statistically-based tests for the number of common factors.* Paper presented at the annual Spring Meeting of the Psychometric Society in Iowa City.

Thompson, B. (2000). Q-technique factor analysis: One variation on the two-mode factor analysis of variables. In L. Grimm & P. Yarnold (Eds.), *Reading and understanding more multivariate statistics* (pp. 207–226). Washington, DC: American Psychological Association.

Velicer, W. F., & Jackson, D. N. (1990). Component analysis versus common factor analysis: Some issues in selecting an appropriate procedure. *Multivariate Behavioral Research, 25,* 1–28.

Velicer, W. F., Eaton, C. A., & Fava, J. L. (2000). Construct explication through factor or component analysis: A review and evaluation of alternative procedures for determining the number of factors or components. In R. D. Goffin & E. Helmes, E. (Eds.), *Problems and solutions in human assessment: A festschrift to Douglas Jackson at seventy,* pp. 47–71. Norwell, MA: Kluwer Academic Publishers.

CHAPTER 7

Clustering and Classification Methods

GLENN W. MILLIGAN AND STEPHEN C. HIRTLE

The purpose of this chapter is to provide a review of the current state of knowledge in the field of clustering and classification as applied in the behavioral sciences. Because of the extensive literature base and the wide range of application areas, no attempt or assurance can be made that all domains of study in this area have been covered. Rather, the main research themes and well-known algorithms are reviewed. In addition, the chapter includes a survey of the issues critical to the analysis of empirical data with recommendations for the applied user.

Clustering and classification methods as discussed here are within a context of exploratory data analysis, as opposed to theory development or confirmation. Some methods or strategies useful for theory confirmation are included as appropriate.

One difficulty in this area is that no unifying theory for clustering is widely accepted. An interesting result in the field of clustering is that the standard statistical assumption of multivariate normality as a basis for the derivation of such algorithms has not automatically led to a superior clustering procedure. Because of derivational difficulties and empirical experience with various approaches, we have today a plethora of methods. Some of these methods work well in certain circumstances, and some of these appear seldom if ever to work as intended. Often, applied users of the methodology are unaware of various issues concerning the performance of clustering and classification methods.

A second problem faced by researchers new to the field is that the literature base is indeed vast and spans virtually all fields of human endeavor. The Classification Society of North America is now in its third decade of publishing an annual bibliographic review called the *Classification Literature Automated Search Service* (Murtagh, 2000). Each issue includes references of upwards of 1,000 scientific articles.

The wide range of application areas creates an additional problem for the applied researcher. Reading scientific articles and textbooks outside of one's own area of expertise can be difficult yet essential to get a good mastery of the topic. Some of the best work in this area has been published in engineering and the biological sciences in addition to outlets normally used by the social sciences community. The reader will see the diversity of disciplines represented in the references section for this chapter. It is useful to note that much of the development of this methodology has appeared in applied journals and less so in the mainstream statistical and mathematical journals.

This chapter continues with a section on data preparation, data models, and representation, including a discussion of distance and similarity measures. Three illustrative applications of classification methods are presented in turn. A section on clustering algorithms covers a wide range of classification methods. In addition, this section includes a discussion of the recovery performance of clustering methods. The fourth section covers a variety of issues important for applied analyses such as data and variable selection, variable standardization, choosing the number of clusters, and postclassification analysis of the results. The chapter concludes with a section that covers a variety of extensions and issues in classification.

DATA PREPARATION AND REPRESENTATION

The basic data for input to a cluster analysis can consist of either a square or rectangular matrix, with or without replications. For a typical cluster analysis scenario, assume there is a matrix of n objects measured on m features. Depending on the context, the objects have been denoted in the literature as items, subjects, individuals, cases, operational taxonomic units (OTUs), patterns, or profiles, whereas the features have been denoted variables, descriptors, attributes, characters, items, or profiles (Legendre & Legendre, 1998). Thus, the reader of multiple articles must be careful in interpretation, as the same terminology has been used in the literature to refer to both the n rows or the m columns in the data matrix, depending on the specific context of the classification problem.

While is it possible for a cluster-analytic approach to analyze the data in the rows and columns of the rectangular matrix directly, it is more typical first to transform the $n \times m$ rectangular matrix into an $n \times n$ symmetric proximity matrix. Each entry x_{ij} in the transformed matrix represents either similarity of item i to j, in which case we call it a *similarity* matrix, or the dissimilarity of item i to j, in which case we call it *dissimilarity* or *distance* matrix. Alternatively, one could convert the $n \times m$ rectangular matrix to an $m \times m$ symmetric matrix to measure the similarity between features. Sneath and Sokal (1973) denoted the analysis of an $n \times n$ matrix *R analysis,* whereas the analysis of an $m \times m$ matrix was denoted *Q analysis.*

It is also possible to collect similarity or dissimilarity measures directly. For example, Shepard (1963) uses a confusion matrix (Rothkopf, 1957) for the identification of Morse code as an indication of the perceptual similarity of each pair of codes. A matrix entry x_{ab} would indicate how many times the transmitted code for letter a is perceived as letter b. Note that such a matrix would most likely be nonsymmetric. Thus, the researcher would first want to construct a symmetric matrix through the average or weighted average of the two cells x_{ab} and x_{ba}, unless the clustering method explicitly represents asymmetries in the solution (Furnas, 1980; Hirtle, 1987; Okada, 1996).

Carroll and Arabie (1980, 1998) denote the $n \times n$ matrix as *two-way, one-mode* data, whereas the $n \times m$ matrix is referred to as *two-way, two-mode* data. That is, the number of

ways reflects the number of dimensions in the data set, while the number of modes reflects the number of conceptual categories represented in the data set. Examples of two-way, one-mode data include confusions, correlations, and similarity ratings (in psychology); frequency of communication between individuals (in sociology); or the subjective distance between locations (in behavioral geography). Examples of two-way, two-mode data include individual responses to questionnaire items (in psychology), n specimens measured on m characteristics (in biology), or ratings of products by consumers (in marketing). This terminology can be extended to include *three-way, two-mode data,* for which two-way, one-mode data is replicated for individual subjects or groups of subjects. Examples of three-way, two-mode data include individual ratings of similarity (in psychology), or the buying patterns of consumer groups (in marketing).

Ultrametric and Additive Inequalities

The results of classification analyses are often represented by tree diagrams, which reflect the inherent relationships in the underlying model. The most common representation is a rooted, valued tree, also called a *dendrogram,* as shown in panel A of Figure 7.1. Here, each node in the tree is joined at a specific height, as indicated by the scale on the right side of the figure. In this case, the set of heights can be shown to satisfy the ultrametric inequality (Johnson, 1967). Specifically, if h_{ij} is the smallest value for which items i and j cluster, then

$$h_{ij} \leq \max(h_{ik}, h_{jk}) \text{ for all } i, j, k.$$

That is, the three heights between each pair of a triple of points can be thought of as an isosceles triangle, with the equal sides being at least as long as the third side.

An alternative tree model is the path-length, or *additive,* tree shown in panel B of Figure 7.1. Here, the dissimilarity

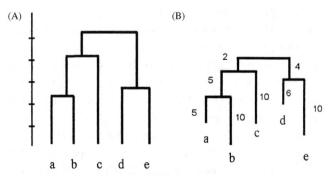

Figure 7.1   Example of two rooted trees. Panel A shows an example of an ultrametric tree, whereas panel B shows an example of a path-length or additive tree.

between items is reflected in length of the paths between the terminal nodes (Buneman, 1971; Corter, 1996; Dobson, 1974). An additive tree is governed by the additive inequality, which states that if d_{xy} is the path length between x and y, then

$$d_{ij} + d_{kl} \leq \max(d_{ik} + d_{jl}, d_{il} + d_{jk}) \text{ for all } i, j, k, l.$$

The ultrametric tree is therefore a special case of the additive tree, where the leaf nodes are all equally distant from the root node. In an additive tree, this restriction does not hold. For example, in the tree shown in panel B of Figure 7.1, $d_{ab} = 15$, $d_{ac} = 20$, and the $d_{bc} = 25$, whereas in panel A the $d_{ac} = d_{bc}$.

In all cases just discussed, only the leaves are explicitly labeled. The researcher may often label the internal nodes on an ad hoc basis to assist in the readability and interpretation of the clusters. The reader, however, should be warned that in such cases the internal labels are arbitrary and not defined by the clustering algorithm.

Classification Data as Tree Models

Corter (1996) argued for the acknowledgment of clustering and trees as models of proximity relationships, rather than as the result of an algorithm for fitting data. The distinction here is subtle but important. Cluster analysis can begin with the notion of some existing underlying clusters. The clusters might be subject to noise and error and vary in dispersion and overlap. The clusters are sampled with measurements taken on a variety of attributes, which are then subjected to a cluster analysis to recover the true clusters. This approach is described in many of the general references in cluster analysis, such as Aldenderfer and Blashfield (1984), Hartigan (1975), or Jain and Dubes (1988).

An alternative framework proposed by Corter (1996) considers the problem of representing a similarity matrix by a structure, such as an additive or ultrametric tree. That is, the information within a matrix has a structure that can alternatively be captured in a representation with fewer parameters than are found in the original data matrix. Pruzansky, Tversky, and Carroll (1982), using this approach, examined the properties of data matrices that would lead to the best fit of spatial or tree representations. Their approach was based on two distinct analyses. First, artificial data were generated by choosing points either randomly from a two-dimensional space or from a randomly generated tree. Noise, at various levels, was then added to some of the data matrices. Not surprisingly, they found that multidimensional scaling algorithms, such as KYST (Kruskal & Wish, 1978), which generated a two-dimensional solution, resulted in a better fit for the spatially generated data, whereas a clustering method,

such as ADDTREE (Sattath & Tversky, 1977), resulted in a better fit for the tree-generated data.

The next step was more interesting. Are there patterns in the data matrix that would lead one to adopt one method or the other? As diagnostic measures, they calculated the skewness of the distances and the number of elongated triples. A triple of distances was said to be elongated if the medium distance was closer to the longer distance than to the shorter distance. The analysis by Pruzansky et al. (1982) showed that spatially generated data tended be less skewed and had fewer elongated triples, while the tree-generated data were more negatively skewed and had a larger percentage of elongated triples. As a final step, these diagnostic measures were confirmed using various empirical data sets, which were thought to be best modeled by a tree or by a spatial representation. Thus, for deciding between spatial and tree-based representations, the analyses of Pruzansky et al. (1982) suggest that appropriate diagnostic techniques might suggest which class of models is more appropriate for a given a data set.

EXAMPLES

At this point, it is useful to consider three examples of cluster analysis from the literature. The first example is based on kinship data from Rosenberg and Kim (1975), which has been analyzed in detail by Carroll and Arabie (1983), De Soete and Carroll (1996), and others. The task that the subjects performed in the initial study was to sort kinship terms into any number of piles so that each pile consisted of related terms and there were at least two piles. By taking the total number of times that a subject put two terms in the same pile, one can construct a similarity matrix between terms. Rosenberg and Kim (1975) asked some subjects to sort the terms once, while others were asked to sort the terms multiple times. Using the data matrix from female subjects, De Soete and Carroll (1996) constructed a dendrogram, as shown in Figure 7.2, using a least-squares ultrametric tree-fitting procedure called LSULT (De Soete, 1984). The resulting ultrametric tree representation, which accounts for 96.0% of the variance in the original data matrix, encapsulates the standard anthropological model of kinship terms (Carroll & Arabie, 1983). The tree divides direct kin, such as grandparents, from collaterals, such as cousins. It further divides the direct kin into the immediate family versus ± 2 generations. Within these clusters, further groupings occur on the basis of generation (e.g., mother and father are clustered). In this case, there is great benefit in considering the entire representation. That is, if one were to truncate the tree and declare that kin terms are best represented as three clusters or seven clusters, much information would be lost.

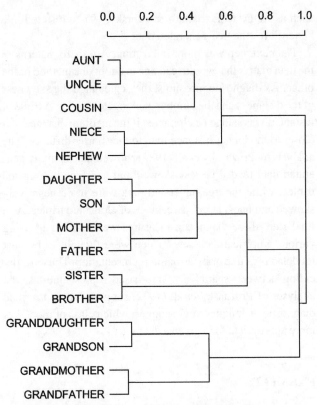

Figure 7.2 Dendrogram for kinship data as produced by a least-squares ultrametric tree-fitting procedure by De Soete and Carroll (1996).

Another example where the entire tree is important is shown in Figure 7.3, which comes from De Soete and Carroll (1996). Figure 7.3 displays an additive tree representation of data collected by Arabie and Rips (1973), based on an earlier study by Henley (1969). In the study, 53 American students were asked to judge the similarity among 30 animals. The representation was generated by LSADT (De Soete, 1984), which is a least-squares additive tree-fitting procedure, and accounts for 87.3% of the variance in the data. As in the previous example, the entire tree representation is interesting, and truncating the tree would be misleading. In addition, some relationships represented by the additive tree would not be represented in an ultrametric tree. For example, *dog* and *cat* are closer to each other in the representation than *tiger* and *wolf,* even though *dog* and *wolf* are in one cluster of canine animals and *cat* and *tiger* are in another cluster of feline animals. An ultrametric representation would force *dog* and *cat* to be the same distance apart as *tiger* and *wolf,* assuming they remained in the canine and feline clusters.

It is also worth emphasizing in both of these examples that only the terminal nodes are labeled. However, implicit labels could be generated for the internal nodes, such as *grandparents* or *felines.* Carroll and Chang (1973) developed one of the few clustering methods for generating a tree representation with labeled internal nodes from a single data set. However, the method has not been widely used, in part because of

the limited number of stimulus sets that contain both terminal and nonterminal item names.

One final example is based on a cluster analysis by Lapointe and Legendre (1994). In their study, they produced a classification of 109 single-malt whiskies of Scotland. In particular, the authors of the study were interested in determining the major types of single malts that can be identified on the basis of qualitative characteristics as described in a well known connoisseur's guide (Jackson, 1989). The primary data consisted of 68 binary variables, which represented the presence or absence of a particular descriptive term, such as a *smoky* palate, a *salty* nose, *bronze* in color. The 109×68 matrix was transformed into a 109×109 lower triangular matrix of proximities using the Jaccard (1901) coefficient of similarity, which is based on the number of attributes that a pair of items has in common. The proximity matrix was used to construct the dendrogram using Ward's method, which is described in the next section. The resulting dendrogram in shown in Figure 7.4. In contrast with

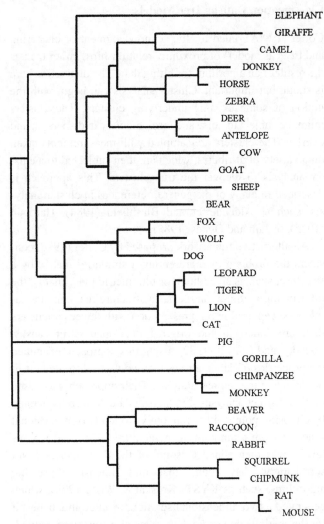

Figure 7.3 Additive tree representation for the animal similarity data as produced by De Soete and Carroll (1996).

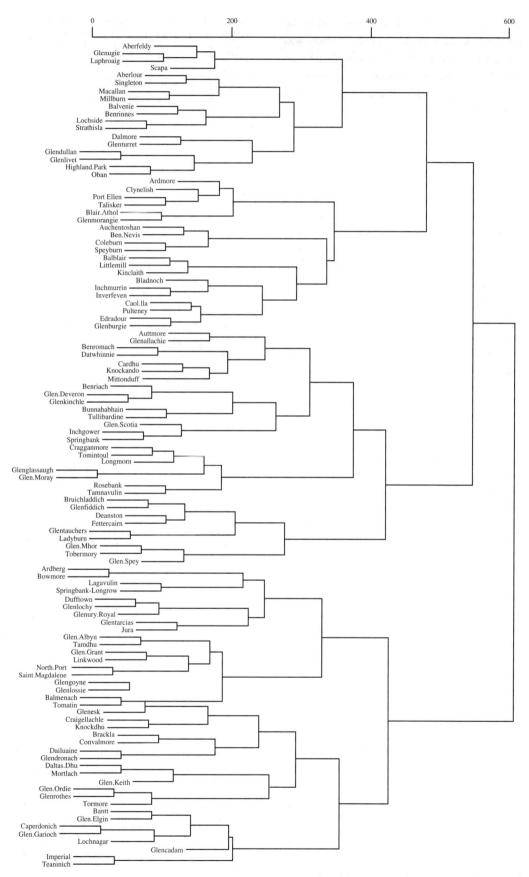

Figure 7.4 The Lapointe and Legendre (1994) classification of single malt scotch whiskies.

the previous examples, the authors are less interested in the structure of the entire tree. Instead, the goal of the study was to identify an unknown number of distinct groups. As a result of the analysis, the dendrogram was truncated to generate 12 identifiable classes of whiskeys, each labeled with a letter of the alphabet in Figure 7.4.

ALGORITHMS

There are several fundamental issues relating to the selection of a suitable clustering algorithm. First, the method must be appropriate for the type of cluster structure that is expected to be present in the data. Different clustering criteria and cluster formation methods yield different types of clusters. Second, the clustering method needs to be effective at recovering the types of cluster structures that it was intended to find. Nearly all clustering methods are heuristics, and there is no guarantee that any heuristic is effective. Finally, software support needs to be available for applied analyses. It is our experience that the latter issue tends to drive method selection with only limited regard for the first two concerns.

For those readers who wish to make a more in-depth study of clustering algorithms, several textbooks and survey articles have been written. These include the texts by Anderberg (1973), Everitt (1993), Gordon (1999), Hartigan (1975), Jain and Dubes (1988), Legendre and Legendre (1998), Lorr (1983), and Späth (1980). Survey articles include Gordon (1987), Milligan and Cooper (1987), and Milligan (1996, 1998). Although some of these sources are more dated than others, they include a wealth of information about the topic.

The next three sections offer a review of the major types of clustering methods that have been proposed in the literature. Included in each section is a discussion concerning the issue of selecting a clustering method appropriate to the type of cluster structure expected to be present in the data. The fourth section reviews the performance of a range of clustering methods in finding the correct clustering in the data.

Agglomerative Algorithms

Agglomerative algorithms are the most common among the standard clustering algorithms found in most statistical packages. Here, each of the n objects is considered to be cluster consisting of a single item. The algorithm then iterates through $n-1$ steps by combining the most similar pair of existing clusters into a new cluster and associating a height with this newly formed cluster (Gordon, 1996). Different algorithms use different methods for defining the most similar pair, associating a height, and defining a proximity measure

TABLE 7.1 Coefficients to Generate Clustering Techniques Based on the Formalization of Lance & Williams (1966)

Clustering Method	α_i	β	γ
Single link	$1/2$	0	$-1/2$
Complete link	$1/2$	0	$1/2$
Group-average link	$\dfrac{n_i}{n_i + n_j}$	0	0
Weighted-average link	$1/2$	0	0
Centroid	$\dfrac{n_i}{n_i + n_j}$	$\dfrac{-n_i n_j}{(n_i + n_j)^2}$	0
Median	$1/2$	$-1/4$	0
β-Flexible	$\dfrac{1-\beta}{2}$	$-1 \le \beta \le 1$	0

between the new cluster and the previously established clusters. In particular, if the new cluster is given by the agglomeration of C_i and C_j, then one can define the new dissimilarities measures by the general formula given by Lance and Williams (1966, 1967) as follows:

$$dissim(C_i \cup C_j, C_k)$$
$$= \alpha_i d(C_i, C_k) + \alpha_j d(C_j, C_k) + \beta d(C_i, C_j)$$
$$+ \gamma |d(C_i, C_k) - d(C_j, C_k)|$$

Different choices of the parameters $\{\alpha_i, \alpha_j, \beta, \gamma\}$ define different clustering algorithms as shown in Table 7.1. For example, $\alpha_i = 1/2, \gamma = -1/2$, defines the single-link algorithm where the new dissimilarity coefficient is given by the smallest distance between clusters. This algorithm tends to generate unstable clusters, where small changes in the data matrix result in large changes in the dendrogram (Gordon, 1996). However, it is one of the few clustering algorithms that would be able to detect clusters that are the result of a long chain of points, rather than a densely packed cluster of points.

Complete link clustering corresponds to $\alpha_i = 1/2$, $\gamma = 1/2$. Single and complete link clustering are based solely on the rank order of the entries in the data matrix and thus can be used with ordinal scale data. Most other algorithms require interval scale data. Of the interval scale techniques, group-average link [$\alpha_i = n_i/(n_i + n_j)$] and weighted-average link ($\alpha_i = 1/2$) demonstrate greater success at cluster recovery, as shown later in this chapter, than do either of the ordinal scale techniques. Group-average link is also commonly denoted as UPGMA (for unweighted pair group mean average), whereas the weighted average link method is commonly denoted as WPGMA (weighted pair group mean average; Sneath & Sokal, 1973). Additional information on combinatorial clustering methods can be found in Podani (1989).

Divisive Algorithms

For divisive algorithms, the reverse approach from agglomerative algorithms is used. Here, all *n* objects belong to a single cluster. At each step of the algorithm, one of the existing clusters is divided into two smaller clusters. Given the combinatorial explosion of the number of possible divisions, divisive algorithms must adopt heuristics to reduce the number of alternative splittings that are considered. Such algorithms often stop well before there are only single items in each cluster to minimize the number of computations needed. Still, the problem of finding an optimal division of clusters for several criteria has been shown to be NP-hard (which implies that the computational time will most likely grow exponentially with the size of the problem) for several clustering criteria (Brucker, 1978; Welch, 1982).

Optimization Algorithms

An alternative approach to iterative algorithms is to reconsider the problem by transforming a dissimilarity matrix (d_{ij}) into a matrix (h_{ij}) whose elements satisfy either the ultrametric or the additive inequality. Optimization algorithms have been developed using a least-squares approach (Carroll & Pruzansky, 1980), a branch-and-bound algorithm (Chandon, Lemaire, & Pouget, 1980), and other approximation approaches (Hartigan, 1967). One promising technique was an approach developed by De Soete (1984). The technique, which is discussed later in this chapter, has been successful at addressing the problem of determining optimal weights for the input variables.

Selecting a Clustering Method

This section focuses on the issue of evaluating algorithm performance. One approach commonly used in the literature is the analysis of real-life data sets. It is not unusual for various articles to attempt to establish algorithm performance by using only one or two empirical data sets. Thus, validating a heuristic method is always questionable. In many cases the results are considered valid because they correspond to some general or intuitive perspective. Several criticisms of this approach exist. First, one must recognize that a very small sample size has been used to establish validity. Second, one can always question the author's a priori grouping of the data. Third, how are we to know that clusters actually exist in the empirical data? Few authors consider a null clustering condition. Finally, assuming that clusters are present, how can we determine that the correct cluster structure was found? These criticisms can seldom if ever be addressed properly through the use of empirical data sets for validation purposes.

Most classification researchers have turned to the use of computer-generated data sets for establishing clustering validity. Simulation or Monte Carlo experiments allow the researcher to know the exact cluster structure underlying the data. This strategy has the advantage that the true clustering is known. The extent to which any given clustering algorithm has recovered this structure can be determined. Because of the use of artificially generated data sets, simulation results can be based on hundreds or thousands of data sets. Thus, sample size is not an issue.

There is a serious weakness in the use of simulation methods. In every case, such results are limited on the basis of generalizability. That is, the Monte Carlo results may be valid only for the types of cluster structures and distributions that were present in the generated data sets. Thus, the effectiveness of the algorithms may not extend to other data structures that are possible in applied analyses. Thus, it is important to establish replicability of simulation results from differing studies. It is especially valuable when different researchers achieve similar results using different strategies for data generation and evaluation. Such replications offer investigators more confidence in the selection of methods for applied analyses.

In terms of results on the recovery of underlying cluster structure, agglomerative hierarchical algorithms have been the most extensively studied. Three reviews of Monte Carlo clustering studies covering various time frames were published by Milligan (1981a), Milligan and Cooper (1987), and Milligan (1996). The validation studies have examined a number of factors that might affect recovery of the underlying clusters. Many studies have included an error-free data condition. The clustering present in the error-free data typically was so distinct that almost any method should have been able to perform well with this sort of simple and obvious data structure. Clustering methods that fail with error-free data would not be suitable for most applied research settings.

A second factor examined has been the introduction of some sort of error, either on the underlying variables or directly to the similarity measures. This condition has the capability of being tuned to a gradient of increasing noise. An effective clustering method should be capable of finding clusters that have been hidden by moderate amounts of error in the data.

A different sort of error involves the introduction of outlying data points to a core set of elements that defines a suitable cluster structure. Unusual observations are not unusual in behavioral research. A clustering method used for applied analyses should have some insensitivity to the presence of such data points.

The population distribution used to conceptualize and generate the clusters themselves need not be multivariate normal. Nonnormality may be present in many empirical data sets, and a clustering method should be able to recover well-defined clusters in such circumstances. Furthermore, alternative population distributions serve to generalize the Monte Carlo results. Few simulation studies have included more than one type of distribution. The generalization exists across different studies using differing underlying population probability models.

The number of clusters in the underlying data can be varied easily and, thus, can serve to ensure that a given clustering method is not sensitive to this factor. The clustering method adopted should not have differential effectiveness on this factor.

The relative sample size of clusters can be systematically varied as well. Some clustering methods do not respond properly to the presence of unequal cluster sizes. This is not a

desirable result, and it has implications for applied analyses. The characteristic can be demonstrated most easily by generating data sets with varying cluster sizes.

Some authors have varied the number of variables that are used to construct the artificial data. Since the data are first transformed to a similarity measure, most clustering methods do not directly analyze the original data. However, the number of variables may influence the information captured by the similarity measure and, hence, influence the method's ability to recover the underlying clusters. Other factors have been included in one or more studies. These include the use of more than one similarity measure for the data and the number of underlying dimensions from a principal component representation of the variable space, among others.

Simulation results for a set of hierarchical methods are presented first. Validation results for five such methods are reported in Table 7.2, adapted from Milligan and Cooper (1987). It is important not to overinterpret the results in the

TABLE 7.2   Monte Carlo Validation Results for Hierarchical Methods

	Method				
Study	Single Link	Complete Link	Group Average	Ward's Method	Beta Flexible
Baker (1974)					
Low error	.605	.968			
Medium error	.298	.766			
High error	.079	.347			
Kuiper & Fisher (1975)					
Medium size	.579	.742	.710	.767	
Five clusters	.444	.690	.630	.707	
Unequal sizes	.663	.705	.702	.689	
Blashfield (1976)	.06	.42	.17	.77	
Mojena (1977)	.369	.637	.596	.840	
Mezzich (1978)					
Correlation	.625	.973			
Euclidean	.648	.943			
Edelbrock (1979)					
Correlation	.90	.80	.96		
Euclidean	.62	.63	.70	.88	
Milligan & Isaac (1980)	.30	.64	.70	.57	
Bayne, Beauchanp, Begovich, & Kane (1980)					
Configuration 1	.53	.68	.66	.70	
Configuration 2	.55	.76	.75	.76	
Edelbrock & McLaughlin (1980)					
Correlation	.858	.813	.880		
Euclidean	.690	.780	.858	.873	
Milligan (1980)					
Zero error	.974	.995	.998	.987	.997
Low error	.902	.970	.997	.989	.994
High error	.777	.880	.948	.940	.945
Scheibler & Schneider (1985)					
Correlation	.43	.49	.81	.78	.73
Euclidean	.04	.38	.16	.79	.77

Note. For details on the nature of the recovery values, see Milligan and Cooper (1987).

table because the recovery index is not the same across all studies. Direct numerical comparisons should be made within a given study, and not across different experiments. The measures do have the common characteristic that recovery performance improves as the index approaches 1.00, which indicates perfect cluster recovery.

The simulation results in Table 7.2 contain some important lessons for the applied user. In most cases, there appears to be an advantage in favor of Ward's (1963) method and the β-flexible approach. Performing somewhat more erratically, the group-average method can be competitive as gauged by cluster recovery, but not always. The effectiveness of the β-flexible approach from these studies led to some improvements on this method by Milligan (1989a) and Belbin, Faith, and Milligan (1992).

A particularly important result seen in Table 7.2 is that the single-link method has consistently performed poorly, even in the case of error-free data where distinct clustering exists. Furthermore, single link is especially sensitive to most any form of error added to the data. Cheng and Milligan (1995a, 1996a) also demonstrated that the single-link method was remarkably sensitive to outliers present in the data. That is, the method can be adversely affected by the presence of only one outlier. An outlier in a clustering context refers to an entity that does not fall within the general region of any cluster. Although some authors have argued that the method possesses optimal theoretical properties (e.g., Fisher & Van Ness 1971; Jardine & Sibson; 1971), simulation and empirical evidence suggest that this is an unsuitable method for most applied research.

Simulation-based research on nonhierarchical partitioning methods has not been as extensive as for the hierarchical routines. K-means (MacQueen, 1967) algorithms have been the most frequently examined methods to date. Simulation results for such methods are presented in Table 7.3. Generally, these studies were based on error-free data sets. The simulation-based literature indicates that the recovery performance of some partitioning methods can be competitive with those found for the best hierarchical procedures. As before, the reader is warned not to overinterpret the numerical recovery values between studies as they are based on different indices.

Most of the generated data sets used to establish the results in Table 7.3 were multivariate normal and should have been the ideal application context for the normal theory-based clustering methods such as the Friedman and Rubin (1967) and Wolfe's (1970) NORMIX procedures. Unfortunately, such methods performed inconsistently in these studies. Less sophisticated methods, such as k-means algorithms, can produce equivalent or superior recovery of cluster structure.

TABLE 7.3   Monte Carlo Validation Results for Nonhierarchical Clustering Methods

Clustering Method	Average Recovery	Recovery With Rational Seeds
Blashfield (1977)		
Forgy k-means	.585	
Convergent k-means	.638	
CLUSTAN k-means	.706	.643
Friedman-Rubin trace **W**	.545	
Friedman-Rubin |**W**|	.705	
MIKCA trace **W**	.560	
MIKCA |**W**|	.699	
Mezzich (1978)		
Convergent k-means: correlation	.955	
Convergent k-means: Euclidean distances	.989	
Ball-Hall ISODATA	.977	
Friedman-Rubin |**W**|	.966	
Wolfe NORMIX	.443	
Bayne et al. (1980)		
Convergent k-means	.83	
Friedman-Rubin trace **W**	.82	
Friedman-Rubin |**W**|	.82	
Wolfe NORMIX	.70	
Milligan (1980): Low error condition		
MacQueen's k-means	.884	.934
Forgy's k-means	.909	.996
Jancey's k-means	.926	.993
Convergent k-means	.901	.996
Scheibler & Schneider (1985)		
CLUSTAN k-means	.67	.78
Späth's k-means	.55	.77

Note. Average recovery for k-means methods corresponds to random starting seeds. "Rational Seeds" were centroids obtained from Ward's or group-average methods.

One characteristic discovered from the set of studies reported in Table 7.2 concerns the nature of the cluster seeds used to start the k-means algorithms. The k-means algorithms appear to have differential recovery performance depending on the quality of the initial configuration. This effect was systematically studied by Milligan (1980). The results reported by Milligan indicated that starting seeds based on randomly selected sample points were less effective than was the use of rational starting configurations. Rational starting seeds markedly improved the recovery performance of all k-means methods. In light of these results, Milligan and Sokol (1980) proposed a two-stage clustering algorithm that was designed to improve the recovery of the underlying clusters. Subsequently, other researchers have endorsed this approach or developed useful refinements (see Punj & Stewart, 1983; Wong, 1982; Wong & Lane, 1983).

Overall, more research on the comparative evaluation of clustering methods is needed. We have good information on certain types of methods. However, for other methods or approaches the current knowledge base on algorithm performance is weak or badly lacking. For example, there have been a number of recent developments. An interesting approach to clustering, called MCLUST, has been proposed by Raftery, Fraley, and associates (see Fraley & Raftery, 1998). To date, an independent evaluation of this approach has not been published.

STEPS IN A CLUSTER ANALYSIS

A fundamental principle in classification is that as the level of error increases in the data, or in the specification of one or more factors relating to the clustering, the ability to recover the underlying cluster structure is reduced. Thus, a number of issues must be addressed while conducting an applied analysis in addition to the choice of clustering method.

Sometimes these decisions are not apparent to the researcher. For example, a researcher may select a clustering software package that makes one or more of these decisions without user intervention. The researcher should be alert to the fact that these decisions were made and that they directly affect the quality of the clustering results.

When applied research is published using clustering methodology, we recommend that the specific actions taken during the classification process be clearly articulated. This practice is essential to allow subsequent researchers the ability to evaluate, compare, and extend the results. Examples abound in the literature where authors have failed to provide such information (see Milligan, 1996). Critical information includes the choice of similarity measure, the clustering algorithm used to form the groups, the determination of the number of clusters, and information on the sample and variables used in the analysis.

Several key elements or decision points in the clustering process are reviewed in this section. Best practical suggestions, based on the current state of knowledge, are offered. These suggestions relate to the selection of the elements to be clustered, the selection of the variables to cluster, issues concerning variable standardization, the selection of the number of clusters, and the validation of empirical analyses.

Selecting the Data Set

The issue of selecting the data elements in a cluster analysis has seen limited research. This issue is critical because it is the sample of data elements selected for study that define the resulting cluster structure. Several fairly simple principles can guide the researcher. Unlike traditional inference-based statistical procedures, random samples are not required for an effective cluster analysis. Certainly, the selected sample should accurately represent the underlying clusters, but not necessarily in proportion to their size in the larger population. In the absence of this consideration, it is likely that small population segments may not be detected in a cluster analysis. Oversampling these small populations would likely serve to enhance their recovery in the cluster analysis. Furthermore, some clustering methods have some bias to find clusters of relatively equal size, and this tendency can be used to good advantage.

Of course, random sampling would be desirable if it is essential for the researcher to be able to generalize the results of the study to a target population. However, doing so would imply a more theoretically driven analysis as opposed to a more exploratory study. Random or stratified sampling would be useful in replication studies or in more advanced studies attempting to validate a contextual theory.

The selection of the sample elements should consider the overall size of the database. A second sample or a split-half sample would be helpful for validation purposes, as discussed later in this chapter. As suggested by Milligan (1996), one possible approach is to place artificially generated ideal-type individuals or subjects in the data set. The researcher specifies the values for each variable of an ideal-type individual. The ideal type would represent a subject or other experimental object that would represent the norm for each group or cluster suspected to be present in the data. One or possibly more ideal types would be specified for each hypothesized cluster. The presence of the correct ideal type or types in a cluster would support the researcher's conceptualization for the hypothesized clustering. On the other hand, if markedly different ideal types appear in the same cluster, then the researcher's theory or the cluster analysis is suspect. The presence of clusters without ideal types may represent groups not yet defined by the researcher's theory, or possibly subgroups of a larger cluster. The user should be warned that the use of ideal types is a temporary process. The presence of ideal types in the final clustering may change the assignment of other elements in the data set. The relative influence of individual data elements has been explored by Cheng and Milligan (1995a, 1995b, 1996a, 1996b).

Related to the issue of influential data points is the issue of outliers. Outliers in a clustering context deserve special consideration. As stated previously, an outlier in a clustering context refers to an entity that does not fall within the general region of any cluster. Note that outliers may or may not have influence on the clustering solution obtained, and some data points near or in a cluster may have an influential effect on the clustering process.

An early simulation study on the effect of outliers in clustering was conducted by Milligan (1980). This research confirmed that as the percentage of outliers increased, the ability of hierarchical clustering methods to recover the underlying structure decreased. Some methods were less affected than others. More recent results concerning the effect of outliers on hierarchical methods can be found in Milligan (1989a) and Belbin et al. (1992). This more recent research suggests that Ward's (1963) method may not be as seriously affected by the presence of outliers as first suspected. Similarly, Belbin et al. (1992) demonstrated desirable characteristics with respect to outliers for two versions of the β-flexible method. Overall, the impact of outliers appears to be less severe for k-means methods.

The applied user of clustering methodology can adopt several different strategies for dealing with outliers. One can eliminate those elements that appear to be outliers to the overall set of data. Alternatively, the relationship between the obtained clusters and the suspected outliers can be investigated after an initial clustering is completed. A third alternative is to use a clustering method resistant to the presence of outliers. Selected parameterizations of the β-flexible hierarchical clustering procedure and Ward's (1963) minimum variance method may be good selections, as well as some of the k-means algorithms.

Variable Selection and Weighting

Clustering methods differ profoundly from traditional statistical inference models. Standard statistical requirements such as the assumption of normally distributed data generally do not apply within the clustering framework. That is, the methods are heuristics, and they were often developed without consideration of an underlying probability model for the data.

Another common misconception is that the presence of correlated variables in the data set is somehow bad or undesirable. Researchers often fail to realize that the correlations among variables may be a result of the natural cluster structure in the data. Attempts to eliminate these correlations would likely serve to distort or hide the structure in the data. Numerous applied analyses have attempted to eliminate intervariable correlation by means of principal components or other multivariate methods. Unfortunately, the routine application of principal components or other factoring techniques prior to clustering is appropriate only in those cases where the clusters are hypothesized to exist in the factor space and not in the original data. Sneath (1980) has shown that clusters embedded in a high-dimensional variable space may not be correctly identified in a reduced number of orthogonal components.

A different issue relates to the selection of variables to include in the cluster analysis. Care must be exercised in selection of the variables. Most reference works in the clustering area fail to offer strong advice on this issue. Only those variables that are believed to help discriminate among the clusters in the data should be included in the analysis. Far too many analyses have been conducted by including every available variable. Some users have gone to great efforts to collect just one more variable without considering its ability to help find the underlying clustering. Instead, the bias should be *not* to include the variable without additional information.

The difficulty in using all available data can result from the added irrelevant variables' serving to mask whatever actual clustering is present in a reduced number of variables. In fact, the addition of only one or two irrelevant variables can dramatically interfere with cluster recovery. Milligan (1980) was the first to demonstrate this effect. In this study only one or two random noise variables were added to data sets where a strong and distinct clustering was present in a reduced set of variables. Fowlkes and Mallows (1983) introduced the term *masking variables,* which is a good description of the effect. Results from the Milligan (1980) study are presented in Table 7.4.

As can be seen in Table 7.4, cluster recovery quickly degraded with even one random noise dimension added to the core data containing distinct clustering. A second dimension continued to diminish the ability to find the true structure in the data. The core dimensions defined a strong clustering in the data. Clearly, there are important implications for applied analyses. The inclusion of just one irrelevant variable may serve to mask or hide the real clustering in the data. It would

TABLE 7.4   Results From Milligan (1980): Mean Recovery Values With Masking Variables

Clustering Method	Error-Free Data	1-Dimensional Noise	2-Dimensional Noise
Hierarchical			
Single link	.974	.899	.843
Complete link	.995	.859	.827
Group average (UPGMA)	.998	.930	.903
Weighted average (WPGMA)	.994	.917	.885
Centroid (UPGMC)	.983	.808	.616
Median (WPGMC)	.976	.808	.661
Ward's method	.987	.881	.855
β-flexible	.997	.904	.863
Average link in cluster	.985	.870	.834
Minimum total SS	.935	.837	.780
Minimum average SS	.993	.900	.865
Partitioning			
MacQueen's k-means	.884	.793	.769
Forgy's k-means	.932	.844	.794
Jancey's k-means	.927	.867	.823
Convergent k-means	.903	.849	.787

Note. Average within-cell standard deviation is .108 and was based on 108 data sets.

be wise to provide a justification for each variable included in the clustering process. The bias should be toward exclusion in the case where doubt exists as to whether the variable may contain information regarding the clustering in the data.

Fortunately, a significant contribution on the problem of masking variables has been made. If Euclidean distances are used with a hierarchical clustering method, then the optimal variable weighting method of De Soete (1986, 1988) may offer helpful protection against masking variables. De Soete's method computes optimal weights for the distance equation:

$$d_{ij} = \left[\sum_{k=1}^{nv} w_k(x_{ik} - x_{jk})^2 \right]^{.5}.$$

The derivation and computation of the weights are complex, and the reader is referred to the work of De Soete (1986, 1988) and Makarenkov and Legendre (2000) for further details. Originally, De Soete's procedure was not intended to detect masking variables. Rather, the purpose was to optimize the fit of the computed distances to an ultrametric structure. The application to masking variables was suggested by one of the example analyses conducted by De Soete (1986). Milligan (1989b) pursued this application and found evidence that the method was effective at dealing with the masking problem. Makarenkov and Legendre (2000) recently have replicated the results concerning the effectiveness of the weights against masking variables. In addition, their work provides an important extension to k-means methods.

The results in Table 7.5 are from Milligan's (1989b) study of De Soete's algorithm. The study compared the recovery performance using equal variable weights to that obtained using optimal weights. As can be seen in the table, recovery performance was greatly enhanced, even when three masking variables were added to the core cluster dimensions. Further research revealed that De Soete's algorithm was assigning effectively zero weights to the masking variables,

thus eliminating their noise contribution to the distance computation.

There have been other attempts to deal with the problem of optimal variable weighting. For example, DeSarbo, Carroll, and Green (1984) proposed a procedure called SYNCLUS. The algorithm uses a nonhierarchical k-means method in the clustering process. To date, there has not been a systematic validation study conducted on the SYNCLUS algorithm. Green, Carmone, and Kim (1990) reported that the starting configuration used for the k-means method appears to be a critical factor for the success of the effectiveness of the variable weighting method. Other approaches to the masking problem do not attempt to provide differential weighting of variables. Rather, the method of Fowlkes, Gnanadesikan, and Kettenring (1988) attempts to include or exclude variables in a manner analogous to that used in stepwise regression.

Variable Standardization

With respect to variable standardization, we again find that applied researchers bring potentially ill-advised biases to the clustering process. First, many researchers assume that variable standardization is required in order to prepare the data for clustering. They assert that variable standardization is necessary when the variances among variables differ to any significant degree. Similarly, some authors will argue that standardization is essential when substantial differences exist in the numerical magnitude of the mean of the variables. Otherwise, it is believed that those variables with the larger scales or variances will have an undue influence on the cluster analysis.

Many researchers fail to consider that if the cluster structure actually exists in the original variable space, then standardization can distort or hide the clustering present in the data. Again, as with principal components, standardization would be appropriate if the clusters were believed to exist in

TABLE 7.5   Results From Milligan (1989b): Mean Recovery for Masking Variables Using De Soete's (1988) Variable Weighting Algorithm

Clustering Method	1 Dimension		2 Dimensions		3 Dimensions	
	Equal Weights	Weighted	Equal Weights	Weighted	Equal Weights	Weighted
β-flexible = −.5	.750	.966	.673	.952	.601	.948
β-flexible = −.25	.788	.979	.716	.962	.657	.961
Single link	.812	.883	.647	.840	.473	.820
Complete link	.668	.977	.595	.955	.555	.930
Group average	.859	.980	.809	.965	.732	.957
Ward's method	.764	.968	.675	.955	.627	.947
Column standard deviation	.263	.128	.295	.163	.307	.180

Note. Each mean was based on 108 data sets.

the transformed variable space. This result was first demonstrated in a simple example by Fleiss and Zubin (1969). Other discussions on this topic appeared in Sneath and Sokal (1973) and in Anderberg (1973).

A different bias brought to the analysis by applied researchers is an assumption as to the form of variable standardization to be used. Researchers with a social science or statistics background often assume that variable standardization would be based on the traditional z score:

$$z_1 = \frac{x - \bar{x}}{s}.$$

It turns out that there are number of other ways in which to standardize data so that the influence of variance and relative numerical values can be controlled. Milligan and Cooper (1988) documented several other approaches to variable standardization:

$$z_2 = \frac{x}{s},$$

$$z_3 = \frac{x}{Max(x)},$$

$$z_4 = \frac{x}{Max(x) - Min(x)},$$

$$z_5 = \frac{x - Min(x)}{Max(x) - Min(x)},$$

$$z_6 = \frac{x}{\sum x},$$

and $z_7 = Rank(x).$

Milligan and Cooper (1988) evaluated the performance of the various forms of standardization in a large-scale simulation study. Included were the traditional z score (z_1), z_2 through z_7, as well as the unstandardized data represented by z_0 in their study.

Selected simulation results from the Milligan and Cooper (1988) article are presented in Tables 7.6 and 7.7. Each entry in the tables represents the average obtained from 864 data sets. Note that the rows in the tables correspond to the various forms of standardization. The columns in Table 7.6 represent different types of artificially generated data structures. The entries are averages across four clustering methods. Table 7.7 presents similar information broken down by clustering method.

The asterisk notation is unique to these tables and requires explanation. An asterisk indicates that the corresponding standardization method was in the statistically equivalent superior group for a given column. This was, in effect, a test of simple main effects in a factorial ANOVA design. Thus, the asterisk indicates the best performing methods for each condition. Across the conditions explored in Milligan and

TABLE 7.6 Results From Milligan & Cooper (1988): Effect of Standardization Procedure and Alternative Data Structures

Standard-ization Formula	Separation Level		Maximum Variance Ratio		Global Variance
	Near	Distant	16	100	Experiment
z_0	.662	.821	.745	.739	.621(L)
z_1 & z_2	.672	.837	.755	.754	.936
z_3	.689*	.854*	.771*	.772*	.984*
z_4 & z_5	.693*	.864*	.778*	.780*	.968*
z_6	.674*	.836	.757	.753	.981*
z_7	.639(L)	.768(L)	.693(L)	.713(L)	.839
Overall	.674	.835	.754	.756	.888

Note. The asterisk indicates membership in the statistically equivalent superior group. (L) indicates that the procedure performed significantly worse than the other methods.

Cooper (1988), the only standardization procedures that were in the superior group in every case were those methods that standardized by range, namely z_4 and z_5. The consistency of the results was unexpected. Since the publication of the 1988 study, anecdotal evidence reported by numerous researchers has supported the Milligan and Cooper results. Recently, Mirkin (2000) has been developing a mathematical theory as to why standardization by range has been consistently effective. Mirkin and other researchers are likely to continue with this line of inquiry.

Selecting the Number of Clusters

The next significant problem faced in the analysis is the determination of the number of clusters to be used in the final solution. Some clustering methods, such as k-means, require the user to specify the number of groups ahead of time. Other methods require the researcher to sort through and select

TABLE 7.7 Results From Milligan & Cooper (1988): Effect of Standardization Procedure and Clustering Method

Standardization Formula	Clustering Method			
	Single Link	Complete Link	Group Average	Ward's Method
z_0	.608*	.750	.811	.798(L)
z_1 & z_2	.577	.778	.800	.864*
z_3	.622*	.793*	.835*	.836
z_4 & z_5	.609*	.815*	.839*	.851*
z_6	.616*	.761	.813	.828
z_7	.494(L)	.730(L)	.810	.781(L)
Overall	.589	.777	.819	.834

Note. The asterisk indicates membership in the statistically equivalent superior group. (L) indicates that the procedure performed significantly worse than the other methods.

from a sequence of different clustering solutions. This is the case when hierarchical algorithms are selected and the purpose is to find a coherent grouping of the data elements as opposed to a tree representation.

Numerous methods have been proposed for selecting the number of clusters, especially in a hierarchical context. As with many aspects of the clustering process, theoretical developments on this problem have been limited to date. Rather, we have a set of ad hoc methods. The formulas are sometimes called stopping rules for hierarchical clustering methods. The most comprehensive study on the selection of a suitable stopping rule in a hierarchical context is the article by Milligan and Cooper (1985). These authors conducted a comparative evaluation of 30 stopping rules within a simulation framework. The authors considered only those rules that were independent of the clustering method. The generated data sets used by Milligan and Cooper (1985) consisted of error-free structure with distinct clustering. Despite the pronounced clustering present in the data, the results of their study revealed that there was a wide range in the effectiveness of the stopping rules. Selected results from the Milligan and Cooper (1985) study are presented in Table 7.8. The reader is referred to the 1985 article for more detailed performance information and for references for each stopping rule.

The results in Table 7.8 indicate the number of times that a given stopping rule selected the correct number of clusters in the data. The maximum performance rate that could be obtained for any specific number of clusters was 108, and 432 overall. The results in the table include a number of well known approaches such as Mojena's (1977) method, Beale's (1969) pseudo F test, and the rule developed by Calinski and Harabasz (1974). As one reaches the least effective methods at the bottom of the table, the chance selection rate for each cluster level is around 9.

Certainly, more research in the area of stopping rules is needed. The Milligan and Cooper results are from one simulation study, and the potential limitation of generalizability is an important consideration. Independent validation of the performance of the rules with other types of simulated data needs to be undertaken. The reader is warned not to take the performance ranking of the stopping rules as an absolute finding. The rankings produced by Milligan and Cooper (1985) may have been a result of the specific characteristics of the simulated data sets. On the other hand, one might argue that those stopping rules found in the upper third of those tested by Milligan and Cooper might be replicated to some degree in an independent study. Similarly, it would seem unlikely that the least effective rules in their report would perform with a degree of distinction in a different experiment. Support for this conjecture was found by Cooper and Milligan (1988) in a

TABLE 7.8   Results From Milligan & Cooper (1985): Stopping Rule Performance

	Number of True Clusters				
Stopping Rule	2	3	4	5	Overall
1. Calinski & Harabasz	96	95	97	102	390
2. Duda & Hart	77	101	103	107	388
3. C-index	71	89	91	96	347
4. Gamma	74	86	83	96	339
5. Beale	57	87	95	92	331
6. Cubic clustering criterion	67	88	82	84	321
7. Point-biserial	94	83	66	65	308
8. $G(+)$	52	70	79	96	297
9. Mojena	20	84	93	92	289
10. Davies & Bouldin	54	72	72	89	287
11. Stepsize	96	56	53	68	273
12. Likelihood ratio	64	72	64	68	268
13. $|\log(p)|$	78	71	45	43	237
14. Sneath	34	51	66	83	234
15. Frey & Van Groenewoud	0	76	79	77	232
16. $\log(SSB/SSW)$	0	104	42	66	212
17. Tau	85	77	30	10	202
18. $\bar{c}/\sqrt{k}$	88	80	25	7	200
19. $n \log(|\mathbf{W}|/|\mathbf{T}|)$	0	104	32	13	149
20. $k^2 |\mathbf{W}|$	0	104	15	27	146
21. Bock	74	15	31	22	142
22. Ball & Hall	0	104	23	1	128
23. Trace Cov($\mathbf{W}$)	0	104	17	0	121
24. Trace $\mathbf{W}$	0	104	16	0	120
25. Lingoes & Cooper	37	30	17	16	100
26. Trace $\mathbf{W}^{-1}\mathbf{B}$	0	52	23	9	84
27. Generalized distance	5	22	11	9	47
28. McClain & Rao	9	5	5	6	25
29. Mountford	1	6	1	2	10
30. $|\mathbf{W}|/|\mathbf{T}|$	0	0	0	0	0

related experiment. In this experiment, the data were subjected to various levels of error perturbation. Although the performance of the rules declined as expected, the relative ranking of the stopping was sustained in the experiment.

For applied analyses, it is recommended that one use two or three of the better performing rules from the Milligan and Cooper (1985) study. The *Statistical Analysis System* (SAS) (Gilmore, 1999) has implemented several of these rules as clustering software options. When consistent results are obtained from the rules, evidence exists for the selection of the specified number of clusters. If partial agreement is found, the user might opt for the larger number of clusters. In this case, one may have an incomplete clustering of the data where two or more groups still need to be merged. Their characteristics will appear to be fairly similar when the researcher is attempting to interpret each cluster. Finally, if no consistency can be found among the rules, the researcher is facing one of several possibilities. Of course, the stopping rules might have failed on the empirical data set at hand. A different outcome is that there is no cluster structure inherent in the data set. Since most clustering routines will produce a partition (or set of partitions) for any data set, a researcher might assume that there is a significant clustering present in the data. This belief induces a bias against a null hypothesis of no significant clustering in the data in empirical research.

Validation of the Clustering Results

Once the clustering results are obtained, the process of validating the resulting grouping begins. Several strategies or techniques can assist in the validation process. This section covers the topics of interpretation, graphical methods, hypothesis testing, and replication analysis.

Interpretation

An empirical classification will contribute to the knowledge of a scientific domain only if it can be interpreted substantively. To begin the evaluation process, descriptive statistics should be computed for each cluster. The descriptive values can be computed both on those variables used to form the clusters as well as on exogenous variables not involved in computing the clusters. The descriptive information can reveal important differences and similarities between clusters, and it can indicate the degree of cohesiveness within clusters. Skinner (1978) refers to such characteristics as level (cluster mean or centroid), scatter (variability), and shape (covariances and distribution of data within clusters). Similarly, if ideal type markers were used in the analysis, their cluster assignments can be examined for interpretive information.

A different approach is to use a block diagonal matrix display (Anderberg, 1973; Duffy & Quiroz, 1991). Although this technique results in a matrix of numbers, the display approaches that of a graphical presentation. The process is based on rearranging the similarity matrix according to the groups obtained by the cluster analysis. The rows and columns are reordered to place elements in the same cluster in consecutive order. The result is ideally a block diagonal matrix where within-block values represent within-cluster distances or similarities. Entries outside of the blocks correspond to between-cluster distances. If distinct clusters have been recovered by the clustering method, the within-block values should be distinctly different in magnitude when compared to those between blocks. The permuted matrix can be converted to a graphical display if the cells or blocks are shaded according to some rule based on the values of the similarity measures.

A variety of graphical displays have been proposed in the classification literature. For example, Andrews (1972) proposed a bivariate plot where data from a high-dimensional variable space are transformed by means of selected transcendental functions. Andrews argued that similar elements should produce similar transformed profiles in the plot. Bailey and Dubes (1982) developed a different type of display called a cluster validity profile. The profiles were intended to allow for the evaluation of the relative isolation and compactness of each individual cluster. Kleiner and Hartigan (1981) presented a set of graphical methods based on natural-appearing "trees" and "castles." These displays are best suited to hierarchical clustering results. An excellent discussion on the use of graphical methods in a clustering context is found in Jain and Dubes (1988).

Hypothesis Testing

Hypothesis testing is possible in a cluster-analytic situation, but it can be tricky and full of pitfalls for the unsuspecting user. Most testing procedures have been developed to determine whether a significant cluster structure has been found. Because clustering algorithms yield partitions, applied researchers who see such results tend to assume that there must be clusters in their data. However, clustering methods will yield partitions even for random noise data lacking structure.

There are some significant limitations in the use of traditional hypothesis-testing methods. Perhaps the most tempting strategy, given the context of the analysis, is to use an ANOVA, MANOVA, or discriminant analysis directly on the variables that were used to determine the clustering. The partitions obtained from the cluster analysis are used to define the groups for the ANOVA or discriminant analysis. An attempt is made to determine whether there are significant differences between the clusters. Unfortunately, such an analysis is invalid. Since the groups were defined by partitions on each variable, an ANOVA or discriminant analysis will almost always return significant results regardless of the structure in the data, even for random noise. The fundamental problem is that one does not have random assignment to the groups independent of the values on the variables in the analysis. This result was noted by Dubes and Jain (1979) and by Milligan and Mahajan (1980). It is unfortunate that many textbooks on clustering do not emphasize this limitation.

There is a way to conduct a valid inference process in a clustering context. Valid testing procedures take on one of several different approaches. The first approach is called an external analysis, and the test is based on variables not used in the cluster analysis. The second approach is called an internal analysis and is based on information used in the clustering process. These two approaches are considered in turn.

External criterion analysis can be performed using standard parametric procedures. One can test directly for significant differences between clusters on variables that were not used in the cluster analysis. It is critical for the validity of the test that the variable not be used in forming the clusters.

A different type of external analysis is based on a data partition generated independently of the data set at hand. The partition can be specified from a theoretical model or obtained from a clustering of a separate data set. Hubert and Baker (1977) developed a method to test for the significance of similarity between the two sets of partitions. The test is based on an assumption of independent assignments to groups in the two partition sets. It is important to note that the Hubert and Baker method cannot be applied to two clusterings of the *same* data set. Doing so would not result in two independent groupings of the objects in the study.

An internal criterion analysis is based on information obtained from within the clustering process. These analyses are based on measures that attempt to represent in some form the goodness of fit between the input data and the resulting cluster partitions. There are numerous ways in which to measure the goodness of fit. Milligan (1981b) conducted a study of 30 internal criterion indices for cluster analysis. For an extended discussion of such indices, see Milligan (1981b). Milligan's research indicated that indices such as the gamma, C-index, and tau measures should make an effective measure of internal consistency.

The advantage to identifying an effective internal criterion index is that it can serve as a test statistic in a hypothesis-testing context. The test can be used to determine whether a significant clustering exists in the data. The main problem with this approach is the specification of a suitable sampling distribution for the test statistic under the null hypothesis of no cluster structure. One can use randomization methods, or bootstrapping, to generate an approximate sampling distribution. Milligan and Sokol (1980), Begovich and Kane (1982), and Good (1982) have all proposed tests based on this strategy. Unfortunately, software support for this form of testing is not widely available.

Replication Analysis

Replication analysis within a clustering context appears to have been developed by McIntyre and Blashfield (1980) and by Morey, Blashfield, and Skinner (1983). Replication analysis is analogous to a cross-validation procedure in multiple regression. The logic behind replication analysis is that if an underlying clustering exists in the data set, then one should be able to replicate these results in a second sample from the same source and set of variables. There are six steps in a replication analysis. First, one obtains two samples. This can be done by taking a random split-half reliability of a larger

data set. Data must be obtained on the same set of variables in both samples. Second, the first sample is subjected to the planned cluster process. Once the clusters have been identified, the cluster centroids are computed from the first sample. These centroids are used in the next step. Third, the distances between the data points in the second sample to the centroids obtained from the first sample are computed. Fourth, each element in the second sample is assigned to the nearest centroid determined from the first sample. This produces a clustering of the second sample based on the cluster characteristics of the first sample. Fifth, the second sample is subjected to the same cluster process as used for the first sample. Note that we now have two clusterings of the second sample. One was obtained from the nearest centroid assignment process, the second from a direct clustering of the data. The final step is to compute a measure of partition agreement between the two clusterings of the second sample. The kappa statistic or the Hubert and Arabie (1985) corrected Rand index can serve as the measure of agreement. The resulting statistic indicates the level of agreement between the two partitions and reflects on the stability of the clustering in the data from two samples.

Breckenridge (1989, 1993) extended this approach to replication analysis and provided performance information on the effectiveness of the approach. The results reported in Table 7.9 are from his 1993 simulation study. The column labeled "Recovery" indicates the degree of agreement between the true cluster assignments and the partitions obtained from the clustering procedure. The column for "Replication" indicates the degree of agreement between the direct clustering of the second sample and the nearest centroid grouping for the same sample. Recall that this grouping was based on the classification from the first sample. The results indicate that the replication means were close in value to average recovery for each method. This finding suggests that replication analysis can be used as a validation tool for applied cluster analysis.

Breckenridge (1993) also reported that replication analysis can be used to help determine the number of clusters in the

TABLE 7.9   Results From Breckenridge (1993): Mean Recovery and Replication Values for Error-Free Data

Clustering Method	Recovery	Replication
β-flexible = −.5	.773	.750
β-flexible = −.25	.761	.738
Single link	.440	.350
Complete link	.695	.654
Group average	.751	.740
Ward's method	.787	.766
Hartigan & Wong k-means: (Ward's method seed points)	.785	.797

Note. Averages based on 960 data sets.

TABLE 7.10 Results From Breckenridge (1993): Number of Clusters Selected by the Scree Test

True Number of Clusters	Number Chosen							
	2	3	4	5	6	7	8	9
2	58	1	0	0	0	0	0	0
3	10	48	1	0	0	0	0	0
4	1	12	45	2	1	0	0	0
5	1	2	11	35	9	1	1	0
6	1	2	5	11	32	5	3	1
7	1	0	6	8	12	22	7	4
8	0	1	0	6	13	8	12	20
9	1	5	5	7	5	5	3	29

TABLE 7.11 Number of Source Articles in Psychology Journals on Clustering and Classification by Subdiscipline for 1999

Subdiscipline	N	%
Social/personality	28	21.5%
Cognitive/experimental	22	16.9%
Applied/organizational	16	12.3%
General	16	12.3%
Methodological	12	9.2%
Counseling	9	6.9%
Developmental	8	6.2%
Clinical	7	5.4%
Educational	6	4.6%
Neuroscience	5	3.8%

data. Results for 480 data sets are presented in Table 7.10. The columns of the table indicate the number of clusters selected by a scree test, and the rows represent the correct number of clusters in the data. Thus, the diagonal of the table corresponds to the correct specification of the number of clusters identified by the scree test. A scree test is a graphical method used for visually identifying the change in level of a statistical measure. In this application the replication values are plotted across the number of groups in the clustering solution. A notable change in level of the statistic may indicate that the correct number of clusters has been found. The replication scree test was able to specify the correct number of clusters in 58% of the cases. When including those cases that were accurate to within ±1 cluster, 82% of the data sets were resolved correctly. Thus, further development of the replication methodology seems warranted.

DISCUSSION AND EXTENSIONS

The recommendations presented in this chapter are simply guidelines and not hard and fast rules in clustering. The authors would not be surprised if an empirical data set can be found for each case that would provide a counterexample to the suggested guidelines. Since the classification area is quite active and new research continues to appear, applied researchers are encouraged to review more recent results as time progresses. The journals listed as references for this chapter can serve as a basis for following the current literature. There is no doubt that further advances will reshape our knowledge with respect to this methodology.

Use of Clustering in Psychology and Related Fields

Clustering continues to be used heavily in psychology and related fields. The 1994–1999 editions of the SERVICE bibliographic database list 830 entries in the psychological

journals alone. Primary areas of application include personality inventories (e.g., Lorr & Strack, 1994), educational styles (e.g., Swanson, 1995), organizational structures (e.g., Viswesvaran, Schmidt, & Deshpande, 1994), and semantic networks (e.g., Storms, Van Mechelen, & De Boeck, 1994). Table 7.11 lists the 130 articles in psychology journals by subdiscipline for the publication year of 1999, as listed in the SERVICE bibliography. One can note that the subdiscipline list in Table 7.11 spans most of psychology with a remarkably even distribution. In addition, although a number of articles about clustering appear in methodological journals, this category represents only 9% of the publications about clustering and classification. Thus, clustering and classification research remains very healthy in psychology with both methodological developments and substantive applications appearing within the literature on a regular basis.

In addition to research within the mainstream psychology journals, there is a large body of psychological research using classification techniques in several closely related areas. Some of the notable areas include environmental geography, where cluster analysis is used to identify neighborhood structures (Hirtle, 1995); information retrieval, where clustering is used to identify groups of related documents (Rasmussen, 1992); marketing, where there remains a close relationship between data analysis techniques and theoretical developments (Arabie & Daws, 1988); social network theory (Wasserman & Faust, 1994); and evolutionary trees (Sokal, 1985). Arabie and Hubert (1996) emphasize the last three areas as particularly notable for their active use of clustering and for their methodological advances. Psychologists with an interest in the development or novel adaptation of clustering technique are urged to look toward these fields for significant advances.

Relationship to Data Mining

With a recent explosion of interest in data mining, there has also been a resurgence of interest in clustering and classification. Data mining applies a variety of automated and statistical tools to the problem of extracting knowledge from large databases. The classification methods used in data mining are more typically applied to problems of supervised learning. In such cases, a training set of preclassified exemplars is used to build a classification model. For example, one might have data on high- and low-risk credit applicants. Such problems are well suited for decision trees or neural network models (Salzberg, 1997). In contrast, unsupervised classification is closer to the topic of this chapter in that a large number of cases are divided into a small set of groups, segments, or partitions, based on the similarity across some n-dimensional attribute space. Data-mining problems can be extremely large, with as many as a half million cases in the case of astronomical data (e.g., Fayyad, Piatetsky-Shapiro, Smyth, & Uthurusamy, 1996) or pharmacological data (e.g., Weinstein et al., 1997). Thus, the use of efficient algorithms based on heuristic approaches may replace more accurate, but inefficient, algorithms discussed previously in this chapter.

Han and Kamber (2000) reviewed extensions and variants of basic clustering methods for data mining, including partitioning, hierarchical, and model-based clustering methods. Recent extensions of k-means partitioning algorithms for large data sets include three related methods, PAM (Kaufman & Rousseeuw, 1987), CLARA (Kaufman & Rousseeuw, 1990), and CLARANS (Ng & Han, 1994), which are based on building clusters around medoids, which are representative objects for the clusters. Extensions to hierarchical methods for large databases include BIRCH (Zhang, Ramakrishnan, & Linvy, 1996) and CHAMELEON (Karypis, Han, & Kumar, 1999), both of which use a multiphase approach to finding clusters. For example, in CHAMELEON, objects are divided into a relatively large number of small subclusters, which are then combined using an agglomerative algorithm. Other datamining clustering techniques, such as CLIQUE (Agrawal, Gehrke, Gunopulos, & Raghavan, 1998), are based on projections into lower dimensional spaces that can improve the ability to detect clusters. CLIQUE partitions the space into nonoverlapping rectangular units and then examines those units for dense collections of objects. Han and Kambar (2000) argued that the strengths of this method are that it scales linearly with the size of the input data and at the same time is insensitive to the order of the input. However, the accuracy of the method may suffer as a result of the simplicity of the algorithm, which is an inherent problem of data-mining techniques.

Software Considerations

Applied researchers may face significant problems of access to user-friendly software for classification, especially for recent advances and cutting-edge techniques. Commercially available statistical packages can seldom keep up with advances in a developing discipline. This observation is especially true when the methodology is not part of the mainstream statistical tradition. It is unfortunate that research-oriented faculty are not able to provide a greater degree of applied software support. Fortunately, the Internet can facilitate access to the research software that is available. For example, the Classification Society of North America maintains a Web site that provides access to an extensive set of software programs that have been made freely available to the research community. The site can be located at http://www.pitt.edu/~csna/. The Web site also provides useful links to commercial software packages, some of which are not widely known. More generally, a wealth of information on the classification community can be found at the Web site.

We still believe that the best advice is for graduate students to develop some skill in writing code in at least one higher level language to support their research activities. In some situations you may just have to write it yourself in order to get the analysis done. One option, among several, is to gain skill at writing macros for the S-Plus (1999) software package. This software package provides a fairly flexible system for handling, manipulating, and processing statistical data.

REFERENCES

Agrawal, R., Gehrke, J., Gunopulos, D., & Raghavan, P. (1998). Automatic subspace clustering of high dimensional data for data mining applications. In *Proceedings of the ACM SIGMOD Conference on Management of Data* (pp. 94–105). New York: Association for Computing Machinery.

Aldenderfer, M. S., & Blashfield, R. K. (1984). *Cluster analysis*. Thousand Oaks, CA: Sage.

Anderberg, M. R. (1973). *Cluster analysis for applications*. New York: Academic Press.

Andrews, D. F. (1972). Plots of high-dimensional data. *Biometrics, 28,* 125–136.

Arabie, P., & Daws, J. (1988). The interface among data analysis, marketing, and knowledge representation. In W. Gaul & M. Schader (Eds.), *Data, expert knowledge and decisions* (pp. 10–15). Heidelberg, Germany: Springer-Verlag.

Arabie, P., & Hubert, L. (1996). Advances in cluster analysis relevant to marketing research. In W. Gaul & D. Pfeifer (Eds.), *From data to knowledge, studies in classification, data analysis, and knowledge organization* (pp. 3–16). New York: Springer.

Arabie, P., & Rips, L. (1973). *A 3-way data set of similarities between Henley's 30 animals.* Unpublished manuscript, Stanford University.

Bailey, T. A., & Dubes, R. (1982). Cluster validity profiles. *Pattern Recognition, 15,* 61–83.

Baker, F. B. (1974). Stability of two hierarchical grouping techniques. Case I: Sensitivity to data errors. *Journal of the American Statistical Association, 69,* 440–445.

Bayne, C. K., Beauchamp, J. J., Begovich, C. L., & Kane, V. E. (1980). Monte Carlo comparisons of selected clustering procedures. *Pattern Recognition, 12,* 51–62.

Beale, E. M. L. (1969). *Cluster analysis.* London: Scientific Control Systems.

Begovich, C. L., & Kane, V. E. (1982). Estimating the number of groups and group membership using simulation cluster analysis. *Pattern Recognition, 15,* 335–342.

Belbin, L., Faith, D., & Milligan, G. (1992). A comparison of two approaches to beta-flexible clustering. *Multivariate Behavioral Research, 27,* 417–433.

Blashfield, R. K. (1976). Mixture model tests of cluster analysis: Accuracy of four hierarchical agglomerative methods. *Psychological Bulletin, 3,* 377–388.

Blashfield, R. K. (1977). *A consumer report on cluster analysis software. Vol. 3: Iterative partitioning methods* (NSF grant DCR No. 74-20007). State College: Pennsylvania State University, Department of Psychology.

Breckenridge, J. N. (1989). Replicating cluster analysis: Method, consistency, and validity. *Multivariate Behavioral Research, 24,* 147–161.

Breckenridge, J. N. (1993, June). *Validating cluster analysis: Consistent replication and symmetry.* Paper presented at the meeting of the Classification Society of North America, University of Pittsburgh, PA.

Brucker, P. (1978). On the complexity of clustering problems. In R. Henn, B. Korte, & W. Oettli (Eds.), *Optimization and operations research* (pp. 45–54). Berlin: Springer-Verlag.

Buneman, P. (1971). The recovery of trees from measures of dissimilarity. In D. Kendall & P. Tautu (Eds.), *Mathematics in archeological and historical science* (pp. 387–395). Edinburgh, Scotland: Edinburgh University Press.

Calinski, R. B., & Harabasz, J. (1974). A dendrite method for cluster analysis. *Communications in Statistics, 3,* 1–27.

Carroll, J. D., & Arabie, P. (1980). Multidimensional scaling. *Annual Review of Psychology, 31,* 607–649.

Carroll, J. D., & Arabie, P. (1983). INDCLUS: An individual differences generalization of the ADCLUS model and the MAPCLUS algorithm. *Psychometrika, 48,* 157–169.

Carroll, J. D., & Arabie, P. (1998). Multidimensional scaling. In M. H. Birnbaum (Ed.), *Handbook of perception and cognition* (Vol. 3, pp. 179–250). San Diego, CA: Academic Press.

Carroll, J. D., & Chang, J. J. (1973). A method for fitting a class of hierarchical tree structure models to dissimilarities data and its application to some "body parts" data of Miller's. *Proceedings of the 81st Annual Convention of the American Psychological Association, 8,* 1097–1098.

Carroll, J. D., & Pruzansky, S. (1980). Discrete and hybrid scaling methods. In E. D. Lantermann & H. Feger (Eds.), *Similarity and choice* (pp. 108–139). Bern, Switzerland: Huber.

Chandon, J. L., Lemaire, J., & Pouget, J. (1980). Construction de l'ultrametrique la plus proche d'une dissimilarité au sens des moindres carrés (Fitting a least-squares ultrametric that is nearest to a given dissimilarity). *Recherche Opérationnelle, 14,* 157–170.

Cheng, R., & Milligan, G. W. (1995a). Mapping influence regions in hierarchical clustering. *Multivariate Behavioral Research, 30,* 547–576.

Cheng, R., & Milligan, G. W. (1995b). Hierarchical clustering algorithms with influence detection. *Educational and Psychological Measurement, 55,* 237–244.

Cheng, R., & Milligan, G. W. (1996a). Measuring the influence of individual data points in a cluster analysis. *Journal of Classification, 13,* 315–335.

Cheng, R., & Milligan, G. W. (1996b). *K*-Means clustering methods with influence detection. *Educational and Psychological Measurement, 56,* 833–838.

Cooper, M. C., & Milligan, G. W. (1988). The effect of measurement error on determining the number of clusters in cluster analysis. In W. Gaul & M. Schader (Eds.), *Data, expert knowledge and decisions* (pp. 319–328). Berlin: Springer-Verlag.

Corter, J. E. (1996). *Tree models of similarity and association.* Thousand Oaks, CA: Sage.

DeSarbo, W. S., Carroll, J. D., & Green, P. E. (1984). Synthesized clustering: A method for amalgamating alternative clustering bases with different weighting of variables. *Psychometrika, 49,* 57–78.

De Soete, G. (1984). A least squares algorithm for fitting an ultrametric tree to a dissimilarity matrix. *Pattern Recognition Letters, 2,* 133–137.

De Soete, G. (1986). Optimal variable weighting for ultrametric and additive tree clustering. *Quality and Quantity, 20,* 169–180.

De Soete, G. (1988). OVWTRE: A program for optimal variable weighting for ultrametric and additive tree fitting. *Journal of Classification, 5,* 101–104.

De Soete, G., & Carroll, J. D. (1996). Tree and other network models for representing proximity data. In P. Arabie, L. J. Hubert, & G. De Soete (Eds.), *Clustering and classification* (pp. 157–198). London: World Scientific Press.

Dobson A. J. (1974). Unrooted trees for numerical taxonomy. *Journal of Applied Probability, 11,* 32–42.

Dubes, R., & Jain, A. K. (1979). Validity studies in clustering methodologies. *Pattern Recognition, 11,* 235–254.

Duffy, D. E., & Quiroz, A. J. (1991). A permutation-based algorithm for block clustering. *Journal of Classification, 6,* 65–91.

Edelbrock, C. (1979). Comparing the accuracy of hierarchical clustering algorithms: The problem of classifying everybody. *Multivariate Behavioral Research, 14,* 367–384.

Edelbrock, C., & McLaughlin, B. (1980). Hierarchical cluster analysis using intraclass correlations: A mixture model study. *Multivariate Behavioral Research, 15,* 299–318.

Everitt. B. S. (1993). *Cluster analysis* (3rd ed.). New York: Wiley.

Fayyad, U. M., Piatetsky-Shapiro, G., Smyth, P., & Uthurusamy, R. (1996). *Advances in knowledge discovery and data mining.* Cambridge, MA: AAAI/MIT Press.

Fisher, L., & Van Ness, J. W. (1971). Admissible clustering procedures. *Biometrika, 58,* 91–104.

Fleiss, J. L., & Zubin, J. (1969). On the methods and theory of clustering. *Multivariate Behavioral Research, 4,* 235–250.

Fowlkes, E. B., Gnanadesikan, R., & Kettenring, J. R. (1988). Variable selection in clustering. *Journal of Classification, 5,* 205–228.

Fowlkes, E. B., & Mallows, C. L. (1983). A method for comparing two hierarchical clusterings. *Journal of the American Statistical Association, 78,* 553–584.

Fraley, C., & Raftery, A. E. (1998). How many clusters? Which clustering method?: Answers via Model-Based Cluster Analysis. *Computer Journal, 41,* 578–588.

Friedman, H. P., & Rubin, J. (1967). On some invariant criteria for grouping data. *Journal of the American Statistical Association, 62,* 1159–1178.

Furnas, G. W. (1980). *Objects and their features: The metric representation of two class data.* Unpublished doctoral dissertation, Stanford University, Palo Alto, CA.

Gilmore, J. (1999). *Painless Windows: A handbook for SAS users.* Cary, NC: SAS Institute.

Good, I. J. (1982). An index of separateness of clusters and a permutation test for its statistical significance. *Journal of Statistical Computing and Simulation, 15,* 81–84.

Gordon, A. D. (1987). A review of hierarchical classification. *Journal of the Royal Statistical Society, Series A, 150,* 119–137.

Gordon, A. D. (1996). Hierarchical classification. In P. Arabie, L. Hubert, & G. De Soete (Eds.), *Clustering and classification* (pp. 65–121). River Edge, NJ: World Scientific Press.

Gordon, A. D. (1999). *Classification: Methods for the exploratory analysis of multivariate data* (2nd ed.). London: Chapman & Hall.

Green, P. E., Carmone, F. J., & Kim, J. (1990). A preliminary study of optimal variable weighting in *k*-means clustering. *Journal of Classification, 7,* 271–285.

Han, J., & Kamber, M. (2000). *Data mining: Concepts and techniques.* San Francisco, CA: Morgan Kaufman.

Hartigan, J. A. (1967). Representation of similarity matrices by trees. *Journal of the American Statistical Association, 62,* 1140–1158.

Hartigan, J. A. (1975). *Clustering algorithms.* New York: Wiley.

Hartigan, J., & Wong, M. (1979). A K-means clustering algorithm. *Applied Statistics, 28,* 100–108.

Henley, N. M. (1969). A psychological study of the semantics of animal terms. *Journal of Mathematical Psychology, 8,* 176–184.

Hirtle, S. C. (1987). On the classification of recall strategies using lattice-theoretic measures. *Journal of Classification, 4,* 227–242.

Hirtle, S. C. (1995). Representational structures for cognitive space: Trees, ordered trees, and semi-lattices. In A. V. Frank & W. Kuhn (Eds.), *Spatial information theory: A theoretical basis for GIS.* Berlin: Springer-Verlag.

Hubert, L. J., & Arabie, P. (1985). Comparing partitions. *Journal of Classification, 2,* 193–218.

Hubert, L. J., & Baker, F. B. (1977). The comparison and fitting of given classification schemes. *Journal of Mathematical Psychology, 16,* 233–253.

Jain, A. K., & Dubes, R. (1988). *Algorithms for clustering data.* Englewood Cliffs, NJ: Prentice-Hall.

Jardine, N., & Sibson, R. (1971). *Mathematical taxonomy.* New York: Wiley.

Karypis, G., Han, E., & Kumar, V. (1999). CHAMELEON: A hierarchical clustering algorithm using dynamic modeling. *Computer, 32,* 68–75.

Kaufman, L., & Rousseeuw, P. J. (1987). Clustering by means of medoids. In Y. Dodge (Ed.), *Statistical data analysis based on the L 1 Norm* (pp. 405–416). New York: North Holland/Elsevier Science.

Kaufman, L., & Rousseeuw, P. J. (1990). Finding groups in data: An introduction to cluster analysis. New York: Wiley.

Kleiner, B., & Hartigan, J. A. (1981). Representing points in many dimensions by trees and castles (with comments and rejoinder). *Journal of the American Statistical Association, 76,* 260–276.

Kruskal, J. B., & Wish, M. (1978). *Multidimensional scaling.* Thousand Oaks, CA: Sage.

Kuiper, F. K., & Fisher, L. (1975). A Monte Carlo comparison of six clustering procedures. *Biometrics, 31,* 777–783.

Lance, G. N., & Williams, W. T. (1966). A generalized sorting strategy for computer classifications. *Nature, 212,* 218.

Lance, G. N., & Williams, W. T. (1967). A general theory for classificatory sorting strategies I. Hierarchical systems. *Computer Journal, 9,* 373–380.

Legendre, P., & Legendre, L. (1998). *Numerical ecology* (2nd ed.). Amsterdam: Elsevier Science.

Lorr, M. (1983). *Cluster analysis for social sciences.* San Francisco: Jossey-Bass.

Lorr, M., & Strack, S. (1994). Personality profiles of police candidates. *Journal of Clinical Psychology, 50,* 200–207.

MacQueen, J. (1967). Some methods for classification and analysis of multivariate observations. In L. M. Le Cam & J. Neyman (Eds.), *Proceedings of the Fifth Berkeley Symposium on Mathematical Statistics and Probability* (Vol. 1, pp. 281–297). Berkeley: University of California Press.

Makarenkov, V., & Legendre, P. (2000). *Optimal variable weighting for ultrametric and additive tree clustering and K-means partitioning: Method and software.* Manuscript submitted for publication.

McIntyre, R. M., & Blashfield, R. K. (1980). A nearest-centroid technique for evaluating the minimum-variance clustering procedure. *Multivariate Behavioral Research, 15,* 225–238.

Mezzich. J. (1978). Evaluating clustering methods for psychiatric-diagnosis. *Biological Psychiatry, 13,* 265–346.

Milligan, G. W. (1980). An examination of the effect of six types of error perturbation on fifteen clustering algorithms. *Psychometrika, 45,* 325–342.

Milligan, G. W. (1981a). A review of Monte Carlo tests of cluster analysis. *Multivariate Behavioral Research, 16,* 379–407.

Milligan, G. W. (1981b). A Monte Carlo study of thirty internal criterion measures for cluster analysis. *Psychometrika, 46,* 187–199.

Milligan, G. W. (1989a). A study of the beta-flexible clustering method. *Multivariate Behavioral Research, 24,* 163–176.

Milligan, G. W. (1989b). A validation study of a variable weighting algorithm for cluster analysis. *Journal of Classification, 6,* 53–71.

Milligan, G. W. (1996). Clustering validation: Results and implications for applied analyses. In P. Arabie, L. Hubert, & G. De Soete (Eds.), *Clustering and classification* (pp. 345–379). River Edge, NJ: World Scientific Press.

Milligan, G. W. (1998). Cluster analysis. In S. Kotz, C. Read, & D. Banks (Eds.), *Encyclopedia of statistical sciences* (Vol. 2, pp. 120–125). New York: Wiley.

Milligan, G. W., & Cooper, M. C. (1985). An examination of procedures for determining the number of clusters in a data set. *Psychometrika, 50,* 159–179.

Milligan, G. W., & Cooper, M. C. (1987). Methodological review: Clustering methods. *Applied Psychological Measurement, 11,* 329–354.

Milligan, G. W., & Cooper, M. C. (1988). A study of variable standardization. *Journal of Classification, 5,* 181–204.

Milligan, G. W., & Isaac, P. (1980). The validation of four ultrametric clustering algorithms. *Pattern Recognition, 12,* 41–50.

Milligan, G. W., & Mahajan, V. (1980). A note on procedures for testing the quality of a clustering of a set of objects. *Decision Sciences, 11,* 669–677.

Milligan, G. W., & Sokol, L. M. (1980). A two-stage clustering algorithm with robust recovery characteristics. *Educational and Psychological Measurement, 40,* 755–759.

Mirkin, B. (2000, June). *Data driven classification and clustering.* Paper presented at the meeting of the Classification Society of North America, University of Montréal, Canada.

Mojena, R. (1977). Hierarchical grouping methods and stopping rules: An evaluation. *Computer Journal, 20,* 359–363.

Morey, L. C., Blashfield, R. K., & Skinner, H. A. (1983). A comparison of cluster analysis techniques within a sequential validation framework. *Multivariate Behavioral Research, 18,* 309–329.

Murtagh, F. (2000). *Classification literature automated search service.* Available at http://www.pitt.edu/~csna.

Ng, R. T., & Han, J. (1994). Efficient and effective clustering methods for spatial data mining. In J. B. Bocca, M. Jarke, & C. Zaniolo (Eds.), *Proceedings of the 20th International Conference on Very Large Data Bases* (pp. 144–155). San Francisco: Morgan Kaufmann.

Okada, A. (1996). A review of cluster analysis research in Japan. In P. Arabie, L. Hubert, & G. De Soete (Eds.), *Clustering and classification* (pp. 271–294). River Edge, NJ: World Scientific Press.

Podani, J. (1989). New combinatorial clustering methods. *Vegetatio, 81,* 61–77.

Pruzansky, S., Tversky, A., & Carroll, J. D. (1982). Spatial versus tree representations of proximity data. *Psychometrika, 47,* 3–24.

Punj, G., & Stewart, D. W. (1983). Cluster analysis in marketing research: Review and suggestions for application. *Journal of Marketing Research, 20,* 134–148.

Rasmussen, E. (1992). Clustering algorithms. In W. B. Frakes & R. Baeza-Yates (Eds.), *Information retrieval: Data structures and algorithms.* Upper Saddle River, NJ: Prentice-Hall.

Rothkopf, E. Z. (1957). A measure of stimulus similarity and errors in some paired-associate learning tasks. *Journal of Experimental Psychology, 53,* 94–101.

Salzberg, S. L. (1997). On comparing classifiers: Pitfalls to avoid and a recommended approach. *Data Mining and Knowledge Discovery, 1,* 317–327.

Sattath, S., & Tverksy, A. (1977). Additive similarity trees. *Psychometrika, 42,* 319–345.

Scheibler, D., & Schneider, W. (1985). Monte Carlo tests of the accuracy of cluster analysis algorithms: A comparison of hierarchical and nonhierarchical methods. *Multivariate Behavioral Research, 20,* 283–304.

Shepard, R. N. (1963). Analysis of proximities as a technique for the study of information processing in man. *Human Factors, 5,* 33–48.

Skinner, H. A. (1978). Differentiating the contribution of elevation, scatter, and shape in profile similarity. *Educational and Psychological Measurement, 38,* 297–308.

Sneath, P. H. A. (1980). The risk of not recognizing from ordinations that clusters are distinct. *Classification Society Bulletin, 4,* 22–43.

Sneath, P. H. A., & Sokal, R. R. (1973). *Numerical taxonomy.* San Francisco: W. F. Freeman.

Späth, M. (1980). *Cluster analysis algorithms for data reduction and classification of objects.* Chichester, UK: Ellis Horwood.

S-Plus. (1999). *S-Plus 2000 modern statistics and advanced graphics.* Seattle, WA: MathSoft Inc.

Storms, G., Van Mechelen, I., & De Boeck, P. (1994). Structural-analysis of the intension and extension of semantic concepts. *European Journal of Cognitive Psychology, 6,* 43–75.

Swanson, H. L. (1995). Effects of dynamic testing on the classification of learning-disabilities: The predictive and discriminant validity of the Swanson cognitive processing test (S-Cpt). *Journal of Psychoeducational Assessment, 13,* 204–229.

Viswesvaran, M., Schmidt, F. L., & Deshpande, S. P. (1994). A metaanalytic method for testing hypotheses about clusters of decision-makers. *Organizational Behavior and Human Decision Processes, 58,* 304–321.

Ward, J. H., Jr. (1963). Hierarchical grouping to optimise an objective function. *Journal of the American Statistical Association, 58,* 236–244.

Wasserman, S., & Faust, K. (1994). *Social networks analysis: Methods and applications.* New York: Cambridge University Press.

Weinstein, J. N., Myers, T. G., O'Connor, P. M., Friend, S. H., Fornace, A. J., Kohn, K. W., Fojo, T., Bates, S. E., Rubinstein, L.V., Anderson, N. L., Buolamwini, J. K., van Osdol, W. W., Monks, A. P., Scudiero, D. A., Sausville, E. A., Zaharevitz, D. W., Bunow, B., Viswesvaran, V. N., Johnson, G. S., Wittes, R. E., & Paull, K. D. (1997). An information-intensive approach to the molecular pharmacology of cancer. *Science, 275,* 343–349.

Welch, W. J. (1982). Algorithmic complexity: Three NP-hard problems in computational statistics. *Journal of Statistical Computation and Simulation, 15,* 17–25.

Wolfe, J. H. (1970). Pattern clustering by multivariate mixture analysis. *Multivariate Behavioral Research, 5,* 329–350.

Wong, M. A. (1982). A hybrid clustering method for identifying high-density clusters. *Journal of the American Statistical Association, 77,* 841–847.

Wong, M. A., & Lane, T. (1983). A kth nearest neighbour clustering procedure. *Journal of the Royal Statistical Society, Series B, 45,* 362–368.

Zhang, T., Ramakrishnan, R., & Linvy, M. (1996). BIRCH: An efficient data clustering method for very large databases. In *Proceedings of the ACM SIGMOD Conference on the Management of Data* (pp. 103–104). New York: Association for Computing Machinery.

PART TWO

RESEARCH METHODS IN SPECIFIC CONTENT AREAS

CHAPTER 8

Clinical Forensic Psychology

KEVIN S. DOUGLAS, RANDY K. OTTO, AND RANDY BORUM

Although clinical and experimental psychologists have made contributions to the legal system since the early 1900s (e.g., see Travis, 1908; Munsterberg, 1908; Wrightsman, 2001) clinical forensic psychology has thrived as a subspecialty only for the past 25 years (Otto & Heilbrun, 2002). For the purposes of this chapter, we adopt the broad definition of forensic psychology that was crafted by the Forensic Psychology Specialty Council (2000) for submission to the American Psychological Association (APA), which was accepted by the APA Council of Representatives in August 2001. Forensic psychology is defined here as "the professional practice by psychologists within the areas of clinical psychology, counseling psychology, neuropsychology, and school psychology, when they are engaged regularly as experts and represent themselves as such, in an activity primarily intended to provide professional psychological expertise to the legal system" (Forensic Psychology Specialty Council, 2000). More specifically, we define clinical forensic psychology as assessment, treatment, and consultation that revolves around clinical issues and occurs in legal contexts or with populations involved within any sphere of the legal system, criminal or civil. Research areas and methods common to other applications of psychology to law (e.g., social psychology, experimental psychology, cognitive psychology, industrial-organizational psychology) are not addressed here;

in this chapter we use the terms *forensic psychology* and *clinical forensic psychology* interchangeably.

With increasing frequency, clinical psychologists have provided assistance to the legal system by assessing persons involved in legal proceedings whose mental state is at issue (e.g., in cases of competence to stand trial, criminal responsibility, guardianship, child custody, personal injury, testamentary capacity) and treating persons who are involved in the legal system in some capacity (e.g., convicted adults and juveniles, crime victims). Indicators that clinical forensic psychology is now a unique subspecialty are numerous and include the recent designation of forensic psychology as a specialty area by the American Psychological Association, development of special interest organizations (e.g., American Psychology-Law Society–Division 41 of the American Psychological Association), implementation of a specialty board that credentials persons who practice forensic work at an advanced level (i.e., American Board of Forensic Psychology), establishment of graduate predoctoral, internship, and postdoctoral specialty training programs in clinical forensic psychology (see Cruise, 2001, and Packer & Borum, in press, for reviews), and publication of professional books (e.g., Melton, Petrila, Poythress, & Slobogin, 1997; Grisso, 1986; Rogers, 1997) and scientific journals (e.g., *Behavioral Sciences and the Law, International Journal of Forensic Mental*

Health Law and Human Behavior, Journal of Forensic Psychology Practice) devoted to research and practice in clinical forensic psychology.

Clinical forensic psychologists typically are involved in one of three pursuits within the legal system—assessment, treatment, and consultation. This chapter focuses on research methods and issues that occur in assessment and treatment contexts, as opposed to those in consultation, which typically involve working with legal bodies or legal professionals (i.e., judges, attorneys). For each task that is unique to clinical forensic psychology research, we provide examples of the clinical challenges confronting the psychologist, identify problems and challenges faced when researching the issues or constructs, and describe research strategies that have been employed, their strengths, and their limitations. We do not discuss in this chapter those research endeavors that may be relevant to clinical forensic psychology but are not unique to the specialty.

Assessment of persons involved in the legal system in some capacity is a major activity for forensic psychologists. Forensic psychological assessment even has been described by some as a cottage industry (Grisso, 1987). The majority of forensic assessment tasks facing psychologists can be classified as descriptive or predictive. Some forensic activities are retrospective in nature, insofar as the psychologist is asked to offer opinions about a person's mental state at a prior point in time, such as in criminal responsibility and contested will evaluations.

DESCRIPTIVE CLINICAL FORENSIC ASSESSMENT

Overview

In a subset of criminal and civil cases, a litigant's mental state or psychological functioning may be at issue. In these cases, triers of fact (i.e., judges or juries) often seek the input of psychologists or other mental health professionals who, as a function of their expertise, can provide the court with information about the person's mental condition that otherwise would be unavailable, based on the assumption that this input results in a better and more accurate legal decision. For example, in criminal cases, a defendant's mental state and emotional functioning may be relevant to his or her criminal responsibility or competence to proceed with the criminal process (i.e., to understand the charges or to assist in one's own defense). Similarly, a plaintiff's mental state and psychological functioning also can become an issue in a variety of civil proceedings, including personal injury litigation, cases of disputed child custody, testamentary capacity, and guardianship.

The assessment task in all of the above cases fundamentally is descriptive—that is, the legal system looks to the psychologist to describe the abilities, capacities, or functioning of the person as they affect or are related to the particular legal issues at hand. The legally relevant behaviors, capacities, and skills that the forensic psychologist assesses have been broadly conceived as psycholegal capacities (e.g., see Grisso, 1986).

Exactly what the psychologist assesses and describes is defined and identified by the law, although the assessment techniques and approach are based on the psychologist's knowledge and expertise in psychopathology and human behavior (see Grisso, 1986, for further discussion of this issue). For example, when assessing a criminal defendant's competence to proceed, although the specific legally relevant elements are determined by the law (i.e., the defendant's understanding of the legal proceedings, the ability to work with counsel as it might be affected by mental disorder or other, related factors), the potentially relevant mental states and evaluation techniques are determined by the psychologist. Similarly, although the law regarding testamentary capacity delineates the abilities, knowledge, and understanding one must have to execute a valid will, the forensic psychologist examining someone in the context of a contested will proceeding determines, based on his or her knowledge of cognitive functioning and mental disorder, what psychological factors will be addressed and how they will be evaluated.

Psychologists use various techniques to assess psycholegal capacities. In addition to employing traditional assessment methods (i.e., clinical interview; record review; and measures of psychopathology, intelligence, academic achievement, and cognitive functioning) psychologists have developed a variety of special assessment techniques, including those specifically designed to assess psycholegal capacities (i.e., forensic assessment instruments; see Grisso, 1986; Heilbrun, Rogers, & Otto, in press).

Psychologists who research psycholegal constructs then are faced with two separate but related tasks: (a) conducting research that operationalizes these psycholegal capacities, and (b) conducting research that examines the utility of various techniques and instruments that are designed to assess these capacities.

Challenges to Researching Psycholegal Capacities

Researching psycholegal capacities presents a number of challenges, some of which are caused by working in a venue that is defined by another discipline (i.e., the law), and some of which are inherent to the task. We describe some of these challenges below, including (a) varying definitions of constructs across jurisdictions, (b) multifaceted constructs, and (c) the lack of a gold standard.

Varying Definitions

A unique problem that may be experienced by clinical forensic psychologists researching psycholegal capacities is that the definition and conceptualization of the constructs they research can vary across jurisdictions and change over time within a particular jurisdiction as the applicable law changes. Research focused on criminal defendants' competence to confess and waive their Miranda rights provides a good example of this difficulty.

In *Miranda v. Arizona* (1966) the Supreme Court determined that the United States Constitution requires that criminal defendants who waive their Fifth Amendment right to avoid self-incrimination must do so knowingly, intelligently, and voluntarily. To meet this requirement, arresting officers typically inform suspects of their constitutional rights in a colloquy that has become well known even to laypersons (*You have the right to remain silent . . .*). Less well known by the lay public is that different jurisdictions employ various "Miranda warnings," although the fundamental elements of the various warnings remain primarily the same (Oberlander & Goldstein, 2001).

Whether waiver of one's right to avoid self-incrimination is valid and the resulting confession admissible is determined on case-by-case basis. The court considers the totality of the circumstances surrounding the waiver and confession in reaching a conclusion about admissibility factors specific to the situation, along with the abilities of the suspect. Grisso (1981) conducted a program of research examining the ability of adults and juveniles to comprehend their Fifth Amendment right to avoid self-incrimination and developed four instruments designed to operationalize these psycholegal capacities as psychological constructs (Comprehension of Miranda Rights, Comprehension of Miranda Rights–True/False, Comprehension of Miranda Vocabulary, and Function of Rights in Interrogation; Grisso, 1998). Grisso subsequently examined the psychometric properties of these instruments and normed them on both adults and juveniles, some of whom were involved in the criminal justice system and some of whom were not. Revised versions of these instruments are now used by psychologists in the context of Miranda waiver evaluations. Of some interest is that the Miranda warning language employed in Grisso's measures is that used by law enforcement officials in St. Louis county in the 1980s. This language, of course, may differ from the Miranda language provided to criminal defendants in other jurisdictions, and this issue has been raised on occasion to challenge the external validity of the instruments and test findings in particular. Researchers need to be aware of these differences as they plan studies to construct and evaluate instruments designed to assess such capacities.

Assessing and Researching Multifaceted Constructs

Another challenge that clinical forensic researchers face is operationalizing and researching multifaceted psycholegal issues or constructs. The child custody arena provides perhaps the best example of this challenge. In those instances when divorcing parents cannot reach agreement about custody of their minor children, judges are left to make decisions about custody and placement based on the "best interests of the children." In these cases, judges and attorneys sometimes look to psychologists to provide the court with a better understanding of the children's needs, the parents, and the parents' abilities to meet their children's needs. Essentially all states have attempted to define and operationalize what they consider to be the best interests of the child, at least insofar as they have identified factors that judges must consider in making custody and placement decisions (i.e., the child's emotional, educational, and physical needs; the emotional functioning and adjustment of the parents; the nature and quality of the relationship between the parents and the child; the stability of the child's current and proposed environments; the willingness of each parent to foster a relationship between the child and the other parent). Nevertheless, different states define the standard in different ways and direct judges to consider different factors. Even the casual observer can conceive of circumstances in which the factors that are to be considered may suggest different outcomes and decisions. For example, the custody decision that might be best for a child's emotional adjustment may not be best with respect to fostering a continuing relationship with the noncustodial parent. Similarly, one parent may do best at meeting a child's educational and academic needs, while the other may most ideally respond to the child's emotional needs. Whether and how the various factors are to be weighed is not specified, and judges are not provided a legal calculus for arriving at an ultimate decision. This makes defining, researching, and assessing this psycholegal construct (the best interests of the child) particularly difficult.

Lack of a Gold Standard

A final problem facing clinical forensic researchers is the lack of a gold standard to define or identify a construct. This problem is not unique to research in clinical-forensic psychology.

For example, there is no gold criterion or absolute standard for any mental disorder, despite what proponents of the *Diagnostic and Statistical Manual–Fourth Edition* (*DSM-IV;* American Psychiatric Association, 1994) might argue. After all, the *DSM-IV* diagnoses represent little more than consensus judgments. Because psycholegal capacities are based on legal constructs, identifying a criterion is difficult. For example, the ultimate threshold judgment of whether a criminal defendant is competent or incompetent, whether a child's best interests are served by living with his or her mother or father after a divorce, whether someone is or is not capable of managing his or her legal and financial affairs, or whether someone is capable of consenting to a proposed psychological or medical intervention are all ultimately moral-legal decisions that are to be made by the legal decision maker (Slobogin, 1989). As is described in more detail in the following section, when developing, researching, and evaluating instruments that are designed to assess these various capacities, forensic psychologists must operationalize abstract constructs and employ proxy criteria.

Research Strategies 1: Operationalizing Psycholegal Constructs and Assessing the Validity of Assessment Techniques

As noted previously, regardless of the psycholegal capacity at issue, the researcher's first task is to operationalize and define a construct that ultimately is a legal one, and that has no true or absolute definition. Next, as researchers develop instruments or approaches designed to assess a particular psycholegal capacity, they must evaluate the validity of their assessment techniques. Researchers employ a variety of strategies as they try both to operationalize psycholegal criteria and to assess the validity of instruments designed to assess particular psycholegal capacities.

Surveys of the Literature

In some cases, researchers have attempted to operationalize or define a particular psycholegal capacity based on a review of the relevant scientific and legal literatures. For example, Ackerman and Schoendorf (1992) developed the Ackerman-Schoendorf Scales for Parent Evaluation of Custody (ASPECT), an assessment battery designed for use in cases of contested custody to identify the parent who is best able to meet the child's needs. So that their battery would identify and assess factors that the legal decision maker (i.e., the court) considered relevant to child custody decision making and the best interests of the child, the authors surveyed the published legal and mental health literatures addressing child

custody. The value of this approach is that it ensures consideration of factors that are likely to be relevant to defining a particular psycholegal capacity. Accordingly, it should result in a conceptualization (and associated assessment approach) that has face validity, which may be particularly important in legal contexts (see Grisso, 1987). This approach, however, requires considerable judgment and discretion on the part of the professional who reviews the literature, particularly in those instances in which there is a lack of consensus or difference of opinion expressed.

Polling Experts

Researchers seeking to operationalize psycholegal capacities also have attempted to do so by surveying professionals whose opinions are thought to be relevant to the issue of interest. Those surveyed can be legal professionals, mental health professionals, or a combination of both. An example of this approach is provided by Jameson, Ehrenberg, and Hunter (1997), who surveyed a sample of psychologists from British Columbia with experience conducting child custody evaluations; the psychologists were asked about their opinions relating to child custody decision making and the standard of *the best interests of the child*. Such surveys can provide helpful information regarding how persons in the field conceptualize a particular issue, but there are several limitations. Perhaps most importantly, the value of such surveys can be limited by the population sampled. In the example just cited, although the opinions of psychologists from British Columbia with respect to matters of child custody are interesting, they certainly do not settle the issue because matters of custody ultimately are moral-legal ones (Slobogin, 1989). But even polling members of the bar (either judges or attorneys) can pose problems, as questions can be raised about the representativeness of the samples utilized. Finally, questions of sample appropriateness aside, test developers or researchers may find themselves in awkward situations when the opinions of the sample polled are discordant with the prevailing law as it is understood.

Theory-Based Development

In some cases researchers attempt to define forensic psycholegal constructs and to develop techniques designed to assess these constructs based on legal theory. As an example, the MacArthur Competence Assessment Tool–Criminal Adjudication (MacCAT-CA; Poythress et al., 1999), which is designed to assess a defendant's competence to participate in the criminal process, is based in part on Bonnie's (1993) theory of adjudicative competence. Like the literature review strategy previously described, this approach benefits from face validity that is particularly important in legal contexts (Grisso, 1987), but it is limited insofar as the assessment approach or technique developed is anchored in a particular theory that may or may not be consistent with the law as it exists or as it may evolve.

Research Strategies 2: Assessing the Utility of Assessment Techniques

Only after a psycholegal capacity is adequately defined and operationalized can psychologists develop approaches to assess the capacity. These assessment approaches then must be assessed and validated before they can be used for decision-making purposes (American Educational Research Association, American Psychological Association, National Council on Measurement in Education, 1999). Many of the basic psychometric properties of these assessment techniques (e.g., scale consistency, inter-rater reliability, test-retest reliability) can be evaluated in much the same way as one evaluates traditional measures of intelligence, academic achievement, and psychopathology. More difficult, however, is assessing the validity of these assessment techniques given the unique nature of the constructs they assess.

Predicting Judges' Decisions or Legal Outcomes

One validation strategy sometimes employed by researchers is to examine the relationship between classifications based on the examinee's test performance and the legal outcome. For example, Ackerman and Schoendorf (1992) offer as support for the validity of the ASPECT (see this chapter's section titled "Surveys of the Literature" for a description) that 75% of the parents identified as the better parent by their instrument were awarded custody by the court. Similarly, as evidence of the validity of the Bricklin Perceptual Scales (BPS), which are used to identify a child's parent of choice in the context of child custody, the author (Bricklin, 1990) cited a high rate of agreement (94%) between BPS classifications and judges' ultimate decisions regarding custody and placement.

Although in some circumstances such analyses can be enlightening (e.g., it may be particularly important to know whether judges' decisions and classification on a particular forensic assessment instrument are highly negatively correlated), high rates of agreement between the legal decision maker's conclusions and classifications based on the forensic assessment instrument do not settle the issue. If such logic is followed and judges' decisions are adopted as the gold standard, then there is little reason to spend time developing assessment techniques to inform or influence judges' opinions.

Of course, when such an approach is used it is particularly important that the decisions of judges or legal decision makers' decisions not be based, in full or in part, on how the litigant performed on the assessment instrument. If such is the case, criterion contamination occurs and renders any positive findings of limited value (see Otto & Collins, 1995, and Otto, Edens, & Barcus, 2000, for further discussion of this issue in the context of the ASPECT and BPS previously described).

Evaluating Agreement Between Test Classification and Clinicians' Assessments of the Psycholegal Construct

Another approach similar to that previously described that has been employed to evaluate the validity of forensic assessment instruments is to examine agreement between the classification offered from the assessment instrument and independent clinical assessments of the relevant capacity. An example of this approach is provided by Bricklin and Elliott (1997) in their discussion of the validity of the Perception of Relationships Test (PORT), which is described by the test developer as a child custody evaluation measure that assesses the types of interactions a child has with each parent and the degree to which a child seeks psychological closeness with each parent. Bricklin and Elliott reported that they administered the PORT to a sample of 30 children in order to identify a primary caretaker, and also had clinicians offer similar opinions based on observed parent-child interactions. In over 90% of the cases there was agreement between the clinicians' identified parent of choice and the parent of choice identified by the PORT results, leading them to conclude that the PORT validly assesses childrens' perceptions of their parents.

In this section, we discussed descriptive forensic psychological assessment tasks and research. These tend to focus on psycholegal capacities at the time of the evaluation (i.e., adjudicative competence) or at some time in the past (i.e., mental status at the time of the offense, testamentary capacity). Some of the challenges to research include varying legal definitions, multifaceted constructs, and the lack of criteria establishing a gold standard. Researchers have attempted to overcome these challenges by conducting surveys of the literature, polling experts, using theory-based development, predicting legal outcomes, and evaluating the correspondence between test classifications and clinicians' judgments.

In other contexts, however, a variety of other research challenges and corresponding research strategies exist. Legal decision makers often ask mental health professionals to inform decisions that are based not on current functioning, but rather on what persons might (or might not) do at some point in the future, how they might (or might not) behave, and how well (or poorly) they will function in one setting versus another. It should be clear even before these tasks are described that there are a number of complexities involved in the research endeavors involved in our next main topic—predictive forensic assessments.

PREDICTIVE CLINICAL FORENSIC ASSESSMENT

Overview

There are many circumstances in which the future behavior or functioning of persons is a defining element of a legal decision, and for which clinicians often are called upon to offer expert opinions. The legal settings in which such decisions are required are varied, including much more than criminal courts and judicial decisions, such as civil courts, family courts, specialty courts (i.e., mental health courts, drug courts), and administrative tribunals of many kinds (i.e., parole boards, workers compensation boards). In addition, clinicians in many applied settings, such as mental health clinics, psychiatric facilities, forensic hospitals, juvenile residential treatment facilities, and correctional institutions, often are asked to forecast the future behavior of their clients-patients, particularly with respect to violence, suicide, and treatment response. Some of the more common clinical questions that require predictive assessments include (a) violence risk; (b) child, parental, and family functioning; and (c) treatment and intervention response. Concerning *violence risk assessment,* which has previously been described by terms such as *violence prediction, risk prediction, prediction of dangerousness,* and *dangerousness assessment,* mental health professionals are asked in dozens of legal settings about the likelihood that persons will act violently in the future. Shah (1978) identified 15 such settings in criminal justice and mental health over 20 years ago. Lyon, Hart, and Webster (2001) recently identified 17 points in Canadian law in which risk assessment is required by statute or regulation. The term *violence risk assessment* is used broadly in this chapter to refer to the assessment of risk for numerous types of antisocial behavior, such as general violence (i.e., homicide, battery, armed robbery), as well as more specialized forms of violence, such as sexual violence, domestic violence, and stalking.

In some contexts, such as civil commitment proceedings for sexual offenders, the question is fairly narrow and specific (is the individual *likely* to commit a violent sexual crime in the future?). There are currently 16 states with such legislation. Although there are variations among these laws, most define sexual predators as persons charged with or convicted of sexually violent offenses who have a mental abnormality, personality disorder, or paraphilia that makes them likely to commit future acts of sexual violence. These laws allow for postsentence civil commitment.

Other contexts require consideration of different types of violence, different severities of violence, or violence that might take place within different time frames (imminent vs. eventual risk). As with descriptive clinical forensic assessment, there typically is some source of legal authority (i.e., statutes, cases, bylaws, and administrative policies) that specifies the types of behavior that are to be forecast. However, beyond this minimum specification, the mental health professional must decide how best to proceed to be optimally informative to the legal decision maker.

In some settings, the legal source is far removed. For instance, the clinical management of a private psychotherapy patient or even the inpatient management of a psychiatric or forensic patient is not carried out in order directly to inform a specific legal decision that must be made (as is the case in many other risk assessment contexts). However, to the extent that service providers have legal duties in such contexts to prevent violence or to provide a safe workplace, then there are existing standards under tort and malpractice law—or perhaps professional practice and ethical standards—that would in effect serve as the legal authority to which clinicians or agencies would be held.

In the *child and family context,* there are several instances in which mental health professionals might be involved in forecasting future circumstances, and the adjustment thereto of children, parents, and families. Child custody cases are one important example. Although involving a strong descriptive assessment element, as reviewed in the previous section, child custody assessments also involve a substantial future-oriented component. The purpose of custody evaluations or, more precisely, legal proceedings to determine custody, is to decide which of numerous possible future scenarios of living arrangements best suits the interests of the child(ren), given the present *and predicted future* adjustment and social functioning of the children and their parents under various conditions (e.g., joint custody, sole custody with mother, sole custody with father).

Forecasting *treatment response* or amenability to certain interventions is relevant in numerous legal contexts, just as it is in nonlegal settings as well. In civil disputes, for example, a plaintiff's (i.e., the person who brings the cause of action and alleges wrongdoing by others that caused injury) projected course of recovery often will be relevant to the legal determinations of injury and damages.

Under tort law, there must be some sort of injury suffered by the plaintiff in order for that person to be compensated.

Most relevant to the present discussion is the concept of psychological injury, also variously known as emotional shock, nervous shock, psychiatric damage, or emotional injury. This is a controversial subject with differing legal standards—ranging from liberal to conservative—in terms of compensability across jurisdictions (see Douglas, Huss, Murdoch, Washington, & Koch, 1999). Most commonly, such injuries would arise from criminal or accidental victimization. In the former cases, a defendant might be held liable for the "intentional infliction of nervous shock," in addition to other injuries (such as the tort of battery). In the latter cases, the law of negligence typically applies to psychological injuries suffered as a result of motor vehicle and other accidents.

In addition to descriptive assessment issues such as the severity of psychological injury, civil courts may want to know the typical course of psychological recovery from the trauma at issue, promising treatment approaches, and whether they will be able to "restore" the person's condition to preinjury status, which is the theoretical purpose of tort law. These questions might relate to emotional functioning (i.e., posttraumatic stress disorder, acute stress disorder, depression) or neurocognitive functioning (i.e., executive dysfunction, memory impairment, and restoration of cognitive function relevant to traumatic brain injury).

Challenges to Researching Predictive Assessment

In this section, we discuss common threats to the validity and reliability of forensic research endeavors that attempt to evaluate predictive assessment tasks. We recommend methodological or statistical procedures to safeguard against these potential pitfalls. The context for this discussion centers primarily around violence risk assessment, one of the more common predictive forensic assessment tasks and research endeavors.

Varying Legal Definitions of Important Outcome Measures

Although forensic research ultimately is about human behavior, there is a very important constraint on its generalizability—the law. In most other research applications, concerns over external validity are based on participant characteristics, cultural factors, or design issues (i.e., how were participants selected for the study?). These concerns exist in forensic assessment research as well. The law, however, imposes on the researcher an additional set of generalizability concerns. As previously noted, research carried out

in one jurisdiction may not generalize to another for the simple reason that the laws differ between them. Similarly, legal principles, standards, and tests may differ between related but different legally substantive settings as well.

To illustrate the problem that this may pose to forensic assessment research (and practice), we can consider the case of violence risk assessment. On its face, the task may seem quite simple conceptually—evaluate a person by some reasonable method and give an opinion about risk for future violence. However, the law introduces a number of complexities that belie this seeming simplicity. For instance, what is the type of violence that is legally relevant in the particular setting and jurisdiction? For some legal issues and in some jurisdictions, only serious physical harm will satisfy the legal test. For instance, although most civil commitment statutes require risk for bodily harm or physical violence, some jurisdictions permit less serious forms of violence to satisfy the legislative requirement (Melton et al., 1997). The complicating nature of jurisdiction is daunting enough within the United States. Given the global nature of research, however, there is really no reason to fail to consider legal contexts beyond the United States; this is particularly so given the tendency for contemporary risk assessment instruments to be translated for use in foreign countries. Ethical principles about researchers' responsibility for how their research is used would suggest at least some cause for being aware of the use of such research in other countries, particularly if permission is granted to translate copyrighted works (implying preknowledge of anticipated use).

In more specialized legal settings, the nature (sexual violence), victim (domestic violence), or context (violence in the context of stalking) of violence is specified. Further, differing legal standards might impose constraints on the imminence or duration of risk that is relevant. In traditional civil commitment proceedings, for instance, there typically must be some concern about a person's imminent risk for violence. Contrast this to civil commitment under sexual predator laws, in which the legally relevant duration for risk can be decades long (e.g., see Florida Statues 394.910–394.931). In certain jurisdictions and settings, the law might require that particular risk factors form part of the assessment. Depending on the context, there might be differing standards concerning the degree of risk (or the likelihood of violence) that is required for the law to be satisfied, and for the degree of certainty that the court must have about this degree of risk.

In essence, risk assessment is clinically and legally complex and multifaceted. Depending on legal jurisdiction and setting, evaluators and researchers must be concerned about different definitions and operationalizations of severity, imminence, duration, frequency, target, likelihood, nature, certainty, context, and specified factors relevant to risk assessment (Hart, 2001, in press; Mulvey & Lidz, 1995). Any of these dimensions can vary across settings and jurisdictions, and researchers and clinicians ought to be aware of those that apply in the settings in which their work is located. This is a problem that is inherent to research and practice activities of clinical psychology situated within the legal context (Ogloff & Douglas, in press).

How do these varying legal standards across settings and jurisdictions translate into clinical forensic assessment practice and research? A first step to tackling the multiplicity of relevant applications of risk assessment (and, in fact, of any forensic assessment application) is to conduct a *psycholegal content analysis* of the germane substantive area in which research (or practice) is to be carried out (Douglas, 2000; McNiel et al., in press; Ogloff & Douglas, in press). This involves (a) identifying the relevant primary legal authority—typically a statute—that governs the assessment task that will be the object of study, (b) isolating the pieces of the legal authority that will apply most directly to the assessment task, (c) evaluating how sources of supporting law—typically cases—have interpreted and applied the primary authority, (d) distilling legal principles from the statute and supporting interpretive sources of law, and (e) applying psychological knowledge to the legal concepts and principles that were derived in steps a through d. This procedure can lay the groundwork for conducting legally relevant and appropriate research within legal or forensic settings.

Researchers and clinicians must bear in mind that the generalizability of their findings will be limited by these legal factors. In some cases, there is little one can do to counter this limiting factor. For instance, research on the long-term recidivism of sexual offenders will have little generalizability to and hence be minimally informative with respect to imminent risk posed by acutely mentally ill persons being considered for involuntary civil commitment. Researchers can, however, promote the generalizability of their findings by incorporating, to the degree that is methodologically feasible, a number of the aspects of risk previously described. For instance, evaluating the relationship between a risk assessment measure and differing severities or types of violence (see Douglas, Ogloff, Nicholls, & Grant, 1999; McNiel & Binder, 1994a, 1994b) over different time periods (Quinsey, Harris, Rice, & Cormier, 1998; Rice & Harris, 1995), and using different classes of persons (Estroff & Zimmer, 1994) could be accomplished in a single research study. Similarly, evaluating the role of different risk factors within single studies has become common in risk assessment research, typically through the construction or evaluation of risk assessment measures

(Douglas et al., 1999; McNiel & Binder, 1994a, 1994b; Monahan et al., 2000, 2001; Quinsey et al., 1998; Steadman et al., 2000).

Insensitive Predictor and Outcome Measures

In the context of violence risk assessment, Monahan (1988; see also Monahan & Steadman, 1994a) wrote that previous research efforts had suffered from "impoverished predictor variables" and "weak criterion variables" (Monahan, 1988; pp. 251, 253). By this he meant that complex clinical phenomena such as psychopathology commonly were reduced to gross categorizations such as psychotic-nonpsychotic. Similarly, outcome measures considered only a single source and were coded simply as violent-not violent. Clearly, such methodological operationalizations oversimplify the constructs they purport to measure. As a result, they obscure meaningful relationships that might exist among the data.

To avoid this shortcoming, Monahan encouraged researchers to define and measure risk factors in more complex ways that more accurately reflect the actual nature of the risk factors (Monahan, 1988; Monahan & Steadman, 1994a). A good example is psychopathology. Rather than define major mental illness grossly as psychotic-nonpsychotic, researchers started to evaluate the role of certain diagnostic classes of disorders (Binder & McNiel, 1988; Eronen, Hakola, & Tiihonen, 1996a, 1996b; Hodgins, Mednick, Brennan, Schulsinger, & Engberg, 1996; McNiel & Binder, 1994a, 1994b, 1995; Räsänen et al., 1998) and certain types of psychotic symptoms (Appelbaum, Robbins, & Monahan, 2000; Link & Stueve, 1994; Monahan et al., 2001; Swanson, 1994; Swanson, Borum, Swartz, & Monahan, 1996). In so doing, a fairly robust relationship has been observed between certain aspects of mental illness, rather than mental illness per se and violence. It is important to note that not all research has observed positive relationships between indexes of disorder and symptoms. Nonetheless, this approach is able to evaluate which aspects of mental disorder are and are not related to violence, at least under certain conditions.

Researchers also have drawn on risk factors that are supported by theory. For instance, contemporary models and measures of psychopathy (Hare, 1991, 1996), anger (Novaco, 1994), psychotic symptoms (Link & Stueve, 1994; McNiel, 1994) and impulsivity (Barratt, 1994) have promoted more thoughtful and systematic evaluation of their contribution to risk for violence (see Monahan & Steadman, 1994b).

Similarly, with respect to violence as an outcome, it has come to be recognized that (a) measurement from a single source and (b) simple operationalizations of violent-nonviolent are not adequate. As risk is multifaceted, so too is violence—it can vary in severity, frequency, rate, timing, target, motivation, and context. Using a single source (e.g., arrest records) to measure violence is guaranteed to underestimate the actual occurrence of violence, and likely its actual severity due to the fact that many violent acts go unreported. Moreover, arrest records are often bereft of detail concerning the nature of violence, context, targets, and so forth. Such difficulties are magnified when other sources are used as indicators of violence (e.g., criminal convictions).

Use of a single source for recording outcome criteria also makes research subject to the peculiar biases of each type of outcome source (Mulvey & Lidz, 1993). For instance, arrest records may underestimate the true nature of violence, self-reports also may underestimate occurrence and severity of violence, and collateral reports may suffer from memory biases. Using multiple sources, each of which compensates for the weaknesses of others, is a sound approach. Some researchers (Monahan et al., 2001) have developed scales for measuring violence that are intended to capture a range of severities. Other researchers incorporate severity in other ways, typically by distinguishing between physical and non-physical violence (Douglas et al., 1999; McNiel & Binder, 1994a). Further, most studies use more than one source to detect violence. For instance, in two large-scale, prospective risk assessment projects using civil psychiatric samples, the researchers were able to use official arrest records, collateral interviews, and self-reports of patients (Lidz, Mulvey, & Gardner, 1993; Monahan et al., 2000, 2001), increasing the likelihood of adequate detection of criterion violence.

The importance of this issue cannot be overemphasized. For instance, using official records as the only source of violence detection among a large sample of civil psychiatric patients who had been released into the community, Mulvey, Shaw, and Lidz (1994) reported a base rate of violence of 12% (73 of 629 individuals). When the methodology was expanded to include self- and collateral reports of violence, this base rate rose dramatically to 47% (293 of 629 subjects). Similarly, in another large-scale sample of close to 1,000 civil psychiatric patients, Steadman et al. (1998) reported a 1-year base rate of serious violence of 4.5% when using agency reports only; when participant and collateral reports were added, the base rate rose to 27.5%. These differences in base rate could affect the statistical analyses used to evaluate the predictive utility of a risk factor or assessment measure. Such differences in base rates will affect the maximum effect size obtainable under most statistical procedures. Rice and Harris (1995), for example, reported that the correlational index (ϕ) used in their research with a large sample of forensic psychiatric patients increased from .25 to .40 under corresponding base rates of 15% and 50%.

Dichotomous Legal Outcomes Versus Continuous Psychological Outcomes

Law and psychology differ on numerous conceptual and epistemological bases. One of these is certainty versus probability (Haney, 1980). That is, the law demands certainty, whereas psychology—particularly academic or research psychology—is inherently probabilistic. Even though legal standards such as *preponderance of evidence, beyond a reasonable doubt,* or *balance of probabilities* certainly imply a probabilistic approach to legal decision making, it is equally clear that decisions and outcomes in law are absolute—persons either are or are not guilty, liable, dangerous, unfit, and so forth. There is no such thing in law as a person being found "likely guilty, within 95% confidence." A person *is* guilty although the evidence that supports this decision only needs proof beyond a reasonable doubt.

In some contexts, the law recognizes the continuous nature of constructs such as risk. For instance, the language used in many statutory regimes contains references to risk and other related concepts. There may be some conceptual overlap between psychology and law in these domains. Even here, however, the law must come to an absolute, dichotomous decision that a person is or is not at such a level of risk that satisfies whatever legal test is relevant, and hence justifies state-sanctioned deprivation of liberty or other restriction of rights. Even though risk is inherently probabilistic and continuous, the law must dichotomize it or cut the continuum into risk that meets statutory requirements and risk that does not.

In general, then, the most *legally* relevant clinical outcomes and criteria are dichotomous (i.e., rearrested or not). In research, however, it is a truism that to dichotomize is to lose information. To retain some legal external validity, however, coding for and analyzing outcomes in legally relevant ways is recommended, in addition to the perhaps more sophisticated and appropriate conceptualization of human behavior as a complex, continuous phenomenon. In this way, research can optimally inform legal reality, as well as contribute to understanding of human behavior on a more basic level.

Low and Varying Outcome Base Rates

Criterion variables that occur infrequently (i.e., low base rates) are difficult to predict. More precisely, base rates that deviate substantially from .50, whether low *or* high, attenuate effect sizes of many statistical procedures. As such, a base rate of .95 would be as problematic as .05 in terms of predicting the occurrence of the criterion. The problem of low base rates was in fact one of the critical focal points in early risk assessment research. Commentators argued that violence by persons with mental illness was simply too rare to permit meaningful analyses. Since that time, methodology has improved substantially, and, as it turns out, base rates are not as low as was previously believed. Steadman et al. (1998), for example, reported that 61% of the patients in their large-scale risk assessment study were violent in the community within 1 year of release, and 28% seriously so. Lidz et al. (1993) reported a 45% base rate of violence over 6 months among 714 patients evaluated in a psychiatric emergency department.

Researchers have developed several methodological and statistical procedures to ensure that the problem of low base rates does not preclude meaningful scientific inquiry. First, as suggested above, methodological procedures surrounding data collection have been strengthened to include multiple sources of information. In early studies, arrest records typically were used as the sole indication of violence. As discussed above, researchers have since recognized the inadequacy of this approach, and commonly employ a combination of sources—such as self-report, collateral report, clinical files, hospital records, and incident reports (Mulvey & Lidz, 1993).

The second general approach to deal with base rate issues is to define outcome criteria broadly. For instance, violence can be defined as any attempted, actual, or threatened harm to a person that is nonconsensual (Boer, Hart, Kropp, & Webster, 1997; Webster, Douglas, Eaves, & Hart, 1997). As Mulvey and Lidz (1993) pointed out, however, such liberal definitions actually may make outcome variables less relevant to legal decisions by incorporating a good deal of fairly trivial behavior that would not satisfy most legal tests. An advisable procedure is to adopt a broad definition of violence, but to distinguish between less and more serious forms of violence in coding and analyses (i.e., Douglas et al., 1999; McNiel & Binder, 1994a, 1994b; Monahan et al., 2000, 2001; Steadman et al., 1998), which permits some flexibility in terms of choosing relevant outcome variables.

Finally, it has been common in the published risk assessment research to use certain statistical procedures that are much less sensitive to base rate problems than are traditional statistical procedures such as correlation or regression. Primary among these are the areas under receiver operating characteristic (ROC) curves (Metz, 1978, 1984; Mossman & Somoza, 1991). Rice and Harris (1995) showed that across differing base rates of violence in their sample, traditional indexes of accuracy and association varied by up to 37.5%, whereas the areas under ROC curves remained stable. This analysis is recommended, and has become standard in the analysis of data in risk assessment research (Douglas et al., 1999; Monahan et al., 2000, 2001; Quinsey et al., 1998; Steadman et al., 2000). In

theory, it could be applied to any data containing a dichotomous outcome and continuous predictor.

Ethical Constraints

In all areas of research, ethical considerations prohibit certain methodological approaches. Although all research ethical guidelines that apply generally in psychology also apply to forensic assessment, some additional ethical factors delimit the scope of research in a manner that directly affects methodological soundness. The first has to do with *restriction of range,* and is really a matter of public policy and law in addition to professional ethics. That is to say, although a given risk assessment measure will be applied to all persons who are, for example, referred for parole, it can only be validated on the portion of that sample that actually is released. This restricts the range of participants and likely of risk factor variance that otherwise would have been observed. Even the best validated risk assessment instruments, then, are based on samples of restricted range.

The extent to which this affects the psychometric properties of instruments is unclear. Little can be done methodologically to combat this problem because to do so would require releasing all persons from correctional and forensic institutions, regardless of concerns about future violence. One strategy is to measure the released and nonreleased persons on key variables (i.e., age, race, important clinical variables and risk factors), and control for these in analyses.

The second methodological limit in predictive research arising from ethical constraints is what we call *intervention effects:* In most settings, when an assessment of high risk is made, intervening steps are (and should be) taken to prevent violence (or whatever the adverse event of concern happens to be). To do otherwise for the sake of research would be ethically impermissible. Despite our agreement with this reality from clinical, ethical, and policy perspectives, the case remains that it seriously hampers the ability to conduct predictive research in forensic settings. In essence, this problem is analogous to obtrusive measurement. By measuring a person's risk, we change his or her later behavior that would serve as the ultimate criterion in terms of validation (because we have to intervene to prevent the behavior we fear might occur).

To circumvent this problem, most research adopts procedures that parallel actual practice as closely as possible, but do not actually form part of clinical practice (Douglas & Kropp, in press). For instance, participants can be evaluated clinically for research purposes, with information being unavailable for decision-making purposes. This is essentially the procedure that has been followed in several contemporary studies of risk assessment measures (Douglas et al., 1999; Monahan et al., 2000, 2001; Quinsey et al., 1998). However, some fruitful research that *has* relied on actual practice has been published. For instance, Dale McNiel and colleagues have led a productive program of research on risk assessment and violence among civil psychiatric patients (see, e.g., Binder & McNiel, 1988, 1990; McNiel & Binder, 1987, 1989, 1991, 1994a, 1994b, 1995; McNiel, Binder, & Greenfield, 1988; McNiel, Sandberg, & Binder, 1998) using the clinical judgments of mental heath professionals in a large psychiatric facility. Lidz et al. (1993) were able to use the actual clinical judgments of psychiatrists in their study of the clinical prediction of violence.

In this subsection, we have identified obstacles to sound research endeavors in predictive assessment, including varying legal definitions of outcome criteria, insensitive predictor and outcome measures, dichotomous versus continuous conceptualizations of outcome criteria, and low or varying base rates, as well as research limitations placed by ethical concerns. We have described several strategies that can be used to overcome—or at least minimize the harm from—these obstacles. In the next subsection relevant to predictive assessment, we describe in more general terms methodological and statistical approaches that forensic researchers have taken or could take to answer common predictive forensic assessment research questions, including evaluations of the relationship between (a) individual predictors and outcome, (b) multiple-variable scales and outcome, or (c) clinical decisions (that are based on the predictors or scales) and outcomes.

Research Methods for Predictive Assessment

Research Strategies

Given that the research task is predictive, one might assume that most research strategies also are predictive or truly prospective. However, given the resources required to conduct a true predictive study, researchers have employed other designs as well, such as retrospective and pseudoprospective designs. The utility of repeated-measures prospective designs and that of case-crossover designs also are discussed.

Retrospective or postdictive designs are perhaps the most limited in terms of validating predictive forensic assessment research questions, although they provide the benefits of low cost and time burden. In these designs, the predictor in question, be it a putative risk factor or a full measure, is evaluated in terms of its ability to predict *past* outcome criteria. As such, this design cannot evaluate actual *pre*diction. However, it can offer preliminary evidence of whether a predictor is at least related in expected ways to outcome variables. For

example, researchers may wish to investigate whether posttraumatic stress disorder (PTSD) subsequent to trauma will predict other emotional problems in the future, so as to be able to forecast, in the context of civil litigation, recovery from such trauma. To do so, they may evaluate the prevalence of depression in the past of persons who do and do not have PTSD following a trauma. This study would permit evaluation of whether the two constructs, PTSD and depression, are at least related. Of course, it would not provide justification, in a pure epidemiological sense, for calling PTSD a risk factor for *subsequent* depression.

Similarly, researchers may wish to know if a certain putative risk factor will predict violence, but are unable to conduct a prospective analysis of the issue. Researchers have used postdictive designs to evaluate the connection between psychosis, variously defined, and violence. Swanson et al. (1996) evaluated whether certain types of psychotic symptoms and disorders were related to violence since the age of 18 in the Epidemiological Catchment Area data set of approximately 10,000 people. They then applied those relationships to an equation in order to estimate the predicted probability of violence, given certain risk factor combinations. Their findings that certain combinations of symptoms and disorders were related to past violence offered support for the position that the constructs are related and that these symptoms and disorders might then predict violence in subsequent investigations. Similarly, Douglas and Webster (1999b) evaluated the relationship between two violence risk assessment measures—both intended to forecast future behavior—and past violence. Their findings provided preliminary support for the position that the measures relate to violence, as they should.

Researchers must be cautious in interpreting findings from such designs because the design is vulnerable to confounding the predictor and the outcome. That is to say, it is possible that because the so-called outcome occurred earlier in time than did the predictor, the outcome actually influenced scores on the predictor, rather than the other way around. For instance, one risk factor on the risk assessment measures used by Douglas and Webster (1999b) is substance misuse. It is possible that a past violent episode (the outcome) could lead a person to drink or use drugs in order to cope with the stressful aftermath of the violence. In this way, the outcome of violence would have actually caused, preceded, or led to the predictor, rather than the other way around. As such, results can only be interpreted as showing a noncausal relationship, or that the variables or measures are associated in some expected way.

Researchers should take steps to remove obviously conflated factors from those identified as predictors if using this design (i.e., Douglas & Webster, 1999b). For instance, most risk assessment measures contain risk factors relating to past violence. Past violence is also the outcome criterion. Having the outcome criterion also contribute to the predictor obviously is problematic and will artificially inflate effect sizes. This is a rather straightforward example. The danger lies in less obvious instances that might not be readily discernible to the researcher, but that do exist.

Another problem that can arise with this research design relates to what might be called either *cohort effects,* or could be considered forms of the threats to validity called *history* and *selection* by Cook and Campbell (1979). Whatever the terminology, the problem stems from changes that might occur through the passage of time. For instance, if a measure is validated postdictively on a group of persons who were admitted to (or released from) a facility in a particular year (e.g., 1990, 1995, or 2000, etc), its application to persons recently admitted or discharged will be suspect if there have been any changes in the admission or discharge criteria (which is often the case due to the modification of law and policy). Different admission and discharge criteria could substantially alter the prevalence among persons of important factors such as type of disorder, history of violence, substance use, and so forth. Given that these factors also correlate with many criterion variables of interest, such as violence or suicide, such a shift likely will affect the relationship between a predictor and the criterion variable. Application of a predictor or measures devised on an earlier sample to a later sample, then, would be tenuous.

Pseudoprospective designs attempt to model true prospective designs in structure, but actually are retrospective. Typically, researchers will rate certain factors or measures based on archival or file data that is several years old, and then conduct what is called a *retrospective follow-up* for outcome criteria. In this design, the predictor is coded from information that existed prior in time to the outcome. However, the actual coding occurs later in time than the outcome does. For instance, Douglas et al. (1999) completed the HCR-20 (Historical-Clinical-Risk Management) risk assessment measure (Webster et al., 1997) and the Hare Psychopathy Checklist: Screening Version (PCL:SV; Hart, Cox, & Hare, 1995) based on file information of civil psychiatric patients who had applied for review panels for discharge in 1994. They used multiple sources of records to track the violence of patients until late 1996. Harris, Rice, and Quinsey (1993; Quinsey et al., 1998) used a similar procedure to construct a risk assessment measure called the Violence Risk Appraisal Guide (VRAG). Although the information upon which the measures were based existed prior to the outcome, the actual completed measures did not. As such, this design allows for proper temporal ordering of the predictor and outcome, but is not truly prospective.

This design is a reasonable alternative to a true prospective design in that it is far less resource intensive and does not require researchers to follow subjects for years before gathering information about the predictive potential of certain factors. It therefore permits somewhat more confident statements about the relationship between a putative predictor and subsequent criteria than do postdictive designs. However, the design suffers some weaknesses. If studies are conducted properly, coders will be blind to outcome status. There is a risk, however, that coders will inadvertently learn of the outcome, creating criterion contamination. Perhaps the larger limitation is that the information upon which the measures are completed is not optimally aligned to the purpose of the study. That is, researchers have to make do with existing data, rather than collect data in a predefined manner. The information that exists—typically medical, psychological, social, legal, and criminal file and report information—was not gathered originally to complete the measures that the researcher is investigating. As such, the rating of some items might be less reliable than it would be if the researcher were able to construct a priori information-gathering mechanisms.

For instance, the assessment measures completed by Douglas et al. (1999) and Harris et al. (1993), respectively, require some degree of clinical inference. Risk factors on the HCR-20 include constructs such as *lack of insight* and *impulsivity.* Both the HCR-20 and the VRAG require ratings of psychopathy on a clinician-rated test. These constructs might be difficult to rate based on preexisting reports. Additionally, because all ratings are done from file information, patients are not present to participate in interviews. This further limits the type or (at least) the reliability of data that can be collected.

Truly prospective designs compensate for the weaknesses of both the postdictive and the pseudoprospective design. As such, they are preferable to these other designs, but also tend to be more time and cost intensive. In this design, collection of all data and completion of all measures are done before participants enter a follow-up phase. As such, there is no risk of confounding outcome and predictor, or of contaminating ratings with knowledge of outcome. Variables and measures can be operationalized in optimal ways, and special-to-purpose data collection procedures can be constructed to allow optimal ratings of constructs. There is no built-in necessity to make do with existing information. Data can be collected that suit the purpose of the study, eliminating the need to conform the purposes and procedures of the study to suit the data. For these reasons, prospective studies yield results that allow the most confidence in the predictive utility of variables or measures.

To illustrate, prospective designs are common in research on trauma secondary to accidents or crime. Ehlers, Mayou, and Bryant (1998), for instance, evaluated approximately 1,000 victims of motor vehicle accidents who were consecutively admitted to a British hospital. They then evaluated the utility of information gathered during the hospital admission (i.e., severity of injury, perception of accident, anger over accident, PTSD symptoms present, trait worry, coping style) to predict PTSD incidence at 3 and 12 months postaccident. In the violence risk assessment field, prospective studies have been used to construct or validate predictive instruments (i.e., Belfrage, Fransson, & Strand, 2000; McNiel & Binder, 1994b; Monahan et al., 2000, 2001; Steadman et al., 2000) and to evaluate the validity of clinical predictions of violence (Lidz et al., 1993; McNiel, Sandberg, & Binder, 1998).

Repeated-measures prospective designs offer yet more potential. For instance, a currently important topic in risk assessment and treatment research is the malleability of risk factors, the relationship of such changes to frequency of violent behavior, and the potential systematically to target such risk factors for intervention (Douglas & Kropp, in press; Hanson & Harris, 2000; Webster, Douglas, Belfrage, & Link, 2000). Using this design permits such analyses. Cox proportional-hazards survival analysis with time-dependent covariates (i.e., the putatively changeable variables that are measured on a repeated basis) would permit evaluation of the relationship between changes in risk factors and the occurrence of violence (or changes in the hazard functions related to changes in risk factors).

Although we are aware of no examples in forensic prediction, a potentially useful methodology is the *case-crossover design*. As Maclure and Mittleman (2000) explained, this design can evaluate whether something notable happened immediately prior to some event of interest (i.e., violence, treatment dropout). The design is so named because at least some of the sample will have crossed over, so to speak, from low to high exposure on a potential trigger or risk factor (Maclure & Mittleman, 2000, p. 196). In this design, the control condition is time rather than participant based (i.e., it is essentially a within-group design). Further, the design is retrospective. It searches for what might have been present just prior to an outcome of interest that was *not* present during some previous time period for the same people. The design attempts to distill precursors to events by retrospectively examining equal-sized time periods: one prior to the event and another at some earlier time point. Acute or sudden events, such as a violent act, might be particularly amenable to this design because time periods could be well defined.

Finally, some researchers have been able to take advantage of *natural field experiments*. These opportunities, although rare, come about through sudden changes in the law or through comparisons between jurisdictions. Two of the more infamous examples in forensic psychology stem from court decisions holding that certain state legislation violated the Constitution. In *Baxstrom v. Herold* (1966), the petitioner, Johnnie K. Baxstrom, sought a writ of habeas corpus concerning his postsentence civil commitment without protections that were afforded to all persons who were subject to civil commitment proceedings in the community. Further, although psychiatrists had opined that he could be placed in a civil institution, he was placed by administrators in a correctional facility.

The U.S. Supreme Court held that this procedure denied Baxstrom equal protection under the Constitution. Following this holding, Baxstrom and close to 1,000 others in his situation were transferred to less secure civil hospitals or released outright in what came to be known as Operation Baxstrom. In the other seminal case, *Dixon v. Attorney General of the Commonwealth of Pennsylvania* (1971), seven plaintiffs brought a class action against the attorney general of the state on their own behalf and the behalf of similarly situated persons institutionalized at Farview State Hospital. The state mental health statute permitted postsentence, indefinite civil commitment of prisoners nearing the ends of their sentences—without a formal hearing or process, without even notification of prisoners or their families, and without the right to counsel or to solicit an independent mental health examination. On top of this, the statute permitted such commitment on the basis that the person appeared to be mentally disabled and in need of care. The United States District Court for the Middle District of Pennsylvania held that "we entertain no doubt that Section 404 of the . . . Act . . . is unconstitutional on its face" (p. 972), having no semblance of due process. As a result, the court ordered that persons were to be discharged, or recommitted under an entirely new and fair procedure that provided patients with the right to notification, to counsel, to present evidence, to cross-examine witnesses, and to retain independent experts. The standard for commitment was changed to require the fact finder to establish "clearly, unequivocally and convincingly that the subject of the hearing requires commitment because of manifest indications that the subject poses a present threat of serious physical harm to other persons or to himself" (p. 974). Again, the result was that numerous persons were released or transferred to less secure facilities.

These legal cases provided natural experiments to researchers. One might infer from their commitment that these patients all had been determined (or predicted) to be dangerous mentally ill prisoners. Despite this, many were released, hence minimizing the ethical concerns and restriction of range problem previously described. Follow-up studies of the *Baxstrom* (Steadman & Cocozza, 1974; Steadman & Halfon, 1971; Steadman & Keveles, 1972) and *Dixon* (Thornberry & Jacoby, 1979) patients revealed a very low rearrest rate for violent crime, leading some to conclude that the original predictions were highly inaccurate, being characterized by very high false-positive errors (Monahan, 1981). These cases and naturalistic research studies were largely responsible for setting in motion the accrual of research and writing as well as the conceptual and methodological developments in the field of violence risk assessment.

Reliability in Prediction

Of course, reliability in forensic prediction is as important as it is in any predictive endeavor. Because most predictive measures are not construct measures, reliability indexes from classical test theory (i.e., internal consistency, item-total correlations, item homogeneity) and modern test theory (i.e., a and b item parameters, differential item functioning, item characteristic curves) typically are not of paramount interest. Rather, inter-rater reliability is most important. If clinicians cannot agree on predictive decisions, then such decisions are of little utility. We recommend that measures of agreement rather than of association are used as reliability indexes. Measures of association, such as the Pearson r or ϕ are not sensitive to additive and multiplicative biases between raters, whereas measures of agreement, such as *intraclass correlation* (ICC) and kappa (κ) are. For instance, on a 10-point scale, a correlation of unity would result from either of the following two pairs of ratings: Rater A: 1, 2, 3, 4, 5; Rater B: 6, 7, 8, 9, 10 (additive bias) *or* 2, 4, 6, 8, 10 (multiplicative bias). Clearly these pairs of ratings are associated with one another. Equally clear, however, is that raters are not in agreement. As such, measures of chance-corrected agreement, such as ICC, κ, or $\kappa_{weighted}$ are recommended.

Common Statistical Approaches

We list here the commonly used statistical approaches in predictive forensic assessment. Traditional indexes of classification accuracy are common, such as false and true negatives and positives, and positive and negative predictive power (e.g., see Douglas et al., 1999; Lidz et al., 1993; McNiel & Binder, 1994b). Discriminant function analyses have been used as well (Klassen & O'Connor, 1989). Linear and logistic regression-based models also are commonly used to test for independent relationships between predictors and outcomes (see, respectively, Douglas et al., 1999; Harris et al., 1993; Kropp & Hart, 2000; Monahan et al., 2000, 2001;

Quinsey et al., 1998; Steadman et al., 2000). Hierarchical regression models have been used to evaluate incremental validity (Douglas et al., 1999; Kropp & Hart, 2000; Swanson et al., 1996). As described above, ROC analysis is now frequently used to estimate predictive accuracy (Douglas et al., 1999; Monahan et al., 2001; Quinsey et al., 1998; Rice & Harris, 1995; Steadman et al., 1998). Survival analysis has been used to evaluate hazard rates relative to predictors (Douglas et al., 1999). This list is not comprehensive, but illustrative.

We have chosen to forego discussion of other methodological aspects of predictive forensic assessment, such as the use of rational versus empirical scale construction, or the evaluation of clinical versus actuarial predictions, because these topics are discussed in other chapters and require much more space than could be allotted here. We can offer a few comments. First, given the numerous variations in forensic predictive tasks created by differing legal standards across settings and jurisdictions, discussed earlier, the generalizability of empirically derived, actuarial instruments *may* be more difficult to achieve than in other fields. This has led to a movement to study rationally derived instruments that promote structured clinical decisions (rather than the traditional clinical decisions that typically are described as informal, impressionistic, and subjective—see Grove & Meehl, 1996). These structured models of decision making (e.g., see Augimeri, Koegl, Webster, & Levene, 2001; Boer, Hart, Kropp, & Webster, 1997; Borum, Bartel, & Forth, 2002; Kropp, Hart, Webster, & Eaves, 1999; Webster et al., 1997) provide operationalized factors that evaluators must consider, and for the scoring of which evaluators must follow standard rules. Initial research suggests that the clinical decisions that are based on these measures are adequately reliable (Douglas, 2001; Kropp & Hart, 2000) and add incremental validity to actuarial predictions (Dempster, 1998; Douglas, 2001; Kropp & Hart, 2000). For fuller treatments of this issue, see Douglas, Cox, and Webster, 1999; Douglas and Kropp, in press; Douglas and Webster, 1999a; Hart, 1998, 2001, in press; Melton et al., 1997; Otto, 2000.

Clinical forensic psychologists often find themselves asked to forecast the future behavior or functioning of their patients and clients. Often the substance of such predictive assessments is violent behavior, future child and family functioning, and response to trauma and treatment. Research efforts to evaluate the reliability and validity of these efforts are challenged by numerous factors, some of which could easily appear in other fields of inquiry (i.e., low or varying base rates of criteria), whereas others are more salient within forensic settings (i.e., influence on criteria of legal standards). We have described several methodological or statistical procedures to compensate for some of these shortcomings (i.e., using multiple sources of outcome, adopting broad definitions of outcome criteria, employing particular statistical approaches, using research strategies that parallel actual clinical practice without influencing it). We also presented the strengths and weaknesses of general research designs used to answer predictive assessment research questions, such as postdictive, pseudoprospective, true prospective, repeated-measures prospective, case-crossover, and natural field experiments.

In the next and final section—dealing with the evaluation and validation of legally relevant diagnostic constructs and response styles—forensic researchers are presented with yet more research challenges. They also employ a variety of methodological and statistical approaches in addition to those discussed previously in order to provide reasonable answers to important research questions. We discuss these issues in the following section.

RESEARCH REGARDING THE ASSESSMENT AND VALIDATION OF LEGALLY RELEVANT DIAGNOSTIC CONSTRUCTS AND RESPONSE STYLES

Overview

In the first section of this chapter, we discussed research efforts designed to evaluate psycholegal constructs, or psychologically related constructs that essentially are defined by law (i.e., best interests of the child, fitness to stand trial). The current section has some similarities in that it concerns psychological constructs rather than the prediction of future behavior or functioning, as in the middle section of this chapter. This third area of research in clinical forensic psychology—although somewhat less distinctive than the others—pertains to the exploration and validation of legally relevant diagnostic constructs. In many ways, the conceptual and methodological issues are the same as those that face any researcher seeking to understand and validate a clinical syndrome, diagnosis, or psychological construct, but the legal context in which subjects are examined or in which the results would be relevant poses some additional challenges for research design (Moore & Finn, 1986). The two primary areas of research in clinical forensic psychology have been (a) the search for personality styles that place persons at risk for negative legal outcomes, and (b) response styles aimed at manipulating certain legal outcomes. As in the previous two sections of this chapter, we provide a brief overview of these topics, discuss some general research challenges within these fields, and

then present specific methodological approaches that researchers have used to evaluate these topics.

In clinical forensic psychology there has been significant interest in identifying a *clinical syndrome or cluster of personality traits* that distinguish individuals who are at particularly high risk for negative legal outcomes (Millon, Simonsen, Birket-Smith, & Davis, 1998; Stoff, Breiling, & Maser, 1997). This research has proceeded along two lines. In the first, researchers have attempted to identify personality traits and characteristics that distinguish individuals who engage in criminal or violent behavior from those who do not. Studies in the second line of research have explored the existence of a personality type, syndrome, or disorder that is reliably associated with criminal or violent behavior.

The research methods or statistical approaches used in the first line are not particularly distinctive or unique to forensic psychology (Lilienfeld, 1994). Most investigations in this tradition have used one or more scales or tests designed to assess a particular construct of interest—such as anger, hostility, or impulsivity—and looked for mean score differences between two criterion groups (e.g., violent offenders vs. nonviolent offenders). Between-group differences are then interpreted by inference to mean that the particular trait is somehow associated with the criterion behavior.

Another issue that has received significant research attention in clinical forensic psychology is the *response style* of individuals who are subjects of forensic examinations when they are asked to complete psychological tests or report their symptoms in interviews. The applied problem in these assessments is that respondents may consciously misrepresent their psychological status or symptoms to achieve some secondary gain. Both underreporting and overreporting of one's symptoms can be problematic in a forensic context. Although it is likely that a hybrid response set, in which the examinee is motivated to deny or minimize some problems and exaggerate or fabricate others, may be the most common response style adopted in forensic evaluations (see Rogers, 1997, for a discussion), specific response styles are more likely to occur in particular types of evaluations.

Concerns about underreporting and minimization—often referred to as defensiveness or *positive malingering*—are most likely to surface in three types of forensic evaluations: fitness for duty, custody-dependency, and release decision making. In evaluations of fitness for duty and in pre-employment screening, examinees may be motivated to deny and minimize problems they may be experiencing in order to gain desired employment or placement. In custody and dependency evaluations, parents may be motivated to present themselves in a positive light so that they can gain custody of their children. And in cases in which persons are being evaluated in order to make decisions about their appropriateness for release from an institution of some type (e.g., in the context of a parole or civil commitment hearing) they also may be motivated to present themselves in a positive light and deny or minimize psychopathology. Concerns about overreporting—often referred to as *malingering*—occur when potential secondary gain may accrue from a patient's having severe psychological impairment. In criminal cases, such incentives may occur for defendants seeking to assert an insanity or other mental-state defense. In civil cases, such incentives may occur when a plaintiff claims to have suffered psychological damages due to the negligence of someone else, and the degree of compensation due will be contingent in part on the degree of severity of those damages.

Challenges to Researching Legally Relevant Diagnostic Constructs and Response Styles

Personality-Diagnosis

As noted in the previous section, two major research challenges have beset these studies: weak predictor variables and weak criterion variables (Monahan, 1988). These are the same issues that have vexed research in violence prediction, and they are problematic for many of the same reasons:

- The constructs selected as predictors are not conceptually or empirically related to the criterion.
- The constructs selected as predictors are related to the criterion, but the relationship is largely nonspecific.
- The scales or tests used are poor (invalid) measures of the construct.
- The scores themselves have very little variability (restricted range) in the samples chosen for study (e.g., delinquent status offenders vs. violent delinquents).
- The criterion behaviors (or scores) have a restricted range in the samples chosen for study.
- The criterion groups are poorly defined or distinguished (e.g., using the instant offense as the sole criterion to distinguish violent offenders and nonviolent offenders, when many nonviolent offenders also have a history of prior violence).

Research attempting to identify a syndrome associated with propensity for criminality has proceeded somewhat differently. Early efforts attempted to discover and discern the elements of a so-called criminal personality (Eysenck, 1964; Howell, 1971). Predictably, these efforts met with limited success because they worked backward from a

multiply-determined behavior and attempted to define and explain its manifestation as a personality style. One would perhaps expect similar results in attempting to define the "addictive personality," or the "bad driving personality." An extensive body of research has shown that in predicting or explaining any form of human behavior—including aggression—that personality variables explain very little of the variance. Situational factors tend to have much greater explanatory power, but they are not the focus of a criminal personality model of behavior.

These early efforts did, however, contribute to further thinking about a disorder that might be associated with a particularly strong propensity for antisocial behavior—even if most people who engaged in such behavior did not possess the disorder. "The viability of a psychopathological construct is based on a range of evidence. A prerequisite is the existence of a coherent syndrome, that is, a cluster of symptoms, signs, and traits that occur together and that are distinct from other clusters" (Cooke & Michie, 2001, p. 171). Based on early conceptual work by Cleckley (1941), several researchers, most notably Robert Hare, attempted to operationally define and measure such a syndrome; they referred to the construct as psychopathy (Hare & Schalling, 1978). Later in this section we use this line of research to illustrate some methodologies for validating these constructs in forensic clinical psychology.

Response Style

The main challenge confronting this line of research easily is evident on the face of the problem—how do you study people who lie? Individuals in the criterion group do not want to be accurately identified and use deception and distortion to avoid identification. In the previous section on researching legally relevant capacities, we discussed the challenges posed by the absence of a gold standard for the criterion. This problem applies here as well. Individuals who successfully exaggerate or minimize their symptoms—by definition—will not be identified in real-world contexts, so that they or their responses cannot be studied. The closest that a researcher can come to having unequivocal evidence of extreme response distortion (e.g., claiming to have severe impairment that is not really present, or denying significant problems that really are present) is either to have an admission of that distortion, or to have compelling factual evidence that directly contradicts the individual's self report (e.g., an individual claims to have been in a particular hospital on three occasions, but there is no record of an admission), or to have evidence of certain criteria that are considered to be highly specific (e.g., performing at a rate significantly below chance on a symptom validity test).

Researching Legally Relevant Diagnostic Constructs and Response Styles

Diagnosis-Personality

A commonly used approach to the study of legally relevant constructs is *factor analysis*. Using concepts derived from Cleckley, Hare and his colleagues attempted initially to validate the construct through the use of exploratory factor analysis (EFA). Their work, as presented in the manual (Hare, 1991), produced three hypothetical factor structures: a model with three so-called facets, a model with two distinct but correlated factors, and a hierarchical structure in which component facets were nested within a higher-order construct. The two-factor model—consisting of a "selfish, callous, and remorseless use of others" factor and a "chronically unstable and antisocial lifestyle" factor (Hare, 1991, p. 38)—gained initial ascendance in the literature on psychopathy and the associated instrument, the Hare Psychopathy Checklist–Revised (PCL-R; Hare, 1991). Hare's interpretation of the two-factor model was guided by a measure of factor similarity referred to as the congruence coefficient, although some critics have argued that this coefficient should not be relied upon as an exclusive measure of factor similarity (Floyd & Widaman, 1995).

Subsequent analyses were conducted using confirmatory factor analysis (CFA), with results of goodness-of-fit measures supporting the two-factor model—although no alternative or competing models were tested (Cooke & Michie, 2001). A subsequent EFA of the data from the instrument's standardization sample by Cooke and Michie (2001) examined the acceptability of the two-factor model using multiple measures of fit, and the analysis found that structure to be notably lacking in support. They then attempted to refine the model by combining theoretical considerations (e.g., the three historical domains of psychopathy and the hierarchical nature of most models of normal and disordered personality) and analytic methods that would produce the largest number of factors for preliminary consideration (e.g., applying direct oblimin criteria to obtain a solution with obliquely rotated factors). Their data were most consistent with a three-factor model (in essence dividing the "selfish, callous, and remorseless use of others" factor into two). Next, they cross-validated the proposed structure within and across cultures, again using multiple fit coefficients, and consistently found strongest support for their three-factor model. Among the research that has

attempted to validate the construct of psychopathy, the data from factor analytic research has received the greatest attention. The evolution from a two-factor to three-factor model being regarded as the dominant model demonstrates some potential advantages to combining theoretical and statistical considerations in model development and to using multiple criteria and indexes of fit to enhance one's confidence in the viability of the solution.

An alternative approach to validate or clarify a diagnostic construct is *prototypical analysis*. This method is based on prototype theory (Dopkins & Gleason, 1997; Hampton, 1995) and is seen as being particularly useful to bring operational clarity to constructs that may otherwise be ambiguous. The basic approach is to generate a pool of nonredundant items based on the empirical and theoretical literature that may potentially characterize the construct. It is recommended that one think broadly about the construct at the initial phase of item selection and to choose items that extend beyond one's own theoretical or conceptual view of the syndrome, and even to include some items that may be only marginally related (Salekin, Rogers, & Machin, 2001). The items are presented to a sample of experts who are asked to consider the most prototypical case of a person with the syndrome that they have seen in the recent past and to rate each item on a Likert scale according to how strongly related or characteristic that trait is of the overall syndrome. This method has been applied to antisocial personality disorder in adults (Rogers, Dion, & Lynett, 1992; Rogers, Duncan, Lynett, & Sewell, 1994) and to the construct of psychopathy in youth (Salekin, Rogers, & Machin, 2001).

Response Style

Given that a definitive known groups design is typically not feasible, researchers typically must resort to *proxy criteria or analogue (or simulation) research designs* to study the problem, but each of these comes with its own set of challenges and limitations. Proxy criteria typically used are cutting scores on other psychometric measures of malingering and deception. For example, the Structured Interview of Reported Symptoms (SIRS; Rogers, Bagby, & Dickens, 1992) is one of the most widely accepted measures for malingered psychotic symptoms. To validate a new instrument that assesses for malingering, an investigator might concurrently administer the SIRS, along with the experimental measure, and designate those with a certain predetermined SIRS score as the *malingering* group (see, e.g., Miller, 2001). This would not be considered a known groups design by conservative standards because the condition can only be inferred indirectly from a psychometric measure. One's psychological impairment, however, cannot definitively be determined in the same way that a physical impairment can be detected by diagnostic imaging techniques, so proxy criteria often are used as alternatives.

Another option frequently used in studies of response distortion is the *analogue study.* In this approach, the investigator randomly assigns the sample to one of two conditions: instructions to respond honestly or instructions to distort responses. In a typical analogue study, the experimenter would administer a scale or measure to a sample. Half of the participants would be given instructions to respond as honestly as possible. The other half would be instructed to use a particular response set (e.g., *you are attempting to convince the evaluator that you have a severe mental illness*). The mean scores of the two groups would be compared to determine whether there were significant differences, and the presence of such a difference would be interpreted as evidence of the scale's ability to distinguish honest from nonhonest (malingering) responders. Rogers (1997) also recommended that subjects in analogue research on malingering and deception be debriefed following their participation in an experiment for two reasons: (a) to ensure they understood and complied with the instructions, and (b) to explore—at least qualitatively—the different strategies that people may use to portray themselves as being more or less troubled than they actually are.

What are the problems with analogue research? It is perhaps not surprising that any reasonably designed scale for assessment of exaggerated symptoms will show large differences between normal participants asked to respond honestly (who presumably would have few if any symptoms), and honest participants asked to appear pathological (who presumably would seek to report a significant number of symptoms). In any applied context, the between-groups distinction is likely to be much more difficult, particularly because some people who minimize or exaggerate their problems do have actual symptoms or disorders. Someone who uses malingering as a response style may still have a serious mental disorder. Thus, on its face the analogue study in this context would not appear to be a very rigorous test for the validity of a measure.

This dilemma is further compounded by two problems—one conceptual and the other motivational—inherent in the analogue design. The conceptual problem is one that some have previously referred to as the *simulation-malingering paradox:* That is, the design uses information obtained from individuals who comply with instructions to respond dishonestly to make inferences about people who do not comply with instructions to respond honestly. Arguably, this raises a question about generalizability. Further threatening external validity are the potential differences in motivation and

incentives between a research situation in which no real consequences accrue to subjects regardless of whether they are successful in dishonestly portraying their psychological status, and a legal situation in which the incentives for avoiding criminal penalties or gaining substantial monetary damages may be quite compelling. It is not difficult to imagine how these differences could affect one's investment, effort, preparation, or performance.

Given that incentives may be high in legal contexts, concerns have been raised that some individuals may seek to learn—or be coached by their attorneys—about the strategies and scales used by mental health professionals to detect the type of deception in which they intend to engage. If that were true, then it might be possible to defeat the detection strategies. Some researchers sought to examine this issue empirically by designing studies in which some subjects were provided with instructions about how particular psychometric measures operated to detect response bias to examine whether this knowledge enhanced one's ability successfully to present a distorted protocol without invalidating the measure or triggering indexes of deception.

In presenting the results of this line of research, a fundamental tension is raised between the ethical obligation to protect the security of and integrity of psychometric measures and tests, and the scientific obligation to describe one's research method and protocol in detail (Ben-Porath, 1994; Berry, Lamb, Wetter, Baer, & Widiger, 1994). For example, if a study finds that a certain instructional set—such as providing detailed information on how a particular validity scale operates to detect dishonest responding—helps dishonest responders to distort the protocol while avoiding detection, to publish those instructions might then compromise the test in applied settings. On balance, a researcher reading these results would likely be interested to know the nature of the instructions that affected the results, not simply that some undefined instruction produced the effect. Berry and colleagues (1994)—after reviewing numerous options—recommended an approach to handle this dilemma by limiting the amount of detail provided in the publication about the specific instructions or strategy that was given to enhance the avoidance of detection.

In summary, then, two primary issues have been the focus of research efforts described in this section—legally relevant diagnostic constructs and response styles. In the former, researchers have been interested in identifying and describing personality styles such as psychopathy that relate to meaningful and important legal outcome criteria. In the latter case, researchers have attempted to describe styles of responding intended to mislead legal decision makers. Some of the research challenges here were similar to those described in the other sections: weak predictor and criterion variables, lack of a gold standard for outcome criteria, and the difficulty of studying persons who are intentionally dishonest and do not want to be detected. Common research approaches have included exploratory and confirmatory factor analysis, prototypicality analysis, use of proxy criteria, and analogue studies.

CONCLUSION

Clinical forensic psychology has become a well-defined subspecialty of clinical psychology. It can be defined as assessment, treatment, or consultation that centers around clinical issues within legal contexts, or with populations involved in the legal system. Psychologists who conduct research in forensic contexts are faced with challenges that present themselves in any research context, as well as with some that are unique to working within another profession's venue. As such, forensic researchers must be well versed in general research design and methodological principles from clinical and experimental psychology, in addition to being alive and responsive to the unique legally related research challenges that they will face. They must be able to apply both (a) the general principles of research design within legal contexts, and (b) forensic-specific approaches to research design and methodology.

In this chapter, we described (a) common areas of inquiry in clinical forensic psychology (descriptive assessment and psycholegal capacities, predictive assessment, and legally relevant diagnostic constructs and response styles); (b) general challenges to conducting research within these areas; and (c) specific research designs and methodological approaches that scholars effectively have employed within these areas.

Concerning the first topic, clinical forensic psychologists who are interested in the assessment of psycholegal capacities must define and operationalize these capacities based on their understanding of both the law and of psychological factors. After these constructs are identified and defined, researchers must develop methods for their description and evaluation. In addition to assessing the standard psychometric properties of these instruments (i.e., normative data, structural reliability), clinical forensic psychologists are presented with the challenge of assessing their validity within the legal contexts in which they are intended to be used. Many of the research challenges that face any researchers are relevant here as well. However, this task presents numerous forensic-specific challenges to research, such as the lack of a gold standard for outcome criteria, varying legal definitions of constructs, and the legally multifaceted nature of many of these constructs. Researchers have used various approaches

to study these issues, such as literature and expert surveys, theory-based development, and evaluating the correspondence between constructs or instruments and either judges' or clinicians' decisions.

Next, clinical forensic psychologists also continue to be called upon to develop assessment protocols designed to predict behaviors of interest. As with the other two main areas of research activity, research on predictive forensic assessment is beset with forensic-specific challenges, such as varying legal definitions of outcome criteria, insensitive predictor and outcome measures, the clash between dichotomous legal outcomes and continuous psychological outcomes, low and varying base rates, and limiting factors stemming from legitimate ethical concerns, such as restriction of range and intervention effects.

Given the sensitive and important issues with which the courts concern themselves in such matters (e.g., risk for violent reoffending, risk for suicide, risk for sexual reoffending, best custody arrangement for a child in the future) as well as the challenges to researching them, psychologists researching these issues must employ a variety of ingenious designs. Researchers have used a variety of designs in this area—ranging from the most simple and perhaps least informative (postdictive) to more sophisticated and informative designs (repeated-measures true prospective designs). Within these designs, researchers attempt to counter the challenges to research by employing multiple sources of outcome data, employing broad but hierarchical and multifaceted definitions of outcome, adopting theoretically informed and complex predictor variables, and using statistical procedures such as ROC analysis to compensate for base rate problems.

In terms of the third area of clinical forensic research—legally relevant constructs and response styles—researchers face some of the same challenges as those who research descriptive psycholegal capacities or predictive measures. These challenges include weak predictor and criterion variables and lack of a gold standard; in addition, taking a "single explanation approach" (i.e., personality) to multiply-determined behavior (criminal behavior) has posed challenges to researchers. A further difficulty in this area has been posed by efforts to study persons who are intentionally attempting to lie, and hence whose self-reports cannot be trusted. Common research methods on this line of research include exploratory and confirmatory factor analysis, prototypicality analysis, and analogue studies.

Clinical forensic psychological research seeks to promote the understanding and optimal legal use of psychological constructs and behaviors as they unfold in legal settings. For a relatively young field, there has been reasonable growth in the quantity and quality of research carried out in the service of this goal. All projections would lead to a forecast of continued growth in clinical forensic research, with the result, we hope, of continued increasing understanding of the role of psychology within law.

REFERENCES

Ackerman, M., & Schoendorf, K. (1992). *Manual for the Ackerman-Schoendorf Scales for Parent Evaluation of Custody*. Los Angeles: Western Psychological Services.

American Educational Research Association, American Psychological Association, National Council on Measurement in Education (1999). *Standards for educational and psychological testing*. Washington, DC: Author.

American Psychiatric Association. (1994). *Diagnostic and statistical manual of mental disorders* (4th ed.). Washington, DC: American Psychiatric Association.

Appelbaum, P. S., Robbins, P. C., & Monahan, J. (2000). Violence and delusions: Data from the MacArthur violence risk assessment study. *American Journal of Psychiatry, 157,* 566–572.

Augimeri, L. K., Koegl, C. J., Webster, C. D., & Levine, K. S. (2001). *Early Assessment Risk List for Boys (EARL-20B): Version 2*. Toronto, Ontario, Canada: Earlscourt Child and Family Centre.

Barratt, E. S. (1994). Impulsiveness and aggression. In J. Monahan & H. J. Steadman (Eds.), *Violence and mental disorder: Developments in risk assessment* (pp. 61–79). Chicago: University of Chicago Press.

Baxstrom v. Herold, 383 U.S. 107 (1966).

Belfrage, H., Fransson, G., & Strand, S. (2000). Prediction of violence using the HCR-20: A prospective study in two maximum security correctional institutions. *Journal of Forensic Psychiatry, 11,* 167–175.

Ben-Porath, Y. (1994). The ethical dilemma of coached malingering research. *Psychological Assessment, 6,* 14–15.

Berry, D., Lamb, D., Wetter, M., Baer, R., & Widiger, T. (1994). Ethical considerations in research on coached malingering. *Psychological Assessment, 6,* 16–17.

Binder, R. L., & McNiel, D. E. (1988). Effects of diagnosis and context on dangerousness. *American Journal of Psychiatry, 145,* 728–732.

Binder, R. L., & McNiel, D. E. (1990). The relationship of gender to violent behavior in acutely disturbed psychiatric patients. *Journal of Clinical Psychiatry, 51,* 110–114.

Boer, D. P., Hart, S. D., Kropp, P. R., & Webster, C. D. (1997). *Manual for the Sexual Violence Risk–20: Professional guidelines for assessing risk of sexual violence*. Vancouver, British Columbia, Canada: British Columbia Institute Against Family Violence.

Bonnie, R. (1993). The competence of criminal defendants; Beyond *Dusky* and *Drope. Miami Law Review, 47,* 539–601.

Borum, R., Bartel, P, & Forth, A. (in press). *Manual for the Structured Assessment for Violence Risk in Youth (SAVRY): Consultation version*. Tampa: Florida Mental Health Institute, University of South Florida.

Bricklin, B. (1990). *Manual for the Bricklin Perceptual Scales*. Furlong, PA: Village Publishing.

Bricklin, B., & Elliott, G. (1997). *Critical child custody evaluation issues: Questions and answers. Test manuals supplement for BPS, PORT, PASS, PPCP*. Furlong, PA: Village Publishing.

Cleckley, H. (1941). *The mask of sanity*. St. Louis, MO: Mosby.

Cook, T. D., & Campbell, D. T. (1979). *Quasi-experimentation: Design and analysis issues for field settings*. Chicago: Rand McNally.

Cooke, D., & Michie, C. (2001). Refining the construct of psychopathy: Towards a hierarchical model. *Psychological Assessment, 13,* 171–188.

Cruise, K. (2001). *Resource directory of forensic psychology predoctoral internship training programs*. Lincoln, NE: American Psychology-Law Society.

Dempster, R. J. (1998). *Prediction of sexually violent recidivism: A comparison of risk assessment instruments*. Unpublished master's thesis, Simon Fraser University, Burnaby, British Columbia, Canada.

Dixon v. Attorney General of the Commonwealth of Pennsylvania, 325 F.Supp. 966 (1971).

Dopkins, S., & Gleason, T. (1997). Comparing exemplar and prototype models of categorization. *Canadian Journal of Experimental Psychology, 51,* 212–223.

Douglas, K. S. (2000, March). *A psycholegal analysis of violence risk assessment: Bringing law, science, and practice closer together*. Paper presented at the 2000 Biennial Meeting of the American Psychology-Law Society (Div. 41 APA), New Orleans, LA.

Douglas, K. S. (2001). *Making structured clinical decisions about violence risk: The reliability and validity of the HCR-20 violence risk assessment scheme*. Unpublished manuscript.

Douglas, K. S., Cox, D. N., & Webster, C. D. (1999). Violence risk assessment: Science and practice. *Legal and Criminological Psychology, 4,* 149–184.

Douglas, K. S., Huss, M. T., Murdoch, L. L., Washington, D. O., & Koch, W. J. (1999). Posttraumatic stress disorder stemming from motor vehicle accidents: Legal issues in Canada and the United States. In E. J. Hickling & E. B. Blanchard (Eds.), *International handbook of road traffic accidents and psychological trauma: Current understanding, treatment and law* (pp. 271–290). New York: Elsevier Science.

Douglas, K. S., & Kropp, P. R. (in press). A prevention-based paradigm for violence risk assessment: Clinical and research applications. *Criminal Justice and Behavior.*

Douglas, K. S., Ogloff, J. R. P., Nicholls, T. L., & Grant, I. (1999). Assessing risk for violence among psychiatric patients: The HCR-20 violence risk assessment scheme and the Psychopathy

Checklist: Screening version. *Journal of Consulting and Clinical Psychology, 67,* 917–930.

Douglas, K. S., & Webster, C. D. (1999a). Predicting violence in mentally and personality disordered individuals. In R. Roesch, S. D. Hart, & J. R. P. Ogloff (Eds.), *Psychology and law: The state of the discipline* (pp. 175–239). New York: Plenum.

Douglas, K. S., & Webster, C. D. (1999b). The HCR-20 violence risk assessment scheme: Concurrent validity in a sample of incarcerated offenders. *Criminal Justice and Behavior, 26,* 3–19.

Ehlers, A., Mayou, R.A., & Bryant, B. (1998). Psychological predictors of chronic posttraumatic stress disorder after motor vehicle accidents. *Journal of Abnormal Psychology, 107,* 508–519.

Eronen, M., Hakola, P., & Tiihonen, J. (1996a). Mental disorders and homicidal behavior in Finland. *Archives of General Psychiatry, 53,* 497–591.

Eronen, M., Hakola, P., & Tiihonen, J. (1996b). Factors associated with homicide recidivism in a 13-year sample of homicide offenders in Finland. *Psychiatric Services, 47,* 403–406.

Estroff, S. E., & Zimmer, C. (1994). Social networks, social support, and violence among persons with severe, persistent mental illness. In J. Monahan & H. J. Steadman (Eds.), *Violence and mental disorder: Developments in risk assessment* (pp. 259–295). Chicago: University of Chicago Press.

Eysenck, H. (1964). *Crime and personality.* New York: Houghton Mifflin.

Floyd, F., & Widaman, K. (1995). Factor analysis in the development and refinement of clinical assessment instruments. *Psychological Assessment, 7,* 286–299.

Forensic Psychology Specialty Council (Heilbrun, K., Bank, S., Follingstad, D., & Frederick, R.) (2000, September). *Petition for forensic psychology as an APA specialization.* Presented to the Committee for the Recognition of Specialties and Proficiencies in Professional Psychology, American Psychological Association, Washington, DC.

Grisso T. (1981). *Juveniles' waiver of rights: Legal and psychological competence.* New York: Plenum.

Grisso, T. (1986). *Evaluating competencies.* New York: Plenum.

Grisso, T. (1987). The economic and scientific future of forensic psychological assessment. *American Psychologist, 42,* 831–839.

Grisso, T. (1998). *Manual for instruments for assessing understanding and appreciation of Miranda rights.* Sarasota, FL: Professional Resource Press.

Grove, W. M., & Meehl, P. E. (1996). Comparative efficiency of informal (subjective, impressionistic) and formal (mechanical, algorithmic) prediction procedures: The clinical-statistical controversy. *Psychology, Public Policy, and Law, 2,* 293–323.

Hampton, J. (1995). Testing the Prototype Theory of concepts. *Journal of Memory & Language, 34,* 686–708.

Haney, C. (1980). Psychology and legal change: On the limits of a factual jurisprudence. *Law and Human Behavior, 6,* 191–235.

Hanson, R. K., & Harris, A. J. R. (2000). Where should we intervene? Dynamic predictors of sexual offense recidivism. *Criminal Justice and Behavior, 27,* 6–35.

Hare, R. D. (1991). *The Hare Psychopathy Checklist–Revised.* Toronto, Ontario, Canada: Multi-Health Systems.

Hare, R. D. (1996). Psychopathy: A clinical construct whose time has come. *Criminal Justice and Behavior, 23,* 25–54.

Hare, R. D., & Schalling, D. (Eds.). (1978). *Psychopathic behavior: Approaches to research.* Chichester, England: Wiley.

Harris, G. T., Rice, M. E., & Quinsey, V. L. (1993). Violent recidivism of mentally disordered offenders: The development of a statistical prediction instrument. *Criminal Justice and Behavior, 20,* 315–335.

Hart, S. D. (1998). The role of psychopathy in assessing risk for violence: Conceptual and methodological issues. *Legal and Criminological Psychology, 3,* 121–137.

Hart, S. D. (2001). *Complexity, uncertainty, and the reconceptualization of risk assessment.* Retrieved from http://www.sfu.ca/psychology/groups/faculty/hart.

Hart, S. D. (in press). Assessing and managing violence risk. In K. S. Douglas, C. D. Webster, S. D. Hart, D. Eaves, & J. R. P. Ogloff (Eds.), *HCR-20 violence risk management companion guide.* Burnaby, British Columbia, Canada: Mental Health Law and Policy Institute, Simon Fraser University.

Hart, S. D., Cox, D. N., & Hare, R. D. (1995). *The Hare Psychopathy Checklist: Screening Version (PCL:SV).* Toronto, Ontario, Canada: Multi-Health Systems.

Heilbrun, K., Rogers, R., & Otto, R. K. (in press). Forensic psychological assessment. In J. Ogloff (Ed.), *Psychology and law: The state of the discipline.* New York: Kluwer/Plenum.

Hodgins, S., Mednick, S. A., Brennan, P. A., Schulsinger, F., & Engberg, M. (1996). Mental disorder and crime: Evidence from a birth cohort. *Archives of General Psychiatry, 53,* 489–496.

Howell, R. (1971). A brief history and some reflections of the criminal personality. *Correctional Psychologist, 4,* 188–202.

Jameson, B. J., Ehrenberg, M. F., & Hunter, M. A. (1997). Psychologists, ratings of the best-interests-of-the-child custody and access criterion: A family systems assessment model. *Professional Psychology: Research and Practice, 28,* 253–262.

Klassen, D., & O'Connor, W. A. (1989). Assessing the risk of violence in released mental patients: A cross-validation study. *Psychological Assessment: A Journal of Consulting and Clinical Psychology, 1,* 75–81.

Kropp, P. R., & Hart, S. D. (2000). The Spousal Assault Risk Assessment (SARA) Guide: Reliability and validity in adult male offenders. *Law and Human Behavior, 24,* 101–118.

Kropp, P. R., Hart, S. D., Webster, C. D., & Eaves, D. (1999). *Manual for the Spousal Assault Risk Assessment Guide* (3rd ed.). Toronto, Ontario, Canada: Multi-Health Systems.

Lidz, C. W., Mulvey, E. P., & Gardner, W. (1993). The accuracy of predictions of violence to others. *Journal of the American Medical Association, 269,* 1007–1111.

Lilienfeld, S. (1994). Conceptual problems in the assessment of psychopathy. *Clinical Psychology Review, 14,* 17–38.

Link, B. G., & Stueve, A. (1994). Psychotic symptoms and the violent/illegal behavior of mental patients compared to community controls. In J. Monahan & H. J. Steadman (Eds.), *Violence and mental disorder: Developments in risk assessment* (pp. 137–159). Chicago: University of Chicago Press.

Lyon, D. R., Hart, S. D., & Webster, C. D. (2001). Violence risk assessment. In R. Schuller & J. R. P. Ogloff (Eds.), *Law and psychology: Canadian perspectives* (pp. 314–350). Toronto, Ontario, Canada: University of Toronto Press.

Maclure, M., & Mittleman, M. A. (2000). Should we use a case-crossover design? *Annual Review of Public Health, 21,* 193–221.

McNiel, D. E. (1994). Hallucinations and violence. In J. Monahan & H. J. Steadman (Eds.), *Violence and mental disorder: Developments in risk assessment* (pp. 183–202). Chicago: University of Chicago Press.

McNiel, D. E., & Binder, R. L. (1987). Predictive validity of judgments of dangerousness in emergency civil commitment. *American Journal of Psychiatry, 144,* 197–200.

McNiel, D. E., & Binder, R. L. (1989). Relationship between preadmission threats and later violent behavior by acute psychiatric inpatients. *Hospital and Community Psychiatry, 40,* 605–608.

McNiel, D. E., & Binder, R. L. (1991). Clinical assessment of the risk of violence among psychiatric inpatients. *American Journal of Psychiatry, 148,* 1317–1321.

McNiel, D. E., & Binder, R. L. (1994a). The relationship between acute psychiatric symptoms, diagnosis, and short-term risk of violence. *Hospital and Community Psychiatry, 45,* 133–137.

McNiel, D. E., & Binder, R. L. (1994b). Screening for risk of inpatient violence: Validation of an actuarial tool. *Law and Human Behavior, 18,* 579–586.

McNiel, D. E., & Binder, R. L. (1995). Correlates of accuracy in the assessment of psychiatric inpatients' risk of violence. *American Journal of Psychiatry, 152,* 901–906.

McNiel, D. E., & Binder, R. L., & Greenfield, T. K. (1988). Predictors of violence in civilly committed acute psychiatric patients. *American Journal of Psychiatry, 145,* 965–970.

McNiel, D. E., Borum, R., Douglas, K. S., Hart, S. D., Lyon, D. R., Sullivan, L., & Hemphill, J. (in press). Risk assessment. In J. R. P. Ogloff (Ed.), *Psychology and law: Reviewing the discipline.* New York: Kluwer/Plenum.

McNiel, D. E., Sandberg, D. A., & Binder, R. L. (1998). The relationship between confidence and accuracy in clinical assessment of psychiatric patients' potential for violence. *Law and Human Behavior, 22,* 655–669.

Melton, G. B., Petrila, J., Poythress, N. G., & Slobogin, C. (1997). *Psychological evaluations for the courts: A handbook for mental health professionals and lawyers* (2nd ed.). New York: Guilford.

Metz, C. E. (1978). Basic principles of ROC analysis. *Seminars in Nuclear Medicine, 8,* 283–298.

Metz, C. E. (1984). Statistical analysis of ROC data in evaluating diagnostic performance. In D. E. Herbert & R. H. Myers (Eds.), *Multiple regression analysis: Applications in the health sciences* (pp. 365–384). Washington, DC: American Institute of Physics.

Miller, H. (2001). *Professional manual for the Miller Forensic Assessment of Symptoms Test.* Odessa, FL: Psychological Assessment Resources.

Millon, T., & Simonsen, E., Birket-Smith, M., & Davis, R. D. (Eds.). (1998). *Psychopathy: Antisocial, criminal, and violent behavior.* New York: Guilford.

Miranda v. Arizona, 484 U.S. 436 (1966).

Monahan, J. (1981). *Predicting violent behavior: An assessment of clinical techniques.* Beverly Hills, CA: Sage.

Monahan, J. (1988). Risk assessment of violence among the mentally disordered: Generating useful knowledge. *International Journal of Law and Psychiatry, 11,* 249–257.

Monahan, J., & Steadman, H. J. (1994a). Toward a rejuvenation of risk assessment research. In J. Monahan & H. J. Steadman (Eds.), *Violence and mental disorder: Developments in risk assessment* (pp. 1–17). Chicago: University of Chicago Press.

Monahan, J., & Steadman, H. J. (Eds.). (1994b). *Violence and mental disorder: Developments in risk assessment.* Chicago: University of Chicago Press.

Monahan, J., Steadman, H. J., Appelbaum, P. S., Robbins, P. C., Mulvey, E. P., Silver, E., Roth, L. H., & Grisso, T. (2000). Developing a clinically useful actuarial tool for assessing violence risk. *British Journal of Psychiatry, 176,* 312–319.

Monahan, J., Steadman, H. J., Silver, E., Appelbaum, P. S., Robbins, P. C., Mulvey, E. P., Roth, L. H., Grisso, T., & Banks, S. (2001). *Rethinking risk assessment: The MacArthur study of mental disorder and violence.* New York: Oxford University Press.

Moore, L., & Finn, P. (1986). Forensic psychology: An empirical review of experimental research. *Journal of Clinical Psychology, 42,* 675–679.

Mossman, D., & Somoza, E. (1991). ROC curves, test accuracy, and the description of diagnostic tests. *Journal of Neuropsychiatry and Clinical Neurosciences, 3,* 330–333.

Mulvey, E. P., & Lidz, C. W. (1993). Measuring patient violence in dangerousness research. *Law and Human Behavior, 17,* 277–288.

Mulvey, E. P., & Lidz, C. W. (1995). Conditional prediction: A model for research on dangerousness to others in a new era. *International Journal of Law and Psychiatry, 18,* 129–143.

Mulvey, E. P., Shaw, E., & Lidz, C. W. (1994). Why use multiple sources in research on patient violence in the community? *Criminal Behaviour and Mental Health, 4,* 253–258.

Munsterberg, H. (1908). *On the witness stand.* Garden City, NY: Doubleday.

Novaco, R. W. (1994). Anger as a risk factor for violence among the mentally disordered. In J. Monahan & H. J. Steadman (Eds.), *Violence and mental disorder: Developments in risk assessment* (pp. 21–59). Chicago: University of Chicago Press.

Oberlander, L., & Goldstein, N. (2001). A review and update on the practice of evaluating Miranda comprehension. *Behavioral Sciences and the Law, 19,* 453–472.

Ogloff, J. R. P., & Douglas, K. S. (in press). Forensic psychological assessments: Defining and shaping a new specialty area of psychology. In J. R. Graham & J. A. Naglieri (Eds.), *Comprehensive handbook of psychology (Volume 10): Assessment Psychology.* New York: Wiley.

Otto, R. K. (2000). Assessing and managing violence risk in outpatient settings. *Journal of Clinical Psychology, 56,* 1239–1262.

Otto, R. K., & Collins, R. (1995). Use of the MMPI-2 in child custody evaluations. In J. Graham, Y. Ben-Porath, & M. Zaragoza (Eds.), *Forensic applications of the MMPI-2* (pp. 222–252). Thousand Oaks, CA: Sage.

Otto, R. K., Edens, J. F., & Barcus, E. (2000). The use of psychological testing in child custody evaluations. *Family and Conciliation Courts Review, 38,* 312–340.

Otto, R. K., & Heilbrun, K. (2002). The practice of forensic psychology: A look toward the future in light of the past. *American Psychologist, 57,* 5–18.

Packer, I., & Borum, R. (in press). Forensic training and practice. In A. Goldstein (Ed.), *Comprehensive handbook of psychology* (Volume 11): Forensic psychology. New York: Wiley & Sons.

Poythress, N., Nicholson, R., Otto, R. K., Edens, J. F., Bonnie, R., Monahan, J., & Hoge, S. K. (1999). *Manual for the MacArthur Competence Assessment Tool: Criminal adjudication.* Odessa, FL: Psychological Assessment Resources.

Quinsey, V. L., Harris, G. T., Rice, G. T., & Cormier, C. A. (1998). *Violent offenders: Appraising and managing risk.* Washington, DC: American Psychological Association.

Räsänen, P., Tiihonen, J., Isohanni, M., Rantakallio, P., Lehtonen, J., & Moring, J. (1998). Schizophrenia, alcohol abuse, and violent behavior: A 26-year followup study of an unselected birth cohort. *Schizophrenia Bulletin, 24,* 437–441.

Rice, M. E., & Harris, G. T. (1995). Violent recidivism: Assessing predictive validity. *Journal of Consulting and Clinical Psychology, 63,* 737–748.

Rogers, R. (1997). (Ed.). *Assessing malingering and deception* (2nd ed.). New York: Guilford.

Rogers, R., Bagby, R. M., & Dickens, S. E. (1992). *Structured Interview of Reported Symptoms (SIRS) and professional manual.* Odessa, FL: Psychological Assessment Resources.

Rogers, R., Dion, K., & Lynett, E. (1992). Diagnostic validity of antisocial personality disorder: A prototypical analysis. *Law and Human Behavior, 16,* 677–689.

Rogers, R., Duncan, J., Lynett, E., & Sewell, K. (1994). Prototypical analysis of antisocial personality disorder: DSM-IV and beyond. *Law and Human Behavior, 18,* 471–484.

Salekin, R., Rogers, R., & Machin, D. (2001). Psychopathy in youth: Pursuing diagnostic clarity. *Journal of Youth and Adolescence, 30,* 173–195.

Shah, S. A. (1978). Dangerousness and mental illness: Some conceptual, prediction, and policy dilemmas. In C. Frederick (Ed.), *Dangerous behavior: A problem in law and mental health* (pp. 153–191). Washington, DC: Government Printing Office.

Slobogin, C. (1989). The 'ultimate issue' issue. *Behavioral Sciences and the Law, 7,* 258–266.

Steadman, H. J., & Cocozza, J. (1974). *Careers of the criminally insane.* Lexington, MA: Lexington Books.

Steadman, H. J., & Halfon, A. (1971). The Baxstrom patients: Backgrounds and outcomes. *Seminars in Psychiatry, 3,* 376–386.

Steadman, H. J., & Keveles, G. (1972). The community adjustment and criminal activity of the Baxstrom patients: 1966–1970. *American Journal of Psychiatry, 129,* 80–86.

Steadman, H. J., Mulvey, E., Monahan, J., Robbins, P. C., Appelbaum, P. S., Grisso, T., Roth, L. H., & Silver, E. (1998). Violence by people discharged from acute psychiatric inpatient facilities and by others in the same neighborhoods. *Archives of General Psychiatry, 55,* 393–401.

Steadman, H. J., Silver, E., Monahan, J., Appelbaum, P. S., Robbins, P. C., Mulvey, E. P., Grisso, T., Roth, L. H., & Banks, S. (2000). A classification tree approach to the development of actuarial violence risk assessment tools. *Law and Human Behavior, 24,* 83–100.

Stoff, D., Brieling, J., & Maser, J. (Eds.). (1997). *Handbook of antisocial behavior.* New York: Wiley.

Swanson, J. W. (1994). Mental disorder, substance abuse, and community violence: An epidemiological approach. In J. Monahan & H. J. Steadman (Eds.), *Violence and mental disorder: Developments in risk assessment* (pp. 101–136). Chicago: University of Chicago Press.

Swanson, J., Borum, R., Swartz, M., & Monahan, J. (1996). Psychotic symptoms and disorders and the risk of violent behavior in the community. *Criminal Behaviour and Mental Health, 6,* 317–338.

Thornberry, T., & Jacoby, J. (1979). *The criminally insane: A community follow-up of mentally ill offenders.* Chicago: University of Chicago Press.

Travis, T. (1908). *The young malefactor: A study in juvenile delinquency.* New York: Crowell.

Webster, C. D., Douglas, K. S., Belfrage, H., & Link, B. (2000). Capturing change: An approach to managing violence and improving mental health. In S. Hodgins & R. Müller-Isberner (Eds.), *Violence among the mentally ill: Effective treatment and management strategies* (pp. 119–144). Dordrecht, Netherlands: Kluwer/Academic.

Webster, C. D., Douglas, K. S., Eaves, D., & Hart, S. D. (1997). *HCR-20: Assessing Risk for Violence (Version 2).* Burnaby, British Columbia, Canada: Mental Health, Law, and Policy Institute, Simon Fraser University.

Wrightsman, L. S. (2001). *Forensic psychology.* Belmont, CA: Wadsworth.

CHAPTER 9

Psychotherapy Outcome Research

EVELYN S. BEHAR AND THOMAS D. BORKOVEC

Between-group outcome research is a scientific approach to evaluating the effectiveness of psychotherapy and the mechanisms of change associated with those treatments for psychological disorders. This area of research is replete with important methodological issues that need to be considered in order for investigators to draw the strongest, most specific cause-and-effect conclusions about the active components of treatments, human behavior, and the effectiveness of therapeutic interventions.

In this chapter, we present the various methodological considerations associated with these experiments. The chapter begins with a discussion of independent variable considerations, including a description of the different experimental designs from which investigators may choose in designing a therapy outcome study, as well as the methodological, client-participant, and therapist concerns that must be taken into account in the design stage. Then we discuss the measurement of change, starting with the considerations surrounding dependent variables and ending with methods of analyzing data and assessing clinically significant change. Finally, after a presentation on small-N experimental designs, we discuss the importance of scientific research in naturalistic settings.

Preparation of this manuscript was supported in part by National Institute of Mental Health Research Grant RO1 MH58593 to the second author.

INDEPENDENT VARIABLE CONSIDERATIONS: BETWEEN-GROUP EXPERIMENTAL DESIGNS

The primary goal of any experimental design is to hold constant all factors among experimental conditions except the single factor under investigation. Such a design allows researchers to draw cause-and-effect conclusions about that factor, and the strength of those conclusions is a direct function of the extent to which variables other than the manipulated variable were equivalent across conditions. In the strong inference approach to scientific research (Platt, 1964), one constructs rival hypotheses about the cause-and-effect relationship observed between variables, accordingly conducts methodologically rigorous experiments designed to rule out one or more of those rival hypotheses, and subsequently conducts experiments aimed at ruling out further rival hypotheses about whatever remained unrejected by the previous experiment. The process is recycled repeatedly, leading to increasingly specific cause-and-effect conclusions.

The beauty of such an approach to scientific investigation lies in its unique ability to discard rejected hypotheses in pursuit of highly specific pieces of knowledge about a single causal relationship. As is the case for any class of scientific investigation, the primary goal of psychotherapy outcome research is to establish such cause-and-effect relationships, and thus the strong inference approach is the most powerful way to pursue this ultimate goal. Through such an approach, investigators are well equipped to identify the mechanisms through which a psychotherapeutic procedure produces change. With the identification of these mechanisms, we are able to acquire specific knowledge about human behavior and simultaneously enable the application of this knowledge in developing increasingly effective psychotherapeutic interventions.

In the various psychotherapy outcome research designs that we describe in this chapter, participants are randomly assigned to different treatment conditions in which variables are held constant (i.e., are equivalent) to varying degrees. Each of these designs allows investigators to draw causal conclusions, but the specificity of those causal conclusions varies with the type of design employed. Factors that are equivalent between conditions cannot explain ways in which the conditions differ in outcome. Differences in outcome can only be causatively explained by the ways in which the conditions differed. Thus, the fewer the dissimilarities and the greater the similarities between comparison conditions, the more specific we can be in identifying the cause of observed differences in their outcome.

This section describes each of these research designs in the order of the scientific rigor and specificity of causal conclusions associated with them. Whereas the no-treatment

and common factors comparison designs allow investigators to draw the weakest, most general cause-and-effect conclusions due to remaining potential differences between compared conditions, the dismantling, additive, catalytic, and parametric designs are best suited to the application of the strong inference approach to scientific investigation because of the close similarities between compared conditions. These designs enable investigators to establish specific cause-and-effect conclusions and thus acquire knowledge about human behavior and the mechanisms of change.

No-Treatment Comparison Design

The no-treatment comparison design compares the degree of change caused by a particular intervention to the change that would occur if no intervention were provided. This approach is often used for new therapeutic techniques that have not yet been tested in a controlled fashion but that clinical experience and related basic scientific research suggest will probably be useful. The design employs a condition in which participants are assessed at pretherapy and posttherapy moments, but they do not receive any form of intervention. Because participants in the no-treatment condition are being denied a treatment that might prove to be helpful for their clinical problem, investigators ordinarily have an ethical obligation to institute a waiting-list (no-treatment) control group in place of a pure no-treatment control group. Participants assigned to this condition are told that they will be given therapy after the waiting period.

As in any experimental investigation, a control group is employed in a research design in order to control for the many variables other than the variable under investigation that might cause change in the participants. In a waiting-list no-treatment design, the waiting-list group is used to control for (i.e., hold constant or equivalent) all potential causes of change other than the reception of therapy. Such potential causes include the effects of (a) history (any event or events other than the independent variable that occur outside of the experiment that may account for the results); (b) maturation (processes within participants that change over time, such as aging); (c) repeated testing (the possibility that being tested once may influence performance on future testing); (d) instrumentation (changes in the instruments or procedures used to measure participants on the dependent variables); (e) statistical regression (the tendency for extreme scores to revert toward the mean when participants are tested again); (f) selection bias (differences in conditions that occur as a result of having different client characteristics due to nonrandomly assigned groups); (g) differential attrition (different rates of dropout between groups); and (h) interactions of selection bias with the other factors (for a more detailed discussion of these variables, see Campbell & Stanley, 1963). Because participants are randomly assigned to treatment and no-treatment conditions, we can rule out these potential causes of change as the explanation of any difference found in the outcome comparison. With random assignment, such variables can be assumed to affect both conditions equally (i.e., the groups will be equivalent in the likely influence of such factors). The reader should, however, realize that there is no guarantee that random assignment will in fact yield equivalent groups; it merely (but importantly) maximizes the probability of equivalence. Note also that the larger the sample size, the greater the likelihood that equivalence will be realized. Hence, whatever gains the experimental group experiences *beyond* the changes observed in the no-treatment condition can be attributed to something about receiving treatment.

Such an experiment has some advantages. This simple design typically results in large between-group effect sizes, thus rendering a small sample size acceptable, and is relatively low in cost. Despite these clear advantages, however, some important ethical, methodological, and practical disadvantages exist. From an ethical standpoint, it is important to consider the ramifications of delaying treatment for a group of individuals, particularly if one is studying severely distressed populations or conditions with the potential for deterioration during the waiting period (e.g., chronically depressed, suicidal, or posttrauma individuals). Moreover, some form of monitoring clients in a waiting-list condition needs to be employed in order to detect any significant worsening of the problem. If deterioration does occur, the client must be removed from the protocol and immediately placed in an appropriate treatment for the disorder. In a similar consideration, there may be a selection problem in this design if the waiting-list control group consists only of clients who *agreed* to delay the reception of treatment. Such a feature would of course result in nonrandom assignment of clients to conditions. The consequential selection bias as well as a potential need to remove deteriorating clients from the waiting-list condition can yield a nonequivalent control group (e.g., symptomatology may be less severe than that displayed by the experimental group at the pretreatment assessment). This presents a serious methodological flaw and a highly plausible alternative hypothesis to explain any results found in the investigation. Additionally, because no-treatment participants must be treated at the conclusion of the study, the employment of such a group does not allow long-term follow-up assessments. It thus becomes impossible to examine the differential effects of treatment over an extended posttherapy period.

Finally, an important practical disadvantage of such a design is that it yields very little knowledge relevant to either empirical or applied goals. Investigators can draw a cause-and-effect conclusion from such a design, but that conclusion is merely that *something* about the provision of therapy caused a change in functioning above and beyond the change caused by such factors as the mere passage of time. What that something is, however, remains a mystery and cannot be determined. The no-treatment comparison group does not control for some other potentially powerful ingredients inherently present in clinical interventions, such as client expectancy to improve, hope and faith, demand characteristics to report improvement at the end of therapy, and the therapeutic relationship that develops between clinician and client. There is also very little applied knowledge to be gained from such a design. It is quite unlikely that an intervention would actually be worse than or equivalent to not being in treatment at all, particularly in light of variables such as the therapeutic relationship, which has been shown to be an important predictor of psychotherapy outcome (Alexander & Luborsky, 1986; Suh, Strupp, & O'Malley, 1986).

In summary, a waiting-list, no-treatment design is a simple, low-cost experimental design that is often used when examining new treatment techniques that have not yet been put to empirical test. However, it is useful for researchers employing this design to recognize its important scientific limitations, including the potential for selection biases, the inability to assess long-term results, and the limited amount of attainable empirical and applied knowledge. (Due to these limitations, we strongly suggest a discontinuation of this type of design and instead recommend the creation of other comparison conditions that incorporate a greater number of potential causative factors in common with the treatment condition under investigation.)

It should be noted at this point that all of the comparison conditions described in the following sections do control for the variables ordinarily held constant by the no-treatment condition (i.e., history, maturation, etc.). They also control for other potentially causative factors inherent to a therapy, and the degree to which those factors are held constant is directly related to the strength of causal conclusions investigators may draw. Throughout this discussion, however, it is important to keep in mind the potential presence of unmeasured variables that may differ between groups—differences that would limit the strength of causal conclusions (for an in-depth discussion of these issues, the reader is referred to this chapter's section entitled "Random Assignment Within Waves").

Common (Nonspecific) Factors or Placebo Comparison Design

Whereas the no-treatment design allows researchers to reject the hypothesis that variables associated with history, maturation, and so on are responsible for any greater change observed in the experimental condition, the strong inference approach dictates the need for ruling out further, more specific rival explanations not addressed by the no-treatment comparison before meaningful theoretical or applied conclusions are possible.

Frank (1971) identified the major elements of psychotherapy shared by all approaches, regardless of theoretical orientation: (a) the therapeutic relationship; (b) facilitation of emotional arousal; (c) a therapist who provides a conceptualization of the presenting problem, as well as a believable rationale for treatment; (d) techniques that are implemented to increase the client's believability in the therapist or therapy; and (e) provision of success experiences. The common factors design provides a control condition in which participants receive only those elements of therapy that are considered to be common in (nonspecific to) nearly all forms of psychotherapy and that are not included in the theoretical foundation of the experimental therapy. This condition was originally termed a *placebo* condition, because its use was thought to be analogous to pharmacological treatment trials in which an inert substance was given to control patients. Parloff (1986), however, has argued that the use of placebo conditions in medical research is not analogous to their use in psychotherapy research, because in psychotherapy research, the so-called inert factors interact with the theory-specific factors in such a way that they are not truly inert. For example, a strong therapeutic relationship, perhaps in the form of trust, may well be necessary for the effective deployment of active intervention methods. Without a strong relationship, a client might not be willing to engage in therapeutic tasks both within and outside of the therapy session, thus rendering the otherwise efficacious treatment less effective or ineffective. In such a circumstance, the therapeutic relationship and the specific therapy techniques may interact in such a way as to cause the observed therapeutic gains; thus, the extent to which an investigator can conclude that the techniques themselves caused the change is compromised (i.e., less specificity in ruling out rival hypotheses).

The term *common factors* refers to those elements that are presumably shared by most forms of psychotherapy. For example, attention to the presenting problem, contact with a caring and supportive individual, personal contact with a trained professional, expectancy effects, hope and faith, suggestion effects, and demand characteristic effects (i.e., reporting an alleviation of symptoms in the absence of actual change, based on client perception that improvement is expected and desired by the clinician) are present in all forms of psychotherapy. The term *common factors* is now often used to replace the older phrase, *nonspecific*

factors (cf. Castonguay, 1993 for the arguments against the use of the latter phrase).

The common factors design employs random assignment to experimental and control treatment conditions, wherein participants in the control group meet with the therapist regularly to receive treatment comprised solely of those common factors previously described. Ideally, the experimental therapy contains equivalent degrees of common factors plus specific and theoretically driven interventions, so that any observed differential effects can be attributed to those presumably active ingredients. This design, in contrast to the no-treatment design, allows more specific cause-and-effect conclusions to be drawn. That is, superiority of the experimental therapy over a common factors condition allows the conclusion that something specific in the former intervention caused that degree of change that exceeded the change observed in the latter condition.

Ethically, the common factors design is more advantageous than the no-treatment (waiting-list) design in that clients are at least being provided with a therapeutic relationship, which contains features known to contribute to the amelioration of psychological problems. Clients are also less likely to decline participation in such a condition; thus potential selection bias is minimized. However, important ethical as well as methodological disadvantages can be present in this design. One important ethical consideration is that in one condition of the experiment, researchers are knowingly providing clients with a treatment that they strongly suspect from a theoretical viewpoint may not be as efficacious as the experimental therapy. Potential methodological limitations also exist, beginning with important threats to internal validity. Therapists, for certain, and possibly even clients, may not be blind to condition (Lettieri, 1992), potentially leading to differing levels of demand characteristics and expectancy effects across groups. As Kazdin (1992) points out, developing a common factors condition that appears equally credible to both the therapist and the client can pose a great challenge. Important threats to external validity can also be present. Parloff (1986) argues that common factors conditions do not necessarily resemble actual therapy in applied settings. Thus, researchers may be comparing theoretically derived therapeutic interventions to a form of control treatment that is in actuality almost never practiced. Most important is that this design has a crucial scientific limitation. The data can lead scientists to conclude that the intervention caused a degree of change superior to that caused by elements common to most forms of treatment, but they are still not able to conclude exactly what the causative ingredients of that therapy were. The best this design can do is provide evidence that specific causal ingredients do indeed exist in the treatment and that subsequent research would profitably aim at identifying what those ingredients are, what mechanisms underlay their causal influence, and what this information tells us about the nature and mechanisms of the disorder being treated. (Given the important ethical and scientific limitations often present in the use of pure psychological placebo conditions, a work group from a National Institute of Mental Health conference has recently recommended a discontinuation of the placebo control condition in psychotherapy outcome research [cf. Borkovec & Onken, in press]).

Although many types of nonspecific control groups that have been used in past research have suffered from the previously described problems, one common factors condition is less severely handicapped by these difficulties. If one does decide to use a common factors control group, perhaps the best type of choice involves the provision of a nondirective or supportive listening condition. In such a condition, the therapist provides supportive and reflective statements in response to the content and affect contained in the client's verbal and nonverbal communications. This condition finds its origins in early Rogerian therapy and thus has theoretical foundations for its change mechanisms. Secondly, the therapeutic relationship factors contained in that theory and represented by supportive listening techniques are widely accepted by the field as critical background elements in any specific therapeutic approach; the condition thus represents a significant core of what is often meant by the phrase *common factors*. Given their ubiquitous nature throughout varying therapeutic approaches, these techniques are thus part of common clinical practice. Finally, in this sense, the use of this particular control condition approximates the employment of the component control (or dismantling) design, which will be described in a moment: An experimental therapy (specific plus common components) is being compared to one of its components (i.e., the set of common components). Specification of the exact active ingredients remains impossible, but at least the other problems previously mentioned are minimized.

In the Penn State research program investigating the treatment of generalized anxiety disorder (GAD), Borkovec and Costello (1993) compared the effectiveness of nondirective therapy (ND), applied relaxation (AR), and a full cognitive-behavioral package (CBT) which consisted of AR plus imagery rehearsal of coping skills and cognitive therapy. Although the investigation employed a dismantling design (described in the next section) by comparing AR to a more complete CBT package, the ND condition was instituted in an attempt to control for common factors. Results indicated that both the component treatment condition (AR) and the full CBT package were superior to ND at posttreatment, and the full CBT package caused greater clinically significant

maintenance of treatment gains over the 12-month follow-up period. Although the ND condition was associated with some degree of change in participants at posttreatment, these improvements deteriorated over the follow-up period. From this design and its outcome, we can conclude that CBT and AR both contain active ingredients causative of change beyond the improvement caused by common factors at posttreatment, and that the addition of cognitive therapy to AR (i.e., the CBT condition) causes an increment in long-term change.

The remaining methodological approaches described in the following sections offer greater control for common factors and simultaneously allow investigators to hold constant several additional variables. By so doing, they are able to isolate exactly what the active ingredients of a therapy are. Scientifically, these designs are more elegant in that they allow investigators to draw more specific cause-and-effect conclusions.

Component Control (Dismantling) Comparison Design

If an investigator wishes to control for the common factors of therapy via a control group, he or she may as well demonstrate efficacy beyond those common factors and at the same time establish more specific cause-and-effect conclusions regarding the elements of a treatment package. The component control design (also called the dismantling design) is a scientifically rigorous method for identifying specific causative elements; it does so by providing some participants with all components of a treatment while providing only some components of the treatment to other participants.

The methodological, scientific, and ethical advantages of such a design are numerous. First, the conditions in a dismantling design control for factors such as history and maturation, repeated testing, and statistical regression just like any other control condition. Moreover, its conditions maximize the likelihood of having equivalent levels of common factors (e.g., credibility, expectancy, and therapeutic relationship) and minimize therapist bias effects. Because the procedures employed across conditions of this design are highly similar to each other, the likelihood that credibility and expectancy will be equivalent across conditions is high. This was empirically demonstrated to be the case for credibility several years ago (Borkovec & Nau, 1972). Furthermore, therapist bias should be minimized because therapists are delivering components of a treatment in which they are fully and equivalently trained while recognizing that the component or combination of components most likely to be effective is currently unknown. Most important for scientific purposes, such a design allows for very specific cause-and-effect conclusions to be drawn because it holds constant all other elements of the therapy except for the intervention's specific comparison component. Thus, investigators are well equipped to identify which ingredients (alone and in combination) are specifically causative of change. For example, if a treatment package consisting of components A and B is dismantled via this design, then the investigator can randomly assign participants to receive only component A, only component B, or both components A and B. If the A + B condition is superior to either element alone, one can conclude that (a) A + B is causative of change beyond common factor effects and history, maturation, and so on; and (b) A + B's combination of elements is additively or interactively causative of change beyond either element alone. If component A, on the other hand, is found to be equivalent to A + B, and component B is inferior to A and A + B, then the evidence indicates that (a) B is not causatively contributing to the effects of A + B, (b) A is the likely explanation of the causative effects of A + B, and (c) both A and A + B contain active, causative ingredients beyond the effects of common factors and of history, maturation, and so on, given their superiority over B, which contains those potential causative variables. In addition to identifying very specific causal relationships, the beauty of the dismantling design from a basic knowledge perspective is that its outcomes point future research in the direction of understanding the nature of the disorder under investigation and the nature of the mechanisms of change. If a particular component is causative, then that component contains a mechanism for further pursuit, and scientists can devise new investigations to explore rival theories about what that mechanism might be and how it generates its therapeutic impact. Notice also how it invites further research and theoretical understandings of the disorder itself: *What is the nature of this disorder and its maintaining conditions such that this particular component or combination of components specifically causes its amelioration?*

In an investigation of treatment for generalized anxiety disorder, Butler, Fennell, Robson, and Gelder (1991) compared the effectiveness of a waiting-list control group (WL); behavior therapy (BT) consisting of relaxation training, graded exposure to feared situations, and confidence-building strategies; and a full cognitive behavior therapy (CBT) package, which consisted of behavior therapy in addition to cognitive therapy techniques targeting anxious thoughts. Results indicated that at posttreatment, the WL condition was inferior to BT on 4 out of 16 main outcome measures and inferior to CBT on 13 out of 16 of those measures. In comparing the two active treatment conditions, CBT was superior to BT on 6 of the 16 main outcome measures at the end of treatment, whereas it was superior to BT on 9 out

of 16 measures at the 6-month follow-up. These findings indicate that in dismantling CBT for the treatment of GAD, behavior therapy was not as causative of change overall as was a more complete package incorporating cognitive therapy, and this was particularly evident at the 6-month follow-up assessment. Notice how this finding invites pursuit of what it is in CBT (e.g., challenging automatic thoughts or decatastrophizing feared outcomes) that causes greater change, and what it is about GAD such that these elements increment its amelioration. Such an implementation of the strong inference approach would allow us to eventually establish increasingly specific cause-and-effect conclusions regarding the treatment of GAD.

In addition to offering considerable basic knowledge about therapeutic change, the dismantling design also potentially yields significant applied implications. Clinicians can discard the elements of the original package found to be inactive or superfluous. Moreover, scientists can attempt to improve or add to the remaining active elements in future empirical investigations designed to identify further causes of change.

The dismantling approach is also advantageous from an ethical perspective. Such a design does not require clinical researchers to employ deception in their investigations because at the outset of the study (and as was the case when considering therapist biases), they do not yet know which elements of a complete therapy package will be identified as active or inactive. Each component is potentially effective, given that it was included in the package by its developer based on clinical experience or prior theoretical and empirical work. Hence, no participants receive an intervention believed to be inactive or for which evidence for lack of effectiveness already exists.

After investigators have identified the inactive ingredients of a treatment package and are left with the components that were found to be active, they may separate the remaining components into even more specific elements and repeat the procedure. Alternatively, they can generate rival hypotheses as to why specific components are active and design experiments to rule out one or more of these rival hypotheses (e.g., in the aforementioned study dismantling the effects of CBT for GAD, one could compare BT + challenging automatic thoughts, BT + decatastrophizing, and BT + challenging automatic thoughts + decatastrophizing). This application of the strong inference approach to psychotherapy research is of crucial importance in the quest to develop the best possible treatments for individuals with clinical problems. By recycling the experimental process in order to refine our treatment packages and to increase our basic knowledge about a disorder, we can determine increasingly specific cause-and-effect relationships that will eventually lead to therapeutic interventions that contain more causes of change.

The disadvantage of the dismantling design is that not all interventions (especially nonbehavioral or noncognitive therapies) are easily broken down into separate components (Basham, 1986). When this is the case, the next two scientifically rigorous experimental designs can be employed.

Additive (Constructive) Comparison Design

The goal of the additive design (also called the constructive design) is to create a new treatment package by adding two or more separate techniques together and then testing the combined effect of those techniques against the original separate techniques. This design is very similar to the dismantling design in its implementation, and it also has exactly the same methodological, scientific, and ethical strengths as the dismantling design; thus, these points are not to be repeated here. The additive design improves on the dismantling design in that it can be utilized with treatment packages in which separating the intervention into separate components is not a feasible option, yet the experimental quest for identifying additional causal change elements and thus for creating more effective therapies for application in clinical settings can continue.

Of special consideration is how researchers decide which techniques to add to the already existing ones in order to carry out this type of experimental approach. This is precisely the step in the research process in which basic knowledge about the disorder under investigation is very useful to the decision of what technique(s) to add to the treatment package. Developers of treatment protocol manuals would ideally have an intimate knowledge of the disorder under investigation. Familiarity with the theoretical and empirical literature in that area can be a key to deciding what elements should be added to the existing treatment.

The additive design is the design of choice for empirical investigations of new components that could potentially be added to previously existing treatment packages. It is also the design of choice for investigations of integrative psychotherapy, which has recently been receiving more attention in both research and applied settings. Psychologists can improve on existing treatment packages by adding techniques derived from other theoretical orientations in the hope of producing the most effective treatments possible. This is a very different, less problematic, and much more promising design approach to evaluating different forms of psychotherapy than the comparative design, which we describe and evaluate later in this chapter.

Based on the hypothesis that binge eating is negatively reinforced by the anxiety-reducing effects of purging behavior,

Agras, Schneider, Arnow, Raeburn, and Telch (1989) employed the additive design in an investigation of the potential additive effects of response prevention on CBT for bulimia nervosa. Participants were randomly assigned to one of four conditions: a waiting-list control group (WL); self-monitoring of caloric intake and purging behavior (SM, a condition which employed the use of nondirective techniques and thus controlled for the common factors of therapy as well as the act of monitoring one's own eating and purging behaviors); cognitive-behavioral therapy (CBT, which included self-monitoring of eating and purging behaviors in addition to the altering of dietary habits, exposure to avoided foods, and challenging of distorted cognitions regarding diet and body image); or CBT plus response prevention of vomiting (CBT + RP). The investigators concluded that after 4 months of treatment, each of the three treatment groups (i.e., SM, CBT, CBT + RP) but not the WL group had shown significant improvement in the frequency of purging. Furthermore, only the CBT group experienced significantly greater reduction in purging behavior as well as overall cessation of purging than did the WL group, while the SM and CBT + RP groups did not differ from the WL group at treatment termination on these two main outcome measures. At the 6-month follow-up assessment, only the CBT group had experienced significantly greater cessation of purging than did the WL group. From this study, we can conclude that (a) treatment gains were not due solely to the passage of time, because the WL group failed to show a significant reduction of symptoms at treatment termination and was significantly inferior to the other treatment conditions, and (b) RP did not offer therapeutic effects above and beyond the effects of CBT alone as had originally been expected. In fact, it may have had a limiting effect on the improvements that clients would have experienced had they received CBT alone. One important limitation in this study was that the CBT + RP condition allotted less time for cognitive behavioral therapy than did the CBT condition, given that part of the session was devoted to the RP component. Thus, the lessened effectiveness of CBT + RP may have been due to the lessened amount of CBT (for a discussion on the importance of allotting equal amounts of time in therapy for each condition, see this chapter's section titled "Session Parameters").

Another example of an additive design can be seen in our current investigation of the additive effects of an interpersonal and emotional processing component to cognitive-behavioral therapy for generalized anxiety disorder (GAD). Although our original dismantling study (Borkovec & Costello, 1993) showed that CBT was more effective in terms of clinically significant change for treating GAD in the long run than was one of its components in isolation (i.e., applied relaxation), only about 50% of the clients in that study who received CBT managed to achieved a "normal" state of functioning on a majority of main outcome measures (i.e., only about 50% receiving CBT achieved high end-state functioning). Extensive research on the nature of GAD led us to conclude that worry is likely characterized by (a) a cognitive avoidance of somatic and emotional experience, and (b) an etiology partially consisting of deficits in interpersonal relationships with early caregivers (for a review of this literature, see Borkovec, Alcaine, & Behar, in press). Such findings led to the decision to add an interpersonal and emotional processing (IEP) segment to the original CBT treatment package for GAD in an attempt to increase the rate of improvement. The current clinical trial is an additive design in which this CBT + IEP condition is being compared to CBT plus a supportive listening component (included to control for the amount of time spent in session). If we find that the combined CBT + IEP is superior to CBT without IEP, we can conclude that IEP is the cause of the incremented improvement. We could potentially pursue such an effect further in a subsequent dismantling of IEP. Clients could be randomly assigned to CBT plus interpersonal therapy, CBT plus emotional processing therapy, and CBT plus IEP. If, on the other hand, the two conditions in our current trial do not differ in outcome, we can conclude that targeting interpersonal problems and emotional processing is unnecessary in the treatment of GAD.

Catalytic Design

When dismantling or additive designs reveal that combined components are superior to any of its individual components, we remain uncertain whether this is because each component causes a degree of improvement by itself and the effects of each component are merely additive, or whether this is because of an interactive effect between the components. Researchers have the opportunity to explore this question through the use of catalytic designs. These designs involve the manipulation of the order of presentation of the components in the combined condition. This paves the way for an understanding of how one component may cause a facilitation effect on the mechanisms of the other component and thus produce a degree of change that is greater than merely the additive effects of each component. For example, in a design consisting of components A and B, the investigator can employ one condition in which component A precedes component B during each therapeutic hour, and another condition in which component A follows component B. An ideal rendition of this design would also include two additional control groups, each containing only one component during

the last half of the session hour with common factor treatment during the first half (thus holding constant total amount of treatment time among all conditions).

In a study designed to test the contributions of relaxation to systematic desensitization, Borkovec and Sides (1979) randomly assigned speech-phobic participants to receive one of four treatment conditions: hierarchy exposure followed by relaxation training (E + R); relaxation training followed by hierarchy exposure (R + E); hierarchy exposure only (E); or no treatment (NT). Results indicated that in contrast to the other three conditions, the R + E condition produced the greatest reductions in subjective fear, as well as greater vividness of imagery, greater autonomic responses to visualizations of scenes in the hierarchy, and greater declines in autonomic reactions to initial visualizations of scenes as well as declines across repetitions of the same scene. Thus, relaxation training had a catalytic effect on phobic image exposures. This effect was not merely due to the additive effects of exposure and learning relaxation techniques, because the condition in which relaxation training followed exposure was inferior to the R + E condition.

If a catalytic effect is observed in an investigation, a possible extension of the study could involve the comparison of two conditions: In one condition, the different components of the treatment are allowed to occur and interact with each other throughout the entire session; in the second condition (like the two studies previously described), separate segments or time periods are devoted to only one component within the session. Similar to the dismantling and additive designs, an important consideration in such a design is the need to ensure that an equal amount of treatment time is allotted to each component despite the fact that they are being alternately used throughout the entire session. Having the different components interact with each other throughout the session may offer greater external validity. Clinicians in applied settings may find it awkward to dedicate a half hour of therapy to behavioral interventions and then quickly shift gears and begin discussing interpersonal concerns. Additionally, having the two components in constant interaction may make the occurrence of a catalytic effect of one component on another more probable.

Suppose, for example, that in an investigation designed to examine the potential catalytic effect of interpersonal and emotional processing (IEP) on cognitive therapy (CT) in the treatment of generalized anxiety disorder, we find that a condition in which IEP precedes CT is superior to a condition in which it follows CT. We could further examine the effects of having these two components in constant interaction with each other. Thus, in one condition, therapists could sensitively deploy cognitive therapy, emotional deepening, or interpersonal interventions depending on their reading of clients' cognitive, affective, and behavioral states moment to moment in the session. In the other condition, the first half of each session would be dedicated to IEP, whereas the second half would be dedicated to administering CT. If the interactional condition caused a degree of change superior to that caused by the condition employing separated components, we could conclude that interpersonal interventions, emotional processing, and cognitive therapy interact with each other in such a way that their interaction causes an even greater degree of change than the catalytic effect of IEP on CT.

The catalytic design offers a very high degree of scientific control across conditions because, like the parametric design discussed in the next section, *the only thing that varies between two of its conditions is the order of presentation of the components of treatment,* and like the additive or dismantling design, single component conditions hold constant one of the two elements in the combined condition. This design thus allows for very specific cause-and-effect conclusions about catalytic effects.

Parametric Design

After an active ingredient of a treatment package has been identified, investigators can pursue further causative knowledge about its specific parameters. As Kazdin (1998) asks, "What [quantitative] changes can be made in the specific treatment to increase its effectiveness?" Knowing, for instance, that cognitive therapy is an active ingredient in a treatment package is certainly helpful and important for theoretical and applied purposes. When administering cognitive therapy, however, scientists and treatment providers might want to know, for example, what level of assertiveness (e.g., low, moderate, or high) in the process of challenging cognitions optimizes cognitive change. Other possible examples of parameters include depth of addressing interpersonal issues, depth of emotional processing, degree of therapist empathy, and length of exposure to feared stimuli, to name just a few. The parametric design addresses such questions by comparing conditions that are created by sampling at least three points along a theoretically important or procedurally present dimension of a particular element of therapy.

Borkovec, Robinson, Pruzinsky, and DePree (1983) randomly assigned high and low worriers to engage in a worry induction for either 0-, 15-, or 30-min intervals. Results indicated a curvilinear causal relationship: Participants who were instructed to worry for 15 min reported increases in negative cognitive intrusions, whereas those who were instructed to worry for 0- or 30-min periods experienced reductions in negative cognitive intrusions on a subsequent

attention-focusing task. Thus, worrying for 15 min produced an incubation of negative cognitive activity. Although this study was not conducted as part of a psychotherapy outcome investigation (indeed, few outcome investigations to date have employed a parametric design), results such as these are obtainable from outcome trials and would significantly add to our basic knowledge about the disorder or therapeutic parameter under investigation.

Like the previously discussed catalytic design, the parametric design achieves a great amount of experimental control across conditions because *the only thing that varies between the conditions is the dimensional level of a single technique.* The content of the technique is identical across conditions; it is simply the quantified level of the technique that varies. Thus, although investigators must conduct a cost-benefit analysis before carrying out this design (given that the nature of the design is such that small effect sizes are likely, thus requiring a larger sample and hence a greater economic expense), this experimental approach allows for highly specific cause-and-effect conclusions to be drawn because so much is held constant across conditions. Moreover, such a design can elucidate laws of behavior that may not be linear in nature, as long as its conditions sample more than two levels of the parameter of interest.

Comparative Design

The comparative design contrasts the effectiveness of two or more interventions that represent different theoretical and historical traditions. Common examples include the comparison of the effects of psychotherapy to psychopharmacological interventions, of one type of psychotherapy to another (e.g., interpersonal psychotherapy and cognitive behavioral therapy), and of a newly developed treatment package to *treatment as usual* (TAU; an approach in which investigators compare the effects of a protocol treatment to the effects of the non–empirically validated methods traditionally used in the practicing community to treat the disorder under investigation).

Society and the mental health profession understandably want to know the answers to the question *Which therapy is best for a particular disorder?* Unfortunately, despite its appearances, we do not believe this question can be answered directly by the comparative design. The comparative trial does not allow specific cause-and-effect conclusions to be drawn, it lacks internal validity, and its outcomes (even if internally valid) would have little useful applied significance. In the following discussion we detail our reasons for these conclusions.

As has been evident throughout our discussion of the different experimental approaches to evaluating the efficacy of treatment packages, the goal of experimental therapy investigations is to hold constant all variables except the manipulated variable, allowing investigators to rule out all rival explanations of differential outcome between conditions and leaving the one manipulated feature as the unambiguous explanation for the cause of that outcome difference. Such causal conclusions can significantly enhance our knowledge about the pathology and about the investigated intervention. Unfortunately, in the case of a comparative design, the two (or more) contrasted treatments are so fundamentally different in terms of their theoretical foundations, historical traditions, and most importantly, their (often myriad) specific techniques, that the scientific ideal of holding all variables constant except one is not even nearly approximated. For example, consider for a moment how many techniques are used in psychodynamic therapy and in cognitive behavioral therapy. If the two conditions are compared and found to differ in outcome, one cannot determine what among those many differences caused the difference in outcome. Although a drug condition may appear to be more simple and straightforward when involved in a comparative trial in its contrast to a psychotherapy condition, there still remain several ways in which the two conditions differ (e.g., who administers the drug, with what types of interpersonal interaction, for how many minutes per session and how many sessions, in what treatment or medical context). Thus, implementation of such a design yields almost no scientific knowledge (i.e., specific cause-and-effect information) because so many rival hypotheses exist; any difference in outcome may be due to any one or a combination of the ways in which the compared conditions differ, including ways that have nothing to do with the specific elements of the interventions.

Even more fundamental problems having to do with the internal validity of comparative designs make their results wholly uninterpretable. One major threat to internal validity is potentially differential quality of treatment across conditions. If one therapy is administered poorly and the other therapy expertly, obviously this is an unfair comparison. Even if researchers employ separate "expert" therapists from each type of therapy, as is often done in comparative trials in an effort to maximize quality, there is no way to know whether the expertise of each set of therapists is equivalent. This is because valid measurements of expertise and quality of treatment are not yet available for any single therapy, much less for two different therapies that might be entered into a comparative trial. Furthermore, even if researchers could ensure by valid measurement equivalence of expertise and quality of the treatments offered by expert therapists, the grave threat of a therapist-by–condition confound would

remain. One would not know whether outcome differences were due to the type of therapy, the type of therapists, or the interaction of these two factors. (For a more detailed discussion on the need to unconfound therapists and therapy conditions, see the section on therapist concerns below). Comparison of a drug to a psychotherapy method might appear to have fewer such problems than when differing types of psychotherapy are compared, given that at least the quality of the medication (by its proscribed ingredients) is assured. However, one still does not know about the quality of the psychotherapy comparison condition. Moreover, as previously mentioned, the attending physicians providing the medication will not likely be the same therapists administering the psychotherapy with the same common factors in the same type of setting for the same amount of time. Consequently, amount of contact time and the personal characteristics of the physicians and the qualities with which they provide common factors will be different from those of the psychotherapists and thus represent significant potential confounds of any outcome differences observed.

The National Institute of Mental Health Treatment of Depression Collaborative Research Program (Elkin et al., 1989) employed a comparative design in an attempt to evaluate the relative effectiveness of cognitive-behavioral therapy (CBT); interpersonal therapy (IPT); a tricyclic antidepressant (imipramine hydrochloride) plus what they called a clinical management component in which patients were provided with a minimal supportive therapy in order to control for common factors (IMI-CM, regarded as the reference condition based on its status as a currently accepted treatment for depression); and a pill placebo condition that likewise included the clinical management component (PLA-CM). Overall results indicated no significant differences between the two psychotherapies and the reference condition (IMI-CM). Additionally, compared to the PLA-CM condition, there was no strong evidence of the specific effectiveness of either IPT or CBT. For the more severely depressed subsample, IMI-CM led to the greatest improvement, and PLA-CM produced the poorest outcome. IPT and CBT fell in between these two conditions, with only IPT leading to significantly more improvement than PLA-CM. In this investigation, the comparison of the two pharmacotherapy conditions in isolation (IMI-CM versus PLA-CM) constitutes an additive design in which the additive effects of imipramine hydrochloride and clinical management were validly tested. From this aspect of the design, we can conclude that for more severely depressed patients, the medication did provide effectiveness above and beyond the effects of clinical management plus pill placebo. However, IPT and CBT are so fundamentally different from each other and from a pharmacological intervention (e.g., theoretical foundations [interpersonal versus cognitive-behavioral versus biological], techniques [identification and modification of interpersonal problems versus identification and modification of intrapersonal thought and behavioral processes versus drug], and sets of therapists administering each condition) that the design yields no valid scientific knowledge, much less any knowledge about mechanisms of change. Thus, although this study does allow for causal conclusions to be drawn about the effectiveness of a particular pharmacological treatment for depression in comparison to a pill placebo, it is not a methodologically valid way to test the relative effectiveness of CBT, IPT, and tricyclic antidepressants.

One ethical advantage to a comparative design is that all participants are placed in a treatment condition—each held by researchers on the basis of past efficacy results, by practicing clinicians on the basis of theory and clinical experience, or both—to be an effective therapy for the disorder. However, this advantage in and of itself is insufficient to warrant the use of this design, given its lack of internal validity. Without internal validity, no scientifically meaningful results can emerge. Moreover, in terms of applied significance, even if the design *could* be carried out with internal validity, the implications of its results would be short-lived. This is because outcome investigations often require 3–5 years just to obtain pre-post assessments on a large number of clients (and this time period is extended even further for obtaining follow-up data). During this time, the techniques would be changing and improving on the basis of growing clinical experience and empirical data. Thus, the design's answer to the question *Which therapy is better?* is at least several years old and of less relevance to existing versions of the therapies. The other, more scientifically rigorous designs described earlier do not suffer from this drawback because they are establishing cause-and-effect relationships and contributing to knowledge about the disorder and the mechanisms of change. Such cause-and-effect links and basic knowledge about the disorder under investigation are timeless, unaffected by the passage of time or by any further developments and improvement of the specific techniques, although further elaborations of their meaning will occur as further research relevant to the underlying principles of behavior proceeds.

It may eventually be the case that some of the criticisms of comparative designs will someday be addressed. For example, the trend in graduate clinical programs is toward greater training in several diverse therapeutic orientations and their integrative use in therapy. Indeed, there is even movement within the American Psychological Association toward the training

of clinical psychologists to administer psychoactive medications. One future consequence of these trends is the potential availability of protocol therapists who have been trained in a large number of therapeutic approaches in which the quality of their services is more likely to be equivalent across these approaches. In such a case, therapists can then be crossed with the treatment factor, thus eliminating the otherwise disastrous therapist confound. The reader is reminded, however, that some of the other problems with the comparative design will remain. Consider the example of a contrast of a pharmacological treatment and a psychotherapy. We will further assume certain crucial methodological features that have never been employed in past such comparisons—for example, practitioners equally trained in both interventions treat an equal number of clients in each condition, amount of in-session contact time and the number of sessions are held constant, and client credibility and expectancy for improvement are found to be equivalent. Assume that the drug yields not only a significantly superior outcome but also a much greater degree of clinically significant change. Although we have eliminated several possible confounds by our methodological features, we still have two important problems remaining. Although such an outcome would suggest that intervening at the biological level has value (we can rule out common factors from explanation of its greater change and conclude that it does contain an active ingredient attributable to pharmacological effects), we have learned nothing about its specific ingredients, nor have we learned about the nature of its change mechanisms, nor about the nature of the pathology other than the vague conclusion that biology plays a role in the disorder. The two conditions simply differ from each other in far too many ways to allow for specificity in conclusions. Second, as described earlier, by the time the investigation is completed with long-term follow-up, its answer to the question of which treatment is better for the disorder is several years old.

Ultimately, in order to answer the urgent questions of what therapies are effective and which therapies are best for a particular psychological problem, we would wisely pursue basic knowledge about a specific therapy using the more valid and powerful designs described earlier and building increasingly effective (causal) therapies based upon that knowledge. Going deeply into a specific therapy (whether psychological or pharmacological), learning everything we can about its techniques' specific cause-and-effect mechanisms, and using such knowledge to increase our understanding about the nature of the pathology and how best to treat it (i.e., how to include increasing numbers of elements causative of change) will ultimately provide answers to society's questions and better therapies for people suffering from psychological problems. Using constructive, dismantling, and parametric designs can accomplish this without pitting two therapies against each other in a comparative design that cannot provide any useful basic or applied knowledge.

Each of the designs described above allows investigators to draw causal conclusions of varying specificity. The no-treatment and common factors conditions yield relatively weak, general causal conclusions, whereas the dismantling, additive, catalytic, and parametric designs, due to the similarity between their conditions, yield highly specific causal conclusions that are conducive to constructing further rival hypotheses to be tested in future experiments. Within each of these designs, several methodological considerations need to be taken into account. The next section describes these considerations in detail.

INDEPENDENT VARIABLE CONSIDERATIONS: METHODOLOGICAL CONCERNS

Determining Sample Size

When determining the number of participants to include in a treatment outcome study, the investigator should conduct power analyses. For a detailed discussion of the use of power analyses in determining sample size, the reader is referred to the chapter in this volume by Behrens and Yu. Additionally, because sample sizes typically decrease due to client dropout (attrition), it may be beneficial for investigators to recruit more clients than are needed so that posttherapy and follow-up data will possess sufficient power to detect condition differences, if indeed they exist.

Random Assignment Within Waves

As mentioned earlier, it is vitally important to the methodology of an efficacy study that the investigator randomly assign participants to conditions. In practice, this is typically done within consecutive temporal waves of clients as they are enrolled in the experiment. Because of the large number of clients required for an outcome study and the limited resources of the therapy project, it is unlikely that all participants in an experiment can begin receiving treatment at the same time. So in random assignment within waves, in a three-condition study, the first three entered clients are randomly assigned to each of the three conditions, the next three clients to each condition, and so forth. This block random assignment also controls for several factors such as seasonal variation, cohort effects, changes in the level of experience or expertise of protocol therapists, changes in

the experience of assessors, and changes in personnel. As always, controlling for any other factor that might affect outcome reduces rival explanations of any relationships observed.

Session Parameters

It is also essential to avoid the potential confound of differential amount of therapy time between conditions. Clearly, if one condition of the experiment provides 2 hours of therapy per week, whereas a comparison condition provides only 1 hour, any difference in outcome between the two conditions may very well be due to the amount of therapist contact, common factors, or exposure to a treatment rather than to the difference in their content and techniques. Thus, an important methodological concern is to hold the number of sessions and the number of minutes per session constant across conditions of the experiment.

This concern raises a particularly salient consideration when conducting a dismantling or additive design investigation. In these two designs, experimenters are testing the effects of elements A and B against the effect of combined elements A and B. Clearly, the combined A and B condition will require a greater amount of time in therapy than will either A or B alone. Because it is important to equate the amount of time devoted to a single component in both of its single component conditions as well as in the total package, experimenters are faced with the question of what to do with the remaining time in the single-component conditions. The most common approach is to fill that time with common factors treatment (e.g., supportive listening). By instituting this "filler," experimenters ensure that each condition receives equal amounts of exposure to each theoretically active ingredient *and* equal amounts of time in each session.

Therapy Manuals

Detailed procedures to be followed in each condition of the experiment should be provided for therapists in the form of a protocol manual. Manuals developed for behavioral and cognitive therapy studies have commonly contained session-by-session outlines of goals to be accomplished and specific techniques to be employed during each meeting with the client participant. Such a manual typically includes the rationale initially given to participants for the type of therapy being administered, a description of the methods to be used for each session, and an explanation of the theory underlying any given technique so that the therapist can exercise flexibility in therapeutic methods depending on the particular client and situation while still being true to protocol. With this combination of contents, the therapy provided is structured and uniform enough to maintain a standardized implementation of the therapy constant across participants and therapists in any given condition, while at the same time being flexible enough to allow for the sundry challenges and individualized circumstances that each participant brings to the therapy room.

Therapies that are not cognitive-behavioral in nature (e.g., interpersonal, psychodynamic, experiential) frequently need to employ manuals that do not outline what is to be done session-by-session, given that these therapies are driven more by theoretical principles than by specific techniques. Strupp and Anderson (1997), furthermore, assert that, given the importance of personality characteristics of the client and therapist as well as the ensuing therapeutic interaction and relationship that elicit change in clients, treatment manuals may be limited in their ability to precisely define the in-session variables that will lead to improvement on the part of patients. In such cases, the alternative type of treatment manual provides specific operational definitions of the theoretical principles guiding treatment, and it allows considerable flexibility for specific in-session interventions while remaining true to those underlying theoretical principles.

The use of detailed protocol manuals has important implications beyond the need to maintain standardized implementation of the independent variables. First, replication of findings by other investigators is facilitated by the use of a protocol manual that can be made available. Furthermore, therapists in applied settings who wish to provide empirically supported treatments for their clients would have protocols to follow to allow them to adhere to the treatment as it was implemented in the study that validated the therapy.

The inclusion of treatment manuals in therapy outcome research has had a major impact on the experimental evaluation of psychotherapy. Any experiment requires clear operational definitions of the independent variable. The use of protocol manuals provides the scientific and methodological rigor necessary to do this in the case of independent variables involving complex psychotherapy methods. Indeed, according to the American Psychological Association Task Force on Promotion and Dissemination of Psychological Procedures, the inclusion of protocol manuals is now a criterion for demonstrating empirical support for a therapy (1995; Chambless et al., 1996).

Integrity and Adherence Checks

After the treatment manual has been developed and therapists have been trained in its use, it is important to ensure that the therapists do not break protocol so that the independent variable is the only factor systematically varied across conditions. Adherence checks evaluate whether cross-contamination occurs between conditions or whether other therapy techniques are inadvertently employed. In performing adherence checks, typically 20–25% of the treatment session tape recordings are randomly selected from each condition. Staff trained in the protocols categorize each therapist's utterances against a checklist of allowed and not-allowed techniques. Checklist items for not-allowed methods include (a) those relating to techniques of the comparison conditions (e.g., if CBT is being compared to CBT plus an interpersonal therapy component, then statements specific to interpersonal therapy are not allowed into the CBT—only portions of therapy) and (b) any other techniques of other psychotherapies not specifically appropriate for the employed therapy condition. Investigators must establish a predetermined rule for how many major and minor breaks in protocol are necessary for exclusion of a client's data from the final analyses, as well as clear definitions of what constitutes a major or minor break of the protocol. The more stringent the criteria, the more likely the therapy conditions will reflect only those techniques defined by the independent variable manipulation.

Several investigations have alternatively employed the practice of condition identification as a means of performing adherence checks. In this approach, raters who are blind to condition listen to therapy audiotapes and then independently determine which condition was being employed on the tape. The percentage of reliably differentiated tapes is then reported. Because it is absolutely essential that the elements of one condition not appear in a contrasted condition, such an approach to ensuring integrity may be too liberal. It is fairly easy for a rater to correctly classify an audiotape if only one or two breaks in protocol are made within a session. If several breaks in protocol are allowed in any one condition (as may be the case in such an approach), the ideal of having the independent variable be the only aspect of treatment that varies between conditions is lost. Thus, we recommend that investigators employ the more conservative practice of categorizing each therapist utterance against a checklist of allowed and not-allowed techniques.

Expectancy and Credibility Checks

Research on drug efficacy in the medical field has yielded important findings concerning the power of client expectancy for improvement, faith, and hope. Such investigations have traditionally found that placebos (i.e., chemically inactive substances used in comparison to active drugs) often yield improvements in health despite their biologically inert natures. Given the psychological mechanisms undoubtedly involved in the pharmacological placebo effect, these factors are also powerfully involved in psychotherapy effects. Thus, all conditions involved in an experimental clinical trial need to be equivalent in the degree to which participants in each condition expect to improve and how credible they believe the rationale for the conditions is. If the conditions differ on these crucial variables, a confound potentially exists, and we cannot rule out differential expectancy or credibility as the sole explanation of any observed outcome differences between conditions.

In measuring how much participants expect to change and perceive the demand to change, investigators often administer expectancy and credibility scales. Because such ratings may increase or decrease over sessions as improvements occur or do not occur, these scales are best administered early in therapy—for example, after the first session when the rationale and description of the therapy's techniques have been provided to the client. Analysis indicating condition equivalence on these variables is critical to ruling out the role of these common factors in contributing to any observed differential outcome among conditions.

Dropout and Attrition

Psychotherapy outcome studies, like all longitudinal studies, are at risk for losing clients who choose to discontinue their participation during or after therapy. Some common reasons for discontinuation include dissatisfaction with the therapy or therapist, failure to experience signs of improvement, discomfort with the emotions elicited in treatment, and a lack of time to devote to sessions or out-of-session activities (e.g., homework).

According to Lettieri (1992), *dropout* refers to participants who discontinue treatment while treatment is still being administered, whereas *attrition* refers to the loss of participants during the follow-up period of assessment. Investigators should have predetermined criteria for what constitutes a dropout (i.e., how many missed sessions) and what constitutes attrition (i.e., how many missed follow-up assessments). Either occurrence potentially compromises the scientific integrity of the investigation. Unambiguous interpretations of between-group differences rest upon the statistically legitimate assumption that random assignment results in groups that are identical on the host of known and unknown client characteristics that might affect outcome, thus holding these variables constant across conditions. Consequently, large dropout or attrition rates undermine the likely validity of that assumption. Separately, differential rates regardless of overall rate particularly reduce confidence in group equivalence, given that these groups are de facto different. Although statistical comparisons between completers and noncompleters on

available pretherapy assessments and demonstration of nonsignificance between these two groups is often used to argue that overall rates or differential rates are less likely to cause this interpretive problem, investigators need to remember that such comparisons are only conducted on existing measures and do not address the many other ways not assessed that might influence outcome.

On the other hand, differential dropout rates also offer an important dependent variable, even though the internal validity of group comparisons is severely compromised. It is important to know whether one intervention will yield higher rates of dropout than will another therapy in applied settings. Investigators should also keep track of and report participants' reasons for dropout because such information might be useful later. For example, if a treatment package requires that participants complete very time-consuming and complex homework assignments between sessions, and dropout clients report this to be a reason for discontinuing participation, although effective for clients who complied with homework demands, such a treatment package may not be at all effective for clients who lacked the desire or time to comply with such demands. With such information, investigators can work on ways to develop interventions that address the problem, are effective, *and* have low rates of dropout. For example, designers of treatment protocols may take steps such as making homework assignments more manageable and realistic or devising ways to strengthen the therapeutic relationship so that clients are more willing to remain in treatment. Kazdin (1998) has suggested further strategies to prevent attrition, including providing reminders for appointments and instituting monetary incentives or compensation. Developing a strong alliance between the principal investigator and participants may also minimize attrition rates.

The methodological concerns outlined in this section are important considerations in designing therapy outcome studies. Their implementation maximizes the likelihood that conditions will be equivalent on numerous factors that would otherwise present rival hypotheses for why between-group differences emerged. In addition to these methodological considerations, several client-participant characteristics also need to be taken into account. The following section outlines these client-participant concerns.

INDEPENDENT VARIABLE CONSIDERATIONS: CLIENT-PARTICIPANT CONCERNS

Sources of Participants

Of special consideration in conducting psychotherapy outcome research are the sources from which clients are drawn. Some common sources of clients include referrals from other mental health agencies or private practitioners in the area, self-referrals, and responses to media advertisements. As with all other independent variable considerations, participant source would ideally be distributed evenly across the conditions of the experiment in order to avoid confounds and maximize the strength of cause-and-effect conclusions at the study's termination. Investigators should keep track of the sources from which clients are drawn so that these figures can be reported and tested for between-group equivalence and so that the generalizability of the findings can be assessed.

Client-Participant Characteristics

The means, standards deviations, ranges, and frequencies of particular client characteristics (especially any variables known to relate to outcome) should be reported, regardless of whether such characteristics are a part of the selection criteria (see next section). Variables such as age, gender, ethnicity, medication status, marital status, educational level, socioeconomic status, and sexual orientation then need to be analyzed for equivalence across conditions in order to rule out potential confounds. Reporting of such variables also aids in evaluating the external validity of the findings and is indeed a criterion for status as an empirically supported treatment (APA Task Force on Promotion and Dissemination of Psychological Procedures, 1995; Chambless et al., 1996).

Selection Criteria

Inclusion and exclusion criteria for admittance into a research study must be specified before selection of clients begins. Efficacy studies typically focus on a particular diagnostic group. However, investigators need to specify which comorbid conditions would or would not preclude admission to the study. As with other variables, relatively equivalent rates of specific comorbid disorders between conditions would optimize internal validity. Comorbidity selection criteria also affect external validity. The more strict the exclusion criteria, the less generalizable the results will be. This is of particular importance to external validity of research on disorders with high comorbidity rates. For example, if the diagnostic group under investigation involves individuals with major depressive disorder, excluding anxiety disorders would severely limit the generalizability of the findings, given that anxiety and depression tend to co-occur (Sanderson, DiNardo, Rapee, & Barlow, 1990). Recent emphasis at the National Institute of Mental Health on the growing importance of effectiveness (naturalistic setting) research (described later) and concerns about the external validity of carefully controlled efficacy studies involving homogeneous samples that are not characteristic of clients seen in typical practice settings has resulted in

recommendations by a recent NIMH work group that selection criteria in efficacy studies be relaxed (cf. Rush, 1998).

When deciding on the selection criteria to be used for a study, investigators face an important trade-off. The more homogeneous the sample due to restrictive selection criteria, the less error variance is likely to be present and thus the greater the likelihood of a strong signal-to-noise ratio for detecting between-condition differences. However, restrictive selection criteria reduces the generalizability of the conclusions.

Representativeness

Investigators should keep track of all referred clients and the reasons for which any were excluded. This practice aids in determining the characteristics of the *entire* sample of potential participants and thus allows for an assessment of generalizability of the final sample. Also important is that such a practice provides heuristic data on the number of individuals who have the target disorder or problem under investigation.

One particularly important limit to generalizability to keep in mind is that the final sample of participants consists of clients who were willing to participate in a research program. This may be indicative of a higher severity of the problem, higher motivation to change, or greater expectancy or credibility than would normally be found in the general population of individuals having the target disorder. There may also be several other client characteristics associated with this willingness that are unknown but potentially related to treatment responsiveness.

Although the previously discussed external validity concerns have important practical implications, it is imperative not to compromise the internal validity of a study in order to improve its external validity. Again, the primary goal of therapy outcome research is to establish specific cause-and-effect relationships by eliminating as many potential rival hypotheses as possible. Researchers certainly want their findings to have significant implications for applied settings, but the ideals of rigorous scientific experimentation cannot be sacrificed in order to achieve this goal. If a study has no or limited internal validity, the issue of external validity becomes moot, regardless of the setting in which the investigation occurred. We discuss this issue in more detail later in this chapter.

Severity and Duration of the Problem

A particularly important methodological concern is that the severity and duration of the problem under investigation be assessed, reported, and balanced across conditions. Severity and duration of the problem are two of the most likely and potent confounding variables if not equated across conditions because they are so likely to affect outcome in and of themselves.

Concurrent and Past Treatment

Acquisition and reporting of information regarding the presence of past or concurrent psychopharmacological or psychological treatment for each of the conditions under investigation allows for the evaluation of possible influences of such treatments on clients' outcomes. Because excluding clients who are currently undergoing pharmacological treatment may introduce a significant threat to the generalizability of findings (clients in naturalistic settings are often medicated), researchers may include such clients as long as this variable is balanced across conditions. However, holding the dosage constant (with the physician's approval) during the treatment period is essential so that any observed changes can be attributed to the independent variable and are not confounded by changes in dosage during the course of psychotherapy or the interaction of dosage change with the psychotherapy effects. It is also customary to allow concurrent pharmacological treatment only if the client has been medicated for 1 month or longer, so that drug effects have stabilized. Finally, daily monitoring and reporting of dosage and frequency can be used to verify unchanging medication levels during the trial.

Concurrent psychosocial treatment is typically an exclusionary criterion based on the probability that such treatment will interfere with the treatment package being administered. Indeed, this is analogous to common clinical practice in applied settings. Clinicians rarely agree to see a client in therapy when that client is in a separate psychotherapeutic relationship. This is due to the potential for conflict or incompatibility of the separate clinicians' advice or therapeutic process. One especially threatening possibility occurs when the concurrent psychosocial treatment addresses issues that the current investigation only addresses in one of its conditions. The result would be tantamount to a breach of protocol integrity. Because investigators cannot know how many of these breaches have occurred, it may be most prudent simply to exclude potential participants who are concurrently being seen in any other psychosocial treatment. However, if such participants are included in the investigation, it is crucial to report this inclusion and balance the presence of concurrent treatment across conditions. For any psychological or medical intervention variables included, the research report should include statistical analyses to assess main and interaction effects involving those variables on outcome measures.

Diagnosis

In psychotherapy studies on the effects of an intervention on a particular disorder, selection criteria for the central presenting problem (typically, the principal diagnosis) are specified at the outset of the study. Investigators need to indicate the system of diagnosis used and the method for obtaining diagnoses. Most therapy outcome studies conducted in the United States and many other countries employ *DSM-IV* criteria and utilize previously developed semistructured interviews (e.g., the Structured Clinical Interview for *DSM-IV* Axis I Disorders: SCID; First, Spitzer, Gibbon, & Williams, 1997; see also the Anxiety Disorders Interview Schedule for *DSM-IV:* ADIS-IV; Di Nardo, Brown, & Barlow, 1994) to arrive at the diagnoses. In order to lower the likelihood of false positive diagnoses, reliability checks and analyses are invaluable in reducing error variance and increasing the validity of conclusions. In order to perform reliability checks, ideally two independent interviews by different interviewers would be administered, and reports should indicate acceptable levels of training and qualifications of the interviewers. Some diagnoses have high interrater reliability, and thus dual interviews may be conducted on only a randomly selected sample of potential clients (commonly around 20%). Other diagnoses, however, have low interrater reliability and thus require dual interviews by separate diagnostic assessors on every potential client. In these cases, inclusion in the research study would be restricted to cases in which both assessors agree on the diagnosis or staff discussion and consensus takes place to resolve any disagreements. An alternative to having two independent interviews is to conduct only one interview and have a separate assessor listen to the audiotaped interviews in order to make a diagnosis. Problems with this approach, however, make this strategy undesirable. First, this practice is insensitive to the possibility that clients may change their answers from one interview to the next. Indeed, in our own research laboratory, we have often found that, upon hearing a question being asked a second time, clients report that being asked the question the first time caused them to think about it more carefully and thus arrive at a response different from the one they originally gave. Second, clients may respond differently to different interviewers. Thus, although dual interviews are more expensive and time consuming, they greatly reduce the possibility of false positive diagnoses and are particularly crucial for diagnostic categories known from past research to have poor interassessor reliability.

When performing diagnoses on potential participants, researchers should also assess the severity of the problem using a valid and reliable measurement. Furthermore, the duration of a problem should be assessed via interview, preferably by more than one interviewer, in order to establish reliability of the client's self-report. When possible, particularly in the case of psychotherapy outcome research using children as participants, corroborating evidence of severity and duration of the problem should be obtained via reports from other individuals who have had regular contact with the client.

The considerations outlined in this section are intended to maximize the probability that client-participant characteristics are equivalent across conditions and thus do not pose rival hypotheses for why differences between conditions were found. Attention to these considerations also helps to increase the external validity of findings so as to make them more generalizable to other settings. In addition to considering these important client-participant characteristics, investigators should similarly pay attention to specific therapist characteristics. These concerns are discussed in the following section.

INDEPENDENT VARIABLE CONSIDERATIONS: THERAPIST CONCERNS

Therapists' characteristics introduce variables worthy of attention in psychotherapy research. Their background, previous training, and prior experience both in general and with regard to the current diagnosis under consideration and the current treatment protocol should all be described. Treatment providers are typically individually supervised by the principal investigator of the research study in order to ensure strict adherence to the protocol and high-quality administration of the interventions.

It is crucial for the internal validity of the investigation that more than one therapist be employed to provide treatment and that these therapists are crossed as a factor with therapy conditions (i.e., each therapist treats an equal number of clients in each condition). Protocol clinicians bring their own (highly numerous) individual qualities and characteristics to the therapeutic process, thus introducing the possibility of main or interaction effects based on those variables. If only a single therapist is employed, limited generalizability exists for the findings, and internal validity would be compromised to the degree that this single set of therapist characteristics interacts with conditions to yield the observed between-condition differences. Employing multiple therapists crossed with conditions increases external validity and internal validity, allowing for the statistical isolation of condition effects collapsed over the therapist characteristics represented by the protocol clinicians. Investigators will also be able to statistically analyze for effects involving the therapist factor. If there are main or interaction effects, clues are provided for the future empirical

pursuit of what therapist characteristics were causatively involved, leading to additional knowledge about mechanisms of change.

Therapist bias in regard to preferences for one condition of the experiment over another also introduces an important potential confound in any intervention outcome study. Such a bias may influence outcome by leading to subtle and unintentional systematic differences in the way treatment or nonspecific processes occur across conditions. Thus, in addition to balancing therapists across experimental conditions, experimenters may want to obtain (early in therapy) therapist ratings of how credible they perceive each treatment condition to be and how much they expect their clients to improve in each condition. Such a practice provides a quantified means of assessing therapist bias, and equivalence of ratings across conditions would increase internal validity. On the other hand, if differential ratings are found, there is also a rare but powerful and exciting possibility that greater change occurs in the condition in which therapists have the lowest expectations. This outcome is quite likely when the therapists are newly trained in one method but well-experienced in comparison conditions. If the unfamiliar experimental condition yields superior gains despite therapist bias in favor of the other condition, then therapist bias can be ruled out as a potential confound (cf. Paul, 1966, for an example). As mentioned previously, differential quality of therapy due to therapist bias or differential experience is less of a danger in dismantling, additive, and parametric designs, due to the fact that clinicians are likely to be equally experienced in all of the components of the design and are cognizant of the fact that it is not yet known which elements or parameters of an intervention are crucial to its efficacy.

So far, we have outlined various independent variable considerations associated with selection of a design, general methodological concerns, as well as client-participant and therapist concerns. The following section outlines considerations associated with the selection and measurement of dependent variables.

DEPENDENT VARIABLE CONSIDERATIONS

Multiple Domain Assessment

When assessing the amount of change exhibited by clients undergoing therapy, it is important to use more than one domain of assessment as well as more than one method of assessment. Although relevance to the disorder and cost in terms of time, expense, or availability will no doubt affect how many measures can be obtained, domains of assessment would ideally include cognition, affect, behavior, and physiology. Ascertaining the level at which participants are functioning in each of these domains constitutes a more thorough, comprehensive approach than does any one level in isolation. By assessing multiple domains, the researcher will also be able to determine whether change is occurring in a broad range of areas or whether change is limited to a specifically defined realm. NIMH has also begun to encourage outcome researchers to investigate the effects of interventions beyond mere symptom reduction. Thus, investigators are asked to assess an intervention's impact on a client's broader functioning in the world, such as physical health and social role functioning.

It is also useful for investigators to rely on different methods of assessing change. Pre- and posttherapy questionnaires, daily diaries, assessor ratings from interviews and sessions, observational measures, third-person reports, and physiological assessments provide just a sample of the options available for a multimethod approach to assessing change. Investigators can assess for a convergence or divergence of findings both across the different domains of assessment and across the different methods. Discrepancies across the domains of assessment may provide important information regarding how best to improve the treatment package in future investigations. For example, if a particular intervention yields significant behavioral changes but fails to produce a change in cognitive or affective functioning, future modifications to the treatment protocol might include previously absent techniques or more potent techniques for targeting cognition (e.g., adding deeper cognitive therapy) and emotion (e.g., adding deeper emotional processing techniques).

In 1994, the American Psychological Association and Vanderbilt University hosted the Core Battery Conference in an effort to develop a standardized battery of measures intended for use by psychotherapy outcome researchers. As part of the conference, special attention was devoted to reaching a consensus on the domains of assessment investigators should measure when determining the efficacy of a therapeutic intervention (see Horowitz, Strupp, Lambert, & Elkin, 1997). These domains of assessment included (a) the severity of the individual's subjective distress; (b) the level of impairment evident in the individual's life functioning (e.g., in interpersonal relationships, self-care, and work); and (c) the frequency of occurrence of an individual's symptoms. An examination of the individual's self-evaluation and maladaptive interpersonal behavior was also recommended for investigators of therapies aimed at anxious and personality disordered populations.

Assessors

Treatment outcome studies often require the employment of several staff members for conducting diagnostic and other assessment sessions as well as for collecting and managing the vast amount of data typically associated with these studies. These individuals also deserve special attention in planning the methodology of an experiment. Assessors and data collectors should always be kept blind to condition to avoid biasing effects on or biased interpretations of the data procured in the experiment. Such individuals should also be balanced across conditions to avoid the potentially confounding factor of assessor characteristics (analogous to crossing therapists with conditions). Furthermore, because assessor characteristics may introduce error variance for a particular client's data, the same individuals should be used to conduct all assessments (i.e., pre-, post-, and follow-up assessments) for any one client-participant in an effort to reduce such variance.

Follow-Up Assessment

In order to assess whether therapeutic changes are sustained over time after treatment has ended, investigators need to conduct follow-up assessments. This crucial phase of the experiment is relatively low in cost and yields important information about whether observed posttreatment changes are maintained. A minimum follow-up period of 1 year is often recommended, although several studies have assessed change up to 2 or 3 years after treatment has ended. It is a good idea to include several follow-up assessments to allow for detection of nonlinear trends. Thorough follow-up measurement is ideal—that is to say, the same multiple domain assessments employed at pretherapy and posttherapy should be used at follow-up periods. Because further psychological or pharmacological treatment subsequent to the experimental trial and outside of the project can obviously affect follow-up improvements, investigators should also assess types and frequencies of such interventions at the follow-up interview. It is particularly important to analyze for between-group differences in these variables; differential rates of subsequent treatment would indicate a potential rival hypothesis regarding follow-up outcome differences (or similarities) between compared conditions. Follow-up outcome analyses may also be conducted comparing participants who did and did not receive further treatment, as well as comparing conditions that in separate analyses include and do not include clients who did receive subsequent therapy.

The dependent variable considerations listed previously help to ensure that the assessment of clients-participants is thorough and not subject to error variance. An additional consideration related to dependent variables has to do with the methods used by investigators when analyzing the data from their studies. The next section details methods of analyzing data from therapy outcome studies.

STATISTICAL ANALYSIS OF DATA

Many traditional and newly emerging statistical analyses exist for the analysis of outcome data. The reader is referred to chapters in this volume that provide a comprehensive overview of those data-analytic techniques. In this section we merely summarize a few traditional approaches commonly used in past therapy research.

Before presenting outcome results, tests for condition equivalence on pretherapy demographic and dependent variables need to be reported in order to ensure the absence of potentially confounding differences between conditions prior to the beginning of treatment. An important consideration when conducting these analyses, however, is that there is often insufficient power to detect moderate effect size differences when comparing groups only on baseline measures. This is due to the reduced group ns that are required as a result of repeated measures designs, such as those employed in therapy outcome research. Thus, investigators are advised to practice caution when concluding that groups did not differ on pretreatment variables, because in fact moderate differences may actually exist.

After one has ensured that groups did not differ on pretherapy variables, primary outcome analyses on base-free measures of change should be conducted and reported. When these analyses are performed, it is advisable to reduce as much error variance as possible by removing the variation shown by clients on pre-therapy scores from later assessment scores. The most common choice is analysis of covariance (ANCOVA). This analysis is advisable when initial tests indicate that there were no differences in pretherapy scores, and it is necessary when the tests indicate that differences did exist. Random assignment typically prevents the emergence of pretherapy differences, but it is unfortunate when such differences do emerge. In these cases, using covariance-adjusted postscores statistically removes the pretherapy score influence. It should be noted, however, that this does not ensure that the clients in the different experimental conditions were not *psychologically* different, even though their scores were made to be mathematically equivalent. If clients differ across conditions on any one characteristic, they may also be different in other psychological processes and may therefore respond to treatment differentially. Thus, when pretherapy differences exist, investigators should exercise caution in drawing conclusions on outcome results.

There are several statistical considerations to take into account when using multiple measures from multiple domains. Some measures show significant condition effects merely because using a large number of measures capitalizes on chance (Type I error), and this likelihood increases as the number of measures utilized increases. Data analysts need to therefore make adjustments. One option is to employ a Bonferroni adjustment (see Miller, 1981) in which the predetermined alpha level is divided by the number of outcome measures to arrive at a new alpha level for all analyses. This adjustment is widely seen as overly conservative. An alternative is to use Simes' (1986) improved approach which provides adjusted alpha levels which protect against Type I error but are less stringent.

The best option, however, is to conduct multivariate analyses of covariance (MANCOVA) on the set of main outcome measures, particularly when the set of measures is being included based on some underlying empirical or theoretical rationale. For example, it would be appropriate to use MANCOVA when assessing multiple self-report measures of anxious symptomatology. Separate MANCOVAs can be run on sets of multiple measures reflecting areas of functioning that are not theoretically or empirically related to each other. If the MANCOVA indicates that a significant condition effect is present, then the investigator has several options from which to choose when conducting post hoc comparisons. Stevens (1996) outlines three possible post hoc procedures, ranging from least to most conservative. The least conservative approach is to analyze Hotelling T^2s and univariate t tests, in which one first conducts all pairwise multivariate tests (T^2s) to determine the pairs of groups that differed on the set of dependent variables, and then conducts individual univariate t tests (each at the .05 level) to determine the specific variables that are contributing to the multivariate pairwise differences from the first step. A moderately conservative approach is to analyze all pairwise multivariate tests as described above, and then construct a confidence interval using Tukey's simultaneous confidence interval technique in order to determine which variables are contributing to each pairwise difference from the first step. Finally, the most conservative approach is to create Roy-Bose simultaneous confidence intervals, a procedure in which all pairwise and complex comparisons are examined for each dependent variable of interest. Use of this more conservative procedure, however, severely minimizes the amount of power in the analyses, and thus Stevens argues against its use. For specific examples of how to employ each of these follow-up procedures, the reader is referred to Stevens (1996).

Within-condition *t* tests are also useful for determining whether a specific condition actually showed significant change for any given dependent measure. This statistical procedure is especially important for follow-up assessments in order to ascertain whether a condition is generating increased, maintained, or decreased improvement relative to posttherapy levels.

Special consideration should be given to participants with missing data. Investigators can usefully analyze the results separately on (a) only clients without any missing data and (b) all clients wherein missing data are replaced either by regression-determined values or by using the client's last available assessment score (*end point analysis*). Of course, the greater the amount of missing data, the less confident one can be about one's conclusions, especially if analyses with and without clients having missing data yield different results. (For a detailed discussion of approaches to handling missing data, the reader is referred to the chapter by Graham, Cumsille, & Elek-Fisk in this volume.)

Finally, power analyses should be conducted in order to verify a low probability of Type II error (see Cohen, 1988). Insufficient power resulting from small sample sizes may help to explain the absence of a difference between any two conditions. (For a detailed discussion of power analyses, the reader is referred to the chapter by Wilcox in this volume.)

As we have described in this section, several considerations factor into the statistical analysis of data in psychotherapy outcome research. An emerging recent concern, however, has been that investigators demonstrate the practical significance of their interventions in addition to showing statistical significance. In the next section, we present considerations associated with demonstrating that a given intervention leads to clinically significant change.

CLINICALLY SIGNIFICANT CHANGE

In psychotherapy outcome research, statistically significant change does not necessarily imply clinical significance. Although the convention in behavioral sciences and particularly in treatment outcome research (Kazdin & Wilson, 1978; Meltzoff & Kornreich, 1970) has been to employ statistical significance tests with primary outcome measures to infer whether differences exist between groups, such a practice ignores the fact that statistical significance often has little relation to the practical importance of the effect (Jacobson, Follette, & Revenstorf, 1984). Furthermore, by relying on statistical significance tests in order to determine the effectiveness of treatment, information about the variability of outcome among clients is de-emphasized, thus leaving no

way to determine the proportion of clients who benefited from the treatment (Jacobson et al., 1984).

Thus, in addition to testing for the statistical significance of a treatment, it is also important to assess to what extent the therapy-induced change is of practical importance for the client. Many researchers have thus advocated using *clinical significance* as a criterion for evaluating the effectiveness of psychotherapy. However, there has been much disagreement in the field in regard to what constitutes clinical significance. Some suggestions have included: improvement shown by a large proportion of the clients (Hugdahl & Ost, 1981); a change that is large in magnitude (Barlow, 1981); an improvement in the everyday functioning of the client (Kazdin & Wilson, 1978); an elimination of the presenting problem (Kazdin & Wilson, 1978); and attaining a level of functioning that is indistinguishable from that of the nondeviant population (Kazdin & Wilson, 1978; Kendall & Norton-Ford, 1982).

One common approach has been to calculate the percentage of clients in each condition who show an operationally defined amount of improvement on a specified set of measures (also termed *responder status*). This measure of clinically significant change is often arbitrarily set at 20% (i.e., clients achieved a 20% change from their scores at pretherapy). Investigators differ in how many posttherapy measures are considered in evaluating whether a given client is a responder, although most commonly investigators require that a client show 20% improvement on the majority of main outcome measures.

Responder status is an effective means of communicating how many clients displayed at least some response to treatment. However, it is a fairly weak means of assessing clinically significant change. If reported, it should be combined with the more stringent criterion of *high end-state functioning,* which is defined as the percentage of clients from each condition that is now functioning at so-called normal levels on a majority of main outcome measures. Here, *normal* is typically defined as a posttherapy or follow-up score falling within the normal or functional range. Operationally defined normal functioning is often a score falling within one standard deviation of normative means or, in the absence of normative data, a score deemed normal on the basis of its face validity (e.g., a daily diary anxiety score of 20 or less on a 0–100 point scale, where 20 was labeled as *slight anxiety*). However, as Jacobson, Roberts, Berns, and McGlinchey (1999) point out, the criteria chosen for such face valid measures are often arbitrary (e.g., Jansson & Ost, 1982) or highly subjective (e.g., Barlow & Mavissakalian, 1981).

Jacobson et al. (1984) have proposed three potential operational definitions of clinically significant change in functioning: (a) the level of functioning at posttherapy falls outside the range of the dysfunctional population such that the posttherapy score falls two standard deviations beyond the mean (in the direction of functionality) for that population; (b) the level of functioning at posttherapy falls within the range of the functional population such that functionality begins at two standard deviations from the mean for the normal population; and (c) the level of functioning at posttherapy suggests that the subject is statistically more likely to be in the functional than in the dysfunctional population (i.e., the posttherapy score is statistically more likely to be drawn from the functional than the dysfunctional distribution). The authors suggest that definition (a) is a more stringent criterion than (b) and that when the dysfunctional and functional distributions overlap, (c) is the best choice. In order to use these criteria, however, norms need to be available on the distributions of functional and dysfunctional individuals. If norms are unavailable (or if norms are available on a random sample of individuals such that both functional and dysfunctional people are represented in the sample), the authors suggest employing definition (a) in deciding the clinical significance of a treatment (Jacobson et al., 1984; Jacobson & Truax, 1991). Importantly, however, Jacobson et al. (1999) stress that any method of determining clinical significance can only be as good as the psychometric properties of the instruments of measurement.

In addition to defining clinically significant change, it is important to know the degree of change that has taken place as a result of therapy. To address this concern, Jacobson and Truax (1991) suggest employing a reliable change index, whereby the index is equal to the difference between the pretest and posttest scores, divided by the standard error of difference between the two test scores. Thus, in conjunction with defining the functional performance of clients according to the criteria above, the reliable change index provides a measure for whether observed change is indicative of more than mere measurement error.

In conclusion, reporting responder status and end-state functioning is an effective means of characterizing the level of clinically significant change from two different perspectives. In addition, one may also want to consider both the appropriate definition of functional performance and the reliable change index for an assessment of the degree of clinically significant change elicited by an intervention. By reporting the amount of clinically significant change, clients as consumers are in a better position to make educated decisions about which therapy will aid them in achieving clinically significant—not merely statistically significant—improvement. Additionally, scientific investigators will be able to ensure that their treatment packages offer significant symptom alleviation for clients while meeting the scientific goal of establishing specific cause-and-effect conclusions about a particular intervention.

Thus far, we have presented the various methodological considerations associated with between-group psychotherapy outcome research in terms of independent and dependent variables as well as data analytic concerns. When combined, these suggestions can yield highly controlled investigations in which highly specific cause-and-effect conclusions can be drawn. However, for various reasons such large studies cannot always be conducted. In the following section, we describe some of the commonly used small-*N* experimental designs and discuss the strength of cause-and-effect conclusions associated with each design.

SMALL-*N* EXPERIMENTAL DESIGNS

Between-group experimental designs are the most commonly used approaches to evaluating the efficacy of a therapy. However, such highly controlled investigations may not be conducive to research in applied settings, in which investigators may not have access to a large number of individuals meeting the criteria for the same disorder or in which resources may be limited. Moreover, scientists may wish to conduct a rigorous scientific investigation with a small number of clients or evaluate the effectiveness of an approach in a preliminary fashion with a few clients before embarking on a large-scale, expensive between-group design. Finally, there are times when the characteristics of the disorder (e.g., rare occurrence in the population) make it unlikely that a sufficient number of participants will be available. For these reasons, small-*N* designs are commonly instituted. It is possible and desirable for practicing clinicians to employ these types of designs whenever possible both to evaluate their therapy interventions and to contribute to science. In small-*N* research, inferences are made about the effectiveness of the treatment based on systematically presenting different conditions to a single client-participant over time or to different clients at systematically different times and tracking the clients' progress during phases of the experiment. Unlike most between-group investigations, small-*N* designs require frequent assessments over time, sometimes as many as several observations per day or week. The reason for this requirement is that the investigator must examine the pattern and stability of performance during each phase of the experiment. Furthermore, because such designs often rely heavily on behavioral assessments, they are most appropriate for treatments targeting operant behavior and less so for emotional (respondent) behavior.

All small-N designs begin with a baseline assessment in which the frequency, duration, and intensity of the behavior under consideration are tracked and measured for several days before treatment is implemented. These baseline data serve as a prediction of what the client's behavior would be in the immediate future if the intervention were not instituted. It is important that the baseline measures show a stable rate (i.e., absence of a slope in the data and little variability). A slope would indicate that there is already a tendency for the behavior to be increasing or decreasing over an assessment period and thus changes observed after treatment implementation would not be clearly interpretable. If there is evidence of large variability (i.e., fluctuation over time) in the baseline data, it will be more difficult to ascertain changes due to treatment in the midst of such "noise." The most common small-N experimental designs include the ABAB design, the multiple baseline design, and the changing criterion design.

ABAB Design

The ABAB design alternates the baseline condition (A) with the intervention condition (B). Cause-and-effect inferences can be drawn if the client's functioning improves during the B phase, reverts back in the direction of the baseline level during the second A phase, and then again improves during the second B phase. Kazdin (1998) offers variations on the ABAB design such that if the implemented treatment (B) fails to produce an improvement in functioning, the clinical scientist may institute a different treatment (B_2). Alternate interventions (B_x) may be tested until a change in behavior is detected. After a change in behavior has emerged, then the no-intervention (A) phase should again be implemented and followed again by the intervention (B_x). In every A or B phase, it is important to wait until the behavior is stable before moving to the next phase.

The ABAB design presents a practical dilemma for the clinical scientist. During the second A (baseline) phase of the design, the client's behavior must revert toward baseline levels if causal inferences are to be unambiguously drawn. However, from a clinical standpoint, this reversion in behavior is undesirable, given that a clinician hopes the client's behavior continues to improve or at least remains stable even without continued intervention. From a scientific standpoint, however, if the client's behavior fails to return to the original baseline during the second A phase, a multitude of rival hypotheses exist for why the problematic behavior improved during the intervention phase and preclude drawing a cause-and-effect conclusion about the intervention.

The most likely candidate for the ABAB design is a problem behavior that is under the control of environmental contingencies (i.e., operant or instrumental behavior). The design is rarely possible with many types of emotional problems (i.e., respondent behavior). The advantage of the next design is that it is suitable for experimental evaluations of treatments for either operant or respondent behaviors.

Multiple Baseline Design

In the multiple baseline design, baseline data are collected concurrently on two or more baseline targets, and the intervention is applied to each target at systematically different points in time. There are three basic versions of the multiple baseline design, differing in what the multiple targets are: (a) different behaviors within the same client; (b) the same behavior among different clients; or (c) the same behavior within the same client across different situations. Thus, depending on the version of the design chosen, the behavior, the client, or the situation is the variable that is targeted for treatment applications at any given phase of therapy. After the initial baselines are stable on all targets, the clinical scientist implements intervention for one behavior, client, or situation while leaving the other behavior(s), client(s), or situation(s) under baseline (nontreated) conditions. After the treated target improves and stabilizes, treatment is then implemented for the next behavior, client, or situation while all measures continue to be administered. The clinician can draw causal inferences if each target changes *only* when the intervention is implemented and fails to change prior to intervention.

Two considerations are important when conducting multiple baseline research. First, one needs to implement at least two baselines, but utilizing three or four baselines may strengthen the validity of causal inferences. For example, an investigator implementing an after-school intervention with emotionally troubled children may choose the same behavior across different children as the target. If one child is administered the intervention, continued baseline assessment must be performed on a minimum of one other child. However, if the investigator collects baseline data on two or three other children and observes that the behavior remains stable in those children while the treated child's behavior improves, the strength of causal inferences is stronger than it would be if only one other child had been employed as a comparison. The investigator can then go on to implement the treatment with a second child while continuing to collect baseline data on the remaining two children and so on until all four children have been treated. By employing more than two baseline participants, the investigator is able to assess whether those behaviors still exposed to the baseline condition remain stable and whether treatment initiation reliably results in improvements in a replicable fashion. Thus, more confidence exists in the inference that the intervention caused the behavior change.

Second, it is essential that the targets be independent. Because this design requires that a behavior changes when and only when the treatment is implemented, investigators need to ensure that change in one target will not likely yield change in another target that is still being exposed to the baseline condition. If the targets are interdependent such that the effects of one target carry over to another, the clinician will have less confidence in the conclusion that the intervention caused the change in behavior.

Changing-Criterion Design

In the changing-criterion design, the baseline assessment is followed by implementation of treatment, at which time a predefined level of performance (i.e., a criterion) is established. After the client's performance meets or surpasses the goal, the criterion is made more stringent. The criterion is continuously changed until the final goal has been reached. If the behavior changes as the criterion is changed, then it is likely that the intervention and not some extraneous variable caused the change. However, because extraneous variables could still account for general change in any one direction, the clinician may make bidirectional changes in the criterion in order to assess whether the behavior follows in the appropriate direction. The disadvantage of this practice is that the client may begin to engage in the unwanted behavior again, a scientifically important change, but potentially harmful clinically. It should be noted that such a design is limited to demonstrating gradual as opposed to rapid changes due to the need for a changing criterion (Kazdin, 1998).

A variety of more complex designs that make use of one or more of the basic designs described previously and that allow for outcome studies analogous to the dismantling, additive, and parametric between-group designs are also available. The interested reader is referred to Hersen and Barlow (1977).

In this section, we have described the small-N ABAB, multiple baseline, and changing-criterion designs, as well as the methodological considerations associated with each of these approaches. The following section provides a discussion of the distinction between and considerations surrounding efficacy and effectiveness research.

SCIENTIFIC RESEARCH IN THE NATURALISTIC SETTING

The present chapter has focused on the various experimental approaches for evaluating the efficacy of therapeutic interventions and the methodological considerations necessary in conducting such investigations. We have emphasized the importance of employing rigorous scientific methodology in the quest for increasingly specific cause-and-effect conclusions from internally valid investigations. The types of studies that we have been describing are often called *efficacy* studies and are characterized by the high degree of methodological rigor typical of clinical research conducted under controlled conditions. Features of this kind of therapy research include the enrollment of carefully screened and diagnosed clients who are given a specific number of therapy sessions in two or more randomly assigned comparison conditions administered by clinicians who have been thoroughly trained in each of the highly operationally defined treatments that are described in detail in protocol manuals, supervised closely by project investigators, and checked for protocol adherence by independent assessors listening to tape recordings of the therapy sessions. All of these features are of course incorporated to ensure the greatest degree of control over the experiment in order to reduce error variance and to provide the most unambiguous conclusions from the investigation.

Among those who believe that therapy research is indeed capable of directly answering applied questions like *Is this therapy effective?* or *Which therapy is most effective?*, some have argued that the results of efficacy investigations are not relevant to the applied setting because they lack external validity (cf. Elliott, 1998). That is, the highly controlled and restrictive circumstances of efficacy studies are so unlike what occurs in the real world of clinical intervention (e.g., heterogeneous clients with frequently complex problems and co-morbid conditions, absence of protocol manuals defining how to intervene, absence of supervision, and variable length of treatment as determined by insurance policies or ability to self-pay) that the results of rigorous efficacy experiments are unlikely to generalize to actual clinical practice. If one is focused on the scientifically unanswerable questions about therapy effectiveness (rather than on causal relationships), then this criticism is well taken.

In the context of this criticism, a distinction is now often made between efficacy investigations and what has been termed *effectiveness* research (e.g., see Seligman, 1995). Effectiveness research refers to therapy studies that are conducted in real-world clinical settings. In such research, there are often fewer or no restrictions on client participants (anyone who comes to a clinic can participate), and participating therapists do not undergo any specialized training but administer their therapies as they usually do. Typically, the main elements of the study that are controlled include the timing and content of assessment materials used to measure outcome and perhaps to measure client and therapist characteristics. Such effectiveness research does have the advantage of possessing greater external validity in the sense that it is more representative of what typically occurs in practice settings than is the case for typical clinical efficacy trials. Additionally, this research approach does have the capability of revealing potentially important correlational relationships (e.g., assessing the predictive value of certain client characteristics, therapist characteristics, and therapy process variables) that can lead the way to discovering critical moderator, mediator, or predictor variables for further pursuit. Based on a work group report (cf. Rush, 1998) arguing for the enormous importance of obtaining valid findings about therapy in actual clinical settings, the National Institute of Mental Health has recently placed high priority on funding this type of research.

Despite its potentially greater external validity, however, three things need to be kept in mind about effectiveness research. First, generalizability problems do not disappear. There is no guarantee that the results discovered in one clinical setting with its types of clients, therapists, and procedures will generalize to other clinical settings that have somewhat different characteristics. Thus, it is critical that the investigator document and report those characteristics and procedures in order to help other researchers and clinicians to evaluate the potential relevance of the results to their own settings. Second, the best that effectiveness research (as it is typically performed) is able to provide is the discovery of correlational, and not cause-and-effect, relationships. Experimental designs and carefully controlled methodologies are required for causative conclusions. Finally, there is a danger in effectiveness studies that any demonstration of significant improvement among client participants may be erroneously attributed to the provision of therapy. As we have seen throughout this chapter, such a conclusion is not possible, given the large number of reasonable alternative explanations for such an outcome. Without a comparison condition that holds certain potential causes (e.g., history, maturation, provision of a sympathetic listener) constant, there is no way to conclude unambiguously that therapy was the actual cause of any of the observed changes. Findings that possess no internal validity are of no use, regardless of how much external validity the study has.

Despite our obvious bias toward carefully controlled therapy investigations that are focused on discovery of causal relationships (because that is indeed the only outcome that

scientific research can yield by its very nature, cf. Borkovec & Castonguay, 1998), it is important to point out a critical role for applied research. Local clinical sites can conduct research studies that are aimed at improving the quality of their services, even if such research is designed in a way that does not allow the types of unambiguous causal inferences generated by the rigorous designs and methodologies described in this chapter. One could, for example, assess client and therapist characteristics and correlate these variables with client outcomes to search for potential predictors of therapeutic gains, compare masters-level therapists to PhD therapists within an agency, contrast the improvements observed in clients who have received psychotherapy as customarily delivered in the agency to clients who are given medication for their psychological problems, or even compare the outcomes of clients who happened to have received (nonrandomly) different forms of psychotherapy (a comparative design) offered by different therapists within the agency. Clinical sites conducting such research can use such information to identify and make increasing use of the types of services that are found to be associated with maximal client outcomes. It may not matter to the researchers what the causal elements are for maximized change; they merely wish to determine the best services for their clientele and to constantly improve those services. In conducting such research, two points need to be kept in mind. First, conclusions reached by such investigations are limited in generality only to the particular clinical site involved. Second, even for these local conclusions, because many rival hypotheses remain, causal conclusions are not possible. Consequently, the results do not contribute to basic knowledge in the field. Even more important, however, is that one cannot be certain that the variables investigated and found to be associated with better outcomes are indeed the reason for (i.e., the cause of) the superior improvements. Thus, maximizing their use in one's clinical service may not actually result in the desired increments in client change. Continued evaluation of those variables would, however, provide the necessary feedback to allow continuing evolution of services being administered. The reader is referred to texts by Newcomer (1997); Shadish, Cook, and Campbell (2002); and Bickman and Rog (1998) for information on designs, methodologies, and considerations pertaining to applied research.

On the other hand, a new and growing movement has been occurring within the field of clinical psychology that gives promise to the creation of psychotherapy research that can maximize both internal and external validity. Practice research networks are being organized within practice communities and mental health agencies wherein a common core assessment battery will be administered and collaborative research efforts between practicing clinicians and clinical scientists will be established. The creation of such a research infrastructure will provide great opportunities for clinically relevant research within the naturalistic setting on a large scale. The greater optimism in this movement comes, however, from a growing recognition that experimental studies are both necessary and possible within such an infrastructure (cf. Borkovec, Echemendia, Ragusea, & Ruiz, 2001). Although it remains to be seen how this approach to clinical research unfolds, there is the real possibility in the near future that well-designed practice research networks will be established maximizing both internal and external validity in their research efforts, and that as a consequence considerable basic knowledge about psychopathology and therapeutic change mechanisms will emerge that can contribute to the development of increasingly effective forms of intervention.

CONCLUSIONS

Like any experiment, the goal of a psychotherapy outcome investigation is to establish cause-and-effect conclusions. Such conclusions are achievable by instituting experimental designs in which all variables are held constant except the single variable of interest. Additionally, through the use of the strong inference approach, investigators can repeatedly construct rival hypotheses about observed relationships between variables and are thus well equipped to uncover increasingly specific cause-and-effect conclusions about those relationships. Ultimately, through the use of this procedure and a methodologically rigorous approach to outcome research, investigators can obtain highly specific pieces of knowledge about a single observed relationship.

Although the no-treatment and common factors comparison designs do hold constant some important variables that may contribute to observed change, we have shown why their employment does not allow for an examination of the active ingredients of a treatment package. Additionally, the comparative design contains a large number of threats to internal validity and thus its use is problematic if one's goal is to establish specific cause-and-effect relationships between variables. We have demonstrated throughout the present chapter that the scientific ideal of holding constant all variables except the single variable of interest is best achieved by instituting the component control (dismantling), additive (constructive), catalytic, and parametric designs in an effort to establish causal conclusions about the mechanisms of change and the basic nature of a particular psychological condition.

We have also described the various methodological considerations that must be taken into account when conducting psychotherapy outcome investigations. The application of these prescriptions (e.g., random assignment within waves, equation of session parameters, the use of detailed therapy manuals, integrity checks, expectancy and credibility checks, a standardized approach to diagnosis, crossing therapists with conditions) strengthens the specificity of causal conclusions by holding important variables constant within and between conditions. Important dependent variable considerations (e.g., assessment multiple domains of functioning, conducting follow-up assessments, assessing clinically significant change) ensure that investigators gather quality data that will reflect the changes caused by a given intervention.

Finally, we have outlined other scientific approaches to assessing change, particularly in smaller groups of individuals. Such investigations are useful in treating infrequently occurring conditions or in conducting preliminary research on potential cause-and-effect relationships in psychotherapy. Finally, conducting methodologically rigorous studies in naturalistic settings may optimize internal and external validity and contribute to basic knowledge about psychological disorders and mechanisms of change.

By using a basic science approach to psychotherapy outcome investigations and thus making the ultimate goal of such investigations the establishment of highly specific cause-and-effect conclusions, we consequently are able to discover increasingly effective ways of treating individuals who are suffering from psychological problems. It is precisely through upholding these rigorous scientific ideals that we are able to uncover the specific nature of disorders and the mechanisms of change necessary to alleviate the symptoms associated with them.

APPENDIX: CHECKLIST OF RECOMMENDATIONS FOR INVESTIGATORS OF PSYCHOTHERAPY OUTCOME RESEARCH

1. Decide what type of design will be employed (no-treatment, common factors, component control, additive, catalytic, or parametric). The more elements held constant across conditions, the more specific the cause-and-effect conclusions that can be drawn from the design.

2. Investigators should conduct power analyses to determine sample size.

3. Participants should be randomly assigned to conditions. Block random assignment within waves should be employed if participants are entering the study over an extended period of time.

4. Conditions should be matched on length, number, and frequency of sessions. For dismantling and additive designs, a common factors component must be added to single-component conditions in order to equate them on length of sessions with the multicomponent condition.

5. Protocol manuals should be used to operationalize the independent variable of the investigation. They should include an outline of the rationale for treatment, theoretical foundations of the therapy, and session-by-session goals and techniques when possible.

6. Integrity and adherence checks should be performed on 20–25% of randomly selected tapes from each condition of the study. Raters blind to condition should categorize each therapist utterance against a checklist of allowed and not-allowed techniques and utterances. Investigators should make a priori decisions regarding the number of protocol breaks allowed before a client's data will be excluded from the analyses.

7. Conditions should not differ in terms of clients' expectancy to change or how credible they think the rationale for treatment is. Thus, credibility-expectancy scales should be administered after the rationale for treatment has been provided (usually after the first session).

8. Conditions should be equal in terms of how many clients have discontinued treatment while it is being administered, as well as how many clients have been lost during the follow-up period of assessment.

9. Sources of participants (i.e., referrals from private practitioners, self-referrals by clients, responses to media advertisements) should be equally distributed across conditions.

10. Demographic characteristics (e.g., age, marital status, level of education, ethnicity) should be equivalent across conditions.

11. Inclusion and exclusion criteria should be specified before patient recruitment begins. Comorbidity of disorders should be equivalent across conditions. Exclusion of comorbid disorders presents a limit to the generalizability of findings; however, a more homogeneous sample reduces the amount of error variance present.

12. To assess the representativeness of the sample under investigation, investigators should track reasons for participant exclusion.

13. Severity and duration of the problem should be assessed, reported, and balanced across conditions.

14. Concurrent or past treatment must be balanced across conditions and reported.

15. For investigations of specific diagnostic groups, operational definitions of the system employed to make diagnoses should be specified, and reliability checks on diagnoses should be conducted and reported.

16. Therapist characteristics should be described, and more than one therapist must be employed.

17. Therapists should treat an equal number of clients in each condition.

18. Therapist bias should be assessed and reported. Such ratings should be equivalent across conditions.

19. Multiple domains of patient functioning (e.g., cognitive, affective, behavioral, physiological) should be assessed, and these assessments should take several forms (e.g., self-report, observational, physiological).

20. Assessors and data collectors should be kept blind to condition and should be balanced across conditions. Furthermore, the same individuals should be used to conduct all assessments for any one client in order to reduce error variance.

21. Follow-up assessment(s) of at least 1 year should be conducted in order to determine the degree of maintenance of change. Several follow-up assessments should be employed to allow for the detection of nonlinear trends, and each assessment should include multiple domains.

22. Statistical tests for condition equivalence on pretherapy variables should be conducted and reported. Nonequivalence on any variables represents a potential rival hypothesis for differential change between conditions.

23. Statistical correction methods for multiple tests (e.g., Bonferroni correction) must be employed when multiple measures from multiple domains are analyzed.

24. Analyze between-condition effects using MANCOVA on the set of main outcome measures.

25. Within-condition statistical tests should be employed to determine the degree of change from pretreatment to posttreatment and follow-up assessment periods.

26. Sufficient power must be demonstrated before an equivalence between conditions is interpreted as indicating a true absence of differences.

27. Operational definitions of clinically significant change should be analyzed and reported.

REFERENCES

Agras, W. S., Schneider, J. A., Arnow, B., Raeburn, S. D., & Telch, C. F. (1989). Cognitive-behavioral and response-prevention treatment for bulimia nervosa. *Journal of Consulting and Clinical Psychology, 57,* 215–221.

Alexander, L. B., & Luborsky, L. (1986). The Penn helping alliance scales. In L. S. Greenberg & W. M. Pinsoff (Eds.), *The psychotherapeutic process: A research handbook.* New York: Guilford.

APA Task Force on Promotion and Dissemination of Psychological Procedures (1995). Training in and dissemination of empirically-validated psychological treatments: Report and recommendation. *The Clinical Psychologist, 48,* 3–23.

Barlow, D. H. (1981). On the relation of clinical research to clinical practice: Current issues, new direction. *Journal of Consulting and Clinical Psychology, 49,* 147–155.

Barlow, D. H., & Mavissakalian, M. (1981). Directions in the assessment and treatment of phobia: The next decade. In M. Mavissakalian & D. H. Barlow (Eds.), *Phobia: Psychological and pharmacological treatments* (pp. 199–245). New York: Guilford.

Basham, R. B. (1986). Scientific and practical advantages of comparative design in psychotherapy outcome research. *Journal of Consulting and Clinical Psychology, 54,* 88–94.

Bickman, L., & Rog, D. J. (Eds.). (1998). *Handbook of applied social research methods.* Thousand Oaks: Sage.

Borkovec, T. D., Alcaine, O., & Behar, E. (in press). Avoidance theory of worry and generalized anxiety disorder. In R. G. Heimberg, C. L. Turk, & D. S. Mennin (Eds.), *Generalized anxiety disorder: Advances in research and practice.* New York: Guilford.

Borkovec, T. D., & Castonguay, L. G. (1998). What is the scientific meaning of "empirically supported therapy"? *Journal of Consulting and Clinical Psychology, 66,* 136–142.

Borkovec, T. D., & Costello, E. (1993). Efficacy of applied relaxation and cognitive-behavioral therapy in the treatment of generalized anxiety disorder. *Journal of Consulting and Clinical Psychology, 61,* 611–619.

Borkovec, T. D., Echemendia, R. J., Ragusea, S. A., & Ruiz, M. (2001). The Pennsylvania Practice Research Network and future possibilities for clinically meaningful and scientifically rigorous psychotherapy research. *Clinical Psychology: Science and Practice, 8,* 155–168.

Borkovec, T. D., & Nau, S. D. (1972). Credibility of analogue therapy rationales. *Journal of Behavior Therapy and Experimental Psychiatry, 3*(4), 257–260.

Borkovec, T. D., & Onken, L. (in press). Recommendations for the use of placebos in clinical trials to test behavioral interventions. In A. Kleinman, H. Guess, L. Engel, & J. Kusek (Eds.), *The science of placebo: Toward an interdisciplinary research agenda.* London: British Medical Journal Press.

Borkovec, T. D., Robinson, E., Pruzinsky, T., & DePree, J. A. (1983). Preliminary exploration of worry: Some characteristics and processes. *Behaviour Research and Therapy, 21,* 9–16.

Borkovec, T. D., & Sides, J. K. (1979). The contribution of relaxation and expectancy to fear reduction via graded, imaginal exposure to feared stimuli. *Behaviour Research and Therapy, 17,* 529–540.

Butler, G., Fennell, M., Robson, P., & Gelder, M. (1991). Comparison of behavior therapy and cognitive behavior therapy in the treatment of generalized anxiety disorder. *Journal of Consulting and Clinical Psychology, 59,* 167–175.

Campbell, D. T., & Stanley, J. C. (1963). *Experimental and quasi-experimental designs for research.* Chicago: Rand-McNally.

Castonguay, L. G. (1993). "Common factors" and "nonspecific variables": Clarification of the two concepts and recommendations for research. *Journal of Psychotherapy Integration, 3,* 267–286.

Chambless, D. L., Sanderson, W. C., Shoham, V., Johnson, S. B., Pope, K. S., Crits-Christoph, P., Baker, M., Johnson, B., Woody, S. R., Sue, S., Beutler, L., Williams, D. A., & McCurry, S. (1996). An update on empirically validated treatments. *The Clinical Psychologist, 49,* 5–18.

Cohen, J. (1988). *Statistical power analysis in the behavioral sciences* (2nd ed.). Hillsdale, NJ: Erlbaum.

DiNardo, P. A., Brown, T. A., & Barlow, D. H. (1994). *Anxiety Disorders Interview Schedule for DSM-IV.* Albany, NY: Graywind.

Elkin, I., Shea, M. T., Watkins, J. T., Imber, S. D., Sotsky, S. M., Collins, J. F., Glass, D. R., Pilkonis, P. A., Leber, W. R., Docherty, J. P., Fiester, S. J., & Parloff, M. B. (1989). National Institute of Mental Health Treatment of Depression Collaborative Research Program: General effectiveness of treatments. *Archives of General Psychiatry, 46,* 971–982.

Elliott, R. (1998). Editor's introduction: A guide to the empirically supported treatments controversy. *Psychotherapy Research, 8,* 115–125.

First, M. B., Spitzer, R. L., Gibbon, M., & Williams, J. B. W. (1997). *Structured Clinical Interview for DSM-IV Axis I Disorders – Clinician Version (SCID-CV).* Washington, DC: American Psychiatric Press.

Frank, J. D. (1971). Therapeutic factors in psychotherapy. *American Journal of Psychotherapy, 25,* 350–361.

Hersen, M., & Barlow, D. H. (1977). *Single case experimental designs: Strategies for studying behavior change.* Oxford, England: Pergamon.

Horowitz, L. M., Strupp, H. H., Lambert, M. J., & Elkin, I. (1997). Overview and summary of the core battery conference. In H. H. Strupp, L. M. Horowitz, & M. J. Lambert (Eds.), *Measuring patient changes in mood, anxiety, and personality disorders: Toward a core battery* (pp. 11–54). Washington, DC: American Psychological Association.

Hugdahl, K., & Ost, L. (1981). On the difference between statistical and clinical significance. *Behavioral Assessment, 3,* 289–295.

Jacobson, N. S., Follette, W. C., & Revenstorf, D. (1984). Psychotherapy outcome research: Methods for reporting variability and evaluating clinical significance. *Behavior Therapy, 15,* 336–352.

Jacobson, N. S., Roberts, L. J., Berns, S. B., & McGlinchey, J. B. (1999). Methods for defining and determining the clinical significance of treatment effects: Description, application, and alternatives. *Journal of Consulting and Clinical Psychology, 67*(3), 300–307.

Jacobson, N. S., & Truax, P. (1991). Clinical significance: A statistical approach to defining meaningful change in psychotherapy research. *Journal of Consulting and Clinical Psychology, 59,* 12–19.

Jansson, L., & Ost, L. (1982). Behavioral treatments for agoraphobia: An evaluative review. *Clinical Psychology Review, 2,* 311–336.

Kazdin, A. E. (1992). *Research design in clinical psychology* (2nd ed.). Needham Heights, MA: Allyn & Bacon.

Kazdin, A. E. (1998). *Research design in clinical psychology* (3rd ed.). Needham Heights, MA: Allyn & Bacon.

Kazdin, A. E., & Wilson, G. T. (1978). *Evaluation of behavior therapy: Issues, evidence, and research strategies.* Cambridge, MA: Ballinger.

Kendall, P. C., & Norton-Ford, J. D. (1982). Therapy outcome research methods. In P. C. Kendall & J. N. Butcher (Eds.), *Research methods in clinical psychology* (pp. 429–460). New York: Wiley.

Lettieri, D. J. (1992). *A primer of research strategies in alcoholism treatment assessment.* Rockville, MD: National Institute on Alcohol Abuse and Alcoholism (NIAAA).

Meltzoff, J., & Kornreich, M. (1970). *Research in psychotherapy.* New York: Atherton.

Miller, R. G. (1981). *Simultaneous statistical inference* (2nd ed.). New York: Springer-Verlag.

Newcomer, K. E. (Ed.). (1997). *Using performance measurement to improve public and nonprofit programs.* Jossey-Bass: San Francisco.

Parloff, M. B. (1986). Placebo controls in psychotherapy research: A sine qua non or a placebo for research problems? *Journal of Consulting and Clinical Psychology, 54,* 79–87.

Paul, G. L. (1966). *Insight vs. desensitization in psychotherapy: An experiment in anxiety reduction.* Stanford, CA: Stanford University Press.

Platt, J. R. (1964). Strong inference. *Science, 146,* 347–353.

Rush, A. J. (1998). *Bridging science and service. The National Advisory Mental Health Council's Clinical Treatment and Services Research Workgroup report.* Washington, DC: National Institute of Mental Health.

Sanderson, W. C., DiNardo, P. A., Rapee, R. M., & Barlow, D. H. (1990). Syndrome comorbidity in patients diagnosed with a DSM-III—R anxiety disorder. *Journal of Abnormal Psychology, 99*(3), 308–312.

Seligman, M. E. P. (1995). The effectiveness of psychotherapy: The Consumer Reports study. *American Psychologist, 50,* 965–974.

Shadish, W. R., Cook, T. D., & Campbell, D. T. (2002). *Experimental and quasi-experimental design for generalized causal inference.* Boston: Houghton Mifflin.

Simes, R. J. (1986). An improved Bonferroni procedure for multiple tests of significance. *Biometrika, 73,* 751–754.

Stevens, J. (1996). *Applied multivariate statistics for the social sciences* (3rd ed.). Hillsdale, NJ: Erlbaum.

Strupp, H. H., & Anderson, T. (1997). On the limitations of therapy manuals. *Clinical Psychology: Science and Practice, 4*(1), 76–82.

Suh, C. S., Strupp, H. H., & O'Malley, S. S. (1986). The Vanderbilt Process Measures: The Psychotherapy Process Scale (VPSS) and the Negative Indicators Scale (VNIS). In L. S. Greenberg & W. M. Pinsoff (Eds.), *The psychotherapeutic process: A research handbook.* New York: Guilford.

CHAPTER 10

Health Psychology

TIMOTHY W. SMITH

Health psychology can be defined as the application of theories, methods, and research findings in basic and applied psychology to the study and promotion of physical health. As in the closely related interdisciplinary field of behavioral medicine, health psychology is founded on the assumption that psychological factors and physical health are reciprocally determined. For example, daily habits (e.g., exercise, diet), psychological processes (e.g., emotions), individual differences (e.g., personality traits), social relationships, and levels of functional activity both influence and are influenced by physical health. Unlike other applied subdisciplines (e.g., clinical and counseling psychology), health psychology concerns emotional health and adjustment only to the extent that they are influences on or consequences of physical diseases or disorders.

Health psychology formally emerged in the 1970s, culminating in the establishment of the Division of Health Psychology (38) of the American Psychological Association in 1978 (Wallston, 1997). It was preceded by and still enjoys close associations with a variety of psychological fields, including pediatric psychology, rehabilitation psychology, and psychophysiology. In its development, health psychology has drawn heavily—in terms of concepts, methods, and existing literature—from these and other psychological fields, especially clinical, social, personality, experimental, and physiological psychology. During the same period, the interdisciplinary field of behavioral medicine was formally established (G. E. Schwartz & Weiss, 1978). It addresses overlapping concerns, but includes methods, accumulated knowledge, researchers, and practitioners from fields beyond psychology, especially medicine, epidemiology, public health, genetics, nursing, and other health professions and sciences. The roots of health psychology and behavioral medicine can be traced through older related fields (e.g., psychosomatic medicine), many specific developments in biomedical and behavioral science over the preceding 50 years, and the steady expansion of psychology's role in medical education and health care. However, research and application at this interface have expanded at a remarkable rate since 1980, to the point that health is a primary focus in psychology and psychological considerations are increasingly common in biomedical research and health services.

Given its evolution from other fields in psychology and its location at the intersection of behavioral and biomedical science, health psychology utilizes a very broad array of research methods. This breadth of topics and methods may indeed be the most daunting challenge to health psychology researchers and consumers of their work. There are few, if any, specific methods that are truly unique to the field. Most of the topics covered in this volume, for example, are relevant to health research. Hence, broad traditional methodological training is a prerequisite for this work. Yet the application of traditional psychological methods to problems of physical health and illness poses many complex challenges.

This chapter provides an overview of these issues. It begins with a discussion of the scope and context of health psychology research, as these are critical background considerations in the design and evaluation of research in the field. Next, key methodological issues in each of the three central topics or domains of the field are addressed—the role of behavior (e.g., smoking, physical activity levels) in the development and prevention of disease, the role of stress and emotion as more direct psychobiological influences on disease, psychological aspects of acute and chronic illness and medical care, and the effects of psychosocial interventions as additions to traditional care. The chapter concludes with a review of classic issues in research design and methodology as they relate to health psychology, followed by a discussion of emerging and future issues. Although a thorough review of research methods in health psychology would itself require a sizable volume and hence is well beyond the scope of this chapter, it is possible to introduce and illustrate the unique methodological challenges and opportunities in this rapidly evolving field. Indeed, one very appropriate goal of this chapter could be to facilitate the application of the other topics covered elsewhere in this volume to the specific domain of health and disease.

THE SCOPE AND COMPLEXITY OF HEALTH PSYCHOLOGY RESEARCH

As this volume describes, methodological principles can be articulated in the abstract, but their effective use requires a nuanced understanding of the specific application. The strengths and weaknesses of any specific study design and the value of its contribution depend heavily on the content and context of the question. That context involves not only the state of the prior literature on the topic, but also the broader issues and perspectives in which it is embedded. Both the

content and context of health research are often unfamiliar to students, practitioners, and consumers of behavioral science. As a result, even researchers with considerable experience in other psychological fields can have considerable difficulty in applying their skills to the interface of the behavioral and biomedical sciences.

Three Domains of Health Psychology

The variety of research questions in health psychology can be organized into three broad and interconnected topics. The first—*health behavior and risk reduction*—examines the effects of daily habits and other behaviors (e.g., smoking, inactivity, diet) on the risk of physical disease. After reliable behavioral risk factors are identified, subsequent research examines possible moderators of their effects (e.g., gender, family history of specific diseases, ethnicity, etc.), in order to identify population subgroups for whom these behavioral risks are particularly dangerous. Other studies examine the multiple determinants of these behavioral risk factors. These determinants of health behavior can include a broad range of factors, ranging from cultural, economic, and social factors (e.g., socioeconomic status, education, ethnicity), to intra-individual psychosocial factors (e.g., belief, attitudes) and even biological influences (e.g., biochemistry of addiction). Research on the nature, moderators, and determinants of behavioral risk factors guides the development and evaluation of risk reducing interventions. Intervention research of this types asks two basic questions. First, *What interventions are effective in changing health behavior and maintaining these changes?* Second, *Do these interventions reduce the incidence of disease?* The most common intervention approaches run the full range from traditional psychological treatments with individuals (e.g., counseling, behavior therapy) to population-based interventions (e.g., public education, policy, or advertising campaigns). Although a few specific behaviors have received the most attention because of their central role in the most common causes of morbidity and mortality (e.g., smoking, diet, exercise), interventions address a very wide variety of end points—from the use of seatbelts and sunscreen to participation in health risk screenings.

In addition to psychological effects on health and illness through the pathway of lifestyle and health behavior, the second major topic in the field—*stress and health,* or *psychosomatics*—concerns more direct psychobiological influences on disease. Perhaps the oldest issue at the interface of biomedical and behavioral science concerns the effect of stress, negative emotions, and related characteristics of people (e.g., personality traits) and their social environments (e.g., isolation vs. support) on the development and course of physical disease. Studies in psychosocial epidemiology examine the effects of such risk factors on the incidence of disease in initially healthy populations, and their impact on the course of disease among individuals with a specific, established condition. These risk factors range from broad—higher-order factors such as socioeconomic status to characteristics of individuals, such as personality and emotional adjustment. After psychosocial risk factors (e.g., social isolation, chronic anger, hostility) have been identified, other research examines the mechanisms underlying these statistical associations. If the behavioral or lifestyle mechanisms described previously do not account fully for these associations, the primary focus of mechanism studies becomes the psychobiological correlates of psychosocial risk factors that could plausibly affect the pathophysiology of a given disease. In a maturing bio-behavioral science, these mechanisms are informed by basic research in medical physiology and closely tied to current research on the pathophysiology of specific diseases. In addition to human epidemiological and clinical research on psychosocial risk factors and human psychobiological research on the underlying mechanisms, research in this area often utilizes animal models that permit stronger experimental tests of psychosocial influences on disease and more definitive albeit invasive evaluations of underlying mechanisms. Animal research permits tests that would be obviously unethical in humans, but the issue of generalizability to human disease is a central concern. Ultimately, psychosomatic research in this area guides the development and evaluation of interventions (e.g., stress management) intended to prevent or manage disease through the disruption of unhealthy psychobiological processes or through the promotion of stress-buffering resources.

This latter type of intervention research could also be considered an example of the third major topic in health psychology—*psychosocial aspects of physical illness and medical care.* Research in this area examines the psychosocial impact (e.g., emotional functioning, functional activity levels, pain) of physical illness and other medical events on patients and their families. Not all people with a given type and severity of disease experience the same psychosocial impact. Hence, the determinants of individual differences in these impacts is an important topic in this area, as it identifies high risk groups in need of assistance and guides the development and evaluation of interventions designed to maximize functioning and well-being. A related topic addresses the psychosocial impact of standard medical and surgical care, again with the ultimate goal of maximizing benefits and minimizing the negative consequences and side effects of these regimens and procedures. In many cases (e.g., diabetes), the standard medical care of a condition is largely behavioral,

such as modifications in diet, activity levels, and adherence to prescribed medical regimens. The effectiveness of these approaches and the identification of potentially modifiable determinants of their effectiveness are important topics in health psychology research, as such research can help to maximize the effectiveness of standard care. Finally, the effects of psychosocial additions or even alternatives to traditional medical and surgical care are an increasingly important topic.

This brief review illustrates the relevance of traditional methodological topics in psychology to research in health psychology. Psychological, behavioral, and psychophysiological assessment, measurement and analysis of determinants of such variables, and the evaluation of behavioral interventions are essential elements of the field. However, transposing these traditional methodologies to the "new key" of health and illness is a complex process, especially in light of the wide range of risk factors, medical conditions, and intervention approaches included in the field.

Levels of Analysis and the Biopsychosocial Model

During the emergence of health psychology and behavioral medicine, Engel (1977) described important limitations of the traditional biomedical model of health and illness as reflecting alterations in biochemistry and the structure and function of organ systems. As an alternative, Engel proposed the *biopsychosocial* model, which describes health and disease as reflecting the reciprocal interplay of biological, psychological, and sociocultural processes. This model quickly became a cornerstone of these fields. Rather than a potentially reductionistic view of health and illness, the biopsychosocial model is based in the broad perspective of systems theory (von Bertalanffy, 1968), depicted in Figure 10.1. Systems theory conceptualizes natural phenomena—including health and disease—as involving hierarchically arranged levels of analysis, ranging in complexity from small, simpler units such as cells to large, complex, and superordinate factors such as communities and even cultures. Each level of analysis involves its own conceptual models and related research methods, but each is influenced by adjacent levels. Therefore, processes within a given level cannot be fully understood without consideration of the neighboring levels. Further, models and methods traditionally belonging to separate levels of analysis must frequently be integrated in order to investigate biopsychosocial perspectives on health and behavior more directly.

The far-reaching criticism of the traditional biomedical model posed by Engel's alternative is clear. Coronary heart disease, for example, cannot be reduced simply to the biology

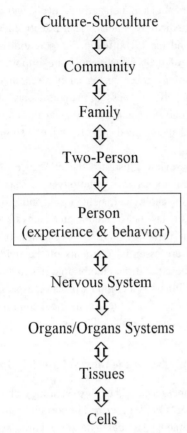

Culture-Subculture

⇕

Community

⇕

Family

⇕

Two-Person

⇕

Person
(experience & behavior)

⇕

Nervous System

⇕

Organs/Organs Systems

⇕

Tissues

⇕

Cells

Figure 10.1   Hierarchical Biophysical Model

of the slow and progressive narrowing of the arteries that supply blood to the heart and the pathophysiology of acute coronary events (e.g., myocardial ischemia, thrombosis, arrhythmia). Rather, these essential considerations must be placed in the context of individual psychosocial, interpersonal, and sociocultural processes. Individual health behaviors, psychobiological processes, and the social, cultural, and economic factors in which they are embedded are equally important in any comprehensive understanding of coronary disease and virtually all of the major sources of morbidity and mortality.

Conventional scientific training and research are usually located comfortably within one of these various levels of analysis. Yet, research in health psychology explicitly eschews the single-level approach, and must be conducted at least with an appreciation of the embeddedness of a given question, if not an active integration of cross-level methodologies. From the perspective of systems theory and the biopsychosocial model, the challenges and burdens for the producers and consumers of health psychology research are obvious. The concepts, accumulated knowledge, and methods of several disciplines are highly relevant to health psychology. The resulting conceptual and methodological

pluralism necessary for the most informative research is inconsistent with many traditional disciplinary identities and conventional approaches to training. Such broad expertise poses major demands on researchers and scholars. These burdens are typically eased in health psychology research through interdisciplinary collaboration. But even this strategy requires broad training and expertise for the individuals comprising a research team, in order to manage the difficulties of cross-disciplinary communication.

Health and Disease Across the Life Span

For each of the major topics in health psychology, the specific questions and methods are heavily influenced by the age of participants and the natural history of disease. Specific manifestations or indications of health change across the lifespan, as do the nature of threats to health and the prevalence of specific diseases and disorders. For example, accidents and violence are the main cause of morbidity and mortality in childhood, adolescence, and young adulthood, but chronic illnesses such as cancer and cardiovascular disease predominate later. Similarly, the determinants of behavioral risk factors, the role of psychosocial risk factors and their underlying psychobiological mechanisms, and the appropriateness of various intervention strategies all change in important and far-reaching ways across the life span and the course of a disease. The determinants of initiation of smoking in adolescence are very different from the key influences on maintenance and cessation of smoking in adulthood, as are the optimal methods for intervention. Similarly, the psychosocial challenges posed by early stages of cancer (e.g., behavioral risk factors, early detection) are very different from those posed by its later stages (psychobiological mechanisms in progression, psychosocial impacts of medical and surgical care, etc.). Further, the outcomes of interest and the optimal methods for assessing them and their determinants vary as well. For example, the effects of chronic headaches on academic functioning are a critical concern among school-age children, whereas vocational functioning is obviously more relevant for adults. In very young children, self-reports of pain and symptoms may be problematic, whereas they are the optimal indicators of the same condition for adults.

Because health psychology can reasonably be seen as including pediatric psychology, geropsychology, and every age group in between, collaborations among types of psychologists are as important and necessary as the interdisciplinary collaborations described previously. Just as health psychologists must be cognizant of the embeddedness of their work in biological and sociocultural levels of analysis, they must also recognize its embeddedness in the life span and related stages and processes of development. The nature of research questions and the methods used to pursue them must be informed accordingly.

Multiple Contexts of Health Psychology Research

Just as age, developmental stages, and phases of disease development and course are key contexts for health research within psychology, there are additional contexts outside of psychology to be considered. They determine the relative importance of research questions, shape the specific focus of those questions, and influence the selection of methodologies. *Public health and epidemiology* are perhaps the most obvious examples of allied disciplines that provide an essential context. The prevalence and incidence of specific threats to health and how these patterns vary across segments of the population shape the research agenda in health psychology. Answers to the question *What afflicts us?* are a driving force in this agenda. This includes not only the most common causes of death, but also the most common sources of morbidity, impairments in functional status or activity (i.e., disability), and threats to well-being (e.g., pain).

The epidemiological perspective explains the central place in the field of some conditions, such as heart disease, cancer, and chronic pain, as well as more recent topics, such as HIV and AIDS. Variations in sources of morbidity and mortality across age, sex, ethnicity, and socioeconomic status provide additional guidance from the epidemiological or public health perspective. One could argue, for example, that the field has paid too little attention to women's health, childhood injuries, the elderly, depression, drug abuse, and violence. If the public health and epidemiology perspective is extended to a worldwide view, the field arguably pays too little attention to many issues, including hunger, access to basic medical care, and infectious disease in nonindustrialized nations (Creer et al., in press). Some of these issues arguably lie near or beyond the boundaries of traditional definitions of health psychology, but this perspective sharpens our appreciation of the field's strengths and limitations.

A second obvious context for health psychology research is *medical science and care*. Increasingly, health psychology research must be informed by an appreciation of the pathophysiology of specific diseases, in order to make certain that the connections between behavior and disease are explicit and plausible. General, black-box models in which the nature of connections between behavior and disease are not specified rarely make valuable contributions to the field in its current state, and if they do it is only in the beginning stage of investigations of a new topic. Much more detailed models of the links between psychological and biological realms are now required as guides to theory-driven research. In studies of predictors of specific diseases, current standards for the assessment and classification of those medical conditions are essential in order to maximize the impact of psychological research. Similarly, studies of the psychosocial consequences of disease must utilize current knowledge and methods of medical science to capture adequately the nature and severity of a given condition. Finally, questions about the value of psychosocial interventions as additions to traditional medical and surgical care must be informed by a clear and current understanding of that care, as well as of the specific ways in which it is delivered. Only then can the additional role of health psychology interventions be adequately addressed.

A final context of increasing importance is *health economics and health care financing*. Additional influences on the prioritizing of topics within the research agenda of health psychology are answers to the questions *How are we spending our money?*, *What are we getting for it?*, and *How can we spend less without a loss of public health?* Obvious and pervasive behavioral and psychosocial influences on sources of health care expenditures (e.g., smoking) highlight the growing importance of the field. Economic impacts of health psychology interventions (e.g., reductions in health care utilization and expenditures) are important frameworks for evaluations of their effects and importance, and behavioral outcomes (e.g., functional activity levels and quality-of-life–adjusted years) are arguably the most important and universally relevant metric for evaluating the effects and relative benefits of all aspects of health care (R. M. Kaplan, 1994). In a period of spiraling health care expenditures and the rapid advance of often terribly expensive medical technologies, this perspective is essential in any substantive role for health psychology research.

Methodological Implications of the Scope and Complexity of Health Psychology

From even this brief review, it should be clear that the concepts and methods of traditional research in psychology are necessary but not sufficient in the study of health and illness. Health psychology research requires breadth of knowledge not only within psychology but also beyond it. Ironically, research in health psychology often suffers equally from inadequate incorporation of methods and perspectives outside psychology and insufficient use of traditional psychological approaches. That is, long-standing concerns in psychological methods (e.g., construct validity, assessment of change) are as common a source of methodological limitations as are failures to adequately incorporate methodological considerations and approaches outside of psychology. Many researchers in the field identify this situation as both a demanding challenge and a source of profound interest. Practically, it requires broad and extensive training, including experiences that facilitate the development of interdisciplinary collaborations and encourage familiarity with ongoing developments in the neighboring fields.

HEALTH BEHAVIOR AND RISK REDUCTION

The nature of threats to the health of industrialized nations changed profoundly during the last century. Advances in public health and medicine (e.g., sanitation, vaccines, antibiotics) reduced dramatically the previous, terrible toll of infectious disease. Replacing these conditions as the major sources of morbidity and mortality were chronic illnesses such as cardiovascular disease and cancer. Importantly, epidemiological research has identified a variety of behavioral factors that confer much of the risk of these conditions. Tobacco use, a diet high in saturated fat, low levels of regular physical activity, and other aspects of the modern lifestyle in industrialized nations increase the risk of heart disease, stroke, cancer, hypertension, diabetes, and several other serious illnesses. Behaviors—specifically, unsafe sexual practices and injection drug abuse—are also the primary modes of transmission of HIV infection. Behavior (e.g., drinking and driving, seat belt use) is also central in the risk of accidental injury and death. Finally, knowledge of and participation in health risk assessments (e.g., mammography, blood pressure screening) can facilitate the potentially lifesaving early detection of serious illnesses. These developments set the stage for much of the current role of health psychology (Matarazzo, 1980). The explication of the determinants of these behaviors and the subsequent design, evaluation, and implementation of related risk-reducing interventions comprise perhaps the greatest potential contribution of the field.

Conceptualizing and Measuring Outcomes in Health Behavior Research

As in all areas of behavioral research, the use of reliable and valid measures of health behavior is essential. Yet, this seemingly basic task is often problematic in health behavior research. Some of the difficulty in this area stems from incomplete or invalid conceptual models of the nature of health behavior. The classic literature on measurement and its more recent refinements underscore the necessity of clear and complete preoperational conceptual specification of the construct to be assessed as an essential prerequisite to valid assessment. Health behavior research has often been limited in this regard.

For example, despite common assumptions, individual health behaviors are not closely correlated (Norris, 1997). People who smoke may or may not consume a high-fat diet. Further, many individual health behaviors are not particularly stable over time. Despite the best of intentions, high levels of regular physical activity may wane. Hence, measurements based on an implicit model of stable, generally healthy (vs. unhealthy) lifestyles are not appropriate, as they may fail to capture much of the specific and changing nature of important health behavior. More frequent assessments of circumscribed behavior provide a more informative approach.

Given the rather straightforward nature of many health behaviors (e.g., smoking vs. nonsmoking; daily vs. infrequent exercise; frequency of inclusion of fruits and vegetables in one's diet), self-reports of health behavior would seem to be an obvious, appropriate, and inexpensive approach to assessment. All of the usual threats to the reliability and validity of self-reports (e.g., inaccuracies in recall) are relevant to this domain. However, social desirability is particularly important, as most health behaviors are well known by the general public and have clear evaluative connotations (Patrick et al., 1994). It is widely believed that smoking is unhealthy and unwise, that exercise is good, that regular consumption of high fat foods is bad, and that unprotected sexual intercourse is potentially dangerous to oneself and to others. Hence, alternative or additional methods of assessment are needed, such as behavioral observations, mechanical measurement (e.g., movement sensitive devices for activity assessments), biochemical validation (e.g., exhaled carbon monoxide, or plasma cotinine validation of smoking status; Glasgow et al., 1993). In most topics in health behavior research, well-validated assessments are available and supported by large measurement literatures (Dubbert, in press; Niaura & Abrams, in press; Wadden, Brownell, & Foster, in press).

In many types of studies of health behavior, technically involved or time-consuming assessments are not feasible, as in the case of large epidemiological studies of the prevalence of these habits, their distribution across segments of the population, and predictors of their relative frequency. Such studies are often very useful, as they have adequate statistical power to detect even small effects, and can help elucidate the determinants and effects of these behaviors. However, when self-reports of health behavior are used in these studies, artifacts associated with social desirability must be considered as alternative explanation of the observed effects. For example, the personality trait of conscientiousness is generally positively valued in Western cultures. Hence, correlations between self-reports of this trait and self-reports of regular exercise, prudent dietary patterns, and engagement in preventive practices (e.g., dental flossing) could be inflated by the common or overlapping variance in socially desirable response styles. Such alternative explanations for potentially important associations among health behaviors and predictor variables obtained through self-reports should be evaluated in smaller or better-funded studies involving more compelling assessments.

This potential artifact is particularly troubling in the context of intervention research. Except for very unusual instances in which the "treatment" is not communicated directly and explicitly to participants (e.g., community or policy-level interventions involving taxes or restrictions in access to cigarettes), health behavior change interventions typically convey a clear message that such change is both highly desirable and possible. Hence, there is a clear demand characteristic inherent in these interventions. If outcomes are assessed primarily through self-reports, then seemingly significant and important treatment outcome effects could be inflated by the tendency to respond to clear demands for healthy behavior with socially desirable self-reports. Of course, this alternative interpretation can be managed in part through the inclusion of comparison conditions that differ on the active ingredients of the intervention but are otherwise equivalent in demands for change. Nonetheless, multimethod assessments that go beyond self-reports are valuable additions to the outcome assessment protocol in health behavior change studies.

More recent research evolving from the cognitive psychology of memory and recall suggests another very important caution in the use of self-reports of health behavior. If individuals already know that they have a specific disease or are at high risk for some reason (e.g., positive family history), then hypothesis-driven recall could bias their self-reports of well-established behavioral risk factors (Croyle & Loftus, 1993). That is to say, knowing that (a) one has a specific disease and (b) a particular behavior is a contributing factor in that disease can lead to a confirmatory bias in which the individual "finds" evidence of his or her elevated standing on this behavioral risk factor. In epidemiological research, comparisons between individuals with known disease and healthy controls on possible behavioral risk factors is a common strategy. However, all such cross-sectional studies of risk contain this potential interpretive limitation if they rely on self-reports of health behavior.

As previously noted, virtually all of the major topics in health behavior have accumulated a fairly advanced assessment literature. Clearly, the design of health behavior research should make extensive use of these literatures (Dubbert, in press; Kelly & Kalichman, in press; Niaura &

Abrams, in press; Wadden et al., in press). Consumers of health behavior research should also be familiar with the optimal methods of assessment in a given domain, as well as with the general issues outlined in the preceding discussion.

Testing Health Behavior Models

Despite its relatively brief history, health psychology includes several highly detailed and quite useful conceptual models of the determinants of health behavior, as well as the processes involved in change and maintenance of such change. The *transtheoretical* or *stages of change model* (Prochaska & DiClemente, 1984), *self-efficacy theory* (Bandura, 1977), *health belief model* (Janz & Becker, 1984), and *relapse prevention model* (Marlatt & Gordon, 1985) are perhaps the most influential perspectives in research on various aspects of the determinants of health behavior, the process of related changes, and influences on maintenance of such changes (Weinstein, Rothman, & Sutton, 1998). Clear theories that generate specific predictions have a positive effect on the quality of research and on the likelihood that it will produce cumulative knowledge (Meehl, 1978). Examples of the key constructs in these models are listed in Table 10.1.

In order to reap the benefits of such theories, the measures of these key constructs must be reliable and valid. Yet, all too often measures are developed for use in a single study and are not subjected to adequate psychometric evaluation. For example, apart from the tests of primary hypotheses in such studies, often there is no independent evidence that measures of the key predictors of health behavior actually assess the specific construct of interest—that is, that they

TABLE 10.1   Psychological Influences on Health Behaviors

Person Variable	Example
Health-relevant encodings	• Internal representations of health and risk. • Attentional strategies in processing health information.
Health beliefs and expectations	• Outcome expectancies for health behaviors. • Self-efficacy for health behaviors.
Affects	• Emotional impact of health information. • Feelings about the self.
Health goals and values	• Desired health outcomes and their subjective importance. • Health-relevant goals and life tasks.
Self-regulatory competencies and skills	• Knowledge and strategies for overcoming barriers to change. • Planning and problem solving for relapse and maintenance.

Note. Adapted from S. M. Miller, Shoda, and Hurley (1996; p. 73).

display convergent and discriminant validity. The latter is of particular concern, given the closely related constructs listed in Table 10.1 (Weinstein, 1993). It is quite possible that distinctly labeled but functionally highly overlapping variables are examined across studies, but this redundancy is not recognized due to a failure to conduct formal studies of convergent and divergent validity (i.e., discriminant validity). The broad theories of determinants of health behavior receive much more attention than do the smaller—but critical—measurement theories implicit in such research. However, the extent to which the measures of health beliefs, self-efficacy, and related constructs specifically assess the intended construct is no less important a component of the nomological net in evaluating the theory than are the primary associations of these measures with health behavior outcomes.

Health behavior theories often specify conditions under which a potential determinant of health behavior (e.g., outcome expectancies) will have a larger or smaller effect on the behavioral outcome. Other elements of these theories often specify additional constructs through which a given determinant exerts its effects. Yet, these questions of moderation and mediation, respectively, are often confused (Weinstein, 1993), and often they are not tested with the appropriate statistical procedures (Baron & Kenny, 1986; Holmbeck, 1997). To have their maximum positive effect on the cumulative value of health behavior research, models of health behavior must generate specific conceptual questions and predictions, which are then tied directly to appropriate statistical hypotheses and tests. These linkages among measurement, design, and analysis should be guided by conceptual models at each step.

Some models of health behavior appropriately include biological determinants of health behavior. For example, a growing body of research has demonstrated that smoking involves genetic predispositions and addictive mechanisms that limit or moderate the effectiveness of behavioral interventions (Niaura & Abrams, in press). Similarly, behavioral interventions for weight loss must contend with genetic predispositions and underlying biological impediments to weight loss (Wadden et al., in press). The same behavioral risk status may reflect varying levels of biological contributions, and hence comprehensive models and studies of the determinants of risk behavior must consider such factors. For many years, traditional biomedical research has been appropriately criticized for failing to include psychosocial factors; health psychology research must avoid the parallel error. Hence, study samples must be carefully assessed and described on relevant biological contributions to health behavior, and their role in moderating or mediating the effects of psychosocial determinants of health behavior examined.

Some of the most influential models of the determinants of health behavior and processes underlying change include critical temporal dimensions. For example, stage models posit a sequence of time-linked processes through which health behaviors change (e.g., Prochaska & DiClemente, 1984). Often, these models are tested in cross-sectional studies, rather than the prospective research designs that provide the strongest and most valid test of such models. In cross-sectional tests, the predictions of stage models regarding the discreteness, nature, and sequence of stages can be artifactually supported (T. Q. Miller, 1994; Weinstein et al., 1998). Hence, cross-sectional tests of stage models and other temporal theories must be seen as preliminary and their findings interpreted as providing limited support.

However, in the design and interpretation of prospective studies, care must be taken to make sure that the timing of assessments corresponds to the underlying model. For example, the highly influential *relapse prevention model* of Marlatt and Gordon (1985) specifies a variety of time-linked influences on the likelihood and implications of initial failures to maintain desired changes in health behavior. Some of the constructs are seen as exerting their effects over both long and short periods of time (e.g., behavioral skills or competencies). Others are equally important in the model, but exert their effects over much briefer, delimited periods (e.g., urges to smoke, exposure to high risk situations or cues for smoking). Designs that assess predictors of relapse initially and health behavior change several weeks or months later would provide strong and sensitive tests of the former class of predictors, but would provide much less sensitive and potentially quite inaccurate tests of the importance of the more fleeting determinants of relapse. As a complement to the more traditional prospective designs, studies that incorporate frequent assessment of these constructs on a daily or even more frequent basis can be analyzed with hierarchical linear modeling (HLM) techniques to provide very sensitive tests (e.g., Shiffman et al., 1994; Shiffman, Paty, Gnys, Kassel, & Hickox, 1996; Shiffman et al., 1997). A typical protocol might assess urges to smoke or overeat on an hourly basis over several days, and examine their concurrent and prospective associations with these unhealthy behaviors. Such designs can be constructed so as to include even advanced questions involving mediators and moderators of these effects, and test both intra-individual (i.e., idiographic) and traditional interindividual (i.e., nomothetic) associations. However, the measurement and analysis challenges in this daily experience, diary, or experience sampling research are considerable (Affleck et al., 1999; J. E. Schwartz & Stone, 1998).

The explanatory value of models of health behavior likely varies across several factors. Notably, gender, ethnicity, and socioeconomic status are themselves important influences on behavioral aspects of risk, but these factors might also alter the effects of key concepts in models of health behavior. For example, concerns about weight gain might be differentially involved in the initiation and cessation of smoking among adolescent girls as opposed to boys, and this difference could alter the importance of other predictors of health behavior (e.g., health beliefs, self-efficacy expectations). Similarly, socioeconomic status and associated living circumstances likely alter access to safe and enjoyable places to exercise. These effects not only likely influence activity levels directly, but would also likely moderate the importance of other determinants of the adoption and maintenance of regular exercise. Thus, the external validity or generalizability of health behavior research is an important but understudied question.

Behavioral Risk Reduction and Preventive Interventions

After important predictors of health behavior have been identified, interventions can be designed and evaluated in a theory-driven manner. The range of intervention approaches in health behavior and prevention research poses obvious methodological challenges. For example, in smoking research, traditional psychological and behavior therapy approaches delivered in individual or small group formats are a mainstay of research (Niaura & Abrams, in press). However, large-scale approaches (e.g., advertising, policy programs, combined approaches) in which organizations (e.g., schools) or communities are the unit of analysis are increasingly common. These latter approaches reflect the fact that researchers, public health officials, and policy makers increasingly recognize that prevalent behavioral risk factors must be addressed not only at the level of individuals, but also in more population-based approaches that incorporate behavior change principles. Such large-scale interventions pose particular challenges in study design and quantitative evaluation, most of which are beyond our present scope.

In the more traditional individual and small group approaches, many issues described above and other methodological considerations quite familiar to intervention researchers are relevant. For example, adequate assessments of health behavior outcomes must be included, especially in cases in which the inherent expectations or demands for change communicated in such interventions could lead to overestimates of treatment effects when outcomes are assessed solely through self-reports. Independent assessments of the

integrity of intervention protocols are important in order to establish that independent variables were implemented appropriately and reliably (Waltz, Addis, Koerner, & Jacobson, 1993). Similarly, comparison conditions must be carefully selected so as to control nonspecific factors potentially influencing health behavior outcomes. In many cases, the intervention research literature has matured to the point at which simple comparisons with no-treatment or waiting-list controls are not appropriate. Rather, designs drawing comparisons between new interventions and standard treatments previously found to be effective are appropriate, as are dismantling designs in which the elements within compound effective interventions are examined to identify the critical component or components (Kendall, Flannery-Schroeder, & Ford, 1999). However, the application of these classic issues in intervention research design (e.g., assessing intervention integrity, selection of comparison groups) must be considered carefully in some types of health behavior change research, as when interventions are very brief (e.g., informational or motivational interventions) and delivered by physicians or other health professionals during routine care. The methodological issues are clearly relevant, but traditional strategies must be adapted to fit the specific intervention approach and context.

Across most health behavior changes (e.g., smoking cessation, exercise, and diet programs) several common problems emerge. First, most people can successfully initiate short-term changes, but the maintenance of these changes is severely limited (Brownell, Marlatt, Lichtenstein, & Wilson, 1986). In some cases (e.g., smoking cessation, weight loss), return to preintervention behavior or conditions are the most common outcome (Dubbert, in press; Niaura & Abrams, in press; Wadden et al., in press). Hence, even in well-controlled randomized designs, initial health behavior changes immediately following treatment are rarely of substantive importance. In many cases, substantive contributions to the literature require follow-up periods of a year or longer.

The need for longer follow-up periods exacerbates a common problem in intervention research—the statistical management of dropouts and missing outcome data. Nonrandom attrition is a clear threat to internal validity in health behavior change intervention, especially in light of the fact that such dropouts can plausibly be attributed to treatment failures or relapse. For example, participants in smoking cessation or weight loss interventions who relapse may not return to treatment for fear of embarrassment. If such failure-driven dropouts are differentially distributed across treatment and comparison conditions, conclusions regarding group differences can be invalid. This likelihood is the justification of traditional intent-to-treat analyses, in which all randomized participants are included and pretreatment levels on key outcomes are substituted for missing data (Flick, 1988; Kendall et al., 1999). However, dropout status may not be equivalent to full relapse, and in applications in which missing data may be common and unavoidable (e.g., large-scale programs) the traditional, conservative approach may produce highly misleading results.

Hence, in recent years, this standard approach has been challenged and a variety of potentially more informative alternatives proposed (Little & Yau, 1998; Shadish, Hu, Glaser, Kownacki, & Wong, 1998). These techniques have in common a goal of estimating the effect on outcome results of a range of assumptions about the status of dropouts. However, none of these techniques are substitutes for valid information on participants. Therefore, in designing and conducting health behavior change research, minimizing dropouts and missing data is a paramount concern. In reporting and evaluating such research, information about the degree of missing data, its distribution across treatment arms, its correlates with pretreatment factors (e.g., demographic characteristics, initial severity, etc.), and the potential impact on the validity of statistical tests and related conclusions about the significance and magnitude of intervention effects (or the lack thereof) must be reported and considered carefully.

When interventions are delivered to more than one individual at a time, the nesting of observations within groups and the resulting potential dependencies among the observations must be considered. Previously unacquainted individuals within small groups, members of a couple or family, students within a given classroom or school, or residents within a community assigned to a treatment and receiving that intervention together do not provide truly independent observations. Hence, treatment of their data as representing independent observations can seriously violate the underlying assumptions of many traditional statistical techniques. Typically this failure to recognize dependencies leads to an overestimate of the significance of intervention effects (Feng, Diehr, Peterson, & McLerran, 2001). The most common version of this problem is when psychosocial interventions are delivered in small groups of previously unacquainted participants. Unique features of individual groups, such as positive versus negative group climate, cohesion, or morale, can alter the effectiveness of treatment (Etringer, Gregory, & Lando, 1984). This issue is problematic in many areas of health behavior change (e.g., Rooney & Murray, 1996) and is quite familiar in other areas of traditional psychological intervention research (Crits-Christoph & Mintz, 1991). Recent HLM models and other techniques can be adapted to this design problem, with additional benefits (e.g., more efficient management of missing observations) beyond the accurate estimate of intervention effects while recognizing dependency among observations across individuals (Feng et al., 2001).

As in all areas of psychological intervention research, valid evidence that a treatment program produces statistically significant changes in health behavior is important, but such evidence begs the question of the magnitude, importance, or clinical significance of those effects (Kendall, 1999). In the case of health behavior change, however, many of the typical methods of quantifying clinically significant change (e.g., comparisons with normal populations) are not ideal when population norms are not necessarily desired states (e.g., degree of overweight, level of regular physical activity, dietary consumption of saturated fat). In some cases, such as smoking cessation, clearly defined outcomes (i.e., nonsmoking status) have obvious clinical significance, given their demonstrated association with future health outcomes. In others, such as weight loss, the levels of risk reduction can be estimated from epidemiological evidence regarding the risk factor. However, the degree of risk associated with excess pounds, frequency and intensity of exercise, and intake of fat as calculated from prospective studies of the health effects of these risk factors provides at best an indirect indication of the likely health benefits accruing from a change in these characteristics of a given magnitude. Hence, some index of effect size and the percentage of intervention participants displaying changes within each of several ranges (e.g., weight losses of 5–10%; 10–15%, etc.) should be regularly reported and compared to what is known about the likely health effects of such changes. It is interesting to note that participant satisfaction with treatment results may be a misleading index for some types of health behavior change. For example, reductions in excess body weight that have clear medical significance for the reduction of serious health risk and improvements in health are actually below the level of weight loss that participants rate as the minimal loss necessary to be satisfactory (Wadden et al., in press).

Ideally, the impact of health behavior interventions could be evaluated on the basis of their effects on morbidity and mortality; in most cases, however, this is not feasible, given that such beneficial consequences of even very effective interventions may take many years to emerge. For example, successful interventions for smoking cessation in young adults would not produce notable effects on cardiac, pulmonary, or cancer morbidity or mortality for decades. Further, it is important to recognize that the associations between even the most well-documented and important risk factors (e.g., smoking) and health outcomes are probabilistic, and even the most effective interventions have effect sizes in the small to moderate range. Hence, the likely—and usually modest—impact of even an effective intervention can be estimated by the product of the effect size for the association of the risk factor with disease and the effect size for the intervention effect on the risk factor (R. M. Kaplan, 1984). This is one reason that even in large trials, significant effects on documented morbidity and mortality have proven elusive (Hancock, Sanson-Fisher, & Redman, 1997). However, this is not to say the preventive interventions are ill-advised, as health behavior changes in a large segment of the population would likely have important effects on the incidence of prevalent diseases that are heavily influenced by behavior.

STRESS AND DISEASE

Perhaps the oldest questions at the interface of behavioral and biomedical science involve long-suspected effects of stress, emotion, and other aspects of *mind* on physiological changes, disease, and other important outcomes of the *body* (McMahon, 1976); Effects of stress, emotion, social relations, and other risk and resilience factors on disease certainly were central in the emergence of health psychology and behavioral medicine, as they were in the earlier field of psychosomatic medicine. A broad array of rapidly evolving methods is brought to bear on such questions, producing increasingly specific and scientifically compelling answers.

The basic model guiding this area of research holds that characteristics of people (e.g., emotions, personality traits) and aspects of the environment (e.g., social networks, job stress) can affect the pathophysiology of disease. In general, these effects are believed to occur through the intervening effects of physiological changes associated with stress and emotion (Lovallo, 1997). Of course, these same characteristics of people and their environments could influence disease through the pathway of health behavior or lifestyle, as described previously. For example, social support could reduce one's risk of heart disease because it attenuates physiological stress responses that would otherwise accelerate atherosclerosis, or because it encourages better health behavior (e.g., a more prudent diet, less alcohol consumption, and more frequent exercise). Hence, this alternative explanation must be addressed in many studies of these more direct psychobiological influences on disease (Adler & Matthews, 1994; Cohen & Rodriguez, 1995; Smith & Gallo, 2001).

Several types of research comprise this general topic in health psychology. *Psychosocial epidemiology* relates personality or social-environmental risk factors to health outcomes. This work is of necessity observational and nonexperimental in nature, and therefore provides evidence of associations between psychosocial variables and health outcomes. *Animal research* provides the opportunity for more compelling experimental manipulations of psychosocial variables and invasive assessments of disease processes and outcomes. However, as previously noted, the generalizability of such studies to human disease is a complex and critical question. *Human mechanism research* tests models of the psychophysiological links between psychosocial inputs and health outcomes. Finally, *intervention research* examines the impact of stress-reducing interventions and related treatments on disease processes and outcomes.

Each of these types of research should be guided by a clear and current model of the pathophysiology of the disease in question, including the ways in which this process changes over the natural history of the specific illness. In some cases, general associations between psychosocial risk factors and longevity or all-cause mortality are potentially quite important. These outcomes are obviously important and any reliable predictor of them is inherently of interest. Further, general associations with health and longevity are quite useful in initial investigations of a potential psychosocial risk factor. However, such associations beg the question of what specific diseases or conditions are affected, during what stage of their development and course, and what mechanisms account for the observed effects. Hence, more general associations, after they are established as reliable, should be followed by tests of more specific associations and mechanisms.

In most cases, the pathophysiology of the disease of interest (e.g., coronary heart disease, cancer, HIV, hypertension) is at least generally articulated in current biomedical research, providing the foundations for this type of research. For example, coronary heart disease begins with fatty deposits at the sites of microscopic injuries to the lining of the coronary arteries, appearing as early as late childhood or early adolescence. The further deposition of lipids, inflammation, and other processes at these sites leads to the slow, progressive, but asymptomatic narrowing of the arteries as the atherosclerotic plaques or lesions intrude into the artery opening. Much later in the natural history of the disease, other events (e.g., myocardial ischemia, thrombosis, arrythmia) produce the overt manifestations of coronary heart disease (e.g., chest pain, myocardial infarction, sudden death). Hence, statistical associations between psychosocial risk factors and coronary heart disease outcomes (e.g., myocardial infarction, coronary death) observed in epidemiological studies could reflect an influence at one or more of the very different stages in this long and complex natural history, affected through one or more of many specific psychobiological mechanisms (Smith & Ruiz, in press). Therefore, models of the potential effects of a psychosocial risk factor on CHD must attend to this complex array of changing, medically plausible connections. Further, the design and timing of risk-reducing interventions would clearly depend on a more refined understanding of the specific processes involved.

Epidemiological Studies of Psychosocial Risk

Reliable associations between psychosocial risk factors and disease are the empirical cornerstone of research in this area. Without such evidence, there is little justification to assert that personality, stress, emotions, or characteristics of the social environment affect health. Studies of this type examine characteristics that might influence the development of disease, but also of interest are the associations of these characteristics with the prognosis of established disease. Studies of both types have common potential methodological limitations, as well as unique ones.

The Limitations of Cross-Sectional Designs

The potential association between psychosocial risk factors and health outcomes has often been examined with very limited research designs and methods of assessment. For example, cross-sectional comparisons of participants' levels of a given risk factor in groups with and without a given disease have been common. However, many psychosocial variables (e.g., negative emotions, coping strategies or styles) could plausibly both influence and be influenced by physical illness (Cohen & Rodriguez, 1995). Hence, the direction of causality is a very serious concern in cross-sectional designs. Further, studies of this type (i.e., cross-sectional case-control designs) often compare patients suffering from a specific condition recruited from a medical clinic of some sort with controls recruited from a convenient population (e.g., hospital employees or medical outpatients on routine visits). Selection processes differ across such groups, and those processes may be associated with the psychosocial risk factor of interest. For example, patients with early stages of asymptomatic cancer undergoing treatment in a specialty clinic may be characterized by a greater degree of health worry than are individuals with a similar level or stage of cancer who have not yet sought medical attention. Hence, health worries and associated variables (e.g., negative emotionality) are likely to be overrepresented in the clinic sample. Therefore, psychosocial differences between cases and controls could reflect selection processes rather than the presence versus absence of the disease.

Given the maturing status of the field, cross-sectional designs should be used only in initial investigations, and they should be interpreted cautiously and replicated with more compelling prospective studies as soon as possible. Some newer cross-sectional approaches are available that are less susceptible to these limitations. For example, noninvasive imaging techniques are available to assess asymptomatic atherosclerosis in population-based samples of outwardly healthy individuals (e.g., Iribarren et al., 2000).

The Assessment of Health End Points

Even in prospective studies, the history of health psychology and behavioral medicine has included recurring problems with the health outcomes assessed in studies of psychosocial risk factors. Self-reports of physical symptoms or related behaviors (e.g., visits to a physician) are often interpreted as reasonable indications of actual disease. This approach to quantifying health outcomes blurs the critical distinction between illness behavior and disease. Illness behavior refers to things that people typically do when suffering from a major or even minor disease or illness (e.g., report symptoms, visit a doctor, etc.), whereas disease refers to the underlying objective condition (e.g., infection, etc.). These indicators are typically highly correlated, and self-reports of symptoms and health status predict future health—including mortality—even when controlling for independently assessed initial health (Idler & Benyamini, 1997; McGee, Liao, Cao, & Cooper, 1999). Hence, self-reports of symptoms and health status clearly contain variance relevant to actual health and disease.

However, illness behavior and actual illness are far from perfectly correlated. More important is that the unique variance in illness behavior that is not associated with actual disease may itself be associated with purported psychosocial risk factors. For example, individual differences in neuroticism or negative affectivity are correlated with the tendency to report physical symptoms in the absence of—or that exceed—actual disease (Costa & McCrae, 1987; Watson & Pennebaker, 1989). These same characteristics also reliably predict actual disease and mortality (Smith & Gallo, 2001). Hence, a statistical association between a measure of negative emotionality and self-reported physical symptoms could reflect an actual psychosocial effect on disease, an effect on unfounded somatic complaints, or some combination of these very different phenomena. When the question of interest involves actual disease, care should be taken to measure it directly. Further, when illness behaviors are assessed as the outcome, generalizations about associations with actual illness and disease are unjustified. In studies of initially healthy populations and groups with established disease, care must be taken to distinguish between end points that might be influenced by illness behavior—such as (re)hospitalizations in response to worrisome symptom presentations—from those that unambiguously reflect actual disease (e.g., documented myocardial infarction).

The Assessment of Psychosocial Predictors

The assessment of psychosocial predictors of health and disease in epidemiological and clinical studies of psychosomatic associations has also been problematic. In one common limitation, measures of personality characteristics or aspects of the social environment are often included without adequate evidence that they assess the predictive construct of interest (i.e., convergent validity) and not a competing construct (divergent or discriminant validity). In developing accurate statistical accounts of risk factors, the meaning of scores on assessments of psychosocial risk factors does not matter—only their predictive utility is of interest. However, unlike actuaries, researchers in health psychology are typically interested in testing theories or models of the potential psychosocial influences on subsequent health and disease. Therefore, the construct validity of these assessments is a primary concern. Obviously, reliable prospective associations between measures of stress, emotion, personality, or social environments and subsequent disease are a critical component of the empirical foundation of the field. However, without independent evidence that measures of these psychosocial factors are valid, the importance of such prospective findings is severely limited.

In a closely related problem, the array of personality characteristics and features of the social environment studied as risk factors has proliferated without adequate attention to the potential overlap or even redundancies among measures purporting to assess distinct risk factors. Scales with very different names may in fact be psychometrically indistinguishable (Smith & Gallo, 2001). For example, measures of individual differences in anxiety and depression may be so highly correlated as to be indistinguishable, and may be more accurately interpreted as assessing the broader trait of neuroticism or negative affectivity (Watson et al., 1995). This issue of overlap with previously established, broad personality traits has even been evident when scales are developed to assess very specific, novel individual differences, such as optimism (Smith, Pope, Rhodewalt, & Poulton, 1989) and hardiness (Funk, 1992). Finally, psychosocial epidemiology implicitly parses the list of risk factors into characteristics of individuals (e.g., personality, emotion) and aspects of the social environments they inhabit (e.g., social support). However, measures of social risk factors often display evidence of heritability in behavioral genetics research (Kendler, 1997; Plomin, Reiss, Heatherington, & Howe, 1994) and substantial associations with measures of well-established personality traits (Pierce,

Lakey, Sarason, Sarason, & Joseph, 1997). Hence, even though a measure of labeled social support or social isolation may have a very consistent predictive association with subsequent health, it is not obvious that it is a characteristic of the social environment that in fact confers that risk. Compelling evidence of convergent and discriminant validity is quite useful in strengthening that interpretation; without it, many very different conclusions are equally plausible.

This literature could be strengthened if widely accepted frameworks and established methods were used in the construct validation process. For example, the traits and inventories associated with the five-factor model of personality could be used to examine the similarities, differences, and potential redundancies of personality characteristics examined as potential risk factors (Smith & Williams, 1992). A version of the five-factor model that includes basic dimensions of interpersonal behavior (Trapnell & Wiggins, 1990) has been used in similar evaluations of measures intended to assess aspects of the social environment (Gallo & Smith, 1999; Trobst, 2000). These well-established nomological nets provide a conceptual and methodological context for a systematic and cumulative literature on psychosocial risk factors, in which construct validity is a central concern and the overlap and alternative interpretation of measures of psychosocial risk are identified routinely. At a minimum, all studies of psychosocial risk should attend directly to the issue of the validity and specificity of the main predictive measures.

Third Variables and Correlated Risk Factors

Many of these issues are inherent in or at least exacerbated by the correlational nature of epidemiological studies. The problem of third variables must always be considered in critical evaluation of the results of such studies. As described previously, many of the alternative third variables are obvious confounds (e.g., initial health status, selection factors) or are conceptually quite different from the predictor of interest (e.g., health behaviors). Such variables provide alternative explanations for associations observed in epidemiological research. Careful assessment of these third variables and their inclusion in multivariate analyses can reduce their plausibility. However, their role cannot be ruled out completely, given the possibility of their imperfect measurement and resulting undercorrection of their contribution to observed associations. Other third variables suggest alternative pathways linking psychosocial risk factors and health outcomes, beyond the hypothesized psychobiological mechanisms in this research area. For example, analyses that control health behaviors associated with a psychosocial risk factor can appropriately be seen as testing alternative models. If personality characteristics and features of the social environment predict subsequent health and disease, but statistical control of smoking, diet, exercise or other lifestyle factors eliminates this effect, then a specific mediational model of the epidemiological association has been supported. Of course, partial mediation in such cases may suggest multiple mechanisms (e.g., health behavior *and* psychobiological pathways) linking risk factors and health outcomes. Other third variables take the form of correlated psychosocial risk factors. For example, both depressive symptoms and low social support are reliable risk factors for the initial development of CHD, and predict recurrent cardiac events and death among patients with established cardiovascular disease (Krantz & McCeney, 2002; Smith & Ruiz, in press). In epidemiology, the standard approach to correlated risk factors is the statistical test of their independent effects, such as in multiple linear or logistic regression models. In some instances, this is quite sensible. For example, if both smoking and low levels of physical activity predict CHD and if these behavior are reliably correlated, then risk stratification and prevention strategies can be effectively designed only after their unique or independent effects are established. However, in the case of psychosocial risk factors like depression and social isolation, the standard approach may be both useful and potentially misleading. At one level, the independent predictive effects of depression and social isolation are interesting and important. If the general approach is accepted, the validity of the findings is threatened only to the extent that the predictors are closely correlated. In such cases, multicollinearity renders the effects of estimates of independent effects unstable. However, there are many reasons that these characteristics are related, as depression is known to be both a cause and a consequence of problematic social relations (Davila, Bradbury, Cohan, & Tochluk, 1997; Johnson & Jacob, 1997). Therefore, the forced statistical separation of the characteristics creates a counterfactual (Meehl, 1970) or artificial circumstance in which the unique variance in either depression or social isolation may not be representative of the construct that confers risk. Further, the shared variance may reflect the process most relevant to disease (e.g., chronic isolation and conflict engendered by and promoting depressive behavior). Therefore, the most familiar strategy of testing statistically created independent effects must be viewed with caution.

Sometimes, the covariation among psychosocial risk factors occurs across levels of analysis in the biopsychosocial model. For example, individual differences in hostility and other negative cognitive or affective processes are associated with low socioeconomic status. It is important to note that low socioeconomic status not only confers risk of serious illness

and early mortality when measured at the level of individuals (e.g., their education or income), but the SES of the individual's place of residence (e.g., average income levels) also confers independent risk (Yen & Kaplan, 1999). These recently documented *place effects* raise a host of alternative interpretations in psychosocial epidemiology. For example, low neighborhood SES could confer risk because it promotes stress and negative emotions. Alternatively, reports of stress and negative emotion could be a noncausal correlate of some other health-threatening aspect of low-SES environments (e.g., low levels of perceived control). Some evidence suggests that religious participation (e.g., church attendance) is associated with reduced risk of serious illness and improved longevity (McCollough et al., 2000). Yet this could reflect either some sort of intra-individual effect (e.g., dampened stress responses stemming from attenuated appraisals of threat in everyday activities) or the operation of a correlated place effect (e.g., increased exposure to supportive and agreeable people).

Alternative strategies for dealing with correlated psychosocial risk factors are increasingly available, but not yet widely used. For example, cluster analytic strategies and some types of factor analysis can be used to group individuals—rather than variables—on the basis of patterns of co-occurring personality and social environmental characteristics (Gallo & Smith, 1999). The covariation among individual differences (i.e., personality traits), individual SES, and the SES of the local environment suggest a variety of causal models. Personality traits could mediate the effects of SES on health, or they could be a noncausal marker for those effects. Hierarchical causal models, such as SES place effects on health mediated by personality or emotional characteristics, can be tested in appropriate statistical models, if the sampling strategy has been designed appropriately (i.e., individuals nested within multiple neighborhoods). The general point to be taken from this discussion is that correlations among psychosocial risk factors—rather than simply a confounding nuisance—reflects the complexities of everyday life. Hence, choices among various statistical approaches to the issue should be based on a clear understanding of their potential limitations and preferably guided by underlying conceptual models. Ideally, the resulting analytic approaches can be used to test directly competing conceptual models of the associations between risk factors and health outcomes.

Sampling in Epidemiological and Clinical Risk Factor Studies

Another common limitation in epidemiological studies involves sampling. Ideally, a large, carefully selected representative sample is recruited, assessed with well-validated psychosocial measures, and then followed for the many years necessary for the emergence of serious illness in sufficient frequency to permit sensitive tests of prospective associations. However, this is a very slow and expensive approach to testing hypotheses about psychosocial influences on disease process. In many instances, small samples of convenience (e.g., medical students, college freshmen, military draftees, etc.) that have undergone psychosocial screenings for other purposes are available in archival data sets. These archives present important opportunities to accelerate the progress of psychosocial epidemiological research through the time-saving process of prospective studies that are available much more rapidly and inexpensively. Current health outcomes (e.g., survival, current diagnoses) can be related to the psychosocial data collected years ago. However, the psychosocial assessments available are quite likely less than ideal, relative to the standards described previously. Further, the selection process not only places the obvious limitations on the generalizability of the results to other groups, but may also be the source of other interpretive limitations. For example, the validity of self-reports of negative psychosocial characteristics may be suspect among individuals who underwent such assessments as part of college admissions or similar procedures. Hence, the scientific value of studies of such convenience samples involves a trade-off between a more rapid development of the literature versus more definitive studies.

Sampling in clinical studies of psychosocial risk factors as predictors of the course of established disease pose other potential limitations. For example, if a risk factor (e.g., depression) exerts an effect on the initial development of a life-threatening disease (e.g., CHD), persons who survive long enough to be recruited into clinical studies will not provide a representative sample for studying this risk factor. Persons who survive despite a high level of the risk factor are likely to be more resilient to its negative effects than are those who did not survive the initial presentation of the disease (T. Q. Miller, Turner, Tindale, Posavac, & Dugoni, 1991; R. B. Williams, 2000). Of course, questions about the psychosocial predictors of the course of a disease are important in and of themselves, and the appropriate sample consists by definition of those who survived its initial presentation. However, if a risk factor has a significant effect in initially healthy samples and not among those with established disease, this may reflect moderation of its effects by the nonrandom selection into clinical populations.

Effect Sizes

Valid evidence of reliable associations between psychosocial risk factors and subsequent disease or mortality raises a final question; is the effect large enough to be of interest or practical concern? Certainly, any significant association is quite likely to be conceptually interesting, as it suggests a potential influence of the mind on the body. But the clinical or practical significance is a different matter. When the indexes of effect size commonly used in epidemiology (e.g., relative risk ratios) are converted to metrics more familiar to psychologists (e.g., R^2), they often appear small. Very important risk factors typically explain less than 10% of the variance in objectively measured morbidity or mortality. However, individual predictors would not be expected to account for a large portion of the variance in complex, multifactorial diseases. Further, even small effects take on added importance when they predict prevalent and potentially serious diseases.

Animal Models

Given the interpretive ambiguities inherent in the observational or correlational nature of epidemiological research, animal models of psychosocial influences on disease provide a valuable complementary methodological approach. Animals can be randomly assigned to experimental manipulations of environmental stress or other purported risk factors, and invasive methods can be used to assess critical end points. The condensed natural history of disease and life span of many species, relative to humans, is also useful. For most of the major diseases (e.g., atherosclerosis, hypertension, cancer, diabetes, etc.), animal models have been developed in basic biomedical research. These models are usually based on rodents or nonhuman primates, and can be readily adapted to examine psychosocial influences on the development and progression of disease. Further, pharmacological or even surgical interventions are available to manipulate the mechanisms believed to link psychosocial risk factors to disease end points. Hence, animal models are a central source of evidence in psychosomatic research (Carroll & Overmier, 2001).

However, this approach contains obvious limitations as well. The most basic involves the equivalence of the animal disease or physiological mechanism and the human phenomenon of interest. Typically, this issue has been addressed in the early stages of development of an animal model of a specific condition, but research should always be designed and evaluated with this issue in mind. Further, even if basic issues of parallel pathophysiology in humans and the animal model are addressed adequately, the equivalence of the human psychosocial influence of interest and its experimental animal analogue must be considered. Species-specific patterns of social behavior, for example, must be considered in developing an experimental analogue of social-environmental stress.

Psychobiological Mechanisms

As noted above, most current models of psychosocial influences on the development and course of disease identify the endocrine and autonomic correlates of stress and negative emotion as the primary pathway or mechanism (Lovallo, 1997). Briefly, through the endocrine responses (e.g., cortisol release), direct neural innervation by the sympathetic or parasympathetic branch of the autonomic nervous system, or both, the physiological effects of stress can initiate or hasten the development of a variety of disease processes if such responses are sufficiently pronounced, frequent, and prolonged. These mechanisms are most clearly identified in the case of the pathophysiological links between psychosocial risk factors and the development of cardiovascular disease (e.g., Krantz & McCeney, in press; Smith & Ruiz, in press) and disease processes mediated by the immune system, such as cancer (Andersen, in press; Andersen, Kiecolt-Glaser, & Glaser, 1994). However, a great variety of psychobiological models have been developed either by extending basic cardiovascular and immunological models to other diseases or by focusing on the physiology of other organ systems. Examples include rheumatoid arthritis (Keefe, Smith, Buffington, Studts, & Caldwell, in press), headache, and other types of chronic pain (Holroyd, in press; Turk & Okifuji, 2002), gastrointestinal disorders (Blanchard & Scharff, in press; Levenstein, in press), diabetes (Gonder-Frederick, Cox, & Ritterband, in press), and wound healing (Kiecolt-Glaser, McGuire, Robles, & Glaser, in press a, in press b).

This lengthy list of conditions with widely varying pathophysiologies underscores issues discussed earlier. Current research must be based on plausible models of the potential specific links between psychosocial processes and the pathophysiology of specific conditions. Older black-box models and those based on general models of stress and physiological arousal are no longer sufficient. Further, because most of these conditions are influenced by health behaviors and elements of lifestyle, behavioral models must be ruled out as alternative explanations, just as in psychosocial epidemiology. For example, effects of chronic stress on the immune system could be due to disrupted sleep or reductions in exercise rather than more direct psychobiological mechanisms (Hall et al., 1998).

Using the cardiovascular and immune mechanisms as examples, the stress responses linking psychosocial inputs and pathophysiological processes are complex. Even simple increases in heart rate in response to experimentally manipulated stressors involve both direct sympathetic and parasympathetic neural innervation, as well as indirect endocrine influences via the circulation. The list of elements of the immune system known to be influenced by stress mechanisms, let alone the actual neural and endocrine pathways involved in these effects, seems to expand exponentially with each passing year (Ader, Felten, & Cohen, 2001; Kiecolt-Glaser et al., in press). In addition to underscoring the importance of current conceptual models of pathophysiology, this complexity poses basic problems in design and analysis. In nearly all cases, state-of-the-art research by necessity assesses multiple correlated features of the stress response of interest. This mosaic of interdependent outcomes often requires multiple statistical tests. Atheoretical approaches to the control of Type I error rates (e.g., Bonferroni corrections) are one option for dealing with multiple dependent variables, but this method results in a potentially severe loss of statistical power. Given the time and expense involved in many studies of this type, overly conservative approaches to the problem are ill-advised. Clear, conceptually driven, a priori organization or prioritization of the list of outcomes can reduce the problem to some extent. Further, the use of multivariate procedures and the interpretation of composite outcomes can be useful (Huberty & Morris, 1989). The least acceptable approach, however, is the assessment of multiple components of a complex system without a priori rank ordering of their importance, followed by consideration of the unadjusted, significant effects among many significance tests computed.

Psychobiological mechanisms are generally conceptualized in two very distinct ways in this area of research. In the first, variation in physiological reactivity in a given system in response to potentially stressful stimuli is seen as reflecting an individual difference. Some individuals, for example, respond to daily stressors with particularly large and prolonged increases in blood pressure and heart rate. This stable individual difference, in turn, is hypothesized to place them at risk for the development of cardiovascular disease (Manuck, 1994). In tests of this conceptual model, basic issues in the assessment of individual differences have proven to be relevant. For example, estimates of this individual difference become more reliable with the addition of multiple stressors and occasions of measurement (Kamarck, Jennings, Pogue-Geile, & Manuck, 1994). Failure of responses to a single task on a single occasion of stress reactivity testing to predict an important health outcome may reflect a basic issue in assessment—single items typically provide unreliable estimates of an individual difference—rather than disconfirming evidence of a psychosomatic hypothesis. Hence, when physiological reactivity is conceptualized as an individual difference mechanism, research protocols should be designed so as to provide a reliable estimate, and evidence of that reliability becomes an important criterion in evaluating such studies.

The second conceptual model in this area considers physiological reactivity not as a stable individual difference variable, but as a mediating mechanism. Briefly, a psychosocial risk factor (e.g., social isolation, trait anger) is believed to affect health through its intervening effects on physiological responses. The most basic research addressing this type of model tests the predicted association between a measured or manipulated psychosocial risk factor—typically previously identified in epidemiological research—with some sort of psychophysiological response to an experimental stressor. This general approach raises other methodological concerns. Of course, the issue of the construct validity of the measure or manipulation of the psychosocial risk factor is a serious concern, as discussed previously, as is the relevance of the physiological response to what is known about the pathophysiology of the disease of interest. However, an often overlooked issue is the relevance of the experimental stressor. It is common for researchers to use easily controlled and standardized stressors, such as reaction time tasks or mental arithmetic. This has obvious advantages for reliability of implementation of independent variables and measurement of physiological responses. Yet the psychosocial risk factors of interest may not be clearly related to these relatively artificial and nonsocial challenges. Modeling the psychophysiological mechanisms underlying psychosocial risk factors arguably requires the use of conceptually relevant laboratory stress paradigms. For example, in tests of the hypothesis that trait anger and hostility confer increased risk of cardiovascular disease through the mechanism of cardiovascular and neuroendocrine reactivity to stressors, mental arithmetic or signaled reaction time tasks may provide a poor stressor in which to examine the expected psychophysiological response. Stressors more clearly relevant to this risk factor (e.g., interpersonal conflict, provocation) are more appropriate. A failure to find the expected association between a risk factor and physiological response may reflect the use of an inappropriate context or type of stressor rather than disconfirming evidence. Hence, a specific conceptual model of the psychosocial risk process is as important as the conceptual description of pathophysiology.

However, this more ecologically valid modeling of risk factors, relevant stressors, and their association with physiological response poses its own problems. In manipulating interpersonal constructs or social interactions in the psychophysiology laboratory, measured psychosocial variables or levels of manipulated stressors may be confounded with artifacts (e.g., speech volume or rate, movement) that alter physiological responses (Smith, Limon, Gallo, & Ngu, 1996;

Smith, Nealy, Kircher, & Limon, 1997). These potential artifacts must be measured or controlled in order to rule them out as alternative explanations for associations between psychosocial risk factors and physiological responses. The ecological validity of such social psychophysiological studies can be heightened further by studying these effects in the context of actual relationship interactions, such as those between spouses or friends. Further, care must be taken to assess the psychological meaning or impact of these complex stressors, in order to provide converging, independent evidence of the successful and specific manipulation of constructs of interest (Smith, Gallo, & Ruiz, in press). Manipulations intended to represent provocation, support, or efforts to exert social dominance are likely to be quite complex and could be interpreted by research participants in a variety of ways. Interpretations of both expected associations between psychosocial risk factors and physiological responses and the failure to find them are strengthened by independent evidence of the effectiveness and specificity of manipulations.

Even the most carefully crafted and assessed laboratory manipulations of factors hypothesized to influence psychophysiological responses will not truly capture the experience of such factors in daily life. Hence, an important complementary approach to studying psychobiological mechanisms involves the assessment of ambulatory physiological responses. Advances in the assessment of physiological responses during daily activities (e.g., salivary cortisol excretion, ambulatory blood pressure monitoring, etc.) can be combined with dairy assessments of daily experiences related to psychosocial risk factors (e.g., episodes of interpersonal conflict or job stress). Covariation between physiological responses and risk factors can be tested using appropriate statistical models (Affleck, Zautra, Tennen, & Armeli, 1999; Jaccard & Wan, 1993; J. E. Schwartz & Stone, 1998). The potential benefits in ecological validity inherent in this approach are obvious, but it is not without limitations. For example, the daily diary assessments of psychosocial risk factors pose their own challenges in terms of reliable and valid measurement. Further, the time frame (i.e., number of days of monitoring) and method (e.g., interval- vs. event-based) for sampling must be designed so as to capture adequately the independent variable of interest. Finally, a variety of complex decisions regarding implementation of the statistical analyses must be addressed in order to reach valid conclusions about the presence and magnitude of covariation between psychosocial processes and ambulatory physiological responses (Affleck et al., 1999).

Each of these issues concerns the validity of tests of the association between a risk factor and a hypothesized mediating mechanism. It is important to note that they do not provide an actual test of the mediational model. Research on such models typically addresses critical strands or pathways in such models, but formal tests of mediation require assessment of psychosocial risk factors, mediating mechanisms, and disease outcomes. Such designs are very rare, given the inherent time and expense involved. Hence, most research related to mediational models of psychosocial risk and underlying mechanisms must be interpreted cautiously. Failures to find predicted relationships would be strong disconfirming evidence, but confirming evidence for components of such model must not be mistaken for support for the full mediational hypothesis. More complete mediational tests of the more influential models will be important for the future of this research area. Until they are available, basic questions must be posed about any mechanism research (Cohen & Rabin, 1998). Are the physiological responses plausibly related to what is known about the specific disease? If they are biologically plausible, are they of sufficient magnitude and frequency as to influence the pathophysiology of disease?

Stress and Risk-Reducing Intervention Research

When reliable psychosocial predictors of disease are identified in epidemiological research and studies of mechanisms support the likely mediating role of the psychophysiology of stress responses, then it is appropriate to develop and test interventions intended to prevent or manage the disease by modifying the psychosocial risk factor or its underlying mechanism(s). Intervention research of this type should address methodological issues common to most treatment research (Kendall et al., 1999), with particular attention to how these issues are altered in the specific context of health research.

For example, all intervention research should carefully document the process by which potential participants are identified and recruited, in order to address issues of the sample's representativeness. In the case of stress-reducing interventions for individuals with established disease, they may come to be recruited after a multistage process of seeking medical attention, possibly limited response to traditional medical care (and hence, in need of additional treatment), and referral to specialty clinics (Turk & Rudy, 1990). This complex sequence of events is difficult to identify, and hence the representativeness of the sample can be quite difficult to document. Therefore, generalization of the results of such treatment studies to other populations must be made very cautiously. In terms of an adequate sample size, the choice of an intervention outcome is a critical consideration. If psychological outcomes (e.g., stress and levels of other risk factors) are the primary focus, prior intervention research can provide a reasonable estimate of likely effect sizes and hence can

guide the necessary power calculations for determining sample sizes. In many cases, however, such as new applications to a physiological mediating mechanism, such information may be difficult to obtain. Further, if intervention effects on medically documented morbidity or even mortality are of interest, sample size requirements for reasonably sensitive statistical tests will likely be considerable. In some cases, intermediate medical outcomes provide a compromise between the need for compelling outcomes and the cost and difficulty in treating and following enough participants for enough time to test effects on rare or slowly changing disease outcomes. For example, Blumenthal, Jiang, Babyak, and Krantz (1997) examined the effects of a stress management intervention for coronary patients on ambulatory ischemia as assessed via Holter monitoring. This index itself predicts risk of recurrent cardiac events and cardiac death, but shows sufficient variability across patients and over time to permit sensitive tests of treatment outcome with a fairly small sample studied for a brief period of time. In evaluating the results of stress or risk-reduction interventions that produce effects on physical disease outcomes, small samples should be an obvious reason to consider the findings tentative, as an a priori power analysis would likely suggest that large samples are needed to detect effects on such variables.

Even after careful randomization, initial differences in the health status of participants in different intervention and control conditions is a potential concern. The evaluation of the initial equivalence of randomized groups should include medical assessments that are established and accepted in the specific disease. Without such information, potentially small initial differences in important prognostic indicators could serve as an explanation for treatment effects (or the lack thereof) on physiological or disease outcomes. As in the case of behavioral risk-reducing interventions (e.g., smoking cessation) described previously, assessment of adherence to carefully described intervention procedures and the use of appropriate analytic strategies when interventions are delivered to more than one individual at a time (i.e., participants nested within therapy groups) are important but often overlooked in psychosocial risk interventions. For the assessment of psychosocial outcomes, the obvious advantages in expense and ease of administration associated with an exclusive reliance of self-report measures of these risk factors should be balanced by consideration of the interpretive limitations imposed by such a strategy. As in the case of health behavior change, most interventions for reducing stress or psychosocial risk factors communicate a clear expectation for change. Differences across treatment and comparison groups in this demand can combine with the limitations of self-reported outcomes to inflate apparent intervention effects. As in most areas of intervention research, multimethod assessments of intervention effects are desirable (e.g., interview or significant other ratings of social support, anger, anxiety, or stress).

The selection of appropriate comparison or control groups can be complicated in this context (C. E. Schwartz, Chesney, Irvine, & Keefe, 1997). Placebo or expectancy effects on physiological outcomes are common, making some sort of nonspecific factor or alternative treatment comparison appropriate (Turner, Deyo, & Loweser, 1994). The length of follow-up and the frequency and timing of assessments of physiological outcomes should be guided by an understanding of the typical course of the disease or physiological outcome of interest. Finally, the magnitude and clinical significance of intervention effects should be examined. Except in the obvious cases of recurrent morbid events or survival, the selection of an approach or metric for evaluating clinical significance can be difficult. Sometimes prior conventions or criteria used for evaluating medical interventions can be adapted for the evaluation of psychosocial interventions. For example, if a reduction in blood pressure of 10 mmHg achieved with antihypertensive medication is considered clinically significant in the medical literature, the same benefit achieved through stress management should be considered clinically significant.

PSYCHOSOCIAL ASPECTS OF MEDICAL ILLNESS AND CARE

Acute and chronic illnesses produce a variety of important effects, such as painful symptoms, emotional distress, and limitations in functioning. Further, the standard medical or surgical management of these conditions can pose further demands, such as adherence to potentially unpleasant medication regimens or significant alterations in lifestyle. Research on these impacts, the identification of potentially modifiable predictors of variation in these effects, and the utility of adjunctive psychosocial interventions must begin with a thorough understanding of the specific medical context—including the disease or health event in question, as well as the standard medical care and the context in which it is delivered (Smith & Nicassio, 1995). These aspects of the context of medical illness and care are far-reaching influences of the patient's experience, the identification of important outcomes, and the feasibility of potential interventions.

Impacts of Acute and Chronic Illness

Most specific acute and chronic conditions have been examined in health psychology research. As a result, the key outcomes of interest (e.g., specific symptoms, limitations in areas of functioning) have been identified in most cases and may

have even been the subject of sophisticated assessment research. In designing or evaluating research on acute and chronic medical illness, a review of the relevant outcome assessment literature is critical. Increasingly, this research is published in the relevant medical outlets in a specific area (e.g., rheumatology, cardiology, oncology). It is important to determine the extent to which psychometric characteristics—especially construct validity—have been examined in the specific medical context (i.e., disease or population) of interest.

Although this assessment literature has matured, several problems are common. Some studies of medical populations utilize measures that were developed for use in physically healthy mental health populations, and their construct validity may not generalize across this dimension. For example, the somatic items on depression inventories are highly diagnostic among individuals who do not have serious illnesses. Yet, in medical populations, such items are likely to tap symptoms or impacts of the disease, rather than indicate affective disorder. A chronically medically ill person could produce an elevated depression score on the MMPI or Beck Depression Inventory, simply by accurately describing the impact of their illness on fatigue, appetite, sleep, and their concerns about appearance (Clark, Cook, & Snow, 1998; McDaniel, Musselman, Porter, Reed, & Nemeroff, 1995; Mohr et al., 1997; O'Donnell & Chung, 1997; Peck, Smith, Ward, & Milano, 1989).

A related assessment problem occurs when measures of emotional adjustment are selected while an inappropriate conceptual model of the domain is implicitly being used. Sometimes reflecting their clinical training, health psychologists often assess the emotional correlates of acute or chronic medical illness exclusively with measures of depression and related negative emotions or general levels of maladjustment. The implicit assumption that measures of maladjustment and emotional distress capture the emotional sequelae of medical conditions is debatable, as few patients suffer diagnosable emotional disorders. Models of the structure on normal variations in mood—such as the two-dimensional model of negative and positive affect proposed by Watson and Tellegen (1985) may be more appropriate. It is important to note that measures of depressive symptoms correlate with both high negative affect and low positive affect. In medical populations, positive and negative affect have distinct correlates (Smith & Christensen, 1996; Zautra et al., 1995). Hence, use of measures of depressive symptoms to assess the emotional impact of acute or chronic illness not only pathologizes normal emotional adaptation, but also may result in a loss of specificity about the determinants of the emotional impact of a given illness or medical crisis.

In many illnesses or medical contexts (e.g., surgery, childbirth, etc.), the most important outcomes (e.g., pain, symptoms, emotional adjustment) are most appropriately assessed via self-reports. Other outcomes (e.g., functional activity levels, adherence) are readily assessed with these methods. Yet, even when self-reports are appropriate, methodological limitations of this method may pose problems, such as overestimates of covariation among outcome domains due to common method variance, or inflated estimates of effect sizes when predictors (e.g., coping styles, social support) are assessed with the same method. Sometimes self-reports of conceptually distinct outcomes or predictors contain very similar item wording, exacerbating this problem. For example, covariation between reports of pain and depressive symptoms may reflect an actual association between these variables, the common effects of social desirability or other response styles (e.g., suppression), or the inclusion of similarly worded items on the corresponding inventories. Multimethod approaches—despite the expense and inconvenience—have much to recommend them in this area of health psychology research.

Predictors of Impact

Similar issues arise in the assessment of predictors of the impact of acute and chronic medical conditions. Cognitive models of adaptation are widespread in this area, and self-reports are typically the main way of assessing the key constructs (e.g., self-efficacy, problem- and emotion-focused coping, cognitive distortions, etc.). Even when interpersonal processes are identified as critical influences on adaptation (e.g., social support, conflict, etc.), self-report methods are the most commonly used. Again, a variety of artifacts can lead to the overestimation of effect sizes when single methods are utilized. Scales intended to assess cognitive or social constructs often contain item wording reflecting affective distress, creating thinly veiled tautologies (Coyne & Gotlib, 1983) in which psychometrically conflated measures are interpreted as providing estimates of substantive associations. Each of these issues becomes a more likely problem when scales intended to assess influences on adaptation to illness and other medical contexts are used without adequate psychometric evaluation and refinement, especially formal studies of convergent and discriminant validity.

Many of the influences on adjustment (e.g., coping responses) and outcomes involve moment-to-moment or day-to-day processes. Yet they are often assessed via general self-reports of typical responses over long or indefinite periods of time. There is growing concern that this approach to assessing coping and other predictors of adaptation (as well as the outcomes of interest themselves) is seriously inaccurate

(Coyne & Gottlieb, 1996; Stone et al., 1998). Participants may simply be unable, by describing retrospective summaries of their responses, to accurately describe processes that vary in important ways over brief periods of time. Daily experience sampling approaches (Affleck et al., 1999; Stone et al., 1998) offer an important alternative, although it is not without its own methodological and quantitative challenges. Some prospective associations between potential influences on adaptation and psychosocial outcomes do operate over long periods of time and are therefore amenable to infrequent assessments. However, many processes are not and therefore require the more intensive approach. In all cases, a careful analysis of the specific medical context can suggest which approaches regarding the frequency of assessment are appropriate.

Design and Evaluation of Adjunctive Interventions

Interventions in this area range from the brief provision of sensory and procedural information (Anderson, 1987; Auerbach, 1989) as a way to reduce distress and facilitate recovery in brief medical procedures to multisession cognitive-behavioral interventions for pain and disability (Keefe et al., in press; Turk & Okifuji, in press). In other cases, increased adherence to the behavioral components of standard medical care are the main foci (e.g., diabetes, renal dialysis; Christensen & Ehlers, in press; Gonder-Frederick et al., in press). In many instances, such as cancer, heart disease, and arthritis, all of these are relevant intervention targets, as is the progression of the underlying disease itself. The selection of outcome measures must begin with a careful consideration of the specific disease and medical intervention context, as these factors determine not only the selection of specific assessments, but also general methodological approaches. In the case of most specific illnesses and medical contexts, well-established measures of clinically relevant outcomes are available, with prior evidence of their sensitivity to interventions (Smith & Ruiz, 1999).

The primary features and considerations of experimental design in psychological intervention research (e.g., choice of comparison conditions, sampling, implementation and assessment of independent variable, etc.; Haaga & Stiles, 2000; Kendall et al., 1999) are obviously relevant in this type of intervention research, but again they will be shaped by the specific medical context. Interventions vary from minutes to many hours in length, and can be delivered by a wide variety of personnel, including family members, nurses, physicians, or psychologists. Similarly, the appropriate follow-up may be a matter of hours, as in the case of the painfulness of medical procedures, to months or years, as in the case of psychosocial interventions intended to reduce the recurrence of cancer or coronary disease. Although appropriate comparison groups often are standard medical practice (i.e., no adjunctive psychosocial treatment), placebo effects are well-established in many areas of acute and chronic illness. This necessitates the consideration of more complex comparison conditions.

A classic issue in psychological intervention research involves the optimal matching of clients or patients and specific interventions. Conceptually, these moderator designs are quite similar in the context of medical illness and care, but the array of individual differences and interventions can be quite different. For example, the interactive or matching effects of psychological differences among patients (e.g., high vs. low preference for involvement in health care) can be crossed with alternative medical treatment options (e.g., home vs. in-center renal dialysis; Christensen & Ehlers, in press). Medical individual differences (high vs. low illness severity) can be crossed with psychosocial interventions (Blumenthal et al., 1997). The quantitative analysis of these moderator designs is similar to traditional intervention research, but the range of relevant person (or condition) by (medical or psychosocial) treatment questions is broad.

As we discuss later in this chapter, the evaluation of the clinical significance of intervention effects is important in this context. Many specific applications or contexts provide easily quantified, clinically meaningful outcomes (e.g., length of labor or incidence of complications during childbirth; days of hospitalization following bypass surgery; reductions in blood pressure). Further, prior research may have identified accepted criteria for clinical success, even when outcomes of interest require subjective reports (e.g., reductions in the frequency of headache; Holroyd, in press). Although specific conditions require specific measures in order to provide optimally sensitive outcome assessment (e.g., pain associated with arthritis vs. cancer pain), standardized measures of pain, emotion distress, and functional activity can be added in order to compare the magnitude and clinical significance of intervention effects across diseases and medical contexts (Bergner, Bobbit, Carter, & Gilson, 1981; Derogatis, Fleming, Sudler, & DellaPietra, 1995; Jensen, Turner, Turner, & Romano, 1996).

GENERAL ISSUES

Clearly, a variety of classic issues in psychological methods are relevant to health psychology, albeit in the new key, so to speak, of the interface between behavioral and biomedical research and practice. Several of these issues are highlighted in the following discussion.

The Active Use of Conceptual Models

Virtually all aspects of psychological research are grounded in theory, even if this grounding is not explicitly recognized. Even the most basic components of the research process are guided in this way, including the small theories about the connections between our research operations and the constructs we hope to understand. This is true even for the most basic and central construct we hope to understand in the field—health. As noted previously, research in the field is often limited by simplistic assumptions about the validity of measures intended to assess actual disease, as in the case of self-reports of physical symptoms or visits to health care professionals. These illness behaviors clearly share variance with the construct of actual disease, but the unique variance may also be systematically related to factors believed to influence actual health and disease. Clearly, there is more to health than the simple presence versus absence of disease. Functional activity levels, physical distress, subjective well-being, and other constructs are important aspects of broad conceptual definitions of health (Ryff & Singer, 1998). However, the individual elements of such multidimensional constructs are not all relevant for a given research question, and researchers (and consumers of their work) should not generalize across these correlated yet distinct elements.

Similar care should be taken in the development and interpretation of other central constructs in psychosocial models of health and disease. In studies of health behavior and its predictors, of more direct psychosocial influences on disease, and of the predictors and outcomes of adjustment to acute and chronic illness and care, clear conceptual models should guide the development and psychometric evaluation of measurement scales and procedures. A key aspect of the conceptual context in this process should be the disease or health outcome in question, as well as its standard medical evaluation and management. That is to say, the grounding conceptual models should attend equally to the relevant psychosocial and biomedical elements. The field has suffered in many instances from inadequate attention to the quality of measurement of key concepts, and the needed improvement in measurement will be facilitated by attending to its grounding in conceptual models.

Opportunities for theory testing are often missed when researchers perform routine tasks. For example, in controlling possible behavioral confounds such as smoking or exercise in prospective tests of the effects of social support or depression on subsequent cardiovascular disease, these analyses can easily be reconceptualized as conceptually driven tests of competing models of the effects of these psychosocial risk factors—specifically, a model in which their effects are mediated by health behaviors relative to one that does not involve behavioral mediation (Smith & Gallo, 2001). Some of the traditions in other disciplines that often collaborate with health psychology in research efforts are not as concerned with theory testing; predictive statistical models are sufficient in these traditions, and the potential slip between construct and research operations may be of less concern. Given their unique methodological tradition, health psychologists can often increase the yield of multidisciplinary research by attending to opportunities for testing conceptual models at each step.

One common opportunity for theory testing that is often overlooked is in the area of intervention research. In evaluating interventions in the area of health behavior change and risk reduction, modification of psychosocial risk factors, and psychosocial adjunctive treatments for acute and chronic illness, the interventions evaluated are often based on conceptual models that otherwise have been tested almost exclusively in observational, nonexperimental designs. As a result, intervention studies provide very rare and valuable opportunities to subject the guiding model to an experimental test. This requires the inclusion of reliable and valid measures of the key constructs hypothesized to influence the outcomes of interest and targeted by the intervention. Traditional tests of the significance and importance of intervention effects can then also be supplemented by formal mediational analyses of the those effects, testing the underlying models. In this way, models of the determinants of health behavior, stress and disease, and adaptation to illness can be tested through experimental manipulations of independent variables that are typically only observed in concurrent and at best prospective correlational designs.

Design and Sampling

In many of the research areas discussed previously, observational designs are an important component of research. Some influences on health either cannot ethically or practically be manipulated experimentally, or the expense of an experimental study must first be justified by consistent supportive findings from observational studies. In cross-sectional observational studies, the potential bidirectional relationship between psychosocial variables and physical health must always be entertained as an alternative hypothesis. Prospective designs can be less ambiguous in this regard, but interpretive ambiguities remain, especially the problem of third variables. For example, the number of times an individual has

voted in presidential elections would likely be a reliable risk factor for CHD over the subsequent decade. Of course, associations between voting history and age, and between age and CHD risk are the likely explanation, rather than any effects of voting per se. Although not all third variables are this obvious, health and disease have multifactorial influences, and each of the relevant factors is likely associated with many other variables. Hence, the universe of alternative explanations for correlational, albeit prospective effects is difficult to define, let alone rule out. Behavioral researchers may need to take particular care to consider medical or health status variables, including aspects of medical treatment.

The prevalence of most serious diseases increases with age, and such diseases reduce life expectancy. As a result, the age of the sample can influence the presence, magnitude, and even direction of association between a behavioral or psychosocial factor and health outcomes. The predictive utility of even well-established risk factors changes over the life span (G. A. Kaplan, Haan, & Wallace, 1999). Behavioral risk factors may not predict disease early in life, simply because the disease has not yet become manifest. The same risk factor may not predict disease late in life, because those who died because of this risk factor may be missing from the sample; only those who are for some reason resilient have the risk factor and have survived long enough to be included in a later adulthood sample (e.g., R. B. Williams, 2000).

As described previously, sampling in clinical studies poses a very difficult challenge, in that entry into clinical samples involves a very complex, multistep process involving access to health care, seeking such service, referral by health professionals, response to prior interventions, and patterns of dropout. It can be virtually impossible to define the population such samples meaningfully represent (Turk & Rudy, 1990). Finally, like other aspects of psychological and biomedical research, health psychology can be fairly accused as studying too many White middle- and upper-class men. Although inclusion of more diverse samples in the field has been improving (Park, Adams, & Lynch, 1998), the problem remains. These demographic factors (i.e., ethnicity, SES, and gender) are themselves associated with the prevalence, incidence, and prognosis of most major health threats, and may also moderate the effects of psychosocial variables and interventions.

Evaluating Intervention Outcomes

In each of the three major topics in health psychology, intervention research is a central focus. Can we modify unhealthy behaviors, and do such changes reduce morbidity or postpone mortality? Can we modify stress, negative emotions, and the psychophysiological mechanisms through which they impact disease, and if so, do these interventions have beneficial effects on morbidity and mortality? Finally, can adjunctive psychosocial treatments reduce the negative impact of acute and chronic medical conditions, improve adherence to medical regimens, or otherwise improve the quality of life among those with medical problems? As described in the preceding discussion, classic issues in psychological and behavioral intervention studies are relevant in each of these areas. However, there are additional methodological issues in health psychology interventions that require consideration in the application of the traditional principles and emerging concerns in intervention research.

First, the overwhelming majority of interventions studies in health psychology take the form of small, well-controlled trials, with careful assessment of intermediate outcomes, such as behavior change, temporary changes in physiology, or specific symptoms. In their recent review, Schneiderman, Antoni, Saab, and Ironson (2001) emphasize that these small studies provide important and scientifically compelling evidence regarding the feasibility of interventions and conditions under which psychosocial factors influence disease processes, quality of life, and other aspects of medical care (e.g., adherence). However, evidence of impacts on morbidity and mortality—the most important end points in traditional medical research—require much larger trials, given the requirements for statistical power to detect effects on such end points. Health psychology interventions will have a greater impact on health care and medical practice if they are supported in such trials. However, unlike those involved in traditional clinical medicine research (e.g., evaluations of new drug treatment protocols or surgical procedures), psychologists are less accustomed to the design, conduct, and analysis of multisite trial designs often required in such research. Further, given their relatively more complex nature as compared to drug trials, the delivery of psychosocial interventions consistently across multiple sites is a daunting challenge.

The recent movement to develop standards for empirically supported therapies in mental health (Chambless & Hollon, 1998; Chambless & Ollendick, 2001) has been applied at least initially in health psychology (Compas, Haaga, Keefe, Leitenberg, & Williams, 1998) and has a clear parallel in the concept of evidence-based medicine (Sackett, Richardson, Rosenberg, & Haynes, 1997). Hence, the application of the concept of empirically supported therapies in health psychology is consistent with trends in the broader field of health care, and it presents the opportunity to compare the benefits of behavioral interventions and traditional medical approaches on the level playing field of established methodological principles. This is likely to have considerable advantages for health psychology if the evidence-based practice movement in health care challenges long-standing beliefs in the medical community about the relative value of behavioral versus traditional medical approaches. An emphasis on evidence-based practice applied equally to behavioral and medical interventions could influence policies regarding reimbursement and other aspects of health care resource allocation.

The criteria for the status of empirically supported therapies distinguish between evidence of efficacy and effectiveness (Kendall et al., 1999). Paralleling the distinction between internal and external validity, *efficacy* refers to evidence of significant effects in carefully controlled trials using highly selected patients or participants and specifically trained therapists or providers. In contrast, *effectiveness* refers to evidence of significant treatment effects in the context of actual clinical or applied settings, with unselected recipients and actual health care providers. The evaluation of efficacy in health psychology intervention research is quite similar to the context of mental health intervention research (e.g., description of sample, random assignment, evaluation of reliability of treatment implementation, etc.), with the exception that it involves a very broad array of intervention targets, types of intervention-delivering personnel, and contexts for delivery. Table 10.2 illustrates this range by describing interventions as falling along two dimensions—(a) the levels of analysis as described in the biopsychosocial model, as described by Engel (1977) and illustrated in Figure 10.1; and (b) the particular stage of the health versus disease, from the prevention of risk, to the reduction of risk, and to the management of the impact of established disease. Hence, the nature of carefully controlled trials that produce evidence of efficacy will vary enormously, as will the real-world studies of effectiveness. In both cases, for example, health psychology interventions may involve treatments delivered by peers, parents, spouses, other health care professionals (e.g., nurses, physicians), or psychologists. Further, these interventions may be targeted toward healthy persons or chronically ill persons, and may be delivered to individuals, families, organizations, or communities.

As noted previously, for interventions in each of the three main content areas, evaluations of the importance or clinical significance of intervention effects is an important concern. In addition to indexes specific to individual behavior change targets (e.g., weight loss, smoking cessation, blood pressure reduction, change in headache frequency), health psychologists should also consider the suggestion of mental health researchers to include quality of life in evaluations of clinical significance (Gladis et al., 1999). As noted above, quality of life is a key element of broader views of health outcomes

TABLE 10.2 Level of Analysis and Phase of Disease Risk as Dimensions in Health Psychology Interventions

Level	Phase		
	Primary	Secondary	Tertiary
Individual	Self-instruction guide for HIV prevention	Screening and behavior-change counseling for mild hypertension	Stress management for individuals with heart disease
Group	Parents' group training in communicating with teens about risk behaviors	Supervised exercise program for sedentary adults	Couples' group for coping with cancer
Organization	Work site education and exercise program for injury prevention	Work site incentive program for smoking cessation	Physical therapy and vocational retraining for injured workers
Community	Neighborhood media campaign to promote exercise in minority populations	Neighborhood support groups for caregivers of chronically ill	Improving access for disabled persons to recreational facilities
Institution-Policy	Enforcing laws banning cigarette sales to minors	Increasing health insurance coverage for smoking cessation treatment	Mandating a course of rehabilitation for stroke victims

(R. M. Kaplan, 1994). It also figures prominently in recent efforts to capture the full impact of intervention effects, relative to their costs.

Increasingly, the effects of health interventions are evaluated relative to their costs. In a climate of limited health care expenditures, the value of interventions with demonstrated efficacy and effectiveness must considered along with the costs associated with the intervention, in order to inform decisions about the distribution or allocation of finite health care resources (Ramsey, McIntosh, & Sullivan, 2001). Several key concepts are often misunderstood in evaluating the effects of interventions relative to their costs (R. M. Kaplan & Groessel, in press). *Cost-effectiveness* refers to the monetary value of resources used, relative to the health effects produced. For example, smoking cessation interventions could be compared in terms of the treatment delivery costs associated with the production of 1 year of smoking abstinence (e.g., costs of delivery a counseling intervention to five smokers, one of whom quits and remains smoke free for a year). This sort of comparison can suggest differing strengths and weaknesses of intervention approaches. Multicomponent, cognitive-behavioral interventions for smoking delivered to individuals or small groups may produce greater initial and maintained cessation rates as compared to a brief interventions consisting of physician advice and self-help manuals dispensed during routine medical visits. However, the very low costs of the latter could make it the more cost-effective approach.

Cost-benefit analyses compare this same monetary value of resources consumed in treatment to the monetary value of all resources saved or created, including the monetary value of impacts on other health care utilization and health outcomes (e.g., economic productivity of recipients). Comprehensive and accurate assessments of both the costs and the benefits pose a significant challenge in this type of analysis (R. M. Kaplan & Groessel, in press). A closely related concept is often referred to as *cost offset,* in which psychosocial interventions can produce reductions in subsequent health care expenditures that exceed the costs associated with the psychosocial treatment (Chiles, Lambert, & Hatch, 1999; Friedman, Subel, Meyers, Caudill, & Benson, 1995). Specifically, this concept compares the cost of the intervention to the costs saved by reductions in other medical care (e.g., reduction in health care utilization or the expense of continuing care), independent of their health benefits.

Finally, a more comprehensive approach has been proposed in which intervention effects for all types of health care are compared in a standard metric for assessing a broad definition of health benefits. *Cost-utility analyses* compare the value of resources used in delivering a specific intervention or service to an outcome that combines mortality and quality of life, including morbidity, functional status, and subjective symptoms (R. M. Kaplan & Groessel, in press). For example, the Quality of Life Adjusted Year (i.e., QALY; R. M. Kaplan, 1994) weights years of life by a summary of ratings of various aspects of morbidity and functional status. The continuum is bounded by a rating of 0.0 for death and 1.0 for asymptomatic, optimal functioning. Interventions with similar effects on mortality could have very different effects on quality of life adjusted years, as when one intervention is associated with significant side effects, incomplete relief of symptoms, or continuing limitations in mobility or other aspects of functional status. This approach permits an overall, comprehensive assessment of intervention effects—both positive and negative—in a metric that is broadly applicable. For example, the cost-utility of coronary artery bypass surgery could be compared to that associated with medical or even behavioral management of coronary disease. Comparisons of apples and oranges, so to speak, in health care research are increasingly important as we face difficult questions involving the allocation of limited health resources. Importantly, such standardized and comprehensive outcome assessments define a level playing field on which psychosocial and traditional medical interventions can be compared objectively.

Communication

An often overlooked issue in discussions of research methods is the dissemination of research findings. In traditional behavioral and psychosocial research, this issue is relatively straightforward; we are generally communicating with similarly trained professionals. The optimal audience for health psychology research is much broader. If only other psychologists hear or read about the findings of such studies, then a major goal of the research will not be obtained. Just as the public health and medical contexts shape the importance and nature of health psychology research, these potential audiences must guide decisions about how and where the findings are reported. Writing for medical or epidemiological audiences is usually quite different than for behavioral scientists. As in the case of research design, interdisciplinary teams are often needed to accomplish this complex task.

METHODOLOGICAL CONSIDERATIONS IN THE FUTURE OF HEALTH PSYCHOLOGY

Given that the context of research questions represents a critical influence on methodological decisions, it is useful to conclude this overview of methods in health psychology by considering the changes in context that will impact methods in the field. For example, as noted previously, increasing pressure on health care financing will both increase the potential importance of health psychology interventions and motivate the comprehensive assessment of their benefits and costs. The concern with cost containment will also prompt studies of the effectiveness in real world health settings of interventions found to be efficacious in carefully controlled trials. Changing demographics represent another contextual influence on future methodological concerns. In industrialized nations, the rising average age of the population and the increasing proportion of the population that is elderly will increase the need for incorporation of methods from gerontology and life span developmental psychology (Siegler et al., 2002). This may also change the relative importance of various health outcomes and identify the need for improved assessments, such as an increased emphasis on functional status and independent living. Yet just as the aging population calls our attention to the later stages of the life span, it is increasingly clear that the most common sources of premature mortality and excess morbidity in later adulthood are heavily influenced by behaviors and related characteristics that emerge in childhood and adolescence (e.g., smoking, inactivity, obesity) (P. G. Williams, Holmbeck, & Greenley, in press). Hence, developmental methods will play an increasing part in the health psychology research across the life span. The growing recognition that women and minorities are underrepresented in all aspects of health research including health psychology will prompt increasing attention to related methodological issues, especially as the ethnic minority population increases in the United States.

Finally, developments in basic biomedical science and clinical medicine will shape health psychology research. Some of these developments will prompt new psychosocial questions, such as psychological aspects of organ transplantation (Olbrisch, Benedict, Ashe, & Levenson, in press) and genetic testing (Lerman, Croyle, Tercyak, & Hamann, in press). Biomedical science will provide new opportunities for answering existing questions at the interface of behavioral and biomedical science, as when new medical imaging technologies provide unprecedented opportunities to examine disease processes noninvasively. Other developments will refine our understanding of the pathophysiology of disease, and in the process pose new questions about the ways in which mind and body are reciprocally related. These developments will make the continuing methodological education of the health psychologist a critical and ongoing concern, but the basic concepts and methods of behavioral research will remain an equally essential foundation.

REFERENCES

Ader, R., Felten, D. L., & Cohen, N. (Eds.). (2001). *Psychoneuroimmunology* (3rd ed.). San Diego, CA: Academic Press.

Adler, N., & Matthews, K. (1994). Health psychology: Why do some people get sick and some stay well? *Annual Review of Psychology, 45,* 229–259.

Affleck, G., Zautra, A., Tennen, H., & Armeli, S. (1999). Multilevel daily process designs for consulting and clinical psychology: A primer for the perplexed. *Journal of Consulting and Clinical Psychology, 67,* 746–754.

Andersen, B. L. (in press). Biobehavioral outcomes following psychological interventions for cancer patients. *Journal of Consulting and Clinical Psychology.*

Andersen, B. L., Kiecolt-Glaser, J. K., & Glaser, R. (1994). A biobehavioral model of cancer stress and disease course. *American Psychologist, 49,* 389–404.

Anderson, E. (1987). Preoperative preparation facilitates recovery, reduces psychological distress, and reduces the incidence of acute postoperative hypertension. *Journal of Consulting and Clinical Psychology, 55,* 513–520.

Auerbach, S. M. (1989). Stress management and coping research in the health care setting: An overview and methodological commentary. *Journal of Consulting and Clinical Psychology, 57,* 388–395.

Bandura, A. (1977). Self-efficacy: Toward a unifying theory of behavioral change. *Psychological Review, 84,* 191–215.

Baron, R. M., & Kenny, D. A. (1986). The moderator-mediator variable distinction in social psychological research: Conceptual, strategic, and statistical consideration. *Journal of Personality and Social Psychology, 51,* 1173–1182.

Bergner, M., Bobbit, R. A., Carter, W. B., & Gilson, B. S. (1981). The sickness impact profile: Validation of a health status measure. *Medical Care, 14,* 57–67.

Blanchard, E. B., & Scharff, L. (in press). Psychosocial aspects of assessment and treatment of irritable bowel syndrome in adults and recurrent abdominal pain in children. *Journal of Consulting and Clinical Psychology.*

Blumenthal, J. A., Jiang, W., Babyak, M. A., & Krantz, D. S. (1997). Stress management and exercise training in cardiac patients with myocardial ischemia. *Archives of Internal Medicine, 157,* 2213–2223.

Brownell, K. D., Marlatt, G. A., Lichtenstein, E., & Wilson, G. T. (1986). Understanding and preventing relapse. *American Psychologist, 41,* 765–782.

Carroll, M. E., & Overmier, J. B. (2001). *Animal research and human health.* Washington, DC: American Psychological Association.

Chambless, D. L., & Hollon, S. D. (1998). Defining empirically supported therapies. *Journal of Consulting and Clinical Psychology, 66,* 7–18.

Chambless, D. L., & Ollendick, T. H. (2001). Empirically-supported psychological interventions. *Annual Review of Psychology, 52,* 685–716.

Chiles, J. A., Lambert, M. J., & Hatch, A. L. (1999). The impact of psychological interventions on medical cost offset: A meta-analytic review. *Clinical Psychology: Research and Practice, 6,* 204–220.

Christensen, A. J., & Ehlers, S. L. (in press). Psychosocial factors in end-stage renal disease: An emerging context for behavioral medicine research. *Journal of Consulting and Clinical Psychology.*

Clark, D. A., Cook, A., & Snow, D. (1998). Depressive symptom differences in hospitalized, medically ill, depressed psychiatric inpatients, and nonmedical controls. *Journal of Abnormal Psychology, 107,* 38–48.

Cohen, S., & Rabin, B. S. (1998). Psychologic stress, immunity, and cancer. *Journal of the National Cancer Institute, 90,* 3–4.

Cohen, S., & Rodriguez, M. (1995). Pathways linking affective disturbances and physical disorders. *Health Psychology, 14,* 374–380.

Compas, B. E., Haaga, D. A., Keefe, F. J., Leitenberg, H., & Williams, D. A. (1998). Sampling of empirically supported psychological treatments from health psychology: Smoking, chronic pain, cancer, and bulimia nervosa. *Journal of Consulting and Clinical Psychology, 66,* 89–112.

Costa, P. T., Jr., & McCrae, R. R. (1987). Neuroticism, somatic complaints, and disease: Is the bark worse than the bite? *Journal of Personality, 55,* 299–316.

Coyne, J. C., & Gotlib, I. (1983). The role of cognition in depression: A critical review. *Psychological Bulletin, 94,* 472–505.

Coyne, J. C., & Gottlieb, B. H. (1996). The mismeasure of coping by checklist. *Journal of Personality, 64,* 959–991.

Crits-Christoph, P., & Mintz, J. (1991). Implications of therapist effects for the design and analysis of comparative studies of psychotherapies. *Journal of Consulting and Clinical Psychology, 59,* 20–26.

Croyle, R. T., & Loftus, E. F. (1993). Recollection in the kingdom of AIDS. In D. G. Ostrow & R. Kessler (Eds.), *Methodological issues in AIDS behavioral research* (pp. 163–180). New York: Plenum.

Davila, J., Bradbury, T. N., Cohan, C. L., & Tochluk, S. (1997). Marital functions and depressive symptoms: Evidence for a stress generation model. *Journal of Personality and Social Psychology, 73,* 849–861.

Derogatis, L. R., Fleming, M. P., Sudler, N. C., & DellaPietra, L. (1995). Psychological assessment. In P. M. Nicassio & T. W. Smith (Eds.), *Managing chronic illness: A biopsychosocial perspective* (pp. 59–116). Washington, DC: American Psychological Association.

Dubbert, P. M. (in press). Physical activity and exercise: Recent advances and current challenges. *Journal of Consulting and Clinical Psychology.*

Engel, G. L. (1977). The need for a new medical model: A challenge for biomedicine. *Science, 196,* 129–136.

Etringer, B. D., Gregory, V. R., & Lando, H. A. (1984). Influence of group cohesion on the behavioral treatment of smoking. *Journal of Consulting and Clinical Psychology, 52,* 1080–1086.

Feng, Z., Diehr, P., Peterson, A., & McLerran, D. (2001). Selected statistical issues in group randomized trials. *Annual Review of Public Health, 22,* 167–187.

Flick, S. N. (1988). Managing attrition in clinical research. *Clinical Psychology Review, 8,* 499–515.

Friedman, R., Subel, D., Meyers, P., Caudill, M., & Benson, H. (1995). Behavioral medicine, clinical health psychology, and cost offset. *Health Psychology, 14,* 509–518.

Funk, S. (1992). Hardiness: A review of theory and research. *Health Psychology, 11,* 335–345.

Gallo, L. C., & Smith, T. W. (1999). Patterns of hostility and social support: Conceptualizing psychosocial risk factors as characteristics of the person *and* the environment. *Journal of Research in Personality, 33,* 281–310.

Glasgow, R. E., Mullooly, J. P., Vogt, T. M., Stevens, V. J., Lichetenstein, E., Hollis, J. F., Lando, H. A., Severson, H., Pearson, K., & Vogt, M. (1993). Biochemical validation of smoking status in public health settings: Pros, cons, and data from four low-intensity intervention trials. *Addictive Behaviors, 18,* 511–527.

Gonder-Frederick, L. A., Cox, D. J., & Ritterband, L. M. (in press). Diabetes and behavioral medicine: The second decade. *Journal of Consulting and Clinical Psychology.*

Haaga, D. A. F., & Stiles, W. B. (2000). Randomized clinical trials in psychotherapy research: Methodology, design, and evaluation. In C. R. Snyder & R. E. Ingram (Eds.), *Handbook of psychological change: Psychotherapy procedure and practices for the 21st century* (pp. 14–39). New York: Wiley.

Hall, M., Baum, A., Buysse, D. J., Prigerson, H. G., Kupfer, D. J., & Reynolds, C. F. (1998). Sleep as a mediator of the stress-immune relationship. *Psychosomatic Medicine, 60,* 48–51.

Hancock, L., Sanson-Fisher, R. W., & Redman, S. (1997). Community action for health promotion: A review of methods and outcomes 1990–1995. *American Journal of Preventive Medicine, 13,* 229–239.

Holmbeck, G. N. (1997). Toward terminological, conceptual, and statistical clarity in the study of mediators and moderators: Examples from the child-clinical and pediatric psychology literatures. *Journal of Consulting and Clinical Psychology, 65,* 599–610.

Holroyd, K. A. (in press). Assessment and psychological management of recurrent headache disorders. *Journal of Consulting and Clinical Psychology.*

Huberty, C. J., & Morris, J. D. (1989). Multivariate analysis versus multiple univariate analyses. *Psychological Bulletin, 105,* 302–308.

Iribarren, C., Sidney, S., Bild, D. E., Liu, K., Markovitz, J. H., Roseman, J. M., & Matthews, K. (2000). Association of hostility with coronary artery calcification in young adults: The CARDIA study. *Journal of the American Medical Association, 283,* 2546–2551.

Jaccard, J., & Wan, C. K. (1993). Statistical analysis of temporal data with many observations: Issues for behavioral medicine data. *Annals of Behavioral Medicine, 15,* 41–50.

Janz, N. W., & Becker, J. H. (1984). The health belief model: A decade later. *Health Education Quarterly, 11,* 1–47.

Jensen, M., Turner, L., Turner, J., & Romano, J. (1996). The use of multiple-item scales for pain intensity measurement in chronic pain patients. *Pain, 67,* 35–40.

Johnson, S. L., & Jacob, T. (1997). Marital interactions of depressed men and women. *Journal of Consulting and Clinical Psychology, 65,* 15–23.

Kamarck, T. W., Jennings, J. J., Pogue-Geile, M., & Manuck, S. B. (1994). A multidimensional measurement model for cardiovascular reactivity: Stability, and cross-validation in two adult samples. *Health Psychology, 13,* 471–478.

Kaplan, G. A., Haan, M. N., & Wallace, R. B. (1999). Understanding changing risk factor associations with increasing age in adults. *Annual Review of Public Health, 20,* 89–108.

Kaplan, R. M. (1984). The connection between clinical health promotion and health status: A critical overview. *American Psychologist, 39,* 755–765.

Kaplan, R. M. (1994). The Ziggy theorem: Toward an outcomes-focused health psychology. *Health Psychology, 13,* 451–460.

Kaplan, R. M., & Groessel, E. J. (in press). Applications of cost-effectiveness methodologies in behavioral medicine. *Journal of Consulting and Clinical Psychology.*

Keefe, F. J., Smith, F. J., Buffington, A. L. H., Gibson, J., Studts, J., & Caldwell, D. S. (in press). Recent advances and future directions in the biopsychosocial assessment and treatment of arthritis. *Journal of Consulting and Clinical Psychology.*

Kelly, J. A., & Kalichman, S. C. (in press). Behavioral research in HIV/AIDS, primary and secondary prevention, recent advances, and future directions. *Journal of Consulting and Clinical Psychology.*

Kendall, P. C. (1999). Clinical significance. *Journal of Consulting and Clinical Psychology, 67,* 283–284.

Kendall, P. C., Flannery-Schroeder, E. C., & Ford, J. D. (1999). Therapy outcome research methods. In P. C. Kendall, J. N. Butcher, & G. N. Holmbeck (Eds.), *Handbook of research methods in clinical psychology* (2nd ed., pp. 330–363). New York: Wiley.

Kendler, K. S. (1997). Social support: A genetic-epidemiologic analysis. *American Journal of Psychiatry, 154,* 1398–1404.

Kiecolt-Glaser, J. K., McGuire, L., Robles, T. F., & Glaser, R. (2002). Emotions, morbidity, and mortality: New perspectives from psychoneuroimmunology. *Annual Review of Psychology, 53,* 83–107.

Kiecolt-Glaser, J. K., McGuire, L., Robles, T. F., & Glaser, R. (in press). Psychoneuroimmunology: Psychological influences on immune function and health. *Journal of Consulting and Clinical Psychology.*

Krantz, D. S., & McCeney, M. K. (2002). Effects of psychological and social factors on organic disease: A critical assessment of research on coronary heart disease. *Annual Review of Psychology, 53,* 341–369.

Lerman, C., Croyle, T. T., Tercyak, K. P., & Hamann, H. (in press). Genetic testing: Psychological aspects and implications. *Journal of Consulting and Clinical Psychology.*

Levenstein, S. (in press). Psychosocial factors in peptic ulcer and inflammatory bowel disease. *Journal of Consulting and Clinical Psychology.*

Little, R. J., & Yau, L. H. Y. (1998). Statistical techniques for analyzing data from prevention trials: Treatment no-shows using Rubin's causal model. *Psychological Methods, 3,* 147–159.

Lovallo, W. (1997). *Stress and health*. Thousand Oaks, CA: Sage.

Manuck, S. B. (1994). Cardiovascular reactivity in cardiovascular disease: "Once more unto the breach." *International Journal of Behavioral Medicine, 1*, 4–31.

Marlatt, G. A., & Gordon, J. J. (1985). *Relapse prevention*. New York: Guilford.

Matarazzo, J. D. (1980). Behavioral health and behavioral medicine: Frontiers for a new health psychology. *American Psychologist, 35*, 807–817.

McDaniel, J. S., Musselman, D. L., Porter, M. R., Reed, D. A., & Nemeroff, C. B. (1995). Depression in patients with cancer: Diagnosis, biology, and treatment. *Archives of General Psychiatry, 52*, 89–99.

McGee, D. L., Liao, Y. L., Cao, G. C., & Cooper, R. S. (1999). Self-reported health status and mortality in a multi-ethnic U.S. cohort. *American Journal of Epidemiology, 149*, 41–46.

McMahon, C. E. (1976). The role of imagination in the disease process: Pre-cartesian medical history. *Psychological Medicine, 6*, 179–184.

Meehl, P. E. (1970). Nuisance variables and the ex post facto design. In M. Radner & S. Winokur (Eds.), *Minnesota studies in the philosophy of science: Vol. 4. Analyses of theories and methods of physics and psychology* (pp. 373–402). Minneapolis: University of Minnesota Press.

Meehl, P. E. (1978). Theoretical risks and tabular asterisks: Sir Karl, Sir Ronald, and the slow progress of soft psychology. *Journal of Consulting and Clinical Psychology, 46*, 806–834.

Miller, S. M., Shoda, Y., & Hurley, K. (1996). Applying social-cognitive theory to health protective behavior: Breast self-examination in cancer screening. *Psychological Bulletin, 119*, 70–94.

Miller, T. Q. (1994). A test of alternative explanations for the stage-like progression of adolescent substance use in four national samples. *Addictive Behaviors, 19*, 287–293.

Miller, T. Q., Turner, C. W., Tindale, R. S., Posavac, E. J., & Dugoni, B. L. (1991). Reasons for the trend toward null findings in research on Type A behavior. *Psychological Bulletin, 110*, 469–485.

Mohr, D. C., Goodkin, D. E., Likosky, W., Beutler, L., Gatto, N., & Langan, M. K. (1997). Identification of Beck Depression Inventory items related to multiple sclerosis. *Journal of Behavioral Medicine, 20*, 407–414.

Niaura, R., & Abrams, D. B. (in press). Smoking cessation: Progress, priorities, and prospectus. *Journal of Consulting and Clinical Psychology*.

Norris, F. H. (1997). Frequency and structure of precautionary behavior in the domains of hazard preparedness, crime prevention, vehicular safety, and health maintenance. *Health Psychology, 16*, 566–575.

O'Donnell, K., & Chung, J. Y. (1997). The diagnosis of major depression in end-stage renal disease. *Psychotherapy and Psychosomatics, 66*, 38–43.

Olbrisch, M. E., Benedict, S. M., Ashe, K., & Levenson, J. L. (in press). Psychological assessment and care of organ transplant patients. *Journal of Consulting and Clinical Psychology*.

Park, T. L., Adams, S. G., & Lynch, J. (1998). Sociodemographic factors in health psychology research: 12 years in review. *Health Psychology, 17*, 381–383.

Patrick, D. L., Cheadle, A., Thompson, D. C., Diehr, P., Koepsell, T., & Kinne, S. (1994). The validity of self-reported smoking: A review and meta-analysis. *American Journal of Public Health, 84*, 1086–1093.

Peck, J., Smith, T. W., Ward, J. J., & Milano, R. (1989). Disability and depression in rheumatoid arthritis: A multi-trait, multi-method investigation. *Arthritis and Rheumatism, 32*, 1100–1106.

Pierce, G. R., Lakey, B., Sarason, I. G., Sarason, B. R., & Joseph, H. J. (1997). Personality and social support processes: A conceptual overview. In G. R. Pierce, B. Lakey, I. G. Sarason, & B. R. Sarason (Eds.), *Sourcebook of social support and personality* (pp. 3–18). New York: Plenum.

Plomin, R., Reiss, D., Heatherington, E. M., & Howe, G. W. (1994). Nature and nurture: Genetic contributions to measures of the family environment. *Developmental Psychology, 30*, 32–43.

Prochaska, J. O., & DiClemente, C. C. (1984). *The transtheoretical approach: Crossing traditional boundaries of change*. Homewood, IL: Irwin.

Ramsey, S. D., McIntosh, M., & Sullivan, S. D. (2001). Design issues for conduction cost-effectiveness analyses along side clinical trails. *Annual Review of Public Health, 22*, 129–141.

Rooney, B. L., & Murray, D. M. (1996). A meta-analysis of smoking prevention programs after adjustment for errors in the unit of analysis. *Health Education Quarterly, 23*, 48–64.

Ryff, C. D., & Singer, B. (1998). The contours of positive human health. *Psychological Inquiry, 9*, 1–28.

Sackett, D. L., Richardson, W. S., Rosenberg, W., & Haynes, R. B. (1997). *Evidence-based medicine*. New York: Churchhill Livingstone.

Schneiderman, N., Antoni, M., Saab, P. G., & Ironson, G. (2001). Health psychology: Psychological and biobehavioral aspects of chronic disease management. *Annual Review of Psychology, 52*, 555–580.

Schwartz, C. E., Chesney, M. A., Irvine, J., & Keefe, F. J. (1997). The control group dilemma in clinical research. Applications for psychosocial and behavioral medicine trials. *Psychosomatic Medicine, 59*, 362–371.

Schwartz, G. E., & Weiss, S. M. (1978). Behavioral medicine revisited: An amended definition. *Journal of Behavioral Medicine, 1*, 249–251.

Schwartz, J. E., & Stone, A. A. (1998). Strategies for analyzing ecological momentary assessment data. *Health Psychology, 17*, 6–16.

Shadish, W. R., Hu, X., Glaser, R. R., Kownacki, R., & Wong, S. (1998). A method for exploring the effects of attrition in randomized experiments with dichotomous outcomes. *Psychological Methods, 3,* 3–22.

Shiffman, S., Fisher, L. A., Paty, J. A., Gnys, M., Kassel, J. D., Hickox, M., & Perez, W. (1994). Drinking and smoking: A field study of their association. *Annals of Behavioral Medicine, 16,* 203–209.

Shiffman, S., Hufford, M., Hickox, M., Paty, J. A., Gnys, M., & Kassel, J. (1997). Remember that? A comparison of real-time versus retrospective recall of smoking lapses. *Journal of Consulting and Clinical Psychology, 65,* 292–300.

Shiffman, S., Paty, J. A., Gnys, M., Kassel, J. D., & Hickox, M. (1996). First lapses to smoking: Within subject analysis of real-time reports. *Journal of Consulting and Clinical Psychology, 64,* 366–379.

Smith, T. W., & Christensen, A. J. (1996). Positive and negative affect in rheumatoid arthritis: Increased specificity in the assessment of emotional adjustment. *Annals of Behavioral Medicine, 18,* 75–78.

Smith, T. W., & Gallo, L. C. (2001). Personality traits as risk factors for physical illness. In A. Baum, T. Revenson, & J. Singer (Eds.), *Handbook of health psychology,* 139–173. Hillsdale, NJ: Erlbaum.

Smith, T. W., Gallo, L. C., & Ruiz, J. M. (in press). Toward a social psychophysiology of cardiovascular reactivity: Interpersonal concepts and methods in the study of stress and coronary disease. In J. Suls & K. Wallston (Eds.), *Social psychological foundations of health and illness.* Oxford, UK: Blackwell.

Smith, T. W., Limon, J. P., Gallo, L. C., & Ngu, L. Q. (1996). Interpersonal control and cardiovascular reactivity: Goals, behavioral expression, and the moderating effects of sex. *Journal of Personality and Social Psychology, 70,* 1012–1024.

Smith, T. W., Nealey, J. B., Kircher, J. C., & Limon, J. P. (1997). Social determinants of cardiovascular reactivity: Effects of incentive to exert influence and evaluative threat. *Psychophysiology, 34,* 65–73.

Smith, T. W., & Nicassio, P. (1995). Psychosocial practice in chronic medical illness: Clinical application of the biopsychosocial model. In P. C. Nicassio & T. W. Smith (Eds.), *Managing chronic illness: A biopsychosocial perspective* (pp. 1–32). Washington, DC: American Psychological Association.

Smith, T. W., Pope, M. K., Rhodewalt, F., & Poulton, J. L. (1989). Optimism, neuroticism, coping, and symptom reports: An alternative interpretation of the Life Orientation Test. *Journal of Personality and Social Psychology, 56,* 640–648.

Smith, T. W., & Ruiz, J. M. (1999). Methodological issues in adult health psychology. In P. C. Kendall, J. N. Butcher, & G. N. Holmbeck (Eds.), *Handbook of research methods in clinical psychology* (2nd ed., pp. 499 536). New York: Wiley.

Smith, T. W., & Ruiz, J. M. (in press). Psychosocial influences on the development and course of coronary heart disease: Current status and implications for research and practice. *Journal of Consulting and Clinical Psychology.*

Smith, T. W., & Williams, P. G. (1992). Personality and health: Advantages and limitations of the five-factor model. *Journal of Personality, 60,* 395–423.

Stone, A. A., Schwartz, J. E., Neale, J. M., Shiffman, S., Marco, C., Hickox, M., Paty, J., Porter, L., & Cruise, L. (1998). A comparison of coping assessed by ecological momentary assessment and retrospective recall. *Journal of Personality and Social Psychology, 74,* 1670–1680.

Trapnell, P. D., & Wiggins, J. S. (1990). Extension of the Interpersonal Adjective Scales to include the big five dimensions of personality. *Journal of Personality and Social Psychology, 59,* 781–790.

Trobst, K. K. (2000). An interpersonal conceptualization and quantification of social support transactions. *Personality and Social Psychology Bulletin, 26,* 971–986.

Turk, D. C., & Okifuji, A. (in press). Psychological factors in chronic pain: Evolution and revolution. *Journal of Consulting and Clinical Psychology.*

Turk, D. C., & Rudy, T. E. (1990). Neglected factors in chronic pain treatment outcome studies—Referral patterns, failure to enter treatment, and attrition. *Pain, 43,* 7–21.

Turner, J. A., Deyo, R. A., & Loweser, J. D. (1994). The importance of placebo effects in pain treatment and research. *Journal of the American Medical Association, 271,* 1609–1614.

von Bertalanffy, L. (1968). *General systems theory.* New York: Braziller.

Wadden, T. A., Brownell, K. D., & Foster, G. D. (in press). Obesity: Responding to the global epidemic. *Journal of Consulting and Clinical Psychology.*

Waltz, J., Addis, M. E., Koerner, K., & Jacobson, N. S. (1993). Testing the integrity of a psychotherapy protocol: Assessment of adherence and competence. *Journal of Consulting and Clinical Psychology, 61,* 620–630.

Watson, D., & Pennebaker, J. W. (1989). Health complaints, stress, and distress: Exploring the central role of negative affectivity. *Psychological Review, 96,* 234–254.

Watson, D., & Tellegen, A. (1985). Toward a consensual structure of mood. *Psychological Bulletin, 98,* 219–235.

Watson, D., Weber, K., Assenheimer, J. S., Clark, L. A., Strauss, M. E., & McCormick, R. A. (1995). Testing a tripartite model: Vol. 1. Evaluating the convergent and discriminant validity of anxiety and depression symptom scales. *Journal of Abnormal Psychology, 104,* 3–14.

Weinstein, N. D. (1993). Testing four competing theories of health-protective behavior. *Health Psychology, 12,* 324–333.

Weinstein, N. D., Rothman, A. J., & Sutton, S. R. (1998). Stage theories of health behavior: Conceptual and methodological issues. *Health Psychology, 17,* 211–213.

Williams, P. G., Holmbeck, G. N., & Greenley, R. N. (in press). Adolescent health psychology. *Journal of Consulting and Clinical Psychology.*

Williams, R. B. (2000). Psychosocial factors, health, and disease: The impact of aging and the life cycle. In S. B. Manuck, R. Jennings, B. S. Rabin, & A. Baum (Eds.), *Behavior, health and aging* (pp. 135–151). Mahwah, NJ: Erlbaum.

Yen, I. H., & Kaplan, G. (1999). Neighborhood social environment and risk of death: Multilevel evidence from the Alameda County study. *American Journal of Epidemiology, 149,* 898–907.

Zautra, A., Burleson, M., Smith, C., Blalock, S., Wallston, K., DeVellis, R., DeVellis, B., & Smith, T. W. (1995). Arthritis and perceptions of quality of life: An examination of positive and negative affect in rheumatoid arthritis patients. *Health Psychology, 14,* 399–408.

CHAPTER 11

Animal Learning

RUSSELL M. CHURCH

The purpose of this chapter is to describe how research in animal learning has been conducted, not what has been discovered. At one time most behavioral research was conducted by individuals whose training was focused on the topics covered by this chapter. Now many neuroscientists, with interest in the functions of the brain, are also conducting research in animal learning. Some of this research, even that published in premier journals in the field, includes behavioral methods that are flawed by problems in behavioral measurement, experimental design, or interpretation. A goal of this chapter is to transfer what is fairly common knowledge in experimental psychology to others who can make use of it. Often, several alternative methods can be used to accomplish a particular goal, and particularly for readers at the graduate level, it is important to be able to make choices among these alternatives wisely. Thus, I have included evaluative comments

about the strengths and weaknesses of the methods that are described.

The organization of this chapter is much like the standard organization of a journal article in experimental psychology as described in the *Publication Manual of the American Psychological Association* (American Psychological Association, 2001a). Such articles have sections devoted to introduction, method, results, and discussion. These sections are designed to answer such questions as, What is the problem? What apparatus is required? What animals should be used? How should the independent and dependent variables be measured? What procedure should be used? What experimental design should be used? How should the data be analyzed? and How should the results be explained? Because computers are being used in all stages of the research process, a separate section is devoted to the use of computers in research in animal learning. The final section is a case study of an experiment that illustrates how each of these questions arose and how they were answered.

WHAT IS THE PROBLEM?

In any experimental study of animal learning it is important to specify the problem under study. In some cases the problem may be simply to describe the typical behavior of animals under well-specified conditions. In other cases the problem may be to describe the capacity of animals to solve well-specified problems. The early attention toward what was called *animal intelligence* was an interest in the capacity of animals (Thorndike, 1898; Washburn, 1936).

The purpose of some studies of animal learning is to develop an apparatus, a procedure, or some measures of behavior that provide a good basis for further experiments. Examples of these include the development and use of the radial arm maze for the study of working memory (Olton & Samuelson, 1976) and the development and use of the operant box for the study of contingencies of reinforcement (Skinner, 1938). The development of such reference experiments, which involve a combination of apparatus, procedure, and measures, can have an enormous influence on subsequent research. Even the development of a procedure such as matching to sample (Blough, 1960) or the development of a behavioral measure such as the time at which the response rate changes from a low to high (Schneider, 1969) can have a substantial influence on subsequent research. The goal is to demonstrate that the new apparatus, procedure, or measure leads to more reliable or valid results than did previous methods.

In some cases the problem is simply to determine if two variables, neither of which is controlled by the experimenter, are related. In such correlational research the causes of the behavior are unclear: Variable *a* may have affected variable *b*, variable *b* may have affected variable *a*, or some unmeasured variable may have affected both variables *a* and *b*. Many studies of the relationship between brain processes are correlational studies. For example, an investigator may record the times of occurrence of spikes of a single neuron and the times of occurrence of a behavioral response. Such a study will reveal the presence of a relationship between the two dependent variables, but not a causal basis for the relationship.

Many studies are designed to identify the causes of behavior. The problem is to determine whether a particular independent variable controlled by the experimenter is related to a behavioral dependent variable. To identify the specific features of the independent variable that were responsible, considerations of experimental design are particularly important. In addition to determining whether a particular variable affects a particular behavior, a more quantitative problem is to specify the functional relationship between an independent variable x and a behavioral dependent variable y. The function may be linear, exponential, or any well-specified form.

Finally, the problem of many studies is to test a particular theory. This requires that the theory be precisely described and that the observed variables be related precisely to the concepts of the theory. Then the results of the experiments can be compared to the predictions of the theory. In some cases the theory may specify only that one treatment will have a greater effect than another, but in others quantitative results of an experiment can be compared to quantitative predictions of the theory. This should include both standard goodness-of-fit measures and considerations of model complexity. An overly complex model may fit a particular set of data but not generalize well to other data (Myung, 2000).

WHAT APPARATUS IS REQUIRED?

Field studies of animal learning provide information about what animals do and what they are capable of learning. They also lead to hypotheses regarding the variables responsible for learning and performance. Tests of these hypotheses can be carried out with field experimentation (Tinbergen, 1953). In field experimentation the investigator manipulates some independent variable in the animal's natural environment; in laboratory experimentation the investigator manipulates some independent variable in an artificial environment. The distinction between a natural and artificial environment is sometimes blurred by the use of artificial environments that have similarities to the natural environment. In some cases these laboratory approximations to naturalistic environments may be close approximations to the naturalistic environment; in other cases researchers may use standard laboratory apparatus. For example, the study of foraging behavior can be conducted with field observation, field experimentation, or laboratory experimentation.

The two main types of laboratory apparatus for the study of animal learning are mazes and boxes. A maze is an apparatus in which the dependent variable is the location of the animal; a box is an apparatus in which the dependent variable is a response of the animal (i.e., what the animal does in a location, not where it is).

Mazes

The first experimental study of learning of the white rat was conducted in a wooden replica of a maze patterned after the hedge maze in the Hampton Court Palace in England (Small, 1900). This was a complex maze with many blocked paths, but with one sequence of correct turns the rat could reach the center of the maze, which contained food. Measures of performance included the time required to reach the food and the number of erroneous paths taken. With successive experiences in the maze, the typical time to reach the goal and the number of errors decrease. Subsequently, investigators used much simpler mazes. A good history of the first 50 years of the use of mazes is provided by Munn (1950).

The simplest of all mazes is the straight runway, often about 4 ft long, with food at the end of the runway. The measures of performance normally recorded are the response latency (time to leave the starting chamber) and the running speed (the time from leaving the starting chamber to reaching the food, divided by the length of the runway). With successive experience in the runway, the typical latency decreases, and the typical running speed decreases.

For the study of choice the simplest type of maze is the T-maze. It consists of a straight runway and two arms to form the shape of a T with food at the end of one of the arms. The measures of performance normally recorded are latency, running speed, and particularly choice of the left or right arm. The food may always be at the same arm, or it may be at the arm that is identified by a particular stimulus that is assigned to the arm on each trial at random.

For the study of working memory, the radial arm maze is frequently used (Olton & Samuelson, 1976). The radial arm maze consists of eight or more arms radiating from a central point located in a room with distinctive cues. A standard procedure is to place food at the end of each of the arms and record the pattern of responding to the various arms. An animal with a perfect working memory of which arms had been visited would enter only those arms that have not yet been visited (i.e., the arms that still have food). This apparatus is also used for the study of reference memory with a modification of the procedure in which some of the arms never have food. Animals readily learn to distinguish between arms that are sometimes baited and those that are never baited (reference memory), and they seldom reenter arms that have already been baited (working memory).

For the study of navigation, the Morris water maze is frequently used (Morris, 1981). This is a large round tub of water that has been made opaque and that contains a small, slightly submerged platform that is located in a room with distinctive cues. The animal is typically released from random locations around the periphery of the tub, and it learns to swim toward the location of the submerged platform and stand on it. The behavior is normally monitored by a video camera that can be analyzed by a computer program that identifies the location of the animal as a function of time.

Although a great deal of research in animal learning has used the maze, three problems are notable. First, in some cases the measure of behavior is dependent on the judgment of the experimenter—as, for example, when time is measured by a stopwatch or when entry into an arm is based on a decision by the investigator. This is a source of random error, and it can lead to a biased measure of the animal's behavior if the experimenter has beliefs about what the animal should be doing in a particular situation. Such measures should be done blindly by an experimenter who cannot identify the previous treatment of the animal and who has no hypothesis about what the animal should be doing. Some mazes have been developed that provide a way for automatic recording of behavior. Second, in most cases the animal must be frequently handled during a session. Because it is not possible to standardize such handling completely, it is a source of random error, and if the experimenter has beliefs about what the animal should be doing in a particular situation, it may lead to biased handling of animals in the different groups. Some mazes have been developed in which the animal does not need to be handled between trials. Third, the stimuli are difficult to describe in physical terms, and even more difficult to describe in terms of the proximal cues received by the animal.

Boxes

About the same time that the first maze studies were being conducted, research on animal learning was being conducted in problem boxes (Thorndike, 1898). A problem box is an enclosure with various features that can be manipulated. One of the manipulations or a combination of several manipulations opens the box, permitting the animal to leave the box and get some food. Thorndike used many different problem boxes with cats, dogs, and chickens. The primary objective measure of performance was the latency to escape from the box.

The operant box developed by Skinner (1938) for rats is a simplified version of a problem box that eliminates the need to handle the animals after food reward. The box contained a lever, a food cup, and a light. Food was delivered according to some schedule of reinforcement based on time intervals and numbers of responses. Four standard schedules of reinforcement are fixed interval, fixed ratio, variable interval, and variable ratio. In a fixed interval schedule of reinforcement the first response after a particular interval of time (such as 1 min) is followed by food; in a fixed-ratio schedule of reinforcement a particular number of responses (such as 20 responses) is followed by food. The variable interval and ratio schedules are specified by a distribution of time intervals or number of responses that are characterized by the mean (such as a 1-min variable interval schedule or a variable ratio schedule of 20 responses). Many other schedules of reinforcement have also been used, but all of them are based on contingencies of reinforcement based on times from well-specified events and number of responses. More than a single lever is used for choice experiments, and many experiments require multiple stimuli or graded control of the dimensions of the stimulus. The basic data consist of the time of occurrence of each stimulus, response, and food delivery. These times are measured automatically when a mechanical or electronic switch is closed with force, contact, breaking of a photobeam, or some other means.

The operant box typically used for pigeons is similar in concept to the one used for rats but differs in many details. The typical response is a peck at a lighted disk, rather than the pressing of a lever. In addition, the box is larger, and the food typically is delivered for a fixed time (such as 3 s) rather than a fixed amount (such as 45 mg). Other adjustments in the details of the box must be made for other species, such as the mouse.

In some animal learning experiments, electric shock has been used instead of food. The shock presentation may be contingent on a response (punishment) or on a stimulus (conditioned emotional response); shock termination may be contingent on a response (escape); or the shock may be omitted contingent on a response (active avoidance).

Basis for Choice of Apparatus

When it is adequate for the problem under investigation, standard equipment should normally be used. Typically, such equipment has gone through a long process of modification guided by the performance by animals. For example, the modern lever box for rats contains a lever of a particular size located in a particular place that requires a particular force to activate. If the lever were located higher on the wall or if it required more force to activate, the performance of the rat would undoubtedly be affected. Sources of fast movement (such as rapid insertion and retraction of a lever) or loud noises (such as solenoid activation of a feeder) have been eliminated. With current standard equipment, there is no need to shape the rat to press the lever—a well-handled rat on a restricted diet that does not encounter frightening events such as loud noises, fast movements, or unusual handlers, treatments, or testing times will quickly learn to press the lever to secure 45-mg pellets of food. The use of standard equipment also facilitates attempts by other researchers to replicate the experimental results. Of course, there are problems for which the investigator must develop a new apparatus, but early versions of a new apparatus are likely to contain some difficulties for the animals.

An apparatus that has typically been used for a particular problem should generally be favored over some alternative apparatus. This increases the comparability of results of multiple experiments within a given laboratory and between laboratories. Of course, when sufficient understanding of a phenomenon has been obtained with one type of apparatus, it is often desirable to test the generality of the conclusions by some investigation of the effect of similar treatments in a very different apparatus.

Another consideration in the selection of testing apparatus is the degree of the experimenter's control of stimuli. This includes not only the control of the physical stimulus at the source (such as the speaker or the light bulb) but also the proximal stimulus at the location of the animal. It is generally easier to control the proximal stimulus in a box than in a maze, so it is better to use a box than a maze in those cases in which either can be used.

An apparatus that requires little or no handling of the animals during the training task is highly desirable. Although investigators should make efforts to handle each animal in the same way every day, this cannot be done precisely, and the degree of variability cannot be properly measured. Typically, animals trained in mazes require handling between successive trials, but animals trained in boxes require handling only at the beginning and end of a long session. Thus, boxes are generally better than mazes in cases in which either can be used.

Finally, there are practical considerations in the choice of apparatus, such as the cost and availability of the equipment and the investigator's experience with the apparatus and with analysis of data obtained from it.

WHAT ANIMALS SHOULD BE USED?

Many investigators do research primarily or exclusively with a single species of animals. This is often a good strategy because it is important to know the animals well. It enables the investigator to recognize conditions that might make the animal frightened or angry, to appreciate the animal's motivational state, and to identify health problems. With extensive experience with a particular species an investigator can develop an understanding of which tasks should be relatively easy or difficult for the animal to learn.

Studies of animal learning have been conducted with many species of mammals, birds, reptiles, amphibians, and invertebrates. Most of the studies have been with mammals, and the most frequently used species has been the rat. A search of the PsychINFO database identifies thousands of studies of learning in the rat—many more than other mammalian species. The laboratory rat has been bred to be well adapted for laboratory environments. With regular handling it is docile, and in a relatively constant environment it is unafraid. Rats are easily trained to make particular responses, to discriminate among stimuli, and to learn contingencies of reinforcement. They have been extensively used both for both behavioral and for neuroscience research. Many other species of mammals have also been used, including nonhuman primates, mice, rabbits, dogs, and cats. The choice of species depends in part on the problem under investigation.

For the goal of extending knowledge of learning mechanisms of animals to humans, nonhuman primates are presumed to be most relevant. Although most of this research has been conducted with monkeys, such as the rhesus monkey, a few laboratories have the ability to conduct learning research with gorillas, orangutans, and, particularly, chimpanzees. The goal of such research often is to develop an animal model of human behavior.

For the goal of understanding genetic mechanisms of behavior, the mouse has been the mammal of choice. Recently, there has been a great increase in understanding the genetics of the mouse, so more investigators have been attempting to study the relationship of genetic manipulations to learning mechanisms. Progress in this field has been impeded by the limited understanding of the effects of various treatments on the behavior of the mouse.

For the understanding of classical conditioning of a discrete response (such as nictitating membrane response of the eye, or the eyelid response), the rabbit has been found to be an excellent animal because of its ability to be relatively motionless under restraint. For animal learning experiments with visual stimuli, the pigeon has been used extensively. Many other species of birds have also been used, typically for comparative purposes. Reptiles and amphibians have been much less frequently used, primarily because of the limited number of behavioral learning procedures that are available.

Invertebrates have been used in animal learning experiments for various purposes. In some cases the genetics is particularly well understood (e.g., *drosophila*); in other cases the neural mechanisms are particular well understood (e.g., *aplysia*). In some cases, the results of conditioning experiments with an invertebrate (e.g., honey bee) are remarkably similar to the results of similar experiments with mammals (e.g., rat). Such findings provide considerable support for the existence of general laws of learning (Bitterman, 2000).

For the purposes of comparison among species it is sometimes desirable for an investigator to conduct research with multiple species of animals. This avoids a concern that

differences in the training conditions in different laboratories, rather than species differences, were responsible for the difference in the results. One approach is to sample a wide range of species informally. When this is done, acquiring similar results from the different species indicates that the phenomenon has wide generality. Another approach is to identify species that are similar genetically but that typically live in different ecological niches. This provides evidence for the relationship between ecology and behavior. Comparative studies are difficult to interpret because of the concern that the impact of the conditions of training were not identical. For example, it is uncertain how to equate the motivational level of different species.

HOW SHOULD THE INDEPENDENT AND DEPENDENT VARIABLES BE MEASURED?

Objective recording of data requires that the behavior activate a transducer with an output that can be stored as a number. A mechanical switch may be used to record a rat's pressing of a lever or a pigeon's pecking at a lighted disk; a photocell circuit may be used to record the location of an animal; and other transducers may be used to record pressures or velocities. Objective recording reduces the possibility that the investigator's expectations can affect the measured behavior. The behavior is usually easy to record, and because it is originally in numbers, it is easy to analyze. The major concern about objective recording is that it does not capture the richness of the behavior that can be observed, although it is usually possible to develop an objective way to measure well-defined behavior.

As an alternative to such objective recording of data, an investigator may use subjective recording of behavior that is observed directly or observed on videotape. One of the advantages of videotaped recordings is that the same behavior can be scored by multiple observers, which permits correlations of the scores to be used as a measure of reliability. The major concerns about subjective recording are that the analysis of the data is time-consuming, that some of the measures may not be highly reliable, and that the measurements may reflect, in part, the expectations of the individuals who are scoring the behavior.

Typically, an objective measure of behavior provides information about three questions: What happened? Where did it happen? and When did it happen? The type of response may be identified by which transducer was activated (e.g., the mechanical switch of the left lever response). The location of the response may also be identified by which transducer was activated (e.g., the photocell circuit at the food cup). The time of the response may be measured by a clock that runs during the session. The resolution of the clock that is used depends on the behavior being measured. For most behavioral purposes there is no need to have resolution greater than 1 ms, and it may be satisfactory to record data to the nearest 10 ms or 100 ms. Thus, a single measure of behavior may consist of a pair of numbers: one representing the behavior (the type of response and its location) and the other representing the time of the behavior. The procedure can also be represented by a pair of numbers: one representing the stimulus (e.g., onset of a light, termination of a light, and delivery of food) and the other representing the time of the event. Thus, what happened to the animal in a session and what the animal did can be represented in this time-event format as a list of times and the events that occurred at each of these times.

The most detailed data that are recorded may be called the raw data. It is now both feasible and desirable to save all of the raw data. It is feasible because of the low cost of storage of information in computer-readable form. Normally the data are initially stored in computer memory and then transferred to some mass storage device (such as magnetic disk or CD-ROM). Storing the raw data is desirable because it makes it possible to perform secondary data analyses that would not be possible if only the summarized data were available. Prior to the general availability of personal computers, the raw data consisted of what would now be considered summary statistics. For example, the number of responses of an animal during a session in the presence of a stimulus and in the absence of a stimulus might be the most detailed data that were recorded. Now it is feasible to record the time of occurrence of each response, stimulus onset, and stimulus termination. From these raw data it is possible to calculate the number of responses of the animal during a session in the presence of a stimulus and in the absence of a stimulus, and it is also possible to calculate many other measures of behavior such as the time from stimulus onset to the next response. The task of the data analyst is to select and use appropriate measures of performance based on the raw data.

Measures of learned behavior are based on time, number, and magnitude. For example, a dependent variable might be the latency to respond at the onset of a stimulus (a time measure), the number of responses during the presence of a stimulus (a number measure), or the extent of closure of the nictitating membrane (a magnitude measure). Other measures involve a combination, such as response rate (a ratio of number to time). Any of these measures can be expressed in absolute or relative units.

Transformations

A transformation of a measure of learned behavior involves a mathematical operation on the raw data. For example, an investigator may record the times of occurrence of response,

calculate the difference between the times of successive responses (interresponse times), calculate the reciprocal of the interresponse times (response speeds), and use the response speeds for further analysis. There are various reasons for transforming a measure. In some cases the distribution of the transformed data may be simpler than the distribution of the raw data. For example, it may be more symmetrical, or the ratio of the standard deviation to the mean (the coefficient of variation) may be more constant in the transformed data than in the raw data. In some cases a theory may make simpler predictions about one dependent variable than about another. Another reason for transforming a measure is to use a dependent variable that is typically used by others in order to permit direct comparison of new results with previous ones. Probably the most important reason for transforming data is to obtain a dependent variable that accounts for a higher percentage of the variance in the data. For example, a discrimination ratio, such as rate of response in the presence of a stimulus relative to the absence of a stimulus, often accounts for treatment effects better than an absolute measure, such as rate of response in the presence of a stimulus (Church, 1969).

Two types of transformations have been found to be particularly useful. One of them is the expression of a dependent variable as a relative, rather than absolute, value. The other is a nonlinear but order-preserving transformation. Examples are the logarithm, reciprocal, square root, and others in a ladder of transformations (Tukey, 1977). Some investigators are reluctant to use any transformations because of concern about distorting the raw data. This concern is misguided because there is no particular reason to believe that the easiest variable to measure is the most fundamental for understanding the learning process. Of course, it is important to specify precisely the transformations that are used because the conclusions that apply to a particular dependent variable may not apply to a transformation of the dependent variable. For example, a significant interaction based on one dependent variable (such as time) may not be present on a transformation of that variable (such as speed).

Summary Measures

A measure of behavior is usually conceptualized as containing a true value plus random error. The random error is assumed to have a mean of zero and a symmetrical (usually normal) distribution with some standard deviation. If one examines the original measure of behavior, the true value can be lost in the random variability. To reduce this random variability, a measure of central tendency is used. The typical measure is the mean or the median, but variants of these measures of central tendency are sometimes used. The median provides a way to reduce the effects of outliers. The measure of central tendency is normally calculated first within animals and then between animals. This provides equal weight for each animal, rather than each response, and it provides multiple independent measures for inferential analyses.

Two main problems have been identified with the use of measures of central tendency. One problem is inherent in the calculation of any summary statistic: There is some loss of information. For example, averaging information across several animals eliminates any individual differences in performance. Thus, the analyst must decide which factors to examine and clearly specify which factors are being ignored.

Another problem is more subtle, and more serious: The mean function may not represent the function of any of the individuals (Bakan, 1954; Estes, 1956; Sidman, 1953). The standard example is the following: Suppose that learning is characterized by an abrupt acquisition of a response, but the number of exposures to the situation required for acquisition is a random variable. If one calculates the mean of a large number of such step functions, with some variability in the number of exposures before the step, one obtains a gradually rising function that is not characteristic of the shape of any individual function. The gradually rising function is sometimes assumed to characterize the shape of the individual functions (with random error reduced), but this is an error. The error becomes serious when theories are designed to account for such behavior in individual animals; obviously, in this case one would need theories that produce step functions in individual animals.

This problem does not mean that one cannot average performance across animals. One solution is to average with respect to some criterion, such as the occasion on which the animal reaches a criterion of learning. Such a backward learning curve, in the step-function example given, would have a low probability of responding prior to the criterion and a high probability of responding after the criterion. Thus, an average function with respect to a criterion may have the same shape as the individual functions.

The same problem with averaging performance across animals applies to averaging performance within an animal. For example, in a fixed interval schedule of reinforcement the first response after a particular time (such as 60 s) is followed by food. Animals often respond at a low rate for about two thirds of the interval and then switch to a fast response rate (Schneider, 1969). If one calculates the mean of a large number of such step functions, with some variability in the number of exposures before the step, one obtains a gradually rising function that is not characteristic of the shape of any individual function. The gradually rising function, often called a fixed-interval scallop, is sometimes assumed to characterize the shape of the individual functions (with random error reduced), but this is an error. The error becomes

serious when theories are designed to account for such behavior on individual intervals; obviously, in this case one would need theories that produce step functions on individual intervals.

In addition to measures of central tendency, it is also important to report measures of variability. This includes both within-animal variability providing evidence regarding the stability of the measure and between-animal variability providing evidence regarding individual differences. If means are used as a measure of central tendency, it is most consistent to use standard deviations or median absolute deviations as a measure of variability; if medians are used as a measure of central tendency, it is most consistent to use an interquartile-range measure of variability. Error bars on figures provide a visualization of the amount of variability. They may be either standard deviations or interquartile ranges to represent the variability of the observations or the standard errors to represent the variability of the estimate of the mean.

WHAT PROCEDURES SHOULD BE USED?

A procedure should be chosen that is appropriate for the problem. In some cases the judicious selection of a critical procedure can be particularly revealing; in other cases a large number of alternative procedures can be revealing. Ideally, a theory would be able to make explicit predictions of performance for any procedure within a well-specified domain.

Simple procedures may be defined in terms of the number of stimuli required (0, 1, or more than 1) and the number of response contingencies (0, 1, or more than 1). The number of stimuli required is self-explanatory. A response contingency refers to the relationship between a response and a reward. In classical conditioning the reward is delivered independently of a response; in instrumental conditioning the reward is delivered contingent on a response; in choice experiments there may be two or more response contingencies. The simplest of all procedures is one in which there are no stimuli or response contingencies. For such a procedure food is delivered at fixed times, random times, or some other distribution. This procedure is known as *context conditioning, magazine training,* and *temporal conditioning.* Many of the other simple procedures also have multiple names and separate histories. Other procedures may involve the probabilistic presentation of events (as in partial reinforcement), presentation of events in a repeating pattern, and concurrent presentation of events.

Many procedures involve the variation of an interval of time between two events, such as the interval between the conditioned and unconditioned stimulus, between the stimulus and the response (in the study of working memory), and between the response and the reward (in the study of delay of reward). Other procedures involve manipulations of the stimulus conditions (in the study of stimulus control of behavior). These procedures often use one of the psychophysical methods that were originally developed for the study of sensory processes.

WHAT EXPERIMENTAL DESIGN SHOULD BE USED?

The planning of an experimental design involves many decisions. These include decisions about whether to use an independent group design, a repeated measure design, or some combination of the two. If all animals are treated alike, it is possible to describe what was done and what was observed, but there is no basis for identifying causal variables. For the identification of causation it is necessary to use one or more control groups, so that comparisons can be made between the effects of different treatment comparisons. A simple untreated control condition can be used to identify that something about the treatment produced the observed differences between an experimental and control condition, but additional control groups are essential to identify the aspects of the treatment that were necessary and sufficient for the observed effects. The art of experimental design is to choose the control conditions that provide information about essential features in an efficient way.

Independent Group Designs

Many standard experimental designs are used in the study of animal learning (see chapter by Wilcox in this volume). To avoid carryover effects of previous treatments, many investigators typically use independent group designs. There are three ways to deal with irrelevant variables: They may be held constant, counterbalanced, or randomized. For example, if the important independent variable in a particular study is the spacing of the trials, how should the investigator deal with possible effects of the time during the day at which the testing occurs? One possibility is to hold the time of day constant by testing all of the animals in both conditions at the same time; another is to counterbalance the time of day by testing half the animals in each condition in a morning session and half the animals in each condition in an afternoon session; and another is to assign the animals to the morning and afternoon sessions randomly. Typically, investigators hold constant as many variables as possible, although it is recognized that this may limit the generality of the conclusions to the specific conditions used in the experiment. Variables that are likely to

have an effect on performance typically will be counterbalanced. All other variables will be randomized.

To randomize all other variables, conditions are randomly assigned to animals, often with the restriction that an equal number are in each of the conditions. A method of doing this is to assign a random number to each animal and put half of the animals with the lowest random numbers in one group and those with the highest random numbers in the other group. This provides a way of randomizing all other factors, both those that can be readily measured and those that cannot. Haphazard assignment of animals to groups should never be done. It is unlikely that a person without access to a randomization device can assign animals to groups in a manner such that each animal has an equal and independent chance of being in a particular group.

Independent group designs for the study of animal learning often involve multiple phases. This is essential for making the important distinction between *learning* and *performance*. The conceptual distinction is that performance refers to the observed behavior but that learning is a theoretical variable referring to what the animal knows rather than what the animal does. For example, rats may be trained to run to the goal box of a straight alley that contains food. If the animals run more rapidly with a particular drug, the drug's effect on performance can be described, but its effect on learning cannot. To make this distinction, a second phase may be added without food in which half the rats in each training group receive the drug and half do not (see Table 11.1).

If mean testing performance depends on the conditions of testing, but not of training (i.e., a difference between the columns in the mean running speed, $a + c$ vs. $b + d$), the drug has influenced performance but not learning. If, on the other hand, the mean testing performance depends on the conditions of training, but not of testing (i.e., a difference between the rows in the mean running speed, $a + b$ vs. $c + d$), the drug has influenced learning. This design was used by Spence (1956) to identify factors affecting learning. Of course, other patterns of results can occur. For example, the performance may depend on the similarity of the conditions of testing to the conditions of training (i.e., a difference between the positive and negative diagonals of the table in

TABLE 11.1   A Two-Phase Design to Identify Factors Affecting Learning and Performance: Mean Running Speed During Testing as a Function of Drug Conditions During Training and Testing

Training	Testing	
	Drug	No Drug
Drug	a	b
No drug	c	d

the mean running speed, $a + d$ vs. $b + c$). This is known as *state-dependent learning*. In addition to distinguishing between learning and performance, transfer designs with multiple phases have been important for the assessment of what was learned in the first phase (Rescorla, 1988).

Repeated Measures Designs

To reduce the effect of individual differences, many investigators typically use repeated measures designs. In a repeated measures design, each of the animals receives each of the conditions. Because of potential carryover effects, different animals receive the conditions in different orders. They may be counterbalanced or randomized. Other potential influencing variables may also be counterbalanced or randomized. In some cases a mixed design may be used, which is a combination of an independent groups design and a repeated measures design.

Single-Subject Designs

Some investigators use what is sometimes called single-subject design (Sidman, 1960). This requires that all of the treatments be given to a single animal. Typically, such research is replicated on two or three other animals to determine the generality of the conclusions. The assumption is that most animals produce similar results, so there is no need for larger samples. But there is also a concern about combining the results of multiple animals because the performance of each of the animals is different. This approach is particularly advocated by the *Journal of the Experimental Analysis of Behavior*. Although such experiments could be conducted with random ordering of treatments, fixed criteria for each phase, and other features of standard experimental designs, the approach actively encourages the decisions of investigators based on the behavior of the animals. This approach is difficult to distinguish from pilot studies that are often conducted in new situations. In a pilot study an investigator may use a small number of animals and a large number of treatments; the purpose is to develop hypotheses, not to produce convincing and interpretable data.

Problems Common to All Experimental Designs

There are some common problems for all experimental designs. These include the rationale for determining the number of animals per group, the number of trials in a phase, and the ways in which errors are handled.

The number of animals in an experiment is usually based on several considerations. In the independent group designs, investigators almost always test an equal number of animals in each condition, and in each combination of conditions. Although analyses can be conducted of data with unequal numbers of animals in each cell, or even missing cells, they require some additional assumptions; in rare cases an investigator may choose to use a larger number of animals in a condition likely to produce more variable data. If only a single animal is used in each combination of conditions, there can be no separation between interaction and random error. If two or more animals are used in each combination of conditions, a measure of variability within cells can be calculated.

Ideally, investigators would determine the number of animals to be tested in each condition based on an analysis of power. To do this the investigator makes an estimate of the within-group variability to be expected and an estimate of the expected size of the effect. These estimates are typically based on previous research. Alternatively, the investigator may decide on the size of the effect that is worth identifying. With this information and some assumptions about the form of the error distribution, the investigator can rationally decide on the number of animals per group. In fact, most investigators do not do a power analysis (or do not report doing so) in deciding on the number of animals per group. Many undoubtedly use the number of animals typically used in similar experiments. If there are many such similar experiments, this approach may be satisfactory because previous investigators will have found by trial and error a number of animals per condition that is sufficient to identify phenomena (i.e., a low Type II error rate), but not many more than necessary (i.e., a number of animals that produces an exceedingly small p value).

The number of animals in repeated-measures designs is based on similar considerations. In the single-subject designs, however, the decisions are based almost entirely on convention. The term *single subject* refers to the fact that separate analyses are done of each animal, not that the experiment consists of only one animal. Because of concern that the behavior of a single animal may not be representative of others, it is typical to use three or five animals. Ideally, all of them will show similar patterns of results. In cases in which the performances of the animals differ, the investigator may comment on the range of possible behaviors of different animals, and because an odd number of animals are typically tested, the investigator may also comment on the typical pattern.

In experiments on animal learning, the investigator typically chooses a number of trials of training sufficient to produce relatively complete learning. This is referred to as asymptotic, steady-state, or stable behavior. This number may be chosen before the beginning of the experiment based on the number used in similar experiments, or it may be based on some formal criterion of stability. Either of these bases is better than the informal ones involved in optional stopping because the latter allow experimenter biases to affect the outcomes. In some experiments the investigator chooses a number of trials that produces incomplete learning. For example, the blocking result is most clearly observed with an intermediate number of presentations of paired reinforced stimuli. The numbers in previous similar experiments are often used because they are assumed to be close to the optimal.

The method section of an article on animal learning describes the procedure that was used, but it seldom describes minor apparatus or human errors in the procedure that are difficult to avoid. Of course, good laboratory practices involve preventive maintenance and daily checking of the apparatus, as well as modification of faulty equipment to reduce errors. Good laboratory practice also involves the recording of all known human errors that occur, such as a dropped animal, a change in the time of testing or feeding, and the recording of unusual events, such as construction noise or injury or sickness of an animal. If these are rare, the reported results will not be affected in any meaningful way by reasonable alternative data analysis decisions.

HOW SHOULD THE DATA BE ANALYZED?

The problems of data analysis in animal learning research are similar to those in other psychological research. In some cases investigators report the central tendency of a single standard dependent variable, usually with a measure of the variability of the variable, and then proceed to test the significance of the difference between conditions. Among the dependent variables that may be used are absolute and relative measures of time, number, or magnitude, and trials to criterion. These studies usually involve a large number of carefully chosen control groups so that it is possible to identify the controlling variables for the observed effects.

Animal learning experiments involve changes in a dependent variable as a function of time or trial. Thus, some investigators describe the learning curve, which is the functional relationship between a behavioral dependent measure and time or trial. Time-series analysis is particularly important for such data (see chapter by Lanza, Flaherty, & Collins in this volume).

Some investigators make extensive use of the techniques of exploratory data analysis for the discovery of effects and for the graphical presentation of phenomena (see chapter by Kirk in this volume). The raw data from a session of learning by an animal may include a large number of events that occur at unique times. For example, a record may be kept of the onset and termination of a light, a tone, a lever response, a head entry into the food cup, a lick on the water bottle, and others. The times can be recorded precisely in milliseconds since the beginning of the session. These data provide a rich basis for exploratory data analysis, and if these data are available in archives on the Web, they may be used by others for secondary data analysis.

The major role of inferential data analysis in research on animal learning is to provide a consistent standard for making conclusions based on results. It also provides a succinct report of the conclusions regarding significance, confidence intervals, and magnitudes of results. Without the conventions of inferential statistics, different investigators might reach different conclusions from the same results. The key intuition is that a result is significant if it is consistently observed.

HOW SHOULD THE RESULTS BE EXPLAINED?

There are several ways to explain animal behavior. They include a description of the controlling variables, statements of principles, and process models based on psychological, biological, or mathematical variables. The results are facts that have been observed; the explanations are alternative ways to understand these results. A good explanation will provide a succinct and accurate description of a wide range of results.

Operational Definitions of Cognitive Factors

An unsatisfactory way to attempt to explain behavior is to identify some particular behavior as an operational definition of a cognitive process and then use this as an explanation. Various measures have been proposed for working memory, attention, fear, and other psychological processes. The psychological terms then can be used instead of the behavioral measures. This provides an alternative term for the behavior that is short and memorable and which may or may not serve to direct the investigator's attention to relevant psychological processes. The term, however, remains equivalent to the particular behavior and is not an explanation of the behavior.

Functional Relationships Between Input and Output Variables

In animal learning experiments, the input variable is some treatment condition, and the output variable is some measure of behavior. Usually, both variables can be expressed on a quantitative scale so that it is possible to describe a functional relationship between the input and the output. This type of explanation is not clearly distinguished from a report of results. Typically, a functional explanation will be more general (such that it applies to several variables), more analytical (such that it will suggest causal variables), and more quantitative (such that it will provide a simple mathematical function).

Principles of Behavior

In an explanation of behavior, it is important to distinguish between the procedure, the results, and the explanation. This is made more difficult when the same word is used to describe what is done (the procedure), what is observed (the results), and the explanation of the results (the explanation). *Blocking* and *subjective shortening* are examples of terms that have been used for a procedure, a result, and an explanation.

The explanation of behavior by principle is based on deductive logic: If A then B, X is an example of A, then B. For example, A = a general blocking procedure, B = a blocking result, and X is a particular blocking procedure. The goal is to identify principles of behavior of the form "If A then B" that apply to many apparently different examples (X). The principles of classical conditioning are explanations of this type.

Process Models

A process model involves input, intervening, and output variables. As in the case of functional explanations, the input variable is some treatment condition, and the output variable is some measure of behavior. The new term is *intervening variable,* and it may be psychological, biological, or mathematical. In a process model, the relationship between an input variable and at least one intervening variable must be specified, and the relationship between at least one intervening variable and the output must also be specified. In addition, there may be multiple intervening variables with relationships that need to be specified.

Some process models involve psychological intervening variables of perception, memory, attention, and decision. Scalar timing theory provides an example of such a psychological information-processing model. Other processes models involve biological intervening variables related to electrical and chemical activity in different parts of the brain. These models involve consideration of electrophysiology, neurochemistry, and anatomy. Finally, the intervening variables may be described in mathematical terms. They may be

stochastic models of learning based on probability theory (Bush & Mosteller, 1955) or neural network learning models based on linear algebra (Haykin, 1999). Of course, a process model can be specified in psychological, biological, and mathematical terms. This provides a way to relate the psychology and biological bases of behavior and to specify them in terms of mathematical functions.

THE USE OF COMPUTERS AT ALL STAGES OF THE RESEARCH PROCESS

In the mid-twentieth century, computers were used in psychological research primarily for data analysis. The few investigators of animal learning who used them transferred their written records into a machine-readable form, such as IBM cards with 10 rows and 80 columns of locations that could be punched out. Other cards would be punched out with the program, perhaps written in FORTRAN. Stacks of such cards would be brought to a central computer center for batch processing. The next day the investigator would be given a report of the results that often indicated that a syntax error had been made. This was superseded by time-shared computers that permitted entries of data and programs from remote entries from a Teletype machine, including paper tape that could transmit data at a rate of about 10 bits per second. The time-shared computers were convenient to access and presented faster reports of errors that could be immediately corrected, but they were still used almost exclusively for data analysis.

A major change in the use of computers in psychological research began in the mid-1960s, when a few investigators began to use laboratory computers for multiple purposes. By current standards, these computers were large, slow, unreliable, expensive, and limited. For example, the classic Link computer had only 1,000 12-bit words of memory, and a magnetic tape was its only permanent storage medium. The revolutionary feature of these computers was that they could be used for control of experiments and recording of results, as well as for the analysis of data.

The modern personal computer is smaller, faster, more reliable, and less expensive than previous ones. It is now widely used by investigators in animal learning, and competence in the use of computers has become essential. Computers are now used for nearly all stages of the research process, including literature search, design of experiments, implementation of the procedure, storage of results, analysis of data, development of quantitative theories, comparison of theory and data, preparation of manuscripts and graphs, and dissemination of results (Church, 1993). As a result, many special-purpose devices that were used for each of these stages have now become curiosities. These include such items as books of tables and random numbers, india-ink lettering sets, graph paper, calculators, counters, relays, and typewriters. Others remain heavily used but are less essential, such as file cabinets, telephones, and reference books.

Literature Search

As the primary literature in animal learning has grown, the expectation that investigators of animal learning would be scholars of this field has decreased. In fact, even the expectation that investigators in a specialized aspect of this field (e.g., learned fear or choice) would be scholars in their more specialized aspect has decreased. A thorough knowledge of previous research, however, is a valuable asset. With only printed versions of the *Psychological Abstracts,* the identification of relevant publications was a time-consuming process. With the increasing availability of electronic access to the published literature, better scholarship is feasible without taking an enormous amount of time from other aspects of the research process. This search of the literature is particularly important in the planning stages of an experiment and in the preparation of the discussion and introduction to the written report.

Probably the most important journals specializing in studies of animal learning are (in alphabetical order) *Animal Learning and Behavior* (Psychonomic Society), *Behavioural Processes* (Elsevier), *Journal of the Experimental Analysis of Behavior* (Society for the Experimental Analysis of Behavior), *Journal of Experimental Psychology: Animal Behavior Processes* (American Psychological Association), *Learning and Motivation* (Academic Press), and *Quarterly Journal of Experimental Psychology B, Comparative and Physiological Psychology* (Experimental Psychology Society). Many other journals, particularly in behavioral neuroscience, psychopharmacology, and ethology, make substantial use of behavioral methods for the study of animal learning.

The most complete source of information about articles in animal learning is found in PsychINFO. This provides complete information about the reference (author, title, source, etc.) and an abstract. An outstanding feature of this database is that it goes back to 1887. Search strategies may involve getting the abstract for a particular reference, finding articles published by a particular investigator during certain years, or finding articles on a particular topic. Searches may be used to find particular words in the title, author, journal, or abstract. The *Thesaurus of Psychological Index Terms* (American Psychological Association, 2001b) is helpful when searching for key words. All of this can still be done with the printed form of *Psychological Abstracts,* but it is generally much easier to do with the electronic database. For searches in biological areas of animal learning, MedLine (the electronic form of *Indicus Medicus*) is an alternative source of information. This information is also available from PubMed without charge at http://www.PubMed.gov/.

One of the problems with typical search methods is that it is much easier to search backward than forward. Thus, if one has identified a particular article of value, one can identify other articles of potential value in its list of references—but how is it possible to know who subsequently referred to the original article? One of the important features of *Science Citation Index* is that one can enter a particular reference to obtain a list of references that subsequently cited it. With this feature one can determine what use, if any, was made of the original article.

Another problem with typical search methods is that one can obtain the abstract but not the content of the article. Research libraries are purchasing more licenses for access to the full-text version of articles controlled by commercial publishers and scientific societies, but most people do not have easy or inexpensive access to most of the published literature in animal learning.

Research scholarship involves a clear understanding of the accomplishments of others. Investigators who now have electronic access to the references and abstracts of the published literature, or, increasingly, even the complete text of the articles, can easily develop a depth of understanding of the literature that was previously possible only with extensive effort. In the future, researchers may be able to retrieve in electronic form data archives that include complex stimuli used in an experiment, videos of performance of the animal, interactive demonstrations of the procedure, and (of particular importance) the original raw data.

Design of Experiments

Randomization is an important feature of experimental designs. In experiments in which different groups of animals receive different treatments, the animals should be assigned to treatments at random. No firm conclusions can be made from an experiment in which animals were assigned to treatments haphazardly because it is impossible to rule out the possibility that the assignment was made in a way that biased the results. In experiments in which each animal receives all of the treatments, the order of treatments for each animal should be assigned at random. No firm conclusion can be made from an experiment in which the order of treatments was selected haphazardly because it is impossible to rule out the possibility that the order of the treatments (such as the characteristics of the previous treatment) affected the performance on the current treatment.

Randomization is easy to implement. Before the extensive use of computers, investigators often relied on physical processes (e.g., flipping coins or pulling numbers out of a hat) or random number tables that were constructed from physical processes, such as the tables constructed by the Rand Corporation (1955), or the combination of many independent numbers from different databases. Now pseudorandom number algorithms are used almost exclusively. These are iterative equations that calculate a random real number between 0 and 1 based on the previous number. This number is represented by a decimal with a fixed number of digits. Of course, the number is based on a deterministic rather than a random process. If the process is always begun with the same number it will always produce the same sequence of numbers, and the inevitable appearance of a second occurrence of a particular finite set of digits means that the sequence of numbers will be repeated forever. But by careful choice of the two constants of the iterative equations of the pseudorandom number algorithms, the random numbers generated by functions in many statistical and mathematical software applications produce sequences of numbers that pass most tests for being random.

In a software application one simply specifies the need for a random number (or many random numbers), and they are supplied. A procedure for randomly assigning 10 animals to two treatment conditions, each consisting of 5 animals, is as follows: Generate 10 random numbers (associated with animals 1 through 10) and then assign the five animals with the highest random numbers to the first treatment condition and the others to the second treatment condition. This is easily generalized for different numbers of animals or treatment conditions. A procedure for randomly ordering five treatments for a particular animal is to generate five random numbers (associated with the five treatment conditions), and assign the five treatments in the order of the size of the random number.

The goal of a random assignment of animals to groups is to equalize the chance for each animal to be in each group and to make the assignment of one animal to a group independent of the assignment of any other animal. Not all assignment plans are successful in fulfilling this goal. Of course, if an investigator does not adhere to the assignments specified by the random process, but makes adjustments to make the assignments "more random," the process is not random and no firm conclusions can be made from the results of the experiment.

Implementation of Procedure

Computers are extensively used in the control of experiments. For the presentation of visual stimuli to an animal, the computer can activate a light, a slide projector, or an external monitor; for the presentation of an auditory stimulus, the computer can activate a hardware sound generator or deliver auditory signals directly to a speaker. For the delivery of food or water rewards, a specialized electromechanical delivery device can be activated by the computer interface. From the animal's point of view, stimuli and rewards are inputs.

In addition to the delivery of stimuli and reinforcers, the implementation of a procedure often involves information regarding the responses of the animal. From the animal's point of view, responses are the output. Particular responses activate a switch or transducer, and this information can be sent to the computer. Switches are often used for detecting lever responses of rats, pecks on a lighted disk by a pigeon, and the location of an animal on a floor that can be tilted, among others. Photocell circuits are also extensively used for response detection. In these circuits, the breaking of a beam of light (often infrared) completes a circuit that is detected by the computer. A single photocell circuit can be used to identify head entry into a food cup or other specific location; multiple photocell circuits can be used to identify the amount and direction of activity of an animal. All of the input and output devices should be checked prior to each session or at least on a daily basis. The check can consist of a simple program that permits the investigator to activate each of the input devices and observe the programmed consequence on each of the output devices.

To use a computer for control of an experiment, it is necessary to have a computer, the input and output devices, and the interface between the computer and the devices. A standard personal computer, with an interface board, is usually sufficient for most experiments. The interface usually consists of a specialized board (such as those made by Computer Boards International) that may include digital and analog input and output and an external timer. Software can be written by the user in a general-purpose language (such as C) or a general application program (such as Matlab). Alternatively, a specific application program may be used. For example, Med-PC provides a software programming language that is well integrated with their hardware input and output devices for operant conditioning experiments.

A real-time programming environment should be evaluated with respect to its simplicity, versatility, and performance. Ideally, a program to implement a procedure would be easy to write and easy for others to read. It should be possible to program any procedure and to modify system functions as desired. Finally, the program should execute quickly and never crash. Such performance features are critical for a real-time program.

Storage of Results

In many experiments, a complete record may consist of the time of occurrence of specific responses. The format of the record may be in terms of a list of paired numbers, one for the time (usually in milliseconds) and the other for the event (in terms of a numerical code or a word). The events include both inputs, such on onset or termination of a particular stimulus, and outputs, such as the closing or opening of a switch and the breaking of a particular photocell. Investigators often record only summary data (such as the number of responses of one kind over some extended time period), but these data do not make it possible for the investigator or others to examine behavior of the animal in other ways.

To facilitate communication, the format should be one that can be readily used by everyone, such as text instead of a proprietary format that requires purchase of particular software. In some cases, the use of open source software for data compression may be justified, but space is not critical in most applications. During the experiment, much of the data may be stored in active memory. If the computer has insufficient memory to hold all the information from an experimental session, a double-buffer technique may be used to record the data on a more permanent storage medium. With this method, one buffer is still recording the data (in foreground) while the other buffer is writing the data on the storage medium (in background). At the end of an experimental session the data should be copied, usually automatically, to a more permanent medium. At present floppy disks, Zip drives, and CD-ROMs are used extensively for data storage. In the future other media will be used, and for archival purposes it is important to maintain the data on a medium that can be readily accessed.

Analysis of Data

Originally, computers were used primarily for the calculation of standard inferential statistical tests. Modern statistical application programs (such as SAS and SPSS) provide investigators with a convenient way to conduct a large number of such tests. The investigator, of course, is responsible for selecting an appropriate test and for interpreting the output correctly. This is only one of several stages of analysis of data, and it is seldom critical in the discovery of phenomena.

Exploratory data analysis is important for the early identification of problems, for the selection of measures that separate systematic from random effects, and for the discovery of relationships between variables. After each session, the investigator can rapidly examine major features of the data of each animal with a program that permits examination of each input and output employed. Substantial changes in the behavior of a particular animal, or of many animals on a particular session, can alert the investigator to possible equipment failures, procedural irregularities, or other factors that could be interfering with the performance. Most of them can be eliminated easily. At the end of the experiment, the investigator should examine the performance on individual trials before combining across trials, the performance on individual sessions before combining across sessions, and the performance of individual animals before combining across animals. Summary measures across trials, sessions, and animals are necessary for succinct quantitative descriptions of performance, but the exploratory data analysis on the original data will guide the selection of summary measures that do not distort the results of inspection of the individual data. This examination of the original data can be greatly facilitated by computer-generated graphs that display measures of the performance.

Many different programming languages and applications can be effectively used for data analysis and permit exploratory data analysis. For smaller data sets, a spreadsheet (such as Excel) may be satisfactory. For larger data sets, a matrix-oriented program (such as MATLAB), a statistical program (such as S+), or a general purpose language (such as C) may be chosen. Most investigators will want to select a single programming language or application for data analysis and thoroughly learn how it can be effectively used for the types of data being analyzed. The characteristics of a good analysis program include speed of execution, readability of programs, and adequacy of graphics.

The main purpose of inferential data analysis as a research method in animal learning is to provide a common standard for investigators to use in making conclusions about their experimental results. Without such a standard, different investigators might reach different conclusions regarding the presence or absence of an effect based on the same information. Their conclusions would then reflect more about their attitude toward their results than about the results themselves.

Development of Theory

The development and evaluation of quantitative theories of learning have been greatly facilitated by the use of computers. Simulation of any well-specified quantitative theory requires the following steps: (a) selection of a programming language or an appropriate application program, (b) specification of the quantitative model in the computer program along with parameters to be estimated, (c) specification of the procedure to be implemented in the computer program, and (d) execution of the computer program that consists of modules for the theory and for the procedure. The output of the simulation is normally compared to the records of the behavior of the animals, and the parameters of the model are adjusted to maximize some measure of goodness of fit. Initially the analyst can adjust the parameters by trial and error, but parameters should be estimated on the basis of some automatic procedure. This may be an exhaustive search of all combinations of parameter values within a certain range and step size, or it may be done by a hill-climbing search procedure.

Explicit solutions have been obtained for some quantitative theories. These are equations that follow from the specifications of the theory. They may require some assumptions of distribution forms that are only approximately correct, and they may be restricted to a particular type of procedure. They do, however, make it possible to explore rapidly and precisely the effect of variations in the parameters on the expected behavior. Symbolic programming languages, such as Mathematica and Maple, provide many useful facilities for the development of explicit solutions.

Comparison of Theory and Data

The selection of a model should be based on its generalizability, as well as its fit to a particular data set. One simple approach is to estimate the parameters on half the data and apply the estimates to the other half of the data. Other approaches have also been used to avoid the choice of a model with many parameters that fit the random noise in a particular set of data but do not reflect a systematic process. A goal is to select a relatively inflexible model that provides a good fit of the data (Zucchini, 2000).

Some quantitative models apply primarily to a particular procedure, or even to a particular dependent variable. Ideally, models should apply to a wide range of procedures and any dependent variable based on the recorded behavior.

Preparation of Manuscripts

Computers are now routinely used for preparation of manuscripts, including tables and figures. This greatly facilitates multiple revisions of a manuscript.

Dissemination of Results, Including Data Archives

Finally, computers are used for the dissemination of results. Many full-text articles are available from scientific societies, commercial publishers, open archives, and individual Web sites. In some cases, the original data are available on the Web. Although many of these resources are now restricted

because of fees, wider dissemination of articles and data without cost to the user will undoubtedly occur in the near future.

A CASE STUDY

In any study of animal learning an investigator must deal with each of these methodological problems. Here is how my colleagues and I dealt with them in research titled "Application of Scalar Timing Theory to Individual Trials" (Church, Meck, & Gibbon, 1994).

What Was the Problem?

The first sentence of the abstract of the article described the problem: "Our purpose was to infer the characteristics of the internal clock, temporal memory, and decision processes involved in temporal generalization behavior on the basis of the analysis of individual trials." We used a standard procedure (the peak procedure), but instead of analyzing performance based on data averaged across many trials, we chose to analyze individual trials. We also used a standard theory (scalar timing theory). The problem of this experiment was to determine if we could identify the intervening variables of the theory (internal clock, temporal memory, and decision processes) based on individual trials rather than the averaged performance.

What Apparatus Was Required?

We decided to use the 10 standard lever boxes that were available and would be satisfactory for this problem. Other experiments may require creativity in the selection or development of the apparatus, but the lever boxes for this experiment were selected primarily because they were convenient.

What Animals Should Be Used?

We decided to use rats because the apparatus and colony room were adapted for rats, and rats would be satisfactory for this problem. Other experiments may require creativity in the selection of the species, but the rats for this experiment were selected primarily because they were convenient.

How Should the Independent and Dependent Variables Be Measured?

As an independent variable we decided to use three stimulus durations (15, 30, and 60 s) to evaluate the scalar property, and two durations of nonreinforced trials (eight times the stimulus duration, or 240 s) to determine whether the absolute or relative duration of the nonreinforced trials was relevant. According to the scalar property, measures of behavior as a function of time since stimulus onset should be similar if time is scaled in relative units (proportion of the interval), but different if time is scaled in absolute units (seconds). Two types of dependent measures were described. One was the mean response rate as a function of time since stimulus onset; the other involved the pattern of responding on individual trials. An algorithm was described that identified the time at which the animal began a fast rate of response (start time) and the time at which it stopped a fast rate of response (stop time). The independent variable and the dependent variable based on mean rates of responding were conventional ones; the dependent variables based on individual trials were the ones that were being evaluated.

What Procedure Should Be Used?

We decided to use the peak procedure because its characteristics were well known for the mean response rate functions. We decided to use 30 rats, with 10 rats randomly assigned to each of the three conditions. No formal power analysis was done to determine this number. Typically we have used six or eight rats per group, and we decided to use a slightly larger number of rats per group to have particularly reliable estimates of the characteristics of individual trials.

What Experimental Design Should Be Used?

An independent groups design was used to eliminate complexities of carryover effects from one condition to another.

How Should the Data Be Analyzed?

The analysis was conducted on the last 10 sessions for which data were available. The most important analyses were done on the correlations of starts, stops, spreads, and middles of the high response rate on individual trials. The treatment on two of the sessions was correct, but the data were unavailable. No advance plans were made for the treatment of such an error.

How Should the Results Be Explained?

Scalar timing theory was used to explain the data. This required that the implications of this theory for the correlations between the starts, stops, spreads, and middles be derived and compared to the observed correlation pattern. The conclusion

was that the individual trial analysis corroborated and extended the previous analyses based on averaged data. Most of the methodological decisions were based on previous research, and this made it possible to compare the results of this experiment with the results of previous research. Some of the methods were not standard, for example, the measures taken on individual trials, the analyses of correlation patterns, and the inferences of cognitive processes based on the correlation patterns. The nonstandard methods led to some advance in knowledge.

REFERENCES

American Psychological Association. (2001a). *Publication manual of the American Psychological Association* (5th ed). Washington, DC: Author.

American Psychological Association. (2001b). *Thesaurus of psychological index terms.* Washington, DC: Author.

Bakan, D. (1954). A generalization of Sidman's results on group and individual functions, and a criterion. *Psychological Bulletin, 51,* 63–64.

Bitterman, M. E. (2000). Cognitive evolution: A psychological perspective. In C. Heyes & L. Huber (Eds.), *The evolution of cognition: Vienna series in theoretical biology* (pp. 61–79). Cambridge, MA: MIT Press.

Blough, D. S. (1960). Delayed matching in the pigeon. *Journal of the Experimental Analysis of Behavior, 2,* 151–160.

Bush, R. R., & Mosteller, F. (1955). *Stochastic models for learning.* New York: Wiley.

Church, R. M. (1969). Response suppression. In B. A. Campbell & R. M. Church (Eds.), *Punishment and aversive behavior* (pp. 111–156). New York: Appleton-Century-Crofts.

Church, R. M. (1993). Uses of computers in psychological research. In G. Keren & C. Lewis (Eds.), *A handbook for data analysis in the behavioral sciences: Statistical issues* (pp. 459–491). Hillsdale, NJ: Erlbaum.

Church, R. M., Meck, W. H., & Gibbon, J. (1994). Application of scalar timing theory to individual trials. *Journal of Experimental Psychology: Animal Behavior Processes, 20,* 135–155.

Estes, W. K. (1956). The problem of inference from curves based on group data. *Psychological Bulletin, 53,* 134–140.

Haykin, S. (1999). *Neural networks* (2nd ed.). Upper Saddle River, NJ: Prentice Hall.

Morris, R. G. M. (1981). Spatial localization does not require the presence of local cues. *Learning and Motivation, 12,* 239–260.

Munn, N. L. (1950). *Handbook of psychological research on the rat.* Boston: Houghton Mifflin.

Myung, J. (2000). The importance of complexity in model selection. *Journal of Mathematical Psychology, 44,* 190–204.

Olton, D. S., & Samuelson, R. J. (1976). Remembrance of places passed: Spatial memory in rats. *Journal of Experimental Psychology: Animal Behavior Processes, 2,* 97–116.

Rand Corporation (1955). *A million random digits with 100,000 normal deviates.* Glencoe, IL: Free Press.

Rescorla, R. A. (1988). Behavioral studies of Pavlovian conditioning. *Annual Review of Neuroscience, 11,* 329–352.

Schneider, B. A. (1969). A two-state analysis of fixed-interval responding in the pigeon. *Journal of the Experimental Analysis of Behavior, 12,* 677–687.

Sidman, M. (1953). A note on functional relations obtained from group data. *Psychological Bulletin, 49,* 263–269.

Sidman, M. (1960). *Tactics of scientific research.* New York: Basic Books.

Skinner, B. F. (1938). *The behavior of organisms.* New York: Appleton-Century-Crofts.

Small, W. W. (1900). An experimental study of the mental processes of the rat. *American Journal of Psychology, 11,* 133–165.

Spence, K. W. (1956). *Behavior theory and conditioning.* New Haven, CT: Yale University Press.

Thorndike, E. L. (1898). Animal intelligence: An experimental study of the associative processes in animals. *Psychological Review Monograph Supplements,* Vol. 2 (No. 4, Whole No. 8).

Tinbergen, N. (1953). *The herring gull's world.* London: Collins.

Tukey, J. W. (1977). *Exploratory data analysis.* Reading, MA: Addison Wesley.

Washburn, M. F. (1936). *The animal mind* (4th ed.). New York: Macmillan.

Zucchini, W. (2000). An introduction to model selection. *Journal of Mathematical Psychology, 44,* 41–61.

CHAPTER 12

Neuropsychology

RUSSELL M. BAUER, ELIZABETH C. LERITZ, AND DAWN BOWERS

The last decade has witnessed a significant explosion of interest in brain research, owing in part to the appearance of exciting new technologies and to funding initiatives made possible by the Presidential designation of the 1990s as the decade of the brain. Research examining the relationship between brain function and complex behavior has exploded and has led to new discoveries about topics of fundamental importance to clinicians, cognitive scientists, and the lay public. The decade of the brain saw the development of new methodological tools for investigating brain function in normal individuals and clinical populations. For example, important advances have been made in supplementing traditional behavioral methods for analyzing normal and disordered information processing with emergent techniques of functional neuroimaging (e.g., positron-emission tomography, or PET; single photon emission computed tomography, or SPECT; functional magnetic resonance imaging, or fMRI; magnetoencephalography, or MEG), electrophysiology, and reversible lesions (e.g., transcranial magnetic stimulation, intracarotid sodium amobarbital technique). The next decade promises

great progress in understanding normal and disordered neuropsychological function by engaging in cross-platform approaches that combine the strengths of these various techniques within the same experimental investigation.

This chapter provides a broad overview of contemporary experimental methods in neuropsychology. We first provide a brief discussion of neuropsychological inference, focusing on basic assumptions and on ways in which neuropsychological research can yield useful information about brain-behavior relationships. We then provide a brief description of major approaches to neuropsychological research, beginning with the traditional information-processing approach and its application to the evaluation of brain dysfunction through group and single-case experiments. We then consider newer techniques, including functional neuroimaging, electrophysiology, magnetoencephalography, and reversible lesion methods. In each section, we describe the conceptual basis of the technique, outline its strengths and weaknesses, and cite some examples of how it has been used in addressing today's problems in neuropsychology.

NEUROPSYCHOLOGICAL INFERENCE

Key Assumptions in Neuropsychological Research

One key assumption of neuropsychological research is that complex abilities represent the combined and interacting activity of several more elementary cognitive processes or subsystems. This assumption holds that each complex ability has a *cognitive architecture*. This assumption leads directly to the prediction that damage to the brain will result in performance impairments that reveal the underlying organization or functional architecture upon which complex abilities are built. As one example, the complex act of recognizing and naming faces can be thought of as being comprised of several constituent visual, mnemonic, and linguistic processes linked together in complex ways. On the behavioral side, we can specify such components in a cognitive model like the one proposed by Bruce and Young (1986), depicted in Figure 12.1. The model contains components that are dedicated to the visual analysis of emotional displays

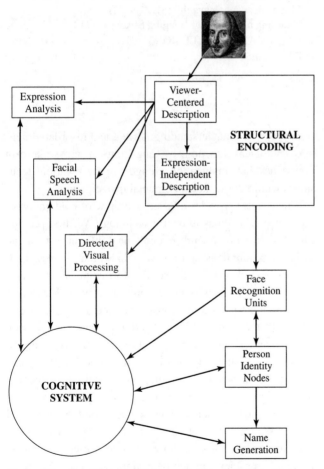

Figure 12.1 Cognitive model of face recognition adapted from Bruce and Young (1986).

(expression analysis), lipreading (facial speech analysis), and face gender, age, and racial characteristics (structural encoding). After visual analysis takes place, the resulting perception is matched to stored representations of familiar faces built up on the basis of prior experience (face recognition units). Access to the face recognition unit unlocks other information about the person who owns the face, including personality, occupation, and other characteristics (person identity nodes). After this information is accessible, the name of the person is accessed (name generation). Connections between these components of the system and other visual (directed visual processing) and cognitive components illustrate interactions with other cognitive processes not specific to faces. Such a model not only decomposes face recognition into its constituent components, but also leads to predictions about how localized damage to such components might result in specific performance deficits. One key goal of neuropsychological research is to determine whether a model like this has any basis in brain structure and function. In other words, the question of how the cognitive components of such a model map onto specific brain structures and systems is of paramount importance in investigating brain-behavior relationships.

A related assumption is that such correspondence does in fact exist. The *modularity* assumption states that complex functions are comprised of more elementary processors (modules) that are dedicated to highly specific tasks and that combine in complex ways to yield cognitive abilities. This assumption is closely linked with the *locality* assumption, which further states that such specialization of processing is regionally localized within the brain rather than being nonspecifically distributed throughout cortical and subcortical systems. Fodor (1983) conceptualized modules as domain-specific (i.e., performing a specific function in response to a particular domain or type of input), innately specified (i.e., not wholly dependent upon experience or learning), informationally encapsulated (i.e., having a limited set of inputs and outputs), and autonomous (i.e., operating on the basis of an internal algorithm) processors. In our face recognition example, the existence of localized brain regions dedicated only to the processing of facial features or facial identity (Perrett, Rolls, & Caan, 1982; Perrett, Hietanen, Oram, & Benson, 1992) is consistent with a modular view of face processing. It is important to recognize that the modularity assumption encompasses thinking on both the behavioral and the anatomical side of the brain-behavior interface. One fundamental challenge to neuropsychological researchers is to uncover the modular organization of complex abilities and to better understand the nature of the computation(s) that take place within the modules that make up the cognitive or brain system. Key questions include whether all complex functions have a modular organization (and if they do, whether they so organized to the same extent), whether modules can be precisely localized in the brain, and whether cognitive models of what occurs within modules bears any direct relationship with the kinds of computations performed by the physical brain.

Despite widespread adherence to the modularity assumption, there is increasing recognition that certain abilities are not represented in regionally localized brain structures, but instead result from activity in *widely distributed* regions at both the cortical and subcortical level. For example, a large number of clinical, electrophysiological, and functional imaging studies have revealed that memory is a distributed process dependent upon structures in the medial temporal lobe, the diencephalon, the basal forebrain, and the frontal lobe (Gabrieli, 1998; Schacter, Wagner, & Buckner, 2000). Additionally, advances in computational neuroscience have led to increasing acceptance of *distributed processing* as a useful way of modeling how the visual system combines complex features to construct an object (Fahle, 1994) or how memory storage is actually enacted at a neural level (Horner, 1990). These data are not necessarily contrary to a view that posits modular organization of cognitive functions. The modularity assumption pertains primarily to assumptions about cognitive and neural *structure,* and assumes little about underlying computational *processes*.

A third assumption is that although there are substantial individual differences in cognitive abilities, all humans share a certain uniformity in underlying brain organization (Coltheart, 2001). This can be referred to as the *uniformity assumption*. Although this seems to be a reasonable assumption, it might be seen as controversial in light of data suggesting that early brain injury can affect cerebral organization due to neuronal plasticity (Arendt, Bruckner, Bigl, & Marcova, 1995; Nadel & Moscovitch, 1998; Poldrack, 2000) and that brain injury can be met with substantial variability in functional adaptation (Geffen, Encel, & Forrester, 1991; Teuber, 1975). These data notwithstanding, this assumption asserts that, all other things being equal, principles of brain organization can be generalized across people. This is a conceptually important assumption in generalizing the results of any study to a broader population of patients.

A final assumption is that for the most part, brain injury results in deficits or impairments, rather than in the introduction of new behavior (Coltheart, 2001). This *subtractivity* assumption asserts that from the standpoint of cognitive

models, brain injury removes boxes or abolishes connections between components of the cognitive system, but does not introduce new boxes or connections. Although brain injury can result in the appearance of behaviors not seen in the normal individual (e.g., intrusions in memory performance, perseveration of a previously effective problem-solving strategy), the subtractivity assumption asserts that these can be understood as deficits or impairments of a normal cognitive model. For example, intrusions can be seen as an impairment in selective retrieval mechanisms (Kixmiller, Verfaellie, Chase, & Cermak, 1995), and at least some varieties of perseveration can be seen as impairments in normal inhibitory processes (Sandson & Albert, 1987).

Associations and Dissociations in Performance

One important goal of neuropsychology is to understand the manner in which complex cognitive processes are represented in the brain—to discover the so-called functional architecture (Anderson, 1983) or behavioral geography (Lezak, 1995) of the brain. Although cognitive psychologists have traditionally studied people with normal cognition as these individuals perform certain mental tasks, neuropsychologists have been more likely to study people with acquired or developmental disorders of cognition (Coltheart, 2001). Suppose a patient develops an inability to recognize objects visually as a result of a bilateral posterior cerebral artery infarction. One important goal in the experimental evaluation of the patient's deficit is to design the evaluation in such a way that the patient's disorder can be understood from the viewpoint of a theory about how the object recognition system operates. Often, such an evaluation utilizes an explicit cognitive model (like the one previously described for face recognition) as a guide (Bruce & Young, 1986; Riddoch & Humphreys, 1993). The model specifies the constituent cognitive abilities that should be tested for purposes of localizing and characterizing the patient's deficit(s) in behavioral terms. Several possible outcomes can emerge from this approach, each of which has implications for understanding the nature of the cognitive process and for localizing the patient's deficit.

A basic heuristic for understanding different possible outcomes from neuropsychological research investigations is depicted in Figure 12.2. Suppose, for example, that patients are asked to perform a visual discrimination task in which they are asked whether two depicted objects are the same or different (Task A) and a semantic judgment task in which they are asked to evaluate whether two simultaneously presented objects belong to the same class of objects (Task B).

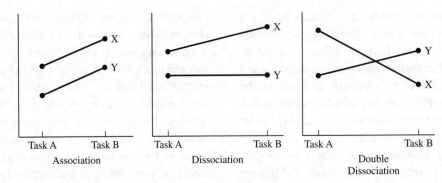

Figure 12.2   Possible outcomes in neuropsychological research with two patients (or groups) and two tests.

If the patient is impaired on both tasks, these deficits are said to be *associated* with one another. A similar situation arises if two patients (or groups) show equal task effects, as depicted in the left panel of Figure 12.2. The implications of this result for understanding the patient's deficit are ambiguous because it could mean that the two tasks both tap the same underlying ability, or it could mean that both are dependent on a third (unmeasured) ability earlier in the cognitive processing chain. Thus, associations, although helpful, may sometimes lead to results that are difficult to interpret (Shallice, 1988).

If our patient (or group) fails Task A but performs well on Task B, or if the patient is significantly more impaired on Task A than on Task B, then a *dissociation* has occurred. This may mean that the patient (or group) is impaired in some cognitive process tapped by Task A but not by Task B, which is potentially useful in our attempt to understand the nature of the measured deficit. A similar situation arises when one group shows task effects, whereas the other does not, as depicted in the central panel of Figure 12.2. Such a dissociation may occur for reasons that are less interesting or informative, such as a difference between tasks in level of difficulty. Thus, single dissociations are also limited in their usefulness.

The strongest evidence for a specific relationship between a brain lesion and behavioral dysfunction exists when a *double dissociation* occurs (Teuber, 1955). Here, suppose we test at least two different patients (or groups) on at least two different tasks. In a double dissociation, Patient (or group) X is impaired on Task A but performs normally on Task B, whereas Patient (or group) Y shows the opposite pattern. In this situation, we can logically conclude that the patients (or groups) differed meaningfully on some cognitive variable that was differentially tapped by the two tasks, and can rule out task difficulty as an alternative explanation of results. This line of reasoning is fundamental to neuropsychological inference in both the clinic and the laboratory (Lezak, 1995),

because most neuropsychological research makes use of patterns of association and dissociation in order to arrive at inferences about the relationship between brain function and behavioral function.

NEUROPSYCHOLOGICAL ANALYSIS OF BRAIN IMPAIRMENT: THE LESION APPROACH

Key Features of the Lesion Approach

Over the last century, the study of brain-behavior relationships has relied extensively on what has come to be known as the *lesion approach,* in which models of cognitive function are developed, verified, and modified through the study of patients with acquired or developmental brain lesions (Selnes, 2001). The lesion method aims at establishing a relationship between "a circumscribed region of brain damage, a lesion, and a pattern of alteration in some aspect of an experimentally controlled cognitive or behavioral performance" (Damasio & Damasio, 1997, p. 69). Because many patients have localized damage to specific brain regions, it is possible, through dissociation logic, to make inferences about brain function by treating the functional damage as an independent variable in experimental investigation. An important premise underlying lesion paradigms is that much can be learned about *normal* function from the study of dysfunction (Damasio & Damasio, 1997; McCloskey, 2001). As a result, insight can be gained into cognitive architecture and, through the analysis of performance associations and dissociations, into the manner in which elementary functions interact to yield complex neuropsychological abilities. This method of ascribing functions to brain regions has yielded much of the basic, fundamental knowledge that currently exists in neuropsychology and cognitive neuroscience. Classic examples of the use of the ablative paradigm in neuropsychology include Broca's (1861) description of the patient Leborgne (Tan), Wernicke's (1874) monograph on aphasic syndromes,

Harlow's (1848, 1868) descriptions of Phineas Gage, who suffered dramatic disturbances of personality and complex behavior after traumatic frontal lobe injury, Scoville & Milner's (1957) description of the amnesic patient H.M., who underwent bilateral resection of the hippocampus and overlying temporal cortex for relief of intractable epilepsy, and Geschwind and Kaplan's (1962) description of left-sided agraphia and apraxia following damage to the anterior four-fifths of the corpus callosum.

A key feature of the lesion paradigm is its emphasis on *deficit measurement*. In order to characterize or quantify behavioral deficits, the researcher establishes some appropriate comparison standard against which to evaluate the patient's performance (cf. Lezak, 1995). Such standards may be derived *within subject* (in which impaired abilities are compared with the patient's spared performances) or may involve *between-subject* comparisons using appropriate control groups or objective normative standards of performance derived from psychometric research. Because many neuropsychological abilities are at least somewhat dependent upon age and education, it has become customary to use normative standards that correct for these variables (Heaton, Grant, & Matthews, 1991). Using appropriately selected control groups and cognitive tasks designed to provide single or double dissociations, strong forms of inference (Platt, 1966) about brain-behavior relationships are possible.

The lesion approach encompasses experimentally induced chemical or surgical lesions as well as so-called accidents of nature in the form of naturally occurring disease processes that result in damage to specific brain structures. In the case of experimental ablation, some degree of control over the extent of the lesion can be achieved, whereas in the case of naturally occurring disease, the degree of control over lesion location and extent is greatly reduced. The intrinsic variability seen in naturally occurring lesions is in many respects a nuisance that complicates inference within the lesion paradigm. Nonetheless, the study of patients with naturally occurring lesions can still lead to meaningful conclusions about the underlying architecture of cognitive functions if steps are taken to document lesion localization through neuroimaging or postmortem analysis. Reporting affected structures using standardized atlases or cytoarchitectonic maps has made it possible for researchers to clearly and precisely communicate lesion localization for purposes of comparing results across patients (Damasio & Damasio, 2000).

Group Versus Single-Case Designs

In the lesion approach, data can be collected from a single case of brain impairment or from a group of subjects with the same disease or anatomical localization. Descriptive or experimental analysis of single cases is often the first step in elucidating a cognitive deficit for purposes of describing its characteristics and boundary conditions. Single-case analysis is often necessary if the disorder under investigation is rare, and single-case reports are particularly effective if they demonstrate an exception to a universally held assumption. For example, case reports of focal retrograde amnesia have caused us to rethink and refine classic concepts of anterograde and retrograde memory loss (Kapur, 1993). Similarly, the widely held notion, that the visual recognition of living things was somehow more vulnerable to impairment in certain visual agnosic syndromes, has been contradicted by single cases showing selective impairments in nonliving objects such as medical implements (Crosson, Moberg, Boone, Rothi, & Raymer, 1997) or artifacts (Moss & Tyler, 2000). Thus, single cases can provide important data that constrain prevailing theory. However, they suffer from the obvious shortcoming that it is always possible that the results from a single case reflect something idiosyncratic about the individual patient, and thus cannot be relied upon (by themselves) to yield conclusions that generalize across subjects.

Group studies rely on the classification of individual patients into groups such that everyone in a group is (theoretically) homogeneous with respect to some criterion variable. Most often, groups are formed on the basis of the presence or absence of a particular disease entity (e.g., Parkinson's disease, single-event stroke, closed head injury) or damage to particular brain structures or systems. Research using this type of methodology can take one of two approaches. One is primarily descriptive in nature, aiming to characterize, within a broad assessment of neuropsychological abilities, those impairments that are correlated with the grouping variable. Indeed, group research is often useful in observing patterns of symptom co-occurrence (so-called *observational science*) and in refining the basis for group classification for later study (Zurif, Swinney, & Fodor, 1991). Much of what we know about neuropsychological correlates of neurological diseases such as Alzheimer's disease, epilepsy, and stroke comes from a multitude of studies that have examined a broad range of cognitive domains.

The other general approach to group research involves structuring group classification around a particular theory or hypothesis regarding the neural architecture of cognitive systems. For example, researchers interested in studying memory may select patients who, through diverse etiologies, have lesions localized to a specific brain region (e.g., the medial temporal lobe memory system; Squire & Zola Morgan, 1991). Alternatively, subjects may be grouped together because they share the same neuropsychological deficit (e.g., a problem in permanently storing new long-term memories). One potential drawback to this approach is that because of variability in the criteria used for group classification, it is sometimes difficult to make comparisons *across* studies. For this reason it has become customary in recent years to provide more operational criteria that can be used to assign patients to groups. For an example of how this has been accomplished in research on amnesia, see Squire and Shimamura (1986).

In recent years, controversy has existed about the relative utility of group versus single-case studies in facilitating progress in clinical neuropsychology. Some have argued that *both* single-case and group studies are appropriate in neuropsychological research, whereas others argue that only single-case studies promote reliable inferences into cognitive structure (McCloskey, 1993; Shallice, 1988). Those who contend that only single-case studies are appropriate criticize group research on a number of grounds. One criticism is based on the use of *syndromes,* or collections of clinical symptoms, as a basis for group classification. Cognitive symptoms can co-occur after damage to the brain because they (a) are each based on the same underlying cognitive mechanism, or (b) depend on regionally adjacent brain structures or systems. The argument against group research is that if one studies a syndrome based on the situation described previously in (b), one runs the risk of confusing functional and structural associations. If such symptoms are related simply through regional proximity, studying them with cognitive methods may tell us little about underlying *functional* architecture. This is an in-principle argument that many neuropsychologists believe applies in general to all syndromes used for group classification (Coltheart, 2001). Proponents of this argument suggest that although the study of syndromes is a useful first step in defining what cognitive processes might be involved in the deficit, real progress is made only through the analysis of individual cases.

An additional problem with group research is that even when patients are grouped in order to be homogeneous with respect to the presence of a localized lesion, they may be behaviorally heterogeneous with respect to the cognitive process under study (Gazzaniga, Ivry, & Mangin, 1998). It is widely known that individual data cannot be derived from an exclusive study of average scores (Sidman, 1952). Thus, even though we are capable of generating point estimates of central tendency (e.g., means, medians, modes) from group data, the individual data points or curves might be quite heterogeneous with respect to these estimates. This heterogeneity might result, for example, from subtle individual differences in brain organization or in the degree of functional compensation. Thus, despite the fact that a group of

individuals may have received identical diagnoses, there can be substantial behavioral variability among group members. As a result, inferences made by averaging across individual patients can be imprecise (Caramazza, 1986; Caramazza & Badecker, 1989). Caramazza and Badecker (1989) argue further that manifestations of lesions can differ across individuals, therefore rendering inferences about normal cognitive function unreliable (see also Shallice, 1988).

Some researchers therefore feel that the only way in which to make conclusions regarding the structure of cognitive systems is to investigate single cases, and to make subsequent comparisons *across* patients. This idea has led to the notion of *multiple* single-case studies as an alternative to group research. In this approach, each patient participates in the same experiment, but techniques such as averaging across individuals are not employed. We believe that a hybrid approach strikes a reasonable compromise between group and single-case advocates on this point. When predicting and analyzing a directional group difference on some cognitive variable, it is useful not only to report measures of central tendency (means, medians, etc.), but also to report how many individual patients show the predicted effect. Arguments in favor of group-based lesion studies advocate that in some instances, group studies can be more effective at distinguishing very discrete components of cognitive systems (Robertson, Knight, Rafal, & Shimamura, 1993; Zurif et al., 1991). Although these researchers do not dismiss the use of single-case studies in drawing inferences about normal cognitive function, they believe that useful information can be obtained from analysis of neuropsychological syndromes (Zurif et al., 1991). One key problem in group research is the variability of symptom presentations seen in most neuropsychological syndromes. Thus, for example, not all patients with Broca's aphasia or Gerstmann's syndrome present with precisely the same symptoms. Thus, in searching for behavioral precision in group studies, the need to establish necessary and sufficient inclusionary and exclusionary criteria is obvious. This issue is similar in kind to the historical controversies in clinical psychiatry that led to the development of research diagnostic criteria for major mental disorders (Spitzer, Endicott, & Robins, 1978). Operationally defined criteria sets have been developed for certain neuropsychological syndromes, such as age-associated memory impairment (Crook, Larrabee, & Youngjohn, 1990), mild traumatic brain injury (Paniak, MacDonald, Toller Lobe, Durand, & Nagy, 1998), and Alzheimer's disease (McKhann et al., 1984) in order to achieve homogeneity in group research.

One important difference between group and single-case approaches involves the use of replication as a tool for validating and strengthening scientific conclusions. In group research, replication is the cornerstone of clinical inference because it helps to rule out error variance as the basis for the finding, and it helps to strengthen the notion that the finding reflects some stable characteristic of the cognitive architecture under study rather than just a chance finding. Radical proponents of single-case methodology not only de-emphasize the importance of replication, but also have directly argued that it is impossible (Coltheart, 2001) because single-case studies concern themselves with unique deficits. It is true that certain meaningful neuropsychological findings cannot be easily replicated, but this does not logically support a wholesale denial of the importance of replication. As before, a compromise position in which both single-case investigations and group studies are used, each capitalizing on its strengths, seems the most appropriate agenda for the next decade of neuropsychological research. It seems clear that a combination of both approaches is relevant to the establishment and support of models depicting the complex relationships between the brain and cognition. For example, it may be appropriate to use results from multiple single-case studies to develop hypotheses, and then to conduct group-based studies in attempt to confirm or disconfirm theories.

Performance Measures

The lesion approach lends itself to an almost unlimited set of dependent variables, including behavioral performance measures, psychophysiological and electrophysiological indices, differences in functional brain activation, and differential treatment response measures. Thus, the lesion approach is distinguished by the presence of a contrast between a group with a brain lesion or disorder and an appropriate control group, not by the use of particular sets of performance measures. This having been said, the majority of studies conducted within the lesion paradigm have used behavioral performance measures. Such measures derive from one of the three great traditions relevant to clinical neuropsychology: the psychometric tradition within clinical psychology (Russell, 1986), the information-processing tradition within cognitive psychology, and cognitive neuropsychology (Ellis & Young, 1986; R. A. McCarthy & Warrington, 1990; Rapp, 2001), or the behavioral neurology tradition of syndrome analysis within clinical medicine (Mendez, Van Gorp, & Cummings, 1995). Aside from basic standards of reliability and validity, there are no explicit standards or acid tests, so to speak, that determine which measures are suitable for a particular experimental investigation. In some cases, measures with large-scale normative bases are selected in order to provide stable measures of deficit. In other cases, researchers might construct an in-house measure to evaluate a function

that is thought to be uniquely affected in a single case. In some situations, measures with a high degree of specificity or sensitivity to the disorder under investigation might be selected, whereas in other situations, the investigator might choose to use measures with a high degree of external or ecological validity.

Regardless of the measure(s) selected, the use of appropriate comparison groups or a control group is critical for interpretation and later conclusions about results. In some cases, it is appropriate to utilize a group comprised of normal, healthy individuals who are matched on relevant demographic variables (e.g., age, education) to compare normal with nonnormal performance. It is also often relevant to use an additional disease comparison group (e.g., a group with neurologic disease not affecting the cognitive component under investigation). This can be particularly helpful when it is important to rule out nonspecific contributions to the patient's deficit, and when researchers are attempting to localize the deficit within some component of a cognitive model. Essentially, this process allows researchers to draw conclusions regarding the differential effects of brain damage on a particular cognitive function.

Strengths and Limitations of the Lesion Method

On the one hand, the basic logic of the lesion paradigm, that an observed cognitive or neuropsychological deficit reflects the contribution normally given to the cognitive function by the damaged brain region (Feinberg & Farah, 2000; Selnes, 2001), is rather straightforward. One important complication, however, is that the behavioral consequences of damage to a particular brain structure reflect the combined outcome of (a) a loss of function in the damaged area and (b) the adaptive response of the undamaged neural substrate. Depending upon the nature of the injury, the adaptive response may entail a large-scale physiological effect (e.g., diaschisis) in which depression of neuronal activity outside the lesion site can occur (von Monakow, 1969). Alternatively, the adaptive response may reflect disconnection of functional areas from one another due to damage to interconnecting structures or white-matter tracts (Geschwind, 1965). These effects may differ widely in importance depending upon the nature, severity, and regional localization of the injury, as well as upon the complexity of interconnections to and from the affected structure(s). It is thus important to have a clear anatomic understanding of the potential effect of a lesion on the remaining brain before attempting to interpret its behavioral implications.

In addition to the aforementioned complexities, the lesion paradigm, at least in its application to naturally occurring lesions in human research, has inherent limitations. One of the most important problems is that as accidents of nature, most lesions do not obey structural or architectonic boundaries, and as such, they function as partially uncontrolled independent variables (Gazzaniga et al., 1998). This limitation constrains the ability to make reliable deductions about normal function or about the contribution made by the damaged structure or brain system. Processes that occur during and after the lesion cannot be controlled either. From a functional standpoint, individuals react differently to injury, in part due to overall level of cognitive ability or cognitive reserve (Satz, 1993; Stern, Albert, Tang, & Tsai, 1999). Functional compensation can occur and may change the observed pattern of deficits, making time after injury a potentially important variable to control.

In recent years, the lesion approach has been enhanced considerably with the advent of imaging technology (Mazziotta & Gilman, 1992). The ability to more precisely characterize the nature and extent of the lesion has enabled more precise interpretations of performance dissociations and has led to the discovery of many specific relationships between behavioral dysfunction and damage to particular brain structures (Damasio & Damasio, 2000; Tranel, 1992). The development of atlases for lesion localization (Damasio & Damasio, 2000) has enhanced the ability to compare results across studies. Researchers can proceed with confidence knowing lesion location more precisely.

REVERSIBLE LESION METHODS

In recent years, methodologies designed to create temporarily abnormal brain function have been employed in neuropsychological research. We call these methods *reversible lesion paradigms*. These methods have the explanatory power of the lesion approach but are without some of the major disadvantages of the lesion method that we highlighted earlier. A particularly important feature of the reversible lesion approach is that it allows for repeated measurement of the individual both in and out of the lesioned state. This allows for a more specific attribution of the observed deficits to the lesion per se, provided that other factors governing performance are adequately controlled. In this section, we describe two representative examples of this approach: repetitive transcranial magnetic stimulation (rTMS) and the intracarotid amobarbital procedure (IAP) or WADA test.

Repetitive Transcranial Magnetic Stimulation (rTMS)

Transcranial magnetic stimulation (TMS) is a relatively new and noninvasive technique that has been increasingly used for activating cortical neurons in normal individuals. TMS involves applying pulses of magnetic stimulation to the brain and examining the effects of this stimulation on motor and cognitive processing. In some respects, TMS is the opposite of MEG, in which magnetic fields from the brain are measured as an individual carries out some cognitive or motor task. As described below, TMS can either transiently disrupt ongoing cognitive processing, thereby inducing a so-called reversible lesion, or it can activate simple motor or visual systems.

Although it is a relatively new technique, magnetic stimulation has its historical roots in the late nineteenth century (for review, see Barker, 1991). D'Arsonval (1896) was the first to describe visual changes (phosphenes) and vertigo when a subject's head was placed inside a brass coil that received an alternating current from a power supply. During the early 1900s, a flurry of research articles appeared in prominent journals, describing visual sensations that were caused by stimulation of the retina due to changing magnetic fields. However, it was not until the early 1980s, when investigators at the University of Sheffield developed a prototype magnetic stimulator, that TMS emerged as a viable research tool for studying brain-behavior relationships (Polson, Barker, & Freeston, 1982). Barker and the Sheffield group (1985) published the first report of magnetic stimulation of the cortex in normally functioning individuals and in clinical populations. They found that magnetic stimulation over the frontal motor cortex could elicit motor-evoked potentials from the hand, and they also noted differences in the latency of motor EPs between normal individuals and patients with multiple sclerosis (Barker et al., 1985; Barker, Freeston, Jalinous, & Jarratt, 1987).

Since the mid-1980s, a virtual explosion in the number of publications on TMS has taken place worldwide, beginning with one article in 1985 to almost 400 published research articles in 2001. In part, this has been prompted by technologic advances, including the development of a device for delivering rapid rate or repetitive trains of magnetic pulses (rTMS), as well as demonstrations that TMS is generally safe, is not painful, and may have clinical utility and promise as a tool for empirical investigation of cognitive and motor ability. In the following sections, the basic principles underlying TMS are briefly described, followed by discussion of methodological considerations (stimulation parameters, dependent variables) and applications of TMS to neuropsychological studies.

Basic Principles of rTMS

The basic principle underlying transcranial magnetic stimulation (TMS) draws from Faraday's idea that electric current passing through a coil of wire produces a magnetic field. If the magnetic field fluctuates in magnitude, a secondary electric current is produced in nearby media. The strength of the induced electric current is directly related to the rate of change (on-off-on) of the magnetic field. It is but a simple step to consider the power of this approach when applied to study brain-behavior relationships in humans. Theoretically, one can stimulate underlying brain tissue in a relatively non-invasive manner and thus use this technique with normal individuals.

In human TMS studies, an insulated coil in the shape of a circle or figure eight is placed over the head and held in place by the investigator or by a mechanical fixation device. When brief pulses of electric energy pass through the coil, a changing magnetic field is created that easily penetrates the scalp and skull. In turn, the magnetic pulses create a secondary electric current in underlying brain and neural tissue. It is this secondary electric current, not the magnetic field, that causes neural excitation by influencing membrane depolarization. In most modern devices, the strength of the magnetic field during TMS ranges from 1 to 3 Tesla, about the same strength as found in most MRI scanners. Although magnetic stimulation is not painful per se, there is a loud clicking noise that is associated with the changing magnetic field. Most subjects experience a nonpainful tapping sensation on the scalp that is related to muscle contraction.

Magnetic stimulation can be applied in single pulses or in repetitive trains of multiple pulses (rTMS). Single-pulse TMS is a relatively safe procedure that has been used extensively in clinical neurophysiology to index central cortico-motor excitability in studies designed to map regions of the motor cortex. Each pulse lasts approximately 100 μs and is presented at a rate of one pulse every 3 to 4 seconds. Generally speaking, single-pulse TMS seems to exert an excitatory effect on behavior when an individual is not engaged in another ongoing behavior. For example, observable twitches of the finger, hand, or arm can easily be elicited when single-pulse TMS is applied over the hand area of the motor cortex.

During rTMS, multiple trains of pulses can be applied at very high rates (up to 60/s) over various periods of time. Repetitive transcranial magnetic stimulation (rTMS) has been used more typically in neuropsychological studies examining language, working memory, and other cognitive processes. In very general terms, rTMS tends to disrupt or interfere with ongoing cognitive behavior, and for this reason it has been viewed as inducing a reversible (virtual) brain lesion. Because rTMS poses some risk for eliciting seizures in normal individuals, very strict safety guidelines have been developed (Wasserman, 1998; Pascual-Leone et al., 1993). These guidelines address various stimulation parameters that can be safely used together during a particular experiment.

Of particular importance with respect to safety issues are the intensity of magnetic stimulation, the number of stimuli per second (frequency) and the duration of the stimulation.

Several important questions arise with respect to TMS. What is the spatial resolution of magnetic stimulation within the brain? How deep does the induced electric current extend into the brain tissue? Are its effects excitatory, inhibitory, or both? Does activation spread to distant brain regions that are anatomically connected with the target site? The answers to these questions are certainly crucial for enabling one to draw inferences about the relationships between anatomic specificity and neurocognitive function. Although they are not fully resolved, some progress has been made in recent years to answer these questions.

Regarding the size of the magnetic field induced by rTMS, it is generally believed that the spatial extent of the magnetic field induced by various TMS coils ranges from .5 to 2 cm wide and from 2 to 3 cm deep (Bohning, He, George, & Epstein, 2001; Rhuohonen et al., 1995). This level of resolution is generally much smaller than are naturally occurring brain lesions that are seen in clinical patient studies. In general, circular magnetic coils affect larger cortical areas, whereas figure eight coils provide more focal stimulation at the point just beneath the intersection of the coil loops.

Although the magnetic field per se may be relatively focal, the electric current it induces may have far-reaching effects both spatially, temporally, and neurochemically. In recent years, multiplatform studies combining rTMS with positron-emission tomography (PET), EEG (electroencephalogram), or even fMRI have attempted to address this issue. In some studies rTMS is applied to a targeted brain areas, while EEG or regional PET activation is simultaneously measured (Paus et al., 1997; Sieber et al., 1998). These studies have revealed that the effects of TMS may extend beyond the immediate area of magnetic perturbation to include regions connected to the stimulated region. For example, Paus et al., (1997) reported that TMS applied over the frontal eye fields elicited increased regional cerebral blood flow in distant regions to which the frontal eye fields are presumably connected (i.e., visual cortex of superior parietal and medical parietal-occipital regions). Fox et al., (1997) stimulated primary motor cortex with TMS and found increased CBF (cerebral blood flow; using PET) over ipsilateral primary and secondary motor and somatosensory cortices and contralateral SMA. Taken together, such findings suggest that rTMS over a focal cortical area may not remain strictly focal, but rather may spread in a neuroanatomically distinct manner to areas to which it is interconnected.

Equally important have been other multiplatform studies suggesting that TMS may exert at least short-term effects on brain neurotransmitter systems. Strafella, Paus, Barrett, and

Dagher (2001) used a dopamine receptor ligand ([C]raclopride) to detect changes in extracellular dopamine after 30 min of rTMS over the left dorsolateral frontal lobe or over the left occipital lobe. The dopamine receptor ligand was injected within 5 min of completion of the rTMS trial, and PET imaging took place within 30 min. The study found decreased dopamine uptake in the ipsilateral caudate following left frontal TMS, with no effects seen in the putamen, nucleus accumbens, or contralateral caudate.

Findings from such combined TMS and PET studies can have important implications for the cognitive neuroscientist–neuropsychologist during experimental design of TMS studies. First, the effects of TMS may extend well beyond the immediate hot spot that was focally stimulated, and this consideration may play a role in the design of control tasks. The flip side of this is that rTMS may be used as a powerful tool for studying local cortical reactivity and functional connectivity (Bailey, Karhu, & Ilmoniumi, 2001; Pascual-Leone, Walsh, & Rothwell, 2000) Finally, although the effects of TMS may be relatively short lasting in many conditions, the temporal course and dissipation of shorter and longer lasting effects (e.g., in treatment of depression) has not been carefully studied.

Methodological Issues

How does one go about designing a TMS study? What important methodological problems must be addressed? Some issues depend on whether TMS or rTMS is being conducted and how the stimulation parameters temporally relate to the particular neurocognitive task under study (e.g., naming, a working memory n-back task, or a motor sequencing task). In rTMS studies, decisions must be made about various *stimulation parameters*. These include (a) the frequency (in Hz) of TMS stimuli, (b) the duration of the train of stimulation, (c) the interval between trains, (d) the total number of trains, (d) the intensity of the stimulation, and (e) the total number of stimuli in a given session, or to a specific brain region. For example, consider the study that involves 50 2-s trains of 40 stimuli delivered at a rate of 20 Hz with an intertrain interval of 28 s. In this study, a subject would receive 2 s of rTMS (40 stimuli) that is delivered every 30 s for 25 min, resulting in 2,000 total stimuli. These various stimulation parameters for rTMS are guided in part by safety considerations.

For both TMS and rTMS, *intensity of magnetic stimulation* is individually determined. Typically, intensity of stimulation is based on the individual's motor-evoked threshold (e.g., intensity = 70% motor-evoked potentials; MEP, or 120% MEP). This can be quantified by attaching surface EMG electrodes over the abductor policis brevis muscles in the hand

and measuring motor-evoked potentials when magnetic stimulation (1 Hz) is applied over the cortical motor hand area. Thus, threshold can be defined as the lowest intensity for eliciting MEPs 50% of the time. Regardless of whether a motor study or cognitive study is planned, the intensity of stimulation is based on the motor-evoked threshold.

A concern common to both TMS and rTMS studies is *selection of the TMS stimulation site*. This can be fairly straightforward in TMS studies of motor cortex in which stimulation grids (i.e., 5 × 5 cm) can be marked on a swimsuit cap that is worn by the participant. Finding the motor hot spot involves stimulating the various grid points in a systematic manner in order to find the site of peak responsivity. In contrast, identifying the hot spot in cognitive studies can be more subjective and unreliable, especially when specific cortical association areas are targeted. In most studies, the site of coil placement is determined in reference to the location of primary motor cortex (M1) or the International 10-20 EEG system. In other studies, behavioral performance during a pilot task has been used to identify the area of stimulation. For example, if one were interested in the effects of TMS on working memory, one could adopt a trial-and-error method for determining the hot spot by finding an area that resulted in the most errors during a pilot run of the working memory task (Mull & Seyal, 2001). Clearly, this approach is highly subjective. A more sophisticated approach might use brain-based coordinate systems that employ external fiducial markers, selecting a stimulation region based on available functional imaging results. In some systems, real-time monitoring of coil position and the person's head is possible (see Paus, 1999).

Equally important to the selection of the TMS stimulation site is *selection of a control stimulation site*. Walsh and Rushworth (1999) have identified three ways in which a control site can be chosen—dissociation, proximity, and time. Following the classic dissociation approach (Teuber, 1955), one selects two brain areas thought to have different neuropsychological functions and applies TMS to these two regions. In the proximity approach, one assumes that Area X is important for Task A, but neighboring areas are not. Thus, selection of the control site is dictated by proximity. This approach is particularly important when MRI structural scans are not available to help with localization. Finally, control sites can be selected based on the idea that TMS might have different effects across different sites, depending on when in the temporal sequence the TMS is applied.

Applications

TMS has been applied to several areas of interest to neuropsychologists. In *motor mapping studies,* single-pulse TMS over the motor cortex have been shown to produce electromyographic responses in the contralateral hand, arm, and face muscles. Presumably, these motor-evoked potentials (MEPs) reflect activation of neuronal networks in the motor cortex that link to spinal motor neurons (Pascual-Leone et al., 1994; Rothwell et al., 1991). Various researchers have used single-pulse TMS to map the size of cortical motor representations (Mills & Nithi, 1992; Triggs et al., 1994; Wasserman, McShane, Hallett, & Cohen, 1992). For example, Triggs, Subramanium, and Rossi (1999) mapped contralateral motor representations of the preferred and nonpreferred hand in right- and left-handed subjects. Although there were no handedness differences in the size or threshold of motor-evoked potentials (MEPs), the number of scalp stimulation sites that elicited MEPs was larger for the preferred hand. This was true for both dextrals and sinistrals, suggesting that handedness is associated with an asymmetry in the area of the cortical motor representations.

Recently, several researchers have reported that single-pulse TMS over the motor cortex can readily induce *ipsilateral* motor-evoked potentials (MEPs) from the hands and face (Ziemann et al., 1999). In general, ipsilateral MEPs require higher-intensity stimulation than do contralateral MEPs, occur more readily if the target muscle is mildly contracted, and are elicited more prominently from sites lateral to the optimal position for producing MEPs in the contralateral hand (Ziemann et al., 1999). An ipsilateral, multisynaptic pathway from the motor cortex to the hand (or face) has been proposed as the route for ipsilateral MEPs from muscles, classically viewed as being under exclusive control of the contralateral cortex.

Following from these observations of ipsilateral pathways are clinical studies that have used rTMS to examine recovery of function following acquired brain lesions (Caramia et al., 2000; Trompetto, Assini, Ducolieri, Marchese, & Abbruzzese, 2000). Trompetto and colleagues (2000) studied recovery following acute stroke by comparing motor responses that had been elicited by TMS when it was applied over the frontal regions of the damaged and nondamaged hemisphere. Three subgroups of patients were identified. The largest subgroup were those with poor recovery of motor function. Their responses (motor-evoked potentials) to TMS were absent over both the damaged and undamaged hemispheres. The two remaining subgroups had good motor recovery. In one, patients had larger MEPs with stimulation of the damaged (ipsilateral) than nondamaged (contralateral) hemisphere. Their good recovery possibly related to the unmasking of ipsilateral motor pathways. In the third recovery group, MEPs were larger in the affected than in nonaffected limb and possibly related to the use of alternate circuits within the damaged hemisphere. Such studies point to the

potential of TMS for providing information about clinical prognosis and mechanisms that might underlie recovery following stroke.

In other clinical studies, high-frequency stimulation of motor cortex has been used to activate the motor system and temporarily improve motor function in patients with Parkinson's disease (Pascual-Leone et al., 1994). In contrast, low-frequency motor cortex rTMS (presumably inhibitory in nature) improves motor function in patients with focal dystonia, a disorder characterized by hyperexcitability of cortical motor circuits (Siebner et al., 1999).

Several studies have used rTMS to induce *interference* in ongoing cortical activity or behavior. When applied over the speech area, *repetitive TMS* (rTMS) has been associated with speech arrest (C. M. Epstein et al., 1996; Pascual-Leone, Gates, & Dhuna, 1991; Wasserman et al., 1998). When applied over the left posterior temporal region (left BA37), rTMS has slowed visual object naming with no effects on word reading, non–word-reading, or color naming (Stewart, Meyer, Frith, & Rothwell, 2001). Within the memory domain, several studies have used rTMS as a probe for studying working and longer term memory (for review, see Grafman & Wasserman, 1999). When applied to the frontal or temporal regions, short- and longer-term recall deficits have been reported by some investigators. Grafman and colleagues (1994) gave a word list learning task to normally functioning individuals and examined the effects of timing of rTMS and the region of stimulation (e.g., frontal, temporal). It is interesting to note that rTMS over the left temporal lobe was more effective in reducing subsequent recall when stimulation was immediately applied at word onset (i.e., during encoding?), whereas the effects of frontal rTMS appeared at longer delays. Such findings imply that timing parameters in rTMS studies may help dissociate temporal and frontal lobe contributions to learning and memory.

In several recent studies, rTMS has been investigated for its efficacy as an intervention for *neuropsychiatric disorders*. The efficacy of rTMS as a treatment modality for major depressive disorder is currently being investigated across various centers around the country (C. Epstein et al., 1998; George et al., 1995; Pascual-Leone, Rubio, Pallardo, & Catala, 1996; Triggs, McCoy, 1999). Early studies administered relatively nonfocal rTMS using large circular coils centered over the scalp vertex and obtained promising but inconclusive evidence of improved mood in patients with severe depression (Hoflich, Kasper, Hufnagel, Ruhrmann, & Moller, 1993; Kolbinger et al., 1995). More recent studies have targeted the left dorsolateral frontal lobe in various treatment studies of depression. The basis for a potential therapeutic effect of rTMS on depression is unknown. Several lines of evidence have implicated hypoactivity of the left prefrontal cortex in the pathophysiology of depression. Even so, it is clear that the prefrontal region is just one component of a distributed network that is important for regulating mood. Although rTMS appears promising, carefully controlled and blinded studies with appropriate "sham" conditions are few and far between, and a variety of methodological issues remain to be addressed before claims about efficacy of rTMS for treating depression can be established (see Wasserman & Lisanby, 2001).

The WADA Technique

The intracarotid amobarbital procedure (IAP) was first developed by Wada to lateralize language function in the evaluation of patients with epilepsy, but it more recently has been used to predict the degree of postoperative amnesia in patients being considered for epilepsy surgery (Trenerry & Loring, 1995). Although the precise procedure varies, the typical IAP involves the injection of sufficient barbiturate (e.g., sodium amytal, sodium brevital) into a catheter placed in the internal carotid artery to produce a contralateral hemiplegia. Memory and language testing is typically conducted before, during, and after the period of drug action. The procedure generally results in a temporary impairment in hemispheric functions subserved by the middle cerebral artery. During injection of the language-dominant hemisphere, the patient becomes globally aphasic. Both hemispheres are studied sequentially in the same procedure. In addition to predicting hemisphere dominance for language, behavioral performance during the WADA procedure has been shown to predict seizure outcome and verbal memory decline after unilateral temporal lobectomy (Loring et al., 1994; Trenerry & Loring, 1995), and is useful for determining whether the nonaffected hemisphere can support memory function in isolation. WADA test results correlate well with hippocampal volume asymmetries in unilateral onset cases (Loring et al., 1993).

One significant drawback of the WADA procedure is that it is highly invasive. Because of this, it is used exclusively in patients undergoing diagnostic evaluation for brain surgery in which determination of language lateralization or memory support is important for predicting outcome. In recent years, there has been substantial interest in determining whether less invasive functional imaging procedures can be used to provide the same information as the IAP. Several studies using fMRI (Binder et al., 1996; Desmond et al., 1995; Lehericy et al., 2000), transcranial Doppler ultrasound (Knecht et al., 1998; Rihs, Sturzenegger, Gutbrod, Schroth, & Mattle, 1999), magnetic source imaging (Breier, Simos,

Zouridakis, Wheless, et al., 1999; Simos, Papamolaon, 2000), and repetitive transcranial magnetic stimulation (C. M. Epstein et al., 2000) to comparatively evaluate language function have been published in the last 5 years. Most studies have shown excellent correlation between language lateralization indices derived from WADA and functional imaging protocols, but perfect agreement has not emerged. For example, C. M. Epstein and colleagues (2000) found more right-sided interruption with vocal speech in surgical epilepsy candidates using transcranial magnetic stimulation than the interruption that would have been predicted by the WADA results. Postsurgical language performance correlated best with WADA results. Thus, these less invasive functional imaging techniques hold promise as alternatives to WADA testing, but the precise relationship between WADA and these other procedures remains to be understood. It should be kept in mind that the WADA technique is a gross inactivation technique, whereas most functional imaging approaches utilize cognitive activation paradigms to provide lateralizing or localizing information (Loring, 1997).

HUMAN LATERALITY PARADIGMS

Dichotic Listening

The dichotic listening task involves the simultaneous presentation of two auditory stimuli, one to each ear (Springer, 1986). The technique has been widely used in neuropsychological research to evaluate hemispheric asymmetries for auditory processing of speech in normal and clinical populations.

In the cognitive psychology literature, the procedure has its roots in early research on attention. Cherry (1953) used dichotic listening to investigate how listeners could extract and attend to one message in the context of many (the so-called cocktail party effect). Cherry presented messages in the same voice to both ears at once, and found that listeners had significant difficulty in separating the two messages. On the basis of these findings, he argued that attention used physical characteristics of the acoustic message to extract the message. In further experiments, Cherry used the technique of *shadowing,* in which one of the two messages had to be repeated back as it was presented. When shadowing instructions were added to the basic dichotic listening task, very little information could be extracted from the nonattended ear. For example, listeners asked to shadow the message in their right ear seldom noticed when the left-ear message was presented in a foreign language or when the speech presented there was garbled or reversed. Later recall tests revealed that there was very little memory for unattended words, even in situations in which the words were presented multiple times (Moray,

1959). These and other findings contributed to the empirical basis for the classic bottleneck theory of attention that presumes an early mechanism whereby unattended information is filtered from further processing and thus does not enter conscious awareness or memory (Broadbent, 1958). Although we now know this theory to be oversimplified, (i.e., there is substantial evidence that unattended information can be processed rather extensively; McGlinchey Berroth et al., 1993) the dichotic listening paradigm played a seminal role in the development of this influential model of selective attention.

In neuropsychological research, the dichotic listening paradigm primarily has been used extensively to study lateralization of cognitive processes in the brain, and more recently as a technique to study disordered brain organization in a wide variety of clinical neurological and psychopathological syndromes. In her seminal work with the technique, Kimura (1961a, 1961b) presented three pairs of spoken digits to each ear and asked subjects with unilateral right or left temporal lobectomies to recall as many of the six digits as possible. Two important findings emerged. First, patients with lefttemporal lobe damage identified fewer digits than did patients with right temporal lobe excisions. Second, regardless of lesion side, stimuli presented to the right ear were more accurately recalled. This right ear advantage (REA) has since been discovered to be related to hemispheric asymmetry for speech perception and production (Springer, 1986), verified by both behavioral and functional imaging techniques (Hugdahl et al., 1999) and with results of language lateralization studies using the WADA (intracarotid amobarbital) technique (Kimura, 1961b).

Subsequent studies have found a left-ear advantage for certain nonverbal stimuli, including emotional prosody (Bryden, Free, Gagne, & Groff, 1991; Erhan, Borod, Tenke, & Bruder, 1998), musical chords (H. W. Gordon, 1970), tonal sequences (Spellacy, 1970), and environmental sounds (Curry, 1967). It is generally more difficult to obtain a left-ear advantage, owing possibly to variations among both stimuli and subject abilities (Springer, 1986).

A recent trend has been to combine the behavioral task of dichotic listening with functional imaging or electrophysiological investigation to understand more precisely the neural basis of dichotic listening effects (Jancke, Buchanan, Lutz, & Shah, 2001). These studies have found the expected REA for linguistic stimuli and LEA for emotional stimuli, and have found lateralized material-specific differences in planum temporale and Heschl's gyrus that are in accordance with the behavioral ear asymmetries (Jancke et al., 2001).

The reliability and validity of the dichotic listening technique has been the topic of several investigations. This has been of some concern because about 70–80% of right-handed normal subjects show an REA for speech stimuli, whereas a much higher percentage (>90%) of such subjects show left-hemisphere language lateralization on WADA testing (Springer, 1986). Because the dichotic listening technique evaluates speech perception (rather than production), this may suggest that different components of language might be differentially lateralized in the brain. Also, subjects might develop strategies for dealing with dichotic listening or shadowing tasks that might alter the degree of lateralization. There are some encouraging data on the validity of dichotic listening for language lateralization, however (Geffen & Caudrey, 1981). In this study, 27 of 28 subjects with left-hemisphere speech showed an REA to speech stimuli, whereas four of seven subjects with right-hemisphere speech showed an LEA. Correct language lateralization was enhanced by the use of a discriminant function taking handedness, hit rates, and reaction time into account, suggesting that a simple correct recognition score may not be sufficient in characterizing dichotic listening performance (Geffen & Caudrey, 1981; Springer, 1986). Test-retest reliability of the dichotic listening test has also been of some concern, as several studies have reported reliabilities in the .70–.80 range, dependent on the number of trials (Blumstein, Goodglass, & Tartier, 1975; Shankweiler & Studdert-Kennedy, 1975).

To the extent that performance on dichotic listening reflects the lateralization of relevant cognitive processes in the brain, the task is useful for assessing abnormalities in brain organization in neurological and psychiatric disorders. In recent investigations, dichotic listening has been used to examine disordered cerebral lateralization in schizophrenia (Bruder et al., 1995; Green, Hugdahl, & Mitchell, 1994), mood disorder (Bruder, Wexler, Stewart, Price, & Quitkin, 1999; Pine et al., 2000), developmental dyslexia (Cohen, Hynd, & Hugdahl, 1992; Hugdahl et al., 1998), attention-deficit disorder (Manassis, Tannock, & Barbosa, 2000; Manassis, Tannock, & Masellis, 1996), and other clinical syndromes. The power of dichotic listening paradigms to discern differences in brain organization in clinical groups is limited by aforementioned limits to the reliability and validity of the technique itself.

Tachistoscopic Visual Presentation

One complicating factor in dichotic listening studies is that each ear sends both contralateral and ipsilateral connections to the cortical receiving areas responsible for sound perception. Because of this, performance on dichotic listening paradigms likely reflects either the dominance of contralateral over ipsilateral connections, or some form of dynamic suppression of ipsilateral connections by contralateral ones. In either event, the behavioral outcome is complex and often difficult to interpret. The anatomic arrangement of the visual system, in contrast, is simpler because each visual half-field (VHF) projects to the contralateral cortical visual area in the occipital lobe. Thus, stimuli exclusively presented to the left visual field (LVF; the left hemiretinal field of each eye) is first received in the right occipital lobe, whereas stimuli projected to the right visual field (RVF) are first processed in the left occipital lobe. If stimulus presentation is arranged so that a single visual field is stimulated, the researcher can at least know which hemisphere receives direct sensory input from the environment. This is the basis of the tachistoscopic visual half-field technique (McKeever, 1986). Tachistoscopic techniques have been prominent in experimental neuropsychological research since the 1940s, but they have not been commonly used in clinical research.

Application of tachistoscopic techniques to questions of hemispheric lateralization and specialization received impetus from studies of split-brain patients who underwent surgical disconnection of the hemispheres for relief of intractable epilepsy (Sperry, 1968), and the technique was subsequently applied to study a broad range of questions relevant to the concept of cerebral asymmetry. Many such studies reported visual half-field asymmetries for verbal (for which the right VHF excels) and nonverbal information (for which the left VHF excels; McKeever, 1986).

Two main explanations for these asymmetries have been offered. The first explanation was that the directional characteristics of language (e.g., whether it is read right-to-left or left-to-right) should determine the cerebral dominance pattern seen when linguistic stimuli were briefly presented to the visual half-field (Mishkin & Forgays, 1952). Thus, initial experiments (reviewed in McKeever, 1986) showed different visual half-field asymmetries for English and Yiddish words. This view was challenged in the 1960s by several studies suggesting RVF asymmetries for letters, words, and other linguistic stimuli, consistent with an alternative explanation—namely, that VHF asymmetries reflected cerebral dominance for language (Bryden, 1964; McKeever, 1986). In the years subsequent to these initial developments, it has become clear that cerebral specialization for language influences VHF asymmetries and that directional scanning does not account for the majority of findings.

Like the literature on dichotic listening, one relatively stable finding in the tachistoscopic recognition literature has been that it has been difficult to devise tasks that yield LVF-right-hemisphere superiority of comparable magnitude to that seen in recognition of linguistic stimuli. For example, studies showing clear RVF asymmetries for object naming showed little if any visual field asymmetry for geometric drawings (Bryden & Rainey, 1963). One significant problem in this regard is finding stimuli that cannot be verbalized. Some studies have shown that visual half-field asymmetries could be reversed (from LVF to RVF) when subjects were required to use an arbitrary name to identify laterally presented forms (Hannay, Dee, Burns, & Masek, 1981). However, some tasks have shown significant LVF asymmetries, including line orientation (Umilta et al., 1974), face recognition (Rizzolatti, Umilta, & Berlucchi, 1971), and emotionally evocative material (Suberi & McKeever, 1977).

Tachistoscopic paradigms are somewhat crude measures of hemispheric specialization or lateralization because it cannot be assumed that the presented stimulus is processed exclusively by the hemisphere to which the stimulus is primarily projected. In fact, it is assumed that all stimuli are processed by both hemispheres to some degree, and that lateralized performance is a function of specialized or privileged processing in the hemisphere to which presentation is directly targeted. However, because of precise timing and control over stimulus presentation, tachistoscopic investigations are capable of answering (at least coarsely) questions about the time course of cognitive operations. For example, systematic variation of the input and output requirements of tachistoscopic recognition tasks can yield important information about the time needed to transfer information across the hemispheres. Suppose that a train of word and nonword stimuli are presented to either the RVHF or the LVHF, and the subject is asked to respond with either the right or left hand. In the RVHF-right-hand (uncrossed) combination using word stimuli, the left hemisphere both receives the input, presumably processes the word, and programs the motor response. In the RVHF-left-hand (crossed) combination, the left hemisphere receives the input, performs appropriate processing, and then must send the processing result to the right hemisphere for motor output. Reaction time differences between these two conditions can be used to provide an estimate of interhemispheric transfer time (Bayshore, 1981). Similarly, by manipulating other aspects of the task, the temporal parameters of input, processing, and output stages of processing can be estimated.

The use of the classical tachistoscopic VHF technique for determining hemispheric specialization or lateralization has waned in recent years. However, variations of the technique have found their way into contemporary cognitive science investigations of several topics of current interest. Prominent examples include investigations of the interface between attention and memory (Bavelier, Prasada, & Segui, 1994; Fagot & Pashler, 1995; Park & Kanwisher, 1994), cognitive processing without awareness (Henke, Landis, & Markowitsch,

1994; Kunimoto, Miller, & Pashler, 2001; Monahan, Murphy, & Zajonc, 2000), and the relationship between emotion and cognition (Kunst-Wilson & Zajonc, 1980; Murphy, Monahan, & Zajonc, 1995; Zajonc, 1980).

Dual-Task Paradigms

One key assumption in the application of information processing models to neuropsychological questions is that the brain is a limited-capacity processor. Cognitive operations consume such information-processing resources and, if sufficient numbers of operations are needed simultaneously, performance may suffer. The idea that limitations or conflicts in cognitive resource allocation might have observable effects on behavior is the basis of dual-task paradigms (Hiscock, 1986). The strategy of having subjects perform multiple simultaneous tasks has a long tradition in the selective attention literature, and has been used in neuropsychology to evaluate cerebral dominance for language and other processes.

The basic paradigm is quite simple: Subjects perform some cognitive or motor task simultaneously with a manual task using either the right or left hand. Interpretation of results is based on the concept of *functional cerebral distance*. This principle states that the degree to which the two tasks affect each other varies inversely with the functional distance between the cerebral regions or systems in which the cognitive processes are represented (Hiscock, 1986; Kinsbourne & Hicks, 1978). Functional cerebral distance does not mean the same thing as anatomical distance, although interference effects *are* generally greater when the cognitive and motor tasks depend on resources from the same cerebral hemisphere. Hiscock (1986) provides an excellent review of the conceptual and methodological issues surrounding dual-task paradigms. His review of the available literature suggests that verbal activity disrupts right-hand performance more than it does left-hand performance, but that nonverbal activity produces more variable effects, sometimes disrupting left-hand performance more than right, and sometimes affecting both hands equally. One problem in this literature is the degree to which factors other than the nature of verbal versus nonverbal processing (e.g., level of task difficulty) are appropriately controlled.

Dual-task paradigms represent fundamentally *indirect* ways of evaluating processing resources, and as such, are subject to limitations based on a lack of knowledge of how performance changes directly reflect differences in resource allocation. For example, it cannot be assumed that performance on one task will increase linearly while performance on the other will decrease linearly as resources are allocated from one to the other (Hiscock, 1986). Also, it cannot be assumed

that the total number of resources needed to perform two tasks concurrently is the simple sum of resources needed to perform them separately (Kinsbourne, 1981; Navon & Gopher, 1979). Although these methodological problems are significant, they do not invalidate the use of dual-task paradigms to investigate laterality questions. Hiscock (1986) provides useful recommendations for improving research design in dual-task experiments, including the use of multiple levels of task difficulty, multiple measures of task performance, or both as a way of establishing reasonable parameters within which the study of verbal and nonverbal processing can proceed.

ELECTROPHYSIOLOGICAL AND PSYCHOPHYSIOLOGICAL APPROACHES

Electrophysiological and psychophysiological approaches make use of the measurement of bioelectrical signals by the placement of sensitive transducers on the body surface. In cognitive neuroscience and neuropsychology research, the term *electrophysiology* has typically referred to investigations that measure brain electrical activity (the EEG) from the scalp (or, more rarely, from the brain itself), whereas *psychophysiology* generally refers to investigations that measure autonomic and somatomotor activity through devices placed on the skin. In both domains, the goal is to define and measure psychologically relevant physiological variables and to relate them in some way to behavioral performance. The basic level of analysis inherent in these techniques is in understanding *organism-environment transactions* (Cacioppo, Tassinary, & Berntson, 2000). Cacioppo and colleagues regard this approach as a "top down approach within the neurosciences that complements the bottom-up approach of psychobiology" (p. 7).

Electrophysiological and psychophysiological investigations have exploded over the past several decades, and increasing attempts are being made to integrate the available findings with results from neuroscientific and neuropsychological investigations. Numerous recent examples of the application of electrophysiological approaches to the study of clinical brain disorders (Honda, Suwazono, Nagamine, Yonekura, & Shibasaki, 1996; Newton, Barrett, Callanan, & Towell, 1989; O'Donnell et al., 1993; Polich & Squire, 1993) are examples of this emerging integration.

Evoked-Potential Investigations

For several decades, measurement of brain electrical activity has been an important component of the overall information-processing approach to cognition (Donchin, 1979). What is seen in the raw EEG signal is generally believed to be the result of summated postsynaptic potentials. To measure these signals, electrodes are placed on the scalp in standard locations and are connected to amplifiers. In special instances, electrodes can be implanted in the brain in the context of a diagnostic workup (Halgren et al., 1980). Modern computer equipment can sample the resulting electrical potentials many thousands of time per second and can digitize the analog readout for later storage and analysis.

The raw EEG signal contains multiple sources of information, some of which are systematic, low voltage changes in potential that are thought to reflect neural events of psychological significance. These *event-related potentials* (ERPs) can be separated from the background EEG by averaging samples of the EEG that are time-locked to the occurrence of a specific event in the experiment, such as the presentation of a stimulus or the initiating or a response (Fabiani, Gratton, & Coles, 2000; Kutas & Dale, 1997). By averaging many such samples, random aspects of the EEG that are not time-locked to the event will average out, leaving the ERP visible. The topographical distribution of ERPs across the brain can yield important information about potential localization of constituent processes. In most experiments, the peaks in the ERP are described in terms of their distribution, their polarity (positive or negative), and their latency. For example, the N400 refers to a negative-going peak that reaches its maximum about 400 ms after stimulus presentation, while the P300 is a positive-going peak that tops out about 100 ms earlier. Alternatively, peaks can be named in ordinal latency (such that P3 is the third positive-going peak in the waveform), for their scalp distribution (e.g., frontal P300), or for the psychological processes presumed to underlie them (e.g., novelty P3, mismatch negativity, etc.; Fabiani et al., 2000).

Some components of the ERP are based primarily on the physical properties of stimuli that elicit them. Because these components are dependent on the characteristics of an outside stimulus, they are referred to as *exogenous* potentials. In contrast, ERP components that more directly reflect cognitive processing or some form of interaction of the subject with the environment are referred to as *endogenous* potentials. It is primarily the latter type of potential that is of interest to neuropsychologists.

ERP data are used in two main ways. First, the effects of specific independent variables or subject characteristics can be analyzed in terms of their separate and interacting effects on specific ERP components. Second, the topographical pattern of ERPs, in terms of latency and magnitude, can be analyzed, either separately or in combination with other imaging methods, to model the source of the waveform.

The concept of an *ERP component* has come to refer to segments of the ERP waveform that covary in response to particular experimental manipulations (Fabiani et al., 2000). Components can be defined as peaks occurring within a certain time window after a specific event. Several classes of components exist, and only those relevant to neuropsychological research are mentioned here. Response-related components include the lateralized readiness potential (LRP) that occurs in advance of executing a motor response (Kutas & Donchin, 1980) , the contingent negative variation (CNV) that occurs in the period before a reaction time task (Rohrbaugh & Gaillard, 1983), and the error-related negativity (ERN) that occurs when subjects make errors in reaction time tasks (Falkenstein, Hohnsbein, Hoormann, & Blanke, 1990). Early negative responses in the ERP waveform have been interpreted to reflect selective attention effects. Several studies have indicated that attended stimuli are associated with more negative ERP between 100–200 ms after stimulus onset (Hilliard, Hink, Schwent, & Picton, 1973). At middle latencies, the mismatch negativity (MMN) effect is seen, which results from subtracting the waveform to frequent stimuli from that generated by the presentation of rare stimuli. The MMN, which can occur as early as 50 ms after stimulus onset with a peak of 100–200 ms, occurs to both attended and unattended stimuli, and is thought to reflect the operation of a preattentive mismatch or novelty detector (Naatanen, 1995). Later components include the P300, a positive peak elicited by attended task-relevant "oddball" stimuli (Donchin & Coles, 1988; Johnson, 1988), and the N400, a negative component that occurs between 200–400 ms poststimulus that appears to reflect the detection of semantic incongruity (Kutas & Hilliard, 1980; Van Petten & Kutas, 1987).

As might be anticipated, there has been significant interest in applying ERP methodology to the study of cognitive disorders to validate claims about impairments at particular stages of information processing in these patients. For example, several recent investigations have been able to distinguish between components of recollection using ERP techniques (Allan, Wilding, & Rugg, 1998; Curran, 1999), and others have shown that false recollection is associated with more negativity in the ERP (Curran, Schacter, Johnson, & Spinks, 2001; Endl, Walla, Lindinger, Deecke, & Lang, 1999). In a complementary approach, there has been interest in applying ERP methods to the study of temporal lobe dysfunction owing in part to evidence that the P300 originates in the temporal cortex or hippocampus (E. Gordon, Rennie, & Collins, 1990). Surprisingly, some investigations have found normal P300 amplitude and latency in patients with amnesia associated with mesial temporal damage (Polich & Squire, 1993; Rugg, Pickles, Potter, & Roberts, 1991). As another example, the N400 has been examined in normally functioning individuals and brain injured subjects to test hypotheses about semantic processing (Deacon, Hewitt, & Tamney, 1998; Grunwald et al., 1999; Tachibana et al., 1999).

Scalp recording of EEG, and the ERP data that can result from it, has certain advantages in neuropsychological research. The primary strength of the approach is its excellent temporal resolution. With sampling rates as high as 10,000 Hz and excellent analog-to-digital resolution common of contemporary computers, determination of latency and peak of ERP components can be determined with millisecond precision. One drawback, however, is that because of the electrical properties of the skull and scalp, spatial resolution is lower than that which can be obtained with brain imaging methods. This issue has received a significant amount attention in recent years. Dense-array electrode montages are now available, together with statistical procedures that allow for better spatial sampling and localization (Tucker, 1993). Also, combining the excellent temporal resolution of ERP with source localization methods or functional brain imaging approaches is emerging as a way of combining the strengths of available paradigms (Absher, Hart, Flowers, Dagenbach, & Wood, 2000; Heinze, Hinrichs, Scholz, Burchert, & Mangun, 1998; Kruggel, Wiggins, Herrmann, & von Cramon, 2000; Pouthas, Maquet, Garnero, Ferrandez, & Renault, 1999). With accumulating data from electrophysiological and functional brain imaging studies, localization of the source of neural activity responsible for characteristic components is now becoming a reality (Alho et al., 1998; Hopf et al., 2000; Tarkka, Stokic, Basile, & Papanicolaou, 1995; Yamazaki et al., 2000). Invasive measurement of electrographic activity, when possible, provides an exciting new approach to the study of neural representation that complements brain imaging methods (Allison, Puce, Spencer, & McCarthy, 1999; Nobre, Allison, & McCarthy, 1994) because it is not subject to limitations in spatial resolution imposed by scalp recording.

Autonomic Psychophysiology

Research paradigms exploring autonomic and somatomotor aspects of cognitive functioning have a long history within the parent field of psychophysiology and have enjoyed similar application to research questions in neuropsychology and cognitive neuroscience (Cacioppo et al., 2000; Sarter, Berntson, & Cacioppo, 1996). Psychophysiological evaluation of normal and clinical populations has contributed substantially to our understanding of a broad array of relevant phenomena, including visual perception (Bauer, 1984; Tranel & Damasio, 1985), memory (Diamond, Mayes, & Meudell, 1996; McGlinchey Berroth, Carrillo, Gabrieli, Brawn, & Disterhoft, 1997), emotion (Bradley & Lang, 2000; Davidson & Sutton, 1995; Tranel & Hyman, 1990), and decision making (Bechara, Tranel, Damasio, & Damasio, 1996). Measurement

of organism-environment interactions can make use of a broad array of response systems, including electrodermal reactivity, pupillary responses, electromyographic changes, cardiovascular changes, and effects on hormonal and endocrine regulation.

Several issues confront the neuropsychological researcher who is considering adopting a psychophysiological approach to investigation. One important issue is whether the research question demands an evaluation of time-locked (phasic) changes in physiological reactivity or an investigation of some generalized (tonic) level of activity in a physiological channel. An example of the former approach would involve questions about the degree to which remembered versus forgotten information was associated with time-locked physiological reactivity at the time of encoding (Diamond et al., 1996; Verfaellie, Bauer, & Bowers, 1991). An example of the latter type of question would be an investigation of the effect of acquired brain damage on nonspecific cardiac or hormonal activity (e.g., Emsley, Roberts, Aalbers, Taljaard, & Kotze, 1994).

A second issue concerns the selection of specific response systems or variables for study. Measurement selection may be governed by a number of factors, including invasiveness, ease of use (e.g., computational intensity), and sensitivity and specificity to the psychological constructs under study. For example, the measurement of electrodermal activity has been popular in a wide range of experiments because it is easy and inexpensive to collect and simple to quantify and because electrodermal activity is sensitive to a wide range of manipulations affecting psychological effort, arousal, surprise, and significance detection (Dawson, Schell, & Filion, 2000). However, within this advantage is a potential limitation: Unless the experimental task is appropriately controlled (for example, controlling for task difficulty across levels of arousal), it is sometimes difficult to precisely interpret the source of increased electrodermal activity. For example, just because some studies suggest that larger electrodermal responses occur in situations in which novel, significant stimuli are detected (Bernstein, Taylor, & Weinstein, 1975) does not mean that electrodermal responding can be simply inferentially applied as a significance detector. An excellent review of inferential concepts in psychophysiological research is given by Cacioppo et al. (2000).

A third issue concerns the selection of an approach to instrumentation and data analysis. There are numerous ways to collect psychophysiological data, and the fact is that many neuropsychologists and cognitive neuroscientists might want to apply these methods without the typical didactic or empirical training that would characterize the mainstream psychophysiological researcher. Consensus statements exist regarding appropriate methods for instrumentation, recording, analysis and reporting of results for a number of response systems (Fowles et al., 1981; Jennings et al., 1981; Picton et al., 2000; Shapiro et al., 1996), and researchers should consult these statements when planning experiments.

A final issue has to do with the fact that changes in specific autonomic or somatomotor response systems do not occur in isolation, but instead occur as part of a complex set of responses. So, for example, manipulations that might increase electrodermal responding might also be expected to have effects on blood pressure, heart rate, respiration rate, or other psychophysiological parameters. Within individuals, these various responses might correlate poorly with one another (particularly at low overall levels of arousal) so that conclusions about the individual's cognitive or affective state might be different depending upon which response system is assessed. Complicating matters is that individuals tend to respond in similar ways to different stimuli, a phenomenon known as *individual response stereotypy* (Engel, 1960; Lacey & Lacey, 1958). Such issues need to be taken into account when evaluating responses of a given magnitude, particularly in group designs.

FUNCTIONAL BRAIN IMAGING

Basis of Functional Brain Imaging

For our purposes, the term *functional brain imaging* refers to any technique that provides information about neurochemical or metabolic activity in the brain, particularly when the study of such processes is applied to an understanding of cognitive activity (Nadeau & Crosson, 1995). Such techniques include direct imaging of metabolic processes by radioisotope tagging of glucose uptake (e.g., [^{18}F]fluorodeoxyglucose PET or FDG PET), indirect imaging of metabolism via markers of cerebral blood flow (e.g., [^{99m}Tc]-hexamethyl-propylene-amine-oxime single photon emission computed tomography or HMPAO SPECT; functional magnetic resonance imaging or fMRI), and imaging of neurotransmitters (e.g., [^{18}F]fluorodopa PET; Nadeau & Crosson, 1995). In general, these techniques image the effects of neuronal energy expenditure, which tends to be greatest at the terminus of the axonal arborization and in the dendritic tree. Thus, resulting images do not reflect activity in the cell bodies per se, but at the projection site (Nadeau & Crosson, 1995). This is a rapidly expanding field within neuroscience, with emerging applications to the scientific study of basic cognitive processes and to clinical research including diagnosis and outcomes assessment.

The ability to image the human brain has been a possibility for many years, beginning with the advent of the X-ray computed tomography (CT). From this basic technique, which allowed researchers to obtain structural images of the brain in order to determine areas of abnormalities based on knowledge of anatomy (Papanicolau, 1998; Perani, 1999), technology has advanced considerably. More sophisticated techniques have enabled the acquisition of anatomical images with clearer resolution, providing investigators with important information when determining correlations or associations between neuropsychological and neurological deficits and dysfunction in localized brain regions. In the past two decades, advances in functional brain imaging have occurred at such a rapid pace that this area can be said to be one of the most rapidly developing in all of neuropsychology and cognitive neuroscience. The opportunity to image in vivo activity of the intact brain provides an exciting alternative to studying neuropsychological function exclusively from the viewpoint of a damaged or lesioned system. Some of the limitations of the ablation approach (e.g., functional reorganization after damage) are eliminated by the opportunity to study the normal, working brain; as we shall see, however, functional imaging methods have limitations of their own. In many areas of inquiry, results from functional imaging studies have served to augment, refine, and constrain the results of lesion and ablation studies, and thus have provided a further basis for determining the relationship between structure and function.

All functional imaging approaches depend on two basic steps: recording (registration) and representation-construction (Papanicolau, 1998). In the simplest possible terms, some type of physiological (e.g., electromagnetic) signal is recorded from the imaged object (brain) by a sensitive device (scanner), and the resulting signal pattern is represented in terms of a model (atlas) of the object constructed from known parameters. Neither recording nor representation is a perfect reflection of reality, so that the results of such studies are, by definition, approximations of what actually occurs in the brain. Papanicolau (1998), in an incisive description of the basis of functional imaging, suggests that what emerges from this enterprise depends on (a) the relationship between the object and the electromagnetic signal derived from it, (b) the specific characteristics of the recording instrument, and (c) the intentions and methods employed by the user of the device. An understanding of the contribution that functional imaging has made (and can make) to neuropsychological research requires at least a basic appreciation of these three domains. Any large-scale functional imaging enterprise depends upon the interdisciplinary cooperation of a number of professionals, including physicists, radiologists, neurologists, neuropsychologists, cognitive scientists, mathematicians, and statisticians, among others. Decisions about which functional imaging approach to use or whether to use functional brain imaging at all are dependent upon many factors, including cost and availability of appropriate equipment, spatial and temporal resolution, intrusiveness of the scanning environment and repeatability of the scanning operation, and artifact susceptibility (Nadeau & Crosson, 1995). Regardless of the specific choices that are made, neuropsychologists are particularly well positioned to contribute such functional imaging studies because of their expertise in cognitive task design and behavioral measurement.

In a typical functional imaging study, metabolic aspects of brain activity (e.g., glucose utilization) are measured indirectly while the subject performs a cognitive task. The resulting pattern of activity is then registered and reconstructed anatomically based either on the use of a stereotactic approach (Talairach & Tournoux, 1988) or by an individual approach based on the establishment of skull-based markers or fiducials (Mazziotta et al., 1982; Shukla, Honeyman, Crosson, Williams, & Nadeau, 1992).

One key aspect of functional imaging studies is the manner by which results are visually displayed and interpreted. For those unaccustomed to viewing such images, it is critical to be mindful of the distinction between images that represent some *direct or indirect readout* of metabolism or CBF and images that represent a *statistical map of differences* in activity between two conditions. In many instances, what is displayed in an image does not bear a simple or direct relationship to actual metabolic activity or CBF occurring at a specified location; instead, what is displayed are *probability values* that describe, on a voxel-by-voxel basis, the likelihood that differences in activity between, say, a cognitive activation condition and a control or resting state occurred by chance. An example of this can be seen in Figure 12.3. This image was taken from a recent

study of memory function we recently completed using a 3 Tesla magnet (Loftis et al., 2000). Here, subjects alternatively engaged in two tasks, one in which they were asked to remember a series of complex pictures (memory condition), and the other in which a single picture was simply repeated over and over (repeat condition). After a number of initial data-analytic steps, signal intensities recorded during these two conditions were compared on a voxel-by-voxel basis using a Bonferroni-corrected t test. The resulting image (Figure 12.3) depicts chance probabilities that depicted voxels were more active in the memory condition than in the repeat condition, using a level of significance of $p < .00001$. Thus, the image is a graphic presentation of probability values, not a direct readout of blood flow or signal intensity. This is important to keep in mind, because such images are often compelling (or sexy, so to speak) and can lead to inaccurate interpretations if the reader does not clearly understand what he or she is viewing.

A number of functional imaging techniques now exist, each of which has its own unique methods of registration and reconstruction. In the following sections, we describe procedural aspects of the major functional imaging paradigms, and we describe their strengths and weaknesses. Regardless of paradigm, the ability of the investigator to develop an effective and well-controlled cognitive task can be thought of as the rate-limiting step of neuroimaging research.

Positron-Emission Tomography (PET)

Rationale

PET imaging depends upon the introduction of a positron-emitting isotope created by bombardment of stable chemical elements with protons (Papanicolau, 1998). Such isotopes

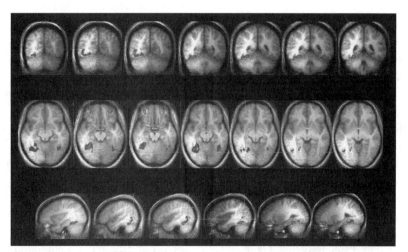

Figure 12.3   Results of voxel-by-voxel t test comparisons of a memory condition (remember five pictures) and a repeat condition (remember one picture presented five times), from Loftis et al. (2000).

can be combined with other elements to create complex molecules that can substitute for naturally occurring compounds like water, glucose, or different neurotransmitters. The resulting compounds are called *tracers* because their tendency to shed their positive charge in the form of positron emissions can be detected by appropriate imaging devices and can thus reveal their relative position and concentration in different regions of the brain (Papanicolau, 1998). Typical compounds include oxygen-labeled (^{15}O) water, or 2-fluoro-2-deoxy-8-glucose (FDG). What is imaged in PET is the collision between an escaping positron and an electron in the adjacent environment; when this interaction occurs, both are annihilated and converted to a pair of high-frequency photons that move at equal speed in diametrically opposite directions. The emitted photons constitute the electromagnetic signal imaged in PET, and the surface distribution of such signals can be reconstructed to build a model of regional activity.

PET using FDG makes use of a ligand that is taken up by the glucose transport mechanism and that then remains trapped until cleared by relatively slow-acting metabolic processes. It produces high-quality images, but the slow rate of FDG uptake requires the subject to engage in the task for a long (30–40 min) time. Although this is a disadvantage, the slow rate of absorption makes it possible for the subject to engage in the cognitive task outside the scanner and to be moved later to the scanning environment. In contrast, ^{15}O-PET uses a radiotracer that is actively circulating within the volume of cerebral blood and that diffuses freely into the cerebral tissue, necessitating much briefer task and scanning times (Nadeau & Crosson, 1995). With this technique, multiple tasks are possible in the same experimental session.

Applications

PET is a leading methodology for the study and measurement of physiological properties within the human brain (Perani, 1999), and is one of the earliest functional imaging techniques to have been employed in studies of cognitive function (Raichle, 2001; Reiman, Lane, Petten, & Bandettini, 2000). The PET technique can be used to measure a variety of different functions, including regional cerebral blood flow (rCBF), glucose metabolism, oxygen consumption, and regional neurotransmission (Paulesu, Bottini, & Frackowiak, 1997; Perani, 1999; Reiman et al., 2000). Within neuropsychology, PET is most commonly utilized for studying blood flow or glucose metabolism, because these are properties that reflect regional neuronal activity. From the cellular level, it is important to note that blood flow to a particular brain region can increase or decrease in response to changes in cellular

activity (Buckner & Logan, 2001; Raichle, 2001). Studies with rCBF usually focus on *brain activation,* in which subjects engage in a particular cognitive task (Perani, 1999) that is thought to call for activity in specific structures or systems. Inferences from these paradigms are based on the idea that when a cognitive function is performed, blood flow will increase in the region responsible for that activity (Frith & Friston, 1997; Papanicolau, 1998). The ability of the PET scanner to detect radiation density is equal throughout the brain, so that the obtained signal can be used in a way that allows for comparisons of rCBF across different regions. A PET scanner takes a series of scans during an experiment, each lasting for approximately 30 s (Papanicolau, 1998). By averaging across the scans, researchers can track patterns of neuronal activity in response to behavioral performance.

Neuropsychological investigations of rCBF involving PET have included studies of working memory (Baddeley, 1998; Jonides et al., 1997; Smith, Jonides, & Koeppe, 1996), long-term memory encoding and retrieval (Beauregard, Gold, Evans, & Chertkow, 1998; Cabeza et al., 1997; Tulving, Habib, Nyberg, Lepage, & McIntosh, 1999; Ungerleider, 1995), language (Bookheimer et al., 1998; Cabeza & Nyberg, 2000; Gabrieli, Poldrack, & Desmond, 1998; Warburton, Price, Swinburn, & Wise, 1999), attention (Lane et al., 1998), and mental imagery (Alivisatos & Petrides, 1997; Vingerhoets et al., 2001). Recently, several group studies have evaluated task-related disturbances in regional CBF in patient populations (Backman, Robins-Wahlin, Lundin, Ginovart, & Farde, 1997; Perani, 1999; Price & Friston, 2001; Zakzanis, 1998), although use of these paradigms in patients can be difficult depending on level of complexity of the particular task.

In a typical experiment, participants perform a control task designed to produce a baseline level of activation against which the experimental task is compared. Researchers then average responses and activation sites across participants in order to interpret and make conclusions regarding activated regions (Raichle, 1997). Sophisticated analyses, the description of which is beyond the scope of this chapter, are utilized in an effort to determine significant activation patterns while controlling for interparticipant differences and variability, as well as incorporating specific hypothesis testing (Perani, 1999).

Development of the appropriate control condition is critical to interpretation of the overall experiment, and great care is needed to equate control and experimental conditions on as many input, processing, and output variables as is possible while varying the specific cognitive process under investigation. For example, an appropriate control task in a picture naming experiment would attempt to equate as many stimulus parameters as possible, would require the same or similar response modality, and would present the subject with a task of equal difficulty that did not engage the specific naming mechanism under investigation. Obviously, these requirements are often difficult to satisfy completely. Although it might seem reasonable to compare the experimental task with a simple *rest* condition in which the participant is asked to *do nothing,* such an approach is not without its complexities. *Do nothing* instructions might be variably interpreted by different individuals, leading to poorly controlled activations in the control condition. For example, one participant may think anxiously about her upcoming examination, while another might be reliving last night's date with much excitement, and still another might take a short nap. If this variability occurs, one cannot say that this so-called control condition controls very much at all.

Still, *resting state studies,* in which subjects are scanned without having to perform a task or function, have provided neuropsychological researchers with important information regarding structure and function. In particular, PET scans conducted on patients with specific lesions (i.e., aphasic patients with lesions to Broca's area, amnesic patients with medial temporal lobe lesion) have allowed researchers to learn more about regional blood flow in impaired brain regions (Price & Friston, 2001). Many resting-state paradigms have utilized PET to study the metabolic properties of select brain regions. Because glucose metabolism is indirectly related to blood flow and can interact with certain types of labeled tracers, it is also possible to study metabolic properties of injured brain tissue. An example is in the case of Alzheimer's disease, in which studies have found abnormal rates of glucose metabolism in temporal-parietal brain regions (Perani, 1999).

Strengths and Limitations

Functional imaging using PET has inherent advantages and disadvantages. Assuming a sufficient number of detectors in the imaging system, PET imaging has relatively high spatial resolution (about 4 mm), meaning that its ability to accurately capture brain structures is superior to that of some other imaging techniques (Papanicolau, 1998). With PET CBF techniques such as ^{15}O, it is relatively simple to obtain absolute measures of CBF. However, temporal resolution, (i.e., the ability to evaluate rapidly evolving cognitive processes) is less than optimal for many experimental paradigms (Buckner & Logan, 2001; Papanicolau, 1998). Like many of the other functional imaging techniques that are discussed in this chapter, PET scanning is incapable of differentiating the *type* of physiological activity that is occurring. Essentially, it is impossible to know whether the activation

patterns represent excitatory or inhibitory neuronal transmission (Buckner & Logan, 2001). The net result, which is depicted in the final image, likely reflects a combination of both excitatory and inhibitory effects. One expensive disadvantage of ^{15}O-PET is the need for an adjacent cyclotron due to the short half-life of the radiotracer.

Single Photon Emission Computed Tomography (SPECT)

Rationale

Single photon emission computed tomography (SPECT) is a technique for studying radioactive tracers introduced into the body, usually by intravenous injection or inhalation. With X-ray CT scanning, the signal used is based on the release of photons, transmitted from an X-ray source, that have passed through the body. The signal detected is the decay of radioactive nuclides inside the body, derived from injection or inhalation of a tracer and distributed throughout the bloodstream. Typical isotopes used in SPECT imaging include xenon 133, technetium 99m-HMPAO, and receptor ligands labeled with iodine 123 (Lassen & Holm, 1992).

HMPAO SPECT makes use of a ligand that binds to endothelial cell membranes and is rapidly transported across the membranes and altered so that it cannot back-diffuse into the blood (Nadeau & Crosson, 1995). Because the ligand is accumulated by endothelial membranes, it serves as an amplified measure of CBF with good signal-to-noise ratio. An advantage of the technique is that because the ligand is rapidly absorbed, short task times are possible. Another advantage is that because the ligand remains stably trapped for several hours, a participant can be injected, can engage in a cognitive task outside the scanner, and can then be later moved to the scanner for imaging. HMPAO SPECT and FDG PET are the only imaging techniques that allow the subject to perform the cognitive task outside the potentially intrusive scanner environment.

Applications

In recent years, SPECT imaging has been widely used in the evaluation of metabolic correlates of seizure activity (Lee et al., 1997; Mastin et al., 1996), and has also been useful in evaluating disordered regional CBF in head injury (Goldenberg, Oder, Spatt, & Podreka, 1992; Varney et al., 1995), dementia (Costa, Ell, Burns, Philpot, & Levy, 1988; Parnetti et al., 1996), and other neurological syndromes (Benson et al., 1996; Chatterjee et al., 1997; Giroud, Lemesle, Madinier, Billiar, & Dumas, 1997) and psychiatric disorders (Camargo, 2001;

Kotrla & Weinberger, 1995; Toone, Okocha, Sivakumar, & Syed, 2000). The psychiatric literature contains several excellent examples of the use of SPECT for imaging of neurotransmitter system activity rather than CBF (Bryant & Jackson, 1998; Heinz et al., 2000; Raedler et al., 1999).

Strengths and Limitations

One strength of SPECT is that it is relatively inexpensive and relies on readily available technology. It has a moderately high signal-to-noise ratio, but compared to other imaging methods, SPECT has inferior spatial resolution (6–7 mm) because of a high degree of attenuation and scatter. One distinct advantage is that the cognitive task used to generate the metabolic image is conducted outside the scanner and is thus not subject to potentially distracting stimuli in the scanner environment or to the restrictions on movement or vocalization imposed particularly by fMRI. Currently, SPECT is used less commonly than are PET or fMRI in neuropsychological studies of associations between physiological properties and behavior. As with PET, it can be used during activation studies, and as a *resting* indicator of cerebral blood flow. SPECT is mainly used for measuring rCBF, and, as a result, its clinical applications have most commonly been in providing evidence of disturbed rCBF in various patient groups as a way of validating behavioral hypotheses.

Functional Magnetic Resonance Imaging (fMRI)

Rationale

The basic principle behind fMRI is based on the fact that changes in neuronal activity produce alterations in oxygen content of local tissue (Papanicolau, 1998; Reiman et al., 2000). Because this increase in blood flow is disproportionate to change in oxygen consumption, the overall content of deoxyhemoglobin is also altered (Raichle, 2000). Reduction in hemoglobin triggers a vascular reaction resulting in an oversupply of oxygenated blood to tissue some seconds later (Papanicolau, 1998). Through effects on hydrogen atoms, this overcompensation results in changes in the MR signal, and this can be estimated and captured as an image. Changes in localized magnetic field properties due to alterations in the ratio of oxyhemoglobin and deoxyhemoglobin are thus detected through fMRI. Although many techniques are used to measure the hemodynamic response, the most commonly utilized is the blood oxygen level dependent (BOLD) contrast signal (Reiman et al., 2000; Turner, Howseman, Rees, & Josephs, 1997). Other techniques, including use of blood flow and blood volume, are also utilized (Reiman et al., 2000).

Applications

Currently, fMRI is the leading technique for imaging local blood flow in conjunction with performance on neuropsychological or cognitive tasks. In the recent literature, fMRI investigations have played a critical role in lesion-deficit paradigms, taking localization of function to a new level. Like PET scanning, fMRI paradigms have been used to investigate a wide variety of cognitive functions (see Cabeza & Nyberg, 2000 for review), including short-term working memory (Baddeley, 1998; Casey et al., 1995; D'Esposito et al., 1995; D'Esposito, Postle, & Rypma, 2000), encoding and retrieval into long-term memory (Gabrieli, 1998; McIntosh, 1998), language generation and comprehension (de Zubicaray et al., 1998; Demb et al., 1995), object recognition (Bartels & Zeki, 2000; Courtney & Ungerleider, 1997; R. Epstein & Kanwisher, 1998), attention (LaBar, Gitelman, Parrish, & Mesulam, 1999; Mangun, Buonocore, Girelli, & Jha, 1998), and emotional processing (Crosson et al., 1999; Maratos, Dolan, Morris, Henson, & Rugg, 2001; Rama et al., 2001). Functional MRI is also enjoying increasing use in studies of brain-impaired patients (Monchi, Taylor, & Dagher, 2000; Rees et al., 2000) and in studies of recovery of function after brain injury (Poldrack, 2000).

Strengths and Limitations

Functional MRI has significant advantages, including the direct mapping of blood-flow images onto anatomic images, the fact that no radioactive tracer is involved, and the relative speed with which images can be acquired. Compared to other imaging methods, the signal-to-noise ratio in BOLD fMRI is quite small, though this is becoming less of a limitation with the development of sophisticated signal-averaging techniques (Bandettini, Jesmanowicz, Wong, & Hyde, 1993; G. McCarthy, Puce, Luby, Reiman, Lane, Van Petten, & Bandettini, 2000). Another limitation is the intrusiveness of the scanner environment and its possible effects on cognitive processing. Although the spatial resolution associated with fMRI is thought to be excellent and one of the highest among functional neuroimaging techniques, temporal resolution, which refers to the ability of the image to reflect adequate sequences of activation, is a significant limitation. Neural activity typically occurs 5–8 s before blood flow is actually observed and recorded, meaning that brain activity (hemodynamics) is longer than the preceding neuronal activity (Frith & Friston, 1997). Essentially, this means that the peak of an activation signal occurs approximately 5–10 s after presentation of an experimental stimulus (Bandettini, Rasmus, & Donahue, 2000; Buckner & Logan, 2001; Perani, 1999). This results in what is often referred to as *temporal blurring,* indicating that it is somewhat difficult to determine the exact sequence of events that happen in response to a probe (i.e., a cognitive task). Investigators have developed techniques to account for this phenomenon, which is referred to as the hemodynamic response function (Miezin, Maccotta, Ollinger, Petersen, & Buckner, 2000).

In addition to the problem of the delayed hemodynamic response, one of the major limitations of fMRI is its high degree of sensitivity to movement artifact. Even slight head movements can produce artifact. There are also artifacts associated with changes in air flow (inside the scanner), as well as with movement associated with cardiac and respiratory processes. As a result, fMRI paradigms are restricted to experiments that contain minimal movement—or in an ideal situation, experiments that contain no movement at all. This presents difficulty for studies designed to image higher-order, complex cognitive properties. Because many experiments have to be performed silently by the participant, investigators can never be certain that participants are actually engaging in the appropriate task. To deal with this, behavioral measures are often taken off-line, so to speak, to ensure that the predicted behavioral effect is obtained. Also, because performance measures are frequently not taken during actual scanning, there is often no direct way of quantifying the relationship between successful performance and brain activation. It is possible, for example, that participants may become more practiced or skilled at the task through the many experimental repetitions that are offered during scanning. To deal with this problem, many experiments contain a training phase prior to the scanning session designed to stabilize task performance prior to the imaging session.

Functional MRI can be used to study a variety of different cognitive and neuropsychological functions. However, some brain regions are more susceptible to artifact and other types of noise than to others. Regions in close proximity to sinuses and air-fluid interfaces, such as the anterior temporal lobes and orbitofrontal cortex, are often difficult to image because of a relatively high signal-to-noise ratio (Buckner & Logan, 2001). The exact level of resolution depends on the particular scanning equipment utilized, with more powerful scanners (i.e., more powerful magnet) producing images with better spatial and temporal resolution (Papanicolau, 1998), but also producing increases in corresponding artifact.

Similar to PET, fMRI is also unable to provide information concerning physiological properties of brain tissue (Buckner & Logan, 2001). An image that captures brain activity is depicting activation of a particular region or structure. What is unknown is what *type* (i.e., excitatory or inhibitory) of activation this is reflecting. This kind of information is vital to delineating cognitive networks in particular for determining the specific effect one region or structure has on another.

Behavioral Task Design in fMRI

In a typical fMRI paradigm, participants perform a behavioral task aimed at engaging the neuropsychological processes in question. As with PET scanning, these are alternated with periods of control tasks, which serve as a reference to which activation in the target tasks is compared (Aguirre & D'Esposito, 1999; Frith & Friston, 1997; Worden & Schneider, 1995). Several common experimental methods for task administration have been developed. One method involves a *blocked* paradigm, in which trials collectively designed to tap a particular cognitive process are presented. Blocks are alternated with control trials, designed to capture identical properties as the experimental trials *except* for the process of interest, and images are taken repeatedly during both conditions (Aguirre & D'Esposito, 1999). Subtracting images obtained in the control condition from the experimental trials or correlating brain activity with a theoretical curve produces an *activation map* or image that reflects regional differences in activity during experimental and control conditions. Limitations of this type of design include the fact that subjects may become able to anticipate trials because of the successive, repetitive nature of the task, and therefore may engage alternative processing strategies that confound what would be expected with a more pure activation pattern. An alternative approach, called *event-related fMRI (ER-fMRI)* utilizes task design in which experimental and control trials are presented alternately and at random to subjects so that the hemodynamic response to individual items or events can be measured (Aguirre & D'Esposito, 1999). The advantage of ER-fMRI is that activation can be contrasted across *trial types,* in addition to averaging *across* trials (as is done in blocked paradigms). For example, ER-fMRI might be used to study hemodynamic response to the encoding of items as a function of whether they are later recalled on a delayed memory test. Studies directly contrasting ER-fMRI with traditional blocked experiments have revealed differing patterns of activation, suggesting that at the very least, different strategies were used (Bandettini et al., 2000).

Magnetoencephalography (MEG)

Rationale

Except for neurotransmission, all forms of signal activity in the brain result in potentially measurable electrical currents. The pattern of activation or neuronal signaling that accompanies psychological processes is contained in seemingly random electrical activity, but gives rise to two forms of electromagnetic energy that can be captured and recorded outside the head. One of these types of energy, *magnetic flux,* can be measured through magnetoencephalography (Papanicolau, 1998). Any current is associated with a magnetic field perpendicular to its direction. The magnetic field strength is proportional to the source currents that generate it, and it dissipates as a function of the square of the distance from the current source. The magnetic flux lines that emanate from the head correspond primarily to dendritic currents in synchronized sets of cells; this is what is imaged during MEG.

The shape of the surface flux distribution can be measured by detectors called magnetometers, which are loops of wire placed parallel to the head surface in which current as magnetic flux lines thread through the loop. If sufficient numbers of such detectors are placed at regular intervals over the entire head surface, then the entire flux distribution created by a brain activity source can be determined (Papanicolau, 1998). Because the measured magnetic field strengths are so small, the magnetometers that record them must offer practically no resistance; in other words, they must be superconductive. Superconductivity is often achieved by cooling the wires to extremely low temperatures (e.g., about 4° Kelvin). The induced current in superconductive magnetometers is weak and must be amplified. Special amplifiers called SQUIDS (superconductive quantum interference devices) are used for this purpose. A modern MEG apparatus may contain nearly 150 magnetometers arranged so as to cover the entire head surface for simultaneous recording of magnetic flux at all surface points simultaneously.

One of the primary goals of MEG imaging is source localization (i.e., localizing the neural source that is generating particular characteristics of the observed distribution of magnetic flux). A detailed description of how this is accomplished is beyond the scope of this chapter, although knowledge of the basic dipolar characteristics of the magnetic flux distribution allow the dipole source to be localized from the pattern of current induced in the magnetometer array. After such an estimate is derived, it can be coregistered with structural MRI to provide localization in brain-anatomical terms. Coregistering results from MEG with structural brain images is known as *magnetic source imaging* (Ganslandt, Nimsky, & Fahlbusch, 2000; Lewine & Orrison, 1995; Roberts, Poeppel, & Rowley, 1998).

Applications

MEG and magnetic source imaging have become increasingly popular in recent years and have been applied to a variety of problems in neuropsychology and in cognitive neuroscience. For example, it has been applied to the lateralization-localization of language functions in surgical planning (Breier, Simos, Zouridakis, Wheless et al., 1999; Roberts, Ferrari, Perry, Rowley, & Berger, 2000), to localization of memory processes in the temporal lobe (Castillo et al., 2001), and elucidation of the processes underlying visual object recognition (Halgren, Raij, Marinkovic, Jousmaki, & Hari, 2000), normal and disordered reading (Breier, Simos, Zouridakis, & Papanicolaou, 1999; Simos et al., 2000), and attention (Assadollahi & Pulvermuller, 2001).

Choosing a Functional Imaging Strategy

The researcher who contemplates using functional brain imaging as an investigative tool must consider a broad range of factors when choosing a particular strategy. Assuming unlimited availability, as well as the extensive financial and personnel resources that such techniques often require, the researcher is faced with evaluating the relative strengths and weaknesses of available methods. A summary of these strengths and weaknesses, adopted from the excellent review by Nadeau and Crosson (1995), is presented in Table 12.1. The notion of

TABLE 12.1 Advantages and Limitations of Functional Imaging Techniques

	O-PET	HMPAO SPECT	BOLD fMRI
Cost	High	Low	Moderate
Availability	Limited	Widespread	Potentially widespread
Spatial resolution	Maximum < 4 mm FWHM, in practice 16 mm	Maximum 6–7 mm	Maximum < 1 mm
Temporal resolution	1–2 min	3–4 min	Seconds
Number of studies per session	Maximum 8–10	Maximum 3–4	Unlimited
Signal-to-noise ratio	Moderate	Moderate	Low
Measurement parameter	Potential for actual CBF; in practice, relative counts	Relative counts	Degree to which CBF is entrained by task
Intrusiveness of environment	Moderate	None	High
Susceptibility to movement	Low	Low	High
Technical support needed	High	Low	High
State of development	Advanced	Limited	Limited

Note. Adapted from Nadeau, S. E., & Crosson, B. (1998). A guide to the functional imaging of cognitive processes. *Neuropsychiatry, Neuropsychology, and Behavioral Neurology, 8,* 143–162.

conducting *cross-platform* research that utilizes multiple imaging modalities or that combines an imaging approach with lesion studies is becoming increasingly popular. Systematic use of the cross-platform approach will be necessary for a full understanding of the comparability of these different methods.

Advances in functional brain imaging have continued to augment lesion-deficit models and behavioral studies of normal human cognition. As our knowledge of complex neuropsychological functions increases, so does the technology capable of imaging them. The bridges between cognitive psychology, neuropsychology, and neuroimaging will continue to strengthen, and should yield exciting new discoveries in the next decade.

SUMMARY AND CONCLUSIONS

The techniques and approaches described in this chapter reflect remarkable evolution over the past few decades. Each approach has identifiable strengths and weaknesses, and each seems particularly well-suited for studying a limited range of questions. The particular strategy chosen for a research investigation is partly driven by logistic factors and partly by the suitability of the approach for the research domain. In the next decade, the limitations posed by individual approaches should be made less significant by the use of cross-platform approaches that utilize multiple methodologies to address specific research questions. For example, combining functional imaging and lesion-based approaches within the same research program can allow the researcher to draw broader conclusions. In the next decade, additional attention will be paid to issues of external validity (generalizability) of findings and to evaluation of the real-world significance of results. Continued attempts to understand how results from one method map onto others will be undertaken. Ongoing interdisciplinary collaboration between neuropsychologists, neuroscientists, cognitive scientists, physicians, and other professionals will continue to yield exciting new approaches to solving research problems in neuropsychology.

REFERENCES

Absher, J. R., Hart, L. A., Flowers, D. L., Dagenbach, D., & Wood, F. B. (2000). Event-related potentials correlate with task-dependent glucose metabolism. *Neuroimage, 11,* 517–531.

Aguirre, G. K., & D'Esposito, M. (1999). Experimental design for brain fMRI. In C. T. W. Moonen, P. A. Bandettini, & G. K. Aguirre (Eds.), *Functional MRI* (pp. 370–380). New York: Springer Verlag.

Alho, K., Winkler, I., Escera, C., Huotilainen, M., Virtanen, J., Jaaskelainen, I. P., Pekkonen, E., & Ilmoniemi, R. J. (1998). Processing of novel sounds and frequency changes in the human auditory cortex: Magnetoencephalographic recordings. *Psychophysiology, 35,* 211–224.

Alivisatos, B., & Petrides, M. (1997). Functional activation of the human brain during mental rotation. *Neuropsychologia, 35,* 111–118.

Allan, K., Wilding, E. L., & Rugg, M. D. (1998). Electrophysiological evidence for dissociable processes contributing to recollection. *Acta Psychologica, 98,* 231–252.

Allison, T., Puce, A., Spencer, D. D., & McCarthy, G. (1999). Electrophysiological studies of human face perception. I: Potentials generated in occipitotemporal cortex by face and non-face stimuli. *Cerebral Cortex, 9,* 415–430.

Anderson, J. R. (1983). *The architecture of cognition.* Cambridge, MA: Harvard University Press.

Arendt, T., Bruckner, M. K., Bigl, V., & Marcova, L. (1995). Dendritic reorganisation in the basal forebrain under degenerative conditions and its defects in Alzheimer's disease: Vol. 3. The basal forebrain compared with other subcortical areas. *Journal of Comparative Neurology, 351,* 223–246.

Assadollahi, R., & Pulvermuller, F. (2001). Neuromagnetic evidence for early access to cognitive representations. *Neuroreport, 12,* 207–213.

Backman, L., Robins-Wahlin, T. B., Lundin, A., Ginovart, N., & Farde, L. (1997). Cognitive deficits in Huntington's disease are predicted by dopaminergic PET markers and brain volumes. *Brain, 120,* 2207–2217.

Baddeley, A. (1998). Recent developments in working memory. *Current Opinion in Neurobiology, 8,* 234–238.

Bailey, C. J., Karhu, J., & Ilmoniumi, R. (2001). Transcranial magnetic stimulation as a tool for cognitive studies. *Scandinavian Journal of Psychology, 42,* 297–306.

Bandettini, P. A., Jesmanowicz, A., Wong, E., & Hyde, J. S. (1993). Processing strategies for time-course data sets in functional MRI of the human brain. *Magnetic Resonance Imaging in Medicine, 30,* 161–173.

Bandettini, P. A., Rasmus, M. B., & Donahue, K. M. (2000). Functional MRI: Background, limits, and implementation. In J. T. Cacioppo, L. G. Tassinary, & G. G. Berntson (Eds.), *Handbook of psychophysiology* (2nd ed., pp. 978–1014). Cambridge, UK: Cambridge University Press.

Barker, A. T. (1991). An introduction to the basic principles of magnetic nerve stimulation. *Journal of Clinical Neurophysiology, 8,* 26–37.

Barker, A. T., Freeston, I., Jalinous, R., & Jarratt, J. A. (1987). Magnetic stimulation of the human brain and peripheral nervous system: An introduction and the results of an initial clinical evaluation. *Neurosurgery, 20,* 100–109.

Barker, A. T., Jalinous, R., & Freeston, I. L. (1985). Non-invasive magnetic stimulation of human motor cortex. *Lancet, 1,* 1106–1107.

Bartels, A., & Zeki, S. (2000). The architecture of the colour centre in the human visual brain: new results and a review. *European Journal of Neuroscience, 12,* 172–193.

Bauer, R. M. (1984). Autonomic recognition of names and faces in prosopagnosia: A neuropsychological application of the Guilty Knowledge Test. *Neuropsychologia, 22,* 457–469.

Bavelier, D., Prasada, S., & Segui, J. (1994). Repetition blindness between words: Nature of the orthographic and phonological representations involved. *Journal of Experimental Psychology: Learning, Memory, and Cognition, 20,* 1–19.

Bayshore, T. R. (1981). Vocal and manual reaction time estimates of interhemispheric transmission time. *Psychological Bulletin, 89,* 356–368.

Beauregard, M., Gold, D., Evans, A. C., & Chertkow, H. (1998). A role for the hippocampal formation in implicit memory: a 3-D PET study. *Neuroreport, 9,* 1867–1873.

Bechara, A., Tranel, D., Damasio, H., & Damasio, A. R. (1996). Failure to respond autonomically to anticipated future outcomes following damage to prefrontal cortex. *Cerebral Cortex, 6,* 215–225.

Benson, D. F., Djenderedjian, A., Miller, B. L., Pachana, N. A., Chang, L., Itti, L., & Mena, I. (1996). Neural basis of confabulation. *Neurology, 46,* 1239–1243.

Bernstein, A. S., Taylor, K. W., & Weinstein, E. (1975). The phasic electrodermal response as a differentiated complex reflecting stimulus significance. *Psychophysiology, 12,* 158–169.

Binder, J. R., Swanson, S. J., Hammeke, T. A., Morris, G. L., Mueller, W. M., Fischer, M., Benbadis, S., Frost, J. A., Rao, S. M., & Haughton, V. M. (1996). Determination of language dominance using functional MRI: A comparison with the Wada test. *Neurology, 46,* 978–984.

Blumstein, S. E., Goodglass, H., & Tartier, V. (1975). The reliability of ear advantage in dichotic listening. *Brain and Language, 2,* 226–236.

Bohning, D., He, L., George, M., & Epstein, C. (2001). Deconvolution of transcranial magnetic stimulation (TMS) maps. *Journal of Neural Transmission, 108,* 35–52.

Bookheimer, S. Y., Zeffiro, T. A., Blaxton, T. A., Gaillard, W. D., Malow, B., & Theodore, W. H. (1998). Regional cerebral blood flow during auditory responsive naming: Evidence for cross-modality neural activation. *Neuroreport, 9,* 2409–2413.

Bradley, M. M., & Lang, P. J. (2000). Affective reactions to acoustic stimuli. *Psychophysiology, 37,* 204–215.

Breier, J. I., Simos, P. G., Zouridakis, G., & Papanicolaou, A. C. (1999). Temporal course of regional brain activation associated with phonological decoding. *Journal of Clinical and Experimental Neuropsychology, 21,* 465–476.

Breier, J. I., Simos, P. G., Zouridakis, G., Wheless, J. W., Willmore, L. J., Constantinou, J. E., Maggio, W. W., & Papanicolaou, A. C. (1999). Language dominance determined by magnetic source imaging: a comparison with the Wada procedure. *Neurology, 53,* 938–945.

Broadbent, D. E. (1958). *Perception and communication.* Oxford, UK: Pergamon.

Bruce, V., & Young, A. (1986). Understanding face recognition. *British Journal of Psychology, 77,* 305–327.

Bruder, G. E., Wexler, B. E., Stewart, J. W., Price, L. H., & Quitkin, F. M. (1999). Perceptual asymmetry differences between major depression with or without a comorbid anxiety disorder: A dichotic listening study. *Journal of Abnormal Psychology, 108,* 233–239.

Bruder, G. E., Rabinowicz, E., Towey, J., Brown, A., Kaufmann, C. A., Amador, X., Malaspina, D., & Gorman, J. M. (1995). Smaller right ear (left hemisphere) advantage for dichotic fused words in patients with schizophrenia. *American Journal of Psychiatry, 152,* 932–935.

Bryant, C. A., & Jackson, S. H. (1998). Functional imaging of the brain in the evaluation of drug response and its application to the study of aging. *Drugs and Aging, 13,* 211–222.

Bryden, M. P. (1964). Tachistoscopic recognition and cerebral dominance. *Perceptual and Motor Skills, 19,* 686.

Bryden, M. P., Free, T., Gagne, S., & Groff, P. (1991). Handedness effects in the detection of dichotically-presented words and emotions. *Cortex, 27,* 229–235.

Bryden, M. P., & Rainey, C. A. (1963). Left-right differences in tachistoscopic recognition. *Journal of Experimental Psychology, 66,* 568–571.

Buckner, R. L., & Logan, J. M. (2001). Functional neuroimaging methods: PET and fMRI. In R. K. Cabeza (Ed.), *Handbook of functional neuroimaging and cognition* (pp. 27–48). Cambridge, MA: MIT Press.

Cabeza, R., & Nyberg, L. (2000). Imaging cognition II: An empirical review of 275 PET and fMRI studies. *Journal of Cognitive Neuroscience, 12,* 1–47.

Cabeza, R., Mangels, J., Nyberg, L., Habib, R., Houle, S., McIntosh, A. R., & Tulving, E. (1997). Brain regions differentially involved in remembering what and when: a PET study. *Neuron, 19,* 863–870.

Cacioppo, J. T., Tassinary, L. G., & Berntson, G. G. (2000). Psychophysiological science. In J. T. Cacioppo, L. G. Tassinary, & G. G. Berntson (Eds.), *Handbook of psychophysiology* (2nd ed., pp. 3–23). Cambridge, UK: Cambridge University Press.

Camargo, E. E. (2001). Brain SPECT in neurology and psychiatry. *Journal of Nuclear Medicine, 42,* 611–623.

Caramazza, A. (1986). On drawing inferences about the structure of normal cognitive systems from the analysis of impaired performance: The case for single-patient studies. *Brain and Cognition, 5,* 41–66.

Caramazza, A., & Badecker, W. (1989). Patient classification in neuropsychological research. *Brain and Cognition, 10,* 256–295.

Caramia, M., Palmieri, M., Giacomini, P., Iani, C., Dally, L., & Silvestrini, M. (2000). Ipsilateral activation of the unaffected motor cortex in patients with hemiparetic stroke. *Clinical Neurophysiology, 111,* 1990–1996.

Casey, B. J., Cohen, J. D., Jezzard, P., Turner, R., Noll, D. C., Trainor, R. J., Giedd, J., Kaysen, D., Hertz-Pannier, L., & Rapoport, J. L. (1995). Activation of prefrontal cortex in children during a nonspatial working memory task with functional MRI. *Neuroimage, 2,* 221–229.

Castillo, E. M., Simos, P. G., Davis, R. N., Breier, J., Fitzgerald, M. E., & Papanicolaou, A. C. (2001). Levels of word processing and incidental memory: Dissociable mechanisms in the temporal lobe. *Neuroreport, 12,* 3561–3566.

Chatterjee, A., Yapundich, R., Mennemeier, M., Mountz, J. M., Inampudi, C., Pan, J. W., & Mitchell, G. W. (1997). Thalamic thought disorder: On being "a bit addled". *Cortex, 33,* 419–440.

Cohen, M., Hynd, G., & Hugdahl, K. (1992). Dichotic listening performance in subtypes of developmental dyslexia and a left temporal lobe brain tumor contrast group. *Brain and Language, 42,* 187–202.

Coltheart, M. (2001). Assumptions and methods in cognitive neuropsychology. In B. Rapp (Ed.), *The handbook of cognitive neuropsychology* (pp. 3–21). Philadelphia: Psychology Press/Taylor & Francis.

Costa, D. C., Ell, P. J., Burns, A., Philpot, M., & Levy, R. (1988). CBF tomograms with [99mTc-HM-PAO in patients with dementia (Alzheimer type and HIV) and Parkinson's disease: Initial results. *Journal of Cerebral Blood Flow and Metabolism, 8,* S109–S115.

Courtney, S. M., & Ungerleider, L. G. (1997). What fMRI has taught us about human vision. *Current Opinion in Neurobiology, 7,* 554–561.

Crook, T. H., Larrabee, G. J., & Youngjohn, J. R. (1990). Diagnosis and assessment of age-associated memory impairment. *Clinical Neuropharmacology, 13*(Suppl. 3), S81–S91.

Crosson, B., Moberg, P. J., Boone, J. R., Rothi, L. J., & Raymer, A. (1997). Category-specific naming deficit for medical terms after dominant thalamic/capsular hemorrhage. *Brain and Language, 60,* 407–442.

Crosson, B., Radonovich, K., Sadek, J. R., Gokcay, D., Bauer, R. M., Fischler, I. S., Cato, M. A., Maron, L., Auerbach, E. J., Browd, S. R., & Briggs, R. W. (1999). Left-hemisphere processing of emotional connotation during word generation. *Neuroreport, 10,* 2449–2455.

Curran, T. (1999). The electrophysiology of incidental and intentional retrieval: ERP old/new effects in lexical decision and recognition memory. *Neuropsychologia, 37,* 771–785.

Curran, T., Schacter, D. L., Johnson, M. K., & Spinks, R. (2001). Brain potentials reflect behavioral differences in true and false recognition. *Journal of Cognitive Neuroscience, 13,* 201–216.

Curry, F. W. K. (1967). A comparison of left handed and right handed subjects on verbal and nonverbal dichotic listening tasks. *Cortex, 3,* 343–352.

Damasio, H., & Damasio, A. R. (1997). The lesion method in behavioral neurology and neuropsychology. In T. E. Feinberg & M. J. Farah (Eds). *Behavioral neurology and neuropsychology* (pp. 69–82). New York: McGraw-Hill.

D'Arsonval, A. (1896). Dispositifs pour la mesure des courants alternatifs de toutes frequences.

Davidson, R. J., & Sutton, S. K. (1995). Affective neuroscience: The emergence of a discipline. *Current Opinion in Neurobiology, 5,* 217–224.

Dawson, M. E., Schell, A. M., & Filion, D. L. (2000). The electrodermal system. In J. T. Cacioppo, L. G. Tassinary, & G. G. Berntson (Eds.), *Handbook of psychophysiology* (2nd ed., pp. 200–223). Cambridge, UK: Cambridge University Press.

de Zubicaray, G. I., Williams, S. C., Wilson, S. J., Rose, S. E., Brammer, M. J., Bullmore, E. T., Simmons, A., Chalk, J. B., Semple, J., Brown, A. P., Smith, G. A., Ashton, R., & Doddrell, D. M. (1998). Prefrontal cortex involvement in selective letter generation: a functional magnetic resonance imaging study. *Cortex, 34,* 389–401.

Deacon, D., Hewitt, S., & Tamney, T. (1998). Event-related potential indices of semantic priming following an unrelated intervening item. *Brain Research. Cognitive Brain Research, 6,* 219–225.

Demb, J. B., Desmond, J. E., Wagner, A. D., Vaidya, C. J., Glover, G. H., & Gabrieli, J. D. (1995). Semantic encoding and retrieval in the left inferior prefrontal cortex: A functional MRI study of task difficulty and process specificity. *Journal of Neuroscience, 15,* 5870–5878.

Desmond, J. E., Sum, J. M., Wagner, A. D., Demb, J. B., Shear, P. K., Glover, G. H., Gabrieli, J. D., & Morrell, M. J. (1995). Functional MRI measurement of language lateralization in Wada-tested patients. *Brain, 118,* 1411–1419.

D'Esposito, M., Detre, J. A., Alsop, D. C., Shin, R. K., Atlas, S., & Grossman, M. (1995). The neural basis of the central executive system of working memory. *Nature, 378,* 279–281.

D'Esposito, M., Postle, B. R., & Rypma, B. (2000). Prefrontal cortical contributions to working memory: Evidence from event-related fMRI studies. *Experimental Brain Research, 133,* 3–11.

Diamond, B. J., Mayes, A. R., & Meudell, P. R. (1996). Autonomic and recognition indices of memory in amnesic and healthy control subjects. *Cortex, 32,* 439–459.

Donchin, E. (1979). Event-related brain potentials: A tool in the study of human information processing. In H. Begleiter (Ed.), *Evoked potentials and behavior* (pp. 13–75). New York: Plenum.

Donchin, E., & Coles, M. G. H. (1988). Is the P300 component a manifestation of context updating? *Behavioral and Brain Sciences, 11,* 357–374.

Ellis, A. W., & Young, A. W. (1986). *Human cognitive neuropsychology.* Hillsdale, NJ: Erlbaum.

Emsley, R. A., Roberts, M. C., Aalbers, C., Taljaard, F. J., & Kotze, T. J. (1994). Endocrine function in alcoholic Korsakoff's syndrome. *Alcohol and Alcoholism, 29,* 187–191.

Endl, W., Walla, P., Lindinger, G., Deecke, L., & Lang, W. (1999). Event-related potential correlates of false recognitions of faces. *Neuroscience Letters, 265,* 115–118.

Engel, B. T. (1960). Stimulus-response and individual-response specificity. *Archives of General Psychiatry, 2,* 305–313.

Epstein, C., Figiel, G., McDonald, W., Amazon-Leece, J., & Figiel, L. (1998). Rapid rate transcranial magnetic stimulation in young and middle-aged refractory depressed patients. *Psychiatric Annals, 28,* 36–39.

Epstein, C. M., Lah, J., Meador, K., Weissman, J., Gaitan, L, & Dihenia, B. (1996) Optimum stimulus parameters for lateralized suppression of speech with magnetic brain stimulation. *Neurology, 47,* 1590–1593.

Epstein, C. M., Woodard, J. L., Stringer, A. Y., Bakay, R. A., Henry, T. R., Pennell, P. B., & Litt, B. (2000). Repetitive transcranial magnetic stimulation does not replicate the Wada test. *Neurology, 55,* 1025–1027.

Epstein, R., & Kanwisher, N. (1998). A cortical representation of the local visual environment. *Nature, 392,* 598–601.

Erhan, H., Borod, J. C., Tenke, C. E., & Bruder, G. E. (1998). Identification of emotion in a dichotic listening task: event-related brain potential and behavioral findings. *Brain and Cognition, 37,* 286–307.

Fabiani, M., Gratton, G., & Coles, M. G. H. (2000). Event-related brain potentials: Methods, theory, and applications. In J. T. Cacioppo, L. G. Tassinary, & G. G. Berntson (Eds.), *Handbook of psychophysiology* (2nd ed., pp. 53–84). Cambridge, UK: Cambridge University Press.

Fagot, C., & Pashler, H. (1995). Repetition blindness: perception or memory failure? *Journal of Experimental Psychology: Human Perception and Performance, 21,* 275–292.

Fahle, M. (1994). Human pattern recognition: parallel processing and perceptual learning. *Perception, 23,* 411–427.

Falkenstein, M., Hohnsbein, J., Hoormann, J., & Blanke, L. (1990). Effects of errors in choice reaction time tasks on the ERP under focused and divided attention. In C. H. M. Brunia, A. W. K. Gaillard, & A. Kok (Eds.), *Psychophysiological brain research,* (pp. 192–195). Tilburg, Netherlands: Tilburg University Press.

Feinberg, T. E., & Farah, M. J. (2000). A historical perspective on cognitive neuroscience. In M. J. Farah & T. E. Feinberg (Eds.), *Patient-based approaches to cognitive neuroscience* (pp. 3–19). Cambridge, MA: MIT Press.

Fodor, J. A. (1983). *The modularity of mind.* Cambridge, MA: MIT Press.

Fowles, D., Christie, M. J., Edelberg, R., Grings, W. W., Lykken, D. T., & Venables, P. H. (1981). Publication recommendations for electrodermal measurements. *Psychophysiology, 18,* 232–239.

Fox, P., Ingham, R., George, M., Mayberg, H., Ingham, J., Roby, J., Marin, C., & Marabou, P. (1997). Imaging human intra-cerebral connectivity by PET during TMS. *Neuroreport, 8,* 2787–2791.

Frith, C. D., & Friston, K. J. (1997). Studying brain function with neuroimaging. In M. D. Rugg (Ed.), *Cognitive neuroscience* (pp. 169–195). Cambridge, MA: MIT Press.

Gabrieli, J. D. (1998). Cognitive neuroscience of human memory. *Annual Review of Psychology, 49,* 87–115.

Gabrieli, J. D., Poldrack, R. A., & Desmond, J. E. (1998). The role of left prefrontal cortex in language and memory. *Proceedings of the National Academy of Sciences, USA, 95,* 906–913.

Ganslandt, O., Nimsky, C., & Fahlbusch, R. (2000). Magnetic source imaging. *Journal of Neurosurgery, 92,* 1079–1080.

Gazzaniga, M. S., Ivry, R. B., & Mangin, G. R. (1998). The methods of cognitive neuroscience. In M. S. Gazzaniga, R. B. Ivry, & G. R. Mangin (Eds.), *Cognitive neuroscience: The biology of the mind* (pp. 82–83). New York: W.W. Norton.

Geffen, G., & Caudrey, R. (1981). Reliability and validity of the dichotic monitoring test for language laterality. *Neuropsychologia, 19,* 413–423.

Geffen, G. M., Encel, J. S., & Forrester, G. M. (1991). Stages of recovery during post-traumatic amnesia and subsequent everyday memory deficits. *Neuroreport, 2,* 105–108.

George, M., Wasserman, E., Willliams, W., Callahan, A., Ketter, T., Basser, P., Hallett, M., & Post, R. (1995). Daily repetitive transcranial magnetic stimulation improves mood in depression. *Neuroreport, 6,* 1853–1856.

Geschwind, N., & Kaplan, E. (1962). A human deconnection syndrome. *Neurology, 12,* 675–685.

Geschwind, N. (1965). Disconnexion syndromes in animals and man. *Brain, 88,* 237–294; 585–644.

Giroud, M., Lemesle, M., Madinier, G., Billiar, T., & Dumas, R. (1997). Unilateral lenticular infarcts: Radiological and clinical syndromes, aetiology, and prognosis. *Journal of Neurology, Neurosurgery, & Psychiatry, 63,* 611–615.

Goldenberg, G., Oder, W., Spatt, J., & Podreka, I. (1992). Cerebral correlates of disturbed executive function and memory in survivors of severe closed head injury: A SPECT study. *Journal of Neurology, Neurosurgery, & Psychiatry, 55,* 362–368.

Gordon, E., Rennie, C., & Collins, L. (1990). Magnetoencephalography and late component ERPs. *Clinical and Experimental Neurology, 27,* 113–120.

Gordon, H. W. (1970). Hemispheric asymmetries in the perception of musical chords. *Cortex, 6,* 387–398.

Grafman, J., & Wasserman, E. (1999). Transcranial magnetic stimulation can measure and modulate learning and memory. *Neuropsychologica, 37,* 159–194.

Grafman, J., Pascual-Leone, A., Alway, D., Nichelli, P., Gomez-Tortosa, E., & Hallett, M. (1994). Induction of a recall deficits by rapid rate transcranial magnetic stimulation. *Neuroreport, 5,* 1157–1160.

Green, M. F., Hugdahl, K., & Mitchell, S. (1994). Dichotic listening during auditory hallucinations in patients with schizophrenia. *American Journal of Psychiatry, 151,* 357–362.

Grunwald, T., Lehnertz, K., Pezer, N., Kurthen, M., Van Roost, D., Schramm, J., & Elger, C. E. (1999). Prediction of postoperative seizure control by hippocampal event-related potentials. *Epilepsia, 40,* 303–306.

Halgren, E., Raij, T., Marinkovic, K., Jousmaki, V., & Hari, R. (2000). Cognitive response profile of the human fusiform face area as determined by MEG. *Cerebral Cortex, 10,* 69–81.

Halgren, E., Squires, N. K., Wilson, C. L., Rohrbaugh, J. W., Babb, T. L., & Randall, P. H. (1980). Endogenous potentials generated in the human hippocampal formation and amygdala by infrequent events. *Science, 210,* 803–805.

Hannay, H. J., Dee, H. L., Burns, J. W., & Masek, B. S. (1981). Experimental reversal of a visual field superiority for forms. *Brain and Language, 13,* 54–66.

Heaton, R., Grant, I., & Matthews, C. (1991). *Comprehensive norms for an Expanded Halstead-Reitan Battery: Demographic corrections, research findings, and clinical applications.* Odessa, FL: Psychological Assessment Resources.

Heinz, A., Jones, D. W., Raedler, T., Coppola, R., Knable, M. B., & Weinberger, D. R. (2000). Neuropharmacological studies with SPECT in neuropsychiatric disorders. *Nuclear Medicine and Biology, 27,* 677–682.

Heinze, H. J., Hinrichs, H., Scholz, M., Burchert, W., & Mangun, G. R. (1998). Neural mechanisms of global and local processing: A combined PET and ERP study. *Journal of Cognitive Neuroscience, 10,* 485–498.

Henke, K., Landis, T., & Markowitsch, H. J. (1994). Subliminal perception of words and faces. *International Journal of Neuroscience, 75,* 181–187.

Hilliard, S. A., Hink, R. F., Schwent, V. L., & Picton, T. W. (1973). Electrical signs of selective attention in the human brain. *Science, 182,* 177–180.

Hiscock, M. (1986). Lateral eye movements and dual-task performance. In H. J. Hannay (Ed.), *Experimental techniques in human neuropsychology* (pp. 264–308). New York: Oxford University Press.

Hoflich, G., Kasper, S., Hufnagel, A., Ruhrmann, S., & Moller, H. (1993). Application of transcranial magnetic stimulation in treatment of drug-resistant major depression: A report of two cases. *Human Psychopharmacology, 8,* 361–365.

Honda, M., Suwazono, S., Nagamine, T., Yonekura, Y., & Shibasaki, H. (1996). P300 abnormalities in patients with selective impairment of recent memory. *Journal of Neurological Science, 139,* 95–105.

Hopf, J. M., Luck, S. J., Girelli, M., Hagner, T., Mangun, G. R., Scheich, H., & Heinze, H. J. (2000). Neural sources of focused attention in visual search. *Cerebral Cortex, 10,* 1233–1241.

Horner, M. D. (1990). Psychobiological evidence for the distinction between episodic and semantic memory. *Neuropsychology Review, 1,* 281–321.

Hugdahl, K., Bronnick, K., Kyllingsbaek, S., Law, I., Gade, A., & Paulson, O. B. (1999). Brain activation during dichotic presenta-

tions of consonant-vowel and musical instrument stimuli: A 15O-PET study. *Neuropsychologia, 37,* 431–440.

Hugdahl, K., Heiervang, E., Nordby, H., Smievoll, A. I., Steinmetz, H., Stevenson, J., & Lund, A. (1998). Central auditory processing, MRI morphometry and brain laterality: Applications to dyslexia. *Scandinavian Audiology, 27*(Suppl. 49), 26–34.

Jancke, L., Buchanan, T. W., Lutz, K., & Shah, N. J. (2001). Focused and nonfocused attention in verbal and emotional dichotic listening: An FMRI Study. *Brain and Language, 78,* 349–363.

Jennings, J. R., Berg, W. K., Hutcheson, J. S., Obrist, P., Porges, S., & Turpin, G. (1981). Committee report. Publication guidelines for heart rate studies in man. *Psychophysiology, 18,* 226–231.

Johnson, J., R. (1988). The amplitude of the P300 component of the event-related potential: Review and synthesis. In P. K. Ackles, J. R. Jennings, & M. G. H. Coles (Eds.), *Advances in psychophysiology* (pp. 69–138). Greenwich, CT: JAI.

Jonides, J., Schumacher, E. H., Smith, E. E., & Lauber, E. J. (1997). Verbal working memory load affects regional brain activation as measured by PET. *Journal of Cognitive Neuroscience, 9,* 462–475.

Kapur, N. (1993). Focal retrograde amnesia in neurological disease: a critical review. *Cortex, 29,* 217–234.

Kimura, D. (1961a). Cerebral dominance and the perception of verbal stimuli. *Canadian Journal of Psychology, 15,* 166–171.

Kimura, D. (1961b). Some effects of temporal-lobe damage on auditory perception. *Canadian Journal of Psychology, 15,* 156–165.

Kinsbourne, M. (1981). Single channel theory. In D. H. Holding (Ed.), *Human skills.* Chichester, UK: Wiley.

Kinsbourne, M., & Hicks, R. E. (1978). Functional cerebral space: A model for overflow, transfer and interference effects in human performance. In J. Requin (Ed.), *Attention and Performance* (Vol. 8). Hillsdale, NJ: Erlbaum.

Kixmiller, J. S., Verfaellie, M., Chase, K. A., & Cermak, L. S. (1995). Comparison of figural intrusion errors in three amnesic subgroups. *Journal of the International Neuropsychological Society, 1,* 561–567.

Knecht, S., Deppe, M., Ebner, A., Henningsen, H., Huber, T., Jokeit, H., & Ringelstein, E. B. (1998). Noninvasive determination of language lateralization by functional transcranial Doppler sonography: A comparison with the Wada test. *Stroke, 29,* 82–86.

Kolbinger, H., Koflinch, G., Hufnagel, A., Moller, H., & Kasper, S. (1995). Transcranial magnetic stimulation (TMS) in treatment of major depression: A pilot study. *Human Psychopharmacology, 10,* 305–310.

Kotrla, K. J., & Weinberger, D. R. (1995). Brain imaging in schizophrenia. *Annual Review of Medicine, 46,* 113–122.

Kruggel, F., Wiggins, C. J., Herrmann, C. S., & von Cramon, D. Y. (2000). Recording of the event-related potentials during functional MRI at 3.0 Tesla field strength. *Magnetic Resonance in Medicine, 44,* 277–282.

Kunimoto, C., Miller, J., & Pashler, H. (2001). Confidence and accuracy of near-threshold discrimination responses. *Consciousness and Cognition, 10,* 294–340.

Kunst-Wilson, W. R., & Zajonc, R. B. (1980). Affective discrimination of stimuli that cannot be recognized. *Science, 207,* 557–558.

Kutas, M., & Dale, A. (1997). Electrical and magnetic readings of mental functions. In M. D. Rugg (Ed.), *Cognitive neuroscience* (pp. 197–242). Cambridge, MA: MIT Press.

Kutas, M., & Donchin, E. (1980). Preparation to respond as manifested by movement-related brain potentials. *Brain Research, 202,* 95–115.

Kutas, M., & Hilliard, S. A. (1980). Reading senseless sentences: Brain potentials reflect semantic incongruity. *Science, 207,* 203–205.

LaBar, K. S., Gitelman, D. R., Parrish, T. B., & Mesulam, M. (1999). Neuroanatomic overlap of working memory and spatial attention networks: a functional MRI comparison within subjects. *Neuroimage, 10,* 695–704.

Lacey, J. I., & Lacey, B. C. (1958). Verification and extension of the principle of autonomic response-stereotypy. *American Journal of Psychology, 71,* 50–73.

Lane, R. D., Reiman, E. M., Axelrod, B., Yun, L. S., Holmes, A., & Schwartz, G. E. (1998). Neural correlates of levels of emotional awareness. Evidence of an interaction between emotion and attention in the anterior cingulate cortex. *Journal of Cognitive Neuroscience, 10,* 525–535.

Lassen, N. A., & Holm, S. (1992). Single photon emission computerized tomography (SPECT). In J. C. Mazziota & S. Gilman (Eds.), *Clinical brain imaging: Principles and applications* (pp. 108–134). Philadelphia: F. A. Davis.

Lee, B. I., Lee, J. D., Kim, J. Y., Ryu, Y. H., Kim, W. J., Lee, J. H., Lee, S. J., & Park, S. C. (1997). Single photon emission computed tomography-EEG relations in temporal lobe epilepsy. *Neurology, 49,* 981–991.

Lehericy, S., Cohen, L., Bazin, B., Samson, S., Giacomini, E., Rougetet, R., Hertz Pannier, L., Le Bihan, D., Marsault, C., & Baulac, M. (2000). Functional MR evaluation of temporal and frontal language dominance compared with the Wada test. *Neurology, 54,* 1625–1633.

Lewine, J. D., & Orrison, W. W. (1995). Magnetic source imaging: basic principles and applications in neuroradiology. *Academic Radiology, 2,* 436–440.

Lezak, M. D. (1995). *Neuropsychological assessment* (3rd ed.). New York: Oxford University Press.

Loftis, C., Zawacki, T., Bauer, R. M., Crosson, B., Briggs, R., Sadek, J., Auerbach, E., Gokcay, D., & Gopinath, K. (2000). Occipital and temporal lobe activation during an explicit memory task. *Journal of the International Neuropsychological Society, 6,* 159.

Loring, D. W. (1997). Neuropsychological evaluation in epilepsy surgery. *Epilepsia, 38*(Suppl. 4), S18–S23.

Loring, D. W., Meador, K. J., Lee, G. P., Nichols, M. E., King, D. W., Gallagher, B. B., Murro, A. M., & Smith, J. R. (1994). Wada memory performance predicts seizure outcome following anterior temporal lobectomy. *Neurology, 44,* 2322–2324.

Loring, D. W., Murro, A. M., Meador, K. J., Lee, G. P., Gratton, C. A., Nichols, M. E., Gallagher, B. B., King, D. W., & Smith, J. R. (1993). Wada memory testing and hippocampal volume measurements in the evaluation for temporal lobectomy. *Neurology, 43,* 1789–1793.

Manassis, K., Tannock, R., & Barbosa, J. (2000). Dichotic listening and response inhibition in children with comorbid anxiety disorders and ADHD. *Journal of the American Academy of Child and Adolescent Psychiatry, 39,* 1152–1159.

Manassis, K., Tannock, R., & Masellis, M. (1996). Cognitive differences between anxious, normal, and ADHD children on a dichotic listening task. *Anxiety, 2,* 279–285.

Mangun, G. R., Buonocore, M. H., Girelli, M., & Jha, A. P. (1998). ERP and fMRI measures of visual spatial selective attention. *Human Brain Mapping, 6,* 383–389.

Maratos, E. J., Dolan, R. J., Morris, J. S., Henson, R. N., & Rugg, M. D. (2001). Neural activity associated with episodic memory for emotional context. *Neuropsychologia, 39,* 910–920.

Mastin, S. T., Drane, W. E., Gilmore, R. L., Helveston, W. R., Quisling, R. G., Roper, S. N., Eikman, E. A., & Browd, S. R. (1996). Prospective localization of epileptogenic foci: Comparison of PET and SPECT with site of surgery and clinical outcome. *Radiology, 199,* 375–380.

Mazziotta, J. C., Phelps, M. E., Meadors, A. K., Ricci, A., Winter, J., & Bentson, J. R. (1982). Anatomical localization schemes for use in positron computed tomography using a specially designed head-holder. *Journal of Computer Assisted Tomography, 6,* 848–853.

Mazziotta, J. C., & Gilman, S. (1992). *Clinical brain imaging: Principles and applications.* Philadelphia: F. A. Davis.

McCarthy, G., Puce, A., Luby, M., Belger, A., & Allison, T. (1996). Magnetic resonance imaging studies of functional brain activation: analysis and interpretation. *Electroencephalography and Clinical Neurophysiology Supplement, 47,* 15–31.

McCarthy, R. A., & Warrington, E. K. (1990). *Cognitive neuropsychology: A clinical introduction.* New York: Academic Press.

McCloskey, M. (1993). Theory and evidence in cognitive neuropsychology: A "radical" response to Robertson, Knight, Rafal, and Shimamura (1993). *Journal of Experimental Psychology: Learning, Memory, and Cognition, 3,* 718–734.

McCloskey, M. (2001). The future of cognitive neuropsychology. In B. Rapp (Ed.), *The handbook of cognitive neuropsychology* (pp. 593–610). Philadelphia: Psychology Press.

McGlinchey Berroth, R., Carrillo, M. C., Gabrieli, J. D., Brawn, C. M., & Disterhoft, J. F. (1997). Impaired trace eyeblink conditioning in bilateral, medial-temporal lobe amnesia. *Behavioral Neuroscience, 111,* 873–882.

McGlinchey Berroth, R., Milberg, W. P., Verfaellie, M., & Alexander, M. (1993). Semantic processing in the neglected visual field: Evidence from a lexical decision task. *Cognitive Neuropsychology, 10,* 79–108.

McIntosh, A. R. (1998). Understanding neural interactions in learning and memory using functional neuroimaging. *Annals of the New York Academy of Sciences, USA, 855,* 556–571.

McKeever, W. F. (1986). Tachistoscopic methods in neuropsychology. In H. J. Hannay (Ed.), *Experimental techniques in human neuropsychology* (pp. 167–211). New York: Oxford University Press.

McKhann, G., Drachman, D., Folstein, M., Katzman, R., Price, D. J., & Stadian, E. (1984). Clinical diagnosis of Alzheimer's disease: report of the NINCDS-ADRDA work group under the auspices of Department of Health and Human Services Task Force on Alzheimer's Disease. *Neurology, 34,* 939–944.

Mendez, M., Van Gorp, W., & Cummings, J. (1995). Neuropsychiatry, neuropsychology, and behavioral neurology: A critical comparison. *Neuropsychiatry, Neuropsychology, and Behavioral Neurology, 8,* 297–302.

Miezin, F. M., Maccotta, L., Ollinger, J. M., Petersen, S. E., & Buckner, R. L. (2000). Characterizing the hemodynamic response: Effects of presentation rate, sampling procedure, and the possibility of ordering brain activity based on relative timing. *Neuroimage, 11,* 735–759.

Mills, K., & Nithi, K. (1992). Corticomotor threshold to magnetic stimulation: Normal values and repeatability. *Muscle and Nerve, 20,* 570–576.

Mishkin, M., & Forgays, D. G. (1952). Word recognition as a function of retinal locus. *Journal of Experimental Psychology, 43,* 43–48.

Monahan, J. L., Murphy, S. T., & Zajonc, R. B. (2000). Subliminal mere exposure: specific, general, and diffuse effects. *Psychological Science, 11,* 462–466.

Monchi, O., Taylor, J. G., & Dagher, A. (2000). A neural model of working memory processes in normal subjects, Parkinson's disease and schizophrenia for fMRI design and predictions. *Neural Networks, 13,* 953–973.

Moray, N. (1959). Attention in dichotic listening: Affective cues and the influence of instructions. *Quarterly Journal of Experimental Psychology, 11,* 56–60.

Moss, H. E., & Tyler, L. K. (2000). A progressive category-specific semantic deficit for non-living things. *Neuropsychologia, 38,* 60–82.

Mull, B., & Seyal, M. (2001). Transcranial magnetic stimulation of left prefrontal cortex impairs working memory. *Clinical Neurophysiology, 112,* 1672–1675.

Murphy, S. T., Monahan, J. L., & Zajonc, R. B. (1995). Additivity of nonconscious affect: Combined effects of priming and exposure. *Journal of Personality and Social Psychology, 69,* 589–602.

Naatanen, R. (1995). The mismatch negativity: a powerful tool for cognitive neuroscience. *Ear and Hearing, 16,* 6–18.

Nadeau, S. E., & Crosson, B. (1995). A guide to the functional imaging of cognitive processes. *Neuropsychiatry, Neuropsychology, and Behavioral Neurology, 8,* 143–162.

Nadel, L., & Moscovitch, M. (1998). Hippocampal contributions to cortical plasticity. *Neuropharmacology, 37,* 431–439.

Navon, D., & Gopher, D. (1979). On the economy of the human information processing system: A model of multiple capacity. *Psychological Review, 86,* 214–225.

Newton, M. R., Barrett, G., Callanan, M. M., & Towell, A. D. (1989). Cognitive event-related potentials in multiple sclerosis. *Brain, 112,* 1637–1660.

Nobre, A. C., Allison, T., & McCarthy, G. (1994). Word recognition in the human inferior temporal lobe. *Nature, 372,* 260–263.

O'Donnell, B. F., Cohen, R. A., Hokama, H., Cuffin, B. N., Lippa, C., Shenton, M. E., & Drachman, D. A. (1993). Electrical source analysis of auditory ERPs in medial temporal lobe amnestic syndrome. *Electroencephalography and Clinical Neurophysiology, 87,* 394–402.

Paniak, C., MacDonald, J., Toller Lobe, G., Durand, A., & Nagy, J. (1998). A preliminary normative profile of mild traumatic brain injury diagnostic criteria. *Journal of Clinical and Experimental Neuropsychology, 20,* 852–855.

Papanicolau, A. C. (1998). *Fundamentals of functional brain imaging.* Lisse, Netherlands: Swets & Zeitlinger.

Park, J., & Kanwisher, N. (1994). Determinants of repetition blindness. *Journal of Experimental Psychology: Human Perception and Performance, 20,* 500–519.

Parnetti, L., Lowenthal, D. T., Presciutti, O., Pelliccioli, G. P., Palumbo, R., Gobbi, G., Chiarini, P., Palumbo, B., Tarducci, R., & Senin, U. (1996). 1H-MRS, MRI-based hippocampal volumetry, and 99mTc-HMPAO-SPECT in normal aging, age-associated memory impairment, and probable Alzheimer's disease. *Journal of the American Geriatric Society, 44,* 133–138.

Pascual-Leone, A., Gates, J. R., & Dhuna, A. (1991). Induction of speech arrest and counting errors with rapid rate transcranial magnetic stimulation. *Neurology, 41,* 697–702.

Pascual-Leone, A., Houser, C. M., Reese, K., Shotland, L. I., Grafman, J., Sato, S., Valls-Sole, J., Brasil-Neto, J. P., Wasserman, E. M., Cohen, L. F. (1993). Safety of rapid-rate transcranial magnetic stimulation in normal volunteers. *Electroencephalography and Clinical Neurophysiology, 89,* 120–130.

Pascual-Leone, A., Rubio, B., Pallardo, F., & Catala, M. (1996). Beneficial effect of rapid-rate transcranial magnetic stimulation of the left dorsolateral prefrontal cortex in drug-resistant depression. *Lancet, 348,* 233–237.

Pascual-Leone, A., Valls-Sole, J., Brasil-Neto, J., Cammarota, A., Grafman, J., & Hallett, M. (1994). Akinesia in Parkinson's disease. II. Effects of subthreshold repetitive transcranial motor cortex stimulation. *Neurology, 44,* 892–98.

Pascual-Leone, A., Walsh, V., & Rothwell, J. (2000). Transcranial magnetic stimulation in cognitive neuroscience: Virtual lesion, chronometry, and functional connectivity. *Current Opinion in Neurobiology, 10,* 232–237.

Paulesu, E., Bottini, G., & Frackowiak, S. J. (1997). Cognitive neurology and the contribution of neuroimaging. In M. R. C.

Trimble, J. L. (Ed.), *Contemporary behavioral neurology*. Boston: Butterworth-Heinemann.

Paus, R. (1999). Imaging the brain before, during, and after transcranial magnetic stimulation. *Neuropsychologia, 37,* 219–224.

Paus, R., Jeck, R., Thompson, C., Comeau, R., Poeters, R., & Evans, A. (1997). Transcranial magnetic stimulation during positron emission tomography: A new method for studying connectivity of the human cerebral cortex. *Journal of Neuroscience, 17,* 3178–3184.

Perani, D. C., S.F. (1999). Neuroimaging methods in neuropsychology. In G. P. Denes, L. (Ed.), *Handbook of Clinical and Experimental Neuropsychology*. East Sussex: Psychology Press.

Perrett, D. I., Hietanen, J. K., Oram, M. W., & Benson, P. J. (1992). Organization and functions of cells responsive to faces in the temporal cortex. *Philosophical Transactions of the Royal Society of London B: Biological Sciences, 335,* 23–30.

Perrett, D., Rolls, E. T., & Caan, W. (1982). Visual neurons responsive to faces in the monkey temporal cortex. *Experimental Brain Research, 47,* 329–342.

Picton, T., Bentin, S., Berg, P., Donchin, E., Hilliard, S. A., Johnson, R., Miller, G. A., Ritter, W., Ruchkin, D. S., Rugg, M. D., & Taylor, M. J. (2000). Guidelines for using human event-related potentials to study cognition: Recording standards and publication criteria. *Psychophysiology, 37,* 127–152.

Pine, D. S., Kentgen, L. M., Bruder, G. E., Leite, P., Bearman, K., Ma, Y., & Klein, R. G. (2000). Cerebral laterality in adolescent major depression. *Psychiatry Research, 93,* 135–144.

Platt, J. R. (1966). Strong interference. *Science, 146,* 347–353.

Poldrack, R. A. (2000). Imaging brain plasticity: Conceptual and methodological issues: A theoretical review. *Neuroimage, 12,* 1–13.

Polich, J., & Squire, L. R. (1993). P300 from amnesic patients with bilateral hippocampal lesions. *Electroencephalography and Clinical Neurophysiology, 86,* 408–417.

Polson, M. J. R., Barker, A. T., & Freeston, I. L. (1982). Stimulation of nerve trunks with time-varying magnetic fields. *Medical and Biological Engineering and Computing, 20,* 243–244.

Pouthas, V., Maquet, P., Garnero, L., Ferrandez, A. M., & Renault, B. (1999). Neural bases of time estimation: a PET and ERP study. *Electroencephalography and Clinical Neurophysiology,* (Suppl.), 50598–50603.

Price, C. J., & Friston, K. J. (2001). Functional neuroimaging of neuropsychologically impaired patients. In R. Cabeza & A. Kingstone (Eds.), *Handbook of functional neuroimaging of cognition* (pp. 379–399). Cambridge, MA: MIT Press.

Raedler, T. J., Knable, M. B., Lafargue, T., Urbina, R. A., Egan, M. F., Pickar, D., & Weinberger, D. R. (1999). In vivo determination of striatal dopamine D2 receptor occupancy in patients treated with olanzapine. *Psychiatry Research, 90,* 81–90.

Raichle, M. E. (1997). Functional imaging in behavioral *Neurology* and neuropsychology. In T. E. F. Feinberg & M. J. Farah (Eds.),

Behavioral neurology and neuropsychology (pp. 83–100). New York: McGraw-Hill.

Raichle, M. E. (2000). Functional imaging in cognitive neuroscience. In M. J. Farah & T. E. Feinberg (Eds.), *Patient-based approaches to cognitive neuroscience* (pp. 35–52). Cambridge, MA: MIT Press.

Raichle, M. E. (2001). Functional neuroimaging: A historical and physiological perspective. In R. K. Cabeza & A. Kingstone (Eds.), *Handbook of functional neuroimaging and cognition* (pp. 3–26). Cambridge, MA: MIT Press.

Rama, P., Martinkauppi, S., Linnankoski, I., Koivisto, J., Aronen, H. J., & Carlson, S. (2001). Working memory of identification of emotional vocal expressions: An fMRI study. *Neuroimage, 13,* 1090–1101.

Rapp, B. (Ed.). (2001). *The handbook of cognitive neuropsychology: What deficits reveal about the human mind.* Philadelphia: Psychology Press/Taylor & Francis.

Rees, G., Wojciulik, E., Clarke, K., Husain, M., Frith, C., & Driver, J. (2000). Unconscious activation of visual cortex in the damaged right hemisphere of a parietal patient with extinction. *Brain, 123,* 1624–1633.

Reiman, E. M., Lane, R. D., Petten, C., & Bandettini, P. (2000). Positron emission tomography and functional magnetic resonance imaging. In J. T. Cacioppo, L. G. Tassinary, & G. G. Berntson (Eds.), *Handbook of psychophysiology* (2nd ed., pp. 85–118). Cambridge, UK: Cambridge University Press.

Riddoch, M. J., & Humphreys, G. W. (1993). *BORB: Birmingham Object Recognition Battery*. Hove, UK: Psychology Press.

Rihs, F., Sturzenegger, M., Gutbrod, K., Schroth, G., & Mattle, H. P. (1999). Determination of language dominance: Wada test confirms functional transcranial Doppler sonography. *Neurology, 52,* 1591–1596.

Rizzolatti, G., Umilta, C., & Berlucchi, G. (1971). Opposite superiorities of the right and left cerebral hemispheres in discriminative reaction time to physiognomical and alphabetic material. *Brain, 87,* 415–422.

Roberts, T. P., Ferrari, P., Perry, D., Rowley, H. A., & Berger, M. S. (2000). Presurgical mapping with magnetic source imaging: Comparisons with intraoperative findings. *Brain Tumor Pathology, 17,* 57–64.

Roberts, T. P., Poeppel, D., & Rowley, H. A. (1998). Magnetoencephalography and magnetic source imaging. *Neuropsychiatry, Neuropsychology, and Behavioral Neurology, 11,* 49–64.

Robertson, L. C., Knight, R. T., Rafal, R., & Shimamura, A. P. (1993). Cognitive neuropsychology is more than single case studies. *Journal of Experimental Psychology: Learning, Memory, and Cognition, 19,* 710–717.

Rohrbaugh, J. W., & Gaillard, A. W. K. (1983). Sensory and motor aspects of the contingent negative variation. In A. W. K. Gaillard & W. Ritter (Eds.), *Tutorials in event-related potential research: Endogenous components* (pp. 269–310). Amsterdam: North-Holland.

Rugg, M. D., Pickles, C. D., Potter, D. D., & Roberts, R. C. (1991). Normal P300 following extensive damage to the left medial temporal lobe. *Journal of Neurology, Neurosurgery, and Psychiatry, 54,* 217–222.

Russell, E. W. (1986). The psychometric foundation of clinical neuropsychology. In S. B. Filskov & T. J. Boll (Eds.), *Handbook of clinical neuropsychology* (2nd ed., pp. 45–80). New York: Wiley.

Sandson, J., & Albert, M. L. (1987). Varieties of perseveration. *Neuropsychologia, 22,* 715–722.

Sarter, M., Berntson, G. G., & Cacioppo, J. T. (1996). Brain Imaging and cognitive neuroscience: Toward strong inference in attributing function to structure. *American Psychologist, 51,* 13–21.

Satz, P. (1993). Brain reserve capacity on symptom onset after brain injury: A formulation and review of evidence for threshold theory. *Neuropsychology, 7,* 273–295.

Schacter, D. L., Wagner, A. D., & Buckner, R. L. (2000). Memory systems of 1999. In E. Tulving & F. I. M. Craik (Eds.), *The Oxford handbook of memory* (pp. 627–643). New York: Oxford University Press.

Selnes, O. A. (2001). A historical overview of contributions from the study of deficits. In B. Rapp (Ed.), *The handbook of cognitive neuropsychology* (pp. 23–41). Philadelphia: Psychology Press.

Shallice, T. (1988). *From neuropsychology to mental structure.* New York: Cambridge University Press.

Shankweiler, D., & Studdert-Kennedy, M. (1975). A continuum of lateralization for speech perception. *Brain and Language, 2,* 212–225.

Shapiro, D., Jamner, L. D., Lane, J. D., Light, K. C., Myrtek, M., Sawada, Y., & Steptoe, A. (1996). Blood pressure publication guidelines. *Psychophysiology, 33,* 1–12.

Shukla, S. S., Honeyman, J. C., Crosson, B., Williams, C. M., & Nadeau, S. E. (1992). Method for registering brain SPECT and MR images. *Journal of Computer Assisted Tomography, 16,* 966–970.

Sidman, M. (1952). A note on functional relations obtained from group data. *Psychological Bulletin, 49,* 263–269.

Siebner, H. R., Tormos, J. M., Ceballos-Baumann, A. O., Auer, C., Catala, M. D., Conrad, B., & Pascual-Leone, A. (1999). Low frequency repetitive transcranial magnetic stimulation of the motor cortex in writer's cramp. *Neurology, 52,* 529–537.

Simos, P. G., Breier, J. I., Wheless, J. W., Maggio, W. W., Fletcher, J. M., Castillo, E. M., & Papanicolaou, A. C. (2000). Brain mechanisms for reading: the role of the superior temporal gyrus in word and pseudoword naming. *Neuroreport, 11,* 2443–2447.

Simos, P. G., Papanicolaou, A. C., Breier, J. I., Fletcher, J. M., Wheless, J. W., Maggio, W. W., Gormley, W., Constantinou, J. E., & Kramer, L. (2000). Insights into brain function and neural plasticity using magnetic source imaging. *Journal of Clinical Neurophysiology, 17,* 143–162.

Smith, E. E., Jonides, J., & Koeppe, R. A. (1996). Dissociating verbal and spatial working memory using PET. *Cerebral Cortex, 6,* 11–20.

Spellacy, F. (1970). Lateral preferences in the identification of pattern stimuli. *Journal of the Acoustic Society of America, 47,* 574–578.

Sperry, R. W. (1968). Hemisphere deconnection and unity in conscious awareness. *American Psychologist, 23,* 723–733.

Spitzer, R. L., Endicott, J., & Robins, E. (1978). Research diagnostic criteria: rationale and reliability. *Archives of General Psychiatry, 35,* 773–782.

Springer, S. P. (1986). Dichotic listening. In H. J. Hannay (Ed.), *Experimental techniques in human neuropsychology* (pp. 138–166). New York: Oxford University Press.

Squire, L. R., & Shimamura, A. P. (1986). Characterizing amnesic patients for neurobehavioral study. *Behavioral Neuroscience, 100,* 866–877.

Squire, L. R., & Zola Morgan, S. (1991). The medial temporal lobe memory system. *Science, 253,* 1380–1386.

Stern, Y., Albert, S., Tang, M. X., & Tsai, W. Y. (1999). Rate of memory decline in AD is related to education and occupation: cognitive reserve? *Neurology, 53,* 1942–1947.

Stewart, L., Meyer, B., Frith, U., & Rothwell, J. (2001). Left posterior BA37 is involved object recognition: A TMS study. *Neuropsychologia, 39,* 1–6.

Strafella, A., Paus, T., Barrett, J., & Dagher, A. (2001). Repetitive transcranial magnetic stimulation of the human prefrontal cortex induces dopamine release in the caudate nucleus. *Journal of Neuroscience, 21,* RC157, 1–4.

Suberi, M., & McKeever, W. F. (1977). Differential right hemispheric memory storage of emotional and non-emotional faces. *Neuropsychologia, 15,* 757–768.

Tachibana, H., Miyata, Y., Takeda, M., Minamoto, H., Sugita, M., & Okita, T. (1999). Auditory event-related potentials in an amnesic patient with a left temporal lobe lesion. *Journal of Neurological Sciences, 168,* 52–56.

Talairach, J., & Tournoux, P. (1988). *Coplanar stereotaxic atlas of the human brain.* New York: Thieme.

Tarkka, I. M., Stokic, D. S., Basile, L. F., & Papanicolaou, A. C. (1995). Electric source localization of the auditory P300 agrees with magnetic source localization. *Electroencephalography and Clinical Neurophysiology, 96,* 538–545.

Teuber, H.-L. (1955). Physiological psychology. *Annual Review of Psychology, 6,* 267–296.

Teuber, H.-L. (1975). Recovery of function after brain injury in man. *Ciba Foundation Symposia, 34,* 159–190.

Toone, B. K., Okocha, C. I., Sivakumar, K., & Syed, G. M. (2000). Changes in regional cerebral blood flow due to cognitive activation among patients with schizophrenia. *British Journal of Psychiatry, 177,* 222–228.

Tranel, D. (1992). Functional neuroanatomy: Neuropsychological correlates of cortical and subcortical damage. In S. C. Yudofsky

& R. E. Hales (Eds.), *The American Psychiatric Press textbook of neuropsychiatry* (2nd ed., pp. 57–88). Washington, DC: American Psychiatric Press.

Tranel, D., & Damasio, A. R. (1985). Knowledge without awareness: an autonomic index of facial recognition by prosopagnosics. *Science, 228,* 1453–1454.

Tranel, D., & Hyman, B. T. (1990). Neuropsychological correlates of bilateral amygdala damage. *Archives of Neurology, 47,* 349–355.

Trenerry, M. R., & Loring, D. W. (1995). Intracarotid amobarbital procedure. The Wada test. *Neuroimaging Clinics of North America, 5,* 721–728.

Triggs, W. J., Calvanio, R., MacDonnell, R. A., Cros, D., & Chiappa, K. H. (1994). Physiological motor asymmetry in human handedness: Evidence from transcranial magnetic stimulation. *Brain Research, 636,* 270–276.

Triggs, W. J., McCoy, K., Greer, R., Rossi, F., Bowers, D., Kortenkamp, S., Nadeau, S., Heilman, K., & Goodman, W. (1999). Effects of left frontal transcranial magnetic stimulation on depressed mood, cognition, and corticomotor threshold. *Biological Psychiatry, 45,* 1440–1446.

Triggs, W. J., Subramanium, B., & Rossi, F. (1999). Hand preference and transcranial magnetic stimulation: Asymmetry of cortical motor representation. *Brain Research, 835,* 324–329.

Trompetto, C., Assini, A., Ducolieri, A., Marchese, R., & Abbruzzese, G. (2000). Motor recovery following stroke: A transcranial stimulation study. *Clinical Neurophysiology, 111,* 1860–1867.

Tucker, D. (1993). Spatial sampling of head electrical fields: The geodesic sensor net. *Electroencephalography and Clinical Neurophysiology, 58,* 519–524.

Tulving, E., Habib, R., Nyberg, L., Lepage, M., & McIntosh, A. R. (1999). Positron emission tomography correlations in and beyond medial temporal lobes. *Hippocampus, 9,* 71–82.

Turner, R., Howseman, A., Rees, G., & Josephs, O. (1997). Functional imaging with magnetic resonance. In R. S. J. Frackowiak, K. J. Friston, C. D. Frith, & R. J. Dolan. (Eds.), *Human brain function* (pp. 467–486). San Diego, CA: Academic Press.

Umilta, C., Rizzolatti, G., Marzi, C., Zamboni, G., Franzini, C., Camarda, R., & Berlucchi, G. (1974). Hemispheric differences in the discrimination of line orientation. *Neuropsychologia, 12,* 165–174.

Ungerleider, L. G. (1995). Functional brain imaging studies of cortical mechanisms for memory. *Science, 270,* 769–775.

Van Petten, C., & Kutas, M. (1987). Ambiguous words in context: An event-related analysis of the time course of meaning activation. *Journal of Memory and Language, 26,* 188–208.

Varney, N. R., Bushnell, D. L., Nathan, M., Kahn, D., Roberts, R., Rezai, K., Walker, W., & Kirchner, P. (1995). NeuroSPECT correlates of disabling mild head injury: Preliminary findings. *Journal of Head Trauma Rehabilitation, 10,* 18–28.

Verfaellie, M., Bauer, R. M., & Bowers, D. (1991). Autonomic and behavioral evidence of "implicit" memory in amnesia. *Brain and Cognition, 15,* 10–25.

Vingerhoets, G., Santens, P., Van Laere, K., Lahorte, P., Dierckx, R. A., & De Reuck, J. (2001). Regional brain activity during different paradigms of mental rotation in healthy volunteers: A positron emission tomography study. *Neuroimage, 13,* 381–391.

von Monakow, C. (1969). Diaschisis. In K. H. Pribram (Ed.), *Brain and behavior: Vol. 1. Mood, states and mind.* Baltimore: Penguin Books.

Walsh, V., & Rushworth, M. (1999). A primer of magnetic stimulation as a tool for neuropsychology. *Neuropsychologia, 37,* 125–135.

Warburton, E., Price, C. J., Swinburn, K., & Wise, R. J. (1999). Mechanisms of recovery from aphasia: Evidence from positron emission tomography studies. *Journal of Neurology, Neurosurgery, and Psychiatry, 66,* 155–161.

Wasserman, E. (1998). Risk and safety of repetitive transcranial magnetic stimulation: Report and suggested guidelines from the International Workshop on the Safety of Repetitive Transcranial Magnetic Stimulation. *Electroencephalography and Clinical Neurophysiology, 108,* 1–16.

Wasserman, E., & Lisanby, S. (2001). Therapeutic application of repetitive transcranial magnetic stimulation: A review. *Clinical Neurophysiology, 112,* 1367–1377.

Wasserman, E., McShane, L., Hallett, M., & Cohen, L. (1992). Noninvasive mapping of muscle representations in human motor cortex. *Electroencephalography and Clinical Neurophysiology, 85,* 108.

Worden, M., & Schneider, W. (1995). Cognitive task design for fMRI. *International Journal of Imaging Systems and Technology, 6,* 253–270.

Zajonc, R. B. (1980). Feeling and thinking: Preferences need no inferences. *American Psychologist, 35,* 151–175.

Zakzanis, K. K. (1998). Quantitative evidence for neuroanatomic and neuropsychological markers in dementia of the Alzheimer's type. *Journal of Clinical and Experimental Neuropsychology, 20,* 259–269.

Ziemann, U., Ishii, K., Borgheresi, A., Yaseen, Z., Battaglia, F., Hallet, M., Cincotta, M., & Wassermann, E. (1999). Dissociation of the pathways mediating ipsilateral and contralateral motor-evoked potential in human hand and arm muscles. *Journal of Physiology, 518,* 895–906.

Zurif, E., Swinney, D., & Fodor, J. A. (1991). An evaluation of assumptions underlying the single-patient-only position in neuropsychological research: A reply. *Brain and Cognition, 16,* 198–210.

CHAPTER 13

Program Evaluation

MELVIN M. MARK

Psychologists from many different specialty areas are involved with evaluation. Often, people are what psychologists evaluate. Clinical psychologists evaluate people in terms of whether they have some psychopathology or another. Industrial-organizational psychologists frequently develop systems for personnel evaluation. Educational psychologists are commonly concerned with the evaluation of student performance or with teacher performance, which is a specialized kind of personnel evaluation. But entities other than people can be evaluated. For example, consumer or human-factors psychologists sometimes evaluate products.

Often, the entity that is evaluated is some sort or program or policy. In fact, psychologists of many of the discipline's subareas are involved in the evaluation of policies and programs. Consider but a few of the myriad possible examples. Many industrial-organizational psychologists have attempted to evaluate training programs that are offered to an organization's employees (e.g., Eckert, 2000). Educational psychologists have evaluated a variety or educational policies and programs. These range from preschool programs such as Head Start (Zigler & Muenchow, 1992) to postsecondary programs such as the Hope Scholarship program (Henry & Rubenstein, 2002). Clinical and counseling psychologists have evaluated a wide range of interventions, from general psychotherapy (e.g., Smith & Glass, 1977) to specialized

forms of therapy for specific disorders (e.g., Borkovec & Ruscio, 2001). Psychosocial interventions also include both prevention and treatment (see, e.g., Christensen & Heavey, 1999, for reviews of both prevention and treatment in the area of marital relations). Social psychologists have evaluated interventions that are designed to improve a wide array of social problems. These include prejudice (Aronson, Blaney, Stephan, Sikes, & Snapp, 1978), the transmission of sexually transmitted diseases (e.g., Alstead et al., 1999), and binge drinking among college students (e.g., Schroeder & Prentice, 1998).

Whatever their specialty area, when psychologists evaluate a program or policy, the question of impact—of the intervention's effects—is often at center stage. Examples abound. Does a particular type of training increase employee's performance? Does preschool increase children's subsequent academic performance? Do certain types of cooperative learning arrangements in schools reduce racial prejudice? Does a specific form of cognitive-behavioral therapy alleviate generalized anxiety disorder? It appears that causal questions usually are central in evaluations of the kinds of interventions that are of interest to psychologists. Given the importance of causal questions, a major focus of this chapter is on key methods for estimating the effects of policies and programs in the context of evaluation.

Causal questions are not, however, the only kind of concern that arises in program and policy evaluation. For example, funders sometimes want to know whether the authorized services have been delivered to the target population. Sometimes, demands for accountability do not require the typically intensive, difficult, and costly methods of causal analysis. In some cases evaluation may be carried out in service of program managers' needs for ongoing feedback to help guide program administration and improve program services and operations, and causal methods may not be appropriate. Given that evaluations should sometimes emphasize issues other than causal questions, this chapter attends in part to other kinds of methods that may be used for evaluation.

Whether an evaluation focuses on estimating a program's effects, the evaluator must consider a set of issues that rarely arise for psychologists working in other areas. Chief among these is that evaluators may need special skills to identify the right evaluation questions. Unlike more basic research, evaluation questions do not necessarily derive from past theory and research leavened with the researcher's interests. Unlike some areas of applied research, there often is not a single client whose concerns can legitimately drive the study. Rather, there are usually multiple groups, with at least partially competing interests, who all have some legitimate interest in the evaluation. In addition, questions are likely to arise as to whether a causal analysis or some alternative will have a better chance of aiding social or organizational improvement. Against this background, identifying the best questions to drive an evaluation can require skillful analysis of stakeholder needs, combined with a sort of policy analytic perspective. Accordingly, this chapter deals also with this ancillary topic, which goes beyond the scope of most methodology treatises.

Finally, this chapter briefly considers possible future developments in the field of evaluations. Four general areas of potential methodological developments are identified. Two additional challenges for the field are discussed, along with a possible common solution. (As an aside, although the remainder of this chapter speaks to the evaluation of policies as well as programs, for the sake of simplicity the terms *program evaluation* or *evaluation* will generally be used.)

THE CONCEPT OF CAUSALITY IN PROGRAM EVALUATION

As just noted, causal questions abound in the evaluation of programs and policies. Knowing what effects, if any, a program has is critical for assessing the program's merit and worth. Whether an organization views an employee training program positively depends, for example, on whether the program improves the performance and retention of its employees. Although this chapter focuses largely on methods of causal analysis, it is important to recognize that these methods are not always absolutely necessary in order to judge the merit and worth of something. Indeed, when things other than policies and programs are evaluated, causal analyses may be far less common. In product evaluations, such as *Consumers Reports'* or *PC Computing*'s assessments of computers, the methods of causal analysis are not generally used. Instead, the evaluator assesses the computer with respect to certain (presumably) valued attributes, such as processing speed, multimedia quality, upgradability, and technical support. Admittedly, in some cases product evaluation does in fact involve causal analysis (as when a car manufacturer studies the effect of a new hood shape on air resistance), often using relatively simple causal methods. On the other hand, causal analyses are not so important when the characteristics that people value can be assessed through simpler, descriptive means. For computers, for example, processing speed can be observed descriptively—by measuring how quickly the computer performs on a standard set of software applications—and with relatively little ambiguity. To take another example, legroom in a car can readily be assessed without causal means.

For social programs and policies, however, decades of practice indicate that the things that people value, the attributes that make a program or policy worthwhile or not, are predominantly causal. This is illustrated in the set of causal questions given earlier, such as whether preschool causes an increase in children's academic success. And unlike observing a computer's processing speed, attributing an effect to a program is usually not a simple matter. It is not as easy as simply seeing how a child performs academically after participating in a preschool program. Myriad influences could affect the child's academic performance other than the program. More generally, because there are many possible causes of change in the kinds of outcomes that are of interest in most program evaluations, causal attribution is challenging. Understanding these challenges, and the ways of dealing with them, can be aided by some understanding of the concept of causation.

However, the literature on causation is voluminous. Philosophers, methodologists, and statisticians have given considerable attention to what causation is and to how one can reasonably draw a causal inference. Although practicing evaluators need not follow every nuance of this literature, some understanding of causation can enhance evaluation practice. One potentially useful view suggests that causation can best be understood through three partially overlapping perspectives: a counterfactualist definition of cause and effect; an emphasis on underlying generative mechanisms; and an explicit representation of the probabalistic nature of causal relations (Mark, Henry, & Julnes, 2000). Subsequent sections shall deal with how these three perspectives can inform evaluation practice.

The Counterfactualist Definition of Cause and Effect

Imagine that we are interested in the effect of a freshman orientation program on the drinking behavior of a new college student named Bob (cf. Schroeder & Prentice, 1998). We want to answer the question, Did participation in the freshman orientation program cause Bob to drink less alcohol? A number of philosophers (e.g., Mackie, 1974) and methodologists (e.g., Mohr, 1995; Reichardt & Mark, 1998; Rubin, 1974; Shadish, Cook, & Campbell, 2002) suggested that a *counterfactualist* perspective is needed to answer this question and, more generally, to define causation. We can of course observe that Bob participated in the program and also measure, at some subsequent point in time, how often and how much he drinks. According to the counterfactualist perspective, to know whether the freshman orientation program caused Bob to drink less we would also need to know whether Bob would have consumed more alcohol than he in fact did after participating in the program *if* Bob had not participated in the program and everything else had been just the same. More generally, we can define an effect, and by implication a cause, as follows: The effect of causal state A (e.g., participating in the program), as compared to causal state B (e.g., not participating), is the difference between (a) the outcome that arose at time 2 after A had been administered at time 1 and (b) the outcome that *would have arisen* at time 2 if, instead, B had been administered at time 1 but (c) everything else at time 1 had been the same. This comparison, between what subsequently happened under condition A and what would have happened if condition B had taken place with everything else initially the same, is called the *ideal comparison.*

Because the ideal comparison, unfortunately, cannot be achieved in practice, Reichardt and Mark (1998) called it the *ideal but unattainable comparison.* It is impossible for everything else to be the same if a program is administered in one condition and not administered in the other (or if Program A is administered in one condition and Program B in the other). Something else must differ when the different treatments are introduced. For example, we could compare (a) the drinking behavior of Bob, who participated in a freshman orientation program, with (b) the drinking behavior of Tom, another college freshman who did not participate in a freshman

orientation program. However, not only would the treatments differ in the two conditions, but the individuals receiving the treatments would also differ. Any observed difference between Bob's and Tom's drinking behavior might be the result of differences between the two individuals, rather than the result of the freshman orientation program.

The ideal but rather impractical way to obtain the ideal but unattainable comparison would be to travel back in time and arrange things so that Bob participated in the freshman orientation in one sequence, but not in another, comparison sequence. The difference in the outcomes would exactly equal the effect of the freshman orientation, according to the counterfactualist definition of the effect of a cause. Any difference in an outcome variable at time 2 could be due only to the treatment differences that were introduced at time 1, because everything else would have been the same. Lacking the ability to travel back in time, however, we cannot have everything else be the same in real-life comparisons. Thus, incorrect conclusions may be drawn about causal relations. Scientists have developed a repertoire of methods that allow us to minimize the likely errors. One important step in the evolution of these techniques has been the identification of several categories of factors, other than the program of interest, that can vary across the treatment conditions in real-life comparisons. These are commonly called *threats to internal validity* (Campbell & Stanley, 1966), several of which are described later in the context of specific research designs.

Another important step in the development of causal methods has been the invention of randomized experiments and various alternatives that, to varying degrees, allow us to approximate the ideal but unattainable counterfactual comparison. The strongest of these methods for causal analysis ask not about effects for a single case such as Bob, but about "average effects" combining over some population or subgroup of individuals (Little & Rubin, 2000; Rubin, 1974). Fortunately, this focus on average effects generally matches the emphasis of policy and program evaluation, in that one cannot usually tailor policies and programs to each individual but must instead offer interventions intended for broader groups.

Underlying Generative Mechanisms, or Mediators

Although the counterfactualist conception of cause has several advantages, including a useful and meaningful definition of cause and effect, it also has important limits. One shortcoming of the standard counterfactualist position is that it does not place sufficient emphasis on addressing *why* the effects have occurred, that is, on the mechanisms through which a cause influences an effect. Working from the counterfactualist perspective, one can, for example, frame the question of a freshman orientation program's effects on drinking behavior simply by reference to the ideal comparison. In practice, one could attempt to approximate the ideal but unattainable comparison by creating two comparable groups of freshman (e.g., by random assignment), having one group participate in the orientation program while the other did not, and subsequently comparing average drinking behavior for the two groups. The counterfactualist perspective, in short, can easily lead researchers to focus on the observable cause and effects of interest, with no attention to the processes that connect them. This process-free approach is often derided as "black-box evaluation," with the underlying mechanism residing within the metaphoric box into which the evaluator has not peered. From one perspective, it is unfair to criticize the counterfactual approach in this way. After all, the counterfactual approach provides a useful and widely accepted way of defining and estimating the effect of some causal variable of interest. On the other hand, to think of causal analysis *only* in terms of estimating the observable effects of specified causal variables is to wear a kind of blinders—blinders that can seriously limit the conduct of program evaluation.

Indeed, psychologists doing program evaluation are likely to be interested in underlying mechanisms, that is, the processes by which the program causes a difference in the outcome of interest. In the freshman orientation case, social psychologists would probably ask whether the program had its effects because it (a) changed participants' subjective norms about the frequency of drinking among other students, (b) changed the impact of subjective norms on behavior (Schroeder & Prentice, 1998), (c) changed their attitudes about the desirability of drinking, or (d) changed their perception of contextual variables that may enhance or inhibit alcohol use (Triandis, 1994). A simple counterfactualist view of causal effects allows investigators to ignore these or other underlying mechanisms.

Admittedly, it can be useful to know only about molar cause-effect relations, such as whether aspirin alleviates headache pain, even without understanding the underlying mechanisms (Cook & Campbell, 1979). Nevertheless, it will typically be even *more* useful to understand the underlying mechanisms (Cronbach, 1982; Mark, Henry, & Julnes, 1998). If we understand the processes that underlie a cause-effect relationship, we can sometimes create more effective or more efficient treatments. We can sometimes better target the intervention to the right cases. We are more likely to be able to fix things if they break. Of great importance to evaluators, a focus on underlying mechanisms can also increase one's confidence that the program made a difference, especially in those cases where it is not possible to have a strong counterfactual

comparison, as we shall see later. In addition, psychologists will generally be more attracted to evaluation projects that focus on underlying mechanisms because it allows for theory testing as well as for valuable applied work (Yeh, 2000).

Moreover, a view of causation that does not emphasize underlying generative mechanisms simply seems deficient as a representation of causal forces in the world: Cause and effect relations happen for reasons. If an orientation program reduces drinking in college freshman, there is some psychological process that mediates the effect, such as changes in perceived norms (Schroeder & Prentice, 1998). In short, the counterfactualist view of causal effects needs to be supplemented, and this supplementation not only enriches our view of causation but also helps guide evaluation design in such a way as to enhance evaluation practice. Although cause and effect can be defined counterfactually, a complete view of causation requires attention to underlying generative mechanisms as well. In addition, at least one more piece is needed for a satisfactory conception of causality.

INUS Conditions: The Contingent Nature of Causal Relations

Cook and Campbell (1979, chap. 1), in what remains one of the most valuable reviews of concepts of causation for social scientists, contended that causation is probabilistic. Mackie (1965, 1974) provided an important conceptualization of the probabilistic nature of causal relations. Mackie claimed that what we call causes are actually *INUS conditions*. That is, they are an *insufficient* but *necessary* part of a condition that is itself *unnecessary* but *sufficient* to cause the result. A classic example is a cigarette that is identified as the cause of a house fire. The cigarette by itself is *insufficient* in that other conditions had to occur, such as the presence of combustible material and the absence of a sprinkler system. But the cigarette was a *necessary* component of the specific causal package that actually caused the fire. Nevertheless, the causal package that included the dropped cigarette was *unnecessary* in the sense that in principle several other causal packages could have led to a fire (involving, say, an electrical short circuit or a forest fire). But the cigarette and its associated package of conditions were *sufficient* to cause the house fire; nothing else was needed. The counterfactualist approach, by emphasizing one "cause" as the manipulable focus of interest, may lead people to miss the other conditions that must be present for *the* cause to produce the effect.

The logic of INUS causes applied nicely to social programs and policies. For example, consider again the question of whether a freshman orientation program is effective in causing Bob, our college freshman, to drink less. Perhaps for

Bob, the freshman orientation program is effective because Bob and his environment include the other needed components of the relevant causal package, which might include (a) a student who is not already alcohol dependent, (b) a local college culture in which binge drinking is not so epidemic as to make lowered subjective norms implausible, and (c) the presence of some alternative social and recreational activities for students. Thus, the freshman orientation program might be effective for Bob, but not be effective for another freshman who is already an alcoholic, or it might not be effective in a different environment where students find nothing else to do on a weekend night. In addition, there may be other causal packages, which do not include a freshman orientation program, that also cause low levels of drinking among other students.

By highlighting the contingencies on which program effectiveness depends, the INUS approach reminds us that a program may be effective in some contexts with some clients, but not be effective elsewhere. The INUS approach thus suggests modesty in our aspirations for social programs. It also suggests modesty in our aspirations for evaluation research, in that we can usually hope to achieve only incomplete knowledge about the effectiveness of programs and policies. But incomplete knowledge of a program's effects is generally much better than no knowledge, and may in fact be of great help in guiding action. Of course, it is also desirable to try to obtain the missing knowledge about the contingencies on which program success depends, and this will often require the use of data-intensive techniques for identifying moderators of program impact (Julnes, 1995; Mark, 2001; Mark, Hofmann, & Reichardt, 1992; Mark, Henry, et al., 2000), which are discussed later in the context of principled discovery.

In sum, a useful and meaningful perspective on causation can be achieved by integrating (a) the counterfactualist definition of cause with (b) an emphasis on underlying generative mechanisms and (c) Mackie's model of the contingent and elliptical nature of causal relations. Having considered this threefold conceptualization of causation, let's see how it plays out in the context of some specific methods for causal analysis.

DESIGNS FOR CAUSAL ANALYSIS: APPROXIMATING THE IDEAL COUNTERFACTUAL

In this section, selected methods for causal analysis are reviewed. The methods reviewed are prominent in evaluation practice. They are reviewed here largely in terms of how well they approximate the ideal but unattainable counterfactual comparison that one would need for completely confident causal inference.

The Randomized Experiment

Randomized experiments are often referred to as the gold standard against which other methods of assessing treatment effects are compared. In a randomized experiment, individuals (or other units) are randomly assigned to treatment conditions. Without random assignment, selection differences are likely to arise, which means that the cases in a treatment group and those in a comparison group differ on the average initially. For example, the college freshmen who choose on their own to attend a freshman orientation would probably differ on average in several ways from those who choose not to attend. Random assignment is beneficial to causal inference largely because it removes systematic bias due to initial selection differences and, thus, creates a fair comparison (Boruch, 1997). In other words, unlike most cases in which participants self-select into treatment, the comparison is unbiased if the treatment and comparison groups are created at random.

Random assignment does not, however, guarantee that there will be *no* initial selection differences. Even randomly assigned treatment and control groups are still likely to differ somewhat initially. That is, even if the true treatment effect is zero, the mean difference between the two groups on an outcome variable is unlikely to be *exactly* zero. Random assignment does, however, mean that the initial selection differences between the groups are completely random. The second great benefit of random assignment thus arises: The classical statistical procedures of confidence intervals and hypothesis tests can take into account whatever random selection differences exist, providing well-grounded statements about the warrant for confidence in one's results (Boruch, 1997; Reichardt & Mark, 1998).

Viewed from the counterfactualist perspective, the response of the people randomly assigned to the comparison group serves to approximate the ideal but unattainable counterfactual comparison. That is, the randomized comparison group represents what would have happened to those in the treatment group if the treatment had not been presented. Let us assume that a randomized experiment is carried out well—even though meeting this assumption in evaluation can be challenging in practice (given such potential problems as attrition, discussed later). If the randomized experiment is carried out well, this comparison of the treatment group's outcomes with those of the randomized comparison group should be a close approximation of the ideal comparison.

Unlike nonequivalent-groups designs, where systematic initial selection differences are likely, random assignment precludes systematic selection in the randomized experiment. Moreover, as just noted, classical statistical procedures provide a way of summarizing and modeling the random selection differences that remain. Because it provides a close approximation to the ideal comparison, a randomized experiment, if carried out well, provides a strong warrant for inferring a cause-effect relationship.

Note, however, that this holds for the global hypothesis that the treatment causes a difference in the outcome. For the more specific hypotheses about the underlying mechanism, the randomized experiment is not *intrinsically* so strong. For example, a randomized evaluation of the impact of a freshman orientation session on drinking behavior can demonstrate a causal relationship while leaving completely unaddressed whether the underlying mechanism involves subjective norms, attitudes, or something else. (Readers familiar with Cook & Campbell's 1979 validity scheme will hear echoes of the distinction between internal and construct validity). In addition, the randomized experiment does not necessarily assist in describing those characteristics, other than the treatment, that were required for the effect to occur, which would allow the researcher to fill in the missing knowledge about the contingencies that apply to the causal relationship. (Here, readers familiar with the Cook & Campbell validity scheme will hear an echo involving external validity).

The randomized experiment has been soundly criticized by some evaluators on these grounds (e.g., Pawson & Tilley, 1997). In fact, randomized experiments do, as these critics suggest, *enable* researchers to examine cause-effect relationships without also examining underlying mechanisms. However, this blind spot is not an inevitable product of the use of randomized experiments (Julnes, Mark, & Henry, 1998; Mark et al., 1998). To the contrary, the randomized experiment can, if appropriately designed, be a powerful tool for studying underlying process as well as for estimating cause-effect relationships. Indeed, the laboratory experiment has been used widely in psychology precisely to study underlying mechanisms, with investigators using different conditions chosen carefully to differentiate between alternative mechanisms. In most evaluation contexts, however, the between-condition differences are so coarse and multifaceted that between-group differences are generally not very revealing about underlying processes.

Nevertheless, even in evaluation contexts, patterns of differential effects (e.g., across client subgroups) can support one underlying mechanism and discount others (Mark, 1990). In addition, as discussed in the next section, mediation can be examined in the context of a randomized experiment.

This will often involve the use of adjunct techniques such as qualitative observation (Maxwell, 1996) or structural equations modeling to test for changes in a sequence of hypothesized mediating variables that occur between the intervention and outcome variables (Fiske, Kenny, & Taylor, 1982; Mark, 1990). For example, one might measure whether students' subjective norms about alcohol use change after participating in a freshman orientation program and whether that change can account statistically for any change in drinking behavior (cf. Schroeder & Prentice, 1998). When underlying mechanisms are tested in these ways within a randomized experiment, one can simultaneously have considerable confidence in the resulting estimate of the magnitude of the treatment effect, assuming that the randomized experiment is carried out reasonably well.

The caveat that the randomized experiment is well carried out is very important. A randomized experiment can fall short in several ways. These include (a) flawed methods of random assignment, whether unintentional or because of subversion of the assignment process by program staff not committed to randomization; (b) differential refusal or attrition across conditions, so that initial randomization is not maintained among the participants who remain in the experiment at the end; (c) substantial amounts of missing data, which may bias results if not random; (d) failure of the treatment and comparison group to be implemented as planned; (e) an inadequate number of cases for sufficiently powerful statistical tests, perhaps because of initial overestimates of client flow; (f) resistance to randomization as a method for assignment to groups, for practical or ethical reasons; (g) restriction of random assignment to unusual circumstances that may hinder generalization to settings of interest; and (h) awareness by control group participants that they did not receive the treatment, which may lead to between-group differences that are instead attributed to the program. These problems, and the potential solutions to them, are discussed in several sources, including Boruch (1997), Boruch and Wothke (1985), Braucht and Reichardt (1993), Conner (1977), Cook and Campbell (1979), Lipsey and Cordray (2000), and Shadish et al. (2002). Some of the most important of these problems are discussed momentarily.

In short, the randomized experiment is in principle an outstanding tool for causal analysis, particularly for estimating the effects or a program or policy, though less so for establishing underlying mechanisms. Random assignment provides a close approximation of the ideal counterfactual, as applied to the estimate of an average treatment effect. In fact, random assignment appears to be common in some areas, especially those that span evaluation and more traditional psychological research. For instance, clinical trials of various forms of therapy commonly involve random assignment. On the other hand, random assignment is admittedly not feasible in every evaluation in which causal analysis is important. Random assignment is not possible when a treatment is applied uniformly across some geographical area, for example. This problem is increasingly present in so-called comprehensive community initiatives (Fullbright-Anderson, Kubisch, & Connell, 1998). And it appears that random assignment is especially likely to be difficult to arrange when the evaluator is not also the developer of the intervention being tested. (This, incidentally, may explain why random assignment to conditions is common in therapy evaluations, where the evaluator has often developed the therapy protocol as well, but is not as common in many other practice areas). Nevertheless, there are a number of circumstances in which random assignment is feasible (Boruch, 1997; Cook & Campbell, 1979; Shadish et al., 2002), perhaps more than many practicing evaluators believe. At the same time, conducting randomized experiments effectively is not simple but entails a number of management responsibilities and challenges, some of which can be quite problematic in some cases (Boruch, 1997; Cook & Campbell, 1979; Shadish et al., 2002).

Attrition

One of the most common problems facing randomized evaluations is attrition, that is, participants who drop out over the life of the evaluation. Attrition can reduce one's ability to generalize to the kind of participants who tend to drop out of an evaluation. Attrition reduces statistical power, and with attrition rates of 40–50% common in some kinds of programs (Ribisl et al., 1996), the loss of power can be considerable. Even more important, when attrition differs across conditions, the estimate of a program's effects becomes biased. When attrition is treatment-related, one loses the equivalence that random assignment is designed to provide. In other words, nonequivalent groups are created through treatment-related attrition.

How does one deal with the possibility of attrition? As may be obvious, the preferred strategy is to work proactively to try to minimize attrition. Ribisl et al. (1996) provided a very useful review of procedures that can be used to try to retain participants and to track them over time (also see Boruch, 1997; Shadish et al., 2002). These include obtaining contact and location information from participants and from their friends or relatives who are likely to know their whereabouts in the future and obtaining permission to search other records and contact agencies that might know their location in the future. In addition, it is important to make involvement in the evaluation and its associated data collection as convenient

as possible (e.g., by offering child care during interviews for working participants, by providing transportation, or by using phone interviews). Incentives for participation may be offered. Funds to support the tracking of participants should be included in evaluation budgets, and lower-cost options should be attempted before moving on to more costly tracking efforts. To prevent condition-related attrition, it is especially important to consider the features of the different conditions that may influence the relative desirability of participation. Sometimes, special incentives can be offered in the otherwise less-attractive condition, as long as this does not obscure the program effect of interest or create any ethical problems (for additional suggestions on reducing attrition and tracking clients over time, see Ribisl et al., 1996).

Despite the best use of preventive steps, some attrition may occur. One after-the-fact approach to attrition is to analyze data as though all participants received the treatment to which they were initially assigned. This approach is often called *intent-to-treat (ITT) analysis*. The ITT approach will typically provide a conservative estimate of the treatment effect because some portion of those assigned to the treatment did not in fact receive it. Obviously, the ITT analysis also requires that outcome measures be available even if the person dropped out of the assigned condition (or switched to another condition). In general, if the ITT approach is used, the results of this analysis should be reported in conjunction with other analyses.

Another approach is to replace missing data. Considerable work has been done in the last two decades on data imputation (e.g., Rubin, 1987; Schafer, 1997). As Graham and Donaldson (1993) demonstrated, taking extra steps to obtain outcome data from a sample of dropouts can greatly aid in the imputation of missing data. In addition, other kinds of analyses, summarized next, can be used in an attempt to adjust for any nonequivalence that is created by attrition. Again, multiple analyses, using alternative ways of dealing with missing data, are suggested as a way to increase confidence that the conclusions of an evaluation do not ride on some single (and perhaps incorrect) set of assumptions that underlie a single form of analysis (Shadish et al., 2002).

Statistical Adjustments

A variety of statistical techniques, including the analysis of covariance (ANCOVA), latent variable structural equation modeling, selection modeling, and propensity scores, can be used to try to adjust for nonequivalencies introduced by attrition in randomized experiments. However, these techniques are more commonly discussed in terms of their use in quasi-experiments, where the absence of random assignment often means that biases will exist even if there is no attrition. We discuss these analyses further in the context of quasi-experiments, to which we now turn.

Quasi-experiments

The term *quasi-experiment* refers to approximations of experiments, to studies that have several but not all of the characteristics of full-scale controlled experiments. Most important, quasi-experiments lack random assignment. When causal questions predominate in an evaluation and random assignment is infeasible, evaluators commonly resort to quasi-experiments. Contemporary knowledge about quasi-experiments derives primarily from the work of Campbell (1957, 1969) and his associates (Campbell & Stanley, 1966; Cook & Campbell, 1979; Shadish et al., 2002), which can be consulted for additional detail.

There are several different quasi-experimental designs, ranging in complexity, and also ranging in how well on average they approximate the ideal but unattainable counterfactual comparison. One relatively simple quasi-experiment, which often can be implemented but almost as often will be inadequate, is the *pretest-posttest one-group design*. Imagine as an example that a freshman orientation program were evaluated by measuring students' self-reported drinking before the program and again after it. In the simple pretest-posttest design, the ideal counterfactual is meant to be approximated with the pretest observation. The posttest observation, obviously, shows what really happened after the intervention. If the pretest observation showed what would have happened at the time of the posttest if the intervention had in fact not occurred, then the treatment effect could validly be estimated as the difference between the pretest and the posttest. The problem, of course, is that the pretest observation may well *not* represent what would have happened at the posttest if the intervention had not taken place. That is, the pretest may be a very poor and biased approximation of the ideal but unattainable comparison. Several generic, alternative mechanisms exist that can lead to changes over time in students' drinking behavior and, more generally, in the kind of outcomes measured by evaluators and others interested in human behavior. These forces have come to be called *internal validity threats*.

History, for instance, is a threat to validity that occurs when some specific event, other than the intended treatment, also occurred between the pretest and posttest and when this other event caused a change in the outcome of interest. Imagine that at the time of the freshman orientation program, the local police began a well-publicized campaign against underage drinking. This (or another historical event) might be responsible for a drop in student drinking that could mistakenly be attributed to the orientation program.

Alternatively, students' drinking behavior could change simply because they are older at the time of the posttest than at the pretest, rather than because of a treatment effect. This threat to internal validity is called maturation and includes a variety of processes that can occur over time within research participants, such as growing older, hungrier, more fatigued, wiser, and the like. For example, it may be a typical maturational pattern for drinking to increase in the first months of college. If so, maturation could obscure any real effect of the orientation program in the pretest-posttest design.

The simple pretest-posttest design is subject to several internal validity threats in addition to history and maturation. These include threats known as instrumentation, regression to the mean, testing, and attrition (see Cook & Campbell, 1979, and Shadish et al., 2002, for descriptions and examples). These various threats do not, however, automatically apply whenever the design is used. For example, Eckert (2000) has argued that these threats often will not be plausible in evaluations of training programs (at least in terms of certain key outcome variables), and that such programs can reasonably be evaluated with this relatively practicable and low cost pretest-posttest one-group design. For instance, Eckert argues that maturation will not plausibly account for improvements in immediate posttests in most training evaluations because knowledge and skills generally would not rise markedly by maturation in a short time. In most instances of policy and program evaluation, in contrast, the threats that apply to the simple pretest-posttest one-group design will be sufficiently plausible that potential users of evaluation would be well served if a more complex design were implemented instead. Eckert's argument stands as a valuable reminder, though, that, as Campbell and Stanley (1966) long ago told us and Cronbach (1982) reminded us, designs should not be selected mindlessly, but instead considered relative to the likely plausibility of validity threats in context.

A more complex design that can sometimes be implemented is the *interrupted time-series (ITS) design*. ITS designs use time-series data, that is, repeated measurement of an outcome variable at (approximately) equally spaced intervals, such as days, months, quarters, or years, to estimate the effect of a treatment. In a simple ITS design, a series of pretest observations is collected, a treatment is introduced, and the series of (posttest) observations continues. In essence, the ideal counterfactual is estimated by projecting the trend in the pretreatment observations forward in time. The treatment effect is then derived from the differences, if any, between the projected and the actual posttreatment trend.

Unlike most other quasi-experimental designs, the ITS designs allow an evaluator to observe the temporal pattern of the effect. This can be important. For example, the value of a freshman orientation program might be judged differently if its effects die out after three or six months, rather than persist over a longer period. Even more important, the simple ITS design, with its series of pretest and posttest observations, can help to strengthen causal inference. As just noted, maturation is often a plausible threat for the pretest-posttest design. If the pattern of maturation is relatively steady over time, then the ITS design allows the evaluator to estimate the pattern of maturation from the trend in the pretreatment observations. In the case of the freshman orientation program, the pretest time-series observations could demonstrate the maturational change that was already underway before the program began. To the extent that the pretreatment trend allows the researcher to model and project correctly the maturational trend into the posttreatment time period, maturation is removed as a threat to internal validity in the ITS design (see Shadish et al., 2002, and Mark, Reichardt, & Sanna, 2000, for further discussion, including the question of possible nonlinear maturation).

Although the simple ITS design helps rule out some threats to valid causal inference, as just illustrated with the threat of maturation, it does not rule out all internal validity threats. In particular, the threat of history is equally as plausible in the simple ITS time-series design as in a pretest-posttest design, assuming that the interval between observations is the same. The plausibility of history and other validity threats can be reduced, however, by the use of more complex ITS designs. For example, one might extend the simple ITS design by adding a control group that is not exposed to the treatment. For more detail on the threats that apply to the simple ITS design, on the ITS with nonequivalent control group, on other complex ITS designs, and on data analysis with time-series observations, see Shadish et al. (2002); Marcantonio and Cook (1994); and Mark, Reichardt, et al. (2000). Although ITS designs can be relatively strong for causal inference, they are infeasible for many evaluations because of the need for repeated pretest and posttest measurements. In some cases, however, measures of interest will already exist in time-series form (e.g., when the outcome variable of interest involves divorce rates, crime rates, or organizational productivity). In still other instances, the evaluator will be able to implement repeated measurement of important outcome variables (e.g., Kazi, 1997). Even if time-series data are available for only one of several outcome variables, the inclusion of an ITS design as part of an evaluation can contribute considerably to overall validity. More generally, evaluators should be attentive to the possible use of different designs for different outcome variables, depending on data availability. Evaluators should recognize, however, that time series in existing archives are not likely to include measures of underlying processes (Mark, Sanna, & Shotland, 1992). In addition, existing time series need to be inspected carefully for possible instrumentation problems (i.e., possible changes in the definition or measurement of the time series variable that may co-occur with the intervention and could obscure the true treatment effect).

Both the simple pretest-posttest one-group and the simple ITS designs use comparisons across time in place of the ideal but unattainable comparison. That is, in those designs a comparison is made of the same individual or aggregate units at different points in time (i.e., before the treatment and after). Alternatively, in other designs researchers substitute for the ideal comparison by comparing different (groups of) individuals at the same time. When assignment to the different conditions is not random, designs of this sort are known as nonequivalent-groups designs. In these quasi-experiments, (a) individuals self-select into the different groups (e.g., individuals may choose to participate in a freshman orientation program or not), (b) individuals are assigned in some nonrandom fashion into the groups by others such as program administrators (e.g., dormitory administrators may exercise their discretion in assigning some students to a freshman orientation program), (c) group assignment is determined by one's location (e.g., the freshman orientation program is implemented in one dorm but not in another one), or (d) assignment to the different treatment groups takes place in some other nonrandom fashion.

The simplest between-group design is the *posttest-only nonequivalent-groups design*. In this design, individuals (or other aggregate units, such as schools or communities) fall into the treatment group, which receives the program, or into the control or comparison group, which does not receive the program (or receives some alternative program). Following the treatment, the members of both groups are measured on one or more outcome variables of interest. The control or comparison group serves as the substitute for the ideal but unattainable comparison.

The fundamental shortcoming of this design is the validity threat known as *selection*. Selection arises when the difference between the treatment group and the control (or comparison) group on an outcome measure results from preexisting differences between the groups, rather than from the effect of the program. That is, the groups may have initial differences that cause subsequent differences on the outcome variable. In general, in most evaluations the threat of initial selection differences will create great uncertainty about the program's effect in the posttest only nonequivalent-groups design. Absent any other information, it is typically quite plausible that the groups would have differed even in the absence of a treatment effect.

In many cases, nonequivalent groups are observed on a pretest as well as a posttest, resulting in what is called the *pretest-posttest nonequivalent-groups design*. With this design, the pretest is used to try to take account of initial se-lection differences. One way to do this would be to estimate the program's effect—not by the difference between treat-ment and control groups at the posttest, but by the difference between the two groups in the amount of change, on the av-erage, between pretest and posttest. This gain-score approach is based on the assumption that if there actually were no treat-ment effect, the treatment group would change over time the same amount as the control group. If this assumption is cor-rect, gain-score analysis works well. The problem, of course, is that the assumption that in the absence of the program the treatment group would have changed the same amount as the control group did may be incorrect. Perhaps, for in-stance, the treatment group starts out 10 points ahead at the pretest, but would have been 15 points ahead at the posttest even if there were no treatment effect. As the old saying goes, sometimes the rich get richer. Many differences increase with time. For example, the difference in running speed between the fastest and slowest eighth-grader is much greater than the difference between the fastest and slowest preschooler. Such possibilities led Campbell and Stanley (1966) to describe the "selection-by-maturation interaction" as a threat to the inter-nal validity of the pretest-posttest nonequivalent-groups de-sign. This threat refers to the possibility that one of the groups would change at a different rate than the other group, even if there actually were no treatment effect. In other words, selection by maturation occurs when one group is ma-turing at a different rate than the other, in the absence of a treatment effect, and this pattern of differential maturation could obscure the true treatment effect.

Several alternatives to gain-score analysis exist for the pretest-posttest nonequivalent-groups design. One long-standing alternative analytic procedure is ANCOVA (e.g., Reichardt, 1979). More recent approaches include structural equation modeling (e.g., Bentler, 1992), selection modeling (e.g., Rindskopf, 1986), and the calculation and use of propensity scores (e.g., Rosenbaum, 1995; Rosenbaum & Rubin, 1983). Each of these involves a different approach to-ward controlling statistically for initial selection differences. In essence, each also involves a different implicit way of substituting for the ideal but unattainable counterfactual comparison. Each approach will give unbiased estimates of the treatment effect if the assumptions underlying it hold. The problem in practice, however, is that it will generally not be possible to be fully confident that the assumptions underlying a specific analysis hold in a particular evaluation (Boruch, 1997; Reichardt, 1979). Consequently, multiple analyses are often recommended for the pretest-posttest nonequivalent-groups design, in order to demonstrate that one's conclusions about the merit of a program are robust across different

analytic assumptions (e.g., Reynolds & Temple, 1995; Wortman, Reichardt, & St. Pierre, 1981). Related analysis issues will be addressed later.

In addition to the possible selection-by-maturation prob-lem, the pretest-posttest nonequivalent-groups design is sus-ceptible to other threats that also are called interactions with selection. Selection by history refers to the possibility that the two groups are subjected to different historical forces, so that history may cause a larger effect in one than in the other. For instance, if we were evaluating the effect of a freshman ori-entation program that is implemented at one college and used a different college as a nonequivalent control group, selection by history might operate if there was a death by alcohol poi-soning that was highly publicized locally at one school at about the same time as the freshman orientation was intro-duced. These and other interactions with selection (Cook & Campbell, 1979; Shadish et al., 2002) may be plausible in the pretest-posttest nonequivalent design.

Some Conclusions About Quasi-experiments

In summarizing and expanding the preceding selective re-view of quasi-experimental designs, several conclusions can be highlighted. First is that modifications in research design can render specific validity threats implausible. For example, the addition of time series to a simple pretest-posttest design can allow an evaluator to assess the plausibility of maturation and to control for (linear) maturation. Second, evaluators should be careful to assess the plausibility of validity threats *in context*. As Eckert (2000) illustrated in the context of World Bank training programs, just because a validity threat can apply to a specific design in general does not mean that it is operating in a particular evaluation using that design (or oper-ating powerfully enough to obscure the true treatment effect). Third, by considering the possible effect of plausible validity threats, one can try to develop more elaborate designs that will better approximate the ideal counterfactual. In the case of the possible selection-by-history problem in the freshman ori-entation evaluation, for example, a treatment effect hypothe-sis would predict large treatment effects among freshman but no effects for upperclassmen who did not experience the program. In contrast, a history effect based on a publicized alcohol-related death would presumably lead to the predic-tion of comparable effects across all grade levels. Careful consideration of validity threats can lead to the development of quasi-experimental designs especially suited to how that threat might operate in that particular evaluation. Fourth, at-tention should be given not simply to the potential presence of a validity threat, such as selection or history, but to the likely magnitude of its effect. Past writings often seem to suggest a dichotomous, valid-or-invalid perspective. Thinking instead of the likely size of the effect of a validity threat can lead to more accurate conclusions about the effects of an intervention (Reichardt, 2002).

Analysis Techniques for Nonequivalent-Groups Designs

Discussion of quasi-experimentation sometimes includes detailed discussion of analysis procedures, such as ANCOVA, selection modeling, and propensity scores (Shadish et al., 2002). These (and other) techniques each have advocates who argue for them as a way to control for selection biases in nonequivalent-groups designs. ANCOVA controls statistically for initial differences, in essence matching individuals across treatment groups based on their pretest (or other initial scores) and essentially taking the average difference between the matched groups on the posttest as the estimate of the treatment effect. Measurement error in the pretest will introduce bias in these estimates (Reichardt, 1979), so *latent-variable structural-equations models* are sometimes used instead. These models use multiple measures of the construct thought to be responsible for any selection bias, and these measures are essentially factor analyzed in an effort to obtain an estimate of the latent variable that effectively is without measurement error. Latent-variable structural-equations models also nicely support the testing of mediational models. However, the validity of the estimates that result from these models depends on the accuracy and thoroughness of the model, and evaluators will rarely know enough to specify a model accurately. An alternative approach, known as *selection modeling,* typically requires the estimation of two equations. In essence, the first equation is designed to predict group membership (e.g., treatment or control), using variables that are thought to be related to the factors that determine selection into groups. In the second equation, treatment effects are estimated as usual, but with the addition of a new variable, which is a score taken from the first equation representing the best prediction of group membership. In a related approach, *propensity score analyses,* the predicted probability of being in the treatment (rather than the control) group is generated by a logistic regression. Cases are then usually stratified into subgroups (commonly five subgroups) based on their propensity scores, and the treatment effect computed as a weighted average based on the treatment and control-group means within each subgroup. Alternatively, the propensity score can be treated as a covariate in ANCOVA. Winship and Morgan (1999) provided a very useful review of several of these techniques, and several other recent sources are also valuable (e.g., Little & Rubin, 2000; Shadish et al., 2002; West, Biesanz, & Pitts, 2000).

No consensus exists yet regarding the preferable approach to statistical analysis for nonequivalent designs. Criticisms of each approach remain and are based on the assumptions, mostly untestable in practice, that are built into the methods. Three recommendations seem especially sensible for the analysis of the pretest-posttest nonequivalent-groups design. First, where possible, it is desirable to conduct sensitivity analyses, that is, analyses that assess how robust a given finding is to different assumptions within a single form of analysis (Rosenbaum, 1995). Second, confidence will be enhanced if different forms of analysis are employed and if the results converge reasonably well on some estimate of the treatment effect (e.g., Reynolds & Temple, 1995). Third, rather than relying exclusively on statistical adjustments, it is preferable to develop a stronger research design that better approximates the ideal but unattainable counterfactual comparison (Shadish et al., 2002).

TESTING MEDIATION: PROBING UNDERLYING GENERATIVE MECHANISMS

As noted in the previous discussion of randomized experiments, having a relatively strong counterfactual comparison does not necessarily result in findings that tell us anything about underlying mechanisms. We could observe, for instance, that a new freshman orientation program causes a reduction in student drinking, relative to a standard orientation program, and not gain any insights as to *why* the new program is more effective. As noted in the earlier section on underlying generative mechanisms, several advantages can result from increased knowledge about the processes that mediate a program's effects.

This is reflected in the attention that many methodologists and statisticians have given to the study of mediation, that is, to the causal chains that connect a cause and an effect. This has been a major focus in work on causal modeling, structural equation modeling, and similar methods (e.g., Baron & Kenny, 1986; Jöreskog & Sörbom, 1993; Kenny, Kashy, & Bolger, 1998). One approach to testing hypotheses about underlying generative mechanisms is to apply such methods in the context of a randomized experiment or quasi-experiment. In addition to the outcome variables of interest, potential mediators are measured, and relationships are assessed to test specific mediational models.

For example, an evaluation might test the impact of an experimental policy that reduces class size in selected grade school classrooms. The relevant theory may suggest that class size reductions improve student achievement because teachers in smaller classes spend more time on instruction and less time on discipline. Measures of these potential mediators can be taken, in addition to the outcome measures of interest (e.g., achievement test scores). If the mediational measures reveal that classroom processes change as expected, with a decline in time on discipline and an increase in time on instruction in the treatment classrooms, and if this change in the mediators can account statistically for (all or some) of the subsequent change in the outcome variables, then the mediational hypothesis would be supported. In addition, demonstrating an expected mediational path can also increase confidence that the difference between the treatment and control group is actually attributable to the treatment. This is because the treatment effect hypothesis specifically predicts the mediational pattern, but most validity threats, such as selection or selection maturation, usually would not.

Mediational tests are strongly recommended by many evaluators, including many of those who advocate theory-driven evaluation (e.g., Donaldson, in press). In fact, some evaluators and other researchers seem to equate the study of underlying mechanisms with the use of mediational tests through structural equation modeling (SEM) or other related methods. This is unfortunate for at least two reasons. First, these quantitative mediational methods, such as SEM, are not without limits (e.g., Freedman, 1987; Kenny et al., 1998). Second, there are alternative approaches that evaluators (and others) should consider.

Tests of moderated relationships can also be important for assessing underlying mechanisms. A moderated relationship is another name for a statistical interaction whereby the effect of a program varies as a function of some other variable. A hypothesized mediational process will often imply differential treatment effects. For example, a freshman orientation program may be expected to work by changing students' subjective norms about how much others at school drink. If so, effects should be lower for those freshman who have strongly held subjective norms (perhaps because of an older sibling) before starting college, compared to other freshman who are more uncertain in their subjective norms. If analyses are conducted to show that the program is less effective for those students who initially have strong subjective norms, we can have somewhat stronger confidence that changes in subjective norms actually are the mechanism that underlies the treatment effect.

In addition, in many instances in evaluation, evidence about underlying generative mechanisms will come from qualitative observation rather than from quantitative measures and statistical tests. Evaluators often employ qualitative methods, sometimes alone but often in conjunction with quantitative approaches such as randomized experiments and quasi-experiments. In some cases the causal path implied by

a program theory may be traced with qualitative observations and interviews, which can be used to assess whether the expected sequence of changes occurred. For example, rather than survey freshman about their subjective norms, in some instances one might have more open-ended interviews, with narrative reporting of representative views.

PRINCIPLED DISCOVERY: BUILDING KNOWLEDGE IN AN INUS WORLD

Evaluations often begin, implicitly at least, with a general form of hypothesis to be tested. For example, an evaluation might be motivated by the general hypothesis that a particular type of freshman orientation will cause a reduction in drinking, relative to no orientation (or relative to some alternative form of freshman orientation). The initial hypotheses may on occasion be somewhat more specific, indicating that the program will work better in some circumstances than in others (e.g., it may be expected that the freshman orientation will be less effective for incoming students who already drink heavily). In many (if not all) cases, however, the initial hypotheses will be woefully inadequate relative to the complexities and contingencies of a world of INUS causes. For the most part, our collective knowledge about social problems and their solutions is rather limited. How can evaluators hope to go beyond relatively simple initial hypotheses and try to fill in some of the missing knowledge about the rest of the causal package within which the program, as an INUS condition, has its effects? And how can they do this without being misled by chance findings that arise only because one has sifted through the data so much? Mark et al. (1998, 2000; Mark, 2001) used the term *principled discovery* to describe methods that can allow for discovery, via induction, of the complexities of an INUS world, but that are principled in the sense of subsequently being disciplined by other data.

The standard statistical models to which quantitatively trained evaluators are exposed in their training emphasize the testing of a priori hypotheses and understate the importance of discovery. As Tukey (1986) put it, "Exploration has been rather neglected; confirmation has been rather sanctified. Neither action is justifiable" (p. 822). Rosenthal (1994) cast the issue in stark terms: "Many of us have been taught that it is technically improper and perhaps even immoral to analyze and reanalyze our data in many ways (i.e., to snoop around in the data). We were taught to test the prediction with one particular preplanned test . . . and definitely not look further at our data. . . . [This] makes for bad science and for bad ethics" (Rosenthal, 1994, p. 130). Failure to explore one's data may especially be bad science and bad ethics in the context of evaluation, where any data set may be costly and difficult to obtain, and where failure to learn inductively may mean foregoing a valuable opportunity to create better or cheaper programs.

Principled discovery has two primary steps. First, the researcher carries out some exploratory analyses that may (a) demonstrate the contingent limits of a causal relationship (i.e., may identify moderators of the effect), (b) suggest an underlying mechanism, or (c) both. Second, the researcher then (a) replicates the initial finding, or, probably more likely in evaluation, (b) conducts a test of a theoretical implication of the new finding, or (c) both. It is important to note that these two steps of principled discovery can be carried out in conjunction with the traditional procedures used to test an a priori hypothesis. For example, one might test the effectiveness of a freshman orientation program using a random experiment or a quasi-experimental design, and also undertake principled discovery with the same data set.

The first step of principled discovery (i.e., the exploratory analyses through which discovery occurs) can be carried out in a wide variety of ways (Mark, 2001; Mark et al., 1998). Indeed, the methods of discovery are as varied as are the methods of systematic inquiry. A few examples should suffice. First, standard statistical techniques such as regression and ANCOVA can be used in an exploratory fashion (Tukey, 1977). In general, this would involve exploratory tests to try to find interactions. That is, one would use ANCOVA or another method to search for moderators of treatment effectiveness, where the potential moderating variables may consist of client characteristics, attributes of different sites where the program is administered, and aspects of the service delivery. The exploratory use of familiar techniques such as regression and ANCOVA may be the easiest approach to the first phase of principled discovery, but many other possibilities exist.

In a second technique for discovery, the exploratory data analyses of Tukey (1977; see also Behrens, 1997) can be used to discover possible moderators of program effects and, therefore, to guide informed speculation about underlying mechanisms. Even if not predicted in advance, the observation that larger effects cluster in one subgroup or in one setting should set off additional investigation and the search for the underlying mechanism that could account for the observed pattern of effects. A third (and conceptually related) method of discovery involves inspecting residuals from the original a priori hypothesis (e.g., the treatment–control group comparison). Based on the residuals, one may be able to identify sites or cases that have larger or smaller outcomes than would be expected from standard predictors. These extreme cases can be contrasted to see whether the variation in outcome appears to be associated with differences in types of

participants or in treatment implementation, relying perhaps on qualitative data from interviews or observations. This technique is analogous to the extreme case analysis employed by some qualitative researchers.

Fourth, in cases in which multilevel modeling is appropriate (e.g., Bryk & Raudenbush, 1992), similar exploratory analyses can be carried out to assess whether higher order variables moderate the treatment effect. For example, in a reading-intensive math program introduced to some but not all classes within several schools, one might use school-level variables to probe for possible moderators (e.g., Seltzer, 1994). Fifth, techniques for classification can be applied in an exploratory fashion. For example, one might use background data on clients in a cluster analysis to see if distinct groups of program clients emerge. If different subtypes of clients are found, one would then conduct additional analyses to see whether the program has differential effects across the client categories. If differential effects are observed, this may in turn lead to new hypotheses about causal mechanisms.

In these and numerous other ways, evaluators can attempt to discover possible variations in treatment effectiveness (see Mark, 2001, and Mark et al., 1998, for more specific methods that can be used for discovery). Based on any observed variations in treatment effectiveness, the evaluator would also attempt to identify possible underlying mechanisms that would generate the discovered patterns of effects. This attempt to identify mechanisms that could account for the discovery might be carried out in conjunction with content area specialists and program staff and stakeholders, which may especially be important if the evaluator has limited content expertise. Of course, an evaluator could stop there. The evaluation report could describe the tests carried out to test the original hypothesis, and then describe the discovery-oriented tests and findings, perhaps with caveats added that the latter work was exploratory and that the findings should be treated as hypotheses that should subsequently be tested in future research. This approach, which may be suitable in basic research, is generally problematic in the context of evaluation. Decisions about a program usually cannot be deferred until after a second evaluation is finished. Indeed, resources may not be available for another major evaluation. In short, the conventional call for future research may be inadequate as a response to discoveries in the context of evaluation. In part, this is because it can be difficult to persuade the consumers of evaluation reports to give the findings of exploratory research the same degree of uncertainty that a researcher thinks is appropriate. The people who will use the evaluation are likely to generate explanatory accounts for any exploratory findings, and these self-generated theories may influence their subsequent actions.

One reason it is dangerous for evaluation consumers to act on an unexpected discovery is that when a discovery occurs, chance generally exists as a plausible alternative explanation (perhaps along with other plausible alternative explanations). The problem that multiple tests may lead to chance findings is sometimes referred to as *multiplicity*. According to Diaconis (1985), "Multiplicity is one of the most prominent difficulties with data-analytic procedures. Roughly speaking, if enough different statistics are computed, some of them will be sure to show structure" (p. 9), that is, to seem to contain something systematic. Or as Stigler (1987, p. 148) put it more metaphorically, "Beware of testing too many hypotheses; the more you torture the data, the more likely they are to confess, but confession obtained under duress may not be admissible in the court of scientific opinion." In the court of evaluation use, the potential problem is that a confession obtained under duress may actually convince the jury but that it should not be convincing without independent collaboration.

Thus, the second step of principled discovery is needed. In essence, this step calls for subjecting any discovery to replication or some other tests. Replication of course is widely recommended as the ideal way to "discipline" discoveries. Replication can in fact be valuable and in certain respects is the preferred way to ensure that a discovery is real and not due to chance or other artifact. On the other hand, replication may not be feasible in evaluation before decisions must be made. Evaluations are often costly and time consuming. It may be politically infeasible to delay action until after a replication has been done. Likewise, in evaluation, costs will generally preclude replication via cross-validation with a split sample (in which discoveries are sought through exploratory analyses in half the sample and then verified in the other half); there are, however, some cases in which evaluation involves large data sets, and cross-validation with a split sample is the ideal disciplining in such instances.

Even if replication is possible in a particular case, ambiguities in causal inference can exist if both the replication and the original evaluation include some unrecognized validity threat that is responsible for the original "discovery." For example, if a selection artifact plagues both evaluations, the replication of a finding may simply be spurious. It can also be difficult, in planning a replication, to decide which aspects of the program services, clientele, and so on should be held constant and which should be allowed to vary.

In the absence of replication, the second step of principled discovery will usually require that other tests be carried out within the same data set. In general, this will require some theory development to undergird the choice of new tests. Although replication enables what might be called black-box disciplining, whereby a finding is confirmed without additional conceptualization, in general other forms of disciplining require theory development. This strategy is illustrated well by what Julnes (1995) calls the *context-confirmatory approach*. In brief, under this approach an empirical discovery (e.g., the discovery of differential effects across subgroups on a key outcome) is used to infer an underlying mechanism. This newly induced mechanism is then used to generate a distinct prediction that should be true *if* the mechanism is operating. This new prediction is then tested using different variables in the same data set.

Julnes (1995) illustrated the context-confirmatory approach in an evaluation of a "resource mother" program, in which staff provided support to new single mothers. In the a priori, planned test that compared program clients' outcomes with those of a comparison group, Julnes found that the program was effective on average. In the discovery phase of the inquiry, exploration revealed that the effects were larger for older than for younger mothers. Julnes then posited that younger mothers' needs were more tangible and task oriented, and not necessarily met by the resource mothers, who often were providing primarily emotional support. To further test this new account, Julnes differentiated the support mothers on the basis of the extent to which they provided tangible support versus emotional support. Subsequent tests confirmed that, as expected, the program was especially ineffective for younger mothers when the support mothers emphasized emotional support.

As another example, imagine an evaluation of a boot camp program for criminal offenders. The overall evaluation design might involve comparing the effects of the boot camp program relative to traditional sentences. If the initial program theory is lacking, as it is likely to be, one should also carry out more exploratory analyses in service of discovery. Suppose that with these exploratory analyses it was discovered that compared to the traditional criminal justice system, the boot camp program reduces recidivism for offenders with minor criminal records but not for offenders with more severe records. From that finding, the evaluator might then generate an explanatory hypothesis, say, that the mechanism underlying the program is "labeling." That is, the boot camp may help prevent minor offenders from being labeled, by themselves and by others, as criminals. Based on the newly hypothesized potential mechanism, the evaluator would then develop another hypothesis, such as that controlling for offense, the program will be more effective for younger than for older offenders because the younger ones will be less likely to have strong labels as criminals.

At this point the disciplining of the original discovery and the associated explanatory account would move to the foreground. In the context of the disciplining step, it is important also to identify any alternative mechanisms—whether drawn from the literature, program staff, clients, or direct observation—that could account for the observed pattern of effects. For example, the original discovery might arise because of motivation or increased work skills instead of labeling. The evaluator's task then would be to find and test predictions that can differentiate among these alternative mechanisms. For example, a simple labeling mechanism would presumably imply that the difference between younger and older offenders should be similar at all sites. On the other hand, if the underlying mechanism involved the acquisition of work skills, the age difference is likely to depend in predictable ways on the specific activities that are carried out at each site to teach work skills.

Some other strategies can be used for the disciplining step of principled discovery. In some cases, the evaluator can add additional measures midway through an evaluation to test the explanatory account generated to explain a discovery. Evaluation contracts often require interim reports. Some exploratory work can be carried out for an interim report, and any discoveries made can guide the selection of new measures. In other cases, a discovery might suggest a more specific test, with the increased specificity of the second test providing greater confidence that the original discovery was not the result of chance. Imagine, for example, that initial exploratory tests reveal that an intervention was more effective when clients and therapists were matched on some background variable, such as parental socioeconomic status (SES), represented simply as low SES and high SES in the initial exploratory testing. This discovery could be disciplined to some extent by carrying out a more specific test of the matching hypothesis, with finer gradations of SES, and with the prediction not only that outcomes will be better when client and therapist match but also that outcomes should decline the worse the match (see Abelson & Prentice, 1997, on contrast coding for such a test).

Principled discovery is valuable because it can help fill in the missing information about the contingencies of an INUS world while reducing the likelihood of being misled by chance findings. Moreover, although the preceding discussion may suggest a sharp dichotomy between principled discovery and traditional a priori hypothesis testing, the two can and often should be integrated in practice. As the Julnes (1995) example suggests, tests of a priori hypotheses can be conducted virtually consecutively with the exploratory step of principled discovery. In addition, although the present discussion has focused on the use of principled discovery to learn about the causal contingencies of an INUS world, principled discovery can also be used to complement the causal analysis methods that are used to assess the overall effects of a program or policy. In particular, some evaluations include a large number of outcome variables, and chance is a plausible explanation when significant differences are obtained on a limited set of outcome measures. The disciplining techniques (of the second step of principled discovery) can help increase—or decrease—confidence that the observed differences are meaningful.

Despite its potential benefits, important practical limits will often apply to principled discovery. First, existing data sets may not include the additional variables needed to conduct a strong test of a new explanatory account. If Julnes (1995) did not have information on service providers, for example, he could not have tested to see whether the treatment was especially ineffective when younger clients received services from resource mothers who emphasized emotional support. Second, statistical power to detect moderator effects may be lacking (Cohen, 1988; McClelland & Judd, 1993). Third, a single validity threat may be shared across the test that provided the initial discovery and the test used to discipline it. Fourth, the potentially complex nature of causality can make the relevant patterns difficult to detect. Mackie's INUS notion raises our awareness that more than one mechanism may be operating simultaneously. Different mechanisms may be operating for different subgroups of clients, or in different circumstances (a condition that Baron & Kenny, 1986, called *moderated mediation*). Although such complexities do not render principled discovery invalid or useless, they may make it more complex. Finally, some aspects of principled discovery as a research strategy are not yet well developed. For instance, it would be useful to have user-friendly procedures for specifying the degree to which a new test is independent of the original discovery. Despite these limitations, principled discovery can be a valuable approach for evaluation, aiding in identifying the rest of the causal package required for a program to work effectively while minimizing false leads that otherwise would arise due to chance.

OTHER METHODS FOR EVALUATION

As previously noted, causal methods will often be the most appropriate methods for evaluation because people need to know what (if any) effects a program has in order to gauge its value. Nevertheless, a wide range of other methods can also be used in evaluation, and there are conditions under which methods other than causal ones are most appropriate. Sometimes evaluators use methods for classification, such as when Kuhn and Culhane (1998) used cluster analysis to identify different types of homeless people. Sometimes evaluators may assist in needs assessments to advise in decisions about whether some new program is needed (Scriven & Roth, 1978). Sometimes evaluators, especially those trained in economics, carry out cost-benefit analyses that, as the name implies, are designed to compare the cost of a program with the estimated benefits.

An increasingly important kind of method for evaluators has come to be known as *performance measurement.* Performance measurement refers to a set of techniques used to measure and record characteristics of the inputs, services, clients, and increasingly the postprogram status of clients on some outcome variables. Performance measurement has been a growth industry in recent years for evaluators and those working in allied areas (Newcomer, 1997). In the public sector, this is because of the Government Performance and Results Act (GPRA) of 1993, which effectively mandates performance measurement in all United States. Performance measurement has been booming in agencies outside of government. In the case of nonprofit agencies, this has been stimulated largely by the requirements of the United Way (Newcomer, 1997).

Although a variety of data sources may be used in performance measurement systems, often the central task is the development of administrative databases. These databases can record a variety of program-related variables ranging from inputs (e.g., budgetary receipts) to short- and long-term outcome indicators (e.g., the health status of clients). Wholey (in press) persuasively illustrated the potential value of using performance measurement systems to inform what he and others call *results-oriented management.* Wholey offered the example of the U.S. Coast Guard, which used a new performance measurement system to discover a surprisingly high fatality rate among commercial towing crews. They then developed interventions targeted specifically at the towing industry. A dramatic decline in fatalities followed, offering a compelling illustration of the potential for performance measurement systems to guide organizational management.

Despite successes such as that of the Coast Guard, there are a number of concerns about performance measurement systems and, correspondingly, about the results-oriented management movement (e.g., Mark, Henry, & Julnes, 2000, chap. 7; Perrin, 1998). One significant concern is whether the complex outcomes that are the target of many programs can be represented adequately by the kinds of indicators that can be repeatedly measured over time in a performance measurement system. A case in point involves the current controversy over the adequacy of standardized tests as measures of learning in primary and secondary schools. A related problem involves the potential for the corruption of indicators and for goal displacement. For example, in the context of high-stakes educational testing, in which test results can determine whether an individual student passes on to the next grade level and whether a local school is taken over by the state, concerns arise about whether teachers are "teaching to the test" rather than more broadly educating their students.

Another potential problem with performance measurement systems is the inability in most cases to draw confident causal inference that the program, rather than other causal forces, is responsible for any observed improvement (or decline) in performance over time. Even though clients' posttreatment standing on outcomes variables may be measured in a performance measurement system, it will generally not be possible to attribute those outcomes to the program. In a sense, performance measurement systems, as commonly used, incorporate at best a weak quasi-experimental design. Of course, knowing that a client has achieved a specific health status after treatment does not mean that the treatment *caused* an improvement in health. Performance measurement systems often provide no control group at all, or at best a quite noncomparable comparison group, and relatively little attention has been given to methods for correcting for selection bias in the context of performance measurement systems.

On the other hand, some recent work has been directed at integrating standard tools for causal analysis, including quasi-experimental design (Harkreader & Henry, 2000) and mediational analysis (Scheirer, 2000), with the use of performance measurement systems. Moreover, performance measurement systems can be useful for program management, even in the absence of strong causal inferences. For example, managers can identify areas where service delivery is relatively low and make adjustments accordingly. In addition, in some contexts, unambiguous attribution of effects to a program may not be required to decide whether things seem to be going in the right direction. Causal analyses can contribute greatly to an assessment of the merit or worth of a program, but at some points in the policymaking and funding process, all that people need to know is whether things are so broke that they need to be fixed. Performance measurement systems should generally suffice for judgments of this kind. In this sense program evaluators need to be policy analytic, thinking about what type of information is needed to contribute maximally to social betterment in light of the information needs of the moment. (See Mark, Henry, & Julnes, 2000, for a planning framework that begins with an analysis of the policy context, generates from that an evaluation purpose, and moves from that—plus an assessment of the degree of methodological rigor required in light of information needs—to a selection of methods.) As part of this planning process, the evaluator needs to consider alternative ways to arrive at the questions that will guide an evaluation.

WHERE SHOULD EVALUATION QUESTIONS COME FROM?

In most psychological research, the driving questions come from theory, from past research, and from the investigator's interests. These are the primary sources of the independent and dependent variables of most basic research, for example. In some cases, evaluators can safely rely on the same sources for the driving questions in an evaluation. For instance, imagine a theory-driven but multicomponent program designed to reduce conduct disorder. The evaluator who chooses to rely on past research to identify outcome measures of conduct disorder and related outcomes would probably not be subject to much criticism. But in many cases, the decisions about the driving questions in an evaluation are not so simple. If you are going to evaluate a preschool program, do the relevant outcomes involve the children's academic skills, their social skills, their affective regulation, the parent's employment, their satisfaction, the magnitude of the achievement gap between children of high and low SES parents, longer term outcomes such as the children's retention in school, delinquency, and employment, or something else altogether? Although it may be possible to measure many outcomes in an evaluation, resource constraints will usually preclude measuring *all* possible outcomes. So how are evaluators to try to identify the driving questions in an evaluation?

Evaluators have tried out many different strategies for doing this (for more detailed reviews of the alternative strategies, see House, 1980, 1993; Mark, Henry, & Julnes, 2000; Patton, 1997). Many early evaluators looked to *explicit program goals*. On the face of it, this approach seems sensible. If a program is supposed to do X, shouldn't the evaluator try to see if in fact it does X? In practice, however, this approach is riddled with problems. Formal statements about program goals may provide a very flawed guide. In some cases, advocates may have oversold what a program might reasonably accomplish in order to acquire political support for the program. Where support was initially strong, program documents may "set the sights low" to increase the likelihood that the program will be considered a success. Some of the program's objectives may be left out of formal policy statements to reduce controversy. Others may be missing because goals change or emerge over time. Formal statements probably do not include side effects that can be critical to judging a program's merit and worth. Thus, for a variety of reasons, formal statements do not provide a compelling map that can guide evaluation questions—although evaluators should of course consult these documents during the planning phase of an evaluation.

Instead of formal goals, some evaluation theorists have suggested that evaluators should focus on *needs* as a guide to specifying evaluation questions (e.g., Scriven, 1993; Scriven & Roth, 1978). This approach may seem eminently sensible: Why not develop evaluation questions to assess a program in terms of the most important human needs that it is meant to address? For example, why not identify the basic human needs that preschool programs may address and then evaluate the program in terms of how well it meets those needs. Again, though, problems arise. First, it is not so easy to identify, or even to define, human needs. For example, are programs for gifted children really directed at any *needs,* or do they involve enrichment well beyond basic needs? In addition, how easy is it to determine what needs a program (e.g., a preschool intervention) does or should address? Second, our conception of needs, both in general and in terms of a given program, may change over time. The history of day care and preschool evaluations presents a striking example. Although early evaluations focused on cognitive skills, it became clear over time that policy makers and the public were also interested in social outcomes, such as staying on grade and avoiding assignment to special education (Zigler & Muenchow, 1992). Third, it can be quite difficult to establish priorities across different needs. Which is more important as a need that universal preschool might meet—increases in traditional academic skills, enhanced social development, decreases in dropout rates, improvements in parents' SES? In short, although it may seem sensible to use needs as a guide to evaluation questions, and although it is reasonable for evaluators to think about needs when identifying evaluation questions, this approach faces important problems.

Another alternative that some evaluators have considered is to use *program theory* as a guide to direct evaluation questions (e.g., Bickman, 1987; Chen, 1990). The idea is to construct, based on local program ideas, general social science theory, or both, a kind of theoretical model of program activities, processes, and outcomes. This program theory would then be used to help guide the evaluation, such as in the choice of outcome measures (e.g., Bickman, 1987; Chen, 1990). Despite the potential usefulness of program theory, theory can also have some undesirable consequences (e.g., Greenwald, Pratkanis, Leippe, & Baumgardner, 1986). Using theory to guide evaluation design is unlikely to be harmful if one's theory is fully correct. But theories are usually only partially correct at best, and the theory-driven evaluation may exclude important outcome measures that the (imperfect) theory did not specify, ignore possible mediators other than those specified in the theory, and fail to search for important moderators of the program's success. Strong adherence to a program theory can even lead one to misinterpret results or overgeneralize conclusions (Greenwald et al., 1986). In addition, just as formal goals may sometimes be set for public relations purposes, so too can the rationale that underlies a program theory. For instance, manufacturing extension programs are based on a theory involving what economists call *market failure,* meaning that the market does not provide certain services that small manufacturers supposedly need. But it is unclear whether this is truly the theoretical justification or just part of a rationale that is required to justify funding (Feller, 1997). Another potentially serious problem comes into better focus once one realizes that there are often fairly different theories that can be applied to a given program. These competing theories may even highlight different outcomes. Whose program theory is to dominate the design of an evaluation?

Indeed, many evaluators have suggested that evaluation should look directly to *stakeholder input,* that is, to the opinions of various interested parties, to find the guiding questions for an evaluation (e.g., Bryk, 1983; Weiss, 1983). Views have differed as to whether one stakeholder group or another should be given a predominant voice. Some have suggested that stakeholders should be involved because they are influential in decision making (see Patton, 1997, and Wholey, 1994), or alternatively because of a desire to give standing to those without voice in the formal policymaking processes (see House, 1995). Although stakeholder involvement is both appropriate and valuable, stakeholder approaches are limited. First, they do not provide guidance about how to differentiate mere stakeholder preferences from stronger needs or values—or even tell evaluators whether this is important. Second, the nature of stakeholder involvement is often unclear, in terms of who should be considered a stakeholder and how they should be involved. Third, stakeholder involvement usually omits the public (Henry, 1996; Henry & Julnes, 1998; Mark, Henry, & Julnes, 2000) despite the important role the public plays in democratic systems—including their holding a stake in public programs as the party that pays the bill.

By helping to clarify the views that stakeholders have about programs and policies, stakeholder involvement is one method to guide evaluation questions. But other methods, which fall under the general rubric of what Mark et al. (2000) called *values inquiry,* can also go somewhat further. Values inquiry refers to attempts to identify the values positions relevant to social programs and policies and to infuse them into evaluations. But what are values? Values can be defined simply as normative beliefs, that is, deeply held beliefs about how things should be. Values may be deeply held and tend to be relatively enduring. At the same time, values must also be subject to reason and must be changeable for democracies to work and for social betterment to occur (Richardson, 1997). In the context of evaluating social programs, the most relevant values

are beliefs about what society's responsibilities are and how government should act. For some people, for example, the belief that government should provide for a decent standard of living after retirement is a strongly held value. Also relevant are the values that people would use to judge the success or failure of a given program. For instance, would the parents of young children see a preschool program as a failure if it did not enhance academic outcomes but promoted social skills?

The concept of values can help in sorting out some of the problems that occur when evaluators try to select evaluation questions. Take the case of an evaluator trying to choose outcome variables based on an analysis of needs. As previously noted, needs can emerge over time and can exceed the minimum required to avoid malfunction. Examined from the perspective of values, it can be argued that perceived needs emerge as values change. Perceived needs can exceed minimums, as in the case of special educational opportunities for talented youth, because of shared values. Bringing values into the picture also helps evaluators to sort out criteria when there are too many to examine, and to make sense if a program meets one perceived need but creates another. When there are too many criteria to examine them all, the most important ones to examine, presumably, are those that are most highly valued. When a program meets one need but creates another, its judged worth depends in large part on the relative importance of the values associated with each need.

Systematic values inquiry can help alleviate some of the more serious problems that have previously been identified with the use of stakeholder input as a guide to evaluation decisions (Greene, 1988; Henry & Julnes, 1998; Mark & Shotland, 1985). As noted earlier, one of the problems with traditional stakeholder approaches is that the public is usually neglected as a stakeholder, even though the public is in fact a stakeholder for any publicly funded program, and even though the public effectively sets the direction for many changes in public policy over time. Methods for values inquiry exist that readily allow the public a role in providing input. For example, sample surveys allow evaluators to assess what kinds of outcomes the public would find most important. Focus groups and other group-process techniques (Krueger, 1994) may allow more detailed consideration and exploration of the values of a small sample of the public.

Another problem with stakeholder approaches in practice is that the choices that are made, and even more so the rationale for making them, are often not reported. These become part of the implicit evaluation process rather than part of the explicit evaluation findings. With systematic values inquiry, stakeholder input is construed as an early finding of the evaluation. When stakeholder input is clearly reported as a finding, the consequence is a kind of transparency about how the key decisions (e.g., the choice of outcome measures) were made. Such transparency in turn is very useful for the purpose of accountability.

Several different methods can be used for systematic values inquiry. As already noted, the views of the public can be examined in sample surveys. For example, one can ask a random sample of voters to rate or rank the importance of a set of possible outcomes of preschool programs. Special population surveys can be conducted to obtain the views of more specialized stakeholder groups (e.g., college administrators could be surveyed to identify what they see as the most valued outcomes of freshman orientation programs). In place of (or in addition to) surveys, group interviews can be held. The relevant group methods are sometimes discussed under the banner of focus groups (Krueger, 1994). Such group interviews may allow more in-depth and detailed assessment of values, including perhaps more thoughtful consideration of tradeoffs across different values. More intense group methods can also be implemented in an attempt to simulate dialog and deliberation across members of different stakeholder groups (House & Howe, 1999), perhaps to try to achieve consensus among the varying groups. In addition, critical review or the application of some formal theory, such as Rawlsian or feminist analysis, might be undertaken to try to identify submerged values issues. For instance, a feminist analysis of a freshman orientation program might indicate inadequate attention to issues of sexual assault (for more details on these and other methods of systematic values inquiry, see Mark, Henry, & Julnes, 2000).

Of course, systematic values inquiry does not magically tell us which questions should drive an evaluation. Just as the original stakeholder-input approach is plagued with the question of how to weight the views of different stakeholders, the values inquiry approach faces the challenge of weighting the reported values of different stakeholders. If disparate value positions are found in a given evaluation, one response is to engage in *more* values inquiry (Mark, Henry, & Julnes, 2000). For example, if survey results show discrepant values across stakeholder groups, then subsequent group discussions with representatives of each stakeholder group might be undertaken to see if some degree of consensus could be achieved in light of the specific empirical evidence about the value positions of each stakeholder group.

Many of the other pragmatic problems that apply to stakeholder input apply also to values inquiry. The identification of who should participate in values inquiry, and the difficulties of successfully recruiting them, are as challenging for values inquiry as for older forms of stakeholder involvement. One important difference, however, comes in the position,

intrinsic within the values inquiry approach, that the procedures and findings of values inquiry should explicitly be reported. When these aspects of the evaluation planning process are reported, any potential bias affecting the subsequent selection of evaluation questions should be more apparent. Moreover, the process underlying the selection of the driving questions in an evaluation can be debated, and the result of this process can be challenged with the same level of rigor as for other aspects of research. Without the transparency advocated by values inquiry, the evaluator in a sense can wrap him- or herself in the cloak of stakeholder participation, with no external accountability for how well stakeholder inquiry was conducted or translated into evaluation questions. By increasing the degree of rigor in the stakeholder input processes and by providing transparent reporting of stakeholder procedures and findings, the values inquiry approach holds some promise of improving the way that the driving questions for an evaluation are selected.

In short, although it will still be important to think about program goals, client needs, and program theory, several different methods for values inquiry can be used to help guide the questions asked in an evaluation, including the question of which outcome variables should be measured. The argument for the use of systematic values inquiry is probably strongest for evaluations of publicly funded programs. Of course, evaluation also takes place in the private sector, as in the fairly widespread evaluation of training programs for employees. An argument can be made that values inquiry still fits well, at least for those private-sector firms that subscribe to contemporary business philosophy. Recent schools of thought in business management often include efforts to reduce hierarchical structure in organizations, initiatives to empower frontline employees as participants in decision making, reconceptualizations of consumers and the public as stakeholders, and efforts to realize values other than the bottom line. Businesses that take such an approach may be responsive to systematic values inquiry. Indeed, some experience suggests that systematic inquiry into different stakeholder groups' perspectives is worthwhile even in the case of training evaluation in the private sector (Michalski & Cousins, 2001). On the other hand, in principle private-sector owners and managers can choose to ignore some stakeholders with impunity. In at least some instances, evaluators may work more efficiently by focusing on Patton's (1997) notion of intended use by intended users, rather than on systematic values inquiry involving a range of stakeholders. Indeed, in some private-sector contexts the process of identifying key evaluation questions may actually simplify to the use of formal program goals or judged needs as a guide to evaluation.

FUTURE DIRECTIONS

The area of program and policy development has, to some extent, been a fertile area for those trying to advance statistical analysis (e.g., Rubin, 1974) and research design (e.g., Shadish et al., 2002). The potential exists for significant future developments. Among the areas where future developments are needed are the following four.

First, the theory and techniques of values inquiry is a fertile ground for additional work. Values inquiry is a relatively recent offshoot of stakeholder approaches. Additional experience is needed both to refine the specific methods of values inquiry and to gain experience about how well the general values inquiry approach works in practice.

Second, conceptual and methodological developments are needed to help us specify what constitutes a given program or type of program (Lipsey, 2001). Typically, we define programs in terms of either (a) a common funding stream (e.g., all local sites funded through Head Start are called "Head Start") or (b) claims that program staff are following some named program (e.g., regardless of the funding source, drug prevention offerings in schools are called DARE, for Drug Abuse Resistance Training, if police officers are involved). But how much deviation should be allowed, and on which dimensions of service delivery, among the activities of local sites while still justifying use of the same program name? For example, should a local school's drug prevention activities be called DARE if someone other than a police officer serves as the program staff? How far can a police officer vary from the DARE curriculum and still have it constitute an instance of DARE? In essence, the fundamental question is, How do we decide that two specific cases are instances of the same category? A related question is, In a world of hierarchically embedded categories, how do we decide which level of categorization is more important? For example, should we be concerned about whether a local school's activity is an instance of DARE or of the more inclusive category, "resistance skills training approaches to drug use prevention"? Further work on how to define the program could have beneficial effects outside of evaluation because similar questions about how to define constructs abound in the social and behavioral sciences.

Third, there is need for the development of better methods for rigorous estimates of the effects of everyday programs (Lipsey, 2001). As Lipsey noted, it appears that, at least in some policy areas, most of the rigorous causal evaluations are directed at demonstration projects—interventions specially set up in order to test their effects—rather than at everyday, ongoing programs. Demonstration programs can facilitate the use of random assignment, for example, in a way that is rarely

the case for everyday, ongoing programs. In part, improving methods to evaluate everyday, ongoing programs will probably involve continued enhancement and refinement of methods for controlling for selection bias. In part, this may involve additional work on the pragmatic problems that can limit the implementation of rigorous methods, including randomized experiments. Other, more creative approaches may also need to be developed.

Fourth, evaluation practice may be enhanced in the future by the development of better methods for combining evidence from different kinds of methods. Although this chapter has focused on the conduct of individual evaluations, the cumulation of evidence from multiple evaluations is critical in order to draw the best possible inferences to guide actions. Meta-analyses of evaluations have become relatively commonplace since Smith and Glass's (1977) seminal work (Lipsey & Wilson, 1993). Meta-analytic techniques, however, are limited in terms of their ability to combine vastly different kinds of evidence that may be obtained either within or across evaluations. These may be quantitative estimates of a program's effects, on the one hand, and qualitative evidence, on the other. Some work has been carried out on cumulating diverse kinds of evidence (e.g., Droitcour, Silberman, & Chelimsky, 1993), but further advances would be welcome.

In addition to these four areas of prospective methodological developments, the practice of evaluation will likely face some challenges in the near future. Two potential challenges stand out. Although these are distinguishable concerns, they may have a common solution.

The first challenge involves recent disagreements about the proper role of stakeholders in the conduct of evaluation. There is a visible trend in one recent stream of evaluation theory that involves a focus on a high level of direct stakeholder participation in the evaluation. This work has occurred under such labels as empowerment, participatory, inclusive, and transformative evaluation (e.g., Fetterman, 2000; Mertens, 1999). Although distinct in some ways, these approaches all give a central emphasis to stakeholder participation in evaluation. Indeed, authors writing under these banners sometimes seem to claim that an evaluation is intrinsically flawed if it is not driven by stakeholders, often by some specific stakeholder group favored by that approach, such as program clients or the disadvantaged. These approaches take stakeholder involvement both as necessary and as an intrinsic good, and many of them seem to suggest that stakeholder involvement should be at a high level throughout the evaluation. Indeed, some recent authors seem to be suggesting that stakeholder dialogue *comprises* evaluation, while others suggest that the professional evaluator's role is that of a consultant to help stakeholders directly carry out all stages of an evaluation. In contrast, other streams of contemporary evaluation theory and practice view stakeholder participation as beneficial, but as instrumental to other evaluation activities and to evaluation use rather than as an intrinsic and necessary good. In addition, while the empowerment and transformative literature emphasizes stakeholder process, the rest of the field emphasizes evaluation findings.

A second potential challenge involves the role of evaluation relative to several related endeavors in service of organizational learning. Several evaluators have suggested that evaluation needs to merge with routine organizational learning and quality improvement methods (Fetterman, 2001; Torres & Preskill, 2001). The long-term challenge raised by this perspective involves whether the practice of evaluation will exist separately, or will instead be subsumed by tools of industrial engineering or quality improvement. As even advocates of integration of evaluation and organizational learning recognize (e.g., Torres & Preskill, 2001), it may be important that evaluation as a practice area is not simply subsumed within these other endeavors. Continuous quality improvement and organizational learning approaches may emphasize ongoing adjustments in organizational practices in order to try to achieve incremental improvements. Although this kind of work certainly has its place, the field of evaluation, as generally practiced by psychologists, also holds in high regard the kind of causal methods that can be used to assess the overall merit and worth of programs and policies. The experience of DARE is illuminating. In the last two decades DARE has come to be widely used as a drug abuse prevention program in schools. A series of evaluations, mostly using quasi-experimental designs, have demonstrated that DARE was not effective and in some circumstances may actually backfire. Attention to underlying mechanisms helped to explain the null and occasional negative effects: By emphasizing the prevalence of drug use, DARE inadvertently made drug use seem to be normative, as something that people generally do and accept. Based on the results of these cause-probing evaluations, major funding has been provided to carry out a complete reformulation of the DARE program. If the evaluation of DARE had focused on organizational learning and continuous quality improvement, the risk is that the evaluation results would have amounted to, as the expression goes, rearranging deck chairs on the Titanic.

In essence, these two challenges—sorting out the proper role of stakeholder participation and defining the role of other forms of evaluation relative to organizational learning and quality improvement—point to the same long-term need. It is a need to develop usable frameworks to try to help evaluators, funders, and stakeholders make reasoned judgments about what kind of evaluation activities are appropriate at a given time in a specific context. Sometimes the methods of causal analysis are appropriate, but certainly not in all cases. In fact, given the complexity, cost, and challenges of rigorous causal methods, it is important not to assume that they should be at the center of all evaluations. Sometimes performance measurement systems are appropriate. Sometimes stakeholder dialogue may be exactly what is needed. Sometimes continuous quality improvement and organizational learning techniques should be at the fore. Sometimes one or another combination of these approaches is called for. Although a case could be made that the field of evaluation should endorse a diversity of approaches and "let a thousand flowers bloom," this would provide precious little direction to those who must commission evaluations (and to those who must conduct them). Thus, theories and conceptual frameworks that aid in making choices among the many available evaluation options will prove increasingly important in the future (see Mark, Henry, & Julnes, 2000, for a tentative and partial framework of this sort).

SUMMARY AND CONCLUSIONS

Evaluation in general aims to provide information about policies and programs with the hope that the information can be used to help make things better. For the kinds of policy and programs psychologists evaluate, the question of effects—of the difference the policy or program makes on valued outcomes—is often central. Accordingly, in this chapter considerable attention has been given to the methods for causal analysis that can be used in evaluation. These methods can be used to approximate the ideal counterfactual in order to estimate a program's effects, to study mediation in order to try to understand the underlying mechanisms through which the program may have its effects, and to probe the moderators of program effectiveness in order to fill in the gaps in our knowledge of an INUS world. When a program's effects are estimated (e.g., with a randomized experiment or the best available quasi-experiment), interested parties can better judge the program's value and decide whether to continue its funding.

But the knowledge of causal methods does not suffice for evaluation practice. Unlike basic research, where research questions reasonably derive from theory and researcher interest, and unlike much applied research, where a sponsor's interests may reasonably guide the research question, the selection of the driving questions in an evaluation can be relatively challenging. Especially for publicly funded policies and programs, there are likely to be competing stakeholders, including the public, who may have differing values and perspectives. Values inquiry, with its emphasis on systematic methods for assessing stakeholder views and on explicit reporting to enhance transparency and accountability, is a promising approach for guiding the choice of evaluation questions. Values inquiry is also one of several promising areas where methodological and theoretical developments are desirable and may be expected in the foreseeable future.

The policies and programs that psychologists and others evaluate are intended to make a positive difference in people's lives. They may be designed, for example, to reduce prejudice (Aronson et al., 1978), to improve the educational attainment of children (Zigler & Muenchow, 1992), and to improve individuals' psychological well-being (Smith & Glass, 1977). But the good intentions of program designers do not automatically translate into effective programs. Thus there is a need for evaluation. High-quality evaluation can contribute in many ways. Ineffective programs can be identified and alternatives developed (as in the case of DARE). Effective programs, on the other hand, can be identified and support for them increased. Underlying mechanisms can be demonstrated, opening up the possibilities of more effective and more efficient interventions. The contextual complexities, that is, the moderators of effectiveness in an INUS world, can be identified, thereby raising the prospect of better targeting interventions to those cases where they are most likely to be effective. In all these and other ways, the ultimate goal of evaluation is to improve the capacity of policies and programs to achieve their intended ends to improve people's lives. If evaluation can achieve this goal, even in some degree, it is no small accomplishment.

REFERENCES

Abelson, R. P., & Prentice, D. A. (1997). Contrast tests of interaction hypotheses. *Psychological Methods, 2,* 315–328.

Alstead, M., Campsmith, M., Halley, C. S., Hartfield, K., Goldbaum, G., & Wood, R. W. (1999). Developing, implementing, and evaluating a condom promotion program targeting sexually active adolescents. *AIDS Education & Prevention, 11*(6), 497–512.

Aronson, E., Blaney, N., Stephan, C., Sikes, J., & Snapp, M. (1978). *The jigsaw classroom.* Beverly Hills, CA: Sage.

Baron, R. M., & Kenny, D. A. (1986). The moderator-mediator variable distinction in social psychological research: Conceptual, strategic, and statistical considerations. *Journal of Personality and Social Psychology, 51,* 1173–1182.

Behrens, J. T. (1997). Principles and procedures of exploratory data analysis. *Psychological Methods, 2,* 131–160.

Bentler, P. M. (1992). *EQS structural equations program manual.* Los Angeles: BMDP Statistical Software.

Bickman, L. (Ed.). (1987). *Using program theory in evaluation* (New Directions for Program Evaluation, No. 33). San Francisco: Jossey-Bass.

Borkovec, T. D., & Ruscio, A. (2001). Psychotherapy for generalized anxiety disorder. *The Journal of Clinical Psychiatry, 62*(Supplement 11), 37–42.

Boruch, R. E. (1997). *Randomized experiments for planning and evaluation: A practical guide.* Thousand Oaks, CA: Sage.

Boruch, R. E., & Wothke, W. (Eds.). (1985). *Randomization and field experimentation.* San Francisco: Jossey-Bass.

Braucht, G. N., & Reichardt, C. S. (1993). A computerized approach to trickle-process, random assignment. *Evaluation Review, 17*(1), 79–90.

Bryk, A. S. (Ed.). (1983). *Stakeholder-based evaluation* (New Directions for Program Evaluation, No. 17). San Francisco: Jossey-Bass.

Bryk, A. S., & Raudenbush, S. W. (1992). *Hierarchical linear models: Applications and data analysis methods.* Thousand Oaks, CA: Sage.

Campbell, D. T. (1957). Factors relevant to the validity of experiments in social settings. *Psychological Bulletin, 54,* 297–312.

Campbell, D. T. (1969). Reforms as experiments. *American Psychologist, 24,* 409–429.

Campbell, D. T., & Stanley, J. C. (1966). *Experimental and quasi-experimental designs for research.* Skokie, IL: Rand McNally.

Chen, H-t. (1990). *Theory-driven evaluations.* Thousand Oaks, CA: Sage.

Christensen, A., & Heavey, C. L. (1999). Interventions for couples. *Annual Review of Psychology, 50,* 165–190.

Cohen, J. (1988). *Statistical power analysis for the behavioral sciences.* Hillsdale, NJ: Erlbaum.

Conner, R. F. (1977). Selecting a control group: An analysis of the randomization process in twelve social reform programs. *Evaluation Quarterly, 1*(2), 195–244.

Cook, T. D., & Campbell, D. T. (1979). *Quasi-experimentation: Design and analysis issues for field settings.* Skokie, IL: Rand McNally.

Cronbach, L. J. (1982). *Designing evaluations of educational and social programs.* San Francisco: Jossey-Bass.

Diaconis, P. (1985). Theories of data analysis: From magical thinking through classical statistics. In D. C. Hoagland, F. Mosteller, & J. W. Tukey (Eds.), *Exploring data tables, trends, and shapes* (pp. 1–36). New York: Wiley.

Donaldson, S. I. (in press). The theory-driven view of evaluation. In S. I. Donaldson & M. Scriven (Eds.), *Evaluating social programs and problems: Visions for the new millennium.* Hillsdale, NJ: Erlbaum.

Droitcour, J., Silberman, G., & Chelimsky, E. (1993). Cross-design synthesis: A new form of meta-analysis for combining results from randomized clinical trials and medical-practice databases. *International Journal of Technology Assessment in Health Care, 9,* 440–449.

Eckert, W. A. (2000). Situational enhancement of design validity: The case of training evaluation at the World Bank. *American Journal of Evaluation, 21*(2), 185–193.

Fetterman, D. M. (2000). *Foundations of empowerment evaluation.* Thousand Oaks, CA: Sage.

Fetterman, D. M. (2001). The transformation of evaluation into a collaboration: A vision of evaluation in the 21st century. *American Journal of Evaluation, 22*, 381–385.

Fiske, S. T., Kenny, D. A., & Taylor, S. E. (1982). Structural models for the mediation of salience effects on attribution. *Journal of Experimental Social Psychology, 18,* 105–127.

Freedman, D. A. (1987). As others see us: A case study in path analysis. *Journal of Educational Statistics, 12,* 101–128.

Fullbright-Anderson, K. Kubisch, A. C., & Connell, J. P. (Eds.). (1998). *New approaches to evaluating community initiatives: Vol. 2. Theory, measurement, and analysis.* Washington, DC: Aspen Institute.

Graham, J. W., & Donaldson, S. I. (1993). Evaluating interventions with differential attrition: The importance of nonresponse mechanisms and use of follow-up data. *Journal of Applied Psychology, 78,* 119–128.

Greene, J. G. (1988). Stakeholder participation and utilization in program evaluation. *Evaluation Review, 12*(2), 91–116.

Greenwald, A. G., Pratkanis, A. R., Leippe, M. R., & Baumgardner, M. H. (1986). Under what conditions does theory obstruct research progress? *Psychological Bulletin, 93,* 216–229.

Harkreader, S. A., & Henry, G. T. (2000). Using performance measurement systems for assessing the merit and worth of reforms. *American Journal of Evaluation, 21*(1), 151–170.

Henry, G. T. (1996). Does the public have a role in evaluation? Surveys and democratic discourse. In M. T. Braverman & J. K. Slater (Eds.), *Advances in survey research* (New Directions for Evaluation, No. 70, pp. 3–15). San Francisco: Jossey-Bass.

Henry, G. T., & Bugler, D. T. (1998). Evaluating an education reform named HOPE. *Educational Evaluation and Policy Analysis.* Manuscript submitted for publication. UPDATE

Henry, G. T., & Julnes, G. (1998). Values and realist evaluation. In G. T. Henry, G. Julnes, & M. M. Mark (Eds.), *Realist evaluation: An emerging theory in support of practice* (New Directions for Evaluation, No. 78, pp. 53–72). San Francisco: Jossey-Bass.

House, E. R. (1980). *Evaluating with validity.* Thousand Oaks, CA: Sage.

House, E. R. (1993). *Professional evaluation.* Thousand Oaks, CA: Sage.

House, E. R. (1995). Putting things together coherently: Logic and justice. In D. Fournier (Ed.), *Reasoning in evaluation: Inferential links and leaps* (New Directions for Evaluation, No. 68, pp. 33–48). San Francisco: Jossey-Bass.

House, E. R., & Howe, K. R. (1999). *Values in evaluation and social research.* Thousands Oaks, CA: Sage.

Jöreskog, K. G., & Sörbom, D. (1993). *LISREL 8: A guide to the program and applications.* Chicago: Scientific Software International.

Julnes, G. (1995, November). *Context-confirmatory methods for supporting disciplined induction in post-positivist inquiry.* Paper presented at the annual meeting of the American Evaluation Association, Vancouver, British Columbia, Canada.

Julnes, G., Mark, M. M., & Henry, G. T. (1998). Promoting realism in evaluation: Realistic evaluation and the broader context. *Evaluation, 4,* 483–504.

Kazi, M. A. F. (1997). Single case evaluation in British social services. In E. Chelimsky & W. R. Shadish (Eds.), *Evaluation for the 21st century: A handbook* (pp. 419–442). Thousand Oaks, CA: Sage.

Kenny, D. A., Kashy, D. A., & Bolger, N. (1998). Data analysis in social psychology. In D. T. Gilbert, S. T. Fiske, & G. Lindzey (Eds.), *The handbook of social psychology* (Vol. 1, 4th ed., pp. 233–265). Boston: McGraw Hill.

Krueger, R. A. (1994). *Focus groups: A practical guide for applied research* (2nd ed.). Thousand Oaks, CA: Sage.

Kuhn, R., & Culhane, D. P. (1998). Applying cluster analysis to test a typology of homelessness by pattern of shelter utilization: Results from the analysis of administrative data. *American Journal of Community Psychology, 26*(2), 207–232.

Lipsey, M. L. (2001). Re: Unsolved problems and unfinished business. *American Journal of Evaluation, 22*, 325–328.

Lipsey, M. L., & Cordray, D. S. (2000). Evaluation methods for social intervention. *Annual Review of Psychology, 51,* 345–375.

Lipsey, M. W., & Wilson, D. B. (1993). The efficacy of psychological, educational, and behavioral treatment: Confirmation from meta-analysis. *American Psychologist, 48,* 1181–1209.

Little, R. J. A., & Rubin, D. B. (2000). Causal effects in clinical and epidemiological studies via potential outcomes: Concepts and analytical approaches. In J. E. Fielding, L. B. Lave, & B. Starfield (Eds.), *Annual review of public health* (Vol. 21, pp. 121–145). Palo Alto, CA: Annual Reviews.

Mackie, J. L. (1965). Causes and conditions. *American Philosophical Quarterly, 2*(4), 245–255, 261–264.

Mackie, J. L. (1974). *The cement of the universe: A study of causation.* Oxford, England: Clarendon.

Marcantonio, R. J., & Cook, T. D. (1994). Convincing quasi-experiments: The interrupted time series and regression-discontinuity designs. In J. S. Wholey, H. P. Hatry, & K. E. Newcomer (Eds.), *Handbook of practical program evaluation* (pp. 133–154). San Francisco: Jossey Bass.

Mark, M. M. (1990). From program theory to tests of program theory. In L. Bickman (Ed.), *Advances in program theory* (New Directions for Program Evaluation, No. 47, pp. 37–51). San Francisco: Jossey-Bass.

Mark, M. M. (2001). *Principled discovery.* Unpublished manuscript. University Park, PA: Pennsylvania State University.

Mark, M. M., Henry, G. T., & Julnes, G. (1998). A realist theory of evaluation practice. In G. T. Henry, G. Julnes, & M. M. Mark (Eds.), *Realist evaluation: An emerging theory in support of practice* (New Directions for Evaluation, No. 78, pp. 3–32). San Francisco: Jossey-Bass.

Mark, M. M., Henry, G. T., & Julnes, G. (2000). *Evaluation: An integrated framework for understanding, guiding, and improving policies and programs*. San Francisco: Jossey Bass.

Mark, M. M., Hofmann, D., & Reichardt, C. S. (1992). Testing theories in theory-driven evaluations: (Tests of) moderation in all things. In H.-t. Chen & P. H. Rossi (Eds.), *Using theory to improve program and policy evaluations* (pp. 71–84). Westport, CT: Greenwood Press.

Mark, M. M., Reichardt, L. S., & Sanna, L. J. (2000). Time series analysis. In H. E. A. Tinsley & S. R. Brown (Eds.), *Handbook of applied multivariate statistics and mathematical modeling* (pp. 353–389). Orlando, FL: Academic Press.

Mark, M. M., Sanna, L. J., & Shotland, R. L. (1992). Time series methods in applied social research. In F. B. Bryant, J. Edwards, R. S. Tindale, E. J. Posavac, L. Heath, E. Henderson, & Y. Suarez-Balcazar (Eds.), *Methodological issues in applied social research: Social psychological applications to social issues* (Vol. 2, pp. 111–133). New York: Plenum.

Mark, M. M., & Shotland, R. L. (1985). Stakeholder-based evaluation and value judgments. *Evaluation Review, 9,* 605–626.

Maxwell, J. (1996). *Qualitative research design: An interactive approach*. Thousand Oaks, CA: Sage.

McClelland, G. H., & Judd, C. M. (1993). Statistical difficulties of detecting interactions and moderator effects. *Psychological Bulletin, 114,* 376–390.

Mertens, D. M. (1999). Inclusive evaluation: Implications of transformative theory for evaluation. *American Journal of Evaluation, 20*(1), 1–14.

Michalski, G. V., & Cousins, J. B. (2001) Multiple perspectives on training evaluation: Probing stakeholder perceptions in a global network development firm. *American Journal of Evaluation, 22*(1), 37–53.

Mohr, L. B. (1995). *Impact analysis for program evaluation* (2nd ed.). Thousand Oaks, CA: Sage.

Newcomer, K. E. (Ed.). (1997). *Using performance measurement to improve public and nonprofit programs* (New Directions for Evaluation, No. 75). San Francisco: Jossey-Bass.

Patton, M. Q. (1997). *Utilization-focused evaluation: The new century text*. Thousand Oaks, CA: Sage.

Pawson, R., & Tilley, N. (1997). *Realistic evaluation*. Thousand Oaks, CA: Sage.

Perrin, B. (1998). Effective use and misuse of performance measurement. *American Journal of Evaluation, 19,* 367–379.

Reichardt, C. S. (1979). The statistical analysis of data from nonequivalent group designs. In T. D. Cook & D. T. Campbell, *Quasi-experimentation: Design and analysis issues for field settings* (pp. 147–205). Skokie, IL: Rand McNally.

Reichardt, C. S., & Mark, M. M. (1998). Quasi-experimentation. In L. Bickman & D. J. Rog (Eds.), *Handbook of applied social research methods* (pp. 193–208). Thousand Oaks, CA: Sage.

Reynolds, A. J., & Temple, J. A. (1995). Quasi-experimental estimates of the effects of a preschool intervention: Psychometric and econometric comparisons. *Evaluation Review, 19,* 347–373.

Ribisl, K. M., Walton, M. A., Mowbray, C. T., Luke, D. A., Davidson, W. S., & Bootsmiller, B. J. (1996). Minimizing participant attrition in panel studies through the use of effective retention and tracking strategies: Review and recommendations. *Evaluation and Program Planning, 19,* 1–25.

Richardson, H. S. (1997). Democratic intentions. In J. Bohman & W. Rehg (Eds.), *Deliberative democracy: Essays on reason and politics* (pp. 349–381). Cambridge, MA: MIT Press.

Rindskopf, D. M. (1986). New developments in selection modeling for quasi-experimentation. In W. M. K. Trochim (Ed.), *Advances in quasi-experimental design and analysis* (New Directions for Program Evaluation, No. 31, pp. 79–89). San Francisco: Jossey-Bass.

Rosenbaum, P. R. (1995). *Observational studies*. New York: Springer-Verlag.

Rosenbaum, P. R., & Rubin, D. B. (1983). The central role of the propensity score in observational studies for causal effects. *Biometrika, 70*(1), 41–55.

Rosenthal, R. (1994). Science and ethics in conducting, analyzing, and reporting psychological research. *Psychological Science, 5,* 127–134.

Rubin, D. B. (1974). Estimating causal effects of treatments in randomized and nonrandomized studies. *Journal of Educational Psychology, 66,* 688–701.

Rubin, D. B. (1987). *Multiple imputation for nonresponse in surveys*. New York: Wiley.

Schafer, J. L. (1997). *Analysis of incomplete multivariate data*. London: Chapman and Hall.

Scheirer, M. A. (2000). Getting more 'bang' for your performance measurement bucks. *American Journal of Evaluation, 21*(1), 139–149.

Schroeder, C. M., & Prentice, D. A. (1998). Exposing pluralistic ignorance to reduce alcohol use among college students. *Journal of Applied Social Psychology, 28,* 2150–2180.

Scriven, M. S. (Ed.). (1993). *Hard-won lessons in program evaluation* (New Directions for Evaluation, No. 58). San Francisco: Jossey-Bass.

Scriven, M. S., & Roth, J. (Eds.). (1978). *Needs assessment: Concept and practice* (New Directions for Program Evaluation, No. 1). San Francisco: Jossey-Bass.

Seltzer, M. H. (1994). Studying variation in program success: A multilevel modeling approach. *Evaluation Review, 18,* 342–361.

Shadish, W. R., Cook, T. D., & Campbell, D. T. (2002). *Experimental and quasi-experimental designs for generalized causal inference*. Boston: Houghton-Mifflin.

Smith, M. L., & Glass, G. V. (1977). Meta-analysis of psychotherapy outcome studies. *American Psychologist, 32,* 752–760.

Stigler, S. M. (1987). Testing hypotheses or fitting models: Another look at mass extinction. In M. H. Nitecki & A. Hoffman (Eds.), *Neutral models in biology* (pp. 145–149). Oxford, England: Oxford University Press.

Torres, R. T., & Preskill, H. (2001). Evaluation and organizational learning: Past, present, and future. *American Journal of Evaluation, 22,* 387–395.

Tukey, J. W. (1977). *Exploratory data analysis.* Reading, MA: Addison-Wesley.

Tukey, J. W. (1986). *The collected works of John W. Tukey: Vol. 4. Philosophy and principles of data analysis: 1965–1986.* Monterey, CA: Wadsworth.

Triandis, H. C. (1994). *Culture and social behavior.* New York: McGraw Hill.

Weiss, C. H. (1983). The stakeholder approach to evaluation: Origins and promise. In A. S. Bryk (Ed.), *Stakeholder-based evaluation* (New Directions for Program Evaluation, No. 17, pp. 3–14). San Francisco: Jossey-Bass.

West, S. G., Biesanz, J. C., & Pitts, S. C. (2000). Causal inference and generalization in field settings: Experimental and quasi-experimental designs. In H. T. Reis & C. M. Judd (Eds.), *Handbook of research methods in personality and social psychology* (pp. 40–84). New York: Cambridge University Press.

Wholey, J. S. (1994). Assessing the feasibility and likely usefulness of evaluation. In J. S. Wholey, H. P. Hatry, & K. E. Newcomer (Eds.), *Handbook of practical program evaluation* (pp. 15–39). San Francisco: Jossey-Bass.

Wholey, J. S. (in press). Improving performance and accountability: Responding to emerging management challenges. In S. I. Donaldson & M. Scriven (Eds.), *Evaluating social programs and problems: Visions for the new millennium.* Hillsdale, NJ: Erlbaum.

Winship, C., & Morgan, S. L. (1999). The estimation of causal effects from observational data. *Annual Review of Sociology, 25,* 659–707.

Wortman, P. M., Reichardt, C. S., & St. Pierre, R. S. (1978). The first year of educational voucher demonstration: A secondary analysis of student achievement test scores. *Evaluation Quarterly, 2,* 193–214.

Yeh, S. S. (2000). Improving educational and social programs: A planned variation cross-validation model. *American Journal of Evaluation, 21*(2), 171–184.

Zigler, E. F., & Muenchow, S. (1992). *Head Start: The inside story of America's most successful educational experiment.* New York: Basic Books.

PART THREE
MEASUREMENT ISSUES

CHAPTER 14

Mood Measurement: Current Status and Future Directions

DAVID WATSON AND JATIN VAIDYA

In this chapter, we provide a basic introduction to the measurement of mood. After decades of neglect, *mood* emerged as a seminal concept within psychology during the 1980s, and its prominence has continued unabated ever since. Indeed, a PsycINFO database survey during the 5-year period from 1996 to 2000 generated 5,563 references with the keyword *mood*. Our survey of this rapidly expanding literature is organized into three broad sections. First, because good instruments obviously should assess the basic constructs in a domain, we examine current thinking and research regarding the underlying structure of mood. Second, we briefly describe and evaluate many of the most important measures in this area. Finally, we discuss several general issues related to the reliability and construct validity of mood measures.

Before turning to these other matters, however, we first need to define the domain itself. What exactly is a mood, and how does it differ from the related concept of emotion? *Moods* can be defined as transient episodes of feeling or affect (Watson, 2000a). As such, moods differ from emotions in several important ways (see Larsen, 2000; Watson, 2000a, 2000b); we will restrict ourselves here to three key differences that have important implications for measurement. First, mood research focuses primarily—indeed, almost exclusively—on subjective, phenomenological experience. In contrast, emotions classically have been viewed as multimodal psychophysiological systems, with at least four differentiable components: (a) the *subjective* (e.g., feelings of fear and apprehension), (b) the *physiological* (e.g., activation of the sympathetic nervous system), (c) the *expressive* (e.g., the

facial expression of fear), and (d) the *behavioral* (e.g., flight away from danger; Watson, 2000a; Watson & Clark, 1992). Thus, in sharp contrast to emotion research, mood measurement essentially involves the assessment of subjective feelings, without any systematic consideration of these other components.

Second, emotions tend to be extremely brief, lasting perhaps only a few seconds (Izard, 1991; Larsen, 2000). One occasionally observes prolonged emotional states, but these extended reactions tend to be dysfunctional manifestations of psychopathology (see Clark & Watson, 1994; Watson, 2000a). In contrast, moods typically are much longer in duration. For example, whereas the full emotion of anger might last for only a few seconds, an annoyed or irritable mood may persist for several hours, or even for a few days. Because of their longer duration, moods are more easily linked to long-term individual differences in temperament and personality. Indeed, some prominent measures in this area—such as the Multiple Affect Adjective Checklist–Revised (MAACL-R; Zuckerman & Lubin, 1985) and the Positive and Negative Affect Schedule–Expanded Form (PANAS-X; Watson & Clark, 1994)—contain alternative versions that permit one to assess either (a) short-term fluctuations in current mood or (b) long-term individual differences in trait affect. Accordingly, we consider both state and trait affect in our review.

Third, the concept of mood subsumes *all* subjective feeling states, not simply those experiences that accompany classical, prototypical emotions such as fear and anger. This has caused some confusion in the literature; writers periodically have criticized mood measures for including nonemotion terms (e.g., *sleepy, calm, alert*) as items (e.g., Lazarus, 1991; Clore, Ortony, & Foss, 1987). This criticism is based on the assumption that mood research should be restricted to clear referents of emotion, which simply is not the case. Because mood researchers seek to understand all aspects of affective experience, it is necessary to go beyond the narrow confines of prototypical emotions and assess a much broader array of feelings (see Watson, 2000a). Accordingly, this does not represent a valid criticism of mood measures.

THE STRUCTURE OF AFFECTIVE EXPERIENCE

Discrete Affect Models

What are the basic constructs that need to be assessed in this domain? Early mood research tended to emphasize the importance of discrete, specific types of affect, such as fear-anxiety, sadness-depression, anger-hostility, and happiness-joy. This approach was supported by an extensive array of evidence; most notably, structural analyses of mood terms repeatedly identified well-defined content factors corresponding to these specific affective states. Moreover, a common core of discrete affects—including fear, sadness, and anger—emerged consistently across factor analyses reflecting different pools of items and diverse samples of respondents (e.g., McNair, Lorr, & Droppleman, 1971; Nowlis, 1965; Watson & Clark, 1994; Zuckerman & Lubin, 1985).

Nevertheless, advocates of this approach eventually encountered a very serious problem, namely, that measures of different specific affects are strongly interrelated and tend to show questionable discriminant validity. Correlations among affects of the same valence tend to be particularly strong. For instance, people who experience significant levels of one type of negative affect (e.g., anger) also tend to report elevated levels of other negative moods (e.g., fear, sadness, guilt); similarly, individuals who report one type of positive mood (e.g., joy) report many others (e.g., energy, enthusiasm, interest) as well. In fact, multitrait-multimethod analyses consistently demonstrate much stronger evidence for nonspecificity (i.e., significant positive correlations among measures of different, similarly valenced affects) than for specificity (i.e., unique relations between indicators of the same target affect) in mood data (see Bagozzi, 1993; Berenbaum, Fujita, & Pfennig, 1995; Diener, Smith, & Fujita, 1995; Watson & Clark, 1992). We should add that cross-valence correlations (e.g., between fear and enthusiasm) tend to be much weaker, but often are not negligible, an issue we shall return to later.

Dimensional Models

This enormous nonspecificity establishes that mood can be characterized by a much smaller number of general dimensions. Accordingly, researchers increasingly have turned to *dimensional models* over the past two decades. Although earlier approaches often posited three major dimensions (e.g., Engen, Levy, & Schlosberg, 1958), affect researchers gradually converged on a two-factor structure. In 1980, Russell made a major contribution to this literature by proposing that these two dimensions define a *circumplex,* that is, a model in which mood descriptors can be systematically arranged around the perimeter of a circle. As it is usually presented, this circumplex actually defines four bipolar dimensions that are spaced 45° apart: *Pleasantness* (pleasure versus misery), *Excitement* (excitement vs. depression), *Activation* (arousal vs. sleepiness), and *Distress* (distress vs. contentment; see Russell, 1980, Figure 1). We must emphasize, however, that Russell always has viewed Pleasantness and Activation as the basic dimensions of affect (see Feldman Barrett & Russell, 1998; Russell & Carroll, 1999).

Although Russell (1980) reported some evidence suggesting that this circumplex could be applied to self-rated mood, most of his evidence actually was based on other types of affect data (e.g., analyses of facial expressions, judged similarities among mood terms). Watson and Tellegen (1985), however, subsequently reanalyzed data from several studies and established that the same basic two-dimensional structure also consistently emerged in self-report data. Furthermore, on the basis of these reanalyzed data, they presented a circular structure that was designed to resemble Russell's circumplex as closely as possible. This structure is displayed in Figure 14.1. Paralleling Russell's model, Watson and Tellegen's circular scheme portrays four bipolar dimensions that are neatly spaced 45° apart: *Pleasantness* (happy vs. sad), *Positive Affect* (excited vs. sluggish), *Engagement* (aroused vs. still), and *Negative Affect* (distressed vs. relaxed). In contrast to Russell, however, Watson and Tellegen emphasized the importance of the Positive Affect and Negative Affect dimensions that are represented by the solid lines in Figure 14.1.

Although it has encountered some significant problems of its own (which we discuss shortly; see also Watson, Wiese, Vaidya, & Tellegen, 1999), this affect circumplex continues to exert a dominant influence on affect assessment at the general, higher order level (see Feldman Barrett & Russell, 1998; Larsen & Diener, 1992; Russell & Carroll, 1999; Tellegen, Watson, & Clark, 1999; Watson et al., 1999). We must emphasize again that although the defined space is itself two-dimensional, the circumplex traditionally is displayed as consisting of four bipolar constructs, which essentially represent

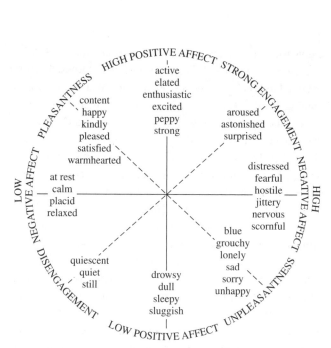

active
elated
enthusiastic
excited
peppy
strong

HIGH POSITIVE AFFECT

PLEASANTNESS

content
happy
kindly
pleased
satisfied
warmhearted

LOW NEGATIVE AFFECT

at rest
calm
placid
relaxed

DISENGAGEMENT

quiescent
quiet
still

LOW POSITIVE AFFECT

drowsy
dull
sleepy
sluggish

STRONG ENGAGEMENT

aroused
astonished
surprised

HIGH NEGATIVE AFFECT

distressed
fearful
hostile
jittery
nervous
scornful

blue
grouchy
lonely
sad
sorry
unhappy

UNPLEASANTNESS

Figure 14.1 The two-dimensional structure of affect. *Source:* From Watson and A. Tellegen (1985, p. 221). Copyright 1985 by the American Psychological Association.

rival two-factor schemes: one based on Pleasantness and Engagement (to use the terminology shown in Figure 14.1), and the other defined by Negative Affect and Positive Affect. We shall review measures of all four constructs later.

A Hierarchical Synthesis

Watson and Tellegen (1985) further clarified the underlying structure of the domain by pointing out that these two basic approaches—that is, general dimensions and discrete affects— are not incompatible or mutually exclusive; rather, they reflect different levels of a single, integrated hierarchical scheme (see also Berenbaum et al., 1995; Diener et al., 1995; Watson & Clark, 1992, 1994, 1997). Specifically, they proposed that the higher order dimensions of Negative Affect and Positive Affect each can be decomposed into several correlated—yet ultimately distinct—affective states; the general dimension of Negative Affect, for instance, can be subdivided into specific negative affects such as fear, hostility, and sadness. In this hierarchical scheme, the lower level reflects the specific *content* of the mood descriptors (i.e., the distinctive qualities of the individual discrete affects), whereas the higher order level reflects their valence (i.e., whether they reflect negative or positive states).

Subsequent studies have reported evidence that strongly supports this hierarchical scheme. Watson and Clark (1992), for example, reported four studies demonstrating the hierarchical arrangement of the negative affects. In their Study 1,

measures of sadness-depression correlated more highly with one another than with indicators of fear-anxiety or anger-hostility. Similarly, Studies 2 and 3 demonstrated that a given Time-1 measure (e.g., Time-1 guilt) correlated more strongly with its Time-2 counterpart (e.g., Time-2 guilt) than with Time-2 measures of other negative affects (e.g., Time-2 sadness). Finally, Study 4 established that self-rated traits (e.g., self-rated sadness) correlated more highly with their peer-rated counterparts (e.g., peer-rated sadness) than with parallel ratings of other target affects (e.g., peer-rated hostility). Berenbaum et al. (1995) later replicated these findings in another series of four studies.

Consequently, both levels of this hierarchical structure must be assessed in any comprehensive assessment of mood. We therefore consider measures of both specific, discrete affects and general dimensions in our review. Finally, it is worth noting that Tellegen et al. (1999) recently proposed an expanded three-level hierarchical scheme that incorporates important features from all of the approaches we have discussed. A general bipolar dimension of Pleasantness versus Unpleasantness (a key construct in Russell's model) comprises the highest level of this structure; this dimension reflects the fact that positive and negative affective states tend to be negatively correlated (albeit somewhat weakly) with one another. The intermediate level of the model consists of the Positive and Negative Affect dimensions that were highlighted by Watson and Tellegen (1985); this level represents the strong within-valence correlations that were discussed earlier. Finally, the lowest level of the hierarchy consists of discrete affects such as fear, anger, and sadness; this level captures the distinctive qualities of these specific types of affect.

REVIEW OF EXISTING MEASURES

Measures of the Higher Order Dimensions

Measures of Pleasantness and Activation

We begin our review by considering measures of Pleasantness (also known as *Valence* or *Evaluation*) and Engagement (also called *Activation* or *Arousal*). This represents a rather puzzling area within the affect assessment literature. As we already have discussed, Pleasantness and Engagement are important constructs that have played an influential role in mood research for several decades. Moreover, measures of these dimensions have been included in numerous studies (e.g., Green, Goldman, & Salovey, 1993; Russell & Carroll, 1999; Watson, 1988; Watson et al., 1999). Almost invariably, however, researchers have relied on ad hoc measures whose psychometric properties have not been thoroughly established.

Because of this, no scales have emerged as standard, widely used measures of these constructs.

For instance, in their recent examination of affect scales, Larsen and Fredrickson (1999) reviewed only one measure of these dimensions, the *Affect Grid* (Russell, Weiss, & Mendelsohn, 1989). The Affect Grid consists of a single item, which is presented to respondents as a 9 × 9 matrix. Participants are instructed to place a check within the cell of this matrix that best reflects their current feelings of pleasantness and activation. One key advantage of this approach is that the Affect Grid can be administered repeatedly over a relatively short interval without taxing the patience of respondents. This makes it ideal for intensive, massed assessments of mood (see Russell et al., 1989). At the same time, however, the Affect Grid suffers from two problems that lessen its value in many assessment contexts. First, because it consists of only a single item, its internal consistency reliability cannot be determined. Second, because the assessment is completely undisguised (i.e., the targeted constructs of Pleasantness and Engagement are explicitly presented to respondents), its validity may be significantly compromised in situations in which responses are likely to be substantially influenced by expectancy effects, demand characteristics, or social desirability concerns.

Feldman Barrett and Russell (1998; see also Yik, Russell, & Feldman Barrett, 1999) recently introduced a promising assessment instrument, the *Current Mood Questionnaire* (CMQ), which includes measures of Pleasantness and Engagement. The CMQ was designed to assess the affect circumplex in a comprehensive manner, and it contains scales assessing all of the octants displayed in Figure 14.1. One unusual feature of the full CMQ is that each octant can be measured using three different rating methods: (a) simple mood adjectives that are rated on a 5-point Likert scale; (b) more elaborate statements that are assessed using a 5-point agree-disagree format; and (c) a similar set of statements that are rated using a 4-point "describes me" format. Feldman Barrett, Russell, and their colleagues also have included a fourth measure of Pleasantness and Engagement in many of their analyses, using six-item semantic differential scales that originally were developed by Russell and Mehrabian (1974). Although the use of multiple methods can be cumbersome and time consuming, it allows one to compute corrected correlations that control for both random and systematic (i.e., method variance) sources of error; we shall consider this important issue in detail later.

The CMQ scales assessing the Pleasantness, Unpleasantness, Engagement, and Disengagement octants tend to be quite short, consisting of only two to four items within each method. Despite their brevity, however, the Pleasantness and Unpleasantness scales typically show excellent reliabilities. In their Studies 2 and 3, Feldman Barrett and Russell (1998) obtained internal-consistency reliabilities (coefficient alphas) ranging from .79 to .91 (*Mdn* = .88) for their Pleasantness scales, and from .83 to .90 (*Mdn* = .88) for the Unpleasantness scales (Feldman Barrett, personal communication, November 13, 2000). Moreover, the reliabilities were even better when the items from both octants were combined into single bipolar measures of Pleasantness versus Unpleasantness, ranging from .88 to .94 (*Mdn* = .91).

The CMQ measures of Engagement versus Disengagement proved to be less satisfactory, however (Feldman Barrett, personal communication, November 13, 2000). Coefficient alphas for the Engagement scales ranged from .63 to .83, with a median value of only .73; similarly, the reliabilities for the Disengagement measures ranged from .50 to .78, with a median value of .71. Moreover, combining the items from both octants into a single bipolar measure of Engagement versus Disengagement did not improve things much: The reliabilities still ranged from .67 to .86, with a median value of .77. We have collected CMQ data (using only the describes-me response format) in a sample of 676 University of Iowa undergraduates, and the results are even more discouraging. Coefficient alphas for the Engagement and Disengagement scales were .59 and .58, respectively; combining the items into a single bipolar dimension still yielded an alpha of only .66.

The CMQ Engagement and Disengagement scales appear to work well when they are used as originally intended, that is, as components in a multimethod approach that is designed to control for various types of measurement error (Feldman Barrett & Russell, 1998; Yik et al., 1999). They are less satisfactory, however, when used separately as stand-alone measures of these constructs. Thus, we cannot advocate their broad use as general measures of Engagement versus Disengagement.

We should emphasize that this problem is by no means unique to the CMQ, but rather reflects a more general issue in mood measurement. Although it is relatively easy to create reliable indicators of Pleasantness versus Unpleasantness, it has proven much more difficult to create good measures of Engagement versus Disengagement (see Watson et al., 1999). The assessment difficulties in this area reflect two basic problems. First, compared to the other three dimensions shown in Figure 14.1, the available supply of good marker terms is relatively limited for this dimension. In this regard, Watson et al. (1999) measured all of the octants in the affect circumplex in three different samples; they analyzed these data using *CIRCUM* (Browne, 1992), a structural modeling technique for testing circumplexity (see also Fabrigar, Visser, & Browne, 1997). Rather than defining a neat circumplex,

TABLE 14.1   Correlations Among Octant Markers of the Affect Circumplex

Correlation	Sample 1	Sample 2	Sample 3	Sample 4	Mean r
Pleasantness-Engagement markers					
Pleasantness vs. Unpleasantness	−.47*	−.37*	−.36*	−.65*	−.50
Engagement vs. Disengagement	−.20*	.02	−.30*	−.35*	−.24
Pleasantness vs. Engagement	.33*	.30*	.46*	.31*	.35
Pleasantness vs. Disengagement	−.07	−.09	−.17*	−.17*	−.13
Unpleasantness vs. Engagement	−.06	.17*	−.15*	−.14*	−.07
Unpleasantness vs. Disengagement	.15*	.31*	.21*	.25*	.23
Positive-Negative Affect markers					
High PA vs. Low PA	−.31*	−.13	−.35*	−.60*	−.41
High NA vs. Low NA	−.41*	−.34*	−.16*	−.52*	−.39
High PA vs. High NA	.15*	.01	.20*	−.20*	.01
High PA vs. Low NA	.04	.15*	.31*	.52*	.30
Low PA vs. High NA	.23*	.52*	.09	.36*	.30
Low PA vs. Low NA	.08	−.14	−.28*	−.38*	−.21

Note. $N = 486$ (Sample 1), 317 (Sample 2), 421 (Sample 3), 676 (Sample 4). PA = Positive Affect. NA = Negative Affect.
*$p < .01$, two-tailed.

however, the data actually revealed the presence of two broad *superclusters* (see Watson et al., 1999, Figure 2). The first (spanning from High Negative Affect to Disengagement) occupied only 100° of the circle (rather than the 135° depicted in Figure 14.1), whereas the second (ranging from Low Negative Affect to Engagement) occupied only 105°. These superclusters were separated by two large gaps at the opposite ends of the space (76° between Engagement and High Negative Affect, 79° between Disengagement and Low Negative Affect); these gaps reflected the fact that no variables fell close to the hypothesized Engagement-Disengagement axis.

Put differently, none of the analyzed variables was affectively neutral; rather, all of them could be characterized as positively or negatively valenced. In light of this situation, mood researchers typically have been forced to use valenced terms in their measures of Engagement versus Disengagement. The CMQ, for instance, includes a number of positively valenced items (e.g., *alert, filled with energy, full of energy*) and negatively valenced items (e.g., *stirred up, keyed up*) in its Engagement scales. Although this practice is problematic, researchers ultimately have little choice. As the Watson et al. (1999) results demonstrate, it has proven very difficult to identify affectively neutral terms that are clear, unambiguous markers of this dimension.

The second problem concerns the relatively weak bipolarity of this dimension. The accumulating data consistently demonstrate strong negative correlations between measures of Pleasantness and Unpleasantness. For instance, Watson and Tellegen (1999) summarized the results of several studies that reported latent correlations (controlling for measurement error) between measures of Pleasantness and Unpleasantness; these correlations ranged from −.84 to −.93, with a

median value of −.91 (see Watson & Tellegen, 1999, Table 1). In contrast, the correlations between measures of Engagement and Disengagement tend to be much lower. Because of this, there is little to be gained (in terms of augmenting reliability) by combining the two ends of the dimension into a single bipolar scale.

To document this important point, Table 14.1 presents data from four samples in which respondents completed measures of all of the octants in the affect circumplex. The first three samples were described previously by Watson et al. (1999). Sample 1 consists of 486 undergraduates at Southern Methodist University (SMU) who rated their current, momentary mood using a 5-point scale (1 = *very slightly or not at all*, 5 = *extremely*); Sample 2 was composed of 317 SMU students who completed a general, trait version of the same questionnaire. Participants in both samples rated themselves on the 38 affect terms shown in Figure 14.1. The descriptors defining each octant then were summed to yield an overall measure of that octant; however, two terms (*placid* and *quiescent*) had to be dropped because many respondents were unfamiliar with them and left them blank. Sample 3 consisted of 421 University of Iowa undergraduates who rated their current, momentary mood on the same 5-point scale. Using the terms presented in Russell (1980) and Feldman Barrett and Russell (1998) as a guide, Watson et al. (1999) created three- or four-item scales to assess each octant (the terms included in each scale are reported in Watson et al., 1999, p. 822). Finally, Sample 4 consisted of the 676 University of Iowa students who rated themselves on the CMQ using the describes-me format. Six of the octant scales were assessed in their original form; however, the CMQ markers of High Positive Affect and High Negative Affect were modified to maximize their similarity to the corresponding scales in the

Positive and Negative Affect Schedule (PANAS; Watson, Clark, & Tellegen, 1988).

Correlations among the Pleasantness and Engagement scales are presented in the top half of Table 14.1. The table shows the individual correlations from each sample, as well as weighted mean coefficients calculated across all of them (these were computed after subjecting the individual sample correlations to an *r* to *z* transformation). Consistent with the evidence reviewed earlier, these data demonstrate moderate to strong bipolarity between markers of Pleasantness and Unpleasantness, with an overall mean correlation of −.50. Corrected for measurement error, these coefficients again would reflect a very strong inverse relation between the two hypothesized poles of this dimension. In sharp contrast, however, the correlations between hypothesized markers of Engagement and Disengagement ranged from .02 to −.35, with a mean coefficient of only −.24. These correlations reflect a rather weak level of bipolarity, and indicate that the two hypothesized poles of this dimension do not neatly define the opposite ends of a single construct. On the basis of these data, we strongly recommend that mood researchers carefully examine the correlations between their Engagement and Disengagement scales before combining them into a single bipolar measure.

It also is noteworthy that the Engagement scales tended to correlate more strongly with markers of Pleasantness (mean *r* = .35) than with indicators of Disengagement (mean *r* = −.24); conversely, the Disengagement measures correlated as highly with Unpleasantness (mean *r* = .23) as with Engagement. These results again demonstrate that it is exceedingly difficult to find mood terms that truly are affectively neutral. In these four samples, the purported markers of Engagement clearly tended to be positively valenced, whereas the Disengagement items tended to be negatively valenced.

In summary, Pleasantness and Engagement represent key constructs within the affect literature. It is rather surprising, therefore, that so little attention has been given to their assessment, such that no scales have emerged as standard, definitive measures of these constructs. Our brief survey of this literature indicates that it is relatively easy to develop reliable measures of Pleasantness and Unpleasantness; the CMQ, for instance, contains three reasonably reliable measures of each construct. Furthermore, in light of the strongly bipolar nature of this dimension, markers of Pleasantness and Unpleasantness can be safely combined into a single index to create an even more reliable measure of the construct. In sharp contrast, the assessment of the Engagement dimension has proven to be much more problematic. As we have seen, the available supply of good marker terms is relatively limited for this dimension. Furthermore, the two hypothesized ends

of the dimension tend to be weakly interrelated, making it problematic to combine them into a single bipolar scale. This is a significant assessment problem that merits far greater attention from affect researchers in the future.

Measures of Positive and Negative Affect

The situation is quite different when one examines the literature related to the Positive and Negative Affect dimensions depicted in Figure 14.1. Multiple measures of these constructs have been created, and several of these scales—including those of Bradburn (1969), Stone (1987), and Diener and Emmons (1984)—were frequently used in the past (for a comparative analysis of these instruments, see Watson, 1988). Gradually, however, the PANAS (Watson et al., 1988) emerged as the standard measure of these constructs. The original PANAS (which later was subsumed into the more comprehensive PANAS-X) contains 10-item scales assessing each dimension. The terms comprising the PANAS Positive Affect scale are *active, alert, attentive, determined, enthusiastic, excited, inspired, interested, proud,* and *strong;* the items included in the Negative Affect scale are *afraid, ashamed, distressed, guilty, hostile, irritable, jittery, nervous, scared,* and *upset.* These terms can be used with several different time instructions (e.g., how one feels right now, how one has felt over the past week, how one feels in general). In each case, respondents rate the extent to which they have experienced each term on a 5-point scale (1 = *very slightly or not at all,* 5 = *extremely*). Since their introduction in 1988, the PANAS scales have been used in hundreds of studies; in fact, an inspection of the Institute for Scientific Information citation database indicates that the original 1988 article now has been cited more than 1,450 times.

The widespread popularity of the PANAS rests, in part, on the rich body of psychometric data that have established the reliability and validity of the scales. With regard to reliability, Watson et al. (1988) reported that the PANAS scales showed excellent internal consistency in six large data sets, with sample sizes ranging from 586 to 1,002. Specifically, the coefficient alphas for the Negative Affect scale ranged from .84 to .87, whereas those for the Positive Affect scale ranged from .86 to .90. Watson and Clark (1994) later reported a more extensive analysis of this issue, examining data from 19 samples (representing eight different time instructions) with a combined *N* of 17,549. Across these samples, the coefficient alphas ranged from .83 to .90 for Negative Affect, and from .84 to .91 for Positive Affect (see Watson & Clark, 1994, Table 4).

With regard to validity, Watson et al. (1988) established that the PANAS scales were excellent measures of the underlying Positive and Negative Affect dimensions. Watson et al. factor-analyzed the data from six large data sets, extracting two factors in each case. They then correlated the PANAS scales with regression-based estimates of these factors. The PANAS Positive Affect scale had correlations ranging from .89 to .95 with the Positive Affect factor scores, and from −.02 to −.17 with the Negative Affect factor. Conversely, the PANAS Negative Affect scale had correlations ranging from .91 to .93 with scores on the Negative Affect factor, and from −.09 to −.18 with the Positive Affect factor. Watson and Clark (1997) subsequently extended these findings in 13 additional data sets. Eleven of these were between-subject data sets with a combined sample size of 8,685. Across these samples, the PANAS Positive Affect scale had correlations ranging from .90 to .95 (Mdn = .93) with its corresponding factor score; similarly, the PANAS Negative Affect scale had convergent correlations ranging from .92 to .95 (Mdn = .94) with its target factor. In the final two samples, respondents rated themselves repeatedly over a large number of occasions: One data set was based on momentary ratings (10,169 observations) and the other on daily ratings (11,322 observations). The data in each sample were standardized on a within-subject basis and then subjected to an overall factor analysis. The PANAS Positive Affect scale had correlations of .93 and .90 with its corresponding factor score in the momentary and daily ratings, respectively; the convergent correlations for the Negative Affect scale were .89 and .89, respectively.

The construct validity of the PANAS is further supported by a diverse array of evidence. For instance, state versions of the scales (in which respondents rate how they are feeling currently, or how they have felt over the course of the day) have been shown to be sensitive to a variety of transient situational and biological factors. Thus, PANAS Negative Affect scores are significantly elevated in response to stress and are reduced following moderate exercise. Conversely, Positive Affect scores are significantly elevated following exercise and social interactions, and show a systematic circadian rhythm over the course of the day; they also have been shown to be highly sensitive to variations in the daily body temperature rhythm and the sleep-wake cycle (see Watson, 2000a; Watson et al., 1999).

Furthermore, trait versions of the scales (in which respondents rate how they have felt over the past year, or how they feel in general) are strongly stable over several months and display substantial levels of stability over retest intervals as long as 7 years (Watson & Clark, 1994; Watson & Walker, 1996). In addition, self-ratings on the scales show significant convergent validity when correlated with corresponding judgments made by well-acquainted peers, such as friends,

roommates, dating partners, and spouses (see Watson & Clark, 1991, 1994; Watson, Hubbard, & Wiese, 2000). Self-ratings on these scales also show strong convergence with the Big Two personality traits of extraversion and neuroticism; for instance, in a combined sample of 4,457 respondents, the general, trait version of the PANAS Negative Affect scale correlated .58 with neuroticism, whereas the Positive Affect scale correlated .51 with extroversion (Watson et al., 1999). We shall examine the construct validity of these general trait ratings in greater detail shortly.

It also is noteworthy that Watson (2002) recently created parallel forms of the PANAS scales. These new scales also are composed of 10 terms each, none of which overlap with those included in the original scales. The parallel form of the Positive Affect scale consists of the terms *bold, cheerful, concentrating, confident, daring, delighted, energetic, fearless, joyful,* and *lively;* the alternate form for the Negative Affect scale includes *angry, angry at self, blameworthy, dissatisfied with self, disgusted, disgusted with self, frightened, loathing, scornful,* and *shaky.* These parallel versions also show excellent psychometric properties. For instance, across 12 large between-subject data sets with a combined sample size of 9,887, the new Positive Affect scale had coefficient alphas ranging from .81 to .89 (Mdn = .88) and the Negative Affect scale had alphas ranging from .85 to .91 (Mdn = .87). Moreover, these new measures are strongly convergent with the original scales. Across the 12 data sets, the two Positive Affect scales had convergent correlations ranging from .79 to .87 (Mdn = .86) and the Negative Affect scales had correlations ranging from .82 to .89 (Mdn = .85). Furthermore, trait versions of these parallel forms showed levels of (a) temporal stability and (b) self-other convergence that were fully as good as the original PANAS scales. The development of these parallel forms represents a significant advance in the assessment of these higher order dimensions; as noted earlier, by using multiple indicators of a construct, one is able to compute corrected, latent correlations that control for measurement error (see Watson, 2002, for more details).

Despite (or perhaps because of) their popularity, however, the PANAS scales have not been immune to criticism. Some of these criticisms are terminological and need not concern us here (for discussions, see Watson & Clark, 1997; Watson et al., 1999). We will focus instead on one very understandable concern, namely, the unipolar nature of the scales. As we have noted, the PANAS scales (and, indeed, virtually all of the commonly used measures of these dimensions) contain only high-end terms, such as *active, interested, enthusiastic* (Positive Affect), *guilty, irritable,* and *scared* (Negative Affect). The dimensions portrayed in Figure 14.1, however, clearly are bipolar in nature: Low Positive Affect is defined by terms reflecting lassitude and lethargy (e.g., *sluggish, dull*), whereas Low Negative Affect is characterized by indicators of serenity (e.g., *calm, relaxed*). Several writers have criticized the PANAS for excluding these low-end terms, arguing quite plausibly that unipolar scales cannot possibly assess bipolar dimensions validly (Larsen & Diener, 1992; Mossholder, Kemery, Harris, Armenakis, & McGrath, 1994; Nemanick & Munz, 1994).

Why were these low-end terms excluded from the PANAS scales? The reason is that they subsequently were found to be factorially complex and to correlate significantly with both of the underlying dimensions. Their factorial complexity is well illustrated in the bottom half of Table 14.1, which reports correlations among scales assessing the High Positive Affect, High Negative Affect, Low Positive Affect, and Low Negative Affect octants of Figure 14.1; these data are based on the same four samples described earlier. Consistent with the structural scheme depicted in Figure 14.1, markers of High and Low Positive Affect do tend to be inversely related, with a weighted mean correlation of $-.41$. Contrary to Figure 14.1, however, the Low Positive Affect terms also are moderately correlated with markers of High Negative Affect (mean $r = .30$). Similarly, the Low Negative Affect scales are moderately related to both High Negative Affect (mean $r = -.39$) and High Positive Affect (mean $r = .30$). These results establish some significant inaccuracies in the original formulation of the affect circumplex (see Watson et al., 1999, for a discussion).

Moreover, they further suggest that the inclusion of these low-end terms actually would lessen the construct validity of the PANAS scales. Watson and Clark (1997) examined this issue by constructing a bipolar form of the PANAS. They created a bipolar Positive Affect scale by reverse-keying ratings on the four items comprising the PANAS-X Fatigue scale (*sleepy, tired, sluggish, drowsy*) and adding them to the 10 regular high-end terms; in parallel fashion, they created a bipolar Negative Affect scale by reverse-scoring the three terms included in the PANAS-X Serenity scale (*calm, relaxed, at ease*) and adding them to the 10 regular high-end descriptors. Both the original unipolar PANAS scales and these alternative bipolar versions then were correlated with regression-based factor scores in each of 13 data sets. The results established that the original PANAS scales were superior measures of the underlying dimensions, in that they consistently showed both better convergent validity (i.e., higher correlations with the target factor score) and superior discriminant validity (i.e., lower correlations with the other factor score). In other words, unipolar scales consistently provide better measures of these dimensions than do bipolar scales. Thus, for most assessment purposes, researchers

should continue to use only the high-end terms to measure these constructs.

In summary, the PANAS scales—including both the original versions and the new parallel forms—provide reliable and valid assessment of the underlying Positive and Negative Affect dimensions. The scales are supported by an impressive array of psychometric evidence and currently represent the standard measures of these constructs. In a subsequent section, we will explore the construct validity of the trait forms of the scales in greater detail.

Measures of the Lower Order Discrete Affects

Description of Individual Measures

We turn now to a consideration of inventories designed to assess the specific, discrete affects within the hierarchical structure. Due to space restrictions, we cannot review all of the available instruments, or even all of the widely used measures of affect. For instance, countless scales have been developed to measure a single target affect, such as anxiety, depression, or hostility. Instead, we will restrict ourselves here to five influential multiaffect instruments that attempt to assess the domain in a reasonably comprehensive manner. We begin with a brief description of each individual instrument, and then follow with a discussion of two general problems in this area.

The earliest of these multiaffect inventories was the Mood Adjective Checklist (MACL), which was based on the pioneering factor-analytic work of Vincent Nowlis and Russel Green (summarized in Nowlis, 1965). It must be emphasized that despite its name, the MACL was not actually a checklist; rather, respondents rated their current feelings using a 4-point response format (*definitely feel, feel slightly, cannot decide, definitely do not feel*) that subsequently was subjected to extensive criticism (see Meddis, 1972; Russell, 1979; Watson & Tellegen, 1985). Nowlis and Green initially created a large pool of 130 mood terms. Extensive factor analyses of these terms identified 12 replicable content dimensions, which were used to create corresponding scales consisting of two to six items apiece: Aggression (e.g., *defiant, rebellious*), Skepticism (e.g., *dubious, skeptical*), Anxiety (e.g., *clutched up, fearful*), Sadness (e.g., *regretful, sad*), Egotism (e.g., *egotistic, self-centered*), Fatigue (e.g., *drowsy, dull*), Surgency (e.g., *carefree, playful*), Elation (e.g., *elated, overjoyed*), Vigor (e.g., *active, energetic*), Social Affection (e.g., *affectionate, forgiving*), Concentration (e.g., *attentive, earnest*), and Nonchalance (*leisurely, nonchalant*).

The work of Nowlis and Green must be accorded a prominent place in the history of affect assessment because of its substantial influence on such important mood researchers as

Thayer (1978, 1986) and Stone (1987). Moreover, their comprehensive pool of mood terms was the starting point for many later factor analyses and scale development projects in this domain (see, e.g., McNair et al., 1971; Zuckerman, 1960). Nevertheless, the MACL itself never became a standard, widely used measure, in large part because much of the supporting psychometric data were buried in Office of Naval Research technical reports and unpublished conference proceedings. Indeed, the basic psychometric properties of the MACL scales—such as their internal consistency—never were clearly established. Hence, we will not consider this instrument further.

A more popular assessment instrument was introduced in 1960 as the Affect Adjective Check List (AACL; Zuckerman, 1960), which provided a single measure of anxiety. The AACL was expanded a few years later into the Multiple Affect Adjective Check List (MAACL; Zuckerman & Lubin, 1965), a 132-item instrument that yielded separate measures of Anxiety, Depression, and Hostility. One innovative aspect of the MAACL was that it included both state and trait versions. In the state format respondents were asked to describe "how you feel now—today," whereas in the trait form they were asked to rate "how you generally feel. Unlike the MACL, the MAACL was a true checklist, in that participants were asked to check only those items that apply to them.

The MAACL quickly became quite popular. In fact, Lubin, Zuckerman, and Woodward (1985) identified 716 published articles or doctoral dissertations that had used one or more of the MAACL scales. With its increased use, however, it also became apparent that the MAACL had serious psychometric problems, many of them stemming from its use of a checklist format. This response format is notoriously susceptible to systematic rating biases that can lead to highly distorted results; because of this, measurement experts now strongly recommend that this format be avoided (see Clark & Watson, 1995; Green et al., 1993; Watson & Tellegen, 1999).

The most obvious problem with the original MAACL was the poor discriminant validity of its scales. The MAACL scales typically showed intercorrelations ranging from .70 to .90 and, moreover, tended to produce identical patterns of results (see Gotlib & Meyer, 1986; Zuckerman & Lubin, 1985). In response to this problem, Zuckerman and Lubin created the revised MAACL (MAACL-R; Zuckerman & Lubin, 1985; see also Lubin et al., 1986; Zuckerman, Lubin, & Rinck, 1983). The most important change in this revision was that positive mood terms were eliminated from the three original scales and used instead to create two new scales: Positive Affect (e.g., *friendly, happy, peaceful, secure*) and Sensation Seeking (*active, adventurous, enthusiastic, wild*). This modification also now permits researchers to compute overall, nonspecific measures of negative mood (by summing the scores on Anxiety, Depression, and Hostility) and positive mood (by summing the responses to Positive Affect and Sensation Seeking).

Although the MAACL-R clearly represents an improvement over its predecessor, it still suffers from two noteworthy problems. First, the correlations among the three negative mood scales remain rather high. An inspection of the data presented in the MAACL-R manual (Zuckerman & Lubin, 1985) indicates that the average correlations among the negative affect scales are .61 (Anxiety vs. Depression), .61 (Anxiety vs. Hostility), and .62 (Depression vs. Hostility; these are weighted mean correlations—after r to z transformation—of the data reported in Zuckerman & Lubin, 1985, Table 2). Second, although the other scales appear to be internally consistent (with coefficient alphas generally in the .70 to .95 range), the reliability of the Sensation Seeking scale is unsatisfactory. Across multiple samples, it has coefficient alphas ranging from only .49 to .81 ($Mdn = .65$) in its state form, and from .69 to .81 ($Mdn = .77$) in its trait version (Lubin, personal communication, August 8, 1997; see also Zuckerman & Lubin, 1985 [In his personal communication, Lubin also reported that the coefficient alphas for the trait version of this scale are incorrectly reported in both the 1985 MAACL-R manual and in the accompanying 1986 article by Lubin et al.])

The Profile of Mood States (POMS; McNair et al., 1971) is another widely used mood inventory; indeed, the keyword *Profile of Mood States* generated 833 references in the PsycINFO database covering the period from 1984 through 2000. The POMS consists of 65 mood terms that are rated on a 5-point scale (*not at all, a little, moderately, quite a bit, extremely*). The POMS terms can be used with various time instructions, although the usual format is to have respondents rate "how you have been feeling during the past week, including today." These responses are used to score six scales (consisting of 7–15 items each): Tension-Anxiety (e.g., *tense, shaky*), Depression-Dejection (e.g., *unhappy, hopeless*), Anger-Hostility (e.g., *angry, peeved*), Fatigue-Inertia (e.g., *worn-out, listless*), Confusion-Bewilderment (e.g., *confused, muddled*), and Vigor-Activity (e.g., *lively, cheerful*).

The POMS scales are the product of an extensive series of factor analyses; not surprisingly, therefore, they generally show impressive reliabilities. McNair et al. (1971), for instance, report coefficient alphas ranging from .84 to .95 across two large patient samples. Similarly, in a sample of 563 undergraduates, Watson and Clark (1994) obtained coefficient alphas ranging from .77 (Confusion-Bewilderment) to .92 (Depression-Dejection), with a median value of .89. Similar to the MAACL and MAACL-R, however, the POMS suffers from one serious problem, namely, that many of its negative mood scales show poor discriminant validity. For instance, across various samples reported in McNair et al. (1971), the POMS Depression-Dejection scale had average correlations of .77 with Confusion-Bewilderment, .75 with Tension-Anxiety, .65 with Anger-Hostility, and .64 with Fatigue-Inertia (these are weighted mean correlations—after r to z transformation—of the data reported in McNair et al., 1971, Table 7). We shall examine the discriminant validity of the POMS negative mood scales in greater detail shortly.

The Differential Emotions Scale (DES) is an important mood measure that is based on Carroll Izard's influential differential emotions theory (see Izard, 1977, 1991; Izard, Libero, Putnam, & Haynes, 1993). The DES also is the product of multiple factor analyses and exists in at least four different versions (see Blumberg & Izard, 1985, 1986; Izard et al., 1993). Similar to the MAACL and MAACL-R, it can be used to assess either state or trait affect by varying the time instructions given to respondents. Izard and his colleagues also have used different response formats in various incarnations of the DES, most commonly employing either a 5-point frequency- or a 5-point intensity-rating format. Earlier versions of the DES contained 10 scales: Interest, Joy, Surprise, Sadness, Anger, Disgust, Contempt, Fear, Shame-Shyness, and Guilt. In the most recent modification (the DES-IV), however, the instrument has been expanded to 12 scales by (a) splitting Shame and Shyness into separate measures and (b) adding a new scale assessing Inner-Directed Hostility (e.g., *feel mad at yourself, feel sick about yourself*) (see Blumberg & Izard, 1985, 1986; Izard et al., 1993).

Throughout these various transformations of the DES, one constant feature is that the scales invariably are quite short, generally consisting of only three items apiece. One unfortunate consequence of their brevity is that several of the scales do not show adequate levels of reliability. Izard et al. (1993, Table 1), for example, report coefficient alphas of .56 (Disgust), .60 (Shame), .62 (Shyness), .65 (Surprise), .73 (Guilt), .75 (Interest), and .75 (Inner-Directed Hostility); in fact, the median reliability across the 12 scales was only .75. These data strongly suggest that several of the DES scales need to be lengthened to increase their reliability.

Finally, the 60-item PANAS-X—which, as noted earlier, subsumes the original PANAS—includes 11 factor-analytically derived scales that assess specific, lower order affects. As with the PANAS, respondents rate the extent to which they have experienced each mood term on a 5-point scale (1 = *very slightly or not at all*, 5 = *extremely*); the items can be used with varying time instructions to assess either state or trait affect. Four scales assess specific negative mood states that are strong markers of the higher order Negative Affect dimension: Fear (six items; e.g., *scared, nervous*), Sadness (five items; e.g., *blue, lonely*), Guilt (six

items; e.g., *ashamed, dissatisfied with self*), and Hostility (six items; e.g., *angry, scornful*). In addition, three scales assess positively valenced states that are strongly linked to the higher order Positive Affect factor: Joviality (eight items; e.g., *happy, enthusiastic*), Self-Assurance (six items; e.g., *confident, bold*), and Attentiveness (four items; e.g., *alert, concentrating*). Finally, four scales are less strongly and consistently related to the higher order dimensions: Shyness (four items; e.g., *bashful, timid*), Fatigue (four items; e.g., *sleepy, sluggish*), Serenity (three items; e.g., *calm, relaxed*), and Surprise (three items; e.g., *amazed, astonished*).

Watson and Clark (1994, 1997) report extensive reliability data on these scales. For instance, Watson and Clark (1997, Table 7) present median internal consistency estimates across 11 samples (nine of students, one of adults, and one of psychiatric patients), with a combined sample size of 8,194; these data reflect eight different time frames. All of the longer (i.e., five- to eight-item) PANAS-X scales were highly reliable, with median coefficient alphas of .93 (Joviality), .88 (Guilt), .87 (Fear), .87 (Sadness), .85 (Hostility), and .83 (Self-Assurance). As would be expected, the reliabilities of the shorter scales tended to be lower, but still were quite good: .88 (Fatigue), .83 (Shyness), .78 (Attentiveness), .77 (Surprise), and .76 (Serenity). We shall examine these lower order scales in greater detail in subsequent sections, considering various types of evidence (e.g., discriminant validity, temporal stability, and self-other agreement) related to their construct validity.

General Issues in Assessment at the Lower Order Level

We conclude this review by discussing two general problems in the lower order assessment of affect. First, except for the introduction of the PANAS-X a few years ago, it appears that little psychometric progress has been made in this area over the past 20 to 30 years. It is particularly disturbing that we still lack a compelling taxonomy of affect at the specific, lower order level (see also Watson & Clark, 1997). That is, even after nearly 50 years of study, mood researchers still show no consensus regarding the basic states that must be included in any complete and comprehensive assessment of affect. Without an organizing taxonomic scheme, it is impossible to determine which of the instruments we have reviewed ultimately provides the most valid and comprehensive assessment of affect.

Our review does suggest two important points of agreement. First, all four instruments in current use (i.e., MAACL-R, POMS, DES, PANAS-X) assess a common core of subjective distress defined by three specific negative affective states: fear-tension-anxiety, sadness-depression-dejection, and anger-hostility-aggression. Second, all of these inventories include at least one measure of positive mood. Beyond that, however, one sees many important differences. For instance, the PANAS-X assesses three different types of positive mood, whereas the MAACL-R and DES include two, and the POMS only one. The POMS, DES, and PANAS-X all include a measure of tiredness-fatigue, whereas the MAACL-R does not. The PANAS-X combines descriptors of anger, disgust, and contempt into a single scale, whereas the DES divides them into three separate scales; moreover, the POMS and MAACL-R focus exclusively on anger and fail to include disgust or contempt terms at all. Finally, it is noteworthy that each of the instruments contains unique content that is not well captured by any of the others. Thus, only the DES contains a measure of Shame, only the POMS assesses Confusion-Bewilderment, only the MAACL-R measures Sensation Seeking, and only the PANAS-X includes a marker of Serenity.

These obvious differences give rise to some important questions: How does one choose among these measures? Which of these assessment approaches is preferable? For instance, is it necessary to include descriptors of contempt and disgust in a comprehensive assessment of mood? If so, should they be combined with terms reflecting anger (as in the PANAS-X) or should they be analyzed separately (as in the DES)? Unfortunately, in the absence of any clear structural consensus, it is impossible to provide any compelling answers to these questions.

The second problem is that remarkably few studies have directly compared the psychometric properties of two or more instruments in the same sample and under the same assessment conditions. Because of this, it is hazardous to offer any definitive conclusions regarding the relative psychometric merits of these inventories. For instance, our survey of the evidence suggests that the brief DES scales typically are less reliable than their counterparts in the other inventories; although this makes good psychometric sense (in that shorter scales generally have lower coefficient alphas; see Clark & Watson, 1995), it still would be reassuring to have this point documented under controlled conditions that eliminate possible alternative explanations.

There have been a few exceptions, however. Zuckerman and Lubin (1985, Tables 16 and 17) report convergent correlations between the POMS scales and trait and state MAACL-R scores. Unfortunately, the sample sizes tend to be small (e.g., one set of correlations is based on the responses of 37 college students), and the results are complex and difficult to interpret. For instance, across four different samples, the state version of the MAACL-R Anxiety scale had convergent correlations of .09, .68, .47, and .08 with POMS

TABLE 14.2   Correlations Among Negative Affect Scales from the PANAS-X and POMS

Scale	1	2	3	4	5	6
PANAS-X Scales						
1. Fear	(.87)					
2. Sadness	.61	(.86)				
3. Hostility	.58	.49	(.85)			
POMS Scales						
4. Tension-Anxiety	**.85**	.57	.62	(.85)		
5. Depression-Dejection	.74	**.85**	.66	.69	(.92)	
6. Anger-Hostility	.59	.51	**.91**	.63	.66	(.90)

Note. Convergent correlations are highlighted; coefficient alphas are in parentheses. All correlations are significant at $p < .01$, two-tailed. PANAS-X = Expanded Form of the Positive and Negative Affect Schedule (Watson & Clark, 1994). POMS = Profile of Mood States (McNair et al., 1971).

Tension-Anxiety. Corresponding correlations between the MAACL-R Depression and POMS Depression-Dejection scales were .13, .38, .50, and .32, respectively. Although these convergent correlations seem quite low, it should be noted that the two instruments reflected different time instructions. Specifically, respondents completed daily affect ratings on the MAACL-R, but rated their moods over the previous week on the POMS.

Watson and Clark (1994, Table 15) provide a more compelling comparison of convergent and discriminant validity in a sample of 563 students who rated their mood over "the past few weeks," using descriptors from both the POMS and PANAS-X. Table 14.2 presents an adapted version of these data, reporting correlations among the fear-anxiety, sadness-depression, and anger-hostility scales from both instruments (it also includes reliability information not previously published). Three aspects of these data are noteworthy. First, Table 14.2 demonstrates that all of these scales are highly reliable, with coefficient alphas ranging from .85 (PANAS-X Hostility) to .92 (POMS Depression-Dejection). Second, the instruments show impressive convergent validity. Specifically, the convergent correlations between scales assessing the same target affect are .85 (fear-anxiety), .85 (sadness-depression), and .91 (anger-hostility); thus, the two instruments provide very similar coverage of these core affects. Third, the PANAS-X scales show substantially better discriminant validity than their POMS counterparts. The average correlation among the PANAS-X scales (after an r to z transformation) is .56, whereas that among the POMS scales is .66. Moreover, two of the three individual correlations (fear-anxiety vs. sadness-depression; anger-hostility vs. sadness-depression) are significantly lower in the PANAS-X than in the POMS. Thus, the PANAS-X scales ultimately provide a more differentiated assessment of essentially the same content domain.

Watson and Clark (1997) partially replicated these results using only the fear-anxiety and sadness-depression scales in two new samples (521 students and 328 adults). Again, the scales showed impressive convergent validity, with correlations ranging from .77 to .89 across the two samples. Moreover, consistent with the Table 14.2 results, the correlation between the Fear and Sadness scales of the PANAS-X was significantly lower (.58 and .59 in the student and adult data, respectively) than that between POMS Tension-Anxiety and Depression-Dejection ($r = .69$ and .69, respectively) in both samples.

We badly need further comparative data of this sort, representing a much broader array of scales, instruments, time instructions, and participants. In the absence of such data, it is impossible to offer any definitive evaluation of the relative psychometric adequacy of these various mood inventories. With such data, however, we finally could begin to resolve some of the measurement differences we have noted and, consequently, move assessment in this area forward.

GENERAL ISSUES IN CONSTRUCT VALIDITY

The Problem of Measurement Error

The Distorting Influence of Measurement Error

We turn now to an examination of several broad issues related to the overall construct validity of mood measures. We begin by discussing the general problem of measurement error. Thus far, the large majority of the findings we have considered are based on raw correlations that have not been corrected for the influence of error. Can such uncorrected correlations be trusted, or do they yield highly distorted results?

Mood researchers have been concerned with the effects of both random and systematic error for more than 3 decades (Bentler, 1969; Diener & Emmons, 1984; Russell, 1979, 1980). The general conclusion from the earlier literature on this topic was that error exerted only a modest effect, assuming that one (a) employed suitably reliable scales and (b) avoided highly problematic response formats such as adjective checklists (e.g., Watson & Tellegen, 1985). In a highly influential paper, however, Green et al. (1993) challenged the prevailing practice of analyzing raw, uncorrected data, arguing that it yielded distorted and highly misleading results. In fact, they argued that raw data could not be trusted at all. Green et al. (1993) were particularly interested in the bipolarity of the Pleasantness versus Unpleasantness dimension (note that they referred to the two poles of this dimension as "positive affect" and "negative affect," respectively). In discussing the nature of this dimension, they made the bold assertion that "When one adjusts for random and systematic error in positive and negative affect, correlations between the

two that at first seem close to 0 are revealed to be closer to -1.00 and support a largely bipolar structure" (p. 1029).

To establish the validity of their claim, Green et al. (1993) reported supportive findings from several studies. In discussing the results of their Study 1, for instance, they pointed out that an observed correlation of $-.25$ was transformed into a latent correlation of $-.84$ after controlling for error (see Green et al., 1993, p. 1033). These seemingly impressive results have been interpreted by subsequent writers as establishing that raw, uncorrected correlations are highly distorted and can be expected to yield misleading results (Feldman Barrett & Russell, 1998; Russell & Carroll, 1999). Feldman Barrett and Russell (1998), for example, concluded that "Green et al. (1993) delivered the *coup de grâce* to all research in which conclusions are based directly on the *observed* correlations between *measures* of affect" (p. 968; emphasis in original).

However, as we document in detail elsewhere (see Watson & Clark, 1997; Watson & Tellegen, 1999; Watson et al., 1999), these critiques have substantially overestimated the actual effect of measurement error on mood ratings. Indeed, corrected correlations will approach 1.00 only when the raw, uncorrected correlations already are quite substantial. For instance, as noted earlier, Watson and Tellegen (1999) summarized the results of several studies that reported latent, corrected correlations between measures of Pleasantness and Unpleasantness; these correlations ranged from $-.84$ to $-.93$, with a median value of $-.91$. It is noteworthy, however, that the mean uncorrected correlations ranged from $-.53$ to $-.78$ across these same studies, with a median value of $-.56$ (see Watson & Tellegen, 1999, Table 1). Thus, the bipolarity of this dimension already is readily apparent in raw, uncorrected data, as we already observed in our own Table 14.1 (weighted mean $r = -.50$). In contrast, measures of High Positive Affect and High Negative Affect had raw correlations ranging from $-.18$ to $-.36$, with a median value of $-.25$; correcting them for measurement error yielded latent correlations ranging from $-.43$ to $-.58$ ($Mdn = -.46$). More generally, analyses of this issue have established that controlling for measurement error can transform (a) low correlations into moderate correlations and (b) strong correlations into very strong correlations, but that it will not turn (c) low correlations into strong correlations (see Watson & Tellegen, 1999).

On the basis of these data, we can conclude that measurement error exerts only a moderate influence on mood ratings, and that raw, uncorrected correlations do not yield highly distorted or misleading results. This conclusion is unsurprising once one understands how these correlations are corrected for measurement error; we therefore will present a brief discussion of this topic. Recent analyses of this issue (e.g.,

TABLE 14.3   Estimated Latent Correlations Between Factors as a Function of the Mean Convergent (Within-Factor) and Discriminant (Between-Factor) Correlations

Mean Convergent Correlation	Mean Discriminant Correlation							
	−.10	−.20	−.30	−.40	−.50	−.60	−.70	−.80
.20	−.50							
.30	−.33	−.67						
.40	−.25	−.50	−.75					
.50	−.20	−.40	−.60	−.80				
.60	−.17	−.33	−.50	−.67	−.83			
.70	−.14	−.29	−.43	−.57	−.71	−.86		
.80	−.13	−.25	−.38	−.50	−.63	−.75	−.88	
.90	−.11	−.22	−.33	−.44	−.56	−.67	−.78	−.89

Note. These correlations are computed from matrices in which (a) all of the convergent (within-factor) correlations are constrained be equal and (b) all of the discriminant correlations are constrained to be equal. See text for details.

Feldman Barrett & Russell, 1998; Green et al., 1993; Tellegen et al., 1999; Yik et al., 1999) have used multiple indicators of each hypothesized construct (e.g., Pleasantness and Unpleasantness) to define latent underlying factors in a confirmatory factor analysis; this allows one to estimate the correlation between these latent factors, which then is interpreted as the corrected correlation between the constructs. For instance, as we discussed earlier, the CMQ provides three different indicators (using three different response formats) to measure both Pleasantness and Unpleasantness; these multiple indicators then can be used to define underlying Pleasantness and Unpleasantness factors, and the correlation between them can be estimated.

How is the correlation between these factors estimated? In essence, confirmatory factor analysis computes a correlation that is corrected for attenuation due to unreliability (Campbell, 1996); in this case, reliability is estimated by treating the multiple indicators as parallel forms of the same instrument. Suppose, for instance, that one has a data set containing six variables: three are markers of Pleasantness, and three assess Unpleasantness. Let us suppose further that (a) each of the Pleasantness measures correlates .80 with the others, (b) each of the Unpleasantness markers correlates .80 with the others, and (c) all of the cross-construct correlations (i.e., those between Pleasantness and Unpleasantness) are exactly −.50. In this simple, idealized case, the disattenuated correlation between the factors would be estimated as −.50/.80, or −.625.

To document this important point, we submitted a large series of idealized correlation matrices of this type to EQS (Bentler & Wu, 1995), a widely used structural modeling program. As in the previous example, all of the correlations between indicators of the same construct (e.g., between two indicators of Pleasantness, or between two markers of Unpleasantness; we refer to these subsequently as *convergent correlations*) were constrained to have the same value; we

tested matrices with convergent correlations ranging from a low of .20 to a high of .90. Similarly, all of the cross-factor correlations (e.g., between measures of Pleasantness and Unpleasantness; we will refer to these as *discriminant correlations*) were restricted to be the same; we tested matrices with discriminant correlations ranging from −.10 to −.80. Finally, we ran parallel series of matrices that included two, three, or four indicators of each construct.

These analyses (which are summarized in Table 14.3) yielded two noteworthy findings. First, the number of indicators had no effect whatsoever on the estimated correlations; in other words, we obtained identical results regardless of whether we used two, three, or four indicators of each construct. Accordingly, Table 14.3 presents a single matrix of correlations collapsed across this parameter. This finding is important because it indicates that using a large number of indicators does not necessarily enhance one's ability to model measurement error; we return to this issue later. Second, as we suggested earlier, the estimated factor intercorrelation can be computed quite simply by dividing the mean discriminant correlation by the average convergent correlation. For example, if the discriminant correlations all are −.20—and the convergent correlations all are .40—then the estimated factor intercorrelation is −.50. Again, this is conceptually analogous to computing the traditional correction for attenuation, using the multiple indicators of each construct as parallel forms to estimate reliability.

Viewed in this light, it is easy to see why mood researchers actually have failed to find instances in which raw correlations of −.25 are transformed into latent correlations of −.84; indeed, if the average discriminant correlation was only −.25, one would need mean convergent correlations of approximately .296 to achieve this result. This was hardly the case in the data reported by Green et al. (1993). In fact, although they had one raw correlation of −.25 in their initial analysis, the average uncorrected correlation was much higher (−.53). Coupled with a mean convergent correlation of .64, this yielded an estimated factor intercorrelation of −.84 (see Green et al., 1993, Tables 1 and 2).

Our remarks should not be interpreted as suggesting that measurement error is unimportant. Error obviously is an important fact of life that exerts a significant influence on mood ratings. Our point, rather, is that sweeping dismissals of raw, uncorrected correlations are not supported by the data. Instead, our review of the evidence indicates that uncorrected correlational data still can play a very useful role in mood research, as long as one uses reliable mood measures and adequate response formats.

Modeling Measurement Error

As we have seen, measurement error can be expected to have a significant effect on mood ratings, and it obviously is important to be able to estimate its impact on one's data. How should one go about modeling the potential effects of measurement error in mood data?

As we have noted, the most popular strategy has been to adopt a multimethod approach in which a variety of different formats (e.g., adjective checklist, Likert rating scales) are used to measure the same constructs. For instance, the CMQ provides three different rating formats that have been used to compute corrected, latent correlations among the higher order dimensions of the affect circumplex (Feldman Barrett & Russell, 1998; Yik et al., 1999). Similarly, Green et al. used four different rating formats (adjective checklist, a 4-point agree-disagree rating scale, a 4-point describes-me format, and 7-point Likert scales) to assess both Pleasantness and Unpleasantness. If properly used, this multiformat approach can provide an excellent way of modeling error.

However, it also suffers from two potentially important problems. First, it requires that researchers create multiple parallel forms of the same constructs, which is not always an easy task. The obvious danger is that systematic differences in content will emerge across the various formats, thereby making the measures nonparallel and, in turn, leading to distorted estimates of the interfactor correlations. As we discuss in detail elsewhere, this appears to be a significant problem in the CMQ's assessment of Low Negative Affect (Watson et al., 1999), and in Green et al.'s (1993) measurement of High Positive Affect and High Negative Affect (Watson & Tellegen, 1999).

Second, the use of multiple formats is cumbersome and time consuming, and it places severe restrictions on the range of content that can be assessed without taxing the patience of respondents. This is a particularly vexing problem in the assessment of highly evanescent phenomena such as current, momentary mood states. It is hardly accidental, for instance,

that Green et al. (1993)—who used four different response formats—restricted themselves to assessing only Pleasantness and Unpleasantness in most of their studies. More generally, it clearly would be quite difficult to use three or four different rating methods to assess the entire range of content subsumed in multiaffect inventories such as the DES, POMS, MAACL, and PANAS-X.

Fortunately, one does not necessarily need to use three or four response formats. Indeed, we already have seen that the estimated factor intercorrelation is unaffected by the sheer number of indicators used to define each construct, assuming that these indicators all show very similar convergent-discriminant properties. To document this important point further, we reanalyzed the correlation matrices reported by Green et al. (1993) and Feldman Barrett and Russell (1998), subjecting them to confirmatory factor analyses using EQS. To simplify these analyses, we restricted ourselves to estimating the interfactor correlation between Pleasantness and Unpleasantness and ignored other aspects of their data. We conducted parallel analyses of four different correlation matrices reported by Green et al. (1993), as well as two relevant matrices presented in Feldman Barrett and Russell (1998).

We began by using only two indicators to define both Pleasantness and Unpleasantness in each of the four Green et al. data sets, using all possible pairwise combinations of formats (e.g., adjective checklist vs. agree-disagree; adjective checklist vs. describes-me); the mean interfactor correlations (averaged across the six possible pairwise combinations) are reported in the first row of Table 14.4. Next, we repeated this process using all possible combinations of three methods; the average correlations (computed across the four possible combinations) are reported in the second row of Table 14.4. Finally, we recreated the results originally reported by Green et al. (1993) by recalculating the interfactor correlations using all four methods; these are shown in the third row of the table. Similarly, we first analyzed the two Feldman Barrett and Russell (1998) data sets using all possible pairwise combinations of indicators to estimate the factor intercorrelations; the mean correlations (averaged across the three possible pairwise combinations) also are reported in the first row of Table 14.4. We then recreated their reported results by recomputing the correlations using all three available methods; these are reported in the second row of the table.

These results clearly establish that one obtains very similar correlations regardless of whether two, three, or four different methods are used to define Pleasantness and Unpleasantness. It is particularly noteworthy that two methods are sufficient to produce very strong corrected correlations between these constructs. Across the six data sets, the mean correlations ranged from −.80 to −.92, with a median value of −.86. Moreover, these values are deflated somewhat by Green

TABLE 14.4   Estimated Latent Correlations Between Pleasantness and Unpleasantness as a Function of the Number of Assessed Methods

| No. of Methods | Green, Goldman, & Salovey (1993) | | | | Feldman Barrett & Russell (1998) | |
| | Study 1 | | | | | |
	Time 1	Time 2	Study 2	Study 3	Study 2	Study 3
All methods						
Two methods	−.80	−.82	−.92	−.81	−.92	−.92
Three methods	−.84	−.85	−.93	−.85	−.93	−.92
Four methods	−.84	−.85	−.92	−.86	—	—
Dropping Adjective Checklist						
Two methods	−.87	−.87	−.97	−.89	—	—
Three methods	−.87	−.86	−.93	−.90	—	—

Note. $N = 139$ (Green et al., 1993, Study 1), 250 (Green et al., 1993, Study 2), 304 (Green et al., 1993, Study 3), 225 (Feldman Barrett & Russell, 1998, Study 2), 316 (Feldman Barrett & Russell, 1998, Study 3).

et al.'s (1993) use of the highly problematic adjective checklist format. We therefore reran these analyses, dropping the checklist data and using only the other three response methods; paralleling the previous analyses, we initially ran all possible pairwise combinations and then recomputed the correlations using all three methods. The factor intercorrelations from these analyses are displayed in the final two rows of the table. These results are especially striking, in that the mean two-method correlation actually exceeded the four-method correlation in every data set. Clearly, one can model measurement error quite well using only two methods.

In fact, it is unclear whether one actually needs two different methods (in the sense of two different response formats) at all. Thus far, we have considered the potential effects of random error only. One purported advantage of the multiformat approach, however, is that it also permits investigators to model the effects of systematic sources of error, such as response biases. This can be done quite easily by allowing the monomethod error terms (e.g., those representing the adjective checklist measures of Pleasantness and Unpleasantness) to be correlated. Somewhat surprisingly, however, Green

et al. (1993) and Feldman Barrett and Russell (1998) both found that modeling systematic error essentially had no effect on the interfactor correlations.

To examine this issue more closely, we reconducted all of the Table 14.4 analyses that used either three or four rating formats. These new analyses were identical to those reported earlier, except that the monomethod error terms now were allowed to be correlated, thereby modeling the effects of both random and systematic error (we could not conduct these reanalyses on the two-method models, however, because they now would be underidentified; this illustrates one important advantage of having more than two indicators per construct). The resulting interfactor correlations are shown in Table 14.5, which also reports the parallel findings from Table 14.4 (labeled here as "random error only") for comparison purposes. The correlations are virtually identical in every case, regardless of whether one controls for systematic error.

All other things being equal, it clearly is preferable to use multiple measures—and multiple methods—to assess all of the key constructs in a study. However, all other things rarely are equal, such that this basic psychometric principle must be

TABLE 14.5   The Effect of Controlling for Systematic Error on Estimated Latent Correlations Between Pleasantness and Unpleasantness

| Type of Correction | Green, Goldman, & Salovey (1993) | | | | Feldman Barrett & Russell (1998) | |
| | Study 1 | | | | | |
	Time 1	Time 2	Study 2	Study 3	Study 2	Study 3
Three Methods						
Random error only	−.84	−.85	−.93	−.85	−.93	−.92
Random and systematic error	−.84	−.84	−.91	−.87	−.93	−.93
Four Methods						
Random error only	−.84	−.85	−.92	−.86	—	—
Random and systematic error	−.84	−.84	−.91	−.87	—	—

Note. $N = 139$ (Green et al., 1993, Study 1), 250 (Green et al., 1993, Study 2), 304 (Green et al., 1993, Study 3), 225 (Feldman Barrett & Russell, 1998, Study 2), 316 (Feldman Barrett & Russell, 1998, Study 3).

weighed against pragmatic considerations. In light of the data we have presented, we must question whether it is worth the time and bother to create multiple parallel measures using a variety of different response formats. In our view, a much quicker and easier approach is to create multiple indicators of each construct within a single rating method (e.g., unipolar Likert rating scales). Moreover, brief validity scales can be created within this same format to allow one to model systematic response biases such as acquiescence. An excellent example of this approach is reported by Tellegen et al. (1999), who constructed brief measures of Pleasantness, Unpleasantness, and acquiescence that were embedded within a single response format. Using this single-format approach, Tellegen et al. (1999) obtained a corrected latent correlation of $-.92$ between Pleasantness and Unpleasantness, a value that exceeds most of those shown in Tables 14.4 and 14.5. We strongly advocate this method as a simple, quick, and effective alternative to the multiformat strategy.

The Problem of Social Desirability

We conclude our discussion of measurement error by considering the problem of social desirability, another potential source of systematic bias in mood ratings. Psychologists long have been concerned that people might have only limited insight into their thoughts, motives, and feelings; furthermore, it has been argued that self-raters may respond defensively and that they may consciously or unconsciously distort their responses in a socially desirable manner (Edwards & Edwards, 1992; Paulhus & Reid, 1991). This would seem to be a particularly serious problem in mood measurement, which typically involves asking participants to respond to face-valid items whose content is completely undisguised.

One way to investigate this issue is to compare overall mean scores on affect self-ratings with the corresponding judgments made by well-acquainted peers. Compared to self-raters, peer judges should be more objective and relatively free of these biasing, self-enhancing tendencies (see McCrae, 1982, 1994, for a discussion of the various biases attributed to self- and other-raters). If this is, in fact, a substantial problem in self-ratings, then one would predict that mean self-ratings should be tipped in the direction of greater social desirability; that is, compared to peer judges, self-raters should report generally higher levels of positive affectivity and relatively lower levels of negative affectivity.

We examined this issue in four dyadic samples in which respondents generated both self- and other-ratings on the complete PANAS-X; all of these responses were made using general, trait instructions (three of these samples are described in greater detail in Watson et al., 2000; the Texas

dating sample is discussed in Watson & Clark, 1994). The first sample consisted of 279 friendship dyads drawn from the Iowa City area; on average, these respondents had known each other for 33.6 months. The second sample was composed of 68 currently dating couples in Dallas, Texas; at the time of assessment, these couples had been dating for an average of 21.5 months. The third sample was composed of 136 currently dating couples from the Iowa City area; these couples had known each other for an average of 36.0 months and had been dating for an average of 18.2 months. Finally, the fourth sample consisted of 74 married couples drawn from the St. Louis, Missouri, area; the mean length of marriage was 202.6 months, that is, slightly less than 17 years.

Table 14.6 presents a comparison of the mean self- versus other-ratings in each sample. Specifically, it indicates whether the mean self-rating was significantly greater than the mean other-rating ($S > O$), whether the mean self-rating was significantly less than the mean other-rating ($S < O$), or whether the two scores did not differ from one another ($S = O$). The only real support for a self-enhancement bias comes from the married sample; here, self-raters rated themselves as less sad, guilty, hostile, and fatigued than did their spouses. In sharp contrast, however, only 2 of 26 comparisons were significant across the two dating samples: Self-raters described themselves as more alert and attentive in the Texas sample, and as less surprised in the Iowa sample. Finally, the friendship dyads did show clear evidence of a systematic bias, but in the direction opposite to prediction; that is, compared to their friends, self-raters consistently described themselves as experiencing *higher* levels of negative affectivity and *lower* levels of positive affectivity.

On the basis of these data, we can reject the argument that affect self-ratings are systematically biased toward greater social desirability in relation to judgments made by well-acquainted peers. More generally, these data lead us to suspect that self-enhancement does not represent a serious problem in mood measurement. Having said that, however, we also must emphasize that our results do not necessarily indicate that social desirability has no discernible impact on affect ratings; that is, it remains possible that both the self-ratings and the other-ratings were biased toward greater social desirability in these samples.

On the Construct Validity of Trait Affect Measures

Temporal Stability

In this section, we consider several issues that are specifically related to the construct validity of trait affect measures. Earlier, we briefly summarized a range of evidence (e.g.,

TABLE 14.6 Comparison of Mean Self- Versus Other-Ratings on the PANAS-X Scales

Scale	Friendship Dyads	Texas Dating Couples	Iowa Dating Couples	Married Couples
Negative Affect scales				
General Negative Affect	S > O	S = O	S = O	S < O
Fear	S > O	S = O	S = O	S = O
Sadness	S > O	S = O	S = O	S < O
Guilt	S > O	S = O	S = O	S < O
Hostility	S = O	S = O	S = O	S < O
Positive Affect scales				
General Positive Affect	S > O	S = O	S = O	S = O
Joviality	S > O	S = O	S = O	S = O
Self-Assurance	S > O	S = O	S = O	S = O
Attentiveness	S > O	S > O	S = O	S = O
Other affect scales				
Shyness	S > O	S = O	S = O	S = O
Fatigue	S > O	S = O	S = O	S < O
Serenity	S < O	S = O	S = O	S = O
Surprise	S > O	S = O	S < O	S = O

Note. $N = 558$ (Friendship Dyads), 136 (Texas Dating Couples), 272 (Iowa Dating Couples), 148 (Married Couples). The entries in the table indicate whether the mean self-rating is significantly greater than the mean other-rating (S > O), the mean self-rating is significantly less than the mean other-rating (S < O), or the two means did not differ from each other (S = O).

temporal stability, self-other convergence) that broadly establishes the validity of such measures. Our goal here is to examine this evidence in greater detail so as to (a) evaluate the relative merits of various approaches to trait assessment and (b) suggest possible areas for improvement.

We begin with an examination of *temporal stability,* which is an essential property of any trait dimension. Specifically, we should expect to see substantial evidence of *rank-order stability:* Individuals who initially score relatively high on the trait should remain relatively high upon retest, whereas those who initially are low should remain low in subsequent assessments. We investigated this issue using two samples who completed general, trait versions of the complete PANAS-X on two different occasions. The first sample (short-term stability) consisted of 409 SMU students who were assessed across a 2-month retest interval (a slightly different version of these data are reported in Watson & Clark, 1994, Table 20). The second sample (long-term stability) was composed of 396 University of Iowa students who initially completed the PANAS-X in September, 1996, and subsequently were reassessed in the spring and early summer of 1999; these data therefore reflect an average retest interval of approximately 32 months (see Vaidya, Gray, Haig, & Watson, 2002, for more details).

Table 14.7 reports stability correlations for the PANAS-X scales in both samples; the table also includes weighted mean correlations (after r to z transformation) across the two data sets. The most noteworthy aspect of these data is that all of the PANAS-X scales show moderate to strong stability in

both samples; the short-term correlations generally fall in the .50 to .65 range, whereas the long-term coefficients tend to be in the .40 to .55 range. Together with other findings in this area (e.g., Watson & Walker, 1996), these data clearly establish that general affect ratings contain a stable, dispositional component; this, in turn, helps to establish their construct validity as trait measures.

Beyond that, however, we also see evidence of consistent differences in stability across the various scales. At the one

TABLE 14.7 Retest Reliabilities of the PANAS-X Scales

Scale	Short-Term	Long-Term	Mean r
Negative Affect scales			
General Negative Affect	.59	.48	.54
Fear	.57	.45	.52
Sadness	.59	.51	.55
Guilt	.66	.46	.57
Hostility	.57	.50	.54
(Mean r)	(.60)	(.48)	
Positive Affect scales			
General Positive Affect	.64	.50	.57
Joviality	.64	.54	.59
Self-Assurance	.68	.51	.60
Attentiveness	.55	.46	.51
(Mean r)	(.63)	(.50)	
Other affect scales			
Shyness	.65	.58	.61
Fatigue	.52	.42	.48
Serenity	.51	.48	.49
Surprise	.51	.43	.47
(Mean r)	(.55)	(.48)	

Note. $N = 409$ (short-term), 396 (long-term). All correlations are significant at $p < .01$, two-tailed.

extreme, Shyness, Joviality, and Self-Assurance all show average stability correlations of approximately .60; at the other extreme, Fatigue, Serenity, and Surprise have mean retest correlations below .50. In fact, the long-term (i.e., 2- to 3-year) retest correlations of the most stable scales tend to be as high or higher than the short-term (i.e., 2-month) correlations of the least stable scales. These consistent differences suggest the intriguing possibility that certain types of affect are more stable and traitlike than others. More fundamentally, they suggest that the notion of trait affect can be more meaningfully applied to some types of mood state (e.g., energy, enthusiasm, confidence, and timidity) than to others (e.g., sluggishness, calmness, surprise). We currently are conducting further stability analyses to investigate the merits of this idea.

Another interesting aspect of these data is that although the temporal stability correlations are substantial in magnitude, they nevertheless tend to be lower than those obtained for other trait measures. In this regard, 392 of the participants in the long-term stability sample also completed the Big Five Inventory (BFI; John, Donahue, & Kentle, 1991) at both assessments. The BFI is a measure of the prominent five-factor model of personality, which consists of the general dimensions of Neuroticism, Extroversion, Openness, Agreeableness, and Conscientiousness (John & Srivastava, 1999; Watson, Clark, & Harkness, 1994). The stability correlations for these broad traits tended to be significantly higher than those of the PANAS-X scales, ranging from .59 (Agreeableness, Neuroticism) to .71 (Extroversion), with a mean value of .64.

What do these comparative data tell us about the construct validity of trait affect scales? To a considerable extent, these retest correlations likely reflect true, valid differences in the actual stability of the underlying constructs. It makes sense, for instance, that affect-centered traits would be somewhat less stable than behavior-based dimensions such as Extroversion and Conscientiousness. Thus, it is hardly surprising that the PANAS-X Positive Affect scale (stability $r = .57$ in this sample) is significantly less stable than BFI Extroversion ($r = .71$).

However, it is surprising that the PANAS-X Negative Affect scale ($r = .48$) is significantly less stable than BFI Neuroticism ($r = .59$). These two scales correlated strongly with each other at both Time 1 ($r = .62$) and Time 2 ($r = .60$). Furthermore, the coefficient alphas for the 10-item PANAS-X Negative Affect scale tend to be somewhat higher than those of the 8-item BFI Neuroticism scale, so this stability difference cannot be attributed to differential reliability. Finally—and most importantly—the content of the two scales is extremely similar. Indeed, the BFI Neuroticism items (e.g., *can be, tense. can be moody, gets nervous easily, is depressed, blue, worries a lot*) are strongly affective in character and assess content that is quite similar to that contained in the PANAS-X Negative Affect scale. This suggests to us that subtle differences in format and presentation (such as the nature of the instructions given to participants) may have a significant impact on the long-term stability of the measures (see Vaidya et al., 2002). If so, then this further suggests that one can enhance the construct validity of trait affect measures by introducing relatively subtle stylistic changes. We currently are conducting research to explore this important possibility.

Self-Other Agreement

Another traditional approach in establishing the construct validity of trait measures is to examine the magnitude of the correlations between self- and peer-ratings of the same targets. To the extent that these two raters agree, one can be confident that trait measures are validly assessing systematic, meaningful individual differences.

Accordingly, Table 14.8 presents self-other agreement correlations in the four dyadic samples described in our earlier discussion of social desirability; in addition, the final column of the table shows weighted mean correlations (after r to z transformation) computed across all of the individual data sets. In many respects, these data closely resemble the stability results in the previous table. Once again, the most noteworthy aspect of these data is that—with the single exception of Surprise—all of the PANAS-X scales show substantial convergent validity, with weighted mean agreement correlations ranging from .25 (Fear) to .42 (Self-Assurance). Moreover, these correlations show clear evidence of the well-established *acquaintanceship effect;* that is, numerous studies have shown that self-other agreement improves with increasing levels of acquaintance (Funder, 1995; Funder & Colvin, 1988, 1997; Watson et al., 2000). In Table 14.8, this effect can be seen in the elevated level of agreement among the married couples; indeed, the convergent correlations generally fall in the .35 to .55 range in this sample.

As in the stability data, we also see consistent differences across the affect scales. At one extreme, Joviality and Self-Assurance (which also showed relatively high stabilities) had weighted mean agreement correlations of .41 and .42, respectively; at the other extreme, Surprise showed an average convergence of only .15 across the four samples, and even failed to display significant self-other agreement in the married couples. These negative findings are consistent with other data that challenge the construct validity of trait ratings of Surprise (Watson & Clark, 1994). In light of these data, we can conclude that this affect does not have a meaningful dispositional component and we recommend that Surprise items not be assessed in the trait version of the PANAS-X.

TABLE 14.8   Self-Other Agreement Correlations for the PANAS-X Scales

Scale	Friendship Dyads	Texas Dating Couples	Iowa Dating Couples	Married Couples	Mean r
Negative Affect scales					
General Negative Affect	.20*	.23*	.22*	.44*	.28
Fear	.20*	.23*	.20*	.36*	.25
Sadness	.31*	.31*	.32*	.47*	.35
Guilt	.27*	.14	.26*	.49*	.30
Hostility	.21*	.30*	.32*	.50*	.34
(Mean r)	(.24)	(.25)	(.26)	(.45)	
Positive Affect scales					
General Positive Affect	.30*	.32*	.33*	.39*	.34
Joviality	.38*	.37*	.38*	.51*	.41
Self-Assurance	.36*	.43*	.38*	.52*	.42
Attentiveness	.28*	.32*	.29*	.26*	.29
(Mean r)	(.33)	(.36)	(.35)	(.43)	
Other affect scales					
Shyness	.37*	.32*	.28*	.36*	.33
Fatigue	.13*	.31*	.17*	.53*	.29
Serenity	.21*	.38*	.17*	.38*	.29
Surprise	.18*	.13	.17*	.10	.15
(Mean r)	(.22)	(.29)	(.20)	(.35)	

Note. N = 558 (Friendship Dyads), 136 (Texas Dating Couples), 272 (Iowa Dating Couples), 148 (Married Couples).
$p < .01$, two-tailed.

In contrast, the rest of the scales show reasonable convergent validity. Paralleling the stability data, however, it again is noteworthy that these agreement correlations tend to be significantly lower than those observed for other traits, such as the Big Five. In this regard, Watson et al. (2000) also assessed self-other convergence on the Big Five traits in the friendship, married, and Iowa-dating samples. Across these samples, the Big Five showed mean agreement correlations ranging from .42 (Agreeableness) to .53 (Openness; see Watson et al., 2000, Table 2).

Consistent with our earlier discussion of stability, these agreement correlations surely reflect true, valid differences in the nature of underlying constructs. In fact, the accumulating data clearly establish the existence of a *trait visibility effect*— that is, easily observable personality traits (those with clear, frequent behavioral manifestations) yield better interjudge agreement and higher self-other correlations than do more internal, subjective traits (e.g., Funder, 1995; Funder & Colvin, 1988, 1997; John & Robins, 1993; Watson et al., 2000). Thus, it is hardly surprising that traits such as Extroversion and Conscientiousness show better self-other agreement that do measures of trait affectivity. Once again, however, it is much more difficult to explain why self-other agreement correlations consistently are higher for measures of Neuroticism than for the negative affect scales of the PANAS-X (see Watson et al., 2000). For instance, the BFI Neuroticism scale produced a significantly higher agreement correlation ($r = .37$) in the friendship sample than did the

PANAS-X Negative Affect scale ($r = .20$). As discussed earlier, this substantial correlational gap cannot be attributed to differential reliability or to substantial differences in item content. Consequently, it again suggests to us that subtle differences in format and presentation may enhance the construct validity of trait affect measures; as noted previously, we currently are conducting research to explore this important possibility.

General Versus Aggregated Ratings of Trait Affect

Thus far, our review indicates that general trait ratings (a) have substantial construct validity but (b) perhaps can be improved somewhat through changes in format and presentation. We conclude this discussion by comparing the relative merits of this approach to an alternative method for assessing trait affect, namely, the use of aggregated, on-line ratings.

This recently has become an important topic in the affect literature. It arose in response to evidence indicating that general affect ratings suffer from a variety of problems that may substantially lessen their validity (Kahneman, 1999; Russell & Carroll, 1999; Schwarz & Strack, 1999; Stone, Shiffman, & DeVries, 1999). Most of these problems arise from the retrospective nature of these global ratings, which require respondents to (a) recall their relevant past experiences and then (b) draw inferences from them. This process is subject to at least three problems. First, Fredrickson and Kahneman (1993) demonstrated that global ratings suffer from *duration neglect,* that is, from an insensitivity to the actual amount of time that an affect was experienced (see also Kahneman, 1999; Russell & Carroll, 1999). Second, several studies have shown that general affect ratings are influenced by the respondents' mood at the time of assessment (e.g., Schwarz & Clore, 1983; Schwarz & Strack, 1999; Stone et al., 1999). Third, retrospective ratings are subject to recency effects, such that more recent experiences have a greater influence than more distant ones (Schwarz & Sudman, 1994; Stone et al., 1999).

In light of these problems, many researchers have argued for an alternative assessment approach based on immediate, on-line ratings of affect (e.g., ratings of one's current, momentary mood). A single rating of current affect obviously cannot provide a valid assessment of long-term individual differences in trait affectivity. However, multiple on-line judgments of this type can be averaged to create more reliable and valid trait measures. Note that this approach to trait assessment neatly circumvents all of the problems associated with retrospective judgments. Moreover, it takes advantage of the well-established benefits of aggregation, which typically yields substantial gains in both reliability and validity (Rushton, Brainerd, & Pressley, 1983). Consequently, after reviewing the advantages and disadvantages associated with both global and aggregated ratings, Stone et al. (1999) encouraged researchers to avoid retrospective ratings and to "target multiple, immediate reports from people in their typical environments" (p. 26; see also Kahneman, 1999; Schwarz & Strack, 1999).

Before proceeding further, we must emphasize that these two approaches to trait affect assessment generally show moderate to strong levels of convergence (see Watson & Tellegen, 1999; Watson, Tellegen, & Cudeck, 2002). To further establish this key point, Table 14.9 reports correlations between general and aggregated mean ratings in two large samples; in both cases, affect was assessed using the complete PANAS-X. The first sample was composed of 251 SMU students who initially completed a general, trait form of the PANAS-X. They then rated their daily mood once per day over a period of 6–7 weeks; these responses were averaged across the entire rating period to yield mean scores on each PANAS-X scale. To be included in the analyses reported here, a respondent had to complete a minimum of 30 daily assessments; overall, the participants produced a total of 11,062 observations ($M = 44.1$ per participant). The second sample was composed of 187 University of Iowa students who first rated their general affect, and then rated their moods each week over a period of 14 weeks. To be included in these analyses, a respondent had to complete a minimum of 10 weekly assessments; overall, these participants produced a total of 2,544 observations ($M = 13.6$ per person).

TABLE 14.9   Convergent Correlations Between General Trait Ratings and Aggregated Mood Scores on the PANAS-X Scales

Scale	Daily Data	Weekly Data	Mean r
Negative Affect Scales			
General Negative Affect	.48	.63	.55
Fear	.46	.63	.54
Sadness	.55	.64	.59
Guilt	.60	.68	.64
Hostility	.44	.52	.48
(Mean r)	(.51)	(.62)	
Positive Affect scales			
General Positive Affect	.54	.49	.52
Joviality	.55	.53	.54
Self-Assurance	.51	.51	.51
Attentiveness	.53	.45	.50
(Mean r)	(.53)	(.50)	
Other affect scales			
Shyness	.47	.61	.53
Fatigue	.44	.59	.51
Serenity	.52	.52	.52
Surprise	.37	.50	.43
(Mean r)	(.45)	(.56)	

Note. $N = 251$ (Daily Data), 187 (Weekly Data). All correlations are significant at $p < .01$, two-tailed.

Consistent with other evidence of this type (see Diener et al., 1995; Watson & Tellegen, 1999), Table 14.9 demonstrates that the two types of ratings converged well in both samples. Specifically, the correlations ranged from .37 to .60 ($Mdn = .51$) in the daily data, and from .45 to .64 ($Mdn = .53$) in the weekly ratings. These results are quite reassuring, in that they indicate that these two assessment approaches can be expected to yield substantially similar results.

Although these two approaches generally converge well, however, the correlations obviously do not approach 1.00. This raises an important question: To the extent that they disagree, which assessment strategy should be given greater credibility? Although general affect ratings clearly suffer from several problems that render them imperfect, it would be a mistake to conclude that aggregated, on-line judgments therefore represent a better, more valid assessment approach. This is because aggregated ratings have some serious problems of their own (see Watson et al., 2002).

One particularly serious problem is the reduced level of discriminant validity among scales assessing specific, lower order affects. Diener et al. (1995) collected both global ratings (in which respondents indicated how they had felt over the past month) and aggregated daily ratings (averaged over 52 consecutive days) from 212 participants who completed measures of four different negative affects: fear, anger, shame, and sadness. The resulting correlations are presented in Table 14.10. It is noteworthy that the two types of ratings again showed good convergent validity; specifically, correlations between parallel measures of the same affect ranged

TABLE 14.10 Correlations Among Negatively Valenced Scales (Diener, Smith, & Fujita, 1995)

	1	2	3	4	5	6	7
Month Ratings							
1. Fear	—						
2. Anger	.61	—					
3. Shame	.56	.54	—				
4. Sad	.59	.60	.57	—			
Aggregated Ratings							
5. Fear	**.69**	.53	.46	.53	—		
6. Anger	.46	**.61**	.44	.51	.76	—	
7. Shame	.39	.41	**.52**	.41	.73	.79	—
8. Sad	.42	.43	.42	**.64**	.70	.77	.71

Note. $N = 212$. Convergent correlations are highlighted. These results are adapted from Diener et al. (1995, Table 4).

from .52 to .69, with a mean value (after r to z transformation) of .62. The discriminant correlations differed dramatically, however. In the global ratings, correlations among the negative affect scales ranged from .54 to .61, with a mean value of .58; note that this average coefficient reflects 33.6% shared variance. In marked contrast, the corresponding correlations in the aggregated ratings ranged from .70 to .79, with a mean value of .75; this average coefficient represents 56.2% common variance. The reduced discriminant validity of aggregated ratings is a very robust phenomenon: We have replicated this finding in several analyses of the negative affect scales of the PANAS-X, and have extended it by showing that it also holds true for positively valenced states (see Watson et al., 2002).

What causes this reduced discriminant validity in aggregated mood ratings? As we discuss in detail elsewhere (Watson et al., 2002), the most likely explanation is that it reflects the augmented influence of systematic measurement errors, such as acquiescence. *Acquiescence* represents a tendency to respond to different items similarly, irrespective of content; thus, it will bias all observed correlations toward greater positivity (i.e., toward +1.00). If the true correlation between two constructs is positive (as in the case of similarly valenced affects such as fear and sadness), acquiescence will artifactually inflate the observed coefficients.

As we already have discussed, systematic error generally has only a modest impact on disaggregated mood ratings. It appears, however, that acquiescence exerts a much greater influence in aggregated ratings, thereby substantially inflating the correlations among similarly valenced affects such as fear and sadness (and, in turn, reducing the discriminant validity of measures of these constructs). This augmented acquiescence component likely is an unintended byproduct of the aggregation process itself. Traditional discussions of aggregation have argued that it progressively eliminates measurement error (e.g., Rushton et al., 1983). However, this generalization

applies only to *random* error. Because random errors are, by definition, uncorrelated across assessments, they can be expected to cancel each other out as more observations are averaged. In marked contrast, however, systematic errors (such as acquiescence) are correlated across assessments; thus, their influence may grow with increasing aggregation. Furthermore, if this error variance expands more rapidly than the true score component, increasing aggregation actually may have the paradoxical effect of lessening the validity of the resulting measure.

An acquiescence-based explanation also can account for a second curious property of aggregated ratings, namely, an almost complete absence of bipolarity. As noted earlier, acquiescence will bias observed correlations toward greater positivity. If the true correlation between two constructs is negative (as in the case of oppositely valenced affects such as happiness and sadness), acquiescence will act to weaken the observed coefficients so that they become more weakly negative—or even slightly positive. Consistent with an acquiescence-based explanation, correlations between measures of negative and positive affectivity repeatedly have been found to be shifted toward greater positivity in aggregated ratings (see Diener & Emmons, 1984; Diener, Larsen, Levine, & Emmons, 1985; Russell & Carroll, 1999; Watson & Clark, 1997; Watson et al., 2002).

In light of these data, it seems reasonable to conclude that response biases such as acquiescence represent a substantially greater problem in aggregated data than in general ratings of trait affectivity. This, in turn, suggests that despite the problems associated with this approach (see Schwarz & Sudman, 1999; Stone et al., 1999), general ratings actually provide more valid and trustworthy data. We certainly are not arguing that aggregated ratings be abandoned. These ratings provide very useful information in a variety of contexts; moreover, as we have seen, they converge well with general trait ratings. Our point, rather, is that to the extent these two approaches disagree, general ratings ultimately appear to have superior construct validity, and therefore should continue to be viewed as the gold standard in trait affect assessment.

RECOMMENDATIONS FOR FUTURE RESEARCH

The mood literature has flourished in recent years, in large part because affect researchers have developed an impressive array of measures to assess most of the key constructs within this domain. Our overall evaluation of the current state of mood assessment is positive. As we have seen, interested researchers have access to a wide range of reliable measures that show both excellent internal consistency and (in the case of trait ratings) adequate temporal stability. Moreover, we now have amassed extensive evidence (e.g., significant correlations between self- and other-ratings of the same individuals) to establish the convergent and discriminant validity of many of these measures. Finally, although measurement error is a universal problem in assessment, we see no evidence that affect measures are especially susceptible to either random or systematic error.

The current situation is particularly good at the higher order level. Assessment in this area has been greatly facilitated by the emergence of a consensual structural scheme—emphasizing the dominance of two general dimensions—during the 1980s (see Feldman Barrett & Russell, 1998; Larsen & Diener, 1992; Russell & Carroll, 1999; Tellegen, et al., 1999; Watson & Tellegen, 1985; Watson et al., 1999). This structural consensus encouraged the development of reliable and valid measures of Positive Affect, Negative Affect, and Pleasantness. As we have seen, however, mood researchers have relied largely on ad hoc Pleasantness measures whose psychometric properties have not been thoroughly analyzed. Accordingly, it would be helpful if future investigators worked to establish standard measures of this construct.

Obviously, however, the Engagement or Activation dimension constitutes the major unresolved problem at this level. Although many theorists have argued that Engagement represents a fundamental dimension of affect (e.g., Feldman Barrett & Russell, 1998; Larsen & Diener, 1992; Russell & Carroll, 1999; Yik et al., 1999), no one has yet developed a fully adequate measure of the construct; thus, we cannot recommend the routine use of any of the existing instruments. Furthermore, as discussed earlier, interested researchers face two formidable—and currently unresolved—assessment problems: (a) a paucity of good marker terms and (b) the weak bipolarity of its two hypothesized ends. In light of these problems, we cannot be optimistic about future attempts to measure this construct. More fundamentally, these problems raise the issue of whether Engagement truly represents a basic dimension of affect. It is particularly disturbing that extensive analyses have identified very few affectively neutral terms representing pure, unambiguous markers of this dimension. Until good, clear markers of the construct can be found, its status as a basic dimension remains suspect. These clearly are crucial issues for future research.

In contrast to assessment at the higher order level, the assessment of lower order, discrete affects remains less satisfactory. As we indicated earlier, the key problem is that we still lack a compelling taxonomy of affect at the specific, lower order level. It is particularly discouraging to note that research in this area appears to have stagnated, such that very little progress has been made in recent years. We emphasize again

that without an organizing structural scheme, it is impossible to evaluate the comprehensiveness and content validity of all existing measures. For instance, should a comprehensive measure contain descriptors related to disgust? If so, should they be assessed separately, or instead combined with markers of anger and contempt? In our view, the absence of a suitable taxonomy is the single most important unresolved issue in mood assessment, and it should be accorded top priority by affect researchers.

In the meantime, it would be enormously helpful if investigators conducted studies that directly compared the reliability and validity of the major instruments in this area (the DES, MAACL-R, PANAS-X, and POMS). The limited evidence that currently is available is sufficient to demonstrate that purported measures of the same construct (e.g., fear-tension-anxiety, sadness-depression-dejection) are not interchangeable and differ widely in their internal consistency, discriminant validity, and other psychometric properties. Comparative research would be invaluable in helping researchers to identify the specific measures that best suited their assessment needs.

Finally, trait affect assessment presents us with a paradoxical situation. On the one hand, extensive recent evidence has firmly established the reliability and construct validity of global trait ratings. Among other things, these global ratings (a) are substantially stable over time, (b) are strongly correlated with general trait measures such as Neuroticism and Extroversion, and (c) show significant levels of self-other convergence. Thus, we can have much more confidence in these measures than we could 10 years ago.

On the other hand, we also are more painfully aware of their limitations than we were 10 years ago. Thus, it now is clear that general affect ratings suffer from a variety of problems—including duration neglect and recency effects—that may substantially lessen their construct validity (Kahneman, 1999; Schwarz & Strack, 1999; Stone et al., 1999). Furthermore, general affect scales show (a) lower temporal stability and (b) weaker self-other agreement than do other types of trait measures, even closely related traits such as neuroticism and extroversion. As discussed previously, these effects cannot be attributed simply to differences in content, but reflect in part subtle influences of format and presentation. Put differently, it appears that we can improve the construct validity of these measures by experimenting with various stylistic changes (see Vaidya et al., 2002; Watson et al., 2000). In this regard, it is noteworthy that contemporary mood researchers still rely primarily on the same basic assessment instrument that was pioneered by Nowlis and Green more than 40 years ago. Although this instrument generally has worked quite well over the years, it now is time to revisit it—and, perhaps, to reinvent it.

REFERENCES

Bagozzi, R. P. (1993). An examination of the psychometric properties of measures of negative affect in the PANAS-X scales. *Journal of Personality and Social Psychology, 65,* 836–851.

Bentler, P. M. (1969). Semantic space is (approximately) bipolar. *Journal of Psychology, 71,* 33–40.

Bentler, P. M., & Wu, E. J. C. (1995). *EQS for Macintosh user's guide.* Encino, CA: Multivariate Software.

Berenbaum, H., Fujita, F., & Pfennig, J. (1995). Consistency, specificity, and correlates of negative emotions. *Journal of Personality and Social Psychology, 68,* 342–352.

Blumberg, S. H., & Izard, C. E. (1985). Affective and cognitive characteristics of depression in 10- and 11-year-old children. *Journal of Personality and Social Psychology, 49,* 194–202.

Blumberg, S. H., & Izard, C. E. (1986). Discriminating patterns of emotions in 10- and 11-year-old children's anxiety and depression. *Journal of Personality and Social Psychology, 51,* 852– 857.

Bradburn, N. M. (1969). *The structure of psychological well-being.* Chicago: Aldine.

Browne, M. W. (1992). Circumplex models for correlation matrices. *Psychometrika, 57,* 469–497.

Campbell, D. T. (1996). Unresolved issues in measurement validity: An autobiographical overview. *Psychological Assessment, 8,* 363–368.

Clark, L. A., & Watson, D. (1994). Distinguishing functional from dysfunctional affective responses. In P. Ekman & R. J. Davidson (Eds.), *The nature of emotion: Fundamental questions* (pp. 131– 136). New York: Oxford University Press.

Clark, L. A., & Watson, D. (1995). Constructing validity: Basic issues in objective scale development. *Psychological Assessment, 7,* 309–319.

Clore, G. L., Ortony, A., & Foss, M. A. (1987). The psychological foundations of the affective lexicon. *Journal of Personality and Social Psychology, 53,* 751–766.

Diener, E., & Emmons, R. A. (1984). The independence of positive and negative affect. *Journal of Personality and Social Psychology, 47,* 1105–1117.

Diener, E., Larsen, R. J., Levine, S., & Emmons, R. A. (1985). Intensity and frequency: Dimensions underlying positive and negative affect. *Journal of Personality and Social Psychology, 48,* 1253–1265.

Diener, E., Smith, H., & Fujita, F. (1995). The personality structure of affect. *Journal of Personality and Social Psychology, 69,* 130–141.

Edwards, A. L., & Edwards, L. K. (1992). Social desirability and Wiggins' MMPI content scales. *Journal of Personality and Social Psychology, 62,* 147–153.

Engen, R., Levy, N., & Schlosberg, H. (1958). The dimensional analysis of a new series of facial expressions. *Journal of Experimental Psychology, 55,* 454–458.

Fabrigar, L. R., Visser, P. S., & Browne, M. W. (1997). Conceptual and methodological issues in testing the circumplex structure of data in personality and social psychology. *Personality and Social Psychology Review, 1,* 184–203.

Feldman Barrett, L., & Russell, J. A. (1998). Independence and bipolarity in the structure of affect. *Journal of Personality and Social Psychology, 74,* 967–984.

Fredrickson, B. L., & Kahneman, D. (1993). Duration neglect in retrospective evaluations of affective episodes. *Journal of Personality and Social Psychology, 65,* 45–55.

Funder, D. C. (1995). On the accuracy of personality judgment: A realistic approach. *Psychological Review, 102,* 652–670.

Funder, D. C., & Colvin, C. R. (1988). Friends and strangers: Acquaintanceship, agreement, and the accuracy of personality judgment. *Journal of Personality and Social Psychology, 55,* 149–158.

Funder, D. C., & Colvin, C. R. (1997). Congruence of others' and self-judgments of personality. In R. Hogan, J. Johnson, & S. Briggs (Eds.), *Handbook of personality psychology* (pp. 617– 647). San Diego: Academic Press.

Gotlib, I. H., & Meyer, J. P. (1986). Factor analysis of the Multiple Affect Adjective Check List: A separation of positive and negative affect. *Journal of Personality and Social Psychology, 50,* 1161–1165.

Green, D. P., Goldman, S. L., & Salovey, P. (1993). Measurement error masks bipolarity in affect ratings. *Journal of Personality and Social Psychology, 64,* 1029–1041.

Izard, C. E. (1977). *Human emotions.* New York: Plenum Press.

Izard, C. E. (1991). *The psychology of emotions.* New York: Plenum Press.

Izard, C. E., Libero, D. Z., Putnam, P., & Haynes, O. M. (1993). Stability of emotion experiences and their relations to traits of personality. *Journal of Personality and Social Psychology, 64,* 847–860.

John, O. P., Donahue, E. M., & Kentle, R. L. (1991). *The Big Five Inventory–Versions 4a and 54.* Technical Report. Berkeley, University of California, Institute of Personality and Social Research.

John, O. P., & Robins, R. W. (1993). Determinants of interjudge agreement on personality traits: The Big Five domains, observability, evaluativeness, and the unique perspective of the self. *Journal of Personality, 61,* 521–531.

John, O. P., & Srivastava, S. (1999). The Big Five trait taxonomy: History, measurement, and theoretical perspectives. In L. A. Pervin & O. P. John (Eds.), *Handbook of personality* (2nd ed., pp. 102–138). New York: Guilford.

Kahneman, D. (1999). Objective happiness. In D. Kahneman, E. Diener, & N. Schwarz (Eds.), *Well-being: The foundations of hedonic psychology* (pp. 3–25). New York: Russell Sage Foundation.

Larsen, R. J. (2000). Toward a science of mood regulation. *Psychological Inquiry, 11,* 129–141.

Larsen, R. J., & Diener, E. (1992). Promises and problems with the circumplex model of emotion. In M. S. Clark (Ed.), *Review of Personality and Social Psychology: Emotion* (Vol. 13, pp. 25–59). Newbury Park, CA: Sage.

Larsen, R. J., & Fredrickson, B. L. (1999). Measurement issues in emotion research. In D. Kahneman, E. Diener, & N. Schwarz (Eds.), *Well-being: The foundations of hedonic psychology* (pp. 40–60). New York: Russell Sage Foundation.

Lazarus, R. S. (1991). *Emotion and adaptation.* New York: Oxford University Press.

Lubin, B., Zuckerman, M., Hanson, P. G., Armstrong, T., Rinck, C. M., & Seever, M. (1986). Reliability and validity of the Multiple Affect Adjective Check List–Revised. *Journal of Psychopathology and Behavioral Assessment, 8,* 103–117.

Lubin, B., Zuckerman, M., & Woodward, L. (1985). *Bibliography for the Multiple Affect Adjective Check List.* San Diego, CA: Educational and Industrial Testing Service.

McCrae, R. R. (1982). Consensual validation of personality traits: Evidence from self-reports and ratings. *Journal of Personality and Social Psychology, 43,* 293–303.

McCrae, R. R. (1994). The counterpoint of personality assessment: Self-reports and observer ratings. *Assessment, 1,* 159–172.

McNair, D. M., Lorr, M., & Droppleman, L. F. (1971). *Manual: Profile of Mood States.* San Diego, CA: Educational and Industrial Testing Service.

Meddis, R. (1972). Bipolar factors in mood adjective checklists. *British Journal of Social and Clinical Psychology, 11,* 178–184.

Mossholder, K. W., Kemery, E. R., Harris, S. G., Armenakis, A. A., & McGrath, R. (1994). Confounding constructs and levels of constructs in affectivity measurement: An empirical investigation. *Educational and Psychological Measurement, 54,* 336–349.

Nemanick, R. C., Jr., & Munz, D. C. (1994). Measuring the poles of negative and positive mood using the Positive Affect Negative Affect Schedule and the Activation Deactivation Check List. *Psychological Reports, 74,* 195–199.

Nowlis, V. (1965). Research with the Mood Adjective Check List. In S. S. Tomkins & C. E. Izard (Eds.), *Affect, cognition, and personality* (pp. 352–389). New York: Springer.

Paulhus, D. L., & Reid, D. B. (1991). Enhancement and denial in socially desirable responding. *Journal of Personality and Social Psychology, 60,* 307–317.

Rushton, J. P., Brainerd, C. J., & Pressley, M. (1983). Behavioral development and construct validity: The principle of aggregation. *Psychological Bulletin, 94,* 18–38.

Russell, J. A. (1979). Affective space is bipolar. *Journal of Personality and Social Psychology, 37,* 1161–1178.

Russell, J. A. (1980). A circumplex model of affect. *Journal of Personality and Social Psychology, 39,* 1161–1178.

Russell, J. A., & Carroll, J. M. (1999). On the bipolarity of positive and negative affect. *Psychological Bulletin, 125,* 3–30.

Russell, J. A., & Mehrabian, A. (1974). Distinguishing anger and anxiety in terms of emotional response factors. *Journal of Consulting and Clinical Psychology, 42,* 79–83.

Russell, J. A., Weiss, A., & Mendelsohn, G. A. (1989). Affect Grid: A single-item scale of pleasure and arousal. *Journal of Personality and Social Psychology, 57,* 493–502.

Schwarz, N., & Clore, G. L. (1983). Mood, misattribution, and judgments of well-being: Informative and directive functions of affective states. *Journal of Personality and Social Psychology, 45,* 513–523.

Schwarz, N., & Strack, F. (1999). Reports of subjective well-being: Judgmental processes and their methodological implications. In D. Kahneman, E. Diener, & N. Schwarz (Eds.), *Well-being: The foundations of hedonic psychology* (pp. 61–84). New York: Russell Sage Foundation.

Schwarz, N., & Sudman, S. (1994). *Autobiographical memory and the validity of retrospective reports.* New York: Springer-Verlag.

Stone, A. A. (1987). Event content in a daily survey is differentially associated with concurrent mood. *Journal of Personality and Social Psychology, 52,* 56–58.

Stone, A. A., Shiffman, S. S., & DeVries, M. W. (1999). Ecological momentary assessment. In D. Kahneman, E. Diener, & N. Schwarz (Eds.), *Well-being: The foundations of hedonic psychology* (pp. 26–39). New York: Russell Sage Foundation.

Tellegen, A., Watson, D., & Clark, L. A. (1999). On the dimensional and hierarchical structure of affect. *Psychological Science, 10,* 297–303.

Thayer, R. E. (1978). Factor analytic and reliability studies on the Activation-Deactivation Adjective Check List. *Psychological Reports, 42,* 747–756.

Thayer, R. E. (1986). Activation-Deactivation Adjective Check List: Current overview and structural analysis. *Psychological Reports, 58,* 607–614.

Vaidya, J. G., Gray, E. K., Haig, J., & Watson, D. (2002). *On the temporal stability of personality: Evidence for differential stability and the role of life experiences.* Manuscript submitted for publication.

Watson, D. (1988). The vicissitudes of mood measurement: Effects of varying descriptors, time frames, and response formats on measures of Positive and Negative Affect. *Journal of Personality and Social Psychology, 55,* 128–141.

Watson, D. (2000a). *Mood and temperament.* New York: Guilford Press.

Watson, D. (2000b). Basic problems in positive mood regulation. *Psychological Inquiry, 11,* 205–209.

Watson, D. (2002). *The development and construct validation of parallel forms of the PANAS Scales.* Manuscript in preparation.

Watson, D., & Clark, L. A. (1991). Self- versus peer-ratings of specific emotional traits: Evidence of convergent and discriminant validity. *Journal of Personality and Social Psychology, 60,* 927–940.

Watson, D., & Clark, L. A. (1992). Affects separable and inseparable: On the hierarchical arrangement of the negative affects. *Journal of Personality and Social Psychology, 62,* 489–505.

Watson, D., & Clark, L. A. (1994). *The PANAS-X: Manual for the Positive and Negative Affect Schedule–Expanded Form.* Unpublished manuscript, University of Iowa, Iowa City, IA.

Watson, D., & Clark, L. A. (1997). Measurement and mismeasurement of mood: Recurrent and emergent issues. *Journal of Personality Assessment, 68,* 267–296.

Watson, D., Clark, L. A., & Harkness, A. R. (1994). Structures of personality and their relevance to psychopathology. *Journal of Abnormal Psychology, 103,* 18–31.

Watson, D., Clark, L. A., & Tellegen, A. (1988). Development and validation of brief measures of positive and negative affect: The PANAS scales. *Journal of Personality and Social Psychology, 54,* 1063–1070.

Watson, D., Hubbard, B., & Wiese, D. (2000). Self-other agreement in personality and affectivity: The role of acquaintanceship, trait visibility, and assumed similarity. *Journal of Personality and Social Psychology, 78,* 546–558.

Watson, D., & Tellegen, A. (1985). Toward a consensual structure of mood. *Psychological Bulletin, 98,* 219–235.

Watson, D., & Tellegen, A. (1999). Issues in the dimensional structure of affect—Effects of descriptors, measurement error, and response formats: Comment on Russell and Carroll (1999). *Psychological Bulletin, 125,* 601–610.

Watson, D., Tellegen, A., & Cudeck, R. (2002). *General versus aggregated ratings of trait affectivity: Analyses of convergent and discriminant validity.* Manuscript in preparation.

Watson, D., & Walker, L. M. (1996). The long-term stability and predictive validity of trait measures of affect. *Journal of Personality and Social Psychology, 70,* 567–577.

Watson, D., Wiese, D., Vaidya, J., & Tellegen, A. (1999). The two general activation systems of affect: Structural findings, evolutionary considerations, and psychobiological evidence. *Journal of Personality and Social Psychology, 76,* 820–838.

Yik, M. S. M., Russell, J. A., & Feldman Barrett, L. (1999). Structure of self-reported current affect: Integration and beyond. *Journal of Personality and Social Psychology, 77,* 600–619.

Zuckerman, M. (1960). The development of an Affect Adjective Checklist for the measurement of anxiety. *Journal of Consulting Psychology, 24,* 457–462.

Zuckerman, M., & Lubin, B. (1965). *Manual for the Multiple Affect Adjective Check List.* San Diego, CA: Educational and Industrial Testing Service.

Zuckerman, M., & Lubin, B. (1985). *Manual for the MAACL-R: The Multiple Affect Adjective Check List–Revised.* San Diego, CA: Educational and Industrial Testing Service.

Zuckerman, M., Lubin, B., & Rinck, C. M. (1983). Construction of new scales for the Multiple Affect Adjective Check List. *Journal of Behavioral Assessment, 5,* 119–129.

CHAPTER 15

Measuring Personality and Psychopathology

LESLIE C. MOREY

TRADITIONAL APPROACHES TO PERSONALITY TEST CONSTRUCTION

Rational-Theoretical Approach

Over the past century, there have been four generations, as it were, of approaches to the construction of personality measures. The oldest of these traditions is the rational or theoretical approach. This form of test construction relies heavily upon the developer's notions of the concept in question, as he or she attempts to design an instrument that reflects a particular theory about the concept. This theoretical reflection can either be implicit or explicit. For example, the items of the Woodworth Personal Data Sheet, assembled in response to needs for psychiatric screening during the U.S. entry into World War I, represented Woodworth's implicit theory about important indicators of psychological adjustment. Alternatively, the items of the Myers-Briggs Type Indicator represent an attempt to implement an explicit psychological theory of personality, that of C. G. Jung.

An important advantage of the rational approach to personality test construction is that it places an important emphasis upon the *content validity* of the resultant measure. As will be discussed in more detail in following sections, this important emphasis has sometimes been lost in more recent approaches to test construction, with unfortunate consequences. However, the early rational approach also suffered from a number of drawbacks. One particular problem was the failure to use any data-driven procedures in the development of the measures. Thus, these measures were entirely dependent upon the assumptions of the test author, and these assumptions may or may not have been well founded. Erroneous assumptions could take place at the level of interpreting the theory or at the level of generating the relevant indicators. At the level of theory, for example, a test author might assume two concepts are related when in fact they are not. At the item level, an item that might appear relevant at first glance may in fact turn out to be measuring something other than what was intended. In the absence of any confirming data prior to the general use of the test, any instrument developed entirely by rational means is likely to contain several such errors.

Empirical Approach

As American psychology became increasingly behavioristic in outlook, a second criticism of the rationally developed measures emerged. These behavioral psychologists were unwilling to base conclusions about personality or psychopathology on the introspections of the respondent.

Rather, the personality measure began to be viewed as simply another mechanism by which to observe the behavior of the respondent. From this framework emerged the next generation of personality test construction, the *empirical approach*. From this perspective, the only aspect of item responses that mattered was their correlates; the content or theoretical applicability of the item was of no interest in construction. Meehl (1945) provided a manifesto for this approach, stating that "it is suggested tentatively that the relative uselessness of most structured personality tests is due more to a priori item construction than to the fact of their being structured" (p. 6).

The empirical approach to test construction is exemplified by the creation of the Minnesota Multiphasic Personality Inventory (MMPI; Hathaway & McKinley, 1967) and the Strong Vocational Interest Blank (Strong, 1927). In these instruments, a single extratest criterion—ability to differentiate members of a criterion group from those in a control group—was used to select items for the final version of these tests. For the Strong, group membership involved persons engaged in particular occupations, whereas for the MMPI, group membership was determined by psychiatric diagnosis. Thus, it was this criterion correlate that determined the composition of test items, and item content was ignored.

The potential advantages of the approach over the rational method, as discussed by Meehl (1945), were numerous. Tests developed from this perspective were unlikely to fall subject to the mistaken theoretical assumptions of the test authors (except perhaps in the generation of the initial pool of items), because the approach was explicitly atheoretical. The approach was initially thought to be much less susceptible to attempts by the respondent to falsify or distort their results, a common concern with the earlier generation of tests that were heavily content based. The use of empirical item selection resulted in the inclusion of a number of so-called subtle items on scales; these items had content with little apparent relationship to the construct for which it was scored. As an example, the MMPI Depression scale included the item "I sweat very easily even on a cool day," which was scored for depression if answered *false*.

Unfortunately, the promise of the empirical approach was often not borne out by subsequent research, because a number of important problems began to surface as research on such instruments accumulated. First, it quickly became apparent that empirical tests were not free from distortions introduced by efforts at impression management; such results led rather quickly to efforts to develop so-called validity scales for the MMPI (e.g., Meehl & Hathaway, 1946) that could assist in identifying such distortion. A second shortcoming was that the selection of items based upon their ability to make a particular discrimination led to problems when these items were called upon to make other discriminations. For example, the MMPI items, selected to contrast normality with psychopathology, tended to have difficulty making distinctions among different forms of psychopathology, leading to efforts by some researchers (e.g., Rosen, 1958) to create empirical MMPI scales designed to make distinctions within clinical populations. Finally, the reliance upon empirical methods to identify subtle items appeared to lead to the inclusion of such items on scales that appeared to have questionable validity upon cross-validation (e.g., Lees-Haley & Fox, 1990). As problems such as these were discovered, the field began to search for more sophisticated, yet still empirically based, strategies that could address these shortcomings.

Statistical Approach

This second alternative to the rational/theoretical approach began to emerge at approximately the same time as the empirical approach, although it gained acceptance more slowly, perhaps because of its greater computational complexity. This approach, sometimes called the *statistical* or *classic psychometric approach,* shared a quantitative emphasis with the empirical perspective. However, the statistical approach received impetus from the development of the classical approach to psychometric theory (e.g., Guilford, 1936) as well as the development of the then-novel set of statistical techniques known as *factor analyses*. Rather than emphasizing external criterion-group membership, as in the empirical approach, the statistical approach emphasized item intercorrelations as its basis for test construction. From this perspective, test construction centered around a statistical search for dimensions that could summarize personality, and items were accordingly selected on the basis of their ability to represent these dimensions. This approach sought to construct scales that were collections of homogeneous indicators of an underlying factor (or factors). In the case of measures of single factors (e.g., trait anxiety), the instruments have sought to maximize item interrelationship, resulting in high internal consistency and factor analysis solutions suggesting a unifactorial structure. Such instruments have often selected items by focusing upon item-scale correlations and choosing those items that demonstrated the largest correlations with the parent scale. This results in high mean interitem correlations and consequently a large coefficient alpha (Cronbach, 1951), which provides an estimate of the average of all possible split-half combinations of items.

Some instruments, particularly multiscale inventories, that were developed from this perspective have tended to rely upon exploratory factor analysis techniques to assign items to scales, selecting and eliminating items as part of creating scales that are internally consistent and factorially pure. In other words, scales for a particular factor are constructed from items that load highly on one factor, and preferably on only one factor. Items with multiple or ambiguous loadings are removed from the instrument. Ideally, this will result in an instrument whose items have what is known as *simple structure* (Thurstone, 1935). One pioneering instrument developed from the statistical perspective was the Guilford-Zimmerman Temperament Survey (Guilford & Zimmerman, 1949), for which the authors factor-analyzed items from many different instruments to create scales representing only those items tapping the resultant dimensions.

One of the most enduring examples of the statistical approach to constructing a personality inventory is the Sixteen Personality Factor Questionnaire (16PF; Cattell, Cattell, & Cattell, 1993). Developed and refined over a number of years, the basis of the instrument was the "lexical" approach advocated by Cattell, who sought to identify a finite number of source traits that explained the various individual differences among people as captured by personality adjective terms in the English language. Based upon factor analyses of various forms of personality data (including behavioral descriptions as well as questionnaire data), Cattell initially concluded that 16 obliquely related source traits appeared to serve as the basis for most observable personality differences, and he sought to construct a questionnaire that could measure these source traits directly. For Cattell, the use of factor analyses to construct the 16PF was a natural extension and replication of the methods that had been used to develop its underlying theory. However, subsequent investigations have generally found that the 16 scales are not factorially independent, and even efforts to replicate Cattell's results using his original data tend to find far fewer factors than 16 (Fiske, 1949; Goldberg, 1993).

One of the most popular models of normal personality in contemporary research is the *five-factor model (FFM)*. The FFM, proposed initially by Tupes and Christal (1961) and refined by Norman (1963), has a number of elements in common with other popular dimensional approaches; in fact, it resembles an integration of the Eysenck (1952) model and the higher order factors of Cattell's (1965) theory. The five factors may be described as follows (Costa & McCrae, 1986): *neuroticism,* characterized by worry, insecurity, and self-pity, as opposed to a calm and self-satisfied nature; *extraversion,* referring to a sociable and affectionate nature in contrast to a sober, reserved one; *openness,* implying an imaginative, independent personality as contrasted to a conforming, orderly nature; *agreeableness,* characterized by a trusting, helpful attitude in contrast to a suspicious, exploitative orientation; and *conscientiousness,* denoting a well-organized, careful, disciplined personality as opposed to a careless, weak-willed personality.

As pointed out by McCrae and Costa (1996), the utility and robust nature of the FFM has been supported in a number of research studies. In addition, there is substantial evidence to suggest that these five factors reflect enduring characteristics that persist throughout much of adult life (Costa and McCrae, 1988). There are a number of instruments available for measuring these five dimensions, with one of the most popular being the NEO Personality Inventory (Costa & McCrae, 1985, 1992b). The emergence of this model is an interesting example of the interaction between theory and measurement in personality, as the emergence of the statistical–factor analytic measurement model provided the foundations for a dimensional theory of personality. As this theory became increasingly well articulated, investigators developed new and refined measures that, while continuing to rely upon factor analysis for development and validation, increasingly did so within a perspective that resembled the construct validation approach.

THE CONSTRUCT VALIDATION APPROACH

During the 1950s, the field of psychological assessment began to move somewhat away from the behaviorally based focus upon *criterion validity,* which used behavioral criteria for test validation, moving toward the notion of *construct validity,* which represented the extent to which a test could be said to reflect a theoretical (and hence not directly observable) construct. A number of seminal articles (Campbell & Fiske, 1959; Cronbach & Meehl, 1955; Loevinger, 1957) began to describe the implications of this shift in emphasis, which included new perspectives on how best to construct psychological measures (Jackson, 1967a, 1970). The *construct validation approach* as delineated in these important works remains the state of the art in test construction today.

In working within a construct validation framework, it is essential to understand that each of the two words—*construct* and *validation*—is there for a reason. Neither is very useful without the other. Constructs without validation tend to be abstractions that typically have little utility in an empirical or in a pragmatic sense; validation in the absence of a construct tends to yield specific-use applications that have little generalizability and do little to further an understanding of what is being measured. The construct validation approach emphasizes the interplay between the theoretical elaboration of the construct and its methodological validation, and both elements deserve some further consideration.

Constructs

Within the construct validation framework, test development cannot proceed without a specification and elaboration of the *construct* to be measured. Although this may seem intuitively obvious to many, the history of psychological assessment is replete with examples to the contrary. The differences can be seen in as basic a level as the names of scales on instruments. Construct validation requires that the scale name reflect the construct being measured; this contrasts with instruments in which scale names are task descriptions (such as the subscales on the Wechsler intelligence scales), factor names (as on the 16PF), or even numerals (such as eventually became the case with the MMPI).

When a scale is designed to measure a particular construct, the scale must be evaluated within the context of a theoretically informed network that makes explicit hypotheses about interrelationships among indicators of various constructs. I have advocated (e.g., Morey, 1991b) that our classifications in personality and psychopathology be viewed simply as a collection of hypothetical constructs that are themselves subject to construct validation procedures. In recent years, there has been increasing recognition that these constructs are best represented by rules that are probabilistic rather than classical (i.e., the use of necessary and sufficient features) in nature. The resulting fuzzy quality of critical constructs in mental health weighs against the success of criterion-referenced approaches (e.g., those tied to specific etiology in a strong sense) to the development and validation of construct indicators. Despite recent efforts to increase the rigor with which certain clinical constructs are identified, the fact remains that no gold standard has been discovered for use as a criterion for membership in any of the major categories of mental disorder or personality since the discovery of the specific qualitative etiology of general paresis around the turn of the twentieth century. Most constructs in psychiatric classification are "open concepts" (Meehl, 1977) with little known about their inner nature. Thus, the construct validation approach is perhaps the only viable strategy with which to tackle this type of measurement problem.

Cronbach and Meehl (1955) suggested that assigning variability in observable behavior to a hypothetical construct requires a theory with respect to that construct that is comprised of an interconnected system of laws (which Cronbach and Meehl called a "nomological network")

relating hypothetical constructs to one another and to behavior observable in the environment. Skinner (1981, 1986) has described a three-stage framework for the elaboration of psychopathological constructs that follows Loevinger's (1957) and Jackson's (e.g., 1971) construct validation frameworks in psychometrics. The stage of *theory formulation* involves an explication of the content domain of the construct, a delineation of the nature of the classification model and the linkages between constructs in the model, and a specification of the relationship of constructs to external variables, such as etiology or treatment outcome. The second stage, *internal validation,* involves the operationalization of the constructs and the examination of various internal properties of the classification; specific properties to be emphasized would depend on the theory elaborated in the initial stage. These properties might include interrater reliability, coverage of the classification, stability of measurement over occasions, internal correlation matrices, internal consistency of features assumed to be indicators of the same construct, or the replicability of classification or factorial structures across different samples. The third stage of construct validation described by Skinner (1981) involves *external validation.* At this stage, links of the constructs to other variables related to etiology, course, or prediction must be tested. This process will involve both convergent and discriminant validation (Campbell & Fiske, 1959). That is, in addition to showing that expected relationships prevail between the construct and to conceptually similar constructs, the process must also involve efforts to demonstrate that observed relationships are not attributable to constructs presumed not to be operating within the theoretical network. As empirical evidence is gathered, the theoretical formulation will likely be revised to accommodate new and unexpected information.

It should be noted that the links among constructs in the theoretical network may be of many types. Historically, classification in medicine has given prominence to etiology as a basis for organization, but there is no reason to presume that theoretically based construct validation research must begin and end with investigations into causation. Meehl (1977) points out that the complexity of causation of most phenomena in the biological and social sciences does not seem compatible with the notion of specific etiology. Consequently, specific etiology may not be a particularly promising candidate to serve as the basis of a scientific classification of mental disorders. Even with the presumption of multiple etiological pathways, there seems to be a need to provide a theoretical link between the observed phenomena and some etiologically proximal final common pathway if the taxonomic construct is to achieve scientific coherence. Thus, efforts directed at establishing theoretical links between constructs and other external validator variables such as treatment response or personality outcome may have as much promise for clarifying these constructs as do etiological investigations. As with etiological research, there is little reason to presume to find specificity (e.g., that disorders should respond specifically to particular treatments) because factors such as treatment response or personality change may involve variables fairly distal to the core of the construct. Nonetheless, more proximal links between certain, presumably malleable, elements of the construct and theoretical mechanisms of treatment or change are reasonable objects of investigation for construct validation. Ultimately, those constructs that are central in a theory that provides such linkages to etiology, description, and intervention should be those that emerge as superordinate in a taxonomy of psychopathology or personality.

Thus, development of construct-validated instruments is possible only for constructs with some depth of elaboration in the theoretical and empirical literature. For example, construction of a measure for passive-aggressive personality is hampered by a lack of theoretical and empirical articulation in the scientific literature. In contrast, depression is useful as an example of a well-articulated construct. Of all mental-disorder concepts, its description is perhaps the most stable, because it has been described consistently at least since the time of the classical Greek physicians. The construct has also received a great deal of theoretical and empirical attention, with a host of instruments available for assessing depression, including the self-report Beck Depression Inventory (BDI; Beck & Steer, 1987), Zung (1965) Depression Scale, and MMPI D scale, as well as the observer rating scales such as the Hamilton Rating Scale for Depression (HAM-D; Hamilton, 1960). Despite the fact that these scales are widely used and tend to be positively correlated, they all have somewhat different characteristics (Lambert, Hatch, Kingston, & Edwards, 1986). For example, the HAM-D is one of the most commonly used instruments in psychopharmacologic trials of antidepressants, perhaps because it emphasizes the measurement of physiological symptoms of depression that are reasonably responsive to such medications (a nomological link to treatment). As an example, 3 distinct items of the 17 items on the original scale inquire about sleep disturbances, but none ask about negative cognitions or expectancies. In contrast, the BDI tends to emphasize cognitive features of depression, such as beliefs about helplessness and negative expectations about the future (Louks, Hayne, & Smith, 1989). This emphasis is not surprising, given Beck's theoretical elaboration (e.g., Beck, 1967) of the role of these factors in the development and maintenance of depression (a nomological link to etiology). Empirically, factor analyses of the BDI support the conclusion that such cognitive elements of depression are a major source of variance on this

instrument, with somatic and affective elements relatively undifferentiated (Steer, Ball, Ranieri, & Beck, 1999). In contrast, other commonly used instruments, such as the MMPI D scale, focus upon affective features such as unhappiness and psychological discomfort, with limited assessment of either the cognitive or physiological features of depression. As a result, they tend to tap more generalized distress and have little specificity in the diagnosis of depression.

Given the consistency of the literature on the indicators of depression, and the convergence of empirical research on the major grouping of these indicators, it is relatively straightforward to pursue the development of depression scales from the construct validation perspective. For example, the construction of the Depression (DEP) scale of the Personality Assessment Inventory (Morey, 1991a) proceeded with the goal of representing these empirically related, but conceptually independent, components of the depression construct, because the empirical and theoretical significance of each had been established in the literature. The initial item pool for these components was generated by examining the literature in each area to identify those characteristics of each that were most central to the definition of the concept. The content of these items was assumed to be crucial to its success, because each item was carefully constructed to measure a reasonably well articulated facet of a complex construct.

The above discussion makes it clear that the construct validation method of test construction differs markedly from atheoretical methods, such as the empirically keyed method of item selection employed in instruments such as the MMPI. In the construct validation view, theory and measurement are inextricably interlinked, and an instrument is viewed as a scientific theory that is open to empirical falsification. Thus, not even instruments such as the MMPI or even the *Diagnostic and Statistical Manual of Mental Disorders, Fourth Edition* (*DSM-IV;* American Psychiatric Association, 1994) are truly atheoretical (e.g., Faust & Miner, 1986; Schwartz & Wiggins, 1987), because each represents an implicit theory about the representation of the constructs and the boundaries between them. However, in such so-called atheoretical methods, the theoretical networks underlying the constructs are typically poorly articulated, and measurement problems invariably result. Thus, for example, in constructing a measure of psychopathology, the investigator may be faced with the choice of developing a direct measure of the *DSM* definitions of a particular disorder or, alternatively, a representation of the disorder that attempts to instantiate contemporary knowledge about the constructs. Each approach has its advantages and disadvantages. The *DSM*-based measurement approach would provide a clear link to a widely used definition of a construct. However, the poor articulation of the constructs potentially complicates interpretation of psychometric properties of the resulting measure. Would properties such as poor internal consistency, limited temporal stability, or poor discriminant validity be a property of the *DSM* definition, or of the measure of that definition?

In the context of a discussion of the utility of theory-based assessment, some mention should be made of the nature of the theories from which assessments may be derived. In general, the nomological network for one construct may look quite different from that for another; for example, it is unlikely that the same set of explanatory principles will hold for introversion, bipolar affective disorder, posttraumatic stress disorder, and dependent personality disorder. Consequently, many of the theories that most help to elaborate psychopathologic constructs tend to be restricted in scope. Theories that are intended to be applicable across the broad expanse of psychopathology (e.g., early applications of psychoanalytic theory, or Millon's 1969 model of syndromes) tend to achieve their expansive coverage at the expense of specificity, and hence falsifiability. Thus, in selecting a theory as a guide to test construction, the developer must consider the relative advantages of breadth of applicability versus specificity of articulation of the theory. For example, the Millon Clinical Multiaxial Inventory (MCMI; Millon, 1994) maintains a particular theoretical focus (Millon's theory) across scales tapping a variety of constructs, whereas the Personality Assessment Inventory (PAI; Morey, 1991a) draws from more circumscribed theoretical models that have shown promise for specific constructs, including models that are psychodynamic, interpersonal, cognitive, or psychopathologic in nature.

Normal Versus Abnormal Constructs

In designing and evaluating a personality instrument, one must take into account the nature of the constructs being assessed, and one aspect of this nature involves whether the constructs reflect normal personality or an abnormal process (i.e., disordered personality or psychopathology). In the psychometric field it is clear that there are differences between instruments depending on whether they are designed to measure normal or abnormal constructs; for example, catalogs from test publishers often present such tests in separate sections. However, the distinction between normal and abnormal aspects of personality has not been well articulated conceptually. For example, the American Psychiatric Association's *DSM,* despite admirable attempts to objectify many critical distinctions, is still unclear on distinctions among normal personality, abnormal personality, and clinical syndromes. Instruments themselves are ambiguous in their terminology;

for example, the MMPI was named a personality inventory despite the fact that it was clearly created as a clinical diagnostic instrument.

To assist in the delineation of personality constructs, Morey and Glutting (1994) discussed a number of empirical criteria that may help to identify whether a construct captures an element of normal personality or whether it represents something abnormal. Each of these criteria will be discussed in some detail, because they serve to highlight some critical differences to anticipate in the design of measures of normality versus abnormality.

1. *Normal and abnormal personality constructs differ in the distribution of their related features in the general population.* Differentiating normal and abnormal personality in this manner is similar to the approach taken by Foulds (1971). Foulds separated what he called *personality deviance* from personal illness (i.e., psychopathology), and he proposed a model of the relationship between these conditions whereby they were viewed as overlapping but conceptually independent domains. In making this distinction, he focused upon quantitative aspects of these conditions, namely the distributions of symptoms (features of personal illness) and traits (features of personality deviance) in various populations.

   In distinguishing between features associated with these conditions, Foulds hypothesized that abnormal symptoms should have distributions that have a marked positive skew (i.e., that occur infrequently) in normal samples, while being roughly normally distributed in clinical samples. In contrast, normative personality traits should be distributed in a roughly Gaussian (i.e., bell-shaped) manner in the general population; a sample of individuals with so-called deviant personalities is distinguished by the personality traits' being manifest to a degree rarely encountered in the general population. It should be noted that both types of constructs may be of clinical interest. Various regions of each type of construct may represent an area of concern; a person can be having difficulties because he or she manifests a particular normative trait (e.g., introversion) to an extreme degree, or because he or she manifests an abnormal construct (e.g., suicidal ideation) to even a slight degree. The primary difference is in the nature of the construct: The individual with a clinical trait (i.e., psychopathology) may be somehow qualitatively different from normals, whereas individuals with what is considered an abnormal amount of a normative personality trait are quantitatively distinct; that is, their trait manifests a difference of degree rather than kind.

These distributional differences will affect the desired properties of the eventual scales. For example, a measure of introversion-extraversion is likely to be bipolar, with a nearly Gaussian distribution, interpretable variance at each end of the scale, and expected scale means that fall somewhere within the middle of the possible range. In contrast, a measure of suicidal ideation is likely to be unipolar, with an absolute zero point, a positively skewed distribution in the general population, and a scale mean in this population that may lie fairly close to this zero point. Interpretations of the suicidal ideation scale are more likely to be made solely in the higher ranges of the scale. Efforts to use a normalizing transformation in standardizing a normal personality measure thus may make sense because the underlying construct may well be normally distributed. However, a similar transformation for a suicidal ideation scale would be problematic, because it would tend to magnify small and perhaps unreliable differences at the low end of the scale and compress differences that might be meaningful at the higher end of the scale.

2. *Normal and abnormal personality constructs differ dramatically in their social desirability.* Assessment investigators have long recognized that self-report personality tests can be vulnerable to efforts at *impression management*. In particular, much concern has been expressed about the influence of efforts to respond in a socially desirable fashion on such tests. Various diverse and creative efforts have been directed at resolving this dilemma, including the empirical keying strategy behind the development of the original MMPI as well as the subsequent use of the *K* correction and the forced-choice matched item alternatives employed in the Edwards Personal Preference Schedule. However, for self-report tests that focus on so-called abnormal constructs, these strategies tend not to work very well. It is suggested that the reason for these problems is that abnormal constructs are inherently socially undesirable. Thus, most measures of social desirability responding will correlate quite highly with measures of abnormal constructs. In contrast, the social desirability of normative personality features is more ambiguous, less evaluative, and more likely to be tied to a specific context. For example, the trait adjective *talkative* might be a socially desirable characteristic in a salesperson but not in a librarian. There is likely to be little consensus among people as to whether *talkative* is a desirable or undesirable characteristic, whereas characteristics such as *depressed* or *delusional* will invariably be viewed consensually as undesirable.

This implies that the social desirability of a construct may be useful as an indicator of its status in capturing normal or abnormal variation between people. The desirability of the construct may be measured in many ways; for example, correlations with measures such as the Marlowe-Crowne social desirability scale (Crowne & Marlowe, 1960) can yield an estimate of the desirability loading of a measure of some construct. Another means by which to assess the desirability of a construct measured by a particular scale is to gauge the impact that efforts at impression management have upon scale scores. In establishing the discriminant validity of a normal personality measure, the test developer may wish for effect sizes of social desirability manipulations that are close to zero, but the author of a measure of an abnormal construct should not have this aim. Instead, discriminant validation of the latter will focus upon the magnitude of social desirability effects *relative to* convergent validity indicators, because some relationship to social desirability should be anticipated.

Another implication of the impact of this assumption is that treatment of social desirability as a nuisance variable should differ in measures of normal and abnormal constructs. As an example, the Edwards Personal Preference Schedule (EPPS; Edwards, 1959) attempts to measure the constructs of Henry Murray's (1938) theory of personality using a forced-choice item response format (e.g., Edwards, 1957), where alternative item responses are equated for social desirability valence. Such an approach makes sense if one assumes that these are normal personality constructs, but it becomes problematic if applied to constructs reflecting abnormality. This assumption may also help clarify why psychometric efforts to correct for stylistic aspects of response variance, such as the MMPI's *K* correction, tend to meet with failure in clinical settings (Archer, Fontaine, & McCrae, 1998). Such strategies essentially treat social desirability as a suppressor variable (Wiggins, 1973) that can be added or subtracted from some substantive indicator to enhance the validity of that indicator. However, in order for this strategy to be successful, it is important that the suppressor variable be minimally correlated with the validity criterion (Wiggins, 1973), and, according to the assumption presented here, this would not be the case for most indicators of abnormal constructs. Such correction strategies may have greater promise for use as suppressor variables in measures of normal personality, which are more likely to meet this requirement.

3. *Scores on measures of abnormal personality constructs differ dramatically between clinical and community samples, whereas scores of normal constructs do not.* This criterion is based upon the assumption that, in dealing with an

abnormal personality construct, more is worse; that is, the more of the construct a person has, the greater the impairment the person manifests and the more likely the person is to come to the attention of mental health professionals. For example, when one considers disordered thinking as a personal characteristic, greater amounts of thought disorder will be associated with greater impairment and need for intervention. Thus, a clinical population should invariably obtain higher scores on measures of such constructs than a community sample. In contrast, for a normative personality trait, the adaptive direction of scores is less clear-cut. Given the assumption that such traits are normally distributed, then the traits are inherently bipolar, and extreme scores at *either* end of the trait may be maladaptive. Thus, even if clinical samples were restricted to persons with problems on a particular normative trait (e.g., extreme scores on introversion-extraversion), there would still be no reason to suspect mean differences between clinical and community subjects, because the extreme scores of the clinical subjects at either end of the continuum would be expected to balance out.

4. *Measures of normative personality traits should demonstrate factorial or correlational invariance across clinical and community samples, whereas measures of abnormal traits may not.* The basic assumption behind this criterion is that the correlation pattern that gives abnormal constructs their syndromal coherence should only emerge in samples where there is adequate representation of individuals manifesting the syndrome (i.e., clinical samples). In community samples, which may include relatively few individuals who have a clinical syndrome, the association between features of the same syndrome may be no greater than that between any two features selected randomly. As an example, if depression were defined by five necessary and sufficient criteria, and these five criteria were intercorrelated in a community sample that contained no depressed subjects, the average correlation between these features might well be zero. In a sample of nondepressed individuals, sleep problems and low self-esteem may be associated only at chance levels because individuals who share the putative causal process that underlies the clinical association of these features have been removed from the sample. It is the convergence of these features in individuals considered to be depressed that lends a correlation pattern to these features. Thus, distinct sets of highly intercorrelated features (i.e., syndromes) might emerge from a factor analysis of clinical subjects that would not be identified in a sample of subjects selected from the community.

In contrast, those traits that describe normal variation in personality would be expected to capture this variability among clinical as well as normal subjects. Even though the clinical subjects may be, as a group, more extreme on normal personality traits, similar correlational patterns among elements of the trait should be obtained. For example, the construct of extraversion/introversion should identify meaningful differences among clinical subjects as well as normal subjects, and the intercorrelation of the behaviors that make up this construct should be similar in the two populations. This should yield predictable empirical results with respect to the factor structure (for multifaceted scales or constructs) and the average item intercorrelation (i.e., coefficient alpha, for unidimensional constructs); for a normative trait, these results should be similar in clinical and nonclinical samples. In contrast, these values may well differ if an abnormal construct is being examined.

The preceding four criteria can be useful for distinguishing between normal and pathological aspects of personality, and also for designing the type of investigations necessary to accumulate evidence of construct validity. The important message is that indicators of validity are not always applicable across different types of constructs. Because of this, a variety of commonly used criteria for scale validity, such as *factorial invariance* or *social desirability loading,* are only useful when justified within the theoretical context of the construct. This points to the importance of the *construct* in construct validation; the discussion now turns to the validation aspect.

Validation

The second part of the construct validation picture is the *validation*. Once a construct has been identified and the major elements of the construct delineated, the putative indicators of the construct need to be examined for validity. Although this sounds simple enough, it is critical to understand that the validation of an indicator is a complex process, and the validity of an indicator cannot be reduced to a single coefficient. The importance of validation has been understood since the beginnings of psychometrics, but the multifaceted nature of validity has not been clearly recognized until relatively recently. In particular, the literature on test development and validation is replete with studies documenting *convergent validity,* or the association between indicators that supposedly measure the same construct. However, two other important aspects of validation often receive short shrift in the test construction literature, and the construct validation approach has been central in highlighting the importance of these overlooked aspects. The following sections examine two of these areas, namely content validity and discriminant validity.

Content Validity

The *content validity* of a measure involves the adequacy of sampling of content across the construct being measured. Often, this characteristic of a test is confused with *face validity,* referring to whether the instrument appears to be measuring what it is intended to measure, particularly as it appears to a lay audience. These are not synonymous terms; a test for depression that consists of a single item such as *I am unhappy* may appear to be highly related to depression (i.e., it has high face validity) but provides a very narrow sampling of the content domain of depression (i.e., it has low content validity). Content validity dictates that scales provide a balanced sampling of the most important elements of the constructs being measured. This content coverage should be designed to include a consideration of breadth as well as depth of the construct. The *breadth* of content coverage refers to the diversity of elements subsumed within a construct. For example, as described earlier, in measuring depression it is important to inquire about physiological and cognitive signs of depression as well as features of affect. Any depression scale that focuses exclusively on one of these elements at the expense of the others will have limited content validity, with limited coverage of the breadth of the depression construct.

The issue of construct breadth brings up one illustration of a situation in which two supposedly desirable aspects of a measure can actually be inversely related. Coefficient alpha (Cronbach, 1951) and its dichotomous version, K-R 20, are measures of internal consistency that provide an estimate of a generalized split-half reliability. Many texts (e.g., Hammill, Brown, & Bryant, 1993) state that a high coefficient alpha (e.g., higher than .80) is a desirable property of a test, and test construction procedures that use part-whole correlations or factor-analytic structures essentially attempt to maximize this psychometric property. However, sometimes internal consistency can be *too* high, an issue described as the "attenuation paradox" by Loevinger (1954) more than 40 years ago. High internal consistency indicates that all test items are measuring the same thing, which at its extreme can result in highly redundant items that address a very narrow portion of a complex construct. As an example, a depression test that consists of 10 questions that all ask about difficulties in falling asleep might be highly internally consistent, but such a test would miss a considerable portion of the breadth of the depression construct, including mood and relevant cognitions.

The *depth* of content coverage refers to the need to sample across the full range of intensity or severity of a particular

element of a construct. Most (if not all) interesting constructs in personality and psychopathology have meaningful dimensional variance with at least ordinal properties; in other words, it makes sense to describe one individual as *more extroverted* or *more depressed* than another. To assure depth of content coverage, the test developer must attempt to capture the differences that exist along the full spectrum of the characteristic. One way that this is commonly done is through the use of response options scaled to address differences in intensity or severity. For example, a question about sociability might provide a range of response options describing differing amounts of social contact during a given time period; a question about hallucinations might capture the frequency with which they occur (as opposed to simply whether they occur). Such questions provide one way to capture dimensional differences among respondents; different response-scaling options are discussed in more detail later in this chapter.

In addition to differences in intensity reflected in the response options, items themselves are often constructed to tap different levels of intensity or severity in the manifestation of a characteristic. Tests have been constructed in this fashion for many years; for example, the harbinger of standardized intelligence tests developed by Binet and Simon in 1905 included items scaled to capture distinctions at different levels of intelligence. In recent years, (Hulin, Drasgow, & Parsons, 1983; Lord, 1980) has made important contributions in representing and utilizing the information inherent in this dimensionality. Item response theory attempts to estimate the value of an individual on some latent trait using information contained in the responses of specific items. Tests developed from an item response approach attempt to provide items that sample information across the entire relevant range of the construct, rather than including items that optimally make a given discrimination. Scales that are developed with reference to an external criterion, such as those on the MMPI, are examples of the latter approach; if items are selected with respect to a particular discrimination (such as schizophrenic vs. normal), they will provide only that information that is optimal for that particular distinction.

To illustrate this issue, consider the hypothetical distributions of three groups on the construct of *thought disorder* shown in Figure 15.1. If items are selected on the basis of their ability to make a discrimination between two particular groups (e.g., schizophrenics vs. controls), those items that provide information at the point of rarity between the distributions of the two groups on the severity continuum will be seen as most useful. For the example in Figure 15.1, in differentiating schizophrenia from normality, items calibrated around point A will provide the most information for

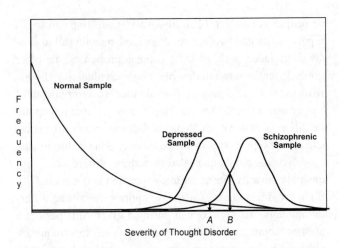

Figure 15.1   Empirical item selection and discrimination.

making this distinction. However, in differentiating schizophrenia from affective disorder, item information should be maximized around point B. If a scale is intended to be useful in making a variety of such distinctions, one would prefer a scale to be composed of items that contain information relevant to discriminations across the entire relevant range—or the full depth—of the construct. In other words, a scale should be composed of items sampling information across the full spectrum of the concept if it is to be able to make a variety of different diagnostic distinctions.

As an example, the item response model was used as a conceptual guide in selecting items for the final version of the PAI (Morey, 1991a), in an attempt to select items that provided information across the full spectrum of the concept in question. Through an examination of the item characteristic curves of potential items, the final items were selected to provide information across the full range of construct severity. The nature of the severity continuum varied across the constructs on the test; for example, for the Suicidal Ideation scale, this continuum involved the imminence of the suicidal threat. Thus, items on this scale varied from vague and ill-articulated thoughts about suicide to immediate plans for self-harm, allowing the examiner to capture information, not only about the presence of suicidal thinking, but about its intensity.

Discriminant Validity

A test is said to have *discriminant validity* if it provides a measure of a construct that is specific to that construct; in other words, the measurement is free from the influence of other constructs. Although discriminant validity has long been recognized as an important facet of construct validity, it has not traditionally played a major role in the construction of

psychological tests. This is unfortunate, because discriminant validity represents one of the largest challenges in the assessment of psychological constructs.

There are a variety of threats to validity where discriminability plays a vital role. Three of the major areas include *discrimination among constructs,* the influence of *response sets and response styles*, and the operation of *test bias*. The following paragraphs review these discriminant validity issues and discuss potential means of handling the issues.

Discrimination Among Constructs

This aspect of discriminant validity is a major challenge to instruments, particularly in the realm of psychopathology. Psychiatric diagnoses tend to be highly *comorbid* (e.g., Maser & Cloninger, 1990), which in essence means that an individual manifesting any type of mental health problem is at greatly increased risk of simultaneously manifesting another such problem. This means that clinical problems are positively correlated in the population at large, and some (e.g., depression and anxiety, or the different personality disorders) are quite highly correlated. This poses an obvious challenge to the discriminant validity of any instrument that seeks to measure such constructs.

One practice that has compromised the discriminant validity of many multiscale inventories involves the use of overlapping items, that is, items that are scored on more than one scale. Overlapping items force a certain correspondence in the measurement of presumably distinct constructs; thus, the relationship between scales can be entirely artifactual rather than representing a true association between distinct characteristics. Given that many constructs are inherently challenging to distinguish, a methodological handicap such as item overlap is ill advised. Even where certain constructs may share particular behavioral manifestations (e.g., social withdrawal), instrument developers should utilize distinct items that capture manifestations typical of the constructs being considered (e.g., social withdrawal due to anxiety vs. withdrawal due to disinterest). Instruments that contain large amounts of item overlap tend to display considerable discriminant validity problems (e.g., Welsh, 1952; Retzlaff & Gilbertini, 1987). Ideally, a test should allow no item overlap in order to reduce this potential source of discrimination problems; each scale should consist of items loading only on that scale.

There are a number of steps in the development of a test in which procedures should be implemented in an attempt to maximize discriminant validity. Items should be written with particular attention to specificity concerns. Tasks involving sorting of items into scale constructs can determine whether the relationship of item content to appropriate constructs is ambiguous. Items should also be examined to insure that they were more highly associated with their parent constructs than with any other constructs measured by the test (e.g., Jackson, 1970, 1971). Such procedures are reviewed in more detail later in this chapter.

Response Styles

Over the past 30 years, the issue of response styles has been a hotly debated topic in the field of objective psychopathology assessment. A classic review of this area by Wiggins (1962) distinguished among three components of variance in responding to self-report questionnaire items: strategic, method, and stylistic variance. *Strategic variance* is directly related to the discriminative purpose of the test and is determined by the subject's true positioning on the construct of interest. *Method variance* is affected by structural aspects of the instrument, such as phrasings of statements, format of response options, and directionality of item keying. Finally, *stylistic variance* consists of response consistencies that exist independent of the test itself, and notions of such as an *acquiescence set* or a *social desirability* set have been proposed as examples. However, there have been many debates as to whether the natures of various constructs represent strategic or stylistic variance in the measurement of personality (Helmes, 2000). For example, the construct of social desirability has been alternatively interpreted as a tendency for individuals to endorse unrealistically positive statements when describing themselves (e.g., Edwards, 1957) or as an indicator of a personality style related to autonomy, extraversion, optimism, and ego strength (Block, 1965; McCrae & Costa, 1983).

One useful approach involves a consideration of the possible influence of response styles as an issue of discriminant validity. In other words, response styles are viewed neither as totally artifactual contributions to variance to be eliminated nor as unimportant features to be ignored. Rather, this influence can be examined at the level of the individual items, with the aim of eliminating items that seem to measure stylistic or method variance to a greater extent than strategic variance (e.g., Jackson, 1971). From this perspective, response styles (either method or stylistic) are treated as independent constructs from which measured constructs should be distinguishable. The idea of eliminating all stylistic variance from a test was neither desirable nor practical, because there is no reason to suspect that response styles such as social desirability will be orthogonal to certain syndromes of mental disorder or to certain personality traits. The psycho-

logical phenomena experienced by the schizophrenic will never be seen as socially desirable, whereas the depressed individual usually manages to see the black cloud surrounding every silver lining. With discriminant validity as an aim, however, items can be evaluated to determine whether they are better measures of their parent constructs than they are of constructs representing method and stylistic variance.

Test Bias

One implication of discriminant validity is that a test that is intended to measure a psychological construct should not be measuring a demographic variable, such as gender, age, or race. This does not mean that psychological tests should never be correlated with age, gender, or race. However, the magnitude of any such correlations should not exceed the theoretical overlap of the demographic feature with the construct. For example, nearly every indicator of antisocial behavior suggests that it is more common in men than in women; thus, it would be expected that an assessment of antisocial behavior would yield average scores for men that are higher than those for women. However, the instrument should demonstrate a considerably greater correlation with other indicators of antisocial behavior than it does with gender; otherwise, it may be measuring gender rather than measuring the construct it was designed to assess.

There are a number of procedures for attempting to examine and identify test bias. Conceptual evaluations of bias can be accomplished by having a panel of individuals representing diverse backgrounds (e.g., both lay and professional individuals, both men and women, of diverse racial and ethnic backgrounds) review items with regard to any potential for bias. Empirical strategies for eliminating test bias typically involve the examination of item psychometric properties as a function of demography. For example, associations between a given item and its corresponding full scale can be evaluated using regression models, and items can be selected that display minimal variation in slope or intercept parameters as a function of demographic variables (Cleary, 1968). Such analyses can help identify and eliminate items that have different meanings for different demographic groups. Thus, if an item inquiring about crying easily seemed to be related to other indicators of depression in women but not in men, then that item should not be included on a depression scale, because interpretation of the item would vary as a function of gender. Note that this strategy will not eliminate mean demographic differences in scale scores. For example, an item inquiring about stealing may have a similar meaning for identifying antisocial personality characteristics for both men and women, yet this behavior may still be more common among men. In this example, the resulting gender difference is not a function of test *bias;* rather, it is an accurate reflection of gender differences in the disorder. It is important to recognize that such differences are not necessarily a sign of bias and that a test with no such differences can in fact be quite biased.

PROCEDURES IN TEST CONSTRUCTION

Once the test developer has arrived at a well-articulated definition of the psychological construct to measure, the next step is to decide how it should be measured. Typically, this involves a two-step process whereby items are generated by the developer and then evaluated to determine whether the items need to be revised or eliminated before the scale is finalized. In both steps, the definition of the construct serves as the blueprint for determining how the items should be presented, the format in which they should appear, and the criteria which should be used to evaluate them.

Item Generation

Items in personality and psychopathology scales typically involve two aspects: a *stimulus aspect* (e.g., the verbal presentation of an item) and a *response method* (e.g., answering an item as either *yes* or *no*). For questionnaire methods, item stems are typically verbal statements or questions, whereas responses are generally constrained to facilitate scoring. Although such methods have the advantage of ease of use, there clearly is a wide array of other forms of assessment. For example, with respect to stimulus properties, items can involve perceptual material, such as the Rorschach inkblots, Thematic Apperception Test (TAT) pictures, or Witkin's Embedded Figures Test; or experimental situations such as the infamous Milgram (1965) shock experiment, which was originally designed as a measure of authoritarianism. Similarly, responses can be open-ended, behavioral, or physiological. However, most measures involve some verbal presentation of material and some need for scaling response alternatives. The following sections describe some issues pertinent to each of these aspects of measurement, particularly as they apply to application in a questionnaire format.

Stimulus Properties of Items

Once the construct has been identified and defined and the major theoretical facets of each construct delineated, items must be generated to tap these constructs. The first step involves creating a preliminary pool of stimulus items. Because a rigorous evaluation of items is likely to reveal considerable variability in the quality of the items, it is recommended that the initial pool of items be considerably larger than the desired final length of the scale. Eliminating items from an item pool in sequential evaluation studies is relatively simple, but adding new items to the pool is often not plausible at later points in the sequence. Although practical and procedural limitations will vary across types of measures, the initial pool should at minimum be twice as long as the desired final scale, and an initial pool five times as large as the final version provides a more comfortable margin for selecting an optimum combination of items.

In generating the initial item pool, it is helpful to keep several guidelines in mind. The following sections describe some of these.

1. *Content of items is critical.* In generating and revising test items, it is always best to assume that the content of a self-report item will be critical to its utility as a measure of some phenomenon. Items should be written so that the content is directly relevant to the construct measured by the test. Empirically derived tests may include items on a scale that have no apparent relation to the construct in question. However, research over the years (e.g., Holden, 1989; Holden & Fekken, 1990; Peterson, Clark, & Bennett, 1989) has continually indicated that such items add little or no validity to self-report tests. The available empirical evidence is entirely consistent with the assumption that the content of a self-report item is critical in determining its utility in measurement. This assumption does not preclude the potential utility of items that are truly subtle (in the sense that a lay audience cannot readily identify the relationship of the item to mental health status). However, the assumption does suggest that the implications of such items for personality or mental health status should at least be apparent to experts in these areas if the item is to prove useful. Thus, the process of item development should be done with a careful eye cast toward the content validity of the resultant scale, with respect to both breadth and depth of the construct, as described previously.

2. *Item self-report must capture phenomenology.* Good items should be written to reflect the phenomenology of various traits and disorders in order to capture the experience of the person manifesting these constructs. Care should be taken not to confuse the experiences of the respondent with those of an outside observer, such as a clinician. For example, the experience of the paranoid individual is not one of being unreasonably suspicious, even though this feature is readily apparent to outside observers and is what is

clinicians consider to be the core of the disorder. Rather, the paranoid individual feels surrounded by obstacles and barriers created by others who may be envious of his or her potential.

3. *Items should be reasonably specific to the construct under consideration.* As described previously, discriminant validity represents one of the largest challenges in the development of a psychological measure. Thus, particular care should be taken in constructing items to insure that they capture aspects that tend to be unique or specific to the construct in question.

   As an example, one of the subscales of the Mania scale from the PAI is Irritability. The literature indicated that irritable mood quality was particularly common in patients presenting during a manic episode (Goodwin & Jamison, 1990), and so this construct was targeted as a facet of mania. However, irritability tends to be associated with many forms of emotional problems—for example, it is often found in people who are depressed, have somatic complaints, or have drinking problems. Thus, an item such as *I am irritable* might prove to converge reasonably well with other indicators of mania, but it would likely have poor discriminant validity. However, extending the item to make it more characteristic of the form of irritability found in this disorder can improve its specificity. Thus, extending this item to something like *I get very irritated when people interfere with my plans* captures the relation of the irritation to the expansiveness and poor frustration tolerance of the manic individual. Such an expansion can thus provide information much more specific to the construct in question, which is likely to enhance discriminant validity.

4. *Items should not reflect only the most extreme manifestations of the trait.* If one assumes that there is meaningful dimensional variability on most constructs of interest in personality and psychopathology, then it is important to have items that make discriminations at various points on this dimension. This fact was described earlier as pertaining to the depth aspect of content validity: Items should sample across the full range of phenomena associated with this dimensional variability. Perhaps the best example appears on ability or intelligence tests, in which questions are typically ordered across different levels of item difficulty. Assuming reasonable validity for the items, this variability of difficulty translates into items that have the capacity to make distinctions at differing levels of ability; so-called easy items distinguish those with low levels of ability from others, whereas so-called difficult items discriminate at higher levels of ability. The same logic can be applied to scales measuring personality or psychopathology; items should capture the less extreme as well as the more extreme forms of characteristics. A collection of items written at the extreme end of a trait will be able to identify only those individuals at that extreme, while making no valid discriminations among individuals at lower levels of the trait.

5. *The item should not be offensive or potentially biased* with respect to any gender, ethnic, economic, religious, or other group. Given the wide array of cultural subgroups, it is difficult to anticipate all possible objections to various items. A useful strategy in this regard is to have a very diverse group of individuals involved in generating the initial pool of items. In such a strategy, items likely to be problematic can be discussed and revised prior to the collection of any data, although it is still important to conduct subsequent data-based evaluations of item bias later in the development process.

6. *The item should be worded simply and unambiguously.* In general, a short and simple item is preferable to one that is complex and contains multiple clauses. To make a scale widely applicable, and to ease any subsequent translations of the scale that might be undertaken, items should be written at a very basic reading level, in the 4th- to 6th-grade range. Also, they should have no more than 10 words if possible, and 20 words at maximum. Scientific or professional jargon should be avoided and reframed in everyday language terms. Items with conjunctions like *and* and *or* make it more difficult to discern the intent of the respondent from the answer, and they also increase the probability that the item can be misinterpreted. No double negations should be used in an item, and single negations should be avoided if possible. Also, no "damned-if-you-do, damned-if-you-don't" items, such as *I have stopped abusing my children,* should be included. The meaning of endorsing an item in a particular manner (as *true, yes,* or *very much like me),* should be readily apparent.

7. *Colloquialisms or slang should be avoided.* Although the use of colloquial terms may appear at first glance to make the test more accessible to respondents, it typically leads to problems in broader applications of a scale that are difficult to anticipate. The popularity of slang terminology tends to wane quickly, resulting in items that sound dated or peculiar in a few years. References to local social or cultural institutions are unlikely to be interpreted similarly in a different part of the country or world, and difficulties are particularly likely to arise in attempts to translate a scale into other languages. For example, the MMPI item *I liked "Alice in Wonderland" by Lewis Carroll* proved difficult to translate into languages such as Chinese, because few Chinese respondents had heard of, let alone read, this particular book. Attempts to reword the item with a similar

book of local importance also prove to be difficult, because there are numerous dimensions along which to equate such works, and attempting to provide a close parallel proves to be a formidable task. It is simply easier to avoid using such terminology at the outset of scale development than to address these problems subsequently.

Response Properties of Items

Another critical step in test construction involves the selection of a response-scaling format for the test stimuli. There are a number of methods for scaling items or combinations of items; some are simple, whereas others are quite complex. Simpler formats often have a number of advantages, including being easy to score and less likely to be misinterpreted by the respondent. However, there may also be important advantages to more complex formats. Completing a more complex scale might be more interesting, particularly for experienced test-takers. Also, many complex response formats can be combined later into simple (e.g., dichotomous) scales if this appears appropriate, whereas the simpler scale cannot be made more complex after data are collected. Finally, larger numbers of response options can allow a scale to capture more true variance per item, meaning that even scales of modest length can achieve satisfactory reliability. The following sections describe some of the advantages and disadvantages of the more commonly used formats.

Binary Summative Method

The binary summative method of item scaling is one of the most common methods used with objective personality tests. It involves a scale score that represents the total number of items endorsed in the direction of the construct; each item is thus scored 1 if so endorsed and 0 if not endorsed in the critical direction. The item response options for this scaling approach are often binary, with *yes-no, true-false,* or *present-absent* being common choices. However, other options are possible as well; a multiple-choice format (with only one of several alternatives indicating a response in the direction of the construct) is frequently used in this type of scaling.

The binary summative method assumes that all items are comparable indicators of the construct in question. It has the advantage of being simple to score, which tends to enhance scorer reliability, and in the case of binary response options, it is also easy for the respondent to understand. The primary disadvantage is that a limited amount of construct variance is captured by each item; thus, to achieve adequate scale reliability, it is typically necessary to include a fairly large number of items for each construct.

Binary Weighted Method

The binary weighted method of item scaling involves the use of items that are initially scored in a binary fashion, and then weighted according to some scaling scheme by their supposed importance for the construct. For example, a personality characteristic might be noted as either present or absent (binary), and then a score for that item is added to the scale total that reflects the weighting of that characteristic. One well-known example of such a scaling method is the Holmes and Rahe (1967) Social Readjustment Rating Scale, which asked respondents to indicate whether certain stressful life events had occurred in the recent past and then weighted these binary responses according to Life Change Units derived by the test authors. Thus, the death of a spouse counts for 100 points in the total Life Change Unit score, whereas a traffic violation counts for 10 points. In the Holmes and Rahe scale, these weights were derived by survey; in other applications, weights are sometimes derived empirically, using regression coefficients, factor loadings, or discriminant function weights.

Unlike the binary summative method, the assumption of the binary weighted method is that not all items are comparable indicators; some are assumed to be more important than others and thus are assigned greater weight in determining the final scale score. In principle, this may seem congruent with theoretical assumptions; in practice, however, experimenter-assigned weights often appear to make little difference in the final result. For example, Skinner and Lei (1980), in studying the Social Readjustment Rating Scale (Holmes & Rahe, 1967) previously described, found that the total Life Change Unit score correlated .97 with an unweighted unit scoring (*present-absent*) of the questionnaire. Other studies have suggested that item weightings based upon regression coefficients or factor scores tend to correlate highly with unit-weighted versions of the scale, with these correlations nearly always higher than the reliability of the scale. Thus, although the binary weighted scaling method may appear to offer the opportunity to capture true score variance more precisely than the binary summative method, it is not clear that it typically does so to a significant extent. Any slight gain that does occur may be offset by greater complexity in scoring and potential scorer reliability problems.

Guttman Scale Method

The Guttman scale is a unidimensional scaling procedure in which items have a monotonic, deterministic pattern. The basic concept is that any individual who endorses an item on one scale will also endorse items lower on the scale. Thus, the scale is deterministic in that, if the evaluator knows how a person answered one item on a scale, the evaluator knows how all items lower on the scale were answered (for the strict Guttman scale, no error in measurement is assumed). The scale is monotonic in the sense that this determinism works in only one direction; one does not know how a respondent will answer any items higher on the scale. For example, consider the following Guttman scale for social activity:

1. I socialize with others more than
   10 times per week.   T   F
2. I socialize with others more than
   7 times per week.   T   F
3. I socialize with others at least
   4 times per week.   T   F
4. I socialize with others at
   least once per week.   T   F

A person answering *true* to Item 3 must also answer *true* to Item 4; in this sense, the scale is deterministic. However, one cannot be certain how this person would answer Item 1 or Item 2, and thus in this sense the determinism is monotonic, applying in only one direction.

The Guttman scale is conceptually useful in thinking about variability of item parameters, but it is generally not very useful in practice. First, the assumption that items are all perfect indicators of the construct being assessed is questionable, particularly in the area of personality and psychopathology measurement. Second, aside from highly artificial constructions such as the scale just presented, it is very difficult to assemble items that fit the model. Third, one can construct a set of items that does fit the model but that is composed of items that almost certainly do not form a unidimensional scale, simply by varying the base rate (i.e., the a priori probability) of endorsing particular items. Finally, the scores provided by such scales tend to be only ordinal in nature, restricting the applicability of the resulting measure.

Thurstone-Type Scales

Thurstone attempted to adapt psychophysical methods to the measurement of attitudinal judgments (Thurstone, 1959). His work led to a number of important developments in psychometrics, including efforts to develop a method of absolute scaling whereby respondents could be placed along a fixed continuum, rather than being scaled against a particular group. The Thurstone-type scales represent an effort to place individuals along such a fixed continuum by identifying the scale values of a number of different items and placing respondents on that continuum according to where agreement with a particular attitude is expressed. This type of scaling is nonmonotonic, in that a respondent would be expected to disagree with items above his or her absolute placement on the scale and to disagree with items below this placement. Thus, ideally each item tends to receive agreement at only one zone of the attribute, although in practice the model is probabilistic in the sense that the probability of agreeing with a particular attitude tends to increase as the scale value of items approaches the actual scale placement of the respondent, and tends to decrease as the scale values get further away.

Although the Thurstone-type scale is important in conceptualizing how items may vary across some absolute continuum, this approach is rarely used in practice. One shortcoming is that it is very difficult to find items that fit the scale model. The pattern of endorsement probabilities is often seen only if items are double-barreled to cut off individuals higher and lower on a continuum; such an item might be *I like to go to parties once in a while, but not too often.* Interpretation of responses to items phrased in this manner can be ambiguous, because some respondents might be responding primarily to the first part of the statement whereas others might be responding to the second part. Also, finding items that fit the model toward the extremes of the scale can be particularly difficult. As a result, Thurstone-type scales are difficult to construct and not commonly used in personality and clinical measurement.

Rasch Scaling and Item Response Theory

The item response models are to some extent a combination of the Thurstone and Guttman approaches to item scaling. These models are based upon the *item characteristic curve (ICC)* that relates probability of endorsement to absolute scale placement of the respondent; they are thus monotonic (at least for valid items) like the Guttman scale, but probabilistic and theoretically distribution free, resembling the Thurstone approach in these respects. The Rasch approach models the ICC with one parameter (the difficulty parameter), whereas two- and three-parameter models (incorporating discrimination and chance or guessing characteristics of items) are also used. In all three approaches, items may be scaled by examining the *item information function,* which is a function of the first derivative of the modeled item characteristic curve. Each item thus contributes information toward making distinctions along the continuum of the latent trait; some items (e.g., those with high endorsement rates) may make this distinction best at the low end of the continuum, and others (e.g., those with low rates of endorsement) may discriminate best at the upper ranges of the trait. In this fashion, individuals are scaled according to the information contained in the patterns of items endorsed.

Likert Scaling Method

The Likert (1932) scaling method involved the use of five-point anchored response choices for a particular item in which each item received a scoring weight from 1 to 5 depending upon the response selected. Items for a scale were selected by examining relationships with the total scale score (e.g., item discrimination or item-total correlations), and items displaying the greatest internal consistency were retained for the final version of the scale. Scale scores were then derived when the total of the item weights was summed. In practice, the term *Likert scale* has come to signify nearly any type of item with nonbinary, graded response alternatives.

Unlike the binary weighted scaling approach, in which the variable item weights are determined by the experimenter, Likert scales use item weights that are dependent upon the respondent's behavior. Because of this, the Likert approach can (and often does) improve the reliability of a scale by capturing more respondent variability per item, particularly with scales composed of relatively few items (Comrey, 1988). Use of this approach can increase the depth of content validity, because each item can capture differences in the intensity or severity of the measured characteristic. If a scale relies upon one or two items, it is recommended that many response alternatives along the scale be offered. Guilford (1954) reported that reliability increases as a function of the number of scale steps, rapidly up to roughly 7 response alternatives, and beginning to asymptote at about 11 alternatives. Nunnally (1978) describes studies that suggest that overuse of a scale midpoint may constitute a response style that may decrease scale reliability; consequently, use of an even number of alternatives may be preferable because it eliminates use of a scale midpoint and facilitates subsequent dichotomization of responses, if desired.

Forced-Choice Method

The forced-choice method (e.g., Edwards, 1957) requires the respondent to select between response alternatives that differ in their relationship to the measured construct but are equated with respect to some nuisance variable. Typically, this nuisance variable is social desirability. For example, the EPPS (Edwards, 1959) attempted to equate item response alternatives based upon indicators of desirability, such as their desirability ratings in a representative group, or the frequency with which an item is endorsed in such groups. The effectiveness of this approach was controversial, with a number of potential shortcomings described. First, the social desirability of a response may be strongly tied to the context of evaluation; for example, the personality traits perceived as desirable for a police officer and a librarian may be quite different. Thus, the use of universal ratings to equate items is unlikely to work across different contexts. Furthermore, it is not clear that use of the forced-choice procedure yields results that are appreciably different from those obtained under a free-response format (Lanyon, 1966). The forced-choice format also potentially loses information about the absolute strength of the characteristic; for example, asking an individual whether he or she would rather hallucinate than contemplate suicide yields little information about the likelihood that the respondent would do either. Finally, for many personality or psychopathological characteristics, social desirability is not a mere nuisance variable, but represents a valid aspect of the construct. For example, many symptoms of schizophrenia or of antisocial personality are inherently undesirable, so efforts to remove variability associated with social desirability are likely to remove valid variance from the scale. Even for personality traits that fall within more normative ranges of functioning, it has been suggested that social desirability represents a substantive dimension of personality (McCrae & Costa, 1983). Perhaps because of such shortcomings, the method has seen little use in recent years, despite its inclusion on some widely used personality measures (e.g., the Myers-Briggs Type Indicator).

Rank-Order Methods

Ranking response-formats ask the respondent to rank a series of items or statements according to some characteristic, typically along dimensions such as personal preference or the extent to which the statement is descriptive of the respondent. On such ranking scales, the score for an item is typically the rank selected for the statement. Number of ranked statements can vary; the standard forced-choice method is essentially a rank-order method with two statements being ranked, whereas other rank order procedures may involve ordering of more than 100 statements. To facilitate comparisons with such large numbers, some investigators use a *Q-sort* technique, in which respondents are asked to sort statements, provided on cards, into piles that conform to the normal distribution. For example, participants would place a relatively large number of statements into a middle pile (which might be labeled *somewhat like me*), while assigning a few statements to the extremes (e.g., *not at all like me* or *very much like me*). Even where items are not sorted into a normal distribution by the participant, they can be converted to *z* scores based upon the percentile score of the rank ordering (Guilford, 1954).

Alternatively, Guilford (1954) has also suggested a *paired-comparison* ranking method, whereby each stimulus statement is paired with every other statement, with the score for a particular statement indicated by the number of times that the statement was selected. Because the number of pairwise comparisons increases exponentially with additional statements, this method quickly becomes impractical with larger items sets.

Rank-order techniques are primarily interpretable as *ipsative* measures, meaning that they are most informative in making comparisons within an individual rather than across individuals. As such, they are most often used in examining change within a particular individual; for example, Carl Rogers popularized the use of the Q-sort technique as a means of describing changes occurring with psychotherapy. However, the rank-ordering techniques are problematic for making absolute comparisons among individuals; there is no way of knowing whether a person who ranks a particular statement first actually has more of that characteristic than another person who ranked it third. Where comparisons across subjects are desired, or where inferences about absolute standings of subjects are being drawn, alternatives to rank-ordering approaches should be considered.

Item Evaluation

After decisions about test format and response options have been made and an initial pool of test items has been developed, the next step typically involves an effort to refine the measure by selecting only the best items for inclusion on the final version of the scale. However, there is no consensual way to identify the so-called best items on a scale, nor should there be. In selecting items, it is important to consider that *no single quantitative item parameter should be used as the sole criterion* for item selection. An overreliance on a single parameter in item selection typically leads to a scale with one desirable psychometric property and numerous undesirable ones. By recognizing this, the application of the construct validation approach can avoid the many pitfalls associated with naive empiricism in test construction. In general, the test developer has the goal of including items that strike a balance between different desirable item parameters, including content coverage as well as empirical characteristics, so that the resulting scale can be useful across a number of different applications.

Because the construct validation approach emphasizes theoretical as well as empirical strategies of test construction, strategies for selecting items should include both conceptual and statistical investigations. It is not necessary that all of these evaluation strategies be applied simultaneously in selecting items; for example, Figure 15.2 presents a sequential strategy for item selection of the type used in constructing the

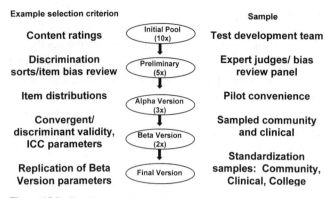

Figure 15.2 Iterative stages in test development.

PAI (Morey, 1991a). In this strategy, the developer begins with an initial pool of items that is 10 times larger than the target length of the final instrument, then successively winnows down this pool using different samples and different selection criteria. The sections that follow describe some useful such criteria for assessing the quality of items on a scale.

Conceptual Evaluation of Items

As mentioned previously, implicit in the construct validation approach is the assumption that the content of a self-report item is critical to its utility as a measure of a subjective phenomenon. Thus, the first stage of evaluation of an initial item pool often consists of studies of the conceptual meaning of item content, preceding any actual data collection from representative respondents. The following procedures are commonly employed in these early stages of item evaluation.

Content Evaluation Ratings

One commonly employed method of evaluating items is to obtain ratings of item quality from individuals familiar with the theoretical domain being measured. It is critical that these raters be given a clear and precise definition of the construct that the items are intended to measure; if there are important facets to the construct, each facet should be defined as well, and the item ratings should be grouped by facet. In these definitions, examples of the characteristics of individuals high and low on the construct might be given. Also, some differentiation of the construct from related but conceptually distinct concepts should be provided as a means of underscoring the importance of discriminant validity to the raters. If possible, raters should be encouraged to provide feedback on items that were rated as being of low quality, because such feedback may be useful in revising the item or in identifying other potential problems with the scale.

Bias-Panel Review

A second conceptual study of potential items involves the use of *bias review panels,* often helpful in identifying items that might be interpreted in different ways depending upon demographic or cultural factors. Every proposed item for a scale can be reviewed by people from a wide variety of backgrounds, both culturally and professionally. The items should be reviewed in the context of the intended construct; for example, items can be presented as supposed indicators of emotional problems, and people from different backgrounds offered an opportunity to raise objections to this explanation of the item. Such bias-panel reviews can reveal interesting and unintended interpretations of items and can circumvent later problems. Again, having these individuals provide feedback on any problem items provides information that can serve as a guide to revising the items.

Blind Sorting Tasks

Another conceptual item evaluation involves the use of external experts in specific fields to appraise items via a blind sorting of item content. A similar procedure, described as "back translation" (Smith & Kendall, 1963), involves using informed judges who were not involved in writing the items to assign the items back to the hypothesized categories. For example, in the construction of the PAI (Morey, 1991), an expert sorting task was used to assess the appropriateness of item content as assessed by a panel of experts in psychopathology; each of these experts was internationally recognized in the assessment of constructs relevant to those measured by the instrument. Preliminary items were divided into contrast groups composed of items from scales on which discriminations were thought to be particularly difficult; for example, the items concerning schizophrenia and anxiety-related disorders were placed within the same contrast group to determine whether the experts could distinguish items tapping schizophrenic social detachment from those tapping heightened social anxiety and phobic avoidance. The percentage agreement among the experts in such studies can be

helpful in determining whether the content of items can be reliably interpreted by leading experts in the field.

Empirical Evaluation of Items

The second aspect of item evaluation involves examining the psychometric properties of items in samples obtained from representative respondents. Because of the time and effort involved in obtaining samples that are sufficiently large to provide stable estimates of important psychometric parameters, it is often most efficient to use the results of conceptual analyses of items (as described previously) to narrow the pool of potential items before gathering these data (although small runs of pilot subjects can be useful in the early stages of scale development to identify problems with administrative aspects of the scale, such as in the instructions or in the response format).

There are a number of empirical properties that may be desirable for certain purposes in a scale, and the scale developer should examine many of these properties for each item in a variety of different samples, to the extent that this is possible. In doing so, the investigator is likely to make a disquieting discovery—that many of these supposedly desirable psychometric items are unrelated or even inversely related! For example, test sensitivity and test specificity are both desirable test properties, and it is well known that each can be altered through changing the cutting scores on which decisions are based (Meehl & Rosen, 1955). Unfortunately, changing the cutting score affects these two desirable test properties inversely—for example, lowering a cutting score will tend to raise sensitivity but lower specificity. Similar effects may be noted at the level of individual items: Those items that are highly sensitive to the presence of some characteristic are often not specific to that characteristic. Other desirable but inversely related psychometric properties are also commonly encountered; for example, items that evidence good convergent validity tend to demonstrate relatively poor discriminant validity. As an example, Table 15.1 lists various item characteristics for five hypothetical items; of these items, Item 4 actually appears to be the most

TABLE 15.1 Empirical Item Characteristics for Five Hypothetical Binary Items

| Item | Selection Criterion | | | | |
	1	2	3	4	5
Item difficulty (endorsement rate)	.10	.22	.37	.48	.45
ICC discrimination threshold	+2.0 SD	+1.3 SD	+0.4 SD	−0.2 SD	−0.3 SD
Item-total correlation	.21	.32	.45	.67	.65
Average discriminant validity (r)	.03	.17	.21	.48	.37
Response-set manipulation F value	14.54	3.21	1.07	0.56	0.75
Squared multiple correlation	.18	.21	.27	.78	.61

expendable item despite having the highest item-total correlation of the five items under consideration. Despite this one desirable property, it appears to provide information in the same range of the construct as Item 5, but with less discriminant validity and contributing less unique information (squared multiple correlation) to the measure. In contrast, Item 1 has a low item-total correlation but provides a useful indicator of the higher range of the construct (with correspondingly attenuated correlations) and does so with good discriminant validity.

Thus, the goal for selecting items is to include items that strike a balance between different desirable item parameters, while avoiding an overreliance on a single parameter as the criterion for item selection. The following psychometric parameters are often useful considerations in selecting test items.

Item Distributions Across Different Samples

In selecting items, the first step generally is to examine distributions, involving endorsement frequency or item difficulty (for binary items) or item means, standard deviations, and skew (for graded items). These distributions should be examined to determine their properties in samples that might be expected to vary with respect to the construct of interest; thus, for a depression measure, it would be important to examine the distributions of items in community and clinical samples. Also, it can be useful to compare distributions in samples that would not be expected to differ. For example, if there is no reason to suspect true gender differences in the construct, different item distributions in men and women might suggest problems in the item.

In general, it is important that there be some variability in the item when examining a sample suspected to be heterogeneous with respect to the construct. Items with markedly unbalanced or skewed distributions will appear problematic in correlational studies of item validity, because the extreme base rates can make such correlations unstable and severely attenuated due to restriction of range. Nonetheless, it is critical to interpret such distributions in light of the sample involved, the nature of the construct, and the place of the item in that construct. For example, items with an endorsement frequency of 1% might appear to be of little use in measuring differences between people. However, it is important to recognize that this requirement must be considered in the contexts of the sample and of the construct. Such an endorsement frequency might well be expected for an item indicating high-intensity symptoms of schizophrenia if the sample was selected at random from the community, because this is roughly the prevalence rate for this disorder.

As has been noted earlier, it is typically advantageous to select items that discriminate along different points on a continuum when attempting to measure a continuous construct. For example, item response theory relies upon the parameters of the ICC to select items for this purpose. In practice, this yields items that tend to have distributions that are quite variable. Thus, in addition to avoiding item distributions that are too extreme, the developer should also try to avoid item distributions for a particular scale that are too similar, because this might be an indication that all items are providing information about the construct at the same point on an intensity or severity continuum. Such a concern is less an issue for responses presented on a continuum (e.g., Likert-type scales) than for dichotomous (binary) scaled items, because the continuous nature of the former provides some allowance for differences in intensity for each item.

Item-Total Correlations/Factor Analyses

This commonly used family of item parameters examines patterns of interitem correlations for item selection. Often, developers examine the corrected part-whole correlation of the item, reflecting the correlation of the item with the sum of other items from the same scale; the correction thus removes the artifactual contribution of the item to the total scale score. Typically, items with negative values or values near zero are considered problematic if obtained in samples with reasonable variability in the construct in question. Scales that use this as the sole criterion for item selection typically will demonstrate high internal consistency (i.e., high K-R 20/ coefficient alpha).

Another related strategy involves the factor analysis of item intercorrelation matrices, with an examination of the factor loadings serving as the basis for item selection. Such factor analyses can involve the use of either exploratory or confirmatory methods, but each is typically conducted to evaluate the hypothesis that the item set is unidimensional. In applications of factor analysis for scale construction, it is typical to retain items displaying a standardized factor loading above some threshold (often .40) for inclusion on the scale. As is the case with the use of item-total correlation, reliance upon factor analysis for item selection results in scales that demonstrate high internal consistency—in fact, coefficient alpha is functionally related to the eigenvalue of the first component extracted from item intercorrelations. However, the factor-analytic approach has the added advantage of potentially identifying problems in discriminant validity, because other factors may emerge from the analyses and certain items may display multiple high loadings, suggesting ambiguity in interpretation of the item.

These types of item selection criteria can lead to the "attenuation paradox" (Loevinger, 1957) whereby increasing item intercorrelation through the inclusion of redundant (and hence highly correlated) items will decrease validity for measurement of complex constructs. Overemphasis on item intercorrelation can also impair the ability of a scale to capture depth as well as breadth in content validity, as described previously. Waller (1999) gives an example in which factor analysis segregates items that reflected a unidimensional construct onto different factors, as a function of differing item difficulties. Thus, overreliance on factor loadings in that instance would have led to retaining only those items with highly similar item difficulties—a problematic outcome, as noted before.

Suggestions for the recommended magnitude of average item intercorrelations tend to vary widely, ranging from .15 to .50 (Briggs & Cheek, 1986; Clark & Watson, 1995). In general, averages for broad constructs typically fall in the .15 to .30 range. As the average item intercorrelation begins to increase above .40, the measurement of the construct is becoming quite narrow, and it is generally advisable to keep this average comfortably below .50 unless the scale is quite brief and highly specific in nature.

Squared Multiple Correlations

As a check upon the possible operation of the attenuation paradox just described, the developer can calculate the squared multiple correlation between each item and all other items from the same scale. Such values are useful in identifying highly redundant items, because the response to a redundant item should be easily predicted from other items in the scale. To maximize the efficiency of the scale, the ideal item should be consistent (but not redundant) with other items from the same scale. Where these values are large (e.g., higher than .70), individual item intercorrelations should be examined to isolate redundancies; where two items are highly redundant, the better of the two items on other parameters can be retained, increasing efficiency without losing any additional information.

Item Characteristic Curve Parameters

As mentioned earlier, ICCs can be modeled by a logistic ogive defined as having up to three parameters. These three parameters include the point of inflection of the curve (sometimes referred to as the *threshold* or *difficulty parameter*), the slope at this point of inflection (the *discrimination parameter*), and the intercept of the logistic function (the *guessing parameter*). Although up to three parameters may be

estimated, the most commonly used procedure involves a one-parameter, or *Rasch,* model (Rasch, 1966) that focuses only upon the threshold parameter. In this model, only respondent ability is assumed to affect responses—items are assumed to be equally discriminating, and guessing is assumed to have no influence upon responses. When a two-parameter item response model is used, typically the guessing parameter is excluded and item threshold and item discrimination are each estimated. In personality and psychopathology, one-parameter and two-parameter models are most useful because the concept of guessing typically has little meaning outside the area of ability testing. With respect to the threshold parameter, it is advisable to select items whose estimated thresholds fall along the full range of the construct, so that the resulting scale can provide discriminations in a wide range of applications; in a one-parameter model, this can be achieved by selecting items with varying levels of item difficulty, as described previously. For the discrimination parameter, the desired values may vary according to the function of the scale. For example, *adaptive testing,* which uses item response theory to tailor test questions to a respondent by selecting the most informative item as estimated from previous responses, works most efficiently when items are sharply discriminating (i.e., have steeper slopes at the point of inflection). On the other hand, a scale with relatively few items may be able to achieve a more even assessment across the continuum by selecting items with a less steep (although still positive) discrimination slope.

Although item response theory is most typically applied to scaling items with binary scoring, models have also been developed for items with graded response options, such as Likert-type scaling (Samijema, 1969). The Samejima graded response model treats the graded item as a series of dichotomies, and models the resulting item information as a function incorporating the component ICCs for these dichotomies. For example, an item rated on a scale of 1 to 4 has three such dichotomies—response 1 versus responses 2, 3, and 4; responses 1 and 2 versus 3 and 4; and responses 1, 2, and 3 versus response 4. The use of the graded approach introduces additional complexities to the interpretation of the results, and a simpler (although less informative) alternative is to dichotomize the graded items in some fashion. In order for the results to be meaningful, the same dichotomizing strategy should be employed for all items on the scale (e.g., responses above vs. below the midpoint of the scale). Also, the dichotomy must be drawn based upon the raw responses rather than on any distributional properties of the items, such as a median split. The latter approach would artificially force all items to appear as if they had similar item difficulties and would seriously distort the estimation of the item parameters.

Operation of Response Styles

The operation of response styles in measures of personality and psychopathology has been a source of concern for many years. For example, efforts to circumvent operation of a social-desirability response style have included strategies such as the forced-choice response format of the EPPS, and the K correction of undesirable characteristics on the MMPI. However, as noted earlier, many of these strategies create more problems than they solve, particularly when they are based upon the assumption that substantive aspects of personality and psychopathology are independent of social desirability. The construct validity approach postulates that substantive constructs may be conceptually independent but still correlated with social desirability. Thus, control of this response style becomes a discriminant validity issue, with the developer seeking to insure that the item is a better measure of the substantive domain than of desirability responding. In constructing the Personality Research Form, Jackson (1971) used a *differential reliability index* to examine this discriminant validity issue, which is computed as follows:

$$\left(r_{is}^2 - r_{id}^2 \right)^{1/2},$$

where the first term reflects the corrected item-total correlation of the item with its parent content scale, and the second term reflects the correlation of the item with a scale measuring social desirability. Thus, the larger the difference between these values, the greater the content saturation of the item and the better the discriminant validity of the item with respect to social desirability. Items are candidates for deletion if the correlation with any such scales approaches or is larger than its corrected part-whole correlation with the parent construct.

Impression Management and Item Transparency

Another approach to examining stylistic aspects of item responses involves studying the influence of experimentally induced response sets. Items that are more transparent with respect to evaluative valence will demonstrate a larger effect of response sets designed to simulate positive or negative impression management. Including items with varying transparency on a scale may be useful for evaluating impression management issues; for example, a comparison of subtle and obvious item content on the MMPI has long been suggested for such purposes (Dubinsky, Gamble, & Rogers, 1985).

If such concerns are an issue for the construct under consideration, the transparency of items can be investigated. Preliminary items on the PAI (Morey, 1991) were evaluated for transparency by examination of the F value of an ANOVA between naive subjects in standard, positive impression, and malingering instructional conditions. Larger F values indicated more transparent items, suggesting that responses to the items could be affected by an examinee's attempts to distort his or her profile in either a positive or negative direction. However, because many key symptoms of mental disorder (such as hallucinations) are easily identified by a naive subject as pathological, transparency alone should not be grounds for deletion of an item from a clinical instrument. Furthermore, the validity of subtle versus obvious distinctions for identifying impression management is clearly questionable (Hollrah, Scholttmann, Scott, & Brunetti, 1995). Although item transparency should never serve as a principal consideration in item selection, insuring a range of transparency may make future research on the topic possible. Thus, where items are equivalent in other respects, developers may seek to include both transparent and nontransparent indicators of a construct.

Acquiescence and Related Sets

Acquiescence refers to the tendency to agree with personality items as being accurate self-descriptions, regardless of the content of the particular item. Similarly, a *nay-saying* set can emerge in clinical instruments, whereby respondents display a set to deny any symptoms regardless of their specific nature. It has become standard practice to address the operation of such sets by balancing the number of true- and false-keyed items. However, this procedure does not insure that the influence of acquiescence has been removed from the scale, as the psychometric properties of the true- and false-keyed subsets of items can (and often will) be different (Jackson, 1967).

Although item content is generally found to be a much more powerful determinant of test results than such response sets (Koss, 1979), some variation in direction of response keying of items is advisable to insure that stimulus items are attended to carefully and that some perseverative response set does not emerge. The operation of response sets on a multiscale inventory can be examined by calculating a score based upon the frequency of use of different response alternatives (Morey, 1991). These scores may then be considered as discriminant validity indicators; items should expected to demonstrate higher correlations with other items from their own scales than with any such indicators of response set tendencies.

Discriminant Validity Correlations

As noted earlier, discriminant validity is one of the most difficult properties for a measure of personality or psychopathology to achieve. The discriminant validity of an instrument can be greatly enhanced by the use of discriminant validity correlations as parameters in item selection. In doing so, the greatest potential threats to discriminant validity of the scale should be considered, and the correlations of potential items with indicators of these discriminant constructs be determined. Items should be related to the other indicators of the parent construct (i.e., convergent validity) to a greater extent than to any other construct. It should be assumed that an item that demonstrates sizable correlations with measures of other constructs will have discrimination problems. Thus, items are candidates for deletion if they demonstrate greater correlation with other scales than with their own scales, or if they are highly correlated with a number of other scales in addition to their own. Jackson's (1971) differential reliability index, described earlier, provides a useful metric for making this discriminative evaluation; however, rather than comparing the corrected item-total correlation to a correlation with an indicator of social desirability, in this index the latter is replaced by correlations with other potential threats to discriminant validity.

Item Bias Analyses

One particularly important threat to test validity is the possibility that some demographic feature may serve as a moderator of test validity. Such a situation can lead to applications of the test that may be biased in some manner. Often, a first step in evaluating this possibility is to look for significant demographic differences in item endorsement. For example, mean endorsement frequencies for items can be examined to determine whether large disparities exist as a function of gender, race, or age. However, it is important to point out that different endorsement rates are neither sufficient nor necessary evidence of item bias. Items can be biased with equivalent endorsement rates between groups, and they can also be unbiased where observed item differences are indicative of actual group differences on the construct. It is not necessary in all instances to equate mean values across demographic features, because certain characteristics are in fact associated with such variables. For example, it is well established that antisocial personality is more frequently observed in men than in women, and also more common in younger than in older patients—as a result, attempting to equate mean scores of these groups would not yield results reflecting the true nature of the disorder. However, in the absence of well-established demographic relationships for a construct, items with no demographic differences are preferable over those with discernible differences.

Rather than focus upon endorsement frequency of an item, efforts should be directed at insuring that items are equally

useful indicators of the construct across different demographic groups. This process typically involves comparing the psychometric performance of the item across groups as gauged against some validity criterion. In some instances, the criterion may be external to the test (as with a widely accepted alternative measure of the construct, or a specific criterion behavior), but can also involve a criterion derived from internal test properties, such as the total scale score. One such approach involves a comparison of ICCs across demographic group membership. Item response theory can be used to estimate item parameters separately for the groups of interest, and the resulting parameters should be linearly related across groups (Allen & Yen, 1979). Items whose parameters are not linearly related are potentially biased and can be revised or deleted from the test. For graded response options, another commonly employed method involves the use of regression, whereby some criterion (total test score, or an external validity indicator) is regressed upon the item response (e.g., Cleary, 1968). Unbiased items should display identical slope and intercept parameters across demographic groups; differences in the slope of the regression line suggest differential item validity in the groups, whereas differences in the intercept may point to problems in test fairness that may require the use of demographic-specific norms to correct. Regardless of whether ICC or regression approaches are used, items that demonstrate parameters differing significantly across demographic groups are potentially biased and should be targets for deletion.

Some authors have proposed the use of factor analysis to investigate consistency of item validity across demographic group membership. For example, differences in factor loadings might be observed in one group versus another, suggesting that the meaning of item endorsement might differ in these groups. However, true frequency differences among demographic groups can result in factor solutions that are not invariant; for example, the factor structure of a measure of antisocial personality might look quite different at different ages, because of restriction of range in the construct among older respondents. Using a criterion of factorial invariance across populations for item selection is probably most useful when no population differences on the construct are either expected or observed.

TEST VALIDATION AND EXTENSION

The final step in the construct validation strategy of test construction involves the gathering of evidence of validity, as gauged against expectations derived from the theoretical nomological network. The validation is never complete, but rather is an ongoing process that provides feedback that is important in refining the use and interpretation of the test. Typically, the test developer is called upon to provide evidence of the reliability and validity of the test, but neither is truly a property of the test itself; they are properties of the resulting scores in a given application of the instrument. Furthermore, reliability and validity are not distinct, but are simply both elements representing nodes in the aforementioned nomological net. The following sections briefly discuss some applications of these constructs, and some potential pitfalls.

Reliability

In classical test theory, *reliability* is considered to be a critical aspect of an instrument inasmuch as it is interpreted as "freedom from random measurement error," and thus as a constraining factor on validity. From this framework, measurement error is assumed to be random, and the reliability coefficient can be interpreted directly as the percentage of variability in performance that could be attributed to variance in the true scores of the individuals tested. A test-taker's observed score on a measure is thus interpreted as reflecting a combination of the person's true score and the influence of random measurement error; tests with lower reliability have a larger contribution of error to determining the observed score.

Estimating the reliability of a measure is typically performed by varying some nonsubstantive facet of the scoring process to evaluate its impact upon the consistency of scores observed. There are four widely used methodological approaches to gathering these estimates. *Test-retest reliability* examines the consistency of scores obtained on two different occasions; thus, *time* is the facet varied using this approach. *Internal consistency reliability* examines the consistency of scores obtained using different subsets of items from a particular scale; this approach varies *items* as a potential facet of error. *Alternate-forms reliability,* less widely used in the field of personality and psychopathology, examines the consistency of scores across different (but supposedly equivalent) forms of the same test, with *form* as a potential source of measurement error. Finally, *scorer reliability* refers to the consistency of scores resulting from an application of the scoring process; for example, differences in scores assigned by different raters would reflect error associated with the facet of *rater*.

One important extension of classical test theory is *generalizability theory* (Cronbach, Gleser, Nanda, & Rajaratnam, 1972), which decomposes the different sources of error variance in a reliability design, allowing the test evaluator to specify the possible facets of measurement error more precisely. Generalizability theory represents a significant advance over classical test theory, because it recognizes that reliability depends upon a number of possible different conditions of measurement, such as time, items, or raters, as noted previously. This approach is particularly useful to the test developer because it can point out strategies to improve reliability estimates. Regardless of whether a classical or generalizability approach is used, it is important to examine critically the assumption that the error associated with the different sources or facets are indeed random and do not reflect substantive constructs. These assumptions must be understood as part of the nomological net that provides the theoretical articulation for the construct. The following sections discuss some of these issues as related to specific procedures for estimating reliability.

Test-Retest Reliability

Any test-retest reliability study must take into account the theoretical stability of the construct in evaluating the meaning of reliability estimates. For example, assumptions about temporal stability in the measurement of mood may be quite different from those assumptions made in measuring intelligence, yet many textbooks fail to differentiate such concepts when discussing optimal levels of reliability for a test.

Although personality traits are typically assumed to be stable over time (an assumption itself the source of some controversy, as witnessed by the debate triggered by Mischel's 1968 book), constructs in psychopathology are diverse with respect to temporal stability. Some constructs refer to states that can be quite fleeting (e.g., acute suicidal ideation, or transient psychotic phenomena in borderline personality), whereas others may involve traits that can be stable over many years (e.g., social deficits in schizophrenia). To further complicate matters, test-retest reliability estimates of clinical phenomena conducted in clinical settings are typically confounded with treatment received during the retest interval, because it is ethically problematic to withhold treatment for the purposes of establishing reliability. Alternatively, reliability studies of such measures are often conducted with nonclinical samples, but this creates a problematic restriction of range; variances in measures of clinical constructs will be smaller in normal than in clinical samples and this restricted variance will attenuate all (including reliability) correlations with scale scores. Given the diverse range of phenomena that the psychopathologist might measure, no single, optimal stability value can be applied equally to such theoretically differing constructs. Textbooks often mistakenly suggest a minimum guideline for test-retest reliability without an adequate specification of the nature of the construct and the conditions of measurement under which the estimate will be obtained.

Internal Consistency

It is also critical to examine the assumption of nonsubstantive facets of error when examining the method of internal consistency as an estimate of reliability. Internal consistency is typically measured by splitting the items of a multi-item scale into two parts and determining the correlations between the parts; hence the use of the term *split-half reliability* to describe this technique. Because the approach depends upon the particular split of items involved (e.g., correlating odd and even items will not necessarily give the same result as correlating the first and last halves of items on the scale), estimates of the results of all possible split-half combinations of items can be provided by the K-R 20 formula or by coefficient alpha, the generalized form of K-R 20 for nonbinary items with calculable item variances. These numbers are a direct function of the average item intercorrelation and the number of items on the scale; higher values for either lead to higher estimates for coefficient alpha.

Conceptually, coefficient alpha is simply a summary metric of the *equivalence* of items, and once again any distinctions between items are assumed to reflect random measurement error. However, there are problems with assuming (or even desiring) item equivalence. Loevinger's classic 1954 article on the attenuation paradox pointed out that high interitem correlations can constrain validity (although they may maximize internal consistency) by narrowing the measurement of complex constructs through a focus upon redundant, albeit valid, variance. As noted previously, the paradox is that, while under the assumptions of classical test theory, reliability is considered to be a necessary condition for that sets an upper bound for validity. Loevinger points out that interitem correlation is not conceptually necessary, and that it can, in fact, *lower* validity. This lowering of validity tends to work through the mechanism of reducing content validity, because highly redundant items cannot capture a broad range of phenomena that might be associated with a complex construct.

There are other instances in which content validity can be compromised by the assumption of item equivalence. One such example is provided by item response theory, whereby items are selected to provide information at differing points on the trait continuum, and thus are specifically assumed *not* to be equivalent. Internal consistency is also influenced by the composition of the sample in which it is determined: Item intercorrelation should be lower in samples that are homogeneous on the trait, and higher in heterogeneous

samples. In fact, this variability of item intercorrelation serves as the basis of some quantitative efforts to identify the taxonic status of a construct, such as the MAXCOV method (Meehl, 1986). Finally, Cronbach and Gleser (1964) discuss the *bandwidth-versus-fidelity* trade-off inherent in scale construction; a developer who wishes to construct an efficient instrument with a broad bandwidth, such as a measure that screens for a wide variety of quite distinct physical or psychological problems, often must sacrifice fidelity to achieve this breadth—particularly if fidelity is defined by coefficient alpha. Thus, high internal consistency could be viewed as an *undesirable* aspect of a broadband screening instrument, because it would involve a sacrifice of efficient content coverage for the sake of redundancy.

In sum, although various references (e.g., Nunnally, 1978; Hammill, Brown, & Bryant, 1993) are often cited stating that a supposedly good coefficient alpha is one above .80, the reality is more complex. A desirable value for internal consistency statistics will vary as a function of the nature of the phenomenon being measured, the length of the scale used to measure it, and the composition of the sample used to calculate it. Thus, the test developer is encouraged to move away from viewing internal consistency estimates as necessarily being an evaluative property of an instrument, and toward viewing it more as a metric that is simply descriptive of a particular data set.

Scorer Reliability

Scorer reliability refers to the consistency of scores resulting from an application of the scoring process. The so-called objective tests are usually so described because the objectivity of the scoring procedures typically results in higher scorer reliability; but this is not always the case. Automated scoring procedures such as optically scannable answer sheets can still result in misread information if a respondent does not use the correct type of pencil or does not erase a stray mark cleanly. As the 2000 U.S. presidential election revealed, use of automated scoring systems will not necessarily result in perfect scorer reliability; thus, even with these systems, scorer reliability should be assessed if a high degree of precision is critical for the measurement. Such procedures could include multiple scans of the same raw data, or in the case of hand-entered information, double-punched data entry, in which the data-entry technicians must enter the same information twice (with identical results) before it is accepted into the data set.

The most common form of scorer reliability comes into play when a human is used as a measuring device. Common applications of this approach include the use of behavioral observations, psychiatric diagnoses, or construct-based rating scales. As with other types of reliability, scorer reliability values for these types of scales are typically expressed with some form of correlation. Early reliability studies of nominal-categorical scales, such as psychiatric diagnoses, often reported *percentage agreement statistics*—that is, statistics describing the percentage of ratings on which scorers agreed—in support of reliability. However, there were significant problems in interpreting these values because differences in the marginal probabilities of the response categories greatly influenced the likelihood of observed agreements; agreement by random chance was much more likely to occur when the probabilities of the different response categories were highly unbalanced. The *kappa coefficient* (Cohen, 1960), a derivative of an intraclass correlation coefficient, has thus become somewhat of a standard for reporting scorer reliability for categorical judgments, because it incorporates an adjustment to percentage agreement that accounts for the probability of chance agreement.

Shrout and Fleiss (1979) provide a general model for the use of intraclass correlation in the study of scorer reliability. They provide reliability calculations for scorer reliability under different assumptions about the nature of the scores. For example, calculations differ depending upon whether the rater variable is assumed to represent a random or a fixed effect. The *random effect* approach assumes that the raters studied are a sampling from the universe of possible raters, and is more useful as an estimate of the generalizability of reliability estimates to other sets of raters; the *fixed effect* approach provides a reliability value for a *particular* set of raters in a particular study. Another calculation distinction can be drawn depending upon whether the final scale score reflects the ratings as provided by the mean of a group of raters, in contrast to a score provided by a single rater. Because individual ratings tend to be less reliable, comparing these estimates can provide the developer with information about the improvements that can be obtained by having multiple raters provide scores for all subjects.

Validity

The process of validating a psychological measure is a cumulative process that is never complete. In part, this is because validity is not a property of a test per se, but rather is a property of a score obtained in a particular context. *Validity* is a process that evolves as evidence begins to accumulate that scores from a particular instrument, gathered in many contexts, are behaving in theoretically anticipable ways. There are many types of evidence, both qualitative and quantitative, that contribute to the process of validation. Messick (1995)

described six aspects of evidence of construct validity that represent a useful starting point for validation. As might be expected, these principles overlap considerably with processes involved in scale construction from the construct validation perspective. The following sections review and discuss Messick's types of validity evidence.

Content Aspects

Evidence of the content aspect of construct validity addresses the relevance and representativeness of the scale content. The content should be relevant in that it falls within the boundaries of the construct in question, and it should be representative in that it captures the processes and experiences of the respondent in an ecologically valid way. Such evidence is typically gathered through the use of tasks involving expert professional judgment, such as the rating or sorting tasks described earlier as item selection strategies.

Substantive Aspects

Evidence for the substantive aspect of construct validity derives from theories around the processes assessed by the scale. Such a task represents a particular challenge for objective assessments of personality, because the respondent is typically asked to comment or introspect about response processes (e.g., interpersonal actions) without specifically engaging those processes. However, certain process aspects are open to investigation. For example, investigators have found that emotionally evocative personality-test items tend to display longer response latencies than neutral items (Tryon & Mulloy, 1993). Such studies suggest that process-based examinations of self-report measures are possible and may hold an important place in the future of construct validation as the theoretical processes that are proximal to self-description become better articulated.

Structural Aspects

Evidence for the structural aspect of construct validity pertains to the validation of the internal structure and scoring of the instrument. The interrelations among elements of a measure (e.g., items or subscales) should be consistent with what is known about the structure of the construct domain. The many item-selection parameters discussed previously will result in items that are related to each other. However, the means by which the items are combined into scale scores (typically through addition) are typically not compared for validity to alternative scorings (e.g., configural or interactive combinations of items).

Researchers often perform factor analyses of instruments, either confirmatory or exploratory, in an attempt to provide evidence of the structural aspect of construct validity. However, as described earlier, the use of factor analysis makes certain assumptions about scale structure that should be considered carefully. Furthermore, such factor analyses (particularly the exploratory variants) are largely useless in the absence of a well-articulated theory of the classificatory relations (Skinner, 1981) among the different elements. Factor analysis represents a means of simplifying scale interrelations and representing them as linear functions, but in the absence of a theory to explicate how the relationships should look, it is simply a data-exploration tool and not a construct validation one. For many tests, such relations can be articulated. The NEO-PI (Costa & McCrae, 1985), for example, is based upon a theory that posits five orthogonal factors that underlie most stable personality characteristics. Thus, one aspect of the construct validity of the NEO-PI can be examined by determining whether the items load on five orthogonal factors (ideally, regardless of one's choice of extraction or rotation methods). Interestingly, even McCrae et al. (1997) has expressed skepticism that a confirmatory approach is very useful for validating measures derived from the five-factor model.

Generalizability Aspects

Generalizability evidence involves the extent to which score properties and interpretations generalize across different groups and contexts. Although many such studies should be conducted in selecting items for the scale, it is typically not possible to sample all population groups or all plausible contexts in which the scale might be used. Thus, further studies involving stability of item or scale parameters across settings, raters, or groups are important. Many of these investigations may conducted under the rubric of *reliability studies,* but as discussed previously, reliability itself falls within the generalizability aspect of construct validation.

External Aspects

The external aspects of construct validity refer to score relationships with other measures and behaviors; these relationships should reflect the relations implicit in the theory of the construct being assessed. The classic paper by Campbell and Fiske (1959) highlighted that both convergent and discriminant patterns of correlations are important. *Convergent validation* involves examining correlations with other indicators of the same construct, and as such typically subsumes the concept of criterion validity; discriminant validation, as

discussed previously, involves elimination of alternative interpretations of test scores through examining correlations with indicators of other constructs. Campbell and Fiske pioneered the use of the multitrait-multimethod matrix as a powerful tool for examining these correlation patterns within a single study. With this approach, the investigator assesses two or more constructs (the *traits*) using two or more measurement techniques (the *methods*) and then evaluates the intercorrelations among the various measures. Campbell and Fiske proposed four classic criteria for interpreting the matrix as supportive of construct validity:

1. The correlations among multiple measures of the same construct (monotrait-heteromethod correlations) should be sufficiently large and significantly different from zero;
2. The correlations described in Criterion 1 should be larger than correlations between differing constructs, measured across different methods (heterotrait-heteromethod);
3. The correlations described in Criterion 1 should be larger than correlations between different constructs as measured by the same method (monomethod-heterotrait), implying that the methods are relatively free from method variance that forces interrelationships among traits; and
4. The pattern of correlations among the different constructs should be similar across measurement methods.

Although the Campbell and Fiske (1959) criteria are important guidelines, they are not explicit and make a number of assumptions that often do not hold (Schmitt & Stults, 1986). In recent years, many investigators have used confirmatory factor analysis to model the multitrait-multimethod matrix. This approach has a number of potential advantages, such as allowing the researcher to distinguish the contributions of trait, method, and error components to score variance. However, analyzing this type of matrix using confirmatory factor analysis tends to be quite difficult in practice, because parameter estimates often fail to converge or yield values that fall out of permissible ranges (Kenny & Kashy, 1992). One confirmatory factor analysis variant that tends to provide interpretable solutions is the *correlated uniqueness* model (Marsh, 1989), which represents method variance as correlation between error terms of indicators derived from the same method. However, this model assumes independence of method factors, which may not be the case when similar methods are used, such as different self-report techniques (Bryant, 2000). Although the confirmatory approach reflects the state of the art in the analyses of matrices composed of external validation correlates, there are important limits to its use, suggesting that a rigorous implementation of the original

Campbell and Fiske (1959) criteria retains a place in construct validation.

Consequential Aspects

Messick's (1995) final aspect of construct validation involves evidence to evaluate the intended and the unintended consequences of score interpretation. Messick points out that the social consequences of testing may be either positive, such as greater identification and hence earlier intervention for mental health problems, or negative, such as restriction of access to services because of biases in interpretation or fairness in use. Research in this area needs to establish that any negative impact that a test score may have on an individual or group does not derive from some failure in test validity, such as the inclusion of construct-irrelevant variance in the scale score that is associated with demographic group membership.

CONCLUSION

The construct validation approach to psychological assessment appears deceptively simple, yet the subtleties become much more apparent in the process of developing and validating an instrument. However, because of the application of these procedures, psychological assessment has more to offer the researcher and clinician today than it did four decades ago. The construct validation approach yields instruments that are straightforward in terms of meaning and interpretation; because the measures are tied explicitly to constructs, the interpretation of a scale score generally corresponds directly to the name of the scale, which, remarkably, has often not been the case in the history of assessment. This parsimony of interpretation should not be viewed as a limit, but rather as a solid beginning point for any individual who seeks to learn more about a particular personality or psychopathology construct. Ultimately, the goal for an assessment instrument is the same as the goal for a more general science of psychology, this being a thorough elaboration of the nomological network relating important constructs and their various indicators. The process of developing and validating an instrument informs this elaboration, and ultimately both theory and method gain from the interaction. This chapter describes some of the approaches and some of the pitfalls that the scale developer can encounter. In constructing scales, as in so many other important areas of inquiry, there is no one approach that is superior. Each assessment problem reflects unique challenges with diverse solutions. The developer's goal must be to assemble a mosaic of indicators and studies of those indicators that together may suggest the optimum route for assessing the target construct.

REFERENCES

American Psychiatric Association (1994). *Diagnostic and statistical manual of mental disorders* (4th ed.). Washington, DC: Author.

Archer, R. P., Fontaire, J., & McCrae, R. R. (1998). Effects of two MMPI-2 validity scales on basic scale relations to external criteria. *Journal of Personality Assessment, 70,* 87–102.

Beck, A. T. (1967). *Depression: Clinical, experimental, and theoretical aspects.* New York: Harper & Row.

Beck, A. T., & Steer, R. A. (1987). *Beck Depression Inventory manual.* San Antonio, TX: Psychological Corporation.

Block, J. (1965). *The challenge of response sets: Unconfounding meaning, acquiescence, and social desirability in the MMPI.* New York: Appleton-Century-Crofts.

Campbell, D. T., & Fiske, D. W. (1959). Convergent and discriminant validation by the multitrait-multimethod matrix. *Psychological Bulletin, 56,* 81–105.

Cattell, R. B. (1965). *The scientific analysis of personality.* Baltimore: Penguin Books.

Cattell, R. B., Cattell, A. K. S., & Cattell, H. E. P. (1993). *16PF,* (5th ed.). Champaign, IL: Institute for Personality and Ability Testing.

Cleary, T. A. (1968). Test bias: Prediction of grades of negro and white students in integrated colleges. *Journal of Educational Measurement, 5,* 115–124.

Comrey, A. L. (1988). Factor-analytic methods of scale development in personality and clinical psychology. *Journal of Counsulting and Clinical Psychology, 56,* 754–761.

Costa, P. T., & McCrae, R. R. (1988). Personality in adulthood: A six-year longitudinal study of self-reports and spouse ratings on the NEO Personality Inventory. *Journal of Personality and Social Psychology, 54,* 853–863.

Costa, P. T., & McCrae, R. R. (1989). *The NEO-PI/FFI manual supplement.* Odessa, FL: Psychological Assessment Resources.

Costa, P. T., & McCrae, R. R. (1992a). Normal personality in clinical practice: The NEO Personality Inventory. *Psychological Assessment, 4,* 5–13.

Costa, P. T., & McCrae, R. R. (1992b). Professional manual: Revised NEO Personality Inventory (NEO-PI-R) and the NEO Five-Factor Inventory (NEO-FFI). Odessa, FL: Psychological Assessment Resources.

Cronbach, L. J. (1951). Coefficient alpha and the internal structure of tests. *Psychometrika, 16,* 297–334.

Cronbach, L. J., & Gleser, G. C. (1964). The signal-noise ratio in the comparison of reliability coefficients. *Educational and Psychological Measurement, 24,* 467–480.

Cronbach, L. J., & Meehl, P. E. (1955). Construct validity in psychological tests. *Psychological Bulletin, 52,* 281–302.

Crowne, D. P., & Marlowe, D. (1960). A new scale of social desirability independent of psychopathology. *Journal of Consulting Psychology, 24,* 349–354.

Edwards, A. L. (1957). *The social desirability variable in personality assessment and research.* New York: Dryden.

Edwards, A. L. (1959). *Manual for the Edwards Personal Preference Schedule* (Rev. ed.). New York: Psychological Corporation.

Eysenck, H. J. (1952). *The scientific study of personality.* London: Routledge & Kegen Paul.

Faust, D., & Miner, R. A. (1986). The empiricist and his new clothes: DSM-III in perspective. *American Journal of Psychiatry, 143,* 962–967.

Fiske, D. W. (1949). Consistency of the factorial structures of personality ratings from different sources. *Journal of Abnormal and Social Psychology, 44,* 329–344.

Foulds, G. A. (1971). Personality deviance and personal symptomatology. *Psychological Medicine, 1,* 222–233.

Goldberg, L. R. (1993). The structure of phenotypic personality traits. *American Psychologist, 48,* 26–34.

Goodwin, F. K., & Jamison, K. R. (1990). Manic-depressive illness. New York: Oxford University Press.

Guilford, J. P. (1936). *Psychometric methods.* New York: McGraw-Hill.

Guilford, J. P. (1954). *Psychometric methods.* New York: McGraw-Hill.

Guilford, J. P., & Zimmerman, W. S. (1949). *The Guilford-Zimmerman temperament survey.* Beverly Hills, CA: Sheridan Supply Co.

Hamilton, M. (1960). A rating scale for depression. *Journal of Neurology, Neurosurgery, and Psychiatry, 23,* 56–62.

Hammill, D. D., Brown, L., & Bryant, B. R. (1993). *A consumer's guide to tests in print.* Austin, TX: Pro-Ed.

Hathaway, S. R., & McKinley, J. C. (1967). *MMPI manual* (Rev. ed.). New York: Psychological Corporation.

Helmes, E. (2000). The role of social desirability in the assessment of personality constructs. In R. D. Goffin & E. Helmes (Eds.), *Problems and solutions in human assessment* (pp. 21–40). Norwell, MA: Kluwer Academic.

Holden, R. R. (1989). Disguise and the structured self-report assessment of psychopathology: II. A clinical replication. *Journal of Clinical Psychology, 45,* 583–586.

Holden, R. R., & Fekken, G. C. (1990). Structured psychopathological test item characteristics and validity. *Psychological Assessment, 2,* 35–40.

Holmes, T. H., & Rahe, R. H. (1967). The social readjustment rating scale. *Journal of Psychosomatic Research, 11,* 213–218.

Hulin, C. L., Drasgow, F., & Parsons, C. K. (1983). *Item response theory: Application to psychological measurement.* Homewood, IL: Irwin.

Jackson, D. N. (1967a). *Personality Research Form manual.* Goshen, NY: Research Psychologists Press.

Jackson, D. N. (1967b). A review of J. Block: The challenge of response sets. *Educational and Psychological Measurement, 27,* 207–219.

Jackson, D. N. (1970). A sequential system for personality scale development. In C. D. Spielberger (Ed.), *Current topics in clinical and community psychology* (Vol. 2, pp. 62–97). New York: Academic Press.

Jackson, D. N. (1971). The dynamics of structured personality tests. *Psychological Review, 78,* 229–248.

Koss, M. P. (1979). MMPI item content: Recurring issues. In J. N. Butcher (Ed.), *New developments in the use of the MMPI* (pp. 3–38). Minneapolis: University of Minnesota Press.

Lambert, M. J., Hatch, D. R., Kingston, M. D., & Edwards, B. C. (1986). Zung, Beck, and Hamilton rating scales as measures of treatment outcome: A meta-analytic comparison. *Journal of Consulting and Clinical Psychology, 54,* 54–59.

Lees-Haley, P. R, & Fox, D. D. (1990). MMPI subtle-obvious scales and malingering: Clinical versus simulated scores. *Psychological Reports, 68,* 203–210.

Likert, R. (1932). A technique for the measurement of attitudes. *Archives of Psychology, 140.*

Loevinger, J. (1954). The attenuation paradox in test theory. *Psychological Bulletin, 51,* 493–504.

Loevinger, J. (1957). Objective tests as instruments of psychological theory. *Psychological Reports, 3,* 635–694.

Lord, F. M. (1980). *Applications of item response theory to practical testing problems.* Hillsdale, NJ: Erlbaum.

Louks, J., Hayne, C., & Smith, J. (1989). Replicated factor structure of the Beck Depression Inventory. *Journal of Nervous and Mental Disease, 177,* 473–479.

Maser, J. D., & Cloninger, C. R. (1990). *Comorbidity of mood and anxiety disorders.* Washington DC: American Psychiatric Press.

McCrae, R. R., & Costa, P. T. (1983). Social desirability scales: More substance than style. *Journal of Consulting and Clinical Psychology, 31,* 882–888.

McCrae, R. R., & Costa, P. T. (1984). *Emerging lives, enduring dispositions: Personality in adulthood.* Boston: Little-Brown.

McCrae, R. R., & Costa, P. T. (1986). Clinical assessment can benefit from recent advances in personality psychology. *American Psychologist, 41,* 1001–1003.

McCrae, R. R., & Costa, P. T. (1996). Toward a new generation of personality theories: Theoretical contexts for the five-factor model. In J. S. Wiggins, (Ed.), *The five-factor model of personality: Theoretical perspectives* (pp. 51–87). New York: Guilford Press.

Meehl, P. E. (1945). The dynamics of structured personality tests. *Journal of Clinical Psychology, 1,* 296–303.

Meehl, P. E. (1977). Specific etiology and other forms of strong influence: Some quantitative meanings. *Journal of Medicine and Philosophy, 2,* 33–53.

Meehl, P. E., & Hathaway, S. R. (1946). The K factor as a suppressor variable in the MMPI. *Journal of Applied Psychology, 30,* 525–564.

Milgram, S. (1965). Some conditions of obedience and disobedience to authority. *Human Relations, 18,* 57–76.

Millon, T. (1994). Manual for the MCMI-III. Minneapolis, MN: National Computer Systems.

Morey, L. C. (1991a). *The Personality Assessment Inventory professional manual.* Odessa, FL: Psychological Assessment Resources.

Morey, L.C. (1991b). The classification of mental disorder as a collection of hypothetical constructs. *Journal of Abnormal Psychology, 100,* 289–293.

Morey, L. C., & Glutting, J. H. (1994). The Personality Assessment Inventory: Correlates with normal and abnormal personality. In S. Strack, & M. Lou (eds.), *Differentiating Normal and Abnormal Personality* (pp. 402–420). New York: Springer.

Murray, H. A. (1938). *Explorations in personality.* New York: Oxford University Press.

Norman, W. T. (1963). Toward an adequate taxonomy of personality attributes: Replicated factor structure in peer nomination personality ratings. *Journal of Abnormal and Social Psychology, 66,* 574–583.

Nunnally, J. C. (1978). *Psychometric theory* (2nd ed.). New York: McGraw-Hill.

Peterson, G. W., Clark, D. A., & Bennett, B. (1989). The utility of MMPI subtle, obvious scales for detecting fake good and fake bad response sets. *Journal of Clinical Psychology, 45,* 575–583.

Retzlaff, P., & Gilbertini, M. (1987). Factor structure of the MCMI basic personality scales and common-item artifact. *Journal of Personality Assessment, 51,* 588–594.

Rosen, A. (1958). Differentiation of diagnostic groups by individual MMPI scales. *Journal of Consulting Psychology, 22,* 453–457.

Schwartz, M. A., & Wiggins, O. P. (1987). Empiricism and DSM-III. *American Journal of Psychiatry, 144,* 837–838.

Skinner, H. A. (1981). Toward the integration of classification theory and methods. *Journal of Abnormal Psychology, 90,* 68–87.

Skinner, H. A. (1986). Construct validation approach to psychiatric classification. In T. Millon & G. L. Klerman (Eds.), *Contemporary directions in psychopathology* (pp. 307–330). New York: Guilford Press.

Skinner, H. A., & Lei, H. (1980). Differential weights in life change research: Useful or irrelevant? *Psychosomatic Medicine, 42,* 367–370.

Smith, P. C., & Kendall, L. M. (1963). Retranslation of expectations: An approach to the construction of unambiguous anchors for rating scales. *Journal of Applied Psychology, 47,* 149–155.

Steer, R. A., Ball, R., Ranieri, W. F., & Beck, A. T., (1999). Dimensions of the Beck Depression Inventory-II in clinically depressed outpatients. *Journal of Clinical Psychology, 55,* 117–128.

Strong, E. R. (1927). Vocational interest test. *Educational Record, 8,* 107–121.

Thurstone, L. L. (1935). *Vectors of the mind.* Chicago: University of Chicago Press.

Thurstone, L. L. (1959). *The measurement of values.* Chicago: University of Chicago.

Tryon, W. W., & Mulloy, J. M. (1993). Further validation of computer-assessed response time to emotionally evocative stimuli. *Journal of Personality Assessment, 61,* 231–236.

Tupes, E. C., & Christal, R. E. (1961). Recurrent personality factors based on trait ratings. USAF ASD Technical Report, No. 61–97.

Welsh, G. S. (1952). A factor study of the MMPI using scales with item overlap eliminated. *American Psychologist, 7,* 341.

Wiggins, J. S. (1962). Strategic, method, and stylistic variance in the MMPI. *Psychological Bulletin, 59,* 224–242.

Wiggins, J. S. (1973). *Personality and prediction: Principles of Personality Assessment.* Reading, MA: Addison-Wesley.

Zung, W. W. (1965). A self-rating depression scale. *Archives of General Psychiatry, 12,* 63–70.

CHAPTER 16

The Circumplex Model: Methods and Research Applications

MICHAEL B. GURTMAN AND AARON L. PINCUS

From the signs of the Zodiac to Jung's mandalas to formal geometric models with precise mathematical specification (e.g., Gurtman & Pincus, 2000; Wiggins & Trobst, 1997), circular representations of a variety of domains of human experience have been conceived and presented throughout human history (Wiggins, 1991, 1996). In the field of psychology and beyond, the appeal of circular models lies in the combination of circle's aesthetic (organizational) simplicity, yet powerful potential to describe data in uniquely compelling substantive and geometric ways. Gurtman (1998) noted that, like the form of the circle itself, circumplex models intrigue by their elegant simplicity, yet at the same time have complex features and hidden unfixed properties that compel further exploration.

Building on the work of Louis Guttman (1954), empirically derived circumplex models describing interpersonal behavior began to formally appear in the psychology literature in the 1950s (e.g., Leary, 1957; Schaefer, 1959). The seminal work of Wiggins (1979, 1980, 1982) stimulated the development of progressively diverse applications and formalized empirical approaches. In the last 20 years, increasingly sophisticated circumplex analytic methods have been developed.

The purpose of this chapter is to review these methods and their research applications. We have chosen to organize the majority of this chapter with reference to basic empirical questions likely to underlie investigators' applications of circumplex models and methods. Thus, after the circumplex is defined and examples from contemporary psychological literature are described, the chapter is divided into sections related to the following basic research questions: (a) *How do I evaluate circular representations in my domain of interest?*, (b) *How do I use the circumplex to describe individuals?*, (c) *How do I use the circumplex to describe and compare groups?*, and (d) *How do I use the circumplex to evaluate*

The authors wish to thank Terence J. G. Tracey for several important contributions to this chapter.

constructs and their measures? We conclude the chapter with a brief discussion of future directions in the development and application of circumplex methodology.

DEFINITION OF A CIRCUMPLEX AND EXAMPLES FROM LITERATURE

Louis Guttman (1954) originated the term *circumplex* to describe a "system of variables which has a circular law of order" (p. 325). He also proposed "a very specialized example of a circumplex" (p. 326), having a structure definable in terms of a uniform system of additive components. This led, in turn, to the exposition of a particular kind of correlation pattern among tests ("the equally-spaced, uniform, perfect, additive circumplex," p. 327), which he characterized on the basis of its form (p. 328) as a *circulant*. Table 16.1 provides an example of such a matrix (Guttman, 1954, p. 329).

Guttman's (1954) work, and developments that followed it (see, e.g., Shepard, 1978), suggest two ultimately compatible conceptualizations of the circumplex model. The *geometric circumplex* (e.g., Conte & Plutchik, 1981) defines the circumplex as a circular array of variables (see Figure 16.1). More technically, the circular curve provides a basis for scaling the set of similarities among variables; thus, the similarity between any two variables is inversely related to their distance apart on the circle (Browne, 1992; Fabrigar, Visser, & Browne, 1997; Shepard, 1978). In an earlier article (Gurtman & Pincus, 2000), and similar to Browne (1992), we have formalized this as a highly general correlation model:

$$\rho_{ij} = inverse \ f(\theta_i - \theta_j) \tag{16.1}$$

where ρ_{ij} is the correlation between variables i and j, and θ_i and θ_j are their respective angular displacements ($0° \leq \theta \leq 360°$) on a circle. It is assumed that the function is monotone in form, and that variables are distributed uniformly throughout the full circular continuum.

From a slightly different perspective (see Gurtman, 1994), we note that a valid circular representation implies three

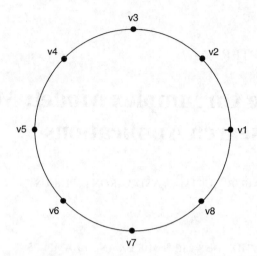

Figure 16.1 A geometric circumplex with eight variables.

defining properties about the set of variable interrelationships: that (a) the differences among variables can be reduced to differences in two dimensions; (b) each of the variables has an equal projection in this plane, as represented by the variable's distance from the origin (of a hypothetical circle); and (c) the variables' distribution around the hypothetical circle is uniform, generally translated into the property of *equal spacing*. These properties are increasingly specific for a circumplex model (see Gurtman, 1994). Indeed, the third criterion (equal spacing) is often used to differentiate between circumplex and simple-structure models (e.g., Hofstee, De Raad, & Goldberg, 1992).

The second way in which the circumplex has been conceptualized in the literature is as a particular kind of correlation matrix. This *circulant correlation model* was first presented by Guttman (1954), as noted earlier, and has been further explored and developed by others (e.g., Browne, 1992; Cudeck, 1986; Rounds, Tracey, & Hubert, 1992; Wiggins, Steiger, & Gaelick, 1981.) This model defines the circumplex as a particular kind of nonrestrictive (i.e., not fully constrained) correlation pattern characterized by a circular, repeating pattern of values in each row and column. Table 16.2 formalizes this model for the eight-variable case;

TABLE 16.1 An Example of an Equally Spaced, Uniform, Perfect, Additive Circumplex

	v1	v2	v3	v4	v5	v6
v1	1.00					
v2	.75	1.00				
v3	.50	.75	1.00			
v4	.25	.50	.75	1.00		
v5	.50	.25	.50	.75	1.00	
v6	.75	.50	.25	.50	.75	1.00

Note. Adapted from Guttman (1954), p. 329.

TABLE 16.2 Circulant Correlation Model for an Eight-Element Circle

	v1	v2	v3	v4	v5	v6	v7	v8
v1	1							
v2	$\rho 1$	1						
v3	$\rho 2$	$\rho 1$	1					
v4	$\rho 3$	$\rho 2$	$\rho 1$	1				
v5	$\rho 4$	$\rho 3$	$\rho 2$	$\rho 1$	1			
v6	$\rho 3$	$\rho 4$	$\rho 3$	$\rho 2$	$\rho 1$	1		
v7	$\rho 2$	$\rho 3$	$\rho 4$	$\rho 3$	$\rho 2$	$\rho 1$	1	
v8	$\rho 1$	$\rho 2$	$\rho 3$	$\rho 4$	$\rho 3$	$\rho 2$	$\rho 1$	1

Note. $\rho 1 > \rho 2 > \rho 3 > \rho 4$.

Table 16.1 provides a numerical example. It may be noted that the circulants presented in Tables 16.1 and 16.2 have the property of *equal spacing* (Guttman, 1954, p. 328), as indicated by the equality of values in each diagonal of the matrix (hence the values are represented by a single parameter, as illustrated in Table 16.2). For equally-spaced circulants, the sum of each column or row of values will be the same (Guttman, 1954).

Examples of Models From the Literature

In our view, the three psychological domains of interpersonal behavior, mood and affect, and vocational preference provide exemplars of the most well developed and empirically evaluated circumplex models in psychology.

The Interpersonal Domain

The most well-established domain for both the application of circumplex models in psychology and the development of circumplex methodology is the study of interpersonal behavior (Wiggins, 1996). Two seminal early lines of research, each employing a different unit of analysis (individuals or dyads), converged in identifying a circular structure in ratings of interpersonal behavior (for a full review, see Pincus, Gurtman, & Ruiz, 1998).

Leary and colleagues (Freedman, Leary, Ossorio, & Coffey, 1951; Leary, 1957) focused on the individual's behavior and catalogued an initial taxonomy of *interpersonal mechanisms* (essentially behavioral verbs) observed in group psychotherapy sessions. Early dimension-reduction techniques were applied to these ratings and to a complementary set of trait adjectives. As noted by LaForge, Freedman, and Wiggins (1985), "Slowly the nodal points or axes of affiliation versus aggression and dominance versus submission emerged" (p. 624).

The *Leary Circle* (Leary, 1957), a circumplex of interpersonal behaviors and traits, organized all interpersonal behaviors in a circular array around the two fundamental dimensions of *Dominance versus Submission* on the vertical axis and *Love versus Hate* on the horizontal axis. This model has been operationalized through a number of objective assessment instruments over the years (see Kiesler, 1996, or Pincus, 1994, for reviews). Although considerably refined across its near-50-year history and most commonly referred to as the *Interpersonal Circle* (IPC; Kiesler, 1983), this basic circumplex model has remained relatively unchanged in its structural underpinnings. From the perspective of the IPC, all interpersonal behavior can be described as a blend of the basic dimensions of *Dominance* and *Nurturance* (Wiggins,

1979), with substantive distinctions ordered around the perimeter of the circle typically segmenting the perimeter's continuum into quadrants, octants, or sixteenths. The IPC structure has generalized across a variety of interpersonal domains, including nonverbal interpersonal behaviors (Gifford, 1991), interpersonal acts (Kiesler, 1985), psychotherapy transactions (Kiesler, 1987; Tracey & Schneider, 1995), interpersonal traits (Gurtman & Pincus, 2000; Wiggins, 1979), interpersonal problems (Alden, Wiggins, & Pincus, 1990; Horowitz, Alden, Wiggins, & Pincus, 2000), social support transactions (Trobst, 2000), and covert interpersonal impact messages (Kiesler, Schmidt, & Wagner, 1997; Wagner, Kiesler, & Schmidt, 1995).

A second early line of research focused on interpersonal behavior within dyads. Schaefer (1959, 1961) observed the interactions of mothers and children and catalogued behaviors of mothers toward their children and the reactions of children to their mothers. His data also suggested that two complementary circumplex models appropriately captured maternal behavior and children's reactions. Schaefer's original circumplexes of maternal behavior and child reactions were similar to the IPC with a single difference. The fundamental dimensions were *Hostility versus Love* (converging with the IPC on the horizontal axes) but *Autonomy versus Control* (diverging with the IPC on the vertical axis). The most detailed circumplex model of interpersonal behavior, originally stemming from Schaefer's work, is Benjamin's (1974, 1996) *Structural Analysis of Social Behavior* (SASB). SASB is a three-circle (or *surface*) model that describes actions toward others (*transitive* behaviors) on one circumplex surface, reactions to others (*intransitive* behaviors) on a second surface, and *introjected* behaviors directed toward the self on a third surface. Each SASB surface describes its focus of behavior in an array of blends of the two dimensions of *Affiliation* and *Interdependence*. SASB has been used widely in investigations of process and outcome in psychotherapy and interpersonal aspects of psychopathology (e.g., Benjamin, 1996; Henry, 1996).

Mood and Affect

Like interpersonal models, circumplex models of affect have emerged from different theoretical perspectives and programs of research. Russell (1980) and Watson and Tellegen (1985) put forth circumplex models of affect that have inspired a significant amount of research and debate. Russell (1980, 1997) proposed that the basic dimensions of affect could be labeled *High Arousal versus Low Arousal* and *Pleasure versus Displeasure,* and demonstrated that discrete emotions arose from blends of these two fundamental dimensions. For example, anxiety reflects of blend of *High Arousal* and *Displeasure,* whereas joy reflects a blend of *High Arousal* and *Pleasure.* Watson and Tellegen (1985) proposed that the basic dimensions of mood could be labeled *Negative Affect* (NA) and *Positive Affect* (PA). Similarly, discrete emotions were suggested to emerge from variation in blends of NA and PA. For example, sadness reflects a blend of high NA and low PA, while surprise reflects a blend of high NA and high PA.

Over the last 20 years, debates among affect researchers have led to the recognition that these two circumplex models, as well as other more recent two-dimensional formulations (Larsen & Diener, 1992; Thayer, 1996), generally converge in terms of the content of circular affect space but often differ in terms of the identified fundamental dimensions or axes underlying the circular models. Although differences in these structural models of affect are not solely an issue of rotation (Cacioppo, Gardner, & Bernston, 1999; Green, Salovey, & Truax, 1999; Russell & Feldman-Barrett, 1999; Watson, Wiese, Vaidya, & Tellegen, 1999), theoretical and empirical efforts at integration of these perspectives continue to support the circumplex as an appropriate structural model for the domain (Yik, Russell, & Feldman-Barret, 1999).

Vocational Interests

A third area in which circumplex models have emerged and flourished is the vocational interests domain, largely on the basis of a reconceptualization of Holland's (1973) hexagonal model of interests (e.g., Tracey & Rounds, 1993). According to Holland's highly influential theory, individuals' occupational preferences, as well as corresponding work environments, can be categorized in terms of six major types: Realistic (R), Investigative (I), Artistic (A), Social (S), Enterprising (E), and Conventional (C). Holland also proposed that these six occupational interests could be arranged as a hexagon on the basis of their strength of relation (the so-called calculus hypothesis). The Holland model, generally referred to in its duality as the RIASEC model, has become the standard for the assessment of occupational preferences, and is represented by all major vocational interests tests.

As Tracey and Rounds (1993) among others (e.g., Hogan, 1983) have duly noted, the hexagonal model is essentially a circular model; moreover, as Prediger (1982) has shown, this circle is situated in a two-dimensional space definable by interests in *People versus Things* and *Data versus Ideas.* A large number of studies have now examined the structure of the RIASEC circumplex across different age, culture, gender, and ethnic groups (e.g., Day & Rounds, 1998; Fouad, Harmon, & Borgen, 1997; Rounds & Tracey, 1996; Tracey &

Ward, 1998). These structure-of-interest studies have not always yielded consistent support for the assumed circular structure of the traditional RIASEC, yet enough to suggest that, perhaps with refinement, the RIASEC space can assume an improved circular form at least in some populations (Tracey & Rounds, 1995; however see Rounds & Day, 1999). Indeed, Tracey and his colleagues (e.g., Tracey & Rounds, 1995) have developed an eight-scale RIASEC type of measure that appears to possess superior circumplex properties; they have also proposed a more elaborate spherical model (Tracey & Rounds, 1996a, 1996b) from which circumplex measures of vocational interests can be derived. Later in this chapter, an updated circumplex version of their measure will be used to illustrate different analytic methods.

Others

A number of additional circular models have been proposed in psychology and related fields, although none is as extensively investigated and evaluated as those models reviewed above. Some circular representations, such as Nobel Laureate Charles Hartshorne's (1980) circular model of the aesthetics of science are purely conceptual, whereas other proposed models are based on moderate amounts of empirical investigation. These include (but are not limited to) family and marital systems (Olson, 1996), personality disorders (Millon, 1987; Plutchik & Conte, 1985; Romney & Byner, 1997), psychological defenses (Benjamin, 1995; Plutchik, Kellerman, & Conte, 1979), psychotic disturbance (Lorr, 1997), and trait structures based on combining all possible pairs of the Five-Factor Model of personality (Hofstee et al., 1992).

HOW DO I EVALUATE CIRCULAR REPRESENTATIONS IN MY DOMAIN OF INTEREST? (EVALUATING DATA FOR GOODNESS-OF-FIT TO A CIRCUMPLEX MODEL)

The issue of how to evaluate whether a particular data set has circumplex properties (i.e., conforms to the circumplex model), and hence mirrors a particular theoretical conception, has now been addressed in a number of worthwhile articles and chapters (e.g., Browne, 1992; Fabrigar et al., 1997; Gaines et al., 1997; Gurtman, 1994; Gurtman & Pincus, 2000; Rounds et al., 1992; Tracey, 2000; Tracey, Rounds, & Gurtman, 1996; Wiggins et al., 1981). Of these, Tracey's (2000) recent chapter stands out as both a technical and practical resource for researchers interested in testing for possible circumplex structure in their measures and in the corresponding domains of interest.

In general, methods of analysis can be divided into two groups. *Exploratory methods,* such as multidimensional scaling and principal components analysis, yield mainly *spatial representations* of the sample data (Gurtman & Pincus, 2000); these representations are then evaluated informally or, in some cases, heuristically (e.g., Pincus et al., 1998) for fit to a circular ideal. *Confirmatory methods,* on the other hand, provide formal tests of circumplex model fit to the data (e.g., to the correlation pattern), and are exemplified by Browne's (1992) CIRCUM routine and by Hubert and Arabie's (1987) tests of order hypotheses. Confirmatory methods often have the added flexibility of allowing different circumplex models to be compared and tested (e.g., Browne, 1992; Gaines et al., 1997; Rounds et al., 1992).

Rather than being considered adversarial approaches to model analysis (e.g., Fabrigar et al., 1997), exploratory and confirmatory methods are arguably complementary in their essential yields. In line with earlier description (also see Gurtman & Pincus, 2000), we see the main role of exploratory methods as providing spatial representations of the data structure. Today, however, any serious test of the circumplex model should also include application of confirmatory methods. Hence, confirmatory methods offer the logical next step in validating the circumplex properties of a given data set.

In the remainder of this section, each method is briefly described and a sample analysis is conducted for illustration. The data for the demonstration consist of scores on a circumplex-based measure of vocational interests, the Personal Globe Inventory–Circumplex (PGI; Kovalski, Tracey, & Darcy, 2000; Tracey, 1998, 2002), a slightly revised version of the Inventory of Occupational Preferences (IOP; Tracey & Rounds, 1995). Figure 16.2 shows the hypothesized structure of this scale, and its relationship to the traditional RIASEC space. For our analysis, data were available for 253 women (henceforth female sample) and 172 men (male sample); respondents were college students enrolled in a career exploration class. We thank Terence Tracey for generously supplying us with these data.

Exploratory Methods

Exploratory Factor Analysis

Perhaps the most widely used method for examining data for circumplex structure is through the application of exploratory factor analysis, notably principal components analysis (PCA). An excellent example is provided by Wiggins, Phillips, and Trapnell (1989), who subjected the Interpersonal Adjective Scales to PCA in an attempt to validate its theoretical structure. The goal of PCA is to identify a small number

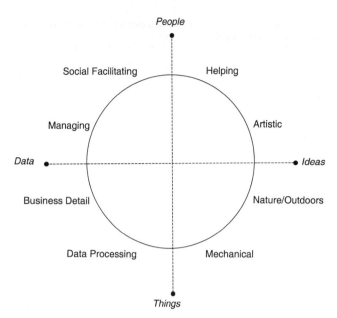

Figure 16.2 The Personal Globe Inventory–Circumplex. *Source:* Adapted from "Personal Globe Inventory: Measurement of the Spherical Model of Interests and Competence Beliefs" by T. J. G. Tracey, *Journal of Vocational Behavior, in press.* Adapted from original source by permission.

of orthogonal components that can account for the obtained correlations among variables. When subjected to PCA, circumplex matrices generally yield a two-factor solution (e.g., Wiggins et al., 1989) or a three-factor solution (e.g., Alden et al., 1990); if a three-factor solution, the first factor is a general factor on which all variables manifest positive and generally high loadings. The two nongeneral factors should be comparable in size (eigenvalue), suggesting a circular rather than elliptical structure (e.g., Pincus et al., 1998). In addition, when the variables are plotted in a two-dimensional plane based on their factor loadings (using the two nongeneral factors), a circular arrangement should exist—caused by variables having roughly equal projections (communalities) in that plane, and roughly equal (i.e., uniform) spacing.

Table 16.3 shows the results of a PCA conducted on the Personal Globe Inventory–Circumplex, as described earlier. (For brevity, only female data are presented, although the results are virtually identical for the two groups.) A scree test of the eigenvalues suggested a three-factor solution, with the first factor clearly a general factor and the next two factors somewhat similar in magnitude, as expected. (The eigenvalues for the first four factors were as follows: 3.47, 1.90, 1.46, and 0.39.) Although not shown, a two-dimensional plot of the variables' loadings on the second and third factors would reveal a roughly circular pattern.

Multidimensional Scaling

As Davison (1985, 1994) among others has shown, multidimensional scaling (MDS) methods are especially well-suited

TABLE 16.3 Factor Loading Matrix Based on Principal Components Analysis of PGI Scales (Females Only)

Scale	Factor		
	1	2	3
Social Facilitating	.55	.72	−.07
Managing	.54	.63	.33
Business Detail	.64	.16	.56
Data Processing	.73	−.36	.39
Mechanical	.75	−.49	.16
Nature/Outdoors	.72	−.52	−.25
Artistic	.68	−.13	−.62
Helping	.57	.46	−.52

Note. $n = 253$; PGI = Personal Globe Inventory.

for recovering circumplex structure from data sets. Such methods seek to identify a minimum number of dimensions that can be used to parsimoniously represent the proximities (e.g., correlations) among variables, and generally use non-metric scaling algorithms. Following Davison (1985), Tracey (2000) has noted that because MDS techniques are "data centered," they effectively eliminate general factors from the obtained solutions, and hence, compared to PCA, can bring greater clarity to the interpretation of the results. This said, MDS and PCA typically produce very similar solutions (i.e., spatial representations), except for how the general factor (if present) is handled (Davison, 1985). A complete example of MDS applied to a circumplex measure (again the Interpersonal Adjective Scales) is provided by Gurtman and Pincus (2000).

For the present example, we subjected each of the PGI correlation matrices to Kruskal's nonmetric MDS procedure. For the female data, *stress values* (smaller values indicating better goodness-of-fit) were .28 in one dimension and .01 in two dimensions, indicating an excellent fit of the proximity data in two dimensions (proportion of variance accounted for = 99.83%). Similarly, for the male data, stress values were .26 in one dimension, and dropped to .02 for the two-dimensional solution (proportion of variance accounted for = 99.60%).

Figures 16.3 and 16.4 show the female and male plots, respectively, of the eight PGI scales based on the scales' obtained dimensional coordinates. Circles are added by fitting the points to a circular model, using a least-squares fit criterion. (For ease of interpretation, the scales' polar coordinates were rotated so that the first scale, *Social Facilitating,* was positioned at its theoretical location on the circle; see Figure 16.2). Although not apparent in the figures, in each solution the scales were perfectly ordered according to the Figure 16.2 model. Visual inspections of the spatial representations reveal a close correspondence to a circular form in each case.

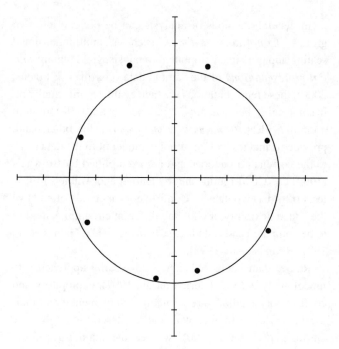

Figure 16.3 Multidimensional scaling plot of Personal Globe Inventory Scales (female sample).

Confirmatory Methods

Covariance Modeling and CIRCUM

As described earlier and shown in Table 16.2, the circumplex is associated with a particular kind of covariance model, referred to by Guttman (1954) as the *circulant matrix.* The circulant is a relatively nonrestrictive model characterized by a circular, repeating pattern of values occurring in each row and column.

Using structural equation modeling (SEM) techniques, it is possible to fit versions of this model to an obtained correlation matrix. Standard SEM programs, such as LISREL (Jöreskog & Sörbom, 1986), can and have been used for this purpose (e.g., Romney & Byner, 1997; Rounds et al., 1992; cf. Gaines et al., 1997). However, perhaps the best current tool for performing this kind of specialized analysis is Browne's (1992) CIRCUM program. Fabrigar et al. (1997) provide a relatively nontechnical introduction to the program; Browne (1992) offers a more technical and detailed description. A growing number of studies have now used CIRCUM to test for circumplex structure in data (e.g., Carroll, Yik, Russell, & Feldman-Barrett, 1999; Gurtman & Pincus, 2000; Pincus et al., 1998; Schmidt, Wagner, & Kiesler, 1999; Tracey, 2000; Watson et al., 1999; Yik et al., 1999).

Described as a *covariance structure modeling* technique (Fabrigar et al., 1997), CIRCUM was developed specifically to evaluate circumplex correlation models, as well as implement tests of Browne's (1992) *circular stochastic model* of

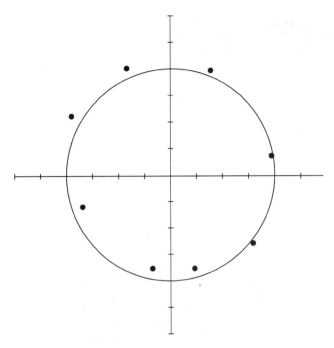

Figure 16.4 Multidimensional scaling plot of Personal Globe Inventory Scales (male sample).

the circumplex. In this regard, Browne has demonstrated that a circulant matrix (see Table 16.2) can be "reparametricized" as a Fourier series having the following general form:

$$\rho_{ij} = \beta_0 + \sum \beta_k \cos (k \times \theta_d) \qquad (16.2)$$

with $k = 1$ to m components in the Fourier series ($m < 4$ for an eight-variable circumplex, such as the circumplex depicted in Table 16.2), and where ρ_{ij} is the common-factor correlation of variables i, j, and θ_d is the angular discrepancy ($0° \leq \theta_d \leq 180°$) between their respective polar angles.

A particular advantage of this reparametricization is that it allows for testing of different geometric versions of the circumplex model. The most restrictive is the *equally spaced* model; it assumes that variables are distributed evenly around the circle. Hence, polar angles are fixed parameters in the equation, and only the βs are estimated. This model

corresponds to Guttman's (1954) equally spaced circumplex, and is given in Table 16.2. CIRCUM can also be used to fit a less restrictive model, the *unequally spaced* circumplex. Here no constraints are placed on the variables' polar angles; they are also estimated, thus the model has more free parameters (i.e., is less parsimonious) than the equally spaced alternative. Finally, it is also possible using CIRCUM to estimate versions of the model in which neither angles nor communalities (i.e., variables' projections) are constrained (*unequally spaced, unequal communalities* model). This is the least parsimonious model, and arguably may not qualify technically as a circumplex (because the variables are not constrained to fall along the circumference of a circle).

As a demonstration, we subjected the two PGI data sets to a CIRCUM analysis. For each data set, we successively tested the three models for fit to the obtained correlation pattern. Model fit was evaluated using multiple indices, as is common practice in the SEM literature. The fit statistics included (a) χ^2; (b) F, the maximum likelihood discrepancy function; (c) *GFI*, the Goodness-of-Fit index (Jöreskog & Sörbom, 1986); (d) *AGFI*, the Adjusted Goodness-of-Fit index (Jöreskog & Sörbom, 1986); and (e) *RMSEA*, the Root Mean Square Error of Approximation (Browne & Cudeck, 1992; Steiger & Lind, 1980). Three of the measures—χ^2, F, and *GFI*—are absolute measures of model fit, whereas two measures—*AGFI* and *RMSEA*—are parsimony-weighted and thus compensate for the model's complexity. (GFI and AGFI were computed from formulas presented in Maiti and Mukherjee (1990), and based on directions generously provided by Michael Browne.)

Table 16.4 presents the results of the CIRCUM analyses. Considering the female sample first, none of the three models had poor fit (e.g., *GFI* and *AGFI* generally > .9, *RMSEA* < .13); but, even with adjustments made for their greater complexity (i.e., more free parameters), the unequally spaced models appeared to offer better fit than the highly constrained equally spaced circumplex. CIRCUM also yields estimates of the variable's polar angles. Examining these (not shown), it is apparent that most of the variables were indeed evenly spaced ≈45° gaps); however, a larger-than-expected gap of

TABLE 16.4 Summary of Model-Fitting Tests for PGI Circulant Correlational Structure

		Model		Goodness-of-fit Measures						
Sample	N	Spacing	Communality	F	χ^2	RMSEA	GFI	AGFI	df	P
Female	253	Equal	Equal	.495	124.83	.129	.918	.877	24	12
		Unequal	Equal	.256	64.39	.105	.967	.929	17	19
		Unequal	Unequal	.065	16.36	.050	.991	.967	10	26
Male	172	Equal	Equal	.239	40.80	.064	.968	.952	24	12
		Unequal	Equal	.098	16.82	<.001	.987	.972	17	19
		Unequal	Unequal	.035	6.02	<.001	.995	.982	10	26

Note. Analyses conducted with CIRCUM (Browne, 1992); PGI = Personal Globe Inventory, F = maximum likelihood discrepancy function, RMSEA = root mean square error of approximation, GFI = goodness-of-fit index, AGFI = adjusted goodness-of-fit index, df = degrees of freedom, P = parameters.

TABLE 16.5   Obtained Correlation Matrix for PGI Scales (Males Only)

Scale	1	2	3	4	5	6	7	8
Social Facilitating	1.00							
Managing	.66	1.00						
Business Detail	.35	.51	1.00					
Data Processing	.13	.24	.55	1.00				
Mechanical	.09	.17	.38	.75	1.00			
Nature/Outdoors	.06	.03	.24	.54	.71	1.00		
Artistic	.28	.11	.14	.28	.43	.68	1.00	
Helping	.59	.35	.19	.12	.12	.23	.57	1.00

Note. $n = 172$; PGI = Personal Globe Inventory.

$63°$ occurred between variables 1 and 2, and a relatively small difference of $19°$ was obtained between variables 4 and 5. This finding is also evident in the earlier MDS depiction of the proximities (Figure 16.3).

Turning to the male sample, the results here suggest a still better overall fit of the circumplex model, with even the highly constrained equally-spaced model approaching a "close fit" (based on RMSEA values near .05; Browne, 1992). Allowing for (slight) unequal spacing (again, for variables 4 and 5), fit is excellent. As further evidence of this, Tables 16.5 and 16.6 show the actual correlation matrix and the reproduced matrix, respectively. (The reproduced values are maximum likelihood estimates provided by CIRCUM and assume an equally-spaced model.) The close correspondence of the two tables is apparent.

In evaluating the results of model-fit tests, Gurtman and Pincus (2000) noted that attention should also be directed toward the issue of whether deviations from model fit also have *practical consequences* for individual assessment. In this case, it can be shown that the slight unequal spacing of the PGI data (female sample) would have virtually no effect on individual assessment results. Gurtman and Pincus (2000) concluded the same was true for the Interpersonal Adjective Scales.

Circular Order Model and the Randomization Test

Tracey, Rounds, and their associates (e.g., Rounds et al., 1992; Tracey & Rounds, 1993) have offered a less restrictive

confirmatory test based on the work of Hubert and Arabie (1987). The test is applied to a derivative of the circumplex model, which they term the *circular order model.* The method has now been used in a number of studies, especially in the literature on structure of vocational interests.

The circular order model involves an essentially ordinal-level interpretation of the circumplex concept: If variables, theoretically, are circularly ordered, it follows that variables closer together on the circle will be more highly correlated than are variables further apart. This prediction is then tested for a given theoretical circle by examining all possible pairwise comparisons of variable intercorrelations. As Rounds et al. (1992) and Tracey (2000) have demonstrated, for an eight-variable circumplex, such as the PGI, this process will lead to 288 comparisons; for a six-variable circle, such as hypothesized for the RIASEC model, 72 possible comparisons are implied. Perfect fit would require that (a) correlations of variables adjacent on the circle should be greater than are correlations of variables more than one step apart; (b) correlations of variables two steps apart on the circle should be greater than are correlations of variables more than two steps apart; and so on. The model does not offer order predictions for correlations based on equidistant pairings of variables.

Generally, the model is evaluated in two ways (see Hubert & Arabie, 1987). The first is through the calculation of a *correspondence index,* or CI (Hubert & Arabie, 1987), which indicates the proportion of order predictions

TABLE 16.6   Reproduced Correlation Matrix for PGI Scales (Males Only)

Scale	1	2	3	4	5	6	7	8
Social Facilitating	1.00							
Managing	.63	1.00						
Business Detail	.35	.63	1.00					
Data Processing	.16	.35	.63	1.00				
Mechanical	.09	.16	.35	.63	1.00			
Nature/Outdoors	.16	.09	.16	.35	.63	1.00		
Artistic	.35	.16	.09	.16	.35	.63	1.00	
Helping	.63	.36	.16	.09	.16	.36	.63	1.00

Note. $n = 172$. Based on results of CIRCUM analysis for equally spaced, equal-communality model.

TABLE 16.7 Summary of Randomization Tests for PGI Circular-Order Model

Sample	Model Predictions			CI	p
	Total	Confirmed	Violated		
Female	288	282	6	.958	.0004
Male	288	277	11	.924	.0004

Note. Randomization tests conducted with RANDALL (Tracey, 1997). CI = correspondence index, P = probability.

confirmed minus the proportion violated. Values can range from 1.0 (all predictions met) to −1.0 (all predictions violated), with 0 indicating a random fit of the data to the model. It is a descriptive index of model-data fit. The second is a significance test for CI based on a *randomization test* strategy (for details see Hubert & Arabie, 1987, or Tracey, 2000). Essentially, the test determines the probability of obtaining the given model fit in comparison to all possible permutations of the rows and columns of the matrix.

Table 16.7 shows the results of the circular model tests of the two PGI correlation matrices. (Terence Tracey kindly performed these analyses for us using RANDALL (Tracey, 1997), a program he designed specifically to do these kinds of tests of the circular order model.) Consistent with the previous results reported, the analyses provided strong support for the circular structure of the PGI. As can be seen, CIs were close to the maximum values of 1 (almost all order predictions confirmed); based on the randomization tests, in both instances, the chance probabilities for the obtained model fit were significantly small ($ps = .0004$).

Circular Order Versus Covariance Modeling

Circular order and covariance modeling are likely to agree when data are a good fit to the equally-spaced circumplex ideal. However, we note that research has yet to directly compare the two approaches, especially with respect to how they handle quasi-circumplex data and data for which the circumplex model is misspecified. Tracey (2000) describes some of the advantages and disadvantages of the two approaches to confirmatory analysis. The interested reader is referred there.

Distribution Tests

Although not a general test of circumplex structure, nor an exploratory technique, distribution tests have recently been used to evaluate a specific criterion for circumplexity in data—namely, whether variables are uniformly distributed, or spaced, when projected onto the circle. Earlier it was noted that this property is often used to distinguish a circumplex structure from a simple structure or other clustered arrangement.

As Upton and Fingleton (1989) note in their authoritative chapter on circular statistics, numerous tests are available for researchers interested in testing for this property. As a class, the least restrictive are generally referred to as *gap tests,* because they concern the pattern of *gaps* (or angular separations) between adjacent variables on the circle. For example, if variables are perfectly uniform in circular spacing, then the gap between adjacent variables will be a constant equal to 360° / *n*, where *n* is the number of variables. Gap tests generally are used to determine the probability that the actual distribution departs from this ideal of uniform spacing.

As an example of applications, Tracey and Rounds (1995) examined the distribution of vocational interest items around a RIASEC circle; using the Neaves-Selkirk gap test (Upton & Fingleton, 1989), they determined that the uniform distribution hypothesis could not be rejected, thereby suggesting that contrary to typology conceptions, vocational interests are not clustered at particular points on the circle. In another example, Gurtman (1997) looked at the distribution of personality items (Q-sort items) in three circumplexes based on combinations of the major personality factors (e.g., Hofstee et al., 1992). Using a test attributed to Rao (Upton & Fingleton, 1989), he found evidence for a uniform distribution in two of three domains.

Gap tests generally require a relatively large number of variables (points on the circle) in order to effectively test the null hypothesis, especially when normal curve approximations are applied. For this reason, gap tests for six- or eight-variable circumplex models (such as the PGI) would usually be severely underpowered, and hence not practical.

HOW DO I USE THE CIRCUMPLEX TO DESCRIBE INDIVIDUALS?

After it is established that a given measure has a circumplex structure, the next issue concerns how data obtained from this measure can be applied in research and assessment contexts. In the next two sections we explore, respectively, two of the more common applications—representing individuals within a circumplex assessment space, then using the circumplex to describe group tendencies based on the accumulation of individual data. Both ventures involve the use of *circular statistics* (e.g., Batschelet, 1981; Mardia, 1972; Upton & Fingleton, 1989), a somewhat novel branch of statistical analysis developed specifically to handle circularly ordered, periodic data of the kind generated by circumplex-based measurements.

With respect to individual assessment, nearly all of the development in this area has been provided by psychologists interested in interpersonal assessment, specifically in relation to the *interpersonal circle* model of personality (e.g., Kiesler, 1996; Leary, 1957; Wiggins & Trapnell, 1996). Recently, Gurtman and Balakrishnan (1998) have provided an in-depth introduction to circular measurement principles in interpersonal assessment. The present section draws heavily on that article. The methods that will be described, however, are general, and go beyond the purposes of interpersonal assessment—although, interestingly, they have not (to our knowledge) been extended yet to other circumplex domains such as affect and vocational interest. (Perhaps the present section can help to realize that possibility.)

Circular Profiles

When circumplex-based measures are used to measure individual tendencies, the result is generally a profile of scores that sample around the circular continuum of that measure. For example, using the PGI to assess vocational interests would lead to a profile of eight scores, each score sampling a specific location on that circumplex. The pattern of scores is appropriately represented by a polar coordinate plot, which has been termed a *circular profile* (Gurtman, 1994; Gurtman & Balakrishnan, 1998). Figure 16.5 shows a circular profile for an individual case example. (We thank Terence Tracey for supplying us with this case data.) Although raw scores can be plotted, generally it makes sense (as we have done in the figure) to standardize (or *center*) scores against the group mean; sometimes, it is also useful to double-center scores by also expressing scores as deviations from the individual mean (i.e., the profile elevation or level). (This was not done here.) Note that in the circular plot of Figure 16.5, the scales are

ordered not by name but by their location—specifically, *angular displacement*—on the circle. (Following the interpersonal tradition, numbering proceeds in a counterclockwise direction from the 3:00 position.)

Dimensional and Polar Coordinate Summaries of Profiles

Circular plots, like other psychological profiles, can be interpreted conventionally—for example, by noting the individual's high-point scores in the configuration and perhaps categorizing individuals on that basis (e.g., Holland, 1973). However, given that the scores are circularly ordered, it becomes possible to use vector arithmetic (e.g., Mardia, 1972) to derive a concise, yet highly effective summary of the score pattern. Applied to the circular profile, this method of analysis yields a resultant vector indicating both the central tendency (i.e., *vector angle*) and variability (*vector length*) of the individual's tendencies (e.g., Wiggins et al., 1989). The Kaiser Research Group (e.g., Leary, 1957) is credited with introducing this general approach for summarizing circular profile data; it was routinely used in their interpersonal assessments. The formulas, rather than being arcane, involve standard trigonometric conversions.

As a demonstration of the calculations involved, Table 16.8 applies this method of circular analysis to the case shown in Figure 16.5. The profile, again, consists of the individual's circularly ordered set of standard scores on the PGI. The first step is to weight each scale score (S_i) according to either the *cosine* (X) or *sine* (Y) of the scale's angular location (θ_i) on the circle, and take their sums. Specifically,

$$X = \sum (S_i \times \cos \theta_i) \qquad (16.3)$$

$$Y = \sum (S_i \times \sin \theta_i) \qquad (16.4)$$

These weighted sums yield the person's resultant X and Y coordinates. To correct for scale, the results are multiplied by a constant factor, c, where c is equal to $2 / n$ and n equal to the number of scores comprising the circular profile (generally 8, hence $c = .25$). As shown in the table, the dimensional coordinates are computed to be .02 and 1.58, respectively. For the last step, these rectangular coordinates are converted to their equivalent polar coordinates, thus defining a resultant vector having an angular direction, δ, and a length, VL. The vector angle (expressed in degrees) can be obtained through the arctangent function, specifically

$$\delta = \tan^{-1}(Y/X) \times 180/\pi \qquad (16.5)$$

Note, however, that due to the periodicity of the sine, cosine, and tangent functions, a correction to this result may need to

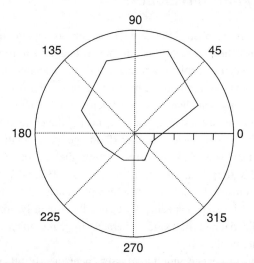

Figure 16.5   Circular profile plot for case analysis (Personal Globe Inventory scores).

TABLE 16.8   Sample Work Sheet for Calculating Vector Angle and Length: PGI Case Study

Scale	θ	Score (s)	$X = s \times \cos(\theta)$	$Y = s \times \sin(\theta)$
Social Facilitating	112.5	0.80	−0.31	0.74
Managing	157.5	−0.10	0.09	−0.04
Business Detail	202.5	−1.30	1.20	0.50
Data Processing	247.5	−1.60	0.61	1.48
Mechanical	292.5	−1.60	−0.61	1.48
Nature/Outdoors	337.5	−2.00	−1.85	0.77
Artistic	22.5	0.50	0.46	0.19
Helping	67.5	1.30	0.50	1.20
		.25 × Sum	0.02	1.58

Note. Angle = $\tan^{-1}(1.58/.02) = 89°$. $VL = sqrt(.02^2 + 1.58^2) = 1.58$.

be applied depending on the respective signs of the X and Y values.

Using the Pythagorean theorem, vector length, *VL*, is easily obtained as

$$VL = sqrt(X^2 + Y^2) \qquad (16.6)$$

Thus, for the profile data presented in the table, $\delta = 89°$ and $VL = 1.58$.

The interpretive significance of vector angle and vector length for profile description has been explored extensively in the interpersonal literature (e.g., Gurtman & Balakrishnan, 1998; Leary, 1957; Wiggins et al., 1989), but not more generally. Computationally, the angle is the *circular mean* of the profile (Mardia, 1972), indicating what may be construed as the center of gravity (Gurtman & Balakrishnan, 1998) of the profile distribution. It thus points to the *predominant theme* of the profile (Gurtman & Balakrishnan, 1998), the blend of the two dimensions that underlie the particular circumplex domain. For example, when based on the interpersonal circumplex, the person's vector angle may be interpreted in terms of the individual's standing on two major dimensions of the interpersonal domain (generally *Dominance* and *Nurturance;* e.g., see Wiggins & Trapnell, 1996). For vocational interests, as in the present example, the circumplex is anchored by two RIASEC dimensions (Prediger, 1982): interests in *People versus Things* (vertical axis) and *Data versus Ideas* (horizontal axis). The case's obtained angle of 89° (between *Helping* and *Social Facilitating* on the circle) suggests a relatively pure interest theme of *People* as a summary of the overall pattern.

Turning to vector length, this summary feature is sometimes thought of as a measure of profile extremity or intensity (e.g., Kiesler, 1996). We regard vector length as more a measure of profile definition, or, as is stated later, *structured patterning* (Gurtman & Balakrishnan, 1998). High vector length indicates a well-articulated profile, with a clear central tendency or directional trend (as in the present case); low vector length suggests poor definition, generally due to low variability in the profile scores (Wiggins et al., 1989). Thus, for a profile with low vector length, little interpretive significance can be attached to the angle parameter.

An Alternative Approach to Profile Analysis: Cosine Curve Model

Recently, Gurtman (1994; Gurtman & Balakrishnan, 1998) suggested an alternative approach for analyzing circular profile data, using curve modeling. Although developed with respect to the interpersonal circumplex and the goals of interpersonal assessment, this method is general enough so that it could be effectively applied to any circular profile data.

The curve modeling approach is predicated on the fact that circumplex measures tend to produce profile patterns that are sinusoidal in form, and hence can be modeled against the prototype of a cosine function. Thus, it is possible to rewrite a given profile of scores as the sum of a structured part (a cosine function) plus a deviation, or more specifically:

$$S_i = e + a \times \cos(\theta_i - \delta) + d_i \qquad (16.7)$$

where S_i is the person's score on scale, i, of a circumplex measure; e is the *elevation*, or mean level, of the profile; a is the *amplitude* of the cosine curve model (the distance from its mean level to its peak value); θ_i is the angle of scale, i; δ is the *angular displacement*, or peak shift, of the cosine curve; and d_i is the *deviation*, generally assumed to be random and pairwise independent. This model then has three parameters—e, a, and δ. The actual profile can be modeled by solving for these three parameters. Finally, a goodness-of-fit index, R^2, can be calculated to indicate how well the cosine model fits the actual profile data, in a sense, quantifying the extent to which the profile can be reduced to its summary features. In an earlier work, Gurtman (1994) noted that elevation, amplitude, angular displacement, and goodness-of-fit constitute what amounts to a *structural summary* of the individual's circular profile. Figure 16.6 provides an illustration

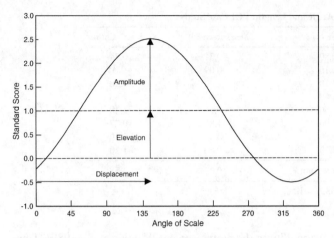

Figure 16.6   Illustration of the cosine curve model.

of the cosine curve model, and Figure 16.7 shows the model applied to the PGI scores of the earlier case study.

Solving for the curve parameters is relatively easy. Gurtman (1994) noted that amplitude will equal vector length, *VL*, as computed by the earlier vector method; and angular displacement will equal the vector's mean direction, or angle. This enables amplitude and angular displacement to be solved for directly, using Equations 16.3 through 16.6 presented previously. Because elevation is simply the profile's mean level, it is also directly obtained. Goodness-of-fit is calculated conventionally as R^2, or $SS_{predicted} / SS_{actual}$.

Gurtman and Balakrishnan (1998) have provided a detailed discussion of the interpretive implications of the summary parameters. The cosine curve method of analysis extends as well as solidifies understandings based on the vector approach. Here we focus specifically on interpretation in the context of the case study (see again Figure 16.7). The

elevation parameter indicates the mean level of the curve, which in this example ($e = -0.5$) denotes a profile level slightly (i.e., 0.5 standard deviations) below the group mean (of 0). Elevation is somewhat ambiguous in interpretation. It may reflect, for example, a nonsubstantive response style (e.g., the individual's idiosyncratic usage of test items) or, depending on the circumplex measure, may have substantive import. In the latter case, if the circumplex includes a general factor (i.e., a factor on which all scales are positively correlated), then elevation may reflect the person's standing on that dimension. The earlier factor analysis (PCA) of the PGI indeed revealed a general factor, but the test is too new for substantive interpretations to be offered.

Turning to amplitude, this indicates the degree of structured patterning of the profile; hence, its meaning is identical to that of vector length, as would be expected. A high value suggests a profile that is highly differentiated to the cosine prototype. In the present example, $a = 1.58$, which thus quantifies the difference between the profile's mean level and its predicted peak value. Angular displacement, like vector angle, indicates the predominant theme of the profile. As the peak-shift of the curve, it shows the point on the circular distribution where the profile is predicted to have its highest value (i.e., the apex of the modeled curve). In this case, $\delta = 89°$, which reveals that the model of the profile peaks at a point on the circular continuum midway between *Social Facilitating* and *Helping*. Dimensionally, as noted before, this identifies a vocational interest in *People* (vs. *Things*). Finally, the goodness-of-fit parameter provides a kind of metasummary of the model, indicating how well the cosine curve fits the actual profile. A high value (here $R^2 = .87$, close to the maximum of 1) shows that the model accounts for a high proportion of the profile's variability; thus, the profile can be effectively reduced to its summary features (e, a, δ) with little loss of information. A low value is ambiguous, but, as suggested elsewhere (Gurtman & Balakrishnan, 1998), may sometimes reflect complex trends within the profile (see also Haslam & Gurtman, 1999).

HOW DO I USE THE CIRCUMPLEX TO DESCRIBE AND COMPARE GROUPS?

After individuals have been assessed and summarized with respect to a circumplex measure, it becomes possible to cumulate these individual data in order to now summarize group characteristics. Groups may consist of individuals who fall into discrete categories—for example, women, pharmacists, or adults meeting diagnostic criteria for social anxiety disorder. Groups may also be created, somewhat arbitrarily,

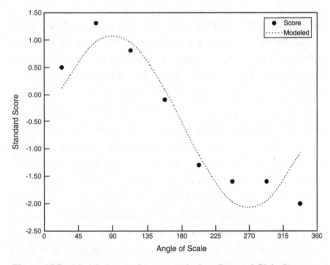

Figure 16.7   Modeled curve for case study data (Personal Globe Inventory scores).

based on a decision applied to a continuous indicator—for example, identifying individuals as depressed or nondepressed according to a cutoff score on certain depression inventory.

Describing Group Tendencies

When cumulating individual data—or more specifically, the circular profiles—there are essentially two approaches that can be taken. Both lend themselves to graphical representation, and fortunately, the two tend to be convergent.

The first method, which we refer to as *profile averaging,* is based on common practice in the psychodiagnostic test literature. Here the circular profiles of group members are averaged on each of the scales to obtain an average or composite group profile. The next step would be to apply the formulas of the vector method described earlier (Equations 16.3 through 16.6) to derive a vector angle and a vector length for the group composite. Alternatively, a cosine curve model can be fit to the group profile, yielding the structural summary parameters also presented earlier. As before, the vector angle (equivalently angular displacement) of the group profile would suggest its predominant substantive theme within the context of the relevant circumplex domain; vector length (equivalently amplitude) would indicate its degree of differentiation. The interpretive implications thus are the same as with individual data, but applied simply at the level of the group.

Although the profile averaging method is serviceable (e.g., Gurtman, 1992b, for an example), its principal shortcoming is that it obscures individual variations. Said another way, the group profile cannot necessarily be generalized to the individual profiles that comprise the group average. For example, the vector length (amplitude) of the group profile may be low because the individuals who make up the group are heterogeneous in their profiles, or because the average (individual) profile is of low amplitude.

Consequently, we prefer a second approach for analyzing group data, one based firmly on established methods of *circular data analysis* (e.g., Mardia, 1972; Upton & Fingleton, 1989). In this approach, each individual profile is represented by its summary projection (point) on the circle (e.g., Leary, 1957). The projection is simply based on the vector angle (described earlier), and ignores the variable of vector length (i.e., each vector is of unit length). This then leads to representing the group as a *circular distribution,* or *circular plot,* as illustrated in Figure 16.8.

The most relevant descriptive features of the circular distribution are its mean and variance. The *circular mean* indicates the average or "preferred direction" (Upton & Fingleton, 1989) of the data points. It is calculated using

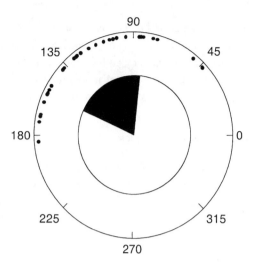

Figure 16.8 Illustration of a circular plot of group data (with insert of iconic representation).

unweighted versions of Equations 16.3 and 16.4 to obtain the relevant coordinates, or

$$X = \sum (\cos \theta_i) \tag{16.8}$$

$$Y = \sum (\sin \theta_i) \tag{16.9}$$

where θ_i is the angle of individual, i, on the circular continuum. The result is then expressed as an angle (Equation 16.5). In this example, the circular mean for the group of individuals is equal to 120°. It can be shown (see Gurtman, 1997) that the circular mean (θ_M) is also the angle that maximizes the *sum of the cosine deviations,* or

$$\sum \cos (\theta_M - \theta_i) \tag{16.10}$$

This implies that the sum of the *sine* deviations from the circular mean will equal 0, a property analogous to that of the familiar, linear mean.

The *circular variance* indicates the dispersion of the data points about this preferred direction, and therefore is an inverse measure of concentration. Following Mardia (1972; see also Gurtman, 1997), and using Equation 16.10 the circular variance can be written as

$$V = 1 - \sum \cos (\theta_M - \theta_i)/n \tag{16.11}$$

where n is equal to the number of data points (i.e., the group n). By taking the arccosine of $\sum \cos (\theta_M - \theta_i)/n$, the variance can be expressed in degrees, which is generally more easily interpreted. In our example, the circular variance is equal to .19, or, in degrees, a dispersion of ±36°. Finally,

Gurtman (1997) suggested *iconic representations* of circular plots; these provide concise, readily understood, depictions of the group's central tendency and variability in the respective circular domain. The relevant iconic representation for this example is presented as an insert to the Figure 16.8 plot.

Comparing Group Tendencies

In research contexts, it is often necessary to compare group tendencies, usually means, to determine whether observed differences are statistically meaningful. Here we briefly consider this kind of hypothesis testing applied to grouped circular-profile data.

The profile averaging method, discussed earlier, suggests profile analysis as an appropriate statistical tool. Relevant to this is that, Tabachnick and Fidell (1989) offered multivariate profile analysis (MPA) as a test of group profile differences. MPA is not specific to circular profile data, and indeed is not optimized for such data. Nevertheless, it can be applied with suggestive results (e.g., see Gurtman, 1992b). The value of MPA is that it allows for comparison of two important features of the group profile data—their mean levels and patterns (or shapes). The test for differences in mean level concerns group profile elevation. The test for differences in profile pattern—or parallelism of profiles (Tabachnick & Fidell, 1989)—is generally more important. The hypothesis of profile parallelism can be rejected, however, on the basis of any profile pattern factor (shape, scatter) that varies reliably between groups; hence, for circular profile data, the test is not sufficiently specific to determine which of the previously discussed profile components contribute to the observed group difference.

When circular profiles are represented as distributions (points) on the circle, then a variety of circular statistics can be used to evaluate group differences. Generally at issue is whether the differences in the mean directions of the respective group distributions are greater than would be expected by chance. Upton and Fingleton (1989) provide a comprehensive survey of statistical tests appropriate for circular data (see pp. 276–295), some quite arcane and complex. For tests of mean differences, these generally fall into one of two categories: (a) nonparametric tests that make no assumptions about underlying (i.e., population) distributions; and (b) more powerful parametric tests that assume the respective group populations follow a von Mises distribution (a circular approximation to the normal distribution; e.g., Mardia, 1972). For grouped individuals, it would seem reasonable generally to assume a von Mises distribution, and hence the class of parametric tests would be appropriate. Stephens *A*-test (see Upton & Fingleton, 1989, p. 289) is a relatively simple,

logical, and straightforward parametric test that is acceptable in many cases, and can be extended beyond the two-group situation; in cases that are not appropriate, corrective modifications have been proposed. Alden and Phillips (1990) used a modified version of the *A*-statistic to compare the interpersonal circle placements of four groups of students characterized on the basis of level of depression and anxiety.

An alternative approach to formal hypothesis testing is to use confidence intervals as a way of identifying reliable differences in group means. Mardia (1972) and Upton and Fingleton (1989) give relevant formulas for computing confidence intervals for circular data. These formulas assume a von Mises distribution for the respective population. We have found that a close approximation to these confidence intervals can often be obtained by using the circular variance (see Equation 16.11) to estimate the standard error of the mean. The 95% confidence interval (ci) would thus equal

$$95\% \ ci = \theta_M \pm 1.96 \times \cos^{-1}(1 - V)/sqrt(n) \quad (16.12)$$

where 1.96 is the multiplier factor based on a two-tailed normal curve probability, and the remaining parameters are as defined previously. For the sample data (Figure 16.8), the confidence interval by this method computes to $\pm 12.00°$, which compares favorably to that provided by a canned program (12.31°).

HOW DO I USE THE CIRCUMPLEX TO EVALUATE CONSTRUCTS AND THEIR MEASURES?

As a research tool, particularly in the areas of clinical, personality, and social psychology, the circumplex model can aid investigators in their efforts to better understand their measures, and, by extension, the constructs that those measures address. This is partly because, as noted earlier, circumplex models often serve to define and represent particular domains of interest to researchers. Thus, by relating a measure (and, indirectly, a construct) to a given circumplex, researchers can gain important insights into that measure's substantive content and underlying structure.

The basic work in refining this method—and perhaps more important, illustrating its potential—was done by Wiggins and Broughton (1985, 1991). In their research, they used the interpersonal circumplex to develop a "geometric taxonomy" of personality test measures by projecting those measures onto the circle. For a given measure, the scale's location on the circular continuum, and its loading in that dimensional space, served to define the scale's "interpersonal-ness." Their work has been succeeded by a large number of other studies that have applied similar methods to objectify the interpersonal meaning of different measures and constructs (e.g., Bartholomew & Horowitz, 1991; Gifford, 1991; Gurtman, 1991, 1999; Pincus & Gurtman, 1995; Pincus et al., 1998; Soldz, Budman, Demby, & Merry, 1993). It is interesting that almost all of the research applying the circumplex in this way has been conducted in the interpersonal domain, using various interpersonal circumplex models and measures. Nevertheless, the methods are (once again) general, and could easily be extended to other circumplex domains.

In this section, we discuss and illustrate three general approaches for using the circumplex to evaluate measures and their implied constructs. In actuality, the methods are simple adaptations of those presented earlier.

Vector Method

Wiggins and Broughton (1985, 1991) suggested that a test variable's coordinates in a circumplex space could be established by correlating the variable with dimensional scores derived from the circumplex measure. This approach starts by creating dimensional scores for each individual, using either the formulas of Equations 16.3 and 16.4 or factor score estimates of these based on a principal components analysis of the circumplex measure (see Wiggins et al., 1989). The variable's correlations (r_X, r_Y) with the dimensional scores yield the X, Y coordinates for the variable's projection in the circumplex space. For interpretive purposes, the rectangular coordinates are converted to their polar equivalents, so that the variable's projection is now expressed as a vector with a given direction (or angle, θ) and length (VL). The direction identifies the variable's substantive content—its blend of the two dimensions that define that space—and the length indicates the degree of its loading in that space, or how much it has in common with that domain. In an example, Wiggins and Broughton (1991) used this technique to categorize the interpersonal quality and loading of a large number of personality test scales that were administered to samples along with a standard circumplex measure of interpersonal traits.

Cosine Curve Modeling

As an alternative, Gurtman (1992a) used the cosine modeling method, described in detail earlier, to assess the structural features of different personality construct measures. In this application, the cosine function is used to model not an individual's pattern of scores, but a given measure's *pattern of correlations* with the (generally) eight octants of a circumplex. The result, essentially, is a kind of structural summary

of the measure, in relation to that circumplex domain. The earlier Figure 16.6 illustrates the nature of the curve (see also Gurtman, 1992a); however, in this adaptation of the method, the dependent variables are a set of correlation coefficients rather than individual scores.

As shown in Gurtman (1992a), there are three parameters in the model, each relevant to understanding the nature of the measure. *Angular displacement* is the peak-shift of the curve, indicating the point on the distribution where the measure achieves its highest predicted correlation in the circumplex continuum. *Amplitude* indicates the degree to which the measure correlates *differentially* with the scales comprising that circumplex, and so assesses a measure's "discriminant validity" (Campbell & Fiske, 1959). *Elevation* is the measure's average correlation with the circumplex domain, and is related then to the measure's correlation with the general factor (if any) that characterizes that domain. Elevation plus amplitude predicts the highest correlation (generally positive), and elevation minus amplitude, the lowest correlation (generally negative) of the measure with the circumplex domain. Table 16.9, adapted from Gurtman (1992a), shows the results of this kind of analysis conducted on a variety of putatively interpersonal measures of adjustment, and in relation to a circumplex of interpersonal problems. For additional information on this method, the interested reader should consult Gurtman (1992a) or Gurtman (1999).

Item-Centric Analyses

Item-centric analysis is a third approach to the circumplex-based study of measures and their constructs. (The term *item-centric* originates here and has not been used previously to describe the approach.) The method is covered in detail by Pincus and Gurtman (1995), who used the approach to analyze the measurement characteristics of different personality tests designed to assess dependency. The basic concepts are discussed in Gurtman (1997).

In an item-centric analysis, a measure's features are evaluated by examining the circular distribution of its items on a given circumplex, as well as the items' loadings in that domain. The first step is to perform a vector analysis (see previous section) on each of the items, which yields, for each item, its angular location (θ) on the circle and its vector length (VL). To illustrate, Figure 16.9, taken from Pincus and Gurtman (1995), shows the circular distribution (projections) for 112 dependency items compiled from a variety of popular measures of that trait.

Using this approach, it is possible to derive three descriptive features of the measure relevant to understanding and characterizing that scale. Following Gurtman (1997), we

TABLE 16.9   Illustration of Cosine Curve Analysis of Interpersonal Characteristics of Measures of Adjustment

Scale	M	SD	Angular Displacement	Amplitude	Elevation	Positive Correlation	Negative Correlation	R^2 Fit
Dependency								
Emotional Reliance	43.02	8.45	16.4	.144	.292	.436	.148	.866
Lack of Self-Confidence	30.94	6.69	269.1	.252	.450	.701	.198	.976
Assertion of Autonomy	26.79	5.30	160.7	.160	.102	.262	−.058	.812
Empathy								
Perspective-Taking	24.17	5.07	321.3	.192	−.078	.114	−.270	.848
Fantasy	24.65	5.83	0.7	.087	.108	.196	.021	.943
Empathic Concern	27.90	4.47	328.9	.290	−.085	.205	−.376	.966
Personal Distress	19.47	4.80	286.5	.180	.242	.423	.062	.970
Narcissism								
Authority	3.84	2.28	86.1	.345	−.188	.157	−.533	.977
Exhibitionism	2.37	1.81	72.1	.265	−.043	.222	−.308	.932
Superiority	1.94	1.32	81.1	.179	−.164	.015	−.343	.943
Entitlement	1.71	1.50	105.2	.268	.086	.354	−.182	.946
Exploitativeness	1.60	1.36	93.3	.264	−.046	.218	−.310	.982
Self-Sufficiency	2.20	1.48	105.0	.177	−.128	.049	−.305	.954
Vanity	0.99	1.05	92.1	.120	−.067	.054	−.187	.929
Leadership-Authority	3.69	2.43	83.6	.364	−.179	.185	−.543	.971
Self-Absorption–Self-Admiration	2.98	2.03	87.2	.183	−.160	.023	−.343	.948
Superiority-Arrogance	2.29	1.80	84.5	.281	−.089	.192	−.370	.987
Exploitativeness-Entitlement	1.77	1.63	108.6	.302	.128	.430	−.174	.955

Note. Adapted from "Construct Validity of Interpersonal Personality Measures: The Interpersonal Circumplex as a Nomological Net" by M. B. Gurtman, *Journal of Personality and Social Psychology, 63,* p. 111. Copyright 1992 by the American Psychological Association.

refer to these as the measure's *thematic quality, breadth of coverage,* and *factorial saturation.* Thematic quality, as before, concerns the trait's predominant descriptive content, in relation to the domain of the circumplex being used. It is indicated by the *circular mean* (mean angular direction) of the set of its items. In calculating the circular mean, each item's contribution may be weighted by the item's vector

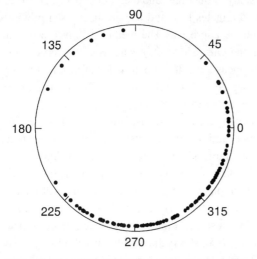

Figure 16.9   Circular plot of 112 dependency items on interpersonal circumplex. *Source:* Adapted from "The Three Faces of Interpersonal Dependency: Structural Analyses of Self-Report Dependency Measures" by A. L. Pincus and M. B. Gurtman, *Journal of Personality and Social Psychology, 69,* p. 749. Copyright 1995 by the American Psychological Association. Adapted by permission.

length (e.g., Pincus & Gurtman, 1995) or each item may be weighted equally (unit weighting) as in Gurtman, 1997. Breadth of coverage concerns how narrowly or broadly the measure samples from that particular circumplex domain. Narrow coverage suggests a cohesive test with "fidelity" of measurement, whereas broad coverage suggests a test that is less cohesive but that has greater "bandwidth." (Cronbach, 1990). Breadth of coverage is indexed by the dispersion of the items around the mean—that is, by its circular variance. Finally, factorial saturation indicates the amount of variance that the measure shares with that particular circumplex domain—for example, how "interpersonal" it is when referenced to an interpersonal circumplex (e.g., Gurtman, 1991). It is calculated as the average vector length (*VL*) of the measure's items.

Figure 16.10, reproduced from Pincus and Gurtman (1995), shows the results of this kind of analysis conducted on eight popular measures of interpersonal dependency. As can be seen, the measures' circular means vary considerably, although most are in the lower right quadrant of the interpersonal circumplex, indicating that the measures generally tap friendly forms of submissiveness. The iconic representations, which are based on the circular variances, suggest that measures also differ in their breadth of coverage. (The circular variances, though not given directly, are related to the values listed in the last two columns.) Finally, each measure's factorial saturation, shown by the mean item vector length,

Dependency Scales		Circular Mean	Mean Item Vector Length	Mean Item Loading	Standardized Item Loading
Dysfunctional Attitudes Scale	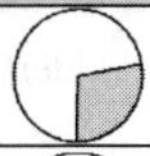	320°	.129	.081	.627
MMPI-Dependent Personality Disorder Scale	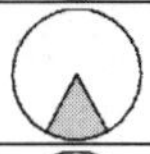	271°	.280	.246	.878
Interpersonal Dependency Scale/ Social Self-Confidence	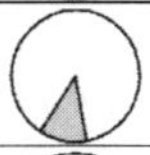	258°	.335	.313	.934
Interpersonal Dependency Scale/ Emotional Reliance	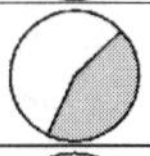	324°	.131	.024	.186
Sociotropy-Autonomy Scale/ Concern about Disapproval	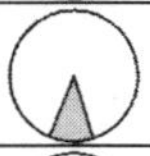	267°	.182	.172	.943
Sociotropy-Autonomy Scale/ Attachment-Concern about Separation	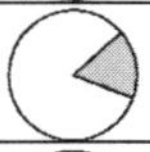	11°	.194	.166	.854
Sociotropy-Autonomy Scale/ Pleasing Others	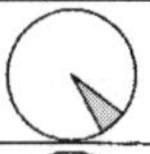	311°	.282	.276	.977
Depressive Experiences Questionnaire/ Dependency	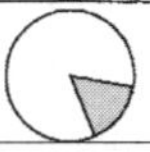	322°	.201	.175	.871

Figure 16.10 Circular analysis conducted on eight dependency scales. *Source:* From "The Three Faces of Interpersonal Dependency: Structural Analyses of Self-Report Dependency Measures" by A. L. Pincus and M. B. Gurtman, *Journal of Personality and Social Psychology, 69,* p. 751. Copyright 1995 by the American Psychological Association. Adapted by permission.

also varies, with some dependency measures more interpersonal (e.g., Social Self-Confidence) than others (e.g., Emotional Reliance).

CONCLUSIONS, FUTURE DIRECTIONS, AND ADDITIONAL RESOURCES

This purpose of this chapter has been to introduce and demonstrate the various methods of analysis associated with circumplex models. For the most part, we have covered the standard ways in which researchers have tested and applied the model in pursuing their research goals. Before closing, however, we would like to briefly suggest two directions for future development of the circumplex model and its methods.

Theory Testing

As was stated early in this chapter, the circumplex correlation model is a relatively nonrestrictive model, in that many correlation patterns ultimately satisfy the requirements of the model (Table 16.2; e.g., Fabrigar et al., 1997). Moreover, in its geometric version, there is no preferred orientation of axes, because variables, by definition, are equally distributed (Hofstee et al., 1992; Tracey, 2000). These unfixed properties of the circumplex put special impetus on investigators to provide appropriate theoretical foundations to support the choice of axes (latent dimensions) and to explain the covariation among variables in the domain of interest.

In a previous article (Gurtman & Pincus, 2000), we have suggested that a necessary next step in circumplex-based research programs is the testing of theories that give rise to alternative circumplex models for a given domain. Within the interpersonal domain, compelling arguments in favor of the dominance-nurturance circumplex system (Wiggins, 1991) and a theoretical account of covariation in traits that proposes a specific correlational pattern (Wiggins, 1979; Wiggins & Trapnell, 1996) have been articulated. However, even with agreement regarding the axes and their orientation, alternative correlational patterns exist for the IPC (Gaines et al., 1997; Gurtman, 1994; Leary, 1957; Wiggins, 1979).

Likewise, investigators interested in the structure of affect (e.g., Carroll et al., 1999; Yik et al., 1999), and of vocational interests (e.g., Tracey & Rounds, 1996a, 1996b), are addressing similar issues with regard to their circumplex models. We suggest that directions for future research should include evaluation of the theoretical bases of alternative circumplex models in any domain in which they are derived and applied.

The Relational Circumplex

We use the term *relational circumplex* to highlight an important potential application of the circumplex model—as a framework for assessing individual relations (i.e., lawful correspondences or interdependencies) between people. For example, in interpersonal psychology, an important theoretical principle is *complementarity* (Benjamin, 1996; Kiesler, 1996; Leary, 1957)—interpersonal behaviors tend to elicit or "invite" certain kinds of consequent behaviors from others (generally, dominance elicits submissiveness and vice versa, love and hate elicit corresponding behaviors). Complementarity thus suggests a kind of fit between the behaviors of the interactants in the dyad. When tied to the circumplex model (e.g., Kiesler, 1996), tests of complementarity theory would require that the circumplex model be used *relationally*—that is, to chart and compare the positions of the two interactants in the common space of the interpersonal circle, and generally across the span of their interaction. A number of studies have now used the circumplex in this way (see Kiesler, 1996, for a review), although until recently (Gurtman, 2001; Tracey, 1994), quantitative methods for indexing relational fit have been relatively crude.

Outside the interpersonal domain, the relational circumplex also has relevance to important research questions and practical applications. Two quick examples are provided here. In the affect domain, an extensive literature exists on the phenomenon of *emotional contagion,* the tendency of individuals to transmit their positive and negative moods to others in their social environment (for a review, see Hatfield, Cacioppo, & Rapson, 1994; for a recent study, see Strack & Neumann, 2000). Application of an affect circumplex (e.g., Russell, 1980) can help bring greater specificity and precision to the assessment of contagion effects. In the vocational interests literature, it is generally assumed that the fit between an individual's vocational interest pattern and the affordances of the work environment is an important determinant of occupational satisfaction (e.g., Holland, 1973). If such assessments are done within the context of the respective RIASEC circles (interests, work environment), then relational fit measures based on the circumplex are both relevant and optimal.

Additional Resources

To further explore the circumplex, its applications, and its methods, the interested reader may consult a number of useful chapters, books, and articles. We especially recommend Kiesler (1996), Tracey (2000), Wiggins and Trapnell (1996), Wiggins and Trobst (1999), as well as a recent volume edited by Plutchik and Conte (1997) and dedicated solely to the circumplex model.

REFERENCES

Alden, L. E., & Phillips, N. (1990). An interpersonal analysis of social anxiety and depression. *Cognitive Therapy and Research, 14,* 499–513.

Alden, L. E., Wiggins, J. S., & Pincus, A. L. (1990). Construction of circumplex scales for the Inventory of Interpersonal Problems. *Journal of Personality Assessment, 55,* 521–536.

Bartholomew, K., & Horowitz, L. M. (1991). Attachment styles among young adults: A test of a four-category model. *Journal of Personality and Social Psychology, 61,* 226–244.

Batschelet, E. (1981). *Circular statistics in biology.* San Diego, CA: Academic Press.

Benjamin, L. S. (1974). Structural analysis of social behavior. *Psychological Review, 81,* 392–425.

Benjamin, L. S. (1995). Good defenses make good neighbors. In H. Conte & R. Plutchik (Eds.), *Ego defense: Theory and measurement* (pp. 38–78). New York: Wiley.

Benjamin, L. S. (1996). *Interpersonal diagnosis and treatment of personality disorders* (2nd ed.). New York: Guilford.

Browne, M. W. (1992). Circumplex models for correlation matrices. *Psychometrika, 57,* 469–497.

Browne, M. W., & Cudeck, R. (1992). Alternative ways of assessing model fit. *Sociological Methods and Research, 21,* 230–258.

Cacioppo, J. T., Gardner, W. L., & Bernston, G. G. (1999). The affect system has parallel and integrative processing components: Form follows function. *Journal of Personality and Social Psychology, 76,* 839–855.

Campbell, D. T., & Fiske, D. W. (1959). Convergent and discriminant validation by the multitrait-multimethod matrix. *Psychological Bulletin, 56,* 81–105.

Carroll, J. M., Yik, M. S. M., Russell, J. A., & Feldman-Barrett, L. (1999). On the psychometric principles of affect. *Review of General Psychology, 3,* 14–22.

Conte, H. R., & Plutchik, R. (1981). A circumplex model for interpersonal personality traits. *Journal of Personality and Social Psychology, 40,* 701–711.

Cronbach, L. J. (1990). *Essentials of psychological testing* (5th ed.). New York: Harper & Row.

Cudeck, R. (1986). A note on structural models for the circumplex. *Psychometrika, 51,* 143–147.

Davison, M. L. (1985). Multidimensional scaling versus components analysis of test intercorrelations. *Psychological Bulletin, 97,* 94–105.

Davison, M. L. (1994). Multidimensional scaling models of personality responding. In S. Strack & M. Lorr (Eds.), *Differentiating normal and abnormal personality* (pp. 196–215). New York: Springer.

Day, S. X., & Rounds, J. (1998). Universality of vocational interest structure among racial and ethnic minorities. *American Psychologist, 53,* 728–736.

Fabrigar, L. R., Visser, P. S., & Browne, M. W. (1997). Conceptual and methodological issues in testing the circumplex structure of data in personality and social psychology. *Personality and Social Psychology Review, 1,* 184–203.

Fouad, N. A., Harmon, L. W., & Borgen, F. H. (1997). Structure of interests in employed male and female members of US racial-ethnic minority and nonminority groups. *Journal of Counseling Psychology, 44,* 339–345.

Freedman, M. B., Leary, T., Ossorio, A. G., & Coffey, H. S. (1951). The interpersonal dimension of personality. *Journal of Personality, 20,* 143–161.

Gaines, S. O., Jr., Panter, A. T., Lyde, M. D., Steers, W. N., Rusbult, C. E., Cox, C. L., & Wexler, M. O. (1997). Evaluating the circumplexity of interpersonal traits and the manifestation of interpersonal traits in interpersonal trust. *Journal of Personality and Social Psychology, 73,* 610–623.

Gifford, R. (1991). Mapping nonverbal behavior on the Interpersonal Circle. *Journal of Personality and Social Psychology, 61,* 279–288.

Green, D. P., Salovey, P., & Truax, K. M. (1999). Static, dynamic, and causative bipolarity of affect. *Journal of Personality and Social Psychology, 76,* 856–867.

Gurtman, M. B. (1991). Evaluating the interpersonalness of personality scales. *Personality and Social Psychology Bulletin, 17,* 670–677.

Gurtman, M. B. (1992a). Construct validity of interpersonal personality measures: The interpersonal circumplex as a nomological net. *Journal of Personality and Social Psychology, 63,* 105–118.

Gurtman, M. B. (1992b). Trust, distrust, and interpersonal problems: A circumplex analysis. *Journal of Personality and Social Psychology, 62,* 989–1002.

Gurtman, M. B. (1994). The circumplex as a tool for studying normal and abnormal personality: A methodological primer. In S. Strack & M. Lorr (Eds.), *Differentiating normal and abnormal personality* (pp. 243–263). New York: Springer.

Gurtman, M. B. (1997). Studying personality traits: The circular way. In R. Plutchik & H. R. Conte (Eds.), *Circumplex models of personality and emotions* (pp. 81–102). Washington, DC: American Psychological Association.

Gurtman, M. B. (1998, August). *In search of the circumplex: A journey inspired by Jerry Wiggins.* Paper presented at the symposium on 40 years of personality assessment: Honoring Jerry S. Wiggins, American Psychological Association annual convention, San Francisco, CA.

Gurtman, M. B. (1999). Social competence: An interpersonal analysis and reformulation. *European Journal of Psychological Assessment, 15,* 233–245.

Gurtman, M. B. (2001). Interpersonal complementarity: Integrating interpersonal measurement with interpersonal models. *Journal of Counseling Psychology, 48,* 97–110.

Gurtman, M. B., & Balakrishnan, J. D. (1998). Circular measurement redux: The analysis and interpretation of interpersonal circle profiles. *Clinical Psychology: Science and Practice, 5,* 344–360.

Gurtman, M. B., & Pincus, A. L. (2000). Interpersonal Adjective Scales: Confirmation of circumplex structure from multiple perspectives. *Personality and Social Psychology Bulletin, 26,* 374–384.

Guttman, L. (1954). A new approach to factor analysis: The radex. In P. F. Lazarsfeld (Ed.), *Mathematical thinking in the social sciences* (pp. 258–348). Glencoe, IL: Free Press.

Hartshorne, C. (1980). Science as the search for the hidden beauty of the world. In D. W. Curtin (Ed.), *The aesthetic dimension of science* (pp. 85–106). New York: Philosophical Library.

Haslam, N., & Gurtman, M. B. (1999). Detecting complex patterns in interpersonal profiles. *British Journal of Medical Psychology, 72,* 23–32.

Hatfield, E., Cacioppo, J. T., & Rapson, R. L. (1994). *Emotional contagion.* Cambridge, England: Cambridge University Press.

Henry, W. P. (1996). Structural Analysis of Social Behavior as a common metric for programmatic psychopathology and psychotherapy research. *Journal of Consulting and Clinical Psychology, 64,* 1263–1275.

Hofstee, W. K. B., De Raad, B., & Goldberg, L. R. (1992). Integration of the Big Five and circumplex approaches to trait structure. *Journal of Personality and Social Psychology, 63,* 146–163.

Hogan, R. (1983). A socioanalytic theory of personality. In M. M. Page (Ed.), *Nebraska symposium on motivation 1982. Personality: Current theory and research* (pp. 55–89). Lincoln: University of Nebraska Press.

Holland, J. L. (1973). *Making vocational choices: A theory of careers.* Englewood Cliffs, NJ: Prentice Hall.

Horowitz, L. M., Alden, L. E., Wiggins, J. S., & Pincus, A. L. (2000). *IIP-64/IIP-32 professional manual.* San Antonio, TX: The Psychological Corporation.

Hubert, L. J., & Arabie, P. (1987). Evaluating order hypotheses within proximity matrices. *Psychological Bulletin, 102,* 172–178.

Jöreskog, K. G., & Sörbom, D. (1986). *Analysis of linear structural relationships by the method of maximum likelihood.* Mooresville, IN: Scientific Software.

Kiesler, D. J. (1983). The 1982 Interpersonal Circle: A taxonomy for complementarity in human transactions. *Psychological Review, 90,* 185–214.

Kiesler, D. J. (1985). *The 1982 Interpersonal Circle: Acts version.* Unpublished manuscript, Richmond, VA: Virginia Commonwealth University.

Kiesler, D. J. (1987). *Revised Check List of Psychotherapy Transactions.* Richmond, VA: Virginia Commonwealth University.

Kiesler, D. J. (1996). Contemporary interpersonal theory and research: Personality, psychopathology, and psychotherapy. New York: Wiley.

Kiesler, D. J., Schmidt, J. A., & Wagner, C. C. (1997). A circumplex inventory of impact messages: An operational bridge between emotion and interpersonal behavior. In R. Plutchik and H. Conte (Eds.), *Circumplex models of personality and emotions* (pp. 221–244). Washington, DC: American Psychological Association.

Kovalski, T. M., Tracey, T. J. G., & Darcy, M. U. (2000, August). *Personal Globe Inventory and an examination of its psychometric properties*. Paper presented at the annual meeting of the American Psychological Association, Washington, DC.

LaForge, R., Freedman, M. B., & Wiggins, J. S. (1985). Interpersonal circumplex models: 1948–1983. *Journal of Personality Assessment, 49*, 613–631.

Larsen, R. J., & Diener, E. (1992). Promises and problems with the circumplex model of emotion. In M. S. Clark (Ed.), *Review of personality and social psychology: Emotion* (Vol. 13, pp. 25–59). Newbury Park, CA: Sage.

Leary, T. (1957). *Interpersonal diagnosis of personality*. New York: Ronald Press.

Lorr, M. (1997). The circumplex model applied to interpersonal behavior, affect, and psychotic syndromes. In R. Plutchik and H. Conte (Eds.), *Circumplex models of personality and emotions* (pp. 47–56). Washington, DC: American Psychological Association.

Maiti, S. S., & Mukherjee, B. N. (1990). A note on the distributional properties of the Jöreskog-Sörbom fit indices. *Psychometrika, 55*, 721–726.

Mardia, K. V. (1972). *Statistics of directional data*. New York: Academic Press.

Millon, T. (1987). *Manual for the MCMI-II* (2nd ed.). Minneapolis, MN: National Computer Systems.

Olson, D. H. (1996). Clinical assessment and treatment using the Family Circumplex Model. In F. W. Kaslow (Ed.), *Handbook of relational diagnosis and dysfunctional family patterns* (pp. 59–80). New York: Wiley.

Pincus, A. L. (1994). The interpersonal circumplex and the interpersonal theory: Perspectives on personality and its pathology. In S. Strack and M. Lorr (Eds.), *Differentiating normal and abnormal personality* (pp. 114–136). New York: Springer.

Pincus, A. L., & Gurtman, M. B. (1995). The three faces of interpersonal dependency: Structural analyses of self-report dependency measures. *Journal of Personality and Social Psychology, 69*, 744–758.

Pincus, A. L., Gurtman, M. B., & Ruiz, M. A. (1998). Structural Analysis of Social Behavior (SASB): Circumplex analyses and structural relations with the Interpersonal Circle and the Five-Factor Model of Personality. *Journal of Personality and Social Psychology, 74*, 1629–1645.

Plutchik, R., & Conte, H. (1985). Quantitative assessment of personality disorders. In R. Nickols, J. O. Cavenar, & H. K. H. Brodie (Eds.), *Psychiatry* (Vol. 7, pp. 1–13). Philadelphia: J. B. Lippincott.

Plutchik, R., & Conte, H. R. (1997). *Circumplex models of personality and emotions*. Washington, DC: American Psychological Association.

Plutchik, R., Kellerman, H., & Conte, H. (1979). A structural theory of ego defenses and emotions. In C. E. Izard (Ed.), *Emotions in personality and psychopathology* (pp. 229–257). New York: Plenum Press.

Prediger, D. J. (1982). Dimensions underlying Holland's hexagon: Missing link between interests and occupations? *Journal of Vocational Behavior, 21*, 259–287.

Romney, D. M., & Byner, J. M. (1997). Evaluating a circumplex model of personality disorders with structural equation modeling. In R. Plutchik & H. Conte (Eds.), *Circumplex models of personality and emotions* (pp. 327–346). Washington, DC: American Psychological Association.

Rounds, J., & Day, S. X. (1999). Describing, evaluating, and creating vocational interest structures. In M. L. Savickas & A. R. Spokane (Eds.), *Vocational interests: Their meaning, measurement and use in counseling* (pp. 103–133). Palo Alto, CA: Davies Black.

Rounds, J., & Tracey, T. J. (1996). Cross-cultural structural equivalence of RIASEC models and measures. *Journal of Counseling Psychology, 43*, 310–329.

Rounds, J., Tracey, T. J., & Hubert, L. (1992). Methods for evaluating vocational interest structural hypotheses. *Journal of Vocational Behavior, 40*, 239–259.

Russell, J. A. (1980). A circumplex model of affect. *Journal of Personality and Social Psychology, 39*, 1161–1178.

Russell, J. A. (1997). How shall an emotion be called? In R. Plutchik & H. Conte (Eds.), *Circumplex models of personality and emotions* (pp. 205–220). Washington, DC: American Psychological Association.

Russell, J. A., & Feldman-Barrett, L. (1999). Core affect, prototypical emotional episodes, and other things called emotion: Dissecting the elephant. *Journal of Personality and Social Psychology, 76*, 805–819.

Schaefer, E. S. (1959). A circumplex model for maternal behaviors. *Journal of Abnormal and Social Psychology, 59*, 226–235.

Schaefer, E. S. (1961). Converging conceptual models for maternal behavior and child behavior. In J. C. Glidwell (Ed.), *Parental attitudes and child behavior* (pp. 124–146). Springfield, IL: Charles C. Thomas.

Schmidt, J. A., Wagner, C. C., & Kiesler, D. J. (1999). Psychometric and circumplex properties of the octant scale Impact Message Inventory (IMI-C): A structural evaluation. *Journal of Counseling Psychology, 46*, 325–334.

Shepard, R. N. (1978). The circumplex and related topological manifolds in the study of perception. In S. Shye (Ed.), *Theory construction and data analysis in the behavioral sciences* (pp. 29–80). San Francisco: Jossey-Bass.

Soldz, S., Budman, S., Demby, A., & Merry, J. (1993). Representation of personality disorders in circumplex and five-factor space:

Explorations with a clinical sample. *Psychological Assessment, 5,* 41–52.

Strack, F., & Neumann, R. (2000). "Mood contagion": The automatic transfer of moods. *Journal of Personality and Social Psychology, 79,* 211–223.

Steiger, J. H., & Lind, J. (1980). *Statistically based tests for the number of common factors.* Paper presented at the meeting of the Psychometric Society, Iowa City.

Tabachnick, B. G., & Fidell, L. S. (1989). *Using multivariate statistics* (2nd ed.). New York: Harper & Row.

Thayer, R. E. (1996). *The origin of everyday moods: Managing energy, tension, and stress.* New York: Oxford University Press.

Tracey, T. J. G. (1994). An examination of the complementarity of interpersonal behavior. *Journal of Personality and Social Psychology, 67,* 864–878.

Tracey, T. J. G. (1997). RANDALL: A Microsoft FORTRAN program for a randomization test of hypothesized order relations. *Educational and Psychological Measurement, 57,* 164–168.

Tracey, T. J. G. (1998, August). *Examination of the Personal Globe Inventory.* Paper presented at the annual meeting of the American Psychological Association, San Francisco.

Tracey, T. J. G. (2000). Analysis of circumplex models. In H. E. A. Tinsley & S. Brown (Eds.), *Handbook of applied multivariate statistics and mathematical modeling.* San Diego: Academic Press.

Tracey, T. J. G. (2002). Personal Globe Inventory: Measurement of the spherical model of interests and competence beliefs. *Journal of Vocational Behavior, 60,* 113–172.

Tracey, T. J. G. (in press). Personal Globe Inventory: Measurement of the spherical model of interests and competence beliefs. *Journal of Vocational Behavior.*

Tracey, T. J. G., & Rounds, J. B. (1995). The arbitrary nature of Holland's RIASEC types: Concentric circles as a structure. *Journal of Counseling Psychology, 42,* 431–439.

Tracey, T. J. G., & Rounds, J. B. (1996a). Spherical representation of vocational interests. *Journal of Vocational Behavior, 48,* 3–41.

Tracey, T. J. G., & Rounds, J. B. (1996b). Contributions of the spherical representation of vocational interests. *Journal of Vocational Behavior, 48,* 85–95.

Tracey, T. J. G., & Rounds, J. B. (1993). Evaluating Holland's and Gati's vocational interest models: A structural meta-analysis. *Psychological Bulletin, 113,* 229–246.

Tracey, T. J. G., Rounds, J. B., & Gurtman, M. (1996). Examination of the general factor with the interpersonal circumplex structure: Application to the Inventory of Interpersonal Problems. *Multivariate Behavioral Research, 31,* 441–466.

Tracey, T. J. G., & Schneider, P. L. (1995). An evaluation of the circular structure of the Checklist of Interpersonal Transactions and the Checklist of Psychotherapy Transactions. *Journal of Counseling Psychology, 42,* 496–507.

Tracey, T. J. G., & Ward, C. C. (1998). The structure of children's interests and competence perceptions. *Journal of Counseling Psychology, 45,* 290–303.

Trobst, K. K. (2000). An interpersonal conceptualization and quantification of social support transactions. *Personality and Social Psychology Bulletin, 26,* 971–986.

Upton, G. J. G., & Fingleton, B. (1989). *Spatial data analysis by example: Vol. 2. Categorical and directional data.* New York: Wiley.

Wagner, C. C., Kiesler, D. J., & Schmidt, J. A. (1995). Assessing the interpersonal transaction cycle: Convergence of action and reaction interpersonal circumplex measures. *Journal of Personality and Social Psychology, 69,* 938–949.

Watson, D., & Tellegen, A. (1985). Toward a consensual structure of mood. *Psychological Bulletin, 98,* 219–235.

Watson, D., Wiese, D., Vaidya, J., & Tellegen, A. (1999). Two general activation systems of affect: Structural findings, evolutionary considerations, and psychobiological evidence. *Journal of Personality and Social Psychology, 76,* 820–838.

Wiggins, J. S. (1979). A psychological taxonomy of trait descriptive terms: The interpersonal domain. *Journal of Personality and Social Psychology, 37,* 395–412.

Wiggins, J. S. (1980). Circumplex models of interpersonal behavior. In L. Wheeler (Ed.), *Review of personality and social psychology* (Vol. 1, pp. 265–294). Beverly Hills, CA: Sage.

Wiggins, J. S. (1982). Circumplex models of interpersonal behavior in clinical psychology. In P. C. Kendall & J. N. Butcher (Eds.), *Handbook of research methods in clinical psychology* (pp. 183–221). New York: Wiley.

Wiggins, J. S. (1991). Agency and communion as conceptual coordinates for the understanding and measurement of interpersonal behavior. In W. M. Grove & D. Cicchetti (Eds.), *Thinking clearly about psychology: Volume 2. Personality and psychopathology* (pp. 89–113). Minneapolis: University of Minnesota Press.

Wiggins, J. S. (1996). An informal history of the interpersonal circumplex tradition. *Journal of Personality Assessment, 66,* 217–233.

Wiggins, J. S., & Broughton, R. (1985). The interpersonal circle: A structural model for the integration of personality research. In R. Hogan & W. Jones (Eds.), *Perspectives in personality* (Vol. 1, pp. 1–47). Greenwich, CT: JAI Press.

Wiggins, J. S., & Broughton, R. (1991). A geometric taxonomy of personality scales. *European Journal of Personality, 5,* 343–365.

Wiggins, J. S., Phillips, N., & Trapnell, P. (1989). Circular reasoning about interpersonal behavior: Evidence concerning some untested assumptions underlying diagnostic classification. *Journal of Personality and Social Psychology, 56,* 296–305.

Wiggins, J. S., Steiger, J. H., & Gaelick, L. (1981). Evaluating circumplexity in personality data. *Multivariate Behavioral Research, 16,* 263–289.

Wiggins, J. S., & Trapnell, P. D. (1996). A dyadic-interactional perspective on the five-factor model. In J. S. Wiggins (Ed.), *The five-factor model of personality: Theoretical perspectives* (pp. 82–162). New York: Guilford.

Wiggins, J. S., & Trobst, K. K. (1997). When is a circumplex an "interpersonal circumplex"? The case of supportive actions. In R. Plutchik & H. Conte (Eds.), *Circumplex models of personality and emotions* (pp. 57–80). Washington, DC: American Psychological Association.

Wiggins, J. S., & Trobst, K. K. (1999). The fields of interpersonal behavior. In L. A. Pervin & O. P. John (Eds.), *Handbook of personality theory and research* (2nd ed., pp. 653–670). New York: Guilford Press.

Yik, M. S. M., Russell, J. A., & Feldman-Barrett, L. (1999). Structure of self-reported current affect: Integration and beyond. *Journal of Personality and Social Psychology, 77,* 600–619.

CHAPTER 17

Item Response Theory and Measuring Abilities

KAREN M. SCHMIDT AND SUSAN E. EMBRETSON

CLASSICAL TEST THEORY

True Score Model

The classical test theory (CTT) approach to measurement is founded on the *true score model* (see Gulliksen, 1950; McDonald, 1999, for discussions). The true score model is based on the observed measurement of a person. This observation is considered a random variable, composed of two other random variables, a true score and an error score, as follows:

$$X = T + E, \qquad (17.1)$$

where X = observed score, with a mean μ_X and a variance σ_X^2; T = true score, with a mean μ_T and a variance σ_T^2; and

E = error score, with a mean μ_E and a variance σ_E^2. The expected value for the error score E is zero, which is the mean, $\mu_E = 0$; hence, the expected value of X equals the expected value of T:

$$E(\mu_X) = E(\mu_T) \qquad (17.2)$$

As with Equation 17.1, the variance of the observed score is the sum of the true score variance and the error score variance, as follows:

$$\sigma_X^2 = \sigma_T^2 + \sigma_E^2. \qquad (17.3)$$

While true score theory acknowledges measurement error, in most approaches it does not generally allow for different levels of measurement error for different levels of ability (but see Feldt & Brennan, 1989, and Lee, Brennan, & Kolen, 2000, for exceptions).

Assumptions

Applying the true and error score model of CTT requires assuming that errors are random and therefore uncorrelated with each other and uncorrelated with true scores. If such errors are a combination of several factors, then a normal distribution of errors can be expected, with a mean of zero and a

Karen M. Schmidt has published under the name of Karen M. Mc-Collam and would like to thank John McArdle, John Nesselroade, Ryan Bowles, Tracy Kline, and Wayne Velicer for helpful comments during the writing of this chapter. She would also like to thank Bill Stell for assistance in editing and writing style. The writing of this chapter was partially funded by grants from the College Board and a sesquicentennial associateship from the University of Virginia to Karen M. Schmidt.

variance of σ_E^2. Random error further implies that error scores are not correlated with other variables. These assumptions about error are necessary to interpret the various indices of reliability.

Notice that the CTT model does not include a test item's characteristics or content, but makes reference to item relationships with other variables. Thus, if the trait or attribute is measured or measurable by more than one test, then *equivalent parallel forms* (e.g., Gulliksen, 1950) or special test-equating methods (Holland & Rubin, 1982) are necessary for making score comparisons. Some characteristics of strictly parallel forms include equal means, variances, and correlations with other variables. To achieve this condition, item properties (discussed later) must be matched across forms.

Score Meaning: Norm-Referenced

In CTT, test scores derive meaning from comparisons to a norm or standard. The normative standard is a large-scale sampling of individuals to which the presently measured person or group is compared. The Wechsler Adult Intelligence Scales–Revised (WAIS-III; Wechsler, 1997), the Beck Depression Inventory (BDI; Beck, Steer, & Brown, 1996), and the Minnesota Multiphasic Personality Inventory–2 (MMPI-2; Butcher, Dahlstrom, Graham, Tellegen, & Kaemmer, 1989) are among the most widely used tests generating the greatest number of references for large-scale, norm-referenced scales (see Murphy, Impara, & Blake, 1999, for a list of tests).

Standard scores are often used in CTT references to norms to indicate the position of test scores in a norm group. Standard scores are based on unit-normal z scores, computed from raw scores for a particular norm group. However, negative scores are generally unacceptable to examinees, so z scores are converted into another metric, for example, a mean of 500 and standard deviation of 100 (e.g., SAT scores), or a mean of 100 and standard deviation of 15 (e.g., WAIS-III scores). A standard score, X_i, involves a target mean, μ_s, and standard deviation, σ_s, which may be computed from a person's z score as follows:

$$X_i = \mu_s + z_i \sigma_s \qquad (17.4)$$

While norm-referenced assessment has dominated the field of psychometrics for many years, the modern test theory approach—IRT—can confer meaning to scores by reference to items as well as to norms. That is, IRT allows person-to-item comparisons because they are on the same measurement scale (e.g., Embretson & Reise, 2000; Wright & Stone, 1979). A norm-referenced score relates, for example, to an age-appropriate group but does not indicate which items a person has successfully mastered. IRT scores also may be referenced to norms, thus allowing for two sources of meaning.

Item Properties

Although the CTT model does not include item characteristics in the basic model, a set of indices and procedures for test development are associated with CTT.

Item Difficulty: p Values

In CTT, p values, defined as the proportion of persons correctly responding to or agreeing with an item, are used to determine an item's difficulty. Values of p_i range from .00 to 1.00. Table 17.1 illustrates common item analysis statistics. In columns 2 and 3 of Table 17.1, the p values and standard deviations are given for 30 dichotomously scored, multiple-choice spatial ability items [SLAT (Spatial Learning Ability Test); Embretson, 1989] for a sample of 178 adults aged 18 to 84 (McCollam, 1997). Note that Item 10 is a relatively easy

TABLE 17.1 Summary Statistics for 30 Spatial Ability Items, N = 178

SLAT Item	p-Value	SD	Point-Biserial Correlation	Biserial Correlation
1	.567	.497	.463	.583
2	.332	.472	.319	.414
3	.506	.501	.252	.316
4	.371	.484	.274	.350
5	.365	.483	.420	.537
6	.500	.501	.406	.509
7	.253	.436	.300	.408
8	.590	.493	.366	.463
9	.438	.498	.574	.723
10	.725	.448	.431	.576
11	.348	.478	.441	.568
12	.697	.461	.467	.614
13	.365	.483	.405	.519
14	.270	.445	.211	.284
15	.242	.429	.158	.217
16	.258	.439	.243	.329
17	.714	.453	.425	.564
18	.573	.496	.324	.409
19	.444	.498	.386	.486
20	.348	.478	.427	.550
21	.399	.491	.278	.353
22	.449	.499	.392	.492
23	.365	.483	.231	.296
24	.534	.500	.418	.525
25	.781	.415	.335	.469
26	.449	.499	.378	.475
27	.438	.498	.496	.624
28	.371	.484	.336	.429
29	.500	.501	.377	.473
30	.584	.494	.344	.435

Note. K-R 20 = .848.

item and Item 7 is a relatively difficult item. Sometimes, observed p values are adjusted for guessing factors in multiple-choice contexts, where the adjusted proportion of people passing the item is not the proportion of persons who know the answer (see Crocker & Algina, 1986).

Item Discrimination: Item to Total Score Correlations

Item discrimination is the correlation between a test item and the total score. Conceptually, good discrimination is evidenced when passing an item positively correlates with individual overall scores. Negative discriminations indicate faulty item design, and items should be eliminated, modified, or examined for possible response strategy differences (e.g., Schmidt McCollam, 1998). With CTT, for a dichotomously scored set of responses to a unidimensionally designed test, an item's effectiveness at discriminating among persons is often indicated by biserial and point-biserial correlations.

Biserial correlations are computed under the assumption that a continuous and normally distributed latent variable underlies the item response. Column 4 of Table 17.1 gives biserial correlations. Note that Item 9 demonstrates relatively good discrimination, and Item 15 relatively poor discrimination. Among the reasons underlying item differences in efficiency are poorly worded items, weak experimental item design, response strategy differences, item multidimensionality, and bias.

The *point-biserial correlation* is a direct, Pearson product-moment correlation of the item response with total score and hence is readily available in standard statistical program packages (e.g., SPSS, SAS). However, the point-biserial correlation is influenced by item difficulty such that items that are very easy or very hard will appear less discriminating. The point-biserial correlation is slightly lower than the biserial correlation for items of moderate difficulty (i.e., .20 to .80) but becomes increasingly smaller as item difficulty becomes more extreme. On Table 17.1, for example, Item 18 and Item 25 have about the same point-biserial correlation, but Item 25 is much easier than Item 18. Notice that the biserial correlation for Item 25 is .469 while the biserial correlation for Item 18 is .409.

Several other CTT indices of discrimination are available for the special case of criterion classification, where individuals are placed into categories from cut scores on test totals. These indices include the index of discrimination, phi correlations, and tetrachoric correlations. The *index of discrimination* computes p-value differences by groups defined from cut scores. Large differences in p values between groups indicate high item discrimination. *Phi correlations* are product-moment correlations between dichotomized total scores and

items. However, like point-biserial correlations, the phi correlation is influenced by item difficulty such that the maximum possible correlation is often substantially less than 1.0. *Tetrachoric correlations* are estimates of the product-moment correlation if both criterion and item were continuous variables. Like the biserial correlation, they can be much higher than the direct product-moment correlation (i.e., phi) for items with extreme difficulties or in small samples.

Both phi and tetrachoric correlations can be computed to intercorrelate items. Such correlations may be used for factor analysis to determine the number of dimensions that are measured by an item set. Tetrachorics usually are preferred over phi correlations because they are not as biased by extreme p values. However, factor analysis using tetrachoric correlations can result in statistical violations such as negative factor variance estimates.

There are generalizations of the biserial correlation and the tetrachoric correlation for polytomously scored items. Polytomously scored items have multiple categories, such as appear in rating scale items. In the ability measurement context, these item responses reflect the relative degree of endorsement, or partial correctness relative to the construct, rather than absolute endorsement or correctness in dichotomous items. *Polyserials* are correlations of continuous variables (such as total scores) with categorical variables (i.e., the items). *Polychoric correlations* correlate two continuous variables that have been divided into at least three categories. For discussions, see McDonald (1999).

Note that adjustments can be made to the item-total correlations by eliminating the item's score from the total score in calculation. This correction is called the *corrected item-total correlation* (see Crocker & Algina, 1986). The need for such adjustment diminishes when considering a relatively large number of items and equally discriminating items.

Test Development With CTT

Item Selection

Earlier, an item's discrimination was described as being indicated by its biserial correlation, and item difficulty as being indicated by its p value. Both of these CTT indices allow for item selection for testing. In general, the goal is to select item difficulties that are appropriate for a target population. If the population is normally distributed and the empirical tryout of items is based on a representative sample, a common rule of thumb is to select most items with p values falling in the range of .40 to .60. Item discriminations should be high. For a test of a single ability (e.g., spatial ability for SLAT) and dichotomous item responses, biserial correlations should be particularly high.

In Table 17.1, no negative or zero biserial correlations were observed, thus indicating at least minimal discrimination for all items. Overall, the set of 30 items shows a good range of difficulty and discrimination and generally appears to be a reliable set. However, if only a subset of the items is needed, then item selection could be applied to yield a set with high psychometric quality. Considering p value and the biserial correlation jointly, Item 9 is the best item overall, with moderate difficulty and high discrimination. Biserial correlations for three items (Item 14, Item 15, and Item 23) fall below .30, which is relatively low for a unidimensional test of ability. One could consider omitting these items. For item difficulty, Table 17.1 shows that 13 items have p values below .40, while only three have p values above .60. A total of 14 items fall in the moderate range. Thus, to better match the population, several hard items should be eliminated. Considering both criteria, Items 14, 15, and 23 are candidates for deletion.

Norms

Since test scores mainly derive meaning from comparisons to norms (reference to a criterion is an alternative approach), it is very important in CTT to have reasonable normative samples available. For example, if SLAT were to be used for selection to military service, then a representative sample of military applicants or young adults should be available. Most tests have multiple norm groups so that scores can be given meaning depending on test use. SLAT may also have high school norms, college norms, engineering student norms, and more.

Test Evaluation With CTT

Reliability and validity are central to evaluating the psychometric quality of a test (e.g., Anastasi & Urbina, 1997; Traub, 1994). Both reliability and validity are theoretical measurement concepts that are not defined by any one study or index.

Reliability

Conceptually, reliability is defined as the proportion of true variance to total variance. Practically, reliability is defined as the consistency of measurement over the conditions of testing. Such conditions include time sampling, content sampling, content heterogeneity, and scorer/rater differences (Anastasi & Urbina, 1997). Since there are many testing conditions, several different types of evidence are needed to support reliability. Further, reliability is also dependent on the population being tested, so multiple studies on a single type of reliability are often needed.

Reliability coefficients are computed for two uses. First, a particular reliability coefficient indicates the proportion of test variance that is due to true variance (see Equation 17.3). Second, the reliability coefficient can be used to compute a standard error of measurement, which thus permits a confidence interval to be set around each score. Some popular reliability indices include the following: split-half (Rulon, 1939); Kuder-Richardson (K-R 20; Kuder & Richardson, 1937); alpha (Cronbach, 1951), which is related to K-R 20; test-retest; alternate or parallel form; and scorer (see Gulliksen, 1950). Index preferences depend on the individual needs of the researcher, available resources, and the test-scoring method.

To estimate the impact of item heterogeneity on reliability, two different indices of internal consistency reliability are often applied. K-R 20 coefficients can be computed on dichotomous items while the Cronbach's alpha coefficients (for which K-R 20 is a special case) can be computed on either dichotomous or polytomous items. The coefficient for K-R 20 is given as follows:

$$r_{tt} = \left(\frac{n}{n-1} \right) \frac{SD_t^2 - \sum pq}{SD_t^2} \qquad (17.5)$$

where r_{tt} is the reliability coefficient, n is the number of items, SD_t^2 is the total score variance, and $\sum pq$ is the sum of the proportion of those passing (p) times those failing (q) each item (and also known as the sum of item variances). At the bottom of Table 17.1 the K-R 20 coefficient is given for the 30-item set, which is a moderately high .848.

Test length and population heterogeneity each affect the size of reliability coefficients. Longer tests and heterogeneous populations, in general, will have higher internal consistency (Anastasi & Urbina, 1997; Traub, 1994). The Spearman-Brown prophecy formula (Gulliksen, 1950) demonstrates and estimates the effect of test length on reliability indices:

$$r_{SB} = \frac{nr_{tt}}{1 + (n-1)r_{tt}} \qquad (17.6)$$

where r_{SB} is the reliability estimate for the increased test length, n is the test length change multiplier (e.g., if the test is to be doubled in length, n is 2), and r_{tt} is the reliability coefficient for the original test length. In the present example, the effect of increasing the test's length by 15 items results in a new reliability estimate of .893. This value is close to .90, and, by strict standards, is often regarded as a minimum for an operational test. Decreasing the test length by 15 items gives a new reliability estimate of .736.

Standard errors of measurement are computed by using a specific reliability coefficient. The general formula for the standard error of measurement is the following:

$$SE_{msmt} = \sigma\pi(1 - r_{tt}), \qquad (17.7)$$

where r_{tt} is the reliability coefficient and σ is the population standard deviation of the test (which is typically from standard scores). Thus, if a test has a standard deviation of 100 and a reliability coefficient of .848, the standard error of measurement is 38.98.

Generalizability Theory. Generalizability theory (G-theory) addresses the separation of different variance sources into components, usually using a linear model (see, e.g., Cronbach, Glaser, Nanda, & Rajaratnam, 1972; Shavelson & Webb, 1991). Typically, one assumes that a unidimensional model underlies the items in the behavior domain, or the set of all items (see McDonald, 1999, for a discussion). Adequate item sampling of the item domain is essential, and inadequate sampling is assumed to be responsible for errors of measurement.

A typical G-study involves determining the *Guttman-Cronbach alpha* (McDonald, 1999), which assesses the score correlation between the item sampling mean and the item domain mean in a given population. This correlation indicates the relationship strength of the item sample with the entire item domain. Next, a decision study (D-study) is made in another population, based on the G-study results. If the new population's alpha is lower than desired, one can use the Spearman-Brown equation in Equation 17.6 to determine the test's more ideal length and increase the number of items sampled, thus reducing measurement error.

Validity

Validity refers to the extent to which theory and evidence support the test as a measure of the construct or attribute that it was designed to measure. This general definition is usually associated with the definition of *construct validity*. The construct may be a latent variable or simply a concept or characteristic of individuals that is inferred from test scores. For example, verbal ability may be considered a construct, defined operationally as facility with language. Construct validation begins with a detailed conceptual framework about what the test measures to describe its scope, extent, and what is represented by the test. It is important to note that this conceptualization of the construct should distinguish it from other constructs (i.e., discriminant validity) and how it is related to other constructs (i.e., convergent validity). Cronbach and Meehl (1955), who first conceptualized construct validity, outlined several relevant types of evidence to support a proposed inference made

from test scores. The current *Standards for Educational and Psychological Tests* (American Psychological Association, American Educational Research Association, National Council on Measurement in Education, 1999) list the following types of evidence: (a) evidence based on test content, which is usually based on expert opinion about the relationship of the construct and the test content domain, item formats, tasks, and so forth; (b) evidence based on response processes, the fit of the construct definition to the processes individuals employ to respond to the task; (c) evidence based on internal structure, the degree to which test component and item interrelationships fit the proposed construct; (d) evidence based on relations to other variables, including the relationship of test scores to performance criteria, measures of other constructs, and group membership; and (e) evidence based on the consequences of test use, such that any discrimination between identifiable groups has its roots only in the intended construct and not in other unintended and irrelevant constructs.

Empirically, construct validity is assessed using a variety of methods. For example, construct validity is assessed using factor analysis, experimental studies, cognitive process studies (Embretson, 1983), experimental studies (Cronbach & Meehl, 1955), structural equation models, and validity generalization (Hunter, 1986). For some discussions of validity and its methodological treatments, see Cook and Campbell (1979), Campell and Fiske (1959), Cronbach and Meehl (1955), Embretson (1983), and Messick (1995).

Prior to the current *Standards for Educational and Psychological Tests,* several subvarieties of validity were distinguished (see Anastasi & Urbina, 1997): predictive validity, concurrent validity, content validity, and construct validity (defined earlier). The current interpretation in the *Standards for Educational and Psychological Tests,* representing the collective wisdom of many measurement experts, considers them all as types of evidence for construct validity, but with an expanded definition of the term *construct.* For completeness, however, we will define these types of validity. *Predictive validity* focuses on the relationship of the test with some outcome measure occurring later in time. *Concurrent validity* examines the correlation between the test and current scores on some test or performance in some specific domain. *Content validity* assesses whether the sampled items represent a content domain adequately. *Construct validity,* in the narrow sense, refers to the appropriateness of inferring standing on a latent construct from the test scores. It can be seen that the first three types of validity are now included as types of evidence (i.e., Examples a and b), and that construct validity has been generalized to include the other types.

Two other validity distinctions, convergent validity and discriminant validity, are included in evidence from relationships with other variables. *Convergent validity* is reflected when tests measuring the same construct are highly correlated, and *discriminant validity* is indicated by low correlations of the test with tests of unrelated constructs.

Summary

Classical test theory has dominated the field of psychometrics for most of the last century. It has provided a foundation for psychological measurement by including (a) an empirical basis for item evaluation and selection, (b) an objective referent for score comparisons (i.e., norms), and (c) the conceptual rationale and empirical basis for evaluating test quality (i.e., reliability and validity).

The CTT model is limited in several ways. First, since the CTT model has no allowance for possibly varying item parameters, item parameters must be regarded as fixed on a particular test. Thus, the generality of true score is limited to tests with parallel or very similar collections of items. Although this limitation is somewhat circumvented by sampling approaches to items (i.e., in generalizability theory and similar approaches), in a practical sense most tests cannot be built as random samples from an item domain. Second, the estimates for item properties and reliability are population-specific; that is, these indices are meaningful only in reference to a particular group of individuals. In reference to another group of individuals, the indices lose meaning. The true and error score model is used to justify estimates of population statistics that require variance estimates. Third, item properties are not directly linked to behavior. That is, knowing a person's score refers to an overall level relative to a group of persons. Nothing is known about which items the person has likely passed or likely failed. Thus, using item difficulty and discrimination to select items is justified by their impact on various population statistics, such as variances and reliabilities.

However, more modern techniques developed since the 1960s have changed measurement methods in several ways. Although item response theory (IRT) methods enhance some CTT methods, perhaps more important is the impact of IRT for a new basis of score meaning, item selection, and design, as well as new methods of testing.

ITEM RESPONSE THEORY

Item response theory methods have two distinct traditions. In the United States, IRT is usually traced to Lord and Novick's (1968) classic book on measurement. Preceding this volume was Lord's (1953) monograph on test theory models and Birnbaum's (see Lord & Novick, 1968, for references) development of estimation methods. In Europe, IRT methods (known as latent trait theory) were first introduced in 1960 by Georg Rasch, a Danish mathematician who developed what is known as the Rasch model. For a historical account of IRT, see Bock (1997).

Since their introduction, IRT models, test procedures, and estimation procedures have developed rapidly. Although IRT can include CTT as a special case, it is based on qualitatively different principles. To provide the reader some insights into IRT, this section begins with a consideration of IRT as model-based measurement, followed by a review of three basic models and their parameters. More complex models, appropriate for a wide range of applications, are also reviewed briefly.

Model-Based Measurement of Ability

Measurements of psychological constructs are usually indirect; latent variables are measured by observing behavior on relevant tasks or items. The properties of both persons and items on a psychological dimension are inferred from behavior. Thus, a measurement theory in psychology must provide a rationale for relating behaviors to the psychological construct. Typically, a measurement theory rationale includes a model of behavior.

In IRT, like CTT, a person's trait level is estimated from responses to test items. However, an IRT model specifies how both trait level(s), as well as item properties, are related to a person's item responses. Since trait level is estimated in the context of an IRT model, IRT is thus a model-based measurement.

IRT is a powerful modeling method because strong assumptions must be met. The following sections describe these assumptions and then present three unidimensional IRT models that are appropriate for tests that measure a single latent trait.

Three Basic IRT Models

The Most Basic Model

In the simplest model, the Rasch model, a person's item responses are modeled from a simple difference between their ability and the item's difficulty in the context of a logistic model. Expressed in the form of conditional probability, giving *item-characteristic curves* (ICCs), the Rasch model (also known as the one-parameter logistic model, or 1PL) is given as follows:

$$P(X_{ij} = 1 \mid \theta_j) = \frac{\exp(\theta_j - \beta_i)}{1 + \exp(\theta_j - \beta_i)} \qquad (17.8)$$

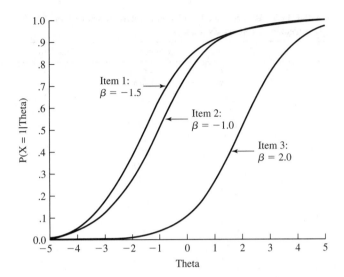

Figure 17.1 Item characteristic curves for a one-parameter IRT model.

where $P(X_{ij} = 1 \mid \theta_j)$ is the probability that person j with ability of θ_j answers item i correctly, θ_j is the ability for person j, β_i is the difficulty for item i, and exp is the exponent of the constant, e (2.7181).

Three ICCs are shown in Figure 17.1. Note the differences among the three items along the theta scale, marked in log-odds units on the abscissa. Items 1 and 2 are centered over values of -1.5 and -1.0, respectively. Item 3 is centered higher on the scale, over 2.0. For the one-parameter dichotomous Rasch model, the *location, threshold,* and *difficulty* of the item refer to the same information: the point along the scale where the probability of endorsing an item is .50. From left to right, the scale ranges from relatively easy to relatively hard items. Similarly, ability values range from low to high trait levels, from left to right. Thus, for most of the ability range, Item 3 requires a higher trait level for correct item endorsement than do Items 1 and 2 and is therefore relatively more difficult than are Items 1 and 2.

Another feature of the ICC is that the probability of correctly endorsing an item, given theta level, never perfectly reaches 1, and never reaches 0. Practically speaking, the possibility of error is specified even for the highest ability, and the possibility of success is specified for even the lowest ability.

More Complex Models

The 1PL model for dichotomous responses, just described, is based on the notion that after ability is considered, the only parameter governing item responses is the difficulty of the item. Item difficulty is symbolized by B, or β. More complex IRT models incorporate more item or person parameters to model the item response data. In this section, we describe two more basic models—the two- and three-parameter (2PL and

3PL) logistic models—that incorporate one more item parameter each. However, much more complex models are available, such as multidimensional IRT models, polytomous IRT models, and IRT models that include mathematical models of item processes (see Andrich, 1978; Masters, 1982, for examples; see Embretson & Reise, 2000, for a survey).

The 2PL model for dichotomous responses incorporates a α parameter, which represents item discrimination. The slope of the logistic ICC varies as a function of α_i, and each item has its own α parameter. The 2PL model is written as follows:

$$P(X_{ij} = 1 \mid \theta_j, \beta_i, \alpha_i) = \frac{\exp \alpha_i(\theta_j - \beta_i)}{1 + \exp \alpha_i(\theta_j - \beta_i)} \quad (17.9)$$

where $P(X_{ij} = 1 \mid \theta_j, \beta_i, \alpha_i)$ is the probability that person j with ability of θ_j answers item I correctly, θ_j is the ability estimate for person j, β_i is the difficulty for item i, α_i is the discrimination (slope) for item i, and exp is the exponent of the constant e. Figure 17.2 shows ICCs for three items estimated from the 2PL model. Notice that α is relatively low for Item 3, indicating that the probability for solving this item is less related to trait level differences than for the other two items. In the Rasch model in Equation 17.8, no α parameter is included because not only are all items assumed to be equally discriminating, but the value is set to 1.0 for all items as well.

The 3PL model for dichotomous responses adds a lower asymptote or guessing parameter, γ, to the terms in the 2PL model as follows:

$$P(X_{ij} = 1 \mid \theta_j, \beta_i, \alpha_i, \gamma) = \gamma + (1 - \gamma)\frac{\exp \alpha_i(\theta_j - \beta_i)}{1 + \exp \alpha_i(\theta_j - \beta_i)} \quad (17.10)$$

The lower asymptote represents the probability of solving an item at the very lowest trait levels and so is thought to

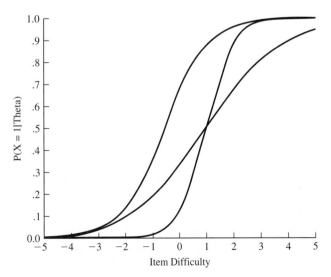

Figure 17.2 Item characteristic curves for a two-parameter IRT model.

represent guessing. Thus the ICCs would not fall below γ in the 3PL model, while for Figure 17.2 the ICCs fall very close to zero for low ability levels.

Assumptions

Two basic assumptions must be made for applying IRT models to a test: (a) The ICCs have a specified form, and (b) local independence has been obtained. The *form* of an ICC describes how changes in trait level relate to changes in the probability of a specified response category. The ICC regresses the probability of item success on trait level. For dichotomously scored items, success is "correct" or "agreement" with an item. The form specified in the 1PL, 2PL, and 3PL models is logistic, which gives the S-shaped curves shown on the figures. The case of multicategory or polytomous items is considered later.

Local independence concerns the sufficiency of an IRT model to characterize the data. Local independence is obtained when the relationships among items (or persons) are adequately reproduced by the IRT model. That is, the principle of local independence states that no further relationships remain between items when the model parameters are controlled. The pattern of correlations among test items is expected to be fully explained by their parameter differences and by the person parameters. Achieving local independence also implies that the number of different person variables (traits) in the model is sufficient to reproduce the data. Thus, if a model with only one person parameter is sufficient, then the data are unidimensional.

Score Meaning: Item or Norm-Referenced

Trait-level scores, θ, are scaled as log-odds ratios, and they are often set so that the mean is zero. Thus, trait level scores are often comparable to z scores in magnitude. However, trait-level scores differ in several ways from z scores, which are CTT-based. First, unlike z scores, θ is not linearly related to the raw score. The intervals between scores differ because the IRT scale generally produces greater distances between extreme scores. Second, for more complex models, such as 2PL and 3PL, θ is not monotonically related to raw score. That is, the item discriminations weight the value of item responses. Individuals at the same raw score will have higher θs if they pass more discriminating items. Third, the standard error of measurement varies over levels of θ, rather than having a constant value as for typical CTT scores. The standard error of measurement is lower for moderate abilities when the test has mostly items of moderate difficulty. The standard error of measurement for a particular θ depends on the

TABLE 17.2   Raw Scores, Trait Levels, and Standard Errors of Measurement for SLAT Examinees

Person	Raw Score	Trait Level	Standard Error
1	14.00	−.6086	.33
2	5.00	−1.6614	.35
3	5.00	−1.5669	.35
4	16.00	.0526	.30
5	4.00	−1.6787	.36
6	5.00	−1.6746	.36
7	16.00	−.0349	.36
8	3.00	−2.0214	.48
9	12.00	−.6194	.32
10	12.00	−.6513	.29
11	6.00	−1.4610	.38
12	9.00	−.7710	.26
13	16.00	.1572	.26
14	7.00	−1.4588	.38
15	7.00	−1.0268	.42

Note. First 15 persons are given.

appropriateness of the items and on other properties, such as item discrimination. Fourth, trait-level scores need not be derived from equivalent forms. In fact, in the case of adaptive testing (discussed later), greater precision is obtained when test forms vary widely in difficulty between examinees (also see Embretson & Reise, 2000). Fifth, the trait-level score has direct meaning for item performance.

Table 17.2 shows raw scores, trait levels (abilities), and standard errors of measurement for the first 15 examinees on SLAT from the 2PL model. Several features of this table illustrate the points just mentioned. Notice that trait-level scores appear similar to z scores. However, note that individuals with the same raw score, such as Person 2 and Person 3, do not have the same estimated trait level. With the 2PL model, ability estimates also depend on which items are passed. Highly discriminating items receive more weight in trait levels. Also notice that the standard errors of measurement differ across examinees and even among examinees with the same total score. Person 9 and Person 10, for example, at a raw score of 12, have slightly different trait levels and standard errors.

Figure 17.3 presents the standard error of measurement corresponding to various SLAT trait levels for the Rasch model. The typical U-shaped curve, with greater measurement error at the extremes, is observed. In general, fewer appropriate items for the extreme scores leads to greater measurement errors.

The last difference from z scores, a direct meaning for item performance, merits further discussion because it provides another basis for interpreting IRT trait levels. Figure 17.4 shows a person-characteristic curve (PCC) for one person. PCCs give the probability that a person with a particular θ level solves items. In the case of the Rasch

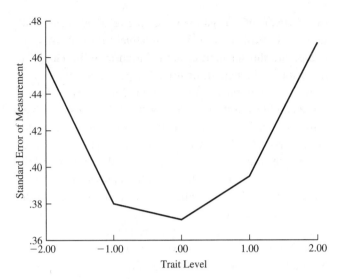

Figure 17.3   Standard error of measurement for trait levels on SLAT.

model, the only item parameter for the PCC is item difficulty. Notice how a probability can be given for any item for which difficulty is known.

Since trait level and item difficulty are on the same scale, it is also possible to make joint distributions of trait-level frequencies in some group and item difficulties. Figure 17.5 shows the joint distribution of persons and items for SLAT. On the person side, the frequency of each trait level in the sample is indicated. On the item side, each item is plotted by its difficulty. The notation for each item indicates its position on the test and two variables to represent the mental folding process—number of surfaces carried and the degrees of rotation. In this plot each trait level can be matched with the items that are at the level (i.e., with a .50 probability). Items

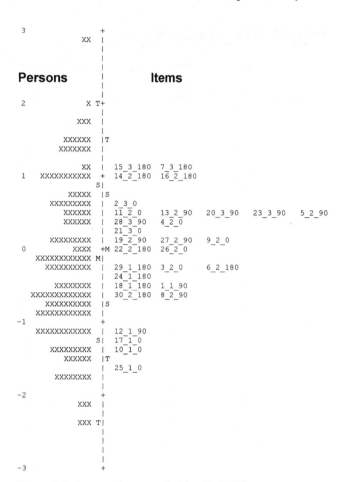

Figure 17.5   Person-to-item map of adults with SLAT items.

falling below the trait level are easy, while items above the trait level are hard.

Like CTT scores, IRT trait levels may be linearly transformed to standard score systems. However, as noted earlier, the standard scores from IRT trait levels will not be linearly related to CTT standard scores. The IRT score intervals are preferable not only because they are optimal for modeling item performance, but also, as in the case of the Rasch model, because justifications for interval-level scale properties can be made (discussed later).

Item Properties

The IRT models just presented are increasingly more complex. In the most complex model, the 3PL, item parameters include item difficulty (β), item discrimination (α), and lower asymptote (guessing, γ).

Table 17.3 presents item parameters from the 1PL (Rasch model) and the 2PL model for the SLAT data. For the 1PL model, all item discrimination parameters are equal and set to 1.0. The mean item difficulty is set to 0, but the individual item difficulties vary substantially, with a standard deviation

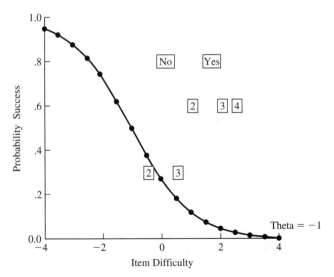

Figure 17.4   Person-characteristic curve.

TABLE 17.3   IRT Item Parameters for SLAT

ITEM	1PL α S.E.	1PL β S.E.	2PL α S.E.	2PL β S.E.
1	1.000	−.530	1.410	−.582
	.040	.169	.272	.190
2	1.000	.636	.819	.672
	.040	.168	.177	.270
3	1.000	−.232	.670	−.341
	.040	.152	.148	.154
4	1.000	.430	.754	.482
	.040	.160	.172	.240
5	1.000	.459	1.094	.315
	.040	.171	.220	.214
6	1.000	−.205	1.114	−.314
	.040	.162	.203	.168
7	1.000	1.088	.806	1.219
	.040	.187	.174	.376
8	1.000	−.639	1.003	−.746
	.040	.163	.201	.191
9	1.000	.093	1.833	−.116
	.040	.177	.341	.201
10	1.000	−1.349	1.575	−1.184
	.040	.190	.317	.300
11	1.000	.546	1.189	.359
	.040	.174	.226	.222
12	1.000	−1.190	1.64	−1.051
	.040	.186	.335	.278
13	1.000	.459	1.113	.307
	.040	.170	.220	.213
14	1.000	.985	.630	1.414
	.040	.176	.151	.444
15	1.000	1.159	.553	1.904
	.040	.182	.136	.569
16	1.000	1.053	.727	1.306
	.040	.178	.180	.439
17	1.000	−1.285	1.385	−1.194
	.040	.187	.288	.282
18	1.000	−.557	.880	−.697
	.040	.158	.191	.186
19	1.000	.066	.977	−.034
	.040	.162	.195	.173
20	1.000	.546	1.213	.351
	.040	.174	.238	.223
23	1.000	.459	.634	.647
	.040	.158	.148	.271
24	1.000	−.367	1.15	−.462
	.040	.163	.214	.174
25	1.000	−1.696	1.188	.236
	.040	.201	−.641	.349
26	1.000	.039	.942	−.054
	.040	.161	.187	.170
27	1.000	.093	1.368	−.073
	.040	.170	.260	.184
28	1.000	.430	.971	.341
	.040	.165	.197	.213
29	1.000	−.205	.992	−.311
	.040	.160	.197	.163
30	1.000	−.612	.901	−.750
	.040	.160	.191	.191

of .75. Items with negative values are relatively easy, while items with positive values are relatively difficult. Also included are the standard errors for each item difficulty. The precision of the item difficulty estimates varies, which indicates the appropriateness of the item difficulties for the observed abilities in the sample. For the 2PL model, both item difficulties and item discriminations vary. Low α parameters are observed for three items, Item 3, 14, and 15. In a direct sense, the value indicates that item-solving probabilities change relatively more slowly with increased trait level of these items. Stated in another way, these items are less discriminating. Item difficulties for the 2PL model, β, differ somewhat from the estimates in the 1PL due to the varying item discriminations. However, the item difficulties have generally the same pattern in the 2PL as in the 1PL model. The 3PL model was not estimated for SLAT because the sample size is too small. Adequately estimating for the 3PL model requires large samples, such as 1,000 persons if a unique lower asymptote is estimated for each item.

Measurement Scale Properties

Two measurement properties that result from applying IRT models are person-free item calibration and item-free person measurement (see Hambleton, Swaminathan, & Rogers, 1991, for a discussion). *Person-free item calibration* means that the distribution of persons used to obtain item indices does not bias the indices. For CTT, item indices, such as *p* values, are directly influenced by the population. For example, if a lower-ability population were used to estimate SLAT *p* values, all values on Table 17.1 would be lower. However, for IRT, comparable estimates for item difficulty can be obtained from the lowest scoring and the highest scoring subpopulations. Whitely and Dawis (1974) show how highly similar item difficulties are obtained when the Rasch model estimates are anchored to the item set (i.e., item mean is fixed to zero).

Other indices, such as the biserial correlation, are influenced by population heterogeneity. More homogeneous populations will have lower estimates. For IRT, however, item parameters are estimated in the context of person ability estimates. That is, a full model of item responses includes abilities and the item parameters. Hence, item parameter estimates are controlled for trait level.

It should be noted, however, that the standard error associated with item parameter estimates is indeed influenced by the population distribution. Higher standard errors will be given for difficult items, for example, when the population's average trait level is low.

Item-free person measurement means that the estimated trait levels for persons are not biased by the characteristics of the items. For CTT, raw scores are directly dependent on item difficulty and other item properties. For example, raw scores on an easy test are much higher than are raw scores on a hard test. Even special equating does not fully handle difficulties arising from differing test difficulties (see Holland & Rubin, 1982). In IRT, item properties such as item difficulty are directly included in the model. Thus, ability is estimated in the context of item parameters. For example, a score of 5 on a test of 10 easy items will receive a much lower trait-level estimate than would the same score on a test of 10 hard items. But as for item parameter calibrations, the standard errors of the person estimates are influenced by item parameters. That is, much larger standard errors will be found when the items are either much too hard or too easy for the person or when the items are not very discriminating.

Item-free person measurement is a central measurement property that makes adaptive testing feasible. In *adaptive testing,* items are selected for each person to provide the most precise measurement. If the item bank is large, few persons receive the same combination of items. IRT can provide equated trait levels in this situation because the item-parameter estimates are controlled for in the estimation of the persons. For adaptive testing, however, measurement error is minimized for everyone because of the optimal selection of items.

Special Properties of the Rasch Model

Wright and colleagues (e.g., Wright & Stone, 1979) have given much attention to *conjoint measurement,* a term first used by Luce and Tukey (1964). Conjoint measurement allows the scores of persons and items to be measured on the same scale (see Linacre & Wright, 2001). Originally, this scale used a logistic function, and the logistic is still the most often used. No other mathematical formulation for the item ogives (ICCs) allows for independent estimation of item difficulty (β_i) and person trait level (θ_j; Rasch, 1961). Other theoretical developments of the Rasch model's measurement properties stem from the European measurement tradition (see Fischer & Molenaar, 1995).

Item-free person calibration for the Rasch model refers to a special relationship for this model and not the other IRT models. Stated simply, the expected difference in performance between two persons on any item is given by the difference in their trait levels. Specifically, its meaning can be readily shown by the following:

$$\ln \frac{P(X_{i1})}{1 - P(X_{i1})} = \theta_1 - \beta_i$$

and

$$\ln \frac{P(X_{i2})}{1 - P(X_{i2})} = \theta_2 - \beta_i, \qquad (17.11)$$

where θ_1 and θ_2 are ability trait level scores for person 1 and 2, β_i is the difficulty of an item, and the left-hand sides of the equations indicate the natural log odds of the item responses, X_{i1} and X_{i2} for persons 1 and 2, respectively. Taking the difference between the two equations results in $\theta_1 - \theta_2$. Note that the item drops from the comparison (see Embretson & Reise, 2000). Restated, for any item the expected difference in log-odds performance is given by the simple difference between their abilities. In this sense, ability differences have justifiable interval-level scale properties.

Person-free item calibration also has a special meaning in the Rasch model. That is, the comparison of items does not depend on the persons used to calibrate them. This concept is illustrated in the following:

$$\ln \frac{P(X_{1s})}{1 - P(X_{1s})} = \theta_s - \beta_1$$

and

$$\ln \frac{P(X_{2s})}{1 - P(X_{2s})} = \theta_s - \beta_2, \qquad (17.12)$$

where θ_s is person s, β_1 is the difficulty of item 1, β_2 is the difficulty of item 2, and the left-hand side of the equation indicates the natural log odds of the item responses, X_{1s} and X_{2s} for person s on items 1 and 2, respectively. Taking the difference between the two equations results in $\beta_1 - \beta_2$. Note that the person drops from the comparison (see Embretson & Reise, 2000). Hence, for any person the difference in performance on two items is due to their difference in item difficulty.

Estimation

Estimating Trait Level

The relationship between item responses and trait level is fundamentally different in IRT compared with CTT. In IRT, determining the person's trait level is *not* a question of how to add up the item responses. Instead, a somewhat different question is asked. That is, given the observed item responses, what is the most plausible ability? Stated in another way, given the properties of the items and knowledge of how item properties influence behavior (i.e., an IRT model), what is the most likely trait level to explain the person's responses?

Some examples help clarify this notion. Consider the response pattern in which a person succeeds on most items in a very difficult test. This response pattern is not very likely if a person has a low trait level. The likelihood that a person with a moderate trait level could pass all the items is higher, but the response pattern is most likely for a person with a high trait level.

Finding the IRT trait level for a response pattern requires a search process instead of a scoring procedure. Trait levels typically are estimated by a maximum likelihood method; specifically, the estimated trait level for person s maximizes the likelihood of his or her response pattern given the item properties. Finding maximum likelihood estimates of trait levels requires a computer program that (a) computes the likelihoods of response patterns under various trait levels and (b) conducts a search process for the trait level that gives the highest likelihood.

To illustrate the concept of searching for a trait estimate that yields the highest likelihood, consider Figure 17.6. This figure shows the likelihoods for four response patterns under various hypothetical abilities. Each likelihood shown is computed by multiplying the probabilities for the five items. In turn, each item probability is computed using a particular IRT model (in this case, the Rasch model in Equation 17.8) with known item parameters and a hypothetical ability. In Figure 17.6, likelihoods are computed for 13 different hypothetical abilities for each response pattern. The ability that gives the highest likelihood would be the maximum likelihood estimate. For response pattern 1, for example, the estimate would be 2.0.

It should be noted that computer programs like BILOG (Mislevy & Bock, 1990), PARSCALE (Muraki & Bock, 1997), and RUMM (Sheridan, Andrich, & Luo, 1996) apply complex numerical procedures to find maximum likelihood estimates. Also, estimation can be conducted using prior information, such as a population ability distribution.

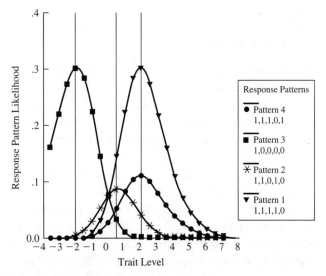

Figure 17.6   Likelihoods for four response patterns.

Estimating Item Parameters

Item parameters for IRT models are usually estimated by a maximum likelihood (ML) method. For ML estimation, error is defined as unlikely observed data, and a search process yields estimates that maximize the total data likelihood. Data likelihoods are defined somewhat differently in the various IRT estimation methods, but in general data likelihoods involve multiplying the response pattern probabilities over persons.

The most frequently used ML estimation methods are (a) joint maximum likelihood (JML), (b) marginal maximum likelihood (MML), and (c) conditional maximum likelihood (CML). In typical IRT applications, both item parameters and trait levels are unknown and must be estimated from the same data. The three ML methods handle the problem of unknown trait levels differently. Many researchers consider MML to be the most statistically adequate and flexible method of the three (Holland, 1990).

Practically speaking, few differences between the estimates will be observed from these different methods for many tests. Perhaps more salient are scale differences, which result from decisions about how to anchor the solution in the case where both person and item parameters are unknown (see Embretson & Reise, 2000).

Test Development With IRT

Model Selection

Test development with IRT models begins with the selection of an appropriate IRT model. Since SLAT is dichotomously scored, the standard models (Rasch, 2PL, and 3PL) are generally appropriate. Selection of an appropriate model depends not only on model fit, but on other considerations as well, such as parsimony and test-scoring philosophy. For example, because of its simplicity and the direct relationship of raw total scores to trait level, the Rasch model may be favored even if it does not fit adequately. In contrast, the 2PL and 3PL models not only contain more parameters but also weight the items by their discrimination in the estimation of trait level.

Several methods exist to evaluate model fit (see Embretson & Reise, 2000). One strategy is to compare the overall fit of alternative IRT models by goodness-of-fit tests and by log-likelihood comparisons. Both of these fit indices, for example, are provided in BILOG. For the goodness-of-fit test, the expected and observed frequencies of passing each item for score groups are compared. The expected frequency is based on predictions from the estimated model parameters. The observed frequency is obtained by dividing the sample into homogeneous groups, based on trait level, and then tabulating the number of persons passing each item. These small calibration samples result in more heterogeneous groups, and maintain a sufficient number of cases for stable estimates of observed frequencies. The fit for each item and for the overall model is indicated by a statistic that is distributed as χ^2. For SLAT, the 1PL model did not fit overall ($\chi^2_{131} = 172.70$, $p = .0086$), and three items did not fit, as indicated by χ^2s with probabilities less than .01. In contrast, the 2PL model did fit ($\chi^2_{129} = 113.00$, $p = .8406$), and only one item failed to fit the model (Item 15). The log-likelihood goodness-of-fit test, which compares the data likelihood between the two models directly, was also statistically significant ($\chi^2_{30} = 66.03$, $p < .01$), indicating a significant difference between models. Therefore, on the basis of model fit, the 2PL model is preferred over the 1PL model.

Person Fit

Another strategy to improve model fit is to exclude persons who do not fit the standard IRT model probabilities. *Person-fit statistics* are available to assess the relative likelihood of a person's response pattern (see Reise & Flannery, 1996). A person whose responses are well predicted from the IRT model parameters—passing items below their trait level and failing items above their trait level—will fit the model. However, some persons fail relatively easy items but then answer correctly much harder items. These persons do not fit the model. The reasons for person misfit are many, including motivational problems, unusual test-taking strategies, language problems, specialized knowledge, and so forth. Eliminating a few poorly fitting persons can improve model fit so that a simpler model fits adequately. Person-fit statistics also may provide useful diagnostic information to accompany test scores in operational tests (see Daniel, 1999). For example, a low score accompanied with poor fit may indicate an invalid test score.

Item Selection

After selecting the most appropriate model, the item fit statistics and parameter estimates can be examined. Item 15 was the only item that failed to fit the 2PL model. Hence, it could be eliminated. The item parameter estimates shown in Table 17.2 indicate that some items have lower discriminations. Whether these should be eliminated depends on the intended use of the items.

Two separate types of tests should be distinguished. A test can be administered as a fixed content test or as an adaptive test. In the *fixed content test* the same items are administered to everyone. Therefore, both the expected population distribution and the goals of measurement are important to consider in item selection. If the goal is to measure the whole population

adequately (vs., say, measuring well near a cut score), then the goal is to minimize the average standard error of measurement in the target population. Or, inversely, the items should be maximally *informative;* thus, selecting items to be maximally informative for the most frequent trait levels is an appropriate strategy.

The person-to-item map of Figure 17.5 shows how items could be selected for SLAT using the Rasch model. Since items and persons are located on the same scale, their distributions can be compared directly. It can be seen directly, for example, that the many difficult items are not well matched by persons at that level. Thus, one could consider deleting some difficult items and developing items appropriate for lower trait levels that have high frequencies but few appropriate items. Although beyond the scope of this overview, IRT permits a very precise targeting of items to a population through test and item information curves (see Hambleton, Swaminathan, & Rogers, 1991), which are applicable to 2PL and 3PL models, as well as the Rasch model.

In an *adaptive test* items are selected from an item bank to provide the smallest standard errors possible for each examinee. To achieve optimal measurement, large numbers of items should be available for most trait levels, including relatively extreme trait levels. Obviously, 30 SLAT items do not constitute an item bank. However, deciding whether to add SLAT items to an existing item bank depends not only on the quality of the SLAT item but also on the need for items at certain difficulty levels in the item bank. Thus, unlike CTT, extreme items may be readily selected because they are needed to provide optimal measurement for extreme trait levels.

Test Evaluation With IRT

Both reliability and validity are relevant and similarly evaluated as for CTT, so an extended discussion is not needed. However, one major difference concerns the evaluation of one type of reliability and its associated standard error of measurement. That is, since IRT provides individual standard errors of measurement for each trait level, the most informative presentation of test quality is a chart showing the standard error at different levels, such as shown in Figure 17.3 for SLAT. Notice that the measurement error is lowest for the more moderate scores.

Composite standard errors for a particular population, Φ_{pop}, may still be estimated using the individual measurement standard errors, Φ_j. The following formula shows the composite standard errors

$$\theta_{msmt} = \sqrt{\left(\sum \theta_j^2 / N \right)} \qquad (17.13)$$

For SLAT with the 2PL model, the average standard error of measurement was .3724.

Reliability may also be estimated from this composite as follows:

$$r_{tt} = 1 - \theta^2_{\text{msmt}}/\theta^2, \qquad (17.14)$$

where θ^2 is the trait-level variance. For SLAT trait levels, the variance is .823. Applying Equation 17.14 with measurement variance $(.3724^2 = .1387)$, the composite reliability is .8315. As for CTT, lengthening the test will improve reliability. However, improving the suitability of the items for the persons will also improve reliability.

Advanced IRT Models

The models just presented have been useful for unidimensional tests with dichotomous item-response variables. However, many measurement problems in psychology are more complex and require complex models to characterize the data (see Embretson & Reise, 2000, for a review). Although space does not permit a full review of these models, the reader may be interested in the following models: (a) those with restrictions on parameters, which are used to relate item difficulty to substantive sources (Fischer, 1973); (b) those for rating scales (e.g., Samejima, 1969); (c) those for partial credit (Masters, 1982); (d) those for multidimensional data (Bock, Gibbons, & Muraki, 1988); (e) those for component processes (Whitely, 1980); (f) those for measuring changes in trait levels (Embretson, 1997; Wang, Wilson, & Adams, 1997); and (g) those for identifying latent classes that differ qualitatively in the nature of test responses (Rost, 1990).

In this section we discuss two of these models: models for rating scales and models with restrictions on parameters.

Models for Rating Scales

Models for rating scales are usually described as models for polytomous data, which means that multiple response categories are scored. Rating scales are important in psychological measurement, and the models for dichotomous data cannot be applied directly to these data.

It is useful to think of polytomous IRT models as extensions of standard IRT models for the multiple response categories. The class of models for rating scales is quite broad. In fact, polytomous IRT models have been developed for many more complex models that were originally available only for dichotomous data, to handle restricted item parameters, multidimensionality, latent classes and much more.

In general, the polytomous model parameters relate the various response categories to a location on the latent trait.

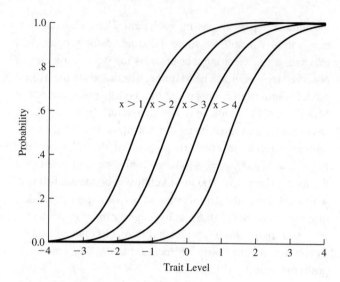

Figure 17.7 Operating-characteristic curves for an item from the graded response model.

The polytomous models vary in specifying how the parameters relate to response probabilities. For example, the *graded response model* (GRM; Samejima, 1969) was proposed to relate the probability of responding in category x or above to category thresholds. Thus, the model requires the categories to be ordered for difficulty, as in typical rating scales. The model looks like the 2PL model presented earlier for dichotomous data, but the item difficulty parameter is defined differently:

$$P(X_{ij} = 1 \mid \theta_j) = \frac{\exp \alpha_i(\theta_j - \beta_{ik})}{1 + \exp \alpha_i(\theta_j - \beta_{ik})} \qquad (17.15)$$

where β_{ik} is the difficulty or location of category threshold k for item i, α_i is item discrimination, and θ_j is trait level. Notice that item difficulty now refers to a response category. In the GRM, Equation 17.15 directly models the probability that a response falls in category k or higher. Figure 17.7 shows the operating-characteristic curves for a rating item with five ordered categories. These curves appear to be ICCs for four items. Instead, they represent the transition between adjacent categories for one rating-scale item. Since the probability of responding in category 1 or higher is 1.0, given no missing data, only four curves are needed to represent the five categories in the item. The four curves model the following response probabilities: category 2 or higher $(x > 1)$, category 3 or higher $(x > 2)$, category 4 or higher $(x > 3)$, and category 5. In Figure 17.7 the intervals between the category thresholds happen to be uniformly ordered on the latent trait, but more often they are not.

Figure 17.8 shows the category response probabilities, which are the probabilities of responding in a particular

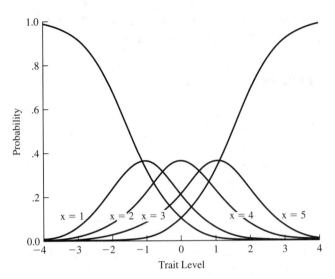

Figure 17.8 Category response curves for an item from the graded response model.

TABLE 17.4 LLTM Weights and Standard Errors for SLAT Items

Complexity Factor	Weight a_k	Standard Error	Significance, t
Degrees, linear	.350	.038	9.211[**]
Degrees, quadratic	−.029	.020	−.145
Surfaces, linear	.715	.039	18.333[**]
Surfaces, quadratic	.098	.020	4.900[**]
Constant	.084		

Note. [**] $p < .01$.

category on an item at various trait levels. These may be computed in the GRM by subtracting adjacent operating characteristic curves. Notice that five curves are given in this case. The lowest category, $x = 1$, has a decreasing probability as trait level increases. The probabilities for the middle categories ($x = 2$, $x = 3$, and $x = 4$) peak at successively higher trait levels and then decrease. For example, a response in category 2 first increases but then decreases with trait levels as responses in the higher categories gain in likelihood. Last, the highest category probability increases steadily with trait level.

Beyond the adaptation to a polytomous item format, the rating scale models have the same advantages and potential as do the binary IRT models described earlier. Item banking, adaptive testing, population-invariance of parameter estimates, and so forth are all applicable to tests built with polytomous IRT models and will not be elaborated further here.

Models With Restricted Parameters: Linear Logistic Test Model

The linear logistic test model (LLTM) was developed by Fischer (1973) to predict item difficulty (b values) from item-complexity design features. These complexity design features can represent stimuli that determine the difficulty of underlying cognitive processes (see Embretson, 1998). Currently, conditional maximum likelihood is used to estimate the LLTM weights, using software such as LPCMWin (Fischer & Pocony-Seliger, 1998) or LINLOG (Whitely & Nieh, 1981). LLTM also has been extended to the polytomous case.

The LLTM contains a model of item difficulty, rather than parameters for item difficulty. The LLTM models item

difficulty as follows:

$$\beta_i^* = a_k q_{ik} + \cdots + d \qquad (17.16)$$

Where β_i^* is the predicted item difficulty, α_k is the LLTM weight on the complexity factor q_{ik}, q_{ik} is the design complexity score for an item i provided by the researcher, and d is a normalization constant, given by LLTM. For example, a test design of four complexity factors has four $a_k q_{ik}$ products.

An illustration for SLAT items is given in Table 17.4. The LLTM weights and their standard errors, as well as significance in the model, are shown. Notice that these weights are very similar to multiple linear regression in which the dependent variable is item difficulty. The weights applied are the design factor scores for Degrees and Surfaces design factors, supplied by the researcher. The predicted b value is a sum of these four products and the normalization constant, using Equation 17.16.

In test analysis the researcher can evaluate a set of design factors by comparing the LLTM to a simple 1PL model using chi-square fit statistics. A fit statistic similar to a multiple correlation coefficient may also be applied (Embretson, 1997). In the example given in Table 17.4, the model comparison indicated a significantly better fit to the data by using the LLTM (see Embretson & Schmidt McCollam, 2000). After discovering a relatively superior LLTM fit to the data, the researcher can use predicted b values to anticipate the difficulty of new items generated by the same design principles.

Summary

IRT differs qualitatively from CTT because it includes a full model of test behavior in terms of person attributes and item properties. Three basic IRT models were introduced, as well as some more complex models that are able to handle the diverse data of psychological research and testing. It was shown that the common scale measurement of persons and items in IRT models allows for an item-referenced basis for score meaning, as well as the more traditional norm-referenced meaning. The item properties for the basic model were described and illustrated with an example. Some major advantages of IRT stem from its measurement scale properties—specifically, invariance of estimates over populations and items. For example, the capability to equate scores over widely different item subsets results from the item invariance property.

Estimation was shown to differ qualitatively from CTT; it involves a search process to maximize data likelihood rather than a direct calculation on the data. Specialized computer programs are available to obtain IRT estimates. Test development with IRT was elaborated, including the issues of model selection, person fit, and item selection. Test evaluation was discussed and, except for internal consistency reliability, was comparable to CTT. Last, two IRT models for complex data were briefly introduced: rating scales and item parameters linked to substantive sources.

IRT differs from CTT in several ways but has three primary advantages. First, IRT measurements need not be based on parallel or equated forms. Trait levels are estimated in the context of an IRT model that includes the properties of the items that were administered. Scores may be estimated on comparable bases. Second, the estimates of reliability for trait-level estimates are individualized, not population-specific. Measurement error depends simply on the appropriateness and quality of the items for individual trait levels. Third, item properties are linked directly to test behavior. Items may be selected to maximize measurement precision for each individual, rather than a population as a whole. These various capabilities allow for adaptive testing, where items are selected individually to minimize measurement error. This results in shorter and more precise measurements. Fourth, special IRT models have capabilities to link substantive aspects of test design to measurement. The LLTM was introduced and illustrated with a spatial ability test for which high levels of prediction of item difficulty were obtained.

OVERALL SUMMARY OF IRT AND ABILITY MEASUREMENT

This chapter overviews two major methods involved in the development and evaluation of psychological measures: CTT and IRT. The former was developed at the beginning of the last century and guided measurement practices for most of the century, whereas the latter was developed in the last part of the century. IRT has many advantages over CTT and is rapidly becoming the method of choice for new or revised tests. Although it was not possible to give extended coverage to IRT, and although the method is admittedly complex, a brief review of major features and some advantages was given. As the specialized computer programs for IRT become more user-friendly and accessible, psychologists will find IRT to be an increasingly valuable basis for their measures.

REFERENCES

American Psychological Association, American Educational Research Association, National Council on Measurement in Education. (1999). *Standards for educational and psychological tests.* Washington, DC: American Psychological Association.

Anastasi, A., & Urbina, S. (1997). *Psychological testing* (7th ed.). Upper Saddle River, NJ: Prentice Hall.

Andrich, D. (1978). A rating formulation for ordered response categories. *Psychometrika, 43,* 561–573.

Beck, A. T., & Steer, R. A., & Brown, G. K. (1996). *The Beck Depression Inventory-II: Manual.* San Antonio, TX: The Psychological Corporation.

Bock, R. D. (1997). A brief history of item response theory. *Educational Measurement: Issues and Practices,* (Winter), 21–33.

Bock, R. D., Gibbons, R., & Muraki, E. J. (1988). Full information item factor analysis. *Applied Psychological Measurement, 12,* 261–280.

Butcher, J. N., Dahlstrom, W. G., Graham, J. R., Tellegen, A., & Kaemmer, B. (1989). *MMPI-2: Manual for administration and scoring.* Minneapolis: University of Minnesota.

Campbell, D. T., & Fiske, D. W. (1959). Convergent and discriminant validity by the multitrait-multimethod matrix. *Psychological Bulletin, 56,* 81–105.

Cook, T. D., & Campbell, D. T. (1979). *Quasi-experimentation: Design & field analysis for field settings.* Boston: Houghton Mifflin.

Crocker, L. M., & Algina, J. (1986). *Introduction to classical and modern test theory.* Orlando, FL: Harcourt-Brace.

Cronbach, L. J. (1951). Coefficient alpha and the internal structure of tests. *Psychometrika, 16,* 297–334.

Cronbach, L. J., & Meehl, P. (1955). Construct validity in psychological tests. *Psychological Bulletin, 52,* 281–302.

Cronbach, L. J., Gleser, G. C., Nanda, H., & Rajaratnam, N. (1972). *The dependability of behavioral measurements: Theory of generalizability for scores and profiles.* New York: Wiley.

Daniel, M. H. (1999). Behind the scenes: Using new measurement methods on the DAS and KAIT. In S. E. Embretson & S. L. Hershberger (Eds.), *The new rules of measurement: What every psychologist and educator should know* (pp. 37–63). Mahwah, NJ: Erlbaum.

Embretson, S. E. (1983). Construct validity: Construct representation versus nomothetic span. *Psychological Bulletin, 93,* 179–197.

Embretson, S. E. (1989). *Spatial Learning Ability Test (SLAT).* Lawrence, KS: University of Kansas.

Embretson, S. E. (1997). Multicomponent response models. In W. J. van der Linden & R. K. Hambleton (Eds.), *Handbook of modern item response theory* (pp. 305–322). New York: Springer.

Embretson, S. E. (1998). A cognitive design system approach to generating valid tests: Application to abstract reasoning. *Psychological Methods, 3,* 300–396.

Embretson, S. E., & Schmidt McCollam, K. M. (2000). A multicomponent Rasch model for measuring covert processes: Application to lifespan ability changes. In M. Wilson & G. Engelhard (Eds.), *Objective measurement: Theory into practice* (Vol. 5, pp. 203–218). Upper Saddle River, NJ: Ablex.

Embretson, S. E., & Reise, S. P. (2000). *Item response theory for psychologists.* Mahwah, NJ: Erlbaum.

Feldt, L.S., & Brennan, R. (1989). Reliability. In R. L. Linn (Ed.), *Educational measurement* (3rd ed., pp. 105–146). New York: Macmillan.

Fischer, G. (1973). The linear logistic test model as an instrument in educational research. *Acta Psychologica, 37,* 359–374.

Fischer, G., & Molenaar, I. (1995). *Rasch models: Foundations, recent developments and applications.* New York: Springer-Verlag.

Fischer, G., & Pocony-Seliger, E. (1998). *LPCMWin manual.* Groningen: Netherlands: ProGAMMA.

Gulliksen, H. (1950). *Theory of mental tests.* New York: Wiley.

Hambleton, R. K., Swaminathan, H., & Rogers, H. J. (1991). *Fundamentals of item response theory.* Newbury Park, CA: Sage.

Holland, P. W. (1990). On the sampling theory foundations of item response theory models. *Psychometrika, 55,* 577–601.

Holland, P., & Rubin, D. (1982). *Test equating.* New York: Academic Press.

Hunter, J. E. (1986). Cognitive ability, cognitive aptitude, job knowledge, and job performance. *Journal of Vocational Behavior, 29,* 340–362.

Kuder, G. W., & Richardson, M. W. (1937). The theory of estimation of test reliability. *Psychometrika, 2,* 151–160.

Lee, W. C., Brennan, R. L., & Kolen, M. J. (2000). Estimators of conditional scale-score standard errors of measurement: A simulation study. *Journal of Educational Measurement, 37,* 1–20.

Linacre, J. M., & Wright, B. D. (2001). A *user's guide to Winsteps.* Chicago: MESA Press.

Lord, F. (1953). The relation of test score to the trait underlying the test. *Educational and Psychological Measurement, 13,* 517–548.

Lord, F. N., & Novick, M. R. (1968). *Statistical theories of mental test scores.* Reading, MA: Addison-Wesley.

Luce, R. D., & Tukey, J. W. (1964). Simultaneous conjoint measurement. *Journal of Mathematical Psychology, 1,* 1–27.

Masters, G. N. (1982). A Rasch model for partial credit scoring. *Psychometrika, 47,* 149–174.

McCollam, K. M. (1997). *The modifiability of age differences in spatial visualization.* Unpublished doctoral dissertation, Lawrence, KS: University of Kansas.

McDonald, R. P. (1999). *Test theory: A unified treatment.* Mahwah, NJ: Erlbaum.

Messick, S. (1995). Validity of psychological assessment: Validation of inferences from persons' responses and performances as scientific inquiry into score meaning. *American Psychologist, 50,* 741–749.

Mislevy, R. J., & Bock, R. D. (1990). *BILOG 3: Item analysis and test scoring with binary logistic models.* Chicago: Scientific Software International.

Muraki, E., & Bock, R. D. (1997). *PARSCALE: IRT Item analysis and test scoring for rating-scale data.* Chicago: Scientific Software International.

Murphy, L. L., Impara, J. C., & Blake, B.S. (1999). *Tests in print V* (vols. 1–2). Lincoln, NE: Buros Mental Measurements Institute.

Rasch, G. (1961). On general laws and the meaning of measurement in psychology. *Proceedings of the Fourth Berkeley Symposium on Mathematical Statistics and Probability, 4,* 321–333.

Reise, S. P,. & Flannery, W. P. (1996). Assessing person-fit on measures of typical performance. *Applied Measurement in Education, 9,* 9–26.

Rost, J. (1990). Rasch models in latent classes: An integration of two approaches to item analysis. *Applied Psychological Measurement, 14,* 271–282.

Rulon, P. J. (1939). A simplified procedure for determining the reliability of a test with split halves. *Harvard Educational Review, 9,* 99–103.

Samejima, F. (1969). Estimation of latent ability using a response pattern of graded scores. *Psychometrika Monograph,* No. 17.

Schmidt McCollam, K. M. (1998). Latent trait and latent class theory models. In G. M. Marcoulides (Ed.), *Modern methods for business research* (pp. 23–46). Mahwah, NJ: Erlbaum.

Shavelson, R. J., & Webb, N. M. (1991). *Generalizability theory: A primer.* Newbury Park, CA: Sage.

Sheridan, B., Andrich, D., & Luo, G. (1996). *RUMM: Rasch unidimensional measurement models.* Duncraig, Western Australia: Rasch Analyst.

Traub, R. E. (1994). *Reliability for the social sciences: Theory and applications* (Vol. 3). Newbury Park, CA: Sage.

Wang, W.-C., Wilson, M., & Adams, R. J. (1997). Rasch models for multidimensionality between and within items. In M. Wilson & G. Engelhard (Eds.), *Objective measurement: Theory into practice, 4,* 139–156.

Wechsler, D. (1997). The *Wechsler Adult Intelligence Scale-III.* San Antonio, TX: The Psychological Corporation.

Whitely, S. E. (1980). Multicomponent latent trait models for ability tests. *Psychometrika, 45,* 479–494.

Whitely, S. E., & Dawis, R. V. (1974). The nature of the objectivity with the Rasch model. *Journal of Educational Measurement, 11,* 163–178.

Whitely, S. E., & Nieh, K. (1981). *Program LINLOG* (National Institute of Education Technical Report No. NIE-81-3). Lawrence: University of Kansas.

Wright, B. D., & Stone, M. H. (1979). *Best test design.* Chicago: MESA Press.

CHAPTER 18

Growth Curve Analysis in Contemporary Psychological Research

JOHN J. McARDLE AND JOHN R. NESSELROADE

PREFACE

The term *growth curve* was originally used to describe a graphic display of the physical stature (e.g., the height or weight) of an individual over consecutive ages. Growth curves have unique features: (a) The same entities are repeatedly observed, (b) the same procedures of measurement and scaling of observations are used, and (c) the timing of the observations is known. The term *growth curve analysis*

denotes the processes of describing, testing hypotheses, and making scientific inferences about the growth and change patterns in a wide range of time-related phenomena. In this sense, growth curve analyses are a specific form of the larger set of developmental and longitudinal research methods, but the unique features of growth data permit unique kinds of analyses.

Contemporary methods of growth curve analysis are considered here. Of course, the techniques to analyze growth data are among the most widely studied and well-developed mathematical and statistical techniques in all scientific research— growth curve analyses have roots in the seventeenth- and eighteenth-century calculus of Newton and probability of Pascal—but this chapter is concerned with more recent historical developments. Techniques for the analysis of growth curves were initiated in the physical sciences and were more

The work described here has been supported since 1980 by the National Institute on Aging (Grant #AG-07137). This research was made possible by the support of our many friends and colleagues, including Steve Aggen, Dick Bell, Steve Boker, Aki Hamagami, Earl Hishinuma, John Horn, Bill Meredith, Carol Prescott, and Dick Woodcock.

fully developed in the biological sciences, where they were used in studies of the size and health of plants, animals, and humans. In the behavioral sciences, growth curve analyses have routinely been applied to a wide range of phenomena—from experimental learning curves, to the growth and decline of intellectual abilities and academic achievements, to changes in other psychological traits over the full life span.

These formal models for the analysis of growth curves have been developed in many different substantive domains, but all share a common goal—to examine and uncover a fundamental set of regularity conditions, or basic functions, responsible for the manifest growth and change. The goals of these models were organized in terms of five "objectives of longitudinal research" and described by Baltes and Nesselroade (1979, pp. 21–27) using the following enumeration:

1. The direct identification of *intra-* (within-) individual change
2. The direct identification of *inter-* (between-) individual differences in intra-individual change
3. The analysis of *interrelationships* in change
4. The analysis of *causes* (determinants) of intra-individual change
5. The analysis of *causes* (determinants) of interindividual differences in intra-individual change

In this chapter, growth curve analyses are related to these objectives of longitudinal research. In current statistical methodology, *intra-individual* is termed *within-person* and *interindividual* is termed *between-person,* but these remain the essential goals of most longitudinal data analyses (e.g., Campbell, 1988; McArdle & Bell, 2000).

This chapter is organized into the following sections: (a) an introduction to growth curves, (b) linear models of growth, (c) multiple groups in growth curve models, (d) aspects of dynamic theory for growth models, and (e) multiple variables in growth curve analyses. The chapter then concludes with a discussion of future issues raised by the current growth models. In all sections we try to present historical perspective to illustrate different kinds of mathematical and statistical issues for the analyses of these data.

The growth curve models are presented in basic algebraic detail, but this presentation is not intended to be overly technical. Instead, we focus on the mathematical formulation, statistical estimation, and substantive interpretation of *latent growth curve* analyses. This focus allows us to show a range of new models and examine why some classical data analysis problems, such as the calculation of difference scores or the unreliability of errors of measurements, are no longer impediments

to development research. Other related techniques such as *time-series* and *dynamical systems* analyses are briefly discussed in the later sections of this chapter. All numerical results are based on a single set of data (the longitudinal data of Figure 18.6), and available computer software for these analyses is described. We use these illustrations to highlight both the benefits and limitations of contemporary growth curve analyses.

INTRODUCTION

Classical Growth Curve Applications

The collection of growth curve data is not a new topic. The first measurements classified as growth curve data appear to have been collected by the French Count de Montbeillard (~1759) and consist of semiannual measurements on the growth of the height of his son over the course of nearly 18 years; these data are plotted as the upper curve of Figure 18.1. As Scammon (1927) reported, "It will be noted that the curve shows the typical four phases which most modern students have observed in the postnatal growth in stature of man, and which are characteristic of the growth of so many parts of the body" (p. 331). The first analysis of these data, by the naturalist Buffon (~1799), "should be given full credit for the discovery of seasonal differences in growth a full hundred years before the modern investigation of this work" (p. 334). The lower growth curve in Figure 18.1 is based on group averages of physical growth obtained by Variot (~1908). As Scammon (1927) suggests, "it is interesting to note that, while the absolute values of the two series are quite different, the general

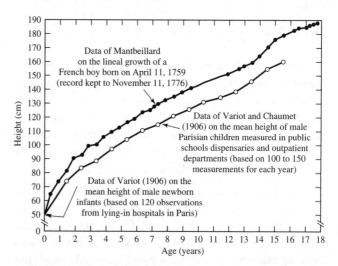

Figure 18.1   The initial growth curves of human height data from Scammon (1927, p. 334); the vertical (*y*) axis represents the height in cm and the horizontal (*x*) axis represents the age in years from birth.

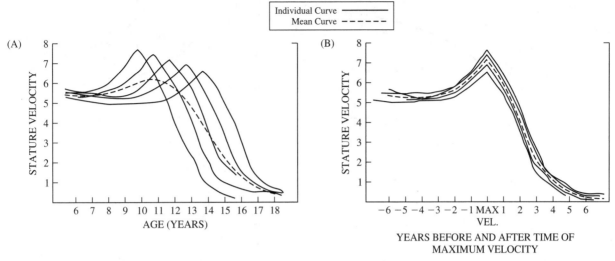

Figure 18.2   Alternative velocity curves of physical stature from Tanner (1960, p. 22); (a) The change in height as a function of the change in time (y) versus the age in years (x); (b) the same curves (y) plotted around the time of maximum change in scores (x) for each individual.

form of the curve is essentially the same in both instances" (p. 335).

These early growth curves were precursors to the collection of an enormous body of biological data on growth and change. More recent illustrations come from the important work of Tanner and his colleagues (1955, 1960). In the individual plots of height in Figure 18.2, (a) the *velocity of change* is plotted at each age, and (b) these curves are plotted against their own *highest peak velocity*. This display demonstrated two interesting features of physical growth: (a) Persons who start growth at the earliest ages also attain the greatest height, but (b) all individuals share a remarkably similar shape in the "adolescent growth spurt." This relationship between chronological time and what has been called *biological time* remains an important substantive issue.

Experimental psychologists have routinely collected different kinds of growth curves. Among the first here were the classical *forgetting curves* collected by Ebbinghaus (~1880), and this introduced the use of quantitative methods in the study of learning and memory and stimulated many experimental data collections. Other classic examples are found in the animal learning curve experiments of Thorndike (~1911), in which *trial-and-error learning* was defined by decreasing response time, and the lack of smooth function over trials was considered error. Thorndike used these growth (or decline) curves to illustrate several classical principles of learning, including the *law of exercise* and the *law of effect* (for review, see Garrett, 1951; Estes, 1959). Other classic examples are found in the *acquisition curves* presented by Estes (1959) and reproduced here in Figure 18.3. The data collected here (i.e., the dots) were measured over the same animals (rats) working

for consistent reward in a free operant Skinner box (a T-maze learning experiment), and the four plots show different aspects of the behaviors (i.e., responses, reinforcements, trials, time). These figures also show how the average probabilities and changes in probabilities were well predicted using mathematical models from statistical learning theory (Estes, 1959). The current emphasis on formal models for growth and change has obvious roots in this kind of experimental research.

Differential psychologists have also contributed growth data in many different substantive areas. One good example of this tradition is given in the plots of Figure 18.4 (from work of Bayley, 1956). Individual growth curves of mental abilities from birth to age 25 are plotted for a selected set of boys and girls from the well-known Berkeley Growth Study. Because mental ability was not easily measured in exactly the same way at each age, these individual curves were created by adjusting the means and standard deviations of different mental ability tests (i.e., Stanford-Binet, Terman-McNemar) at different ages into a common metric. As Bayley says,

They are not in "absolute" units, but they do give a general picture of growth relative to the status of this group at 16 years. These curves, too, are less regular than the height curves, but perhaps no less regular than the weight curves. One gets the impression both of differences in rates of maturing and of differences in inherent capacity." (p. 66)

This application of "linked" measurement scales created a novel set of growth data, raised many issues about the comparability of measurement over time, and permitted the use of

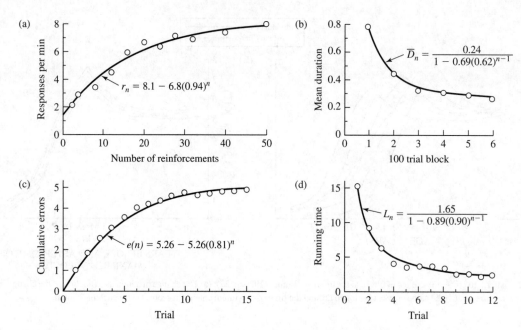

Figure 18.3 Selected acquisition curves of memory from statistical learning theory by Estes (1959).

growth curve analyses initially derived in other scientific areas.

Early work in biological research was directed at characterizing the parallel properties of different growth variables. Models were originally developed to deal with the size of two different organs, and early nineteenth-century work was used by Huxley (~1924, 1932) to form a classical *alometric*

model—two variables having a constant ratio of growth rates throughout the growth period—and many physical processes were found to grow in parallel, or in an ordered time-sequence. A good example is found in the multivariate research of Tanner (1955): Figure 18.5 is a plot of growth and change in four physical variables that were found to follow a fundamental pattern over time (i.e., a relatively invariant

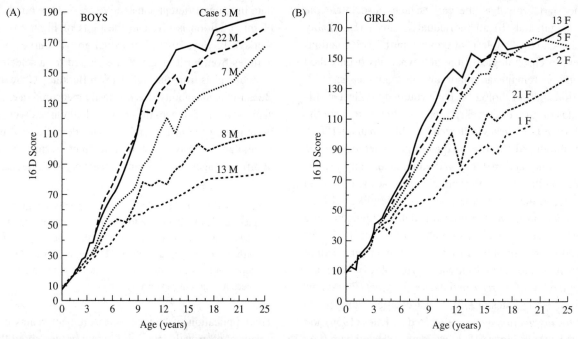

Figure 18.4 Growth curves of intellectual abilities in selected boys and girls from the Berkeley Growth Studies of Bayley (1956, p. 67); age 16 D scores (y) plotted as a function of age at measurement (x) for (a) five boys and (b) five girls.

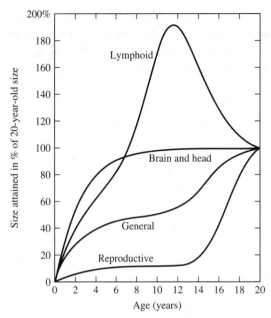

Figure 18.5 Growth curves of tissues and different parts of the body from Tanner (1955).

time-based sequence within an individual). As a result, these physical variables were thought to be indicators of some fundamental time-based dynamic processes. These basic multivariate findings, and questions about the underlying dynamics of multiple growth processes, are still key features of current research.

Classical Growth Curve Analyses

Techniques for the analysis of growth curve analyses are not novel. A classical paper by Wishart (1938) was one of the first to deal with these growth curve analysis problems in an exploratory and empirical fashion. Here, Wishart extended the classical analysis of variance (ANOVA) models to form a linear growth model with group and individual differences. Wishart also showed how power polynomials could be used to better fit the curvature apparent in growth data. The individual growth curve (consisting of $t = 1, T$ occasions) is summarized into a small set of linear orthogonal polynomial coefficients based on a power-series of time $(t, t^2, t^3, \ldots t^p)$ describing the general nonlinear shape of the growth curve. In Wishart's models, the basic shape of each individual's curve could be captured with a small number of fixed parameters and random variance components, and the average of the individual parameters could represent the group growth curve (see Cohen & Cohen, 1983; Joosens & Brems-Heynes, 1975).

More complex forms of mathematical and statistical analyses were developed to deal with growth curve data.

In his initial growth curve analyses, Ebbinghaus (~1880) described his forgetting curves using a form of the classic *exponential growth model* (see Figure 18.3) in which the rate of change is defined as a linear function of the percentage of initial size (e.g., compound interest). The Velhurst (~1839) curve of population growth, an **S**-shaped *logistic curve,* was used by Pearl (~1925) for many forms of cognitive growth. In related work, Thurstone (~1919) found that a *hyperbolic curve* of learning best fit the norms of many different tests; Peters (~1930) advocated an *ogival curve* of growth in ideational learning; and Ettlinger (~1926) and Valentine (~1930) demonstrated the relationships among these functions (see Bock & Thissen, 1980; Seber & Wild, 1989).

A popular model for physical growth was initially presented by Gompertz (~1825), who described the *derivative* (instantaneous rate of change) of the growth curve in terms of two exponential accumulations of different rates toward different asymptotes. This flexible model was studied by Winsor (~1932), used by Medwar (~1940) to study the growth of chicken hearts, and used by Deming (~1957) for human physical growth. Another popular growth model was introduced by von Bertalanffy (1938, 1957) and proposed that the individual's change in a physical variable (e.g., weight) was the direct result of the difference in opposing forces of anabolism and catabolism. Although the exact relationship among these forces was not known, von Bertalanffy used a fixed *alliometric* value (of $\gamma = 2/3$) based on prior research.

In related work on nonlinear growth models, Richards (1959) criticized and expanded the original von Bertalanffy model by demonstrating how all prior models can be seen as specific solutions of a "family" of deterministic differential equations (i.e., specific restrictions led to the exponential, logistic, Gompertz, and von Bertalanffy equations). This work was extended by Nelder (1961) and Sandland and McGhilcrest (1978; for reviews, see Sieber & Wild, 1989; Zeger & Harlow, 1987). Attempts to fit a single growth model to observations over a wide range of ages with a minimal set of parameters led researchers to combine aspects of other models. A more recent expansion based on the logistic model was developed by Preece and Baines (1978), who suggested that all previous models could be written as a derivative based on some predefined function of time and some asymptotic value. This kind of model is related to the *partial adjustment model* used in sociometrics (e.g., Coleman, 1968; Tuma & Hannan, 1984), and has proven useful in recent studies of physical growth (see Hauspie, Lindgren, Tanner, & Chrzastek-Spruch, 1991).

More complex linear (and nonlinear) models have been used to represent growth. Some of these share the common feature of a piecewise model applied to different age or time segments. These kinds of segmented or composite models have also been a mainstay of nonlinear modeling. One of the first truly nonlinear composite forms was the *Jenss curve* (or *normal exponential*), in which a linear part (to fit the early rapid-growth phase) was added at a particular age to an exponential part (to fit negative acceleration of the later slowing-down phase) by Jenss and Bayley (~1937). A more complex composite model, the sum of multiple logistic curves, was suggested by Robertson (~1908) and Burt (~1937), and fully developed by the work of Bock and his colleagues (see Bock, 1991; Bock & Thissen, 1980; Bock et al., 1973). These composite models allowed for different dynamics at different ages and represent a practically important innovation.

The logic of fitting model segments was also apparent in more recent extensions of Wishart's (1938) polynomial model. One model, based on the summations of latent curves, was proposed simultaneously by both Rao (1958) and Tucker (1958, 1966). In the early descriptions of this model, principal components analysis of the raw growth data led to the sum of a small number of unspecified linear functions. In the interpretation of these components, the shapes of the latent curves are determined by the component loadings, and the individual curve parameters are the component scores. The summation of latent curves has roots in the classical work of Fourier (~1822), but the principal components representation included individual differences. These kinds of linear growth models can offer a relatively parsimonious organization of individual differences, and we highlight these models in later applications.

This brief historical perspective demonstrates that there are many different approaches to the analysis of growth curve data. We find a tendency to introduce more general and flexible forms of growth models, but these models are often complex and each model has slightly different theoretical and practical features. One common feature that does emerge is that most growth models can be written explicitly as a set of dynamic change equations, and we return to this issue later in the chapter. Also, we consistently find efforts made to relate the growth parameters to biologically or psychologically meaningful concepts—this is a difficult but most useful goal for any growth curve analysis.

Contemporary Issues in Statistical Data Analysis

Additional kinds of growth curve analyses are presented in the next few sections. These models include classical linear and nonlinear models as well as some newer models adapted from multivariate analyses. Most of these growth models are designed to deal with the practical issues involving (a) alternative models of change, (b) unequal intervals, (c) unequal numbers of persons in different groups, (d) nonrandom attrition, (e) the altering of measures over time, and (f) multiple outcomes.

This contemporary, model-based description of change can be used to clarify some problems inherent in *observed rates of change*. The potential confounds in difference scores have been a key concern of previous methods using observed change scores or rate-of-change scores (e.g., Bereiter, 1963; Burr & Nesselroade, 1990; Cronbach & Furby, 1970; Rogosa & Willett, 1985; Willett, 1990). This research has shown that when observed rates are used as outcomes in standard regression analyses, the results can be biased by several factors, including residual error, measurement error, regression to the mean, and egression from the mean (e.g., Allison, 1990; Nesselroade & Bartsch, 1977; Nesselroade & Cable, 1974; Nesselroade, Stiegler, & Baltes, 1980; Raykov, 1999; Williams & Zimmerman, 1996). These problems can be severe when using standard linear regression with time-dependent variables (e.g., Boker & McArdle, 1995; Hamagami & McArdle, 2000).

One of the key reasons we present the contemporary modeling approach is to move beyond these classical problems. Modern statistical procedures have been developed to minimize some of these problems by fitting the model of an *implied trajectory over time* directly to the observed scores. Alternative mathematical forms of growth can be considered using different statistical restrictions. From such formal assumptions we can write the set of expectations for the means, variances, and covariances for all observed scores, and use these expectations to identify, estimate, and examine the goodness-of-fit of latent variable models representing change over time. Most of these models discussed here are based on fitting observed raw-score longitudinal growth data to a theoretical model using likelihood-based techniques (as in Little & Rubin, 1987; McArdle & Bell, 2000). In general, we find it convenient to *describe* the data using the observed change scores (defined as $\Delta Y_n / \Delta t$), but we make *inferences* about the underlying growth processes by directly estimating parameters of the latent change scores (defined as $\Delta y_n / \Delta t$).

In a recent and important innovation, Meredith and Tisak (1990) showed how the *Tuckerized curve models* (so named in recognition of Tucker's seminal contributions) could be represented and fitted using structural equation modeling of common factors. These growth modeling results were important because this made it possible to represent a wide range of alternative growth models. This work also led to interest in methodological and substantive studies of growth processes using structural equation modeling techniques (McArdle, 1986, 1997; McArdle & Anderson, 1990; McArdle & Bell, 1980; McArdle & Epstein, 1987; McArdle & Hamagami, 1991, 1992). These latent growth models have since been expanded upon and used by many others (Duncan & Duncan, 1995; McArdle & Woodcock, 1997; Metha & West, 2000; B. O. Muthen & Curran, 1997; Willett & Sayer, 1994). The contemporary basis of latent growth curve analyses can also be found in the recent developments of *multilevel models* (Bryk & Raudenbush, 1987, 1992; Goldstein, 1995) or *mixed-effects models* (Littell, Miliken, Stoup, & Wolfinger, 1996; Singer, 1999). Perhaps most important is that the work by Browne and du Toit (1991) showed how the nonlinear dynamic models could be part of this same framework (see Cudeck & du Toit, 2001; McArdle & Hamagami, 1996, 2001; Pinherio & Bates, 2000). For these reasons, the term *latent growth models* seems appropriate for any technique that describes the underlying growth in terms of latent changes using the classical assumptions (e.g., independence of residual errors).

The model-based fitting of structural assumptions about the group and individual differences holds the key to later substantive interpretations. These theoretical restrictions may not hold exactly in the examination of real data, and this leads to the general issues of model testing and goodness-of-fit. Recent research has also produced a variety of new statistical and computational procedures for the analysis of latent growth curves, and their unique features are somewhat difficult to isolate. This means that the likelihood-based approach to the estimation and fitting of growth curve analyses can be accomplished using several widely available computer packages (e.g., SAS: Littell et al., 1996, Singer, 1998, and Verneke & Molenberghs, 2000; SPlus: Pinherio & Bates, 2000; MIXREG: Hedecker & Gibbons, 1996, 1997). A few available computer programs (e.g., Mx: Neale, Boker, Xie, & Maes, 1998; AMOS: Arbuckle & Wotke, 1999, and Mplus: L. K. Muthen & Muthen, 1998), can be used to estimate the parameters of all analyses described herein.

The Bradway-McArdle Longitudinal Growth Data

To illustrate many of the issues and models in this chapter, we use some longitudinal growth data in Figure 18.6. These are age-plots of data from a recent study of intellectual abilities—the *Bradway-McArdle Longitudinal* study (see McArdle & Hamagami, 1996; McArdle, Hamagami, Meredith, & Bradway, 2000). The persons in this study were first measured in 1931, when they were aged 2 to 7 years, as part of the larger standardization sample of the Stanford-Binet test ($N = 212$). They were measured again about 10 years later

by Katherine P. Bradway as part of her doctoral dissertation in 1944 ($N = 138$). Many of these same persons were measured twice more by Bradway as adults at average ages of 30 and 42 using the Wechsler Adult Intelligence Scales (WAIS, $N = 111$; for further details, see Bradway & Thompson, 1962; Kangas & Bradway, 1971). About half ($n = 55$) of the adolescents tested in 1944 were measured again in 1984 (at ages 55 to 57), and between 1993 and 1997 at ages ranging from 64 to 72; 34 were tested in 1993 through 1997 on the WAIS (McArdle, Hamagami, et al., 2001).

These plots illustrate further complexity that needs to be dealt with in longitudinal growth curve analyses. The first plot (Panel A of Figure 18.6) gives individual growth curve data for verbal ability (Rasch scaled) at each age at testing for $n = 29$ individuals who were measured at each time of testing, and for the $n = 82$ persons who were measured at some (but not all) ages of testing. The second plot of Figure 18.6 (Panel B) is a similar plot for data from nonverbal measurements. The comparison of Panels A and B is informative, and leads to important practical issues in subject recruitment and attrition in longitudinal studies. Although not depicted here, multiple variables from the Stanford-Binet and the WAIS have been repeatedly measured, including separate measures of *verbal* (or *knowledge*) ability, and of nonverbal (or *reasoning*) ability (for details, see McArdle, Hamagami, Horn, & Bradway, 2002).

Table 18.1 is a listing of numerical information from this study to be used in subsequent examples of growth curve analyses. The overall subject participation is listed in Panel A of Table 18.1, and here we can see the nearly continual loss of participants over time. The means and standard deviations for two composite variables are listed in Panel B, and here we find early increases followed by less change in the later years. The correlations of these measures over six occasions are listed in Panel C, and here we find a complex pattern of results, with some correlations suggesting high stability of individual differences (e.g., $r > .9$) and others suggesting low stability ($r < .1$). The summary information presented in Panels B and C is limited to those $n = 29$ participants with complete data at all six time points of measurement, but information on $N = 111$ available through adulthood is used in the growth curve examples to follow.

As with any data-oriented study, the information in this data set has some clear limitations (e.g., Pinneau, 1961). Among these, the participants are all from one birth cohort (~1928), in the same geographical area (San Francisco), of one ethnicity (Caucasian), and come from volunteer families with above-average socioeconomic status; moreover, most of them score above average on most cognitive tasks. Whereas

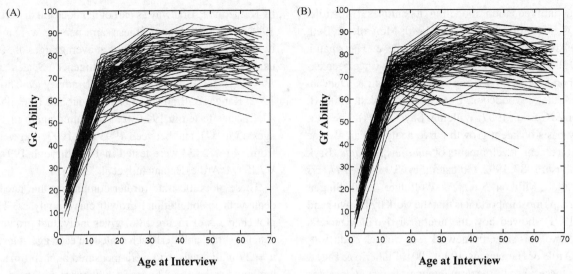

Figure 18.6   Growth curves of verbal (Gc) and nonverbal (Gf) abilities in complete and incomplete data from the Bradway Longitudinal Growth Study (see McArdle, Hamagami, Bradway & Meredith, 2001); Rasch scaled scores (*y*) plotted as a function of age at measurement (*x*) for (a) *N* = 29 participants with complete data and (b) *N* = 82 participants with incomplete data.

TABLE 18.1   Description of the Bradway-McArdle Longitudinal Study Data

A. Subject Ascertainment History

Category	Time 1 Age 2–7 *N* (%)	Time 2 Age 12–17 *N* (%)	Time 3 Age 28–32 *N* (%)	Time 4 Age 40–43 *N* (%)	Time 5 Age 55–58 *N* (%)	Time 6 Age 63–66 *N* (%)
Tested	212 (100.)	138 (65.)	111 (80.)	48 (43.)	53 (48.)	51 (46.)
Inaccessible	0 (0.)	0 (0.)	0 (0.)	7 (6.)	5 (5.)	6 (5.)
Deceased	0 (0.)	0 (0.)	0 (0.)	2 (2.)	9 (8.)	19 (17)
Refused testing	0 (0.)	0 (0.)	0 (0.)	7 (6.)	1 (1.)	12 (11.)
Not located	0 (0.)	74 (35.)	27 (20.)	47 (42.)	43 (39.)	23 (21.)

B. Means and Standard Deviations (*N* = 29)

Variables	Time 1 Age 4	Time 2 Age 14	Time 3 Age 30	Time 4 Age 42	Time 5 Age 57	Time 6 Age 65
Nonverbal mean	25.55	70.40	80.06	82.99	80.60	78.64
(nonverbal S.D.)	(12.61)	(5.89)	(7.87)	(7.84)	(7.53)	(7.80)
Verbal means	22.22	65.84	75.65	78.76	80.70	77.97
(verbal S.D.)	(8.80)	(7.37)	(9.20)	(8.23)	(7.86)	(7.59)

C. Correlations of Nonverbal and Verbal Scores (*N* = 29)

	NV_4	NV_{14}	NV_{30}	NV_{42}	NV_{57}	NV_{65}	V_4	V_{14}	V_{30}	V_{42}	V_{57}	V_{65}
NV_4	1.00											
NV_{14}	.12	1.00										
NV_{30}	−.10	.37	1.00									
NV_{42}	−.04	.19	.81	1.00								
NV_{57}	−.02	.20	.85	.82	1.00							
NV_{65}	.02	.25	.78	.85	.83	1.00						
V_4	.92	.16	−.03	−.08	.03	.02	1.00					
V_{14}	.28	.68	.18	.05	.03	.16	.36	1.00				
V_{30}	−.02	.25	.56	.45	.41	.57	.09	.43	1.00			
V_{42}	.07	.26	.53	.37	.42	.50	.24	.27	.83	1.00		
V_{57}	−.01	.21	.50	.37	.36	.44	.15	.38	.91	.89	1.00	
V_{65}	.02	.24	.52	.46	.41	.56	.10	.35	.85	.77	.90	1.00

the longitudinal age span and the number of measures taken are large, the number of occasions of measurement was limited by practical concerns (e.g., cooperation, fatigue, and practice effects). The benefits and limitations of these classic longitudinal data make it possible to examine both the benefits and limitations of the new models for the growth and change discussed in this chapter.

THE BASIC STRUCTURE OF GROWTH MODELS

Growth Models of Within-Person Changes

Growth curve data are characterized as having multiple observations based on *longitudinal* or *repeated measures.* Assume we observe variable Y at multiple occasions (in brackets, $t = 1$ to T) on some persons (in subscripts, $n = 1$ to N), and we write

$$Y[t]_n = y_{0,n} + A[t]\,y_{s,n} + e[t]_n \qquad (18.1)$$

where the y_0 are scores representing an individual's initial level (e.g., intercept); the y_s are scores representing the individual *linear change over time* (e.g., slopes); the set of coefficients $A[t]$ are termed *basis weights,* used to define the timing or shape of the change over time for the group (e.g., age at testing); and the $e[t]$ are error scores at each measurement.

The latent-change model is constant *within* an individual but it is not assumed to be the same *between* individuals (with subscripts n). The unobserved variables that presumably do not change over time are written in lowercase (y_0, y_s) are similar to the predicted (i.e., nonerror) scores in a standard regression equation. We can write

$$y_{0,n} = \mu_0 + e_{0,n} \quad \text{and} \quad y_{s,n} = \mu_s + e_{s,n}, \qquad (18.2)$$

where the group means (μ_0, μ_s) are fixed effects for the intercept and the slopes and the new scores are deviations (e_0, e_s) around these means. We can define additional features of these scores using standard expected value ($E\{y\}$) notation. First we presume the means of all deviations scores are zero (i.e., $E\{e\} = 0$). Next, we define the nonzero variance and covariance terms as

$$E\{e_0, e_0\} = \sigma_0^2, \quad E\{e_s, e_s\} = \sigma_s^2, \quad E\{e_0, e_s\} = \sigma_{0s}, \quad \text{and}$$

$$E\{e[t], e[t]\} = \sigma_e^2, \qquad (18.3)$$

so these individual differences around the means are termed *random effects* (σ_0^2, σ_s^2, σ_{0s}). In many applications we assume only one random error variance (σ_e^2) at all occasions of

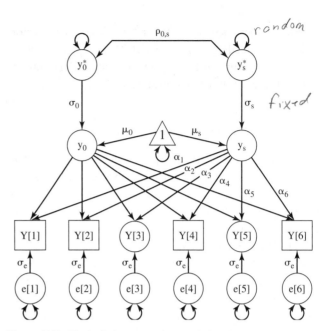

Figure 18.7 The basic latent growth structural model as a path diagram from McArdle & Epstein (1987) and McArdle & Hamagami (1992).

measurement. As in classical regression analyses, the validity of the interpretations is are limited by the most basic model assumptions—for example, linearity, additivity, independence of residuals, independence of other effects, no interactions, and so on.

In order to clarify growth models, we can use a *path diagram* such as the one displayed as Figure 18.7. These kinds of diagrams were originally only used with regression models, but more recently have been used in the context of growth and change (e.g., see McArdle, 1986; McArdle & Aber, 1990; Wright, 1934). In this representation the observed variables are drawn as squares, the unobserved variables are drawn as circles, and the implied unit constant (i.e., scores of 1 before the intercept parameter in Equation 18.1) is included as a triangle. Model parameters representing fixed or group coefficients are drawn as one-headed arrows, while random or individual features are drawn as two-headed arrows. The observed variables ($Y[t]$) are seen to be produced by latent intercepts (y_0) with unit weights, by the latent slopes (y_s) with weights ($A[t] = [\alpha[1], \alpha[2], \ldots \alpha[T]]$), and by an individual error term ($e[t]$).

Following Equations 18.2 and 18.3, the initial level and slopes are often assumed to be random variables with fixed means (μ_0, μ_s) but random variances (σ_0^2, σ_s^2) and covariances ($\sigma_{0,s}$). The standard deviations (σ_0, σ_s) are sometimes drawn in the picture to permit the direct representation of the covariances as scaled correlations ($\rho_{0,s}$). The error terms are assumed to be distributed with a mean of zero, a single variance (σ_e^2), and no correlation with any of the other latent scores (further statistical tests may assume these errors follow a normal distribution as well). These formal structural assumptions distinguish these latent growth models from the other kinds of analyses of growth data.

Considering Alternative Growth Models

As in any form of data analysis, a growth model can be evaluated only in relation to other possibilities. A first set of alternative models might be based on simplifications of the previous model parameters. In this kind of *trajectory equation*, the $Y[t]$ is formed for each group and individual from the $A[t]$ basis coefficients. These coefficients also determine the metric or scaling and interpretation of these scores, so alterations of $A[t]$ can lead to many different models.

As a simple example, suppose we require all coefficients $A[t] = 0$, and effectively eliminate all slope parameters. This leads to a simple additive model

$$Y[t]_n = y_{0,n} + e[t]_n, \tag{18.4}$$

where only the intercept y_0 and the $e[t]$ error terms are included. As later shown, this model is termed a *baseline* or *no-growth alternative* because it is consistent with observations only where there is no change over time in the means, variances, or correlations.

Other simple growth curve analyses are based on simple mathematical functions, and the fitting of a straight line to a set of measures is a standard procedure in scientific research. So, as a next example, let us assume there are $T = 4$ time points and we have set the basis $A[t] = [0, 1, 2, 3]$. Following Equation 18.1, this leads to a set of linear equations where

$$\begin{aligned} Y[1]_n &= y_{0,n} + 0y_{s,n} + e[1]_n, \\ Y[2]_n &= y_{0,n} + 1y_{s,n} + e[2]_n, \\ Y[3]_n &= y_{0,n} + 2y_{s,n} + e[3]_n, \quad \text{and} \\ Y[4]_n &= y_{0,n} + 3y_{s,n} + e[4]_n. \end{aligned} \tag{18.5}$$

At the first time point the specific coefficient $a[1] = 0$, so the slope term drops out of the expression and the score at the first time point is composed of only the intercept plus an error. At the second time point, $a[2] = 1$, so the score is the sum of the intercept (y_0) plus a change over time (y_s) plus a new error score ($e[2]$). At the third time point, $a[3] = 2$, so the score is the sum of the intercept (y_0) plus 2 times the prior change over time ($2y_s$) plus a new error ($e[3]$). At the fourth time point, $a[4] = 3$, so the score is the sum of the intercept

(y_0) plus three times the prior change over time ($3y_s$) plus a new error ($e[4]$). Each additional score would add another weighted change and a new error term. The basic interpretation would change only slightly if we altered the linear basis to be $A[t] = [1, 2, 3, 4]$, because now the intercept (where $t = 0$) is presumably prior to the first time point. A different change of the linear basis to be $A[t] = [0.00, 0.33, 0.67, 1.00]$, would have the effect of shifting the units of the slope to units to be a proportion of the entire range of time but we would still be considering straight-line change.

In contrast, other alterations of the basis coefficients can alter the interpretation of the shape of the changes. For example, if we redefine $A[t] = [1, 2, 2, 1]$, then the model does not represent straight-line change—instead, the basis represents a curve that starts up (1 to 2), flattens out (2 to 2), and then goes back down (2 to 1). Other, more complex alterations of the basis will lead to more complex trajectory models.

As in all linear models, the set of loadings ($A[t]$) defines the shape of the group curve over time. In a latent basis model approach (Meredith & Tisak, 1990), we allow the curve basis to take on a shape based on the empirical data. We fit a factor model based on the standard linear model (Equation 18.1) as before, with two common factor scores, an intercept (y_0) with unit loadings, a linear slope (y_s), and independent unique factor scores ($e[t]$); but the factor loadings ($A[t]$) are now estimated from the data. The two common factor scores account for the means and covariances, and the estimated factor loadings each describe a weight or *saturation* of the slope at a specific time of measurement. The $A[t]$ are estimated as factor loadings and have the usual mathematical and statistical identification problems of any factor analysis. This means we fit the latent basis model as

$$\begin{aligned} Y[1]_n &= y_{0,n} + 0y_{s,n} + e[1]_n, \\ Y[2]_n &= y_{0,n} + 1y_{s,n} + e[2]_n, \\ Y[3]_n &= y_{0,n} + \alpha[3]y_{s,n} + e[3]_n, \quad \text{and} \\ Y[4]_n &= y_{0,n} + \alpha[4]y_{s,n} + e[4]_n. \end{aligned} \tag{18.6}$$

In the typical case, at least one entry of the $A[t]$ will be fixed as, say, $a[1] = 1$, to provide a reference point for the other model parameters. If a nonzero covariance (σ_{0s}) among common factors is allowed, then two fixed values (e.g., $a[1] = 0$ and $a[2] = 1$), can be used to distinguish the factor scores and assure overall model identification (as in McArdle & Cattell, 1994). The other parameters are allowed to be freely estimated (e.g., Greek notation for the estimated parameters $\alpha[3]$ and $\alpha[4]$), so we obtain what should be an *optimal shape* for the group curve. Change from any one time to another ($\Delta y_n / \Delta t$) is a function of the slope score (y_s) and the change in the factor loadings ($\Delta A[t]$).

We may now consider a variety of more complex models. One simple version of a quadratic polynomial growth model can be written as

$$Y[t]_n = y_{0n} + A[t]y_{1n} + \frac{1}{2}A[t]^2 y_{2n} + e[t]_n, \quad (18.7)$$

where the $A[t]$ are fixed at known values, and a new component (y_2) is introduced to represent the change in the change (i.e., the *acceleration*). This implies the expected growth curve may turn direction at least once in a nonlinear (i.e., parabolic) fashion. The additional latent score (y_2) is allowed to have a mean (μ_2) and a variance (σ_2^2) and to be correlated with the other latent scores ($\rho_{0,2}$, $\rho_{1,2}$). Any set of growth data might require a second-order (quadratic), third-order (cubic), or even higher order polynomial model. In each of these alternatives, however, more complexity is added because any pth-order model includes p latent means, $p + 1$ latent variances and $p(p - 1)/2$ covariance terms for the group and individual differences across all observations.

A variety of other growth models can now be studied using this general linear framework. For example, the linear polynomial model (Equation 18.7) could be fitted with orthogonal polynomial constraints, or in an alternative form (e.g., Stimpson, Carmines, & Zeller, 1978), or even with a latent basis (i.e., $\alpha[t]$ and $\frac{1}{2}\alpha[t]^2$). Also, in each model listed previously, it is possible to add assumptions about the structure of the relationships among the residual terms ($e[t]$). We can consider specific-factor terms and consider alternative mechanisms for their construction (e.g., autoregressive, increasing over time, etc.). These *structured residual models* are valuable in statistical efforts to improve the precision, fit, and forecasts of the model, but they do not provide the substantive information we use here (but see Cnaan, Laird, & Slasor, 1997; Littell et al., 1996).

Expectations and Estimation in Linear Growth Models

The parameters of any growth model lead to a set of expectations for the observed data, and these expectations will be used in subsequent model fitting. The previous assumptions can be combined to form the expected trajectories over time. This can be calculated from the *algebra of expectations* (with sums of average cross-products symbolized as $E\{YX'\}$) or from the tracing rules of path analysis (see McArdle & Aber, 1990; Wright, 1934). Using either approach, the observed mean at any occasion can be written in terms of the linear

model parameters as

$$\mu_{Y[t]} = E\{Y[t]1'\} = \mu_0 + A[t]\mu_s, \quad (18.8)$$

(where the constant vector **1** is again used). This implies the mean at any time ($\mu_{Y[t]}$) is the initial-level mean (μ_0) plus the slope mean (μ_s) weighted by the specific basis coefficient ($A[t]$) that is either fixed or estimated. This also implies that changes in the basis weights determine all changes in the mean trajectory.

The expectation of the observed score variance at any occasion can be written as

$$\sigma_{Y[t]}^2 = E\{(Y[t] - \mu_{Y[t]})^2\} = \sigma_0^2 + \sigma_{y[t]}^2 + \sigma_e^2$$
$$= \sigma_0^2 + (A[t]\sigma_s^2 A[t] + A[t]\sigma_{0s} + \sigma_{0s}A[t]) + \sigma_e^2. \quad (18.9)$$

This implies the observed variance at any time ($\sigma_{Y[t]}^2$) is the sum of the initial-level variance (σ_0^2) plus the variance of the latent changes ($\sigma_{y[t]}^2$; with lowercase y) plus the error variance (σ_e^2). Again we find changes in the basis weights account for all the changes in the variance over time. Following this same logic, we can write the expected values for the covariances among the same variable at two occasions, $Y[i]$ and $Y[j]$, as

$$\sigma_{Y[i,j]} = E\{(Y[i] - \mu_{Y[i]})(Y[j] - \mu_{Y[j]})\} = \sigma_0^2 + \sigma_{y[i,j]}$$
$$= \sigma_0^2 + (A[i]\sigma_s^2 A[j] + A[i]\sigma_{0s} + \sigma_{0s}A[j]). \quad (18.10)$$

This implies the observed covariance at any time ($\sigma_{Y[i,j]}$) is the sum of the initial-level variance (σ_0^2) plus the covariance of the latent changes ($\sigma_{y[i,j]}$); changes in the basis weights account for all changes in the covariances over time. Each of these Equations 18.8 through 18.10 can be traced in the diagram (e.g., Equation 18.9 is from any $Y[t]$ back to itself).

These growth model expectations are useful because they can be compared to the observed growth statistics for the estimation of model parameters and the evaluation of goodness-of-fit. Whereas the summary statistics form the basis of the expectations, recent computational techniques can be used to estimate the model parameters directly from the entire collection of raw data. Following standard theory in this area (e.g., Lange, Westlake, & Spence, 1976; Lindsey, 1993), the *multivariate normal model* for an observed vector $Y[t]$ is used to define the *maximum likelihood estimates* (MLEs) of the parameters, and a single numerical value termed the *model likelihood* (L) can be calculated to index the *misfit* of the model expectations to the observed data.

Assuming we have one or more alternative models (see next section), we can compare these models using the differences in log-likelihood ($\Delta L = L_1 - L_2$) and the difference in the numbers of parameters estimated ($\Delta NP = NP_1 - NP_2$). Under standard normal theory assumptions about the distribution of the errors, we can compare model differences to a chi-square distribution ($\Delta L \sim \chi^2$, $\Delta NP \sim df$) and determine the accuracy (i.e., significance) of our comparison. To index the multivariate effect sizes, we can calculate a noncentrality index and provide the statistical power ($P = 1 - \beta$) for all likelihood-based comparisons (e.g., based on $\alpha = .01$ test size). These likelihood-based calculations can answer basic questions phrased as *To what degree do the data conform to the model expectations?* We can also use this same likelihood approach to answer more complex questions, such as *Which is the best model for our data* and *Do the fit statistics indicate that the same dynamic patterns exist in different sub-groups?* Although we do not need to make a rigorous use of probability tests, we do provide information to calculate alternative indices of fit, including test statistics for perfect or close fit (e.g., Browne & Cudeck, 1993; Burnham & Anderson, 1998; McArdle, Prescott, Hamagami, & Horn, 1998).

The resulting parameter estimates allow us to form expected group growth curves for both the observed and true scores (for details, see McArdle, 1986, 2001; McArdle & Woodcock, 1997). We can also characterize the relative size of these parameters by calculating time-specific ratios of the estimated variances

$$\eta^2_{[t]} = \left(\sigma^2_{Y[t]} - \sigma^2_e\right) / \sigma^2_{Y[t]} = \sigma^2_{y[t]} / \sigma^2_{Y[t]}, \quad \text{and}$$

$$\Delta\eta^2_{[i-j]} = \eta^2_{[i]} - \eta^2_{[j]}. \qquad (18.11)$$

These *growth-reliability* ratios can be useful in investigating the changes in the true score variance ($\sigma^2_{y[t]}$) and changes in the reliability of the variable at different points in time (for examples, see McArdle, 1986; McArdle & Woodcock, 1997; Tisak & Tisak, 1996). These simple formulas also suggest that the parameters of the changes are difficult to consider in isolation—that is, the *variance of the changes* is not equal to the *changes in the variance*. In the same way, the expectations of the observed correlations over time ($\rho_{Y[i, j]}$) can be calculated from the basic expressions (the ratio of Equation 18.10 to a function of Equation 18.9), but the resulting expected correlations are usually a complex ratio of the more fundamental parameters. In many growth models, it is complicated to express patterns of change using only correlations.

In general, the growth pattern depends on basic model parameters that may have no isolated interpretation.

Initial Results From Fitting Linear Growth Models

The complete and incomplete data from the six-occasion Bradway-McArdle longitudinal study (Figure 18.6) have been fitted and reported in McArdle & Hamagami (1996) and McArdle et al. (McArdle, Hamagami, et al., in press, 2002). A selected set of these results is presented for illustration here. On a computational note, the standard HLM, MLn, VARCL, MX, and SAS PROC MIXED programs produced similar results for all models with a fixed basis. The models with estimated factor loadings ($A[t]$) were fitted using the general Mx unbalanced raw data option (e.g., the variable length approach) and with SAS PROC NLMIXED and the results are similar. All of these programs follow the same general procedures, so we will consider these as equivalent procedures unless otherwise stated.

The first model (labeled $M0$) was a no-growth model (Equation 18.4) fitted to the nonverbal scores of the Bradway-McArdle data. This simple model was fitted estimated with only three parameters, and we obtained a baseline for fit ($L = 4440$). The parameters estimated include an initial-level mean ($\mu_0 = 46.4$), a small initial-level standard deviation ($\sigma_0 = 0.01$), and a large error deviation ($\sigma_e = 49.8$).

The second model fitted was a linear growth model ($M1$) with a fixed basis (Equation 18.5) and six free parameters. This basis was first formed by using the actual age of the persons at the time of measurement $A[t] = [4, 14, 30, 42, 56, 64]$. Estimates were obtained yielded a fit ($L = 4,169$) that represented a clear improvement over the baseline ($\chi^2 = 271$ on $df = 3$) model, and the error variance has been reduced substantially (to $\sigma_e\{M1\} = 18.1$). The resulting parameters lead to a straight line of expected means that increases rapidly over age; $\mu[t] = [45.4, 52.9, 64.7, 74.1, 84.7, 90.6]$. The variance estimates of the intercept and slope parameters were small, so we refit the model with a simpler basis: That is, $A[t] = [(\mathbf{Age}[t] - 4)/56] = [0.00, 0.19, 0.49, 0.73, 1.00, 1.15]$, so the weights are proportional to the range of data between the *early* age of 4 and the *middle* age of 56. This resulted in identical mean expectations, but the latent variances were still too small to interpret.

This latent basis model ($M2$) was fitted next. For the purposes of estimation, the $A[1] = 0$ (at Age = 4) and $A[5] = 1$ (at Age = 56) were fixed (as proportions) but the four other coefficients were estimated from the data. This resulted in a likelihood ($L = 3,346$) which is substantially better than the baseline model ($\chi^2 = 1,094$ on $df = 7$) and the linear model ($\chi^2 = 823$ on $df = 4$), and the error variance has been

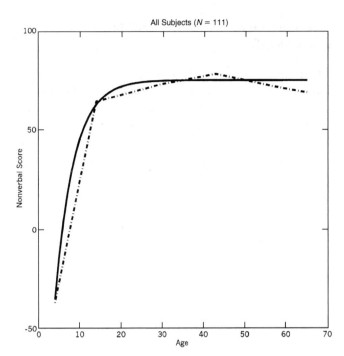

All Subjects ($N = 111$)

Figure 18.8   Alternative latent growth curve model expectations for the average growth curve of nonverbal abilities fitted to the complete and incomplete data from the Bradway-McArdle data (see Figure 18.7; see McArdle & Hamagami, 1996).

substantially reduced (from $\sigma_e\{M1\} = 18.1$ to $\sigma_e\{M2\} = 5.1$). The estimated basis coefficients were $A[t] = [= 0, 0.93, 1.01, 1.06, = 1, .97]$, and the estimated latent means were $\mu_1 = 23.8$ and $\sigma_s = 52.8$. This leads to a group trajectory $\mu[t] = [23.8, 69.2, 76.6, 80.8, 76.6, 75.0]$ that rises quickly between ages 4 and 14, peaks at age 42, and starts a small decline at ages 56 to 65. This group curve is plotted as a dashed line in Figure 18.8 and it is very similar to the general features of the raw data in Figure 18.6. The individual differences in this model are not seen in the means but in the large variances for the level ($\sigma_0 = 10.1$) and the slope ($\sigma_s = 12.3$) parameters, and the latent level and slope scores have a high correlation ($\rho_{1s} = -0.82$).

The improved fit of this latent basis compared to the linear basis model suggests the need for some form of a nonlinear curve. To explore the addition of fixed higher-order growth components, the quadratic polynomial model ($M3$, Equation 18.10) was fitted to these data using the same procedures. The goodness-of-fit was slightly improved over the linear ($\chi^2 = 7$ on $df = 4$, $\sigma_e\{M3\} = 18.0$). Although the latent basis ($M2$) and quadratic basis ($M3$) models are not nested, the quadratic model did not seem as useful as the latent basis model did. Also, problems arose in the estimation of all variance terms, so the polynomial approach was not considered further.

ADDING GROUP INFORMATION TO GROWTH CURVE ANALYSES

Latent Path and Mixed-Effects Models

We next consider analyses which include more detailed information about group differences. In the basic growth model (Equations 18.1–18.4), the latent variance terms in the model tell us about the size of the between group differences at each age (Equation 18.11), but this does not tell us the sources of this variation. To further explore the differences between persons, we can expand the basic growth model. Let us assume a variable termed X indicates some measurable characteristic of the person (e.g., sex, educational level, etc.). If we measure this variable at one occasion we might like to examine its influence in the context of a growth model for $Y[t]$. One popular model is written

$$Y[t]_n = y_{0:x,n} + A[t]y_{s:x,n} + \omega X_n + e[t]_n \quad (18.12)$$

where the ω are fixed (group) coefficients with the same-sized effect on the measured $Y[t]$ scores at all occasions, and the X is an independent observed (or assigned) predictor variable. It is useful to recognize that this model implies the latent score change over time is independent of the X variable(s). That is, the other growth parameters ($\mu_{0:x}$, $\mu_{s:x}$, $\sigma_{0:x}$, $\sigma_{s:x}$, $\sigma_{0,s:x}$) are conditional on the expected values of the measured X variable. This use of adjusted growth parameters is popularly represented in the techniques of the analysis of covariance, and the reduction of error variance from one model to the next ($\sigma_e^2 - \sigma_{ex}^2$) is often considered as a way to understand the impact (see Snyders & Boskers, 1995).

An alternative but increasingly popular way to add another variable to a growth model is to write expressions in which the X variable has a direct effect on the individual differences scores of the growth curve. This can be stated as

$$Y[t]_n = y_{0n} + A[t]y_{sn} + e[t]_n \quad \text{with}$$
$$y_{0n} = v_{00} + v_{0x}X_n + e_{0n}, \quad \text{and} \quad (18.13)$$
$$y_{sn} = v_{s0} + v_{sx}X_n + e_{sn},$$

where the regression of the latent variables (y_0, y_s) on X includes intercepts (v_{00}, v_{s0}) and slopes (v_{0x}, v_{sx}). We can rewrite this model into a compact reduced form,

$$Y[t]_n = [v_{00} + v_{0x}X_n + e_{0n}] + A[t][v_{s0} + v_{sx}X_n + e_{sn}] + e[t]_n$$
$$= v_{00} + v_{0x}X_n + e_{0n} + A[t]v_{s0} + A[t]v_{sxs}X_n + A[t]e_{sn} + e[t]_n$$

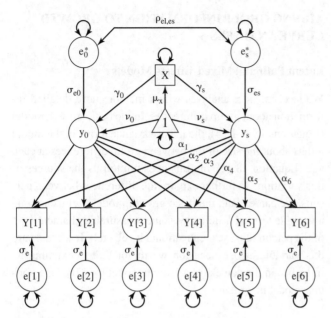

Figure 18.9 Latent growth as a path diagram with mixed-effects or multi-level predictors (from McArdle & Epstein, 1987; McArdle, 1989).

$$= [v_{00} + A[t]v_{s0} + v_{0x}X_n + A[t]v_{sx}X_n]$$
$$+ [e_{0n} + A[t]e_{sn} + e[t]_n], \quad (18.14)$$

and this separates the fixed-effects (first four terms) from the random components (last three terms). This model is drawn as a path diagram in Figure 18.9. This diagram is the same as Figure 18.7, except here we have included the X as a predictor of the levels and slope components. This diagram gives the basic idea of external variable models, and other more complex alternatives are considered in later sections.

In this simple latent growth model, as in more complex models to follow, we can always add other predictors X for the intercepts and the slopes because these models are simply latent growth models with "extension variables" (e.g., McArdle & Epstein, 1987). This kind of model (Equation 18.13 or 18.14) can also be seen as having two levels—a first-level equation for the observed scores, and a second-level equation for the intercepts and slopes. For these reasons, such models have been termed *random-coefficients* or *multilevel models, slopes as outcomes,* or *mixed-effects models* (Bryk & Raudenbush, 1987, 1992; Littell et al., 1996). Variations on these models can be compared for goodness-of-fit indices, and we can examine changes in the model variance explained at both the first and second levels (see Snyders & Boskers, 1995). In any terminology, the between-group differences in the within-group changes can be represented by the parameters in the model of Figure 18.9.

Group Differences in Growth Using Multiple Group Models

The previous models used the idea of having a measured variable X characterizing the group differences and then examining the effect of X on the model parameters. However, this method is limiting in a number of important ways. For example, some of the classical forms of growth processes, such as examining different amplitudes and phase shifts (e.g., Figure 18.2) are not easy to account for within the single-group latent growth framework. A more advanced treatment of the group problem model uses concepts derived from multiple-group factor analysis (e.g., Jöreskog & Sörbom, 1999; Honr & McArdle, 1992; McArdle & Cattell, 1994). In these kinds of models, each group, $g = 1$ to G, is assumed to follow some kind of latent growth model, such as

$$Y[t]_n^{(g)} = y_{0,n}^{(g)} + A[t]^{(g)}y_{1,n}^{(g)} + e[t]_n^{(g)}$$
$$\text{for } g = 1 \text{ to } G, \quad (18.15)$$

with basis parameters $A[t]^{(g)}$ defined by the application. Figure 18.10 gives a path diagram representing several kinds of multiple-group growth models (McArdle, 1991; McArdle & Epstein, 1987; McArdle & Hamagami, 1992). The persons in the groups are assumed to be independent, so this kind of grouping can only be done for observed categorical variables (i.e., sex). The first two groups in Figure 18.10 can be considered as data separated into males or females (or experimentals and controls). Although not necessary, in Figure 18.10 we assume some of the $Y[t]$ occasions were considered incomplete, possibly to represent a collection gathered at unequal intervals of time. In structural modeling diagrams (and programs), the unbalanced data for $Y[3]$ and $Y[5]$ are simply included as latent variables (see McArdle & Aber, 1990). In any case, this multiple-group model now allows us the opportunity to examine a variety of invariance hypotheses.

The multiple-group growth model permits the examination of the presumed invariance of the latent basis functions,

$$A[t]^{(1)} = A[t]^{(2)} = \ldots A[t]^{(g)} = \ldots A[t]^{(G)}. \quad (18.16)$$

The rejection of these constraints (based on χ^2/df) implies that some independent groups have a different basic shape of the growth curve. This is one kind of model that is not easy to represent using standard mixed-effects or multilevel models (Equation 18.13). If a reasonable level of invariance is found, we can further examine a sequence of other group differences. For example, we may examine the equality of the

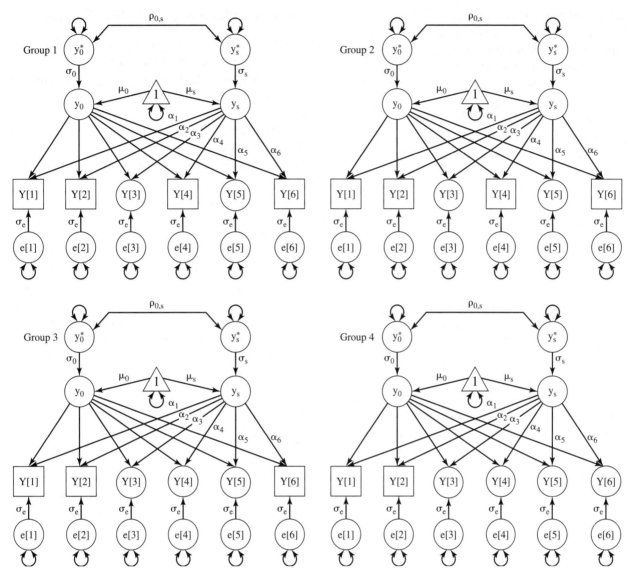

Figure 18.10   A path diagram of a multiple-group latent growth model (Groups 1 and 2) and the inclusion of with patterns of incomplete data (Groups 3 and 4; from McArdle & Hamagami, 1991, 1992).

variances of the latent levels and slopes by writing

$$\sigma_0^{(1)} = \sigma_0^{(2)} = \ldots \sigma_0^{(g)} = \ldots \sigma_0^{(G)} \quad \text{and}$$
$$\sigma_s^{(1)} = \sigma_s^{(2)} = \ldots \sigma_s^{(g)} = \ldots \sigma_s^{(G)}. \tag{18.17}$$

Other model combinations could include the error deviations ($\sigma_e^{(g)}$), the total slope variance and covariances, and functions of all the other parameters. We may still consider the typical mixed-effects group difference parameters when we examine the invariance of the latent means for initial levels and slopes. If we assume invariance of latent shapes (Equation 18.16) and latent variances (Equation 18.17), we

can meaningfully examine

$$\mu_0^{(1)} = \mu_0^{(2)} = \ldots \mu_0^{(g)} = \ldots \mu_0^{(G)} \quad \text{and}$$
$$\mu_s^{(1)} = \mu_s^{(2)} = \ldots \mu_s^{(g)} = \ldots \mu_s^{(G)}. \tag{18.18}$$

Group differences in the fixed effects can even be coded in the same way as in the typical mixed-effects analyses. Each of these multiple-group hypotheses represent a nonlinearity that may not be possible to examine using a standard mixed-effects approach.

Multiple-group models can be a useful way to express problems of incomplete data. Longitudinal data collections often include different numbers of data points for different people and different variables, and one good way to deal with these kinds of statistical problems is to include multiple-group models that permit different numbers of data points on each person (e.g., Little & Rubin, 1987; McArdle, 1994). The third and fourth groups of Figure 18.10 represent persons with incomplete data on some occasions. In other cases, the data from any one age may not overlap very much with those of another group of another age. In order to uniquely identify and estimate the model parameters from this collection of data (all four groups), all parameters are *forced to be invariant over all groups*. This kind of multiple-group model can be symbolized as

$$Y[t]_n = \sum_{g=1,G} \left(F^{(g)}\{y_{0,n} + y_{1,n}A[t] + e[t]_n\} \right), \quad (18.19)$$

where the $F^{(g)}$ is a binary filter-matrix for each group that defines the pattern of complete (1) and incomplete (0) data entries (for further details, see McArdle & Anderson, 1990; McArdle & Hamagami, 1992). This multiple-group incomplete patterning approach is identical to the statistical models in which we fit structural models to the *raw score information for each person on each variable at each time*. The available information for any subject on any data point (i.e., data at any occasion) is used to build up a likelihood function, and the numerical routine is used to optimize the model parameters with respect to the available data (Neale et al., 1999; Hamagami & McArdle, 2001).

This method assumes the invariance of all growth parameters across different patterns of data is a rigid form of "longitudinal convergence" (after Bell, 1954; see McArdle & Bell, 2000). Although invariance is a reasonable goal in many studies, it is not necessarily a hypothesis that can be tested with all incomplete patterns (McArdle & Anderson, 1990; Miyazaki & Raudenbush, 2000; Willet & Sayer, 1995). One key assumption in our use of these *MLE*-based techniques is that the incomplete data are *missing at random* (*MAR;* Little & Rubin, 1987). This assumption does not require the data to be *missing completely at random* (*MCAR*), but *MAR* does assume there is some observed information that allows us to account for and remove the bias in the model estimates created by the lack of complete data (e.g., Hedecker & Gibbons, 1997; McArdle, 1994; McArdle & Hamagami, 1992). In many cases, this *MAR* assumption is a convenient starting point, and allows us to use all the available information in one analysis. In other cases, invariance of some parameters may fail for a number of reasons and it is important to evaluate the adequacy of this helpful *MAR* assumption whenever possible (e.g., Hedecker & Gibbons, 1997; McArdle, 1994).

Latent Groups Based on Growth-Mixture Models

Another fundamental problem is the discrimination of (a) models of multiple curves for a single group of subjects from (b) models of multiple groups of subjects with different curves. For example, we could have two clusters of people, each with a distinct growth curve, but when we summarize over all the people we end up with poor fit because we need multiple slope factors. One clue to this separation is based on the higher-order distribution of the factor scores—groups are defined by multiple peaked distributions in the latent factor scores. In standard linear structural modeling, these higher-order moments are not immediately accessible, so the multiple-factor versus multiple-group discrimination is not easy. These and other kinds of problems require an a priori definition of the groups before we can effectively use the standard multigroup approach.

These practical problems set the stage for a new and important variation on this multiple-group model—models that test hypotheses about *growth curves between latent groups*. The recent series of models termed *growth mixture models* have been developed for this purpose (L. K. Muthen & Muthen, 1998; Nagin, 1999). In these kinds of analyses, the distribution of the latent parameters is assumed to come from a mixture of two or more overlapping distributions. Current techniques in mixture models have largely been developed under the assumption of a small number of discrete or probabilistic "classes of persons" (e.g., two classes), often based on mixtures of multivariate normal distributions. More formally, we can write this kind of a model as a weighted sum of curves

$$Y[t]_n = \sum_{c=1,C} \left(P\{c_n\} \cdot \{y_{0,n}^{(c)} + A[t]^{(c)} y_{1,n}^{(c)} + e[t]_n^{(c)}\} \right),$$
$$\text{with} \quad \sum_{c=1,C} (P\{c_n\}) = 1, \quad (18.20)$$

where $P\{c_n\}$ is constrained to sum to unity so that it acts as a probability of class membership for the person in $c = 1$ to C classes.

Using growth-mixture models we can estimate the most likely threshold parameter for each latent distribution (τ_p, for the pth parameter) while simultaneously estimating the separate model parameters for the resulting latent groups. The concept of an unknown or latent grouping can be based on a succession of invariance hypotheses about the growth parameters. We can initially separate latent level means and variances, then separate latent slope means and variances, then both the level and slope, then on the basis loadings, and so on. The resulting maximum likelihood estimates yield a fit that can be compared to the results obtained from more restrictive single class models, so the concept of a mixture distribution of multiple classes can be treated as a hypothesis to be investigated.

In essence, this growth-mixture model provides a test of the invariance of growth model parameters without requiring exact knowledge of the group membership of each individual. It follows that, as we do in standard discriminant or logistic analysis, we can also estimate the probability of assignment of individuals to each class in the mixture, and this estimation of a different kind of latent trait can be a practically useful device. A variety of new program scripts (e.g., Nagin, 1999) and computer programs (e.g., Mplus, by L. K. Muthen & Muthen, 1998) permit this analysis.

Results From Fitting Group Growth Models

We have studied a variety of mixed-effect or multilevel models of the Bradway data. To allow some flexibility here, we used the same latent basis curve model (M2) but now we add a few additional variables as predictors. These variables included various aspects of demographic (e.g., gender, educational attainment by age 56, etc.), self-reported health behaviors (e.g., smoking, drinking, physical exercise, etc.), health problems (e.g., general health, illness, medical procedures, etc.), and personality measures (e.g., 16 PF factors). As one example, in a mixed-effects model (see Figure 18.9), we added gender as an effect-coded variable (i.e., females = -0.5 and males = $+0.5$). The results obtained for nonverbal scales included the latent basis $A[\mathbf{t}] = [= 0, 0.93, 1.01, 1.06, = 1, .97]$ as before. But now, in the same model, we found the males start at slightly lower initial levels ($\nu_{0x} = -0.06$) but had larger positive changes over time ($\nu_{sx} = 0.30$). The addition of gender does not produce large changes in fit ($\chi^2 = 10$ on $df = 4$), so all gender mean differences may be accounted for using the latent variables, but gender does not account for much the variance of the latent scores (.03, .05). To account for more of this variance we proceed using basic principles of multiple regression: In a third model we added educational attainment, in a fourth model we added both gender and education, and in a fifth model we added an interaction of sex and education.

Group differences in the Bradway-McArdle data were also studied using multiple-group growth curves. In a general model the latent means, deviations, and basis shape of the changes were considered different for the males and the females. The key results for males and females show a lack of invariance for the initial basis hypothesis ($A[\mathbf{t}]^{(m)} = A[\mathbf{t}]^{(f)}$, $\chi^2 = 40$ on $df = 5$). The separate group results show that the females have a higher basis function, and this implies more growth over time (e.g., McArdle & Epstein, 1987). This last

result does not deal only with mean differences, but rather includes both mean and covariance differences, and it may be worth pursuing.

Multiple-group growth models have been used in all prior analyses described here to fit the complete and incomplete subsets of the Bradway-McArdle data (Figure 18.6). We compared the numerical results for the complete data (Figure 18.6, Panel A) versus the complete and incomplete data together (Figure 18.6, Panel A plus Panel B), and the parameters remain the same. As a statistical test for parameter invariance over these groups, we calculated from the difference in the model likelihoods, and these differences were trivial ($\chi^2 < 20$ on $df = 20$). This suggests that selective dropout or subject attrition can be considered random with respect to the nonverbal abilities. This last result allows us to combine the complete and incomplete data sets in the hopes for a more accurate, powerful, and unbiased analysis.

In our final set of multiple-group models, we used the latent mixture approach to estimate latent groupings of models results for the verbal scores, and some results are graphed in Figure 18.11. The latent growth model using all the data was fitted with free basis coefficients and the same fits as were reported earlier (M2). In a first latent mixture model, we allowed the additional possibility of two latent classes ($C = 2$) with different parameters for the latent means and variance but assuming the same growth basis. The two-class growth model (Figure 18.11, Panel A) assumed the same free basis coefficients as previously, smaller latent variances, and an estimated class threshold ($z = 2.48$) separating (a) Class 1 with 92% of the people with high latent means ($\mu_0 = 25$, $\mu_s = 58$), from (b) Class 2 with 8% of the people with lower latent means ($\mu_0 = 16$, $\mu_s = 53$). This two-class model yielded an likelihood that (assuming these two models are nested) represents a substantial change in fit ($\chi^2 = 30$ on $df = 3$). This result suggests that a small group of the Bradway persons may have started at a lower average score with a smaller change. A sequence of parameters were compared under the assumption of two classes, and the final result is presented in Figure 18.11, Panel B. The two-class growth model yielded an estimated class threshold ($z = -0.72$) separating two classes with 33% and 67% of the people. The first class seems to have a higher starting point and lower variability, but the plots of Figure 18.11b seem to show the two curves converge in adulthood. Although this is an interesting possibility, this complete two-class growth-mixture model yielded only a small improvement in fit ($L = -1628$, $\chi^2 = 34$, on $df = 12$), so we conclude that only one class of persons is needed to account for the basic growth curves underlying these data.

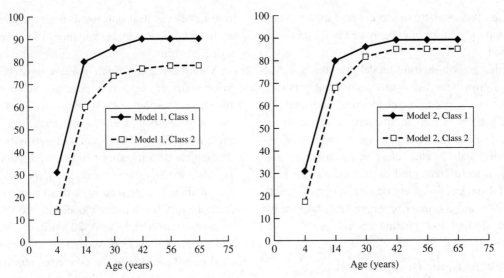

Figure 18.11 Bradway-McArdle verbal score expectations from latent growth-mixture models; Model 1 includes two classes with free means and covariances, and Model 2 is the same with adds four free basis coefficients.

GROWTH CURVE MODELS FROM A DYNAMIC PERSPECTIVE

Growth Models Based on Dynamic Theory

The linear models previously presented can be used to describe a variety of nonlinear shapes, but other models have explicitly included nonlinear functions of the parameters. The development of many of these nonlinear models was based on *differential equations* as an expression of changes as a function of time: that is, dynamic changes. For example, we can write an exponential growth model (see Figure 18.3) as

$$dy/dt = \pi y[t] \quad \text{so} \quad y[t] = y[0] + \exp(-\pi t). \quad (18.21)$$

where the instantaneous derivative (dy/dt) of the score (y) is a proportional function (π) of the current size of the score ($y[t]$). This change model leads to the integral equation with change over time in the score based on an initial starting point ($y[0]$, sometimes set to zero) with an exponential accumulation (**exp**) based directly on the *growth rate parameter* (π). In classical forms of this model, the rate of change is defined as a linear function of the percentage of initial size (e.g., compound interest).

In contemporary nonlinear model fitting, we can add individual differences to this model in several ways. One approach that is consistent with our previous growth models is to simply rewrite the derivative and integral equations as

$$dy_n/dt = \pi y[t]_n \quad \text{so} \quad Y[t]_n = y_{0,n} + A[t]y_{s,n} + e[t]_n$$
$$\text{with} \quad A[t] = 1 - \exp(-\pi t). \quad (18.22)$$

In this approach, the classic nonlinear exponential model (Equation 18.21) is now in the form of a latent growth curve *with structured loadings* (as in Browne & duToit, 1991; McArdle & Hamagami, 1996). Individual trajectories start at different initial levels, but then rise or fall in exponential fashion towards some asymptotic values. In this approach, the group curve is based on the latent means and is not based on an averaging of exponential functions (cf. Keats, 1983; Tucker, 1966). This common factor approach allows us to use current computing techniques to examine the empirical fit of this nonlinear model.

A related approach has been used with a form of the von Bertalanffy model,

$$dy_n/dt = (\alpha_n g[t]_n) - (\beta_n - d[t]_n^{\gamma}), \quad \text{so}$$
$$Y[t]_n = y_{0,n} + [\exp(-\alpha t) - \exp(-\beta t)]y_{s,n} + e[t]_n, \quad (18.23)$$

where $\alpha =$ the rate of growth, $\beta =$ the rate of decline, and $\gamma =$ some relationship between the two components. In this simplified form (i.e., $\gamma = 1$), there is only one slope (y_s) and one nonlinear set of $A[t]$, but we interpret this as separate growth and decline phases of an underlying continuous latent process. The parameters also yield estimated score peaks ($dy/dt = 0$) and valleys ($d^2y/dt^2 = 0$) with individual differences (e.g., McArdle, Ferrer-Caja, Hamagami, & Woodcock, in press; Simonton, 1989).

Several alternative growth curve models have been developed from dynamic change equations with more parameters. A *logistic curve* can be written as

$$dy_n/dt = \alpha_n y[t]_n(\beta_n - y[t]_n) \quad \text{so}$$
$$Y[t]_n = y_{0,n} + \alpha_n/[1 + \exp\{\beta_n - \gamma_n t\}] + e[t]_n \quad (18.24)$$

with α = the asymptote, β = an influence on the slope (i.e., the slope is $\alpha\beta/4$), and γ = the location of maximum velocity. The expression allows for three individual differences terms with structured loadings (see Browne & du Toit, 1991). A related model is the Gompertz growth curve, written as

$$dy_n/dt = \alpha_n\, y[t]_n \exp(\beta_n - y[t]_n) \quad \text{so}$$
$$Y[t]_n = y_{0,n} + \alpha_n \exp(-\beta_n \exp\{[t-1]\gamma_n\}) + e[t]_n,$$
$$(18.25)$$

with α = the asymptote, β = the distance from the asymptote on the first trial, and γ = the rate of change. Browne and duToit (1991) clearly showed how this model could be rewritten as a latent growth curve with structured loadings, including interpretations of individual differences in the rates of growth.

The Preece-Baines family of models start with a derivative based on some predefined function of $\mathbf{t}$ ($f\{\mathbf{t}\}$) and some asymptotic value ($y[\theta]$). To obtain logistic models (Equation 18.24), the functional form used a proportional distance from the starting point ($f\{t\} = \gamma\{y_{0,n} - y[t]\}$). In other models, this function was the simple rate parameter $f\{t\} = \pi$, so

$$dy_n/dt = \pi\{y[t]_n - y[\theta]_n\} \quad \text{so}$$
$$Y[t]_n = y_{0,n} + (\exp\{-(t-1)\pi\})y[\theta]_n + e[t]_n$$
$$(18.26)$$

where the amount of change is a function of the distance from the asymptote. This approach allows us to obtain a form of the partial adjustment model of Coleman (1968; McArdle & Hamagami, 1996). These models seem to have practical features for the description of individual changes over long periods of time (see Hauspie et al., 1991; Nesselrode & Boker, 1994).

Growth Curve Models Using Connected Segments

Complex linear and nonlinear models can be used to represent growth. Some models share the common feature of a piecewise analysis applied to different age or time segments—that is, the model considers the possibility that a specific dynamic process does not hold over all time periods. In the simplest cases, we may assume that growth is linear over specific periods of time, and these times are connected by a critical *knot point*—this leads to a conjoined or linear *spline* model (e.g., Bryk & Raudenbush, 1992; Smith, 1979). If we assume one specific cutoff time ($t = C$), we can write

if ($\mathbf{t} = C$), then $Y[t]_n = y_{0,n} + e[t]_n$ but

if ($\mathbf{t} < C$), then $Y[t]_n = y_{0,n} + A1[t]\,y_{1,n} + e[t]_n$ but

if ($\mathbf{t} > C$), then $Y[t]_n = y_{0,n} + A2[t]\,y_{2,n} + e[t]_n.$ (18.27)

where the latent growth basis is different before ($A1[\mathbf{t}]$) and after ($A2[\mathbf{t}]$) the cut point. This piecewise linear model assumes the first component (y_0) is the score at the cutoff, the second component (y_1) is the slope score before the cutoff, and the third component (y_2) is the slope score after the cut point. As before, the fixed effects (means μ_0, μ_1, μ_2) describe the group curve, but the random coefficients (y_0, y_1, y_2) have variances and covariance and account for the individual differences in curves across all observations.

In some growth data sets, it is possible to estimate optimal cut points ($t = C_n$) as an operationally independent random component (see Cudeck, 1996). Unless the cut points are estimated, this model may require a relatively large number of fixed and random parameters to achieve adequate fit. In a recent mixed-effects analysis, Cudeck & du Toit (2001) followed previous work (e.g., Seber & Wild, 1989) and used a "segmented polynomial" nonlinear mixed model based on an individual a *latent transition point* for each individual. This model can be written in our notation as

$$Y[t]_n = y_{0,n} + y_{1,n}A[t] + y_{2,n}(A[t] - y_{3,n})^2 + e[t]_n,$$
$$|A[t] \leq y_{3,n} \quad \text{and} \quad (18.28)$$
$$Y[t]_n = y_{0,n} + y_{1,n}A[t] + e[t]_n, \quad |A[t] > y_{3,n},$$

where the parameter y_3 is the value of $A[\mathbf{t}]$ when the polynomial of the first phase changes to the linear component of the second phase. Important practical suggestions about fitting multilevel nonlinear curves were presented by Cudeck and DuToit (2001).

These segmented or composite models have also been a mainstay of nonlinear modeling. For example, the segmented logistic model (see Bock, 1975; Bock & Thissen, 1980) can be written as a trajectory where

$$Y[t]_n = \sum_{k=1,K} [\alpha_{k,n}/(1 + \exp\{\beta_{k,n} - \gamma_{k,n}t\})] + e[t]_n$$
$$(18.29)$$

is the sum of $k = 1$ to K logistic age-segments. Within each segment, α_k = the asymptote, β_k = an influence on the slope (i.e., the slope is $\alpha_k\beta_k/4$), γ_k = the location of maximum velocity, and no intercept is fitted. Within each segment, the rate of growth exhibits early increases, reaches a maximum (peak growth velocity), and decreases towards the asymptote; the final value of one segment is used as the starting value of the next segment. While each segment has a simple logistic curve, the overall curve fitted (e.g., over the full life span) has a particularly complex nonlinear form. These composite models allow for different dynamics at different ages, and this represents an important innovation.

Growth Models Based on Latent Difference Scores

The complexities of fitting and extending the previous dynamic models have limited their practical utility. In recent research we have considered some ways to retain the basic dynamic change interpretations but use conventional analytic techniques. This has led us to recast the previous growth models using *latent difference scores* (see McArdle, 2001). This approach is not identical to that represented by the differential equations considered earlier (e.g., Arminger, 1987; Coleman, 1968), but it offers a practical approximation that can add clear dynamic interpretations to traditional linear growth models.

In the latent difference approach, we first assume we have a pair of observed scores $Y[t]$ and $Y[t-1]$ measured over a defined interval of time ($\Delta t = 1$), and we write

$$Y[t]_n = y[t]_n + e[t]_n, \quad Y[t-1]_n = y[t-1]_n + e[t-1]_n$$
$$\text{and} \quad y[t]_n = y[t-1]_n + \Delta y[t]_n \quad (18.30)$$

with corresponding latent scores $y[t]$ and $y[t-1]$, and error of measurements $e[t]$ and $e[t-1]$. It follows that by simple algebraic rearrangement, we can define

$$y[t]_n = y[t-1]_n + \Delta y[t]_n \quad \text{so}$$
$$\Delta y[t]_n = (y[t]_n - y[t-1]_n) \quad (18.31)$$

where the additional latent variable is directly interpreted as a *latent difference score*. This simple algebraic device allows us to generally define the trajectory equation as

$$Y[t]_n = y_{0,n} + \left(\sum_{i=1,t} \Delta y[i]_n \right) + e[t]_n \quad (18.32)$$

where the summation ($\sum_{i=1,t}$) or accumulation of the latent changes ($\Delta y[t]$) up to time t is included. In this latent difference score approach, we do not directly define the $A[t]$ coefficients, but instead we directly define changes as an accumulation of the first differences among latent variables.

This latent difference score ($\Delta y[t]_n$) of Equation 18.31 is not the same as an observed difference score ($\Delta Y[t]_n$) because the latent score is considered after the removal of the model-based error component. Although this difference $\Delta y[t]_n$ is a theoretical score, it has practical value because now we can write any structural model for the latent change scores without immediate concern about the resulting trajectory (as in McArdle, 2001; McArdle & Hamagami, 2001; McArdle & Nesselrode, 1994). For example, Coleman

(1968) suggests we write a change model for consecutive time points as

$$\Delta y[t]_n = \pi(y_{a,n} - y[t-1]_n), \quad (18.33)$$

where y_a is a latent asymptote score that is constant over time, and the π describes the proportional change based on the current distance from the asymptote (i.e., partial adjustment; see Equation 18.26). A slightly more general change expression model is written as

$$\Delta y[t]_n = \alpha y_{s,n} + \beta y[t-1]_n \quad (18.34)$$

where the y_s is a latent slope score that is constant over time, and the α and β are coefficients describing the change. This second expression (Equation 18.34) is more general because we can add restrictions ($\alpha = \pi$, $\beta = -\pi$) and obtain the first expression (Equation 18.33). We refer to this as a *dual change score* (DCS) model because it permits both a systematic constant change (α) and a systematic proportional change (β) over time, and no stochastic residual is added (i.e., $z[t]$; see McArdle, 2001). This is an interesting linear model because the expectations lead to a mixed-effects model trajectory with a distinct nonlinear form (e.g., $A[t]$ in Equation 18.22), but the corresponding accumulation of differences (Equation 18.32) remains unchanged.

One advantage of this approach is that this dynamic model can fitted using standard structural modeling software. The structural path diagram in Figure 18.12 illustrates how the latent change score model (Equations 18.30–18.34) can be directly represented using standard longitudinal structural equation models. This set of equations is drawn in Figure 18.12 by using (a) *unit-valued regression weights* among variables by fixed nonzero constraints (as in McArdle & Nesselrode, 1994), (b) a *constant time lag* by using additional latent variables as placeholders (as in Horn & McArdle, 1980), (c) each *latent change score as the focal outcome variable,* and (d) a repetition (by equality constraints) of the α and β structural coefficients. Following the standard linear growth models, we assume the unobserved initial-level component (y_0) has a mean and variance (i.e., μ_0 and σ_0^2), while the error of measurement has mean zero, has constant variance $\sigma_e^2 > 0$), and is uncorrelated with every other component. As in the linear change model of Figure 18.7, the constant change component (y_s) has a nonzero mean (i.e., μ_s, the average of the latent change scores), a nonzero variance (i.e., σ_s^2, the variability of the latent change scores), and a nonzero correlation with the latent initial levels (i.e., ρ_{0s}). As in other latent growth models, the numerical values of the parameters α and β can now be combined to form

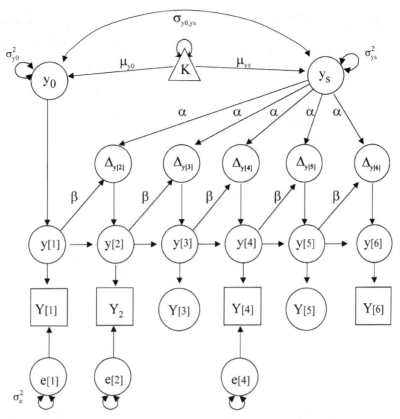

Figure 18.12   A reinterpretation and extension of the latent growth model as a latent difference score structural model, including both additive (α) and proportional (β) change parameters (see McArdle, 2001).

many different kinds of individual and group trajectories over age or time, including the addition of covariates. All these features are apparent without directly writing or specifying a model for the full trajectory over time.

Results From Fitting Dynamic Growth Models

To illustrate some of these dynamic growth models, the Bradway-McArdle Non-Verbal data were fitted (using Mx and NLMIXED). A new model (*M4*) based on the partial adjustment model (as described in Equation 18.26) required four free parameters with individual differences in the initial-level variance (an asymptote) and in the latent slope (the distance from asymptote) parameters. This model requires all loadings to have be an exponential function formed from a single rate parameter (estimated at $\pi = -0.16$), and the resulting expected trajectory is drawn as the solid line in Figure 18.9. In contrast to the shape of previous latent basis model, this is an exponential shape that rises rapidly and then stays fairly constant at the asymptote (or equilibrium point) from age 42 to age 65.

This model fit was not as good as that of the latent basis model, but the difference is relatively small compared to the difference in degrees of freedom ($\chi^2 = 59$ on $df = 3$), the error variance is similar (from $\sigma_e\{M2\} = 5.1$ to $\sigma_e\{M4\} = 6.5$). Unlike the latent basis model, this negative exponential model makes explicit predictions at all ages (e.g., Equation 18.26 for $\mu[22] = 82.7$). A second model was fit allowing individual stochastic differences (random coefficients) in the rate parameter (π_n). The resulting fitted curves show only a small change in the average rate ($\pi = -0.15$), the random variance of these rates is very small ($\sigma_\pi < .01$), and the fit is not much better than that of the simpler partial adjustment model ($\chi^2 = 14$, $df = 4$, $\sigma_e\{M5\} = 5.8$).

The comparison of the latent basis (*M2*) and the partial adjustment models (*M4* or *M5*) suggests that the decline in nonverbal intellectual abilities by age 65 is relatively small. The expectations from these two models yield only minor departures of the exploratory latent basis model (*M2*) from the partial adjustment model (*M4*). The further comparison of the stochastic adjustment (*M5*) and the partial adjustment (*M4*) model suggests that the same shape of change in nonverbal intellectual abilities call be applied to all persons. Although these analyses illustrate only a limited set of substantive hypotheses about dynamic growth processes, these are key questions in aging research.

An example of the segmented models fitted to the Bradway-McArdle data has been published by Cudeck & DuToit (2001). Using data from persons who had data on at least one of the last three occasions ($N = 74$), these authors fit a nonlinear mixed model based on Equation 18.32 and found an estimated transition age ($\boldsymbol{\beta_3} = 18.6$, $\boldsymbol{\sigma_3} = 0.60$) where the polynomial of the first phase changes to the linear decline component ($\boldsymbol{\beta_1} = -.141$, $\boldsymbol{\sigma_3} = 0.05$; $\boldsymbol{\beta_2} = -.571$) of the second phase. The estimated mean response shows a growth curve with rapid increases and gradual decline (after $Age[t] = 18.6$). The variability of these estimated parameters allows for a variety of different curves, and some of these are drawn in Figure 18.13. "Although the trend is decreasing overall, a few individuals actually exhibit increases, while for others the response is essentially constant into old age. . . . The two individuals in Figure (A) had large differences in intercepts, $\boldsymbol{\beta_{i0}}$ (70.8 versus 91.9); those in Figure (B) had large differences in slopes, $\boldsymbol{\beta_{i1}}$ ($-.32$ versus 0.04); those in Figure (C) had large differences in transition age, $\boldsymbol{\beta_{i3}}$ (14.1 versus 23.6)" (Cudeck & duToit, 2001; p. 13). The addition of individual differences in transition points contributes to our understanding of these growth curves.

Four alternative latent difference score models (Figure 18.12) were fitted to the nonverbal scores (Figure 18.6). To facilitate computer programming (e.g., Mx) the original data were rescaled into 5-year age segments (i.e., 30 to 35, 35 to 40, etc.). A baseline no-change model (NCS) was fitted with only three parameters and the results using this approach were comparable to those of the baseline growth model ($M0$). This was also true for a constant change score (CCS; α only) model, and the result was identical to that of the linear basis model ($M1$). The proportional change model (PCS; β only), not fit earlier, shows a minor improvement in fit ($\chi^2 = 5$ on $df = 1$).

To fit the dual change model (Equation 18.34), the additive slope coefficient was fixed for identification purposes ($\alpha = 1$), but the mean of the slopes was allowed to be free (μ_s). This allowed estimation of the effects for nonverbal with (a) inertial effects ($\beta = -1.38$), (b) initial-level means ($\mu_0 = 32$) at Age = 5, and (c) a linear slope mean ($\mu_s = 81$) for each 5-year period after Age = 5. The goodness-of-fit of the DCS model can be compared to that of every other nested alternative, and these comparisons show the best fit was achieved using this model ($\chi^2 = 785$ on $df = 2$; $\chi^2 = 485$ on $df = 1$; $\chi^2 = 385$ on $df = 1$). From these results we calculate the expected group trajectories and the 5-year latent change accumulation as the combination of Equations 18.32

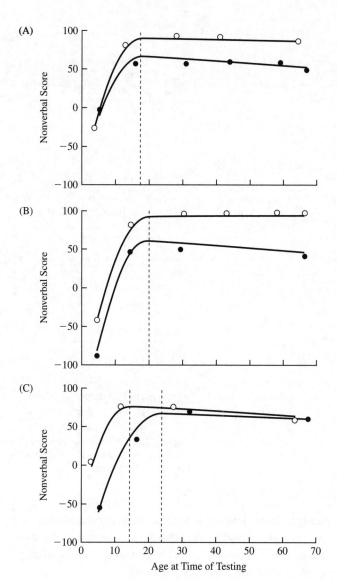

Figure 18.13   Fitted curves for selected individuals from the segmented growth model (from Cudeck & du Toit, 2001).

and 18.34, and we find the expected trajectory over time for the nonverbal variable represented in this way is the same as the previous nonlinear solid line in Figure 18.9 (see Hamagami & McArdle, 2001). This dynamic result is explored more in the next section.

MULTIPLE VARIABLES IN LATENT GROWTH CURVE MODELS

Including Measurement Models Within Latent Growth Analyses

Previous research on growth models for multiple variables has considered the application of standard multivariate models to growth data (e.g., Harris, 1963; Horn, 1972). A parsimonious alternative that has been explored in prior work is the inclusion of a so-called measurement model embedded in these dynamic structural models (for references, see McArdle, 1988; McArdle & Woodcock, 1997). This can be fitted by including common factor scores ($f[t]$), proportionality via factor loadings (λ_y, λ_x), and uniqueness (u_y, u_x). We could write a model as

$$
\begin{aligned}
Y[t]_n &= v_y + \lambda_y f_n + u_{y,n}, \quad \text{and} \\
X[t]_n &= v_x + \lambda_x f_n + u_{x,n},
\end{aligned}
\tag{18.35}
$$

so that each score is related to a common factor ($f[t]$) with time-invariant factor loadings (λ_j), unique components (u_j), and scaling intercepts (v_j). We can then consider whether all latent changes in these observed scores are characterized by the growth parameters of the common factor scores

$$
f[t]_n = f_{0,n} + Af[t] f_{s,n} + ef[t]_n. \tag{18.36}
$$

This common factor growth model is drawn as a path diagram in Figure 18.14. We can also recast these common factor scores into a latent difference form of

$$
\begin{aligned}
f[t]_n &= f[t-1]_n + \Delta f[t]_n \quad \text{and} \\
\Delta f[t]_n &= \alpha f f_{s,n} + \beta f f[t-1]_n,
\end{aligned}
\tag{18.37}
$$

so that the dynamic features of the common factors are estimated directly (e.g., Figure 18.12).

The expectations from this kind of a model can be seen as *proportional growth curves,* even if the model includes additional variables or factors. If this kind of restrictive model of changes in the factor scores among multiple curves provides a reasonable fit to the data, we have evidence for the dynamic construct validity of the common factor (as in McArdle & Prescott, 1992). To the degree multiple measurements are made, this common factor hypothesis about the change pattern is a strongly rejectable model (e.g., McArdle, Ferrer-Caja et al., in press; McArdle & Woodcock, 1997). In either form (Equation 18.36 or Equation 18.37) this multivariate dynamic model is highly restrictive, so it may serve as a *common cause* baseline that can help guide the appropriate level of analysis (as in McArdle & Goldsmith, 1990; Nesselroade & McArdle, 1997).

One explicit assumption made in all growth models is that the scores are adequate measures of the same construct(s) over all time and ages. This assumption may be evaluated whenever we fit the measurement hypothesis (i.e., is $\Lambda[t] = \Lambda[t+1]$?). It may be useful to examine the assumption of *metric factorial invariance* over occasions without the

necessity of a simple structure basis to the measurement model (Horn & McArdle, 1992; McArdle & Cattell, 1994; McArdle & Nesselroade, 1994). However, in long-term longitudinal data collections, we often use repeated measures models when different variables measuring the same constructs were used at different ages. The basic requirements of meaningful and age-equivalent measurement models are a key problem in the behavioral sciences, and future research is needed to address these fundamental concerns (see Burr & Nesselroade, 1990; Fischer & Molenaar, 1995).

Modeling Interrelationships Among Growth Curves

The collection of multiple variables at each occasion of measurement leads naturally to questions about relationships among growth processes and multivariate growth models. The early work on this topic led to sophisticated models based on systems of differential equations for the size of multiple variables. In one comprehensive multivariate model, Turner (1978) extended the simple growth principles to more variables, and permitted an examination of biologically important interactions based on the size and sign of the estimated parameters (see Griffiths & Sandland, 1984). Multivariate research in the behavioral sciences has not gone as far yet, and seems to have relied on advanced versions of the linear growth models formalized by Rao (1958), Pothoff and Roy (1964), and Bock (1975).

Some recent structural equation models described in the statistical literature have emphasized the examination of *parallel growth curves,* including the correlation of various components (McArdle, 1988, 1990; Willett & Sayer, 1994). The models fitted here can be represented in latent growth notation for two variables by

$$
\begin{aligned}
Y[t]_n &= y_{0,n} + A_y[t] y_{s,n} + e_y[t]_n \quad \text{and} \\
X[t]_n &= x_{0,n} + A_x[t] x_{s,n} + e_x[t]_n,
\end{aligned}
\tag{18.38}
$$

where $Y[t]$ and $X[t]$ are two different variables observed over time, there are two basis functions ($A_y[t]$ and $A_x[t]$), and

$$
\begin{aligned}
E\{y_0, x_0\} &= \sigma_{y0,x0}, \quad E\{y_0, x_s\} = \sigma_{y0,xs}, \\
E\{y_s, x_0\} &= \sigma_{ys,x0}, \quad \text{and} \quad E\{y_s, x_s\} = \sigma_{ys,xs},
\end{aligned}
\tag{18.39}
$$

and all covariances ($\sigma_{y[i],x[j]}$) are allowed among the common latent variables. A path diagram of this bivariate growth model is presented in Figure 18.15.

This set of structural equations has been used to examine a variety of substantive hypotheses. One hypothesis relies on the equality of the basis coefficients (e.g., $A_y[t] = A_x[t]$) to

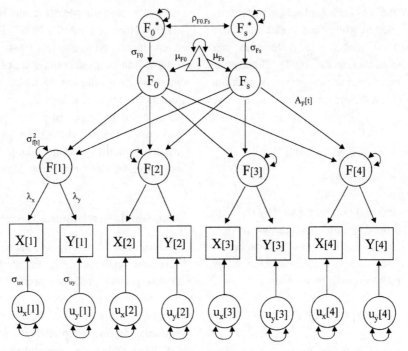

Figure 18.14   A path diagram of a multiple variable measurement model with a latent "curve of factor scores" (McArdle, 1988).

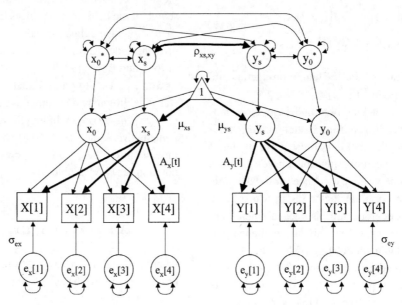

Figure 18.15   A path diagram representing a bivariate latent growth model for multiple variables (from McArdle, 1989).

examine the overall shape of the two curves. Interpretations have also been made about the size and sign of nonzero covariance of initial levels (i.e., $|\sigma_{y0,x0}| > 0$) and *covariance of slopes* (i.e., $|\sigma_{ys,xs}| > 0$), but these interpretations are limited. These random coefficients reflect individual similarities in the way persons start and change over time across different

variables, and these are key features for some researchers (e.g., Duncan & Duncan, 1995; Raykov, 1999; Willet & Sayer, 1994). However, it should be noted that this simple relationship is not time-dependent, so it may not fully characterize the interrelationships over time. This might lead us to consider other, more elaborate models for the time-dependent interrelationships among the measures. That is, if we think one of these variables is responsible for the growth in the other, then we might need to fit a related but decidedly different set of models. The next section presents some advanced models used to solve these kinds of problems.

Multivariate Dynamic Models of Determinants of Changes

The previous models use information about the time-dependent nature of the scores, and there are several extension of these models of interest in multivariate growth curve analysis (Arminger, 1987; Nesselroade & Boker, 1994). One of the most basic extensions is the combination of a measurement model with a dual change score model among common factor scores. This kind of model was displayed earlier in Figure 18.14 but can now be extended into Figure 18.15. In other extensions, we may be interested in a combination of several previous models, including parallel growth curves and time-varying covariates.

Suppose a new variable $X[t]$ is measured at multiple occasions and we want to examine its influence in the context of a growth model for $Y[t]$. One popular model used in multilevel and mixed-effects modeling is based on the analysis of covariance (Equation 18.13) with $X[t]$ as a time-varying predictor. In our notation we can write

$$Y[t]_n = y_{0:xn} + A[t]y_{s:x,n} + \delta X[t]_n + e[t]_n \quad (18.40)$$

where the δ are fixed (group) coefficients with the same effect on $Y[t]$ scores at all occasions. In this case the growth parameters ($\mu_{0:x}$, $\mu_{s:x}$, $\sigma_{s:x}$, etc.) are conditional on the expected values of the external $X[t]$ variable. By taking first differences we find that this model implies the true score change over time is

$$\Delta y[t]_n = \Delta A[t] y_{s:x,n} + \delta \Delta X[t]_n, \quad (18.41)$$

so the basis coefficients still reflect changes based on a constant slope ($y_{s:x}$) independent of $X[t]$, and the new coefficient (δ) represents the effect of changes in X (i.e., $\Delta X[t]$) on changes in Y (i.e., $\Delta y[t]$). This time-varying covariate model is relatively easy to implement using available mixed-effects software (e.g., Sliwinski & Buchele, 1999; Sullivan, Rosenbloom, Lim, & Pfefferman, 2000; Verbeke & Molengerghs, 2000; cf. McArdle, Hamagami, et al., in press).

Modeling for multiple variables over time has been considered in the structural modeling literature. For many researchers, the most practical solution is to fit a cross-lagged regression model (see Cook & Campbell, 1977; Rogosa,

1978). This model can be written for latent scores as

$$y[t]_n = \nu_y + \phi_y y[t-1]_n + \delta_{yx} x[t-1]_n + e_y[t]_n, \quad \text{and}$$

$$x[t]_n = \nu_x + \phi_x x[t-1]_n + \delta_{xy} y[t-1]_n + e_x[t]_n, \quad (18.42)$$

where we assume a complementary regression model for each variable with auto-regressions (ϕ_y, ϕ_x) and cross-regressions (δ_{yx}, δ_x) for time-lagged predictors. This model yields a set of first difference equations that are similar to Equation 18.41, where each change model has zero intercept and the lagged changes. The cross-lagged coefficients (δ) are interpreted as the effect of changes (e.g., $\Delta x[t]$) on changes (e.g., $\Delta y[t]$), and form the basis for the critical hypotheses (e.g., $\delta_{yx} > 0$ but $\delta_{xy} = 0$).

The literature on nonlinear dynamic models has also dealt with similar multivariate issues, but clear examples are not easy to find. One dynamic bivariate model based on the partial adjustment concept was proposed by Coleman (1968) and Arminger (1987) using different techniques for estimation. This model can be written in difference score form as a set of simultaneous equations where

$$\Delta y[t]_n = \pi_y(y_{a,n} - y[t-1]_n) \quad \text{with}$$

$$y_{a,n} = \alpha_y + \gamma_{yx} x[t-1]_n,$$

and

$$\Delta x[t]_n = \pi_x(x_{a,n} - x[t-1]_n) \quad \text{with}$$

$$x_{a,n} = \alpha_x + \gamma_{xy} y[t-1]_n. \quad (18.43)$$

In this model we include pairs of latent asymptotes (y_a and x_a), rates of adjustment (π_y and π_x), intercepts (α_y and α_x), and cross-effects (γ_{yx} and γ_{xy}). The partial adjustment system has some features of a multilevel model for intercepts and slopes (Equation 18.13).

Now, following our previous latent difference scores model, we can also write a *bivariate dynamic change score* model as

$$\Delta y[t]_n = \alpha_y y_{s,n} + \beta_y y[t-1]_n + \gamma_{yx} x[t-1]_n, \quad \text{and}$$

$$\Delta x[t]_n = \alpha_x x_{s,n} + \beta_x x[t-1]_n + \gamma_{xy} y[t-1]_n, \quad (18.44)$$

where we assume a complementary dual change score model for each variable. In the first part of each change score we assume a dual change score model represented by parameters α and β. This model also permits a *coupling* parameter (γ_{yx}) representing the time-dependent effect of latent $x[t]$ on $y[t]$, and another coupling parameter (γ_{xy}) representing the time-dependent effect of latent $y[t]$ on $x[t]$. If we restrict the

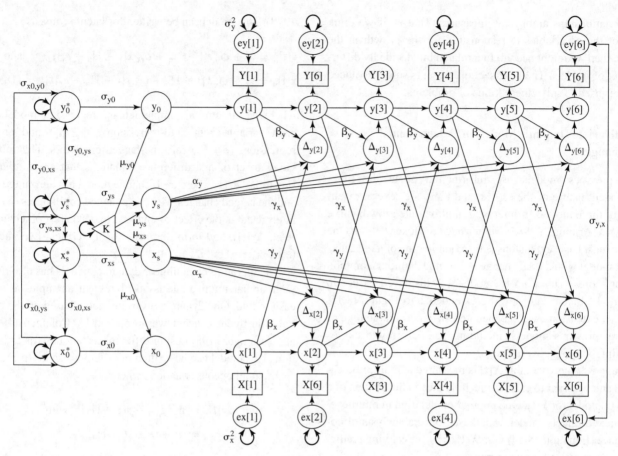

Figure 18.16   A path diagram representing a bivariate latent difference score structural model; each variable is allowed dual changes within variables (α = additive and β = proportional) as well as covariance (σ) and coupling (γ) across variables (from McArdle & Hamagami, 2001).

parameters of Equation 18.44 so that $\alpha = -\beta$, then this model is a reduced form of the partial adjustment system (Equation 18.43). This model is close to the partial adjustment system (Equation 18.43) but is not the same as time-varying covariate models (Equation 18.41) or cross-lagged models (Equation 18.42)—the latent changes in this system of equations have an intercept (α) and the coupling parameters (γ) are direct effects from prior time-varying levels ($x[t-1]$ and $y[t-1]$). Results from these alternative models can be quite different (see McArdle & Hamagami, 2001).

This bivariate dynamic model is described in the path diagram of Figure 18.16. Again the key features of this model include the used of fixed unit values (to define $\Delta y[t]$ and $\Delta x[t]$) and equality constraints (for the α, β, and γ parameters). These latent difference score models can lead to more complex nonlinear trajectory equations (e.g., nonhomogeneous equations) but these can be described simply by writing the respective bases ($A_j[t]$) as the linear accumulation of first differences (Equation 18.31) for each variable.

On a formal basis, however, this bivariate dynamic model of Equation 18.44 permits hypotheses to be formed about (a) parallel growth, (b) covariance among latent components, (c) proportional growth, and (d) dynamic coupling over time. That is to say, in addition to the previous restrictions on the dynamic parameters ($\alpha = 0$, $\alpha = 1$, and/or $\beta = 0$) we can focus on evaluating models in which one or more of the coupling parameters is restricted (i.e., $\gamma_{yx} = 0$ and/or $\gamma_{xy} = 0$). If only one of these coupling parameters is large and reliable, we may say we have estimated a coupled dynamic system with leading indicators in the presence of growth. To the degree these parameters are zero, we can say we have estimated an uncoupled system. Additional descriptions of the relevant dynamic aspects of these model coefficients, including the stability or instability of long run behaviors, can be evaluated from additional calculations (e.g., eigenvalues and equilibrium formulas; Arminger, 1987; Tuma & Hannan, 1984). Additional information can also come from a visual inspection of the bivariate expectations (after Boker & McArdle, 1995).

By combining some aspects of the previous sections, we can now represent a *group difference dynamic change score* model in at least three different ways. Assume C is a observed vector describing some kind of group differences (e.g., effect or dummy codes, for g = 1 to G groups.). If so, we can consider a model whereby the group contrasts (C_n) have a direct effect on the latent change

$$\Delta y[t]_n / \Delta t = \alpha_y \, y_{s,n} + \beta_y \, y[t - \Delta t]_n$$
$$+ \gamma_{yx} x[t - \Delta t]_n + \kappa_y \, C_n, \quad (18.45)$$

with group coefficient κ_y. Alternatively, we can write a model in which the contrasts have direct effects on the latent slopes

$$\Delta y[t]_n / \Delta t = \alpha_y \, y_{s,n} + \beta_y \, y[t - \Delta t]_n + \gamma_{yx} x[t - \Delta t]_n$$
$$\text{with} \quad y_{s,n} = \kappa_0 + \kappa_c C_n + e_z[t]_n. \quad (18.46)$$

Finally, we can write a model in which multiple groups (superscripts g) are used to indicate independent group dynamics,

$$\Delta y[t]_n^{(g)} / \Delta t = \alpha_y^{(g)} \, y[s]_n^{(g)} + \beta_y^{(g)} \, y[t - \Delta t]_n^{(g)}$$
$$+ \gamma_{yx}^{(g)} x[t - \Delta t]_n^{(g)}. \quad (18.47)$$

In the first model (Equation 18.45), we add the group contrasts as a covariate in the difference model. In the second model (Equation 18.46), we add a multilevel prediction structure of the dynamic slopes. In the third model (Equation 18.47), we indicate a potentially different dynamic parameter for each group. This third model can be fitted and used in the same way as any multiple-group models can (e.g., McArdle & Cattell, 1995; McArdle & Hamagami, 1996).

Results From Fitting Multiple Variable Growth Models

Measurement problems arise in the fitting of any statistical model with longitudinal data, and these issues begin with scaling and metrics. Our first problem with the Bradway-McArdle data comes from the fact that the Stanford-Binet (SB) was the measure administered at early ages (4, 14, 30) and the Wechsler Adult Intelligence Scale (WAIS) was used at the later ages (30, 42, 56, 64). Although these are both measures of intellectual abilities, they are not scored in the same way, and they may measure different intellectual abilities at the same or at different ages. These data were examined using a set of structural equation models with common factors for composite scores from the SB and the WAIS.

The initial structural equation model was based on information from the age 30 data in which both measurements were made, and assumed invariance across all measures at other occasions. In model fitting, the factor loading of the first variable was fixed ($\lambda_y = 1$) to identify the factor scores,

and the other loading ($\lambda_x = .84$) was estimated and required to be invariant over all times of measurement. The results quickly showed a single common factor model does not produce a good fit ($\chi^2 = 473$, $df = 34$) even though most of the parameter estimates seem reasonable ($\sigma_x = 1.39$; $\sigma_f = .06$; $\sigma_{sf} = 5.3$). In subsequent analyses, the items in each scale (SB & WAIS) were separated on a theoretical basis—some were considered as verbal items, and these were separated from the items that were considered as nonverbal items in each scale (memory and number items were separated; see Hamagami, 1998; McArdle et al., 2002). The single-factor model was refitted to each new scale, and these models fit much better than before ($\chi^2 = 63$, $df = 32$). At least two separate constructs were needed to reflect the time-sequence information in the interbattery data.

Next we followed the early work of Bayley (1956; see Figure 18.4), and we created longitudinal scores with equal intervals by using some new forms of *item response theory* (IRT) and *latent trait models* (Embretson, 1996; Fisher, 1995; McDonald, 1999). From these analyses, we formed a scoring system or translation table for each construct from the SB and WAIS measures by using IRT calibration (using the MSTEPS program) based on the data from the testing at age 30, in which both the SB & WAIS were administered. These analyses resulted in new and (we hope) age-comparable scales for the verbal and nonverbal items from all occasions (as displayed in Table 18.1 and Figure 18.6).

Several alternative verbal-nonverbal bivariate coupling models were fitted to the data (for details, see McArdle, Hamagami, et al., in press). A first model included all the bivariate change parameters described previously (Equation 18.44). This includes six dynamic coefficients (two each for α, β, γ), four latent means (μ), six latent deviations (σ), and six latent correlations (ρ). This model was fitted with $N = 111$ individuals with at least one point of data and 498 individual data observations, and it yields an overall fit ($L = 7118$) that was different from that of a random baseline ($\chi^2 = 379$ on $df = 16$). The group {and individual} trajectories of the best-fitting model can be written for the verbal ($V[t]$) and nonverbal ($N[t]$) scores in the following way

$$V[t]_n = 15.4 \, \{\pm 1.3\} + \left(\sum_{i=1,t} \Delta V[t]_n \right) + 0 \, \{\pm 4.7\}, \quad \text{and}$$

$$N[t]_n = 33.4 \, \{\pm 7.8\} + \left(\sum_{i=1,t} \Delta N[t]_n \right) + 0 \, \{\pm 11.5\}, \quad \text{with}$$

$$\sigma_{y0x0} = .77, \quad \sigma_{y0xs} = .90, \quad \sigma_{ysx0} = .08, \quad \sigma_{ysxs} = -.05. \quad (18.48)$$

More fundamentally, the respective latent change scores were modeled as

$$\Delta V[t]_n = -\mathbf{10.1}\{\pm 11.2\}V_{s,n} + -\mathbf{0.99}\,V[t-1]_n$$
$$+ \mathbf{1.02}N[t-1]_n, \quad \text{and}$$
$$\Delta N[t]_n = \mathbf{34.6}\{\pm 4.3\}N_{s,n} + -\mathbf{0.28}N[t-1]_n$$
$$+ -\mathbf{0.16}\,V[t-1]_n$$

(18.49)

The fitting of a sequence of alternative models suggested some systematic *coupling* across the V[t] and N[t] variables. Three additional models were fit to examine whether one or more of the coupling parameters (γ) were different from zero. In the first alternative model, the parameter representing the effect of N[t] on $\Delta V[t]$ was fixed to zero ($\gamma_x = 0$), and this led to a notable loss of fit ($\chi^2 = 123$ on $df = 1$). The second alternative assumed no effect from V[t] on $\Delta N[t]$ ($\gamma_y = 0$), and this is a much smaller loss of fit ($\chi^2 = 27$ on $df = 1$). Another model was fit in which no coupling was allowed ($\gamma_x = 0$ and $\gamma_y = 0$), and this resulted in a clear loss of fit ($\chi^2 = 126$ on $df = 2$). These results suggest a dynamic system in which *the nonverbal ability is a positive leading indicator of changes on verbal ability, but the negative effect of verbal ability on the nonverbal changes is not as strong.* The parameters listed previously are specific to the time interval chosen (i.e., $\Delta t = 5$), and any calculation of the explained latent variance requires a specific interval of age. These seemingly small differences can accumulate over longer periods of time, however, so the N[t] is expected to account for an increasing proportion of the variance in $\Delta V[t]$ over age.

These mathematical results of these kinds of models can be also displayed in the pictorial form of a *vector field plot* of Figure 18.17 (for details, see McArdle, Hamagami, et al., in press). This allows us to write the model expectations in a relatively scale-free form: Any pair of coordinates is a starting point (y_0, x_0), and the directional arrow is a display of the expected pair of 5-year changes (Δy, Δx) from this point. These pictures show an interesting dynamic property—*the change expectations of a dynamic model depend on the starting point.* From this perspective, we can also interpret the positive level-level correlation ($\rho_{y0,x0} = .77$), which describes the placement of the individuals in the vector field, and the small slope-slope correlation ($\rho_{ys,xs} = -.05$), which describes the location of the subsequent scores for individuals in the vector field. In any case, the resulting flow shows a dynamic process in which scores on nonverbal abilities have a tendency to impact score changes on the verbal scores, but there is no notable reverse effect.

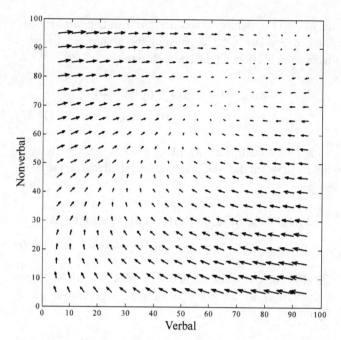

Figure 18.17 A vector field diagram representing the expected trajectories from the bivariate latent difference score model for nonverbal (*y*-axis) and verbal (*x*-axis) changes (i.e., each pair of points is a starting point, and the arrow is the directional change over the next 5 years (for details, see McArdle, Hagamani, et al., in press; McArdle et al., 2002).

Additional models were fit to examine a common growth factor model proportionality hypothesis. In this case, the factor model has two indicators at each time, V[t] and N[t], and it was combined with the previous dual change model (Equation 18.36). The basic model required only nine parameters in common factor loadings ($\lambda_y = 1, \lambda_x = .35$) and common factor dynamic parameters ($\alpha_z = 1, \beta_z = .14, \mu_{sz} = -0.13$, with no γ) and achieved convergence. However, the fit of this common factor DCS was much worse than that of the bivariate DCS model ($\chi^2 = 1262$ on $df = 11$), and this is additional evidence that separate process models are needed for verbal and nonverbal growth processes.

Differences between various Bradway demographic groups were examined using the multiple-group dynamic growth models (Equation 18.47). First we examined results when the data for males and females were considered separately. Here we found that an overall test of invariance across groups now yielded only a small difference ($\chi^2_{(m+f)} = 21$ on $df = 20$). We also find no difference in the coupling hypothesis across gender groups ($\chi^2_{(m)} = 10$ on $df = 2$). The same kinds of dynamic comparisons were calculated for participants with some college experience (ce) versus those with no college education (nc). Here we find that an overall test of invariance across groups yields another small difference ($\chi^2_{(ce+nc)} = 32$ on $df = 20$). However, when we pursue this result in more detail, we do find a large difference in the coupling hypothesis across these groups—the nonverbal to verbal coupling effect is enhanced in the group with some college education ($\gamma = -.28$, $\chi^2_{(ce)} = 25$ on $df = 1$) even though both groups started at similar initial levels.

The final group model was designed to answer several questions about nonrandom attrition. This was addressed by comparing results for participants with complete six-occasion longitudinal data ($n = 29$) from those with some incomplete data ($n = 82$). The differences in fit due to the assumption of invariance of the dynamic process over data groups is relatively small, but nontrivial ($\chi^2_{(c+i)} = 54$ on $df = 20$). This means we did alter the results by using all available data rather than just that for the persons with all data at all time points. This leaves us with a complex issue that requires further investigation.

FUTURE RESEARCH USING GROWTH CURVE ANALYSES

Future Bases of Growth Curve Analyses

The study of behavioral development and change has come a long way in the past few decades. After many years of debating whether and how to measure and represent change, it became clear that a promising solution to many of the problems of change measurement lay in collecting multiple rather than just two occasions of measurement. There had long been a mystique surrounding longitudinal methods in general, but this became translated into a much more functional approach to the representation and assessment of change. Change could be conceptualized as a function defined across time, rather than being based on a single difference score. This meant that a researcher could gather data on 3, 4, 5, or 10 occasions, often within a very short time frame, and instead of getting bogged down in an array of different kinds of change scores, could think in terms of fitting a curve over the multiple time points to represent the course of change. Moreover, concerns regarding individual differences could be cast in terms of the resemblance between these idealized functions and each person's actual trajectory.

These realizations about how to represent change processes were accelerated by the development of the variety of methods we have been referring to as latent growth curves, mixed-effect and multilevel models, and dynamic systems models. The developments in growth curve analysis have provided a number of key substantive and methodological contributions, as have been referenced previously. These developments can be classified by features of the models themselves: (a) the degree of mathematical specification, (b) the way these statistical models are fitted, and (c) the clarity and substantive meaning of the results. These issues have not been completely resolved, so we end with some comments about each of these topics.

The Mathematical Basis of Growth Curve Analyses

Most current growth curve models can be written in a common symbolic form (Seber & Wild, 1992). That is, a general model for a change in the scores over time (often using derivatives dy/dt or differences $\Delta y/\Delta t$) can be based on some mathematical functional form ($f\{x, t\}$) with unobserved scores ($x[t]$) and with unknown parameters ($A[t]$) to be estimated. Additional forms not discussed here can be included, such as auto-regressive residual structures, Markov chains, and Poisson processes. The list of growth functions described here is not exhaustive, and future extensions to other generalized functions (e.g., Ramsey & Silverman, 1997) and dynamic and chaotic formulations (May, 1997) are likely.

It is now clear that growth curve models of arbitrary complexity can be fitted to any observed trajectory over time (i.e., the integral), and the unknown parameters can be estimated to minimize some statistical function (e.g., weighted least squares, maximum likelihood) using, for example, nonlinear programming. Several different computer programs were used for the growth curve analyses discussed here. For many of the initial analyses, standard SAS programs were used, including PROC MIXED and PROC NLMIXED. The Mx-SEM computer program used herein was based on a simplified matrix approach to model expectations. All of these programs can deal with incomplete data patterns using the likelihood-based incomplete data approach presented earlier. The SEM programming is not as convenient as the mixed-effects program input scripts are, but SEM is far more flexible for programming the dynamic models (McArdle, 2001).

Growth curve modeling as an important step—but only a step—in the long progression toward better and better ways to represent behavioral development and change. Indeed, it is important to keep in mind the limitations as well as the strengths of growth curve modeling. Growth curve analysis per se results in a curve or curves defined over concrete measurement intervals—that is, a particular curve or curves. We have moved this towards a more dynamic representation that is defined across the abstract occasions (t, t + 1, t + 2, etc.) that can be integrated and solved for a particular solution. This kind of *dynamic generalizability* seems every bit as central as the more traditional concerns of subject and variable sampling.

The Statistical Basis of Growth Curve Analyses

The generic statistical approach featured here avoids some problems in older techniques, such as fitting a model to a log-scale, or directly to the velocity, or to the analysis of difference score data. These new techniques make it possible to address the critical problems of forecasting future observations, and further research on Bayesian estimation is a proper focus of additional efforts (for details, see Sieber & Wild, 1989).

The present model-fitting approach also permits a wide range of new possibilities for dealing directly with unbalanced, incomplete, or missing data. In classical work, linear polynomials were used extensively to deal with these kinds of problems (e.g., Joossens & Brems-Heyns, 1975). But the more recent work on linear and nonlinear mixed- and multi-level models indicates that it is possible to estimate growth curves and test hypotheses by collecting only small segments of data on each individual (McArdle, Ferrer-Caja, et al., in press; Pinherio & Bates, 2000; Verbeke & Molenberghs, 2000). These statistical models are being used in many longitudinal studies to deal with self-selection and subject attrition, multivariate changes in dynamic patterns of development, and the trade-offs between statistical power and costs of person and variable sampling. The statistical power questions of the future may not be *How* many *occasions do we need?*, but rather *How* few *occasions are adequate?* and *Which persons should we measure at which occasions?* (McArdle & Bell, 2000; McArdle & Woodcock, 1997).

In much the same way, the issues surrounding goodness-of-fit and the choice of an appropriate model are not simply formal statistical issues (see Burnham & Anderson, 1998). The way we conceptualize the relationships among these variables and the substantive issues involved has a great deal to do with the choice of model fitted. If we think our key variables represent substantively different growth processes, we would fit a specific growth model representing this idea (Figure 18.15). However, if we think our key variables are simply indicators of the same underlying common latent variables, then we would fit a different growth model (Figure 18.14). If we think our variables are growing and have time-lagged features, we would fit another model (Figure 18.16). If we do not know the difference, we might fit all kinds of models, examine the relative goodness-of-fit, and make some decisions about the further experiments needed. Although this exploratory approach is probably not optimal and probably requires extensive cross-validation, it certainly seems better to examine a large variety of possibilities rather than to limit our perspective on theories of growth and change (as in McArdle, 1988).

The multiple-group models presented here challenge the current approaches to an important theoretical area in behavioral science research—the study of group dynamics. Although simpler models are more common in popular usage, they seem to be special cases in a multiple-group dynamic framework. Variations of these models can be used to examine combinations of variables, even in the context of latent classes based on mixture models. In the future, we should not be surprised if our best models are checked against exploratory searches for latent-mixtures within dynamic models (Equation 18.42).

The Substantive Basis of Growth Curve Analyses

Some of the most difficult problems for future work on growth curves do not involve statistical analyses or computer programming, but rather deal with the elusive substantive meaning of the growth model parameters. As it turns out, these issues are not new but are unresolved controversies that have important implications for all other areas (Seber & Wild, 1993):

> "It is customary to say we are 'model-making.' Whether or not our model is biologically meaningful can only be tested by experiments. Here and in subsequent models we share G. F. Gause's View [Gause, 1934, p. 10]: 'There is no doubt that [growth, etc.] is a biological problem, and that it ought to be solved by experimentation and not at the desk of a mathematician. But in order to penetrate deeper into the nature of these phenomena, we must combine the experimental method with the mathematical theory, a possibility which has been created by [brilliant researchers]. The combination of the experimental method with the quantitative theory is in general one of the most powerful tools in the hands of contemporary science.' " (p. xx)

Of course, the growth parameters will only have substantive meaning if the measurements themselves and the changes that can be inferred from these measurements have a clear substantive interpretation and meaning. Thus, the basic requirements of meaningful age-equivalent measurement models are fundamental, and future measurement research is needed to address these concerns (see Fischer & Molenaar, 1995). Some of the multivariate models presented here may turn out to be useful, but these will need to be further extended to a fully dynamic time-dependent form. Empirical information will be needed to judge the utility of any growth curve model.

As students of behavior and behavioral change continue to improve their theoretical formulations, there will be a continued need to further strengthen the stock of available methods.

As the late Joachim Wohlwill (1972, 1991) argued, theory and method are partners eternally locked in a dance, with one of them leading at one time and the other leading at another time—neither partner leads all the time. Growth curve modeling has resulted in significant substantive findings that have further bolstered theories about development and change. We can expect in the not-too-distant future that strengthened theory will request even stronger methods. Until that time, however, the promise and power of these modeling techniques should be exploited.

Given the long history of elegant formulations from mathematics and statistics in this area, it is somewhat humbling to note that major aspects of the most insightful growth curve analyses have been based on careful visual inspection of the growth curves. The insight gained from visual inspection of a set of growth curves is not in dispute now; in fact, obvious visual features should be highlighted and emphasized in future research (e.g., Pinherio & Bates, 2000; Wilkinson, 1999). Much as in the past, the best future growth curve analyses are likely to be the ones we can all see most clearly.

REFERENCES

Allison, P. D. (1990). Change scores as dependent variables in regression analysis. In C. C. Clogg (Ed.), *Sociological methodology* (pp. 93–114). San Francisco: Jossey-Bass.

Arminger, G. (1986). Linear stochastic differential equation models for panel data with unobserved variables. In N. Tuma (Ed.), *Sociological methodology* (pp. 187–212). San Francisco: Jossey-Bass.

Arbuckle, J. L., & Wotke, W. (1999). AMOS 4.0 User's Guide [Computer program manual]. Chicago: Smallwaters.

Baltes, P. B., & Nesselroade, J. R. (1979). History and rationale of longitudinal research. In J. R. Nesselroade & P. B. Baltes (Eds.), *Longitudinal research in the study of behavior and development* (pp. 21–27). New York: Academic Press.

Bayley, N. (1956). Individual patterns of development. *Child Development, 27*(1), 45–74.

Bell, R. Q. (1954). An experimental test of the accelerated longitudinal approach. *Child Development, 25,* 281–286.

Bereiter, C. (1963). Some persistent problems in measuring change. In C. W. Harris (Ed.), *Problems in measuring change* (pp. 3–21). Madison: University of Wisconsin Press.

Bradway, K. P., & Thompson, C. W. (1962). Intelligence at adulthood: A 25 year follow-up. *Journal of Educational Psychology, 53*(1), 1–14.

Browne, M., & Cudeck, R. (1993). Alternative ways of assessing model fit. In K. Bollen & S. Long (Eds.), *Testing structural equation models* (pp. 136–162). Beverly Hills, CA: Sage.

Browne, M., & du Toit, S. H. C. (1991). Models for learning data. In L. Collins & J. L. Horn (Eds.), *Best methods for the analysis of change* (pp. 47–68). Washington, DC: American Psychological Association.

Bock, R. D. (1975). *Multivariate statistical methods in behavioral research.* New York: McGraw-Hill.

Bock, R. D. (1991). Prediction of growth. In L. Collins & J. L. Horn (Eds.), *Best methods for the analysis of change* (pp. 126–136). Washington, DC: American Psychological Association.

Bock, R. D., & Thissen, D. (1980). Statistical problems of fitting individual growth curves. In F. E. Johnston, A. F. Roche, & C. Susanne (Eds.), *Human physical growth and maturation: Methodologies and factors* (pp. 265–290). New York: Plenum.

Bock, R. D., Wainer, H., Peterson, A., Thissen, D., Murray, J., & Roche, A. (1973). A parameterization for individual human growth curves. *Human Biology, 45,* 63–80.

Boker, S. M., & McArdle, J. J. (1995). A statistical vector field analysis of longitudinal aging data. *Experimental Aging Research, 21,* 77–93.

Bryk, A. S., & Raudenbush, S. W. (1987). Application of hierarchical linear models to assessing change. *Psychological Bulletin, 101,* 147–158.

Bryk, A. S., & Raudenbush, S. W. (1992). *Hierarchical linear models: Applications and data analysis methods.* Newbury Park, CA: Sage.

Burnham, K. P., & Anderson, D. R. (1998). *Model selection and inference: A practical information-theoretic approach.* New York: Springer.

Burr, J. A., & Nesselroade, J. R. (1990). Change measurement. In A. von Eye (Ed.), *New statistical methods in developmental research* (pp. 3–34). New York: Academic Press.

Campbell, R. T. (1988). Integrating conceptualization, design, and analysis in panel studies of the life course. In K. W. Schaie, R. T. Campbell, W. Meredith, & S. C. Rawlings (Eds.), *Methodological issues in aging research* (pp. 43–69). New York: Springer.

Cnaan, A., Laird, N. M., & Slasor, P. (1997). Using the general linear mixed model to analyse unbalanced repeated measures and longitudinal data. *Statistics in Medicine, 16,* 2349–2380.

Cohen, J., & Cohen, P. (1983). Applied multiple regression/correlation analysis for the behavioral sciences (2nd ed.). Hillsdale, NJ: Erlbaum.

Coleman, J. (1968). The mathematical study of change. In H. M. Blalock & A. B. Blalock (Eds.), *Methodology in social research* (pp. 428–475). New York: McGraw-Hill.

Cook, T. D., & Campbell, D. T. (1979). *Quasi-experimentation design and analysis issues for field settings.* Skokie, IL: Rand-McNally.

Cronbach, L. J., & Furby, L. (1970). How we should measure change—or should we? *Psychological Bulletin, 74,* 68–80.

Cudeck, R., & du Toit (2001). Mixed-effects models in the study of individual differences with repeated measures data. *Multivariate Behavioral Research, 31,* 371–403.

Cudeck, R., & du Toit (in press). Nonlinear multilevel models for repeated measures data. In Duhon & Reise (Eds.).

Duncan, S. C., & Duncan, T. E. (1995). Modeling the processes of development via latent variable growth curve methodology. *Structural Equation Modeling: A Multidisciplinary Journal, 2,* 187–213.

Embretson, S. E. (1996). The new rules of measurement. *Psychological Assessment, 4,* 341–349.

Estes, W. K. (1959). The statistical approach to learning theory. In S. Koch (Ed.), *Psychology: A study of a science* (Vol. 2, pp. 380–491). New York: McGraw-Hill.

Fischer, G. H., & Molenaar, I. (Eds.). (1995). Rasch models: Foundations, recent developments, and applications. New York: Springer.

Garrett, H. E. (1951). *Great experiments in psychology.* New York: Appleton-Century-Crofts.

Griffiths, D., & Sandland, R. (1984). Fitting generalized allometric models to multivariate growth data. *Biometrics, 40,* 139–150.

Goldstein, H. (1995). *Multilevel statistical models* (2nd ed.). New York: Oxford University Press.

Hamagami, F. (1998). A developmental-based item factor analysis. In J. J. McArdle & R. W. Woodcock (Eds.), *Human abilities in theory and practice* (pp. 231–246). Mahwah, NJ: Erlbaum.

Hamagami, F., & McArdle, J. J. (2000). Advanced studies of individual differences linear dynamic models for longitudinal data analysis. In G. Marcoulides & R. Schumacker (Eds.), *Advanced structural equation modeling: Issues and techniques* (pp. 203–246). Mahwah, NJ: Erlbaum.

Harris, C. W. (Ed.). (1963). *Problems in measuring change.* Madison: University of Wisconsin Press.

Hauspie, R. C., Lindgren, G. W., Tanner, J. M., & Chrzastek-Spruch, H. (1991). Modeling individual and average growth data from childhood to adulthood. In D. Magnusson, L. R. Bergman, G. Rudinger, & B. Törestad (Eds.), *Problems and methods in longitudinal research: Stability and change.* Cambridge, UK: Cambridge University Press.

Hedecker, D., & Gibbons, R. (1996). MIXOR: A computer program for mixed-effects ordinal regression analysis. *Computer Methods and Programs in Biomedicine, 49,* 157–176.

Hedecker, D., & Gibbons, R. (1997). Application of random-effects pattern-mixture models for missing data in longitudinal studies. *Psychological Methods, 2,* 64–78.

Horn, J. L. (1972). The state, trait, and change dimensions of intelligence. *British Journal of Educational Psychology, 2,* 159–185.

Horn, J. L., & McArdle, J. J. (1980). Perspectives on Mathematical and Statistical Model Building (MASMOB) in research on aging. In L. Poon (Ed.), *Aging in the 1980s: Psychological issues* (pp. 503–541). Washington, DC: American Psychological Association.

Horn, J. L., & McArdle, J. J. (1992). A practical guide to measurement invariance in research on aging. *Experimental Aging Research, 18*(3), 117–144.

Joossens, J. J. & Brems-Heyns, E. (1975). High power polynomials for studying the growth of a child. *Human Biology, 9,* 556–563.

Jöreskog, K. G., & Sörbom, D. (1999). LISREL: Structural equation modeling with the SIMPLIS command language (Version 8.30) [Computer program]. Hillsdale, NJ: Scientific Software International.

Kangas, J., & Bradway, K. P. (1971). Intelligence at middle age: A thirty-eight year follow-up. *Developmental Psychology, 5*(2), 333–337.

Keats, J. A. (1983). Ability measures and theories of cognitive development. In H. Wainer & S. Messick (Eds.), *Principals of modern psychological measurement.* Hillsdale, NJ: Erlbaum.

Lange, K., Westlake, J., & Spence, M. A. (1976). Extensions to pedigree analysis: Pt. 3. Variance components by the scoring method. *Annals of Human Genetics, 39,* 485–491.

Lindsey, J. K. (1993). *Models for repeated measures.* Oxford, UK: Clarendon.

Littell, R. C., Miliken, G. A., Stoup, W. W., & Wolfinger, R. D. (1996). *SAS system for mixed models.* Cary, NC: SAS Institute.

Little, R. T. A., & Rubin, D. B. (1987). *Statistical analysis with missing data.* New York: Wiley.

May, R. M. (1987). Chaos and the dynamics of biological populations. *Proceedings of the Royal Society of London, Series A, 413,* 27–44.

McArdle, J. J. (1988). Dynamic but structural equation modeling of repeated measures data. In J. R. Nesselroade & R. B. Cattell (Eds.), *The handbook of multivariate experimental psychology* (Vol. 2, pp. 561–614). New York: Plenum.

McArdle, J. J. (1991). Structural models of developmental theory in psychology. In P. Van Geert & L. P. Mos (Eds.), *Annals of theoretical psychology* (Vol. 7, pp. 139–160).

McArdle, J. J. (1994). Structural factor analysis experiments with incomplete data. *Multivariate Behavioral Research, 29*(4), 409–454.

McArdle, J. J. (2001). A latent difference score approach to longitudinal dynamic structural analyses. In R. Cudeck, S. du Toit, & D. Sorbom (Eds.), *Structural equation modeling: Present and future* (pp. 342–380). Lincolnwood, IL: Scientific Software International.

McArdle, J. J., & Aber, M. S. (1990). Patterns of change within latent variable structural equation modeling. In A. von Eye (Eds.), *New statistical methods in developmental research* (pp. 151–224). New York: Academic Press.

McArdle, J. J., & Anderson, E. (1990). Latent variable growth models for research on aging. In J. E. Birren & K. W. Schaie (Eds.), *The handbook of the psychology of aging* (pp. 21–43). New York: Plenum.

McArdle, J. J., & Bell, R. Q. (2000). Recent trends in modeling longitudinal data by latent growth curve methods. In T. D. Little, K. U. Schnabel, & J. Baumert (Eds.), *Modeling longitudinal and multiple-group data: Practical issues, applied approaches, and scientific examples* (pp. 69–108). Mahwah, NJ: Erlbaum.

McArdle, J. J., & Cattell, R. B. (1994). Structural equation models of factorial invariance in parallel proportional profiles and oblique confactor problems. *Multivariate Behavioral Research, 29*(1), 63–113.

McArdle, J. J., & Epstein, D. B. (1987). Latent growth curves within developmental structural equation models. *Child Development, 58*(1), 110–133.

McArdle, J. J., Ferrer-Caja, E., Hamagami, F., & Woodcock, R. W. (in press). Comparative longitudinal structural analyses of the growth and decline of multiple intellectual abilities over the lifespan. *Developmental Psychology.*

McArdle, J. J., & Goldsmith, H. H. (1990). Some alternative structural equation models for multivariate biometric analyses. *Behavior Genetics, 20*(5), 569–608.

McArdle, J. J., & Hamagami, E. (1991). Modeling incomplete longitudinal and cross-sectional data using latent growth structural models. In L. M. Collins & J. L. Horn (Eds.), *Best methods for the analysis of change: Recent advances, unanswered questions, future directions* (pp. 276–304). Washington, DC: American Psychological Association.

McArdle, J. J., & Hamagami, E. (1992). Modeling incomplete longitudinal and cross-sectional data using latent growth structural models. *Experimental Aging Research, 18*(3), 145–166.

McArdle, J. J., & Hamagami, F. (1996). Multilevel models from a multiple group structural equation perspective. In G. Marcoulides & R. Schumacker (Eds.), *Advanced structural equation modeling techniques* (pp. 89–124). Hillsdale, NJ: Erlbaum.

McArdle, J. J., & Hamagami, F. (2000). Linear dynamic analyses of incomplete longitudinal data. In L. Collins & A. Sayer (Eds.), *Methods for the analysis of change* (pp. 137–176). Washington, DC: American Psychological Association.

McArdle, J. J., Hamagami, F., Meredith, W., & Bradway, K. P. (in press). Modeling the dynamic hypotheses of Gf-Gc theory using longitudinal life-span data. *Learning and Individual Differences.*

McArdle, J. J., Hamagami, F., Horn, J. L., & Bradway, K. P. (2002). *A 70-year follow-up study on dynamic of growth and change in intellectual abilities.* Unpublished manuscript, University of Virginia.

McArdle, J. J., & Nesselroade, J. R. (1994). Structuring data to study development and change. In S. H. Cohen & H. W. Reese (Eds.), *Life-span developmental psychology: Methodological innovations* (pp. 223–267). Hillsdale, NJ: Erlbaum.

McArdle, J. J., & Prescott, C. A. (1992). Age-based construct validation using structural equation models. *Experimental Aging Research, 18*(3), 87–115.

McArdle, J. J., Prescott, C. A., Hamagami, F., & Horn, J. L. (1998). A contemporary method for developmental-genetic analyses of age changes in intellectual abilities. *Developmental Neuropsychology, 14*(1), 69–114.

McArdle, J. J., & Woodcock, J. R. (1997). Expanding test-rest designs to include developmental time-lag components. *Psychological Methods, 2*(4), 403–435.

McDonald, R. P. (1999). *Test theory: A unified treatment.* Mahwah, NJ: Erlbaum.

Meredith, W., & Tisak, J. (1990). Latent curve analysis. *Psychometrika, 55*, 107–122.

Metha, P. D., & West, S. G. (2000). Putting the individual back into individual growth curves. *Psychological Methods, 5*(1), 23–43.

Miyazaki, Y., & Raudenbush, S. W. (2000). Tests for linkage of multiple cohorts in an accelerated longitudinal design. *Psychological Methods, 5*(1), 24–63.

Muthen, B. O., & Curran, P. (1997). General longitudinal modeling of individual differences in experimental designs: A latent variable framework for analysis and power estimation. *Psychological Methods, 2*, 371–402.

Muthen, L. K., & Muthen, B. O. (1998). Mplus, the comprehensive modeling program for applied researchers user's guide [Computer program manual]. Los Angeles, CA: Muthen & Muthen.

Nagin, D. (1999). Analyzing developmental trajectories: Semiparametric. Group-based approach. *Psychological Methods, 4*, 139–177.

Neale, M. C., Boker, S. M., Xie, G., & Maes, H. H. (1999). Mx Statistical Modeling (5th ed.). Unpublished computer program manual, Virginia Institute of Psychiatric and Behavioral Genetics, Medical College of Virginia, Virginia Commonwealth University, Richmond, VA.

Nelder, J. A. (1961). The fitting of a generalization of the logistic curve. *Biometrics, 17*, 89–110.

Nesselroade, J. R., & Bartsch, T. W. (1977). Multivariate perspectives on the construct validity of the trait-state distinction. In R. B. Cattell & R. M. Dreger (Eds.), *Handbook of modern personality theory* (pp. 221–238). Washington, DC: Hemisphere.

Nesselroade, J. R., & Boker, S. M. (1994). Assessing constancy and change. In T. F. Heatherton & J. L. Weinberger (Eds.), *Can personality change?* Washington, DC: American Psychological Association.

Nesselroade, J. R., & Cable, D. G. (1974). Sometimes it's okay to factor difference scores: The separation of state and trait anxiety. *Multivariate Behavioral Research, 9*, 273–282.

Nesselroade, J. J., & McArdle, J. J. (1996). On the mismatching of levels of abstraction in mathematical-statistical model fitting. In M. D. Franzen & H. W. Reese (Eds.), *Life-span developmental psychology: Biological and neuropsychological mechanisms.* Hillsdale, NJ: Erlbaum.

Nesselroade, J. R., Siegler, S. M., & Baltes, P. B. (1980). Regression towards the mean and the study of change. *Psychological Bulletin, 88*(3), 622–637.

Pinherio, J. C., & Bates, D. M. (2000). *Mixed-effects models in S and S-PLUS.* New York: Springer.

Pothoff, R. F., & Roy, S. N. (1964). A generalized multivariate analysis model useful especially for growth curve problems. *Biometrics, 51*, 313–326.

Preece, M. A., & Baines, M. J. (1978). A new family of mathematical models describing the human growth curve. *Annals of Human Biology, 5*(1), 1–24.

Ramsey, J., & Sliverman, (1997). *A functional approach to data analysis.* New York: Springer.

Rogosa, D. (1978). Causal models in longitudinal research: Rationale, formulation, and interpretation. In J. R. Nesselroade & P. B. Baltes (Eds.), *Longitudinal research in the study of behavior and development.* New York: Academic Press.

Rogosa, D., & Willett, J. B. (1985). Understanding correlates of change by modeling individual differences in growth. *Psychometrika, 50,* 203–228.

Rao, C. R. (1958). Some statistical methods for the comparison of growth curves. *Biometrics, 14,* 1–17.

Raykov, T. (1999). Are simple change scores obsolete? An approach to studying correlates and predictors of change. *Applied Psychology Measurement, 23*(2), 120–126.

Richards, F. J. (1959). A flexible growth function for empirical use. *Journal of Experimental Botany, 10,* 290–300.

Sandland, R. L., & McGilchrist, C. A. (1979). Stochastic growth curve analysis. *Biometrics, 35,* 255–271.

Seber, G. A. F., & Wild, C. J. (1989). *Nonlinear models.* New York: Wiley.

Scammon, R. E. (1927). The first seriatim study of human growth. *American Journal of Physical Anthropology, 10,* 329–336.

Simonton, D. K. (1989). Age and creative productivity: Nonlinear estimation of an information processing model. *International Journal of Aging and Human Development, 29*(1), 23–37.

Singer, J. D. (1998). Using SAS PROC MIXED to fit multilevel models, hierarchical models, and individual growth models. *Journal of Educational and Behavioral Statistics, 24*(4), 323–355.

Sliwinski, M., & Buschke, H. (1999). Cross-sectional and longitudinal relationships among age, cognition, and processing speed. *Psychology and Aging, 14*(1), 18–33.

Smith, P. L. (1979). Splines as a useful and convenient tool. *The American Statistician, 32*(2), 57–63.

Snijders, T. A. B., & Bosker, R. (1994). Modeled variance in two-level models. *Sociological Methods & Research, 22,* 342–363.

Stimson, J. A., Carmines, E. G., & Zeller, R. A. (1978). Interpreting polynomial regression. *Sociological Methods & Research, 6*(4), 515–524.

Sullivan, E. V., Rosenbloom, M. J., Lim, K. O., & Pfefferman, A. (2000). Longitudinal changes in cognition, gait, balance in abstinent and relapsed alcoholic men: Relationships to changes in brain structure. *Neuropsychology, 14*(2), 178–188.

Tanner J. M. (1955). *Growth at adolescence.* Oxford, UK: Blackwell Science.

Tanner J. M. (Ed.). (1960). *Human growth.* New York: Pergamon.

Tisak, J., & Tisak, M. S. (1996). Longitudinal models of reliability and validity: A latent curve approach. *Applied Psychological Measurement, 20*(3), 275–288.

Tuma, N., & Hannan, M. (1984). *Social dynamics.* New York: Academic Press.

Tucker, L. R. (1958). Determination of parameters of a functional relation by factor analysis. *Psychometrika, 23,* 19–23.

Tucker, L. R. (1966). Learning theory and multivariate experiment: Illustration by determination of generalized learning curves. In R. B. Cattell (Ed.), *Handbook of multivariate experimental psychology.* Chicago, IL: Rand-McNally.

Turner, M. E. (1978). Allometry and multivariate growth. *Growth, 42,* 434–450.

Verbeke, G., & Molenberghs, G. (2000). *Linear mixed models for longitudinal data.* New York: Springer.

von Bertalanffy, L. (1938). A quantitative theory of organic growth. *Human Biology, 10,* 181–243.

von Bertalanffy, L. (1957). Quantitative laws in metabolism and growth. *Quart. Rev. Biology, 32,* 217–231.

Willett, J. B. (1990). Measuring change: The difference score and beyond. In H. J. Walberg & G. D. Haertel (Eds.), *The international encyclopedia of education evaluation* (pp. 632–637). Oxford, UK: Pergamon.

Willett, J. B., & Sayer, A. G. (1994). Using covariance structure analysis to detect correlates and predictors of individual change over time. *Psychological Bulletin, 116,* 363–381.

Williams, R. H., & Zimmerman, D. W. (1996). Are simple gain scores obsolete? *Applied Psychological Measurement, 20*(1), 59–69.

Wilkenson, L. (1999). *Graphics.* New York: Spinger.

Wishart, J. (1938). Growth rate determinations in nutrition studies with the bacon pig, and their analyses. *Biometrika, 30,* 16–28.

Wright, S. (1934). The method of path coefficients. *Annals of Mathematical Statistics, 5,* 161–215.

Zeger, S. L., & Harlow, S. D. (1987). Mathematical models from laws of growth to tools for biologic analysis: Fifty years of growth. *Growth, 51,* 1–21.

PART FOUR
DATA ANALYSIS METHODS

CHAPTER 19

Multiple Linear Regression

LEONA S. AIKEN, STEPHEN G. WEST, AND STEVEN C. PITTS

WHAT IS MULTIPLE REGRESSION ANALYSIS?

Multiple regression analysis (MR) is a general system for examining the relationship of a collection of independent variables to a single dependent variable. It is among the most extensively used statistical analyses in the behavioral sciences. Multiple regression is highly flexible and lends itself to the investigation of a wide variety of questions. The independent variables may be quantitative measures such as personality traits, abilities, or family income; or they may be categorical measures such as gender, ethnic group, or treatment condition in an experiment. In the most common form of multiple regression analysis, which we consider here, the dependent variable is continuous. The basic ideas of multiple regression can be extended to consider other types of dependent variables such as categories, counts, or even multiple dependent variables. The relationship between an independent

variable and the dependent variable may be linear, curvilinear, or may depend on the value of another independent variable.

In the context of multiple regression analysis, the independent variables are termed *predictors;* the dependent variable is termed the *criterion.* These terms reflect the fact that scores on the predictors can be used to make a statistical prediction of scores that will later accrue on the criterion: for example, how good an employee's job performance (the criterion) will be after 2 months on the job, based on the employee's characteristics measured at the outset of the job (the predictors). Multiple regression analysis provides an assessment of how well a set of predictors taken as a whole account for the criterion. It also provides assessments of the unique contribution of each individual predictor within the set, as well as of the contribution of one subset of predictors above and beyond another subset. Assessment of the *unique contribution* of each individual predictor within a set of predictors and of subsets of predictors is a hallmark of multiple regression analysis.

Three Uses of Multiple Regression Analysis: Description, Prediction, and Theory Testing

Multiple regression analysis can be used for *description,* simply to summarize the relationships of a set of predictors to a criterion at a single point in time, (e.g., to summarize the relationship of a set of employee characteristics to job performance). Further, multiple regression analysis can be used for *prediction,* (e.g., to predict the job performance of a set of job applicants based on their characteristics measured during the job application process). The use of MR in *theory testing* is perhaps the most important application for the development of psychology as a science: Ideas derived from theory and from previous research can be translated into hypotheses that are tested using multiple regression analysis, (e.g., testing whether each of a set of predictors of job performance identified by theory or previous empirical research actually predict job performance across a variety of employment settings).

Two Foci of This Chapter

The testing of theoretical predictions through multiple regression is the key focus of this chapter. Theory and prior research lead to *identification* of predictors of interest, and, in addition, characterization of the *form of their relationships* (e.g. linear, curvilinear, interactive) to the criterion. Together, identification of predictors and characterization of forms of relationship are referred to as *model specification.* After a model has been specified, multiple regression can be employed to test each aspect of the specification.

The second focus of the chapter is the identification of problems with the implementation of regression analyses, both from the perspective of the model and the perspective of the data themselves. Problems with the model include, for example, the incorrect specification of the form of relationship of a predictor to the criterion. Problems with the data may arise due to the distributions of the predictors or criterion, or to the presence of a few extreme data points that distort the analysis outcomes. Approaches to problem identification include both modern *statistical graphics* and a class of statistical measures called *regression diagnostics.*

We begin this chapter with an overview of multiple regression as a general system for data analysis, limiting our technical presentation to the most common form of regression analysis, *multiple linear regression analysis.* We then introduce a numerical example drawn from health psychology, which we use to illustrate the foci of our chapter, as well

as many of the kinds of questions that can be answered with multiple regression.

THE STRUCTURE OF MULTIPLE REGRESSION ANALYSIS

The Multiple Regression Equation

Multiple regression (MR) analysis involves the estimation of a *multiple regression equation* that summarizes the relationship of a set of predictors to the observed criterion. One general form of the regression equation written for an individual case i is as follows:

$$\hat{Y}_i = b_0 + b_1 X_{i1} + b_2 X_{i2} + \cdots + b_j X_{ij} + \cdots + b_p X_{ip}.$$

(19.1)

where $X_{i1}, X_{i2}, \ldots X_{ip}$ are the scores of case i on the $j = 1$, $2, \ldots p$ predictors; $b_1, b_2, \ldots b_j \ldots b_p$ are *partial regression coefficients* (or *regression weights*) and b_0 is the *regression intercept.* The regression equation combines the values of the predictors into a single summary score, the predicted score $\hat{Y}$ (*Y hat*). Specifically, $\hat{Y}$ is a *linear combination* of the predictors: Each predictor X_j is multiplied by its regression weight b_j and these products are then summed across all the predictors. The regression intercept b_0 gives the arithmetic mean value of $\hat{Y}$ when each of the predictors has a value of zero and serves to scale the predicted scores so that their mean equals the mean of the observed criterion scores. The predicted score $\hat{Y}$ is the best statistical estimate of the observed criterion score Y, based on the set of predictors. Each person receives a single predicted score $\hat{Y}_i$ based on his or her scores on each of the predictors; the predicted score $\hat{Y}_i$ can be compared directly to the observed criterion score Y_i for that person. The regression equation expresses the unique linear contribution of each X to $\hat{Y}$, above and beyond the contribution from all other predictors in the regression equation. As a single predictor X_j increases in value by one unit, the predicted score increases by b_j units, (i.e., by the value of the partial regression coefficient). The MR equation is thus said to be *linear in the coefficients.*

The Least Squares Criterion for Selection of Regression Coefficients

How are the values of the intercept and regression weights calculated? To understand this, we present a second general form of the MR equation:

$$Y_i = b_0 + b_1 X_{i1} + b_2 X_{i2} + \cdots + b_p X_{ip} + e_i.$$ (19.2)

Note that there are two differences between Equations 19.1 and 19.2. First, the observed value of Y has replaced the predicted value $\hat{Y}$ on the left side of the equation. Second, the residual e_i has been added to the right side of the equation. For each person in the study, the residual e_i is the difference between that person's observed criterion value and predicted value, $e_i = Y_i - \hat{Y}_i$ for person i; the sum of these residuals over all individuals is zero. In multiple regression, the values of each regression weight $b_0, b_1, \ldots, b_p$ are chosen so as to minimize the sum of the squared residuals across the participants. That is, the regression weights $b_0, b_1, \ldots, b_p$ are chosen so that

$$\sum_{i=1}^{n} e_i^2 = \sum_{i=1}^{n} (Y_i - \hat{Y}_i)^2 \quad \text{is minimum.} \quad (19.3)$$

This criterion is termed *ordinary least squares*. MR that employs this criterion is also known as *ordinary least squares regression* (OLS regression). Multiple regression computed using ordinary least squares produces optimal estimates of the regression weights in that the correlation between the predicted score $\hat{Y}$ and the observed criterion Y is maximized. The weights also have desirable properties for use in testing theoretical hypotheses when several statistical assumptions, to be presented later in the chapter, are met. Residuals play a special role in the detection of problems with the hypothesized regression model. Examination of special plots and diagnostic statistics based on the residuals help identify ways in which the regression model can be modified and improved to better capture the relationships in the data.

Nonlinear Relationships and OLS Regression

Although Equation 19.1 might seem to limit multiple regression only to the study of linear relationships, this is not the case. We can also replace any of the X_j terms with a variety of mathematical functions of the predictor variables in Equation 19.1 to represent other forms of relationships. For example, a psychologist studying perceptions of the area of square objects (Y) as a function of their width (X_j) would include a $b_j X_j^2$ term in the regression equation given the known physical relationship for the area of squares, $area = (width)^2$. In general, any mathematical expression involving one or more predictor variables may be used—$\sqrt{X_j}$, $\log(X_j)$, $X_j \sqrt{X_k}$, and so forth. So long as the regression weight simply serves to multiply the mathematical expression, the regression equation is *linear in the coefficients* and can be estimated using ordinary least squares. Thus, although the results would almost certainly not be theoretically meaningful, the equation $\hat{Y} = b_0 + b_1 X_1 + b_2 \sqrt{X_2} + b_3 X_1^2 + b_4 X_1 \sqrt{X_2}$ could be estimated using OLS regression. In contrast, regression equations that are not linear in the coefficients like $Y = b_0 X^{b_1} + e$ cannot be estimated using OLS regression procedures. Such equations require more advanced nonlinear regression techniques that are beyond the scope of this chapter (see Draper & Smith, 1998; Neter, Kutner, Nachtsheim, & Wasserman, 1996; Ryan, 1997, for accessible accounts of nonlinear regression).

Measures of Contribution to Prediction Accuracy

In MR, we measure contributions of predictors to overall prediction at three different levels. First, we measure the overall accuracy of prediction from the full set of predictors. Second, we measure the unique contribution of each predictor to overall prediction. Third, we measure how subsets of predictors contribute above and beyond other sets of predictors.

The Squared Multiple Correlation

The correlation between the predicted score $\hat{Y}$ and the observed criterion score Y is called the *multiple correlation*. It is the maximum possible correlation that can be attained between Y and any linear combination of the predictors. The OLS regression coefficients not only yield the minimum sum of squared residuals; they also maximize the multiple correlation. The multiple correlation provides a single number summary of overall accuracy of prediction—that is, how well the regression equation accounts for the criterion. Typically, the *squared multiple correlation,* the square of this correlation, is reported. The squared measure assesses the proportion of variation in the criterion accounted for by the set of predictors and ranges between 0.0 indicating no linear relationship to 1.00 indicating a perfect linear relationship (100% of the variation in Y is explained). By variation we mean specifically the sum of squared deviations of Y scores about the Y mean:

$$SS_Y = \sum (Y - M_Y)^2 \quad (19.4)$$

The notation for the squared multiple correlation varies across sources: (a) simply R^2, (b) R^2_{multiple}, or (c) $R^2_{Y\hat{Y}}$ to show the correlation between Y and $\hat{Y}$, or (d) $R^2_{Y.12\ldots p}$ to denote that the criterion Y has been predicted by a set of predictors $X_1, X_2, \ldots, X_p$, (e.g., $R^2_{Y.123}$ for a three-predictor regression equation). We use R^2 unless we need to indicate the specific predictors in the equation, in which case we use $R^2_{Y.12\ldots p}$. The squared multiple correlation provides a measure of *effect size* for overall prediction. Cohen (1988) provided guidelines for effect sizes in multiple regression: .02, .13, and .26 for small, moderate, and large effect sizes, respectively.

Partialed Relationships for Individual Predictors: Partial Regression Coefficients, Partial and Semipartial Correlations

Three closely related measures assess the unique contribution of individual predictors to prediction. All three measures call upon the concept of *partialing out* or *holding constant* the overlapping parts of predictors. The term *partial* in MR signifies that the influence of the other predictor(s) has been removed. Insight into partialing is gleaned from the notion of holding constant a second predictor: We can think of measuring the impact of X_2 on Y for individuals all of whom have the same score on X_1, so that the unique contribution of X_2 on Y is measured with no confounding from the impact of X_1. We illustrate the three measures of contribution of individual predictors with two correlated predictors X_1 and X_2 and the criterion Y.

First, the *squared semipartial correlation of X_1 with Y*, noted $R_{Y(2.1)}^2$, measures the proportion of *total variation* in the criterion Y—that is, SS_Y that is uniquely accounted for by X_2, with X_1 partialed out of X_2 but not out of Y (this correlation is also called the squared *part* correlation). Put another way, $R_{Y(2.1)}^2$ measures the gain in prediction from adding X_2 to a regression equation that already contains X_1. We compute R_{Y1}^2, the squared multiple correlation or proportion of variation in Y accounted for by predictor X_1 alone. Then we compute $R_{Y.12}^2$, the squared multiple correlation or proportion of variation in Y accounted for by predictors X_1 and X_2 together. Then the squared semipartial correlation of X_2 with Y holding X_1 constant is given as $R_{Y(2.1)}^2 = R_{Y.12}^2 - R_{Y1}^2$. The second measure, *squared partial correlation*, goes a step further in partialing out the influence of X_1. The influence of X_1 is partialed from both predictor X_2 and from the criterion Y. Thus the *squared partial correlation* measures the proportion of *residual variation* in the criterion Y (not accounted for by other predictors) that is uniquely accounted for by the predictor in question. Again, for X_2 with Y in the two predictor case, X_1 is partialed both from X_2 and Y. The standard notation for this squared partial correlation is $R_{Y2.1}^2$ and is given as $R_{Y2.1}^2 = (R_{Y.12}^2 - R_{Y1}^2)/(1 - R_{Y1}^2)$. Because the residual variation in Y typically will be smaller than the total variation, the squared partial correlation will typically be larger in value than the squared semipartial correlation. Both the squared semipartial and squared partial correlations can range in value from 0.00 to 1.00. Finally, the *partial regression coefficient* for X_2 in a regression equation also containing X_1 measures the unique influence of X_2 on Y with X_1 partialed out. The full notation for the b_2 partial regression coefficient for X_2 in a two-predictor regression equation is $b_{y2.1}$ to reflect the influence of a one-unit change in X_2 on Y with X_1 partialed out.

In sum, the partial regression coefficient, squared semipartial correlation, and the squared partial correlation all assess the unique contribution of a predictor in a regression equation containing other predictors. They all reflect the *conditional relationship* of a predictor to the criterion; the relationship is conditional in that it depends specifically on what other predictor(s) are partialed or held constant. In fact, all three lead to precisely the same value of the test statistic for significance of the predictor's contribution.

Sets of Predictors

The notion of unique contribution of a single predictor above and beyond other predictor(s) can be extended to the unique contribution of a set of predictors beyond other predictor(s)—for example, from a second set of predictors X_4 and X_5, above and beyond a baseline set consisting of X_1, X_2, and X_3. A measure of gain in prediction by the addition of the second set of predictors to the baseline set is computed. First $R_{Y.123}^2$ is computed for the baseline set of predictor variables. Then $R_{Y.12345}^2$ is computed for the baseline plus second set of predictors. The gain in prediction is the difference between the R^2 based on the combined sets and the R^2 based on the baseline set of predictor variables, here $R_{Y.12345}^2 - R_{Y.123}^2$. This difference is the *squared multiple semipartial correlation* $R_{Y(45.123)}^2$ of X_4 and X_5 with Y with X_1, X_2, and X_3 partialed out. The squared partial correlation can also be extended to sets of predictors. However, partial regression coefficients only pertain to the unique contribution of individual variables.

NUMERICAL EXAMPLE: PREDICTING INTENTION TO OBTAIN A MAMMOGRAM

To provide a concrete basis for illustrating the use of multiple regression in the behavioral sciences, we introduce an artificial data set from the health psychology area. Health psychologists have conducted considerable empirical research and have developed theory to explain the extent to which individuals take actions to protect their health (see Aiken, Gerend, & Jackson, 2001). Our example focuses on women's intentions to obtain a screening mammogram, a test that detects breast cancer in its very early, treatable stages (Aiken, West, Woodward, & Reno, 1994). The criterion Y is a scale score on a 6-point multi-item scale of intention to obtain a mammogram, measured on a group of $N = 240$ women who are not in compliance with screening guidelines of the National Cancer Institute at the time of data collection. There are four predictor variables that fall into two sets. The first set (predictor variables 1 and 2) are based on medical factors.

The second set (predictor variables 3 and 4) are based on psychological factors.

1. *Recommendation.* Recommendation for mammography screening by a health professional is a powerful predictor of screening compliance (Aiken, West, Woodward, & Reno et al., 1994). Here we used a three-category recommendation predictor: (a) physician recommended a mammogram, (b) another health professional recommended a mammogram (e.g., nurse, physician assistant), (c) the woman received no recommendation for a mammogram.

2. *Medical risk.* We expected intention to take health-protective action to be related to the woman's objective medical risk of getting the disease. Thus we included a 10-point measure of medical risk for developing breast cancer (see Gail et al., 1989 for an actual measure of risk for breast cancer).

3. *Perceived benefits.* Based on the Health Belief Model (Rosenstock, 1990), a well-researched model of the determinants of health protective behavior, we expected that the likelihood of protective health action would increase with increases in the perception of the benefits of the health action. We included scale scores on a 6-point multi-item scale of benefits.

4. *Worry.* Finally, fear or worry about disease may also affect protective health actions. There is disagreement as to whether protective health behavior increases linearly with fear or worry (Aiken et al., 2001). According to some theorizing (Janis & Feshbach, 1953), this relationship may not be linear, but rather curvilinear. Health protective actions may increase as the level of fear increases only up to a point. Beyond this point, compliance with health recommendations begins to diminish as the individual increasingly focuses on coping with overwhelming emotions rather than taking health-protective actions. We included scale scores on a 6-point multi-item scale of breast cancer worry.

Descriptive statistics for our simulated data set are provided for each continuous predictor and the criterion in Table 19.1. Panel A presents the possible range, mean, standard deviation, skewness, and kurtosis for the scale variables. Of note, risk and worry are both severely nonnormal, which can affect the ability to detect relationships and to test hypotheses. Panel B presents the frequency and proportion of responses in each of the three categories of the recommendation variable, as well as the arithmetic mean intention score in each category. Panel C presents the correlation matrix and Panel D presents the covariance matrix for the continuous

variables, including the relation between each pair of predictors and of each predictor with the criterion. Because it is not meaningful to correlate a variable with three categories with the criterion, we have created two predictors from *recommendation,* our first variable. A full explanation of the rationale for creating the predictors is provided below. The first categorical predictor *any recommendation* (ANYREC) contrasts the intention of women who receive a recommendation from either a physician or other health professional with the intention of women who receive no recommendation. The second categorical predictor, *physician versus other professional* (PHYSOTHR), contrasts those women who received a recommendation from a physician with those who received a recommendation from another health professional. The correlations and covariances of the ANYREC and PHYSOTHR contrast variables with the other predictors and criterion are included in Table 19.1, Panels C and D, respectively.

NUMERICAL EXAMPLE: MULTIPLE REGRESSION ANALYSES

Overview

Our strategy in this section is to work through a number of commonly encountered types of analyses that are performed using multiple regression. Each of these analyses is presented in the context of testing hypotheses from health psychology using our simulated data set. In the course of these analyses, we introduce useful statistics that are computed in multiple linear regression. We also introduce the use of regression graphics and diagnostic statistics to identify problems with the regression model.

One-Predictor Regression: Continuous Predictor Variable—Hypothesis 1

Our first hypothesis from the medical literature is that increases in medical risk increase protective health actions. Following the precedent provided by much previous research, we make the simple prediction that the relationship between risk (X_1) and intention to get a mammogram (Y) will be linear (straight line). This leads to the specification of the following single predictor regression equation:

$$\hat{Y} = b_0 + b_1 X_1 \tag{19.5}$$

The results of the regression analysis to test our first hypothesis are summarized in Table 19.2, Panel A. In the following discussion we explain how these values are obtained.

TABLE 19.1   Descriptive Statistics, Correlation, and Covariance Matrix for All Variables,
N = 240

A. Descriptive Statistics, Continuous Variables

Variable	Mean	Standard Deviation	Skew	Kurtosis	Range
Risk	3.989	.750	2.146	19.634	1–10
Benefit	3.321	.900	−.027	−.515	1–6
Worry	2.373	.520	2.080	11.542	1–6
Intent	3.612	.914	−.180	.018	1–6

B. Descriptive Statistics, Categorical Variable, Recommendation

Category	Frequency	Proportion	Intentions Mean
Recommendation by physician	96	.40	3.8949
Recommendation by other health professional	48	.20	4.1025
No recommendation	96	.40	3.0845

C. Correlation Matrix

	INTENT	RISK	ANYREC[a]	PHYSOTHR[b]	BENEFIT	WORRY
INTENT	1.000	.283	.472	.022	.380	.122
RISK	.283	1.000	.139	−.090	.371	.523
ANYREC	.472	.139	1.000	.218	.281	.072
PHYSOTHR	.022	−.090	.218	1.000	−.006	−.016
BENEFIT	.380	.371	.281	−.006	1.000	.402
WORRY	.122	.523	.072	−.016	.402	1.000

D. Covariance Matrix

	INTENT	RISK	ANYREC[a]	PHYSOTHR[b]	BENEFIT	WORRY
INTENT	.835	.194	.212	.008	.313	.058
RISK	.194	.563	.051	−.025	.251	.204
ANYREC	.212	.051	.241	.040	.124	.018
PHYSOTHR	.008	−.025	.040	.141	−.002	−.003
BENEFIT	.313	.251	.124	−.002	.810	.188
WORRY	.058	.204	.018	−.003	.188	.270

[a]ANYREC is computed from Recommendation by the following coding: Physician recommendation = .333333; other health professional recommendation = .333333; no recommendation = −.666667.
[b]PHYSOTHR is computed from Recommendation by the following coding: Physician recommendation = .50; Other health professional recommendation = −.50; no recommendation = 0.0.

The form of Equation 19.5 is very familiar from high-school mathematics: an equation for a straight line with slope b_1 and intercept b_0. The slope b_1 (the regression coefficient) indicates the change in $\hat{Y}$ for a one unit increase in X. The intercept b_0 indicates the value of $\hat{Y}$ when $X = 0$. The values of b_1 and b_0 are chosen to meet the least squares criterion, given in Equation 19.3. The least squares criterion leads to the following expressions for b_1 and b_0:

$$b_1 = r_{XY} \frac{s_Y}{s_X} \tag{19.6}$$

and

$$b_0 = M_Y - b_1 M_X \tag{19.7}$$

where r_{XY} is the correlation between the predictor X and the criterion Y; s_X and s_Y are the standard deviations of predictors X and Y, respectively; and M_X and M_Y are the arithmetic means of X and Y, respectively.

Table 19.1 provides the needed values for computation of b_1 and b_0 for the prediction of intention from risk. From the correlation matrix we have $r_{XY} = .283$, with standard deviations $s_X = .750$, $s_Y = .914$, so that $b_1 = (.283)(.914/.750) = .344$. From the means, we have $b_0 = 3.612 - (.344) \times (3.989) = 3.612 - 1.376 = 2.238$, yielding the regression equation $\hat{Y} = 2.238 + .344$ RISK. For every one unit of medical risk on the 10-point medical risk scale, intention to obtain a mammogram increases by .344 points on the 6-point intention scale. The intercept of 2.238 is the predicted value of intention when risk = 0, here a nonsensical value, because the minimum value on the risk scale = 1.

Centering Predictors

One way to produce an interpretable intercept is through *centering* the predictor—that is, putting the predictor into deviation form by subtracting the arithmetic mean of the predictor

TABLE 19.2   Regression Analyses to Test Hypotheses Concerning Relationship of Medical Factors to Intention to Obtain a Mammogram

A. Hypothesis 1: Linear Relationship of Medical Risk to Intention

R^2 .07989

Analysis of Regression

	df	Sum of Squares	Mean Square	F	p
Regression	1	15.95103	15.95103	20.665	.001
Residual	238	183.70555	.77187		

Regression Equation

Variable	b	s_b	95% Confidence Interval		$b\star$	t	p
RISK	.344424	.075766	.195167	.493681	.282652	4.545	.001
INTERCEPT	2.238386	.307494	1.632628	2.844143			

B. Hypotheses 2 and 3: Relationships of Recommendation From Physician or From Other Health Professional and Intention to Obtain a Mammogram, With Contrast Coded Predictors

R^2 .23012

Analysis of Regression

	df	Sum of Squares	Mean Square	F	p
Regression	2	45.94591	22.97296	35.421	.001
Residual	237	153.71067	.64857		

Regression Equation

Variable	b	s_b	95% Confidence Interval		$b\star$	t	p
ANYREC	.914219	.108733	.700012	1.128425	.491043	8.408	.001
PHYSOTH	−.207604	.142365	−.488066	.072858	−.085166	−1.458	.146
INTERCEPT	3.693959	.054796	3.586009	3.801909			

Note. b is the unstandardized regression coefficient; $b\star$ is the standardized regression coefficient; s_b is the estimate of the standard error of the regression coefficient; 95% confidence interval is on the unstandardized regression coefficient.

from each score. The predictor variable X_1 is linearly transformed to a centered predictor X_{1C}, where $X_{1C} = X_1 - M_{X1}$ for each participant (Aiken & West, 1991; Wainer, 2000). Centering a predictor renders the value of 0 on the predictor meaningful; it is the mean of the centered predictor across all participants. Once again, we estimate the basic regression equation (Equation 19.4) now using X_{1C} as the predictor,

$$\hat{Y} = \tilde{b}_0 + b_1 X_{1C}, \qquad (19.8)$$

with $\tilde{b}_0$ and b_1 respectively representing the intercept and slope in this new equation. For our example $X_{1C} = \text{RISK}_{\text{CENTERED}}$, and the result is $\hat{Y} = 3.612 + 0.344\,\text{RISK}_{\text{CENTERED}}$. Note that following centering of X_1, the slope is unchanged, but the intercept now equals the mean of Y, intention to get a mammogram. An examination of Equation 19.7 shows that when $M_X = 0$ (which occurs when X_1 is centered), b_0 will always be equal to M_Y. As we will see later in the chapter, centering is often a useful procedure for improving the interpretability of lower-order regression coefficients, here b_0, in regression equations that contain more complex higher-order terms. As a final note, the changes in the value of X_1 to X_{1C} and of b_0 to $\tilde{b}_0$ are such that the predicted scores are identical before and after centering.

Returning to our original regression equation using X_1 as the predictor (Equation 19.5), how well does this equation account for variation in the observed criterion score? To answer this question, we compute two values based on the predicted scores. The first is $SS_{\text{regression}}$, the variation of the predicted scores around the mean of the predicted scores ($M_{\hat{Y}} = M_Y$):

$$SS_{\text{regression}} = \sum (\hat{Y}_i - M_{\hat{Y}})^2 \qquad (19.9)$$

The larger this value, the better the differential prediction from the regression equation. The maximum value that $SS_{\text{regression}}$ can achieve is SS_Y, the variation of the observed criterion scores around the mean of the observed scores (M_Y), given in Equation 19.4. If $SS_{\text{regression}}$ were to equal SS_Y, this would signify that the regression equation had reproduced all the differences among the individual scores on the observed criterion. The second computation is the residual variation SS_{residual}, a measure of failure to reproduce the observed criterion scores:

$$SS_{\text{residual}} = SS_{Y-\hat{Y}} = \sum(Y_i - \hat{Y}_i)^2 \qquad (19.10)$$

For the present data $SS_Y = 199.657$, $SS_{\text{regression}} = 15.951$, and $SS_{\text{residual}} = 183.706$. We note that $SS_Y = SS_{\text{regression}} + SS_{\text{residual}}$, an additive partition. This is directly analogous to the partition of $SS_{\text{total}} = SS_{\text{between}} + SS_{\text{within}}$ in the analysis of variance (ANOVA).

The squared multiple correlation R^2 measures the proportion of criterion variation accounted for by the predictor (or predictors in the case of multiple regression). R^2 is calculated as follows:

$$R^2 = \frac{SS_{\text{regression}}}{SS_Y} = \frac{15.951}{199.657} = .07989 \qquad (19.11)$$

We learn that approximately 8% of the variation in intention is accounted for by medical risk. Each regression equation, regardless of number of predictors, yields a single R^2 as an omnibus measure of overall fit. Note that centering X_1 as we did in Equation 19.8 has no effect on the value of R^2 that is obtained.

To test whether R^2 differs from 0 (no prediction), we test the null hypothesis that this value $= 0$ in the population: $H_0 : \rho^2 = 0$. If the null hypothesis is true, then the risk scores provide no increase in accuracy of prediction of intentions above simply predicting the arithmetic mean of intentions for each person. The test is an F test,

$$F = \frac{MS_{\text{regression}}}{MS_{\text{residual}}} = \frac{15.951/1}{183.706/238} = \frac{15.951}{.772} = 20.665 \qquad (19.12)$$

where $MS_{\text{regression}} = SS_{\text{regression}}/p$ and $MS_{\text{residual}} = SS_{\text{residual}}/(n - p - 1)$ and the degrees of freedom are $df_{\text{numerator}} = p$ and $df_{\text{denominator}} = (n - p - 1)$. Here, with $p = 1$ df for the numerator and $(n - p - 1) = 240 - 1 - 1 = 238$ df for the denominator, we reject the null hypothesis and conclude that medical risk contributes to our differential prediction of intentions across individuals. The computations involved in the test of R^2 are summarized in an *analysis of regression*, illustrated in Table 19.2, Panel A. In the case of multiple regression with more than one predictor, the test of R^2 is an omnibus test of the contribution of the set of predictors taken together to prediction accuracy.

When we use regression analysis to test theoretical hypotheses, our focus is often on the question of whether specific variables contribute to the overall prediction. In the one predictor case, the test of b_1 coefficient will always be equivalent to the overall test of R^2. Nonetheless, we illustrate how this test is conducted here for pedagogical purposes. We first specify the null hypothesis that the population regression coefficient β_1 is zero—that is to say, $H_0 : \beta_1 = 0$. For this test we require an estimate of the *standard error of the regression coefficient*, s_{b1}. The standard error is a measure of instability of the regression coefficient (i.e., how much variability we would expect in the regression coefficient if we estimated the same regression equation in repeated random samples from a single population). The standard error depends upon MS_{residual} and on the variation of the predictor $SS_X = \sum(X_i - M_X)^2$ and is given as

$$s_{b1} = \sqrt{\frac{MS_{\text{residual}}}{SS_x}} = \sqrt{\frac{.772}{134.557}} = .076 \qquad (19.13)$$

The denominator of this expression is informative for the stability of the regression coefficient: The more variation in the predictor X, the more stable the regression coefficient. In some settings, the stability of the regression coefficient may be improved by systematically sampling over a wide range of the predictor X (Pitts & West, 2001).

The t test for the significance of the individual predictor is given as

$$t_{b_1} = \frac{b_1}{s_{b_1}} = = \frac{.344}{.076} = 4.546 \qquad (19.14)$$

With $(n - p - 1) = 238$ degrees of freedom, we reject the null hypothesis that this regression coefficient is zero. Given the positive sign of b_1, we conclude that medical risk has a positive linear relationship with intention to obtain a mammogram.

Several authors (e.g., Cohen, 1990, 1994; Wilkinson & the Task Force for Statistical Significance, 1999) have encouraged the reporting of confidence intervals (CIs) because they directly provide information about the precision of the estimate. Here we consider the sample regression coefficient as an estimator of the population regression coefficient of the slope. We form a 95% confidence interval around the individual regression coefficient using the following expression,

$$C[b_1 - A \leq \beta_1 \leq b_1 + A] = 1 - \alpha, \qquad (19.15)$$

where $A = t_{.975}(df)s_{b1}$. With $df = 238$, $t_{.975}(238) = 1.97$, and $A = (1.97)(.076) = .150$, the CI is $C[.344 - .150 \leq \beta_1 \leq .344 + .150] = .95$, or $C[.194 \leq \beta_1 \leq .494] = .95$. Otherwise stated, the researcher can have 95% confidence that the population regression coefficient falls between approximately .19 and .49. Because the confidence interval does not include zero, there is a positive effect of risk on intention, consistent with Hypothesis 1.

Single Categorical Predictor Variable: Regression with Code Predictors—Hypotheses 2 and 3

Our next two hypotheses address two comparisons within the recommendation categorical predictor variable, a nominal variable comprised of $G = 3$ categories. To represent a categorical predictor variable in MR we must convert the variable to a series of $(G - 1)$ terms to represent the G categories. The set of $(G - 1)$ terms serve as predictors in the regression equation to represent the recommendation predictor variable. The code terms may be specified in several different ways, depending on the researcher's specific hypotheses (see Cohen, Cohen, West, & Aiken, 2003, and West, Aiken, & Krull, 1996, for complete presentations).

Here, Hypotheses 2 and 3 address the impact of the recommendations of health professionals on intention to obtain a mammogram. Hypothesis 2 indicates that recommendation by a physician or other health professional will increase intention. Hypothesis 3 indicates that the physician's recommendation will have a more powerful effect than will those of other health professionals.

Contrast Codes

The hypotheses are easily translated into a coding scheme of *two orthogonal contrast codes*: C_1: ANYREC, and C_2: PHYSOTHR, for Hypotheses 2 and 3, respectively. The coding scheme for each contrast code is shown in the following table (we specify many decimal points to minimize rounding error).

Recommendation	C_1: ANYREC	C_2: PHYSOTHR
Group 1: Recommendation from physician	.333333	.500000
Group 2: Recommendation from other health professional	.333333	−.500000
Group 3: No recommendation	−.666667	0.000000

Following the requirements for contrast coding, the sum of the code values equals zero for each contrast, (e.g., $.333333 + .333333 − .666667 = 0$). We test the two hypotheses in a single regression equation that contains both code terms C_1 and C_2. In general, the two-predictor regression equation is written as follows:

$$\hat{Y} = b_0 + b_{Y1.2}X_1 + b_{Y2.1}X_2 \qquad (19.16)$$

The notation for the regression coefficients has been expanded here to emphasize the fact that these are partial regression coefficients. The coefficient b_1 has been expanded to $b_{Y1.2}$ to indicate the regression of Y on X_1 with X_2 held

constant or partialed out. For the two contrast codes, the regression equation is as follows:

$$\hat{Y} = b_0 + b_{Y1.2}C_1 + b_{Y2.1}C_2. \qquad (19.17)$$

In general, in the two-predictor regression equation, the regression coefficient for each predictor assesses the impact of that predictor when the effect of the other predictor is held constant or partialed out. Any redundancy in prediction from the predictor in question with the other predictor is taken out, (i.e., not credited to the predictor in question). In the case of uncorrelated predictors, there is no effect of partialing, because there is no redundancy. From the coding of ANYREC and PHYSOTHR, it appears on the surface as if the two predictors would be uncorrelated, because the coding schemes form orthogonal contrasts. However, because there are unequal sample sizes in the three categories of the recommendation variable, the code terms are, in fact, correlated, $r(238) = .218$. The inclusion of the two code terms in one equation is critical. The PHYSOTHR contrast actually compares the physician recommendation with other health professional recommendation only if ANYREC is partialed out.

Use of code terms bridges our thinking from regression analysis in which group membership predicts the criterion Y to an analysis of differences between means on the criterion Y as a function of group membership. Hypothesis 2 can be restated to say that the average of the arithmetic means of intention in Groups 1 and 2 (having a recommendation) will exceed the mean intention in Group 3 (no recommendation). With the specific numerical codes employed for ANYREC, the unstandardized regression coefficient for ANYREC will, in fact, equal $b_{Y1.2} = .5M_{Y1} + .5M_{Y2} − M_{Y3} = \frac{(M_{Y1}+M_{Y2})}{2} − M_3 = \frac{(3.8949+4.1025)}{2} − 3.0845 = 0.9142$, where M_{Y1}, M_{Y2}, and M_{Y3} are the mean intention in Groups 1 to 3, respectively, as given in Table 19.1, Panel B. *To achieve this equivalence between the regression coefficient and the particular contrast of means requires that the difference in numerical value between the codes assigned to the groups being contrasted equal exactly one unit.* For ANYREC, the difference is $[.33333 − (−.666667)] = 1.00$. The reason for this requirement is that the regression coefficient represents the change in Y for a *one-unit* change in the predictor. In general, with K_1 groups in the first set being contrasted, and K_2 groups in the second set being contrasted, the appropriate code for the first set is $K_2/(K_1 + K_2)$. The code for the second set is $−K_1/(K_1 + K_2)$. Here, for the $K_1 = 2$ groups in the first set and the $K_2 = 1$ group in the second set, $K_2/(K_1 + K_2) = 1/(2 + 1) = .333333$, and $−K_1/(K_1 + K_2) = −2/(2 + 1) = −.666667$, respectively. The codes used in PHYSREC, that is $+.500000$ and $−.500000$, respectively, yield a one-unit difference between the groups. Thus the regression coefficient for PHYSREC will equal $b_{Y2.1} = M_{Y1} - M_{Y2} = -0.2076$. Finally the intercept $b_0 = \frac{(M_{Y1} + M_{Y2} + M_{Y3})}{3} = \frac{(3.8949 + 4.1025 + 3.0845)}{3} = 3.6940$. Thus, the regression equation is $\hat{Y} = 3.6940 + 0.9142 \text{ ANYREC} - 0.2076 \text{ PHYSREC}$.

The regression analysis for the contrast coding is summarized in Table 19.2, Panel B. From the section on analysis of regression, we see that $R^2 = 0.23$ is statistically significant, meaning that the overall prediction using the two contrast codes exceeds 0 in the population. Otherwise stated, there is an overall effect of the recommendation variable on intention. The tests of the individual regression coefficients reveal that this prediction arises from the ANYREC contrast, $t(237) = 8.41$, $p < .01$, but not the PHYSOTHR variable, $t(237) = -1.46$, ns. Equivalently, we can use Equation 19.15 to estimate the 95% confidence interval for the population regression coefficient for each code variable. For ANYREC, the 95% confidence interval of .70 to 1.23 does not include 0, whereas the 95% confidence interval for the population regression coefficient for PHYSOTHR of -0.49 to 0.07 does include 0. Hypothesis 2 is supported, but Hypothesis 3 is not.

Model Respecification

Based on these results, we collapse the three-category recommendation variable into the two categories of recommendation versus no recommendation defined by the ANYREC contrast. This decision was made primarily for ease of presentation in the remainder of this chapter. In practice, researchers should be cautious about collapsing categories when contrasts indicate they do not differ, unless sample sizes are very large. This caution is particularly important when further analyses involving interactions of other predictor variables with the categorical variable are planned.

Dummy Coding

Dummy coding is a second approach to developing code predictors for a categorical predictor variable. We illustrate dummy coding here for pedagogical purposes, although in this particular instance, the use of dummy coding does not directly test Hypotheses 2 and 3. In dummy variable coding, we specify a *reference group* to which we wish to compare the $G - 1$ other groups. Here, we choose the no recommendation group as the reference group. For the first code variable D_1, each person who received a recommendation from a physician would be given a value of 1, and everyone else would be given a value of 0. For the second code variable D_2,

each person who received a recommendation from another health professional would given a value of 1, and everyone else would be given a value of 0. Each category of the recommendation variable is coded as follows:

	Recommendation Category	D_1	D_2
Group 1	Physician	1	0
Group 2	Other health professional	0	1
Group 3	No recommendation (reference group)	0	0

Note that the reference group is assigned a value of 0 on each dummy variable, here D_1 and D_2. The regression equation is specified as

$$\hat{Y} = b_0 + b_{Y1.2}D_1 + b_{Y2.1}D_2. \qquad (19.18)$$

In Equation 19.18, the intercept b_0 represents the mean value of Y when both D_1 and D_2 equal 0, which is the mean intention in the reference group (no recommendation, $M = 3.0845$). With both D_1 and D_2 in the equation, D_1 is the difference between the mean in the physician group versus the no recommendation group $(3.8949 - 3.0845 = .8104)$ and D_2 is the difference between the mean in the other health professional group versus the no recommendation group $(4.1025 - 3.0845 = 1.018)$. Thus, the regression equation is $\hat{Y} = 3.0845 + .8104\, D_1 + 1.018\, D_2$. The dummy codes test the hypotheses that each recommendation group differs from the no recommendation group. These are not the tests required for Hypotheses 2 and 3.

Unweighted Effects Coding

A third coding scheme, unweighted effects coding, contrasts group means with the unweighted grand mean of all the groups. Each effects code tests the hypotheses that a recommendation group differs from the unweighted grand mean. Again, these are not the tests required for Hypotheses 2 and 3. Readers familiar with ANOVA will recall that the building blocks of the various sums of squares in ANOVA are the differences between each treatment mean and the grand mean. Unweighted effects coding is, in fact, the basis of ANOVA.

The choice among the three coding schemes depends on the specific hypotheses being tested. As we have illustrated, contrast codes can be developed to test any specific hypotheses whatsoever about differences between groups or combinations of groups. Dummy codes are useful if one wishes to compare groups to a base reference group. Effects codes provide a parallel to ANOVA.

Two Continuous Predictors: High Interpredictor Correlation—Hypothesis 4

We now turn to the two continuous psychological predictors, benefits and worry. We can easily test the linear relationship between each predictor and intention separately. Two versions of Equation 19.4, $\hat{Y} = b_0 + b_1 X_1$, are estimated, the first using scores on benefits as X_1 and the second using scores on worry as X_1. The results of these one-predictor regression analyses are given in Table 19.3, Panels A and B, respectively. We note that the slope $b_1 = 0.39$, $t(238) = 6.34$, $p < .001$ for benefits and that the slope $b_1 = 0.21$, $t(238) = 1.89$, $p = .060$ for worry.

TABLE 19.3 Regression Analyses to Test Hypothesis Concerning the Linear Relationships of Benefits and Worry to Intention

A. Intention Predicted From Benefits Alone

R^2 .14453

Analysis of Regression

	DF	Sum of Squares	Mean Square	F	p
Regression	1	28.85571	28.85571	40.209	.001
Residual	238	170.80088	.71765		

Regression Equation

Variable	b	s_b	b*	t	p
BENEFIT	.386013	.060876	.380167	6.341	.001
INTERCEPT	2.330203	.209447		11.125	.001

B. Intention Predicted From Worry Alone

R^2 .01480

Analysis of Regression

	DF	Sum of Squares	Mean Square	F	p
Regression	1	2.95565	2.95565	3.576	.060
Residual	238	196.70093	.82647		

Regression Equation

Variable	b	s_b	b*	t	p
WORRY	.213877	.113097	.121670	1.891	.060
INTERCEPT	3.104729	.274716		11.302	.001

C. Hypothesis 4: Unique Contribution of Benefits and Worry to Prediction of Intention in a Regression Equation Containing Both Predictors

R^2 .14569

Analysis of Regression

	DF	Sum of Squares	Mean Square	F	p
Regression	2	29.08884	14.54442	20.209	.001
Residual	237	170.56774	.71970		

Regression Equation

Variable	b	s_b	b*	t	p
BENEFIT	.401262	.066590	.395184	6.026	.001
WORRY	−.065612	.115281	−.037326	−.569	.570
INTERCEPT	2.435255	.279395		8.716	.001

At this point, we need to carefully consider exactly what hypothesis the researcher wishes to test about the relation of worry and benefits to intention. As shown in Table 19.1, Panel C, worry and benefits are not independent predictors; indeed $r_{12} = .40$, a magnitude between moderate and large in terms of Cohen's (1988) norms for the size of correlation coefficients. These two predictors will overlap in their prediction of intention with each providing partially redundant information. Unless theory specifies that each predictor should be considered separately, then more useful information may often be found by considering both predictors simultaneously in a single regression equation.

Hypothesis 4 is that benefits (X_1) and worry (X_2) each provide unique prediction of intention. This hypothesis has two parts: (a) Over and above the effects of worry, benefits is expected to have a positive linear relationship with intention, and (b) over and above the effects of benefits, worry is also expected to have a positive linear relationship with intention. We specify the two-predictor regression equation $\hat{Y} = b_0 + b_{Y1.2}$ BENEFIT $+ b_{Y2.1}$ WORRY. As shown in Table 19.3, Panel C, when we estimate this equation, we find $\hat{Y} = 2.44 + 0.40$ BENEFIT $- 0.07$ WORRY. Once again, the intercept is the predicted value of intention when both benefits and worry $= 0$, not an interpretable value. The coefficient $b_{Y1.2}$ represents the linear effect of benefits on intention when worry is held constant. The coefficient $b_{Y2.1}$ represents the linear effect of worry on intention when benefits is held constant.

Comparing this result with the results of the two separate one-predictor regressions, we see that the slope for benefits hardly changes from the one-predictor to the two-predictor model (slope $= 0.39$ and 0.40, respectively). In contrast, the slope for worry decreases markedly (slope $= 0.21$ and -0.07, respectively) and no longer even approaches statistical significance. To understand the change in results for worry, recall that the one predictor regression estimates the overall linear effect of worry on intention ignoring the effects of any other variables. The two-predictor regression describes the *conditional relationship* between worry and intention when the value of benefits is held constant. For example, we might select only people who have a benefits score $= 3$ and study the relationship between worry and intention in this subpopulation. The obtained pattern suggests that benefits is contributing essentially all of the unique prediction to intention. This is apparent from $R^2_{Y.12}$ from the two predictors of .146, versus the squared correlation of benefits with intention of $R^2_{Y.1} = .145$. The squared semipartial correlation of worry with intentions $R^2_{Y.(2.1)} = R^2_{Y.12} - R^2_{Y.1} = (.146 - .145) = .001$, showing essentially no contribution of worry to prediction in an equation already containing benefits.

Standardized Regression Coefficients

Although benefits and worry are each measured on similar 7-point scales, some regression problems have predictor variables that are measured in strikingly different units. For example, imagine that height and weight are used to predict a measure of physical fitness. Height (millimeters) and weight (kilograms) are in strikingly different units, so it may be difficult to interpret the meaning of the regression coefficients, particularly in cases in which the units of the scale are not familiar to the researcher. In such cases, it can be useful to report *standardized regression coefficients*.

Conceptually, to compute standardized regression coefficients the researcher first converts X_1, X_2, and Y to z scores, where $z_{X_i} = \frac{(X_i - M_{X_i})}{s_{X_i}}$ and $z_Y = \frac{(Y - M_Y)}{s_Y}$. The standardized regression coefficient in the two predictor case is then

$$\hat{z}_Y = b^*_{Y1.2} z_{X_1} + b^*_{Y2.1} z_{X_2}. \tag{19.19}$$

In this equation, $\hat{z}_Y$ is the predicted score in standardized (z score) form, $b^*_{Y1.2}$ is the standardized regression coefficient corresponding to z_{X_1} and $b^*_{Y2.1}$ is the standardized regression coefficient corresponding to z_{X_2}. For our example, $\hat{z}_Y = 0.40z_{X_1} - .04z_{X_2}$ (see Table 19.3, Panel C). Reflecting the similarity of the rating scales for benefits and worry, the unstandardized and standardized regression coefficients differ only slightly. The standardized regression Equation 19.19 does not include an intercept. In general, in the two-predictor regression equation, the intercept $b_0 = M_Y - b_1 M_{X_1} - b_2 M_{X_2}$. However, because the mean z scores for X_1, X_2, and Y are all 0, $b_0 = 0 - b_1(0) - b_2(0) = 0$. The standardized regression coefficient indicates by how many standard deviations the criterion changes for a one standard deviation change in the predictor. Thus, the predicted value of intention changes by .40 standard deviations for each one standard deviation change in benefits when the value of worry is held constant. Note that in the case of categorical predictors, with contrast codes or dummy codes like those given previously, the idea of a change of one standard deviation in the predictor typically makes little sense.

Further insight into two-predictor regression can be gained from examining another set of formulas for the standardized regression coefficients.

$$b^*_{Y1.2} = \frac{r_{Y1} - r_{Y2}r_{12}}{1 - r_{12}^2} \quad \text{and} \quad b^*_{Y2.1} = \frac{r_{Y2} - r_{Y1}r_{12}}{1 - r_{12}^2} \tag{19.20}$$

where r_{Y1} and r_{Y2} are the correlations of Predictors 1 and 2 with the criterion, respectively, and r_{12} is the correlation between the predictors. The expression for $b^*_{Y1.2}$ includes both the correlation of predictor in question (r_{Y1}) and the correlation of the

other predictor with the criterion (r_{Y2}). The correlation between the predictors, r_{12}, plays a strong role in determining the magnitude and even the sign of each standardized regression coefficient. Note that the standardized regression coefficient is undefined (cannot be computed) if the correlation between the predictors equals 1.0. In fact, there is no solution whatsoever to the regression analysis if two predictors are correlated 1.0. High correlation between the predictors introduces instability into the regression coefficients. On the other hand, when $r_{12} = 0$, then the standardized regression coefficient exactly equals the correlation of the predictor with the criterion (i.e., $b^*_{Y1.2} = r_{Y1}$ and $b^*_{Y2.1} = r_{Y2}$).

Standard Errors of Partial Regression Coefficients and Interpredictor Correlation

An examination of the expression for the standard error of each regression coefficient in the two-predictor case is also informative as to how the correlation between two predictors affects the stability of each regression coefficient. The standard error s_{b_1} of the unstandardized regression coefficient b_1 is a measure of instability of b_1; it may be expressed as

$$s_{b_1} = \sqrt{\frac{MS_{\text{residual}}}{SS_{X_1}}} \sqrt{\frac{1}{1 - r_{12}^2}}. \tag{19.21}$$

Comparison of this equation to Equation 19.13 for the one predictor case reveals that the expressions are the same, except that Equation 19.21 contains a second term that reflects the correlation between the two predictors. The higher this correlation, the larger the standard error. The expression under the square root of this second term, $\frac{1}{1 - r_{12}^2}$, is known as the *variance inflation factor* (VIF). VIF or its reciprocal, $(1 - r_{12}^2)$, which is known as *tolerance*, are commonly used as indices of *multicollinearity*, the extent of overlap or redundancy of predictors. As the value of the VIF for variable X_j increases, the corresponding regression coefficient b_j becomes increasingly unstable. The VIF appears in the expression for the standard error of the standardized regression coefficient as well.

Detecting and Testing Nonlinear Relationships— Hypothesis 5

Thus far, our regression models have only tested linear relationships between the predictors and the criterion. However, past theorizing (see Janis & Feshbach, 1953) has suggested that there may be an inverted U-shaped relationship of worry to intention, with people at the highest levels of worry avoiding screening tests.

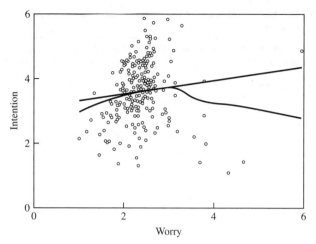

Figure 19.1   Scatter plot of raw data: intention as a function of worry. The straight line is the OLS regression line from the equation, $\hat{Y} = 3.10 + 0.21$ WORRY. The curved line is the lowess fit line. The lowess line suggests a curvilinear relationship between worry and intention.

In Hypothesis 5, we test the prediction of an inverted U-shaped relationship of worry to intention. We begin our exploration of this possibility with a graphical display. We initially focus only on the relationship between worry and intention, ignoring the potential contribution of benefits. Figure 19.1 displays a scatter plot of worry versus intention. We have superimposed two lines on this scatter plot. First is the best-fitting straight line from the regression analysis in Table 19.3, Panel B, $\hat{Y} = 3.10 + 0.21X$. Second is a *lowess smooth* (Cleveland, 1979; Fox, 2000). The lowess smooth is a nonparametric line that follows the trend in the data. If the true relationship in the data is linear, then the lowess smooth should roughly approximate the straight line. Examination of the scatter plot indicates that the data are highly right skewed, with relatively few participants having worry scores above about 3 (see also Table 19.1, Panel A). The lowess line indicates that as worry increases up to about the value of 3.5, intention also increases. Above this point, intention begins to decrease consistent with the hypothesized curvilinear relationship, although we acknowledge the *sparseness* of the data (i.e., few data points) at the high end of the worry distribution.

Figure 19.2 provides a scatter plot of the residuals from the regression equation $\hat{Y} = 3.10 + .021$ WORRY against WORRY. Again a lowess curve is superimposed. The lowess curve highlights the curvilinearity to be modeled after the linear trend in the data has been removed.

Polynomial Regression

The lowess smooth in Figure 19.1 and in Figure 19.2 leads us to explore the curvilinear relationship further using a form of

multiple regression called *polynomial regression*. In polynomial regression we create functions of an individual predictor X that carry a curvilinear relationship of the predictor to the criterion. In general the polynomial regression equation is of the form

$$\hat{Y} = b_0 + b_1 X + b_2 X^2 + b_3 X^3 + \cdots + b_t X^t \quad (19.22)$$

Equation 19.22 is a polynomial of order t, which describes a relationship with $(t - 1)$ bends. In psychology, at least, we expect that our curvilinear relationships will be typically quadratic so that $t = 2$. The specific relationships with one bend include both U-shaped and inverted U-shaped relationships, such as the one that appears to exist between worry and intention. They also include monotonic relationships of X to Y that accelerate or decelerate as X increases in value.

The second order polynomial is given as

$$\hat{Y} = b_0 + b_1 X + b_2 X^2 \quad (19.23)$$

This equation contains a linear $b_1 X$ term and a curvilinear (quadratic) $b_2 X^2$ term. The curvilinear term $b_2 X^2$ measures the extent of curvilinearity in the relationship of X to Y, if and only if the linear $b_1 X$ term is included in the equation. In other words, the curvilinear effect is a partialed effect with the linear effect partialed out (see Cohen, 1978, for an extended discussion of partialed effects). The coefficient b_2 will be positive for U-shaped relationships; negative for inverted U-shaped relationships. Hence, Hypothesis 5 predicts that b_2 will be negative. The reader is cautioned that the b_1 coefficient

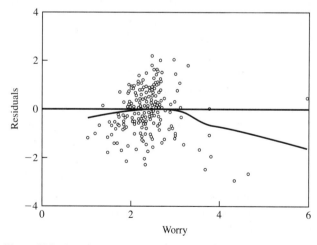

Figure 19.2   Scatter plot of residuals as a function of worry. The residuals presented are from the linear regression equation, $\hat{Y} = 3.10 + 0.21$ WORRY. For each case, the residual $e_i = Y_i - \hat{Y}_i$. The horizontal line is the point where the residuals $= 0$. The curved line is the lowess fit to the residuals. The lowess line suggests the presence of a curvilinear relationship of worry to intentions.

in Equation 19.23 has a very specific interpretation as the linear regression of Y on X at the value $X = 0$. That is, b_1 *is a conditional effect of Y on X only at $X = 0$*, even if $X = 0$ is not part of the actual scale. In this example, none of our scales includes zero.

As we noted earlier, lower-order coefficients become meaningfully interpretable when each of the predictors is *centered*. In the present context, we again center X so that $X_C = (X - M_X)$. This results in the regression equation.

$$\hat{Y} = \tilde{b}_0 + \tilde{b}_1 X_C + b_2 X_C^2 \qquad (19.24)$$

Once again, we use $\tilde{b}_0$ and $\tilde{b}_1$ to indicate that these regression coefficients will typically differ in value from the corresponding regression coefficients in Equation 19.23. In contrast, the b_2 coefficient will be identical in the two equations. The $\tilde{b}_1$ coefficient still represents the regression of Y on X at $X = 0$, but now $X = 0$ is rendered meaningful as the arithmetic mean of the centered predictor. When predictor X is centered, we gain a second interpretation for the $\tilde{b}_1$ coefficient. The $\tilde{b}_1$ coefficient represents the average linear regression of Y on X across the range of the data. The b_2 coefficient represents the extent of curvature.

Table 19.4 presents the second-order polynomial regression equation predicting intention. A new centered predictor represented as WORRYC is employed as the linear predictor, computed as WORRYC = (WORRY − M_{WORRY}). The square of WORRYC, WORRYC2, computed as WORRYC2 = (WORRY − M_{WORRY})^2, serves as the curvilinear predictor. Centering has a second advantage in that it decreases the correlation between X and X^2, yielding a smaller standard error for the $\tilde{b}_1$ coefficient. Here, the correlation between raw (uncentered) X and X^2 is .97, whereas the correlation between X_C and X_C^2 is .567. Aiken and West (1991) discuss the effects of centering on interpredictor correlation in regression equations containing polynomial and interaction terms.

From Table 19.4, we see that the second-order polynomial regression with both the linear and curvilinear terms accounts for $R_{Y.12}^2 = R^2 = .071$ of the variation in intention, $F(2,237) = 9.07$, $p = .001$. The regression coefficient for WORRYC2 is negative, $b_2 = -0.27$, $t(237) = -3.79$, $p < .001$, capturing the inverted U-shaped component of the relationship and confirming Hypothesis 5. The regression coefficient for the linear predictor WORRYC is positive, $b_1 = 0.50$, $t(237) = 3.75$, $p < .001$, capturing the average overall linear trend in the data that intention increases as worry increases.

Note that in the present case we hypothesized a curvilinear relationship between worry and intention, thus making the interpretation of the results straightforward. Such interpretation

TABLE 19.4 Exploration of Curvilinear Relationship of Worry to Intention

Panel A. Hypothesis 5: Inverted-U-Shaped Relationship of Worry to Intention, Examined in a Second-Order (Quadratic) Polynomial Regression Equation

R^2 .07112

Analysis of Regression

	DF	Sum of Squares	Mean Square	F	p
Regression	2	14.19876	7.09938	9.072	.001
Residual	237	185.45782	.78252		

Regression Equation

Variable	b	s_b	b*	t	p
WORRYC	.501137	.133619	.285087	3.750	.001
WORRYC2	−.267887	.070674	−.288127	−3.790	.001
INTERCEPT	3.684393	.060189		61.214	.001

Panel B. Revisiting Hypothesis 4: Unique Contribution of Benefits and Worry to Prediction of Intention in a Regression Equation Containing Both Predictors

R^2 .16299

Analysis of Regression

	DF	Sum of Squares	Mean Square	F	p
Regression	3	32.54122	10.84707	15.318	.001
Residual	236	167.11537	.70812		

Regression Equation

Variable	b	s_b	b*	t	p
BENEFITC	.353639	.069484	.348283	5.090	.001
WORRYC	.135010	.146053	.076805	.924	.356
WORRYC2	−.156159	.070723	−.167958	−2.208	.028
INTERCEPT	3.654315	.057560		63.487	.001

becomes more complex when the form of relationship has not been hypothesized or the form may not have been correctly specified. On one hand, using the lowess smooth provides a powerful method of exploring the data and describing the form of the relationship. On the other hand, powerful graphical methods like lowess can detect chance relationships that only exist in the particular sample at hand. Unpredicted relationships detected through exploratory analyses should be replicated using a new sample to rule out the possibility that the results reflect relationships that are unique to the current sample. In the present example, sampling participants so as to include a larger number of cases with high scores on worry would greatly improve the ability of the regression model to distinguish between the linear and quadratic effects of worry on intention (see Pitts & West, 2001). When a new sample cannot be collected, a variety of resampling procedures can be used to probe the stability of the findings across permutations of the sample. Diaconis (1985) presents an excellent discussion of statistical inference in the context of exploratory data analysis.

Revisiting the Unique Effects of Worry and Benefits

In our earlier section on Hypothesis 4, we showed that when benefits and worry were both included in the regression equation, the regression coefficient for worry no longer approached statistical significance (see Table 19.3, Panel C). However, the regression Equation 19.16 only specified that benefits and worry would have linear effects, and we have seen that worry has a quadratic relationship to intention. We now respecify Equation 19.16 so that it includes both a linear and quadratic relationship of worry to intention. Again, for ease of interpretation of the lower-order regression coefficients, we center both predictor variables (here, benefits and worry, respectively): $X_{1C} = X_1 - M_{X_1}$ and $X_{2C} = X_2 - M_{X_2}$. This results in the following regression equation:

$$\hat{Y} = \tilde{b}_0 + \tilde{b}_1 X_{1C} + \tilde{b}_2 X_{2C} + b_3 X_{2C}^2, \quad (19.25)$$

Here $\tilde{b}_1$ is the linear effect of benefits, $\tilde{b}_2$ is the average linear effect of worry, and b_3 represents the extent of curvature for worry. As is shown in Table 19.4, Panel B, benefits has a statistically significant linear relationship with intention, and worry has a statistically significant quadratic relationship with intention. This example illustrates that testing a regression model with only linear terms does not address the potential existence of higher-order relationships between a predictor and the criterion variable. Hypothesis 4, that both benefits and worry predict intention, is in fact supported, but the unique relationship between worry and intention is quadratic in form. We note the great flexibility of MR in uniquely specifying the shape of the relationship of each variable to Y.

Sets of Predictors: Increment in Prediction—Hypothesis 6

The predictor variables fall into two distinct sets: (a) Set 1, consisting of medical variables of risk (RISK) and recommendation from a health professional (ANYREC), and (b) Set 2, consisting of psychological variables of perceived benefits of screening (BENEFITS) and worry about breast cancer, now characterized by two uncentered predictors (WORRY and WORRY²). In testing the increment in prediction, centered and uncentered predictors will produce identical results. Hypothesis 6 predicts that Set 2 of psychological variables will account for variance in intention over and above Set 1 of medical variables; that is, even with level of medical risk and input from a health professional accounted for (partialed out, held constant), psychological factors will still play a role in whether women are screened.

We use a *hierarchical regression strategy* in which the contribution of Set 2 of variables to an equation already containing

TABLE 19.5   Gain in Prediction of Intention From Psychological Variables Above and Beyond Medical Variables

A. Prediction of Intention From Medical Variables (Set 1)

R^2	.27132

Analysis of Regression

	DF	Sum of Squares	Mean Square	F	p
Regression	2	54.16999	27.08500	44.122	.001
Residual	237	145.48659	.61387		

B. Hypothesis 6: Prediction From Psychological Variables (Set 2) Over and Above Medical Variables (Set 1)

R^2	.33131
R^2 change	.06001 = .33131 − .27132
F for change	F(3,234) = 6.99, p < .01

Analysis of Regression

	DF	Sum of Squares	Mean Square	F	p
Regression	5	66.14839	13.22968	23.188	.001
Residual	234	133.50819	.57055		

Note. The regression equation in Panel A includes predictors RISK and ANYREC. The regression equation in Panel B includes RISK, ANYREC, BENEFIT, WORRY, and WORRY². Since uncentered predictors were used in B, the regression coefficients for the individual predictors should not be interpreted and are hence not reported.

Set 1 is tested. Table 19.5 (Panel A) provides a regression analysis with Set 1 predictors only; this yields $R^2_{Y.12} = .271$. A second regression analysis in Table 19.5 (Panel B) gives the regression analysis from both sets of predictors. This yields $R^2_{Y.12345} = .331$. The squared semipartial correlation of Set 2 with the criterion, over and above Set 1, is $R^2_{Y.(345.12)} = R^2_{Y.12345} - R^2_{Y.12} = .331 - .271 = .06$. There is a 6% gain in prediction by the addition of the psychological variables (between a small and moderate effect size gain according to Cohen, 1988).

We may test whether the squared semipartial correlation, (i.e., the increment in prediction by Set 2 of variables over and above Set 1) is significant, using the expression

$$F_{\text{gain}} = \frac{R_{\text{all}}^2 - R_{\text{set1}}^2}{1 - R_{\text{all}}^2} \frac{(n - k - m - 1)}{m}$$
$$\text{with} \quad [m, (n - k - m - 1)] \, df \quad (19.26)$$

where k is the number of terms in Set 1 (here $k = 2$) and m is the number in Set 2 (here $m = 3$ because worry is coded with two variables, WORRY and WORRY2, in addition to BENEFITS). R_{all}^2 is the multiple correlation for prediction from both sets of predictors (all five terms) and R_{Set1}^2 is the prediction from Set 1 only.

$$F_{\text{gain}} = \frac{.331 - .271}{1 - .331} \frac{240 - 2 - 3 - 1}{3}$$
$$= \frac{.060}{.669} \left(\frac{234}{3} \right) = 6.99$$

This test with (3, 234) degrees of freedom indicates significant gain in prediction with the addition of the psychological predictors ($p < .01$). Note that Equation 19.26 can be extended to any number of predictors in Set 1 and Set 2.

Interaction Between Two Continuous Predictors—Hypothesis 7

In our considerations of what motivates individuals to protect their health, we have argued that individuals perceive the benefits of particular health protective actions more strongly if they are more at risk (or perceive themselves to be more at risk) for the disease in question (Aiken et al., 2001; Aiken, West, Woodward, Reno & Reynolds, 1994; West & Aiken, 1997). Thus Hypothesis 7 predicts a positive or *synergistic interaction* between risk and benefit. As risk increases, the effect of benefits on intention increases as well, such that the total effect of risk plus benefits on intention is greater than the sum of the impacts of the two individual predictors— hence the term *synergistic interaction*. Put in other terms, risk serves as a *moderator* of the relationship of benefits to intention (Baron & Kenny, 1986); for each value of the moderator (here risk), the regression of the outcome variable (here intention) on the predictor in question (here benefits) takes on a different value.

To represent an interaction in MR, we create a new term that is a function of the two variables that are hypothesized to interact. The interaction term is constructed as the product of the predictors entering the interaction. In general, with X and Z as the two predictors, the term carrying the interaction is the product of X and Z—that is, XZ. The regression equation containing the XZ interaction is given as follows:

$$\hat{Y} = b_0 + b_1 X + b_2 Z + b_3 XZ \qquad (19.27)$$

The interaction is a partialed effect. The b_3 partial regression coefficient represents the interaction between X and Z if and only if the two first order terms $b_1 X$ and $b_2 Z$ are included in the equation. In general, all lower-order terms for each variable involved in the interaction must be included in a regression equation containing an interaction, in order that the regression coefficient for the interaction represent pure interaction variation—that is, unconfounded by first-order (main effect) variation of the individual predictors involved in the interaction.

Centering Predictors and Forming the Interaction Term

For our example, the interaction term is the product of risk and benefit. Much interpretational benefit is gained by first centering the individual predictors involved in the interaction (by subtracting their means) and then forming the product of the centered predictors. Here we compute centered RISKC = (RISK − M_{RISK}) and BENEFITC = (BENEFIT − $M_{BENEFIT}$). Then we form the crossproduct term RISKC∗BENEFITC. The regression equation containing the interaction is $\hat{Y} = b_0 + b_1$ BENEFITC $+ b_2$ RISKC $+ b_3$ RISKC∗BENEFITC. (At this point we assume that all the predictors entering the regression equation containing an interaction have been centered and drop the tilde notation previously introduced).

Table 19.6 summarizes the analysis of the interaction between centered risk and benefits. Panel A gives the means and standard deviations of each predictor. We see that even if the two predictors entering the interaction have been centered and have means of zero, their crossproduct RISKC∗BENEFITC will not generally be centered. The correlation matrix in Panel B shows that there are quite low correlations between RISKC, BENEFITC, and the crossproduct term RISKC∗ BENEFITC—that is to say, $r = .148$, $r = −.008$, respectively. If we had not centered the predictors, then these correlations would have been $r = .760$, and $r = .872$, for RISK, BENEFIT with the crossproduct term, respectively. Centering eliminates correlation due to scaling of the predictors. We strongly recommend centering predictors involved in interactions.

If only RISKC and BENEFITC are included as predictors, without the interaction, the resulting $R^2_{Y.12} = .168$; the regression equation is $\hat{Y} = 3.612 + .324$ BENEFITC $+ .200$ RISKC. The regression equation containing the interaction is

$$\hat{Y} = 3.569 + .334 \text{ BENEFITC} + .170 \text{ RISKC}$$
$$+ .175 \text{ RISKC∗BENEFITC}$$

with resulting $R^2_{Y.123} = .186$, about a 2% increment in prediction ($.186 − .168$) due to the interaction. Although this is a small effect size interaction, we will see that the pattern of relationships of benefits to intention is modified by level of risk. Consistent with Hypothesis 7, the existence of the interaction is supported. Having centered the predictors allows us to interpret the regression coefficients for BENEFITC and RISKC as the regressions of intention on these predictors at the respective means of benefits and intention in the sample. The reader is warned that these first-order coefficients should only be interpreted if predictors are centered (see Aiken & West, 1991, chap. 3, for a full explanation).

Having found a significant interaction, our next step is to characterize its specific nature. For those familiar with analysis of variance (ANOVA), the characterization of the interaction in MR parallels the characterization of interactions in ANOVA through the use of simple effects analysis (e.g., see Kirk, 1995; Winer, Brown, & Michels, 1991). We begin by

TABLE 19.6   Interaction Between Two Continuous Variables Benefits and Risk; RISKC*BENEFITC Is the Crossproduct Term of RISKC With BENEFITC

A. Means and Standard Deviations of Predictors

	Mean	Standard Deviation
INTENT	3.612	.914
RISKC	.000	.750
BENEFITC	.000	.900
RISKC*BENEFITC	.250	.725
N of Cases = 240		

B. Correlation Matrix Among Predictors and Criterion

	INTENT	RISKC	BENEFITC	RISKC*BENEFITC
INTENT	1.000	.283	.380	.157
RISKC	.283	1.000	.371	.148
BENEFITC	.380	.371	1.000	−.008
RISKC*BENEFITC	.157	.148	−.008	1.000

C. Hypothesis 7: Synergistic Interaction Between Risk and Benefits

R^2 .18647

Analysis of Regression

	DF	Sum of Squares	Mean Square	F	p
Regression	3	37.23002	12.41001	18.031	.001
Residual	236	162.42657	.68825		

Regression Equation

Variable	b	s_b	b*	t	p
RISKC	.170410	.078090	.139848	2.182	.030
BENEFITC	.334469	.064357	.329403	5.197	.001
RISKC*BENEFITC	.174760	.075001	.138657	2.330	.021
INTERCEPT	3.568648	.056729		62.907	.001

D. Covariance Matrix of the Regression Coefficients

b_1	b_2	b_3			BENEFITC	RISKC	RISKC*BENEFITC
b_1 s_{11}	s_{12}	s_{13}		BENEFITC	.00414	−.00189	.0003325
b_2 s_{21}	s_{22}	s_{23}	=	RISKC	−.00189	.00610	−.0009527
b_3 s_{31}	s_{32}	s_{33}		RISKC*BENEFITC	.0003325	−.0009527	.00563

rearranging the overall regression equation to show the regression of the criterion on the predictor X in question as a function of the moderator Z. Rearranging Equation 19.27, we have

$$\hat{Y} = (b_1 X + b_3 XZ) + (b_2 Z + b_0)$$
$$\hat{Y} = (b_1 + b_3 Z)X + (b_2 Z + b_0) \qquad (19.28)$$

Equation 19.28 is a *simple regression equation* that shows the regression of the criterion on predictor X as a function of the value of another predictor Z, the moderator. The *simple regression coefficient* for X, given by the expression $b_{YX \text{ at } Z} = (b_1 + b_3 Z)$, and the *simple intercept* $(b_2 Z + b_0)$ both depend on the value of Z. Substituting our variables, we have

$$\hat{Y} = (b_1 + b_3 \text{ RISKC}) \text{ BENEFITC} + (b_2 \text{ RISKC} + b_0), \text{ or}$$

$$\hat{Y} = (.334 + .175 \text{ RISKC}) \text{ BENEFITC}$$
$$+ (.170 \text{ RISKC} + 3.569). \qquad (19.29)$$

We may now compute the simple regressions of intention on benefits at different levels of risk. By convention (Aiken & West, 1991), we explore how benefits impacts intention one standard deviation above and one standard deviation below the mean of centered risk, which we term $\text{RISKC}_{\text{HIGH}}$ and $\text{RISKC}_{\text{LOW}}$, or in general Z_{HIGH} and Z_{LOW}, respectively. The standard deviation of RISKC = .7501. We substitute this value of $\text{RISKC}_{\text{HIGH}}$ = .7501 into Equation 19.29 and find

$$\hat{Y} = [.334 + .175(.7501)] \text{ BENEFITC}$$
$$+ [.170(.7501) + 3.569]$$

$$\hat{Y} = .466 \text{ BENEFITC} + 3.696, \text{ one standard deviation above the mean of risk.}$$

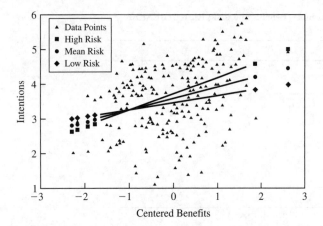

Figure 19.3 Regression of intentions on benefits at three levels of risk: low risk, one standard deviation below the mean of risk; mean risk, at the mean of risk; and high risk, one standard deviation above the mean of risk.

If we substitute the value $\text{RISK}_{\text{LOW}} = -.7501$, we have

$$\hat{Y} = .203 \text{ BENEFITC} + 3.440, \quad \text{one standard deviation below the mean of risk.}$$

Finally, we substitute $\text{RISKC} = 0$ at the mean of centered risk into Equation 19.29 to assess the regression of Y on BENEFITC at the mean of centered risk. This yields the simple regression equation $\hat{Y} = .334 \text{ BENEFITC} + 3.569$. The simple slope and intercept equal the corresponding terms from the overall regression equation.

In general, the regression of Y on benefits increases as risk increases, as is predicted by Hypothesis 7, with simple slope coefficients $b_{YX \text{ at ZLOW}} = .203$, $b_{YX \text{ at ZMEAN}} = .334$, and $b_{YX \text{ at ZHIGH}} = .466$, at low, moderate, and high levels of risk, respectively. The synergistic nature of the interaction is supported. The interaction is illustrated in Figure 19.3; the simple slopes are shown along with the raw data.

The simple slopes may be tested for significance following a method developed in Aiken and West (1991, chap. 2). We require a covariance matrix of the regression coefficients, which is given in Table 19.6, Panel D. Using the notation given in Panel D, we have that the standard error of a simple slope is given as

$$s_{b \text{ at } Z} = \sqrt{s_{11} + 2Z s_{13} + Z^2 s_{33}} \qquad (19.30)$$

where Z is the moderator variable (here, risk), s_{11} and s_{33} are the variances of the b_1 and b_3 regression coefficients, respectively, and s_{13} is the covariance between these regression coefficients. A t test for the significance of the simple slope is given as

$$t_{b \text{ at } Z} = b_{\text{at } Z} / s_{b \text{ at } Z} \qquad (19.31)$$

with degrees of freedom equal to the degrees of freedom of MS_{residual} from the full design, $(n - p - 1)$, where p is the number of predictors including the interaction.

For the regression of intention on benefits at $\text{RISKC}_{\text{HIGH}} = .7501$, one standard deviation above the mean of risk, using the values from Table 19.6, Panel D, we have

$$
\begin{aligned}
&S_{b \text{ at HIGH RISK}} \\
&= \sqrt{[.00414 + 2(.7501)(.0003325) + (.7501)^2(.00563)]} \\
&= .088
\end{aligned}
$$

Then a t test for the simple slope is given as $t_{b \text{ at RISKC HIGH}} = .466/.088 = 5.30$ with $df = (240 - 3 - 1) = 236$, $p < .01$. At $\text{RISKC}_{\text{LOW}} = -.7501$, we have $s_{b \text{ at RISKC LOW}} = .083$, and $t_{b \text{ at RISK LOW}} = .203/.083 = 2.45$, $p < .01$. The t test of simple slope at $\text{RISKC} = 0$ equals that from the overall equation, $t = 5.197$, $p < .001$. We conclude that there is a positive effect of benefits on intention at each level of risk, and that, as predicted, the impact of benefits on intention increases with increasing risk. We note that the particular values of $\text{RISKC}_{\text{LOW}}$ and $\text{RISKC}_{\text{HIGH}}$ arise from this particular sample and, of course, contain sampling error. Thus, the sample simple effects computed here are approximations to the simple effects at corresponding points in the population. Finally, we warn that the standard error expression in Equation 19.30 only pertains to the simple slope in Equation 19.28; Aiken and West (1991) provide standard error expressions for a variety of simple slopes.

We have presented an example of the treatment of interactions in MR. We provide a full presentation, which includes three-variable interactions and interactions involving curvilinear relationships in Aiken and West (1991). A method for estimating and testing simple regression equations by computer is also provided in Aiken and West (1991).

Interaction Between A Categorical and A Continuous Variable—Hypothesis 8

Researchers often hypothesize that categorical variables may modify the relationship between two continuous variables. These hypotheses may be proposed both when the categorical variable represents an experimental treatment and when the categorical variable represents a natural category (e.g., ethnic group). Such hypotheses may be proposed even if there is also an overall relationship between the continuous variable and the dependent variable, or between the categorical variable and the dependent variable, or both. We have already seen in our example (Table 19.3, Panel A) that there is an overall relationship between benefits and intention. We have also seen evidence (Table 19.2, Panel B) that there is also a relationship between receiving a recommendation from a doctor or other health care professional (ANYREC) and intention.

We hypothesize (Hypothesis 8) that there is a *synergistic interaction* between benefits and recommendation such that, if a woman has both received a recommendation and has strong beliefs in the personal benefits of mammography, she is more likely to obtain a mammogram.

The general procedure of specifying a regression equation to represent an interaction between a categorical and a continuous variable draws on several lessons from previous sections. First, the group variable is represented by $G - 1$ code terms. In line with our earlier presentation, we collapse the physician recommendation and other health care professional recommendation groups into a single recommendation group (REC) that is contrasted with the no recommendation group (NOREC). With $G = 2$ groups, we have one code variable. Second, the continuous independent variable is centered, $BENEFITC = BENEFIT - M_{BENEFIT}$, where $M_{BENEFIT} = 3.321$. As we indicated in the previous section, centering is used to render the lower-order coefficients interpretable in a regression equation containing interactions. Third, the interaction is represented by a set of terms corresponding to the product of each of the $G - 1$ code variables and the centered continuous variable.

Because the interpretation of interactions involving categorical variables can be challenging, we present two preliminary analyses for pedagogical purposes that help provide a foundation for our understanding. Our first preliminary analysis examines the regression of intention on centered benefits only for the 144 participants in the REC group (i.e., the combined physician and other health professional recommendation groups),

$$\hat{Y} = b_0 + b_1 \text{ BENEFITC} = 3.903 + .297 \text{ BENEFITC}$$
$$\text{(REC group only)} \quad (19.32)$$

BENEFITC is centered at the mean of the *full* sample of 240 people, $M_{BENEFIT} = 3.321$. Thus, $b_0 = 3.903$ represents the predicted value of intention in the REC group, given that the person's score on benefits equals the mean benefits of the full sample, (i.e., at $M_{BENEFIT} = 3.321$). Further, $b_1 = 0.297$ represents the regression of intention on benefits in the REC group only—that is, the predicted amount of change in intention for each one unit change in benefits for individuals who received a recommendation from a health professional.

Our second preliminary analysis examines the regression of intention on centered benefits for only the 96 participants in the NOREC group:

$$\hat{Y} = b_0 + b_1 \text{ BENEFITC} = 3.157 + .234 \text{ BENEFITC}$$
$$\text{(NOREC group only)} \quad (19.33)$$

Again, since benefits is centered at the mean of all 240 cases, $b_0 = 3.157$ represents the predicted value of intention in the NOREC group, given that the person's score on benefits equals the mean of the full sample, $M_{BENEFIT} = 3.321$. Here, $b_1 = 0.234$ represents the slope in the NOREC group. We note that as we predicted, the slope of the regression of intention on benefits is larger in the group that received the recommendation; yet these two analyses provide no test of whether the difference in slopes is large enough to achieve conventional levels of statistical significance, a test provided by specifying a regression equation containing the interaction between the recommendation variable and benefits.

Contrast Code and the Interaction Test

We now examine the interaction between recommendation and benefits to test Hypothesis 8 directly. We create a contrast code CONTRREC for the respecified two-group recommendation predictor (REC vs. NOREC). We use the formulae we used previously to construct contrast codes for sets of groups. With $K_1 = 1$ group in the first set (the REC group) and $K_2 = 1$ group in the second set (the NOREC group), we assign the code $K_2/(K_1 + K_2) = .50000$ to the REC group and $-K_1/(K_1 + K_2) = -.50000$ to the NOREC group. Note that these codes are one unit apart, following the rule we previously specified. We form the crossproduct term between the categorical CONTRREC and continuous BENEFITC variable as BENEFITC*CONTRREC, which yields the regression equation

$$\hat{Y} = b_0 + b_1 \text{ BENEFITC} + b_2 \text{ CONTRREC}$$
$$+ b_3 \text{ BENEFITC*CONTRREC} \quad (19.34)$$

A significant interaction (b_3 coefficient) would signify that the regression of intention on benefits differs in the two groups. The numerical example using this equation is given in Table 19.7, Panel A, with the resulting regression equation

$$\hat{Y} = 3.5300 + .2653 \text{ BENEFITC} + .7461 \text{ CONTRREC}$$
$$+ .0619 \text{ BENEFITC*CONTRREC} \quad (19.35)$$

The b_3 coefficient represents the interaction and is the difference between the slopes for the two groups, $b_3 = .2963 - .2344 = .0619$. The absence of a significant interaction, $t(236) = 0.52$, *ns*, indicates that the simple regression slopes for the regression of intention on benefits in the two groups are essentially parallel within sampling error. This is also clear from Figure 19.4. The b_2 coefficient for CONTRREC is the difference in mean intention in the two groups, $b_2 = 3.9030 - 3.1569 = .7461$, *conditioned on* both groups' being at the

TABLE 19.7   Interaction Between a Continuous Variable (Benefits) and a Categorical Variable (Recommendation From a Health Professional)

A. Hypothesis 8: Synergistic Interaction Between Recommendation and Benefits; Contrast-Coded Recommendation CONTRREC (REC = .5, NOREC = −.5); BENEFITC*CONTRREC Is the Crossproduct Term Between BENEFITC and CONTRREC

| R^2 | .29050 | | | | |

Analysis of Variance

	DF	Sum of Squares	Mean Square	F	p
Regression	3	57.99968	19.33323	32.209	.001
Residual	236	141.65691	.60024		

Regression Equation

Variable	b	s_b	b*	t	p
BENEFITC	.265325	.059763	.261307	4.440	.001
CONTRREC	.746142	.107228	.400766	6.958	.001
BENEFITC*					
CONTRREC	.061943	.119527	.029324	.518	.605
INTERCEPT	3.529992	.053614		65.841	.001

B. Hypothesis 8: Synergistic Interaction Between Recommendation and Benefits; Dummy-Coded Recommendation DUMMREC (REC = 1, NOREC = 0); BENEFITC*DUMMREC Is the Crossproduct Term Between BENEFITC and DUMMREC

| R^2 | .29050 | | | | |

Analysis of Regression

	DF	Sum of Squares	Mean Square	F	p
Regression	3	57.99968	19.33323	32.209	.001
Residual	236	141.65691	.60024		

Regression Equation

Variable	b	s_b	b*	t	p
BENEFITC	.234354	.094133	.230804	2.490	.014
DUMMREC	.746142	.107228	.400766	6.958	.001
BENEFITC*					
DUMMREC	.061943	.119527	.046616	.518	.605
INTERCEPT	3.156921	.084257		37.468	.001

Note. The continuous variable is centered benefits. The categorical variable is the respecified categorical variable that contrasts all individuals who received a recommendation for a mammogram with those who did not receive a recommendation. This variable is characterized in Panel A with a contrast code and in Panel B with a dummy code.

arithmetic mean of benefits, $M_{BENEFIT} = 3.321$. This difference is significant, $t(236) = 6.96$, $p < .001$ and is reflected in the difference in elevations of the two simple regression lines in Figure 19.4. Due to our use of a contrast code for group, and, moreover, to the choice of the particular values of the codes, the b_0 and b_1 coefficients give specific information about overall sample of $N = 240$ cases of which the groups are comprised. The intercept b_0 equals the unweighted mean of the intercepts of the regression equations within the REC and the NOREC groups, $b_0 = (3.9030 + 3.1569)/2 = 3.5299$. The b_1 coefficient represents the unweighted mean of the slopes in the REC and NOREC groups so that $b_1 = (0.2963 + 0.2344)/2 =$

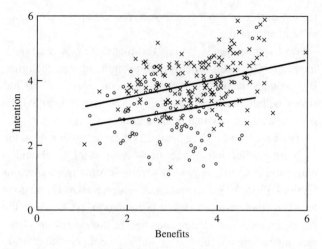

Figure 19.4 Regression of intentions on benefits within each recommendation group. The upper regression line is for the REC group, which received a recommendation from a physician or other health professional for a mammogram; the lower line is for the NOREC group. Raw data points are represented by *Xs* for the REC group and open *Os* for the NOREC group.

0.2653. As we showed above, the b_2 coefficient provides information about the difference between intercepts (means) of the two groups; the b_3 coefficient provides information about the differences between the slopes of the two groups.

Had the interaction been significant, we could have performed simple slope analyses, testing whether the slope in each group was different from zero. We might also ask at what particular values of benefits, if any, the two groups differed in their intention. The test of difference in intentions across groups at particular values of benefits is given by the Johnson-Neyman procedure, which is explained in Aiken and West (1991, chap. 7), Pedhazur (1997), and West, Aiken, and Krull (1996).

Dummy Coding and the Interaction

Instead of using the contrast code CONTRREC, we could have employed a dummy code DUMMREC to represent the respecified two-group recommendation variable, where DUMMREC = 1 for the REC group and 0 for the NOREC group. (Recall that the group coded 0 in a dummy-coded scheme is the reference group.) The crossproduct term is BENEFITC*DUMMREC. The regression equation to be estimated in this instance is

$$\hat{Y} = b_0 + b_1 \, \text{BENEFITC} + b_2 \, \text{DUMMREC}$$
$$+ \, b_3 \, \text{BENEFITC*DUMMREC} \qquad (19.36)$$

The resulting regression equation, given in Table 19.7,

Panel B, is

$$\hat{Y} = 3.1569 + 0.2343 \text{ BENEFITC} + 0.7461 \text{ DUMMREC}$$
$$+ 0.0619 \text{ BENEFITC*DUMMREC} \qquad (19.37)$$

In Equation 19.37, b_2 and b_3, which are associated with the DUMMREC variable, have the same numerical value as in Equation 19.35 containing the contrast-coded CONTRREC; again, they give the difference in intercept and slope, respectively, in the two groups. The b_0 and b_1 coefficients give information about the reference group at centered BENEFITC = 0. Here b_0 is the intercept in the reference group (NOREC) for people for whom BENEFITC = 0; b_1 gives the regression of intention on benefits in the reference (NOREC) group.

The choice of contrast versus dummy codes for the categorical by continuous variable interaction is a matter of interpretational ease and preference. Changing from contrast code to dummy code yields the following general change: With contrast coding, we obtain overall information about the average of the groups, both average intercept and average slope; with dummy coding, we obtain information about the intercept and slope in the reference group. Only in the two-group case do both coding schemes give identical information about the difference in slopes (i.e., the interaction) and about the difference between the means of the two groups on the outcome variable when the formulas presented for establishing the values of the contrast codes are followed. West, Aiken, and Krull (1996) include an extensive presentation of the interpretation of regression coefficients given various schemes for coding the categorical variable when there are more than two groups.

MODEL CHECKING AND DETECTING REGRESSION PROBLEMS

Model Respecification

Models we examine in regression analysis may be incorrectly specified in terms of either the predictors included or the form of the relationship of predictors to the criterion. In two instances we respecified our original regression model during the course of analysis: (a) We collapsed two of the three categories of the recommendation variable into one because we found no statistical evidence of difference between these categories, and (b) We moved from a linear to a curvilinear specification of the relationship of worry to intention based on the data as well as on Janis and Feshbach's (1953) earlier theoretical and empirical work. A combination of statistical tests and graphical displays led us to these model revisions. When model respecification is accomplished in this manner, *cross-validation*—that is, testing of the respecified model in a new sample, is highly desirable.

Shrinkage of R^2

Even when the regression equation has been properly specified, the sample R^2 is a positively biased estimator of the population squared multiple correlation ρ^2—that is, R^2, on average, is larger than ρ^2. An adjusted value of R^2 is computed in the sample; R^2_{adjusted} provides a more accurate estimate of ρ^2. It is given as

$$R^2_{\text{adjusted}} = 1 - (1 - R^2)\frac{(n-1)}{(n-p-1)} \qquad (19.38)$$

This value is given in standard regression analysis software, including SPSS and SAS. The difference between R^2 and R^2_{adjusted} is an estimate of how much R^2 would drop if the sample regression equation were applied to the whole population; the drop is referred to as *shrinkage*. There is a second use of the term *shrinkage*. In cross-validation, we apply a regression equation developed in one sample to the data from another sample. We again expect R^2 to drop from the first to second sample, due to the idiosyncrasies of each sample. The *shrinkage on cross-validation* is expected to be larger than the shrinkage from sample to population; (see Schmitt, Coyle, & Rauschenberger, 1977, for estimates of the cross-validated multiple correlation).

Assumptions of Regression Analysis and Detection of Violations

The OLS regression model makes a series of assumptions, which, if they are met, yield regression coefficients that are optimal statistically in that the coefficients have the smallest standard errors of all linear unbiased coefficients (i.e., are said to be *best linear unbiased*). These assumptions include that the predictors are fixed, (i.e, that cases have been sampled at fixed values on the predictors), that all predictors are measured without error, that the relationships of predictors to the criterion are linear (or can be cast into linear form, as we saw in polynomial regression). The residuals $(Y_i - \hat{Y}_i)$ are the focus of an additional series of assumptions: (a) that they are independent of one another, (b) that they exhibit homoscedasticity (i.e., their variance is constant for all values of X), and (c) for purposes of statistical inference, that they are normally distributed. Violation of these assumptions may lead to bias in regression coefficients. Moreover, violation may lead to bias in the standard errors of the regression coefficients, which, in turn, yield biased significance tests and confidence intervals. Treatments of these assumptions can be found in regression texts such as Cohen et al. (2003, chap. 4) or Neter et al. (1996). A number of graphical displays and statistical tests are used in the detection of violations of assumptions.

Multicollinearity

Multicollinearity, or high redundancy among predictors, causes great instability of regression coefficients. We have already encountered the variance inflation factor (VIF), a measure of the extent to which each predictor is redundant with (can be predicted from) the other predictors in the set. Predictor sets should be screened for variables with very high VIF values. These variables may be eliminated or combined with other variables with which they are very highly correlated. An extensive discussion of multicollinearity and its potential remedies is given in Cohen et al. (2003, chap. 10).

Errant Data Points and Regression Diagnostics

Within a data set there may exist errant or extreme data points that have an unduly strong effect on the outcome of a regression analysis. By outcome we mean the actual values of the regression coefficients, including the intercept, and the size of R^2. It is possible that a single data point is responsible for the presence of an effect (significant regression coefficient). In contrast, a single data point may mask an effect that would be statistically significant if the point were removed. A set of statistical measures, termed *regression diagnostics,* are employed to detect such data points and to measure their potential or actual impact on the regression analysis. The diagnostic measures are *case statistics*—that is, they yield a set of scores assigned to each individual case that characterize a variety of potential or actual impacts of that case on the regression analysis. Regression diagnostic measures are of three types. The first type, measures of *leverage,* assesses the potential of a point to influence the outcome of a regression analysis; measures of leverage are based on the predictors only. The second type, measures of *distance* or *discrepancy,* assesses how far the observed criterion score Y for each case is from the predicted score $\hat{Y}$. Points with high discrepancy are data points whose Y scores are unexpected, given their X scores or position in the predictor space. The third type, measures of *influence,* assesses the actual impact of each case on the outcome of the regression analysis. Following a regression analysis, it is strongly recommended that regression diagnostics be examined to determine whether there are cases that are having an undue influence on the outcome of the

analysis, perhaps leading to conclusions that would not stand a test of replication in the absence of the errant case.

There are a number of measures of each type of regression diagnostic. We present a recommended choice of measure of each type, and illustrate its use with our numerical example. More complete treatments are given in Fox (1991) and in Cohen et al. (2003, chap. 10).

Leverage

Measures of leverage are based on the distance between an individual point and the centroid of the sample. The centroid of the sample is the point representing the mean on each predictor variable. In a simple regression equation containing only the risk and benefits predictors, the centroid is the point at the means of these two predictors: $M_{\text{RISK}} = 3.989$; $M_{\text{BENEFIT}} = 3.321$, as given in Table 19.1, Panel A. The farther an individual observation is from the centroid of the predictors, the greater the potential of that case to change the outcome of the regression analysis. We consider a measure of leverage, referred to as h_{ii}, which is commonly employed.

Distance or Discrepancy

Measures of distance (discrepancy) are all based on the residual for a case $(Y_i - \hat{Y}_i)$. We focus on one of a number of these measures, the *externally studentized residual* (or *studentized deleted residual*). This measure has two characteristics. First, it is a standardized residual that follows a t distribution (residual/standard deviation of residual). Second, it is based on a regression equation derived from an analysis in which the case in question has been deleted. The reason for the deletion of the case during computation of the regression model is that if the case is in the sample and if the case is unduly affecting the regression analysis, then the regression line (or regression plane) will be pulled toward the point. In such cases, the residual will be small because the point is so influential, even though the point may be grossly unrepresentative of the remainder of the sample.

Influence

Measures of influence assess the extent to which a single case determines the outcome of the regression analysis. The measure DFFITS is a standardized measure (in z score form) of the difference in the predicted score for a case if the case is included in the analysis versus if the case is excluded from the analysis. Finally, a series of measures, DFBETAS, one for each regression coefficient, are standardized measures of the change in each regression coefficient if the case is included versus deleted from the analysis (i.e, they indicate by how many standard deviations each point changes each of the regression coefficients).

We turn to our numerical example and examine the measures of leverage, discrepancy, and influence for each case. Table 19.8 summarizes the findings. To limit the demonstration, we adopt the strategy of identifying the case which is most extreme on each of the three diagnostic measures. (In usual practice, we would adopt the strategy of identifying a few extreme cases on each diagnostic measure and examining them in detail or following some rules of thumb for selecting potential problematic cases.) We also simplify matters by focusing on the limited regression equation of intention on centered risk, benefits, and their interaction, summarized in Table 19.6, and given as

$$\hat{Y} = 3.569 + .170 \text{ RISKC} + .334 \text{ BENEFITC}$$
$$+ .175 \text{ RISKC*BENEFITC}$$

The diagnostic measures identify two extreme cases, Cases 239 and 240 that together exhibit the most extreme scores on the three diagnostic measures. Information about these cases is given in Table 19.8, Panel A. As shown in Panel A(1), Case 240 is most extreme on the measures of leverage (h_{ii}) and overall influence (DFFITS); Case 239 is most extreme on discrepancy (studentized deleted residual). Panel A(2) provides raw scores on risk, benefit, and intention. Case 239 has the second-highest risk score in the sample (7.47 on a 10-point scale), a benefits score at the 74th percentile of the sample, and a very low intention score (1.45 on a 6-point scale) at the 2nd percentile of intention in the sample. Case 240 has the highest risk score in the sample (9.99 on a 10-point scale), a perceived benefits score at the 90th percentile, and an intention score (4.90 on a 6-point scale) at the 93rd percentile. Given the remarkably high risk score, we might have expected a higher intention score (the highest in the sample is 5.89 on the 6-point scale). Panel A(3) gives the DFBETAS for the intercept and the three predictors for Cases 239 and 240. Each case has the effect of reducing the positive regression coefficient for risk—that is, making the coefficient more than one standard deviation closer to zero than it would be if the case were deleted. This is shown by the large negative DFBETAS$_1$ for risk (-1.313, -1.504, for Cases 239 and 240, respectively). The reason is that each case has a very high risk score relative to its lower intention score. Case 240 also has a similar effect on the positive interaction between risk and benefit, with a DFBETAS$_3$ for the interaction of -1.786.

To illustrate the impact of Case 240 on the regression equation, we repeat the regression analysis with the case eliminated. The result is given in Table 19.8, Panel B, and

TABLE 19.8 Regression Diagnostics and the Impact of Individual Cases on Regression Analysis

A. Extreme Cases 239 and 240

1. Overall diagnostic measures of leverage (h_{ii}), discrepancy (Studentized Deleted Residual), and influence (DFFITS)

CASE	h_{ii}	Studentized Deleted Residual	DFFITS
239	.11163	−4.41127	−1.59640
240	.54688	−2.32443	−2.57518

2. Scores of cases on predictors and criterion

CASE	RISK	BENEFIT	INTENT
239	7.47	3.96	1.45
240	9.99	4.47	4.90

3. Diagnostic measures of impact on individual regression coefficients (DFBETAS)

CASE	Intercept DFBETAS0	Risk DFBETAS1	Benefit DFBETAS2	Interaction DFBETAS3
239	−.08686	−1.31349	.28886	−.60307
240	.37806	−1.50425	.28541	−1.78621

B. Estimation of regression model with case 240 removed

R^2	.19807

Analysis of Regression

	DF	Sum of Squares	Mean Square	F	p
Regression	3	39.21527	13.07176	19.347	.001
Residual	235	158.77608	.67564		

Regression Equation

Variable	b	s_b	b*	t	p
RISKC	.286797	.092160	.202081	3.112	.002
BENEFITC	.316269	.064244	.311714	4.923	.001
RISKC* BENFITC	.307495	.093718	.197115	3.281	.001
INTERCEPT	3.547398	.056946		62.294	.000

should be compared with that in Table 19.6, Panel C, which gives the same analysis with Case 240 included. Both the regression coefficient for RISKC and for the interaction RISKC*BENEFITC are larger when Case 240 is removed. We find this result comforting in that our interpretations of positive impact of risk on intention and the synergistic interaction between risk and benefits from Table 19.6, Panel D are only enhanced by the deletion of this case. We warn the reader, however, that there can be instances in which the removal of an influential case can completely eradicate an effect.

What should be done about extreme errant data points? Consideration must be made of the source of the extreme cases. The very low intentions score for Case 239 may simply represent a clear recording or data entry error that can be rectified. In other cases, the case may represent a rare subpopulation that is different from the general population of interest. For example, Case 239 may belong to a religious group that does not believe in any form of medical testing or intervention. If so, Case 239 and any other cases representing this religious group should be removed from the analysis. The analyst should then present a full explanation of the rationale for the removal and clearly indicate that the results of the analysis can be generalized only to a population of eligible women for whom religious beliefs do not prohibit medical tests. In still other cases, the analyst will have no clear understanding of the source of the outliers. In such instances, the analyst might repeat the analysis without the errant case(s) and report the results of both analyses. Alternatively, the analyst might transform the data or use robust estimation methods that reduce the influence of the outliers on the results relative to OLS regression (Cohen et al., 2003; Wilcox, 1997). McClelland (2000) notes that some substantive psychologists are concerned about the potential that unscrupulous scientists could abuse these methods; however, many statisticians tend to be more concerned about the possibility that misleading conclusions could be reached based on a small number of aberrant cases in the data set. Given these conflicting concerns, we encourage researchers to make their raw data available for secondary analysis and to follow Kruskal's (1960) classic advice: Always provide full information about outliers in published research reports, "even when one feels that their causes are known or rejects them for whatever good rule or reason" (p. 257).

Missing Data

Throughout our presentation we have assumed that data are complete on all variables. Certain forms of missing data may produce sample regression coefficients that are biased estimates of corresponding population values, as well as increased standard errors. Graham, Cumsille, and Elek-Fisk (this volume) and Allison (2001) provide introductions to the treatment of missing data. Little and Rubin (1987) and Shafer (1997) provide advanced treatments.

SUMMARY

Regression analysis is a broad data analytic system for relating a set of independent variables (or predictors) to a single dependent variable (or criterion) or to a set of dependent variables. We have presented the structure of regression analysis in general and focused in detail on ordinary least squares regression analysis with a single continuous dependent variable. We have examined the squared multiple correlation as a measure of overall fit of a regression model. We have explained

the central concept of examining the effect of individual predictors with the impact of other predictors held constant or partialed out. Using a simulated numerical example designed to follow closely theorizing and empirical findings in health psychology, we have illustrated the use of multiple regression to examine relationships of both continuous and categorical predictors to a criterion, the impact of interpredictor correlation on regression results, the detection of curvilinear relationships through graphical analysis, the respecification of the regression model to accommodate empirically derived forms of relationship, and the detection and interpretation of interactions between continuous variables and between a continuous and a categorical variable. We have also presented methods for detecting errant data points that may have undue influence on regression analysis results and thus undermine conclusions. Throughout the numerical example, we have attempted to serve the aim of illustrating the interplay between theory and empirical findings in the specification, testing, and revision of regression models.

REFERENCES

Aiken, L. S., Gerend, M. A., & Jackson, K. M. (2001). Subjective risk and health protective behavior: Cancer screening and cancer prevention. In A. Baum, T. Revenson, & J. Singer (Eds.), *Handbook of health psychology* (pp. 727–746). Mahwah, NJ: Erlbaum.

Aiken, L. S., & West, S. G. (1991). *Multiple regression: Testing and interpreting interactions.* Newbury Park, CA: Sage.

Aiken, L. S., West, S. G., Woodward, C., & Reno, R. R. (1994). Health beliefs and compliance with mammography screening recommendations. *Health Psychology, 13,* 122–129.

Aiken, L. S., West, S. G., Woodward, C., Reno, R. R., & Reynolds, K. (1994). Increasing screening mammography in asymptomatic women: Evaluation of a second-generation, theory-based program. *Health Psychology, 13,* 526–538.

Allison, P. D. (2001). *Missing data.* Sage University Papers Series on Quantitative Applications in the Social Sciences, 07-136. Thousand Oaks, CA: Sage.

Baron, R. M., & Kenny, D. A. (1986). The moderator-mediator variable distinction in social psychological research: Conceptual, strategic, and statistical considerations. *Journal of Personality and Social Psychology, 51,* 1173–1182.

Cleveland, W. S. (1979). Robust locally weighted regression and smoothing scatter plots. *Journal of the American Statistical Association, 74,* 829–836.

Cohen, J. (1978). Partialed products are interactions; Partialed powers are curve components. *Psychological Bulletin, 85,* 858–866.

Cohen, J. (1988). *Statistical power analysis for the behavioral sciences.* Hillsdale, NJ: Erlbaum.

Cohen, J. (1990). Things I have learned (so far). *American Psychologist, 45,* 1304–1312.

Cohen, J. (1994). The earth is round (*p < .05*). *American Psychologist, 49,* 997–1003.

Cohen, J., Cohen, P., West, S. G., & Aiken, L. S. (2003). *Applied multiple regression/correlation analysis for the behavioral sciences* (3rd ed.). Hillsdale, NJ: Erlbaum.

Diaconis, P. (1985). Theories of data analysis: From magical thinking through classical statistics. In D. C. Hoaglin, F. Mosteller, & J. W. Tukey (Eds.), *Exploring data tables, trends, and shapes* (pp. 1–36). New York: Wiley.

Draper, N. R., & Smith, H. (1998). *Applied regression analysis* (3rd ed.). New York: Wiley.

Fox, J. (1991). *Regression diagnostics.* Sage University Papers Series on Quantitative Applications in the Social Sciences, 07–79. Newbury Park, CA: Sage.

Fox, J. (2000) . *Nonparametric simple regression: Smoothing scatterplots.* Sage University Papers Series on Quantitative Applications in the Social Sciences, 07–130. Thousand Oaks, CA: Sage.

Gail, M. H., Brinton, L. A., Byar, D. P., Corle, D. K., Green, S.B., Schairer, C., & Mulvihill, J. J. (1989). Projecting individualized probabilities of developing breast cancer for white females who are being examined annually. *Journal of the National Cancer Institute, 81,* 1879–1886.

Janis, I. L., & Feshbach, S. (1953). Effects of fear-arousing communications. *Journal of Abnormal and Social Psychology, 48,* 78–92.

Kirk, R. E. (1995). *Experimental design: Procedures for the behavioral sciences* (3rd ed.). Pacific Grove, CA: Brooks Cole.

Kruskal, W. H. (1960). Discussion of the papers of Messrs. Anscombe and Daniel. *Technometrics, 2,* 257–258.

Little, R. J. A., & Rubin, D. B. (1987). *Statistical analysis with missing data.* New York: Wiley.

McClelland, G. H. (2000). Nasty data: Unruly, ill-mannered observations can ruin your analysis. In H. T. Reis & C. M. Judd (Eds.), *Handbook of research methods in social and personality psychology* (pp. 393–411). New York: Cambridge.

Neter, J., Kutner, M. H., Nachtsheim, C. J., & Wasserman, W. (1996). *Applied linear regression models* (3rd ed.). Chicago: Irwin.

Pedhazur, E. J. (1997). *Multiple regression in behavioral research* (3rd ed.). Fort Worth, TX: Harcourt Brace.

Pitts, S. C., & West, S. G. (2001). *Alternative sampling designs to detect interactions in multiple regression.* Unpublished manuscript.

Rosenstock, I. M. (1990). Explaining health behavior through expectancies. In K. Glanz, F. M. Lewis, & B. K. Rimer (Eds.), *Health behavior and health education* (pp. 140–157). San Francisco: Jossey-Bass.

Ryan, T. P. (1997). *Modern regression methods.* New York: Wiley.

Schafer, J. L. (1997). *Analysis of incomplete multivariate data.* London: Chapman and Hall.

Schmitt, N., Coyle, B. W., & Rauschenberger, J. A. (1977). A Monte Carlo evaluation of three formula estimates of cross-validated multiple correlation. *Psychological Bulletin, 84,* 751–758.

Wainer, H. (2000). The centercept: An estimable and meaningful regression parameter. *Psychological Science, 11,* 434–436.

West, S. G., & Aiken, L. S. (1997). Toward understanding individual effects in multiple component prevention programs: Design and analysis strategies. In K. Bryant, M. Windle, & S. G. West (Eds.), *The science of prevention: Methodological advances from alcohol and substance abuse research* (pp. 167–209). Washington, DC: American Psychological Association.

West, S. G., Aiken, L. S., & Krull, J. (1996). Experimental personality designs: Analyzing categorical by continuous variable interactions. *Journal of Personality, 64,* 1–47.

Wilcox, R. R. (1997). *Introduction to robust estimation and hypothesis testing.* San Diego, CA: Academic Press.

Wilkinson, L., & the Task Force on Statistical Inference. (1999). Statistical methods in psychology journals: Guidelines and explanations. *American Psychologist, 54,* 594–604.

Winer, B. J., Brown, D. R., & Michels, K. M. (1991). *Statistical principles in experimental design* (3rd ed.). New York: McGraw Hill.

CHAPTER 20

Logistic Regression

ALFRED DeMARIS

Categorical response variables are common in social and behavioral research. Researchers are frequently interested in modeling such phenomena as the initiation of sexual activity by a certain age, whether individuals have been the victims of various types of crimes, whether couples have experienced violence in their relationship, and so forth. In these instances the response variable may be binary (initiated sexual activity by age 16, did not initiate such activity), unordered categorical (not a crime victim, victim of a property crime, victim of a violent crime, victim of a white-collar crime), or ordered categorical (nonviolent relationship, relationship characterized by minor violence, relationship characterized by severe violence). For various reasons, to be detailed later, linear regression is not the optimal statistical procedure for modeling categorical data. Instead, logistic or probit regression is preferred. In this chapter I provide a thorough introduction to logistic regression. (For probit regression, the reader is referred to the works by Aldrich and Nelson, 1984, and Long, 1997.)

I begin with a discussion of binary response variables. Here, I outline the pitfalls of using linear regression and develop the logistic regression model. Subsequent sections focus on model estimation, the interpretation of model coefficients, various inferential tests used in this type of analysis, and analogues of R^2 for assessing the discriminatory power of a model. Discussion of binary responses then proceeds to more advanced issues, such as modeling and interpreting interaction effects, comparing models across groups, and comparing coefficients of focus variables across nested models. I then treat unordered categorical variables, detailing the use of the multinomial logistic regression model and the test of collapsibility of response categories. Finally, I address the ordered categorical model and how to proceed when the model is not appropriate for the data. The chapter concludes with suggested readings for those interested in pursuing the topic with greater rigor. It is assumed that readers are reasonably familiar with multiple linear regression. Knowledge of matrix algebra is not a requirement; however, matrix notation is introduced in places to facilitate the compact presentation of material.

MODELS FOR A BINARY RESPONSE

Why a Linear Model Is Inappropriate

Suppose that the researcher is interested in modeling a binary response variable, Y, coded 1 for those in the category of interest, and 0 otherwise, using a set of explanatory variables,

Data for this chapter are from the National Survey of Families and Households, which was funded by a grant (HD21009) from the Center for Population Research of the National Institute of Child Health and Human Development and by a grant from the National Institute on Aging. The author wishes to thank William H. Greene for his contribution to the section on R^2 analogues and Wendy D. Manning for her contribution to the section on comparing coefficients across models.

$X_1, X_2, \ldots, X_K$. One possibility is to use multiple linear regression. The model for each sample observation is (omitting the i subscript indicating each individual case):

$$Y = \beta_0 + \beta_1 X_1 + \beta_2 X_2 + \cdots + \beta_K X_K + \varepsilon, \quad (20.1)$$

where the εs, or conditional errors, are usually assumed to be independent and identically distributed random variables with a mean of zero, a variance of σ^2 that is constant across values of the Xs, and, in small samples, a normal distribution. The model can also be expressed in terms of the conditional mean of the response:

$$E(Y) = \beta_0 + \beta_1 X_1 + \beta_2 X_2 + \cdots + \beta_K X_K. \quad (20.2)$$

In that Y is dummy coded, its mean is π, the proportion of individuals in the category coded 1. Alternatively, it is the probability that the ith case is in the category of interest. Because this is being modeled as a linear function of the explanatory variables (more accurately, a linear function of the model parameters), Equation 20.2 is referred to as the linear probability model (LPM; Long, 1997). What is wrong with this approach? There are two major problems: heteroscedastic errors and incorrect functional form. As discriminant analysis is equivalent to multiple linear regression with a dummy response when the dependent variable is binary (Kerlinger & Pedhazur, 1973; Stevens, 1986), it suffers from the same drawbacks.

First, we rewrite Equation 20.2, substituting π for $E(Y)$:

$$\pi = \beta_0 + \beta_1 X_1 + \beta_2 X_2 + \cdots + \beta_K X_K. \quad (20.3)$$

Here it is clear that what is being modeled is the probability that $Y = 1$. Now Equation 20.1 becomes $Y = \pi + \varepsilon$. Consider the error term. Because Y is binary, the error takes on only two values: $1 - \pi$ when Y is 1, and $-\pi$ when Y is 0. The ordinary least squares (OLS) estimators of the βs are still unbiased because the mean of the errors is still zero. To see this, note that the mean of the errors is $E(\varepsilon) = \sum_\varepsilon \varepsilon p(\varepsilon) = (1 - \pi)\pi + (-\pi)(1 - \pi) = 0$. But the variance of the errors is no longer constant over levels of X. This is evident in the expression for the error variance: $V(\varepsilon) = \sum_\varepsilon (\varepsilon - E(\varepsilon))^2 p(\varepsilon) = \sum_\varepsilon \varepsilon^2 p(\varepsilon) = (1 - \pi)^2 \pi + (-\pi)^2 (1 - \pi) = \pi(1 - \pi)[(1 - \pi) + \pi] = \pi(1 - \pi)$. Because Equation 20.3 shows π to be a function of the Xs, the error variance is, too. Thus, the LPM is inherently heteroscedastic. This condition has two consequences. First, the OLS estimators are no longer efficient—there exist other estimators with smaller sampling variance. More important, OLS estimates of the standard errors of the coefficients are

biased (see Greene, 1997, for a discussion of standard-error bias in the presence of heteroscedasticity). That is, the standard-error estimates printed out by regression software are incorrect. These problems are not insurmountable. An alternative to OLS in this situation is to use weighted least squares to estimate the regression coefficients, where the weight is the inverse of the estimated error variance (see Aldrich & Nelson, 1984, for details on using this alternative).

A more serious problem, however, is the implicit assumption in Equation 20.3 that the probability is a linear function of the explanatory variables. The difficulty is that the left-hand side of Equation 20.3, being a probability, is bounded between the values of zero and one. The right-hand side has no such restriction. It is free to take on any real value. The practical consequences of this are coefficient estimates that often give nonsensical predicted probabilities (values less than zero or greater than one) or indicate nonsensical impacts of predictors. An example of the latter is found in Long (1997). He presents an analysis using the LPM in which the response is whether a married woman is in the labor force. Data are from the 1976 Panel Study of Income Dynamics. The OLS coefficient for the number of children under 5 in the household is $-.295$. This means that each additional child in the household reduces the probability of the wife's being employed by .295. However, the reduction in the probability of employment for having four additional children in the household is 1.18, which, of course, is impossible. These caveats aside, conclusions reached regarding the sign and significance of predictor effects using the LPM will typically be consistent with those arrived at using the more sophisticated analytic strategies discussed later.

The Logistic Regression Model

Both logistic and probit regression employ functions of the Xs that are restricted to fall between zero and one. With one X in the equation, the logistic regression model for the probability that $Y = 1$ is

$$\pi = \frac{e^{\beta_0 + \beta_1 X}}{1 + e^{\beta_0 + \beta_1 X}}. \quad (20.4)$$

Figure 20.1 shows the difference between the linear and logistic functions for $P(Y = 1)$. The logistic function (as well as the probit function) is called a *sigmoid*, meaning S-shaped, curve. It should be clear that the right-hand side of Equation 20.4 can never fall outside the 0,1 range. The function approaches 0 as $\beta_0 + \beta_1 X$ becomes increasingly negative, and approaches 1 as $\beta_0 + \beta_1 X$ becomes increasingly positive, as shown in the figure. (For illustration purposes, it is assumed that β_1 is positive.) In the linear specification for

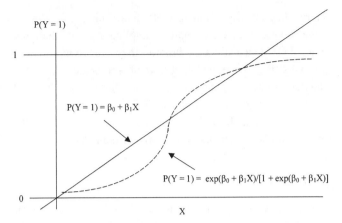

P(Y = 1)

P(Y = 1) = β₀ + β₁X

P(Y = 1) = exp(β₀ + β₁X)/[1 + exp(β₀ + β₁X)]

X

Figure 20.1 $P(Y = 1)$ as a linear, vs. a logistic, function of an explanatory variable.

$P(Y = 1)$, the impact of a unit increase in X on the probability is a constant, β_1, at every value of X. In the logit specification, X has maximum impact on the probability in the middle range of X values, whereas at the extremes of X, increases in X have little effect. This is substantively reasonable. For example, suppose that X is annual income in thousands of dollars and Y is home ownership. We would expect that a unit (i.e., thousand-dollar) increase in income would effect a noticeable increase in the probability of home ownership for people with annual incomes in the range of, say, \$20,000 to \$100,000. However, for those with incomes below \$20,000 annually, home ownership is relatively unlikely, and another \$1,000 probably will not make much difference. Similarly, those making more than \$100,000 per year almost certainly own a home, and \$1,000 is not likely to matter much. In sum, the logistic curve is an appealing function for modeling a probability, from a mathematical as well as a conceptual standpoint.

Motivation to use the logit or probit formulation also follows if we consider Y to be a binary proxy for a latent continuous variable that follows the multiple linear regression model. Suppose, for example, that the propensity for violence toward an intimate is a continuous, unobserved variable, denoted Y^*, ranging from minus infinity to plus infinity. When Y^* is greater than some threshold, say, 0, we observe violence toward an intimate partner. Otherwise, no violence is observed. The model for Y^* is: $Y^* = \sum \beta_k X_k + \varepsilon$, where $\sum \beta_k X_k = \beta_0 + \beta_1 X_1 + \beta_2 X_2 + \cdots + \beta_K X_K$, and the distribution of ε is assumed to be symmetric about zero (not necessarily normal, however). Now the probability that violence is observed to occur is $P(Y = 1) = P(Y^* > 0) = P(\sum \beta_k X_k + \varepsilon > 0) = P(\varepsilon > -\sum \beta_k X_k) = P(\varepsilon < \sum \beta_k X_k)$. This last result follows from the symmetry of the distribution for ε (i.e., the probability that $\varepsilon > -c$ is equal to the

probability that $\varepsilon < c$). The probability of the event of interest is therefore the probability that the error term is less than the value given by $\sum \beta_k X_k$. Whether logistic or probit regression is used depends on the distribution assumed for the errors. If the standard normal distribution is assumed, probit analysis would be used. If instead we assume a logistic distribution for ε (also a distribution symmetric about 0, but with a variance of $\pi^2/3$ instead of 1, where in this case π is the constant 3.14159), the analysis becomes a logistic regression. In general, the logistic regression model for the probability of an event, using K regressor variables, is

$$\pi = \frac{e^{\sum \beta_k X_k}}{1 + e^{\sum \beta_k X_k}}. \qquad (20.5)$$

Modeling the Logit

Equation 20.5 is a model for probabilities. The model can also be expressed in terms of odds. The odds of event occurrence is $\pi/(1 - \pi)$. This is the ratio of the probability of event occurrence to the probability of event nonoccurrence. For example, if the probability that an event occurs is .2, the odds of event occurrence is $.2/.8 = .25$, or 1 in 4. That is, the event is about one fourth as likely to occur as not to occur. In terms of model parameters, the equation for the odds is

$$\frac{\pi}{1 - \pi} = e^{\sum \beta_k X_k} = e^{\beta_0} e^{\beta_1 X_1} e^{\beta_2 X_2} \cdots e^{\beta_K X_K}. \qquad (20.6)$$

In other words, the odds is a multiplicative function of model parameters, where each term in the product is $\exp(\beta_k X_k)$. If we take natural logarithms (denoted "log" throughout the chapter) of both sides of Equation 20.6, we have

$$\log\left(\frac{\pi}{1 - \pi}\right) = \beta_0 + \beta_1 X_1 + \beta_2 X_2 + \cdots + \beta_K X_K. \qquad (20.7)$$

Here the resemblance to the linear regression model should be obvious. The right-hand side is the same as in Equation 20.3. The left-hand side is the log odds of event occurrence, also called the *logit* of event occurrence. The logit can take on any value from minus to plus infinity, and is therefore unrestricted in value, just like the right-hand side. The betas are interpreted just as in linear regression: A unit increase in X_k changes the logit by β_k units, controlling for other covariates in the model. However, in that changes in log odds are difficult to translate into intuitive terms, we will find it easier to interpret variable effects in terms of Equation 20.6 (discussed later).

Estimation

In linear regression, parameter estimates are obtained by minimizing the sum of squared errors with respect to the parameters. In logistic regression, estimates are arrived at by maximizing the likelihood function for the observed data with respect to the parameters. The likelihood function plays an important role in logistic regression and is therefore worth discussing in some detail. Recall that the response variable Y is coded 1 if the ith case has experienced the event of interest (or is in the category of interest) and 0 otherwise, and the probability that Y equals 1 is π. The probability function for the random variable Y is then $p(y) = \pi^y(1-\pi)^{1-y}$. This function gives the probability that Y takes on either value in its range: $p(0) = \pi^0(1-\pi)^{1-0} = 1-\pi$, and $p(1) = \pi^1(1-\pi)^{1-1} = \pi$. A particular collection of Y scores for N cases can be denoted by $\mathbf{y}$, indicating a vector, or collection, of Y scores. The probability of observing a specific set of Y scores, assuming independence of observations, is: $p(\mathbf{y}) = \prod \pi^y(1-\pi)^{1-y}$, where the product is over all N cases in the sample. To write this function in terms of the model parameters, we substitute the right-hand side of Equation 20.5 for π:

$$L(\beta \mid \mathbf{y}, \mathbf{x}) = \prod \left(\frac{e^{\sum \beta_k X_k}}{1 + e^{\sum \beta_k X_k}} \right)^y \left(\frac{1}{1 + e^{\sum \beta_k X_k}} \right)^{1-y}.$$

(20.8)

Equation 20.8 is the likelihood function. For a given sample of Xs and Ys, the value of this expression depends only on the model parameters. Maximum likelihood estimation (MLE) routines find the values of the parameters that result in the largest possible value for this function. These are then the parameter values that make the sample data most likely to have been observed.

Asymptotic Properties

Maximum likelihood estimators have several desirable asymptotic, or large-sample, properties (technically, properties that hold as the sample size tends toward infinity) that make them optimal in statistical applications (Bollen, 1989). First, they are consistent, which means that they converge to the true parameter value as the sample size gets ever larger. (Technically, consistency means that the probability that the MLE is further than some arbitrarily small distance from the parameter value tends to zero as the sample size approaches infinity.) Second, they are unbiased—again, in large samples.

Third, they are asymptotically efficient. This means that in large samples they have smaller sampling variance than any other consistent estimator. Finally, they are asymptotically normally distributed, enabling tests of significance using the standard normal distribution. However, these properties hold only in larger samples. Long (1997), for example, recommends having at least 10 observations per parameter estimated, and never using samples smaller than 100 cases.

An Example

In the following pages I present a series of logistic regression models for the occurrence of intimate violence among 4,401 married and unmarried cohabiting couples for the period 1987–1994. Data are from the National Survey of Families and Households (NSFH), a two-wave panel study of a national probability sample of U.S. households conducted by the University of Wisconsin (details of the initial survey can be found in Sweet, Bumpass, & Call, 1988). The sample for analyses in this chapter consists of couples who were married or living together unmarried in the first wave of the survey (1987–1988) who were still together in the second wave (1992–1994). My interest is in examining what characteristics of couples at time 1 are predictive of violence during the 5- to 7-year period in which the couples were followed. Descriptive statistics for all variables used in the following analyses are shown in Table 20.1. The binary dependent variable in the first set of analyses is whether violence was reported to have occurred in at least one wave of the survey. (In multinomial models I distinguish between two different types of violence; for now, both types are combined into one category, called "Violence" in the table.) Violence is coded as having occurred if at least one of the partners reported perpetrating or being the victim of physical aggression in the relationship. (Details of survey items on which the coding of violence is based can be found in DeMaris, 2000a, 2001.) Of the 4,401 couples, 586, or 13.3%, report violence in their relationship in at least one survey wave.

Independent variables were measured in the first wave of the survey and pertain to sociodemographic characteristics of couples (age at inception of the union, minority status, completed education), relationship stressors (alcohol or drug problems in the household, the relationship of household income to financial need), interdependence factors (duration of the relationship, cohabiting status, number of children), and aspects of the couples' style of conflict resolution (frequency of open disagreements, communication style, nonassertiveness). Generally, I expect couples to be more prone to violence if they were younger when they wed or moved in

TABLE 20.1 Descriptive Statistics for Characteristics of 4,401 Married and Cohabiting Couples in the National Survey of Families and Households

Variable	Description (range)	Mean	SD
Intense male violence[D]	1 if his violence is greater than her violence, or she is the only injured partner	.050	.218
Common couple violence[D]	1 if violence is other than "intense male" kind	.083	.276
Violence[D]	1 if either type of violence occurred	.133	.340
Female's age at union	Female's age at inception of union	24.705	7.429
Cohabiting couple[D]	1 if couple is cohabiting unmarried	.021	.143
Relationship duration	Length of relationship, in years	16.120	13.815
Substance abuse[D]	1 if either partner abuses alcohol/drugs	.057	.231
Minority couple[D]	1 if either partner is a minority	.295	.456
Number of children	Number of children <18 in household	1.178	1.278
Male's education	Male's education in years	13.216	3.115
Female's education	Female's education in years	12.979	2.716
Income-to-needs ratio	Household income divided by poverty line for the household	4.870	4.759
Open disagreement	Scale of frequency of open disagreements in past year	10.990	3.965
Communication style	Scale of positive communication style	7.354	1.384
Male nonassertiveness	Frequency with which male keeps opinions to himself	2.593	.979
Female nonassertiveness	Frequency with which female keeps opinions to herself	2.453	1.032

[D]Dummy variable.

together, if either partner is a minority (Leonard & Senchak, 1996), or if partners are characterized by lower education (Leonard & Senchak, 1996). Similarly, I expect violence to be more likely in relationships experiencing more financial stress (Dutton, 1988), as indexed by a low income-to-needs ratio, and in those in which one or both partners are abusing drugs or alcohol (Heyman, O'Leary, & Jouriles, 1995). On the other hand, I expect violence to be less likely when couples have more resources invested in their relationship (Rusbult & Buunk, 1993), that is, when they have been together longer, are married instead of cohabiting (Stets, 1991), and have more children in the household (MacMillan & Gartner, 1999). Finally, several scholars have found couples' styles of resolving conflict to be a key predictor of whether arguments erupt in violence, as well as whether the couple remains together over the long term (Gottman, Coan, Carrere, & Swanson, 1998; Margolin, John, & Gleberman, 1988). Hence, I expect less violence to the extent that couples have fewer open disagreements, argue in a reasoned fashion when they do have disagreements (i.e., have a "positive" communication style), and bring their opinions out into the open when a difference of opinion occurs (i.e., refrain from being "nonassertive").

Table 20.2 presents the results of three logistic regression models of intimate violence for these couples. (All analyses for this chapter were performed using SAS, version 6.12 for the PC, with procedure LOGISTIC used for the Table 20.2

results.) The response variable is the log odds of Violence (as in Equation 20.7); the coefficients in the table are estimates of the betas in the model. Except for the number of children, all continuous variables have been centered, or deviated from their means. That is, for each continuous variable X, I substitute the variable $X - \overline{X}$. Centered variables therefore have means of zero. Model 1 includes only the focus variables in the study—the sociodemographic, relationship stressor, and interdependence factors. Because of centering, the intercept is interpretable as the estimated log odds of violence for married, nonminority couples with no children under 18 at home, who have no substance abuse problems, and who are average in age at entry into the union, length of relationship, education, and income-to-needs ratio. Its value is −2.141, implying that the odds of violence for this group is exp(−2.141), or .118. The probability is recovered from the odds by the formula probability = odds/(1 + odds). Thus, the probability of violence for this group is .118/(1 + .118) = .106; in other words, this group has about a 10% chance of exhibiting relationship violence.

Interpreting the Betas

At the simplest level, the signs of the coefficients reveal at a glance whether increases in the predictor values raise or lower the probability of event occurrence. Because of the monotonic relationship between the log odds, the odds, and

TABLE 20.2 Logistic Regression Results for Three Models of Intimate Violence

Explanatory Variable	Model 1	Model 2	Model 3	Standardized Coefficients for Model 3
Intercept	−2.141***	−2.222***	−2.210***	
Female's age at union[a]	−.021**	−.006	−.006	−.024
Cohabiting couple	.877***	.982***	1.000***	.079
Relationship duration[a]	−.045***	−.034***	−.035***	−.268
Substance abuse	1.095***	.766***	.766***	.098
Minority couple	.234*	.221*	.161	.041
Number of children	−.038	−.113**	−.128**	−.090
Male's education[a]	−.033	−.031	−.029	−.049
Female's education[a]	.005	.014	.019	.029
Income-to-needs ratio[a]	−.005	−.007	.002	.004
Open disagreement[a]		.080***	.079***	.173
Communication style[a]		−.410***	−.412***	−.315
Male nonassertiveness[a]		−.041	−.035	−.019
Female nonassertiveness[a]		−.113*	−.115*	−.065
Minority couple × income-to-needs ratio			−.091*	−.091
Model Chi-Squared	208.560***	472.915***	480.561***	
Model df	9	13	14	
R^2 analogues:				
$\hat{\Delta}$	.052	.126	.128	
R^2_{MZ}	.123	.240	.243	

Note. $N = 4{,}401$.
[a]Centered predictor.
*$p < .05$. **$p < .01$. ***$p < .001$.

the probability, any factor that increases or decreases the log odds also increases or decreases the odds or the probability. So, for example, couples who were older when entering into the union (female's age at union is a proxy for the age of the couple) or who have been together longer have lower probabilities (odds) of violence, whereas minority couples or those with substance abuse problems have higher probabilities (odds) of violence.

Odds Ratios

Beta values indicate the change in the log odds for each unit increase in a predictor, net of other predictors in the model. However, the log odds has no intuitive meaning for most analysts. Effects are more easily understood if couched in terms of the odds of violence. Equation 20.6 shows that if we exponentiate the coefficients, they indicate the multiplicative impact (Agresti, 1989) on the odds for each unit increase in the predictors. To make this clearer, consider an equation with just two predictors, X and Z. The ratio of the odds of the event for those who are a unit apart on X, controlling for Z, is

$$\psi_{x+1} = \frac{e^{\beta_0} e^{\beta_1(x+1)} e^{\beta_2 Z}}{e^{\beta_0} e^{\beta_1 x} e^{\beta_2 Z}} = \frac{e^{\beta_1(x+1)}}{e^{\beta_1 x}} = e^{\beta_1}, \quad (20.9)$$

where ψ_{x+1} represents the odds ratio for those who are a unit apart on X, controlling for all other covariates in the model. Equation 20.9 shows that the odds of the event for those with an X value of $x + 1$ is higher by a factor of e^{β_1} than for those with an X value of x. In logistic regression, the odds ratio is the multiplicative analogue of the unstandardized coefficient in linear regression. Like the latter, it indicates a constant change in the response for a unit increase in a given predictor, except in this case it is the multiplicative, rather than additive, change in the odds.

Because the odds ratio is such a staple of interpretation in logistic regression, it is worth exploring further. Consider the zero-order impact of substance abuse on violence: Of the 4,151 couples with no substance abuse, 509 reported violence. For this group, then, the probability of violence is $509/4151 = .123$, and the odds of violence is therefore $.123/(1 − .123) = .140$. Among the 250 couples with substance abuse problems, 77 reported violence. Their probability of violence is therefore $77/250 = .308$, implying an odds of violence of $.308/(1 − .308) = .445$. To quantify the "effect" of substance abuse on violence, we take the ratio of the odds, or $.445/.140 = 3.179$. That is, substance abuse raises the odds of violence by a factor of 3.179. Or, the odds of violence is 3.179 times higher for those with substance abuse problems. Notice that it is incorrect to say that those with substance abuse problems are "3.179 times as likely" to be violent, implying that their probability of violence is 3.179 times higher. In fact, their probability of violence is only $.308/.123 = 2.504$ times higher. This ratio of probabilities, called the *relative risk*, is only equivalent to the odds ratio if the probabilities are both very small (Hosmer & Lemeshow, 1989). In sum, the odds ratio is the preferred metric for quantifying effects of predictors in logistic regression. In general, a unit increase in X_k raises the odds of the response by e^{β_k}.

Additionally, it is the case that $\psi_{x+c} = e^{\beta_k c}$. That is, a c-unit increase in X elevates (reduces) the odds by a factor of $\exp(\beta_k c)$. Hence, in Model 1, each 1-year increase in age the female was upon entering the union lowers the odds of violence by a factor of $\exp(-.021)$ or $.979$, whereas being 5 years older at entry lowers the odds of violence by a factor of $\exp(-.021 \times 5) = .900$. Effects can be expressed also in terms of percent changes in the odds: $100(e^{\beta_1} - 1)$ indicates the percent change in the odds for a unit increase in X in Equation 20.9. So, again in Model 1, each 1-year increase in time that the couple has been together changes the odds of violence by $100(e^{-.045} - 1) = -4.4$, or effects a 4.4% reduction in the odds of violence. Exponentiating the coefficient for a dummy variable gives the odds ratio for those in the interest category, compared to the reference group. So the odds of violence for minority couples is $\exp(.234) = 1.264$ times higher (or 26.4% higher) than for nonminority couples. Also, the odds of violence for couples with a substance abuse problem (adjusted for other model covariates) is $\exp(1.095) = 2.989$ times higher (or 198.9% higher) than for those without such problems.

Impacts on Probabilities

The odds ratio neatly encapsulates the impact of a predictor on the odds of event occurrence, an impact that is invariant to the values of other covariates in the model. There is no comparable measure for effects on the probability of event occurrence. The reason for this is that the logistic regression model, unlike the linear one, is nonlinear in the parameters. Therefore the partial derivative of π with respect to, say, X_k—representing the effect of X_k net of other covariates—is not a constant, as it is in the linear probability model (Equation 20.3). In fact, we saw earlier that the assumption of a constant effect on the probability can result in nonsensical estimates of predictor effects. In Equation 20.5 the partial derivative of π with respect to X_k is $\beta_k[\pi(\mathbf{x})(1 - \pi(\mathbf{x}))]$, where $\pi(\mathbf{x})$ indicates the probability of an event at a particular setting of the Xs in the model. Because $\pi(\mathbf{x})$ depends on model parameters, this expression shows that the impact of

X_k on π depends on the values of all Xs in the model, including X_k. In other words, the model is inherently interactive in the probability of event occurrence.

This phenomenon is easy to see using Model 1 in Table 20.2. Recall that the estimated probability of violence for married, nonminority couples with no children under 18 at home, who have no substance abuse problems, and who are average in age at entry into the union, length of relationship, education, and income-to-needs ratio, is .106. If a couple with these characteristics were together for 1 year longer, their odds of violence would be $.113 (= e^{-.045} \times .118)$, implying that their probability of violence would be $.113/(1 + .113) = .102$. The change in probability for a 1-year increase in relationship duration is therefore $.106 - .102 = .004$. Now consider a minority couple with the same initial characteristics. Their odds of violence would be $.149 (= e^{.234} \times .118)$, implying a probability of violence of .130. If they were together a year longer, their odds of violence would drop to .142, implying a new probability of .124. For these couples, a 1-year increase in relationship duration therefore results in a change of .006 in the probability of violence. These results illustrate that the change in probability corresponding to a unit increase in a given predictor (e.g., relationship duration) depends on the values of other variables in the model—even though there are no interaction terms in the model.

Interpretational issues are further complicated by another problem. Even at a particular setting of model covariates, there is no simple expression for the change in π given a *unit* increase in a particular predictor. Some have suggested that the partial derivative, $\beta_k[\pi(\mathbf{x})(1 - \pi(\mathbf{x}))]$, has that interpretation (see, e.g., Cleary & Angel, 1984). Although the partial derivative may closely approximate this change, it does not represent the change exactly. In general, for an equation linking Y with X, the partial derivative of Y with respect to X is the rate of change of Y with change in X at the point x. Specifically, it is the slope of the line tangent to the curve of the function linking Y with X, at the point x. In simple linear regression, the "curve" linking $E(Y)$ with X is already a straight line, so the tangent line and the curve are synonymous. Correspondingly, the partial derivative of $E(Y)$ with X is β at every x. This means that unit changes in X add β to $E(Y)$ everywhere along the line. Figure 20.2 shows the tangent line to the logistic curve at the point x, with just one X in the equation. If we let $P(x)$ indicate $P(Y = 1)$ given $X = x$, then $\Delta P = P(x + 1) - P(x)$ is the actual change in probability along the logistic curve for a unit increase in x. The derivative of $P(x)$ with respect to X at the point x, $P'(x)$, indicates the change in $P(x)$ along the tangent line— not along the function—for a unit increase in X. Thus, $P'(x)$

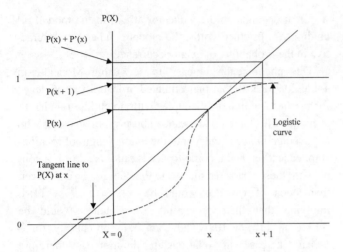

Figure 20.2 Change in probability along the logistic curve for a unit increase in X: exact change vs. change estimated by the partial derivative.

is not generally equal to ΔP. If one wants to compute the precise change in π for a unit increase in X, one generally must evaluate $P(x+1) - P(x)$; see DeMaris (1993) for an extended discussion of this issue.

Standardized Coefficients

In linear regression, standardized coefficients are used to compare the relative impacts of different predictors in the same equation. The standardized coefficient is the product of the unstandardized coefficient times the ratio of the standard deviation of X_k to the standard deviation of Y. In logistic regression, calculating a standardized coefficient is not as straightforward. Recall the latent-variable formulation for the logistic regression model, discussed earlier. The logistic regression coefficient, β_k, can, of course, be interpreted as the change in Y^* for each unit increase in X_k. If we had an estimate of the standard deviation of Y^*, we could compute the standardized version of this coefficient as

$$\beta_k^s = \beta_k \left(\frac{s_{Xk}}{s_{Y^*}} \right).$$

But Y^* is unobserved, so its standard deviation is not readily estimated. One solution, which is found in SAS, is to standardize the coefficients partially by multiplying them by the factor $\frac{s_{Xk}}{\sigma_\varepsilon}$, where σ_ε is the standard deviation of the conditional errors, or approximately 1.814 (since the variance of the errors is assumed to be $\pi^2/3$ in the logistic distribution). These are shown in the last column of Table 20.2 and apply to the full model for violence—one containing the focus variables, the conflict resolution factors, and an interaction of minority status with the income-to-needs ratio. For example, the standardized coefficient for relationship duration is

$-.035(13.815/1.814) = -.267$, which agrees with the figure of $-.268$ in the table (within rounding error). These coefficients perform the same function as the standardized coefficients in linear regression of indicating the relative magnitude of predictor effects within any given equation. From their values, it appears that communication style has the strongest impact on the log odds of violence, followed by relationship duration and then open disagreement.

Inferences in Logistic Regression

Several statistical tests that have counterparts in linear regression are of interest in logistic regression. First, it is usually important to test whether one's model is of any utility in predicting the response. The null hypothesis for this test is that all of the coefficients other than the intercept equal 0. That is, we test H_0: $\beta_1 = \beta_2 = \cdots = \beta_K = 0$. If this is rejected, we conclude that at least one of the β_ks is nonzero. In linear regression, the F test is used to assess this hypothesis. The comparable test statistic in logistic regression is called the model chi-squared. It is based on evaluating the likelihood function (Equation 20.8) at the MLEs for two models. The first is a model that excludes all predictors except the intercept, which is the correct model if the null hypothesis is true. The likelihood function for this model is denoted L_0. The second is the hypothesized model with intercept plus regression coefficients, and its likelihood is denoted L_1. If the null hypothesis is true, the statistic $-2\log(L_0/L_1)$ is distributed asymptotically (i.e., in large samples) as chi-squared with degrees of freedom equal to the number of parameters (excluding the intercept) in the model. As this statistic is based on the ratio of two likelihoods, it is also referred to as the likelihood-ratio chi-squared. Table 20.2 shows that the model chi-squared for Model 1 is 208.560, which, with 9 degrees of freedom, is a highly significant result.

Given a model with predictive utility, we usually wish to know which regressors have significant effects on the response. In linear regression, the coefficient divided by its estimated standard error provides a t test for the null hypothesis that the population coefficient is zero. Similarly, in logistic regression, the coefficient divided by its estimated standard error is a z test for the null hypothesis that the parameter is zero. That is, under H_0: $\beta_k = 0$, the statistic $z = \frac{b_k}{\hat{\sigma}_{b_k}}$ has approximately the standard normal distribution in large samples. Some software programs, such as SAS, print out the square of this statistic, which is labeled the "Wald Chi-square" on SAS printouts. Under the null hypothesis that $\beta_k = 0$, this statistic has the chi-squared distribution with 1 degree of freedom. Significant coefficients, according to these tests, are starred in Table 20.2. It is evident that the significant predictors of violence in Model 1 are the female's age at union, whether the couple is cohabiting or married, relationship duration, whether either partner has a substance abuse problem, and whether the couple is a minority.

It is frequently of interest to test whether a block of variables makes a significant contribution to the model over and above a set of initial variables. More generally, we may wish to test whether there is a difference in predictive utility between two *nested* models. Formally, model B is nested inside model A if the parameters of B can be produced by placing constraints on those of A. The most common constraint is to set a parameter to zero, although more complex constraints are possible. In linear regression, we use a partial F test to test the null hypothesis that model B fits as well as model A or that the constraints imposed on A to create B are true (Long, 1997). In logistic regression, we use a likelihood-ratio chi-squared test. This time, however, the test statistic is $-2\log(L_B/L_A)$, where L_B is the likelihood for the constrained model and L_A is the likelihood for the unconstrained model. Mathematically, this is equivalent to the difference in model chi-squareds for the two models. Under the null hypothesis that the constraints are valid, this statistic has the chi-squared distribution with degrees of freedom equal to the number of constraints imposed (e.g., the number of parameters set to zero).

Model 2 in Table 20.2 shows the result of adding the block of four conflict resolution variables to Model 1. The difference in model chi-squareds for Models 1 and 2 is $472.915 - 208.56 = 264.355$. With four degrees of freedom, this difference is highly significant ($p < .0001$), suggesting that one or more of the additional coefficients is different from zero. In fact, three of the four are significant by individual tests: open disagreement, communication style, and female nonassertiveness. As expected, the greater the frequency of open disagreements, and the poorer the communication between partners (e.g., the partners argue heatedly and shout at each other), the greater the probability of violence. Contrary to expectation, on the other hand, nonassertiveness is associated with a lower chance of aggression: In particular, the more the female partner keeps her opinions to herself, the less likely the couple is to experience violence.

Wald Test versus Likelihood-Ratio Chi-Squared

Model 3 in Table 20.2 adds one more term to those in Model 2: the crossproduct of minority status with the (centered) income-to-needs ratio. This term is designed to capture interaction effects between minority status and the income-to-needs ratio in their effects on the log odds of violence.

Although the interpretation of interaction effects is postponed until a later section, let's focus on the test of this term for the moment. There are two tests for the addition of a single parameter to the model. One is the likelihood-ratio chi-squared, calculated as the difference between model chi-squareds for models with and without the term. Comparing Models 2 and 3, its value is $480.561 - 472.915 = 7.646$. With 1 degree of freedom, this result is significant at $p < .006$. The other test is the Wald chi-squared, whose value is 6.461, also significant, at $p < .02$. These tests will typically agree fairly closely. Both have asymptotic chi-squared distributions with 1 degree of freedom under the null hypothesis that the added term is zero in the population. However, Wald's test can behave in an aberrant manner if the effect of the term in question is too large. Hauck and Donner (1977) showed that this problem occurs because whereas the likelihood-ratio chi-squared is a monotone increasing function of the magnitude of the parameter estimate, the Wald statistic is not. In fact, for any sample size, the Wald test statistic decreases to zero as the absolute value of the parameter estimate tends toward infinity. Moreover, when the parameter estimate becomes too large, the power of the test decreases to the alpha level for the test, which is typically .05. In practical terms, this implies that the researcher could underestimate the importance of a given effect if he or she were to rely solely on the Wald test. When in doubt, the likelihood-ratio test is always to be preferred over the Wald test for testing individual coefficients (Hauck & Donner, 1977).

Numerical Problems

Estimation of logistic regression models is frequently plagued by numerical difficulties. Some of these are also common to estimation with least squares. For example, multicollinearity creates the same kinds of problems in logistic regression that it does in OLS: inflation in the magnitudes of estimates as well as in their standard errors, or, in the extreme case, counterintuitive signs of coefficients (Schaefer, 1986). Collinearity diagnostics are not necessarily available in logistic regression software—for example, none are provided in SAS's LOGISTIC procedure. However, in that collinearity is strictly a problem connected with the explanatory variables, it can also be addressed with linear regression software. In SAS, I use collinearity diagnostics in the OLS regression procedure (PROC REG) to evaluate linear dependencies in the predictors. The best single indicator of collinearity problems is the variance inflation factor (VIF) for each coefficient. This is the reciprocal of the tolerance, which is the proportion of variation in the kth predictor that is not shared with the other predictors in the model. VIFs above 10 (or tolerances smaller than .1) generally signal problematic multicollinearity (Myers, 1986). In the current example, the VIFs for all coefficients in Model 3 in Table 20.2 were inspected for signs of collinearities. As all VIFs were well under 2, no such problems were evident.

Other problems are more unique to MLE. The first pertains to zero cell counts. If the cross-tabulation of the response variable with a given categorical predictor results in zero cells, it will not be possible to estimate effects associated with those cells in a logistic regression model. In an earlier article (DeMaris, 1995) I presented an example using the 1993 General Social Survey in which the dependent variable is happiness, coded 1 for those reporting being "not too happy" and 0 otherwise. Among categorical predictors, I employed marital status, represented by four dummy variables (widowed, divorced, separated, never married) with married as the reference group, and race, represented by two dummies (Black, other race), with White as the reference group. Among other models, I tried to estimate one with the interaction of marital status and race. The problem is that among those in the "other race" category who are separated, all respondents report being "not too happy," leaving a zero cell in the remaining category of the response. I was alerted that there was a problem by the unreasonably large coefficient for the "other race × separated" term in the model and by its associated standard error, which was about 20 times larger than any other. Running the three-way cross tabulation of the response variable by marital status and race revealed the zero cell. An easy solution, in this case, was to collapse the categories of race into White versus non-White and then to estimate the interaction again. If collapsing categories of a categorical predictor is not possible, it could be treated as continuous, provided that it is at least ordinal scaled (Hosmer & Lemeshow, 1989).

A much rarer problem occurs when one or more predictors perfectly discriminate between the categories of the response. Suppose, as a simple example, that all couples with incomes under $10,000 per year report violence, and all couples with incomes over $10,000 per year report being nonviolent. In this case, income completely separates the outcome groups. Correspondingly, the problem is referred to as *complete separation*. When this occurs, the MLEs do not exist (Hosmer & Lemeshow, 1989). Finite MLEs exist only when there is some overlap in the distribution of explanatory variables for groups defined by the response variable. If the overlap is only marginal—say, at a single or a few tied values—a problem of quasi-complete separation develops. In either case, the analyst is again made aware that something is amiss by unreasonably large coefficient estimates and associated standard errors. SAS also provides a warning if the program can detect this data configuration. Surprisingly, the suggested solution for this problem is to revert to OLS regression. One advantage of the LPM over logit or probit is that estimates of coefficients are available under complete or quasi-complete separation (Caudill, 1988).

An Alternative Modeling Strategy

The models examined in Table 20.2 demonstrate one type of modeling strategy—purposive, sequential entry of variables according to a specific theoretical framework. The entry of sociodemographic, relationship stressor, and interdependence factors (the focus variables) as the first predictor set in the model reflects their role as more distal influences on violence. The subsequent entry of conflict management factors (open disagreement, communication style, and male and female nonassertiveness) is consistent with their role as mediators of the impact of the focus variables on violence. For example, I expected substance abuse to elevate the likelihood of violence by leading to more frequent heated arguments between the partners. And such arguments, in turn, become the proximal causes of violence. To assess whether this chain of events is plausible, I must add the conflict management factors *after* the focus variables and then examine whether the impact of, say, substance abuse is reduced once conflict management factors are controlled. The fact that the coefficient for substance abuse is indeed reduced in Model 2 suggests that this causal chain may be supported (below I explain how to test whether this drop in the effect of substance abuse is, in fact, a significant reduction in the coefficient). Finally, after all the main effects of interest are in the model, I test whether there is an interaction between minority status and the income-to-needs ratio.

At times, however, the analyst has no clear idea which explanatory variables are likely to be important in the prediction of the response. Instead, he or she may wish to engage in a more exploratory approach to model fitting. In this case, there is a stepwise model-fitting approach in logistic regression that is much like stepwise linear regression. This technique is particularly useful when the analyst wishes to screen a large number of variables quickly to discern which are the most compelling predictors of the dependent variable (Hosmer & Lemeshow, 1989). As an example, I apply stepwise logistic regression to Model 3 in Table 20.2 to see if a more parsimonious set of regressors can be selected from the 14 shown there. First, however, I examine the functional form of the relationship between the log odds of violence and each continuous predictor (except for the cross-product term) to ensure that any nonlinear associations are adequately captured.

There are several ways to examine potential nonlinearities in the relationship between X and the logit of Y (see Hosmer & Lemeshow, 1989, for a thorough discussion). Perhaps the simplest approach is to use the Box-Tidwell transformation (Hosmer & Lemeshow, 1989). This involves simply adding a term of the form $x \log(x)$ (i.e., x times the natural logarithm of x) to the model in addition to x itself, for each continuous x in the model. If the coefficient of $x \log(x)$ is significant, then there is nonlinearity in the relationship between x and the logit. As all continuous predictors in Table 20.2 are centered—and thus have both negative as well as positive values—the natural log would not always be defined for these variables. Therefore, I used a quadratic term (x^2) in place of $x \log(x)$ to assess non-linearity. Quadratic terms will capture any type of nonlinearity that can be described as a curve with one bend. Of all continuous predictors, only relationship duration evinced a significant quadratic effect, suggesting a nonlinear trend in the relationship between relationship duration and the log odds of violence. A quadratic term for relationship duration was therefore added to the regressors in Model 3 prior to the stepwise run.

Stepwise logistic regression begins with a model containing only the intercept and no regressors. In the first step, the variable is added that results in the largest model chi-squared, compared to the intercept-only model, provided that the p value for that chi-squared is smaller than some preset value. (In the current example, I chose .15 as the minimum p value for entry of variables.) In the next step, the variable is added that produces the largest change in the model chi-squared, compared to the model with just the first predictor entered. Again, that variable is added if the p value for the change is less than the preset value. At this point, there are two predictors in the model. The program now checks whether, with the second variable in the model, the first is still significant. This is accomplished by examining the change in model chi-squared resulting from deleting the first variable entered. If the p value for that change is larger than a second criterion value—the p value for removal of a term—the first variable would be removed from the model. Typically, the p value for removal is set higher than the p value for entry to prevent adding and then dropping the same variable in one step. For this procedure, I chose a p value of .20 for removal of terms. The procedure continues in this fashion, checking each subsequent variable in the candidate pool, adding the variable resulting in the largest change in the model chi-squared— provided that p for chi-squared is less than the preset entry value—and dropping any variables that do not remain significant at the p value for removal of variables, at each step. The procedure terminates when no more variables can be entered—the p value for the largest change in chi-squared is greater than the entry criterion—and when

TABLE 20.3 Results of Stepwise Logistic Regression Applied to Explanatory Variables in Model 3 in Table 20.2, Plus a Quadratic Effect of Relationship Duration

Summary of Stepwise Procedure

Step Variable Entered	Number in	Change in Score χ^2	p Value
1 Open disagreement[a]	1	261.300	.0001
2 Communication style[a]	2	108.900	.0001
3 Relationship duration[a]	3	65.187	.0001
4 Relationship duration^2	4	31.181	.0001
5 Substance abuse	5	22.588	.0001
6 Cohabiting couple	6	17.753	.0001
7 Minority couple × income-to-needs ratio	7	7.251	.0071
8 Female nonassertiveness[a]	8	6.039	.0140
9 Minority couple	9	2.852	.0912
10 Number of children	10	2.246	.1339

Final Model Selected by Stepwise Procedure

Explanatory Variable	b
Intercept	−2.537***
Cohabiting couple	.956***
Relationship duration[a]	−.043***
Relationship duration^2	.001***
Substance abuse	.766***
Minority couple	.185
Number of children	−.065
Open disagreement[a]	.082***
Communication style[a]	−.423***
Minority couple × income-to-needs ratio	−.086*
Female nonassertiveness[a]	−.113*

Note. $N = 4,401$.
[a]Centered predictor.
*$p < .05$. **$p < .01$. ***$p < .001$.

no more variables can be dropped—the p value for removal of the least significant variable is smaller than the removal criterion.

Table 20.3 presents the results of the stepwise procedure for the candidate variables in Model 3 in Table 20.2—plus the quadratic effect of relationship duration. Shown are variables entered in each step, the resulting change in the score chi-squared statistic for variable entry, and the p value for that change. As is evident, open disagreement produces the largest change in the likelihood function, and therefore results in the largest model chi-squared in the first step. Next, in order, are entered communication style, relationship duration, relationship duration squared, substance abuse, cohabitation, the interaction of minority status with income-to-needs ratio, female nonassertiveness, minority couple status, and number of children. After the entry of number of children, no other variables cause a change in the model chi-squared at a p value less than .15, so no further variables are entered. Once entered, all variables appear to retain their importance, as none of the entered variables is removed in a later step. The final model selected by the stepwise procedure retains 10 of the original 15 variables considered.

In the current example, stepwise selection is not a particularly desirable approach. To begin, several factors are omitted that have theoretical importance. For example, male and female education and the age at which the union was formed—tapped by the female's age at union—are important background variables that could affect the couple's style of conflict management, and, therefore, violence. Also, male nonassertiveness is an element in the conflict management group that is posited to mediate the effects of other variables on violence, and should therefore be entered with that group. Finally, the model contains an illegitimate nonhierarchical interaction because the cross product of minority status by the income to needs ratio is present, but the main effect of income to needs is omitted. The interaction term and its component effects, could, of course, be forced into the model in advance. Still, stepwise selection of variables should probably not be used when analyses are guided by theoretical considerations.

Analogues of R^2

Much work in linear regression relies on R^2 to index a model's *discriminatory power*—the ability of a model to discriminate among scores on the response. Many counterparts have been proposed for use in logistic regression (see, e.g., Long, 1997), but no single measure is consistently used. Two difficulties are paramount in fashioning a counterpart for logistic regression. In linear regression, R^2 in any given sample is a function of the discrepancy between the observed response, Y, and the response predicted by the model, $\hat{Y}$. In particular, $R^2 = 1 - \left[\sum(Y - \hat{Y})^2 / \sum(Y - \overline{Y})^2 \right]$. In this case the observed score is directly modeled: $Y = \sum \beta_k X_k + \varepsilon$. In logistic regression, we model the *probability* of an event. This is a mathematical abstraction, not an observable entity. What we *do* observe is only whether an event has occurred. And although we typically assign scores of 1 and 0 to denote the occurrence or nonoccurrence of the event, respectively, these values are purely arbitrary—although mathematically convenient—and have no real quantitative meaning. Constructing an R^2 analogue for the logistic regression model is, therefore, less straightforward.

A second concern revolves around the identity of the parameter that R^2 is intended to estimate in logistic regression. Recall the latent variable development of the logistic regression model, as articulated earlier. If Y is a proxy for a latent scale, Y^*, then it seems that the explained variance in Y^*, or ρ^2 (rho-squared), is the parameter to be estimated. On the other hand, if Y represents a qualitative change in state (e.g., becoming pregnant before age 18), then the explained variance in the binary indicator of event occurrence—Y itself—is the parameter of interest. I refer to this latter quantity as the *explained risk* of the event (following the terminology used by Korn & Simon, 1991) and use Δ to represent this quantity.

In a recent simulation study (DeMaris, 2000b), I investigated the performance of eight popular R^2 analogues as estimators of each of these criteria. Of the eight measures, two emerge as best—one for each criterion—based on the criteria of consistency and mean-squared error. To understand these measures, it is necessary to review the concept of explained variance briefly.

The general expression for the decomposition of variance in a joint distribution of Y and $X_1, X_2, \ldots, X_K$ (Greene, 1997) is

$$\text{Var}(Y) = \text{Var}_x[E(Y \mid X)] + E_x[\text{Var}(Y \mid X)]. \quad (20.10)$$

That is, the variance in Y equals the variance of the conditional mean of Y, given X (the first term in the sum on the right-hand side of Equation 20.10), plus the mean of the conditional variance of Y, given X (the second term on the right), where X represents the vector of covariates $X_1, X_2, \ldots, X_K$. In linear regression, for example, $E(Y \mid X) = \beta_0 + \beta_1 X_1 + \beta_2 X_2 + \cdots + \beta_K X_K$, and $\text{Var}(Y \mid X) = \sigma^2$. Dividing both sides of Equation 20.10 by $\text{Var}(Y)$ results in

$$1 = \frac{\text{Var}_x[E(Y \mid X)]}{\text{Var}(Y)} + \frac{E_x[\text{Var}(Y \mid X)]}{\text{Var}(Y)}. \quad (20.11)$$

The first term on the right-hand side of Equation 20.11 is ρ^2, the proportion of variance in Y that is due to the structural part of the model, or the *explained variance* in Y. Equation 20.11 can also be expressed as follows:

$$\rho^2 = 1 - \frac{E_x[\text{Var}(Y \mid X)]}{\text{Var}(Y)} = 1 - \frac{\sigma^2}{\text{Var}(Y)}. \quad (20.12)$$

That is, ρ^2 is 1 minus the ratio of the average conditional variance of Y to the marginal variance of Y. (Note that the conditional variance of Y is the same as the variance of the conditional errors. And in the classic linear regression model with constant error variance, the average of σ^2 is, of course, just σ^2.) ρ^2 ranges between the values of 0 (indicating that all of the variance in Y is due to error variance) to 1 (suggesting that all of the variance in Y is due to the model covariates).

An analogous decomposition can be applied to a binary response variable, Y, taking on the values 0 and 1 for mathematical convenience. Such a variable has the Bernoulli distribution with mean π and variance $\pi(1 - \pi)$ (Hoel, Port, & Stone, 1971), where π is the marginal probability that the variable takes on the value 1. Assuming a model for π, based on X, of the form $\pi \mid X = F(X)$ (where, e.g., $F[X]$ is the cumulative logistic distribution function), the conditional mean of Y given X is $\pi \mid X$, while the conditional variance of Y given X is $\pi(1 - \pi) \mid X$. Equation 20.12 can be applied to this situation, resulting in a measure of explained variance (Δ) for a dichotomous variable. The formula for Δ is

$$\Delta = 1 - \frac{E_x[\pi(1 - \pi)|X]}{\pi(1 - \pi)}. \qquad (20.13)$$

Assuming a correctly specified model, consistent estimators of P^2 and Δ are as follows. The estimator of P^2 is the McKelvey-Zavoina (1975) pseudo-R^2, or R^2_{MZ}, defined as

$$R^2_{MZ} = \frac{V\left(\sum b_k X_k\right)}{V\left(\sum b_k X_k\right) + \frac{\pi^2}{3}}, \qquad (20.14)$$

where the b_k are the logistic regression estimates, and $\pi^2/3$ is, by assumption, the underlying error variance for the logistic regression model. Because the logistic regression coefficients are estimates of the betas in $Y^* = \sum \beta_k X_k + \varepsilon$, the numerator is a consistent estimator of the variance of the conditional mean of the Y^* and the denominator is a consistent estimator of the marginal variance of Y^*. R^2_{MZ} is therefore a consistent estimator of P^2.

A consistent estimator of Δ is $\hat{\Delta}$, defined as

$$\hat{\Delta} = 1 - \frac{\frac{\sum \hat{\pi}(1 - \hat{\pi})|X}{N}}{p(1 - p)} \qquad (20.15)$$

where the estimated probabilities in the numerator of the second term on the right-hand side of Equation 20.15 are the estimated conditional probabilities of event occurrence, based on the model, and p is the sample marginal probability that Y equals 1.

Values for R^2_{MZ} and $\hat{\Delta}$ for the models in Table 20.2 are shown at the bottom of the table. Which measure to use depends, of course, on whether violence is to be regarded as a qualitative change in state or a proxy for a latent continuous variable. If the former, then $\hat{\Delta}$ suggests that the different models account for between 5% and 13% of variance in the occurrence of violence. If a latent scale underlies the binary indicator of violence, on the other hand, the range of variation explained in that latent scale is between 12% and 24%. (A SAS program that estimates one's model and prints out R^2_{MZ}, $\hat{\Delta}$, and six other R^2 analogues is available on request from the author.)

ADVANCED TOPICS IN BINARY LOGISTIC REGRESSION

Modeling Interaction Effects

Interaction effects occur when the impact of one variable depends on the values of another variable or variables. The other variables are said to interact with, moderate, or condition the impact of the first variable. In this section I discuss the modeling of first-order interaction effects—the case in which the focus variable interacts with only one other variable. These are the most commonly modeled types of interaction effects. I also discuss the case in which the model as a whole might differ depending on group membership—that is, the effects of possibly all model predictors depend on levels of a grouping variable.

Interaction effects in the log odds are modeled using cross-product terms just as in linear regression. The logistic regression model for two predictors, X and Z, with interaction between the predictors is therefore

$$\log\left(\frac{\pi}{1 - \pi}\right) = \beta_0 + \beta_1 X + \beta_2 Z + \beta_3 XZ. \qquad (20.16)$$

To see that the impact of X (the focus variable) is dependent upon the level of Z (the moderator variable) we write equation 16 isolating the impact of X:

$$\log\left(\frac{\pi}{1 - \pi}\right) = \beta_0 + \beta_2 Z + (\beta_1 + \beta_3 Z)X. \qquad (20.17)$$

The partial slope for X is therefore $(\beta_1 + \beta_3 Z)$, which clearly depends on the value of Z. Recall that exponentiating the partial slope gives us the impact on the odds of a unit increase in the predictor. Similarly, $e^{\beta_1 + \beta_3 Z}$ is the impact on the odds for a unit increase in X in the interaction model. Here it is clear that the odds ratio for those who are a unit apart on X is a function of the value of Z. As an example, Model 3 in Table 20.2 contains the cross product of minority status with the income-to-needs ratio, a significant interaction effect. To interpret the effect, it is helpful to choose one of the two variables involved in the interaction as the focus variable. Say we pick the income-to-needs ratio. The impact of this predictor on the log odds is $.002 - .091 \times$ minority couple. For nonminorities, the impact is therefore .002—the impact on the odds is $\exp(.002) = 1.002$. For minorities, on the other hand, it is $.002 - .091 = -.089$—the impact on the odds is $\exp(-.089) = .915$. Thus, a unit increase in the income-to-needs ratio reduces the odds of violence by 8.5% for minorities but has virtually no effect for nonminorities. Because this interaction effect is significant, we know that the difference in the effect of income to needs for each group is significant.

However, is the impact of income to needs significant *within* either group? To answer this question, we need to test the significance of the partial slope for the focus variable at each level of the moderator. In the abstract, the estimated partial slope for the focus variable has the form $b + cZ$, where b is the sample coefficient of the focus variable, c is the sample coefficient of the cross product, and Z is the moderator variable. Under the assumption that values of Z are fixed over repeated sampling, the variance of the partial slope is $V(b + cZ) = V(b) + 2Z\text{Cov}(b, c) + Z^2 V(c)$ (Aiken & West, 1991). The square root of this quantity is the standard error of the partial slope at a particular value of Z. Asymptotically, the partial slope divided by its standard error is a z test for the null hypothesis that the partial slope is zero, as noted previously.

The test for the effect of income to needs for nonminorities is just the test for the main effect of income to needs (because $Z = 0$ for nonminorities), which is nonsignificant in the table. For minorities, we need to use the sample estimates of variances and covariances among parameter estimates found in the "variance-covariance matrix of parameter estimates" (optionally output in SAS using the model option COVB). The variances of the parameter estimates for the income-to-needs ratio and the interaction term are, respectively, .000106 and .0012883, while the covariance of these terms is $-.000083$. The variance of the effect for minorities (keeping in mind that Z is now 1), is therefore, $.000106 + 2(1)(-.000083) + 1^2(.0012883) = .0012283$. The standard error is therefore .035, and the test is $-.089/.035 = -2.54$, which is significant at $p < .02$.

On the other hand, letting minority status be the focus variable, its partial slope on the log odds is $.161 - .091 \times$ the income-to-needs ratio. Aside from rendering the intercept interpretable, centering continuous predictors has the additional advantage of making the main effects interpretable in interaction models. Hence, .161 is the impact of minority status on the log odds of violence at the average income-to-needs ratio (because the mean of the centered income-to-needs ratio is zero), a nonsignificant effect. At this level of the moderator, minority couples are no different from nonminorities in the odds of violence. But at one standard deviation below average income to needs the impact of minority status is $.161 - .091(-4.759) = .594$, implying an increase of 81% in the odds of violence. At this setting of the moderator, the variance of the partial slope is $.0119173 + 2(-4.759)(.0010906) + (-4.759)^2(.0012883) = .0307145$. The standard error is therefore .175, and the test of this effect is $z = .594/.175 = 3.39$, which is significant at $p < .001$. A more complete discussion of first-order interaction in logit models, in general, can be found in DeMaris (1991).

Two other points should be mentioned about interaction effects in logistic regression. First, as in linear regression, cross-product terms typically induce multicollinearity among the regressors involved because the cross product tends to be highly correlated with its component parts. One final advantage of centering continuous predictors, as outlined by Aiken and West (1991), is that it tends to reduce this collinearity substantially. Second, in that the model is inherently interactive in the probabilities, what changes with a cross-product term in the model? The principal difference is that using a cross-product term allows interaction effects in the probabilities to be disordinal, whereas without it the interaction is constrained to be ordinal. The descriptors "ordinal" and "disordinal" (Kerlinger, 1986) refer to degrees of interaction. When the impact of the focus variable differs only in magnitude across levels of the moderator, the interaction is ordinal. If the nature (or direction) of the impact changes over levels of the moderator, the interaction is disordinal. Without a cross-product term, the partial slope of X_k on the probability is, as noted earlier, $\beta_k[\pi(\mathbf{x})(1 - \pi(\mathbf{x}))]$. Because $[\pi(\mathbf{x})(1 - \pi(\mathbf{x}))] > 0$, the impact of X_k on the probability always has the same sign, regardless of the settings of the Xs in the model; that is, $\beta_k[\pi(\mathbf{x})(1 - \pi(\mathbf{x}))]$ takes on whatever sign β_k takes. Hence, the effect of X_k can only differ in magnitude, but not direction, with different values of the Xs. With a cross product in the model of the form $\gamma X_k X_j$, however, the partial slope for X_k on the probability becomes $(\beta_k + \gamma X_j)[\pi(\mathbf{x})(1 - \pi(\mathbf{x}))]$. In this case, because β_k and γ could be of opposite signs, the impact of X_k on the probability could change direction at different levels of X_j, producing a disordinal interaction.

Comparing Models Across Groups

A variation on the interaction theme involves asking whether a given model applies equally in different groups. For example, my sample consists of minority and nonminority couples. We have seen that the impact of income to needs is different in each group. Suppose that we wish to test the hypothesis that the impacts of all predictors are different in each group. There are two equivalent ways to proceed. Both strategies assume that the underlying error variance is the same in each group (Allison, 1999). That is, in the latent variable formulation of the model, $Y^* = \sum \beta_k X_k + \varepsilon$ (outlined earlier), it is assumed that the variance of ε is the same for minority as for nonminority couples. (See Allison, 1999, for procedures to be used when this assumption may not be tenable.) One strategy is to form cross products of all predictors with minority status and to test whether this block of interaction terms is significant when added to Model 2 in Table 20.2.

The model chi-squared for this complete-interaction model (results not shown) is 500.177, with 25 degrees of freedom. The test for the interaction block is therefore $(500.177 - 472.915) = 27.262$. With $25 - 13 = 12$ degrees of freedom, this is significant at $p < .01$. Individual cross-product terms that are significant in the interaction model are the cross products of minority status with income to needs (as already discovered), communication style, and male nonassertiveness.

An equivalent way to proceed for those who want to know only whether the model is different across groups is to test for group differences using an equivalent of the Chow test (Chow, 1960) in linear regression. As outlined by Allison (1999), the procedure is as follows. First, we estimate the model for the combined sample with minority status as one of the predictors (this allows the intercept to differ across groups, as is the case in the first procedure). This is Model 2 in Table 20.2. Then we estimate the same model, minus the dummy for minority status, in each separate sample— minority couples versus nonminority couples. The results are shown in Table 20.4, with Model 2 in Table 20.2 repeated as the first column of the table (under the heading "Combined Sample") for comparison. The test for group differences is then $-2 \log L_c - [-2 \log L_m + (-2 \log L_{nm})]$, where L_c is the likelihood for the combined sample, L_m is the likelihood for the minority sample, and L_{nm} is the likelihood for the nonminority sample, all evaluated at the MLEs. Under the null hypothesis that model coefficients (excluding the intercept) are the same across groups, this statistic is distributed as

chi-squared with degrees of freedom equal to the difference in the number of parameters (including the intercept) estimated in the combined model versus the two separate models. From Table 20.4, the test is $2980.409 - (971.412 + 1981.735) = 27.262$, with $(13 + 13) - 14 = 12$ degrees of freedom, which agrees with the first result. In the table I have noted which effects are significantly different in each group. Apparently, income to needs reduces the odds of violence only among minority couples (as noted previously). Communication style appears to be more effective in reducing the odds of violence among nonminority couples. And male nonassertiveness has opposite effects in each group, enhancing the odds of violence for minority couples but reducing the odds of violence for nonminority couples. The advantage of using the first approach, of course, is that it allows examination of which particular effects differ across groups, whereas the second approach provides only an omnibus test of group difference.

Comparing Coefficients Across Models

It is often the case in regression models that interest centers on changes in coefficients when other variables are added to a model. Theoretically, the analyst may expect the additional variables to confound, mediate, or suppress the effects of variables already in the model. He or she therefore wishes to know whether the effects of existing variables undergo significant changes when additional variables are added. In particular, several of the focus variables in Model 1 in Table 20.2

TABLE 20.4 Logistic Regression Results for Model 2 in Table 20.2, Estimated for the Combined Sample As Well As for Minorities and Nonminorities, Separately

Explanatory Variable	Combined Sample	Minority Couples	Nonminority Couples
Intercept	−2.222***	−1.990***	−2.259***
Female's age at union[c]	−.006	−.009	−.004
Cohabiting couple	.982***	.993**	.938**
Relationship duration[c]	−.034***	−.035***	−.035***
Substance abuse	.766***	.830**	.732***
Minority couple	.221*	—	—
Number of children	−.113**	−.119	−.135*
Male's education[c]	−.031	.013	−.052*
Female's education[c]	.014	−.030	.059*
Income-to-needs ratio[c]	−.007	−.085*	−.000[ab]
Open disagreement[c]	.080***	.071***	.083***
Communication style[c]	−.410***	−.312***	−.473[a]***
Male nonassertiveness[c]	−.041	.211*	−.115[a]*
Female nonassertiveness[c]	−.113*	−.014	−.156**
−2 Log L	2980.409	971.412	1981.735
Number of parameters	14	13	13
N	4,401	1300	3101

[a]Coefficient is significantly different for minority vs. nonminority couples.
[b]Coefficient is less than .0005 in absolute value.
[c]Centered predictor.
*$p < .05$. **$p < .01$. ***$p < .001$.

are seen to change when the conflict resolution variables are added in Model 2. Theoretically, I would expect the extent of relationship conflict and style of conflict resolution to mediate some of the effects of the focus variables. For example, those who marry at younger ages or have been together for a shorter period of time are more likely to fight physically because they are too inexperienced in relationships or have spent too little time together to have learned how to argue constructively. Similarly, those characterized by substance abuse problems are likely to argue more frequently and perhaps more heatedly over *those* difficulties. In other words, I expect that entering the union at a younger age, being together for less time, and having substance abuse problems elevates the probability of physical aggression *because* they increase the frequency of conflict and detract from good conflict resolution skills. Evidence for this hypothesis is that all three effects are reduced when the conflict resolution block is entered into the model. But, are these effects *significantly* lower in model 2? In general, what is needed is a test for significance of the changes in coefficients across models. The issue is complicated by the fact that coefficients in the initial model are not independent of the same coefficients after variables have been added (Clogg, Petkova, & Haritou, 1995). Fortunately, such a test has recently been developed by Clogg et al. (1995).

Formally, we consider two models. The reduced model (H_R) is

$$\log\left(\frac{\pi}{1 - \pi}\right) = \beta_0^* + \beta_1^* X_1 + \cdots + \beta_p^* X_p, \quad (20.18)$$

whereas the full model (H_F) is

$$\log\left(\frac{\pi}{1 - \pi}\right) = \beta_0 + \beta_1 X_1 + \cdots + \beta_p X_p$$
$$+ \gamma_1 Z_1 + \cdots + \gamma_q Z_q. \quad (20.19)$$

We are interested in whether the β_k^*, the coefficients of the focus variables in the reduced model, are significantly different

from the β_k—the coefficients of the same focus variables in the full model—after the other variables (the $Z_1, Z_2, \ldots, Z_q$) have been included. Therefore, we wish to test whether the coefficient differences, $\delta_k = \beta_k^* - \beta_k$, for $k = 1, 2, \ldots, p$, are different from zero. Under the assumption that the full model is the true model that generated the data, the statistic $\frac{d_k}{\hat{\sigma}_{dk}}$ (where $d_k = b_k^* - b_k$ is the sample difference in the kth coefficient and $\hat{\sigma}_{dk}$ is the estimated standard error of the difference) is distributed asymptotically as standard normal (i.e., it is a z test) under H_0: $\delta_k = 0$ (Clogg et al., 1995).

Unfortunately, the standard errors of the d_k are not a standard feature of logistic regression software. However, they can be recovered via a relatively straightforward matrix expression. If we let $V(\hat{\delta})$ represent the estimated variance-covariance matrix of the coefficient differences, then the formula for this matrix is

$$V(\hat{\delta}) = V(\hat{\beta}) + V(\hat{\beta}^*)(V(\hat{\beta}))^{-1} V(\hat{\beta}^*) - 2V(\hat{\beta}^*), \quad (20.20)$$

where $V(\hat{\beta})$ is the sample variance-covariance matrix for the b_ks in the full model, $V(\hat{\beta}^*)$ is the sample variance-covariance matrix for the b_k^*s in the reduced model, and $(V(\hat{\beta}))^{-1}$ is the inverse of the variance-covariance matrix for the b_ks in the full model (Clogg et al., 1995). (A copy of a SAS program that estimates the reduced and full models, computes $V(\hat{\delta})$, and produces z tests for coefficient changes across models is available on request from the author.)

For the focus variables of Model 1 in Table 20.2, Table 20.5 shows the coefficients in the reduced and full models, their differences, the standard errors of the differences, and z tests for the significance of the differences. Due to the large sample size for the current problem, all but two of the coefficient changes (for minority status and male's education) are significant. As expected, the effects of age at union, relationship duration, and substance abuse are significantly reduced when conflict factors are added to the model.

TABLE 20.5 **Comparison of Logistic Regression Coefficients for Focus Variables of Model 1 in Table 20.2 Before and After Adding Conflict Resolution Factors in Model 2**

Focus Variable	(Before) Model 1	(After) Model 2	$\hat{\delta}$	SE($\hat{\delta}$)	z
Female's age at union[a]	−.021**	−.006	−.015	.001	−15.000
Cohabiting couple	.877***	.982***	−.105	.028	−3.750
Relationship duration[a]	−.045***	−.034***	−.011	.001	−11.000
Substance abuse	1.095***	.766***	.329	.020	16.450
Minority couple	.234*	.221*	.013	.009	1.444
Number of children	−.038	−.113**	.074	.007	10.570
Male's education[a]	−.033	−.031	−.002	.002	−1.000
Female's education[a]	.005	.014	−.009	.002	−4.500
Income-to-needs ratio[a]	−.005	−.007	.002	.001	2.000

Note. $N = 4,401$.
[a]Centered predictor.
*$p < .05$. **$p < .01$. ***$p < .001$.

Unexpectedly, the effects of unmarried cohabitation and number of children are significantly enhanced with controls for conflict resolution. Apparently, conflict resolution factors acted as suppressors for these latter variables.

MULTINOMIAL MODELS

Response variables may consist of more than two values but still not be appropriate for linear regression. Unordered categorical, or nominal, variables are those in which the different values cannot be rank ordered. Ordered categorical variables have values that represent rank order on some dimension, but there are not enough values to treat the variable as continuous (e.g., there are fewer than, say, five levels of the variable). Logistic regression models, addressed in the following section, are easily adapted to these situations.

Unordered Categorical Variables

To this point I have been treating intimate violence as a unitary phenomenon. However, in that violence by males typically has graver consequences than violence by females (Johnson, 1995; Morse, 1995), it may be important to make finer distinctions. For this reason, I distinguish between two types of violence in couples. The first is "intense male violence," which refers to any one of the following scenarios: The male is the only violent partner; both are violent but he is violent more often; both are violent but only the female is injured. All other manifestations of violence are referred to as "common couple violence," after the terminology introduced by Johnson (1995). My interest in this section is in examining how characteristics of couples in the initial survey might discriminate intense male from common couple violence, and both from nonviolence. I begin by treating the trichotomous categorization—no violence, common couple violence, intense male violence—as unordered categorical. That is, these three levels are treated as qualitatively different types of physical aggression (or the lack of it). However, it can be argued that they represent increasing degrees of violence severity, with intense male violence being more severe than common couple violence. In a later section, these categories are therefore treated as ordered.

Of the 4,401 couples in the current example, 3,815 (86.7%) are nonviolent, 366 (8.3%) have experienced common couple violence, and 220 (5%) are characterized by intense male violence. There are three possible nonredundant odds that can be formed to contrast these three categories. Each of these is conditional on being in one of two categories (Theil, 1970). For example, there are 4,181 couples who experienced no violence or common couple violence. Given

location in one of these two categories, the odds of common couple violence is $366/3815 = .096$. This odds is also the ratio of the probability of common couple violence to the probability of nonviolence, or $.083/.867 = .096$. Similarly, given that a couple is characterized by either nonviolence or intense male violence, the odds of intense male violence is $220/3815 (= .05/.867) = .058$. Only two of the odds are independent: Once they are recovered, the third is just the ratio of the first two. Thus, given some type of violence, the odds that it is intense male violence are $.058/.096 = .604$. In general, for an M-category variable, there are $M(M-1)/2$ nonredundant odds that can be contrasted, but only $M-1$ independent odds.

Modeling $M - 1$ Log Odds

As before, we typically wish to model the log odds as functions of one or more explanatory variables. However, this time we require $M - 1$ equations, one for each independent log odds. Each equation is equivalent to a binary logistic regression model in which the response is a conditional log odds—the log odds of being in one versus being in another category of the response variable, given location in one of these two categories. (Indeed, the multinomial logistic regression model can be estimated as a series of binary logistic regressions—see, e.g., Begg and Gray, 1984—but it is more efficient to estimate it by maximizing a single likelihood function.) Each odds is the ratio of the probabilities of being in the respective categories. Equations for all of the other $M(M-1)/2 - (M-1)$ dependent log odds are functions of the parameters for the independent log odds, and therefore do not need to be estimated from the data. Typically, we choose one category, say the Mth, of the response variable as the baseline and contrast all other categories with it (i.e., the probability of being in this category forms the denominator of each odds). With $\pi_1, \pi_2, \ldots, \pi_M$ representing the probabilities of being in category 1, category 2, ..., category M, of the response variable, respectively, the multinomial logistic regression model with K predictors is

$$\log\left(\frac{\pi_1}{\pi_M}\right) = \beta_0^1 + \beta_1^1 X_1 + \cdots + \beta_K^1 X_K$$

$$\log\left(\frac{\pi_2}{\pi_M}\right) = \beta_0^2 + \beta_1^2 X_1 + \cdots + \beta_K^2 X_K$$

$$\vdots$$

$$\log\left(\frac{\pi_{M-1}}{\pi_M}\right) = \beta_0^{M-1} + \beta_1^{M-1} X_1 + \cdots + \beta_K^{M-1} X_K,$$

$$(20.21)$$

where the superscripts on the betas indicate that effects of the regressors can change, depending on which log odds is being modeled.

Estimation

As before, parameters are estimated via maximum likelihood. In this case, however, the likelihood being maximized is the joint likelihood function for *all* of the parameters (across the $M - 1$ equations), given the data (see Hosmer & Lemeshow, 1989, for details). In SAS, one uses the procedure CATMOD for estimating this model. As SAS automatically chooses the highest value of the response variable as the baseline, one controls the choice of baseline by coding the variable accordingly. In the current example, I wanted nonviolence to be the baseline category, so the variable *violence type* was coded 0 for intense male violence, 1 for common couple violence, and 2 for nonviolence. Results are shown in Table 20.6. Coefficients in the first two columns are for the two independent log odds contrasting each type of violence with the baseline category of nonviolence. The last equation contrasts intense male with common couple violence. The coefficients in this column are just the differences (within rounding error) between coefficients in the first two columns.

Interpretation

Model coefficients are interpreted just as they are in the binary case, except that now more than two outcome categories are being compared. For example, cohabitants are significantly different in the odds of both intense male and common couple violence, compared to marrieds. In particular, cohabitants' odds of intense male violence (vs. nonviolence) is $\exp(1.104) = 3.016$ times higher than for marrieds, while their odds of common couple violence (vs. nonviolence) is $\exp(.885) = 2.423$ times higher. The odds of occurrence of intense male violence versus common couple violence, however, is not significantly different for cohabitants, compared to marrieds. Each additional child significantly reduces the odds of common couple violence (vs. nonviolence) by a factor of $\exp(-.248) = .780$, or effects a 22% reduction in the odds of this type of violence. On the other hand, the odds of intense male violence (vs. nonviolence) is not significantly affected by the number of children. Relative to common couple violence, however, the odds of intense male violence is enhanced by a factor of $\exp(.301) = 1.351$ for each additional child. This seemingly anomalous effect is due to the fact that the number of children only slightly increases the odds of intense male violence but markedly reduces the odds of common couple violence. Hence, the odds of intense male

TABLE 20.6   Multinomial Logistic Regression Results for the Prediction of Intense Male Violence, Common Couple Violence, and Nonviolence

Explanatory Variable	Intense Male Violence vs. Nonviolence	Common Couple Violence vs. Nonviolence	Intense Male Violence vs. Common Couple Violence
Intercept[a]	−3.723***	−2.444***	−1.278***
Female's age at union[b]	−.010	−.004	−.006
Cohabiting couple[a]	1.104***	.885**	.218
Relationship duration[ab]	−.058***	−.027***	−.031**
Substance abuse[a]	.940***	.661***	.279
Minority couple	.274	.097	.176
Number of children[a]	.053	−.248***	.301***
Male's education[b]	−.064*	−.008	−.057
Female's education[b]	.063	−.003	.066
Income-to-needs ratio[b]	.007	−.003	.009
Open disagreement[ab]	.070***	.086***	−.017
Communication style[ab]	−.476***	−.377***	−.099
Male nonassertiveness[b]	−.159*	.036	−.195*
Female nonassertiveness[ab]	−.012	−.176**	.164
Minority couple × income-to-needs ratio[a]	−.105	−.078	−.027
Model Chi-Squared	527.999***		
Model df	28		

Note. $N = 4{,}401$.

[a]Predictor has a significant global effect on the response variable.

[b]Centered predictor.

*$p < .05$. **$p < .01$. ***$p < .001$.

versus common couple violence grows correspondingly larger with each additional child. Other variables that enhance either type of violence (vs. nonviolence) are substance abuse and open disagreement. Factors that reduce the odds of either type of violence are a longer relationship duration and a positive communication style. Only a couple of factors appear to discriminate intense male violence from common couple violence. The longer couples have been together, and the more that the male partner keeps his opinions to himself, the lower the odds that their violence (if it occurs) will be of the intense male type. The more children they have, on the other hand, the greater the odds that their violence will be of the intense male kind. Whether these two types of violence are really discriminated by model predictors will be examined in more detail later.

Inferences

There are several statistical tests of interest in multinomial logistic regression. First, as in binary logistic regression, there is a test for whether the model as a whole exhibits any predictive efficacy. The null hypothesis is that all $K(M-1)$ of the regression coefficients (i.e., the betas) in Equation 20.21 equal zero. Once again, the test statistic is the model chi-squared, equal to $-2\log(L_0/L_1)$, where L_0 is the likelihood function evaluated for a model with only the MLEs for the intercepts and L_1 is the likelihood function evaluated at the MLEs for the hypothesized model. This test is not automatically output in CATMOD. However, as the program always prints out $-2\log L$ for the current model, it can be readily computed by first estimating a model with no predictors, and then recovering $-2\log L_0$ from the printout (it is the value of "$-2\,$Log Likelihood" for the last iteration on the printout). This test can then be computed as $-2\log L_0 - (-2\log L_1)$. For the model in Table 20.6, $-2\log L_0$ was 4228.9316, while $-2\log L_1$ was 3700.9325. The test was therefore $4228.932 - 3700.933 = 527.999$, with $14(2) = 28$ degrees of freedom, a highly significant result.

Second, the test for the global effect on the response variable of a given predictor, say X_k, is not a single degree of freedom test, as in the binary case. For multinomial models, there are $(M-1)\beta_k$s representing the global effect of X_k, one for each of the log odds in Equation 20.21. Therefore the test is for the null hypothesis that all $M-1$ of these β_ks equal zero. There are two ways to construct the test. One is to run the model with and without X_k and note the value of $-2\log L$ in each case. Then, if the null hypothesis is true, the difference in $-2\log L$ for the models with, and without, X_k is asymptotically distributed as chi-squared with $M-1$ degrees of freedom. This test requires running several

different models, however, and excluding one of the predictors on each run. Instead, most software packages—including SAS—provide an asymptotically equivalent Wald chi-squared test (see Long, 1997, for its formula) that performs the same function. Predictors having significant global effects on violence types, according to this test, are flagged with a superscript a in Table 20.6.

A third test is the test of the effect of a predictor on a particular log odds. This is simply the ratio of a given coefficient to its asymptotic standard error, which—as in the binary case—is a z test. Fourth, it may be desirable to test effects of predictors on the nonindependent log odds—the odds of intense male violence versus common couple violence in the current example. As SAS prints only coefficients and associated tests for the independent log odds in a given run (the first two columns of Table 20.6), these are not automatically output. However, it is a simple matter to obtain these tests, simply by rerunning the program and changing the coding of the response variable. Fifth, tests of nested models are accomplished the same as in the binary case. That is, if model B is nested inside model A (because, e.g., the predictors in B are a subset of those in A), then $-2\log(L_B/L_A) = -2\log L_B - (-2\log L_A)$ is a chi-squared test for the significance of the difference in fit of the two models.

Last, there is a test of collapsibility of outcome categories. Two categories of the outcome variable are *collapsible* with respect to the predictors if the predictor set is unable to discriminate between them. In the current example, it was seen that very few of the predictors discriminate between intense male and common couple violence. A chi-squared test for the collapsibility of these two categories of violence can be conducted as follows. First, I select only the couples experiencing one or the other of these types of violence, a total of 586 couples. Then I estimate a binary logistic regression model for the odds of intense male versus common couple violence. The test of collapsibility is the usual likelihood-ratio chi-squared test that all of the betas in this binary model are zero. Under the null hypothesis that the predictors do not discriminate between these types of violence, this statistic is asymptotically distributed as chi-squared (Long, 1997). The test turns out to have the value 44.835, which, with 14 degrees of freedom, is significant at $p < .001$. Apparently, the model covariates do discriminate between intense male and common couple violence. Previously, I commented on which predictors seem to be important in this regard.

Estimating Probabilities

The probabilities of being in each category of the response are readily estimated based on the sample log odds. That is, if

U is the estimated log odds of intense male violence for a given couple and V is the estimated log odds of common couple violence for that couple, then the estimated probabilities of each response for that couple are

$$P \text{ (intense male violence)} = \frac{e^U}{1 + e^U + e^V},$$

$$P \text{ (common couple violence)} = \frac{e^V}{1 + e^U + e^V},$$

$$P \text{ (nonviolence)} = \frac{1}{1 + e^U + e^V}.$$

$$(20.22)$$

Table 20.7 presents the probabilities of each response category based on selected profiles of the predictors, using the coefficient estimates in Table 20.6 and Equation 20.22. One purpose in examining the probabilities is to compare the conclusions reached with probabilities rather than odds ratios. In the table I show the probabilities associated with having 0, 1, 2, and 3 children for nonminority married couples without substance abuse problems, while setting all continuous predictors to either their mean values, 1 standard deviation below the means, or 1 standard deviation above the means. I also show the probabilities associated with being a minority couple versus being a nonminority couple, for marrieds without substance abuse problems, at the three settings

of the continuous predictors. The exception in the latter case is that 0 children is used in place of 1 standard deviation below the mean number of children.

Odds ratios convey a different impression than probabilities. It is therefore important to exercise care in interpreting odds ratios because it is easy to be misled unless one understands their conditional nature. For example, each additional child raises the odds of intense male versus common couple violence by $\exp(.301)$, or 35%, even though the probability of intense male violence is almost always lower than the probability of common couple violence. *Given* violence, however, the odds that it is of the intense male kind are comparatively higher with an additional child. As another example, compared to nonminority couples, minority couples generally have higher odds of intense male violence versus common couple violence. At the mean level of income to needs, the odds is $\exp(.176) = 1.192$ times higher. At 1 standard deviation below mean income to needs it is $\exp[.176 - .027(-4.759)] = 1.356$ higher. And at 1 standard deviation above mean income to needs it is $\exp[.176 - .027(4.759)] = 1.049$ higher. One might be led to conclude that minorities have higher probabilities of intense male violence compared to nonminorities. However, this is not true at 1 standard deviation above the mean of other covariates (including income to needs). At that setting, in fact, the probability of either type of violence is actually

TABLE 20.7   Predicted Probabilities of Intense Male Violence, Common Couple Violence, and Nonviolence for Unit Changes in the Number of Children and for Minority vs. Nonminority Couples, Based on Multinomial Logit Model Estimates in Table 20.5

Number of Children	Minority Status of Couple	Values of Other Predictors[a]	Probability of Intense Male Violence	Probability of Common Couple Violence	Probability of Nonviolence
1	nonminority	mean	.023	.062	.915
0	nonminority	mean	.022	.078	.900
1	nonminority	mean − 1 SD	.080	.115	.805
0	nonminority	mean − 1 SD	.074	.143	.783
1	nonminority	mean + 1 SD	.006	.031	.963
0	nonminority	mean + 1 SD	.006	.039	.955
3	nonminority	mean	.026	.039	.935
2	nonminority	mean	.025	.049	.926
3	nonminority	mean − 1 SD	.092	.073	.835
2	nonminority	mean − 1 SD	.086	.092	.822
3	nonminority	mean + 1 SD	.007	.019	.974
2	nonminority	mean + 1 SD	.007	.024	.969
1.178	minority	mean	.031	.065	.904
1.178	nonminority	mean	.024	.059	.917
0	minority	mean − 1 SD	.136	.196	.668
0	nonminority	mean − 1 SD	.074	.143	.783
2.456	minority	mean + 1 SD	.006	.017	.977
2.456	nonminority	mean + 1 SD	.007	.022	.971

Note. $N = 4{,}401$.

[a]Substance abuse and cohabiting couple are each set to 0 (for "no substance abuse," and "married," respectively).

slightly lower for minorities (.006 vs. .007 for intense male violence; .017 vs. .022 for common couple violence). But the odds of intense male violence is nevertheless higher for minorities because given any type of violence, the probability of intense male violence is higher in comparison to the probability of common couple violence than it is for nonminorities. As long as one understands that higher odds do not always mean higher probabilities, no confusion is likely to result. (Note that odds ratios computed using the probabilities in Table 20.7 may seem at variance with those based on coefficients in Table 20.6, but this is due only to rounding error. For example, the impact on the odds of intense male violence versus nonviolence for each additional child is, according to Table 20.6, $\exp(.053) = 1.054$. Yet using rows 5 and 6 of Table 20.7, one gets $(.006/.963)/(.006/.955) = .992$. However, if the probabilities in Table 20.7 are carried out to five significant digits, we actually get $(.0063/.96282)/(.00593/.95483) = 1.054$.)

Ordered Categorical Variables

When the values of a categorical variable are ordered, it is usually wise to take advantage of that information in model specification. For example, the trichotomous categorization of violence used for the analyses in Tables 20.6 and 20.7 represents different degrees of violence severity, as mentioned previously. In this section I treat it as an ordinal variable. The ordered logit model is a variant of logistic regression specifically designed for ordinal-level dependent variables. Although there is more than one way to form logits for ordinal variables (see, e.g., Agresti, 1984, 1989, for other formulations), I shall focus on cumulative logits. These are especially appropriate if the dimension represented by the ordinal measure could theoretically be regarded as continuous (Agresti, 1989). Cumulative logits are defined as follows. Suppose that the response variable consists of J ordered categories coded $1, 2, \ldots, J$. The jth cumulative odds is the ratio of the probability of being in category j or lower on Y to the probability of being in category $j + 1$ or higher. That is, if $O_{\leq j}$ represents the jth cumulative odds and π_j is the probability of being in category j on Y, then

$$O_{\leq j} = \frac{\pi_1 + \pi_2 + \cdots + \pi_j}{\pi_{j+1} + \pi_{j+2} + \cdots + \pi_J}.$$

Cumulative odds are therefore constructed by utilizing $J - 1$ bifurcations of Y. In each one, the probability of being lower on Y (the sum of probabilities that $Y \leq j$) is contrasted with the probability of being higher on Y (the sum of probabilities that $Y > j$). This strategy for forming odds makes sense only if the values of Y are ordered. With regard to violence, the first cumulative odds, $O_{\leq 0}$, is the ratio of the probability that *violence type* is 0 (intense male) to the probability that *violence type* is 1 (common couple) or 2 (none). Using the marginal probabilities of each type of violence from Table 20.1, the marginal sample value is $.05/(.083 + .867) = .053$. The second cumulative odds, $O_{\leq 1}$, is the ratio of the probability that *violence type* is 0 or 1 to the probability that it is 2, with marginal value $(.05 + .083)/.867 = .153$. In other words, each odds is the odds of more severe versus less severe violence, with "more severe" and "less severe" being defined using different values of j, the cut point (Agresti, 1989), in either case. The jth cumulative logit is just the log of this odds. For a J-category variable, there are a total of $J - 1$ such logits that can be constructed. These logits are ordered because the probabilities in the numerator of the odds keep accumulating as we go from the first through the $(J - 1)$th logit. That is, if U_j is the jth cumulative logit, then it is the case that $U_1 \leq U_2 \leq \cdots \leq U_{J-1}$.

One model for the cumulative logits, based on a set of K explanatory variables is

$$\log O_{\leq j} = \beta_0^j + \beta_1^j X_1 + \beta_2^j X_2 + \cdots + \beta_K^j X_K, \quad (20.23)$$

where the superscripts on the coefficients of the regressors indicate that the effects of the regressors can change, depending on the cut point. This model is easily estimated using binary logistic regression software, as Equation 20.23 is just a binary logistic regression based on bifurcating Y at the jth cut point. Table 20.8 presents the results of estimating this model for *violence type*. Estimates in the second column, for the log odds of violence versus nonviolence, are just the estimates from Model 3 in Table 20.2, repeated here for completeness. Estimates in the first column are for the log odds of intense male violence versus any other response.

Invariance to the Cut Point

For the most part, results suggest that predictors have the same effect on the log odds of more severe versus less severe violence, regardless of the cut point used to make this distinction. For example, substance abuse elevates the odds of intense male violence versus any other response by a factor of $\exp(.800) = 2.226$, whereas it raises the odds of any violence versus no violence by a factor of $\exp(.766) = 2.151$. If the effects of predictors are invariant to the cut point, then a more parsimonious specification of Equation 20.23 is possible. This is what we usually think of as the ordered logit model:

$$\log O_{\leq j} = \beta_0^j + \beta_1 X_1 + \beta_2 X_2 + \cdots + \beta_K X_K. \quad (20.24)$$

TABLE 20.8   Ordered Logit Model Results for the Prediction of Intense Male Violence, Common Couple Violence, and Nonviolence

Explanatory Variable	Intense male Violence vs. Other Response	Violence vs. Nonviolence	More vs. Less Violence
Intercept	−3.8144***	−2.210***	—
Intercept 1	—	—	−3.418***
Intercept 2	—	—	−2.224***
Female's age at union[a]	−.011	−.006	−.006
Cohabiting couple	.876**	1.000***	.946***
Relationship duration[a]	−.055***	−.035***	−.035***
Substance abuse	.800***	.766***	.767***
Minority couple	.246	.161	.150
Number of children	.094	−.128**	−.107**
Male's education[a]	−.062*	−.029	−.030
Female's education[a]	.065	.019	.022
Income-to-needs ratio[a]	.007	.002	.004
Open disagreement[a]	.052**	.079***	.077***
Communication style[a]	−.410***	−.412***	−.404***
Male nonassertiveness[a]	−.161*	−.035	−.058
Female nonassertiveness[a]	.020	−.115*	−.097*
Minority couple × income-to-needs ratio	−.093	−.091*	−.090*
Model Chi-Squared	245.643***	480.561***	484.895***
Model *df*	14	14	14
Score test	—	—	44.866***
Score *df*	—	—	14

Note. $N = 4,401$.

[a]Centered predictor.

$*p < .05. **p < .01. ***p < .001.$

In this model, the effects of predictors are the same regardless of the cut point for the odds. The results of estimating this model (using procedure LOGISTIC in SAS) are shown in the last column of Table 20.8. Notice that the intercept is allowed to depend on the cut point, so there are two intercepts in the equation. (In fact, there are two different equations, but the coefficients are being constrained to be the same in each.) In that predictors are assumed to be invariant to the cutpoint, there is only one set of regression coefficients. Effects are interpreted just as in binary logistic regression, except that the response is the log odds of more versus less severe violence, rather than, as in Table 20.2, violence per se. Thus, substance abuse is seen to raise the odds of more severe violence by $\exp(.767) = 2.153$, or about 115%, whereas each additional child lowers the odds of more severe violence by about 10%.

Test of Invariance

In the first two columns of Table 20.8, where effects are allowed to depend on the cut point, some predictors appear to have different effects on the odds of intense male violence, compared to violence per se. Particularly noticeable are the effects of number of children, which are opposite in sign and only significant for violence per se, and nonassertiveness,

which has a differential impact on each odds, depending on gender. Are these effects significantly different, or just the result of sampling error? This can be tested using the score test for the proportional odds assumption (automatically provided in SAS). The test is for the null hypothesis that regressor effects are the same across all $J − 1$ possible cut points (i.e., H_0 is that, for each of the K regressors in the model, $\beta_k^j = \beta_k$, for $j = 1, 2, \ldots, J − 1$). Under the null hypothesis, this statistic is asymptotically distributed as chi-squared with degrees of freedom equal to $K(J − 2)$. This is the difference in the number of parameters required to estimate the model in Equation 20.23 versus Equation 20.24: $K(J − 1) − K = K(J − 1 − 1) = K(J − 2)$. As shown in Table 20.8 for the current example, its value is 44.866, which, with 14 degrees of freedom, is quite significant. Apparently, predictor effects in Table 20.8 are not invariant to the cut point.

In the event that the score test proves significant, the researcher has several options. First, he or she can use the ordered logit model anyway, especially if noninvariant effects are only peripheral to the study. As an example, if I am primarily interested in how cohabitation, substance abuse, or relationship duration affect violence net of conflict resolution factors, the invariance model in column 3 of Table 20.8 summarizes those effects in an elegant fashion. Particularly when there are several categories of the response variable, Equation 20.24 is a substantially more parsimonious description of the data than is any of the alternatives. Nevertheless, it is frequently desirable to use a different modeling strategy when invariance is rejected. One alternative is therefore to choose the most informative bifurcation of the response variable and proceed with binary logistic regression. For example, either column 1 or 2 in Table 20.8 could be a legitimate model to estimate. However, if it is especially important to preserve the distinctions among different response categories, the multinomial analysis (as presented in Tables 20.6 and 20.7) is a viable strategy. Of course, if the response variable has at least 5 levels, its sample distribution is not too skewed, and the sample is large, the researcher may just want to treat it as continuous and employ OLS.

SUGGESTIONS FOR FURTHER STUDY

This chapter has been intended as an introduction to a topic with many complex facets. To become more familiar with logistic regression, the reader may want to consult many of the sources that have been cited throughout the chapter. Two volumes that are especially informative are those by Hosmer and Lemeshow (1989) and Long (1997). One major use of logistic regression not covered in this chapter is in survival analysis. This technique is used whenever one is examining the unfolding of events in time. For example, one may be investigating the factors that predict the onset of sexual intercourse among at-risk youth or the timing of entrance into or egress from marital unions. In these analyses, the response variable can be cast in two equivalent forms. First, it can be the length of time people survive in a given state (celibacy, singlehood, marriage) until the occurrence of the event of interest (sexual intercourse, marriage, divorce). Or it can be the hazard of event occurrence. The latter is approximately the instantaneous probability of event occurrence at time t, given that no event has occurred prior to t, for a group of cases at risk for the event. Logistic regression is a convenient statistical tool for estimating survival or hazard models. For those wishing to learn about this use of the technique, Allison (1982, 1995) and Singer and Willett (1993) are especially good source materials.

REFERENCES

Agresti, A. (1984). *Analysis of ordinal categorical data.* New York: Wiley.

Agresti, A. (1989). Tutorial on modeling ordered categorical response data. *Psychological Bulletin, 105,* 290–301.

Aiken, L. S., & West, S. G. (1991). *Multiple regression: Testing and interpreting interactions.* Thousand Oaks, CA: Sage.

Aldrich, J. H., & Nelson, F. D. (1984). *Linear probability, logit, and probit models.* Beverly Hills, CA: Sage.

Allison, P. D. (1982). Discrete-time methods for the analysis of event histories. In S. Leinhardt (Ed.), *Sociological methodology 1982* (pp. 61–98). San Francisco, CA: Jossey-Bass.

Allison, P. D. (1995). *Survival analysis using the SAS system: A practical guide.* Cary, NC: SAS Institute.

Allison, P. D. (1999). Comparing logit and probit coefficients across groups. *Sociological Methods & Research, 28,* 186–208.

Begg, C. B., & Gray, R. (1984). Calculation of polychotomous logistic regression parameters using individualized regressions. *Biometrika, 71,* 11–18.

Bollen, K. A. (1989). *Structural equations with latent variables.* New York: Wiley.

Caudill, S. B. (1988). An advantage of the linear probability model over probit or logit. *Oxford Bulletin of Economics and Statistics, 50,* 425–427.

Chow, G. (1960). Tests of equality between sets of coefficients in two linear regressions. *Econometrica, 28,* 591–605.

Cleary, P. D., & Angel, R. (1984). The analysis of relationships involving dichotomous dependent variables. *Journal of Health and Social Behavior, 25,* 334–348.

Clogg, C. C., Petkova, E., & Haritou, A. (1995). Statistical methods for comparing regression coefficients between models. *American Journal of Sociology, 100,* 1261–1293.

DeMaris, A. (1991). A framework for the interpretation of first-order interaction in logit modeling. *Psychological Bulletin, 110,* 557–570.

DeMaris, A. (1993). Odds versus probabilities in logit equations: A reply to Roncek. *Social Forces, 71,* 1057–1065.

DeMaris, A. (1995). A tutorial in logistic regression. *Journal of Marriage and the Family, 57,* 956–968.

DeMaris, A. (2000a). 'Till discord do us part: The role of physical and verbal conflict in union disruption. *Journal of Marriage and the Family, 62,* 683–692.

DeMaris, A. (2000b). *Explained variance in logistic regression: A Monte Carlo study of proposed measures.* Manuscript submitted for publication.

DeMaris, A. (2001). The influence of intimate violence on transitions out of cohabitation. *Journal of Marriage and the Family, 63,* 235–246.

Dutton, D. G. (1988). *The domestic assault of women: Psychological and criminal justice perspectives.* Boston: Allyn & Bacon.

Gottman, J. M., Coan, J., Carrere, S., & Swanson, C. (1998). Predicting marital happiness and stability from newlywed interactions. *Journal of Marriage and the Family, 60,* 5–22.

Greene, W. H. (1997). *Econometric analysis* (3rd ed.). Upper Saddle River, NJ: Prentice-Hall.

Hauck, W. W., & Donner, A. (1977). Wald's test as applied to hypotheses in logit analysis. *Journal of the American Statistical Association, 72,* 851–853.

Heyman, R. E., O'Leary, K. D., & Jouriles, E. N. (1995). Alcohol and aggressive personality styles: Potentiators of serious physical aggression against wives? *Journal of Family Psychology, 9,* 44–57.

Hoel, P. G., Port, S. C., & Stone, C. J. (1971). *Introduction to probability theory.* Boston: Houghton Mifflin.

Hosmer, D. W., & Lemeshow, S. (1989). *Applied logistic regression.* New York: Wiley.

Johnson, M. P. (1995). Patriarchal terrorism and common couple violence: Two forms of violence against women. *Journal of Marriage and the Family, 57,* 283–294.

Kerlinger, F. N. (1986). *Foundations of behavioral research* (3rd ed.). New York: Holt, Rinehart, and Winston.

Kerlinger, F. N., & Pedhazur, E. J. (1973). *Multiple regression in behavioral research.* New York: Holt, Rinehart, and Winston.

Leonard, K. E., & Senchak, M. (1996). Prospective prediction of husband marital aggression within newlywed couples. *Journal of Abnormal Psychology, 105,* 369–380.

Long, J. S. (1997). *Regression models for categorical and limited dependent variables.* Thousand Oaks, CA: Sage.

MacMillan, R., & Gartner, R. (1999). When she brings home the bacon: Labor-force participation and the risk of spousal violence against women. *Journal of Marriage and the Family, 61,* 947–958.

Margolin, G., John, R. S., & Gleberman, L. (1988). Affective responses to conflictual discussions in violent and nonviolent couples. *Journal of Consulting and Clinical Psychology, 56,* 24–33.

McKelvey, R. D., & Zavoina, W. (1975). A statistical model for the analysis of ordinal dependent variables. *Journal of Mathematical Sociology, 4,* 103–120.

Morse, B. J. (1995). Beyond the conflict tactics scale: Assessing gender differences in partner violence. *Violence and Victims, 10,* 251–272.

Myers, R. H. (1986). *Classical and modern regression with applications.* Boston: Duxbury.

Rusbult, C. E., & Buunk, B. P. (1993). Commitment processes in close relationships: An interdependence analysis. *Journal of Social and Personal Relationships, 10,* 175–204.

Schaefer, R. L. (1986). Alternative estimators in logistic regression when the data are collinear. *Journal of Statistical Computing and Simulation, 25,* 75–91.

Singer, J. D., & Willett, J. B. (1993). It's about time: Using discrete-time survival analysis to study duration and the timing of events. *Journal of Educational Statistics, 18,* 155–195.

Stets, J. E. (1991). Cohabiting and marital aggression: The role of social isolation. *Journal of Marriage and the Family, 53,* 669–680.

Stevens, J. (1986). *Applied multivariate statistics for the social sciences.* Hillsdale, NJ: Erlbaum.

Sweet, J. A., Bumpass, L. L., & Call, V. (1988). *The design and content of the National Survey of Families and Households.* Madison, WI: University of Wisconsin, Center for Demography and Ecology.

Theil, H. (1970). On the estimation of relationships involving qualitative variables. *American Journal of Sociology, 76,* 103–154.

CHAPTER 21

Meta-Analysis

FRANK L. SCHMIDT AND JOHN E. HUNTER

The small-sample studies typical of psychological research produce seemingly contradictory results, and reliance on statistical significance tests causes study results to appear even more conflicting. Meta-analysis integrates the findings across such studies to reveal the simpler patterns of relations that underlie research literatures, thus providing a basis for theory development. Meta-analysis can correct for the distorting effects of sampling error, measurement error, and other artifacts that produce the illusion of conflicting findings. This chapter discusses these artifacts and the procedures used to correct for them. Different approaches to meta-analysis are discussed. Applications of meta-analysis in industrial-organizational (IO) psychology and other areas are discussed and evidence is presented that meta-analysis is transforming research in psychology.

WHY WE NEED META-ANALYSIS

The goal in any science is the production of cumulative knowledge. Ultimately this means the development of theories that explain the phenomena that are the focus of the scientific area. One example would be theories that explain how personality traits develop in children and adults over

time and how these traits affect their lives. Another would be theories of what factors cause job and career satisfaction and what effects job satisfaction in turn has on other aspects of one's life. But before theories can be developed, we need to be able to pin down the relations between variables. For example, what is the relation between peer socialization and level of extroversion? Or the relation between job satisfaction and job performance?

Unless we can precisely calibrate such relations among variables, we do not have the raw materials out of which to construct theories. There is nothing for a theory to explain. For example, if the relationship between extroversion and popularity of children varies capriciously across different studies from a strong positive to strong negative correlation and everything in between, we cannot begin to construct a theory of how extroversion might affect popularity. The same applies to the relation between job satisfaction and job performance.

The unfortunate fact is that most research literatures do show conflicting findings of this sort. Some research studies in psychology find statistically significant relationships and some do not. In many research literatures, this split is approximately 50–50 (Cohen, 1962, 1988; Schmidt, Hunter, & Urry, 1976; Sedlmeier & Gigerenzer, 1989). This has been the traditional situation in most areas of the behavioral and social sciences. Hence it has been very difficult to develop understanding, theories, and cumulative knowledge.

The Myth of the Perfect Study

Before meta-analysis, the usual way in which scientists attempted to make sense of research literatures was by use of the narrative subjective review. In many research literatures, however, there were not only conflicting findings, there were also large numbers of studies. This combination made the standard narrative-subjective review a nearly impossible task—one far beyond human information-processing capabilities (Hunter & Schmidt, 1990b, pp. 468–469). How does one sit down and make sense of (for example) 210 conflicting studies?

The answer as developed in many narrative reviews was what came to be called the myth of the perfect study. Reviewers convinced themselves that most—usually the vast majority—of the studies available were methodologically deficient and should not even be considered in the review. These judgments of methodological deficiency were often based on idiosyncratic ideas: One reviewer might regard the Peabody Personality Inventory as lacking in construct validity and throw out all studies that used that instrument. Another might regard use of that same inventory as a prerequisite for methodological soundness and eliminate all studies *not* using this inventory. Thus any given reviewer could eliminate from consideration all but a few studies and perhaps narrow the number of studies from 210 to seven, for example. Conclusions would then be based on these seven studies.

It has long been the case that the most widely read literature reviews are those appearing in textbooks. The function of textbooks, especially advanced-level textbooks, is to summarize what is known in a given field. But no textbook can cite and discuss 210 studies on a single relationship. Often textbook authors would pick out what they considered to be the one or two best studies and then base textbook conclusions on just those studies, discarding the vast bulk of the information in the research literature—hence the myth of the perfect study.

But in fact there are no perfect studies. All studies contain measurement error in all measures used, as discussed later. Independent of measurement error, no study's measures have perfect construct validity. And there are typically other artifacts that distort study findings. Even if a hypothetical (and it would have to be hypothetical) study suffered from none of these distortions, it would still contain sampling error—typically a substantial amount of sampling error, because sample sizes are rarely very large. Hence no single study or small selected sub-

group of studies can provide an optimal basis for scientific conclusions about cumulative knowledge. As a result, reliance on so-called best studies did not provide a solution to the problem of conflicting research findings. This procedure did not even successfully deceive researchers into believing it was a solution—because different narrative reviewers arrived at different conclusions because they selected a different subset of "best" studies. Hence the so-called conflicts in the literature became conflicts in the reviews.

Some Relevant History

By the middle 1970s the behavioral and social sciences were in serious trouble. Large numbers of studies had accumulated on many questions that were important to theory development, social policy decisions, or both. Results of different studies on the same question typically were conflicting. For example, are workers more productive when they are satisfied with their jobs? The studies did not agree. Do students learn more when class sizes are smaller? Research findings were conflicting. Does participative decision making in management increase productivity? Does job enlargement increase job satisfaction and output? Does psychotherapy really help people? The studies were in conflict. As a consequence, the public and government officials were becoming increasingly disillusioned with the behavioral and social sciences, and it was becoming more and more difficult to obtain funding for research. In an invited address to the American Psychological Association in 1970, then-Senator Walter Mondale expressed his frustration with this situation:

> What I have *not* learned is what we should do about these problems. I had hoped to find research to support or to conclusively oppose my belief that quality integrated education is the most promising approach. But I have found very little conclusive evidence. For every study, statistical or theoretical, that contains a proposed solution or recommendation, there is always another, equally well documented, challenging the assumptions or conclusions of the first. No one seems to agree with anyone else's approach. But more distressing I must confess, I stand with my colleagues confused and often disheartened.

Then in 1981, the Director of the Federal Office of Management and Budget, David Stockman, proposed an 80% reduction in federal funding for research in the behavioral and social sciences. (This proposal was politically motivated in part, but the failure of behavioral and social science research to be cumulative created the vulnerability to political attack.) This proposed cut was a trial balloon sent up to see how much political opposition it would arouse. Even when proposed cuts are much smaller than a draconian 80%, constituencies can usually be counted on to come forward and protest the proposed cuts. This usually happens, and many behavioral and social scientists expected it to happen. But it did not. The behavioral and social sciences, it turned out, had no constituency among the public; the public did not care (see "Cuts Raise New Social Science Query," 1981). Finally, out of desperation, the American Psychological Association took the lead in forming the Consortium of Social Science Associations to lobby against the proposed cuts. Although this superassociation had some success in getting these cuts reduced (and even, in some areas, getting increases in research funding in subsequent years), these developments should make us look carefully at how such a thing could happen.

The sequence of events that led to this state of affairs was much the same in one research area after another. First, there was initial optimism about using social science research to answer socially important questions. Do government-sponsored job training programs work? We will do studies to find out. Does Head Start really help disadvantaged kids? The studies will tell us. Does integration increase the school achievement of Black children? Research will provide the answer. Next, several studies on the question are conducted, but the results are conflicting. There is some disappointment that the question has not been answered, but policymakers—and people in general—are still optimistic. They, along with the researchers, conclude that more research is needed to identify the supposed interactions (moderators) that have caused the conflicting findings—for example, perhaps whether job training works depends on the age and education of the trainees. Maybe smaller classes in the schools are beneficial only for children with lower levels of academic aptitude. It is hypothesized that psychotherapy works for middle-class but not working-class patients. That is, the conclusion at this point is that a search for moderator variables in needed.

In the third phase, a large number of research studies are funded and conducted to test these moderator hypotheses. When they are completed, there is now a large body of studies, but instead of being resolved, the number of conflicts increases. The moderator hypotheses from the initial studies are not borne out, and no one can make sense out of the conflicting findings. Researchers conclude that the question that was selected for study in this particular case has turned out to be hopelessly complex. They then turn to the investigation of another question, hoping that this time the question will turn out to be more tractable. Research sponsors, government officials, and the public become disenchanted and cynical. Research funding agencies cut money for research in this

area and in related areas. After this cycle has been repeated enough times, social and behavioral scientists themselves become cynical about the value of their own work, and they publish articles expressing doubts about whether behavioral and social science research is capable *in principle* of developing cumulative knowledge and providing general answers to socially important questions (e.g., see Cronbach, 1975; Gergen, 1982; Meehl, 1978).

Clearly, at this point there is a critical need for some means of making sense of the vast number of accumulated study findings. Starting in the late 1970s, new methods of combining findings across studies on the same subject were developed. These methods were referred to collectively as *meta-analysis,* a term coined by Glass (1976). Applications of meta-analysis to accumulated research literatures showed that research findings are not nearly as conflicting as had been thought, and that useful and sound general conclusions can in fact be drawn from existing research. Cumulative theoretical knowledge is possible in the behavioral and social sciences, and socially important questions can be answered in reasonably definitive ways. As a result, the gloom and cynicism that had enveloped many in the behavioral and social sciences has been lifting.

META-ANALYSIS VERSUS SIGNIFICANCE TESTING

A key point in understanding the effect that meta-analysis has had is that the illusion of conflicting findings in research literatures resulted mostly from the traditional reliance of researchers on statistical significance testing in analyzing and interpreting data in their individual studies (Cohen, 1994). These statistical significance tests typically had low power to detect existing relationships. Yet the prevailing decision rule has been that if the finding was statistically significant, then a relationship existed; and if it was not statistically significant, then there was no relationship (Oakes, 1986; Schmidt, 1996). For example, suppose that the population correlation between a certain familial condition and juvenile delinquency is .30. That is, the relationship in the population of interest is $\rho = .30$. Now suppose 50 studies are conducted to look for this relationship, and each has statistical power of .50 to detect this relationship if it exists. (This level of statistical power is typical of many research literatures.) Then approximately 50% of the studies (25 studies) would find a statistically significant relationship; the other 25 studies would report no significant relationship, and this would be interpreted as indicating that no relationship existed. That is, the researchers in these 25 studies would most likely incorrectly state that because the observed relationship did not reach statistical significance, it probably occurred merely by chance. Thus half the studies report that the familial factor was related to delinquency and half report that it had no relationship to delinquency—a condition of maximal apparent conflicting results in the literature. Of course, the 25 studies that report that there is no relationship are all incorrect. The relationship exists and is always $\rho = .30$. Traditionally, however, researchers did not understand that a statistical power problem such as this was even a possibility, because they did not understand the concept of statistical power (Oakes, 1986; Schmidt, 1996). In fact, they believed that their error rate was no more than 5% because they used an alpha level (significance level) of .05. But the 5% is just the Type I error rate (the alpha error rate)—the error rate that would exist if the null hypothesis were true and in fact there was no relationship. They overlooked the fact that if a relationship did exist, then the error rate would be 1.00 minus the statistical power (which here is $1.00 - .50 = .50$). This is the Type II error rate: the probability of failing to detect the relationship that exists. If the relationship does exist, then it is impossible to make a Type I error; that is, when there is a relationship, it is impossible to falsely conclude that there is a relationship. Only Type II errors can occur—and the significance test does not control Type II errors.

Now suppose these 50 studies were analyzed using meta-analysis. Meta-analysis would first compute the average r across the 50 studies; all rs would be used in computing this average regardless of whether they were statistically significant. This average should be very close to the correct value of .30, because sampling errors on either side of .30 would average out. So meta-analysis would lead to the correct conclusion that the relationship is on the average $\rho = .30$.

Meta-analysis can also estimate the real variability of the relationship across studies. To do this, one first computes the variance of the 50 observed rs, using the ordinary formula for the variance of a set of scores. One next computes the amount of variance expected solely from sampling error variance, using the formula for sampling error variance of the correlation coefficient. This sampling variance is then subtracted from the observed variance of the rs; after this subtraction, the remaining variance in our example should be approximately zero if the population correlations are all .30. Thus the conclusion would be that all of the observed variability of the rs across the 50 studies is due merely to sampling error and does not reflect any real variability in the true relationship. Thus one would conclude correctly that the real relationship is always .30—and not merely .30 on the average.

This simple example illustrates two critical points. First, the traditional reliance on statistical significance tests in interpreting studies leads to false conclusions about what the study results mean; in fact, the traditional approach to data analysis makes it virtually impossible to reach correct conclusions in most research areas (Hunter, 1997; Hunter & Schmidt, 1990a; Schmidt, 1996). Second, meta-analysis leads, by contrast, to the correct conclusions about the real meaning of research literatures. These principles are illustrated and explained in more detail in Hunter and Schmidt (1990a); for a shorter treatment, see Schmidt (1996).

The reader might reasonably ask what statistical methods researchers should use in analyzing and interpreting the data in their individual studies. If reliance on statistical significance testing leads to false conclusions, what methods should researchers use? The answer is point estimates of effect sizes (correlations and d values) and confidence intervals. The many advantages of point estimates and confidence intervals are discussed in Hunter and Schmidt (1990b), Hunter (1997), and Schmidt (1996). A recent APA Task Force report on statistical methods in research also discusses the advantages of confidence intervals over significance tests (Wilkinson & the Task Force on Statistical Inference, 1999).

Our example here has examined only the effects of sampling error variance and low statistical power. There are other statistical and measurement artifacts that cause artifactual variation in effect sizes and correlations across studies—for example, differences between studies in amount of measurement error, range restriction, and dichotomization of measures. Also, in meta-analysis, mean correlations (and effect sizes) must be corrected for *downward bias* due to such artifacts as measurement error and dichotomization of measures. There are also artifacts such as coding or transcriptional errors in the original data that are difficult or impossible to correct for. These artifacts and the complexities involved in correcting for them are discussed later in this chapter and are covered in more detail in Hunter and Schmidt (1990a, 1990b) and Schmidt and Hunter (1996). This section is an overview of why traditional data analysis and interpretation methods logically lead to erroneous conclusions and why meta-analysis can solve this problem and provide correct conclusions.

A common reaction to the preceding critique of traditional reliance on significance testing goes something like this: *Your explanation is clear but I don't understand how so many researchers (and even some methodologists) could have been so wrong so long on a matter as important as the correct way to analyze data? How could psychologists and others have failed to see the pitfalls of significance testing?* Over the years, a number of methodologists have addressed this question (Carver, 1978; Cohen, 1994; Guttman, 1985; Meehl, 1978; Oakes, 1986; Rozeboom, 1960). For one thing, in their statistics classes young researchers have typically been taught a lot about Type I error and very little about Type II error and statistical power. Thus they are unaware that the error rate is very large in the typical study; they tend to believe the error rate is the alpha level used (typically .05 or .01). In addition, empirical research suggests that most researchers believe that the use of significance tests provides them with many nonexistent benefits in understanding their data. For example, most researchers believe that a statistically significant finding is a reliable finding in the sense that it will replicate if a new study is conducted (Carver, 1978; Oakes, 1986; Schmidt, 1996). For example, they believe that if a result is significant at the .05 level, then the probability of replication in subsequent studies (if conducted) is $1.00 - .05 = .95$. This belief is completely false. The probability of replication is the statistical power of the study and is almost invariably much lower than .95 (e.g., typically .50 or less). Most researchers also falsely believe that if a result is nonsignificant, one can conclude that it is probably just due to chance—another false belief, as illustrated in our delinquency research example. There are other widespread but false beliefs about the usefulness of information provided by significance tests (Carver, 1978; Oakes, 1986). A recent discussion of these beliefs can be found in Schmidt (1996).

During the 1980s and accelerating up to the present, the use of meta-analysis to make sense of research literatures has increased dramatically, as is apparent from reading research journals. Lipsey and Wilson (1993) found over 350 meta-analyses of experimental studies of treatment effects alone; the total number is many times larger, because most meta-analyses in psychology and the social sciences are conducted on correlational data (as was our hypothetical example above). The overarching metaconclusion from all these efforts is that cumulative, generalizable knowledge in the behavioral and social sciences not only is possible but also is increasingly a reality. In fact, meta-analysis has even produced evidence that cumulativeness of research findings in the behavioral sciences is probably as great as in the physical sciences. Psychologists have long assumed that their research studies are less replicable than those in the physical sciences. Hedges (1987) used meta-analysis methods to examine variability of findings across studies in 13 research areas in particle physics and 13 research areas in psychology. Contrary to common belief, his findings showed that there was as much variability across studies in physics as in psychology. Furthermore, he found that the physical sciences used methods to combine findings across studies that were essentially identical to meta-analysis. The research literature in both areas—psychology and physics—yielded cumulative knowledge

when meta-analysis was properly applied. Hedges's major finding is that the frequency of conflicting research findings is probably no greater in the behavioral and social sciences than in the physical sciences. The fact that this finding has been so surprising to many psychologists points to two conclusions. First, psychologists' reliance on significance tests has caused our research literatures to appear much more inconsistent than they are. Second, we have long overestimated the consistency of research findings in the physical sciences. In the physical sciences also, no research question can be answered by a single study, and physical scientists must use meta-analysis to make sense of their research literature, just as psychologists do.

Another fact is relevant at this point: The physical sciences, such as physics and chemistry, do not use statistical significance testing in interpreting their data (Cohen, 1990). It is no accident, then, that these sciences have not experienced the debilitating problems described earlier that are inevitable when researchers rely on significance tests. Given that the physical sciences regard reliance on significance testing as unscientific, it is ironic that so many psychologists defend the use of significance tests on grounds that such tests are the objective and scientifically correct approach to data analysis and interpretation. In fact, it has been our experience that psychologists and other behavioral scientists who attempt to defend significance testing usually equate null hypothesis statistical significance testing with scientific hypothesis testing in general. They argue that hypothesis testing is central to science and that the abandonment of significance testing would amount to an attempt to have a science without hypothesis testing. They falsely believe that null hypothesis significance testing and hypothesis testing in science in general are one and the same thing. This belief is tantamount to stating that physics, chemistry, and the other physical sciences are not legitimate sciences because they are not built on hypothesis testing. Another logical implication of this belief is that prior to the introduction of null hypothesis significance testing by R. A. Fisher (1932) in the 1930s, no legitimate scientific research was possible. The fact is, of course, that there are many ways to test scientific hypotheses—and that significance testing is one of the least effective methods of doing this (Schmidt & Hunter, 1997).

IS STATISTICAL POWER THE SOLUTION?

Some researchers believe that the only problem with significance testing is low power and that if this problem could be solved there would be no problems with reliance on significance testing. These individuals see the solution as larger sample sizes. They believe that the problem would be solved if every researcher before conducting each study would calculate the number of subjects needed for so-called adequate power (usually taken as power of .80) and then use that sample size. What this position overlooks is that this requirement would make it impossible for most studies ever to be conducted. At the start of research in a given area, the questions are often of this form: *Does Treatment A have an effect?* (e.g., *Does interpersonal skills training have an effect?* or *Does this predictor have any validity?*). If Treatment A indeed has a substantial effect, the sample size needed for adequate power may not be prohibitively large. But as research develops, subsequent questions tend to take this form: *Is the effect of Treatment A larger than the effect of Treatment B?* (e.g., *Is the effect of the new method of training larger than that of the old method?*, or *Is Predictor A more valid than Predictor B?*). The effect size then becomes the *difference* between the two effects. Such effect sizes will often be small, and the required sample sizes are therefore often quite large—often 1,000 or 2,000 or more (Schmidt & Hunter, 1978). And this is just to attain power of .80, which still allows a 20% Type II error rate when the null hypothesis is false—an error rate most would consider high. Many researchers cannot obtain that many subjects, no matter how hard they try; either it is beyond their resources or the subjects are just unavailable at any cost. Thus the upshot of this position would be that many—perhaps most—studies would not be conducted at all. (Something like this has apparently occurred in IO psychology in the area of validation studies of personnel selection methods. After the appearance of the Schmidt et al. (1976) article showing that statistical power in criterion related validity studies probably averaged less than .50, researchers began paying more attention to statistical power in designing studies. Average sample sizes increased from around 70 to more than 200, with corresponding increases in statistical power. However, the *number* of studies conducted declined dramatically, with the result the total amount of information created per year or per decade for entry into meta-analyses (validity generalization) studies probably decreased. That is, the total amount of information generated in the earlier period from large numbers of small sample studies may have been greater than that generated in the later period from a small number of larger sample studies.)

People advocating the power position say this would not be a loss. They argue that a study with inadequate power contributes nothing and therefore should not be conducted. But in fact such studies contain valuable information when combined with others like them in a meta-analysis. In fact, very precise meta-analysis results can be obtained based on studies that *all* have inadequate statistical power individually.

The information in these studies is lost if these studies are never conducted.

The belief that such studies are worthless is based on two false assumptions: (a) the assumption that every individual study must be able to justify a conclusion on its own, without reference to other studies, and (b) the assumption that every study should be analyzed using significance tests. One of the contributions of meta-analysis has been to show that no single study is adequate by itself to answer a scientific question. Therefore each study should be considered as a data point to be contributed to a later meta-analysis. And individual studies should be analyzed using not significance tests but point estimates of effect sizes and confidence intervals.

How, then, *can* we solve the problem of statistical power in individual studies? Actually, this problem is a pseudoproblem. It can be solved by discontinuing the significance test. As Oakes (1986, p. 68) notes, statistical power is a legitimate concept only within the context of statistical significance testing. If significance testing is not used, then the concept of statistical power has no place and is not meaningful. In particular, there need be no concern with statistical power when point estimates and confidence intervals are used to analyze data in studies and meta-analysis is used to integrate findings across studies.

Our critique of the traditional practice of reliance on significance testing in analyzing data in individual studies and in interpreting research literatures might suggest a false conclusion: the conclusion that if significance tests had never been used, the research findings would have been consistent across different studies examining a given relationship. Consider the correlation between job satisfaction and job performance. Would these studies have all had the same findings if researchers had not relied on significance tests? Absolutely not: The correlations would have varied widely (as indeed they did). The major reason for this variability in correlations is simple sampling error—caused by the fact that the small samples used in individual research studies are randomly unrepresentative of the populations from which they are drawn. Most researchers severely underestimate the amount of variability in findings that is caused by sampling error.

The law of large numbers correctly states that large random samples are representative of their populations and yield parameter estimates that are close to the real (population) values. Many researchers seem to believe that the same law applies to small samples. As a result they erroneously expect statistics computed on small samples (e.g., 50 to 300) to be close approximations to the real (population) values. In one study we conducted (Schmidt, Ocasio, Hillery, & Hunter, 1985), we drew random samples (small "studies") of $N = 30$ from a much larger data set and computed results on each

$N = 30$ sample. These results varied dramatically from study to study—and all this variability was due solely to sampling error (Schmidt et al., 1985). Yet when we showed these data to researchers they found it hard to believe that each study was a random draw from the larger study. They did not believe simple sampling error could produce that much variation. They were shocked because they did not realize how much variation simple sampling error produces in research studies.

A major advantage of meta-analysis is that it controls for sampling error. Sampling error is random and nonsystematic—over- and underestimation of population values are equally likely. Hence averaging correlations or d values (standardized mean differences) across studies causes sampling error to be averaged out, producing an accurate estimate of the underlying population correlation or mean population correlation. As noted earlier, we can also subtract sampling error variance from the between-study variance of the observed correlations (or d values) to get a more accurate estimate of real variability across studies. Taken together, these two procedures constitute what we call bare bones meta-analysis—the simplest form of meta-analysis. Bare bones meta-analysis is discussed in more detail in a later section.

Most other artifacts that distort study findings are systematic rather than random. They usually create a downward bias on the obtained study r or d value. For example, all variables in a study must be measured and all measures of variables contain measurement error. (There are no exceptions to this rule.) The effect of measurement error is to downwardly bias every correlation or d value. However, measurement error can also contribute to *differences* between studies: If the measures used in one study have more measurement error than those used in another study, the observed rs or ds will be smaller in the first study. Thus meta-analysis must correct for both the downward bias and the artifactually created differences between different studies. Corrections of this sort are discussed in this chapter under the heading "More Advanced Forms of Meta-Analysis."

ORGANIZATION OF REMAINDER OF THIS CHAPTER

Different methodologists have developed somewhat different approaches to meta-analysis (Glass, McGaw, & Smith, 1981; Hedges & Olkin, 1985; Hunter, Schmidt, & Jackson, 1982; Hunter & Schmidt, 1990b; Rosenthal, 1991). We first examine the Hunter-Schmidt methods, followed by an examination of the other approaches. Finally, we look at the impact of meta-analysis over the last 20 years on the research enterprise in psychology.

BARE BONES META-ANALYSIS

Bare bones meta-analysis corrects only for the distorting effects of sampling error. It ignores all other statistical and measurement artifacts that distort study findings. For this reason we do not recommend bare bones meta-analysis for use in final integration of research literatures. Its primary value is that it allows illustration of some of the key features of more complete methods of meta-analysis. We illustrate bare bones meta-analysis using the data shown in Table 21.1. Table 21.1 shows 21 observed correlations, each based on a sample of 68 U.S. Postal Service letter sorters. Each study presents the estimated correlation between the same aptitude test and the same measure of accuracy in sorting letters by zip code. Values range from .02 to .39 and only 8 of the 21 (38%) are statistically significant. Both of these facts suggest a great deal of disagreement among the studies.

We first compute the average correlation using the following formula:

$$\bar{r} = \frac{\sum [N_i r_i]}{\sum N_i} = \hat{\bar{\rho}}_{xy} = .22 \qquad (21.1)$$

where $\bar{r}$ (the average observed correlation) estimates $\bar{\rho}_{xy}$, the population mean correlation. Note that this formula weights each correlation by its sample size—because studies with larger Ns contain more information. (However, in this case all $N = 68$, so all studies are weighted equally.) The mean value of .22 is the meta-analysis estimate of the mean population correlation.

We next compute the variance of the observed correlations using the following formula:

$$S_r^2 = \frac{\sum \lfloor N_i (r_i - \bar{r})^2 \rfloor}{\sum N_i} = .0120 \qquad (21.2)$$

This formula also weights by sample size. The next step is to compute the amount of variance in the observed correlations

TABLE 21.1   Validity Studies ($N = 68$ Each)

Study	Observed Validity	Study	Observed Validity
1	.04	12	.11
2	.14	13	.21
3	.31*	14	.37*
4	.12	15	.14
5	.38*	16	.29*
6	.27*	17	.26*
7	.15	18	.17
8	.36*	19	.39*
9	.20	20	.22
10	.02	21	.21
11	.23		

*$p < .05$, two-tailed.

expected across these studies due solely to sampling error variance:

$$S_e^2 = \frac{\left(1 - \bar{r}^2\right)^2}{\bar{N} - 1} = .0135 \qquad (21.3)$$

where $\bar{N}$ is the average sample size across studies.

Finally, we estimate the amount of between-study variance that is left after we subtract out expected sampling error variance:

$$S_{\rho_{xy}}^2 = S_r^2 - S_e^2 \qquad (21.4)$$

where $S_{\rho_{xy}}^2$ estimates $\sigma_{\rho_{xy}}^2$, the population value.

$$S_{\rho_{xy}}^2 = .0120 - .0135 = -.0015$$

In this case there is slightly *less* variance in the observed r than is predicted from sampling error. (This deviation from zero is called second-order sampling error. Negative variance estimates also occur in ANOVA and other statistical models in which estimates are produced by subtraction; see Hunter & Schmidt, 1990b, chap. 9). Hence we conclude that $\bar{\rho}_{xy} = .22$ and $SD_{\rho_{xy}} = 0$. That is, we conclude that sampling error accounts for all the observed differences between the studies. We conclude that the population ρ_{xy} value underlying every one of the studies is .22.

This example illustrates how meta-analysis sometimes reveals that all of the apparent variability across studies is illusory. Frequently, however, there is considerable variability remaining after correcting for sampling error. Often this remaining variability will be due to other variance-producing artifacts that have not been corrected for. But sometimes some of it might be "real." Suppose the researcher hypothesizes (e.g., based on evolutionary psychology theory) that the results are different for males and females. He or she can then check this hypothesis by subgrouping the studies into those conducted on males and those conducted on females. If sex is indeed a real moderator, then the mean correlations will be different for males and females. The average within group $SD_{\rho_{xy}}$ will also be smaller than the overall $SD_{\rho_{xy}}$. Later in this chapter we discuss other methods of checking for moderator variables.

OTHER ARTIFACTS AND THEIR EFFECTS

Bare bones meta-analysis is deficient and should not be used without further refinement in integrating research literatures. It is deficient because there is no research literature in which the only source of distortion in study findings is sampling error. Because there are no scales that are free of measurement error, the findings of every study are distorted by measurement error—in both the independent variable measure and the dependent variable measure. In addition, independent of measurement error, no measure has perfect construct validity; all measures, even good ones, have at least some construct deficiency (something left out) and some construct contamination (something included that should not be). The findings of most studies are also distorted by other artifacts.

Table 21.2 lists 10 of these additional artifacts. (For notational simplicity, we consider each of these as population values.) Measurement error in the independent and dependent variable measures biases obtained correlations or d values downward, with the amount of downward bias depending on

TABLE 21.2 Study Artifacts Beyond Sampling Error That Alter the Value of Outcome Measures, With Examples From Personnel Selection Research

1. Error of measurement in the dependent variable. Example: Study validity will be systematically lower than true validity to the extent that job performance is measured with random error.

2. Error of measurement in the independent variable. Example: Study validity for a test will systematically understate the validity of the ability measured since the test is not perfectly reliable.

3. Dichotomization of a continuous dependent variable. Example: Turnover—the length of time that worker stays with the organization—is often dichotomized into *more than . . .* or *less than . . .* , whereby the cutoff point is some arbitrarily chosen interval such as 1 year or 6 months.

4. Dichotomization of a continuous independent variable. Example: Interviewers are often told to dichotomize their perceptions into *acceptable* versus *reject.*

5. Range variation in the independent variable. Example: Study validity will be systematically lower than true validity to the extent that hiring policy causes incumbents to have a lower variation on the predictor than is true of applicants.

6. Attrition artifacts: Range variation in the dependent variable. Example: Study validity will be systematically lower than true validity to the extent that there is systematic attrition in workers on performance, as when good workers are promoted out of the population or when poor workers are fired for poor performance, or both.

7. Deviation from perfect construct validity in the independent variable. Example: Study validity will vary if the factor structure of the test differs from the usual structure of tests for the same trait.

8. Deviation from perfect construct validity in the dependent variable. Example: Study validity will differ from true validity if the criterion is deficient or contaminated.

9. Reporting or transcriptional error. Example: Reported study validities may differ from actual study validities due to a variety of reporting problems: inaccuracy in coding data, computational errors, errors in reading computer output, typographical errors by secretaries or by printers. These errors can be very large in magnitude.

10. Variance due to extraneous factors. Example: Study validity will be systematically lower than true validity if incumbents differ in job experience at the time their performance is measured.

the size of the reliabilities of the measures. For example, if both measures have reliability of .70, the downward bias from this artifact alone will be 30%. In addition, *differences* in reliability between studies will cause differences in findings between studies.

Either or both of the continuous independent and dependent variable measures may be dichotomized (typically at the median). If both measures are dichotomized at the median or mean, the underlying correlation will be reduced by the factor .80 × .80 or .64 (Hunter & Schmidt, 1990a).

Either or both of the variables may be affected by range variation. For example, only the top 50% of test scorers might be hired, producing a downward bias of around 30% due to range restriction on the independent variable. In addition, those with poor job performance might be fired, producing range restriction on the dependent variable, resulting in a further downward bias.

Deviation from perfect construct validity in the two measures produces an additional independent downward bias. Construct validity is defined as the correlation between the actual construct one is attempting to measure and true scores on the scale one uses to measure that construct (Hunter & Schmidt, 1990b). Although this correlation cannot be directly observed, there is much empirical evidence to indicate it is rarely perfect.

Errors in the data are not systematic in their effect on the mean correlation or mean *d* value. The distortion produced in the correlation can be in either direction. Across studies such errors do have a systematic effect: They increase the amount of artifactual variation. Sometimes data errors can be detected and corrected, but usually this is not possible in meta-analysis.

An Example

Consider an example. Suppose the construct-level correlation between two personality traits A and B is .60. ($\rho_{AB} = .60$.) This is the correlation that we as researchers are interested in, the correlation between the two constructs themselves. Measure *x* is used to measure trait A and measure *y* is used to measure trait B. Now suppose we have the following situation:

$a_1 = .90 =$ the square root of the reliability of *x*; $r_{xx} = .81$;

$a_2 = .90 =$ the square root of the reliability of *y*; $r_{yy} = .81$;

$a_3 = .90 =$ the construct validity of *x*;

$a_4 = .90 =$ the construct validity of *y*;

$a_5 = .80 =$ the attenuation factor for splitting *x* at the median; and

$a_6 = .80 =$ the attenuation factor for splitting *y* at the median.

This is not an extreme example. Both measures have acceptable reliability (.81 in both cases). Both measures have

high construct validity; for each measure, its true scores correlate .90 with the actual construct. Both measures have been dichotomized into low and high groups, but the dichotomization is at the median, which produces less downward bias than any other split.

The total impact of the six study imperfections is the total attenuation factor *A*

$$A = (.90)(.90)(.90)(.90)(.80)(.80) = .42 \qquad (21.5)$$

Hence the attenuated study correlation—the expected observed study correlation—is

$$\rho_{xy} = .42\rho_{AB} = .42(.60) = .25 \qquad (21.6)$$

That is, the study correlation is reduced to less than half the value of the actual correlation between the two personality traits.

This realistic example illustrates the power of artifacts other than sampling error to severely distort study results. These artifacts produce serious distortions and must be taken seriously. This example contains six artifacts; the first four of these are *always* present in every study. Dichotomization does not occur in every study, but in many studies in which it does not, other artifacts such as range restriction do occur, and the overall attenuation factor, *A*, is often smaller than our .42 here.

This example illustrates a single study. The different studies in a research literature will have different levels of artifacts and hence different levels of downward bias. Hence these artifacts not only depress the overall mean observed correlation, they also create additional variability in correlations across studies beyond that created by sampling error.

MORE ADVANCED METHODS OF META-ANALYSIS

More advanced forms of meta-analysis correct for these artifacts. First, they correct for the overall downward bias produced by the artifacts. Second, they correct for the artifactual differences between studies that these artifacts create. These more advanced meta-analysis methods take two forms: methods in which each observed study correlation (or *d* value) is corrected individually, and methods in which distributions of artifact values are used to correct the entire distribution of observed correlations (or *d* values) at one time. As discussed later, both of these advanced meta-analysis methods are referred to as psychometric meta-analysis methods. These methods are discussed in the following two sections.

Methods That Correct Each *r* or *d* Value Independently

We will describe this form of meta-analysis for correlations but the same principles apply when the statistic being used is the *d* value. The method that corrects each statistic individually is the most direct form of the more complete methods of meta-analysis. In this method, each individual observed correlation is corrected for each of the artifacts that have biased it. This is most easily illustrated using our example from the last section. In that example, the underlying construct-level correlation is .60 ($\rho_{AB} = .60$). But the total downward bias created by the six artifacts operating on it reduced it to .25:

$$\rho_{xy} = .42\rho_{AB} = .42(.60) = .25 \qquad (21.7)$$

The total attenuating or biasing factor is .42. Now in a real study if we can compute this total biasing factor, we can correct our observed value of .25 by dividing it by this factor:

$$\rho_{AB} = .25/.42 = .60 \qquad (21.8)$$

A correction of this sort is applied to each of the observed correlations included in the meta-analysis. This correction reverses the downwardly biasing process and restores the correlation to its actual construct-level value. In the population (that is, when *N* is infinite), this correction is always accurate, because there is no sampling error. In real studies, however, sample sizes are not infinite, so there is sampling error. The effect of this sampling error is that corrections of this kind are accurate only *on the average*. Because of sampling error, any single corrected value may be randomly too large or too small, but the average of such corrected values is accurate. It is the average of these corrected values across all the studies in the meta-analysis that is the focus of the meta-analysis. So our estimate of $\overline{\rho}_{AB}$ is accurate in expectation. There will be no downward or upward bias in $\overline{\rho}_{AB}$.

Meta-analysis also has a second focus—on the variability of these corrected correlations. The variance of these corrected correlations is inflated by sampling error variance. In fact, the corrections actually *increase* the amount of sampling error variance. This sampling error variance is subtracted from the variance of the corrected *r*s to estimate the real variance of the construct-level correlations:

$$S^2_{\rho_{AB}} = S^2_{\hat{\rho}_{AB}} - S^2_{e_{\hat{\rho}_{AB}}} \qquad (21.9)$$

In this equation, $S^2_{\hat{\rho}_{AB}}$ is the variance of the corrected correlations. This variance contains sampling error, and the amount of that sampling error is $S^2_{e_{\hat{\rho}_{AB}}}$. Hence the difference between these two figures, $S^2_{\rho_{AB}}$, estimates the real (i.e., population) variance of ρ_{AB}. The square root of $S^2_{\rho_{AB}}$ is the estimate of

$SD_{\rho_{AB}}$. Hence we have $\overline{\rho}_{AB}$ and $SD_{\rho_{AB}}$ as the product of the meta-analysis. That is, we have estimated the mean and the *SD* of the underlying construct-level correlations. This is a major improvement over bare bones meta-analysis, which estimates the mean and *SD* of the downwardly biased correlations ($\overline{\rho}_{xy}$ and $SD_{\rho_{xy}}$) and hence does not tell us anything about the correlation between actual constructs or traits.

If $SD_{\rho_{AB}}$ is zero or very small, this indicates that there are no moderators (interactions) producing different values of ρ_{AB} in different studies. Hence there is no need to test moderator hypotheses. If $SD_{\rho_{AB}}$ is larger, this variation may be due to other artifacts—such as data errors—that you have not been able to correct for. However, some of the remaining variation may be due to one or more moderator variables. If there is theoretical evidence to suggest this, these hypotheses can be tested by subgrouping the studies and performing a separate meta-analysis on each subgroup. It may turn out that $\overline{\rho}_{AB}$ really is different for males and females, or for higher versus lower management levels. If so, the moderator hypothesis has been confirmed. Another approach to moderator analysis is correlational: The values of $\hat{\rho}_{AB}$ can be correlated with study characteristics (hypothesized moderators). Multiple regression can also be used. Values of $\hat{\rho}_{AB}$ can be regressed on multiple study characteristics. In all forms of moderator analysis, there are statistical problems in moderator analysis that the researcher should be aware of. We discuss these problems later in this chapter.

What we have presented here is merely an overview of the main ideas in this approach to meta-analysis. A detailed discussion can be found in Hunter and Schmidt (1990b). In that book, chapter 3 discusses application of this method to correlations and chapter 7 to *d* values. The actual formulas are considerably more complicated than in the case of bare bones meta-analysis and are beyond the scope and length limitations of this chapter. Several computer programs have been created for these methods. These programs are in the public domain and are available to anyone. They are presented in the appendix to Hunter and Schmidt (1990b) and are available on request from the authors.

Meta-Analysis Using Artifact Distributions

Most meta-analyses do not use the method described in the previous section. Most meta-analyses do not correct each *r* or *d* statistic individually for the artifactual biases that have affected it. Probably less than 10% of advanced-level meta-analyses correct each *r* or *d* value individually. The reason for this is that most studies do not present all of the information on artifacts that is necessary to make these corrections. For example, many studies do not present information on the reliability of the scales used. Many studies do not present information on the degree of range restriction present in the data. The same is true for the other artifacts.

However, artifact information is usually presented sporadically in the studies included in the meta-analysis. Some studies present reliability information on the independent variable measures and some on the dependent variable measures. Some present range restriction information but not reliability information. In addition, information on artifact levels typical of the research literature being analyzed is often available from other sources. For example, test or inventory manuals often present information on scale reliability. Information on typical levels of range restriction can be found in the personnel selection literature. Using all such sources of artifact information, it is often possible to compile a *distribution* of artifacts that is representative of that research literature; for example, a distribution of interrater reliabilities of supervisory ratings of job performance; a distribution of reliabilities typical of spatial ability tests; or a distribution of reliabilities of job satisfaction measures.

Artifact distribution meta-analysis is a set of quantitative methods for correcting artifact-produced biases using such distributions of artifacts. Correlations are not corrected individually. Instead, a bare bones meta-analysis is first performed and then the mean $(\bar{\rho}_{xy})$ and SD $(SD_{\rho_{xy}})$ produced by the bare bones analysis are corrected for artifacts other than sampling error. The formulas for this form of meta-analysis are even more complex than those used when each correlation is corrected individually. These methods are presented in detail in Hunter and Schmidt (1990b), in chapter 4 for correlations and in chapter 7 for the *d* value statistic. Approximately 90% of advanced-level meta-analyses use artifact distribution meta-analysis methods. Again, several public domain computer programs are available for implementing this method of meta-analysis.

In addition to methods developed by the present authors, meta-analysis methods based on artifact distribution have been developed by Callender and Osburn (1980) and Raju and Burke (1983). Computer simulation studies have shown that all of these methods are quite accurate. In data sets in which artifact information is available for each correlation, it is possible to apply both methods of advanced-level meta-analysis to the same set of studies. That is, each correlation can be corrected individually *and* artifact distribution based meta-analysis can also be applied in a separate analysis. In such cases, the meta-analysis results have been essentially identical, as would be expected.

Moderator hypotheses may also be examined when using artifact distribution meta-analysis. With this method of meta-analysis, subgrouping of studies is the preferred method of moderator analysis. Regression of study correlations onto study characteristics (potential moderators) works less well because the study correlations in this case have not been (and cannot be) individually corrected for artifacts and hence the correlations are (differentially) biased as indices of actual study findings. Hence they lack construct validity as measures of true study correlations or effect sizes.

CLASSIFICATION OF META-ANALYSIS METHODS

Meta-analysis methods can be divided into three categories: (a) methods that are purely descriptive (and do not address sampling error); (b) methods that address sampling error but not other artifacts; and (c) methods that address both sampling error and other artifacts that distort findings in individual studies. Figure 21.1 illustrates this classification system and references publications that explicate each type of method.

Descriptive Meta-Analysis Methods

Glass (1976) advanced the first meta-analysis procedures and coined the term meta-analysis to designate the analysis of analyses (studies). For Glass, the purpose of meta-analysis is descriptive; the goal is to paint a very general, broad, and inclusive picture of a particular research literature (Glass, 1977; Glass et al., 1981). The questions to be answered are very general; for example, does psychotherapy—regardless of type—have an impact on the kinds of outcomes that therapy researchers consider important enough to measure, regardless of the nature of these outcomes (e.g., self-reported anxiety, count of emotional outbursts, etc.)? Thus Glassian meta-analysis often combines studies with somewhat different independent variables (e.g., different kinds of therapy) and different dependent variables. As a result, some critics have criticized these methods as combining apples and oranges. However, Glassian meta-analysis does allow for separate meta-analyses for different independent variables (e.g., different types of psychotherapy). But this is rarely done for different dependent variables. Glassian meta-analysis has three primary properties:

1. *A strong emphasis on effect sizes rather than significance levels.* Glass believed the purpose of research integration is more descriptive than inferential, and he felt that the most important descriptive statistics are those that indicate most clearly the magnitude of effects. Glassian meta-analysis typically employs estimates of the Pearson *r* or

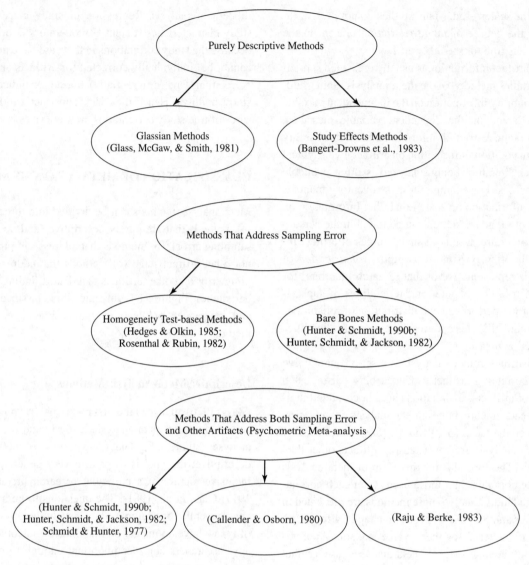

Figure 21.1   Schematic illustrating methods of meta-analysis.

estimates of *d*. The initial product of a Glassian meta-analysis is the mean and standard deviation of observed effect sizes or correlations across studies.

2. *Acceptance of the variance of effect sizes at face value.* Glassian meta-analysis implicitly assumes that the observed variability in effect sizes is real and should have some substantive explanation. There is no attention to sampling error variance in the effect sizes. The substantive explanations are sought in the varying characteristics of the studies (e.g., sex or mean age of subjects, length of treatment, and more). Study characteristics that correlate with study effect are examined for their explanatory power. The general finding in applications of Glassian meta-analysis has been that few study characteristics correlate significantly with study outcomes. Problems of capitalization on

chance and low statistical power associated with this step in meta-analysis are discussed in Hunter and Schmidt (1990b, chap. 2).

3. *A strongly empirical approach to determining which aspects of studies should be coded and tested for possible association with study outcomes.* Glass (1976, 1977) felt that all such questions are empirical questions, and he deemphasized the role of theory in determining which variables should be tested as potential moderators of study outcome (see also Glass, 1972).

One variation of Glass's methods has been labeled *study effects meta-analysis* by Bangert-Drowns (1986). It differs from Glass's procedures in several ways. First, only one effect size from each study is included in the meta-analysis, thus ensuring statistical independence within the meta-analysis. If a study has multiple dependent measures, those that assess the same construct are combined (usually averaged), and those that assess different constructs are assigned to different meta-analyses. Second, study effects meta-analysis calls for the meta-analyst to make some judgments about study methodological quality and to exclude studies with deficiencies judged serious enough to distort study outcomes. In reviewing experimental studies, for example, the experimental treatment must be at least similar to those judged by experts in the research area to be appropriate, or the study will be excluded. This procedure seeks to calibrate relationships between specific variables rather than to paint a broad Glassian picture of a research area. In this sense it is quite different from Glassian methods and is more focused on the kinds of questions that researchers desire answers to. However, this approach is like the Glass method in that it does not acknowledge that much of the variability in study findings is due to sampling error variance. That is, it takes observed correlations and d values at face value. Some of those instrumental in developing and using this procedure are Mansfield and Busse (1977), Kulik and his associates (Bangert-Drowns, Kulik, & Kulik, 1983; Kulik & Bangert-Drowns, 1983–1984), Landman and Dawes (1982), and Wortman and Bryant (1985). In recent years, fewer published meta-analyses have used Glassian methods or study effects meta-analyses.

Meta-Analysis Methods That Focus on Sampling Error

As noted earlier, numerous artifacts produce the deceptive appearance of variability in results across studies. The artifact that typically produces more false variability than any other is sampling error variance. Glassian meta-analysis and study effect meta-analysis implicitly accept variability produced by sampling error variance as real variability. There are two types of meta-analyses that move beyond Glassian methods in that they attempt to control for sampling error variance.

Homogeneity Test-Based Meta-Analysis

The first of these methods is *homogeneity test-based meta-analysis*. This approach has been advocated independently by Hedges (1982b; Hedges & Olkin, 1985) and by Rosenthal and Rubin (1982).

Hedges (1982a) and Rosenthal and Rubin (1982) proposed that chi-square statistical tests be used to decide whether study outcomes are more variable than would be expected from sampling error alone. If these chi-square tests of homogeneity are not statistically significant, then the

population correlation or effect size is accepted as constant across studies and there is no search for moderators. Use of chi-square tests of homogeneity to estimate whether findings in a set of studies differ more than would be expected from sampling error variance was originally proposed by Snedecor (1946).

The chi-square test of homogeneity typically has low power to detect variation beyond sampling error (National Research Council, 1992). (Hedges and Olkin (1985) recommend that if theory suggests the existence of moderators, a moderator analysis should be conducted even if the homogeneity test is not significant. However, those using their methods typically ignore this recommendation.) Hence the meta-analyst will often conclude that the studies being examined are homogenous when they are not; that is, the meta-analyst will conclude that the value of ρ_{xy} or δ_{xy} is the same in all the studies included in the meta-analysis when, in fact, these parameters actually vary across studies. A major problem here is that under these circumstances, the fixed effects model of meta-analysis is then used in almost all cases. Unlike random effects meta-analysis models, fixed effects models assume zero between-study variability in ρ_{xy} or δ_{xy} in computing the standard error of the $\bar{r}$ or $\bar{d}$, resulting in underestimates of the relevant standard errors of the mean. This in turn results in confidence intervals around the $\bar{r}$ or $\bar{d}$ that are erroneously narrow—sometimes by large amounts. This creates an erroneous impression that the meta-analysis findings are much more precise than in fact they really are. This problem also results in Type I biases in all significance tests conducted $\bar{r}$ or $\bar{d}$, and these biases are often quite large (Hunter & Schmidt, 2000). As a result of this problem, the National Research Council (1992) report on data integration recommended that fixed effects models be replaced by random effects models, which do not suffer from this problem. We have also made that recommendation (Hunter & Schmidt, 2000). However, the majority of published meta-analyses using the Rosenthal-Rubin methods and the Hedges-Olkin methods have used their fixed effects models. For example, most of the meta-analyses that have appeared in *Psychological Bulletin* are fixed effects meta-analysis. Most of these analyses employ the Hedges and Olkin (1985) fixed effect meta-analysis model.

Both Rosenthal and Rubin and Hedges and Olkin have presented random effects meta-analysis models as well as fixed effects methods, but meta-analysts have rarely employed their random effects methods. The Hunter-Schmidt methods, described earlier in this chapter, are all random effects methods.

Hedges (1982b) and Hedges and Olkin (1985) extended the concept of homogeneity tests to develop a more general procedure for moderator analysis based on significance testing. It calls for breaking the overall chi-square statistic down into the sum of within- and between-group chi-squares. The original set of effect sizes in the meta-analysis is divided into successively smaller subgroups until the chi-square statistics within the subgroups are nonsignificant, indicating that sampling error can explain all the variation within the last set of subgroups.

Homogeneity test-based meta-analysis represents an ironic return to the practice that originally led to the great difficulties in making sense out of research literatures: reliance on statistical significance tests. As noted previously, the chi-square test typically has low power. Another problem is that the chi-square test has a Type I bias. Under the null hypotheses, the chi-square test assumes that all between-study variance in study outcomes (e.g., rs or ds) is sampling error variance; but there are other purely artifactual sources of variance between studies in effect sizes. As discussed earlier, these include computational, transcriptional, and other data errors, as well as differences between studies in reliability of measurement and in levels of range restriction—and others, as discussed earlier. Thus, even when true study effect sizes are actually the same across studies, these sources of artifactual variance will create variance beyond sampling error, sometimes causing the chi-square test to be significant and hence to falsely indicate heterogeneity of effect sizes. This is especially likely when the number of studies is large, increasing statistical power to detect small amounts of such artifactual variance. Another problem is that even when the variance beyond sampling error is not artifactual, it often will be small in magnitude and of little or no theoretical or practical significance. Hedges and Olkin (1985) recognized this fact and cautioned that researchers should not merely look at significance levels but should evaluate the actual size of the variance; unfortunately, however, after researchers are caught up in significance tests, the usual practice is to assume that if it is statistically significant it is important (and if it is not, it is zero). When the major focus is on the results of significance tests, effect sizes are usually ignored.

Bare Bones Meta-Analysis

The second approach to meta-analysis that attempts to control only for the artifact of sampling error is what we referred to earlier as *bare bones meta-analysis* (Hunter & Schmidt, 1990a; Hunter et al., 1982; Pearlman, Schmidt, & Hunter, 1980). This approach can be applied to correlations, *d*-values, or any other effect size statistic for which the standard error is known. For example, if the statistic is correlations, $\bar{r}$ is first computed. Then the variance of the set of correlations is computed. Next the amount of sampling error variance is computed and subtracted from this observed variance. If the result is zero, then sampling error accounts for all the observed variance, and the r value accurately summarizes all the studies in the meta-analysis. If not, then the square root of the remaining variance is the index of variability remaining around the mean r after sampling error variance is removed. Earlier in this chapter we presented examples of bare bones meta-analysis.

Because there are always other artifacts (such as measurement error) that should be corrected for, we have consistently stated in our writings that the bare bones meta-analysis method is incomplete and unsatisfactory. It is useful primarily as the first step in *explaining* and *teaching* meta-analysis to novices. However, studies using bare bones methods have been published; the authors of these studies have invariably claimed that the information needed to correct for artifacts beyond sampling error was unavailable to them. In our experience, this is in fact rarely the case. Estimates of artifact values (e.g., reliabilities of scales) are usually available from the literature, from test manuals, or from other sources, as indicated earlier. These values can be used to create distributions of artifacts for use in artifact distribution-based meta-analysis (described earlier in this chapter).

Psychometric Meta-Analysis

The third type of meta-analysis is *psychometric meta-analysis*. These methods correct not only for sampling error (an unsystematic artifact) but for other, systematic artifacts, such as measurement error, range restriction or enhancement, dichotomization of measures, and so forth. These other artifacts are said to be systematic because, in addition to creating artifactual variation across studies, they also create systematic downward biases in the results of all studies. For example, measurement error systematically biases all correlations downward. Psychometric meta-analysis corrects not only for the artifactual variation across studies, but also for the downward biases. Psychometric meta-analysis is the only meta-analysis method that takes into account both statistical and measurement artifacts. Two variations of these procedures were described earlier in this chapter in the section titled "More Advanced Methods of Meta-Analysis." A detailed presentation of these procedures can be found in Hunter and Schmidt (1990b) or Hunter et al. (1982). Callender and Osborn (1980), and Raju and Burke (1983) also developed methods for psychometric meta-analysis. These methods differ slightly in computational details but have been shown to produce virtually identical results (Law, Schmidt, & Hunter, 1994a, 1994b).

UNRESOLVED PROBLEMS IN META-ANALYSIS

In all forms of meta-analysis, there are unresolvable problems in the search for moderators. First, when effect size estimates are regressed on multiple-study characteristics, capitalization on chance operates to increase the apparent number of significant associations for those study characteristics that have no actual associations with study outcomes. Because the sample size is the number of studies and many study properties may be coded, this problem is often severe (Hunter & Schmidt, 1990b, chap. 2). There is no purely statistical solution to this problem. The problem can be mitigated, however, by basing choice of study characteristics and final conclusions not only on the statistics at hand, but also on other theoretically relevant empirical findings (which may be the result of other meta-analyses) and on theoretical considerations. Results should be examined closely for substantive and theoretical meaning. Capitalization on chance is a threat whenever the (unknown) correlation or regression weight is actually zero or near zero. When there is in fact a relationship, there is another problem: Power to detect the relation is often low (Hunter & Schmidt, 1990b, chap. 2). Thus, true moderators of study outcomes (to the extent that such exist) may have only a low probability of showing up as statistically significant. In short, this step in meta-analysis is often plagued with all the problems of small-sample studies. Other things being equal, conducting separate meta-analyses on subsets of studies to identify a moderator does not avoid these problems and may lead to additional problems of confounding of moderator effects (Hunter & Schmidt, 1990b, chap. 13).

Although there are often serious problems in detecting moderator variables in meta-analysis, there is no approach to moderator detection that is superior to meta-analysis. In fact, alternative methods (e.g., quantitative analyses within individual studies, narrative reviews of literatures) have even more serious problems and hence are inferior to meta-analysis. Moderator detection is difficult because a large amount of information is required for clear identification of moderators. Even sets of 50–100 studies often do not contain the required amounts of information.

Another issue in meta-analysis that is widely regarded as unresolved is the issue of judgments about which studies to include in a meta-analysis. There is widespread agreement that studies should not be included if they do not measure the constructs that are the focus of the meta-analysis. For example, if the focus is on the correlation between job performance and the personality trait of conscientiousness, correlations based on other personality traits should be excluded from that meta-analysis. Correlations between conscientiousness and measures of other dependent variables—such as tenure—should also be excluded. In addition, it should be explicitly decided in advance exactly what kind of measures qualify as measures of job performance. For many purposes, only measures of *overall* job performance will qualify; partial measures, such as citizenship behaviors on the job, are deficient in construct validity as measures of overall job performance. Hence there is general agreement that meta-analysis requires careful attention to construct validity issues in determining which studies should be included.

Most meta-analysis studies published today contain multiple meta-analyses. To continue our example from the previous paragraph, the meta-analysis of the relation between conscientiousness and job performance would probably be only one of several reported in the article. Others would include the relationship with job performance for the other four of the Big Five personality traits. In addition, other meta-analyses would probably be reported separately for other dependent variables: citizenship behaviors, tenure, absenteeism, and so on. That is, one meta-analysis is devoted to each combination of constructs. Again, there appears to be little disagreement that this should be the case. Hence the total number of meta-analyses is much larger than the total number of meta-analysis publications.

The disagreement concerns whether studies that do meet construct validity requirements should be excluded on the basis of other alleged methodological defects. One position is that, in many literatures, most studies should be excluded a priori on such grounds and that the meta-analysis should be performed only the remaining, often small, set of studies. This position reflects the myth of the perfect study, discussed at the beginning of this chapter. The alternative that we advocate is to include all studies that meet basic construct validity requirements, and to treat the remaining judgments about methodological quality as hypotheses to be tested empirically. This is done by conducting separate meta-analyses on subgroups of studies that do and do not have the methodological feature in question and comparing the findings. If the results are essentially identical, then the hypothesis that that methodological feature affects study outcomes is disconfirmed and all conclusions should be based on combined meta-analysis. If the results are different, then the hypothesis that that methodological feature is important is confirmed. (This position takes it as axiomatic that any methodological feature that has no effect on study findings is not important and can be disregarded.) In our experience, most methodological hypotheses of this sort are disconfirmed. In any case, this empirical approach helps to settle disputes about what methodological features of studies are important. That is, this approach leads to advances in methodological knowledge.

THE ROLE OF META-ANALYSIS IN THEORY DEVELOPMENT

As noted at the beginning of this chapter, the major task in the behavioral and social sciences, as in other sciences, is the development of theory. A good theory is a good explanation of the processes that actually take place in a phenomenon. For example, what actually happens when employees develop a high level of organizational commitment? Does job satisfaction develop first and then cause the development of commitment? If so, what causes job satisfaction to develop and how does it have an effect on commitment? How do higher levels of mental ability cause higher levels of job performance? Only by increasing job knowledge? Or also by directly improving problem solving on the job? The researcher is essentially a detective; his or her job is to find out why and how things happen the way they do. To construct theories, however, researchers must first know some of the basic facts, such as the empirical relations among variables. These relations are the building blocks of theory. For example, if researchers know there is a high and consistent population correlation between job satisfaction and organization commitment, this will send them in particular directions in developing their theories. If the correlation between these variables is very low and consistent, theory development will branch in different directions. If the relation is highly variable across organizations and settings, researchers will be encouraged to advance interactive or moderator-based theories. Meta-analysis provides these empirical building blocks for theory. Meta-analytic findings tell us what it is that needs to be explained by the theory. Meta-analysis has been criticized because it does not directly generate or develop theory (Guzzo, Jackson, & Katzell, 1986). This is like criticizing typewriters or word processors because they do not generate novels on their own. The results of meta-analysis are indispensable for theory construction, but theory construction itself is a creative process distinct from meta-analysis.

As implied in the language used here, theories are causal explanations. The goal in every science is explanation, and explanation is always causal. In the behavioral and social sciences, the methods of path analysis (e.g., see Hunter & Gerbing, 1982) can be used to test causal theories when the data meet the assumptions of the method. The relationships revealed by meta-analysis—the empirical building blocks for theory—can be used in path analysis or structural equation modeling to test causal theories even when all the delineated relationships are observational rather than experimental. Experimentally determined relationships can also be entered into path analyses along with observationally based relations by transforming d values to correlations. Path analysis can be

a very powerful tool for reducing the number of theories that could possibly be consistent with the data, sometimes to a very small number, and sometimes to only one theory (Hunter, 1988). For examples, see Hunter (1983) and Schmidt (1992). Every such reduction in the number of possible theories is an advance in understanding.

META-ANALYSIS IN INDUSTRIAL-ORGANIZATIONAL PSYCHOLOGY AND OTHER APPLIED AREAS

There have been numerous applications of meta-analysis in industrial-organizational (IO) psychology. The most extensive and detailed application of meta-analysis in IO psychology has been the study of the generalizability of the validities of employment selection procedures (Schmidt, 1988; Schmidt & Hunter, 1981). The findings have resulted in major changes in the field of personnel selection. Validity generalization research is described in more detail in the following section.

The meta-analysis methods presented in this chapter have been applied in other areas of IO psychology and organizational behavior. Between 1978 and 1998, there have been approximately 80 published nonselection applications. The following are some examples: (a) correlates of role conflict and role ambiguity (C. D. Fisher & Gittelson, 1983; Jackson & Schuler, 1985); (b) relation of job satisfaction to absenteeism (Hackett & Guion, 1985; Terborg & Lee, 1982); (c) relation between job performance and turnover (McEvoy & Cascio, 1987); (d) relation between job satisfaction and job performance (Iaffaldono & Muchinsky, 1985; Petty, McGee, & Cavender, 1984); (e) effects of nonselection organizational interventions on employee output and productivity (Guzzo, Jette, & Katzell, 1985); (f) effects of realistic job previews on employee turnover, performance, and satisfaction (McEvoy & Cascio, 1985; Premack & Wanous, 1985); (g) evaluation of Fiedler's theory of leadership (Peters, Harthe, & Pohlman, 1985); and (h) accuracy of self-ratings of ability and skill (Mabe & West, 1982).

The applications have been to both correlational and experimental literatures. As of the mid-1980s, sufficient meta-analyses had been published in IO psychology that a review of meta-analytic studies in this area was published. This lengthy review (Hunter & Hirsh, 1987) reflected the fact that this literature had already become quite large. It is noteworthy that the review denoted considerable space to the development and presentation of theoretical propositions; this was possible because the clarification of research literatures produced by meta-analysis provides a foundation for theory development that previously did not exist. It is also noteworthy that the findings in one meta-analysis were often found to be theoretically relevant to the interpretation of the findings in other meta-analyses. A second review of meta-analytic studies in IO psychology has since been published (Tett, Meyer, & Roese, 1994).

The examples cited here applied meta-analysis to research programs. The results of such programs can sometimes be used as a foundation for policy recommendations. But meta-analysis can be applied more directly in the public policy arena. Consider one example. The Federation of Behavioral, Psychological, and Cognitive Sciences sponsors regular science and public policy seminars for members of Congress and their staffs. In one seminar, the speaker was Eleanor Chelimsky, for years the director of the General Accounting Office's (GAO) Division of Program Evaluation and Methodology. In that position she pioneered the use of meta-analysis as a tool for providing program evaluation and other legislatively significant advice to Congress. Chelimsky (1994) stated that meta-analysis has proven to be an excellent way to provide Congress with the widest variety of research results that can hold up under close scrutiny under the time pressures imposed by Congress. She stated that General Accounting Office has found that meta-analysis reveals both what is known and what is not known in a given topic area, and distinguishes between fact and opinion without being confrontational. One application she cited as an example was a meta-analysis of studies on the merits of producing binary chemical weapons (nerve gas in which the two key ingredients are kept separate for safety until the gas is to be used). The meta-analysis did not support the production of such weapons. This was not what officials in the Department of Defense wanted to hear, and the Department of Defense disputed the methodology and the results. But the methodology held up under close scrutiny, and in the end Congress eliminated funds for binary weapons. By law it is the responsibility of the General Accounting Office to provide policy-relevant research information to Congress. So the adoption of meta-analysis by the General Accounting Office provides a clear and even dramatic example of the impact that meta-analysis can have on public policy.

As noted above, one major application of meta-analysis to date has been the examination of the validity of tests and other methods used in personnel selection. Meta-analysis has been used to test the hypothesis of situation-specific validity. In personnel selection it had long been believed that validity was specific to situations—that is, it was believed that the validity of the same test for what appeared to be the same job varied from employer to employer, region to region, across time periods, and so forth. In fact, it was believed that the same test could have high validity (i.e., a high correlation with job performance) in one location or organization and be completely invalid (i.e., have zero validity) in another. This belief was based on the observation that observed validity coefficients for similar tests and jobs varied substantially across different studies. In some such studies there was a statistically significant relationship, and in others there was no significant relationship—which, as noted earlier, was falsely taken to indicate no relationship at all. This puzzling variability of findings was explained by postulating that jobs that appeared to be the same actually differed in important but subtle (and undetectable) ways in what was required to perform them. This belief led to a requirement for local or situational validity studies. It was held that validity had to be estimated separately for each situation by a study conducted in that setting; that is, validity findings could not be generalized across settings, situations, employers, and the like (Schmidt & Hunter, 1981). In the late 1970s, meta-analysis of validity coefficients began to be conducted to test whether validity might in fact be generalizable (Schmidt & Hunter, 1977; Schmidt, Hunter, Pearlman, & Shane, 1979); these meta-analyses were therefore called *validity generalization* studies. If all or most of the study-to-study variability in observed validities was due to sampling error and other artifacts, then the traditional belief in situational specificity of validity would be seen to be erroneous, and the conclusion would be that validity did generalize.

Meta-analysis has now been applied to over 500 research literatures in employment selection, each one representing a predictor–job performance combination. These predictors have included nontest procedures, such as evaluations of education and experience, employment interviews, and biographical data scales, as well as ability and aptitude tests. As an example, consider the relation between quantitative ability and overall job performance in clerical jobs (Hunter & Schmidt, 1996). This substudy was based on 223 correlations computed on a total of 18,919 people. All of the variance of the observed validities was traceable to artifacts. The mean validity was .50. Thus, integration of these of data leads to the general (and generalizable) principle that the correlation between quantitative ability and clerical performance is .50, with no true variation around this value. Like other similar findings, this finding shows that the old belief that validities are situationally specific is false.

Today many organizations use validity generalization findings as the basis of their selection-testing programs. Validity generalization has been included in standard texts (e.g., Anastasi, 1988) and in the *Standards for Educational and Psychological Tests* (1999). A report by the National Academy of Sciences (Hartigan & Wigdor, 1989) devoted a chapter (chapter 6) to validity generalization and endorsed its methods and assumptions.

WIDER IMPACT OF META-ANALYSIS ON PSYCHOLOGY

Some have viewed meta-analysis as merely a set of improved methods for doing literature reviews. Meta-analysis is actually more than that. By quantitatively comparing findings across diverse studies, meta-analysis can discover new knowledge not inferable from any individual study and can sometimes answer questions that were never addressed in any of the individual studies contained in the meta-analysis. For example, no individual study may have compared the effectiveness of a training program for people of higher and lower mental ability; but by comparing mean d value statistics across different groups of studies, meta-analysis can reveal this difference. That is, moderater variables (interactions) never studied in any individual study can be revealed by meta-analysis. But even though it is much more than that, meta-analysis is indeed an improved method for synthesizing or integrating research literatures. The premier review journal in psychology is *Psychological Bulletin*. In viewing that journal's volumes from 1980 to 2000, the impact of meta-analysis is apparent. Over this time period, a steadily increasing percentage of the reviews published in this journal are meta-analyses, and a steadily decreasing percentage are traditional narrative subjective reviews. Most of the remaining narrative reviews published today in *Psychological Bulletin* focus on research literatures that are not well enough developed to be amenable to quantitative treatment. Several editors have told us that it is not uncommon for narrative review manuscripts to be returned by editors to the authors with the request that meta-analysis be applied to the studies reviewed.

As noted above, most of the meta-analyses appearing in *Psychological Bulletin* have employed fixed-effects methods, resulting in many cases in overstatement of the precision of the meta-analysis findings (Hunter & Schmidt, 2000). Despite this fact, these meta-analyses produce findings and conclusions that are far superior to those produced by the traditional narrative subjective method. Many other journals have shown the same increase over time in the number of meta-analyses published. Many of these journals, such as *Journal of Applied Psychology,* had traditionally published only individual empirical studies and had rarely published reviews up until the advent of meta-analysis in the late 1970s. These journals began publishing meta-analyses because meta-analyses came to be viewed not as mere reviews, but as a form of empirical research in themselves. Between 1978 and 1997 *Journal of Applied Psychology* published 60 meta-analysis-based articles. These 60 articles contained a total of 1,647 separate meta-analyses. As a result of this change, the quality and accuracy of conclusions from research literatures improved in a wide variety of journals and in a corresponding variety of research areas in psychology. This improvement in the quality of conclusions from research literatures has expedited theory development in a wide variety of areas in psychology.

The impact of meta-analysis on psychology textbooks has been positive and dramatic. Textbooks are important because their function is to summarize the state of cumulative knowledge in a given field. Most people—students and others—acquire most of their knowledge about psychological theory and findings from their reading of textbooks. Prior to meta-analysis, textbook authors faced with hundreds of conflicting studies on a single question subjectively and arbitrarily selected a small number of their preferred studies from such a literature and based the textbook conclusions on only those few studies. Today most textbook authors base their conclusions on meta-analysis findings—making their conclusions and their textbooks much more accurate. It is hard to overemphasize the importance of this development in advancing cumulative knowledge in psychology.

The realities revealed about data and research findings by the principles of meta-analysis have produced changes in our views of the individual empirical study, the nature of cumulative research knowledge, and the reward structure in the research enterprise.

Meta-analysis has explicated the role of sampling error, measurement error, and other artifacts in determining the observed findings and statistical power of individual studies. In doing this, it has revealed how little information there is in any single study. It has shown that, contrary to previous belief, no single primary study can provide more than tentative evidence on any issue. Multiple studies are required to draw solid conclusions. The first study done in an area may be revered for its creativity, but sampling error and other artifacts in that study will often produce a fully or partially erroneous answer to the study question. The quantitative estimate of effect size will almost always be erroneous. The shift from tentative to solid conclusions requires the accumulation of studies and the application of meta-analysis to those study results.

Furthermore, adequate handling of other study imperfections such as measurement error—and especially imperfect construct validity—may also require separate studies and more advanced meta-analysis. Because of the effects of artifacts such as sampling error and measurement error, the data in studies come to us encrypted, and to understand their meaning we must first break the code. Doing this requires meta-analysis. Therefore any individual study must be considered only a single data point to be contributed to a future meta-analysis. Thus the scientific status and value of the individual study is necessarily reduced. Ironically, however, the value of individual studies in the aggregate is increased.

Because multiple studies are needed to solve the problem of sampling error, it is critical to ensure the availability of all studies on each topic. A major problem is that many good replication articles are rejected by our primary research journals. Journals currently put excessive weight on innovation and creativity in evaluating studies and often fail to consider either sampling error or other technical problems such as measurement error. Many journals will not even consider what they see as mere replication studies or mere measurement studies. Many persistent authors eventually publish such studies in journals with lower prestige, but they must endure many letters of rejection and publication is delayed for a long period.

To us this clearly indicates that we need a new type of journal—whether paper-based or electronic—that systematically archives all studies that will be needed for later meta-analyses. The American Psychological Association's Experimental Publication System in the early 1970s was an attempt in this direction. However, at that time the need subsequently created by meta-analysis did not yet exist; the system apparently met no real need at that time and hence was discontinued. Today, the need is so great that failure to have such a journal system in place is retarding our efforts to reach our full potential in creating cumulative knowledge in psychology and the social sciences. The Board of Scientific Affairs of the American Psychological Association is currently studying the feasibility of such a system.

Finally, we note that meta-analysis has had important effects on other areas of research beyond psychology; finance, marketing, economics, and medical research are examples. The impact has been especially great in medical research (e.g., see Altman, Lau, Kupelnick, Mosteller, & Chalmers, 1992). The following Web site provides information on meta-analysis in medical research: http://www.update-software.com/ccweb/cochrane/general.htm. The impact of meta-analysis in these and other areas is discussed in Hunter and Schmidt (1990b, 1996) and Schmidt and Hunter (1995).

CONCLUSIONS

Until recently, psychological research literatures appeared conflicting and contradictory. As the number of studies on each particular question became larger and larger, this situation became increasingly frustrating and intolerable. This situation stemmed from reliance on defective procedures for achieving cumulative knowledge: the statistical significance test in individual primary studies in combination with the narrative subjective review of research literatures. Meta-analysis principles have now correctly diagnosed this problem, and, more important, have provided the solution. In area after area, meta-analytic findings have shown that there is much less conflict between different studies than had been believed, that coherent, useful, and generalizable conclusions can be drawn from research literatures, and that cumulative knowledge is possible in psychology and the social sciences. These methods have also been adopted in other areas such as medical research. A prominent medical researcher, Thomas Chalmers (as cited in Mann, 1990), has stated, "[Meta-analysis] is going to revolutionize how the sciences, especially medicine, handle data. And it is going to be the way many arguments will be ended" (p. 478). In concluding his oft-cited review of meta-analysis methods, Bangert-Drowns (1986, p. 398) stated:

> Meta-analysis is not a fad. It is rooted in the fundamental values of the scientific enterprise: replicabililty, quantification, causal and correlational analysis. Valuable information is needlessly scattered in individual studies. The ability of social scientists to deliver generalizable answers to basic questions of policy is too serious a concern to allow us to treat research integration lightly. The potential benefits of meta-analysis seem enormous.

REFERENCES

Anastasi, A. (1988). *Psychological testing* (7th ed.). New York: Macmillan.

Altman, E. M., Lau, J., Kupelnick, B., Mosteller, F., & Chalmers, T. C. (1992). A comparison of results of meta-analyses of randomized control trials and recommendations of clinical experts. *Journal of the American Medical Association, 268,* 240–248.

Bangert-Drowns, R. L. (1986). Review of developments in meta-analytic method. *Psychological Bulletin, 99,* 388–399.

Bangert-Drowns, R. L., Kulik, J. A., & Kulik, C.-L. C. (1983). Effects of coaching programs on achievement test performance. *Review of Educational Research, 53,* 571–585.

Callender, J. C., & Osburn, H. G. (1980). Development and test of a new model for validity generalization. *Journal of Applied Psychology, 65,* 543–558.

Carver, R. P. (1978). The case against statistical significance testing. *Harvard Educational Review, 48,* 378–399.

Chelimsky, E. (1994, October 14). *Use of meta-analysis in the General Accounting Office.* Paper presented at the Science and

Public Policy Seminars, Federation of Behavioral, Psychological and Cognitive Sciences. Washington, DC.

Cohen, J. (1962). The statistical power of abnormal-social psychological research: A review. *Journal of Abnormal and Social Psychology, 65,* 145–153.

Cohen, J. (1988). *Statistical power analysis for the behavioral sciences* (2nd ed.). Hillsdale, NJ: Erlbaum.

Cohen, J. (1990). Things I learned (so far). *American Psychologist, 45,* 1304–1312.

Cohen, J. (1994). The earth is round ($\rho < .05$). *American Psychologist, 49,* 997–1003.

Cronbach, L. J. (1975). Beyond the two disciplines of scientific psychology. *American Psychologist, 30,* 116–127.

Cuts raise new social science query: Does anyone appreciate social science? (1981, March 27). *Wall Street Journal,* p. 54.

Fisher, C. D., & Gittelson, R. (1983). A meta-analysis of the correlates of role conflict and ambiguity. *Journal of Applied Psychology, 68,* 320–333.

Fisher, R. A. (1932). *Statistical methods for research workers* (4th ed.). Edinburgh, Scotland: Oliver and Boyd.

Gergen, K. J. (1982). *Toward transformation in social knowledge.* New York: Springer-Verlag.

Glass, G. V. (1972). The wisdom of scientific inquiry on education. *Journal of Research in Science Teaching, 9,* 3–18.

Glass, G. V. (1976). Primary, secondary and meta-analysis of research. *Educational Researcher, 5,* 3–8.

Glass, G. V. (1977). Integrating findings: The meta-analysis of research. *Review of Research in Education, 5,* 351–379.

Glass, G. V., McGaw, B., & Smith, M. L. (1981). *Meta-analysis in social research.* Beverly Hills, CA: Sage.

Guttman, L. (1985). The illogic of statistical inference for cumulative science. *Applied Stochastic Models and Data Analysis, 1,* 3–10.

Guzzo, R. A., Jackson, S. E., & Katzell, R. A. (1986). Meta-analysis analysis. In L. L. Cummings & B. M. Staw (Eds.), *Research in organizational behavior* (Vol. 9, pp. 407–442). Greenwich, CT: JAI Press.

Guzzo, R. A., Jette, R. D., & Katzell, R. A. (1985). The effects of psychologically based intervention programs on worker productivity: A meta-analysis. *Personnel Psychology, 38,* 275–292.

Hackett, R. D., & Guion, R. M. (1985). A re-evaluation of the absenteeism-job satisfaction relationship. *Organizational Behavior and Human Decision Processes, 35,* 340–381.

Hartigan, J. A., & Wigdor, A. K. (1989). *Fairness in employment testing: Validity generalization, minority issues, and the General Aptitude Test Battery.* Washington, DC: National Academy Press.

Hedges, L. V. (1982a). Estimation of effect size from a series of independent experiments. *Psychological Bulletin, 92,* 490–499.

Hedges, L. V. (1982b). Fitting categorical models to effect sizes from a series of experiments. *Journal of Educational Statistics, 7,* 119–137.

Hedges, L. V. (1987). How hard is hard science, how soft is soft science: The empirical cumulativeness of research. *American Psychologist, 42,* 443–455.

Hedges, L. V., & Olkin, I. (1985). *Statistical methods for meta-analysis.* Orlando, FL: Academic Press.

Hunter, J. E. (1983). A causal analysis of cognitive ability, job knowledge, job performance, and supervisory ratings. In F. Landy, S. Zedeck, & J. Cleveland (Eds.), *Performance measurement and theory* (pp. 257–266). Hillsdale, NJ: Erlbaum.

Hunter, J. E. (1988). A path analytic approach to analysis of covariance. Unpublished manuscript, Department of Psychology, Michigan State University, East Lansing.

Hunter, J. E. (1997). Needed: A ban on the significance test. *Psychological Science, 8,* 3–7.

Hunter, J. E., & Gerbing, D. W. (1982). Unidimensional measurement, second order factor analysis and causal models. In B. M. Staw & L. L. Cummings (Eds.), *Research in organizational behavior* (Vol. 4, pp. 267–320), Greenwich, CT: JAI Press.

Hunter, J. E., & Hirsh, H. R. (1987). Applications of meta-analysis. In C. L. Cooper & I. T. Robertson (Eds.), *International review of industrial and organizational psychology 1987* (pp. 321–357). London: Wiley.

Hunter, J. E., & Schmidt, F. L. (1990a). Dichotomization of continuous variables: The implications for meta-analysis. *Journal of Applied Psychology, 75,* 334–349.

Hunter, J. E., & Schmidt, F. L. (1990b). *Methods of meta-analysis: Correcting error and bias in research findings.* Newbury Park, CA: Sage.

Hunter, J. E., & Schmidt, F. L. (1994). The estimation of sampling error variance in meta-analysis of correlations: The homogenous case. *Journal of Applied Psychology, 79,* 171–177.

Hunter, J. E., & Schmidt, F. L. (1996). Cumulative research knowledge and social policy formulation: The critical role of meta-analysis. *Psychology, Public Policy, and Law, 2,* 324–347.

Hunter, J. E., & Schmidt, F. L. (2000). Fixed effects vs. random effects meta-analysis models: Implications for cumulative knowledge in psychology. *International Journal of Selection and Assessment, 8,* 275–292.

Hunter, J. E., Schmidt, F. L., & Jackson, G. B. (1982). *Meta-analysis: Cumulating research findings across studies.* Beverly Hills, CA: Sage.

Iaffaldono, M. T., & Muchinsky, P. M. (1985). Job satisfaction and job performance: A meta-analysis. *Psychological Bulletin, 97,* 251–273.

Jackson, S. E., & Schuler, R. S. (1985). A meta-analysis and conceptual critique of research on role ambiguity and role conflict in work settings. *Organizational Behavioral and Human Decision Processes, 36,* 16–78.

Kulik, J. A., & Bangert-Drowns, R. L. (1983–1984). Effectiveness of technology in precollege mathematics and science teaching. *Journal of Educational Technology Systems, 12,* 137–158.

Landman, J. T., & Dawes, R. M. (1982). Psychotherapy outcome: Smith and Glass' conclusions stand up under scrutiny. *American Psychologist, 37,* 504–516.

Law, K. S., Schmidt, F. L., & Hunter, J. E. (1994a). Nonlinearity of range corrections in meta-analysis: A test of an improved procedure. *Journal of Applied Psychology, 79,* 425–438.

Law, K. S., Schmidt, F. L., & Hunter, J. E. (1994b). A test of two refinements in meta-analysis procedures. *Journal of Applied Psychology, 79,* 978–986.

Lipsey, M. W., & Wilson, D. B. (1993). The efficacy of psychological, educational, and behavioral treatment: Confirmation from meta-analysis. *American Psychologist, 48,* 1181–1209.

Mabe, P. A., III, & West, S. G. (1982). Validity of self evaluations of ability: A review and meta-analysis. *Journal of Applied Psychology, 67,* 280–296.

Mann, C. (1990). Meta-analysis in the breech. *Science, 249,* 476–480.

Mansfield, R. S., & Busse, T. V. (1977). Meta-analysis of research: A rejoinder to Glass. *Educational Researcher, 6,* 3.

McEvoy, G. M., & Cascio, W. F. (1985). Strategies for reducing employee turnover: A meta-analysis. *Journal of Applied Psychology, 70,* 342–353.

McEvoy, G. M., & Cascio, W. F. (1987). Do poor performers leave? A meta-analysis of the relation between performance and turnover. *Academy of Management Journal, 30,* 744–762.

Meehl, P. E. (1978). Theoretical risks and tabular asterisks: Sir Karl, Sir Ronald, and the slow process of soft psychology. *Journal of Consulting and Clinical Psychology, 46,* 806–834.

National Research Council. (1992). *Combining information: Statistical issues and opportunities for research.* Washington, DC: National Academy of Science Press.

Oakes, M. (1986). *Statistical inference: A commentary for the social and behavioral sciences.* New York: Wiley.

Pearlman, K., Schmidt, F. L., & Hunter, J. E. (1980). Validity generalization results for tests used to predict job proficiency and training success in clerical occupations. *Journal of Applied Psychology, 65,* 373–406.

Peters, L. H., Harthe, D., & Pohlman, J. (1985). Fiedler's contingency theory of leadership: An application of the meta-analysis procedures of Schmidt and Hunter. *Psychological Bulletin, 97,* 274–285.

Petty, M. M., McGee, G. W., & Cavender, J. W. (1984). A meta-analysis of the relationship between individual job satisfaction and individual performance. *Academy of Management Review, 9,* 712–721.

Premack, S., & Wanous, J. P. (1985). Meta-analysis of realistic job preview experiments. *Journal of Applied Psychology, 70,* 706–719.

Raju, N. S., & Burke, M. J. (1983). Two procedures for studying validity generalization. *Journal of Applied Psychology, 68,* 382–395.

Rosenthal, R. (1991). *Meta-analytic procedures for social research* (2nd ed.). Newbury Park, CA: Sage.

Rosenthal, R., & Rubin, D. B. (1982). Comparing effect sizes of independent studies. *Psychological Bulletin, 92,* 500–504.

Rozeboom, W. W. (1960). The fallacy of the null hypothesis significance test. *Psychological Bulletin, 57,* 416–428.

Schmidt, F. L. (1988). Validity generalization and the future of criterion-related validity. In H. Wainer & H. I. Braun (Eds.), *Test validity* (pp. 173–292). Hillsdale, NJ: Erlbaum.

Schmidt, F. L. (1992). What do data really mean? Research findings, meta-analysis, and cumulative knowledge in psychology. *American Psychologist, 47,* 1173–1181.

Schmidt, F. L. (1996). Statistical significance testing and cumulative knowledge in psychology: Implications for the training of researchers. *Psychological Methods, 1,* 115–129.

Schmidt, F. L., & Hunter. J. E. (1977). Development of a general solution to the problem of validity generalization. *Journal of Applied Psychology, 62,* 529–540.

Schmidt, F. L., & Hunter, J. E. (1978). Moderator research and the law of small numbers. *Personnel Psychology, 31,* 215–232.

Schmidt, F. L., & Hunter, J. E. (1981). Employment testing: Old theories and new research findings. *American Psychologist, 36,* 1128–1137.

Schmidt, F. L., & Hunter, J. E. (1995). The impact of data analysis method on cumulative knowledge: Statistical significance testing, confidence intervals, and meta-analysis. *Evaluation and the Health Professions, 18,* 408–427.

Schmidt, F. L., & Hunter, J. E. (1996). Measurement error in psychological research: Lessons from 26 research scenarios. *Psychological Methods, 1,* 199–223.

Schmidt, F. L., & Hunter, J. E. (1997). Eight common but false objections to the discontinuation of significance testing in the analysis of research data. In L. Harlow, S. Muliak, & J. Steiger (Eds.), *What if there were no significance tests?* (pp. 37–64). Mahwah, NJ: Erlbaum.

Schmidt, F. L., Hunter, J. E., Pearlman, K., & Shane, G. S. (1979). Further tests of the Schmidt-Hunter Bayesian validity generalization procedure. *Personnel Psychology, 32,* 257–281.

Schmidt, F. L., Hunter, J. E., & Urry, V. E. (1976). Statistical power in criterion-related validation studies. *Journal of Applied Psychology, 61,* 473–485.

Schmidt, F. L., Ocasio, B. P., Hillery, J. M., & Hunter, J. E. (1985). Further within-setting empirical tests of the situational specificity hypothesis in personnel selection. *Personnel Psychology, 38,* 509–524.

Sedlmeier, P., & Gigerenzer, G. (1989). Do studies of statistical power have an effect on the power of the studies? *Psychological Bulletin, 105,* 309–316.

Snedecor, G. W. (1946). *Statistical methods* (4th ed.). Ames: Iowa State College Press.

Terborg, J. R., & Lee, T. W. (1982). Extension of the Schmidt-Hunter validity generalization procedure to the prediction of absenteeism behavior from knowledge of job satisfaction and organizational commitment. *Journal of Applied Psychology, 67,* 280–296.

Tett, R. P., Meyer, J. P., & Roese, N. J. (1994). Applications of meta-analysis: 1987–1992. In *International review of industrial and organizational psychology* (Vol. 9, pp. 71–112). London: Wiley.

Wilkinson, L., & the Task Force on Statistical Inference. (1999). Statistical methods in psychology journals: Guidelines and explanations. *American Psychologist, 54,* 594–604.

Wortman, P. M., & Bryant, F. B. (1985). School desegregation and black achievement: An integrative review. *Sociological Methods and Research, 13,* 289–324.

CHAPTER 22

Survival Analysis

JUDITH D. SINGER AND JOHN B. WILLETT

Psychologists often study *whether* and, if so, *when* events occur. Researchers investigating the course of eating disorders, for example, have examined the age of initial onset (Stice, Killen, Hayward, & Taylor, 1998), the time to first recovery (Herzog, Schellberg, & Deter, 1997), the time to relapse among successfully treated individuals (Strober, Freeman, & Morrell, 1997), and whether participation in a treatment program shortens recovery time (Wilson et al., 1999). Similar questions about event occurrence arise in numerous fields of psychological research, including the study of addictive behaviors (e.g., illicit drugs, smoking, gambling, and crime), the onset and course of depression, the efficacy of psychotherapy and other clinical interventions, and employee turnover.

Research questions about event occurrence present unique design and analytic difficulties. The core problem is that no matter when data collection begins, and no matter how long any subsequent follow-up lasts, some people may not experience the target event before data collection ends—many adolescents will not develop an eating disorder, some who do

will not recover, and some who recover will not relapse. Should a researcher assume that none of these people will ever experience the focal event? All a researcher knows is that by the end of data collection, usually an arbitrary point in time, the event had not yet occurred. Statisticians say that such observations are *censored.*

The prospect of censoring complicates research design; the presence of censoring complicates statistical analysis. Some researchers have responded to these complications with a variety of ad hoc strategies, none entirely satisfactory: (a) creating a dichotomous outcome that contrasts individuals with observed and censored event times (Condiotte & Lichtenstein, 1981); (b) restricting attention to noncensored cases (Lelliott, Marks, McNamee, & Tobena, 1989); (c) deleting censored cases (Litman, Eiser, & Taylor, 1979); or (d) using the censored outcome as a categorical predictor of another outcome that varies over time (Coelho, 1984). Other researchers avoid the "when" question and ask only the "whether" question: Does the event occur by a particular point in time (Grey, Osborn, & Reznikoff, 1986) or by each of several successive points in time (Glasgow, Klesges, Klesges, & Somes, 1988)?

As early as the 1970s, psychologists recognized the severe limitations of these strategies, most notably their sensitivity

---

The order of the authors was determined by randomization.

to the length of data collection (e.g., Hunt, Barnett, & Branch, 1971; Nathan & Lansky, 1978; Sutton, 1979). But it is only since the 1990s, with the widespread availability of statistical software for analyzing event occurrence, that psychologists have begun to use more appropriate methods. The class of methods, known variously as survival analysis, event history analysis, and hazard modeling, were originally developed by biostatisticians modeling human lifetimes (Cox, 1972; Kaplan & Meier, 1958). Over the years, improvements in survival methodology have come from biostatisticians (e.g., Therneau & Grambsch, 2000), economists (e.g., Heckman & Singer, 1985; Lancaster, 1990), and sociologists (e.g., Tuma & Hannan, 1984). Differences in terminology aside, these techniques use similar mathematical roots to reach similar goals: to help researchers simultaneously explore *whether* events occur (do people start using illicit drugs, stop smoking, begin drinking again?) and, if so, *when*. Using specific techniques within the broad class of methods, researchers can describe patterns of occurrence, compare these patterns among groups, and build statistical models of the risk of occurrence over time.

Owing to its genesis in modeling human lifetimes, where the target event is death, survival analysis is shrouded in dark foreboding terms. But beyond the terminology lies a powerful methodology that appropriately uses data from all observations, noncensored and censored cases alike. Data collection can be prospective or retrospective, experimental or observational. Time can be measured continuously or discretely. The only requirements are (a) that at every time point of interest, each individual be classified into one of two or more mutually exclusive and exhaustive states; and (b) that the researcher know, for at least some of these individuals, when the transition from one state to the next occurs.

In this chapter we present a nonmathematical introduction to survival analysis. After describing the basic concepts, we focus on two topics—study design and data analysis—and for each we identify the key issues researchers face and provide guidelines for making informed decisions about them. In the process, we review how psychologists have used the methods to date and point towards new directions for their application. In the final section we provide additional information for readers who want to learn more.

THE CONCEPTS UNDERLYING SURVIVAL ANALYSIS

The concepts underlying survival analysis differ markedly from the familiar means, standard deviations, and correlations of traditional parametric statistics. We develop these concepts here using data reported by Stevens and Hollis (1989), who evaluated the efficacy of supplementing a smoking cessation program with follow-up support sessions designed to help ex-smokers cope with abstinence. The researchers randomly assigned 587 adults who successfully completed a 4-day program to one of three conditions: (a) no supplemental sessions, (b) 3 weeks of coping skills training, or (c) 3 weeks of support sessions without skills training. For 1 year after quitting, participants returned a monthly postcard noting their smoking status. Defining abstinence as smoking no more than five cigarettes per month, Stevens and Hollis asked *whether* the follow-up support helped people remain abstinent and if it did not, *when* people were most likely to relapse.

Survivor Function

Survival analysis begins with the survivor function. When studying abstinence after smoking cessation, as in this example, the population survivor function assesses the probability that a randomly selected ex-smoker will remain abstinent over time. Given a representative sample from a target population, the sample survivor function estimates the population probability that a randomly selected person will remain abstinent longer than each time assessed—in this example, 1 month, 2 months, and so on—until everyone relapses or data collection ends (whichever comes first).

The top panel of Figure 22.1 presents the sample survivor function for the 198 people in Stevens and Hollis's control group. At the beginning of the study (the beginning of "time"), the estimated survival probability is 1.00. As time passes and people relapse, the sample survivor function drops toward 0. In this study, 82% successfully abstain from smoking ("survive") more than 1 month following cessation, 66% abstain more than 2 months, 60% abstain more than 3 months, and so forth. By 12 months, when data collection ends, 38% remain abstinent. These individuals have censored relapse times, either because they never relapse or because if they do, it will be after data collection ends. Because of censoring, sample survivor functions rarely reach zero.

The sample survivor function helps us answer a descriptive question: On average, how many months pass before the abstinent smoker relapses? When the sample survivor function reaches 0.50, half the ex-smokers have relapsed, half have not. The estimated *median lifetime* identifies this midpoint, which indicates how much time passes before half the sample experiences the target event. As shown in Figure 22.1, among ex-smokers without follow-up support, the answer is 4 months. The median lifetime statistic incorporates

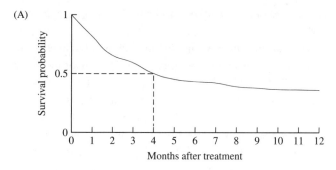

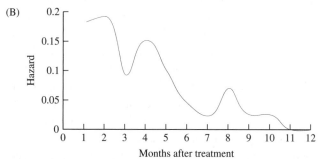

Figure 22.1 Sample survivor (panel A) and hazard (panel B) functions for 198 ex-smokers (based on data from Stevens and Hollis, 1989). *Note:* We estimated the sample survivor function in this figure using summary data kindly supplied by Dr. Victor J. Stevens (Stevens & Hollis, 1989, Figure 1, p. 422) using the Kaplan-Meier product limit method (Kalbfleisch & Prentice, 1980). We then smoothed the obtained discrete estimates using a spline function (after the recommendation of Miller, 1981). The same method was used to create Figures 22.2, 22.3, and 22.4. Our intentions were strictly pedagogic—we wished to use continuous-time survivor and hazard functions to introduce the concepts of survival analysis before discussing the differences between continuous-time and discrete-time methods.

data from both the 123 uncensored individuals who relapsed within the 12 months of data collection and the 75 censored individuals who did not.

All survivor functions have a shape similar to that displayed in Figure 22.1—a negatively accelerating extinction curve, a monotonically nonincreasing function of time. This generalization was noted by Hunt and colleagues well before the advent of modern survival methods (Hunt et al., 1971; Hunt & Bespalec, 1974; Hunt & Matarazzo, 1970). After finding similarly shaped survivor functions in nearly 100 studies of smoking, heroin, and alcohol cessation, Hunt et al. (1971) presaged the utility of another plot (to which we now turn) when they wrote that they "hoped to use the differences in slope between individual curves as a differential criterion to evaluate various treatment techniques" (p. 455).

Hazard Function

If a large proportion of successful abstainers suddenly relapses in a given month, the survivor function drops sharply, as

happens in Figure 22.1 during each of the first few months after smoking cessation. When this happens, ex-smokers are at greater risk of relapse. Examining the changing slope of the survivor function is one way to identify such "risky" time periods. But a more sensitive way to assess the risk of event occurrence is to examine the *hazard function,* a mathematical function related to the survivor function that registers these changing slopes of the (negative log) survivor function.

Mathematical definitions of hazard differ depending on whether time is measured discretely or continuously. In discrete time, events happen during finite intervals, such as months, semesters, or years. In continuous time, events happen at precise instants, and event occurrence is recorded using units such as days or weeks (or perhaps even minutes or hours). If time is measured discretely, hazard is defined as the conditional probability that an ex-smoker will relapse in a particular time interval, given that the person has not relapsed prior to the interval. As the interval length decreases, the probability that an event will occur during any given interval decreases as well. In the limit, when time is measured continuously, we must modify the definition of hazard because the probability that an event occurs at any "infinitely thin" instant of time will approach zero (by definition). So continuous time hazard is defined as the instantaneous rate of relapse, given uninterrupted abstinence until that time. While hazard is always nonnegative, when time is measured discretely, it can never exceed 1; when time is measured continuously, it can assume any value greater than, or equal to, 0.

Like the survivor function, the hazard function can be plotted against time, yielding a profile of the risk of relapsing each month, given uninterrupted abstinence until that month. The magnitude of each month's hazard indicates the risk of relapsing in that month—the higher the hazard, the greater the risk. Each month's hazard is calculated using data on only those individuals still eligible to experience the event during the month (the *risk set*); individuals who have already relapsed are not included.

The lower panel of Figure 22.1 presents the sample hazard function corresponding to the sample survivor function in the top panel. The risk of relapse is high in each of the first few months of the study and then declines over time. Ex-smokers are at greatest risk of relapse immediately after they quit; those who successfully abstain for several months are likely to abstain for at least a year.

The hazard function is an invaluable analytical tool because it effectively portrays variation in risk of event occurrence over time. We identify the moments of this variation by locating the hazard function's distinctive peaks and troughs. Peaks pinpoint periods of elevated risk; troughs pinpoint periods of low risk. We illustrate this approach in Figure 22.2.

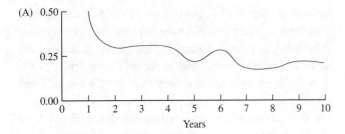

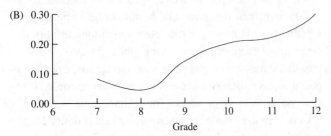

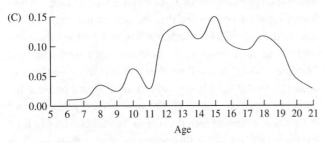

Figure 22.2 Three illustrative hazard functions: (A) duration of wars (based on data from Horvath, 1968); (B) first suicide ideation (based on data from Bolger et al., 1989); (C) first heterosexual intercourse (based on data from Capaldi et al., 1996).

The hazard function in the top panel comes from Horvath's (1968) classic study of the duration of wars. Using an extensive database describing 315 conflicts that occurred between 1820 and 1949, Horvath was able to assess how long after initiation wars are likely to end. As in Figure 22.1, this hazard function peaks immediately and declines thereafter. Conflicts are most likely to end shortly after they begin. Over time, as countries stridently maintain their position, the risk of ending a war declines. Monotonically decreasing hazard functions are common, especially when studying recurrence and relapse. Whether the target event is substance abuse (Hall, Havassy, & Wasserman, 1991), mental illness (e.g., Mojtabai, Nicholson, & Neesmith, 1997), child abuse (e.g., Fryer & Miyoshi, 1994), or incarceration (e.g., Harris & Koepsell, 1996), risk of recurrence is highest immediately after treatment, identification, or release. Monotonically decreasing hazard functions arise when studying other events as well. Two contrasting examples are Hurlburt, Wood, and Hough's (1996) study of whether and when homeless individuals find housing and Diekmann, Jungbauer-Gans, Krassnig, and Lorenz's (1996) study of whether and when

drivers respond aggressively to being blocked by a double-parked car.

The hazard function in the middle panel comes from Capaldi, Crosby, and Stoolmiller's (1996) study of the grade of first heterosexual intercourse among 180 at-risk boys. When data collection ended in 12th grade, 54 (30.0%) were still virgins (censored). This hazard function is also monotonic but in the opposite direction: It begins low and increases over time. Few boys had heterosexual intercourse in 7th or 8th grade. Beginning in 9th grade, the risk of initiation increases annually among those who remain virgins. In 9th grade, for example, an estimated 15.0% of the boys who had not yet had sex do so for the first time; by 12th grade, 31.7% of the remaining virgins (admittedly only 45.1% of the original sample) do likewise. Monotonically increasing hazard functions are common when studying events that are ultimately inevitable (or near universal). At the beginning of time few people experience the event, but as time progresses, the decreasing pool of individuals who remain at risk succumbs. Keifer (1988), for example, found this pattern when characterizing the time it takes to settle a labor dispute, as did Campbell, Mutran, and Parker (1987), who studied how long it takes workers to retire.

The hazard function in the bottom panel comes from Bolger, Downey, Walker, and Steininger's (1989) study of age at first suicide ideation. Among 406 undergraduates, 287 reported having previously thought about suicide; 119 (29.3%) were censored (had not yet had a suicidal thought). The risk of suicide ideation is low during childhood, peaks during adolescence, and then declines to near (but not quite) early childhood levels in late adolescence. A similar hazard function was found by Diekmann and Mitter (1983), who also used a young adult sample to examine event occurrence retrospectively, but of a very different type: shoplifting. They found that the age at first shoplift varied widely, from age 4 to 16, with a peak during early adolescence (ages 12 to 14). In a different context, Gamse and Conger (1997) found a similar shape when following the academic careers of recipients of a postdoctoral research fellowship. The hazard function describing time to tenure was low in the early years of the career, peaked in years 6 through 8, and declined thereafter.

What happens if the hazard function displays no peaks or troughs? When hazard is flat, risk is unrelated to time. Under these circumstances, event occurrence is independent of duration in the initial state, implying that events occur (seemingly) at random. Because of age, period, and cohort effects—all of which suggest duration dependence—flat hazard functions are rare in the social and behavioral sciences. Two interesting examples, however, are whether and when couples divorce following the birth of a child (Fergusson,

Horwood, & Shannon, 1984) and whether and when elementary school children shift their attention away from their teacher (Felmlee & Eder, 1983).

Incidence and Prevalence: An Analogy for Hazard and Survival

Because hazard and survival functions may be unfamiliar concepts, we offer an epidemiological analogy to concepts that some readers may find more familiar—incidence and prevalence. Incidence measures the number of new events occurring during a time period (expressed as a proportion of the number of individuals at risk), while prevalence cumulates these risks to the total number of events that have occurred by a given time (also as a proportion; see, e.g., Kleinbaum, Kupper, & Morgenstern, 1982; Lilienfeld & Lilienfeld, 1980). Incidence and prevalence correspond directly to hazard and survival: Hazard represents incidence, and survival represents cumulative prevalence.

This analogy reinforces the importance of examining both the survivor and hazard functions. Epidemiologists have long recognized that while prevalence assesses the extent of a problem at a particular point in time, incidence is the key to disease etiology (Mausner & Bahn, 1974). Why? Because prevalence confounds incidence with duration. Conditions with longer durations may be more prevalent, even if they have equal or lower incidence rates. To determine *when* people are at risk, epidemiologists study incidence. And when they study incidence, they are actually studying hazard.

DESIGN: COLLECTING SURVIVAL DATA

The conduct of survival analysis requires data summarizing the behavior of a sample of individuals over time. Data can be collected prospectively (as in Stevens and Hollis's smoking cessation study) or retrospectively (as in Bolger's suicide ideation study). The best studies tailor the time frame to the target event. When studying the side effects of a nicotine patch, 10-day or 10-week segments might suffice; but when studying the link between personality traits and coronary heart disease, even a 10-year window might not. In the following sections we discuss nine questions that arise when designing a study of event occurrence.

Whom Will You Study?

As with any statistical method, the full advantages of survival analysis require a representative sample of individuals selected from an appropriate target population. Although data can be collected from convenience samples can be used, probabilistic statements, population generalizations of sample summary statistics, or statistical inferences may be rendered incorrect. Because some psychologists work with sociologists and epidemiologists accustomed to using probabilistic sampling schemes, there are many excellent examples of survival analyses using data collected from representative samples (e.g., Andrade, Eaton, & Chilcoat, 1996; Harris & Koepsell, 1996; Rosenbaum & Kandel, 1990). We hope this standard will persist as survival methods find their way into other substantive areas.

A more problematic issue concerns the need to define carefully the target population from which the sample will be selected. Subtle variations in population definitions can inadvertently distort the distribution of time—the very quantity of interest. Consider the tempting strategy of eliminating censoring altogether by restricting the target population to only those individuals with known event times. A simple example from the research literature on the duration of foster care arrangements illustrates the problems that can arise. When studying discharge times for children in foster care, Milner (1987) defined his target population as the 222 children in a state agency who were released from care between 1984 and 1985 (thus disregarding those who were not discharged). Among a random sample of 75 of these children, he found that 37% had entered care within 5 months of discharge, 29% had entered care within 6 to 11 months of discharge, 14% had entered care within 12 to 24 months of discharge, and the remaining 20% had entered care over 25 months before discharge.

The estimated median time to discharge in this sample was 6 to 11 months. Should we conclude that the "average" child stayed in foster care for under a year? Although this study used a probability sample from a well-defined target population, we do not know the answer to this question because the target population is unsuitable for answering it. Milner knew about discharge times only among children *already discharged;* he ignored those who remained in care. Children in foster care for long periods of time were most likely to be excluded from his study. Determining how long the *average* child stayed in care requires a random sample of *all* children in care. It is likely that Milner's sampling strategy led to an underestimate of the average duration of foster care in the full population.

Some definitions of the target population create more subtle biases. Hidden biases are especially common in retrospective studies because a population defined at a particular point in time excludes people who already experienced an event that made it impossible for them to enter the target population. If a researcher conducted a retrospective study of age at first cocaine use based on a random sample of high school seniors, for example, he or she would necessarily exclude students who had already died because of cocaine use or students who had already dropped out of school.

When a sample excludes individuals who have already experienced the event of interest before data collection began, statisticians say that the sample is *left truncated*. Left truncation has received little attention in the methodological literature, perhaps because the nature of the problem—the omission of any information—makes its difficult to evaluate the extent or impact of the truncation. As Hutchison (1988a, 1988b) noted, many methodologists ignore left truncation entirely or fail to distinguish it from another methodological difficulty discussed later (left censoring). To avoid the complications arising from left truncation, we offer some design advice: Whenever possible, define the target population using delimiters unrelated to time; if this is impossible, fully explore the potential biases created by whatever definition you use.

What Is the Target Event?

At every time point of interest, each individual under study must occupy one, and only one, of two or more states. The states must be mutually exclusive (nonoverlapping) and exhaustive (of all possible states). Each individual is either depressed or well, smoking or abstinent, unemployed or working. The target event occurs when an individual moves from one state to the next.

States must be defined precisely, with clear guidelines indicating the specific behaviors, responses, or scores constituting each state. The definition of states is always difficult, even when clinical definitions of event occurrence exist. When reviewing the literature on the onset, recovery, relapse, and recurrence of depression, for example, members of the MacArthur Foundation Research Network on the Psychobiology of Depression concluded that "one investigator's relapse is another's recurrence" (Frank et al., 1991, p. 851).

Fortunately for psychologists, the specification of criteria for defining states precisely has received much attention in recent years (see, e.g., Langenbucher & Chung, 1995; Lavori et al., 1996). In the drug abuse literature, for example, it is common to use multiple classification systems based on a combination of biochemical assays, clinical judgment, and self-reports. Many researchers who once relied solely on a clinical criterion, such as total abstinence, for example, now augment this definition with a less rigid one that permits temporary lapses (Baer & Lichtenstein, 1988). Similarly, many researchers who once relied solely on self-report now augment their definition with biochemical data (Swan, Ward, & Jack, 1996).

Regardless of the source of data, researchers must strike a balance between restrictive definitions, which lead to underestimates of the time to relapse, and less rigorous definitions, which bias estimates toward late relapse. Brownell, Marlatt, Lichtenstein, and Wilson (1986), for example, argued that researchers routinely consider at least two definitions when studying recurrence: lapse (a temporary slip that may or may not lead to relapse) and relapse. Velicer, Proschaska, Rossi, and Snow (1992) provided a helpful review of the issues arising in the definition of outcome in smoking cessation studies.

Why do we, as methodologists, dwell on these definitional issues? We do so because of their serious methodological ramifications. It is clear, for example, that some of the observed variation in relapse rates reported in the literature is attributable not to the differential effectiveness of various interventions, but to variation in the definition of event states. Consider the different conclusions that a research reviewer could cull from just the first month of data on unaided smoking cessation collected by Marlatt, Curry, and Gordon (1988). By the end of the month, 23% of the sample had never actually quit (they smoked again within 24 hours), 36% had quit for at least 24 hours but subsequently relapsed within the month, 16% had been primarily abstinent but smoked one or two cigarettes, and only 25% had been successfully abstinent. In no time at all, a research reviewer could reasonably calculate at least three different "relapse" rates: by setting aside individuals who never really quit, by pooling the primarily abstinent individuals with the relapsers, or by pooling them with the successfully abstinent individuals.

Given the important role of substantive issues in the definition of event states, we cannot review here all the measurement considerations necessary for deriving reliable and valid definitions of event states. Instead we offer more modest general advice: Collect your data with as much precision as possible so that you can appropriately code transitions from one state to the next. With refined data, you can always collapse individuals together to derive broader definitions; with coarse categorized data, it is difficult (and often impossible) to recoup more differentiated definitions. And when describing your results, operationalize your definitions as precisely as possible (specifying the criteria for onset, recovery, relapse, and recurrence as clearly as possible in terms of the number, intensity and duration of symptoms) so that others can compare their findings to yours.

When Does "Time" Begin?

The problem of starting the clock is more complex than it may appear. Because birth is handy and often meaningful, it is a popular start time, especially in studies that track developmental sequences and milestones. Although it may seem awkward to report it this way, any study that uses age as the metric for time is actually using birth to denote time's beginning. So, for example, when Singer, Fuller, Keiley, and Wolf (1998) examined the age at first entry into child care, the beginning of time was the child's birth.

The other common way of identifying the beginning of time is to set it at the occurrence of a precipitating event— one that places all individuals in the population at risk of experiencing the target event. In a series of studies conducted as part of the Fort Bragg Child and Adolescent Mental Health Demonstration Project, the clock was started at different points in time depending on the event being studied. When assessing whether different types of care reduce inpatient length of stay, Foster (1998) started the clock when patients were first admitted to the hospital, but when assessing whether aftercare services reduce inpatient readmissions, Foster (1999) started the clock when patients were first released. The choice of precipitating event varies widely across research questions. Some options include entry into a particular level of schooling (Rayman & Brett, 1995; Roderick, 1994), release from jail (Henning & Frueh, 1996), divorce or separation (Wu, 1995), or report of child maltreatment (Fryer & Miyoshi, 1994).

Consideration of the process under study usually leads to a defensible decision. When it does not, an arbitrary time can be used as long as that time is itself unrelated to event occurrence. Researchers conducting randomized clinical trials, for example, typically use the date of randomization or intervention (Hurlburt et al., 1996; Greenhouse, Stangl, Kupfer, & Prien, 1991). But beware of the measurement imprecision created when the chosen precipitating event only approximates the conceptual beginning of time. When modeling illnesses, for example, the conceptual beginning of time is the onset of the illness episode, yet medical researchers often use the date of evaluation or diagnosis. Because the time between onset and entry into treatment can vary greatly across individuals (Monroe, Simons, & Thase, 1991) and the magnitude of this lag time may be an important predictor of a treatment's efficacy, use of these more easily measured dates may actually add even more errors into the definition of event occurrence.

What happens if the start date is unknown for some individuals under study? Statisticians say that such observations are *left censored* (to distinguish them from *right-censored* observations in which the event times are unknown). Left censoring presents challenges not easily addressed using even the most sophisticated of survival methods. Little progress has been made in this area since Turnbull (1974, 1976) offered some basic descriptive approaches and Flinn and

Heckman (1982) and Cox and Oakes (1984) offered some guidelines for fitting statistical models under a very restrictive set of assumptions. Most methodologists dismiss the topic soon after introducing the terminology (see, e.g., Blossfeld, Hamerle, & Mayer, 1989, p. 29; Tuma & Hannan, 1984, p. 135). The most common advice is that researchers should define the beginning of time so that left censoring never arises or set the left-censored spells aside from analysis (Allison, 1984; Tuma & Hannan, 1984).

When Should You Collect Data?

Few researchers have the luxury of monitoring subjects continuously. Financial and logistical constraints usually demand that researchers contact subjects at a finite number of preselected intervals. Using these "chunky" data, researchers then try to reconstruct pseudocontinuous event histories retrospectively. Reconstruction can be made more effective if researchers judiciously select the preselected intervals when study subjects will be contacted.

The collection of data in discrete time can add measurement imprecision. If transitions occur in continuous time but data are collected in discrete time, for example, a researcher will never know an individual's mental state at the moment of transition. Such imprecision has serious consequences if information about the transition moment is critical for predicting the timing of events, as when the coping skills of the ex-smoker, gambler, drinker, eater, or drug abuser may determine whether the person succumbs to temptation. Shiffman (1982) used an innovative design to overcome this restriction; he interviewed 183 ex-smokers who called a smoking cessation hotline because they were in crisis. His design may be useful in other studies requiring data collected at the precise moment of transition.

Carefully constructed interview questions can improve the quality of the event history data. Bradburn, Rips, and Shevell (1987) provided strategies for helping respondents construct temporal autobiographies. They recommended letting respondents create their own time lines based on personally salient anchors (birthdays, anniversaries, holidays) and then sequentially placing other events (and symptoms) on this time line (see Young, Watel, Lahmeyer, & Eastman, 1991, for an application). In multiwave studies, bounded-recall probes can enrich the quality of data describing behavior between interviews.

Where should you target your limited data collection resources? Although collection at equally spaced time intervals is systematic, this strategy may omit information about the periods of greatest interest. A simple but effective strategy that maximizes information on the occurrence of the target event is to collect data more frequently when events are most likely to occur.

Information on the anticipated shape of the hazard function provides helpful information for selecting times for data collection. The idea is to collect data more frequently when hazard is high and less frequently when hazard is low. This allocation strategy was used effectively, for example, by Hall, Rugg, Tunstall, and Jones (1984), who in their 1-year prospective study of smoking abstinence following behavioral skills training placed their four data-collection periods at 3, 6, 26, and 52 weeks after treatment. If they had spaced data-collection episodes equally, waiting until week 13 to collect the first follow-up data, they would have been unable to determine that the risk of relapse was highest in the few weeks immediately following cessation.

Can You Reconstruct Event Histories From Retrospective Data Collection?

In 1837 William Farr wrote, "Is your study to be retrospective or prospective? If the former, the replies will be general, vague, and I fear of little value" (cited in Lilienfeld & Lilienfeld, 1980). His words remain true today. Whenever possible, researchers should collect data prospectively. But in the study of infrequent events—depression onset, initiation into opiate drug use, child maltreatment—prospective data collection may be infeasible. Many researchers therefore opt for a different approach: Interview people and ask, "Has the event *ever* occurred?" and if so, "*When* did it first occur?" Retrospective data collection has been used successfully by researchers studying the age at first use of many different addictive substances and remains a fruitful strategy for research (see, e.g., Adler & Kandel, 1983).

Researchers contemplating a retrospective data collection effort should be forewarned, however, that their data will be imperfect. Although rare events (e.g., suicide attempts or hospitalization) may be remembered indefinitely and highly salient events (e.g., initial use of drugs or first symptoms of an illness) may be remembered for two or three years, habitual events (e.g., ongoing symptoms and substance use) are too embedded in an individual's life to be remembered precisely (Bradburn, 1983; Sudman & Bradburn, 1982). The longer the time period is, the greater the error. (And, as noted earlier, if the target event can lead to death, the collection of retrospective data from a cohort ensures that sampling will be biased by the omission of those who have already succumbed.)

Three errors are common in retrospective data collection: (a) *memory failures,* in which respondents forget events entirely; (b) *telescoping,* in which events are remembered as having occurred more recently than they actually did; and (c) *rounding,* in which respondents drop fractions and report even numbers or numbers ending in 0 or 5. These errors create different biases: Memory failures lead to underreporting, telescoping to overreporting, and rounding to both. Lin, Ensel, and Lai (1996) presented an informative thorough study of the reliability and validity of recall data.

If retrospective recall is the only alternative, is it worth the effort? We believe it is. In their retrospective study of suicide ideation, Bolger et al. (1989) successfully used several approaches to improve recall. Although studying a "threatening" event, they couched the study in less threatening terms, that is, about the development of the concept of death and suicide. They never asked about respondents' mental health or suicidal behavior—only about thoughts and knowledge about others. Questionnaires were anonymous and self-administered in a group setting. Respondents were college students—close enough in age to the time period of interest (adolescence) but old enough to be removed.

How Can You Minimize Attrition?

Given the expense and difficulty of prospective data collection, researchers want to keep every case they can. It is well known that statistical power decreases as sample size decreases and that generalizability may also suffer if attrition is nonrandom. Hansen, Collins, Malotte, Johnson, and Fielding (1985) clearly demonstrate that studies on drug abuse prevention, for example, have been plagued by attrition problems. In their review of this literature, Biglan et al. (1991) noted several studies with attrition rates in excess of 50%!

Researchers who are most successful at minimizing attrition have used some of the following strategies: Explain to respondents why you need to follow them; ask them to contact you if they move; visit their homes and ask neighbors for information about them; pay them for participation in each interview; have them pay you an earnest deposit refundable at the end of the last interview; offer lottery prizes for those who successfully compete all required interviews; mail a newsletter at regular intervals; record the names and addresses of several relatives or friends not living with them; record each respondent's Social Security number; convene reunion meetings; maintain contact at regular intervals even if you are not recording data as frequently; send birthday and seasonal greetings cards; and consult official records (jail, hospital, welfare, driver registration). Farrington, Gallagher, Morley, St. Ledger, and West (1990) and M. Murphy (1990) offered many helpful strategies for minimizing attrition.

Despite diligent effort, most researchers lose some individuals to follow-up. Researchers attempting to improve their study by using a long follow-up period face a further conundrum: The longer the follow-up is, the greater the attrition. At first sight, attrition seems nonproblematic for survival analysis because it leads to additional right-censored event times—a problem that survival analysis was designed to handle. But censoring due to attrition may not be the noninformative censoring for which survival methods are valid. Individuals lost to follow-up can differ substantially from individuals who continue to participate. In their longitudinal study of drug abusers, for example, Biglan et al. (1991) presented clear evidence that those who remain in the sample differed from those who did not.

What should a researcher do with the data on individuals lost to follow-up? While multiple imputation methods offer much promise (Little & Rubin, 1987), three simple strategies can sometimes suffice. One is to assign each case a censored event time equal to the length of time the person was observed (without the event occurring). If an individual participated for the first 6 months of a 12-month study before attrition, censor the event time at 6 months. A second approach is to use a worst-case scenario: Assume that the event actually occurred when the case was lost to follow-up. Under this strategy, the event time is not censored. The findings from analyses carried out under both types of recoding can then be contrasted with each other in a sensitivity analysis. Persistence of findings obtained under multiple strategies, or explainable differences between the findings, reinforces the strength of the analytic results. The third approach is to conduct a competing-risks survival analysis, in which study attrition is treated as another event that competes to end an individual's lifetime (Singer & Willett, 1991).

The appropriateness of these alternative strategies depends in part on the target behavior under study. Be especially careful when assuming that the event occurred at the time when the observation is censored because this converts a nonevent into an event. Of course, when studying relapse, this conclusion may be sound because former drug abusers are notoriously unfaithful subjects and those who are clean are more likely to stay in touch. The key idea is to let reason be your guide. Within 12 weeks after beginning a study of 221 treated alcoholics, opiate users, and cigarette smokers, for example, Hall, Havassy, and Wasserman (1990) lost 73 people (one third of their sample) to follow-up, despite valiant attempts to minimize attrition. To ascertain the impact of attrition on their findings, the researchers conducted extensive sensitivity analyses, including (a) coding of relapse as occurring the week after the last interview completed and (b) setting aside these cases from analysis. All the analytic

findings were similar in sign and magnitude, although the standard errors of parameter estimates were higher under the second strategy because of a loss of statistical power.

How Can You Deal With Repeated Events?

Many events of interest to psychologists are repeatable. Indeed, with the exception of initial onset, most other events—ongoing use, abuse, hospitalization, treatment, relapse, employment, unemployment—can occur over and over throughout an individual's lifetime. When studying the timing of potentially repeatable events, make every attempt to note the spell number under study because the natural course of a first spell may differ from the natural course of second and subsequent spells. So, too, the efficacy of treatment may vary depending on how many prior spells the individual has experienced.

Recognizing the difficulties associated with this issue, Kupfer, Frank, and Perel (1989) designed a study to investigate differential recovery patterns across multiple spells when studying patients with recurrent depression. Separately analyzing the time to stabilization in two consecutive episodes, they found virtually identical median lifetimes (between 11 and 12 weeks). But they also found that the efficacy of treatment varied across spells: Early intervention in the second episode, as opposed to the first episode, worked particularly well.

We believe that the unidentified presence of multiple spells in a single data set may help explain some of the major puzzles in psychological research. Researchers studying addiction relapse, for example, have noted renewed abstinence on the part of formerly abstinent people who relapsed early after quitting. They argue that previous treatment, even unsuccessful treatment, may increase the probability of success of subsequent treatments. Similarly, when reviewing the literature on depression, Klerman (1978) demonstrated that some of the observed variation in relapse rates was attributable to researchers' failure to note how many prior episodes of depression each subject had.

For How Long Should You Collect Data?

Once the clock starts, it must eventually stop. Clocks in retrospective studies stop on the date of interview; clocks in prospective studies can, at least in theory, continue indefinitely. As a practical matter, though, most prospective studies follow a sample for a finite period of time. The length of data collection determines the amount of right censoring (hereafter referred to as censoring). Because longer data collection periods yield fewer censored observations, the simple maxim is the longer, the better. But beware—longer studies are more expensive, have more missing data, and may lead to outdated results.

When deciding on the length of follow-up, remember that before you can determine *when* the event is likely to occur, it must actually occur for enough people under study. If the target event never occurs during data collection, all observations are censored. The researcher has little information, knowing only that it generally takes longer than this period for the event to occur.

There is no universally appropriate length of follow-up. The answer depends on many factors. To decide on a reasonable follow-up period, you must consider the shape of the anticipated hazard function, the probable median lifetime, the sample size, and your proposed statistical analyses. As we show later in the section on determining sample size, a good rule of thumb is to follow participants long enough for at least half of them to experience the target event during data collection. This ensures sufficient information for estimating a median lifetime and provides reasonable statistical power.

What have researchers done in practice? Noting that ex-smokers often start smoking again soon after quitting, McFall (1978) suggested that smoking relapse studies use a 6- to 12-month follow-up. And in our review of studies on smoking relapse published during the 1980s (Singer & Willett, 1991), we found that this guideline is widely accepted; the modal follow-up period was 1 year, and this period yielded an average censoring rate below 50%. However, Nathan and Skinstad (1987) noted that "3- or 6-month post-treatment follow-ups are likely to be insufficient . . . ; 2 years or more are probably necessary to determine the long-term effects of a treatment program" (p. 333). When studying infrequent events, even 5 years of data collection may be insufficient. In their review of the link between alcoholism and suicide, for example, G. E. Murphy and Wetzel (1990) lamented the fact that many of the available studies "are relatively short: less than 10 years" (p. 387).

Before deciding on the length of data collection, be sure to consider the substantive ramifications of your choice. It is clear that variation across studies in the length of follow-up explains some of the seemingly discrepant conclusions about treatment efficacy that arise in the literature. Length of follow-up has been identified as a major explanatory factor in several literature reviews, including G. E. Murphy and Wetzel's (1990) review of suicidality among alcoholics. And even when it has not been identified as a key explanatory factor, its impact seems certain. In their review of 26 longitudinal studies of teenage alcohol and other drug use, for example, Flay and Petraitis (1991) found that the length

of follow-up varied from a low of 5 months to a high of 19 years. Although they did not investigate the link between length of follow-up and study findings, we suspect that this design feature may explain why some studies successfully predicted subsequent outcomes while others did not.

Because of the effect of design on conclusions, a researcher must always note the length of follow-up. Any relapse rate cited must be linked to a specific time period. What can we conclude, for example, from Seltzer, Seltzer, and Sherwood's (1982) statement that 65% of the adults with mental retardation under study were not reinstitutionalized, given that we do not know the time frame being referenced? How can we know whether this percentage is low or high? How can we compare this rate to those found in other studies? Even well-documented longitudinal studies using sophisticated analytic techniques occasionally omit this important piece of information (Zatz, 1985). The length of data collection is key to understanding the ultimate course of survival.

How Many People Should You Study?

Having specified in broad outline the design of a study, the final step is to determine how many people to include in the sample. Statisticians determine the minimum number of people a researcher should study by conducting a statistical power analysis (Cohen, 1990; Kraemer & Theimann, 1988). This requires specification of the particular hypothesis to be tested, the desired Type I and Type II error rates, and the minimum effect size considered important; for survival analysis, it also requires presaging the anticipated distribution of the hazard function and the proposed length of follow-up.

Biostatisticians have derived many methods for determining sample size for survival analysis, each applicable under different circumstances. Donner (1984) and Lachin (1981) reviewed the literature; Freedman (1982) provided tables for two group comparisons; Makuch and Simon (1982) provided formulas for multiple group comparisons; and Rubinstein, Gail, and Santner (1981), Moussa (1988), and Lachin and Foulkes (1986) provided formulas for complex designs with stratification, covariate information, or allowances for loss of individuals to follow-up. In the presentation that follows, we have computed minimum sample sizes using the computer program of Dupont and Plummer (1990).

No single table or formula can cover all possible design configurations. Here we provide ballpark estimates of sample size, similar to those we have provided elsewhere for more familiar statistical analyses (Light, Singer, & Willett, 1990). Our discussion does not replace consultation with a statistician *before* data collection, or in Kraemer and Pruyn's (1990) words:

> Answers to questions as to what the optimal approach is depend on the specific research question to be addressed and can and do not have simple answers. How to demonstrate adequate power and how to assess power when there are multiple outcomes are questions that must be addressed, perhaps differently, in each research study, and these questions require the participation of experts at addressing such issues. (p. 1169)

Rather, we hope this discussion will provide researchers with a better sense of the factors affecting the power of survival analyses, a general sense of how many people they must study to ensure a reasonable chance of detecting an effect that really exists, and a language for talking with a statistical consultant. The need for improved design is clear. As Kazdin and Bass (1989) noted, too many studies of differences between alternative treatments lack sufficient statistical power to detect the small-to-medium effect sizes likely to occur in practice.

To conduct a power analysis, you must first specify the smallest effect size deemed important for detection. Although biostatisticians have developed several measures of effect size, perhaps the simplest is the ratio of median lifetimes in the two groups, denoted by R. Letting m_1 be the median lifetime in one group and m_2 the median lifetime in the other, $R = m_1/m_2$. When $R = 1.25$, the median lifetime of one group is 25% longer than the median lifetime of the other; when $R = 1.50$, the median lifetime of one group is 50% longer; when $R = 2.00$, the median lifetime of one group is twice as long (100%) as the other group.

How can you specify the minimum detectable effect size in advance of data collection? One way is to use prior research. Consider a two-group experiment that might follow from Stevens and Hollis's smoking relapse study. The median survival time in the control group of this experiment was 4 months ($m_2 = 4$). If the median survival time in a new experimental group is expected to be as high as 8 months ($m_1 = 8$), the new study can be designed to detect an R of 2.00; if the median survival time in the new experimental group is expected to be only 6 months ($m_1 = 6$), the study should be designed to detect an R of 1.50. In the absence of such prior information, Schoenfeld and Richter (1982) suggested that $R = 1.50$ be used because a 50% increase in survival is "clinically important and biologically feasible" (p. 163).

After specifying the minimum detectable effect size, you must specify the length of follow-up. Because the length of follow-up can vary greatly across studies, we need a standardized measure that is applicable to a variety of settings and metrics. We achieve this goal by dividing the length of follow-up by the average anticipated median lifetime in the two groups. More precisely, letting $A = (m_1 + m_2)/2$ be the average median lifetime in the two groups, and T be the total length of follow-up, our standardized measure of follow-up, F, is T/A. If a study follows individuals to only half the average median lifetime, $F = 0.5$; if a study follows individuals to the average median lifetime, $F = 1.0$; if a study follows individuals for twice as long as the average median lifetime, $F = 2.0$. Creation of a standardized measure of the length of follow-up allows us to use the same power tables with studies of widely varying length. We need not worry whether the average median lifetime is 6 min, 6 days, 6 months, or 6 years. If the average median lifetime (A) is 6 (in any of these units), a follow-up (T) of 3 yields an F of 0.5; a follow-up of 6 yields an F of 1.0; a follow-up of 9 yields an F of 1.5; and a follow-up of 12 yields an F of 2.0. The particular time units cancel each other out in the standardization.

Table 22.1 presents the minimum total sample sizes necessary to achieve a power of .80 for a simple two-group comparison at the .05 level (two-tailed). The rows of the table indicate minimum detectable effect sizes (R); the columns indicate the length of follow-up (F); and the cell entries indicate the minimum total sample size used in the analysis (N). Researchers should inflate these sample-size estimates appropriately to adjust for cases lost to follow-up. The calculations were made assuming a flat hazard function—a restrictive assumption, indeed, but the simplest, and the one that researchers generally assume in the absence of more detailed information.

Examine the minimum sample sizes presented in Table 22.1, focusing first on differences in effect size displayed across the rows. Small effects ($R = 1.25$) are difficult to detect. Regardless of the length of follow-up, a study must include many hundreds or well over a thousand individuals to have a reasonable chance of detecting such effects. Medium-sized effects ($R = 1.50$ to $R = 1.75$) can be detected with moderate-sized samples; somewhere between 200 to 400 individuals will generally suffice, depending on the length of follow-up. Large effects ($R = 2.00$) are relatively easy to

TABLE 22.1   Minimum Total Sample Size Needed to Detect Differences in Survival Between Two Groups

Effect Size	Follow-up Period				
	0.5	1.0	1.5	2.0	2.5
1.25	>2162	1260	976	840	766
1.50	654	382	296	254	232
1.75	344	200	156	134	122
2.00	224	130	102	88	80

Note. Assuming a two-tailed test at the 0.05 level, power of 0.80, exponentially distributed survival times, all individuals followed for the same period of time.

detect, even using small samples. If the median lifetime in one group is twice as long as the median lifetime in the other, you have an 80% chance of detecting this difference using only 100 to 200 individuals.

Table 22.1 can also be used for another purpose: to decide on the length of data collection. Reexamine the table, focusing now on the variation in sample sizes across the columns, corresponding to follow-ups of widely differing lengths. The great variation in minimum sample sizes for a given effect size emphasizes the importance of following individuals under study for as long as possible.

Consider, for example, how the minimum sample size needed to detect an R of 1.50 depends on the length of follow-up. If you follow a sample only halfway to the average median lifetime, $F = .50$, you require 654 people to detect the 50% difference in median lifetimes. But if you follow people for longer periods of time, you need fewer people. If you can extend the follow-up to the average median lifetime ($F = 1.00$), you can achieve the same power of .80 with almost half as many individuals ($N = 382$). And if you extend the follow-up further to twice the average median lifetime ($F = 2.00$), the same power can be achieved with only a third as many individuals ($N = 254$).

The message for research design is clear. Much statistical power can be gained by following people for longer periods of time. Researchers would do well to follow people for at least as long as the average median lifetime ($F = 1.00$). By doubling the length of follow-up, you can achieve the same statistical power with approximately one-third fewer individuals. If the length of follow-up is less than the average median lifetime, only studies of many hundreds of individuals will have adequate statistical power.

ANALYZING SURVIVAL DATA

Most researchers begin their analyses with exploratory and descriptive approaches; they move on to fitting statistical models and testing hypotheses only after a full exploration of the data. In the following sections we present an array of strategies for analyzing survival data, beginning with simple descriptive approaches and moving on to statistical model building.

How Can You Describe Survival Data?

There is much to be learned by straightforward eyeball analysis. Inspection of sample survivor and hazard profiles and comparison of these profiles computed separately for substantively interesting subsamples can be very informative.

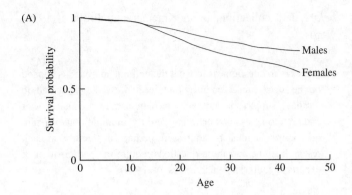

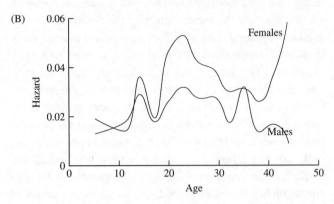

Figure 22.3 Sample survivor (panel A) and hazard (panel B) functions describing risk of first depression onset for 1,303 adults (based on data from Wheaton, Roszell, & Hall, 1996).

Figure 22.3 presents data from Wheaton, Hall, and Roszell (1996), who examined the link between stressful life experiences and the risk of psychiatric disorder. After selecting a random sample of adults, ages 17 to 59, in metropolitan Toronto, Canada, the researchers conducted a structured interview that allowed them to determine whether, and if so at what age (in years), each individual first experienced a depressive episode. Among the 1,393 respondents, 387 (27.8%) experienced a first onset between ages 4 and 39. The figure presents the sample survivor and hazard functions, by gender, describing the age at first depression onset.

These sample survivor and hazard profiles contain a great deal of information. At birth, all individuals are "surviving": Not one has yet experienced a depressive episode, so the survival probabilities for both groups are 1.00. Over time, as individuals experience depressive episodes, the survivor functions drop. Because most adults do not experience a depressive episode at any time in their lives, the functions do not reach 0, ending in this sample at 0.77 for men and 0.62 for women. By subtraction, we conclude that 23% of men and 38% of women *have* experienced a depressive episode at some point before their sixties.

The subsample hazard profiles disentangle these temporal patterns and provide a more sensitive magnifying glass for identifying when men and women are at risk of depression onset. For both groups, the risk of experiencing an initial episode of depression is relatively low in childhood, increases during adolescence, and then peaks in the early twenties. After this point, the risk of initial onset of depression among those individuals who have not yet had a depressive episode is much lower. By the early forties, it declines to preadolescent levels for men, although it rises again for women.

Over and above these temporal patterns, the figure also suggests a sex differential: In general, women are at greater risk than men of experiencing a depressive episode. When we compare hazard profiles for two groups of people, we implicitly treat gender as a predictor of the entire hazard profile. The comparison of profiles illustrates how the risk of onset is related to gender. We could divide the sample in other ways and treat these divisions as predictors of hazard as well.

Exploratory comparisons of sample survivor and hazard profiles provide simple persuasive descriptions of when events occur and how the timing of event occurrence varies across groups. Descriptive statements can then be buttressed by simple statistical tests of between-group differences. Lee (1992) provided a compendium of tests for comparing survivor and hazard profiles among groups, including tests that are the survival-analytic equivalent of the t test and one-way analysis of variance. The most popular are the Wilcoxon and log-rank tests of homogeneity of survivor function across populations, the former test placing more weight on early survival times, the latter on later survival times, when the test statistic is computed.

Graphical displays and multigroup comparisons are limited, however, because they do not help us address the complex questions arising in prevention research. The examination of the effects of continuous predictors on hazard would yield a cumbersome collection of profiles, one per predictor value. Simple bivariate methods are ill suited for exploring the effects of several predictors simultaneously, or for evaluating the influence of interactions among predictors. Borchardt and Garfinkel (1991) encountered these problems in their study of the relationship between adolescents' lengths of stay in a psychiatric hospital and two categorical predictors, diagnostic category (affective, organic, conduct) and number of prescribed medications (none, one, two or more). While the authors elegantly displayed survival profiles for each of these two predictors separately, they did not examine the joint effect of both variables simultaneously or the effects of each after controlling statistically for the other. They did not investigate the possibility of a two-way interaction

between the predictors. Nor did they extend their survival analyses to explore the effects of other predictors, such as funding sources, even though their preliminary exploration suggested that such additional variables were associated with length of stay. To conduct further analysis, researchers require a comprehensive approach to the modeling of event occurrence, a topic to which we now turn.

How Can You Build Statistical Models of Hazard?

Statistical models of hazard express hypothesized population relationships between entire hazard profiles and one or more predictors. To clarify our representation of these models, examine the two sample hazard profiles in the bottom panel of Figure 22.3 and think of sex as a dummy variable, FEMALE, which can take on two values (0 for men, 1 for women). From this perspective, the entire hazard function is the conceptual outcome, and FEMALE is a potential predictor of that outcome.

Ignoring minor differences in shape, now consider how the predictor seems to affect the outcome. When FEMALE $= 1$, the sample hazard function is higher relative to its location when FEMALE $= 0$. Conceptually, then, the predictor FEMALE somehow displaces or shifts one sample hazard profile vertically relative to the other. A population hazard model formalizes this conceptualization by associating this vertical displacement with variation in predictors in much the same way as an ordinary linear regression model associates differences in mean levels of a continuous (noncensored) outcome with variation in predictors.

The difference between a hazard model and a linear regression model, of course, is that the entire hazard profile is no ordinary outcome. The continuous-time hazard profile is a profile of risks bounded by 0. Methodologists postulating a statistical model to represent a bounded outcome as a function of a linear combination of predictors generally transform the outcome so that it becomes unbounded. Transformation prevents derivation of fitted values that fall outside the range of theoretical possibilities—in this case fitted values of hazard less than 0. When time is measured continuously, we build statistical models of the *natural logarithm* of hazard. When time is measured discretely, hazard is a conditional probability bounded by both 0 and 1; we therefore use a *logit* transformation—$\log[p/(1 - p)]$—for the same reason.

The effect of the logarithmic transformation on hazard is illustrated in Figure 22.4, which presents sample log-hazard functions corresponding to the plots in the bottom panel of Figure 22.3. The log transformation has its largest effect on rates near 0, expanding the distance between values at this extreme. Nevertheless, in the transformed world of log

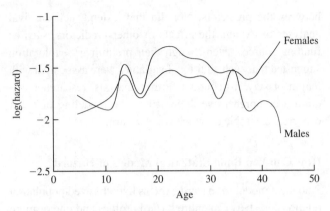

Figure 22.4   Sample log-hazard functions for men and women.

hazard, we recognize that the predictor FEMALE works as it did before. When FEMALE = 1, the log-hazard function is generally higher relative to its location when FEMALE = 0, indicating that among individuals who have yet to experience a depressive episode, women are at greater risk of doing so than are men. Still ignoring the minor differences in the shapes of the profiles, then, the predictor FEMALE essentially displaces the log-hazard profiles vertically relative to each other.

Inspection of the sample relationship between the predictor FEMALE and the entire log-hazard profile in Figure 22.4 leads to a reasonable specification for a population model of the hazard profile as a function of predictors. Letting $h(t)$ represent the entire population hazard profile, a statistical model that captures this vertical displacement relates the log transformation of $h(t)$ to the predictor FEMALE as follows:

$$\log h(t) = \beta_0(t) + \beta_1 \text{ FEMALE} \qquad (22.1)$$

The model parameter $\beta_0(t)$ is known as the *baseline log-hazard profile*. It represents the value of the outcome (the entire log-hazard function) in the population when the predictor (FEMALE) is 0 (i.e., because of the way we have coded FEMALE, it specifies the profile for men). We write the baseline as $\beta_0(t)$, a function of time, and not as β_0, a single term unrelated to time (as in regression analysis), because the outcome, $\log h(t)$, is a temporal profile. The model specifies that differences in the value of FEMALE "shift" the baseline log-hazard profile up or down. The slope parameter, β_1, captures the magnitude of this shift; it represents the vertical shift in log-hazard attributable to a one-unit difference in the predictor. Because the predictor in this example (FEMALE) is a dichotomy, β_1 captures the differential risk of onset between men and women. If the model were fit to these data, the obtained estimate of β_1 would be positive because women are generally at greater risk of first depression onset.

Hazard models closely resemble familiar regression models. Several predictors can be incorporated by including additional variables expressed as linear (or nonlinear) functions of additional unknown slope parameters on the right-hand side of the equation. This model expansion allows examination of one predictor's effect while controlling statistically for others'. Inclusion of cross-product terms enables examination of statistical interactions between predictors. It does not seem excessive to argue that hazard models provide the powerful, flexible, and sensitive approach to analyzing event occurrence that many psychologists should be using. The goodness of fit of a hypothesized population model can be evaluated with data, allowing inferences about population relationships between hazard and predictors. As we show later, reconstructed survivor and hazard functions and estimated median lifetimes can depict the effects of predictors, providing answers to research questions in the original metric of interest—time.

Are the Hazard Profiles Proportional or Nonproportional?

Simple hazard models like that in Equation 22.1 implicitly assume that all the log-hazard profiles corresponding to successive values of a predictor differ only by their relative elevation (described here by β_1). Under such models, but in the antilogged world of raw hazard, all the hazard profiles are simply magnifications or diminutions of each other; that is, they are proportional. Under this *proportionality assumption,* which in continuous-time survival analysis is called the *proportional-hazards assumption,* the entire family of log-hazard profiles represented by all possible values of the predictors share a common shape and are mutually parallel. Singer and Willett (1991, 1993) drew an analogy between this assumption and the assumption of homogeneity of regression slopes in the analysis of covariance.

Proportional-hazards models are the most popular survival analysis approaches used today in part because all major statistical packages now provide programs for estimating their parameters using methods initially developed by Cox (1972). This ingenious strategy allows estimation of parameters such as β_1 without the specification or estimation of the shape of the baseline hazard function, $\beta_0(t)$. For this reason, analogous to traditional nonparametric methods (which make no distributional assumptions), Cox regression is called *semiparametric.*

However, the tremendous boon of the semiparametric method—its ability to evaluate the effects of predictors without estimating the shape of baseline hazard profile—is also its principal disadvantage. The method is so general that it works for an unspecified baseline hazard profile of any shape. Without needing to explore the baseline hazard, investigators can examine effects of predictors without exploring absolute levels of risk. Because the baseline hazard function can be easily ignored, researchers may fail to recognize substantively and statistically important information contained only in the baseline hazard function.

What kinds of information can be found? The baseline hazard function and, under the proportionality assumption, its magnified and diminished cousins describe the pattern and magnitude of risk over time; they indicate *when* the target event will occur and *how likely* that occurrence is (as in Figure 22.2). The hazard profiles in Figure 22.3, for example, show that women are still at greater risk of first depression onset even in their forties. All the predictor does is magnify or diminish this basic pattern of risk.

The ease with which the hazard function's shape can be ignored under the semiparametric method has a further ill consequence: It promotes the unthinking and dubious acceptance of the proportional-hazards assumption. The ease with which a researcher can fit a proportional-hazards model makes it all too easy to examine effects of predictors without examining the tenability of the underlying proportional-hazards assumption. Notice, for example, that the sample log-hazard profiles in Figure 22.4 are neither identical in shape nor parallel, suggesting that the proportional-hazards assumption might not be tenable.

We believe that the tenability of the proportional hazards assumption must be viewed with some circumspection because those few researchers who have examined its tenability have found clear evidence of its violation. In our own research on age at entry into child care (Singer, Fuller, et al., 1998), teacher turnover (Murnane, Singer, Willett, Kemple, & Olsen, 1991), and physician turnover (Singer, Davidson, Graham, & Davidson, 1998), we have found that violations of the proportionality assumption are the rule rather than the exception.

We raise this issue because violation of the proportional hazards assumption is far more than a methodological nuisance. The magnitude and direction of the effects of predictors may be estimated incorrectly if the hypothesized statistical model inappropriately constrains the log-hazard profiles to be parallel with identical shapes. Ignoring such underlying failures can lead to incorrect substantive conclusions. In an early informative paper, Trussel and Hammerslough (1983) documented differences in interpretation that arise when the proportional-hazards assumption is injudiciously assumed to be tenable in a study of child mortality (compare their Tables 3 and 4, particularly the effects of gender, birth order, and age of mother at birth). So uncertain is the veracity of the proportional-hazards assumption

that we always begin our own data analyses with the entirely opposite view. Along with unicorns and normal distributions (Micceri, 1989), we regard the proportional-hazards assumption as mythical in any set of data until proven otherwise. Before adopting a proportional-hazards model, researchers should at least subdivide their sample by substantively important values of critical predictors and inspect the shapes of the sample hazard profiles within these subgroups. Arjas (1988), Grambsch and Therneau (2000), Hosmer and Lemeshow (1999), and Willett and Singer (1993) provided methods for exploring the tenability of the proportionality assumption. Finally, as we discuss next, researchers can easily adopt a broader analytic approach—one that tests the proportional-hazards assumption and fits nonproportional hazard models if they are required.

What Types of Predictors Can Be Included in Hazard Models?

One important advantage of the hazard modeling framework is that it permits the simultaneous study of both *time-invariant* and *time-varying* predictors. As befits their label, time-invariant predictors describe immutable characteristics of individuals; the values of time-varying predictors, in contrast, may fluctuate over time. When investigating the monthly risk of initiating marijuana use in late adolescence, for example, Yamaguchi and Kandel (1984) examined predictors of both types. In the study, 1,325 adolescents were interviewed once in high school and reinterviewed 9 years later at ages 24 to 25. In the follow-up interview, respondents retrospectively reconstructed monthly charts of their drug and life histories. The researchers examined the effects of truly time-invariant predictors such as *race* whose values are immutable over time, but other variables such as *friends' use of marijuana, involvement in delinquent activities,* and *belief that marijuana use is not harmful* were also treated as time-invariant predictors of the risk of initiation of marijuana use because they were measured on a single occasion during the initial high school interview. The researchers also examined the effects of time-varying predictors such as *current alcohol use* and *current cigarette use* whose monthly values were obtained during life-history reconstruction at follow-up. Using hazard models, the researchers were able to present convincing evidence that the "current use of alcohol and cigarettes has strong effects on the initiation of marijuana use among men and women" and "controlling for selected antecedent behavioral, attitudinal, and environmental factors measured in adolescence, . . . friends' use of marijuana has the strongest positive influence on initiation of marijuana" (p. 675). It is interesting to note that when the initiation of prescribed psychoactive drug use was examined later in the paper, Yamaguchi and Kandel found that "multiple factors are involved in the progression to prescribed drugs, with adolescent depressive symptomatology and use of other illicit drugs important for both sexes, and maternal use of psychoactive drugs, dropping out of school, and prior use of marijuana of additional importance for women" (p. 673). These same authors have also used hazard modeling to study links between time-varying drug consumption and the risk of premarital pregnancy (Yamaguchi & Kandel, 1985) and the risk of job turnover (Kandel & Yamaguchi, 1987).

The hazard model in Equation 22.1 includes a single time-invariant predictor, FEMALE. The value of this predictor obviously remains constant over time. The variable β_1 quantifies the time-invariant effect of this time-invariant predictor on the risk of initial depression onset. Hazard models like that in Equation 22.1 can be easily extended to include time-varying predictors. Such extensions can be particularly helpful in psychology, where the values of important predictors vary naturally over time.

Hazard models with time-varying predictors closely resemble the model in Equation 22.1. In Yamaguchi and Kandel's study of the risk of marijuana initiation, for example, one possible population hazard model might include (a) FEMALE and (b) ALCOHOL, a time-varying predictor whose monthly values assess the number of drinks consumed per month. Such a model might be

$$\log h(t) = \beta_0(t) + \beta_1 \text{FEMALE} + \beta_2 \, \text{ALCOHOL}(t)$$
$$(22.2)$$

The parenthetical t in the predictor ALCOHOL(t) indicates that the values of this predictor may vary over time. Unit differences in ALCOHOL correspond to shifts in the log-hazard profile of β_2. Although the values of the predictor ALCOHOL may differ over time, each one-unit difference anywhere produces the same shift of β_2 in the appropriate part of the log-hazard profile. So although the model includes a time-varying predictor, the per-unit effect of that predictor on log hazard is constant over time.

Another way to understand the effects of time-varying predictors is to regard the outcome in Equation 22.2—the log-hazard profile—conceptually as a temporally sequenced list (a vector) of marijuana initiation risks. The predictors also can be viewed as an ordered list of values that for each person describe the values of FEMALE and ALCOHOL over time. Each element in the hazard list corresponds to an element in each predictor's list. For a time-invariant predictor, such as FEMALE, all elements in each person's predictor list are identical: 1 for each girl, 0 for each boy. In contrast, for a time-varying predictor such as ALCOHOL, the values in the predictor list may differ from month to month. If an individual does not use alcohol initially, the early elements in the ALCOHOL vector are 0; when alcohol use begins, the values change. Each person has his or her own alcohol use pattern; the number of patterns across individuals is limited only by the number of possible values and occasions of measurement. The hazard model simply relates the values in one list (the hazard vector) to the values in the other (the predictor vector), regardless of whether the elements in the latter list are identical to each other.

Time itself is the fundamental time-varying predictor. Conceptually, at least, one might argue that it, too, should be included as a time-varying predictor in Equation 22.2, mapping intrinsic changes in the risk of marijuana initiation over time. Although intuitively appealing, this approach produces complete redundancy in the model because this time-varying effect is already captured by the baseline log-hazard function, $\beta_0(t)$, which describes the chronological pattern of baseline risk—the differences in log hazard attributable solely to time. Estimation of the baseline hazard function is tantamount to estimation of the main effect of time. This analogy reinforces the need to examine the shape of the baseline hazard, for it provides information about the effects of the fundamental time-varying predictor, time itself.

Can Predictors in Hazard Models Interact With Time?

Not only can predictors themselves be time-invariant or time-varying, but their effect on hazard can also be constant or vary over time. By including a main effect of the predictor FEMALE in Equation 22.2, we assume that the vertical displacement associated with gender is the same at age 16 and age 24 (and equal to β_1). But the assumption of temporally immutable effects may not hold in reality: The effects of some predictors will vary over time. The gender differential might decline as time passes and individuals mature. If so, the distance between hazard profiles associated with different values of the predictor FEMALE would narrow over time.

When the effect of one predictor on an outcome differs by levels of another predictor, statisticians say that the two predictors *interact*. If the effect of a predictor like FEMALE on an outcome like the risk of marijuana initiation differs across time, we say that the predictor FEMALE *interacts with time*. Predictors that interact with time have important substantive interpretations, allowing researchers to build complex models of the relationship between predictors and risk. If a predictor affects primarily early risks, the hazard profiles will be widely separated in the beginning of time and converge as time passes. If a predictor affects primarily late hazards, it will have little effect at the beginning of time but will widen the distance between hazard functions on each subsequent occasion.

One's understanding of event occurrence can be vastly improved by exploring whether the effects of predictors remain constant or vary over time. As Verhulst and Koot (1991) noted, "what may be a risk factor at one developmental phase may not be at another" (p. 363). Some recent studies that look for such interactions are indeed finding their presence. In their study of the age at first suicide ideation, for instance, Bolger et al. (1989) detected interactions between two key predictors and time. Dividing time into two broad periods—adolescence and preadolescence—they found that the effects of *respondent race* and *parental absence in childhood* both differed across these periods. With regard to race, during preadolescence Caucasian children were less likely to consider suicide than were non-Caucasian children, but during adolescence they were more likely to do so; with regard to parental absence, the authors found that during preadolescence children who experienced a parental absence were more likely to consider suicide than were those who did not experience such absence, but during adolescence parental absence had little impact on the risk of suicidal thought. In addition, in a reanalysis of the National Institutes of Mental Health Collaborative Study of Maintenance Treatment of Recurrent Affective Disorders, Greenhouse et al. (1991) found that the efficacy of selected antidepressants in preventing recurrence was pronounced only during the first few weeks after treatment initiation. By including interactions between predictors and time, researchers can better identify the predictors of risk over time.

If a predictor interacts with time, the proportionality assumption is violated, and models such as the proportional hazards model introduced in Equations 22.1 and 22.2 do not represent reality. The proportionality assumption is easily tested by adding an interaction with time to the hazard model and assessing the effect of this new predictor. If the assumption holds, the interaction term will have no effect and can be removed. If the interaction term proves to be an important predictor of the hazard profile, then a violation of the proportionality assumption has been detected, and the interaction with time must remain in the model to ensure the appropriate estimation of predictor effects. We recommend that researchers routinely examine the effects of such interactions in their hazard models, just as they would routinely examine interactions among other predictors in traditional linear models.

What Is Discrete-Time Survival Analysis?

The hazard models just posited, which assume that time can take on any nonnegative value, represent the hazard profile as a *continuous* function of time (as reflected, e.g., in the parenthetical inclusion of the symbol t in the expression for the baseline hazard function, $\beta_0(t)$). When data are collected in *discrete* time, however, either because the events only occur, or are only measured, at specific times—perhaps every week, month, academic semester, or year—researchers should consider a different class of survival methods known as *discrete-time survival analysis*. The method is easy to apply, facilitates the estimation of the baseline hazard function, encourages the testing of the proportionality assumption, and enables researchers to fit hazard models using procedures available in most statistical computer packages. For all these reasons, we encourage its wider application to studying questions about time.

We describe the discrete-time survival analysis approach in detail in two papers (Singer & Willett, 1993; Willett & Singer, 1993) and in a forthcoming book (Singer & Willett, in press); here, we simply give an overview. A researcher conducts a discrete-time survival analysis by altering the data structure, transforming the standard one-person, one-record data set (the *person data set*) into a one-person, multiple-period data set (the *person-period data set*). In the new person-period data set, a dichotomous variable is created to summarize the pattern of event occurrence in each discrete time period for every person in the sample. If relapse into cocaine use were being studied, for instance, in each discrete time interval this variable (RELAPSE) would be coded 0 if no relapse occurred and 1 if it did occur. So, for instance, an ex-addict who relapsed in the sixth month after treatment would have six lines of data in the new person-period data set, and in each line RELAPSE would take on a value specific to that interval—the first five being 0, the last being 1. The researcher also creates a set of time indicators that index and distinguish the discrete time intervals themselves.

Under the discrete-time approach, the relationship between the dichotomous event summary (RELAPSE) and predictors (including the time indicators) can be fit using a modification of standard logistic regression programs. Interactions among predictors, and between predictors and the time indicators, are easily included by forming cross products in the person-period data set and using them as predictors. Adding these interactions to main-effects models facilitates easy testing of the proportional-hazards assumption, and if the assumption is violated, retention of the interactions in the fitted model ensures the appropriate estimation of the effects.

The ability to use standard logistic regression software to fit discrete-time hazard models brings this methodology within easy grasp of all empirical researchers. The logistic regression parameter estimates, standard errors, and goodness-of-fit statistics are exactly those required for testing hypotheses about the effect of predictors on the discrete-time hazard profile (Singer & Willett, 1993). Allison (1982) commented that these estimates are "consistent, asymptotically efficient, and asymptotically normally distributed" and that, despite the apparent inflation of sample size on creation of the person-period data set, the estimated standard errors are consistent estimators of the true standard errors (p. 82).

Because of the frequency with which psychologists use discrete-time data collection strategies, we encourage readers to learn more about discrete-time survival methods. In the Yamaguchi and Kandel (1984) study of drug use described earlier, for example, participants reconstructed their life histories on a month-by-month basis. Many other researchers follow subjects at discrete points in time. Somers (1996) assessed employee turnover in 1-month intervals; Singer, Fuller, et al. (1998) assessed child care entry in 3-month intervals; and Capaldi et al. (1996) assessed age at first intercourse in annual intervals (grade in school).

How Can Fitted Models Be Interpreted?

Fitting statistical models is of little use unless the researcher can interpret the resultant information clearly and persuasively. Interpretation includes at least three components: identification of statistically significant effects, computation of numerical summaries of effect size, and graphical display of the magnitude and direction of the effects. In traditional analysis of variance, for example, a researcher might first determine whether the difference in average outcome between two groups is statistically significant; if it is, he or she might then express one group's advantage in standard deviation units and provide data plots comparing the distribution of the outcome across groups.

The interpretation of survival analysis must also include the same three components. But because hazard models may be difficult to conceptualize (describing, as they do, variation in entire hazard profiles), we believe that graphical techniques provide a better vehicle for reporting findings. Graphics can help communicate complex and unfamiliar ideas about whether an event occurs, and, if so, when. Yet even the most effective graphical displays must be supported by documentation of parameter estimates and associated standard errors. So we begin our discussion of interpretation with the computer output commonly generated by statistical packages.

Computer output documenting the results of fitting hazard models closely resembles output documenting the results of other statistical techniques. Most programs output estimates of the slope parameters, the standard errors of these estimates, the ratio of each parameter estimate to its standard error (a t statistic), and a p value based on the t statistic for testing the null hypothesis that the corresponding parameter is zero in the population (given that the other predictors are in the model). Some programs output a chi-square statistic in lieu of a t statistic; the accompanying p value assesses the improvement in fit resulting from adding the predictor to a reduced model containing all the other predictors.

Researchers frequently provide tables of some, or all, of these summary statistics in the accounts of their analyses (see, e.g., Ilardi, Craighead, & Evans, 1997, Tables 3 and 4). When you do so, however, do not ignore the sign and magnitude of the slope estimate by focusing on the associated p values. Although p values can help identify critical predictors, they tell us nothing about the direction and relative magnitude of effects.

Because hazard models represent relationships between the entire hazard profile and predictors, specifying an understandable effect size is not easy. One useful approach is to interpret the parameter estimate associated with each predictor in a way that is similar to interpreting a regression coefficient. In continuous-time survival analysis the parameter estimate represents a difference in elevation of the log-hazard profile corresponding to predictor values one unit apart. The parameter estimate's sign indicates the direction of the movement, telling us whether positive differences in the value of the predictor correspond to positive or negative differences in the risk of event occurrence. We find it helpful to imagine the profile on a log-hazard plot moving up (or down, if the estimate is negative) for a one-unit difference in the predictor. Predictors with larger parameter estimates produce larger elevation differences per unit difference in the predictor. (In discrete-time survival analysis, the conceptualization is identical, but the interpreter of the findings is dealing with differences in the elevation of the logit, rather than log, hazard profile.)

Even after considerable experience with hazard models, however, ready visualizations in the transformed world of log hazard may remain tortured. A mathematically complex but intuitively simple approach involves the transformation of the outcome back into the more familiar metric of risk, antilogging parameter estimates as necessary. Of course, a researcher must use different transformations and interpretations depending on whether continuous- or discrete-time models have been fitted.

We illustrate these ideas with the continuous-time hazard model in Equation 22.1. Antilogging both sides, we have

$$h(t) = e^{\beta_0(t)} e^{\beta_1 \text{FEMALE}}.$$

Because FEMALE = 1 for women and 0 for men, the hazard functions corresponding to these two groups are

$$Men: \quad h(t) = e^{\beta_0(t)}$$
$$Women: \quad h(t) = e^{\beta_0(t)} e^{\beta_1}.$$

Notice that the risk profile for women is just the risk profile for men multiplied by e^{β_1}. This multiplicative rule applies to both categorical and continuous predictors. Thus, in continuous-time hazard models, antilogged parameter estimates yield numerical multipliers of risk per unit difference in the predictor. If the antilogged parameter estimate is greater than 1, risk is higher in the reference group; if it is less than 1, risk is lower. (Note that this is not an odds ratio; it is a risk ratio.)

This transformation strategy enabled Burton, Johnson, Ritter, and Clayton (1996) to document the strong effect of early marijuana use on the risk of initiating cocaine use. After controlling statistically for selected family and demographic covariates, the authors obtained a parameter estimate of 2.354 for a predictor indicating whether the respondent had used marijuana by age 17 ($p < .0001$). Antilogging this estimate ($e^{2.354} = 10.5$), we find that the risk of initiating cocaine is 10.5 times for those whose first use of marijuana occurred at age 17 or younger, relative to those who had never used marijuana.

Another way to interpret hazard-model parameter estimates is in terms of *percentage difference in risk*. Doubling the baseline risk (multiplying by a factor of 2) is equal to a 100% increase in risk; halving the baseline risk (multiplying by a factor of .5) is equal to a 50% decrease. So in the cocaine initiation study of Burton et al. (1996), multiplying the baseline hazard by 10.5 corresponds to a 950% (!) increase in the risk of initiation for those who use marijuana by age 17. The general rule is simple: The percentage difference in risk per unit difference in the predictor is $100(e^\beta - 1)$. Some researchers automatically include these estimates of e^β (or $100(e^\beta - 1)$) in tables reporting parameter estimates, standard errors, t statistics, and p values.

Similar, but modified, interpretations can be made after fitting discrete-time hazard models. Since discrete-time hazard is the conditional probability that an event will occur in a particular time interval given that it has not yet occurred before the interval, the discrete-time hazard model, which uses logit hazard as the outcome, expresses the relationship between predictors and the log odds of event occurrence. Estimates of e^β or $100(e^\beta - 1)$ are therefore multipliers of, or percentage increases or decreases in, the odds of an event occurring (see, e.g., Singer, Fuller, et al., 1998).

As these illustrations document, numeric and algebraic strategies are not the last word in the clear communication of the findings of survival analysis. Apart from being arithmetically convoluted, they have at least two other drawbacks. First, they ignore the shape of the baseline hazard function—they indicate only the extent to which one risk profile is a magnification or diminution of another. As argued earlier, the shape of the hazard profile—the temporal placement of its peaks and valleys—tells us much about the survival process under investigation. Second, algebraic interpretations are useful only if the proportionality assumption is met. If the effect of predictors differs over time, risk profiles will be no longer parallel in log or logit space, so it makes little sense to talk about one profile being rescaled to generate the other. If the shapes of the risk profiles differ dramatically, algebraic interpretations may not only oversimplify findings, but may even misrepresent them completely.

Presenting fitted hazard plots, fitted survival plots, and estimated median lifetimes resolves these problems. Most computer programs provide procedures for recovering fitted profiles from parameter estimates. By appropriately substituting back into the hazard model, a researcher can generate fitted hazard profiles at substantively interesting values of the predictors for the range of time values spanning the period of data collection. The use of fitted hazard profiles is clear, comprehensive, and intuitively meaningful. Fitted profiles demonstrate the effect of predictors on risk and pinpoint whether these effects rise, fall, or remain constant with the passage of time. By presenting fitted hazard functions, we need not struggle to describe effects using abstract scaling factors and percentage increases that ignore important interactions with time.

We illustrate the advantages of this graphical approach in Figure 22.5 using data from Hall et al. (1991), who studied the risk of relapse to cocaine use among 104 former users who participated in a treatment program. Among the many predictors Hall and her colleagues studied, there was a strong and statistically significant effect of the route of administration prior to entry into treatment (ROUTE), here divided into two groups: those who used cocaine intranasally and all others. Figure 22.5 presents fitted hazard and survivor functions based on a discrete-time hazard model that included this single predictor. Because we have fit a discrete-time hazard model, we join the fitted values of the survivor function and hazard function using line segments, rather than a smooth curve.

Comparison of the two fitted hazard functions in Figure 22.5 demonstrates the large differential in risk of relapse associated with route of administration. In every week after treatment, intranasal users are far less likely to relapse than are other users. These fitted functions have the same basic

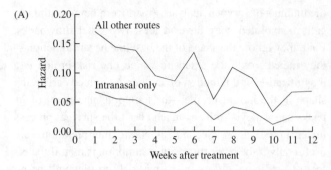

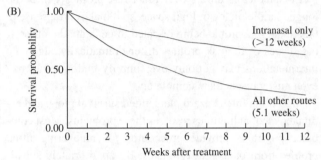

Figure 22.5 Fitted hazard functions (top panel) and survivor functions (bottom panel) describing the risks of relapse for 104 former cocaine abusers following treatment, by route of cocaine administration prior to treatment (intranasal versus all others; based on data reported by Hall et al., 1991).

shape, and one appears to be a magnification of the other. Strictly speaking, however, this apparent magnification of one hazard profile to give the other is only approximate in the discrete-time hazard model and only holds when hazard is small (see Willett & Singer, 1993). Were we to replot these hazard functions on a logit hazard scale, they would have a constant vertical separation. The functions have been constrained to appear this way by the proportionality assumption, which we tested and found to be met.

Fitted survivor functions and estimated median lifetimes can be reconstructed from fitted hazard profiles in order to illustrate the magnitude and direction of important effects. We believe, however, that fitted hazard profiles are generally more informative because they identify the specific times when the events of interest are most likely to occur. It is usually more difficult to discern differences between fitted survivor profiles than between fitted hazard profiles because the survivor function is smoothed by the cumulation of risk over time. The fitted survivor plots in the bottom panel of Figure 22.5 show the cumulative effects of the large weekly differentials in risk. Unlike the fitted hazard functions that emphasize large and consistent differences in risk, the fitted survivor functions condense the effects of these weekly risk differentials together to reveal a substantial difference between the groups. Focusing on the last fitted survival probability, for example, we estimate that 12 weeks after treatment ended, 63% of the intranasal users remained abstinent as compared with 28% of other users.

A third perspective on the divergent relapse patterns of these two groups comes from comparison of the estimated median lifetimes displayed in the bottom panel of Figure 22.5: more than 12 weeks for intranasal users versus 5.1 weeks for all other users. Even though censoring prevents us from estimating a median lifetime precisely for intranasal users, the large difference between these average relapse times powerfully communicates the analytic results.

When selecting predictor values for constructing fitted plots like these, consider your original questions and analytic findings. Questions to ask include: Which predictors did I emphasize in my research questions? and Which predictors were significantly associated with hazard? Use predictors that are substantively and statistically important when generating the fitted profiles; lesser variables can be included as controls by equating their value to their sample averages.

IS SURVIVAL ANALYSIS REALLY NECESSARY?

The methods of survival analysis provide a powerful and flexible set of tools for studying many questions arising in psychological research. Although increasing numbers of researchers are using the methods, many others studying onset, duration, recovery, recidivism, relapse, and recurrence have yet to exploit this new analytic tool.

We believe that one reason why survival methods have not yet been used widely when studying questions about event occurrence is that many researchers still wonder whether the methods are really necessary. Although this view is rarely expressed explicitly, reading between the lines suggests that many researchers believe that traditional analytic approaches will usually suffice.

We agree that some skepticism is healthy. Why bother with complex methods if simpler methods will do? But the problem when studying event occurrence is that simpler methods will not always suffice. To illustrate this point, we conclude by describing five ways in which traditional methods can obscure important information about event occurrence, information that is sensitively and assuredly revealed by survival analysis methods.

First, answers obtained by researchers using traditional methods are inextricably linked to the particular time frame chosen for data collection and analysis, yet these time frames are rarely substantively motivated. Researchers comparing 6-month, 1-year, or 5-year relapse rates for individuals participating in different treatment programs, for example, are simply describing *cumulative* differences in behavior until these times. All other variation over time in the risk of relapse is lost. The literature is filled with examples of disparate risk profiles that lead to comparable relapse rates at specific points in time (e.g., Figure 1 of Cooney, Kadden, Litt, & Getter, 1991; Table 2 of Harackiewicz, Sansone, Blair, Epstein, & Manderlink, 1987). Just because two groups of subjects have identical relapse rates at one point in time does not mean that they followed similar trajectories to get there; most of those in one group might have relapsed in the first month, whereas those in the other might have been equally likely to relapse at all points in time. The 6-month, 1-year, and 2-year cut points used in the past are convenient, but not purposeful. By documenting variation in risk over time and by discovering what predicts variation in risk, we can better understand why people relapse. Traditional methods disregard this information; with survival methods, variation in risk becomes the primary analytic focus.

Disregard for variation in risk over time leads to a second problem with traditional methods: Seemingly contradictory conclusions can result from nothing more than variations in the particular time frames studied. Had Stevens and Hollis (1989) computed only 1-month and 12-month relapse rates when evaluating the efficacy of their individually tailored skills-training technique for preventing relapse to smoking, for example, they would have reached opposite conclusions: The 1-month rates would have shown that subjects in the skills group were *more* likely to relapse (in comparison to those in a discussion-oriented group), whereas the 1-year rates would have shown that they were *less* likely. By thoughtfully presenting sample survivor functions, they showed that the effectiveness of the skills-training approach revealed itself only after several months. Researchers using traditional methods must constantly remind themselves that conclusions can change as the time frame changes. While such caveats usually appear in the "Methods" section of an article, they often disappear by the "Discussion" section. In survival analysis, the time frame itself is integral to the answer; it highlights, rather than obscures, variation over time.

Third, traditional analytic methods offer no systematic mechanism for incorporating censored observations in the analyses. If all the censored observations occur at the same point in time, traditional data analysis can collapse the sampled individuals into two groups: those who experienced the event before the censoring point and those who did not. In their longitudinal study of unaided smoking cessation, for example, Marlatt et al. (1988) compared ex-smokers who relapsed and those who did not at each of four points in time: 1 month, 4 months, 1 year, and 2 years. But if the first days and weeks following cessation are the hardest, individuals who relapse soon after cessation may differ systematically from those who relapse subsequently. Dichotomization

conceals such differences; survival methods, which focus on the risk of event occurrence over time, bring such differences to light.

If censoring does not occur at the same time point for every individual under study (as when researchers follow cohorts of patients admitted over time until a single fixed point in time), traditional methods create a fourth problem: If censoring times vary across people, the risk periods vary as well. People followed for longer periods of time have more opportunities to experience the target event than do those followed for shorter periods of time. This means that observed differences in rates of event occurrence might be attributable to nothing more than research design. In Goldstein, Black, Nasrallah, and Winokur's (1991) study of suicidality among 1,906 Iowans with affective disorders, the follow-up period ranged from 2 to 13 years. As they note, "The highly variable period of follow-up is also a potential limitation, because those patients followed up for the shortest periods may not have been given the opportunity for their suicidal outcome to emerge" (p. 421). Had the researchers used survival methods instead of logistic regression, they would have been better able to address this concern because each person who did not commit suicide would simply have been censored at follow-up.

Fifth, traditional analytic methods offer few mechanisms for including predictors whose values vary over time or for permitting the effects of predictors to fluctuate over time. To overcome this limitation, researchers studying the effects of time-varying variables tend to use predictor values corresponding to a single point in time, the average of predictor values over time, or the rate of change in predictor values over time. This is not necessary in survival analysis. The analytic effort is identical whether including predictors that are static over time or predictors that change over time; so, too, it is easy to determine whether the *effects* of predictors are constant over time or whether they differ over time. There is no need to create a single-number summary of the temporal behavior of a changing predictor. Traditional methods force researchers into building static models of dynamic processes; survival methods allow researchers to model dynamic processes dynamically.

We encourage psychologists to investigate the design and analytic possibilities offered by survival methods. When these methods were in their infancy and statistical software was either not available or not user-friendly, researchers reasonably adopted other approaches. But experience in medicine and elsewhere in the social sciences shows that these methods, originally developed to model human lifetimes, lend themselves naturally to the study of other phenomena as well.

Researchers rarely ask questions that they do not have the analytic methods to answer. We suspect that many researchers interested in the timing of events have modified their questions because they did not know how to build appropriate statistical models. We hope that our presentation of survival analysis will help researchers reframe these modified questions and provide them with strategies for answering those questions as simply and as directly as possible.

WHERE TO GO TO LEARN MORE ABOUT SURVIVAL ANALYSIS

In the body of this chapter, we have purposefully avoided the discussion of technical statistical issues that arise in survival analysis; indeed, we have gone to great pains to ensure that the text is relatively free of technicality. Our goal has been to make a strong case for the use of survival methods in psychological research. For readers considering actually using survival methods, this section provides references to written materials that they might want to consult before embarking on a study.

Readers interested in acquiring a more sophisticated background in these methods can choose among a wide range of published material, both in books and in scholarly journals. Allison's (1984) introductory monograph and his more recent guidebook for conducting survival analysis using the SAS statistical package (Allison, 1995) provide excellent starting points for readers familiar with regression. These are well-documented, accessible, and largely nontechnical introductions to a broad range of survival methods. Allison touches on most of the important issues facing the user of survival analysis, including discrete- versus continuous-time methods, the proportional hazards model and partial likelihood estimation ("Cox regression"), and the analysis of competing risks and repeated events.

Readers wishing to supplement these introductions with greater technical detail should consult one of the several standard texts. The two major classics are Kalbfleisch and Prentice (1980) and Cox and Oakes (1984). In recent years, different teams of biostatisticians have written several more practically oriented books, including Hosmer and Lemeshow (1999), Klein and Moeschberger (1997), and Therneau and Grambsch (2000). We, too, are in the process of writing a book on the analysis of longitudinal data that discusses both survival methods and individual growth modeling (Singer & Willett, in press).

Researchers collecting data in discrete time rather than continuous time should learn more about discrete-time survival analysis. In addition, because discrete-time hazard models are easy to apply, facilitate the recapturing of the baseline hazard and survivor functions, can be estimated with standard logistic regression software, and allow the testing and, if necessary, the relaxation of the proportionality assumption, even researchers with continuous-time data might also want to explore this approach more fully. In a pair of papers, we provide an overview of discrete-time methods written for empirical researchers. Willett and Singer (1993) is the place to start for those seeking a data analytic perspective; Singer and Willett (1993) offers a more mathematical presentation.

REFERENCES

Adler, I., & Kandel, D. B. (1983). Adolescence in France and Israel: Application of survival analysis to cross-sectional data. *Social Forces, 62,* 375–397.

Allison, P. D. (1982). Discrete-time methods for the analysis of event histories. In S. Leinhardt (Ed.), *Sociological methodology* (pp. 61–98). San Francisco, CA: Jossey-Bass.

Allison, P. D. (1984). *Event history analysis: Regression for longitudinal event data.* Sage University Paper Series on Quantitative Applications in the Social Sciences No. 07-046. Beverly Hills, CA: Sage.

Allison, P. D. (1995). *Survival analysis using the SAS system: A practical guide.* Cary, NC: SAS Institute.

Andrade, L., Eaton, W. W., & Chilcoat, H. D. (1996). Lifetime comorbidity of panic attacks and major depression in a population-based study: Age of onset. *Psychological Medicine, 26,* 991–996.

Arjas, E. (1988). A graphical methods for assessing goodness of fit in Cox's proportional hazards model. *Journal of the American Statistical Association, 83,* 204–212.

Baer, J. S., & Lichtenstein, E. (1988). Classification and prediction of smoking relapse episodes: An exploration of individual differences. *Journal of Consulting and Clinical Psychology, 56,* 104–110.

Biglan, A., Hood, D., Brozovsky, P., Ochs, L., Ary, D., & Black, C. (1991). Subject attrition in prevention research. In W. Bukoski & K. Leukefeld (Eds.), *Drug abuse prevention intervention research: Methodological issues* (pp. 213–234). National Institute on Drug Abuse Research Monograph Series No. 107.

Blossfeld, H. P., Hamerle, A., & Mayer, K. U. (1989). *Event history analysis: Statistical theory and application in the social sciences.* Hillsdale, NJ: Erlbaum.

Bolger, N., Downey, G., Walker, E., & Steininger, P. (1989). The onset of suicide ideation in childhood and adolescence. *Journal of Youth and Adolescence, 18,* 175–189.

Borchardt, C. M., & Garfinkel, B. D. (1991). Predictors of length of stay of psychiatric adolescent inpatients. *Journal of the*

American Academy of Child and Adolescent Psychiatry, 30(6), 994–998.

Bradburn, N. M. (1983). Response effects. In P. H. Rossi, J. D. Wright, & A. A. Anderson (Eds.), *Handbook of survey research* (pp. 289–328). New York: Academic Press.

Bradburn, N. M., Rips, L. J., & Shevell, S. K. (1987). Answering auto-biographical questions: The impact of memory and inference on surveys. *Science, 236,* 157–161.

Brownell, K. D., Marlatt, G. A., Lichtenstein, E., & Wilson, G. T. (1986). Understanding and preventing relapse. *American Psychologist, 41,* 765–782.

Burton, R. P. D., Johnson, R. J., Ritter, C., & Clayton, R. R. (1996). The effects of role socialization on the initiation of cocaine use: An event history analysis from adolescence into middle adulthood. *Journal of Health and Social Behavior, 37,* 75–90.

Capaldi, D. M., Crosby, L., & Stoolmiller, M. (1996). Predicting the timing of first sexual intercourse for at-risk adolescent males. *Child Development, 67,* 344–359.

Coelho, R. J. (1984). Self-efficacy and cessation of smoking. *Psychological Reports, 54,* 309–310.

Cohen, J. (1990). *Statistical power analysis for the behavioral sciences* (2nd ed.). Hillsdale, NJ: Erlbaum.

Cooney, N. L., Kadden, R. M., Litt, M. D., & Getter, H. (1991). Matching alcoholics to coping skills or interactional therapies: Two-year follow-up results. *Journal of Consulting and Clinical Psychology, 59,* 598–601.

Condiotte, M. M., & Lichtenstein, E. (1981). Self-efficacy and relapse in smoking cessation programs. *Journal of Consulting and Clinical Psychology, 49,* 648–658.

Cox, D. R. (1972). Regression models and life tables. *Journal of the Royal Statistical Society, Series B, 34,* 187–202.

Cox, D. R., & Oakes, D. (1984). *Analysis of survival data.* London: Chapman and Hall.

Diekmann, A., Jungbauer-Gans, M., Krassnig, H., & Lorenz, S. (1996). Social status and aggression: A field study analyzed by survival analysis. *Journal of Social Psychology, 136*(6), 761–768.

Diekmann, A., & Mitter, P. (1983). The sickle-hypothesis: A time dependent Poisson model with applications to deviant behavior. *Journal of Mathematical Sociology, 9,* 85–101.

Donner, A. (1984). Approaches to sample size estimation in the design of clinical trials: A review. *Statistics in Medicine, 3,* 199–214.

Dupont, W. D., & Plummer, W. D., Jr. (1990). Power and sample size calculations: A review and computer program. *Controlled Clinical Trials, 11,* 116–128.

Farrington, D. P., Gallagher, B., Morley, L., St. Ledger, R. J., & West, D. J. (1990). Minimizing attrition in longitudinal research: Methods of tracing and securing cooperation in a 24-year follow-up study. In D. Magnusson & L. R. Bergman (Eds.), *Data quality in longitudinal research* (pp. 122–147). New York: Cambridge University Press.

Felmlee, D., & Eder, D. (1983). Contextual effects in the classroom: The impact of ability groups on student attention. *Sociology of Education, 56,* 77–87.

Fergusson, D. M., Horwood, L. J., & Shannon, F. T. (1984). A proportional hazards model of family breakdown. *Journal of Marriage and the Family, 46,* 539–549.

Flay, B. R., & Petraitis, J. (1991). Methodological issues in drug use prevention research: Theoretical foundations. In W. Bukoski & K. Leukefeld (Eds.), *Drug abuse prevention intervention research: Methodological issues* (pp. 81–109). National Institute on Drug Abuse Research Monograph Series No. 107.

Flinn, C. J., & Heckman, J. J. (1982). New methods for analyzing individual event histories. In S. Leinhardt (Ed.), *Sociological methodology* (pp. 99–140). San Francisco, CA: Jossey-Bass.

Foster, E. M. (1998). Does the continuum of care influence time in treatment: Evidence from the Fort Bragg evaluation. *Evaluation Review, 22*(4), 447–469.

Foster, E. M. (1999). Do aftercare services reduce inpatient psychiatric readmissions? *Health Services Research, 34*(3), 715–736.

Frank, E., Prien, R. F., Jarrett, R. B., Keller, M. B., Kupfer, D. J., Lavori, P. W., Rush, A. J., & Weissman, M. M. (1991). Conceptualization and rationale for consensus definition of terms in major depressive disorder. *Archives of General Psychiatry, 48,* 851–855.

Freedman, L. S. (1982). Tables of the number of patients required in clinical trials using the logrank test. *Statistics in Medicine, 1,* 121–129.

Fryer, G. E., & Miyoshi, T. J. (1994). A survival analysis of the revictimization of children: The case of Colorado. *Child Abuse and Neglect, 18*(12), 1063–1071.

Gamse, B. C., & Conger, D. (1997). *An evaluation of the Spencer post-doctoral dissertation fellows program.* Cambridge, MA: Abt Associates.

Glasgow, R. E., Klesges, R. C., Klesges, L. M., & Somes, G. R. (1988). Variables associated with participation and outcome in a worksite smoking control program. *Journal of Consulting and Clinical Psychology, 56,* 617–620.

Goldstein, R. B., Black, D. W., Nasrallah, A., & Winokur, G. (1991). The prediction of suicide: Sensitivity, specificity, and predictive value of a multivariate model applied to suicide among 1906 patients with affective disorders. *Archives of General Psychiatry, 48,* 418–422.

Greenhouse, J. B., Stangl, D., Kupfer, D. J., & Prien, R. F. (1991). Methodologic issues in maintenance therapy clinical trials. *Archives of General Psychiatry, 48,* 313–318.

Grey, C., Osborn, E., & Reznikoff, M. (1986). Psychosocial factors in two opiate addiction treatments. *Journal of Clinical Psychology, 42,* 185–189.

Hall, S. M., Havassy, B. E., & Wasserman, D. A. (1990). Commitment to abstinence and acute stress in relapse to alcohol, opiates and nicotine. *Journal of Consulting and Clinical Psychology, 58,* 175–181.

Hall, S. M., Havassy, B. E., & Wasserman, D. A. (1991). Effects of commitment to abstinence, positive moods, stress, and coping on relapse to cocaine use. *Journal of Consulting and Clinical Psychology, 59,* 526–532.

Hall, S. M., Rugg, D., Tunstall, C., & Jones, R. T. (1984). Preventing relapse to cigarette smoking by behavioral skill training. *Journal of Consulting and Clinical Psychology, 52,* 372–382.

Hansen, W. B., Collins, L. M., Malotte, C. K., Johnson, C. A., & Fielding, J. E. (1985). Attrition in prevention research. *Journal of Behavioral Medicine, 8,* 261–275.

Harackiewicz, J. M., Sansone, C., Blair, L. W., Epstein, J. A., & Manderlink, G. (1987). Attributional processes in behavior change and maintenance: Smoking cessation and continued abstinence. *Journal of Consulting and Clinical Psychology, 55,* 372–378.

Harris, V., & Koepsell, T. D. (1996). Criminal recidivism in mentally ill offenders: A pilot study. *Bulletin of the American Academy of Psychiatry Law, 24*(2), 177–186.

Heckman, J., & Singer, B. (Eds.). (1985). *Longitudinal analysis of labor market data.* New York: Cambridge University Press.

Henning, K. R., & Frueh, B. C. (1996). Cognitive-behavioral treatment of incarcerated offenders: An evaluation of the Vermont Department of Corrections' cognitive self-change program. *Criminal Justice and Behavior, 23*(4), 523–541.

Herzog, W., Schellberg, D., & Deter, H.-C. (1997). First recovery in anorexia nervosa patients in the long-term course: A discrete-time survival analysis. *Journal of Consulting and Clinical Psychology, 65*(1), 169–177.

Horvath, W. J. (1968). A statistical model for the duration of wars and strikes. *Behavioral Science, 13,* 18–28.

Hosmer, D. W., Jr., & Lemeshow, S. (1999). *Applied survival analysis: Regression modeling of time to event data.* New York: Wiley.

Hunt, W. A., Barnett, W., & Branch, L. G. (1971). Relapse rates in addiction programs. *Journal of Clinical Psychology, 27,* 455–456.

Hunt, W. A., & Bespalec, D. A. (1974). An evaluation of current methods of modifying smoking behavior. *Journal of Clinical Psychology, 30,* 431–438.

Hunt, W. A., & Matarazzo, J. D. (1970). Habit mechanisms in smoking. In W. A. Hunt (Ed.), *Learning mechanisms in smoking* (pp. 40–72). Chicago: Aldine.

Hurlburt, M. S., Wood, P. A., & Hough, R. L. (1996). Providing independent housing for the homeless mentally ill: A novel approach to evaluating long-term longitudinal housing patterns. *Journal of Community Psychology, 24*(3), 291–310.

Hutchison, D. (1988a). Event history and survival analysis in the social sciences: Vol. 1. Background and introduction. *Quality and Quantity, 22,* 203–219.

Hutchison, D. (1988b). Event history and survival analysis in the social sciences: Vol. 2. Advanced applications and recent developments. *Quality and Quantity, 22,* 255–278.

Ilardi, S. S., Craighead, W. E., & Evans, D. D. (1997). Modeling relapse in unipolar depression: The effects of dysfunctional cognitions and personality disorders. *Journal of Consulting and Clinical Psychology, 65*(3), 381–391.

Kalbfleisch, J. D., & Prentice, R. L. (1980). *The statistical analysis of failure time data.* New York: Wiley.

Kaplan, E. L., & Meier, P. (1958). Non-parametric estimation from incomplete observations. *Journal of the American Statistical Association, 53,* 457–481.

Kazdin, A. E., & Bass, D. (1989). Power to detect differences between alternative treatments in comparative psychotherapy outcome research. *Journal of Consulting and Clinical Psychology, 57,* 138–147.

Kleinbaum, D. G., Kupper, L. L., & Morgenstern, H. (1982). *Epidemiologic research: Principles and quantitative methods.* Belmont, CA: Lifetime Learning Publications.

Klerman, G. L. (1978). Long-term maintenance of affective disorders. In M. A. Lipton, A. DiMascio, & K. Killam (Eds.), *Psychopharmacology: A generation of progress* (pp. 1303–1311). New York: Raven Press.

Klein, J. P., & Moeschberger, M. L. (1997). *Survival analysis: Techniques for censored and truncated data.* New York: Springer.

Kraemer, H. C., & Pruyn, J. P. (1990). The evaluation of different approaches to randomized clinical trials. *Archives of General Psychiatry, 47,* 1163–1169.

Kraemer, H. C., & Theimann, S. (1988). *How many subjects?* Beverly Hills, CA: Sage.

Kupfer, D. J., Frank, E., & Perel, J. M. (1989). The advantage of early treatment intervention in recurrent depression. *Archives of General Psychiatry, 46,* 771–775.

Lachin, J. M. (1981). Introduction to sample size determination and power analysis for clinical trials. *Controlled Clinical Trials, 2,* 93–113.

Lachin, J. M., & Foulkes, M. A. (1986). Evaluation of sample size and power for analyses of survival with allowance for nonuniform patient entry, losses to follow-up, noncompliance and stratification. *Biometrics, 42,* 507–519.

Lancaster, T. (1990). *Econometric analysis of transition data.* New York: Cambridge University Press.

Langenbucher, J. W., & Chung, T. (1995). Onset and staging of DSM-IV alcohol dependence using mean age and survival-hazard methods. *Journal of Abnormal Psychology, 104*(2), 346–354.

Lavori, P. W., Dawson, R., Mueller, T. I., Marshaw, M., Swartz, A., & Leon, A. (1996). Analysis of course of psychopathology: Transitions among states of health and illness. *International Journal of Methods in Psychiatric Research, 6,* 321–334.

Lawless, J. F. (1982). *Statistical models and methods for lifetime data.* New York: Wiley.

Lee, E. T. (1992). *Statistical methods for survival data analysis* (2nd ed.). New York: Wiley.

Lelliott, P., Marks, I., McNamee, G., & Tobena, A. (1989). Onset of panic disorder with agoraphobia. *Archives of General Psychiatry, 46,* 1000–1004.

Light, R. J., Singer, J. D., & Willett, J. B. (1990). *By design.* Cambridge, MA: Harvard University Press.

Lilienfeld, A. M., & Lilienfeld, D. E. (1980). *Foundations of epidemiology* (2nd ed.). New York: Oxford University Press.

Lin, N., Ensel, W. M., & Lai, G. W.-F. (1996). Construction and use of the life history calendar: reliability and validity of recall data. In I. H. Gotlib & B. Wheaton (Eds.), *Stress and adversity over the life course: Trajectories and turning points.* New York: Cambridge University Press.

Litman, G. K., Eiser, J. R., & Taylor, C. (1979). Dependence, relapse and extinction: A theoretical critique and a behavioral examination. *Journal of Clinical Psychology, 35,* 192–199.

Little, R. J. A., & Rubin, D. B. (1987). *Statistical analysis with missing data.* New York: Wiley.

Makuch, R. W., & Simon, R. M. (1982). Sample size requirements for comparing time-to-failure among k treatment groups. *Journal of Chronic Diseases, 35,* 861–867.

Marlatt, G. A., Curry, S., & Gordon, J. R. (1988). A longitudinal analysis of unaided smoking cessation. *Journal of Consulting and Clinical Psychology, 55,* 715–720.

Mausner, J. S., & Bahn, A. K. (1974). *Epidemiology.* Philadelphia: W. B. Saunders.

McFall, R. M. (1978). Smoking-cessation research. *Journal of Consulting and Clinical Psychology, 46,* 703–712.

Micceri, T. (1989). The unicorn, the normal curve, and other improbable creatures. *Psychological Bulletin, 103,* 156–166.

Milner, J. L. (1987). An ecological perspective on duration of foster care. *Child Welfare, 66,* 113–123.

Mojtabai, R., Nicholson, R. A., & Neesmith, D. H. (1997). Factors affecting relapse in patients discharged from a public hospital: Results from survival analysis. *Psychiatric Quarterly, 68*(2), 117–129.

Monroe, S. M., Simons, A. D., & Thase, M. E. (1991). Onset of depression and time-to-treatment entry: Roles of life stress. *Journal of Consulting and Clinical Psychology, 59,* 566–573.

Moussa, M. A. A. (1988). Planning the size of survival time clinical trials with allowance for stratification. *Statistics in Medicine, 7,* 559–569.

Murnane, R. J., Singer, J. D., Willett, J. B., Kemple, J. J., & Olsen, R. J. (1991*). Who will teach?: Policies that matter.* Cambridge, MA: Harvard University Press.

Murphy, G. E., & Wetzel, R. D. (1990). The lifetime risk of suicide in alcoholism. *Archives of General Psychiatry, 47,* 383–392.

Murphy, M. (1990). Minimizing attrition in longitudinal studies: Means or end? In D. Magnusson & L. R. Bergman (Eds.), *Data quality in longitudinal research* (pp. 122–147). New York: Cambridge University Press.

Nathan, P. E., & Lansky, O. (1978). Common methodological problems in research on the addictions. *Journal of Consulting and Clinical Psychology, 46,* 713–726.

Nathan, P. E., & Skinstad, A. (1987). Outcomes of treatment for alcohol problems: Current methods, problems, and results. *Journal of Consulting and Clinical Psychology, 55,* 332–340.

Rayman, P., & Brett, B. (1995). Women science majors: What makes a difference in persistence after graduation? *Journal of Higher Education, 66*(4), 388–414.

Roderick, M. (1994). Grade retention and school dropout: Investigating the association. *American Educational Research Journal, 31*(4), 729–759.

Rosenbaum, E., & Kandel, D. B. (1990). Early onset of adolescent sexual behavior and drug involvement. *Journal of Marriage and the Family, 52,* 783–798.

Rubinstein, L. V., Gail, M. H., & Santner, T. J. (1981). Planning the duration of a comparative clinical trial with loss to follow-up and a period of continued observation. *Journal of Chronic Diseases, 34,* 469–479.

Seltzer, M. M., Seltzer, G. B., & Sherwood, C. C. (1982). Comparison of community adjustment of older vs. younger mentally retarded adults. *American Journal of Mental Deficiency, 87,* 9–13.

Shiffman, S. (1982). Relapse following smoking cessation: A situational analysis. *Journal of Consulting and Clinical Psychology, 50,* 71–86.

Singer, J. D., Davidson, S., Graham, S., & Davidson, H. S. (1998). Physician retention in community and migrant health centers: Who stays and for how long? *Medical Care, 38,* 1198–1213.

Singer, J. D., Fuller, B., Keiley, M. K., & Wolf, A. (1998). Early child-care selection: Variation by geographic location, maternal characteristics, and family structure. *Developmental Psychology, 34*(5), 1129–1144.

Singer, J. D., & Willett, J. B. (1991). Modeling the days of our lives: Using survival analysis when designing and analyzing studies of duration and the timing of events. *Psychological Bulletin, 110*(2), 268–290.

Singer, J. D., & Willett, J. B. (1993). It's about time: Using discrete-time survival analysis to study duration and the timing of events. *Journal of Educational Statistics, 18*(2), 155–195

Singer, J. D., & Willett, J. B. (in press). *Applied longitudinal data analysis: Modeling change and event occurrence.* New York: Oxford University Press.

Somers, M. J. (1996). Modeling employee withdrawal behaviour over time: A study of turnover using survival analysis. *Journal of Occupational and Organizational Psychology, 69,* 315–326.

Stevens, V. J., & Hollis, J. F. (1989). Preventing smoking relapse using an individually tailored skills training technique. *Journal of Consulting and Clinical Psychology, 57,* 420–424.

Stice, E., Killen, J. D., Hayward, C., & Taylor, C. B. (1998). Age of onset for binge eating and purging during late adolescence: A 4-year survival analysis. *Journal of Abnormal Psychology, 107*(4), 671–675.

Strober, M., Freeman, R., & Morrell, W. (1997). The long-term course of severe anorexia nervosa in adolescents: Survival analysis of recovery, relapse, and outcome predictors over 10–15 years in a prospective study. *International Journal of Eating Disorders, 22*, 339–360.

Sudman, S., & Bradburn, N. (1982). *Asking questions: A practical guide to questionnaire design.* San Francisco, CA: Jossey-Bass.

Sutton, S. R. (1979). Interpreting relapse curves. *Journal of Consulting and Clinical Psychology, 47*, 96–98.

Swan, G. E., Ward, M. M., & Jack, L. M. (1996). Abstinence effects as predictors of 28 day relapse in smokers. *Addictive Behaviors, 21*(4), 481–490.

Therneau, T. M., & Grambsch, P. M. (2000). *Modeling survival data: Extending the Cox model.* New York: Springer.

Trussel, J., & Hammerslough, C. (1983). A hazards-model analysis of the covariates of infant and child mortality in Sri Lanka. *Demography, 20*, 1–26.

Tuma, N. B., & Hannan, M. T. (1984). *Social dynamics: Models and methods.* New York: Academic Press.

Turnbull, B. W. (1974). Non-parametric estimation of a survivorship function with doubly censored data. *Journal of the American Statistical Association, 69*, 169–173.

Turnbull, B. W. (1976). The empirical distribution function with arbitrarily grouped, censored and truncated data. *Journal of the Royal Statistical Society, Series B, 38*, 290–295.

Velicer, W. F., Proschaska, J. O., Rossi, J. S., & Snow, M. G. (1992). Assessing outcome in smoking cessation studies. *Psychological Bulletin, 111*, 23–41.

Verhulst, F. C., & Koot, H. M. (1991). Longitudinal research in child and adolescent psychiatry. *Journal of the American Academy of Child and Adolescent Psychiatry, 30*(3), 361–368.

Wheaton, B., Roszell, P., & Hall, K. (1996). The impact of twenty childhood and adult traumatic stressors on the risk of psychiatric disorder. In I. H. Gotlib & B. Wheaton (Eds.), *Stress and adversity over the life course: Trajectories and turning points* (pp. 27–49). New York: Cambridge University Press.

Willett, J. B., & Singer, J. D. (1993). Investigating onset, cessation, relapse and recovery: Why you should, and how you can, use discrete-time survival analysis to examine event occurrence. *Journal of Consulting and Clinical Psychology, 61*, 952–965.

Wilson, G. T., Loeb, K. L., Walsh, B. T., Labouvie, E., Petkova, E., Liu, X., & Waternaux, C. (1999). Psychological versus pharmacological treatments of bulimia nervosa: Predictors and processes of change. *Journal of Consulting and Clinical Psychology, 67*, 451–459.

Wu, X. (1995). Premarital cohabitation and postmarital cohabiting union formation. *Journal of Family Issues, 16*, 212–232.

Yamaguchi, K., & Kandel, D. B. (1984). Patterns of drug use from adolescence to young adulthood: Predictors of progression. *American Journal of Public Health, 74*, 673–681.

Yamaguchi, K., & Kandel, D. B. (1987). Drug use and other determinants of premarital pregnancy and its outcome: A dynamic analysis of competing life events. *Journal of Marriage and the Family, 49*, 257–270.

Young, M. A., Watel, L. G., Lahmeyer, H. W., & Eastman, C. I. (1991). The temporal onset of individual symptoms in winter depression: Differentiating underlying mechanisms. *Journal of Affective Disorders, 22*, 191–197.

Zatz, M. S. (1985). Los Cholos: Legal processing of Chicano gang members. *Social Problems, 33*, 13–30.

CHAPTER 23

Time Series Analysis

WAYNE F. VELICER AND JOSEPH L. FAVA

Time series analysis is a statistical methodology appropriate for an important class of longitudinal research designs. Such designs typically involve single subjects or research units that are measured repeatedly at regular intervals over a large number of observations. Time series analysis can be viewed as the exemplar of a longitudinal design. A time series analysis can help us to understand the underlying naturalistic process, the pattern of change over time, or evaluate the effects of either a planned or unplanned intervention. This chapter discusses time series analysis as it is commonly employed in psychological research, detailing both the past history and future directions of the technique. Advances in information systems technology make time series designs an increasingly feasible method for studying important psycho-

logical phenomena. The chapter is divided into eight sections that carry the reader from the theoretical underpinnings of the methodology through applied examples of time series applications to new applications and directions within time series analysis.

The second section provides a general *overview* and describes the most prevalent methodology used in time series analysis. This section provides an introduction to the major concepts, issues, and terminology. The major classes of research questions that can be addressed by time series analysis are also discussed. These include process analysis, intervention analysis, and the analysis of treatment effects over time. Some general guidelines are suggested to aid in determining when a time series study and analysis might offer specific advantages over alternative methodologies.

The third section presents a more complete and technical discussion of the class of time series known as autoregressive integrated moving average (ARIMA) models. These models

---

Grants CA27821, CA63045, CA71356, and CA50087 from the National Cancer Institute supported this work.

consist of several parameters that describe and provide insight into the basic process of a specific time series. Definitions of parameters (p, d, q) and important terms (order, dependency) within ARIMA models are given. A more technical discussion of the model identification process is also presented. Simulated and applied examples of time series are used to clarify this discussion.

The fourth section provides a detailed examination of interrupted time series analysis. This aspect of time series analysis is especially important when an intervention is the focus in a research study. Typically an examination of the effects of an intervention will be concerned with changes in the overall level or the slope of the time series, or both the level and the slope of the measured series. Statistical tests of significance for the intervention parameters of interest are also available. The provision of accurate statistical tests is dependent on transforming the time series to remove the dependency that is usually present in the data. Selection of an appropriate transformation matrix is a crucial aspect of interrupted time series analysis and several approaches to transforming a time series are presented. The discussion and mathematical treatment of interrupted time series analysis is facilitated with simple examples of time series.

The fifth section examines issues related to the generalization of results to a larger population than the single individual or unit that may be the focus of a time series. Informal methods are contrasted with the more recent formal methodologies of pooled times series and meta-analysis. A description of the various methodologies is provided along with the limitations and benefits of the different methods.

The sixth section addresses the extension of traditional univariate time series analysis to procedures that allow for multivariate time series analysis. These multivariate techniques are still evolving and are generally at the forefront of current time series analysis development. Multivariate applications of time series analysis may examine the role of covariates, involve formal modeling within a structural equation modeling format, or examine patterns of intra-individual differences across time within a dynamic factor analysis model.

The seventh section reviews several important and diverse issues that can affect the meaning and interpretation of a time series analysis solution. The first discusses the cyclic or seasonal nature of some time series. The second reviews missing data and the effects of alternative methods of imputation within time series analysis. The last examines various computational issues within time series analysis.

The eighth section provides a summary discussion of the material on time series analysis presented in this chapter and some general observations on this methodology.

OVERVIEW OF TIME SERIES ANALYSIS

Modern time series analysis and related research methods represent a sophisticated leap in the ability to analyze longitudinal data gathered on single subjects or units. Early time series designs, especially as used within psychology, relied heavily on graphical analysis to describe and interpret results. Although graphical methods are useful and still provide important ancillary information to the understanding of a time series process, the ability to bring a sophisticated statistical methodology to bear on this class of data has revolutionized the area of single subject research.

ARIMA Models

Time series analysis had been more generally developed in areas such as engineering and economics before it came into widespread use within social science research. The prevalent methodology that has developed and been adapted in psychology is the class of models known as *ARIMA models* (Box & Jenkins, 1976; Box, Jenkins, & Reinsel, 1994; Box & Tiao, 1965, 1975). Time series analysis belongs to the class of new methods of data analysis that require the use of modern high-speed computers. The estimation of the basic parameters cannot be performed by precomputer methods.

One of the major characteristics of the data in most time series is the inherent dependency present in a data set that results from repeated measurements over time on a single subject or unit. All longitudinal designs must take the potential relationship between observations over time into account. For time series analysis, the dependency precluded the use of traditional statistical tests. An important assumption for statistical testing, the independence of the error in the data, was usually not met. Methods of handling this dependence appropriate for large sample procedures could not be used. ARIMA models have proven especially useful within time series analysis because they provide a basic methodology to model the effects of dependency from the data series (Glass, Willson, & Gottman, 1975; Gottman, 1973; Gottman & Glass, 1978) and allow valid statistical testing.

Research Applications

As the methodology for time series analysis has evolved, there has also been an emergence of interest among applied researchers. Many behavioral interventions occur in applied settings such as businesses, schools, clinics, and hospitals. More traditional between-subject research designs may not always be the most appropriate, or in some instances can be very difficult if not impossible to implement in such settings.

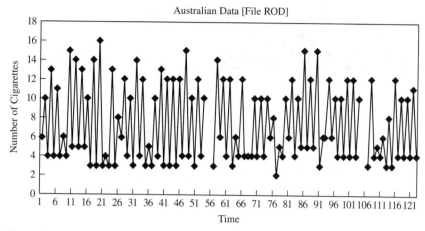

Figure 23.1   Smoking behavior measured on 124 occasions: an example of time series data for a single individual (ROD; from Velicer, Redding, et al., 1992).

In some cases, data appropriate for time series analysis are generated on a regular basis in the applied setting, like the number of hospital admissions. In other cases, a complete understanding of the process that can explain the acquisition or cessation of an important behavior may require the intensive study of an individual over an extended period of time. The advances in information systems technology have facilitated the repeated assessment of individuals in natural settings.

Figure 23.1 (from Velicer, Redding, Richmond, Greeley, & Swift, 1992) illustrates the type of data that would be appropriate for time series analysis. The dependent variable is the number of cigarettes smoked by a single individual, code name ROD. The data were obtained twice a day over a period of two months ($N = 124$ with 3 observations missing). Four parameters were fit to the data: The *level* of the series was estimated to be 7.30, the *error variance* was estimated to be 15.13, the *slope* of the series was not statistically significant and estimated to be 0.0, and the *dependence* was estimated to be −0.67. The first two parameters are directly analogous to parameters estimated in traditional cross-sectional statistical analysis. Because the slope is 0.0, the level of this series is the same as the mean. In cases in which the slope is not equal to zero, then the level is interpreted as an intercept would be in a regression analysis. In this case, it is the same as the mean and the average number of cigarettes consumed in a half day was 7.30. (Both observation periods involved approximately the same length of time when the smoker was awake.) The estimate of error variance represents the variability about the level of the series. As in cross-sectional designs, this is employed in the denominator of a statistical test. The second two parameters represent unique aspects of longitudinal designs. The lagged correlation between the observations provides an estimate of the dependence in the data. The high negative autocorrelation indicates that if the smoker consumes an excessive number of cigarettes during one time period, consumption during the next time period is likely to be low. (In the next section, the direction and magnitude of this parameter will be related to different theoretical models of smoking behavior.) The slope indicates if there is a pattern of systematic change over time. If the series is stable, as in this case, the average consumption is neither increasing nor decreasing over the time period studied.

Process Analysis

Several important classes of research questions can be investigated using ARIMA models applied to time series data. The first class involves using ARIMA modeling to investigate the naturalistic process of change across time. Investigations of this type focus on the dependency parameter and attempt to identify the underlying nature of the series from the dependency parameter. Such process investigations are strongest if they can be linked to a priori hypotheses or established theories. Investigations of this type can lead to a basic understanding of the process under investigation and may provide a foundation to attempt an intervention to alter the process under investigation.

Intervention Analysis

A second important class of questions that can be investigated involves the analysis of the effects of an intervention that is applied to an individual subject or unit. Such an investigation is commonly referred to as an *interrupted time series analysis*. The *interruption* refers to the intervention that is applied at some fixed point in a process. Repeated measurements are

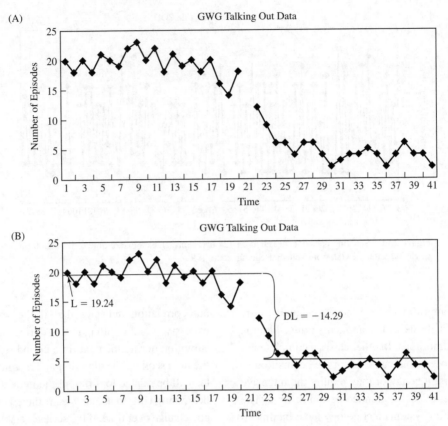

Figure 23.2   Example of an interrupted time series example: the talking out example (from Hall et al., 1971; Glass et al., 1975).

taken before and after the intervention in order to provide a sufficient number of data points to conduct a statistical analysis to evaluate the effects of the intervention. Such investigations can be very useful in trying to understand causality within the process and as a result of the intervention.

Figure 23.2 illustrates the "talking out" data from Glass Willson, and Gottman (1975), an example of an interrupted time series design. The Glass et al. (1975) text introduced time series analysis to the behavioral sciences and includes multiple numeric examples in the appendix that can be used for practice examples. The original talking out data (Hall et al., 1971) represented 40 daily observations of disruptive behavior (talking out) in a second-grade class. The first 20 observations were the baseline and the second 20 observations occurred after an intervention involving praise and access to a favorite activity had been implemented. The first panel illustrates the observed data. The second panel illustrates the same data with the estimate of the *level* and *change in level* parameters. A first-order moving averages model was fit to the data. The level of the series before intervention was estimated to be 19.24. After the intervention, the estimated level of the series was changed by -14.29 to 4.95. The parameter estimate for the error variance was 4.47. The parameter

estimate for the dependence was -0.34. If the analysis includes estimation of slope and change in slope, these parameters are found to be not significant. The analysis indicates that the intervention resulted in a large and sustained decrease in amount of inappropriate behavior in the classroom.

Analysis of Patterns Across Time

Time series analysis allows for a broadening of the range of questions that can be asked in a study beyond a simple investigation of whether the intervention has had an effect. Time series analysis has some important advantages over other methodologies in that it provides the opportunity to investigate the pattern of intervention effects across time. These patterns can be quite varied and some questions that can be investigated in this context include (a) Are the effects of intervention temporary or permanent?, (b) Does the intervention cause a change in the slope of the behavior process as well as the overall level?, (c) Does the intervention cause a change in any cycling that is present in the underlying behavior process?, (d) Does the intervention cause the variance to change?, and (e) Does the intervention cause a change in the nature of the dependency that is present in the time series process?

Caveats

There are also several difficulties and weaknesses associated with standard time series analysis that must be recognized. First, generalizability should not be inferred from a single study. The researcher needs to engage in systematic replication in order to demonstrate generalizability. Second, the traditional measures employed in cross-sectional studies in many content areas may not be appropriate for time series designs. For time series analysis, the best measures are those that can be repeated a large number of times on a single subject at intervals of short duration. Third, within the context of ARIMA models a large number of equally spaced observations are required for accurate model identification. Model identification, discussed in detail in the next section, is an important and necessary step. Advances in time series analysis over the last decade have attempted to address these problems, and these new methodological developments are discussed in a later section of this chapter.

MODEL IDENTIFICATION

Overview of ARIMA Modeling Procedures

Time series analysis, within the ARIMA model framework, involves two important steps that can vary in importance, depending on the goals of the analysis. The first step is *model identification,* in which the researcher tries to identify which underlying mathematical model is appropriate for the data. Model identification focuses on the dependency parameters, one of the types of parameters unique to longitudinal designs. This step can sometimes be a very difficult, complicated, and problematic task. Model identification can represent the primary goal of the analysis, especially if a researcher is trying to identify the basic underlying process represented in a time series data set, and perhaps link this process with important theoretical underpinnings.

When the goal of the analysis involves evaluating the effects of an intervention, as in interrupted time series analysis, then model identification represents a first step. It is preliminary to estimating and testing pre- and postintervention parameters (Box, Jenkins, & Reinsel 1994; Box & Tiao, 1965, 1975; Glass et al., 1975; McCleary & Hay, 1980; Velicer & Colby, 1997; Velicer & McDonald, 1984, 1991). After the model identification step, the researcher moves on to the second step and implements a specific transformation appropriate for the identified model that reconfigures the dependent observed variable into a serially independent variable. After transformation, the dependent variable or effects of intervention can then be evaluated by a generalized least squares estimate of the model parameters.

There has been extensive research developing and comparing procedures to aid the model identification process (Akaike, 1974; Beguin, Courieroux, & Monfort, 1980; Bhansali & Downham, 1977; Glass et al., 1975; Grey, Kelly, & McIntire, 1978; Hannan & Rissanen, 1982; Kashyap, 1977; McCleary & Hay, 1980; Parzen, 1974; Pukkila, 1982; Rissanen, 1978, 1986a, 1986b; Schwartz, 1978; Tsay, 1984; Tsay & Tiao, 1984). Unfortunately there is not yet a clear consensus on a best method for this important task. A simulation study by Velicer and Harrop (1983) studied the model identification process. Some of the reasons for difficulty with this step include the large number of data points required for accurate identification, the complexity of the procedures, and problems with accuracy and reliability of some methods, even under ideal circumstances. Alternative procedures that avoid formal model identification have been proposed (Algina & Swaminathan, 1977, 1979; Simonton, 1977; Swaminathan & Algina, 1977; Velicer & McDonald, 1984, 1991) and are discussed in a later section.

Definition of ARIMA Parameters

The ARIMA model represents a family of models characterized by three parameters (p, d, q) that describe the basic properties of a specific time series model. The value of the first parameter, p, denotes the order of the autoregressive component of the model. If an observation can be influenced only by the immediately preceding observation, the model is of the first order. If an observation can be influenced by both of the two immediately preceding observations, the model is of the second order. The value of the second parameter, d, refers to the order of differencing that is necessary to stabilize a nonstationary time series. This process is described as nonstationary because values do not vary about a fixed mean level; rather, the series may first fluctuate about one level for some observations, and then rise or fall about a different level at a different point in the series. And the value of the third parameter, q, denotes the order of the moving averages component of the model. Again, the order describes how many preceding observations must be taken into account. The values of each of the parameters (p, d, q) of the model may be designated as Order 0, 1, 2, or greater, with a parameter equal to zero indicating the absence of that term from the model. Higher-order models, four and above, are generally rare in the behavioral and social sciences (Glass et al., 1975). Box, Jenkins, and Reinsel (1994) provide a more complete discussion of these parameters.

The *order* of a time series parameter reflects how far into the past one must go to predict a present observation and thus refers to how many preceding observations must be taken into account to accurately describe the dependency present in the data series. Accuracy in determining the exact order can be quite difficult because higher-order autocorrelation terms are generally closer to zero than terms of earlier order. In effect, the higher-order terms become more likely to be included within the interval that would include an error estimate.

Dependency and Autocorrelation

In time series analysis, dependence is assessed by calculating the values of the autocorrelations among the data points in the series. In contrast to a correlation coefficient, which is generally used to estimate the relationship between two different variables measured at the same time on multiple subjects, an autocorrelation estimates the relationships within one variable that is measured at regular intervals over time on only one subject.

The degree of dependency in a time series is determined by the magnitude of the autocorrelations that can vary between -1.00 and 1.00, with a value of 0.00 indicating no relationship. These values can be interpreted as the strength of relationship between consecutive measurements. The accuracy of estimation improves as the number of observations increase. Generally, 50 or more observations provide reasonably accurate estimates (Box & Pierce, 1970; Glass et al., 1975; Ljung & Box, 1978). In practical terms, the degree of dependency indicates the extent to which an observation at any point in time is predictable from one or more preceding observations.

The direction of dependency in a time series refers to whether an autocorrelation is positive or negative. The direction can be determined with a high degree of accuracy when there is strong dependency in the data. As the degree of dependency approaches zero, the direction becomes less important. With strong dependency, the direction has clear implications. When the sign of the autocorrelation is negative, a high level for the series on one occasion predicts a lower level for the series on the next occasion. When the sign is positive, a high level of the series on one occasion predicts a higher level on the next occasion.

In calculating an autocorrelation, the data points of the series are paired off in a lagged manner against each other. Figure 23.3 illustrates this process using the first 20 observations for Lag 1, Lag 2, and Lag 3. Note that for Lag 1 in this example, the second observation is paired with the first, the third observation is paired with the second, and so on, until the last observation is paired with the second from the last observation. If we now calculate the correlation between these paired observations, we will have calculated the Lag 1 autocorrelation. If we were to pair the third observation with

Example. Lag 1			Example. Lag 2			Example. Lag 3		
Time	X	X−1	Time	X	X−2	Time	X	X−3
1	6	--	1	6	--	1	6	--
2	10	6	2	10	--	2	10	--
3	4	10	3	4	6	3	4	--
4	13	4	4	13	10	4	13	6
5	4	13	5	4	4	5	4	10
6	11	4	6	11	13	6	11	4
7	4	11	7	4	4	7	4	13
8	6	4	8	6	11	8	6	4
9	4	6	9	4	4	9	4	11
10	15	4	10	15	6	10	15	4
11	5	15	11	5	4	11	5	6
12	14	5	12	14	15	12	14	4
13	5	14	13	5	5	13	5	15
14	13	5	14	13	14	14	13	5
15	5	13	15	5	5	15	5	14
16	10	5	16	10	13	16	10	5
17	3	10	17	3	5	17	3	13
18	14	3	18	14	10	18	14	5
19	3	14	19	3	3	19	3	10
20	16	3	20	16	14	20	16	3

Figure 23.3 Illustration of arrangement of data to calculate autocorrelations for first three lags using first 20 observations from ROD example.

the first, the fourth observation with the second, and so on, we could then calculate the Lag 2 autocorrelation. The lag of an autocorrelation refers to how far in the past the dependency among measurements is examined. In the behavioral sciences, the size of the autocorrelation generally decreases as the lag increases. An exception would be with seasonal or cyclic data, which are relatively common and are discussed in more detail in a later section. The interpretation of the pattern of autocorrelations within a time series provides one diagnostic step of the model identification process.

The calculation and interpretation of the pattern of the related partial autocorrelations calculated at each lag is employed as a second diagnostic step to aid in the identification of the specific ARIMA model that describes the process underlying the time series. Partial autocorrelations are mathematically complex and are not formally defined here. They are estimated from a solution of the Yule-Walker equation system, and the interested reader should examine Box, Jenkins, and Reinsel (1994), Glass et al. (1975), or West and Hepworth (1991) for a detailed description. The interpretation of partial autocorrelations is that of a measure of the correlation between specific lags of the time series values after the correlation at the intervening lags has been partialled out or controlled for. Figure 23.4 illustrates the autocorrelations and partial autocorrelations for the ROD data from Figure 23.1.

Time Series Model Identification

Model identification ultimately seeks to determine whether autoregressive terms or moving average terms must be included

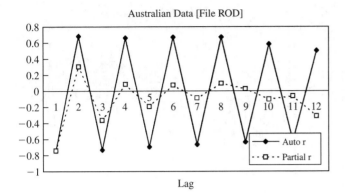

Figure 23.4 Correlogram of the autocorrelations and partial autocorrelations for the ROD example.

to fully describe the time series data. Taken together, the distributional pattern of the autocorrelations and partial autocorrelations provides a visual basis for making these decisions. However, accuracy using traditional visual analysis of the autocorrelations and partial autocorrelations conventionally requires the consensus of three raters. The listing and graphic plots of the autocorrelations and the partial autocorrelations are provided in the printed output of most time series analysis programs. For example, if an autoregressive component is predominant, the autocorrelations will decay slowly to zero for increasing lags and the partial autocorrelations will drop abruptly to zero when the appropriate lag (p) is reached. The residuals of a first-order autoregressive model, i.e., an ARIMA $(1, 0, 0)$ model, with negative autocorrelation will bounce from negative to positive and back. For the moving average component, the autocorrelations will drop abruptly to zero when the appropriate lag (p) is reached, and the partial autocorrelations will drop slowly to zero. Models that demonstrate no dependence will have autocorrelations and partial autocorrelations of approximately zero and are called *white noise models* or ARIMA $(0, 0, 0)$ models. The data from an ARIMA $(0, 0, 0)$ model could be analyzed for slope and change in slope with a standard analysis of variance. Table 23.1 provides a useful heuristic into the interpretation of the most common patterns and identifying the ARIMA model that best represents a particular time series.

TABLE 23.1 Relationship Between ARIMA Models and Auto- and Partial Autocorrelation Patterns

Model	Autocorrelations	Partial Autocorrelations
ARIMA $(p, 0, 0)$	Decays slowly	$= 0$ after p
ARIMA $(0, 0, q)$	$= 0$ after q	Decays slowly
ARIMA $(p, 0, q)$	Decays slowly	Decays slowly
ARIMA $(0, d, 0)$	Does not decay	Does not decay
ARIMA $(0, 0, 0)$	$= 0$	$= 0$

Four different automated methods for order identification have also been found useful in the model identification process: (a) PMDL (predictive minimum descriptive length; Rissanen, 1986a); (b) PLS (predictive least squares; Rissanen, 1986b); (c) PLAV (predictive least absolute value; Djuric & Kay, 1992); and (d) PDC (predictive density criterion; Djuric & Kay, 1992). Two additional methods have been considered less useful: (a) AIC (Akaike information criterion; Akaike, 1974); and (b) MDL (minimum descriptive length; Rissanen, 1978; Schwartz, 1978). A recent simulation study that evaluated these six automated procedures (Djuric & Kay, 1992) found that the AIC and MDL tended to overestimate the order of series. One drawback of all the automated procedures is that they are not commonly available in standard computer packages.

Although the overall goal of the model identification process seems straightforward—that is, to determine the specific values of the ARIMA (p, d, q) parameters that most parsimoniously describe the time series—this can be a very difficult task in practice because the different model families are mathematically linked. For example, a first-order autoregressive model $(1, 0, 0)$ can also be represented as an infinite order moving averages model $(0, 0, \infty)$, or this representation can be reversed such that a first-order moving averages model $(0, 0, 1)$ can also be represented as an infinite-order autoregressive model $(\infty, 0, 0)$.

Illustrations of Alternative Time Series

Figure 23.5 illustrates four different types of models using computer-generated data ($N_1 = N_2 = 60$). The first graph (A) represents an ideal interrupted time series example initially at Level $= 5.0$ with no error and an immediate Change in Level of 2.0 units at the time of intervention. The next three graphs represent an ARIMA $(1, 0, 0)$ model (i.e., an Order 1 autoregressive model). The second graph (B) is the same model with the same change in level but with a random error component added. The variance of the random error is 1.00. There is no autocorrelation in this model. The third graph (C) is a model with the same change in level and error variance as (B) but with a large *negative* autocorrelation (-0.80). The fourth graph (D) is a model with the same change in level and error variance but with a large *positive* autocorrelation ($+0.80$). The impact of dependency can be easily observed. The negative dependency results in an exaggerated sawtooth graph with increased apparent variability. The positive dependency results in a smoother graph with decreased apparent variability. The inclusion of an intervention effect (the change in level) illustrates how difficult it is to determine whether an intervention had an effect by visual inspection alone.

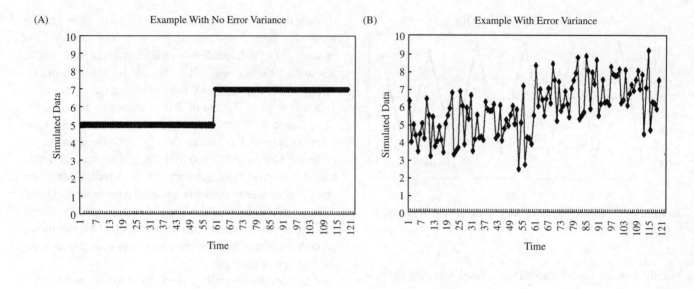

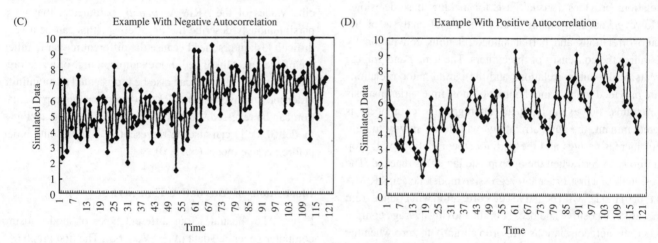

Figure 23.5 Computer-generated data for ARIMA (1, 0, 0) models for level = 5.0 and change in level = 2.0 for four time series illustrating different degrees of dependency.

Example of Model Identification and Theory Testing

To illustrate the use of model identification in theory testing, in this section we present briefly the results of a study (Velicer, Redding, et al., 1992) designed to determine which of three models of nicotine regulation best represented most smokers. These models seek to explain the mechanism that determines how many cigarettes are smoked in any given time period. It is posited that smoking rate controls the level of nicotine in the systems. Three measures were employed in the study but only one, number of cigarettes, is described here.

Nicotine Regulation Models

Three alternative models have been employed to account for nicotine's effectiveness in maintaining smoking: (a) the fixed

effect model, (b) the nicotine regulation model, and (c) the multiple regulation model. Leventhal and Cleary (1980) provide a review of the literature and description of each of the three models. Velicer, Redding, et al. (1992) identified each of the three models with one of three broad classes of time series models: (a) a positive dependency model, (b) a white noise model (no dependency), and (c) a negative dependency model.

The *nicotine fixed effect model* assumes that smoking is reinforced because nicotine stimulates specific reward inducing centers of the nervous system. These have been identified as either autonomic arousal or a feeling of mental alertness and relaxation or both. Following this model, an increase on one occasion should be followed by an increase on the next occasion or a decrease on one occasion should be followed by decreased consumption on a subsequent occasion if the same level of arousal is to be maintained. In time series model terms, this would result in a *positive* autocorrelation.

The *nicotine regulation model* assumes that smoking serves to regulate or titrate the smoker's level of nicotine. Departures from the optimal level (the set point) will stimulate an increase or decrease in smoking to return to this optimal nicotine level. Jarvik (1973) presents a review of a large body of evidence that supports this model (also see Russell, 1977, and Schachter, 1977). The model suggests that any increase or decrease in smoking caused by events in a person's environment should be temporary. The person should immediately return to their personal set point when the environment permits. In this model, only the set point or level is under biological control. All variations are due to the environment. This would result in a white noise model with an autocorrelation of *zero*.

The *multiple regulation model* represents a more complex model designed to overcome some of the problems of the nicotine regulation model—specifically, how the nicotine set point develops and how deviations from the set point generate a craving for cigarettes. Leventhal and Cleary (1980) summarize some of the evidence that the nicotine regulation model cannot adequately account for and suggest the multiple regulation model as an alternative. This model is an elaboration of similar models by Tomkins (1966, 1968) and Solomon and Corbit (1973, 1974; also see Solomon, 1980). This model assumes that the smoker is regulating emotional states. Drops in nicotine level stimulate craving. One way to link craving to nicotine level is the opponent-process theory (Solomon, 1980; Solomon & Corbit, 1973, 1974), which posits that nicotine gives rise to an initial positive affect reaction, which is automatically followed by a slave opponent negative affect reaction. The opponent state becomes stronger with repeated activation and can be eliminated by reinstating the initial positive state. External stimulus provides an alternative source for craving. The theory would predict that an increase (or decrease) in smoking rate caused by events in a person's environment should be followed by an opposite decrease (or increase) in smoking rate. This would result in a negative autocorrelation at Lag 1 and alternating positive and negative autocorrelations at subsequent lags.

Participants

In order to achieve stable autocorrelations, time series analysis requires a minimum of 50 data points (Box & Jenkins, 1976; Glass et al., 1975). The design of the study employed 10 smokers (4 male and 6 female), from whom measures were collected twice daily for 2 months (62 days) for a maximum total of 124 observations.

Measure: Number of Cigarettes

Having participants monitor their own smoking behavior is one of the most commonly employed measures in smoking research (McFall, 1978; Velicer, Prochaska, Rossi, & Snow, 1992; Velicer, Rossi, Prochaska, & DiClemente, 1996). This is an inexpensive and convenient means of gathering data. The accuracy and reliability of data gathered through self-monitoring are not always as high as that of data gathered through other techniques. However, the advantages of using self-monitoring typically outweigh the disadvantages.

Model Identification Procedures

Five procedures were employed for model identification: (a) traditional visual analysis, (b) PMDL (Rissanen, 1986a), (c) PLS (Rissanen, 1986b), (d) PLAV (Djuric & Kay, 1992), and (e) PDC (Djuric & Kay, 1992). For the majority of cases, all five procedures converged on the same answer. When disagreement occurred, it was typically a difference of 1 in order, and all models were reviewed. Disagreements typically involved a low autoregressive coefficient that was approximately equal to the critical value for statistical significance. The more parsimonious fit (lower order) was employed when the evidence for the higher-order model was weak.

Results

Seven of the participants were described by a first-order autoregressive model with a moderate to high degree of *negative* dependence (−.30 to −.80). All participants reported on their smoking behavior in the morning and afternoon. The data resulted in a very clear, easily identified model with a high degree of autocorrelation. This pattern is consistent with the multiple regulation model and the study was interpreted as supporting that model.

Three of the participants did not show the same pattern. One of the participants worked some weeks during the day and some weeks at night. This individual also missed a number of sessions and terminated prematurely. One participant was a very controlled smoker, smoking 15 cigarettes at predetermined intervals. All three averaged less than a pack a day. However, two subjects who demonstrated the pattern of high negative dependence also smoked less than a pack a day.

(A)
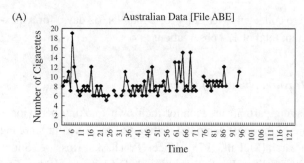

(B)
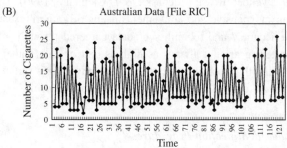

(C)
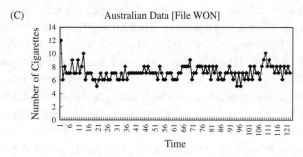

Figure 23.6 Three examples of smoking behavior illustrating different patterns (from Velicer, Redding, et al., 1992).

The data for one participant (ROD) were presented in Figure 23.1. Figure 23.6 presents the data graphically for three additional subjects. Two of the participants (ROD and RIC) were representative of the participants characterized by a high negative dependence. The exaggerated sawtooth shape of this type of time series is clearly observable. Two participants (ABE and WON) were representative of the three individuals who demonstrated either a zero or low positive dependence. The time series graphs for these two participants are much smoother and more regular.

Findings from this study were partially replicated in a similar study conducted in Spain (Rosel & Elósegui, 1994). This study of 29 smokers (9 men and 20 women) examined daily records of cigarettes smoked over a 12-week period. Virtually all of the data series (97%) were best described by autoregressive-type models, and most (75%) of these were Order 1 models; only one participant's data represented a white noise (i.e., no dependency) model.

Other findings from Rosel and Elósegui (1994) apparently conflict with the Velicer, Redding, et al. (1992) results. The data from the 29 smokers apparently supported the fixed-effect model, with 21 participants' data (73%) being described by

that model (i.e., their series had positive autocorrelations); 7 participants (24%) supported the nicotine regulation model (i.e., no autocorrelation detected); and only 1 participant fit a multiple-regulation model. One explanation for the differences between the two studies is the different time intervals used. Velicer, Redding, et al. (1992) collected data twice each day, whereas Rosel and Elósegui (1994) collected data only once each day. A negative autocorrelation at Lag 1, such as that found in the Velicer, Redding, et al. (1992) study, would be a positive autocorrelation at Lag 2, since $r_1^2 = r_2$ for an ARIMA (1, 0, 0) model. A more direct comparison of the two studies would be to compare the r_2 value of the Velicer, Redding, et al. (1992) with the r_1 values of the Rosel and Elosegui (1994) because these two statistics reflect the same time period. The two are both positive and of comparable magnitude.

These apparently conflicting results highlight an important methodological issue—what is the "correct" interval at which to collect data? The answer to this question will depend on one's theoretical framework—for example, the hypothesized influences on the behavior in question and the rate or cycle in which a given influence affects that behavior. In this case, the conclusion about the appropriate nicotine regulation model is clearly affected by the choice of time interval between observations. Clearly, it is critical to pay attention to the time interval when interpreting time series studies.

The other difference between the two studies was the presence of a weekly cyclic in the Spanish study. Rosel and Elósegui (1994) opined that "tobacco consumption is sustained not only because of the effect of nicotine, but also because of the effect of personal and social demand variables, which are reflected in weekly cyclical habits" (p. 1640). Their study found that 45% of the sample fit different 7-day lag models (i.e., weekly smoking patterns), which had not been seen in the previous research. The findings of these two studies are not necessarily at odds. Perhaps nicotine regulation processes influence smoking on a more microlevel, *within* broader cycles of personal and social influence. The presence or absence of a 7-day cyclic might reflect cultural differences. These two studies provide an excellent illustration of the potential contribution that can be made by the time series approach to understanding the processes underlying an addictive behavior.

INTERRUPTED TIME SERIES ANALYSIS

Often the goal of research with single subjects or units is to determine the efficacy of a specific intervention. This can be accomplished by employing various techniques that fall under the nomenclature of interrupted time series analysis. A simple example of an interrupted time series analysis is a design that involves repeated and equally spaced observations on a single subject or unit followed by an intervention. The intervention would then be followed by additional repeated and equally spaced observations of the subject or unit. The intervention could be an experimental manipulation such as a smoking cessation intervention for adolescents, or it could be a naturally occurring event such as a national change in the law regulating tobacco advertising. In order to determine whether the intervention had an effect, an analysis of the data series would first necessitate some preprocessing of the data series to remove the effects of dependence. In addition to the traditional data transformation method, several alternative procedures for removing dependency in the data are also described in the following discussion. The actual statistical analysis used in an interrupted time series analysis employs a general linear model analysis using a generalized least squares or Aitken estimator (Aitken, 1934; Morrison, 1983; see Equation 23.12).

If the intervention effect is found to be statistically significant, an important and related question concerns an evaluation of the nature of the effect. One of the great advantages of time series analysis is the ability to assess the pattern of the change over time, which can involve both change in the mean level of a measured dependent variable, change in the slope over time of the dependent variable, or both. We present the most common variant forms of change over time and the methodology to evaluate these forms of change within this section.

Box-Jenkins Intervention Analysis

The most common methodology employed to examine the effects of a specific interrupted time series intervention is the Box-Jenkins procedure. This methodology is described in detail by Glass et al. (1975) and utilizes a two-step process. As described in the previous section, the autocorrelations and partial autocorrelations are calculated for various lags, and this information is used for identification of the specific ARIMA (p, d, q) model parameter values. Accurate model identification is necessary to determine the specific transformation matrix to be used to remove the dependency from the data series so that it meets the assumptions of the general linear model. The remainder of this section and parts of the next two sections employ some matrix algebra to enhance the discussion of this and some other key aspects of time series analysis within the context of the general linear model. The general linear model is the general analytic procedure that includes the statistical techniques of multiple regression, analysis of variance, and analysis of covariance as special cases. After transforming the data series to remove the dependency in the data, the analysis follows standard estimation and testing procedures, and can be analyzed with a modified general linear model program in which the parameters of interest are estimated and tested for significance. Several variations on the procedure of choosing a data transformation matrix have been proposed to eliminate the problematic model identification step, and are described later in this section.

A basic interrupted time series problem would be to determine whether the average level of the series has changed as a result of the intervention. In such an analysis, two parameters are estimated: L, the level of the series, and DL, the change in level after intervention. A test of significance would then examine the hypothesis of prime interest, H_0: $DL = 0$. In algebraic terms this can be expressed in terms of the general linear model as

$$\mathbf{Z} = Xb + a \tag{23.1}$$

where $\mathbf{Z}$ is an $N \times 1$ vector of observed variables, such that N is the total number of observations, with the first z_i observations occurring prior to the intervention, or

$$\mathbf{Z} = \begin{bmatrix} z_1 \\ z_2 \\ . \\ . \\ z_i \\ . \\ . \\ z_N \end{bmatrix} \tag{23.2}$$

and $\mathbf{X}$ is an $N \times p$ design matrix (see Table 23.2, described in the following discussion, for examples), where p is the number of parameters estimated, $\mathbf{b}$ is the $p \times 1$ vector of parameters, or

$$\mathbf{b} = \begin{bmatrix} L \\ DL \end{bmatrix} \tag{23.3}$$

and $\mathbf{a}$ is the $N \times 1$ vector of residuals, or

$$\mathbf{a} = \begin{bmatrix} a_1 \\ a_2 \\ . \\ . \\ a_i \\ . \\ . \\ a_N \end{bmatrix} \tag{23.4}$$

The general linear model is an approach to data analysis that includes many familiar statistical procedures as special cases. In a multiple regression analysis, the $\mathbf{X}$ matrix contains the numeric observations for each of the p predictor variables for the N subjects, the $\mathbf{Z}$ vector contains the criterion scores for

TABLE 23.2   Examples of Common Design Matrices for Single Unit Analysis ($N_1 = N_2 = 6$)

(A) Immediate and constant changes in level		(B) Immediate and constant changes in level and slope			
1	0	1	0	1	0
1	0	1	0	2	0
1	0	1	0	3	0
1	0	1	0	4	0
1	0	1	0	5	0
1	0	1	0	6	0
1	1	1	1	7	1
1	1	1	1	8	2
1	1	1	1	9	3
1	1	1	1	10	4
1	1	1	1	11	5
1	1	1	1	12	6

(C) Decaying change in level		(D) Delayed change in level	
1	0	1	0
1	0	1	0
1	0	1	0
1	0	1	0
1	0	1	0
1	0	1	0
1	1	1	0
1	.5	1	0
1	.25	1	0
1	.13	1	1
1	.07	1	1
1	.03	1	1

the N subjects, the **b** vector contains the regression weights, and the **a** vector contains the error of prediction and represents the difference between the actual score on the criterion and the predicted score on the criterion. In an analysis of variance, the **X** matrix would consist of indicator variables, such as the numeric values 1 or 0, which indicate group membership, and the **Z** vector contains the dependent variable observations.

For this example, the vector of parameters contains two components, namely L, and DL. This design matrix is presented as (A) in Table 23.2.

The usual least squares solution, which minimizes the sum of the squared errors, is

$$\mathbf{b} = (\mathbf{X'X})^{-1}\mathbf{X'Z}, \tag{23.5}$$

and a test of significance for the null hypothesis H_0: $b_i = 0$ (i.e., H_0: $DL = 0$) is given by

$$t_{bi} = b_i / s_{bi} \tag{23.6}$$

where

$$s_{bi}^2 = s_a^2 C^{ii} \tag{23.7}$$

and s_a^2 is the estimate of the error variance and C^{ii} is the ith diagonal element of $(\mathbf{X'X})^{-1}$. The test statistic would have a **t** distribution with degrees of freedom $N - p$. This is the same test of significance that is used for testing if the regression weight for a predictor is significant in multiple regression.

Transformation of Time Series Data

The general linear model cannot be directly applied to time series analysis because of the presence of dependency in the residuals. It is necessary to perform a transformation on the observed variable, Z_t, to remove dependency, prior to the statistical analysis. A transformation matrix **T** must be found, yielding

$$\mathbf{Y} = \mathbf{TZ}, \tag{23.8}$$

and

$$\mathbf{X^*} = \mathbf{TX} \tag{23.9}$$

The purpose of the model identification step is to determine the appropriate transformation of **Z** into **Y**. Table 23.3 presents mathematical descriptions and relevant comments on six commonly identified ARIMA models. After model identification, an estimation procedure is employed to determine the specific numeric values of ϕ and θ that will be used in the appropriate transformation matrix.

The particular ARIMA (p, d, q) model will determine the specific content of the transformation matrix **T**. Because the correction for dependency involves previous observations, all transformation matrices will have a similar form, a lower triangular matrix. For example, an ARIMA (1, 0, 0) model with five observations would have the following transformation matrix

$$\mathbf{T} = \begin{bmatrix} 1 & 0 & 0 & 0 & 0 \\ \phi_1 & 1 & 0 & 0 & 0 \\ 0 & \phi_1 & 1 & 0 & 0 \\ 0 & 0 & \phi_1 & 1 & 0 \\ 0 & 0 & 0 & \phi_1 & 1 \end{bmatrix} \tag{23.10}$$

that indicates that only the previous observation is necessary to explain the dependency in the data. For an ARIMA (2, 0, 0) model with five observations, the transformation matrix would be

$$\mathbf{T} = \begin{bmatrix} 1 & 0 & 0 & 0 & 0 \\ \phi_1 & 1 & 0 & 0 & 0 \\ \phi_2 & \phi_1 & 1 & 0 & 0 \\ 0 & \phi_2 & \phi_1 & 1 & 0 \\ 0 & 0 & \phi_2 & \phi_1 & 1 \end{bmatrix} \tag{23.11}$$

TABLE 23.3   Common ARIMA Models

Label	(p, d, q)	Descriptive Formula	Comment
White noise	$(0, 0, 0)$	$Z_t = L + a_t$	No dependency in the data
Autoregressive Order One	$(1, 0, 0)$	$Z_t - L = \phi_1(Z_{t-1} - L) + a_t$	Predicted from previous observations
Autoregressive Order Two	$(2, 0, 0)$	$Z_t - L = \phi_1(Z_{t-1} - L) + \phi_2(Z_{t-2} - L) + a_t$	Predicted from previous two observations
Moving Averages Order One	$(0, 0, 1)$	$Z_t - L = a_t - \theta_1 a_{t-1}$	Proportion of previous shock affect observations
Moving Averages Order Two	$(0, 0, 2)$	$Z_t - L = a_t - \theta_1 a_{t-1} - \theta_2 a_{t-2}$	Proportion of two previous shocks affect observations
Integrated Moving Averages	$(0, 1, 1)$	$Z_t - Z_{t-1} = a_t - \theta_1 a_{t-1}$	Stochastic drift and proportion of previous shock affect observations

which indicates that the previous two observations are necessary to explain the dependency in the data. Glass et al. (1975) present an inductive derivation of the necessary transformation for these two models and other common models.

Given **T**, the estimate of the parameters, **b**, may be expressed as a generalized least squares problem—that is to say,

$$\mathbf{b} = (\mathbf{X'T'TX})^{-1}\mathbf{X'T'TZ} = (\mathbf{X^{*'}X^*})^{-1}\mathbf{X^{*'}Y}. \quad (23.12)$$

Parameters of Interest

For an interrupted time series analysis, there are typically four parameters of interest, the level of the series (L), the slope of the series (S), the change in level (DL), and the change in slope (DS). The slope parameters represent one of the other unique characteristics of a longitudinal design, the pattern of change over time. Investigating the pattern of change over time represents one of the real advantages of employing a longitudinal design.

Figure 23.7 illustrates eight different outcomes for a simple one-intervention design. In a typical experimental design, only one follow-up assessment occurs after treatment. By inspecting the different patterns of change over time, we can see that selecting different points in time for the single assessment would result in very different conclusions for four of the examples (C, F, G, and H). For example, ignoring the slope in C would lead the researcher to incorrectly conclude that the intervention was effective. The evolutionary effect (H) is a good example of where the intervention results in a temporary negative effect, perhaps while a response pattern is unlearned, followed by a positive effect. An early assessment would conclude that the treatment had a negative effect; a somewhat later assessment would find no treatment effect, whereas an even later assessment would find a positive treatment effect.

Alternative specifications of the design matrix permit the investigation of different hypotheses concerning the nature of the intervention. Table 23.2 presents some illustrative examples for an $N = 12$ ($n_1 = n_2 = 6$) case. Only changes in level and slope parameters are presented in Table 23.2 because these are the most commonly examined effects in interrupted time series designs. It should also be noted that other representations for specific design matrices have been presented for investigating these parameters. Huitema and McKean (2000) present a detailed discussion of some of the issues related to design specification for the analysis of interventions in time series. As noted earlier, Table 23.2 (A) is the design matrix for an immediate and constant treatment effect that tests for a change in the level of the data series. Table 23.2 (B) is the design matrix for testing both a change in level and a change in slope. Table 23.2 (C) is the design matrix for examining a decaying treatment effect. Table 23.2 (D) is the design matrix for testing a delayed treatment effect. In addition to the designs presented in Table 23.2, alternative time series designs can provide an opportunity to examine additional change parameters that may be impacted by the intervention (e.g., changes in cycles, variance, and pattern or serial dependency). Although less common, such alternative applications can help to more fully elucidate the nature of the effects of an intervention.

Although it is the most prevalent time series methodology, the Box-Jenkins approach to intervention analysis suffers from a number of difficulties. First, gathering the number of data points required for accurate model identification is often prohibitive for research in applied settings. Second, even with the required number of points in hand, correct identification is problematic (Velicer & Harrop, 1983). Third, the method is complex, making applications by the mathematically unsophisticated researcher difficult. Three alternative approaches are described in the next section, all of which attempt to avoid the problematic model identification step.

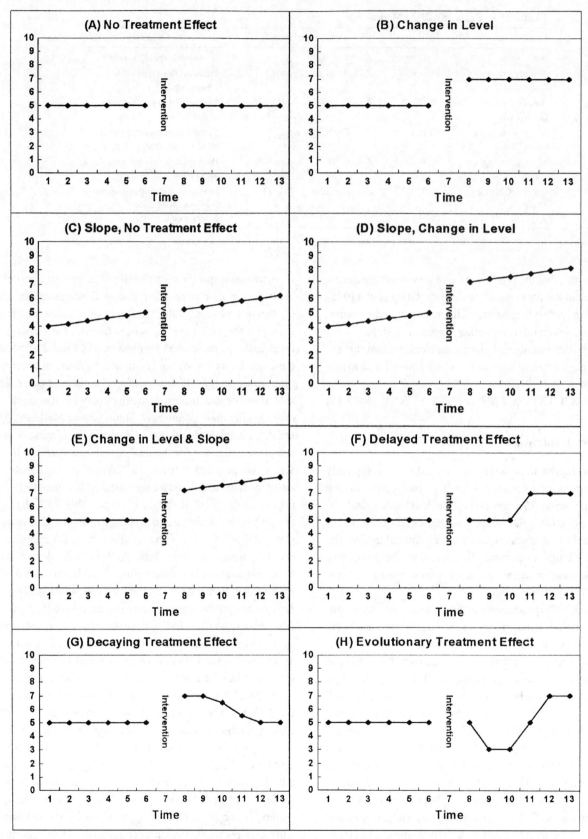

Figure 23.7 Examples of eight different patterns of intervention effects.

Alternative Approaches

Simonton (1977) proposed a procedure that avoids the problem of model identification by using an estimate of the variance-covariance matrix based on pooling the observations across all subjects observed. This approach also requires a basic assumption, namely that all series are assumed to be an ARIMA (1, 0, 0) model. Although this assumption seems to be theoretically indefensible, empirical investigations indicate that this procedure works well in a wide variety of cases (Harrop & Velicer, 1985).

Algina and Swaminathan (1977, 1979; Swaminathan & Algina, 1977) have proposed an alternative in which the sample variance-covariance matrix is employed as an estimator for $\mathbf{T}'\mathbf{T}$ in the modified least squares solution (see Equation 23.7). This approach, however, requires the assumption that the number of subjects is greater than the number of observations per subject. This is not a condition that is likely to be met in most applied research settings, where time series approaches are most appropriate.

Velicer and McDonald (1984) have proposed a third alternative. Instead of trying to determine the specific matrix, they have proposed the use of a *general* transformation matrix with the numerical values of the elements of **T** being estimated for each problem. The rationale for a general matrix is that all transformation matrices, **T**, have an identical form and use a lower triangular matrix with equal subdiagonals. Weight vectors with five nonzero weights were found to be accurate for most cases. A greater number of weights can be employed where indicated by appropriate diagnostics (Velicer & McDonald, 1984). The accuracy of this approach has been supported by two simulation studies (Harrop & Velicer, 1985, 1990b), and it can be implemented with most existing computer programs by specifying a high-order autoregressive model, such as an ARIMA (5, 0, 0) model.

GENERALIZABILITY ISSUES

One of the issues involved in time series analysis is generalizability. How can the results from a single individual or unit be generalized to a larger population? Barlow and Herson (1984) discuss the problem in terms of systematic replication. This approach relies on logical inference rather than formal statistical inference. In another context, this type of approach has been characterized as a qualitative review. Typically, a qualitative review relies primarily on a count of the number of studies that support a hypothesis (Light & Smith, 1971) and the quality of the data is not weighted. Furthermore, the

judgment of the reviewer plays a critical role in the conclusions reached. Two quantitative approaches have been developed that combine multiple replications of a time series study: pooled time series designs and meta-analysis.

Pooled Time Series Analysis

Pooled time series analysis is a large topic with an extensive literature. A complete coverage of the topic is beyond the scope of this chapter. For a more complete coverage of this topic, the reader should see Hsiao (1986) and Dielman (1989). In this section, only one approach is described, an extension of the general transformation approach (Velicer & McDonald, 1991). An advantage of this approach is that it can be adapted with only minor alterations to implement either the Box-Jenkins (1976; Glass et al., 1975) or Simonton (1977) procedures. The method requires only the use of a patterned transformation matrix. The specific choice of the design matrix **X** and the number of units are dictated by the particular questions of interest. The procedure will be illustrated by a two-unit example ($K = 2$), in which the design employed involves only level and change in level (Design Matrix A in Table 23.2).

The observations for all the units are represented in a single vector. This vector contains the set of subvectors for the individual units combined in the form of a single vector rather than a matrix with multiple columns. In this case, the vector **Z** is composed of a subvector of N observations (pre- and postintervention) for each of the experimental units. For example, where there are two experimental units or individuals, with n_1 observations before intervention and n_2 observations after intervention on both Unit 1 and Unit 2, the vector could be represented as

$$\mathbf{Z} = \begin{bmatrix} \mathbf{Z}_1 \\ - \\ \mathbf{Z}_2 \end{bmatrix} = \begin{bmatrix} z_{11} \\ z_{21} \\ \cdot \\ z_{N1} \\ - \\ z_{12} \\ z_{22} \\ \cdot \\ z_{N2} \end{bmatrix} \quad (23.13)$$

Table 23.4 presents an example of the patterned general transformation matrix that could be employed to transform the serially dependent Z_i variables to the serially independent variables Y_i. In this example, there are two experimental units, each with four observations before intervention and four observations after intervention. The w_i entries represent

TABLE 23.4   Example of General Transformation Matrix (T) for Cross-Sectional Analysis

1	0	0	0	0	0	0	0	0	0	0	0	0	0	0	0
W_1	1	0	0	0	0	0	0	0	0	0	0	0	0	0	0
W_2	W_1	1	0	0	0	0	0	0	0	0	0	0	0	0	0
W_3	W_2	W_1	1	0	0	0	0	0	0	0	0	0	0	0	0
W_4	W_3	W_2	W_1	1	0	0	0	0	0	0	0	0	0	0	0
W_5	W_4	W_3	W_2	W_1	1	0	0	0	0	0	0	0	0	0	0
0	W_5	W_4	W_3	W_2	W_1	1	0	0	0	0	0	0	0	0	0
0	0	W_5	W_4	W_3	W_2	W_1	1	0	0	0	0	0	0	0	0
0	0	0	0	0	0	0	0	1	0	0	0	0	0	0	0
0	0	0	0	0	0	0	0	W_1	1	0	0	0	0	0	0
0	0	0	0	0	0	0	0	W_2	W_1	1	0	0	0	0	0
0	0	0	0	0	0	0	0	W_3	W_2	W_1	1	0	0	0	0
0	0	0	0	0	0	0	0	W_4	W_3	W_2	W_1	1	0	0	0
0	0	0	0	0	0	0	0	W_5	W_4	W_3	W_2	W_1	1	0	0
0	0	0	0	0	0	0	0	0	W_5	W_4	W_3	W_2	W_1	1	0
0	0	0	0	0	0	0	0	0	0	W_5	W_4	W_3	W_2	W_1	1

Note. $k = 2$; $n_{11} = n_{12} = n_{21} = n_{22} = 4$.

the values of ϕ and θ required for any ARIMA (p, d, q) model. For example, if an ARIMA $(1, 0, 0)$ model was identified, the values would be $w_1 = \phi_1$ and $w_2 = w_3 = w_4 = w_5 = 0$. Alternatively, if the general transformation approach is employed, only the numeric values for w_1, w_2, w_3, w_4, and w_5 are estimated with no attempt to identify them as values of ϕ or θ.

This transformation matrix will always take the form of a partitioned matrix with repeating transformation matrices in diagonal blocks and null matrices elsewhere. For six units, this could be represented as

$$T = \begin{bmatrix} T^* & O & O & O & O & O \\ O & T^* & O & O & O & O \\ O & O & T^* & O & O & O \\ O & O & O & T^* & O & O \\ O & O & O & O & T^* & O \\ O & O & O & O & O & T^* \end{bmatrix} \quad (23.14)$$

where each T^* is an $N \times N$ lower diagonal transformation matrix $(N = n_1 + n_2)$ and O is an $N \times N$ null matrix. The example in Table 23.4 presents all the elements for a two-unit example. The occurrence of the null matrices in all positions except the diagonal reflects the assumption of independence of the different units.

The use of a properly parameterized design matrix will permit comparisons between different units. Table 23.5 presents an illustrative example. Design Matrix A includes four parameters that reflect level and change in level for both units and the difference between the two units on preintervention and postintervention change in level. If the last parameter (i.e., the difference between the units on the postintervention

change in level) is not significant, Design Matrix B would be adopted, reflecting no difference between the two units in intervention effects (change in level). Differences between units would seem likely to be fairly common for most problems. However, if no such differences exist, Design Matrix C would be appropriate. Design Matrix D is appropriate if no intervention effects or differences between units exist.

The procedure can be generalized to any number of units and any choice of design matrix. Implicit is the assumption that a common transformation matrix is appropriate for all

TABLE 23.5   Example of Design Matrix (X) for Cross-Sectional Problem With Level and Change in Level Analysis

A. Full Model	B. No Difference in Intervention Effects	C. No Difference in Individual Effects	D. No Intervention Effects
1 0 0 0	1 0 0	1 0	1
1 0 0 0	1 0 0	1 0	1
1 0 0 0	1 0 0	1 0	1
1 0 0 0	1 0 0	1 0	1
1 1 0 0	1 1 0	1 1	1
1 1 0 0	1 1 0	1 1	1
1 1 0 0	1 1 0	1 1	1
1 1 0 0	1 1 0	1 1	1
1 0 1 0	1 0 1	1 0	1
1 0 1 0	1 0 1	1 0	1
1 0 1 0	1 0 1	1 0	1
1 0 1 0	1 0 1	1 0	1
1 1 1 1	1 1 1	1 1	1
1 1 1 1	1 1 1	1 1	1
1 1 1 1	1 1 1	1 1	1
1 1 1 1	1 1 1	1 1	1

units. This assumption seems reasonable if the nature of the series is viewed as determined by an underlying process specific to the construct under investigation. As with any of the analytic approaches, diagnostic indicators such as the Ljung and Box test (1978) may be used to test the fit of the model (see Dielman (1989) for a more extensive discussion of testing model assumptions). The basic form of the design matrix should be based on the analyses of the individual units, a priori knowledge when available, or both.

The approach described here has a number of advantages. First, it represents a direct extension of the general transformation approach developed by Velicer and McDonald (1984). This approach avoids the problematic model identification step and has received a favorable evaluation in several simulation studies (Harrop & Velicer, 1985, 1990b).

Second, the approach described here can also be adapted to two of the alternative methods of analysis. For the Glass et al. (1975) approach, a specific transformation matrix corresponding to a particular ARIMA (p, d, q) model would replace the general transformation matrix. Following the Simonton (1977) approach, the ARIMA $(1, 0, 0)$ transformation matrix would be used for all cases instead of the general transformation approach.

Third, the approach is a simple direct extension of existing procedures. It can be implemented by a slight modification of existing computer programs. The problems of adaptation will involve problems of size and speed created by the use of long vectors and resulting large matrices instead of a more complex analysis.

Meta-Analysis

An alternative procedure to combining data from several individuals or units is meta-analysis. Procedures for performing a meta-analysis have been well developed for traditional experimental designs (Glass, McGaw, & Smith, 1981; Hedges & Olkin, 1985; Hunter & Schmidt, 1990; Tobler, 1994). However, meta-analysis procedures have not been widely applied to single-subject designs. Busk and Serlin (1992) present a discussion of the problems of applying meta-analysis to this area. Two problems are (a) primary research reports have often relied on visual analysis (Parsonson & Baer, 1992) rather than time series analysis, resulting in a lack of basic statistical information in the published research reports (O'Rourke & Detsky, 1989); and (b) alternative definitions of effect size must be developed that are appropriate for time series data. Allison and Gorman (1992) and Busk and Serlin (1992) review some alternative effect size calculations appropriate for time series designs.

MULTIVARIATE TIME SERIES ANALYSIS

Cross-Lagged Correlations

Time series analysis on a single dependent measure involves many of the procedures common to multivariate statistics because two vectors of unknowns must be estimated simultaneously: the vector of parameters and the vector of coefficients that represent the dependency in the data. However, when assessing a single unit or subject on multiple occasions, two or more variables can be observed on each occasion. The term *multivariate time series* is used here to denote the observation of more than one variable at each point in time. The variables may be viewed conceptually as including both dependent and independent variables or just dependent variables. If some of the observed variables are appropriately viewed as independent variables, the appropriate analysis is the time series equivalent of an analysis of covariance. If the variables can be viewed as a set of dependent variables—that is to say, multiple indicators of one or more constructs that form the outcome space of interest—the appropriate analysis would be the time series equivalent of a multivariate analysis, sometimes described as a dynamic factor analysis. The next two sections discuss these two approaches in detail.

One of the unique aspects of any time series analysis involving multiple variables observed on each occasion involves the extension of the correlation coefficient. The cross-lagged correlation coefficient for lag $= 0$ is calculated the same way as the pairwise correlation coefficient, using the number of observations over time in place of the number of subjects as the basis. The term *lag* refers to the time relationship between the two variables. Lag zero means that the observation at time t on Z_i is matched with the observation at time t on Z_j. However, the appropriate relationship between the variables may involve one variable at time t and the other variable at time $t - 1$; that is, there may be a delay between a change in one variable and the associated change in the other variable. If Z_i lags Z_j, the maximum correlation would occur between Z_i at time $t + 1$ and Z_j at time t. Alternatively, Z_i could lead Z_j, producing the maximum correlation between Z_i at time $t - 1$ and Z_j at time t.

A critical decision for any multivariate time series analysis is determining the appropriate lag between the set of observed variables. There are generally three alternative methods. First, the lag could be determined on the basis of theory. In some areas, well-established theoretical models exist like the supply and demand models in economics. Second, the lag could be determined on the basis of previous empirical findings. If a set of variables has been extensively investigated, the accumulated empirical evidence could serve as a guide to the appropriate order of the lag. Third, the appropriate lag could be estimated as part of the model estimation procedure. This would involve calculating the cross-lagged correlations for a reasonable set of lags—for example, from +5 to −5. The lag that produces the highest numeric value for the correlation would be assumed to be the appropriate lag.

Covariates

When two variables are observed on each occasion, one of the variables (Z_i) may be conceptualized as the dependent variable and any additional variables (X_j, X_k, etc.) may be viewed as covariates. A covariate should be related to the dependent variable but be unable to be influenced by the intervention. This analysis has been labeled a *concomitant variable time series analysis* (Glass et al., 1975) and is a direct analogue of the analysis of covariance. The covariate is employed to statistically remove some variation from the dependent measure, thus increasing sensitivity. The design matrix and parameter vector are presented in Equation 23.15 for a $N_1 = N_2 = 4$ observation example. The first two parameters estimate the level and change in level, and the last parameter, β, estimates the relationship between the covariate and dependent variable.

$$\mathbf{Xb} = \begin{bmatrix} 1 & 0 & X_1 \\ 1 & 0 & X_2 \\ 1 & 0 & X_3 \\ 1 & 0 & X_4 \\ 1 & 1 & X_5 \\ 1 & 1 & X_6 \\ 1 & 1 & X_7 \\ 1 & 1 & X_8 \end{bmatrix} \begin{bmatrix} \mathbf{L} \\ \mathbf{DL} \\ \beta \end{bmatrix} \quad (23.15)$$

Although similar to the analysis of covariance, there are two problems that are unique to multivariate time series analysis. First, the investigator must determine the appropriate lag between the covariate(s) and the dependent variables. This is the same issue as discussed with the cross-lagged correlation above. Second, there may be dependency present in the covariate. It may be necessary to transform the covariate before performing the analysis. One application of this procedure is to control the effects of seasonality in the data (discussed later in this chapter).

Time Series Analysis Using Structural Equation Modeling

Time series data can be represented as a special case of structural equation modeling (SEM). Although the use of a structural equation modeling program to perform a time series analysis is not recommended, conceptualizing time

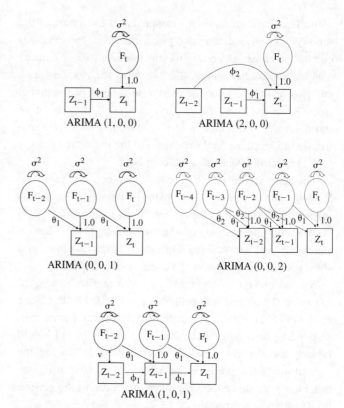

Figure 23.8   Five different ARIMA models represented as structural equation models.

series models in this manner can provide researchers who are familiar with SEM representations a way to better understand ARIMA models. This type of representation, initially described by van Buuren (1997), also provides a bridge to dynamic factor analysis described in the next section.

Figure 23.8 presents the representation of five basic ARIMA models as SEM diagrams. In SEM, unobserved or latent variables are represented as circles and observed or manifest variables are represented as squares. The path coefficients on direct or indirect paths between variables indicate the strength of the relationships. For time series data, the manifest variables are the dependent variables, Z_t. The error term is the latent variable and can be divided into two parts, the unique or uncorrelated part, and the dependent or correlated part. For an ARIMA (1, 0, 0) model, the path between F_t and Z_t is fixed at 1.00 and the path between Z_{t-1} and Z_t is estimated by ϕ_1. This reflects the conceptualization of an autoregressive model as involving prediction from the preceding observation. For an ARIMA (0, 0, 1), the relationship between Z_{t-1} and Z_t is set to 0 and the relationship between F_{t-1} and Z_t is estimated by θ_1. This reflects the conceptualization of a moving averages model as retaining a proportion of the previous shock or error term. The other three panels of Figure 23.8 present the representations for ARIMA (2, 0, 0), (0, 0, 2), and (1, 0, 1) models.

Dynamic Factor Analysis

Another promising and relatively new statistical technique for the analysis of multivariate time series employs dynamic factor models. This method involves a merging of the longitudinal data approaches employed in time series analysis with the use of latent variables or factors to organize a set of observed variables. This methodology represents a very sophisticated extension of P-technique factor analysis (Cattell, 1963, 1988). P-technique factor analysis represents a type of time series analysis that utilizes common factor analysis methodology to examine a multivariate data set collected on a single individual on multiple occasions. However, strong concerns have been raised about the appropriate use of P-technique factor analysis. The major concern centers on the typical dependent nature of data that are gathered on a single individual on multiple occasions and the consequent violation of the underlying traditional factor analysis model with P-technique factor analysis when such data are analyzed (Wood & Brown, 1994). Empirically, one consequence of using P-technique methodology with data with positive serial correlations at the latent variable level would be a bias that results in substantially lowered estimates of the factor loadings compared to the true loading values (Wood & Brown, 1994).

The recently developed dynamic factor analysis (Hershberger, 1998; Hershberger, Molenaar, & Corneal, 1996; Molenaar, 1985, 1987; Molenaar, De Gooijer, & Schmitz, 1992) permits serial dependency in the data and includes P-technique factor analysis as a special case. Dynamic factor analysis may prove especially useful to behavioral researchers interested in questions of growth or change over time, and their underlying processes, because complex serial relationships among variables can be explored utilizing this methodology. Practically, it can be difficult to apply this model. Wood and Brown (1994) provide a detailed description of an implementation of the dynamic factor model, present an evaluation of this approach, and provide a set of SAS macros that make this technique much more accessible to the research community.

One of the limitations to implementing a dynamic factor analysis in practice is the number of observations required to provide an adequate sample estimate of the population covariance matrices. Nesselroade and Molenaar (1999) propose pooling short multivariate time series from a group of individuals and provide an interesting example of this methodology using real data. Pooling has the advantage of utilizing shorter data series that may be more easily gathered and that are not typically examined using traditional time series methods. Although promising, the method requires that a pattern of correlations at the individual level be sufficiently homogeneous such that the individuals can be treated as representing a common model.

Despite improvements in both methodology and the dissemination of program modules developed by individual researchers and available as shareware, conducting a dynamic factor analysis is still a significant, difficult, and somewhat ambiguous undertaking. Aspects of the analyses are still in the development stage (Nesselroade & Molenaar, 1999; Wood & Brown, 1994). Issues to be resolved include determining the correct number of factors to extract, determining the correct lags between the variables in the final model, and statistically testing whether a group of individuals can be legitimately pooled. However, the use of multiple indicators measuring one or more latent variables represents a very promising means of extending the focus of time series analysis from univariate to multivariate outcome spaces.

OTHER ISSUES

Cyclic Data

The presence of cyclic or seasonal data is a potential confounding variable in time series data. Daily data gathered on individuals often have a weekly or monthly cycle. Three alternative procedures have been proposed to deal with cyclic data.

Deseasonalization

In some content areas, the cyclic nature of the data is well known. For example, in the economic area, much of the data is adjusted for seasonal effects before it is reported. These seasonal adjustments, based on *a priori* information, remove cyclic trends from the data prior to any time series analysis.

Statistical Control

An alternative method of adjusting for seasonal effects is to find some variable that is sensitive to the same seasonal effects as the dependent measure but cannot be affected by the intervention in the case of an interrupted series. This variable could then be used as a covariate. The cyclic effects would be statistically controlled. Some of the problems in using a covariate are discussed later in this chapter.

Combined Models

A third alternative approach involves the use of combined models. McCleary and Hay (1980) discuss this approach in detail. As an example, suppose we have a time series that is represented by a lag one moving averages model, that is a (0, 0, 1) model

$$Z_t - L = A_t - \theta_1 A_{t-1}. \quad (23.16)$$

Furthermore, assume that a seasonal component of Lag 7 is present. This could be modeled as

$$Z_t - L = A_t - \theta_7 A_{t-7}. \quad (23.17)$$

The time series would therefore be described as an ARIMA $(0, 0, 1)$ $(0, 0, 1)_7$ model or

$$Z_t - L = (A_t - \theta_1 A_{t-1})(A_t - \theta_7 A_{t-7}). \quad (23.18)$$

Unlike the first two approaches, the combined model approach presents difficulties for the extension of this procedure to either pooled procedures or multivariate time series approaches and would require longer series.

Missing Data

Missing data are an almost unavoidable problem in time series analysis and present a number of unique challenges. Life events will result in missing data even for the most conscientious researchers. In the model identification study on nicotine regulation (Velicer, Redding, et al., 1992) described previously, missing data were a relatively minor problem. Four participants had no missing data—that is, all 124 observations were available. For four other participants, four or fewer observations were missing. Only two participants showed significant amounts of missing data (115 and 97 observations available).

Little and Rubin (1987) provide the most thorough theoretical and mathematical coverage of handling missing data in time series analysis. However, the missing data problem for time series designs has received little attention in the applied behavioral sciences area. Rankin and Marsh (1985) assessed the impact of different amounts of missing data for 32 simulated time series, modeled after 16 real-world data examples. They concluded that with up to 20% missing data there was little impact on model identification, but the impact is pronounced when more than 40% is missing.

In an extensive simulation study, Velicer and Colby (2001) compared four different techniques of handling missing data in an ARIMA (1, 0, 0) model: (a) deletion of missing observations from the analysis, (b) substitution of the mean of the series, (c) substitution of the mean of the two adjacent observations, and (d) maximum likelihood estimation (Jones, 1980). Computer-generated time series data of length 100 were generated for 50 different conditions representing five

levels of autocorrelation ($\phi = -.80, -.40, 0.0, .40,$ or $.80$), two levels of slope (slope $= 0$ or a positive slope of $15°$), and five levels of proportion of missing data (0%, 10%, 20%, 30%, or 40%). Methods were compared with respect to the accuracy of estimation for four parameters (level, error variance, degree of autocorrelation, and slope).

The choice of method had a major impact on the analysis. The maximum likelihood procedure for handling missing data outperformed all others. Although this result was expected, the degree of accuracy was very impressive. The method provided accurate estimates of all four parameters in the ARIMA (1, 0, 0) model, namely level, error variance, degree of autocorrelation, and slope. Furthermore, the method provided accurate parameter estimates across all levels of missing data, even when 40% of the data had been randomly eliminated. Imputing the mean of the series is an *unacceptable* method for handling missing data. Whenever a slope parameter was introduced into the data, the imputed mean method led to very inaccurate estimates of all four parameters. Severe overestimates of error variance and level were obtained, which would result in very inaccurate tests of significance. These results reflect the fact that this procedure ignores the ordinal position of the observations. The other two ad hoc methods also produced inaccurate estimates for some of the parameters. The *mean of adjacent observations* produced reasonable estimates of level and slope. However, the method produced extremely inaccurate estimates of the dependency parameter. *Deletion* was generally accurate for the estimation of level and error variance but was inaccurate for the longitudinal parameters. Deletion led to an overestimate of the slope, and was also inaccurate for moderate and high degrees of negative dependency. The results of this study demonstrated that the maximum likelihood estimation method for handling missing data represents a substantial improvement over the available ad hoc procedures and should be employed in all analyses when missing data occur.

The Velicer and Colby (2001) study investigated missing data procedures when all assumptions were met. Colby and Velicer (2001) extended this approach to cases where one of three assumptions was violated: (a) the ARIMA model was not correctly specified; (b) the pattern of missing data was systematic, rather than random; and (c) the data were not normally distributed. For the model misspecification study, three alternative models were fitted to all data sets: the correct model, an ARIMA (1, 0, 0) model, and an ARIMA (5, 0, 0) model. For the systematically missing data study, three conditions were investigated: missing at random, systematically missing with an odd-even pattern, and systematically missing with a block of sequential data pattern. For the nonnormality study, two distributions were considered: normal and lognormal. The maximum likelihood method with the ARIMA (5, 0, 0) model specified produced very accurate results across all conditions. It was generally as good or better than the correct model identification. The maximum likelihood with the ARIMA (1, 0, 0) model generally produced a very good approximation. Violations of the distribution assumptions had no effect.

Computational Issues

Analysis of time series data requires the use of a computer program. Fortunately, a large number of programs have become available in the last two decades. Harrop and Velicer (1990a, 1990b) evaluated five programs: BMDP (Dixon, 1985), GENTS (Velicer, Fraser, McDonald, & Harrop, 1986), ITSE (Williams & Gottman, 1982), SAS (SAS Institute, 1984), and TSX (Bower & Glass, 1974; Glass, Bower, & Padia, 1974). Simulated data from 44 different ARIMA models were employed to assess the accuracy of the programs (Harrop & Velicer, 1990b). Three programs produced generally satisfactory results (TSX, GENTS, and SAS). One was inaccurate across a wide range of models (ITSE), and one was occasionally inaccurate and occasionally failed to complete the analysis (BMDP). The original ITSE contained incorrect formulas and an amended version of this program, ITSACORR, is available (Crosbie, 1993). The overall evaluation of the computation features and quality of documentation was not very favorable (Harrop & Velicer, 1990a). Some of the programs evaluated in the Harrop and Velicer (1990a, 1990b) studies have been substantially modified since inclusion in the study and time series analysis has since been added to widely used statistical packages, such as SPSS Trends (SPSS, Inc., 1988) and SYSTAT (Wilkinson, 1986). SAS remains one of the best programs, with extensive supporting features. However, a new comparative evaluation of time series programs is needed because the Harrop and Velicer studies are dated.

Measurement Issues

One of the impediments to the widespread use of time series in the behavioral sciences has been the problem associated with obtaining appropriate quantitative measures on a large number of occasions. Measures previously employed for time series analysis include physiological and behavioral measures such as blood pressure, the number of cigarettes smoked per day, and the number of standard drinks per day. Many of the measures that have been employed in cross-sectional research studies are simply not appropriate for time series designs. Assessment batteries were often lengthy and

could not be repeated regularly at short intervals. Assessments have also typically required contact between the researcher and the subject, placing a further burden on the research and limited the number of assessments. Self-report measures, repeated in close proximity, may elicit recall of the subject's previous response rather than an accurate assessment of current status. However, advances in information systems technology are overcoming some of these barriers. This section reviews some of the sources of data appropriate for time series designs and some of the advances in technology that will improve access to this type of data.

Available Data

Some types of data appropriate for time series analysis are gathered regularly by public or private agencies. For example, information on stock market values, number of deaths due to cancer, and incidents of violations of laws are generally available and can be employed to assess the effectiveness of policy decisions. One of the more unusual examples of this approach is Simonton's (1998a) application of time series analysis to a well-studied problem, the recurrent attacks of mental and physical illness experienced by King George III of Great Britain. Although this problem has long been of interest to historians and psychiatrists, the approach employed in this paper is unique and represents an innovative new approach, which was labeled the *historiometric method*. Simonton (1998a) proposes the reasonable hypothesis that changes in stress level precipitated dietary changes such as increased alcoholic consumption that in turn activated changes in liver function that activated *porphyria hepatica*. Using coded historic records, the study describes the pattern of changes over time, proposes a causal mechanism that explains the 9-month lag, and is consistent with the known facts. (See Simonton, 1998b, Velicer & Plummer, 1998, and Read & Nasby, 1998 for related commentary.)

Daily Diary Methods

Self-monitoring a target behavior by recording in a daily diary is a commonly employed method of data collection. Participants use a diary or calendar to record the extent to which they engage in a target behavior for specific intervals of time. Exact dates and amounts (i.e., for drinking behavior) will be more accurate using daily recording than those obtained by retrospective assessment. However, noncompliance with daily diary methods is often a significant problem. Researchers have attempted to overcome the lack of compliance by combining the use of diaries with frequent appointments at the laboratory to turn in data (e.g., every 12 hours; every day) but the utility of this approach is likely to be limited to special populations (e.g., college students). For most populations, transportation and time constraints are likely to result in lack of compliance. Daily telephone calls to participants (or call-ins by participants) can help verify compliance with minimal additional burden on participants.

Technologically Assisted Measurement

In order to assess individuals' naturalistic behavior over extended periods of time, yet still retain more experimental control than daily diaries permits, researchers have employed small computers that participants can carry with them. One of the more extensively developed examples is *ecological momentary assessment* (EMA) developed by Shiffman and colleagues (Shiffman, 1998; Shiffman et al., 1997; Shiffman, Paty, Gnys, Kassel, & Hickcox, 1996; Stone & Shiffman, 1994). In the *experience sampling* paradigm, participants are supplied with a handheld computer that beeps them at random intervals, prompting them to complete an assessment at that time. In addition, participants may be instructed to initiate an assessment on the computer in response to the occurrence of some event (e.g., smoking a cigarette). This paradigm is a high-tech version of self-monitoring; participants enter their data into the computer's interactive framework rather than writing in a diary or log.

Data from EMA would generally be appropriate for time series analysis. One caution, however, is that EMA can present problems for time series analysis, depending on the extent to which the prompting beeps are nonrandomly spaced. A potential solution is to treat the intervals in which no assessment occurred as missing at random and use a missing data procedure. With advances in information systems technology, variations on the EMA approach are being developed that rely on two-way pagers and digital cell phones.

Telemetrics

One of the limitations of physiological monitors has been the restriction of the subject to the confines in the laboratory. Data produced under such settings has limited generalizability to the natural environment. Recent advances in telemetrics have the potential to overcome these limitations. Computers and monitoring devices can now be miniaturized and can continually transmit information to a central source. An example of this approach is provided by the use of so-called wearable computers for such purposes as assessing emotional intelligence (Healy & Picard, 1998; Picard, 1997; Picard & Healey, 1997). Some of the wearable computers that have been developed include sensors and transmitters that are incorporated into articles of clothing—for example, an

earring that can assess blood volume pressure; rings, bracelets, and shoes than can monitor galvanic skin responses; a jacket that can monitor the gestural signals of a conductor; glasses that can record a graphical display of the wearer's facial expressions; and miniaturized cameras and microphones embedded in clothing that can record what a person is seeing and hearing. The combination of such devices can also facilitate the collection of data to study the relationship of physiological responses to environmental cues within the detailed context of the individual's personal and objective environment. This is a rapidly evolving area, with the first IEEE International Symposium on Wearable Computers being held in 1997. These devices produce time series data appropriate for analysis and are likely to be a primary area of application for multivariate time series procedures as the emotional and physiological responses are related to the environmental stimulus and context.

Time as a Critical Variable

One of the critical but often overlooked aspects of longitudinal designs is the importance of the choice of the units of the time variable. Time series analysis assumes that the observations are taken in equally spaced intervals. This is a critical assumption. Unfortunately, there is very little information available in the behavioral sciences to guide the choice of interval size. Sometimes the interval is predetermined, such as when existing data were employed. Other times the choice of interval is determined by the convenience of the experimenter or the subject. As less obtrusive methods of data collection become available, the choice of interval will be able to better reflect the needs of the research question.

The interval employed could strongly influence the accuracy of the conclusions that can be drawn. For example, in Figure 23.1, the choice of two 8-hour intervals (parts of the day when the subject was awake) strongly influenced the results. A negative autocorrelation of −.70 would become a positive autocorrelation of .49 if the observations had occurred once a day and .24 if assessed every 48 hours. In general, longer intervals can be expected to produce lower levels of dependency in the data. Perhaps this explains the basis for Huitema's (1985) problematic observation that autocorrelations should be expected to be zero. (Time series should still be employed if the dependency is near zero.) However, if a cyclic component is present in the data of 30 days and data gathering occurred several times a day for 28 days, the cyclic component would be missed.

If the focus is on the functional relationship between two variables, the time interval can also be critical. If a change in x produces a change in y with a 48-hour lag, observation taken at weekly intervals might erroneously conclude that the variables are not related and observations taken at 24-hour daily intervals would detect the relationship. The longer interval might detect that some relationship exists between the two variables if accumulated across subjects, but would not be able to determine the direction of relationship. Until we have adequate theoretical models and accumulate empirical finding for the variables of interest, shorter intervals will be preferable to longer intervals because it is always possible to collapse multiple observations. It is also important that any statements about the presence or degree of a relation between variables based on autocorrelations and cross-lagged correlations always reference the interval employed in the study.

SUMMARY AND CONCLUSIONS

Time series analysis has a tremendous potential in the behavioral sciences. Longitudinal data analysis methods have the potential to address research questions that could not be addressed, or only addressed indirectly, by cross-sectional methods. Time series analysis is one of the large number of computational procedures that have been developed specifically for the analysis of longitudinal data during the last 30 years. In fact, time series analysis can be viewed as the prototypical longitudinal method. All these recently developed procedures share the common characteristic of requiring a high-speed computer to perform the analysis. For time series analysis, advances in computer technology are also producing more sources of data for which the method is appropriate. The combination of computational advances and new sources of data has increased the range of potential applications. Two of the early drawbacks to time series analysis, the large sample size required for model identifications and problems with generalizability have been largely overcome in the last decade. There are clearly areas in which more work is still needed, such as pooled time series analysis and multivariate time series analysis. Time series analysis should now be viewed as representing one of a number of potential methods of data analysis available to all researchers, rather than as a novel and difficult procedure. We are now reaching the point in the behavioral sciences at which the data analysis method will be matched to the research problem rather than the research problems being determined by the available methods of data analysis.

REFERENCES

Aitken, A. C. (1934). On least squares and lineal combination of observations. *Proceedings of the Royal Society of Edinburg H, 55,* 42–47.

Akaike, H. (1974). A new look at the statistical model identification. *IEEE Transactions on Automatic Control, 19,* 716–723.

Algina, J., & Swaminathan, H. A. (1977). A procedure for the analysis of time series designs. *Journal of Experimental Education, 45,* 56–60.

Algina, J., & Swaminathan, H. A. (1979). Alternatives to Simonton's analysis of the interrupted and multiple-group time series designs. *Psychological Bulletin, 86,* 919–926.

Allison, A. B., & Gorman, B. S. (1992, August). *Calculating effect sizes for meta-analysis: The case of the single case.* Paper presented at the meeting of the American Psychological Association, Washington, DC.

Barlow, D. H., & Hersen, M. (1984). *Single case experimental designs: Strategies for studying behavior change* (2nd ed.). New York: Pergamon.

Beguin, J. M., Courieroux, C., & Monfort, A. (1980). Identification of a mixed autoregressive-moving average process: The corner method. In O. D. Anderson (Ed.), *Time Series: Proceedings of the International Conference held at Nottingham University* (pp. 423–436). Amsterdam: North-Holland.

Bhansali, R. J., & Downham, D. Y. (1977). Some properties of the order of an autoregressive model selected by a generalization of Aiaike's FPE-Criterion. *Biometrika, 64,* 547–551.

Bower, C., & Glass, G. V. (1974). TSX [Computer program]. Boulder, CO: University of Colorado.

Box, G. E. P., & Jenkins, G. M. (1976). *Time-series analysis: Forecasting and control.* San Francisco: Holden Hay.

Box, G. E. P., Jenkins, G. M., & Reinsel, G. C. (1994). *Time series analysis: Forecasting and control* (3rd ed.). Englewood Cliffs, NJ: Prentice-Hall.

Box, G. E. P., & Pierce, W. A. (1970). Distribution of residual autocorrelations in autoregressive-integrated moving average time series models. *Journal of the American Statistical Association, 65,* 1509–1526.

Box, G. E. P., & Tiao, G. C. (1965). A change in level of nonstationary time series. *Biometrika, 52,* 181–192.

Box, G. E. P., & Tiao, G. C. (1975). Intervention analysis with application to economic and environmental problems. *Journal of the American Statistical Association, 70,* 70–92.

Busk, P. L., & Serlin, R. C. (1992). Meta-analysis for single-case research. In T. R. Kratochwill & J. R. Levin (Eds.), *Single-case research designs and analysis* (pp. 187–212). Hillsdale, NJ: Erlbaum.

Cattell, R. B. (1963). The structure of change by P- and incremental r-technique. In C. W. Harris (Ed.), *Problems in measuring change* (pp. 163–198). Madison: University of Wisconsin Press.

Cattell, R. B. (1988). The data box. In J. R. Nesselroade & R. B. Cattell (Eds.), *Handbook of multivariate experimental psychology* (pp. 69–130). New York: Plenum.

Colby, S. M., & Velicer, W. F. (2001). *A comparison of procedures for handling missing data in time series analysis under violation of assumption.* Manuscript under review, University of Rhode Island.

Crosbie, J. (1993). Interrupted time-series analysis with brief single-subject data. *Journal of Consulting and Clinical Psychology, 61,* 966–974.

Dielman, T. E. (1989). *Pooled cross-sectional and time series data analysis*. New York: Marcel-Dekker.

Dixon, W. J. (1985). BMDP statistical software [Computer program manual]. Berkeley: University of California Press.

Djuric, P. M., & Kay, S. M. (1992). Order selection of autoregressive models. *IEEE Transactions on Acoustics, Speech, and Signal Processing, 40,* 2829–2833.

Glass, G. V., Bower, C., & Padia, W. L. (1974). TSX [Computer program]. Boulder, CO: University of Colorado.

Glass, G. V., McGaw, B., & Smith, M. L. (1981). *Meta-analysis in social research*. Beverly Hills, CA: Sage.

Glass, G. V., Willson, V. L., & Gottman, J. M. (1975). *Design and analysis of time series experiments*. Boulder, CO: Colorado Associate University Press.

Gottman, J. M. (1973). N-of-one and N-of-two research in psychotherapy. *Psychological Bulletin, 80,* 93–105.

Gottman, J. M., & Glass, G. V. (1978). Analysis of interrupted time-series experiments. In T. R. Kratochwill (Ed.), *Single subject research: Strategies for evaluating change* (pp. 197–235). New York: Academic Press.

Grey, H. L., Kelly, G. D., & McIntire, D. D. (1978). A new approach to ARMA modeling. *Communications in Statistics, B7,* 1–77.

Hall, R. V., Fox, R., Willard, D., Goldsmith, L., Emerson, M., Owen, M., Davis, F., & Porcia, E. (1971). The teacher as observer and experimenter in the modification of disputing and talking-out behaviors. *Journal of Applied Behavior Analysis, 4,* 141–149.

Hannan, E. J., & Rissanen, J. (1982). Recursive estimation of mixed autoregressive moving average order. *Biometrika, 69,* 81–94.

Harrop, J. W., & Velicer, W. F. (1985). A comparison of three alternative methods of time series model identification. *Multivariate Behavioral Research, 20,* 27–44.

Harrop, J. W., & Velicer, W. F. (1990a). Computer programs for interrupted time series analysis: Pt. I. A qualitative evaluation. *Multivariate Behavioral Research, 25,* 219–231.

Harrop, J. W., & Velicer, W. F. (1990b). Computer programs for interrupted time series analysis: Pt. II. A quantitative evaluation. *Multivariate Behavioral Research, 25,* 233–249.

Healey, J., & Picard, R. (1998). StartleCam: A cybernetic wearable camera. (Technical Report No. 468). Cambridge, MA: M.I.T. Media Laboratory Perceptual Computing Section.

Hedges, L. V., & Olkin, I. (1985). *Statistical methods for meta-analysis*. Orlando, FL: Academic Press.

Hershberger, S. L. (1998). Dynamic factor analysis. In G. A. Marcoulides (Ed.), *Modern methods for business research* (pp. 217–249). Mahwah, NJ: Erlbaum.

Hershberger, S. L., Molenaar, P. C. M., & Corneal, S. E. (1996). A hierarchy of univariate and multivariate structural time series models. In G. A. Marcoulides & R. E. Schumacker (Eds.), *Advanced structural equation modeling: Issues and techniques* (pp. 159–194). Mahwah, NJ: Erlbaum.

Hsiao, C. (1986). *Analysis of panel data*. Cambridge, UK: Cambridge University Press.

Huitema, B. E. (1985). Autocorrelation in applied behavior analysis: A myth. *Behavioral Assessment, 7,* 107–118.

Huitema, B. E., & McKean, J. W. (2000). Design specification issues in time-series intervention models. *Educational and Psychological Measurement, 60,* 38–58.

Hunter, J. E., & Schmidt, F. L. (1990). *Methods for meta-analysis*. Newbury Park, CA: Sage.

Jarvik, M. E. (1973). Further observations on nicotine as the reinforcing agent in smoking. In W. L. Dunn, Jr. (Ed.), *Smoking behavior: Motives and incentives* (pp. 33–49). Washington, DC: V. H. Winston.

Jones, R. H. (1980). Maximum likelihood fitting of ARMA models to time series missing observations. *Technometrics, 22,* 389–396.

Kashyap, R. L. (1977). A Bayesian comparison of different classes of dynamic models using empirical data. *IEEE Transactions on Automatic Control, 22,* 715–727.

Leventhal, H., & Cleary, P. D. (1980). The smoking problem: A review of the research and theory in behavioral risk modification. *Psychological Bulletin, 88,* 370–405.

Little, R. J. A., & Rubin, D. B. (1987). *Statistical analysis with missing data*. New York: Wiley.

Ljung, G. M., & Box, G. E. P. (1978). On a measure of lack of fit in time series models. *Biometrika, 65,* 297–303.

McCleary, R., & Hay, R. A., Jr. (1980). *Applied time series analysis for the social sciences*. Beverly Hills, CA: Sage.

McFall, R. M. (1978). Smoking cessation research. *Journal of Consulting and Clinical Psychology, 76,* 703–712.

Molenaar, P. C. M. (1985). A dynamic factor model for the analysis of multivariate time series. *Psychometrika, 50,* 181–202.

Molenaar, P. C. M. (1987). Dynamic factor analysis in the frequency domain: Causal modeling of multivariate psychophysiological time series. *Multivariate Behavioral Research, 22,* 329–353.

Molenaar, P. C. M., De Gooijer, J. G., & Schmitz, B. (1992). Dynamic factor analysis of nonstationary multivariate time series. *Psychometrika, 57,* 333–349.

Morrison, D. F. (1983). *Applied linear statistical methods*. Englewood Cliffs, NJ: Prentice-Hall.

Nesselroade, J. R., & Molenaar, P. C. M. (1999). Pooling lagged covariance structures based on short, multivariate time series for dynamic factor analysis. In R. H. Hoyle (Ed.), *Statistical strategies for small sample research* (pp. 223–250). Thousand Oaks, CA: Sage.

O'Rourke, K., & Detsky, A. S. (1989). Meta-analysis in medical research: Strong encouragement for higher quality in individual research efforts. *Journal of Clinical Epidemiology, 42,* 1021–1024.

Parsonson, B. S., & Baer, D. M. (1992). The visual analysis of data and current research into the stimuli controlling it. In T. R. Kratochwill & J. R. Levin (Eds.), *Single-case research designs and analysis* (pp. 15–40). Hillsdale, NJ: Erlbaum.

Parzen, E. (1974). Some recent advances in time series modeling *IEEE Transactions on Automatic Control, 19,* 723–729.

Picard, R. W. (1997). *Affective computing.* Cambridge, MA: MIT Press.

Picard, R. W., & Healey, J. (1997). *Affective wearables.* (Technical Report No. 432). Cambridge, MA: M.I.T. Media Laboratory Perceptual Computing Section.

Pukkila, T. M. (1982). On the identification of ARIMA (p, q) models. In O. D. Anderson (Ed.), *Time Series Analysis: Vol. 1. Theory and Practice. Proceeding of the International Conference held at Valencia, Spain* (pp. 81–103). Amsterdam: North-Holland.

Rankin, E. D., & Marsh, J. C. (1985). Effects of missing data on the statistical analysis of clinical time series. *Social Work Research and Abstracts, 21,* 13–16.

Read, N. W., & Nasby, N. (1998). In search of personality: Reflections on the case of King George. *Journal of Personality, 66,* 467–476.

Rissanen, J. (1978). Modeling by shortest data description. *Automatica, 14,* 465–478.

Rissanen, J. (1986a). Stochastic complexity and modeling. *Annals of Statistics, 14,* 1080–1100.

Rissanen, J. (1986b). Order estimation by accumulated prediction errors. *Journal of Applied Probability, 12A,* 55–61.

Rosel, J., & Elósegui, E. (1994). Daily and weekly smoking habits: A Box Jenkins Analysis. *Psychological Reports, 75,* 1639–1648.

Russell, M. A. (1977). Nicotine chewing gum as a substitute for smoking. *British Medical Journal, 1,* 1060–1063.

SAS Institute. (1984). SAS/ETS user's guide (Version 5) [Computer program manual]. Cary, NC: SAS Institute.

Schachter, S. (1977). Nicotine regulation in heavy and light smokers. *Journal of Experimental Psychology: General, 106,* 5–12.

Schwartz, G. (1978). Estimating the dimension of a model. *Annals of Statistics, 6,* 461–469.

Shiffman, S. (1998). Real-time self-report of momentary states in the natural environment: Computerized ecological momentary assessment. In A. A. Stone, J. Turkkan, J. Jobe, C. Bachrach, H. Kurtzman, & V. Cain (Eds.), *The science of self-report: Implications for research and practice* (pp. 277–296). Malwah, NJ: Erlbaum.

Shiffman, S., Hufford, M., Hickcox, M., Paty, J. A., Gnys, M., & Kassel, J. D. (1997). Remember that? A comparison of real-time versus retrospective recall of smoking lapses. *Journal of Consulting and Clinical Psychology, 65,* 292–300.

Shiffman, S., Paty, J. A., Gnys, M., Kassel, J. D., & Hickcox, M. (1996). First lapses to smoking: Within-subjects analysis of real-time reports. *Journal of Consulting and Clinical Psychology, 64,* 366–379.

Simonton, D. K. (1977). Cross-sectional time-series experiments: Some suggested statistical analyses. *Psychological Bulletin, 84,* 489–502.

Simonton, D. K. (1998a). Mad King George: The impact of personal and political stress on mental and physical health. *Journal of Personality, 66,* 443–466.

Simonton, D. K. (1998b). Historiometry and a historic life. *Journal of Personality, 66,* 487–493.

Solomon, R. L. (1980). The opponent-process theory of acquired motivation. *American Psychologist, 35,* 691–712.

Solomon, R. L., & Corbit, J. D. (1973). An opponent-process theory of motivation: Pt. II. Cigarette addiction. *Journal of Abnormal Psychology, 81,* 158–171.

Solomon, R. L., & Corbit, J. D. (1974). An opponent-process theory of motivation: Pt. I. Temporal dynamics of affect. *Psychological Review, 81,* 119–145.

SPSS, Inc. (1988). SPSS-X Trends [Computer program manual]. Chicago, IL: SPSS, Inc.

Stone, A. A., & Shiffman, S. (1994). Ecological momentary assessment (EMA) in behavioral medicine. *Annuals of Behavioral Medicine, 16,* 199–202.

Swaminathan, H., & Algina, J. (1977). Analysis of quasi-experimental time series designs. *Multivariate Behavioral Research, 12,* 111–131.

Tobler, N. (1994). Meta-analytic issues for prevention intervention research In L. M. Collins & L. A. Seitz, (Eds.), *Advances in data analysis for prevention Intervention Research* (NIDA Research Monograph 142, pp. 342–403). Rockville, MD: National Institute on Drug Abuse.

Tomkins, S. S. (1966). Psychological model for smoking behavior. *American Journal of Public Health, 68,* 250–257.

Tomkins, S. S. (1968). A modified model of smoking behavior. In E. F. Borgatta & R. R. Evans (Eds.), *Smoking, health and behavior* (pp. 165–186). Chicago: Aldine.

Tsay, R. S. (1984). Regression models with time series errors. *Journal of the American Statistical Association, 79,* 118–124.

Tsay, R. S., & Tiao, G. C. (1984). Consistent estimates of autoregressive parameters and extended sample autocorrelation function for stationary and nonstationary ARIMA models. *Journal of American Statistical Association, 79,* 84–90.

van Buuren, S. (1997). Fitting ARMA time series models by structural equation models. *Psychometrika, 62,* 215–236.

Velicer, W. F., & Colby, S. M. (1997). Time series analysis for prevention and treatment research. In K. J. Bryant, M. Windle, & S. G. West (Eds.), *The science of prevention: Methodological advances from alcohol and substance abuse research* (pp. 211– 249). Washington, DC: American Psychological Association.

Velicer, W. F., & Colby, S. M. (2001). *A comparison of missing data procedures in Time Series Analysis.* Manuscript under review, University of Rhode Island.

Velicer, W. F., Fraser, C., McDonald, R. P., & Harrop, J. W. (1986). GENTS [Computer program]. Kingston: University of Rhode Island.

Velicer, W. F., & Harrop, J. W. (1983). The reliability and accuracy of time series model identification. *Evaluation Review, 7,* 551–560.

Velicer, W. F., & McDonald, R. P. (1984). Time series analysis without model identification. *Multivariate Behavioral Research, 19,* 33–47.

Velicer, W. F., & McDonald, R. P. (1991). Cross-sectional time series: A general transformation approach. *Multivariate Behavioral Research, 26,* 247–254.

Velicer, W. F., & Plummer, B. A. (1998). Time series analysis in Historiometry: A comment on Simonton. *Journal of Personality, 66,* 477–486.

Velicer, W. F., Prochaska, J. O., Rossi, J. S., & Snow, M. (1992). Assessing outcome in smoking cessation studies. *Psychological Bulletin, 111,* 23–41.

Velicer, W. F., Redding, C. A., Richmond, R., Greeley, J., & Swift, W. (1992). A time series investigation of three nicotine regulation models. *Addictive Behaviors, 17,* 325–345.

Velicer, W. F., Rossi, J. S., Prochaska, J. O., & DiClemente, C. C. (1996). A criterion measurement model for health behavior change. *Addictive Behaviors, 21,* 555–584.

West, S. G., & Hepworth, J. T. (1991). Statistical issues in the study of temporal data: Daily experiences. *Journal of Personality, 59,* 609–662.

Wilkinson, L. (1986). *SYSTAT: The system of statistics.* Evanston, IL: SYSTAT, Inc.

Williams, E. A., & Gottman, J. M. (1982). A user's guide to the Gottman-Williams time-series analysis computer programs for social scientists [Computer program manual]. Cambridge, UK: Cambridge University Press.

Wood, P., & Brown, D. (1994). The study of intraindividual differences by means of dynamic factor models: Rationale, implementation, and interpretation. *Psychological Bulletin, 116,* 166–186.

CHAPTER 24

Structural Equation Modeling

JODIE B. ULLMAN AND PETER M. BENTLER

Structural equation modeling (SEM) is a collection of statistical techniques that allow a set of relationships between one or more independent variables (IVs), either continuous or discrete, and one or more dependent variables (DVs), either continuous or discrete, to be examined. Both IVs and DVs can be either measured variables (directly observed) or latent variables (unobserved, not directly observed). Structural equation modeling is also referred to as causal modeling, causal analysis, simultaneous equation modeling, analysis of covariance structures, path analysis, or confirmatory factor analysis. The latter two are actually special types of SEM.

At the most basic level, SEM allows questions to be answered that involve multiple regression analyses. At the simplest level, a researcher posits a relationship between a single measured variable (perhaps acceptance of risky behavior) and other measured variables (perhaps gender, academic achievement, and weak institutional bonds). This simple model is just a multiple regression model presented in diagram form in Figure 24.1. All four of the measured variables appear in boxes connected by lines with arrows indicating that gender, academic achievement, and weak institutional bonds (the IVs) predict acceptance of risky behaviors (the DV). Lines with arrows at each end indicate a covariance among the IVs. The presence of a residual indicates imperfect prediction.

A more complicated model of acceptance of risky behavior appears in Figure 24.2. In this model, Acceptance of Risky Behavior is a latent variable (a factor) that is not directly measured but rather assessed indirectly, using two measured variables: degree of endorsement with "It is OK to drink" and "It is OK to smoke." Acceptance of Risky Behavior is, in turn, predicted by gender and by Weak Institutional Bonds, a second factor that is assessed through two measured variables: bonds to family and bonds to teachers. For clarity in the text, initial capitals are used for names of factors and lowercase letters for names of measured variables.

Figures 24.1 and 24.2 are examples of *path diagrams*. These diagrams are fundamental to SEM because they allow the researcher to diagram the hypothesized set of relationships—the model. The diagrams are helpful in clarifying a researcher's

The authors sincerely thank Wayne Velicer and four anonymous reviewers for helpful comments on an earlier draft. This chapter was supported in part by NIDA grant DA 01070-28.

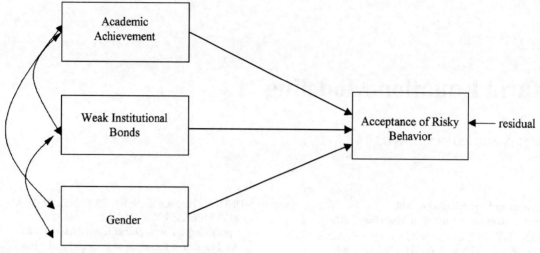

Figure 24.1   Path diagram of a multiple regression model.

ideas about the relationships among variables, and they can be directly translated into the equations needed for the analysis.

Path Diagrams and Terminology

Several conventions are used in developing SEM diagrams. Measured variables, also called *observed variables, indicators,* or *manifest variables,* are represented by squares or rectangles. In the figure, they have verbal labels as well as V designations. Factors have two or more indicators and are also called *latent variables, constructs,* or *unobserved variables.* Factors are represented by circles or ovals in path diagrams and are shown with verbal labels as well as F designations. Relationships between variables are indicated by lines; lack of a line connecting variables implies that no direct relationship has been hypothesized. Lines have either one or two arrows. A line with one arrow represents a hy-

pothesized direct relationship between two variables. The variable with the arrow pointing to it is the DV. A line with an arrow at both ends indicates a covariance between the two variables with no implied direction of effect.

In the model of Figure 24.2, Acceptance of Risky Behavior is a latent variable (factor) that is predicted by gender (a measured variable) and Weak Institutional Bonds (a factor). Notice the line with the arrow at both ends connecting Weak Institutional Bonds and gender. This line with an arrow at both ends implies that there is a relationship between the variables but makes no prediction regarding the direction of the effect. Also notice the direction of the arrows connecting the Acceptance of Risky Behavior construct (factor) to its indicators: The construct *predicts* the measured variables. The implication is that the underlying construct, Acceptance of Risky Behavior, drives the degree of agreement with the statements "It is OK to drink" and "It is OK to smoke." It is

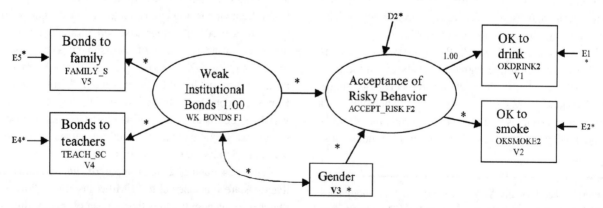

Figure 24.2   Example of a structural equation model of Acceptance of Risky Behavior.

impossible to measure this construct directly, so we do the next best thing and measure indicators of Acceptance of Risky Behavior. We hope that we are able to tap into adolescents' Acceptance of Risky Behavior by measuring several observable indicators. In this example we use just two indicators.

In Figure 24.2, bonds to family, bonds to teachers, degree of endorsement of smoking and drinking, and the latent variable, Acceptance of Risky Behaviors, all have one-way arrows pointing to them. These variables are dependent variables in the model. Gender and Weak Institutional Bonds are IVs in the model; as such they have no one-way arrows pointing to them. Notice that all the DVs, both observed and unobserved, have arrows labeled E or D pointing toward them. Es (errors) point to measured variables; Ds (disturbances) point to latent variables (factors). As in multiple regression, nothing is predicted perfectly; there is always a residual or error. In SEM the residual not predicted by the IV(s) is included in the diagram with these paths.

The part of the model that relates the measured variables to the factors is sometimes called the *measurement model*. In this example, the two constructs (factors), Weak Institutional Bonds and Acceptance of Risky Behavior, and the indicators of these constructs (factors) form the *measurement model*. The hypothesized relationships among the constructs—in this example, the one path between Weak Institutional Bonds and Acceptance of Risky Behavior—is called the *structural model*. Predictive relationships are examined in SEM. For example, in this model we are interested in whether each latent variable (Acceptance of Risky Behavior and Weak Institutional Bonds) predicts the measured variables associated with it. Additionally, it is hypothesized that the latent variable, Acceptance of Risky Behavior, is predicted by Weak Institutional Bonds. Note that both models presented so far include hypotheses about relationships among variables (covariances) but not about means or mean differences. Mean differences associated with group membership can also be tested within the SEM framework but are not demonstrated in this chapter.

Advantages of Structural Equation Modeling

There are a number of advantages to the use of SEM. When relationships among factors are examined, the relationships are free of measurement error because the error has been estimated and removed, leaving only common variance. Reliability of measurement can be accounted for explicitly within the analysis by estimating and removing the measurement error. Additionally, as was seen in Figure 24.2, complex relationships can be examined. When the phenomena of interest are complex and multidimensional, SEM is the only analysis that allows complete and simultaneous tests of all the relationships. In the social sciences we often pose hypotheses at the level of the construct. With other statistical methods these construct-level hypotheses are tested at the level of a measured variable (an observed variable with measurement error). Mismatching the level of hypothesis and level of analysis—although problematic, and often overlooked—may lead to faulty conclusions. A distinct advantage of SEM is the ability to test construct-level hypotheses at the appropriate level.

Another critical advantage of SEM over the basic general linear model or simple regression is that variables that are dependent variables also can play the role of predictor variables in the model as a whole. So, in Figure 24.2 Acceptance of Risky Behavior is a dependent variable with respect to Weak Institutional Bonds and gender. Yet it is also a predictor of "It is OK to drink" and "It is OK to smoke." This feature uniquely allows SEM to model mediation effects. Here, Acceptance of Risky Behavior is a mediator of the effect of Weak Institutional Bonds and gender on degree of endorsement with "It is OK to smoke" and "It is OK to drink."

THREE GENERAL TYPES OF RESEARCH QUESTIONS THAT CAN BE ADDRESSED WITH STRUCTURAL EQUATION MODELING

Adequacy of Model

The fundamental question that is addressed through the use of SEM techniques involves a comparison between a data set, an empirical covariance matrix, and an estimated population covariance matrix that is produced as a function of the model parameter estimates. The major question asked by SEM is, Is the covariance matrix that is estimated from the model equal to the true population covariance matrix? Of course, we do not have the true population covariance matrix, so in practice the question is modified to, Does the model produce an estimated population covariance matrix that is consistent with the sample (observed) covariance matrix? If the model is good the parameter estimates will produce an estimated matrix that is close to the sample covariance matrix. In turn, the sample covariance matrix is assumed to be representative of the population covariance matrix, so it can be assumed that the model describes the population. "Consistent" is evaluated primarily with the chi-square test statistic and fit indices.

Another question addressed regards adequacy of the factor structure. It is possible to estimate a model, with a factor structure, at one time point and then test whether the factor structure remains the same across time points. For example, we could assess the strength of the indicators of children's Acceptance of Risky Behaviors (endorsement of smoking and drinking) and Weak Institutional Bonds (bonds to family and bonds to teachers) when children are 12 and then assess the same factor structure when the children are 14, 16, and 18. Using this longitudinal approach we could assess whether the factor structure, the construct itself, remains the same across this time period or whether the relative weights of the indicators change as children develop.

In addition to examining the factor structure longitudinally, it is also possible to examine the rate of individual change in a construct over time. Using latent growth curve modeling we can test the hypothesis that children's degree of Acceptance of Risky Behavior changes at different rates. We can also test hypotheses about the shape of change; that is, is the change over time linear or quadratic? Other questions that might be addressed with this approach could be, Do children have the same rate of change in Acceptance of Risky Behavior? or Are children's initial starting levels of Acceptance of Risky Behavior associated with their rate of change in the construct?

Significance of Parameter Estimates

Model estimates for path coefficients and their standard errors are generated under the implicit assumption that the model fit is very good. If the model fit is very close, then the estimates and standard errors may be taken seriously, and individual significance tests on parameters (path coefficients, variances, and covariances) may be performed. Using the example illustrated in Figure 24.2 we could test the hypothesis that Weak Institutional Bonds predicts Acceptance of Risky Behavior. This would be a test of the path coefficient between the two latent variables, Acceptance of Risky Behavior and Weak Institutional Bonds (the null hypothesis for this test would be $H_0: \gamma = 0$, where γ is the symbol for the path coefficient between an IV and a DV). This parameter estimate is then evaluated with a z test (the parameter estimate divided by the estimated standard error).

Comparison of Nested Models

In addition to evaluating the overall model fit and specific parameter estimates, it is also possible to compare nested models to one another statistically. Nested models are models that are subsets of one another. Each model might represent a different theory. These nested models are statistically compared, thus providing a strong test for competing theories (models). From the example in Figure 24.2, we could pose a nested model that could be compared to the fuller model that is illustrated. A possible nested model could remove the path from Weak Institutional Bonds to Acceptance of Risky Behavior. This nested model would hypothesize that gender is the only predictor of Acceptance of Risky Behavior. To test this hypothesis, the chi-square from the fuller model depicted in Figure 24.2 would be subtracted from the chi-square for the nested model that removed the path from Weak Institutional Bonds to Acceptance of Risky Behavior. The corresponding degrees of freedom for these two models would also be subtracted. The difference in chi-squares, based on the difference in degrees of freedom, would be evaluated for significance using a chi-square table of significance. If the difference is significant, the fuller model that includes the removed path is needed to explain the data. If the difference were not significant, the nested model, which is more parsimonious than the fuller model, would be accepted as the preferred model. This would imply that Weak Institutional Bonds is not needed when predicting Acceptance of Risky Behavior.

A FOUR-STAGE GENERAL PROCESS OF MODELING

The process of modeling could be thought of as a four-stage process: model specification, model estimation, model evaluation, and model modification. In this section each of these stages will be discussed and illustrated with an example based on data collected as part of an ongoing Drug Abuse Resistance Education (D.A.R.E.) evaluation (see Dukes, Ullman, & Stein 1995, for a full description of the study). This example uses data from students' responses immediately following completion of the D.A.R.E. program (see Dukes, Ullman, & Stein, 1995).

Model Specification/Hypotheses

The first step in the process of estimating an SEM model is model specification. This stage consists of (a) stating the hypotheses to be tested in both diagram and equation form, (b) statistically identifying the model, and (c) evaluating the statistical assumptions that underlie the model. This section contains discussion of each of these components using the

Acceptance of Risky Behavior model (Figure 24.2) as an example. The section concludes with discussion and illustration of the computer process of model specification using the EQS SEM software program.

Model Hypotheses and Diagrams

In this phase of the process, the model is specified; that is, the specific set of hypotheses to be tested is given. This is done most frequently through a diagram. The Acceptance of Risky Behavior diagram given in Figure 24.2 is an example of hypothesis specification. This example has five measured variables: (a) FAMILY_S, the average of three responses to statements about bonds to family, (b) TEACH_SC, the average of three responses to statements that query bonds to teachers, (c) OKDRINK2, a Likert scale measure (1–5) of degree of endorsement of the statement "It is OK to drink," (d) OKSMOKE2, a Likert scale (1–5) measure of degree of agreement with the statement "It is OK to smoke," and (e) gender (boys = 1, girls = 2).

The example of Figure 24.2 contains some asterisks and a 1. The asterisks indicate parameters (variances and covariances of IVs and regression coefficients) to be estimated. The variances of IVs are parameters of the model and are estimated or fixed to a particular value. The number 1 indicates that a parameter, either a path coefficient or a variance, has been set (fixed) to the value of 1. (The rationale behind "fixing" paths is discussed later in the section about identification.)

Our example contains two hypothesized latent variables (factors): Weak Institutional Bonds (WK_BONDS), and Acceptance of Risky Behavior (ACCEPT_RISK). The Weak Institutional Bonds (WK_BONDS) factor is hypothesized to have two indicators, bonds to family (FAMILY_S) and bonds to teachers (TEACH_SC). Weaker Institutional Bonds predicts weaker bonds to both family and teachers. Note that the direction of the prediction matches the direction of the arrows. The Acceptance of Risky Behavior (ACCEPT_RISK) factor also has two indicators; degree of endorsement to two statements, "It is OK to drink" (OKDRINK2) and "It is OK to smoke" (OKSMOKE2). Greater Acceptance of Risky Behavior predicts higher scores on both the alcohol- and tobacco-use statements. This model also hypothesizes that both Weak Institutional Bonds and gender are predictive of Acceptance of Risky Behavior. Also notice the line with the doubled-headed arrow that directly connects Weak Institutional Bonds and gender. This path indicates a hypothesized covariance between these variables. Note that this is a covariance and that it does not imply directionality.

Bentler-Weeks Model Specification

The relationships in the diagram are directly translated into equations, and the model is then estimated. The analysis proceeds by specifying a model as in the diagram and then translating the model into a series of equations or matrices. One method of model specification is the Bentler-Weeks method (Bentler & Weeks, 1980). In this method every variable in the model, latent or measured, is either an IV or a DV. The parameters to be estimated are the (a) regression coefficients and (b) variances and covariances of the independent variables in the model (Bentler, 2001). In Figure 24.2 the regression coefficients, variances, and covariances to be estimated are indicated with an asterisk.

In the example, ACCEPT_RISK, OKSMOKE2, OKDRINK2, FAMILY_S, and TEACH_SC are all DVs because they all have at least one line with a single-headed arrow pointing to them. Notice that ACCEPT_RISK is a latent variable and also a DV. Whether a variable is observed makes no difference as to its status as a DV or IV. Although ACCEPT_RISK is a factor, it is also a DV because it has arrows from both WK_BONDS and gender. The seven IVs in this example are gender, WK_BONDS, D2, E1, E2, E4, E5.

Residual variables (errors) of measured variables are labeled E and errors of latent variables (called disturbances) are labeled D. It may seem odd that a residual variable is considered an IV, but remember the familiar regression equation:

$$Y = X\beta + e, \tag{24.1}$$

where Y is the DV and X and e are both IVs.

In fact, the Bentler-Weeks model *is* a regression model, expressed in matrix algebra:

$$\eta = B\eta + \gamma\xi, \tag{24.2}$$

where, if q is the number of DVs and r is the number of IVs, then η (eta) is a $q \times 1$ vector of DVs, B (beta) is a $q \times q$ matrix of regression coefficients between DVs, γ (gamma) is a $q \times r$ matrix of regression coefficients between DVs and IVs, and ξ (xi) is a $r \times 1$ vector of IVs.

In the Bentler-Weeks model only independent variables have variances and covariances as parameters of the model. These variances and covariances are in Φ (phi), an $r \times r$ matrix. Therefore, the parameter matrices of the model are B, γ, and Φ. Unknown parameters in these matrices need to be estimated. The vectors of dependent variables, η, and independent variables, ξ, are not estimated.

The diagram for the example is translated into the Bentler-Weeks model, with $r = 7$ and $q = 5$, as below,

$$
\boldsymbol{\eta} \quad = \quad \mathbf{B} \quad \boldsymbol{\eta} \quad + \quad \boldsymbol{\gamma} \quad \boldsymbol{\xi}
$$

$$
\begin{bmatrix} \text{V1 or } \eta_1 \\ \text{V2 or } \eta_2 \\ \text{V4 or } \eta_3 \\ \text{V5 or } \eta_4 \\ \text{F2 or } \eta_5 \end{bmatrix} = \begin{bmatrix} 0 & 0 & 0 & 0 & 1 \\ 0 & 0 & 0 & 0 & * \\ 0 & 0 & 0 & 0 & 0 \\ 0 & 0 & 0 & 0 & 0 \\ 0 & 0 & 0 & 0 & 0 \end{bmatrix} \begin{bmatrix} \text{V1 or } \eta_1 \\ \text{V2 or } \eta_2 \\ \text{V4 or } \eta_3 \\ \text{V5 or } \eta_4 \\ \text{F2 or } \eta_5 \end{bmatrix} + \begin{bmatrix} 0 & 0 & 1 & 0 & 0 & 0 & 0 \\ 0 & 0 & 0 & 1 & 0 & 0 & 0 \\ 0 & * & 0 & 0 & 1 & 0 & 0 \\ 0 & * & 0 & 0 & 0 & 1 & 0 \\ * & * & 0 & 0 & 0 & 0 & 1 \end{bmatrix} \begin{bmatrix} \text{V3 or } \xi_1 \\ \text{F1 or } \xi_2 \\ \text{E1 or } \xi_3 \\ \text{E2 or } \xi_4 \\ \text{E4 or } \xi_5 \\ \text{E5 or } \xi_6 \\ \text{D2 or } \xi_7 \end{bmatrix}.
$$

Notice that $\boldsymbol{\eta}$ is on both sides of the equation. This is because DVs can predict one another in SEM. The diagram and matrix equations are identical. Notice that the asterisks in Figure 24.2 correspond directly to the asterisks in the matrices and that these matrix equations correspond directly to simple regression equations. In the matrix equations the number 1 indicates that we have "fixed" the parameter, either a variance or a path coefficient to the specific value of 1. Parameters are generally fixed for identification purposes. Parameters can be fixed to any number; most often, however, parameters are fixed to 1 or 0. The parameters that are fixed to zero are also included in the path diagram but are easily overlooked because the zero parameters are represented by the *absence* of a line in the diagram.

As stated earlier, what makes this model different from ordinary regression is the possibility of having latent variables as DVs and predictors, as well as the possibility of DVs predicting other DVs. The latter occurs with nonzero elements in **B**. When all elements in **B** are zero, no DVs are predicted by other DVs, and the only coefficients needed are in $\boldsymbol{\gamma}$; these give weights for the IVs in predicting the DVs. In such a case the model is a set of regression equations, albeit possibly with latent variables. But when **B** has nonzero elements, certain DVs are predicted by other DVs, and the model is no longer just regression-like. In the example, there are two nonzero elements in **B** (a fixed 1 and a free parameter, *), so this is not just a regression model. In more complex models (so-called nonrecursive models), free parameters exist in some symmetric elements of **B**, such as the 1,2 and the 2,1 elements (which here would indicate that V1 predicts V2 while V2 also predicts V1).

Carefully compare the diagram in Figure 24.2 with this matrix equation. The 5×1 vector of values to the left of the equal sign, the eta ($\boldsymbol{\eta}$) vector, is a vector of DVs listed in the following order, OKDRINK2 (V1), OKSMOKE2 (V2), TEACH_SC (V4), FAMILY_S (V5), and ACCEPT_RISK (F2). The beta matrix (**B**) is a 5×5 matrix of regression coefficients among the DVs.

The 5×7 gamma matrix ($\boldsymbol{\gamma}$) contains the regression coefficients that are used to predict the DVs from the IVs. The five DVs that are associated with the rows of this matrix are in the same order as earlier. The seven IVs that identify the columns are, in the order indicated, GENDER (V3); WK_BONDS (F1); the four E(errors) for V1, V2, V4, and V5; and the D(disturbance) of F2. The 7×1 vector of IVs is in the same order.

The matrix equation summarizes compactly all the equations in the model. Each row of the matrix equation gives one regression-like equation; with five rows there are five equations. To illustrate, the third row gives

$$
\begin{aligned}
\text{V4} = \; & 0\text{V1} + 0\text{V2} + 0\text{V4} + 0\text{V5} + 1\text{F2} + 0\text{V3} \\
& + 0\text{F1} + 0\text{E1} + 0\text{E2} + 1\text{E4} + 0\text{E5} + 0\text{D2},
\end{aligned}
$$

where the numbers in front of the variable names are coefficients taken from the row of **B** and $\boldsymbol{\gamma}$ in turn and the variables are the dependent and then the independent variables in the sequence we have listed them. Therefore this equation simplifies to V4 = 1F2 + 1E4, where 1 is a fixed path from F2 to V4, and E4 to V4, in the model. (Later, Table 24.2 shows this equation as one of the five equations in the EQS model file setup.) The 7×7 symmetric phi matrix contains the variances and covariances that are to be estimated for the IVs,

$$
\boldsymbol{\Phi} = \begin{array}{c} \text{V3 or } \xi_1 \\ \text{F1 or } \xi_2 \\ \text{E1 or } \xi_3 \\ \text{E2 or } \xi_4 \\ \text{E4 or } \xi_5 \\ \text{E5 or } \xi_6 \\ \text{D2 or } \xi_7 \end{array} \begin{bmatrix} * & 0 & 0 & 0 & 0 & 0 & 0 \\ * & 1 & 0 & 0 & 0 & 0 & 0 \\ 0 & 0 & * & 0 & 0 & 0 & 0 \\ 0 & 0 & 0 & * & 0 & 0 & 0 \\ 0 & 0 & 0 & 0 & * & 0 & 0 \\ 0 & 0 & 0 & 0 & 0 & * & 0 \\ 0 & 0 & 0 & 0 & 0 & 0 & * \end{bmatrix}.
$$

These equations form the basis of an EQS (a popular SEM computer package) syntax file used to estimate the model. The syntax for this model is presented in Table 24.1. As seen in the table, the model is specified in EQS using a series of regression equations. In the /EQUATIONS section, as in ordinary regression, the DV appears on the left side of the equation, and its predictors are on the right-hand side. But unlike regression, the predictors may be IVs or other DVs. Measured variables are referred to by the letter V and the number corresponding to the variable given in the /LABELS section.

TABLE 24.1 EQS Syntax for Acceptance of Risky Behavior Model

```
/TITLE
  basic one group model
/SPECIFICATIONS
  DATA='D:\EQS6\dare_kids.ESS';
  VARIABLES=5; CASES=4578; GROUPS=1;
  METHODS=ML,ROBUST;
  MATRIX=RAW;
  ANALYSIS=COVARIANCE;
/LABELS
  V1=OKDRINK2; V2=OKSMOKE2; V3=GENDER2; V4=TEACH_SC; V5=FAMILY_S;
  F1=WK_BONDS; F2=ACCEPT_RISK;
/EQUATIONS
  !ACCEPTANCE OF RISKY BEHAVIOR
    V1 = + 1F2 + 1E1;
    V2 = + *F2 + 1E2;
  !WEAK INSTITUTIONAL BONDS
    V4 = + *F1 + 1E4;
    V5 = + *F1 + 1E5;
    F2 = + *F1 + *V3 + 1D2;
/VARIANCES
    V3 = *;
    F1 = 1;
    E1,E2,E4,E5 = *;
    D2 = *;
/COVARIANCES
    F1,V3 = *;
/PRINT
    FIT=ALL;
    TABLE=EQUATION;
/LMTEST
/WTEST
/END
```

Errors associated with measured variables are indicated by the letter E and the number of the variable. Factors are referred to with the letter F and a number given in the /LABELS section. The errors, or disturbances, associated with factors are referred to by the letter D and the number corresponding to the factor. An asterisk indicates a parameter to be estimated. Variables included in the equation without asterisks are considered parameters fixed to the value 1. The variances of IVs are parameters of the model and are indicated in the /VAR paragraph. In the /PRINT paragraph, FIT=ALL requests all goodness-of-fit indices available. Take a moment to confirm that the diagram relationships exactly match the regression equations given in the syntax file.

Identification

In SEM a model is specified, parameters for the model are estimated using sample data, and the parameters are used to produce the estimated population covariance matrix. But only models that are identified can be estimated. A model is said to be identified if there is a unique numerical solution for each of the parameters in the model. For example, say that

the variance of $y = 10$ and the variance of $y = \alpha + \beta$. Any two values can be substituted for α and β as long as they sum to 10. There is no unique numerical solution for either α or β; that is, there are an infinite number of combinations of two numbers that would sum to 10. Therefore, this single equation model is not identified. However, if we fix α to 0, there is a unique solution for β, 10, and the equation is identified. It is possible to use covariance algebra to calculate equations and assess identification in very simple models; however, in large models this procedure quickly becomes unwieldy. For a detailed, technical discussion of identification, see Bollen (1989). The following guidelines are rough but may suffice for many models.

The first step is to count the number of data points and the number of parameters that are to be estimated. The data in SEM are the variances and covariances in the sample covariance matrix. The number of data points is the number of nonredundant sample variances and covariances:

$$\text{Number of data points} = \frac{p(p+1)}{2}, \qquad (24.3)$$

where p equals the number of measured variables. The number of parameters is found by adding together the number of regression coefficients, variances, and covariances that are to be estimated (i.e., the number of asterisks in a diagram).

If there are more data points than parameters to be estimated, the model is said to be overidentified, a necessary condition for proceeding with the analysis. If there are the same number of data points as parameters to be estimated, the model is said to be just-identified. In this case, the estimated parameters perfectly reproduce the sample covariance matrix, the chi-square test statistic and degrees of freedom are equal to zero, and the analysis is uninteresting because hypotheses about the model's adequacy cannot be tested. However, hypotheses about specific paths in the model can be tested. If there are fewer data points than parameters to be estimated, the model is said to be underidentified, and parameters cannot be estimated. The number of parameters needs to be reduced by fixing, constraining, or deleting some of them. A parameter may be fixed by setting it to a specific value or constrained by setting the parameter equal to another parameter.

In the Acceptance of Risky Behavior example of Figure 24.2, there are 5 measured variables and thus 15 data points: $5(5 + 1)/2 = 15$ (5 variances and 10 covariances). There are 12 parameters to be estimated in the hypothesized model: 5 regression coefficients, 6 variances, and 1 covariance. The hypothesized model has 3 fewer parameters than data points, so the model may be identified.

The second step in determining model identifiability is to examine the measurement portion of the model. The measurement part of the model deals with the relationship between the measured indicators and the factors. It is necessary both to establish the scale of each factor and to assess the identifiability of this portion of the model.

To establish the scale of a factor, the variance for the factor is fixed to 1, or the regression coefficient from the factor to one of the measured variables is fixed to 1. Fixing the regression coefficient to 1 gives the factor the same variance as the measured variable. If the factor is an IV, either alternative is acceptable. If the factor is a DV, most researchers fix the regression coefficient to 1. In the example, the variance of the Weak Institutional Bonds factor was set to 1 (normalized) while the scale of the Acceptance of Risky Behavior factor was set equal to the scale of the "It is OK to drink variable" (OKDRINK2) measured variable.

To establish the identifiability of the measurement portion of the model, look at the number of factors and the number of measured variables (indicators) loading on each factor. If there is only one factor, the model may be identified if the factor has at least three indicators with nonzero loading and if the errors (residuals) are uncorrelated with one another. If there are two or more factors, again consider the number of indicators for each factor. If each factor has three or more indicators, the model may be identified if errors associated with the indicators are not correlated, if each indicator loads on only one factor, and if the factors are allowed to covary. If there are only two indicators for a factor, the model may be identified if there are no correlated errors, if each indicator loads on only one factor, and if none of the covariances among factors is equal to zero.

In the example, there are two indicators for each factor. The errors are uncorrelated, and each indicator loads on only one factor. Additionally, the covariance between the factors is not zero. Therefore, this part of the model may be identified. Please note that identification may still be possible if errors are correlated or if variables load on more than one factor, but it is more complicated.

The third step in establishing model identifiability is to examine the structural portion of the model, looking only at the relationships among the latent variables (factors). Ignore the measured variables for a moment; consider only the structural portion of the model that deals with the regression coefficients relating latent variables to one another. If none of the latent DVs predict each other (the beta matrix is all zeros), the structural part of the model may be identified. The Acceptance of Risky Behavior example has only one latent DV, so this part of the model may be identified. If the latent DVs do predict one another, look at the latent DVs in the model and ask whether they are recursive or nonrecursive. If the latent DVs are recursive, there are no feedback loops among them and no correlated disturbances (errors) among them. (In a feedback loop, DV1 predicts DV2 and DV2 predicts DV1; i.e., there are two lines linking the factors, one with an arrow in one direction and the other with an arrow in the other direction. Correlated disturbances are linked by single curved lines with double-headed arrows.) If the structural part of the model is recursive, it may be identifiable. These rules apply also to path analysis models with only measured variables. The Acceptance of Risky Behavior example is a recursive model and therefore may be identified.

If a model is nonrecursive, there are feedback loops or correlated disturbances among the DVs, or both. Two additional conditions are necessary for identification of nonrecursive models, each applying to each equation in the model separately. Looking at each equation separately, for identification it is necessary that each equation has at least the number of latent DVs − 1 excluded from it. The second condition is that the *information matrix* (a matrix necessary for calculating standard errors) is full rank and can be inverted. The inverted information matrix can be examined in the output from most SEM programs. If after examining the model the number of data points exceeds the number of parameters estimated and both the measurement and structural parts of the model are identified, there is good evidence that the whole model is identified.

Sample Size and Power

Covariances are less stable when estimated from small samples. Structural equation modeling is based on covariances. Parameter estimates and chi-square tests of fit are also very sensitive to sample size. Therefore, SEM is a large sample technique. MacCallum, Browne, and Sugawara (1996) presented tables of minimum sample size needed for tests of goodness of fit based on model degrees of freedom and effect size.

Missing Data

Problems of missing data are often magnified in SEM due to the large number of measured variables employed. The researcher who relies on using complete cases only is often left with an inadequate number of complete cases to estimate a model. Therefore, adequate missing data computation is particularly important in many SEM models. When there is evidence that the data are missing at random (MAR; missingness may depend on the IVs but not DVs) or missing completely at random (MCAR; missingness is unrelated to the IVs or the DVs), a preferred method is to use the expectation maximization (EM) algorithm to obtain maximum likelihood (ML) estimates (R. J. A. Little & Rubin, 1987). Some of the software packages now include procedures for estimating missing data, including the EM algorithm. EQS 6 (Bentler, 2001) produces the EM-based ML solution automatically, based on the Jamshidian-Bentler (1999) computations. It should be noted that if the data are not normally distributed, ML test statistics—including those based on the EM algorithm—may be quite inaccurate.

Additionally, a missing data mechanism can be modeled explicitly within the SEM framework. Treatment of missing data patterns through SEM is not demonstrated in this chapter, but the interested reader is referred to Allison (1987) or Muthén, Kaplan, and Hollis (1987). All of these authors assume that the data are multivariately normally distributed, a very restrictive assumption in practice, as is discussed next. The more general case on how to deal with missing data when the parent distribution is possibly nonnormal is discussed in Yuan and Bentler (2000b). They provided a means for accepting the EM-based estimates of parameters but correcting standard errors and test statistics for nonnormality in an approach reminiscent of Satorra-Bentler (1994). Their approach has been uniquely incorporated into the EQS 6 program (Bentler, 2001).

Multivariate Normality and Outliers

Most of the estimation techniques used in SEM assume multivariate normality. To determine the extent and shape of nonnormally distributed data, examine the data for evidence of outliers, both univariate and multivariate, and evaluate the skewness and kurtosis of the distributions for the measured variables. If significant skewness is found, transformations can be attempted; however, variables are often still highly skewed or highly kurtotic even after transformation. Additionally, multivariate normality can be examined through the use of Mardia's coefficients of multivariate skewness and kurtosis. Some variables, such as drug-use variables, are not expected to be normally distributed in the population anyway. If transformations do not restore normality, or if a variable is not expected to be normally distributed in the population, an estimation method can be selected that addresses the nonnormality.

Residuals

After model estimation, the residuals should be small and centered around zero. The frequency distribution of the residual covariances should be symmetric. Residuals in the context of SEM are residual *covariances,* not residual *scores.* Nonsymmetrically distributed residuals in the frequency distribution may signal a poorly fitting model; the model is estimating some of the covariances well and others poorly. Sometimes, one or two residuals remain quite large even though the model fits reasonably well and the residuals appear to be symmetrically distributed and centered around zero. Typically, more informative than the ordinary residuals are the residuals obtained after standardizing the sample covariance matrix to a correlation matrix and similarly transforming the model matrix. In this metric, it is correlations that are being reproduced, and it is easy to see whether a residual is small and meaningless or too large for comfort. For example, if a sample correlation is .75 and the corresponding residual is .05, the correlation is largely explained by the model. In fact, an average of these standardized root mean square residuals (SRMS) has been shown to provide one of the most informative guides to model adequacy (Hu & Bentler, 1998, 1999).

The Computer Process

So far in this section we have outlined the components (specification of hypotheses, identification, and evaluation of assumptions underlying the model) of the model specification stage of the SEM process. Now we provide a brief tutorial on the software (EQS) implementation of this stage.

The first step of the model-fitting process, model specification, is nicely summarized in the EQS syntax table seen in Table 24.1. The data file is specified after the keyword DATA =. The number of measured variables is given after VARIABLES =, the sample size is indicated after CASES =, and the number of samples is given after GROUPS =. The estimation method, type of data matrix, and type of analysis are also indicated. Labels are provided for each measured (V) and latent (F) variable. As we stated previously, the /EQUATIONS section specifies each predictive relationship in the model. Notice that there are as many equations as DVs. The asterisks indicate parameters to be estimated. Note that in the equation for V1 the parameter estimating the relationship between V1, F2 has been fixed to one for identification. The scale of the F2 latent variable (Acceptance of Risky Behavior) has been set equal to the variance of "It is OK to drink" (OKDRINK2). The next section, /VARIANCES, specifies the variances to be estimated. Notice that the variance of F1, Weak Institutional Bonds, has been fixed to 1 for identification purposes.

Model Estimation Techniques and Test Statistics

After the model specification component is completed, the population parameters are estimated and evaluated. In this section we discuss several popular estimation techniques and provide guidelines for selection of the appropriate estimation technique and test statistic. As with the prior section we conclude with a computer procedure section that provides implementation guidelines using EQS.

The goal of estimation is to minimize the difference between the observed and estimated population covariance matrices. To accomplish this goal, a function, F, is minimized where

$$F = (\mathbf{s} - \boldsymbol{\sigma}(\boldsymbol{\Theta}))'\mathbf{W}(\mathbf{s} - \boldsymbol{\sigma}(\boldsymbol{\Theta})), \qquad (24.4)$$

where $\mathbf{s}$ is the vector of data (the observed sample covariance matrix stacked into a vector); $\boldsymbol{\sigma}$ is the vector of the estimated population covariance matrix (again, stacked into a vector); and $(\boldsymbol{\Theta})$ indicates that $\boldsymbol{\sigma}$ is derived from the parameters (the regression coefficients, variances, and covariances) of the model. $\mathbf{W}$ is the matrix that weights the squared differences between the sample and estimated population covariance matrix.

In factor analysis the observed and reproduced correlation matrices are compared. This idea is extended in SEM to include a statistical test of the differences between the observed covariance matrix and the estimated population covariance matrix that is produced as a function of the model. If the

weight matrix, $\mathbf{W}$, is chosen correctly, at the minimum with the optimal $\hat{\boldsymbol{\Theta}}$, F multiplied by $(N-1)$ yields a chi-square test statistic.

The trick is to select $\mathbf{W}$ so that the sum of weighted squared differences between observed and estimated population covariance matrices has a statistical interpretation. In an ordinary chi-square, the weights are the set of expected frequencies in the denominator of the chi-square test statistic. If we use some other numbers instead of the expected frequencies, the result might be some sort of test statistic, but it would not be a chi-square statistic; that is, the weight matrix would be wrong.

In SEM, estimation techniques vary by the choice of $\mathbf{W}$. Unweighted least squares (ULS) estimation does not standardly yield a chi-square statistic or standard errors though these are provided in EQS. Nor does it usually provide the best estimates, in the sense of having the smallest possible standard errors, and hence it is not discussed further (see Bollen, 1989, for further discussion of ULS).

Maximum likelihood (ML) is usually the default method in most programs because it yields the most precise (smallest variance) estimates when the data are normal. Generalized least squares (GLS) has the same optimal properties as ML under normality. When the data are symmetrically but not normally distributed, an option is elliptical distribution theory (EDT; Bentler, 1990; Shapiro & Browne, 1987), which allows different variables to be nonnormal but symmetric in different ways. Another option in EQS is heterogeneous kurtosis (HK) theory (Kano, Berkane, & Bentler, 1990), which allows different variables to be nonnormal but symmetric in different ways. The asymptotically distribution free (ADF) method has no distributional assumptions and hence is most general (Browne, 1984), but it is impractical with many variables and inaccurate without very large sample sizes.

Satorra and Bentler (1988, 1994, in press) and Satorra (2000) have also developed an adjustment for nonnormality that can be applied to the ML, GLS, EDT or HK chi-square test statistics. Briefly, the Satorra-Bentler scaled χ^2 is a Bartlett-type correction to the chi-square test statistic. EQS also corrects the standard errors for parameter estimates to adjust for the extent of nonnormality (Bentler & Dijkstra, 1985).

The performance of the chi-square test statistic derived from these different estimation procedures is affected by several factors, among them (a) sample size; (b) nonnormality of the distribution of errors, factors, and errors and factors; and (c) violation of the assumption of independence of factors and errors. The goal is to select an estimation procedure that, in Monte Carlo studies, produces a test statistic that neither rejects nor accepts the true model too many times. Several studies provide guidelines for selection of appropriate estimation methods and test statistics. The following sections summarize the performance of estimation procedures examined in Monte Carlo studies by Hu, Bentler, and Kano (1992) and Bentler and Yuan (1999).

Hu et al. (1992) varied sample size from 150 to 5,000, and Bentler and Yuan (1999) examined samples sizes ranging from 60 to 120. Both studies examined the performance of test statistics derived from several estimation methods when the assumptions of normality and independence of factors were violated.

Estimation Methods/Test Statistics and Sample Size

Hu and colleagues found that when the normality assumption was reasonable, both the ML and the Scaled ML performed well with sample sizes over 500. When the sample size was less than 500, GLS performed slightly better. Interestingly, the EDT test statistic performed a little better than ML at small sample sizes. It should be noted that the EDT estimator considers the kurtosis of the variables and assumes that all variables have the same kurtosis although the variables need not be normally distributed. (If the distribution is normal, there is no excess kurtosis.) The HK method, which allows varying kurtosis, performed similarly. Finally, the ADF estimator was poor with sample sizes under 2,500.

In small samples in the range of 60 to 120, when the number of subjects was greater than the number, (p^*), of nonredundant variances and covariances in the sample covariance matrix—that is, $p^* = [p(p+1)]/2$, where p is the number of variables—Bentler and Yuan found that a test statistic based on an adjustment of the ADF estimator and evaluated as an F statistic was best. This test statistic (Yuan & Bentler, 1999a) adjusts the chi-square test statistic derived from the ADF estimator as

$$T_l = \frac{[N - (p^* - q)]T_{ADF}}{[(N-1)(p^* - q)]}, \qquad (24.5)$$

where N is the number of subjects, q is the number of parameters to be estimated, and T_{ADF} is the test statistic based on the ADF estimator.

Estimation Methods and Nonnormality

When the normality assumption was violated, Hu et al. found that the ML and GLS estimators worked well with sample sizes of 2,500 and greater. The GLS estimator was a little better with smaller sample sizes but led to acceptance of too many models. The EDT and HK estimators accepted far too many models. The ADF estimator was poor with sample

sizes under 2,500. Finally, the scaled ML performed about the same as the ML and GLS estimators and better than the ADF estimator at all but the largest sample sizes. (This is interesting in that the ADF estimator has no distributional assumptions and, theoretically, should perform quite well under conditions of nonnormality.) With small samples sizes the Yuan-Bentler test statistic performed best.

Estimation Methods and Dependence

The assumption that errors are independent underlies SEM and other multivariate techniques. Hu et al. also investigated estimation methods and test statistic performance when the errors and factors were dependent but uncorrelated. Factors were dependent but uncorrelated by creating a curvilinear relationship between the factors and the errors. Correlation coefficients examine only linear relationships; therefore, although the correlation is zero between factors and errors, they are dependent.

ML and GLS performed poorly, always rejecting the true model. ADF was poor unless the sample size was greater than 2,500. EDT was better than ML, GLS, and ADF but still rejected too many true models. The scaled ML was better than the ADF estimator at all but the largest sample sizes. The scaled ML performed best overall with medium to larger samples sizes, and the Yuan-Bentler performed best with small samples.

Some Recommendations for Choice of Estimation Method/Test Statistic

Sample size and plausibility of the normality and independence assumptions need to be considered in selection of the appropriate estimation technique. ML, Scaled ML, or GLS estimators may be good choices with medium to large samples and evidence of the plausibility of the normality assumptions. The independence assumption cannot be routinely evaluated. The Scaled ML is fairly computer intensive. Therefore, if time or cost is an issue, ML and GLS are better choices when the assumptions seem plausible. ML estimation is currently the most frequently used estimation method in SEM. In medium to large samples the scaled ML test statistic is a good choice with nonnormality or suspected dependence among factors and errors. In small samples with nonnormality the Yuan-Bentler test statistic seems best. The test statistic based on the ADF estimator (without adjustment) seems like a poor choice under all conditions unless the sample size is very large (>2,500). Similar conclusions were found in studies by Fouladi (2000), Hoogland (1999), and Satorra (1992).

TABLE 24.2   Test Statistic and Fit Indices for Acceptance of Risky Behavior Model

```
GOODNESS OF FIT SUMMARY FOR METHOD = ROBUST

INDEPENDENCE MODEL CHI-SQUARE =        757.123 ON       10 DEGREES OF FREEDOM

INDEPENDENCE AIC =    737.12323    INDEPENDENCE CAIC =   663.51316
       MODEL AIC =      8.37746           MODEL CAIC =   -13.70556

SATORRA-BENTLER SCALED CHI-SQUARE =      14.3775 ON        3 DEGREES OF FREEDOM
PROBABILITY VALUE FOR THE CHI-SQUARE STATISTIC IS        .00243

FIT INDICES
-----------
BENTLER-BONETT     NORMED FIT INDEX =        .981
BENTLER-BONETT NON-NORMED FIT INDEX =        .949
COMPARATIVE FIT INDEX (CFI)         =        .985
BOLLEN   (IFI) FIT INDEX            =        .985
MCDONALD (MFI) FIT INDEX            =        .999
ROOT MEAN-SQUARE ERROR OF APPROXIMATION (RMSEA)  =      .030
90% CONFIDENCE INTERVAL OF RMSEA (        .016,        .046)
```

Computer Procedure and Interpretation

The model in Figure 24.2 is estimated using ML estimation and the Satorra-Bentler Scaled chi-square test statistic because the data are not normally distributed, thus violating multivariate normality. In this model Mardia's normalized multivariate kurtosis estimate is 224.25. This can be interpreted like a z score. Therefore, the probability level associated with a normalized estimate of 224.25 is less than .001. Output for the model estimation and chi-square test statistic is given in Table 24.2.

Several chi-square test statistics are given in the full output. In this severely edited output, only the chi-squares associated with the Satorra-Bentler scaled chi-square are given. The INDEPENDENCE MODEL CHI-SQUARE = 757.123, with 10 dfs tests the hypothesis that the measured variables are orthogonal. Therefore, the probability associated with this chi-square should be small, typically less that .05. The model chi-square test statistic is labeled CHI-SQUARE = 14.3775 BASED ON 3 DEGREES OF FREEDOM. This chi-square tests the hypothesis that the difference between the estimated population covariance matrix and the unstructured population covariance matrix (as represented by the sample covariance matrix) is not significant. Ideally, the probability associated with this chi-square should be large, greater than .05. In Table 24.2 the probability associated with the model chi-square equals $p = .00243$. Strictly interpreted, this indicates that the estimated model-based population covariance matrix and the unstructured population covariance matrix, viewed through the sample covariance matrix, do differ significantly; that is, the model does not fit the data. However, the chi-square test statistic is strongly affected by sample size.

The function minimum multiplied by $N - 1$ equals the chi-square. Therefore, we will examine additional measures of fit before we draw any conclusions about the adequacy of the model.

Model Evaluation

In this section we examine three aspects of model evaluation. First, we discuss the problem of assessing fit in a SEM model. We then present several popular fit indices. The section concludes with a discussion of evaluating direct and indirect parameter estimates.

Evaluating the Overall Fit of the Model

The model chi-square test statistic is highly dependent on sample size; that is, the model chi-square test statistic is $(N - 1)F_{min}$, where N is the sample size and F_{min} is the value of F_{min}, Equation 24.4, at the function minimum. Therefore, the fit of models estimated with large samples, as seen in the Acceptance of Risky Behavior model with $N = 4,578$, is often difficult to assess. Fit indices have been developed to address this problem. There are five general classes of fit indices: comparative fit, absolute fit, proportion of variance accounted for, parsimony adjusted proportion of variance accounted for, and residual-based fit indices. A complete discussion of model fit is outside the scope of this chapter; therefore we will focus on two of the most popular fit indices: the comparative fit index (CFI; Bentler, 1990) and a residual-based fit index, the root mean square error of approximation (RMSEA; Browne & Cudeck 1993; Steiger, 2001; Steiger &

Lind, 1980). See Ullman (2001) and Hu and Bentler (1999) for more detailed discussions of fit indices.

One type of model fit index is based on a comparison of nested models. Nested models are models that are subsets of one another. At one end of the continuum is the uncorrelated variables or independence model: the model that corresponds to completely unrelated variables. This model would have degrees of freedom equal to the number of data points minus the variances that are estimated. At the other end of the continuum is the saturated (full or perfect) model with zero degrees of freedom. Fit indices that employ a comparative fit approach place the estimated model somewhere along this continuum, with 0.00 indicating fit equivalent to that of the independence model (i.e., that no covariances are being explained) and 1.00 indicating perfect fit.

The normed fit index is the easiest index to understand. It summarizes the improvement in chi-square going from the independence model to the model of interest, relative to the starting point. That is, NFI $= (757.1 - 14.4)/757.1 = .98$, indicating excellent fit. This index underestimates fit in small samples. The comparative fit index (CFI: Bentler, 1990) assesses fit relative to other models, as the name implies, and uses an approach based on the noncentral chi-square distribution with the noncentrality parameter, τ_i. If the estimated model is perfect, $\tau_i = 0$ and the larger the value of τ_i, the greater the model misspecification:

$$\text{CFI} = 1 - \frac{\tau_{\text{est. model}}}{\tau_{\text{indep. model}}} \qquad (24.6)$$

Clearly, the smaller the noncentrality parameter, τ_i, is for the estimated model relative to the τ_i, for the independence model, the larger the CFI and the better the fit. The τ value for a model can be estimated by

$$\begin{aligned} \hat{\tau}_{\text{indep. model}} &= \chi^2_{\text{indep. model}} - \text{df}_{\text{indep. model}} \\ \hat{\tau}_{\text{est. model}} &= \chi^2_{\text{est. model}} - \text{df}_{\text{est. model}} \end{aligned}, \qquad (24.7)$$

where $\hat{\tau}_{\text{est. model}}$ is set to zero if negative.

For the example,

$$\tau_{\text{indep. model}} = 757.123 - 10 = 747.123 \quad \text{and}$$

$$\tau_{\text{est. model}} = 14.3775 - 3 = 11.3775 \quad \text{so that}$$

$$\text{CFI} = 1 - \frac{11.3775}{747.123} = .985$$

CFI values greater than .95 are often indicative of good-fitting models (Hu & Bentler, 1999). The CFI is normed to the 0–1 range and does a good job of estimating model fit even in small samples (Hu & Bentler, 1998, 1999).

The RMSEA (Steiger, 2001; Steiger & Lind, 1980) estimates the lack of fit in a model compared to a perfect or saturated model by

$$\text{estimated RMSEA} = \sqrt{\frac{\hat{\tau}}{Ndf_{\text{model}}}}, \qquad (24.8)$$

where $\hat{\tau} = \hat{\tau}_{\text{est. model}}$, as defined in Equation 24.7. As noted earlier, when the model is perfect, $\hat{\tau} = 0$, and the greater the model misspecification, the larger $\hat{\tau}$. Hence, RMSEA is a measure of noncentrality relative to sample size and degrees of freedom. For a given noncentrality, large N and df imply a better fitting model (i.e., a smaller RMSEA). Values of .06 or less indicate a close-fitting model (Hu & Bentler, 1999). Values larger than .10 are indicative of poor-fitting models (Browne & Cudeck, 1993). Hu and Bentler (1999) found that in small samples the RMSEA overrejected the true model (i.e., its value was too large). Because of this problem, this index may be less preferable with small samples. As with the CFI the choice of estimation method effects the size of the RMSEA.

For the example, $\hat{\tau} = 11.3775$; therefore,

$$\text{RMSEA} = \sqrt{\frac{11.3775}{(4277)(3)}} = .03$$

Both the CFI and RMSEA values of .98 and .03, respectively, well exceed guideline cutoff values for evidence of good fit, CFI .95 and RMSEA .06. Thus we can conclude that we have adequate evidence that the model fits the data despite the significant chi-square.

Interpreting Parameter Estimates: Direct Effects

The model fits, but what does it mean? The hypothesis is that the observed covariances among the measured variables arose because of the linkages between variables specified in the model. We conclude that we should retain our hypothesized model because the fit indices provide evidence of good fit.

Next, researchers usually examine the statistically significant relationships within the model. Table 24.3 contains edited EQS output for evaluation of the regression coefficients for the example. If the unstandardized parameter estimates are divided by their respective standard errors, a z score is obtained for each estimated parameter that is evaluated in the usual manner:

$$z = \frac{\text{parameter estimate}}{\text{std error for estimate}}. \qquad (24.9)$$

Because of differences in scales, it is sometimes difficult to interpret unstandardized regression coefficients; therefore,

TABLE 24.3   Parameter Estimates, Standard Errors, Test Statistics, and Standardized Solution for Hypothetical Example

```
MEASUREMENT EQUATIONS WITH STANDARD ERRORS AND TEST STATISTICS
STATISTICS SIGNIFICANT AT THE 5% LEVEL ARE MARKED WITH @.
(ROBUST STATISTICS IN PARENTHESES)

OKDRINK2=V1    =       1.000 F2      +    1.000 E1

OKSMOKE2=V2    =       1.584*F2      +    1.000 E2
                        .109
                      14.499@
                     (  .159)
                     ( 9.949@

TEACH_SC=V4    =        .490*F1      +    1.000 E4
                        .021
                      22.929@
                     (  .027)
                     ( 18.287@

FAMILY_S=V5    =        .406*F1      +    1.000 E5
                        .018
                      22.026@
                     (  .023)
                     ( 17.404@


CONSTRUCT EQUATIONS WITH STANDARD ERRORS AND TEST STATISTICS
STATISTICS SIGNIFICANT AT THE 5% LEVEL ARE MARKED WITH @.
(ROBUST STATISTICS IN PARENTHESES)

ACCEPT_R=F2    =      -.013*V3      +    .181*F1  +  1.000 D2
                       .012               .013
                     -1.036            13.870@
                     (  .012)          (  .018)
                     (-1.065)          ( 10.110@


STANDARDIZED SOLUTION:                                        R-SQUARED

OKDRINK2=V1    =   .533 F2  + .846 E1                           .284
OKSMOKE2=V2    =   .760*F2  + .650 E2                           .577
TEACH_SC=V4    =   .572*F1  + .820 E4                           .327
FAMILY_S=V5    =   .517*F1  + .856 E5                           .268
ACCEPT_R=F2    =  -.021*V3  + .583*F1 + .811 D2                 .342
```

researchers often examine standardized coefficients. Both the standardized and unstandardized regression coefficients for the final model are in Table 24.3 and Figure 24.3. In Figure 24.3 the standardized coefficients are in parentheses. In the section labeled MEASUREMENT EQUATIONS WITH STANDARD ERRORS AND TEST STATISTICS in Table 24.3, for each dependent variable there are five pieces of information: the unstandardized coefficient is given on the first line; the standard error of the coefficient, given the assumption of normality, is given on the second line; and the test statistic for the coefficient, given normality, is given on the third line. The fourth line contains the standard error after

adjustment for nonnormality (Bentler & Dijkstra, 1985), and the fifth line gives the test statistic after adjustment for the nonnormality. For example, for FAMILY_S (V5) predicted from Weak Institutional Bonds (F1), if normal theory methods are used,

$$\frac{.406}{.018} = 22.026, \qquad p < .05,$$

with an adjustment to the standard error for the nonnormality:

$$\frac{.406}{.023} = 17.404, \qquad p < .05.$$

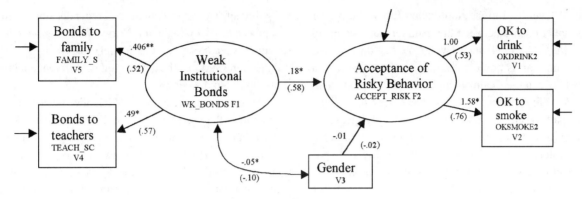

Figure 24.3 Example with unstandardized and standardized coefficients.

It could be concluded that bonds to family (FAMILY_S) is a significant indicator of Weak Institutional Bonds (WK_BONDS); the weaker the Weak Institutional Bonds is, the weaker the bonds to family (unstandardized coefficient = .406). Bonds to teachers (TEACH_SC) is a significant indicator of Weak Institutional Bonds (unstandardized coefficient = .49). Endorsement of smoking (OKSMOKE2) is a significant indicator of Acceptance of Risky Behavior (ACCEPT_RISK), and greater Acceptance of Risky Behavior predicts stronger agreement with the acceptability of smoking (unstandardized coefficient = 1.584). Because the path from ACCEPT_RISK to OKDRINK2 is fixed to 1 for identification, a standard error is not calculated. If this standard error is desired, a second run is performed with the OKSMOKE2 path fixed to 1 instead.

As seen in Table 24.3, the relationships between the constructs appears in the EQS section labeled CONSTRUCT EQUATIONS WITH STANDARD ERRORS AND TEST STATISTICS. Weak Institutional Bonds significantly predicts greater Acceptance of Risky Behavior (unstandardized coefficient = .181). Gender does not predict Acceptance of Risky Behavior (unstandardized coefficient = −.013).

Indirect Effects

A particularly strong feature of SEM is the ability to test not only direct effects between variables but also indirect effects. Mediational hypotheses are not well illustrated in the Acceptance of Risky Behavior example, so a better example is shown in Figure 24.4. Imagine that students are assigned to one of two teaching methods for a statistics class (coded 0 and 1). Final exam scores are recorded at the end of the quarter. The direct effect of teaching method on exam score is path *a*. But is it reasonable to suggest that mere assignment to a teaching method creates the change? Perhaps not. Maybe, instead, the teaching method increases a student's

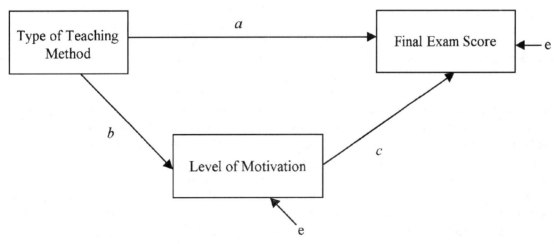

Figure 24.4 Path analysis with indirect effect.

motivational level, and higher motivation leads to a higher grade. The relationship between the treatment and the exam score is *mediated* by motivation level. Note that this is a different question than is posed with a direct-effect "Is there a difference between the treatment and control group on exam score?" The indirect effect can be evaluated by testing the product of paths *b* and *c*. This example uses only measured variables and is called *path analysis;* however, mediational hypotheses can be tested using both latent and observed variables and can involve quite long chains of mediation across many variables. A more detailed discussion of indirect effects can be found in Baron and Kenny (1986); Collins, Graham, and Flaherty (1998); MacKinnon, Krull, and Lockwood (2000); and Sobel (1987).

Model Modification

There are at least two reasons for modifying a SEM model: to test hypotheses (in theoretical work) and to improve fit (especially in exploratory work). Structural equation modeling is a confirmatory technique; therefore, when model modification is done to improve fit, the analysis changes from confirmatory to exploratory. Any conclusions drawn from a model that has undergone substantial modification should be viewed extremely cautiously. Cross validation should be performed on modified models whenever possible.

The three basic methods of model modification are the chi-square difference, Lagrange multiplier (LM), and Wald tests. All are asymptotically equivalent under the null hypothesis but approach model modification differently. In this section each of these approaches is discussed with reference to the Acceptance of Risky Behavior example, and examples will be shown where relevant.

Chi-Square Difference Test

If models are nested (i.e., models are subsets of each other), the chi-square value for the larger model is subtracted from the chi-square value for the smaller, nested model, and the difference, also a chi-square, is evaluated with degrees of freedom equal to the difference between the degrees of freedom in the two models. In the Acceptance of Risky Behavior model we could test whether gender predicted Acceptance of Risky Behavior using the chi-square difference test. The model chi-square from the full model would be subtracted from the chi-square from a model estimated without the path from gender to Acceptance of Risky Behavior. This smaller model has one more degree of freedom and is nested within the larger model. If the chi-square difference test is

significant, we could conclude that gender does predict Acceptance of Risky Behavior. Notice that we did not delete the gender *variable* from the model, just the path. Had we deleted the variable the data would be different, and the models would not be nested.

At least two potentially problematic issues arise that are specific to the use of chi-square difference tests. Because of the relationship between sample size and chi-square, it is hard to detect a difference between models when sample sizes are small. Additionally, and perhaps somewhat less important given current computer capabilities, two models must be estimated to use the chi-square difference test.

Lagrange Multiplier Test

The LM test also compares nested models but requires estimation of only one model. The LM test asks whether the model would be improved if one or more of the parameters in the model that are currently fixed were estimated. Or, equivalently, what parameters should be added to the model to improve the model's fit?

The LM test applied to the Acceptance of Risky Behavior example indicates that if a path were added predicting bonds to teachers (TEACH_SC) from gender, the expected drop in chi-square value would be 12.617. This is one path, so the chi-square value of 12.617 is evaluated with 1 *df*. The *p* level for this difference is $p < .001$, implies that over and above the covariance between gender and Weak Institutional Bonds there is a unique, significantly nonzero relationship between gender and bonds to teachers. If the decision is made to add the path, the model is reestimated. In this example the decision is made not to add this path.

The LM test can be examined either univariately or multivariately. There is a danger in examining only the results of univariate LM tests because overlapping variance between parameter estimates may make several parameters appear as if their addition would significantly improve the model. All significant parameters are candidates for inclusion by the results of univariate LM tests, but the multivariate LM test identifies the single parameter that would lead to the largest drop in model chi-square and calculates the expected change in chi-square. After this variance is removed, the next parameter that accounts for the largest drop in model chi-square is assessed, similarly. After a few candidates for parameter additions are identified, it is best to add these parameters to the model and repeat the process with a new LM test, if necessary. Ideally, with this set of procedures a new sample should be used each time to avoid capitalizing on chance variation in the data and to replicate the findings.

Wald Test

While the LM test asks which parameters, if any, should be added to a model, the Wald test asks which, if any, could be deleted. Are there any parameters that are currently being estimated that could, instead, be fixed to zero? Or, equivalently, which parameters are not necessary in the model? The Wald test is analogous to backward deletion of variables in stepwise regression, where one seeks a nonsignificant change in R^2 when variables are left out.

When the Wald test is applied to the example, the only candidate for deletion is the regression coefficient predicting Acceptance of Risky Behavior (ACCEPT_RISK) from gender. If this parameter is dropped, the chi-square value increases by 1.134, a nonsignificant change ($p = .287$). The model is not significantly degraded by deletion of this parameter. The decision is made to keep the path because this path was central to the hypothesis. However, if the goal is development of a parsimonious model, it might also be reasonable to drop the path. Notice that unlike the LM test, *nonsignificance* is desired when using the Wald test. When only a single parameter is evaluated, the Wald test is just the square of the z test given previously ($1.134 = 1.065^2$).

Some Caveats and Hints on Model Modification

Because both the LM test and Wald test are stepwise procedures, Type I error rates are inflated with the exception of the Scheffe-like procedure suggested by Hancock (1999). There are, as yet, no available adjustments as in analysis of variance (ANOVA). A simple approach is to use a conservative probability value (say, $p < .01$) for adding parameters with the LM test. Cross validation with another sample is also highly recommended if modifications are made. If numerous modifications are made and new data are not available for cross validation, compute the correlation between the estimated parameters from the original, hypothesized model and the estimated parameters from the final model using only parameters common to both models. If this correlation is high ($> .90$), relationships within the model have been retained despite the modifications.

Unfortunately, the order that parameters are freed or estimated can affect the significance of the remaining parameters. MacCallum (1986) suggested adding all necessary parameters before deleting unnecessary parameters. In other words, do the LM test before the Wald test.

A more subtle limitation is that tests leading to model modification examine overall changes in chi-square, not changes in individual parameter estimates. Large changes in chi-square are sometimes associated with very small changes in parameter estimates. A missing parameter may be statistically needed, but the estimated coefficient may have an uninterpretable sign. If this happens, it may be best not to add the parameter although the unexpected result may help to pinpoint problems with one's theory. Finally, if the hypothesized model is wrong, tests of model modification, by themselves, may be insufficient to reveal the true model. In fact, the "trueness" of any model is never tested directly, although cross validation does add evidence that the model is correct. Like other statistics, these tests must be used thoughtfully.

If model modifications are done in hopes of developing a good-fitting model, the fewer modifications there are, the better, especially if a cross-validation sample is not available. If the LM test and Wald tests are used to test specific hypotheses, the hypotheses will dictate the number of necessary tests.

MULTIPLE GROUP MODELS

The example shown in this chapter uses data from a single sample. It is also possible to estimate and compare models that come from two or more samples, called multiple group models (Jöreskog, 1971; Sörbom, 1974). The basic null hypothesis tested in multiple group models is that the data from each group are from the same population with the hypothesized model structure. For example, if data are drawn from a sample of boys and a sample of girls for the Acceptance of Risky Behavior model, the general null hypothesis tested is that the two groups are drawn from the same population. If such a restrictive model were acceptable, a single model and model-reproduced covariance matrix would approximate the two sample covariance matrices for girls and boys. Typically, identical models do not quite fit, and some differences between models must be allowed.

The analysis begins by developing good-fitting models in separate analyses for each group. The models are then tested in one overall analysis with none of the parameters across models constrained to be equal. This unconstrained multiple-group model serves as the baseline against which to judge more restricted models. Following baseline model estimation, progressively more stringent constraints are specified by constraining various parameters across all groups. When parameters are constrained, they are forced to be equal to one another. In EQS, an LM test is available to evaluate whether the constraint is acceptable or needs to be rejected. The same result can be obtained by a chi-square difference test. The goal is not to degrade the models by constraining parameters across the groups; therefore, you want a *nonsignificant* chi-square. If a significant difference in chi-square is found between the models at any stage, the LM test can be examined to locate the specific parameters that are different in the groups. Such parameters should remain estimated separately in each group; that is, the specific *across-group* parameter constraints are released.

Hypotheses are generally tested in a specific order. The first step is usually to constrain the factor loadings (regression coefficients) between factors and their indices to equality across groups. In our hypothetical two-group model of Acceptance of Risky Behavior this would be equivalent to testing whether the factor structure (the measurement model) of Weak Institutional Bonds and Acceptance of Risky Behavior is the same for girls and boys. If these constraints are reasonable, the chi-square difference test between the restricted model and the baseline model will be nonsignificant for both groups. If the difference between the restricted and nonrestricted models is significant, we need not throw in the towel immediately; rather, results of the LM test can be examined and some equality constraints across the groups can be released. Naturally, the more parameters that differ across groups, the less alike the groups are. Consult Byrne, Shavelson, and Muthén (1989) for a technical discussion of these issues.

If the equality of the factor structure is established, there are options in terms of the order in which to proceed to test the equality of the samples. Often a reasonable second step is to ask whether the factor variances and covariances are equal. If these constraints are feasible, the third step examines equality of the factor regression coefficients. Again, in our hypothetical two-group model this is equivalent to testing whether the coefficient predicting Acceptance of Risky Behavior from Weak Institutional Bonds is the same for girls and boys. If all of these constraints are reasonable, the last step is to examine the equality of residual variances across groups, an extremely stringent hypothesis not often tested. If all of the regression coefficients, variances, and covariances are the same across groups, it is concluded that these two samples arise from the same population. An example of multiple group modeling of program evaluation that utilizes a Solomon Four-Group design can be found in Dukes, Ullman, and Stein (1995).

Until this point we have discussed modeling only variances and covariances. Means and intercepts can also be modeled using SEM techniques. Mean structures can be employed in single group models; however, modeling means and intercepts is perhaps most commonly done in the context of a multiple group model. In the next section we discuss incorporating a mean structure within an SEM model. Following this brief discussion we present a second example that incorporates a completely different type of model that utilizes a mean and covariance structure.

Incorporating a Mean and Covariance Structure

Modeling means in addition to variances and covariances requires no modification of the Bentler-Weeks model. Instead a constant, a vector or 1s, (labeled V999 in EQS) is included in the model as an independent variable. As a constant, this independent "variable" has no variance and no covariances with other variables in the model. Regressing a variable (either latent or measured) on this constant yields an intercept parameter. The model-reproduced mean of a variable is equal to the sum of the direct and indirect effects for that variable. Therefore, if a variable is predicted only from the constant, the intercept is equal to the mean; otherwise, the mean is a function of path coefficients. In the hypothetical two-group Acceptance of Risky Behavior model, using a mean structure we could test the hypothesis that boys and girls have different average levels of Acceptance of Risky Behavior.

Another type of model that incorporates a mean structure is a latent growth curve model. Using intercept parameters, growth curve models allow questions to be examined about individual rate of change and average level of construct. These are outside the scope of this chapter, but the interested reader may want to consult Curran (2000), Duncan, Duncan, Strycker, Li, and Alpert (1999), Khoo and Muthén (2000), McArdle (1986), McArdle and Epstein (1987), and Mehta and West (2000).

MULTILEVEL MODELS: AN EXTENSION OF A BASIC MULTIPLE GROUP MODEL

A completely different type of multiple group model is called a multilevel model. In this analysis, separate models are developed for different levels of nested data. For example, you might be interested in evaluating an intervention given to several classrooms of students in several different schools. One model is estimated for the schools, another for the classrooms that are nested within the schools, and a third for the children nested within the classrooms and schools. Predictors at each level are employed to test various within-level and across-level hypotheses.

Specifying a Hierarchical Linear Model

There are several methods of specifying hierarchical linear models (HLMs) within a structural modeling framework. As with general structural equation modeling there are many types and hypotheses relevant to HLM models (Heck & Thomas, 2000; Snijders & Bosker, 1999). A full discussion of these different model specification methods and hypotheses is outside the scope of this chapter. Only one approach, with a very simple model, will be illustrated in this example. For in-depth discussion of multilevel approaches see Muthén (1994, 1997), Chou, Bentler, and Pentz (1998), Bentler and Liang (in press), and Reise (2001).

Multilevel models are appropriate with clustered data. For example, when an intervention, such as the D.A.R.E. (Drug Abuse Resistance Education) program, is given to classroom of students, students are nested within the classroom. If traditional methods are employed to analyze this data, problems may arise. If the data from an evaluation such as D.A.R.E. are analyzed at the student level and there is a sizable intraclass correlation, the standard errors may be too small, and inaccurate conclusions may be drawn. If the data are analyzed only at the level of the classroom then power is substantially reduced. Traditional methods also do not allow for cross-level predictors (i.e., predictors from one level predicting outcomes at another level). For example, participation in D.A.R.E. (a classroom-level variable) may predict students' Acceptance of Risky Behavior (an individual-level variable).

HLM models are specified in a multistage process. A good-fitting model is established hierarchically. After good-fitting models are established at each phase, a multiple group model is tested that allows prediction across levels of measurement. This ability is one of the strongest advantages of multilevel modeling. In the example to follow, a multilevel model will be employed to examine a two-group model of children nested within classrooms. After establishing a good-fitting model for the children (level 1), the second-level model (the classrooms) is added to the model, and a multiple group model is tested. Specifically, a level 1 (children) model is tested for each unit (in this example, each classroom). Then, hypothesized parameters from the individual level 1 models (regression coefficients, variances and covariances of independent variables, and intercepts) are used as dependent variables for second-level (classroom level) predictors.

An Empirical Example of Hierarchical Linear Models

A simple example using data from program evaluations of Drug Abuse Resistance Education (D.A.R.E.) in Colorado Springs will be used to illustrate an HLM model (Ullman, Stein, & Dukes, 2001). D.A.R.E. is a drug use prevention program that is given to classrooms of children in late elementary school. Children are nested within classrooms. The four components that the D.A.R.E. program targets (Self-Esteem,

Institutional Bonds, Acceptance of Risky Behavior, and Resistance to Peer Pressure) as well as two D.A.R.E. curriculum knowledge questions ("Changing the subject is a good way to say no" and "Taking a deep breath is a good way to relax") were employed in this model. The primary hypothesis of interest in this model is whether participation in D.A.R.E. predicts differences in these concepts and curriculum questions. Note that although we conceptualize these components as constructs, due to small sample sizes in some of the classrooms, in this model D.A.R.E. core concepts were treated as measured variables. D.A.R.E. is given to classrooms of children (groups); therefore, D.A.R.E. participation is considered a level 2 (classroom level) predictor. Additionally, other classroom predictors such as (a) size of class and (b) percentage of minority students in the class could also be hypothesized to predict D.A.R.E. effectiveness. These all are hypotheses involving prediction of average student-level outcomes from class-level predictors.

It is also hypothesized that variables measured at the child level also predict changes in these components. At the child level, the four core concepts and the two D.A.R.E. curriculum questions were predicted from (a) ethnicity of child (White, non-White), (b) gender of child, and (c) expected grades for child.

Model Estimation and Evaluation

We use data from 4,578 children in 144 classrooms. Further details about these data and the D.A.R.E. program evaluations can be found in Ullman, Stein, and Dukes (2000). First, a model was estimated with only the child-level data, the four D.A.R.E. core concepts, and two curriculum variables predicted from gender, ethnicity, and grades. The data for children were nonnormally distributed (Mardia's standardized coefficient for multivariate kurtosis $= 92.76$, $p < .001$); therefore, maximum likelihood estimation and the Satorra-Bentler (S-B) Scaled chi-square were used to evaluate the model (Bentler & Yuan, 1999; Satorra & Bentler, 1994). There was evidence that the model fit the data: $\chi^2(N = 4578, 11) = 2.90$, $p = .99$. Although the model fit the data well, none of the regression paths significantly predicted the D.A.R.E. core concepts/curriculum after adjustment to the standard errors for nonnormality. This pattern of nonsignificance is typical of research on the D.A.R.E. program (Dukes, Ullman, & Stein, 1995).

Fundamental to a D.A.R.E. evaluation is whether D.A.R.E. is effective in increasing Self-Esteem, Institutional Bonds, and Resistance to Peer Pressure and in reducing Acceptance of Risky Behaviors. D.A.R.E. is implemented at the classroom level; therefore, participation is a level 2 (classroom level) predictor. In addition to participation status in D.A.R.E., it was also hypothesized that size of the class and proportion of minority students in the class might predict differences in the D.A.R.E. core concepts. This full, multi-level model uses data collected at the classroom level to predict the intercepts of the D.A.R.E. core concepts (Self-Esteem, Institutional Bonds, Resistance to Risky Behavior, and Acceptance of Risky Behavior) and the curriculum questions from the student-level model. The EQS syntax for this model is presented in the appendix. The classroom data were also nonnormally distributed (Mardia's standardized coefficient = 7.07); therefore, the multiple group model was evaluated with the Satorra-Bentler scaled chi-square. There was evidence that the HLM model fits the data, $S\text{-}B\chi^2(N_{children} = 4578, N_{classrooms} = 144, 3) = 4.49$, $p = .21$, CFI = 98. However, none of the class-level variables—participation in D.A.R.E. (yes/no), class size, and percentage of non-White students—significantly predicted the core concepts/curriculum variables. Again, these nonsignificant results are consistent with the prior D.A.R.E. literature.

A GUIDE TO SOME RECENT LITERATURE AND FUTURE DEVELOPMENTS

In this section we provide a guide to some recent publications in the SEM literature, organized by a few topics that are currently the focus of methodological research. While SEM has provided new ways to conceptualize and analyze multivariate data, especially non- or quasi-experimental data, the methodology still has technical pitfalls that need resolution. In the next several years we expect to see improvements in methods for dealing with small samples, for dealing with missing data, for handling outliers and unusual cases, for extending multilevel models to less standard situations, and for dealing with latent variable interactions and nonlinear models. We will say a few words about these selected problems, recognizing that our summary cannot cover many important recent developments in this growing field. For example, we do not review important classes of methods such as growth curve modeling (e.g., Curran, 2000; Duncan et al., 1999; Khoo & Muthén, 2000; Mehta & West, 2000), bootstrap methodology (Bollen & Stine, 1993; Efron, 2000; Nevitt & Hancock, in press; Yung & Bentler, 1996), or specialized applications in dozens of fields (e.g., genetic modeling; Van den Oord, 2000). General reviews of the field are provided by Bentler and Dudgeon (1996) and MacCallum and Austin (2000). Excellent collections of applications can be found in T. D. Little, Schnabel, and Baumert (1999) and Rose, Chassin, Presson, and Sherman (2000). An overview of recent technical developments

can be found in Marcoulides and Schumacker (2001). For work having a LISREL focus, see Cudeck, du Toit, and Sörbom (2001).

Improved Methods for Small Samples

As noted earlier, SEM methodology is often applied when sample size is small: "About 18% of the studies we reviewed used samples of fewer than 100 individuals" (McCallum & Austin, 2000, p. 215). The quality of results that may occur from a given study with small samples will depend on the features of the model of interest (parameter estimates, standard errors, z tests, test statistics, mediational effects) as well as characteristics of the model such as the communality level of the variables (MacCallum, Widaman, Zhang, & Hong, 1999) and the degree and kind of nonnormality that might exist (e.g., Boomsma & Hoogland, 2001; Finch, West, & MacKinnon, 1997; Hoogland, 1999; Yuan & Bentler, 1999b). Ideally, SEM methods would perform well across all the design features just mentioned, but this is not the case (e.g., Bentler & Yuan, 1999). At a minimum, one would like to have enough power to reject alternative models (Hancock, Lawrence, & Nevitt, 2000; MacCallum et al., 1996), but even the estimation of power depends on having a test statistic that can be relied upon under the given circumstances (i.e., typically, that correctly can be referred to the hypothesized noncentral chi-square distribution). Because various test statistics that are presumed to have central chi-square distributions do not behave this way under realistic data-gathering conditions (e.g., violation of normality in the case of normal maximum likelihood), it is likely that the noncentral distributions used to calculate power also may not suffice. Clearly, better small sample methods are needed.

Given the model characteristics, some methods are better able to cope with small samples than are other methods. For example, Bentler and Yuan (1999) studied the normal theory-based likelihood ratio statistic T_{ML}, the Satorra-Bentler rescaled statistic T_{SB}, the Yuan and Bentler version T_{YB} of Browne's (1984) residual-based ADF statistic T_B, and their F statistic derived from the residual-based ADF statistic. They found that the F statistic performed best of all these mentioned at the smallest sample sizes. It also performed very well in Yuan and Bentler's (1999a) and Nevitt's (2000) study, and is available in EQS 6 (Bentler, 2001). However, Fouladi (1999) recommended using a Bartlett (1950) correction and applying it to the Satorra-Bentler (1994) scaled and adjusted statistics. She found that the Bartlett-corrected adjusted statistic performed best. In a related paper Fouladi (2000) found that Bartlett and Swain rescaling was best with small samples and very mild nonnormality, but that SB scaled and adjusted procedures were better with more severe nonnormality. Nevitt (2000) also found that a Bartlett-corrected statistic performed best in his study, which was more extensive than that of Fouladi. Nevitt's final conclusion was that the *k*-factor-corrected Satorra-Bentler scaled (not adjusted) test statistic is best used to evaluate model fit in small samples. This recent work, while very promising, deserves extension and incorporation into standard packages.

Another interesting development that may help in small samples is that of two-stage least squares. Although the method is old, new implementations are distribution free and imply some robustness to misspecification that is not available in full information methods (Bollen, 2001). Bollen's approach may also yield better performance with small sample size.

Improved Methods for Missing Data

In our presentation we did not go into detail on missing data methodology. Yet missing data are inevitable. Two promising methods for dealing with missing data are a direct maximum likelihood (e.g., Neale, 2000; Wothke, 2000) and a two-stage approach based on the unstructured mean and covariance estimates obtained by the EM-algorithm (e.g., Graham & Hofer, 2000; see also Jamshidian & Bentler, 1999, 2000). Enders (2001) provided a good summary. Typical assumptions under these two methods are ignorable nonresponse and normality of data. Unfortunately, there is no effective way of verifying these conditions in practice. When these conditions are not satisfied, normal theory methods generally lead to incorrect model and parameter evaluation and misleading substantive conclusions even in complete data cases (e.g., Curran, West, & Finch, 1996; Hu et al., 1992; Yuan & Bentler, 1998a), and it is unlikely that one can avoid such incorrectness with an added missing data problem. As an improvement over current methods, Yuan and Bentler (2000b) built on Arminger and Sobel (1990) and dropped the normal distribution assumption and thus were able to develop several more accurate procedures for model inference. Based on the theory of generalized estimating equations (see Yuan & Jennrich, 2000), they provided a way to obtain consistent standard errors of the two-stage estimates. They also proposed a minimum chi-square approach and showed that the estimator obtained by this approach is asymptotically at least as efficient as the two likelihood-based estimators for either normal data or nonnormal data. Both the ML and generalized approaches are implemented in EQS 6.

Ad hoc methods have been used in data analysis for decades and provide another option in handling incomplete data. These include mean imputation, listwise deletion, pairwise computations, stochastic regression imputation, and hot deck imputation as well as more recently developed methods such as similar response pattern imputation or person mean imputation (Bernaards & Sijtsma, 2000). In these approaches a modified data set or a covariance matrix is created that subsequently can be analyzed by any existing standard method designed for complete data. An advantage of these approaches is that they are relatively practical to implement; indeed, such methods for dealing with incomplete data can be found in most well-known statistical program packages. Furthermore, nonnormality can be routinely handled when an imputed data matrix is analyzed with a distribution-free method. These methods are all appropriate when the amount of missing data is extremely small. In fact, under some conditions there may be only marginal loss of accuracy or efficiency when compared to maximum likelihood (see Gold & Bentler, 2000). However, there exist several drawbacks of these nonprincipled methods. For example, listwise deletion can render a longitudinal study with few cases left, resulting in grossly inefficient estimates (e.g., Brown, 1994). When the missing data mechanism is so called missing at random (MAR), existing simulation results indicate that listwise deletion causes parameter estimates to be biased even for normal data (R. J. A. Little & Rubin, 1987; Schafer, 1997). We suspect that some technical work can render some of these ad hoc methods more principled and hence potentially competitive with the currently technically advanced methods, especially with nonnormal data.

A problem raised by incomplete data is whether a sample may be a missing completely at random (MCAR) sample from a single population with a given mean vector and covariance matrix. If this can be established, a single SEM model for the population can be considered; if means and covariances are not homogeneous, this may not be advisable. There have been developments that test MCAR in several different areas (e.g., generalized estimating equations; Chen & Little, 1999). In the area of multivariate normal data, there are currently two proposed test statistics for analyzing whether incomplete data patterns are MCAR (R. J. A. Little, 1988; Tang & Bentler, 1998). Both R. J. A. Little and Tang-Bentler use the EM algorithm to impute incomplete data, obtain ML estimates of free parameters under the MCAR assumption, and propose a test statistic to evaluate an MCAR null hypothesis. R. J. A. Little's (1988) MCAR test is based on evaluating the homogeneity of available means for different patterns of incomplete data. R. J. A. Little also mentioned, but did not study, a test based on both means and covariances, in which the homogeneity of available covariance matrices is simultaneously studied with homogeneity of means. He expected that this test might not perform well due to its typically large degrees of freedom. In quite a different context, Tang and Bentler (1998) studied covariance structures, such as factor analysis models, for incomplete data. When their test is specialized to that of an unstructured but common covariance matrix for all patterns of incomplete data, it provides a test of the MCAR assumption. In fact, their test can be shown to specialize to a test that can be constructed based on a chi-square difference rationale applied to R. J. A. Little's two proposed tests. A serious problem with these likelihood approaches is that they break down when the number of subjects for a given pattern of incomplete data is very small. Kim and Bentler developed a new method, included in EQS 6, that uses a generalized least squares rationale to develop tests that should be more stable in small samples.

Extended Use of Robust Methods

Standard linear modeling methods such as ANOVA and SEM are susceptible to catastrophic breakdown in nonregular situations. Unfortunately, those are the very situations encountered in many research situations. As noted by Wilcox (1995, p. 57), "It should be stressed that outliers are not the only reason for considering robust methods. Small shifts in a distribution can have a large impact on the mean, which might render it a potentially misleading measure of the typical individual." He also raises the provocative question of whether discoveries have been lost due to nonuse of robust methods (Wilcox, 1998). It is known that the influence function associated with the sample covariance is quadratic, so that a few influential cases or outliers can lead to inappropriate solutions for virtually all standard statistical methods that rely on sample covariances (Hampel, Ronchetti, Rousseeuw, & Stahel, 1986; Yuan & Bentler, in press). SEM methods, of course, rely heavily on means and covariances as their basic data to be modeled. It is well known that methods for handling data in nonstandard situations, such as methods that have bounded influence functions and can tolerate a high proportion of bad data before breaking down, have existed for a long time (e.g., Hoaglin, Mosteller, & Tukey, 1983). However, in the past these methods have been presented primarily as exploratory and graphical methods, with little attention paid to standard problems of inference in the multivariate case. These issues were solved in a series of papers by Yuan and his colleagues (Yuan & Bentler, 1998b, 1998c, 2000a; Yuan, Chan, & Bentler, 2000). In general, these methods seek to weight cases or observations differentially. By giving a proper weight to each case, the influence of outliers on a robust procedure is minimal. As an example of this approach, Yuan et al. proposed to use the robust procedure as a transformation technique,

generating a new data matrix that can be analyzed by a variety of multivariate methods. The sample covariance matrix of the transformed data then becomes the robust covariance matrix, which is generally more efficient when the sampling distribution has heavy tails. Because the transformation makes the data approximately normal, classical normal theory–based procedures applied to the transformed data give more accurate evaluations regarding model structure. In their approach, Mardia's multivariate skewness and kurtosis statistics are used to measure the effect of the transformation in achieving approximate normality. Examples showed the useful effect of the transformation on model evaluation.

In general, these robust methods work with a weight function that in turn generates the final case weights. Because there are in principle a lot of potential weight functions (see, e.g., Table 11-1 of Hoaglin et al., 1983), there are also many different case weight vectors that could be used. Examples are Maronna's (1976) M-estimator weights, Huber's (1977) type weights, multivariate-t weights (Lange, Little, & Taylor, 1989), and Campbell's (1980) weights. Based on good simulation performance, the Campbell weighting is available in EQS 6. However, because the distribution of the data is not known a priori, it is hard to have a clear a priori rationale as to which weight to use in what circumstance. In fact, this is probably an Achilles' heel of robust methods: Because there are so many possibilities, consensus on the use of a single method has not been achieved, and hence their use in more applied settings has been hindered. In the next few years one can hope that consensus will be achieved as to the best way to do robust mean and covariance structure modeling.

Methods for Multilevel Nonnormal Data

As we noted earlier, data sets often have a hierarchical structure; for example, students are nested within classes, classes are nested within schools, and schools are further nested within school districts. Strenio, Weisberg, and Bryk (1983) noted that growth curve models and models for repeated measures are special cases of a two-level model (see also Chou et al., 1998). Because of such a hierarchical structure, cases within a cluster are generally correlated. Thus, to achieve accurate results, statistical models must explicitly account for these correlations. Using a two-level model applied to educational data, Aitkin and Longford (1986) demonstrated that ignoring the hierarchical structure could be misleading. Assuming that data are normal, Goldstein (1986) and Longford (1987) considered algorithms for obtaining maximum likelihood estimates in an HLM, a hierarchical linear model. Other early developments in multilevel modeling are summarized in Bock (1989). More recent results can be found in Bryk and Raudenbush (1992), Goldstein (1995), and Kreft and deLeeuw (1998). Paralleling the development of HLM, multilevel SEM also has grown rapidly (Goldstein & McDonald, 1988; Lee, 1990; Longford, 1993a, 1993b; McDonald & Goldstein, 1989; Muthén, 1994, 1997; Muthén & Satorra, 1995; Rovine & Molenaar, 2000). An HLM-like approach is given in Chou et al. (2000). The most popular approach is Muthén's MUML method. This is an approximation to maximum likelihood, and it is equivalent to it when the data are balanced. While its "within" parameters are well behaved, the "between" parameters and model tests with MUML may have some bias (e.g., Hox & Maas, 2001). A practical, true ML approach was developed by Bentler and Liang (in press) and is incorporated into the EQS 6 program.

Unfortunately, most approaches to multilevel models currently require a multivariate normality assumption for the hierarchical data or its error structure. An exception is the distribution free approach of Lee and Poon (1994), which, however, is mainly applicable to data with a small number of variables and huge sample sizes. Current research by Yuan and Bentler is aimed at providing statistics that are robust to violation of the normality assumption. The intent is to provide a scaling correction akin to the Satorra-Bentler (1994) correction and to generate more adequate standard error estimates with a triple product, sandwich-type matrix. These have been found to work well in the standard situation of independent observations.

Latent Variable Interactions and Nonlinear Models

The idea of interactions is a standard one in linear models and ANOVA. Yet such ideas continue to be out of reach to practical SEM work. Although introduced many years ago (e.g., Kenny & Judd, 1984; Mooijaart & Bentler, 1986), only recently has a huge and technical literature on this topic developed. See, for example, Schumacker and Marcoulides (1998) or Yang-Wallentin (2001). It is clear from this work that proposed approaches to handling interactions are very complicated to implement and not yet routinely available for applied researchers because no one has figured out how to make this methodology convenient and easy to use in a program package using a few simple commands. It is hoped that the technical issues will soon be solved and that practical implementations will become available (see, e.g., Wood, 2000). Even though nonlinear models with polynomial relations go back several decades (e.g., McDonald, 1967), today "the most challenging problems are generalizations of structural equation modeling that involve nonlinear functions of latent variables" (Browne, 2000, p. 663). According to Wall and Amemiya (2000), the challenge is basic: The Kenny-Judd (1984) approach and its extension by others produces inconsistent parameter estimates unless the latent variables are normally distributed. Although the Bollen (1995, 1996) approach is consistent, Wall and Amemiya found that it could not be extended to general polynomial models such as they have developed. It is possible that their approach is both general and practical enough that if programmed in a way to hide its own complexity, it might be amenable to use by nonspecialists.

As discussed in this chapter, SEM is a technique for dealing with linear relations among variables. Clearly this is a strong and, no doubt, sometimes unreasonable assumption. We hope that practical approaches will become available for nonlinear SEM (and related) models in the next few years. The recent literature uses advanced statistical methods to address such problems. These are based on Bayesian theory using the Gibbs sampler and the Metropolis-Hastings algorithm (e.g., Arminger & Muthén, 1998; Lee & Zhu, 2000; Scheines, Hoijtink, & Boomsma, 1999; Zhu & Lee, 1999). These procedures typically involve estimation of individual specific parameters, such as factor scores, and also take into account the uncertainty in such estimates. Because Bayesian theory is not generally known to applied researchers, producing a practical implementation of any of these methods that is meaningful and accurate will be a big challenge that the field still needs to undertake.

CONCLUSIONS

In this chapter we attempted to introduce the reader to a powerful statistical technique, structural equation modeling (SEM). This technique allows examination of complex systems of variables that are both observed and unobserved. Our goal was to provide a general overview of SEM using applied examples. Therefore, we began the chapter with a brief introduction to the method. We used a real data example to demonstrate basic modeling techniques and issues. After introducing the fundamental theoretical underpinnings and basic modeling techniques, we presented a very simple example of an exciting new extension of basic SEM models, multilevel modeling. Finally, we concluded the chapter with a section that discussed future research directions in SEM, providing a guide to current research as well as presenting exciting areas for further study. Given these promising new research endeavors, the next several years should see continued rapid growth in the development and use of SEM techniques.

APPENDIX: EQS SETUP FOR HLM MULTILEVEL MODEL SPECIFICATION

```
/TITLE
  Kids - Level 1
/SPECIFICATIONS
DATA='c:\program files\spss\kidsema17.ess';
  VARIABLES=68; CASES=4578;
  multilevel=hlm; level = v64; analysis =
   moment;
  METHODS=ML,ROBUST;
  MATRIX=RAW;
  ANALYSIS=moment;
/Equations
  !Self-Esteem
  V57 = *v999 + *V65 + *V43 + *V42 + e57;

  !Institutional Bonds
  V66 = *V999 + *V65 + *V43 + *V42 + E66;

  !Acceptance of Risky Behaviors
  V67=*V999 + *V65 + *V43 + *V42 + E67;

  !Resistance to Peer Pressure
  V68=*V999 + *V65 + *V43 + *V42 + E68;

  V32 = *v999 + *v65 + *v43 + *v42 + e32;
  V33 = *v999 + *v65 + *v43 + *v42 + e33;
  V65 = *V999 + E65;
  V43 = *V999 + E43;
  V42 = *V999 + E42;
/VARIANCES
    E32,E33 = *;
    E65,E43,E42 = *;
    E57,E66,E67,E68=*;
/COVARIANCES
    E32,E33 = *;
    E66 TO E68 =*;
    E57,E66 = *;
    E57,E67=*;
    E57,E68=*;
/END
/TITLE
  Classes - Level 2
/SPECIFICATIONS
DATA='c:\program files\spss\classes.ess';
  VARIABLES=20; CASES=144;
  METHODS=ML;
  MATRIX=RAW;
  ANALYSIS=COVARIANCE;
```

```
/DEFINE                      !This paragraph
pulls in parameters from the prior level
  V21 = (V57,V999);
  V22 = (V66,V999);
  V23 = (V67,V999);
  V24 = (V68,V999);
  V25 = (V32,v999);
  V26 = (V33,v999);
/EQUATION
  V21 = *V13 + *V5 + *V12 + E21;
  V22 = *V13 + *V5 + *V12 + E22;
  V23 = *V13 + *V5 + *V12 + E23;
  V24 = *V13 + *V5 + *V12 + E24;
  v25 = *v13 + *v5 + *v12 + e25;
  v26 = *v13 + *v5 + *v12 + e26;
/VARIANCE
  V13,V5,V12 = *;
  E21 TO E26 = *;
/COVARIANCES
  E21 TO E26 = *;
/PRINT
  FIT = ALL;
/LMTEST
/END
```

REFERENCES

Allison, P. D. (1987). Estimation of linear models with incomplete data. In C. Cogg (Ed.), *Sociological methodology* (pp. 71–103). San Francisco: Jossey Bass.

Aitkin, M., & Longford, N. (1986). Statistical modeling issues in school effectiveness studies. *Journal of the Royal Statistical Society, Series A, 149,* 1–43.

Arminger, G., & Muthén, B. O. (1998). A Bayesian approach to nonlinear latent variable models using the Gibbs sampler and the Metropolis-Hastings algorithm. *Psychometrika, 63,* 271–300.

Arminger, G., & Sobel, M. E. (1990). Pseudo-maximum likelihood estimation of mean and covariance structures with missing data. *Journal of the American Statistical Association, 85,* 195–203.

Baron, R. M., & Kenny, D. A. (1986). The moderator-mediator variable distinction in social psychological research: Conceptual, strategic, and statistical considerations. *Journal of Personality and Social Psychology, 51,* 1173–1182.

Bartlett, M. S. (1950). Tests of significance in factor analysis. *British Journal of Psychology, Statistical Section, 3,* 77–85.

Bentler, P. M. (1990). Comparative fit indexes in structural models. *Psychology Bulletin, 107,* 256–259.

Bentler, P. M. (2001). *EQS 6 structural equations program manual* [Computer program manual]. Encino, CA: Multivariate Software.

Bentler, P. M., & Dijkstra, T. (1985). Efficient estimation via linearization in structural models. In P. R. Krishnaiah (Ed.), *Multivariate analysis* (Vol. 6, pp. 9–42). Amsterdam: North-Holland.

Bentler, P. M., & Dudgeon, P. (1996). Covariance structure analysis: Statistical practice, theory, and directions. *Annual Review of Psychology, 47,* 541–570.

Bentler, P. M., & Liang, J. (in press). Two-level mean and covariance structures: Maximum likelihood via an EM algorithm. In N. Duan & S. Reise (Eds.), *Multilevel modeling: Methodological advances, issues, and applications.* Mahwah, NJ: Erlbaum.

Bentler, P. M., & Weeks, D. G. (1980). Linear structural equation with latent variables. *Psychometrika, 45,* 289–308.

Bentler, P. M., & Yuan, K.-H. (1999). Structural equation modeling with small samples: Test statistics. *Multivariate Behavioral Research, 34*(2), 181–197.

Bernaards, C. A., & Sijtsma, K. (2000). Influence of imputation and EM methods on factor analysis when item nonresponse in questionnaire data is nonignorable. *Multivariate Behavioral Research, 35,* 321–364.

Bock, R. D. (1989). *Multilevel analysis of educational data.* San Diego, CA: Academic Press.

Bollen, K. A. (1989). *Structural equations with latent variables.* New York: Wiley.

Bollen, K. A. (1995). Structural equation models that are nonlinear in latent variables: A least squares estimator. *Sociological Methodology, 25,* 223–251.

Bollen, K. A. (1996). An alternative two stage least squares (2SLS) estimator for latent variable equations. *Psychometrika, 61,* 109–121.

Bollen, K. A. (2001). Two-stage least squares and latent variable models: Simultaneous estimation and robustness to misspecifications. In R. Cudeck, S. du Toit, & D. Sörbom (Eds.), *Structural equation modeling: Present and future* (pp. 119–138). Lincolnwood, IL: Scientific Software International.

Bollen, K. A., & Stine, R. (1993). Bootstrapping goodness-of-fit measures in structural equation models. In K. A. Bollen & J. S. Long (Eds.), *Testing structural equation models* (pp. 111–135). Newbury Park, CA: Sage.

Boomsma, A., & Hoogland, J. J. (2001). The robustness of LISREL modeling revisited. In R. Cudeck, S. du Toit, & D. Sörbom (Eds.), *Structural equation modeling: Present and future* (pp. 139–168). Lincolnwood, IL: Scientific Software International.

Brown, R. L. (1994). Efficacy of the indirect approach for estimating structural equation models with missing data: A comparison of five methods. *Structural Equation Modeling, 1,* 287–316.

Browne M. W. (1984). Asymptotically distribution-free methods for the analysis of covariance structures. *British Journal of Mathematical and Statistical Psychology, 37,* 62–83.

Browne, M. W. (2000). Psychometrics. *Journal of the American Statistical Association, 95,* 661–665.

Browne, M. W., & Cudeck R. (1993). Alternative ways of assessing model fit. In K. A. Bollen & J. S. Long (Eds.), *Testing structural models* (pp. 136–162). Newbury Park, CA: Sage.

Bryk, A. S., & Raudenbush, S. W. (1992). *Hierarchical linear models.* Newbury Park, CA: Sage.

Byrne, B. M., Shavelson, R. J., & Muthén, B. (1989). Testing for the equivalence of factor covariance and mean structures: The issue of partial measurement invariance. *Psychological Bulletin, 105,* 456–466.

Campbell, N. A. (1980). Robust procedures in multivariate analysis: Pt. 1. Robust covariance estimation. *Applied Statistics, 29,* 231–237.

Chen, H. Y., & Little, R. (1999). A test of missing completely at random for generalised estimating equation with missing data. *Biometrika, 86,* 1–13.

Chou, C.-P., Bentler, P. M., & Pentz, M. A. (1998). Comparisons of two statistical approaches to study growth curves: The multilevel model and the latent curve analysis. *Structural Equation Modeling, 5,* 247–266.

Collins, L. M., Graham, J. W., & Flaherty, B. P. (1998). An alternative framework for defining mediation. *Multivariate Behavioral Research, 33,* 295–312.

Cudeck, R., du Toit, S., & Sörbom, D. (Eds.). (2001). *Structural equation modeling: Present and future.* Lincolnwood, IL: Scientific Software International.

Curran, P. J. (2000). A latent curve framework for the study of developmental trajectories in adolescent substance use. In J. R. Rose, L. Chassin, C. C. Presson, & S. J. Sherman (Eds.), *Multivariate applications in substance use research: New methods for new questions* (pp. 1–42). Mahwah, NJ: Erlbaum.

Curran, P. J., West, S. G., & Finch, J. F. (1996). The robustness of test statistics to nonnormality and specification error in confirmatory factor analysis. *Psychological Methods, 1,* 16–29.

Duncan, T. E., Duncan, S. C., Strycker, L. A., Li, F., & Alpert, A. (1999). *An introduction to latent variable growth curve modeling: Concepts, issues, and applications.* Mahwah, NJ: Erlbaum.

Efron, B. (2000). The bootstrap and modern statistics. *Journal of the American Statistical Association, 95,* 1293–1296.

Enders, C. K. (2001). A primer on maximum likelihood algorithms available for use with missing data. *Structural Equation Modeling, 8,* 128–141.

Finch, J. F., West, S. G., & MacKinnon, D. P. (1997). Effects of sample size and nonnormality on the estimation of mediated effects in latent variable models. *Structural Equation Modeling, 4,* 87–107.

Fouladi, R. T. (1999, April). *Model fit in covariance structure analysis under small sample conditions: Modified maximum likelihood and asymptotically distribution free generalized least squares procedures.* Paper presented at American Educational Research Association meetings, Montreal, Canada.

Fouladi, R. T. (2000). Performance of modified test statistics in covariance and correlation structure analysis under conditions of multivariate nonnormality. *Structural Equation Modeling, 7,* 356–410.

Gold, M. S., & Bentler, P. M. (2000). Treatments of missing data: A Monte Carlo comparison of resemblance-based hot-deck imputation, iterative stochastic regression imputation, and expectation-maximization. *Structural Equation Modeling, 7,* 319–355.

Goldstein, H. (1986). Multilevel mixed linear model analysis using iterative generalized least squares. *Biometrika, 73,* 43–56.

Goldstein, H. (1995). *Multilevel statistical models* (2nd ed.). London: Edward Arnold.

Goldstein, H., & McDonald, R. P. (1988). A general model for the analysis of multilevel data. *Psychometrika, 53,* 435–467.

Graham, J. W., & Hofer, S. M. (2000). Multiple imputation in multivariate research. In T. D. Little, K. U. Schnabel, & J. Baumert (Eds.), *Modeling longitudinal and multilevel data* (pp. 201–218). Mahwah, NJ: Erlbaum.

Hampel, F. R., Ronchetti, E. M., Rousseeuw, P. J., & Stahel, W. A. (1986). *Robust statistics: The approach based on influence functions.* New York: Wiley.

Heck, R. H., & Thomas, S. L. (2000). *An introduction to multilevel modeling techniques.* Mahwah, NJ: Erlbaum.

Hoaglin, D. C., Mosteller, F., & Tukey, J. W. (1983). *Understanding robust and exploratory data analysis.* New York: Wiley.

Hoogland, J. J. (1999). *The robustness of estimation methods for covariance structure analysis.* Unpublished doctoral dissertation, Rijksuniversiteit Groningen, Groningen, The Netherlands.

Hu, L.-T., & Bentler, P. M. (1998). Fit indices in covariance structure equation modeling: Sensitivity to underparameterized model misspecification. *Psychological Methods, 3,* 424–453.

Hu, L.-T., & Bentler, P. M. (1999). Cutoff criteria for fit indexes in covariance structure analysis: Conventional criteria versus new alternatives. *Structural Equation Modeling, 6,* 1–55.

Hu, L.-T., Bentler, P. M., & Kano Y. (1992). Can test statistics in covariance structure analysis be trusted? *Psychological Bulletin, 112,* 351–362.

Huber, P. J. (1977). Robust covariances. In S. S. Gupta & D. S. Moore (Eds.), *Statistical decision theory and related topics* (Vol. 2, pp. 165–191). New York: Academic Press.

Jamshidian, M., & Bentler, P. M. (1999). ML estimation of mean and covariance structures with missing data using complete data routines. *Journal of Educational and Behavioral Statistics, 24,* 21–41.

Jamshidian, M., & Bentler, P. M. (2000). Improved standard errors of standardized parameters in covariance structure models: Implications for construct explication. In R. D. Goffin & E. Helmes (Eds.), *Problems and solutions in human assessment* (pp. 73–94). Dordrecht, The Netherlands: Kluwer Academic.

Jöreskog, K. G. (1971). Simultaneous factor analysis in several populations. *Psychometrika, 57,* 409–442.

Kano, Y., Berkane, M., & Bentler, P. M. (1990). Covariance structure analysis with heterogeneous kurtosis parameters. *Biometrika, 77,* 575–585.

Kenny, D. A., & Judd, C. M. (1984). Estimating the nonlinear and interactive effects of latent variables. *Psychological Bulletin, 96,* 201–210.

Khoo, S.-T., & Muthén, B. (2000). Longitudinal data on families: Growth modeling alternatives. In J. S. Rose, L. Chassin, C. C. Preston, & S. J. Sherman (Eds.), *Multivariate applications in substance use research: New methods for new questions* (pp. 43–78). Mahwah, NJ: Erlbaum.

Kreft, I., & deLeeuw, J. (1998). *Introducing multilevel modeling.* London: Sage.

Lange, K. L., Little, R. J. A., & Taylor, J. M. G. (1989). Robust statistical modeling using the t distribution. *Journal of the American Statistical Association, 84,* 881–896.

Lee, S.-Y. (1990). Multilevel analysis of structural equation models. *Biometrika, 77,* 763–772.

Lee, S.-Y., & Poon, W.-Y. (1994). A distribution free approach for analysis of two-level structural equation model. *Computational Statistics & Data Analysis, 17,* 265–275.

Lee, S.-Y., & Zhu, H.-T. (2000). Statistical analysis of nonlinear structural equation models with continuous and polytomous data. *British Journal of Mathematical and Statistical Psychology, 53,* 209–232.

Little, R. J. A. (1988). A test of missing completely at random for multivariate data with missing values. *Journal of the American Statistical Association, 83,* 1198–1202.

Little, R. J. A., & Rubin, D. B. (1987). *Statistical analysis with missing data.* New York: Wiley.

Little, T. D., Schnabel, K. U., & Baumert, J., (Eds.). (1999). *Modeling longitudinal and multilevel data: Practical issues, applied approaches, and specific examples.* Mahwah, NJ: Erlbaum.

Longford, N. T. (1987). A fast scoring algorithm for maximum likelihood estimation in unbalanced mixed models with nested random effects. *Biometrika, 74,* 817–827.

Longford, N. T. (1993a). Regression analysis of multilevel data with measurement error. *British Journal of Mathematical and Statistical Psychology, 46,* 301–311.

Longford, N. T. (1993b). *Random coefficient models.* Oxford, UK: Clarendon.

MacCallum, R. C. (1986). Specification searches in covariance structure modeling. *Psychological Bulletin, 100,* 107–120.

MacCallum, R. C., & Austin, J. T. (2000). Applications of structural equation modeling in psychological research. *Annual Review of Psychology, 51,* 201–226.

MacCallum, R. C., Browne, M. W., & Sugawara, H. M. (1996). Power analysis and determination of sample size for covariance structure modelling. *Psychological Methods, 1,* 130–149.

MacCallum, R. C., Widaman, K. F., Zhang, S., & Hong, S. (1999). Sample size in factor analysis. *Psychological Methods, 4,* 84–99.

MacKinnon, D. P., Krull, J. L., & Lockwood, C. M. (2000). Equivalence of mediation, confounding and suppression effect. *Prevention Science, 1,* 173–181.

Marcoulides, G. A., & Schumacker, R. E. (Eds.). (2001). *Advanced structural equation modeling: New developments and techniques.* Mahwah, NJ: Erlbaum.

Maronna, R. A. (1976). Robust M-estimators of multivariate location and scatter. *Annals of Statistics, 4,* 51–67.

McArdle, J. J. (1986). Latent variable growth within behavior genetic models. *Behavior Genetics, 16,* 163–200.

McArdle, J. J., & Epstein, D. (1987). Latent growth curves within developmental structural equation models. *Child Development, 58,* 110–133.

McDonald, R. P. (1967). *Nonlinear factor analysis* (Psychometric Monograph No. 15). The University of New England, Armidale, New South Wales, Australia.

McDonald, R. P., & Goldstein, H. (1989). Balanced versus unbalanced designs for linear structural relations in two-level data. *British Journal of Mathematical and Statistical Psychology, 42,* 215–232.

Mehta, P. D., & West, S. G. (2000). Putting the individual back into individual growth curves. *Psychological Methods, 5,* 23–43.

Mooijaart, A., & Bentler, P. M. (1986). Random polynomial factor analysis. In E. Diday (Eds.), *Data analysis and informatics* (Vol. 4, pp. 241–250). Amsterdam: Elsevier Science.

Muthén, B. O. (1994). Multilevel covariance structure analysis. *Sociological Methods & Research, 22,* 376–398.

Muthén, B. O. (1997). Latent variable modeling of longitudinal and multilevel data. In A. Raftery (Ed.), *Sociological methodology* (pp. 453–480). Boston: Blackwell.

Muthén, B. O., Kaplan, D., & Hollis, M. (1987). On structural equation modeling with data that are not missing completely at random. *Psychometrika, 52,* 431–462.

Muthén, B. O., & Satorra, A. (1995). Complex sample data in structural equation modeling. In P. V. Marsden (Ed.), *Sociological methodology* (pp. 267–316). Cambridge, MA: Blackwell.

Neale, M. C. (2000). Individual fit, heterogeneity, and missing data in multigroup structural equation modeling. In T. D. Little, K. U. Schnabel, & J. Baumert (Eds.), *Modeling longitudinal and multilevel data* (pp. 249–267). Mahwah, NJ: Erlbaum.

Nevitt, J. (2000). *Evaluating small sample approaches for model test statistics in structural equation modeling.* Unpublished doctoral dissertation, University of Maryland, College Park.

Nevitt, J., & Hancock, G. R. (in press). Performance of bootstrapping approaches to model test statistics and parameter standard error estimation in structural equation modeling. *Structural Equation Modeling.*

Rose, J. S., Chassin, L., Presson, C. C., & Sherman, S. J. (2000). *Multivariate applications in substance use research: New methods for new questions.* Mahwah, NJ: Erlbaum.

Rovine, M. J., & Molenaar, P. C. M. (2000). A structural modeling approach to a multilevel random coefficients model. *Multivariate Behavioral Research, 35,* 51–88.

Satorra, A. (1992). Asymptotic robust inferences in the analysis of mean and covariance structures. *Sociological Methodology, 22,* 249–278.

Satorra, A. (2000). Scaled and adjusted restricted tests in multi-sample analysis of moment structures. In D. D. H. Heijmans, D. S. G. Pollock, & A. Satorra (Eds.), *Innovations in multivariate statistical analysis: A Festschrift for Heinz Neudecker* (pp. 233–247). Dordrecht, The Netherlands: Kluwer Academic.

Satorra, A., & Bentler, P. M. (1988). Scaling corrections for chi-square statistics in covariance structure analysis. *Proceedings of the American Statistical Association, 36,* 308–313.

Satorra, A., & Bentler, P. M. (1994). Corrections to test statistics and standard errors in covariance structure analysis. In A. von Eye & C. C. Clogg (Eds.), *Latent variables analysis: Applications for developmental research* (pp. 399–419). Thousand Oaks, CA: Sage.

Satorra, A., & Bentler, P. M. (in press). A scaled difference chi-square test statistic for moment structure analysis. *Psychometrika.*

Schafer, J. L. (1997). *Analysis of incomplete multivariate data.* London: Chapman & Hall.

Scheines, R., Hoijtink, H., & Boomsma, A. (1999). Bayesian estimation and testing of structural equation models. *Psychometrika, 64,* 37–52.

Schumacker, R. E., & Marcoulides, G. A. (Eds.). (1998). *Interaction and nonlinear effects in structural equation modeling.* Mahwah, NJ: Erlbaum.

Shapiro, A., & Browne, M. W. (1987). Analysis of covariance structures under elliptical distributions. *Journal of the American Statistical Association, 82,* 1092–1097.

Snijders, T. A. B., & Bosker, R. J. (1999). *Multilevel Analysis: An introduction to basic and advanced multilevel modeling.* London: Sage.

Sobel, M. E. (1987). Direct and indirect effects in linear structural equation models. *Sociological Methods & Research, 16,* 155–176.

Sörbom, D. (1974). A general method for studying differences in factor means and factor structures between groups. *British Journal of Mathematical and Statistical Psychology, 27,* 229–239.

Steiger, J. H. (2001). Driving fast in reverse: The relationship between software development, theory, and education in structural equation modeling (review of 3 texts). *Journal of the American Statistical Association, 96,* 331–338.

Steiger, J. H., & Lind, J. (1980, May). *Statistically based tests for the number of common factors.* Paper presented at the meeting of the Psychometric Society, Iowa City, IA.

Strenio, J. L. F., Weisberg, H. I., & Bryk, A. S. (1983). Empirical Bayes estimation of individual growth curve parameters and their relationship to covariates. *Biometrics, 39,* 71–86.

Tang, M.-L., & Bentler, P. M. (1998). Theory and method for constrained estimation in structural equation models with incomplete data. *Computational Statistics & Data Analysis, 27,* 257–270.

Ullman, J. B. (2001). Structural equation modeling. In B. G. Tabachnick & L. S. Fidell (Eds.), *Using multivariate statistics* (4th ed., pp. 653–771). Boston: Allyn & Bacon.

Ullman, J. B., Stein, J. A., & Dukes R. L. (2001). *Student and classroom level effects of D.A.R.E.: A multilevel model.* Manuscript in preparation.

Ullman, J. B., Stein, J. A., & Dukes, R. L. (2000). Evaluation of D.A.R.E. (Drug Abuse Resistance Education) with latent variables in the context of a Solomon Four Group Design. In J. S. Rose, L. Chassin, C. C. Presson, & S. J. Sherman (Eds.), *Multivariate applications in substance use research: New methods for new questions* (pp. 203–232). Mahwah, NJ: Erlbaum.

Van den Oord, E. J. (2000). Framework for identifying quantitative trait loci in association studies using structural equation modeling. *Genetic Epidemiology, 18,* 341–359.

Wall, M. M., & Amemiya, Y. (2000). Estimation for polynomial structural equations. *Journal of the American Statistical Association, 95,* 929–940.

Wilcox, R. R. (1995). ANOVA: A paradigm for low power and misleading measures of effect size? *Review of Educational Research, 65,* 51–77.

Wilcox, R. R. (1998). How many discoveries have been lost by ignoring modern statistical methods? *American Psychologist, 53,* 300–314.

Wood, P. K. (2000). Estimation and equivalent models for quadratic and interactive latent variable models. In J. S. Rose, L. Chassin, C. C. Presson, & S. J. Sherman (Eds.), *Multivariate applications in substance abuse research: New methods for new questions* (pp. 161–202). Mahwah, NJ: Erlbaum.

Wothke, W. (2000). Longitudinal and multigroup modeling with missing data. In T. D. Little, K. U. Schnabel, & J. Baumert (Eds.), *Modeling longitudinal and multilevel data* (pp. 219–240). Mahwah, NJ: Erlbaum.

Yang-Wallentin, F. (2001). Comparisons of the ML and TSLS estimators for the Kenny-Judd model. In R. Cudeck, S. du Toit, & D. Sörbom (Eds.), *Structural equation modeling: Present and future* (pp. 425–442). Lincolnwood, IL: Scientific Software International.

Yuan, K.-H., & Bentler, P. M. (1998a). Normal theory based test statistics in structural equation modeling. *British Journal of Mathematical and Statistical Psychology, 51,* 289–309.

Yuan, K.-H., & Bentler, P. M. (1998b). Robust mean and covariance structure analysis. *British Journal of Mathematical and Statistical Psychology, 51,* 63–88.

Yuan, K.-H., & Bentler, P. M. (1998c). Structural equation modeling with robust covariances. In A. Raftery (Ed.), *Sociological methodology* (pp. 363–396). Malden, MA: Blackwell.

Yuan, K.-H., & Bentler, P. M. (1999a). F tests for mean and covariance structure analysis. *Journal of Educational and Behavioral Statistics, 24,* 225–243.

Yuan, K.-H., & Bentler, P. M. (1999b). On asymptotic distributions of normal theory MLE in covariance structure analysis under some nonnormal distributions. *Statistics & Probability Letters, 42,* 107–113.

Yuan, K.-H. & Bentler, P. M. (2000a). Robust mean and covariance structure analysis through iteratively reweighted least squares. *Psychometrika, 65,* 43–58.

Yuan, K.-H., & Bentler, P. M. (2000b). Three likelihood-based methods for mean and covariance structure analysis with nonnormal missing data. *Sociological methodology* (pp. 165–200). Washington, DC: American Sociological Association.

Yuan, K.-H., & Bentler, P. M. (in press). Effect of outliers on estimators and tests in covariance structure analysis. *British Journal of Mathematical and Statistical Psychology.*

Yuan, K.-H., Chan, W., & Bentler, P. M. (2000). Robust transformation with applications to structural equation modeling. *British Journal of Mathematical and Statistical Psychology, 53,* 31–50.

Yuan, K.-H., & Jennrich, R. I. (2000). Estimating equations with nuisance parameters: Theory and applications. *Annals of the Institute of Statistical Mathematics, 52,* 343–350.

Yung, Y.-F., & Bentler, P. M. (1996). Bootstrapping techniques in analysis of mean and covariance structures. In G. A. Marcoulides & R. E. Schumacker (Eds.), *Advanced structural equation modeling techniques* (pp. 195–226). Hillsdale, NJ: Erlbaum.

Zhu, H.-T., & Lee, S.-Y. (1999). Statistical analysis of nonlinear factor analysis models. *British Journal of Mathematical and Statistical Psychology, 52,* 225–242.

CHAPTER 25

Ordinal Analysis of Behavioral Data

JEFFREY D. LONG, DU FENG, AND NORMAN CLIFF

MOTIVES FOR ORDINAL ANALYSIS

Statistical methods that make use of ordinal information have many desirable properties that argue for their general use. First, much data in the social sciences has only ordinal justification. Ordinal methods are based on operations consistent with ordinal data. Second, many research questions in the social sciences are ordinal in nature. Ordinal methods provide answers to ordinal questions. Third, ordinal methods are invariant under monotonic transformations. Results of ordinal methods obtained on raw data are exactly the same under any order-preserving transformation. Fourth, ordinal methods can be more robust than traditional methods when the latter's assumptions are violated. Ordinal methods require fewer distributional assumptions, are not as vulnerable to extreme values, and are valid for nonlinear but monotonic relationships. After discussing these merits in detail, we present two classes of methods useful in applied analyses, ordinal measures of correlation and ordinal measures for group comparisons.

Many Variables Are Ordinal

Interval-level scales are very desirable in scientific investigation because they allow the relations among empirical variables to be represented with highly specific mathematical expressions. However, few variables in the social sciences can be said to have interval-level scales. The reason is that most scales do not meet the stringent conditions necessary to attain interval status.

According to *axiomatic measurement theory* (Krantz, Luce, Suppes, & Tversky, 1971), the defining characteristic of an interval scale is the representation of the empirical properties of *order* and *additivity*. The property of order means that amounts of an empirical construct can be empirically realized and compared according to the ordinal rules *less than, greater than,* and *equal to*. For example, consider three blobs of clay, α, β, and γ, as empirical realizations of the construct *weight* (note that for constant downward acceleration, i.e., gravity, weight is proportional to mass). We might take certain pairs of blobs of clay, (α, β), (β, γ), weigh them against each other on a beam balance (also known as a pan balance), and determine their ordinal relation by observing which blob pan hangs lower. Suppose that the results of this operation show that $\alpha \succ \beta$ (α is greater than β) and $\beta \succ \gamma$. By transitivity we know that $\alpha \succ \gamma$ (although we can check it) and we have the empirical ordering of the blobs by weight, $\alpha \succ \beta \succ \gamma$.

Additivity is the empirical representation of mathematical addition. This means that an arbitrary unit of a construct is selected and all other amounts of the construct are measured in relation to the cumulative addition of the unit. For example, let us arbitrarily define γ as the unit. Suppose that two replicas of γ were in one pan of a beam balance and β was in the other pan. If the beam was perfectly horizontal (i.e., the blob pans were perfectly level with each other), we could say that $\beta = \gamma + \gamma = 2\gamma$. If γ was arbitrarily small, then the weights of all other blobs could be expressed by successively adding together replicas of γ.

It is an understatement to say that in most areas of the social sciences, the demonstration of empirical additivity is very difficult, perhaps owing to the abstract nature of many of the constructs. A significant step forward in measurement theory was the demonstration by Luce and Tukey (1964) that interval scales could be constructed based on an axiomatic definition of additivity (additivity of differences) without the requirement of empirical additivity. This is known as *simultaneous conjoint measurement*. The essential idea of simultaneous conjoint measurement is that given certain relational conditions known as conjoint axioms, we can take three interrelated variables whose numbers represent at least distinct categories and simultaneously derive interval scales for all the variables through monotonic transformation, provided certain conditions are met. To illustrate, suppose we have three variables, A, B, and Y that we arrange in a factorial design, with A and B as the factors (with many levels) and Y as the dependent variable. Given that the conjoint axioms are satisfied, it is possible to find a monotonic transformation of Y that will induce a *no interaction* model (i.e., a model in which the effects of A and B are additive). A and B are not themselves additive in the sense of weights, but *changes* on A and *changes* on B are. Under this additivity condition, $Y = A + B + k$, where k is an arbitrary constant. The monotonic transformation serves as a basis for an interval scaling of all the variables.

A difficulty with simultaneous conjoint measurement is that it is not stochastic. The conjoint axioms are deterministic and do not allow for errors when investigating the conditions in sample data (Nygren, 1986). An alternative to literal condition checking is to *assume* an additive model, then use the monotonic transformation that will best eliminate any interaction, and then evaluate the goodness of fit of the transformed data to the model. One method that does this is *Rasch scaling* (Rasch, 1980), but there are others (see Cliff, 1973, 1992 for reviews).

Rasch scaling is widely used in mental testing (Wright, 1999). It begins with an additive conjoint model and uses a specific monotonic transformation, a single-parameter logistic transformation, as a basis for interval scaling (strictly speaking, this is only possible for a dichotomous response; see Fischer, 1995). Operating under some assumptions (e.g., unidimensionality), an additive model is fit to item responses (the data) and evaluated for goodness-of-fit using probability-based statistics. Sufficient fit is evidence that the probability of a response can be expressed as an additive function of a person parameter (usually an index of ability) and an item parameter (usually an index of item difficulty; Wright, 1999). The logistic transformation serves as a basis for an interval scale of the latent person variable on which we can locate individuals (the items are simultaneously scaled as well). Assuming the Rasch model holds (which may be a rare occurrence in applied research; see Embretson & Hershberger, 1999), individuals can be assigned interval-scale scores on the latent variable that are monotonically related to raw scores, yet have more desirable properties (e.g., extreme score unbiasedness, sample independence, and linearity). There are problems with Rasch scaling. The most common one is that items vary in discrimination, so that more than one item parameter is necessary. This usually leads to a violation of one or more of the axioms of conjoint measurement and compromises the interval properties of the scale. Another problem is the controversy over evaluating the goodness-of-fit of the model to sample data (see Hambleton, 1989). Nevertheless, Rasch scaling can be a useful tool for determining whether batches of empirical data are at least consistent with a type of additive model.

The foregoing discussion should make it clear that careful thought and planning are required for the creation of an interval scale. Data collected under an additive model (either an empirical additive model, an additive conjoint model, or an additive scaling model) have the best chance of reflecting the characteristics of empirical order and additivity. Such data are amenable to highly parametric model-based methods because these methods provide explicit expressions about unit-based functional relationships between variables. In the great majority of instances, however, the data contradict interval scaling. Where there is no direct contradiction, the data are usually too sparse: They have too few levels to inspire confidence in their interval properties.

Most data in the social sciences are not collected under an additive model, nor are they scaled in accordance with such a model (Cliff, 1992, offers various reasons for this neglect). Therefore, it is unlikely that most scales represent additivity in either an empirical, conjoint, or scaled sense. On the other hand, it seems reasonable that the property of order is represented in many cases. Order is much more easily justified than additivity because one need only argue that two individuals with different scores on a measure can be ordered in terms of the empirical amount of the construct in question, provided the scores are reasonably consistent. This ordering seems sensible in many situations, even when we cannot determine meaningful distance between the ordered individuals. Therefore, it seems realistic to assume that much of the data in the social sciences are ordinal.

The advantage of ordinal methods is that they deal explicitly with the order of the data. Most of the methods to be presented later are based on ordinal comparisons between scores. Pairs of scores on a variable are compared in terms of the order relations *less than, greater than,* and *equal to.* This is the most appropriate treatment when order is the only justified scaling property of the data.

Many Research Questions Are Ordinal

Many of the types of research questions commonly posed tacitly acknowledge that many data are ordinal. When forming research questions, few researchers take seriously the specific interpretations provided for by highly parametric methods. For example, rather than expressing questions about the correlation between two variables in unit-based functional terms, most researchers simply want to know "if high scores on one variable tend to go with high (or low) scores on the other variable" (Long & Cliff, 1997). The same can be said in the case of group comparisons. Instead of expressing questions about group difference in terms of the unit difference between two parameters, researchers often simply want to know "if people in one group tend to score higher on a variable than people in the other group" (Cliff, 1996a, 1996b). These common types of research questions are ordinal in nature. An advantage of ordinal methods is that they directly provide answers to ordinal questions. In addition, there is some protection from overinterpreting results. Ordinal methods do not tempt us to the unit-based interpretations that are not warranted when highly parametric methods are applied to ordinal data.

Invariance Under Monotonic Transformation

Affine Transformation

In his seminal work, Stevens (1951) defined various scales of measurement in terms of what he called admissible transformations that maintain the important information of a scale. He proposed four main categories of scale level based on admissible transformations: *nominal, ordinal, interval,* and *ratio.* Because a ratio scale is an interval scale with an empirically justified origin, and a nominal scale is not quantitative (at least on the surface), we focus on the important distinction between ordinal and interval scales. We have already shown that the information to be maintained for an interval scale is empirical order and additivity, which for a scale means maintaining the rank order of scale values and the relative distances between scale values. The transformation that maintains this scale information is the affine transformation, $Y = bX + a$.

To illustrate the affine transformation, assume we have an interval scale with values x_h, x_i, defined in arbitrary α units, such that $x_i > x_h$. The distance between two scale values is $x_i - x_h$. Suppose we apply the affine transformation $Y = bX + a$ to the values on the original scale. Replacing the x values with the new y values, we have $y_h = bx_h + a$, and $y_i = bx_i + a$. The affine transformation maintains the property of order because a and b are constants that do not affect inequalities. Therefore, given that $(x_i, x_h > 0)$, when $(x_i > x_h)$, it is always the case that $(y_i > y_h)$.

To see that the meaning of distance is maintained by the affine transformation, we compute the difference between the values of the transformed scale, $y_i - y_h = (bx_i + a) - (bx_h + a) = b(x_i - x_h)$. This means that for any given original difference, the transformed distance is equal to the original distance times the arbitrary scaling constant. The nature of two differences is unchanged because the same constant multiplies both. Therefore, the meaning of a fixed distance *anywhere* along the original scale is maintained and simply rescaled by b.

Monotonic Transformation

The order of a scale is preserved with a monotonic transformation. A monotonic transformation has the form $Y = f(X)$, where $f(X)$ is a one-to-one strictly increasing or decreasing function. To illustrate, suppose in the previous example we used the monotonic transformation $Y = (X)^2$ instead of the affine transformation. In this case the transformed values are $y_h = (x_h)^2$, and $y_i = (x_i)^2$. Assuming that x_i and x_h are positive, the property of order is maintained by the monotonic transformation because given that $x_i > x_h$, it must be the case that $(x_i)^2 > (x_h)^2$.

Information about scale distance is not maintained with a monotonic transformation. This is evident by the fact that when we use $Y = (X)^2$ as our transformation, $(y_i - y_h)$ is not equal to $(x_i - x_h)$ times a scaling constant. Rather, $(y_i - y_h) = [(x_i)^2 - (x_h)^2] = (x_i - x_h)(x_i + x_h)$. For any fixed original distance, the transformed distance increases as the values of x_h and x_i increase. Therefore, the meaning of any fixed original distance is not maintained along the transformed scale.

Monotonic Transformation and Data Analysis

A monotonic transformation of a scale maintains the property of order but not that of distance. This fact has important implications when using monotonic transformations with highly parametric methods because such methods make use of the distances of the variables (see the section in this chapter entitled "Pearson's Correlation Coefficient"). When the distances of the variables are changed through monotonic transformations, the results of the parametric methods (including test statistics) will be different. Mild changes in distance produce small changes in the values of the parametric methods, whereas extreme changes can result in very different values. It is important for researchers to be aware of these facts because monotonic transformations are fundamental in two important applications: transforming to meet statistical assumptions, and item response theory (IRT; Rasch scaling is a special case of IRT).

With careful thought and application, monotonic transformations can be very useful in clarifying relationships and interpreting variables (see Emerson & Stoto, 1983). A more arbitrary use of monotonic transformations is to induce sample data to be consistent with parametric assumptions (e.g., normality). The arbitrariness arises from the fact that a transformation is often determined by the sample data without regard for replication or comparison with other analyses (Games, 1984). Consider results of research using reaction time measured in milliseconds (ms). It could be the case that the transformation $f(\text{ms}) = \text{ms}^{(.835)}$ is used to induce normality in one data set, whereas the very different transformation $f(\text{ms}) = \text{ms}^{(-.5)}$ is used to induce normality in another data set. Comparing parametric results based on these two transformations is difficult. The two transformations produce different distances between scale values and lead to different parametric results. In contrast, the ordinal information is the same regardless the monotonic transformation, so that results based on ordinal methods are comparable. Furthermore, ordinal methods make it unnecessary to use monotonic transformations to meet statistical assumptions because results will be the same whether raw or transformed scores are the basis of analysis.

Monotonic relationships and monotonic transformations are also important in the stochastic item response models (IRT) that underlie most of modern test theory. A fundamental premise of IRT is that manifest and latent variables have a nonlinear but monotonic functional relationship (usually ogival).

Highly parametric methods, such as structural equation modeling (SEM), assume linear relations between manifest and latent variables. If IRT is taken seriously, analyzing raw scores with methods such as SEM must lead to a misspecification of the manifest-latent relationships. This contradiction has led some observers to suggest that the results of highly parametric methods can be spoiled when raw scores are analyzed (Embretson, 1996). A dilemma arises when IRT is applied inconsistently with highly parametric methods. Because IRT proposes that manifest (raw) scores be monotonically transformed to estimate latent scores, the results of parametric analyses using latent scores are not comparable to analyses with manifest scores. Ordinal methods have an advantage in this context. Because of the monotonic relation, the ordinal information of the manifest variable is identical to the information of the latent construct. Ordinal results will be identical regardless of whether manifest or latent scores are the basis of the analysis. This means that the misspecification problem with the analysis of raw scores is avoided, and results of ordinal analyses can be compared regardless of whether manifest scores or latent scores are used.

Robustness

Under optimal conditions, parametric statistics generally have larger absolute values than their ordinal counterparts, and parametric inferential methods perform better than ordinal inferential methods, usually in terms of higher power (but see a contrary example in the following discussion). Higher power under optimal conditions is probably the justification for many applied researchers' using parametric methods rather than ordinal methods (Zimmerman & Zumbo, 1993). However, the differences in power can be very small, and when conditions are not optimal, ordinal methods can have many superior properties, including higher power. Because there are reasons to believe that optimal conditions rarely hold in applied research (Micceri, 1989; Sawilowsky & Blair, 1992; Wilcox, 1990), ordinal methods may be a better choice than are parametric methods for general use.

The ordinal methods presented in this chapter tend to be less influenced than are parametric methods by changes in the characteristics of the data such as nonnormality, outliers, and monotonic nonlinearity. In this sense, the ordinal methods are said to be more *robust* than their parametric counterparts. Distributional variations in the data can considerably distort values of parametric statistics, test values, and confidence intervals. For example, monotonic transformation away from bivariate normality can drastically reduce the value of Pearson's r and its t test (Long & Cliff, 2001). In contrast, the values of ordinal statistics and their inferential methods are invariant under monotonic transformations, so that transforming away from normality does not change their values. Thus, ordinal methods are applicable to a wider class of distributions than are parametric methods.

Parametric methods are vulnerable to extreme changes in single scores. A single extreme score can drastically affect the value of a parametric method due to the large distance that is introduced in the computation (see the comments regarding Pearson's *r* later in this chapter). Ordinal methods are much more resistant to extreme values because distances are not considered in computation (only order). A very large outlier, for example, is simply treated as the largest rank value, and its distance to the next-to-lowest score is irrelevant. It does not matter if the largest value is close to the next-to-smallest value or very far above it.

Finally, parametric methods can be adversely affected by nonlinear but monotonic relationships (both in the population and the sample). Nonlinear but monotonic relationships tend to inflate parametric standard errors and lead to lower power (Birkes & Dodge, 1993, chap. 1). Ordinal methods can perform much better with such relationships, due to the fact that the ordinal information is identical for monotonic and linear functions. Suppose we take a linear bivariate relationship and induce a nonlinear but monotonic relationship via monotonic transformation. The parametric standard error for the transformed relationship would tend to be larger than the original and the power of a parametric method would tend to be lower. On the other hand, the standard error and power of an ordinal method would not change. The functional relationship is continuously increasing or decreasing (barring ties) in both situations, and thus the ordinal information is the same.

Ordinal Methods to Be Presented

The methods of ordinal analysis to be presented fall into two categories: measures of correlation and measures for group comparison. We first consider the bivariate situation, and then show how the methods can be extended for use in more complex analyses. We believe that the ordinal statistics presented in the following discussion have clear substantive interpretations, in contrast to traditional nonparametric methods. These statistics should be considered as estimates of meaningful population counterparts and not simply as devices for testing null hypotheses. Another distinction of our presentation from that of traditional nonparametric methods is an emphasis on inferential methods that apply in the non-null case. Many traditional nonparametric inferential methods rely on distributional assumptions that only hold in the null case. In contrast, we present inferential methods based on estimating

properties of sampling distributions from sample data that have more general applications. In this parametric emphasis, the chapter follows earlier publications such as Cliff (1993, 1996a, 1996b), Long (1999), and Long and Cliff (1997).

ORDINAL CORRELATION METHODS

General Form of Correlation

Most of the ordinal correlation methods presented in this section are based on Kendall's tau. Although it is not commonly known, Kendall's tau has a direct connection to the more widely known Pearson and Spearman correlations. In fact, all three are special cases of a general form of correlation based on the comparison of pairs of scores. It is instructive to present the three correlations in a general form involving *pairs* of scores in order to show that their computational formulas are directly related to assumptions about scale level.

To introduce the general form of correlation based on paired comparisons, let us assume we have a set of *n* scores on X and Y. For any pair of scores, say the *i*th and the *h*th, we can assign a score on X, denoted as a_{ih}, representing the comparison between the *i*th and *h*th observations. Likewise, we can also assign a score on Y, denoted as b_{ih}, representing the comparison on Y. Then general form of a correlation coefficient derived from score comparisons is

$$\Gamma = \frac{\sum_{i>h}\sum a_{ih}b_{ih}}{\sqrt{\sum_{i>h}\sum a_{ih}^2 \sum_{i>h}\sum b_{ih}^2}}, \qquad (25.1)$$

where both *i* and *h* run from 1 to *n*, and there are $(1/2)\, n\,(n-1)$ comparisons of scores on each variable for $i > h$. The Pearson, Kendall, and Spearman correlations are defined by the choice of the a_{ih} and b_{ih} comparisons in Equation 25.1. When the *i*th raw score is equal in value to the *h*th raw score on a variable, then the pair is tied. The treatment of tied values can be important, so comments regarding ties are selectively included.

Pearson's Correlation Coefficient

If interval variables can be assumed, then Pearson's ρ is considered an appropriate measure of bivariate correlation. The formulas for ρ and its sample counterpart, *r*, are very familiar. However, our present purposes are served better if we introduce an unnecessary complexity. Let a_{ih} and b_{ih} be differences between raw scores. We define

$$a_{ih} = x_i - x_h, \qquad (25.2)$$

where x_i and x_h are the ith and hth raw scores on X. Similarly,

$$b_{ih} = y_i - y_h, \qquad (25.3)$$

where y_i and y_h are the ith and hth raw scores on Y.

Making substitutions into Equation 25.1, we can compute the sample Pearson correlation, r,

$$r = \frac{\sum\sum_{i>h}(x_i - x_h)(y_i - y_h)}{\sqrt{\sum\sum_{i>h}(x_i - x_h)^2 \sum\sum_{i>h}(y_i - y_h)^2}}. \qquad (25.4)$$

With a bit of algebraic manipulation, it can be shown that Equation 25.4 is equivalent to the traditional formula of Pearson's r. Equation 25.4 shows that r is based on the literal distances between values on X and Y. As was argued previously, these distances are only meaningful with interval data. Therefore, r has an ambiguous interpretation when computed on ordinal data. In addition, changing the distances on one or both of the variables (e.g., by monotonic transformation) also changes the value of r.

Spearman's Rho

A correlation coefficient that uses ordinal information is Spearman's ρ_s, which is based on the differences between pairs of ranks. We define

$$a_{ih} = q_{ix} - q_{hx}, \qquad (25.5)$$

where q_{ix} and q_{hx} are the ranks of the ith and hth scores on X. Similarly,

$$b_{ih} = q_{iy} - q_{hy}, \qquad (25.6)$$

where q_{ix} and q_{hx} are the ranks of the ith and hth scores on Y. Substituting these values into Equation 25.1 yields the sample Spearman correlation, r_s,

$$r_s = \frac{\sum\sum_{i>h}(q_{ix} - q_{hx})(q_{iy} - q_{hy})}{\sqrt{\sum\sum_{i>h}(q_{ix} - q_{hx})^2 \sum\sum_{i>h}(q_{iy} - q_{hy})^2}}. \qquad (25.7)$$

Perhaps an advantage of Spearman's r_s is that it is a bridge, so to speak, between Pearson's r and the tau correlation because it incorporates properties of both. Like Pearson's r, Spearman's r_s uses distances between numbers, and like Kendall tau, the computation of Spearman's r_s is based on the order of the variables.

The Spearman correlation can be shown to be equivalent to a Pearson correlation applied to ranks. Assuming no ties,

several equivalent forms of Spearman's correlation can be derived based on simplifying identities (see Cliff, 1996b, pp. 51–54 for details). Algebraic manipulation of Equation 25.7 yields another form of Spearman's correlation,

$$r_s = \frac{12\left[\sum_i (q_{ix} - \mu_{qx})(q_{iy} - \mu_{qy})\right]}{n^3 - n}, \qquad (25.8)$$

where μ_{qj} is the mean of the ranks of the jth variable. With further algebra, Equation 25.8 can be expressed in its traditional form,

$$r_s = 1 - \frac{6\sum_i (q_{ix} - q_{iy})^2}{n^3 - n}. \qquad (25.9)$$

It is possible to adjust Equations 25.8 and 25.9 for tied pairs. However, when the number of ties is small, the adjusted equations are closely approximated by the unadjusted equations (Kendall & Gibbons, 1990). Most often in applied research, ties are ignored when computing Spearman's correlation. This means that Equation 25.7 is used with tied rank values computed by taking the average of the corresponding ranks for identical raw scores.

Spearman's rho has a theoretical relationship to ρ. In bivariate normal populations,

$$\rho_s = \frac{6}{2\pi} \sin^{-1} \rho, \qquad (25.10)$$

where ρ_s is the population form of Equation 25.9 and ρ is the population form of Equation 25.4. Equation 25.10 indicates that ρ_s is very close in value to ρ (approximately .01 smaller) over the medium values that are common in applied research.

Correlations Based on Kendall's Tau

When one has only ordinal information, a comparison of pairs of scores can be performed that is consistent with the empirical operations of *greater than, less than,* and *equal to*. This is the basis for a class of correlations based on Kendall's tau, τ_{xy}. For Kendall's tau, the a_{ih} and b_{ih} of Equation 25.1 are the signed difference between raw scores, known as the *dominance* of X and Y. We define

$$a_{ih} = d_{ihx} = \text{sign}(x_i - x_h), \qquad (25.11)$$

where $d_{ihx} = +1$ when $x_i > x_h$, $d_{ihx} = -1$ when $x_i < x_h$, and $d_{ihx} = 0$ when $x_i = x_h$. Similarly,

$$b_{ih} = d_{ihy} = \text{sign}(y_i - y_h), \qquad (25.12)$$

where $d_{ihy} = +1$ when $y_i > y_h$, $d_{ihy} = -1$ when $y_i < y_h$, and $d_{ihy} = 0$ when $y_i = y_h$. Substituting the dominance into

Equation 25.1, we can compute the sample Kendall's tau, t_{xy}, as

$$t_{xy} = \frac{\sum_{i>h}\sum d_{ihx}d_{ihy}}{\sqrt{\sum_{i>h}\sum d_{ihx}^2 \sum_{i>h}\sum d_{ihy}^2}}. \quad (25.13)$$

The numerator of Equation 25.13 represents the sum of the order agreement between corresponding pairs of scores. If the order of the pair is the same on both variables, then $(d_{ihx})(d_{ihy}) = +1$. If the order is not the same, $(d_{ihx})(d_{ihy}) = -1$. Finally, if one or both pairs are tied, $(d_{ihx})(d_{ihy}) = 0$.

There are a number of forms of Kendall's tau that can be defined by altering the denominator of Equation 25.13. When there are no ties on X or Y, then the sum of squared dominance scores is equal to the number of pairs for the $(i > h)$ comparisons, which is $(1/2) n (n - 1)$. Therefore, tau may be expressed in the form Kendall (1970) calls *tau-a*,

$$t_a = \frac{\sum_{i>h}\sum d_{ihx}d_{ihy}}{\frac{1}{2}n(n-1)}. \quad (25.14)$$

Tau-a can be expressed in an alternate form. Suppose we let P = the number of dominance products that are positive (i.e., the number of corresponding pairs with the same order on both variables) and N = the number of dominance products that are negative (i.e., the number of corresponding pairs with opposite order on the variables). Then using # to indicate *number of*,

$$t_a = \frac{P - N}{\text{total \# pairs}}. \quad (25.15)$$

Equation 25.15 shows that tau-a can be interpreted as the proportion of pairs of scores that are in the same order minus the proportion of scores that are in the opposite order. The corresponding population probability interpretation is

$$\tau_a = \Pr[(x_i > x_h) \text{ and } (y_i > y_h)]$$
$$- \Pr[(x_i > x_h) \text{ and } (y_i < y_h)]. \quad (25.16)$$

Note that if X and Y are independent (and uncorrelated), in the long run the left-hand and right-hand probabilities will be equal and τ_a will be zero. If X and Y are at least monotonically related, then the probabilities will not be equal and τ_a will not be zero. For bivariate normal populations, tau has a theoretical relation with Pearson's correlation coefficient,

$$\tau_a = \frac{2}{\pi}\sin^{-1}\rho, \quad (25.17)$$

meaning that τ_a is approximately two-thirds the size of ρ over the range of moderate values most commonly found in applied research.

When there are ties on X or Y or both, tau-a cannot attain the limits of ± 1. In this case, tau-a still has a clear interpretation: It is the ordinal correlation among the pairs relative to the total possible number of pairs. When the number of ties is very large, the largest absolute value of tau-a may be uncomfortably small for some researchers. There are other forms of tau that can be computed that attain the limits of ± 1 in the presence of ties. One option is to simply use Equation 25.13 for t_{xy} when ties are present. Kendall (1970) calls this form *tau-b*, and we can write $t_b = t_{xy}$. Because of the possibility of ties, $|t_b| \geq |t_a|$. Tau-b is attractive because its form is similar to the familiar Pearson's correlation. The problem with tau-b is that its definition is not as simple as that of the Pearson correlation. The geometric interpretation of a Pearson correlation as the angle of separation of X and Y (i.e., $\cos\theta_{xy}$) holds in tau-b between the pairwise dominance scores, not between the values of the variables themselves.

A tie-adjusted measure that has a more attractive theoretical definition is a form of tau known as Yule's Q (Yule, 1900), which is also known as Goodman-Kruskal gamma (Goodman & Kruskal, 1959). The sample version of Yule's Q, t_Q, is

$$t_Q = \frac{\sum_{i>h}\sum d_{ihx}d_{ihy}}{\sum_{i>h}\sum d_{ihx}^2 d_{ihy}^2}. \quad (25.18)$$

The numerator of Equation 25.18 is the same as that of the previous tau correlations, but the denominator is equal to the number of pairs of scores that are untied on *both* variables. Thus, t_Q indicates the average ordinal (dis)agreement ignoring ties (or adjusting for ties) on both variables.

Similar to tau-a, t_Q can also be expressed as

$$t_Q = \frac{P - N}{\text{total \# untied pairs}}, \quad (25.19)$$

which is the proportion of corresponding pairs of scores with the same order minus the proportion in the opposite order for those pairs not tied on either variable. The population probability interpretation is

$$\tau_Q = \Pr[(x_i > x_h) \text{ and } (y_i > y_h) \mid (x_i \neq x_h)$$
$$\text{and } (y_i \neq y_h)]$$
$$- \Pr[(x_i > x_h) \text{ and } (y_i < y_h) \mid (x_i \neq x_h)$$
$$\text{and } (y_i \neq y_h)]. \quad (25.20)$$

This probability is similar to tau-a but has the condition of no ties on both variables.

Unlike t_a and t_b, t_Q is not strictly monotonic. This means that very different arrays of scores, or pairs of arrays based on different ns, may produce the same value for t_Q. Therefore, t_Q does not discriminate between certain subsets of relations for which t_a and t_b do (see Agresti, 1984, chapter 9). In terms of values of the coefficients, this means that $|t_Q| \geq |t_b| \geq |t_a|$.

Yet another type of tau correlation can be computed, one that corrects for ties only on the response variable, Y. This correlation is Somers' d, which is symbolized as τ_{dyx}. The yx in the subscript indexes the fact that the correlation adjusts for ties on Y but not X. The sample t_{dyx} is computed as

$$t_{dyx} = \frac{\sum\sum_{i>h} d_{ihx}d_{ihy}}{\sum\sum_{i>h} d_{ihy}^2}, \quad (25.21)$$

and can be interpreted as the average ordinal (dis)agreement adjusting for ties on Y. Alternatively, t_{dyx} can be expressed as

$$t_{dyx} = \frac{P - N}{\text{total \# untied on } Y}, \quad (25.22)$$

which is the proportion of corresponding pairs of scores that are in the same order minus the proportion of corresponding pairs that are in the opposite order for those pairs not tied on Y. The population probability interpretation is

$$\tau_{dyx} = \Pr[(x_i > x_h) \text{ and } (y_i > y_h) \mid (y_i \neq y_h)]$$
$$- \Pr[(x_i > x_h) \text{ and } (y_i < y_h) \mid (y_i \neq y_h)]. \quad (25.23)$$

If one variable is arbitrarily designated the response, it may not make sense to only adjust for ties on it (it is tempting to use the larger of t_{dyx} and t_{dxy}). A situation in which the response is not arbitrarily assigned is in group-comparison problems. In this case, τ_{dyx} can be used as a basis for a type of ordinal measure of location (discussed later in this chapter).

Examples of Calculations

Table 25.1 shows some hypothetical data sorted on Y and calculations using the paired comparisons formulas for all the correlation coefficients. The results illustrate a typical relationship among the correlation coefficients: $|r| \geq |r_s| \geq |t_Q| \geq |t_{dyx}| \geq |t_b| \geq |t_a|$.

Inference in Ordinal Correlation

The focus of this section is inferential methods based on tau-a, but methods for Spearman's rho are also discussed. We feel tau-a is the most interpretable of the ordinal correlations and has favorable statistical properties such as invariance under monotonic transformation. Although we briefly discuss

TABLE 25.1 Computation of Various Correlation Coefficients Based on Paired Comparisons

i,h	Raw Scores		Ranks	
	X	Y	q_X	q_Y
1	41	5	5	1
2	12	8	1	2
3	26	11	4	3
4	17	14	2	4.5
5	19	14	3	4.5

Computation of Pearson correlation

i,h	$(x_i - x_h)$	$(y_i - y_h)$	$(x_i - x_h)(y_i - y_h)$	$(x_i - x_h)^2$	$(y_i - y_h)^2$
2,1	−29	3	−87	841	9
3,1	−15	6	−90	225	36
4,1	−24	9	−216	576	81
5,1	−22	9	−198	484	81
3,2	14	3	42	196	9
4,2	5	6	30	25	36
5,2	7	6	42	49	36
4,3	−9	3	−27	81	9
5,3	−7	3	−21	49	9
5,4	2	0	0	4	0
	Sums:		−525	2530	306
	$r =$		−0.597	(Equation 25.4)	

Computation of Spearman correlation

i,h	$(q_{ix} - q_{hx})$	$(q_{iy} - q_{hy})$	$(q_{ix} - q_{hx}) \times (q_{iy} - q_{hy})$	$(q_{ix} - q_{hx})^2$	$(q_{iy} - q_{hy})^2$
2,1	−4	1	−4	16	1
3,1	−1	2	−2	1	4
4,1	−3	3.5	−10.5	9	12.25
5,1	−2	3.5	−7	4	12.25
3,2	3	1	3	9	1
4,2	1	2.5	2.5	1	6.25
5,2	2	2.5	5	4	6.25
4,3	−2	1.5	−3	4	2.25
5,3	−1	1.5	−1.5	1	2.25
5,4	1	0	0	1	0
	Sums:		−17.5	50	47.5
	$r_s =$		−0.359	(Equation 25.7)	

Computation of Kendall's correlations

i,h	d_{ihx}	d_{ihy}	t_{ihxy}	$(d_{ihx})^2$	$(d_{ihy})^2$	t_{ihxy}^2
2,1	−1	1	−1	1	1	1
3,1	−1	1	−1	1	1	1
4,1	−1	1	−1	1	1	1
5,1	−1	1	−1	1	1	1
3,2	1	1	1	1	1	1
4,2	1	1	1	1	1	1
5,2	1	1	1	1	1	1
4,3	−1	1	−1	1	1	1
5,3	−1	1	−1	1	1	1
5,4	1	0	0	1	0	0
	Sums:	−3		10	9	9

$t_a =$	−0.300	(Equation 25.14)
$t_b =$	−0.316	(Equation 25.13)
$t_Q =$	−0.333	(Equation 25.18)
$t_{dyx} =$	−0.333	(Equation 25.21)

traditional approaches to hypothesis testing, we stress inferential methods that can be used in the non-null case as well, and expanded to provide the basis for a much broader range of application than is generally realized. Cliff (1996b, pp. 55–88) provides a more extensive discussion than can be provided here.

Traditional Randomization Approach

Kendall's Tau-a

The most common inferential method for tau-a is the z test of independence of X and Y. Note that independence implies $\tau_a = 0$, but is a more general assumption than is the latter. Independence assumes that for a given order of one variable, all possible permutations of the other are equally likely. In this case, Kendall (1970) shows that the asymptotic variance of t_a under random permutations of X and Y is

$$\text{var}(t_a) = \frac{2(2n+5)}{9n(n-1)}. \qquad (25.24)$$

Under H_0: $\tau_a = 0$, the normal distribution variate is the sample tau-a over the square root of Equation 25.24,

$$z = \frac{t_a}{\sqrt{\frac{2(2n+5)}{9n(n-1)}}}. \qquad (25.25)$$

The z test statistic of Equation 25.25 has some favorable properties. It is invariant under monotonic transformation of the variables, it does not require the variables to have a specific distributional shape, and it is insensitive to outlying values. The weakness of the test is the assumption of complete independence of X and Y, which has limited applicability. Later in this chapter we discuss a variance term that forms the basis for methods with wider applicability.

Spearman's Rho

Inferential methods for r_s are hampered by the fact that its sampling properties are difficult to specify. Among other things, there is no straightforward method for determining the standard error of r_s, even assuming independence of X and Y (Kendall, 1970). The inferential methods that do appear to have adequate performance require some strong assumptions. For example, if one is willing to test for independence (as previously with tau), then as n increases, r_s is approximately normally distributed with variance $1/(n-1)$. Cliff (1996b) provides a table of critical values of r_s for n up to 37, reproduced from Ramsey (1989). Using the variance term based on Pearson's r, a more general test of

H_0: $\rho_s = 0$ is

$$z = \frac{r_s'}{\sqrt{\frac{1}{n-3}}} \qquad (25.26)$$

where r_s' is Fisher's z transformation of r_s,

$$r_s' = \left(\frac{1}{2}\right) \ln \left| \frac{1+r_s}{1-r_s} \right|. \qquad (25.27)$$

Caruso and Cliff (1997) studied a number of inferential methods based on r_s and found the Equation 25.26 z test performed the best in terms of actual Type I error rate and power. Although Equation 25.26 assumes bivariate normality, it does have at least one advantage over its counterpart based on Pearson's r (which requires the same assumption). Equation 25.26 will yield the same result for any data that is or can be monotonically transformed to bivariate normality because r_s is invariant under such a transformation. In this regard, Equation 25.26 is more general than is the corresponding test based on Pearson's r.

Recently, Bonett and Wright (2000) presented interval estimates based on r_s (and t_a) under rather general assumptions. They base their interval estimate for ρ_s on the variance term $[(1+r_s)/2]/(n-3)$ and offer evidence for its accuracy.

Non-Null Inference With Tau-a

The variance term for tau-a presented previously assumes that X and Y are completely independent. Complete independence is usually of limited interest to the applied researcher because it is not possible to test a general null hypothesis such as H_0: $\tau_a = c$, nor is it possible to compute a confidence interval for τ_a. These failings are in conflict with general recommendations for statistical analysis in psychology and education (Cohen, 1994; Wilkinson & the Task Force on Statistical Inference, 1999).

It is possible to proceed as we do with parametric methods and estimate the characteristics of the sampling distribution of t_a from sample data. Specifically, when $\tau_a \neq 0$, we can compute t_a, estimate its variance, and use these quantities as a basis for a general hypothesis test or a confidence interval.

A number of estimates of the variance of t_a have been developed for use when $\tau_a \neq 0$ (Cliff & Charlin, 1991; Daniels & Kendall, 1947; Kendall, 1970). One such variance estimate is the consistent estimate. It is simpler to discuss the consistent estimate if we first define the dominance product

$$t_{ihxy} = (d_{ihx})(d_{ihy}), \qquad (25.28)$$

which is 1 if d_{ihx} and d_{ihy} have the same sign, -1 if they are opposite, and 0 if one or both are 0. Also used is $t_{i.xy}$, the average consistency of i,

$$t_{i.xy} = \frac{\sum_h t_{ihxy}}{(n-1)}. \quad (25.29)$$

The consistent estimate of $\text{var}(t_a)$ is

$$\text{Est}[\text{var}(t_a)] = \frac{4(n-2)s_{t_{i.xy}}^2 + 2s_{t_{ihxy}}^2}{n(n-1)}, \quad (25.30)$$

where

$$s_{t_{i.xy}}^2 = \frac{\sum_i(t_{i.xy} - t_a)^2}{(n-1)}, \quad (25.31)$$

and

$$s_{t_{ihxy}}^2 = \frac{2\sum_{i>h}\sum t_{ihxy}^2 - n(n-1)t_a^2}{[n(n-1)]-1}. \quad (25.32)$$

The appendix to this chapter illustrates the calculation of the $\text{Est}[\text{var}(t_a)]$ using the data in Table 25.1.

The estimated variance can be used in a significance test of H_0: $\tau_a = c$, or in a confidence interval of the form

$$t_a \pm x_{1-\alpha/2}\sqrt{\text{Est}[\text{var}(t_a)]}, \quad (25.33)$$

where $x_{1-\alpha/2}$ is the appropriate value from Student's distribution based on $(n-2)$ degrees of freedom. Long and Cliff (1997) studied the sampling behavior of the Equation 25.33 confidence interval. A simulation study was conducted in which samples of different sizes were drawn from populations with various values of τ_a. Interest was in the coverage probability, defined as the proportion of times the τ_a parameter was in the confidence interval, and in power, defined as the proportion of times in which zero was not in the confidence interval (the proportion of times H_0: $\tau_a = 0$ was rejected). Results showed that the confidence interval had excellent coverage, never dropping below $(1-\alpha)$ even when the sample size was as small as 10. Power was relatively high as compared to a number of other confidence intervals computed with different variance estimates (for details, see Long and Cliff, 1997). It appears that the Equation 25.33 confidence interval based on the consistent estimate of the variance of t_a is both accurate and relatively powerful under a wide number of conditions.

Extensions of Ordinal Correlation

Comparing Two Independent Taus

The methods of the last section can be extended to other situations involving taus, as described by Cliff (1996a, 1996b). One such situation arises when a researcher seeks to compare tau-a correlations from two independent samples, asking whether the correlation is equal in the two groups. When more than one tau is considered, we must alter our previous subscript notation to allow for multiple coefficients. Specifically, we drop the a in t_a and use difference numerical subscripts to designate taus from two different samples, for example t_1 and t_2.

Inferential methods based on $(t_1 - t_2)$ use the variance of the sum of two independent taus, which is the sum of the individual variances. We can use the formulas from the last section to compute estimates of the variances of the individual taus, $\text{Est}[\text{var}(t_1)]$ and $\text{Est}[\text{var}(t_2)]$. The square root of the sum of variances can be used as a basis to test H_0: $\tau_1 - \tau_2 = 0$, or to compute the 95% CI for $(\tau_1 - \tau_2)$, which is

$$\begin{aligned} &95\% \text{ CI for } (\tau_1 - \tau_2) \\ &= (t_1 - t_2) \pm 1.96\sqrt{\text{Est}[\text{var}(t_1)] + \text{Est}[\text{var}(t_2)]}. \end{aligned} \quad (25.34)$$

Comparing Two Dependent Taus

Suppose we want to see which of two predictors, X_1 and X_2, correlates more highly with a dependent variable, Y. When two taus are computed with the same sample data, they are dependent. In this case, the $\text{var}(t_{1y} - t_{2y}) = \text{var}(t_{1y}) + \text{var}(t_{2y}) - 2\text{cov}(t_{1y}, t_{2y})$, which is parallel to comparing two means from the same sample. We have already shown how to compute the estimates of the variances of the individual taus. The estimate of the covariance between two nonindependent taus, t_{1y} and t_{2y}, is similar in logic to the variance.

In this case there are two sets of t_{ihjk}—namely, t_{ih1y} and t_{ih2y}, which are arranged in the symmetric matrices, $\mathbf{T}_{1y}$ and $\mathbf{T}_{2y}$. Using the formulas of Cliff and Charlin (1991), the estimate of the covariance between t_{1y} and t_{2y} is

$$\text{Est}[\text{cov}(t_{1y}, t_{2y})] = \frac{4(n-2)s_{t_{i.1y}, t_{i.2y}} + 2s_{t_{ih1y}, t_{ih2y}}}{n(n-1)}. \quad (25.35)$$

Consistent with our previous definition of $t_{i.xy}$, the $t_{i.1y}$ are the row totals of $\mathbf{T}_{1y}$ divided by $(n-1)$, and the $t_{i.2y}$ are the row totals of $\mathbf{T}_{2y}$ divided by $(n-1)$. The first term in the numerator, $s_{t.1y, t.2y}$, is the covariance between the $t_{i.1y}$ and $t_{i.2y}$, formally defined as

$$s_{t_{i.1y}, t_{i.2y}} = \frac{\sum_i(t_{i.1y} - t_{1y})(t_{i.2y} - t_{2y})}{(n-1)}. \quad (25.36)$$

The second term in the numerator of Equation 25.35, $s_{t_{ih1y}, t_{ih2y}}$, is the covariance of the t_{ih1y} and t_{ih2y}, formally defined as

$$s_{t_{ih1y}, t_{ih2y}} = \frac{\sum_{i \neq h}\sum(t_{ih1y} - t_{1y})(t_{ih2y} - t_{2y})}{n(n-1)-1}. \quad (25.37)$$

which also uses the individual elements of $\mathbf{T}_{1y}$ and $\mathbf{T}_{2y}$.

To illustrate the computation of the covariance between two dependent taus with Equations 25.35–25.37, the additional variable, X_2,

$$X_2: 9, 5, 2, 8, 7$$

is used with the X and Y of Table 25.1. The samples are too small for a really meaningful comparison, but merely illustrate the computational process. Table 25.2 shows the $\mathbf{D}_{ih2}$ matrix, the $\mathbf{T}_{ih2y}$ matrix, and the $\sum_h t_{ih2y}$. The tau correlation between X_1 and X_2 is $t_{12} = (2/10) = .20$, the tau correlation between X_2 and Y is $t_{2y} = (-1/10) = -.10$, $\mathbf{t}_{i.2y} = [-1, 0, 0, .25, .25]$, and finally, Est$[\text{var}(t_{2y})] = .2550$.

To compute the estimated covariance between t_{1y} and t_{2y}, we solve Equation 25.35 by substituting the results of Equation 25.36 and Equation 25.37. Equation 25.36, $s_{t.1y,t.2y}$, is the covariance between the $t_{i.jk}$ of both pairs of variables. Working with the elements of the $\mathbf{t}_{i.1y}$ and the $\mathbf{t}_{i.2y}$ vectors and recalling that $t_{1y} = -.3$ and $t_{2y} = -.1$, the data at the end of Table 25.2 used in Equation 25.36 yields

$s_{t.1y,t.2y}$

$$= \frac{[(-1 - (-.3))(-1 - (-.1)) + \cdots + (-.25 - (-.3))(.25 - (-.1))]}{4}$$

$$= .1813. \tag{25.38}$$

Equation 25.37, $s_{tih1y,tih2y}$, is the covariance between the t_{ihjk} of both variables. Working with the t_{ih1y} and t_{ih2y}, we compute

$s_{tih1y,tih2y}$

$$= \frac{[(-1 - (-.3))(-1 - (-.1)) + \cdots + (0 - (-.3))(0 - (-.1))]}{5(4) - 1}$$

$$= .1421. \tag{25.39}$$

Finally, substituting all the elements into Equation 25.35, the estimated covariance between t_{1y} and t_{2y} is

$$\text{Est}[\text{cov}(t_{1y}, t_{2y})] = \frac{4(n-2)s_{t_{i.1y},t_{i.2y}} + 2s_{t_{ih1y},t_{ih2y}}}{n(n-1)}$$

$$= \frac{4(3)(.1813) + 2(.1421)}{5(4)}$$

$$= .1230. \tag{25.40}$$

Using Equation 25.30, we find Est$[\text{var}(t_{1y})] = .2615$ (see the appendix), and Est$[\text{var}(t_{2y})] = .2549$. Therefore,

$$\text{var}(t_{1y} - t_{2y}) = \text{var}(t_{1y}) + \text{var}(t_{2y}) - 2\,\text{cov}(t_{1y}, t_{2y})$$

$$= .2615 + .2549 - 2(.1230) = .2704. \tag{25.41}$$

Thus, the standard error of the difference is $\sqrt{.2704} = .52$, making the CI for the difference $t_{1y} - t_{2y} \pm (1.96)$ (standard error of the difference) $= -.2 \pm 1.02$, which is very wide because of the small sample size. The estimated covariance and variances are also the basis of an inferential method in a type of ordinal multiple regression, to which we now turn.

Ordinal Multiple Regression

In addition to the situations just discussed, ordinal correlation can be extended to the multivariate case in a type of ordinal multiple regression (OMR; Cliff, 1994, 1996b). OMR has some advantages over the traditional least squares multiple regression (LSMR). OMR is based on ordinal operations, and its results address the ordinal questions that researchers often pose in multiple regression. Both the descriptive and inferential results of OMR are invariant under monotonic transformation. OMR can be more powerful than LSMR when predictor correlations are moderate to high, and when LSMR assumptions are violated.

LSMR is a method in which the information of a set of predictors (X_j) is combined to optimally predict the scores on a response variable, Y. A weighted combination of predictors is formed, $\hat{Y}_i = \sum b_i X_{ij}$, which minimizes a loss function based on the sum of squared residuals, $\sum(Y_i - \hat{Y}_i)^2$, thereby maximizing the sample multiple correlation. The highly specific mathematics of LSMR means that the relationships between the predictors and the response can be expressed in very explicit, unit-based terms. For example, it is common to interpret an unstandardized regression weight as the predicted increase in Y for a one-unit increase in predictor X_j holding all other predictors constant (Howell, 1997, p. 516). The other predictors are actually held constant only in the case of strict multivariate normality, or when the predictors have fixed values as in ANOVA. In more common situations, the condition satisfied is that the contribution of X_j is uncorrelated with the contributions of all other predictors. Furthermore, raw scores can be composed (or decomposed) from proportions of predictors (and constants). Suppose that $Y_i = b_1 X_{i1} + b_2 X_{i2} + b_0 + e_i$, where $b_1 = .8$ and $b_2 = .4$. This means that the ith response score is .8 of X_1, plus .4 of X_2, plus a constant and a leftover.

It is rare that research questions are consistent with the highly specific nature of LSMR. Rather, most research questions are vague, along the lines of *Given a set of predictors, can we predict who will be high and who will be low on the response?* This type of question is ordinal in nature and is perhaps best answered with a corresponding ordinal method. OMR is based on ordinal operations that provide results consistent with these ordinal questions commonly asked in multiple regression.

TABLE 25.2   Computation of the Estimated Covariance of Two Dependent Taus

i, h	X_1	X_2	Y
1	41	9	5
2	12	5	8
3	26	2	11
4	17	8	14
5	19	7	14

Pair	d_{ih1}	d_{ih2}	d_{ihy}	t_{ih12}	t_{ih1y}	t_{ih2y}	$(t_{ih1y} - t_{1y})$	$(t_{ih2y} - t_{2y})$	$(t_{ih1y} - t_{1y}) \times (t_{ih2y} - t_{2y})$
1,2	−1	−1	1	1	−1	−1	−0.7	−0.9	0.63
1,3	−1	−1	1	1	−1	−1	−0.7	−0.9	0.63
1,4	−1	−1	1	1	−1	−1	−0.7	−0.9	0.63
1,5	−1	−1	1	1	−1	−1	−0.7	−0.9	0.63
2,3	1	−1	1	−1	1	−1	1.3	−0.9	−1.17
2,4	1	1	1	1	1	1	1.3	1.1	1.43
2,5	1	1	1	1	1	1	1.3	1.1	1.43
3,4	−1	1	1	−1	−1	1	−0.7	1.1	−0.77
3,5	−1	1	1	−1	−1	1	−0.7	1.1	−0.77
4,5	1	−1	0	−1	0	0	0.3	0.1	0.03
Sums:			2		−3	−1			2.7
$t_{jk} =$			0.2		−0.3	−0.1		$s_{t_{ih1y},t_{ih2y}} =$	0.1421

$\mathbf{T}_{1y}$		h				$\sum_h t_{ih1y}$	$t_{i.1y}$	$(t_{i.1y} - t_{1y})$	$(t_{i.1y} - t_{1y})^2$
	0	−1	−1	−1	−1	−4	−1	−0.7	0.49
	−1	0	1	1	1	2	0.5	0.8	0.64
i	−1	1	0	−1	−1	−2	−0.5	−0.2	0.04
	−1	1	−1	0	0	−1	−0.25	0.05	0.0025
	−1	1	−1	0	0	−1	−0.25	0.05	0.0025
				Sums:		−6	−1.5	0	1.175

$\mathbf{T}_{2y}$		h				$\sum_h t_{ih2y}$	$t_{i.2y}$	$(t_{i.2y} - t_{2y})$	$(t_{i.2y} - t_{2y})^2$
	0	−1	−1	−1	−1	−4	−1	−0.9	0.81
	−1	0	−1	1	1	0	0	0.1	0.01
i	−1	−1	0	1	1	0	0	0.1	0.01
	−1	1	1	0	0	1	0.25	0.35	0.1225
	−1	1	1	0	0	1	0.25	0.35	0.1225
				Sums:		−2	−0.5	0	1.075

$(t_{i.1y} - t_{1y})$	$(t_{i.2y} - t_{2y})$	$(t_{i.1y} - t_{1y}) \times (t_{i.2y} - t_{2y})$
−0.7	−0.9	0.63
0.8	0.1	0.08
−0.2	0.1	−0.02
0.05	0.35	0.0175
0.05	0.35	0.0175
	Sum:	0.725
	$s_{t_{i.1y},t_{i.2y}} =$	0.18125
Est[covar(t_{1y}, t_{2y})] =	0.1230	(Equation 25.40)

In OMR, information on the predictors is combined to optimally predict the order on Y, where order is defined by the dominance on Y, d_{ihy}. Cliff (1994, 1996b) shows that the information on the predictors can be either raw differences, $a_{ihj} = (x_{ij} - x_{hj})$, rank differences, $a_{ihj} = (q_{ixj} - q_{hxj})$, or dominances, $a_{ihj} = d_{ihxj} = \text{sign}(x_{ij} - x_{hj})$. Similar to LSMR, the information on the predictors is combined by means of a weighted composite, $\hat{d}_{ihy} = \sum w_j a_{ihj}$. However, unlike LSMR, the weights are chosen so as to optimize an ordinal loss function rather than a least-squares loss function.

Treating the problem as a discriminant analysis with the groups defined by the values of d_{ihy}, Cliff (1994) showed that weights for computing the $\hat{d}_{ihy}$ can be obtained that approximately optimize the ordinal loss function,

$$\phi = \frac{\sum\sum_{i>h} (d_{ihy})(\text{sign}[\hat{d}_{ihy}])}{\frac{1}{2}n(n-1)}, \tag{25.42}$$

where $\text{sign}[\cdot] = -1$ when $\hat{d}_{ihy} < 0$, $\text{sign}[\cdot] = +1$ when $\hat{d}_{ihy} > 0$, and $\text{sign}[\cdot] = 0$ when $\hat{d}_{ihy} = 0$ (this last value rarely occurs in practice). ϕ is analogous to a multivariate tau correlation because it is the sum of the product of dominance scores divided by the total number of pairs. When there are tied pairs on Y, it may be desirable to alter the denominator of Equation 25.42 as was done with the bivariate tau correlation.

The equations that are solved to obtain weights that optimize Equation 25.42 are similar in form to those of LSMR. In predicting dominances from raw score differences, we use $a_{ihj} = (x_{ij} - x_{hj})$, and the weights are similar to OMR weights,

$$\mathbf{w}_1 = (2/n)\mathbf{S}_x^{-1}\mathbf{s}_{rxy}, \tag{25.43}$$

where $\mathbf{S}_x$ is the $(p \times p)$ variance-covariance matrix among the p predictors, and $\mathbf{s}_{rxy}$ is the $(p \times 1)$ vector of covariances between the predictors and the ranks of Y. When predicting from the difference between ranks, we use $a_{ihj} = (q_{ixj} - q_{hxj})$, and the weights are

$$\mathbf{w}_2 = \mathbf{R}_{sx}^{-1}\mathbf{r}_{sxy}, \tag{25.44}$$

where $\mathbf{R}_{sx}$ contains the Spearman r_s correlations among the predictors, and $\mathbf{r}_{sxy}$ contains the Spearman r_s correlations between the predictors and Y. In the case of predicting from dominances, we use $a_{ihj} = d_{ihxj} = \text{sign}(x_{ij} - x_{hj})$, and the weights are

$$\mathbf{w}_3 = \mathbf{T}_x^{-1}\mathbf{t}_{xy}, \tag{25.45}$$

where $\mathbf{T}_x$ contains the tau-a correlations among the predictors, and $\mathbf{t}_{xy}$ contains the tau-a correlations between the predictors and Y.

Issues Regarding OMR Weights

Although the weights obtained with Equations 25.43, 25.44, and 25.45 are guaranteed to yield the most signed agreements and maximize ϕ only when the $\hat{d}_{ihy}$ are normally distributed conditional on the d_{ihy}, they work well in practice (Long, 1999). It should be noted that least squares based methods

such as discriminant analysis also yield approximate weights in any applied analysis because normality can never exactly hold in sample data (nor in the population; e.g., see Wilcox, 1991).

In the case of predicting from dominances, a truly optimal solution is possible. For any set of p predictors, there are a finite number of possible dominance patterns across the predictors (3^p if there are ties on the predictors, 2^p if not). In principle, these can be used to define a set of inequalities on the weights (Cliff, 1994). The least squares weights have been found to satisfy all, or nearly all, of these inequalities in the examples tested. However, the number of inequalities rises rapidly with the number of predictors. A curious consequence of the inequalities is that in the two-predictor case without ties, using two predictors cannot improve on the better of the individual predictors by the criterion of Equation 25.42.

No Partial Tau

In the case of predicting from two dominances, the numerator of the first OMR weight can be shown to equal $t_{1y} - t_{2y}t_{12}$. This numerator is identical in form to the numerator of the LSMR standardized regression coefficient and the numerator of the Pearson partial correlation. Given this similarity, it is tempting to interpret OMR weights in terms of partial relationships as is common in LSMR. However, such interpretations are problematic when dealing with dominances. The reason is that the investigation of partial relationships is based on the analysis of residuals, and a residualized dominance makes no sense. A residual of a dominance score obtained with the regular least squares methods can take on any real value. This violates the very nature of dominance as an index of the order relations *greater than, less than,* and *equal to.* More important is that the residuals of dominances do not behave like residuals of raw interval scores and can cause some curious results for partial tau correlations. For example, in situations in which two variables are completely dependent on a third, the partial Pearson correlation will always be zero, but the value of a partial tau correlation can be nonzero (see Nelson & Yang, 1988).

The qualifications just discussed indicate the OMR weights should be interpreted only as practical devices for predicting the order on the criterion. In OMR, the functional relationship between the dominance on Y and the information on the predictors, $d_{ihy} = f(a_{ihj})$, is much more vague than in LSMR. Therefore, the OMR weights cannot be interpreted in any causal or explanatory sense. We can safely say that the size of an OMR weight represents the relative importance of a predictor to the overall prediction system. A variable with a large weight has a relatively large influence in prediction, and a variable with a small weight has a smaller influence in prediction. However, substantive interpretations beyond this have little or no justification. It should be noted that LSMR weights are not without their own interpretational complications, especially when the predictors are correlated (see Cliff, 1987; Mosteller & Tukey, 1977).

Confidence Intervals for OMR Weights

Given that the order on Y can be predicted in the sense that ϕ is not zero, an applied researchers may want to know which variable(s) is(are) important to that prediction. Descriptively, this can be addressed by observing the decrease in ϕ (if any) omitting X_j. If a researcher wants to go beyond description, this can be accomplished by computing a confidence interval for an OMR regression weight.

The OMR CI for a single population weight, π_j is

$$w_j \pm z_{1-\alpha/2}\,\hat{\sigma}_{w_j}, \tag{25.46}$$

where w_j is a sample weight from Equation 25.45 (predicting from dominances), $z_{1-\alpha/2}$ is the appropriate critical value from the standard normal distribution at α, and $\hat{\sigma}_{w_j}$ is the estimated standard error of w_j.

Computing the Estimated Standard Error.   In order to compute the estimated standard error, $\hat{\sigma}_{w_j}$, we assume a fixed effects regression model (this is a common assumption in multiple regression; see Long, 1999). Under the OMR fixed effects model, the elements of the matrix of predictor tau correlations, $\mathbf{T}_x$, are constants, and so are the elements of $\mathbf{T}_x^{-1}$. Given these assumptions, any sample weight, w_j, can be viewed as a linear combination,

$$w_j = \sum_{k=1}^{p} t_{jk}^* t_{ky}, \tag{25.47}$$

where t_{jk}^* is an element from the $\mathbf{T}_x^{-1}$ matrix, t_{jk} is the tau-a correlation between X_j and X_k and t_{ky} is the tau-a correlation between X_k and the criterion, Y.

When an OMR sample weight is defined as a linear combination, then the variance of the weight can be obtained by computing the variance of a linear combination (see Cliff, 1987, pp. 53–60). The formula for the variance of a linear combination of w_j is

$$\sigma_{w_j}^2 = \sum_k (t_{jk}^*)^2 \operatorname{var}(t_{ky}) + 2\sum_{k<m} t_{jk}^* t_{jm}^* \operatorname{cov}(t_{ky}, t_{my}). \tag{25.48}$$

In this equation, $\operatorname{var}(t_{ky})$ is the variance of the tau validity between X_k and Y, $\operatorname{cov}(t_{ky}, t_{my})$ is the covariance between the two respective tau validities, and the t_{jk}^* are known elements

from the $\mathbf{T}_x^{-1}$ matrix, so the task here is to compute estimates of the variances using Equation 25.30 and covariances using Equation 25.35. After this is done, the square root of Equation 25.48 can be used in the CI formula, Equation 25.46.

As an example, suppose we wanted to computed the 95% CI for π_1 based on the data in Table 25.2. The solution for the estimated standard error of the first OMR weight, $\hat{\sigma}_{w_1}^2$, is

$$\hat{\sigma}_{w_1}^2 = (t_{11}^*)^2\, \operatorname{Est}[\operatorname{var}(t_{1y})] + (t_{12}^*)^2\, \operatorname{Est}[\operatorname{var}(t_{2y})]$$
$$+ 2\{t_{11}^* t_{12}^*\, \operatorname{Est}[\operatorname{cov}(t_{1y}, t_{2y})]\}. \tag{25.49}$$

From above we know that

$$\mathbf{T}_x^{-1} = \begin{bmatrix} 1.0 & .2 \\ .2 & 1.0 \end{bmatrix}^{-1} = \begin{bmatrix} 1.0417 & -.2083 \\ -.2083 & 1.0417 \end{bmatrix}. \tag{25.50}$$

The variances of the t_{1y} and t_{2y} and the covariances between them are

$$\hat{\Sigma} = \begin{bmatrix} .2615 & .1230 \\ .1230 & .2549 \end{bmatrix} \tag{25.51}$$

Substituting all the appropriate values,

$$\hat{\sigma}_{w_1}^2 = (1.0417)^2(.2615) + (-.2083)^2(.2550)$$
$$+ 2[(1.0417)(-.2083)(.1230)] = .2414, \tag{25.52}$$

and $\hat{\sigma}_{w_1} = \sqrt{.2414} = .4914$.

Having computed $\hat{\sigma}_{w_1}$, we can use Equation 25.46 to compute the 95% CI for π_1. It can be shown that Equation 25.45 yields $w_1 = -.2917$ and $w_2 = -.0417$. Using all the relevant information, the 95% CI for π_1 is

$$w_1 \pm 1.96\,\hat{\sigma}_{w_1} = -.2917 \pm (1.96)(.4914)$$
$$= [-1.2548, 0.6714]. \tag{25.53}$$

This CI covers zero, so we would not reject H_0: $\pi_1 = 0$, but note that $n = 5$ is very small, contributing to the lack of power in detecting a false null hypothesis.

Performance of the OMR Confidence Interval.   Long (1999) studied the sampling behavior of the CI of Equation 25.46. The results of his stimulation study showed that when sampling from population data that meet the assumptions of fixed effects LSMR, the OMR CI performed well in terms of probability coverage, with the exception that coverage tended to be conservative as effect size increased.

The results for power were noteworthy and showed some important contrasts with the LSMR CI. When the predictors were not correlated, the OMR CI had slightly lower power than the LSMR CI, which seems to confirm the conventional wisdom that ordinal methods are not as powerful as parametric methods when data conditions are optimal for the latter. However, power of the OMR CI was superior to the LSMR CI when the predictors were moderately to highly correlated. This is an especially favorable finding for the OMR CI, given that predictor correlations are usually nonzero and can be quite substantial in applied research (Cohen, 1994; Meehl, 1997).

Omnibus Hypothesis Testing in OMR

If one wants to test whether any of a group of predictors is significantly related to the criterion, one can construct a test of the omnibus null hypothesis

$$H_0: \tau_{1y} = \tau_{2y} = \cdots = \tau_{py} = 0, \qquad (25.54)$$

where τ_{ky} is the population tau-a correlation between the kth predictor and Y.

Assuming that we are predicting from the dominances, let us define the test statistic,

$$H = \mathbf{t}_y'(\mathbf{V}^{-1})\mathbf{t}_y, \qquad (25.55)$$

where $\mathbf{t}_y$ is the ($p \times 1$) vector of tau validities, and $\mathbf{V}$ is the ($p \times p$) variance-covariance matrix of the tau validities. Using the formulas from the past sections,

$$\mathbf{V} = \begin{bmatrix} \text{Est}[\text{var}(t_{1y})] & \text{Est}[\text{cov}(t_{1y}t_{2y})] & \cdots & \text{Est}[\text{cov}(t_{1y}t_{py})] \\ & \text{Est}[\text{var}(t_{2y})] & & \vdots \\ & & \ddots & \text{Est}[\text{cov}(t_{p-1y}t_{py})] \\ & & & \text{Est}[\text{var}(t_{py})] \end{bmatrix},$$

$$(25.56)$$

where $\mathbf{V}$ is symmetric.

Under the null hypothesis, if the elements of $\mathbf{t}_y$ are normally distributed, then $H \sim \chi^2(p)$. The distribution of t_{ky} tends towards normality as n increases. Therefore, under the null, as n increases, $H \rightarrow \chi^2(p)$. H can be computed from the sample data, and with a sufficiently large sample size, we would reject H_0 if $H >$ tabled $\chi^2_\alpha(p)$. When n is not large, we might use the rejection criterion of $pF(p, n - p - 1)$ for a fixed α (see McKean & Sheather, 1991).

An alternative approach to omnibus testing is based on a chi-square analysis of the contingency table defined by the d_{ihy} and the predictor dominance patterns. Assuming no ties on Y, we can compute the entire $n(n - 1)$ dominance vector of Y and call it $\mathbf{d}_y$. In this case, half of $\mathbf{d}_y$ will be $d_{ihy} = +1$ and the other half will be $d_{ihy} = -1$ because $d_{ihy} = -d_{hiy}$. If

we also assume no ties on the predictors, we can form a contingency table defined by the two values of d_{ihy} (i.e., $-1, +1$) and the 2^p possible predictor dominance patterns. The cell frequencies are the tallies of the co-occurrence of a value of d_{ihy} and one of the 2^p patterns. If Y is unrelated to the predictors, then half the number of a given predictor dominance pattern should be associated with $d_{ihy} = +1$ and the other half associated with $d_{ihy} = -1$. To test this hypothesis, we can compute $\chi^2[n(n - 1)]^{-1}$ as a test statistic, which can be evaluated against $\chi^2_\alpha(p)$. A similar test can be computed allowing for ties.

Long (2001) is currently investigating the performance of the omnibus methods. Preliminary investigation indicates that using $pF(p, n - p - 1)$ to evaluate H yields good actual Type I error rate and power, but more investigation is needed before definitive statements can be made.

ORDINAL ALTERNATIVES TO MEAN COMPARISON: DOMINANCE ANALYSIS

Dominance Analysis for Independent Data

The Delta Measure and the d Statistic

One of the most important and frequently encountered problems in psychological and behavioral research is the so-called *two-sample problem,* or *location comparison.* For example, we are often interested in whether scores from one group tend to be higher than those from the other (e.g., treatment effects). This research question is usually answered by the two-sample t test comparing means of the two groups or the parallel one-way ANOVA. The t test requires (a) interval level of measurement for the variables, and (b) the assumptions of normality and homogeneity of variance. However, as argued earlier in the chapter, many behavioral and social variables have only ordinal justification. Although some studies show that Type I error rates and empirical power of the t test are preserved for Likert-scaled data (Hsu & Feldt, 1969; Nanna & Sawilowsky, 1998), ordinal methods can be more powerful than the t test for data of less than interval level. In addition, the parametric assumptions are always violated to a greater or lesser extent in applied research. Nonnormality and heterogeneity of variance can inflate the actual Type I error rate and severely reduce the power of normal-based mean comparison procedures (e.g., Barnard, 1984; Cressie & Whitford, 1986; Gronow, 1953; Pearson & Please, 1975; Ramsey, 1980; Tan, 1982; Wilcox, 1990, 1991, 1992). The t test and the corresponding CI for a mean difference are highly quantified procedures. However, as previously discussed, the question of the researcher is often formulated in a looser, ordinal fashion, such as *Do individuals in this group or under this condition tend to score higher than do those in the other?*

In this section we describe a measure, δ often written Δ, for answering research questions about central tendency of two groups, conditions, or occasions. δ and its sample counterpart, d, directly reflect the tendency for one set of scores to be higher than the other, which a mean difference does not, unless the later is converted to some kind of correlational index. In addition to describing d analysis, ways in which this ordinal measure can be applied in more complex research designs are suggested.

δ is a direct quantification of the extent to which scores in one set are higher than scores in the other. This measure has been discussed in nonparametric statistics books for years (Agresti, 1984; Hettmansperger, 1984; Randles & Wolfe, 1979), but it has not been widely employed. Its application was emphasized and extended recently by Cliff (1991, 1993, 1996b). For a score X_1 sampled from one population and a score X_2 from another, δ is the probability that X_1 is higher than X_2, minus the reverse probability:

$$\delta = \Pr(X_{1i} > X_{2j}) - \Pr(X_{1i} < X_{2j}). \quad (25.57)$$

That is, each observation of the first population is compared to each observation of the second population. There is a probability that the observation of the first population is higher, and a probability that the observation of the second group is higher. δ is the difference between these two probabilities. It runs from -1.0 (nonoverlapping distributions with the X_2 observations higher) to 1.0 (nonoverlapping distributions with the X_1 observations higher). δ is essentially equivalent to $p = \Pr\{X_1 > X_2\}$ (cf. Birnbaum, 1956; McGraw & Wong, 1992; Mee, 1990). When there are no ties between X_1 and X_2 observations,

$$p = (\delta + 1)/2. \quad (25.58)$$

(Note that p in Equation 25.58 is not to be confused with the number of predictors discussed above.) However, we believe δ is preferable to p, particularly when there are ties in the data. By taking the difference between the two probabilities, the formula defining δ includes ties but does not count them as either higher or lower. Therefore, further modifiers to communicate the probability of ties are not necessary. Also, δ is equivalent to the form of Kendall's τ called Somer's d (Somer, 1968) for the special case in which one variable is a dichotomy (see section in this chapter entitled "Ordinal Correlation Methods").

An unbiased sample estimate of δ, the ordinal statistic d, is the proportion of times a score from one group is higher than a score from the other minus the proportion of times when the reverse is true:

$$d = \frac{\#(x_i > x_j) - \#(x_i < x_j)}{mn}, \quad (25.59)$$

where x_i represents any observation in the first group, x_j in the second, n and m represent the respective sample sizes, and # denotes *the number of times*. That is, each of the n scores in the first group is compared to each of the m scores in the second, and counts are made of how many times a score of the first group is higher and how many times it is lower. Ties are included in the denominator, mn, but are not counted in the numerator as either higher or lower.

Faced with a two-sample problem, an investigator is likely to be advised to choose between the well-known t test and the Wilcoxon-Mann-Whitney test (Mann & Whitney, 1947; Wilcoxon, 1945). A less restrictive null hypothesis, that two independent samples of observations have come from the same population, is one of the reasons often cited by those who favor the Wilcoxon-Mann-Whitney U statistic. The d statistic is a simple transformation of U. Let n and m be the sample sizes of the two groups being compared, and the r_1 be the ranks of the first group's scores among all the $m + n$ observations, ties being given the average rank. Then $U = \sum r_1 - n(n + 1)/2$, and

$$d = 2U/nm - 1. \quad (25.60)$$

In fact, the Wilcoxon-Mann-Whitney test provides a test of the null hypothesis that $\delta = 0$, assuming that the two population distributions are identical. However, the distributions could differ in shape or in spread, with or without having δ equal to 0. In other words, the Wilcoxon-Mann-Whitney test is testing the hypothesis that the two groups represent random samples from the same distribution, but rejection of the hypothesis is sometimes taken as reflecting a difference in the location of the two distributions. Differences between the two distributions in shape or in spread may invalidate inferences from the Wilcoxon-Mann-Whitney test. On the other hand, the d statistic tests the H_0 that $\delta = 0$ without assuming identical distributions.

Inferences About Delta

If identical distributions are assumed, the variance of d or U in the null case depends only on the sample sizes of the two groups being compared, it being $\sigma_d^2 = (n + m + 1)/3mn$. For large samples, the ratio d^2/σ_d^2 has a chi-square distribution with $df = 1$. Tables are widely available for the U statistic in small samples. However, this kind of inference has limited applicability because it only allows a test of the null hypothesis that two random samples are from the same distribution. A more useful approach is to treat d as a sample estimate of δ, regardless of the population distributions. Then characteristics of the sampling distribution of d can be used in making inferences regarding δ. Because the sampling distribution of d is asymptotically normal, normal-based inferences can be made with σ_d^2 being estimated from the sample. It should be noted that asymptotic normality of d is distinct from normality of data. Extensive simulation studies (Feng & Cliff, 1995) revealed that even when the distribution of the data is far from normal, the distribution of d approaches normality pretty quickly. In fact, the distribution of the average of d across subjects or across variables is generally platykurtic rather than leptokurtic.

Discussions of the sampling properties of d are aided by the use of dominance variables that represent the direction of differences between scores. The dominance in the two-group case has a slightly different definition from that of the case of ordinal correlation. Suppose that x_i is a score from the first group and x_j a score from the second group, the dominance is defined as

$$d_{ij} = \text{sign}(x_i - x_j). \tag{25.61}$$

The dominance, d_{ij}, simply represents the direction of differences between the x_i scores and the x_j scores. A score of 1 is assigned if $x_i > x_j$, a score of -1 is assigned if $x_i < x_j$, and a score of 0 is assigned if $x_i = x_j$. Then a second definition of δ is the expected value of d_{ij}

$$\delta = \text{E}(d_{ij}). \tag{25.62}$$

In the matrix in which d_{ij} are the elements, the row averages are called $d_i.$, and the column averages are called $d_{.j}$. In samples, the $d_i.$ can be estimated as the proportion of the x_i being higher than the x_j minus the proportion of the reverse:

$$d_i^* = \frac{\#(x_i > x_j) - \#(x_i < x_j)}{m}, \tag{25.63}$$

where "*" indicates an estimate. There is a similar definition for the d_j^*. Obviously, $\text{E}(d_i^*) = d_i.$, and $\text{E}(d_j^*) = d_{.j}$. The sample statistic d can be calculated as

$$d = \sum\sum \frac{d_{ij}}{mn}. \tag{25.64}$$

It can be seen that $\delta = \text{E}(d_i^*) = \text{E}(d_j^*) = \text{E}(d)$.

Because it is a kind of mean, d is asymptotically normally distributed with a sampling variance that can be expressed as

$$\sigma_d^2 = \frac{(m-1)\sigma_{d_i.}^2 + (n-1)\sigma_{d_{.j}}^2 + \sigma_{d_{ij}}^2}{mn}, \tag{25.65}$$

where $\sigma_{d_i.}^2 = \text{E}(d_i. - \delta)^2$, $\sigma_{d_{.j}}^2 = \text{E}(d_{.j} - \delta)^2$, and $\sigma_{d_{ij}}^2 = \text{E}(d_{ij} - \delta)^2$. If there are no ties, the variance of d_{ij}, $\sigma_{d_{ij}}^2$, is $1 - \delta^2$. In large samples, the variance will resemble the variance of the difference between means, becoming approximately $\sigma_{d_i.}^2/n + \sigma_{d_{.j}}^2/m$. As m and n increase, $d_i^* = d_i.$ and $d_j^* = d_{.j}$, so $\sigma_{d_i.}^2$, $\sigma_{d_{.j}}^2$, and δ can be estimated from the sample and substituted in Equation 25.65 to give a consistent estimate of σ_d^2. Alternatively, without relying on asymptotic properties, the unbiased sample estimate of σ_d^2 is

$$s_d^2 = \frac{m^2 \sum(d_i^* - d)^2 + n^2 \sum(d_j^* - d)^2 - \sum\sum(d_{ij} - d)^2}{mn(m-1)(n-1)}. \tag{25.66}$$

In practice, the negative sign on the last term of the numerator makes it possible for the estimate of variance of d to be negative. Thus, it is suggested that $(1 - d^2)/(mn - 1)$ is used as the minimum allowable value for s_d^2. This substitution introduces a bias, but such modification eliminates impossible values and usually increases the efficiency of an estimate. In large samples, the last term of the numerator is negligible compared to the other terms of Equation 25.66.

Adjustments to the Confidence Interval of Delta

Using a sample estimate of the variance of d, the null hypothesis that $\delta = 0$ can be tested without assuming identical distributions, and CIs for δ can be formed. The CI for δ is traditionally computed as $(d - z_{\alpha/2} s_d, d + z_{\alpha/2} s_d)$, using Equation 25.66 for s_d. However, this CI was found in a Monte Carlo study (Feng & Cliff, 1995) to be unsatisfactory for two reasons. First, when $d = \pm1$ (at the edge of the parameter space), there is a zero estimated variance for d. Thus, the conventional CI reduces to the point $\delta = \pm1$. But $d = \pm1$ can occur when $\delta \neq \pm1$, particularly when δ is fairly high and the sample sizes are small. Second, the traditional construction of the CI does not take into account the fact that σ_d^2 and δ are negatively correlated. Adjustments are suggested that take account of these so as to improve the CI for δ.

As discussed in the earlier section, the consistent estimate of the variance of t gives an improved CI for τ and obviates the necessity of using a minimum allowable variance. A similar modification can be made in estimating σ_d^2. Individually, $s_{d_i.}^2$ and $s_{d_{.j}}^2$ are unbiased estimates of $\sigma_{d_i.}^2$ and $\sigma_{d_{.j}}^2$, respectively. Let us define the sample estimate of $\sigma_{d_{ij}}^2$ as $\sum(d_{ij} - d)^2/(nm - 1)$. Then we can substitute $\sigma_{d_i.}^2$, $\sigma_{d_{.j}}^2$, and $s_{d_{ij}}^2$ in Equation 25.65, and using their sample estimates,

$$\hat{\sigma}_d^2 = \frac{(m-1)s_{d_i.}^2 + (n-1)s_{d_{.j}}^2 + \sigma_{d_{ij}}^2}{mn} \tag{25.67}$$

This gives the consistent estimate of σ_d^2, which was found to improve the inferential performance of d (Feng & Cliff, 1995).

To take account of the negative correlation between σ_d^2 and δ, an asymmetric adjustment to the CI for δ was suggested (Feng & Cliff, 1995). It was found that

$$\sigma_d^2 \approx \frac{s_d^2(1 - \delta^2)}{(1 - d^2)} \tag{25.68}$$

Again, assuming that $(d - \delta)/\sigma_d \sim N(0, 1)$, $z_{\alpha/2}^2 = (d - \delta)^2/\sigma_d^2$. Inserting Equation 25.68 for σ_d^2, the boundaries for the CI are taken as the roots of

$$z_{\alpha/2}^2 = \frac{(d - \delta)^2}{[(1 - \delta^2)/(1 - d^2)]s_d^2}. \tag{25.69}$$

Equation 25.69 can be solved to give the asymmetric CI with the adjusted lower and upper bounds

$$\delta = \frac{d - d^3 \pm z_{\alpha/2}\sigma_d\left(1 - 2d^2 + d^4 + z_{\alpha/2}^2\sigma_d^2\right)^{1/2}}{1 - d^2 + z_{\alpha/2}^2\sigma_d^2} \tag{25.70}$$

For example, for $d = .5$, $s_d^2 = .04$, $n = m = 10$, and $\alpha = .05$, the standard method, $\delta \in (d - z_{\alpha/2}s_d, d + z_{\alpha/2}s_d)$ would give a symmetric CI of $(.08, .92)$. With the adjustment, however, the CI would be $(.05, .78)$, which is a little longer on the lower end and shorter on the upper end. Note that Type I error rate under H_0: $\delta = 0$ and power are also affected because H_0: $\delta = 0$ is retained if 0 is within the CI.

Example of Delta for Independent Groups

In this section we use an artificial example to illustrate the independent groups dominance analysis. Suppose that we are interested in the relationship between mental psychological impairment and alcoholism, and we compared 25 female alcoholics with 25 female nonalcoholics on time to complete a performance test. Artificial data from the two groups are sorted and shown in Table 25.3. The mean for the 25 alcoholics is 23.03 min, whereas the mean for the 25 nonalcoholics is 15.65 min.

As a useful visual aid to the analysis of d, a dominance diagram is constructed. In this dominance matrix, the columns represent scores of the nonalcoholic group sorted in ascending order, with the rows representing scores of the alcoholic group sorted in the same way. The elements of the dominance diagram represent the dominance variable. The symbol $+$ stands for the $d_{ij} = +1$, $-$ stands for $d_{ij} = -1$, and 0 stands for $d_{ij} = 0$, as shown in Table 25.3 in the upper right corner. Notice that the frequency of $+$ is much higher than that of $-$, indicating scores from the alcoholic group are generally

higher than those from the nonalcoholic group. The $d_{i.}^*$ and $d_{.j}^*$ are shown and it can be seen that their variation is moderate.

As a comparison with traditional methods, an independent t test with Welch's adjustment of degrees of freedom was performed for the same data. The quantitative results of the d analysis including inferences about δ and the components of variance of d, as well as the inference about Welch's t test, are summarized in the second part of Table 25.3. The statistical decision of whether to reject the null hypothesis that δ is zero is made based on the z score for d, or on whether the CI contains zero. For this example, d for alcoholics versus nonalcoholics on time to complete the performance test is .389, showing that it tends to take the female alcoholics longer to complete the test, but the two sample distributions have some overlap.

The components of the variance of d are also given in the table. Beside each raw score in the table is $d_{i.}$ (for the alcoholic participants) and $d_{.j}$ (for the nonalcoholic participants). The former are the proportion of nonalcoholic scores that are above this alcoholic score, minus the proportion that is below. The latter is the proportion of alcoholic scores that are above this nonalcoholic score, minus those that are below. The three variances that are combined to make up the variance of d are given in the lower part of Table 25.3. According to Equation 25.67, the variance of the observed d is .0237, so the standard deviation of d is .154, leading to a 95% confidence interval for δ of .081 to .696. The z score for the significance of d is 2.530, slightly larger than the observed t score for mean difference ($t = 2.322$ with 44.484 Welch's adjusted df). Both the CI for δ and the z score for d indicate that the null hypothesis $\delta = 0$ should be rejected. It should be noted that although the d and t statistics lead to consistent statistical decisions of rejecting the null hypotheses, the d method has descriptive superiority and provides a more direct answer to the research question of whether female alcoholics tend to take more time to complete the performance test.

Extensions of d Analysis

Extension to Multiple Groups

The d analysis can be extended to multiple groups contexts by estimating a δ for each possible pairwise group comparison. Making inferences about multiple δs raises the issue of controlling the experimentwise Type I error rate. When there is a theoretical or practical basis, one should perform planned comparison and test each hypothesis separately rather than performing post hoc comparisons. Therefore, in many cases in which more than one δ is estimated, one should use a comparisonwise (or parameterwise) α level based on theoretical or important practical issues. When there are several groups

TABLE 25.3   An Example of *d* Analysis for Small Samples From Two Independent Groups

Ordered Scores				
Alchoholic		Nonalchol.		
Score	$d_{i.}$	Score	$d_{.j}$	Dominance Diagram
1	−1.00	3	.92	− −
4	−.72	3	.92	+ + + 0 −
6	−.56	3	.92	+ + + + + 0 − − − − − − − − − − − − − − − − − −
7	−.52	4	.88	+ + + + + + − − − − − − − − − − − − − − − − − −
7	−.52	5	.84	+ + + + + + − − − − − − − − − − − − − − − − − −
14	−.24	6	.80	+ + + + + + + + + 0 − − − − − − − − − − − − − −
14	−.24	12	.60	+ + + + + + + + + 0 − − − − − − − − − − − − − −
18	.40	12	.60	+ + + + + + + + + + + + + + + + 0 0 0 − − − − − −
19	.52	13	.60	+ + + + + + + + + + + + + + + + + + + − − − − − −
20	.52	14	.52	+ + + + + + + + + + + + + + + + + + + − − − − − −
21	.52	15	.44	+ + + + + + + + + + + + + + + + + + + − − − − − −
24	.68	15	.44	+ − − − −
25	.68	15	.44	+ − − − −
26	.68	15	.44	+ − − − −
26	.68	15	.44	+ − − − −
26	.68	16	.44	+ − − − −
27	.72	18	.40	+ 0 − − −
28	.84	18	.40	+ 0 0 −
28	.84	18	.40	+ 0 0 −
30	.92	23	.12	+ −
33	.92	23	.12	+ −
33	.92	27	−.32	+ −
44	1.00	28	−.44	+ +
45	1.00	28	−.44	+ +
50	1.00	43	−.76	+ +

Inferences about δ	
d	.389
s_d	.154
.95 confidence interval	(.081, .696)
z for d	2.530
Components of s_d^2	
$s_{d_{i.}}^2$	.394
$s_{d_{.j}}^2$	.207
$s_{d_{ij}}^2$	.831
Mean comparisons	
t for means	2.322
Welch's df for t	44.484

and it is necessary to control familywise α in a *d* analysis, one can use the Bonferroni procedure.

Extension to Factorial Designs

A common situation that occurs in behavioral and biological science is the factorial design in which the main effects and interactions are tested. Although the additive model that underlies the full analysis of a factorial experiment is not applicable to ordinal data, Cliff (1994, 1996a, 1996b) suggests that the *d* method can be easily extended to multiple groups situations in order to answer research questions that are typically answered by factorial ANOVA.

Suppose there are two factors, A and B, in the factorial design, the main-effect sum of squares for Factor A is equivalent to the between-groups sum of squares that would have been obtained if the groups had been combined across Factor B. The main-effect of A is often interpreted as *scores on X at A_1 tend to be higher than at A_2, regardless of the level of B.* In a *d* analysis, the main-effect of A is tested by calculating the average *d* with respect to different levels of A, averaged across all levels of B. That is, a d_1 is computed by comparing scores on X at A_1 to those at A_2 at B_1, and a d_2 is computed by comparing scores on X at A_1 to those at A_2 at B_2. The average of d_1 and d_2, which we will call *d*-bar, reflects the overall tendency for scores at A_1 to be higher than those at A_2, holding B constant. For independent data, $\sigma^2_{d\text{-bar}}$, the variance of d-bar, can be estimated by $s^2_{d\text{-bar}} = (s^2_{d_1} + s^2_{d_2})/4$. Then this sample estimate of $\sigma^2_{d\text{-bar}}$ can be used to test the null hypothesis that δ-bar $= 0$ with any d-bar, and to form a CI for δ-bar. The main effect of B can be tested in the same manner.

When interaction is of interest, the research question is: *Are the differences due to Factor A the same at all levels of B?* This can be addressed by testing the null hypothesis that $\delta_1 = \delta_2$, or H_0: $\delta_1 - \delta_2 = 0$. Obviously, the unbiased sample estimate of $\delta_1 - \delta_2$ is $d_1 - d_2$ with a sampling variance $\sigma^2_{d_1 - d_2}$, which can be estimated by $s^2_{d_1 - d_2} = (s^2_{d_1} + s^2_{d_2})$. Therefore the null hypothesis can be tested with the variance of $d_1 - d_2$ estimated from the sample, and the CI for $\delta_1 - \delta_2$ can be formed.

Supposed that in an altered version of the study of psychological impairment from alcoholism, the researcher is interested whether alcoholism has an effect on participants' performance on the psychological test independent of gender, and whether alcoholism affects males' and females' performance differently. The first question is a question of the *main-effect* of alcoholism, and the latter is a question of the *interaction* of gender and alcoholism. Suppose that in addition to the data presented in Table 25.3, 25 male alcoholics and 25 male nonalcoholics are also given the same performance test.

To test the main-effect of alcoholism, a dominance analysis is performed for males by comparing male alcoholics and male nonalcoholics, and a similar d analysis is performed for females. As seen, for the simulated data, d_f, which shows the tendency for female alcoholics to take a longer time to complete the performance test than female nonalcoholics, is .389. The sample estimate of the variance of d_f is $s^2_{d_f} = (.154)^2 = .0237$. Analysis for male participants (data not shown) yields $d_m = .425$ and $s^2_{d_m} = .0328$. Then, d-bar $= (.389 + .425)/2 = .407$, and $s^2_{d\text{-bar}} = (.0237 + .0328)/4 = .0141$. The CI for δ-bar can be obtained by inserting these quantities into Equation 25.14. Carrying out the calculation, we found the CI for δ-bar to be $(.126, .674)$, which does not contain zero. Therefore, the H_0: δ-bar $= 0$ should be rejected. The conclusion is that male and female alcoholics tend to be slower in completing the performance test than are male and female nonalcoholics.

To answer the question of whether there is a gender difference in the effect of alcoholism on performance, the null hypothesis $\delta_m - \delta_f = 0$ is tested. Here, $d_m - d_f = (.425 - .389) = .036$, $s^2_{d_1 - d_2} = (.0237 + .0328) = .0565$. Inserting these quantities into Equation 25.70 gives a CI for $\delta_m - \delta_f$ as $(-.075, .147)$. Because the CI contains zero, the null hypothesis is not rejected, and it is concluded that a gender difference in the effect of alcoholism on subjects' performance is not found.

Extension to Multiple Dependent Variables

When the analysis involves multiple correlated dependent variables, MANOVA is traditionally performed. The d analysis can be extended to this situation and an overall conclusion can be drawn, although the predicted direction of differences on all the dependent variables must be determined in advance on a theoretical or practical basis. Let u be the number of variables on which two groups are compared. An overall null hypothesis states that the sum of the δs is zero: That is to say, H_0: $\sum \delta_u = 0$. To test this null hypothesis, we need to obtain an estimate of the variance of $\sum d_u$, var$(\sum d_u)$, and then we can use $\sum d_u / \text{var}(\sum d_u)^{1/2}$ as a z test. Like any other sum, the variance of $\sum d_u$ can be expressed as

$$\text{var}\left(\sum d_u\right) = \sum \text{var}(d_u) + \sum \sum \text{cov}(d_u, d_v), \quad (25.71)$$

where u and v represent the dependent variables. To estimate the covariance term, the expression for the variance of d can be generalized:

$$\text{cov}(d_u, d_v)$$
$$= \frac{(m-1)\text{cov}(d_{i.u}, d_{i.v}) + (n-1)\text{cov}(d_{.ju}, d_{.jv}) + \text{cov}(d_{iju}, d_{ijv})}{mn}$$
$$(25.72)$$

The quantities in this expression can be estimated by substituting sums of squares of products of d-hat for their sums of squares in Equation 25.66 or (preferably) Equation 25.67. When several ds are summed, the complications involved in constructing the asymmetric CI that are used for small-sample ds are unlikely to be important. Therefore, the CI for $\sum \delta_u$ can be constructed in the traditional way.

Robustness and Power Relative to t

Feng and Cliff (1995) performed simulations to evaluate the distributional behavior of d under various circumstances, and compared d with the t test with Welch's adjusted degrees of freedom (t_w). Their results are generally favorable to d, which was found to behave well in terms of size, power, and coverage of the CI for δ in most cases. But the CI coverage can be lower than the nominal .95 when δ is high, especially when a high δ is paired with small sample size. Comparing the dominance analysis with mean comparison, d and t_w both behave well for normal data, although t_w showed slight superiority. For skewed data and for data that are bounded at one or both sides, d behaves well in almost all cases, but t_w showed empirical size that is higher than the nominal level, and CI coverage that is lower than the nominal level, in several cases. Because empirical data often are nonnormal, have heterogeneous variances, or both, d analysis seems preferable as the method of choice.

DOMINANCE ANALYSIS FOR CORRELATED DATA

Paired Data d Analysis

This section discusses the application of d to correlated data (e.g., repeated measures or dependent groups), as described by Cliff (1993, 1996a, 1996b). For paired observations, δ can be used to measure the probability that a score from one occasion is higher than a score from another occasion, just as in the independent groups context. With the dominance variable d_{ih} defined as $\text{sign}(x_i - x_h)$, where x_i represents any observation on the first occasion, x_h in the second, δ can be defined as $E(d_{ih})$. For n pairs of observations, δ can be estimated by $d = \sum\sum d_{ih}/n^2$. In other words, this definition of δ combines information about within-pair changes with information about between-pair changes. The calculation of d involves comparison of each of the scores on one occasion to each of the scores on the other occasion. In practice, the probability that an individual changes in a certain direction could be different from the probability that a random score from the first occasion is higher than a random score from the second. Therefore, for paired observations, it is necessary to distinguish the within-pair (or within-subject) difference from the between-pair (or between-subject) difference. Cliff (1996b) defined a δ_w reflecting the probability that individuals change in a certain direction as:

$$\delta_w = E(d_{ii}). \qquad (25.73)$$

Here, the subscript, ii, indicates that the ith subject's score from the first occasion is compared to the same subject's score from the second occasion. The unbiased sample estimate of δ_w is the average within-pair dominance:

$$d_w = \sum \frac{d_{ii}}{n}. \qquad (25.74)$$

It is the difference between the proportion of individuals who change in one direction and the proportion that change in the opposite direction. When there are no ties in the paired observations, d_w would be equivalent to the Friedman (1937) statistic.

Separately, δ which is a measure of the extent to which the overall distribution has moved, except for the self-comparisons, is estimated by d_b, the average between-pair dominance. In the repeated measure case, d_b is the proportion that individual scores on one occasion are higher than scores of *other* individuals on the *other* occasion, minus the

proportion of the reverse:

$$d_b = \frac{\displaystyle\sum_{i \neq h}\sum d_{ih}}{n(n-1)}. \qquad (25.75)$$

That is to say, d_b is a U statistic with expectation δ^2. A d that was defined to include the self-comparisons has expectation $[\delta_w + (n-1)\delta]/n$.

Inferences about Dependent Groups δ

The sampling distributions of d_b and d_w are asymptotically normal (because they are average scores), with means δ and δ_w, and sampling variances $\sigma_{d_b}^2$ and $\sigma_{d_w}^2$, respectively. Similar to the case of deriving the variances of t, the approach to deriving the variances of d_b and d_w is based on the dominance variables d_{ij}. By taking the expectation of d_b^2, Cliff (1993) showed that

$$\sigma_{d_b}^2 = \\ \frac{\sigma_{d_{ih}}^2 + \text{cov}(d_{ih}, d_{hi}) + (n-2)\left[\sigma_{d_i.}^2 + \sigma_{d_{.i}}^2 + 2\,\text{cov}(d_{i.}, d_{.i})\right]}{n(n-1)}. \qquad (25.76)$$

In the Equation 25.76, $d_{i.}$ and $d_{.i}$ both have i as the subscript because they refer to the same set of subjects. Given the way the dominance variable d_{ih} has been defined, $d_{i.}$ represents the proportion of pretest scores that are lower than subject i's posttest scores, and $d_{.i}$ represents the proportion of posttest scores that are higher than subject i's pretest scores. When pre- and posttest scores are positively correlated with each other, which is usually the case in practice, the covariance of $d_{i.}$ and $d_{.i}$ is negative. Thus, unlike in the case of paired t test, the last term of Equation 25.76 is positive. The variance of d_w is

$$\sigma_{d_w}^2 = \sigma_{d_{ii}}^2/n, \qquad (25.77)$$

where $\sigma_{d_{ii}}^2 = E(d_{ii} - \delta_w)^2$. When there are no ties, $\sigma_{d_{ii}}^2 = 1 - \delta_w^2$. Let p be the probability of a randomly selected subject changing in one direction without ties of pre- and posttest scores. Then $1 - \delta_w^2 = 4p(1-p)$.

Similar to the variance of d in the independent groups case, and to that of t, unbiased estimates of $\sigma_{d_b}^2$ and $\sigma_{d_w}^2$ can be obtained based on the sample. Defining $d_{i.}^* = d_{i.} - d_b$, $d_{.i}^* = d_{.i} - d_b$, and $d_{ih}^* = d_{ih} - d_b$, it is shown that an unbiased estimate of $\sigma_{d_b}^2$ is

$$s_{d_b}^2 = \\ \frac{(n-1)^2\left(\sum d_{i.}^{*2} + \sum d_{.i}^{*2} + 2\sum d_{i.}^* d_{.i}^*\right) - \sum\sum d_{ih}^{*2} - \sum\sum d_{ih}^* d_{hi}^*}{n(n-1)(n-2)(n-3)} \qquad (25.78)$$

The unbiased estimate of $\sigma_{d_w}^2$ is derived in a similar way:

$$s_{d_w}^2 = \frac{\sum(d_{ii} - d_w)^2}{(n - 1)}. \tag{25.79}$$

Then, $s_{d_b}^2$ can be used to form the CI for δ as $(d_b - z_{\alpha/2}s_{d_b}, d_b + z_{\alpha/2}s_{d_b})$, and a hypothesis that $\delta = \delta_0$ can be tested by using $(d_b - \delta_0)/s_{d_b}$ as a standard normal deviate. An asymmetric CI for δ was suggested earlier to compensate for the positive correlation between independent d and its variance in small samples. A Monte Carlo study found that when a similar asymmetric adjustment was applied to correlated data, the CI coverage of d_b tended to be conservative, resulting in reduced power. Therefore, it is suggested that the ordinary $d_b \pm z_{\alpha/2}s_{d_b}$ should be used in constructing a CI for δ in the paired data case. Similarly, a CI for δ_w can be formed, and $H_0: \delta_w = \delta_0$ can be tested, in the traditional way.

In addition to tests of within-pair changes and between-pair changes separately, the dominance analysis provides a test of the combined effect. That is, a null hypothesis that $\delta + \delta_w = \delta_0$ can be tested. Because the two statistics d_w and d_b are not independent, the test of the combined effect involves their covariance $\text{cov}(d_w, d_b)$. The variance of the sum of the two dominance variables d_w and d_b is

$$\text{var}(d_w + d_b) = \sigma_{d_w}^2 + \sigma_{d_b}^2 + 2\,\text{cov}(d_w, d_b). \tag{25.80}$$

It can be shown that the covariance of d_w and d_b is

$$\text{cov}(d_w, d_b) = [\text{cov}(d_{ii}, d_{i.}) + \text{cov}(d_{ii}, d_{.i})]/n, \tag{25.81}$$

and the unbiased estimate of this covariance is

$$\text{Est}[\text{cov}(d_w, d_b)]$$

$$= \frac{\sum_i \left(\sum_h d_{ih} + \sum_j d_{hi}\right) d_{ii} - 2n(n-1)d_b d_w}{n(n-1)(n-2)} \tag{25.82}$$

Substituting the unbiased sample estimates of variances and the covariance for their corresponding terms in Equation 25.80, we can form a CI for the sum $\delta + \delta_w$, and test the null hypothesis about $\delta + \delta_w$.

The d method for paired data is closely related to the widely applied Wilcoxon's signed rank test (WSR), but has some additional advantages. The WSR rank-based inference procedure was originally proposed as a one-sample test of the median, and has been used to test a null hypothesis of random changes. However, because it is applied to the differences on the dependent variable, conclusions based on the WSR test are not invariant under monotonic transformation of the dependent variable. When WSR is used with raw data that are transformed into ranks, the rank transform also makes substantive interpretation difficult. The d statistic, on the other hand, can be used on the raw scores, and thus a rank transformation is not necessary. The d statistic also lends itself to parameter estimations, and does not rely on the identical distribution assumption.

Example of Delta for Paired Groups

The dominance analysis for correlated data can be illustrated by an artificial example of repeated measures. Suppose that in a hypothetical experiment, the experimenter is interested in whether intentional study and incidental study differ in effectiveness for subsequent remembering. First, the experimenter presents a list of 40 common words to 20 participants and instructs them to rate each word as pleasant, neutral, or unpleasant. Then the participants are asked to recall as many words as they can in any order (*incidental remembering*). Three days later, the same 20 participants are presented another list of 40 common words of the same complexity and popularity, but are instructed to study each word carefully for a subsequent memory test (*intentional remembering*). On both occasions, the dependent measure is the number of words each participant can recall correctly. Simulated data are presented in the upper left part of Table 25.4, sorted by incidental remembering scores. The upper right part of Table 25.4 shows the dominance diagram generated based on these artificial data. Here, a + indicates that a subject recalls more words correctly with intentional study, a − indicates the opposite, and a 0 indicates a tie.

Again, to compare with traditional methods, a paired t test was performed for the same data. The d statistics and the inferences about $\delta + \delta_w$ of the dominance analysis for this artificial example are summarized in the second part of Table 25.4. In this example, d_w is .750 with a standard error of .143, indicating that comparing the same participants under two experimental conditions, there is a strong tendency for the subjects to recall more words with intentional study. This d_w is highly significant; the z score for d_w is 5.25, and the .95 CI for δ_w is .470 to 1.0. The tendency of the movement of the whole group is reflected by d_b, which is .329 with a standard error of .123. The d_b shows that compared with each other, participants tend to recall more words under the intentional remembering condition. The between-subject change is significant with a z score 2.67, leading to CI for δ of .088 to .570. The sum of d_w and d_b, reflecting the combined effect of intentional study on remembering is 1.079. These results suggest that null hypotheses $\delta = 0$, $\delta_w = 0$, and $\delta + \delta_w = 0$ all should be rejected. It is significant with a z score of 4.37. For comparison, the paired t test of correlated means yields a significant t score for mean difference ($t = 3.09$, $df = 19$).

TABLE 25.4 An Example of d Analysis for Repeated Measures Data

Subject	Raw Scores Incidental	Raw Scores Intentional	Dominance Diagram
1	2	4	+ ------------------
2	6	11	+ + +++++++++++00-----
3	6	8	++ + ++00-------------
4	7	9	+++ + +++000---------
5	7	10	++++ + +++++000-------
6	8	11	+++++ + +++++++00-----
7	8	11	++++++ + ++++++00-----
8	9	5	+------ - ------------
9	9	14	++++++++ + ++++++++0--
10	9	12	+++++++++ + +++++0----
11	10	13	++++++++++ + +++++0---
12	10	10	++++++++++0 0 0-------
13	10	14	+++++++++++ + ++++0--
14	11	16	++++++++++++ + +++++0
15	11	14	+++++++++++++ + ++0--
16	12	13	++++++++++++++ + 0---
17	13	15	+++++++++++++++ + +0-
18	14	15	++++++++++++++++ + 0-
19	15	16	+++++++++++++++++ + 0
20	16	10	++++++++++000------ -

Inferences about δ_w

d_w	.750
s_{d_w}	.143
.95 confidence interval	(.470, 1.0)
z	5.25

Inferences about δ

d_b	.329
s_{d_b}	.123
.95 confidence interval	(.088, .570)
z	2.67

Components of $s^2_{d_b}$

$s^2_{d_{i\cdot}}$	.332
$s^2_{d_{\cdot j}}$	.323
$cov(d_{i\cdot}, d_{\cdot j})$	−.184
$s^2_{d_{ij}}$	.816
$cov(d_{ih}, d_{hi})$	−.282

Combined inferences

$d_w + d_b$	1.079
$cov(d_w, d_b)$	.013
$s(d_w + d_b)$	.247
z	4.37

Mean comparisons

Mean difference	1.90
s_{diff}	2.751
SE of mean difference	.615
T	3.09
Df	19

Extensions of Paired d Analysis

Extension to Multiple Groups With Repeated Measures

Cliff (1996b) suggested that the paired d analysis can be extended beyond the simple case of one-sample paired observations, including many situations usually analyzed by repeated measures ANOVA. For instance, it may be used for two or

more groups with repeated measures, which is typically analyzed by a mixed ANOVA. Suppose two independent groups are measured on X at two occasions (e.g., pre- and posttest), and the investigator is interested in whether there is a group difference in how subjects change from pretest to posttest—that is, whether the δs for the two groups are the same. Clearly, for each group, δ_w, δ, $(\delta_w + \delta)$, and the variances of d_w and d_b can be estimated from its sample. For two independent groups, the variance of the difference of the two ds, whether two d_ws or two d_bs, or two sums of d_w and d_b, is simply the sum of the variances of the two ds:

$$s^2_{d_1-d_2} = s^2_{d_1} + s^2_{d_2}, \tag{25.83}$$

where the subscripts 1 and 2 represent the group membership. Hence the CI for $\delta_1 - \delta_2$ can be found by $(d_1 - d_2) \pm z_{\alpha/2}(s^2_{d_1} + s^2_{d_2})^{1/2}$, and null hypotheses H_0: $\delta_1 - \delta_2 = 0$, H_0: $\delta_{w1} - \delta_{w2} = 0$, and H_0: $(\delta_1 + \delta_{w1}) - (\delta_2 + \delta_{w2}) = 0$ can be tested.

Suppose that in an altered version of the hypothetical experiment comparing the effectiveness of intentional and incidental study on subsequent remembering, an additional factor, the complexity of the words is examined. The design of the experiment is the same as described earlier, except that two groups of participants are tested. One group is presented with a list of 40 words of high complexity, and the other group is presented with a list of 40 words of low complexity. Based on simulated data, the dominance analysis for the group that is presented with simple words yields $d_{w_1} = .750$, $s_{dw_1} = .143$, $d_{b_1} = .329$, $s_{db_1} = .123$, $d_{w_1} + d_{b_1} = 1.079$, and $s_{dw_1+db_1} = .247$; the analysis for the group presented with highly complex words yields $d_{w_2} = .326$, $s_{dw_2} = .105$, $d_{b_2} = .227$, $s_{db_2} = .098$, $d_{w_2} + d_{b_2} = .653$, and $s_{dw_2+db_2} = .215$. Then, the *main-effect* of type of study can be tested by averaging ds across different levels of word complexity. For within-subject comparisons, d_w-bar $= (.750 + .326)/2 = .538$, $s^2_{d_w\text{-bar}} = [(.143)^2 + (.105)^2]/4 = .0079$, $s_{d_w\text{-bar}} = .089$, and z score for d_w-bar is 6.04. The CI for δ_w-bar formed in the traditional way, d_w-bar $\pm z_{\alpha/2}s_{d_w\text{-bar}}$, is .364 to .712, not containing zero. For between-subject comparisons, d_b-bar $= (.329 + .227)/2 = .278$, $s^2_{d_b\text{-bar}} = [(.123)^2 + (.098)^2]/4 = .0062$, and $s_{d_b\text{-bar}} = .079$. Thus, z score for d_b-bar is 3.52, and the CI for δ-bar is .123 to .433, which does not contain zero. For the combined effect, $[(d_{w_1} + d_{b_1}) + (d_{w_2} + d_{b_2})]/2 = .816$, standard error of the averaged sum of d_w and d_b is $\{[(.143)^2 + (.105)^2]/4\}^{1/2} = .164$, and the z score for this averaged summed d is 4.98, significant at the .05 level. Therefore, the hypotheses that δ_w-bar $= 0$, δ-bar $= 0$, and δ_w-bar $+ \delta$-bar $= 0$, all should be rejected. The conclusion is that averaging across two levels of word complexity, individuals tend to recall more words with intentional study.

When the interaction of word complexity and type of study is of interest, the difference of the ds obtained based on two groups should be calculated, and inferences about the difference of ds should be made. For instance, an interaction of word complexity and type of study for within-subject comparison can be examined by testing the null hypothesis $\delta_{w_1} - \delta_{w_2} = 0$. For this example, $d_{w_1} - d_{w_2} = (.750 - .326) = .424$, $s^2_{dw_1 - dw_2} = (.143)^2 + (.105)^2 = .0315$, $s_{dw_1 - dw_2} = .177$, leading to a CI for $\delta_{w_1} - \delta_{w_2}$ as $(.077, .771)$. Because the CI does not contain zero, the null hypothesis is rejected, and it is concluded that there is a difference in the effect of type of study on recall due to word complexity. Specifically, intentional study results in better subsequent recall, and this is particularly true with recall of complex words. Tests of interaction for between-subject comparisons, or for the combined effect, can be obtained in the same manner.

It should be noted that when there are more then two groups, an omnibus test is not available to test the null hypothesis that all δs are equal. But multiple pairwise comparisons can be made, which may be more closely related to the typical research question about group differences over time.

Extension to Multiple Repeated Measures

Often of interest is whether scores on a certain measure are expected to increase or decrease systematically over time. When there are multiple repeated measures (e.g., a pretest, a posttest, and one or more follow-ups), one may compute a d_w and a d_b between each pair of measurements, and make inferences about each δ and δ_w. The ordinary α should be used if there is a separate interest in each planned comparison. Otherwise, the Bonferroni procedure can be used to control the familywise Type I errors.

Other, perhaps more interesting research questions can be investigated by calculating sums, averages, or differences in ds (whether d_ws or d_bs). For example, when a single group is measured on variable X on three occasions, there are three pairwise ds, d_{12}, d_{23}, and d_{13}, where the pairs of subscripts refer to conditions being compared. Then the amount of overall trend can be represented by $d_{12} + d_{23}$. The question of whether trends are consistent, as opposed to leveling off or even reversing, can be represented by $d_{12} - d_{23}$. The same reasoning can be applied when the various conditions reflect different levels of some ordinal variable. In either case, one must be careful to state conclusions in terms of δs rather than *quantitative* differences.

It is conceptually simple to make inferences about sums or averages or differences of δs. As discussed earlier, the variance of the sums (equivalently, averages) or difference of ds

can be expressed as

$$\text{var}\left(\sum d_u\right) = \sum \text{var}(d_u) \pm \sum \sum \text{cov}(d_u, d_v). \quad (25.84)$$

Here, the subscripts u and v refer to pairs of occasions. We already discussed how to obtain an unbiased estimate of d_u in the two-times-of-measurement context. Again, as seen earlier, the expression for the variance of d can be generalized to estimate the covariance of two ds:

$$\text{cov}(d_u, d_v) =$$

$$\frac{\text{cov}(d_{ihu}, d_{ihv}) + \text{cov}(d_{ihu}, d_{hiv}) + (n-2)\,\text{cov}[(d_{i.u} + d_{.iu}), (d_{i.v} + d_{.iv})]}{n(n-1)}$$

$$(25.85)$$

The unbiased sample estimate of $\text{cov}(d_u, d_v)$ is

$$s_{d_u, d_{bv}} = \frac{(n-1)\left[\sum(d^*_{i.u} + d^*_{.iu})(d^*_{i.v} + d^*_{.iv})\right]}{n(n-2)(n-3)}$$

$$-\frac{\sum\sum d^*_{ihu}d^*_{ihv} + \sum\sum d^*_{ihu}d^*_{hiv}}{n(n-1)(n-2)(n-3)}, \quad (25.86)$$

where subscripted d^*s represent the deviation of that quantity from the corresponding mean, which here is d_u or d_v.

The same strategy can be applied to extend the use of d in more complex research designs, including those traditionally analyzed by factorial or mixed ANOVA. As seen earlier, the main-effect of a factor can be expressed by the average of the ds for this factor at all levels of other factor (or factors). An interaction can be tested by taking the difference of two ds. In other words, there are corresponding d analyses that can be applied to answer various research questions that the investigator has in mind.

CONCLUSION

In this chapter, we have tried to make the case that many research questions in the social sciences can best be answered by use of ordinal methods. Ordinal methods have the benefit that they can be more statistically robust than traditional methods, and the conclusions of ordinal methods do not change under monotonic transformations of the data.

The methods presented should be viewed as valuable in their own right, not simply as methods to be used in place of the traditional ones. They should be regarded as parametric in that parameters of populations are estimated with the sample data. Furthermore, the estimation procedures are not simply convenient devices conditional on unrealistic population assumptions. Standard errors can be estimated from the data and used as the basis for inferences about the parameters in question.

When only the ordinal aspects of data are considered, we have statistical methods in which the statistical and verbal conclusions are very close. Many parametric models are now available for testing highly specific parametric hypotheses. If a researcher has a carefully planned hypothesis that fits into the framework of a highly parametric model, then he or she should use such a model. However, we very often have more loosely formulated hypotheses and use the highly parametric models as a default. There usually is some sort of Procrustean translation of the original research ideas into questions that fit with the sophisticated models. The problem is that an analysis based on a highly parametric model may not provide answers that are fitting for the researcher's original questions. We have given a number of reasons that ordinal statistics provide results that are consistent with common types of research questions. The added benefit is that the conclusions and inferences from the ordinal methods are valid under a wide variety of conditions. Furthermore, the results are unchanged under monotonic transformations: They generalize to scores of latent variables as well as observed ones.

There are SPSS macros and Fortran programs available for a number of the methods described in this chapter. These may be accessed through the website of J. D. Long, http://education.umn.edu/edpsych/Faculty/long.html.

APPENDIX: COMPUTING THE ESTIMATED VARIANCE OF t_a

Here we illustrate the computation of Est[var(t_a)] for the raw data in Table 25.1. The last section of Table 25.1 shows the calculation of the t_{ihxy}, t_{ihxy}^2, and t_a that are required to compute Equations 25.31 and 25.32, and finally, the estimated variance of Equation 25.30. Using the information from Table 25.1, Equation 25.32 is computed as

$$s_{t_{ihxy}}^2 = \frac{2\sum\sum_{i>h} t_{ihxy}^2 - n(n-1)t_a^2}{[n(n-1)] - 1}$$

$$= \frac{2(9) - 5(4)(-.3^2)}{5(4) - 1} = .8526. \quad \text{(A25.1)}$$

The $t_{i.xy}$ in Equation 25.31 are defined by summing the t_{ihxy} in a row of the $(n \times n)$ symmetric matrix. For the t_{ihxy} in Table 25.1, we have

$$\mathbf{T}_{xy} = i \begin{bmatrix} 0 & -1 & -1 & -1 & -1 \\ -1 & 0 & +1 & +1 & +1 \\ -1 & +1 & 0 & -1 & -1 \\ -1 & +1 & -1 & 0 & 0 \\ -1 & +1 & -1 & 0 & 0 \end{bmatrix}^h, \quad \text{(A25.2)}$$

For each row (i) of the above matrix, we sum over columns (h) and divide by $(n-1)$ yielding

$$t_{i.xy}: (-4/4), (2/4), (-2/4), (-1/4), (-1/4), \quad \text{(A25.3)}$$

or

$$t_{i.xy}: -1, .5, -.5, -.25, -.25. \quad \text{(A25.4)}$$

Once we have the $t_{i.xy}$ we can compute Equation 25.31,

$$s_{t_{i.xy}}^2 = \frac{\sum_i (t_{i.xy} - t_a)^2}{(n-1)}$$

$$= \frac{(-1 - (.3))^2 + \cdots + (-.25 - (.3))^2}{4}$$

$$= \frac{1.175}{4} = .2938. \quad \text{(A25.5)}$$

Now we are able to substitute all the relevant results into Equation 25.30. Doing so, we have the consistent estimate of the variance of t_a,

$$\text{Est}[\text{var}(t_a)] = \frac{4(n-2)s_{t_{i.xy}}^2 + 2s_{t_{ihxy}}^2}{n(n-1)}$$

$$= \frac{4(3)(.2938) + 2(.8526)}{5(4)} = \frac{5.2308}{20} = .2615. \quad \text{(A25.6)}$$

(This is an unusually high value even for such a small sample.)

REFERENCES

Agresti, A. (1984). *Analysis of ordinal categorical data*. New York: Wiley.

Barnard, G. (1984). Comparing the means of two independent samples. *Applied Statistics, 33,* 266–271.

Birnbaum, Z. W. (1956). On a use of the Mann-Whitney statistic. In J. Neyman (Ed.), *Proceedings of the Third Berkeley Symposium on Mathematical Statistics* (pp. 13–17). Berkeley CA: University of California Press.

Birkes, D., & Dodge, Y. (1993). *Alternative methods of regression*. New York: Wiley.

Bonett, D., & Wright, T. (2000). Sample size requirements for estimating Pearson, Kendall, and Spearman correlations. *Psychometrika, 65*(1), 23–28.

Caruso, J., & Cliff, N. (1997). Empirical size, coverage, and power of confidence intervals for Spearman's rho. *Educational and Psychological Measurement, 57,* 637–654.

Cliff, N. (1973). Scaling. *Annual Review of Psychology, 24,* 473–506.

Cliff, N. (1987). *Analyzing multivariate data.* New York: Harcourt Brace Javanovich.

Cliff, N. (1991). Ordinal methods in the study of change. In L. M. Collins & J. Horn (Eds.), *Best methods for the analysis of change* (pp. 34–46). Washington, DC: American Psychological Association.

Cliff, N. (1992). Abstract measurement theory and the revolution that never happened. *Psychological Science, 3*(3), 186–190.

Cliff, N. (1993). Dominance statistics: Ordinal analyses to answer ordinal questions. *Psychological Bulletin, 114,* 494–509.

Cliff, N. (1994). Predicting ordinal relations. *British Journal of Mathematical and Statistical Psychology, 47,* 127–150.

Cliff, N. (1996a). Answering ordinal questions with ordinal data using ordinal statistics. *Multivariate Behavioral Research, 31*(3), 331–350.

Cliff, N. (1996b). *Ordinal methods for behavioral data analysis.* Mahwah, NJ: Erlbaum.

Cliff, N., & Charlin, V. (1991). Variances and covariances of Kendall's tau and their estimation. *Multivariate Behavioral Research, 26,* 693–707.

Cohen, J. (1994). The earth is round (p < .05). *American Psychologist, 49,* 997–1003.

Cressie, N. A. C., & Whitford, H. J. (1986). How to use the two sample t-test. *Biometric Journal, 28,* 131–148.

Daniels, H., & Kendall, M. (1947). The significance of rank correlation where parental correlation exits. *Biometrika, 34,* 197–208.

Embretson, S. (1996). Item response theory models and spurious interaction effects in multiple group comparisons. *Applied Psychological Measurement, 20,* 201–212.

Embretson, S., & Hershberger, S. (1999). Summary and future of psychometric method in testing. In S. Embretson & S. Hershberger (Eds.), *The new rules of measurement* (pp. 243–247). Mahwah, NJ: Erlbaum.

Emerson, J. D., & Stoto, M. A. (1983). Transforming data. In D. C. Hoaglin, F. Mostreller, & J. W. Tukey (Eds.), *Understanding robust and exploratory data analysis* (pp. 97–128). New York: Wiley.

Feng, D., & Cliff, N. (1995). *Comparisons of power and size of d and t statistics.* Unpublished manuscript, University of Southern California.

Fischer, G. H. (1995). Derivations of the Rasch model. In G. H. Fischer & I. W. Molenaar (Eds.), *Rasch models: Foundations, recent developments, and applications* (pp. 57–78). New York: Springer-Verlag.

Friedman, M. (1937). The use of ranks to avoid the assumption of normality in the analysis of variance. *Journal of the American Statistical Association, 32,* 675–701.

Games, P. A. (1984). Data transformation, power, and skew: A rebuttal to Levine and Dunlap. *Psychological Bulletin, 95,* 345–347.

Goodman, L., & Kruskal, W. (1959). Measure of association for cross-classification. *Journal of the American Statistical Association, 49,* 732–804.

Gronow, D. G. C. (1953). Nonnormality in two sample t-tests. *Biometrika, 40,* 222–225.

Hambleton, R. (1989). Principles and selected applications of item response theory. In R. Linn (Ed.), *Educational measurement* (3rd ed., pp. 147–200). New York: American Council On Education/Macmillan.

Hettmansperger, T. P. (1984). *Statistical inferences based on ranks.* New York: Wiley.

Howell, D. (1997). *Statistical methods for psychology* (4th ed., chap. 15). Belmont, CA: Wadsworth.

Hsu, T. C., & Feldt, L. S. (1969). The effect of limitations on the number of criterion score values on the significance level of the F-test. *American Educational Research Journal, 6,* 515–527.

Kendall, M. G. (1970). *Rank correlation methods* (4th ed.). London: Charles Griffin.

Kendall, M. G., & Gibbons, J. D. (1990). *Rank correlation methods* (5th ed.). New York: Oxford University Press.

Krantz, D. H., Luce, R. D., Suppes, P., & Tversky, A. (1971). *Foundations of measurement: Vol. 1. Additive and polynomial representations.* New York: Academic Press.

Long, J. D. (1999). A confidence interval for ordinal multiple regression weights. *Psychological Methods, 4,* 315–330.

Long, J. D. (2001). *Omnibus hypothesis testing in ordinal multiple regression.* Manuscript submitted for publication.

Long, J. D., & Cliff, N. (1997). Confidence intervals for Kendall's tau. *British Journal of Mathematical and Statistical Psychology, 50,* 31–41.

Long, J. D., & Cliff, N. (2001). *The performance of Pearson's correlation under non-normality.* Unpublished manuscript, Department of Educational Psychology, University of Minnesota, Twin Cities.

Luce, R., & Tukey, J. (1964). Simultaneous conjoint measurement: A new type of fundamental measurement. *Journal of Mathematical Psychology, 1,* 1–27.

Mann, H. B., & Whitney, D. R. (1947). On a test of whether one of two random variables is stochastically larger than the other. *Annals of Mathematical Statistics, 18,* 50–60.

McGraw, K. O., & Wong, S. P. (1992). A common language effect size statistic. *Psychological Bulletin, 111,* 361–365.

McKean, J. W., & Sheather, S. J. (1991). Small sample properties of robust analyses of linear models based on R-estimates: A survey. In W. Stahel & S. Weisberg (eds.), *Directions in Robust Statistics and Diagnostics, Part II* (pp. 1–19). New York: Springer-Verlag.

Mee, R. W. (1990). Confidence intervals for probabilities and tolerance regions based on a generalization of the Mann Whitney statistics, *Journal of the American Statistical Association, 85,* 793–800.

Meehl, P. E. (1997). The problem is epistemoloty, not statistics: replace significance tests by confidence intervals and quantify accuracy of risky numerical predictions. In L. L. Harlow, S. A. Muliak, & J. H. Steiger (Eds.) *What If There Were No Significance Tests?* Hillsdale, NJ: Lawrence Erlbaum.

Micceri, T. (1989). The unicorn, the normal curve, and other improbable creatures. *Psychological Bulletin, 105,* 156–166.

Mosteller, F., & Tukey, J. (1977). *Data Analysis and Regression* (Ch. 13). Menlo Park, CA: Addison-Wesley.

Nanna, M. J., & Sawilowsky, S. S. (1998). Analysis of Likert scale data in disability and medical rehabilitation research. *Psychological Methods, 3,* 55–67.

Nelson, P., & Yang, S. (1988). Some properties of Kendall's partial rank correlation coefficient. *Statistics & Probability Letters, 6,* 147–150.

Nygren, T. E. (1986). A two-stage algorithm for assessing violations of additivity via axiomatic and numerical conjoint analysis. *Psychometrika, 51,* 483–491.

Pearson, E. S., and Please, N. W. (1975). Relation between the shape of population distribution and the robustness of four simple statistics. *Biometrika, 62,* 223–241.

Ramsey, P. H. (1980). Exact Type I error rates for robustness of Student's test with unequal variances. *Journal of the Educational Statistics, 5,* 337–349.

Ramsey, P. H. (1989). Critical values for the Spearman rank correlation. *Journal of Educational Statistics, 14,* 245–253.

Rasch, G. (1980). *Probabilistic models for some intelligence and attainment tests.* Chicago: University of Chicago Press.

Randles, R. H., & Wolfe, D. A. (1979). *Introduction to the theory of nonparametric statistics.* New York: Wiley.

Sawilowsky, S. S., & Blair, R. C. (1992). A more realistic look at the robustness and Type II error properties of the *t* test to departures from population normality. *Psychological Bulletin, 111,* 352–360.

Stevens, S. S. (1951). Mathematics, measurement, and psychophysics. In S. S. Stevens (Ed.), *Handbook of experimental psychology* (pp. 1–49). New York: Wiley.

Tan, W. Y. (1982). Sampling distribution and robustness of t, F and variance ratio of two samples and ANOVA models with respect to departure from normality. *Communications in Statistics: Theory and Computation, 11,* 2485–2511.

Wilkinson, L. & the Task Force on Statistical Inference. (1999). Statistical methods in psychology journals: Guidelines and explanations. *American Psychologist, 54*(8), 594–604.

Wilcox, R. R. (1990). Comparing the means of two independent groups. *Biometrical Journal, 32,* 771–780.

Wilcox, R. R. (1991). Why can methods for comparing means have relatively low power, and what can you do to correct the problem? *Current Directions in Psychological Science, 1,* 101–105.

Wilcox, R. R. (1992). Comparing the medians of dependent groups. *British Journal of Mathematical and Statistical Psychology, 45,* 151–162.

Wilcoxon, F. (1945). Individual comparisons by ranking methods. *Biometrics, 1,* 80–83.

Wright, B. (1999). Fundamental measurement for psychology. In S. Embertson & S. Hershberger (Eds.), *The new rules of measurement* (pp. 65–104). Mahwah, NJ: Erlbaum.

Yule, G. U. (1900). On the association of attributes in statistics. *Transactions of the Philosophical Society of London, Series A, 194,* 257–319.

Zimmerman, D. W., & Zumbo, B. D. (1993). The relative power of parametric and nonparametric statistical methods. In G. Keren & C. Lewis (Eds.), *A handbook for data analysis in the behavioral sciences: Methodological issues* (pp. 481–518). Hillsdale, NJ: Erlbaum.

CHAPTER 26

Latent Class and Latent Transition Analysis

STEPHANIE T. LANZA, BRIAN P. FLAHERTY, AND LINDA M. COLLINS

Often quantities of interest in psychology cannot be observed directly. These unobservable quantities are known as latent variables. In addition to being unobservable, latent variables tend to be complex, often multidimensional, constructs. Unlike height, which can be measured with a single assessment, depression or temperament cannot be adequately measured with only one questionnaire item. This complexity can be dealt with by using multiple items as indicators of the latent variable; this approach provides a more complete picture of the construct and allows estimation of measurement error. Examples of latent variables in the psychological literature include temperament, psychological diagnoses, attachment, health behaviors, and attitudes. The best that researchers can do to measure latent variables is to collect data on manifest indicators, knowing that the available indicators are imperfect measures of the latent variables. When several manifest indicators are used to assess an underlying latent variable, we have a basis for removing measurement error, leading to better measurement of the latent variable.

The fundamental premise of any latent variable model is that the covariation among manifest variables is explained by the latent variable. There are four latent variable frameworks that model the relationship between manifest variables and a latent variable. Figure 26.1 depicts this relationship for the four frameworks. Which framework is appropriate depends on whether the manifest variables and latent variable are considered to be continuous or categorical. In *factor analysis* or *covariance structure analysis,* observed variables, usually continuous, map onto continuous latent variables assumed to be normally distributed (Jöreskog & Sörbom, 1996). *Latent trait analysis* (Spiel, 1994) refers to discrete observed variables mapping onto a continuous latent variable. For example, a set of aptitude test items coded as correct or incorrect might be seen as indicators of the underlying latent trait, in this case ability. In *latent profile analysis,* continuous observed variables map onto a discrete latent variable. *Latent class analysis* (LCA) models the relationship between discrete observed variables and a discrete latent variable.

The present chapter focuses on this last framework, LCA. The first section introduces the concept of a latent class and then presents the mathematical model. This is followed by a discussion of parameter restrictions, model fit, and the

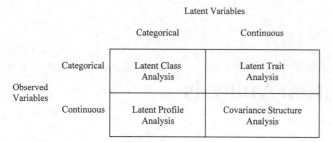

Figure 26.1 Latent variable frameworks.

measurement quality of categorical items. The second section demonstrates LCA through an examination of the prevalence of depression types in adolescents. This empirical example is meant to help clarify concepts presented in the first section and help the reader to understand the latent class model. In the third section we present longitudinal extensions of LCA. This section also contains an empirical example on adolescent depression types; in this example we extend the previous analysis to examine the stability and change in depression types over time. In the final section we turn our attention to several advanced topics in latent class models. Here several recent developments that further extend the latent class model are introduced.

LATENT CLASS ANALYSIS

The Concept of a Latent Class

Latent classes can be thought of as a classification system for groups of individuals when we are classifying individuals according to some construct that is not directly measurable. Suppose, for example, a researcher interested in the construct *temperament* hypothesizes that this construct is made up of qualitatively different categories. The researcher can measure several indicators of temperament, and then use latent class analysis to try to identify two or more temperamental types in which people might be classified. In the following discussion, several examples are presented in which latent class models have been applied in the study of psychological and behavioral phenomena. Note that for some constructs (such as temperament) an individual's latent class membership is generally expected to remain the same over time, whereas for other constructs (such as substance use), it is possible for individuals to move between latent classes over time.

Theory suggests that there are two main temperamental types of children: namely, inhibited and uninhibited, characterized by avoidance or approach to unfamiliar situations

(Kagan, 1989). Stern, Arcus, Kagan, Rubin, and Snidman (1995) used LCA to test this theory empirically, comparing a model with two temperamental types of children to models with three and four types. Infants in two cohorts of sample sizes 93 and 76 were measured on three categorical variables: motor activity, fret-cry, and fear. Two-, three-, and four-class models were fit for each cohort. For both cohorts, a two-class solution appeared to represent the data adequately, although the sample size may not have provided enough power to detect additional classes.

Latent class models have also been used to explore the onset of substance use behaviors during adolescence. Following Kandel's (1975) introduction of the concept of stages in substance use, Collins and colleagues (Collins, Graham, Rousculp, & Hansen, 1997; Hyatt & Collins, 2000) have explored this construct as a categorical latent variable. Using data from the Adolescent Alcohol Prevention Trial (Hansen & Graham, 1991), Collins et al. (1997) identified a stage-sequence of substance use made up of the following eight latent classes: no use; alcohol use; alcohol use with drunkenness; tobacco use; alcohol and tobacco use; alcohol use with drunkenness and advanced use; alcohol, tobacco, and advanced use; and alcohol use with drunkenness, tobacco use, and advanced use. This model specifies that adolescents can first move from the no use latent class to either the alcohol use or the tobacco use latent class, and then progress to latent classes characterized by more advanced substance use. Notice that not all possible combinations of substances are represented in this latent class model. For example, a latent class characterized by alcohol and marijuana use without tobacco use does not exist. The eight latent classes specified by this model were sufficient to represent the data. In this study, a relationship between heavy caffeine use during adolescence and substance use onset was established.

This approach has been applied to various educational studies, including an examination of the number of different classes of teaching style in the United Kingdom conducted by Aitkin, Anderson, and Hinde (1981). Teaching style was characterized by the presence or absence of 38 different teaching behaviors in 468 fourth-grade teachers. A latent class approach to modeling this type of data is appealing because it summarizes data from many different questionnaire items in a parsimonious way. Although only two teaching styles were originally predicted, formal and informal, evidence was found for a three-class model. The first class was a more formal style, in which the teachers were expected to stick to a firm timeline and restrict the students' behaviors. The data suggested that 48% of teachers had a formal style. The second class represented an informal teaching style, in which teachers tended to have less strict classroom organization,

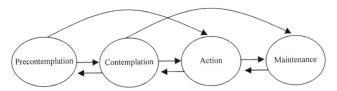

Figure 26.2 Stages of change construct from the transtheoretical model.

to integrate subjects, and to encourage individual work. This class encompassed 32% of teachers. The remaining 20% of teachers fell in the third latent class, a mixed teaching style, in which certain behavior restrictions were enforced as in the formal group, but grading and homework were similar to those of the informal group.

LCA has been used to apply the transtheoretical model of behavior change to various types of health behaviors, including smoking cessation (Martin, Velicer, & Fava, 1996), condom use (Evers, Harlow, Redding, & LaForge, 1998), and exercise (Gebhardt, Dusseldorp, & Maes, 1999). Velicer and colleagues used a latent class approach to test competing models of the stages of change in smoking behavior (Martin et al., 1996; Velicer, Martin, & Collins, 1996). Figure 26.2 shows the model that was found to represent the data best. This model posits that individuals can move both forwards and backwards through the stages of change, and that forward movement between any two adjacent times does not extend beyond a maximum of two stages.

Bulik, Sullivan, and Kendler (2000) used LCA to classify eating disorders in a population-based sample. All individuals in the sample reporting some eating disorder symptom were included in the analysis. Nine eating disorder symptoms were included in the latent class model, including items such as *ever had eating binges* and *excessive concerns with shape and weight*. Three of the six latent classes that were identified clearly reflected the main *DSM-IV* clinical eating disorders: anorexia nervosa, bulimia nervosa, and binge eating disorder. An interesting finding was that three additional latent classes emerged: shape-weight preoccupied, low weight with binging, and low weight without binging. These results suggest that the three *DSM-IV* categories of eating disorders alone did not fully explain the observed data; rather, all six unobserved latent classes were needed.

Several studies have explored subtypes of depression using latent class analysis (e.g., Parker, Wilhelm, Mitchell, Roy, & Hadzi-Pavlovic, 1999; Sullivan, Kessler, & Kendler, 1998). For example, Sullivan et al. (1998) used 14 *DSM-III-R* depressive symptoms in an epidemiological data set to identify six latent classes: severe typical, mild typical, severe atypical, mild atypical, intermediate, and minimal symptoms. Although the particular latent classes identified and the

number of classes found depend on both the sample and the items included in the model, a latent class approach provides a means of empirically testing competing theories about depressive subtypes for a given data set. In a later section an empirical example is presented of LCA applied to data on adolescent depression.

The LCA Mathematical Model and Related Issues

Latent class theory is a measurement theory for a categorical latent variable that divides a population into mutually exclusive and exhaustive latent classes (Goodman, 1974; Lazarsfeld & Henry, 1968). The latent variable is measured by multiple categorical indicators. During the 1970s, two important papers were published that together provided researchers with the theoretical and computational tools for estimating latent class models. First, Goodman (1974) described a maximum likelihood estimation procedure for latent class models. Second, a broadly applicable presentation of the use of the expectation-maximization (EM) algorithm when there is incomplete data was introduced (Dempster, Laird, & Rubin, 1977). The EM algorithm is an iterative technique that yields maximum likelihood estimates from incomplete data. In LCA the latent (unobserved) variables can be considered to be missing data. Several software packages are available for conducting latent class analysis and its extensions, including WinLTA (Collins & Wugalter, 1992; Hyatt & Collins, 2000), ℓem (Vermunt, 1993; Vermunt, Langeheine, & Bockenholt, 1999), PANMARK (Langeheine, 1994; Langeheine, Pannekoek, & van de Pol, 1996; van de Pol & Langeheine, 1990), and Mplus (Muthén & Muthén, 2001).

Latent class models are particularly useful when the theoretical construct of interest is made up of qualitatively different groups, but the group membership of individuals is unknown and therefore must be inferred from the data. Although it might be tempting to try to classify individuals based on their manifest data, LCA has several important advantages over simple cross-tabulation methods. First, a latent variable approach to identifying qualitatively different classes of individuals involves using multiple indicators of the latent variable. The use of multiple indicators provides a basis for estimating measurement error, yielding a clearer picture of the underlying latent variable. Second, LCA can be a confirmatory procedure. For a set of discrete manifest items, the user must specify the number of latent classes. LCA then estimates the parameters and provides a fit statistic. A confirmatory procedure provides a means of testing a priori models and comparing the fit of different models. Third, when measurement error is present, many individuals' responses do not point unambiguously to membership in one particular group. A latent variable approach can help the researcher interpret large contingency tables, providing a sense of both the underlying group structure and the amount of measurement error associated with particular items.

In latent class models, the data are used to estimate the number of classes in the population, the relative size of each class, and the probability of a particular response to each item, given class membership. In this section the LCA statistical model is presented for problems involving three manifest indicators, or variables. The model can be extended directly to problems involving fewer or more indicators. Suppose that Item 1 has response categories $i = 1, \ldots, I$; Item 2 has response categories $j = 1, \ldots, J$; Item 3 has response categories $k = 1, \ldots, K$; and the latent variable has $c = 1, \ldots, C$ latent classes. Let $y = \{i, j, k\}$ represent a particular response pattern (i.e., a vector of possible responses to the three items), and let Y represent the array of all possible ys. Each response pattern y corresponds to a cell of the contingency table formed by cross-tabulating all of the manifest items, and the length of the array Y is equal to the number of cells in this table.

The estimated proportion of a particular response pattern, $P(Y = y)$, can be expressed as a function of two types of parameters. First, the *latent class probabilities,* which are referred to here as γ parameters, represent the proportion of the population that falls in each latent class. Because the latent classes are mutually exclusive and exhaustive (i.e., each individual is placed in one and only one latent class), the γ parameters sum to 1. Second, the *conditional response probabilities,* which we refer to here as ρ parameters, represent the probability of a particular response to a manifest variable, conditioned on latent class membership. These ρ parameters express the relationship between the observed variables and the latent variable. The conditional parameters bear a close conceptual resemblance to factor loadings in that they provide a basis for interpretation of the meaning of the latent classes. However, it is important to remember that they represent probabilities rather than regression coefficients. A probability near 0 or 1 represents a strong relationship between the item and the latent construct. This would mean that, given latent class, we can predict with near certainty how an individual would respond to that item. On the other hand, for dichotomous items, a probability near .5 means that the item does not provide any information above random chance in placing the individual in the latent class.

The probability of a particular response pattern, or cell in the contingency table cross-classifying the three items, can be written as

$$P(Y = y) = \sum_{c=1}^{C} \gamma_c \rho_{i|c} \rho_{j|c} \rho_{k|c} \qquad (26.1)$$

where

- γ_c represents the probability of being in latent class c.
- $\rho_{i|c}$ represents the probability of response i to Item 1, conditional on membership in latent class c.
- $\rho_{j|c}$ represents the probability of response j to Item 2, conditional on membership in latent class c.
- $\rho_{k|c}$ represents the probability of response k to Item 3, conditional on membership in latent class c.

The preceding parameter definitions appear in Appendix A for later reference. The latent class model is defined by making two critical assumptions. First, all individuals in a latent class are assumed to have the same conditional response probabilities for the items. For example, all individuals in the latent class associated with an inhibited temperament type are assumed to have the same probability of displaying high motor activity. Second, there is an assumption of conditional independence given latent class. This implies that within each latent class, the three indicators are independent of one another. For example, individuals' temperament type explains any relationship among their reports of motor activity, fret-cry, and fear. This second assumption allows us to express the probability of a particular response pattern as shown in Equation 26.1, without conditioning on anything in addition to latent class.

Estimation

The EM algorithm is usually used to estimate the parameters of latent class models (Dempster et al., 1977; Goodman, 1974). This algorithm alternates between the E-step, or expectation step, and the M-step, or maximization step. At each step of the EM algorithm, the current set of estimates is compared with the set from the previous step. When the difference between the estimates becomes smaller than a specified criterion, the program has converged on a maximum of the likelihood function. Depending on the likelihood function of a given model, there may be a distinct global maximum, or there may be one or more local maxima. The issue of local maxima is critical in latent class models. If there are several local maxima, which local maximum is reached will depend on the set of starting values used. It is important to explore multiple solutions to ensure that the maximum likelihood estimates represent the best solution. This can be done by estimating the parameters based on several different sets of random start values. Although we hope that only one mode is identified, several different solutions corresponding to different local maxima may be found. In this case there are several possible ways to proceed. One choice is to examine the distribution of solutions and assume that the solution reached most often is the best one, and that one can be selected as the final model. A second approach is to select the solution with the best fit, which corresponds to the highest likelihood. A third way to proceed is to simplify the model being fit, which will reduce the number of parameters being estimated. This often is enough to ensure that just one solution is reached. Any combination of these approaches can be used together in deciding upon a final solution. Fortunately, for many latent class analyses only one solution will be identified.

Missing Data

As has been reviewed extensively in the missing data literature (e.g. Collins, Schafer, & Kam, 2001; Schafer, 1997), there are three major classifications of missing data. If missingness on a variable Y depends on the variable itself, such as when a drug user in a drug use prevention study avoids a measurement session because he is using drugs, this is referred to as *missing not at random* (MNAR). If missingness on Y does not depend on Y itself, this is referred to as *missing at random* (MAR). One example of this would be missingness caused by poor readers' failing to finish a questionnaire. The special case of MAR in which the cause of missingness is completely unrelated to Y is referred to as *missing completely at random* (MCAR). For a thorough introduction to modern missing data procedures, see the chapter by Graham, Cumsille, and Elek-Fisk in this volume.

Most LCA procedures, including WinLTA (Collins & Wugalter, 1992; Hyatt & Collins, 2000), employ a maximum likelihood routine that adjusts for missing data. This approach adjusts for MAR missingness, but not for MNAR missingness. Several simulation studies have documented the success of parameter recovery under various conditions. When the ρ parameters clearly define the latent classes (for example, probabilities above .8 or below .2 for dichotomous indicators), parameter recovery for data that are MCAR or MAR is not substantially biased regardless of the amount of missing data, the sample size, or the latent class model (Hyatt & Collins, 1998; Kolb & Dayton, 1996). It is important to point out that the maximum likelihood missing data procedure will be fully successful only if all variables relevant to missingness are included in the model being fit. If there are variables relevant to missingness that cannot be included in the model being fit, it may be preferable to use a multiple imputation approach in order to include these variables (Collins et al., 2001). The impact of missing data on assessment of model fit is discussed below in the section in this chapter entitled "Advanced Topics in Latent Class Models."

The Use of Parameter Restrictions

Restricted parameters include those that are *fixed,* in which the value is set to a particular value and not estimated, and those that are *constrained* to be equal to other parameters in an equivalence set, so that only one parameter is estimated for the entire set. In a classic article, Goodman (1974) presented the estimation of restricted latent class models using the EM algorithm. Often latent class models are fit without the use of any parameter restrictions. Such unrestricted models can be quite informative, and are especially useful for exploring new models. However, parameter restrictions serve two important roles in latent class models.

First, parameter restrictions can be used to help in achieving identification. Both fixing and constraining parameters reduces the number of parameters to be estimated, which helps in achieving identification. Underidentification refers to a situation in which there are too many parameters to estimate given the information available in a certain data set. One necessary condition for identification is that the *number of independent parameters to be estimated* be less than the *number of possible response patterns*. However, satisfying this condition does not ensure an identified model. Having a large sample size relative to the number of response patterns helps in identification. When the sample size is small relative to the number of response patterns (i.e., the contingency table is *sparse*), parameter restrictions can greatly aid in identification.

Second, parameter restrictions are useful tools for specifying or testing various features of a model. For example, the ρ parameters define the meaning of the latent classes. If we have measurement invariance across groups, meaningful comparisons of the latent class probabilities can then be made. Structural invariance across groups in the measurement of the latent variable is a testable hypothesis. The parameter estimates can be freely estimated in one analysis, and constrained equal across groups in another, and the fit of the two models can be compared. As an example, a researcher interested in comparing sex differences in the prevalence of two temperament types in a sample of infants may wish to start by comparing a model with all parameters freely estimated to one in which the conditional response patterns are constrained to be equal across the two classes. If measurement invariance can be established across classes, this is evidence that the same construct is being measured in males and females, and therefore meaningful cross-sex comparisons of the prevalence of the inhibited and uninhibited types can be made.

Another example of a latent class model for which there is a theoretical justification to impose parameter restrictions is a hierarchical, or Guttman, model (Rindskopf, 1983).

In Guttman models, it is assumed that there is an order among the items in a scale. In models of learning, this order corresponds to the difficulty of passing each item. For example, if three skills are measured and assumed to be hierarchical in level of difficulty, and a pass is denoted 1 and a fail denoted 0, we might restrict the parameters so that the only latent classes correspond to the patterns 000, 100, 110, and 111. The fit of such a model can then be compared to the fit of an unrestricted model to see if the Guttman scale holds in the data.

Model Selection and Goodness-of-Fit

An important issue regarding latent class models is *how many latent classes are there?* Choosing the number of latent classes can be somewhat subjective, and the choice can be driven by both empirical evidence and theoretical reasoning. For example, if theory suggests that there are only two temperament types, the fit of a two-class model can be assessed. A more empirical approach would be to examine models with two, three, and four latent classes to see which solution is most interpretable or provides the best fit. The typical approach to model fit in latent class analysis is to compare the response pattern frequencies predicted by the model with the response pattern frequencies observed in the data. The predicted response pattern frequencies are computed based on the parameter estimates produced in the LCA. The two most common measures of fit in a contingency table analysis are the Pearson chi-square statistic, X^2, and the likelihood ratio statistic, G^2. The likelihood ratio statistic has the advantage that nested models can be compared by a likelihood ratio test, with the resulting statistic distributed as chi-square, and thus is often preferred to the Pearson chi-square. The likelihood ratio statistic is calculated by

$$G^2 = 2 \sum_y obs \log\left(\frac{obs}{\exp}\right) \qquad (26.2)$$

where *y* represents a response pattern (i.e., a cell in the contingency table formed by cross-tabulating all items). This statistic expresses the degree of agreement between these predicted frequencies and the observed frequencies. The G^2 is asymptotically distributed as a chi-square, with degrees of freedom equal to *number of possible response patterns* minus *number of parameters estimated* minus 1. The term *asymptotically* means that a chi-square distribution is a good approximation when the number of observations in each cell is sufficiently large. However, latent class models can often involve large contingency tables, resulting in a contingency table with many sparsely populated cells. For sparse contingency tables, the expected counts can be very small for many cells, and thus the distribution of the G^2 is not well approximated by the chi-

squared distribution. Under such conditions, overall hypothesis testing of model fit using the G^2 can be done in only a rough way (Collins, Fidler, Wugalter, & Long, 1993; Read & Cressie, 1988). A good rule of thumb is that having the value of the fit statistic close to or less than the degrees of freedom is an indication that the model fits the data reasonably well. For a G^2 difference test comparing two nested models, however, the distribution usually is better approximated by the chi-squared distribution, and thus hypothesis testing is more reliable.

A pair of nested models consists of a simpler model and a more complex model. The more complex model can be considered a version of the simpler model, in which some parameters constrained in the simpler model are estimated in the more complex model. Two nested latent class models can be compared statistically by taking the difference of their G^2 values. This difference is distributed as a chi-square with degrees of freedom equal to the difference in the degrees of freedom associated with the two G^2s. If the difference in G^2 is nonsignificant, it means that the more parsimonious model fits about as well as the more complex model, and thus there is no benefit to estimating the parameters in the more complex model. If the difference in G^2 is significant, it means that the additional parameters estimated in the more complex model are necessary to achieve adequate fit. The G^2 difference test can be quite useful when comparing various patterns of parameter restrictions for latent class models with a given number of classes. For example, if we are interested in conducting an omnibus test for sex differences in the prevalence of temperament types in infants, we can constrain the γ parameters (the probability of membership in each temperament type) to be equal across males and females in one model, and freely estimate the γ parameters in a second model. The G^2 difference test will tell us whether it is reasonable to impose this equality restriction. If the difference test reaches statistical significance, then we can conclude that the probabilities of membership in the temperament types vary by sex. Ideally we would like to be able to use this approach to help determine the appropriate number of latent classes by comparing the fit of two models. For example, we might want to compare a model with two temperament types to a model with three temperament types. Unfortunately, two models with different numbers of latent classes are not nested because parameters of the simpler model take on boundary values of the parameter space (Everitt, 1988; Rubin & Stern, 1994). *Boundary values* refer to the maximum and minimum values a parameter can take on. Because all parameters in the latent class model are probabilities, the boundary values are 0 and 1. For example, in order to compare a model with two latent classes and one with three latent classes, the simpler two-class model would have to contain three latent classes, one with probability of membership fixed at zero. Because zero is a boundary value, these two models are not nested.

Various model selection information criteria have been proposed for comparing models with different numbers of classes, including the Akaike information criterion (AIC; Akaike, 1974) and the Bayesian information criterion (BIC; Schwarz, 1978). The AIC and BIC are penalized log-likelihood test statistics, where the penalty is two times the number of parameters estimated for the AIC and the log of N times the number of parameters estimated for the BIC. Results of a simulation study conducted by Lin and Dayton (1997) suggest that, although the AIC performs better than the BIC and the Consistent AIC (CAIC) (Bozdogan, 1987), the AIC tends to select models that are more complex than the true model. Another drawback to this approach is that these methods serve only to compare the relative fit of several models under consideration, but do not help in determining whether a particular model has sufficiently good fit. A Bayesian approach to model monitoring using a posterior predictive check distribution has been proposed as a method for comparing models with different numbers of classes (Rubin & Stern, 1994). This approach is discussed in the section entitled "Goodness-of-Fit Issues," under "Advanced Topics in Latent Class Models." Bootstrapping the goodness-of-fit measures has also been proposed for latent class models (Collins et al., 1993; Langeheine et al., 1996). This method, also referred to as Monte Carlo sampling, involves repeatedly sampling from the model-based parameter estimates to get a distribution of the fit statistic under the assumption that the model is true. This method yields an empirical distribution of the fit statistic, forgoing the use of a theoretical distribution altogether.

It may be helpful to draw a comparison between LCA and factor analysis. In factor analysis, multiple continuous items are mapped onto several factors. In contrast, the latent class model maps multiple categorical items onto several categories of a latent variable. In factor analysis, both exploratory and confirmatory approaches can be used in selecting the number of factors. All factors with eigenvalues greater than 1 are often selected in an exploratory factor analysis. An exploratory approach to LCA might involve the user's fitting a two-class solution to a data set, then a three-class solution, and so on, and comparing the various solutions and fit statistics in a rough way. In this framework there is no rule of thumb for selecting the smallest number of latent classes that can adequately explain the structure in the data. The closest analogue might be to create a table that summarizes the G^2 value and degrees of freedom for each number of classes fit to the data. The most parsimonious model (the model with the smallest number of classes) that provides adequate fit could be selected as the one with the most appropriate number of latent classes. This approach is taken in the empirical example on adolescent depression presented later in this chapter.

Assessing the Quality of Categorical Measures

Latent class models provide a basis for assessing the reliability of categorical items (Clogg & Manning, 1996; Collins, 2001). Psychometric theory for instruments intended to measure continuous latent variables is inappropriate for instruments measuring categorical latent variables (Collins, 2001). However, reliability of such instruments can be examined by means of the parameters in the latent class model.

Clogg and Manning (1996) present two types of reliability for categorical items, item-specific reliability and item-set reliability. Item-specific reliability refers to pairwise relations between single items and the latent class variable. For example, consider the ρ parameters. These values quantify how well membership in a latent class predicts item response, which is one form of reliability. An item that is highly associated with a latent class is a reliable indicator of that class. Another item-specific form of reliability presented by Clogg and Manning (1996) is how well an item response predicts membership in a latent class. Additional methods Clogg and Manning present for assessing item-specific reliability include using odds ratios and transformed odds ratios that are similar to correlations.

Item-set reliability, in contrast to item-specific reliability, refers to the reliability of a set of items with respect to each latent class—that is, how well a particular response pattern predicts latent class membership. Flaherty (in press) uses both item-specific and item-set reliability to examine the measurement quality of four measures of tobacco use in a national survey.

Collins (2001) has developed a reliability index that is similar conceptually to the familiar Cronbach's α. Rather than examine reliability for item and class pairs, or for response patterns and each latent class, Collins (2001) takes the information contained in the item-set reliabilities and develops a single number that summarizes the reliability of the items. Collins (2001) also extends this notion of reliability to the assessment of the reliability of dynamic (changing) categorical latent variables.

Reliability analysis is closely related to item development and selection. Biemer and Wiesen (2002) use the latent class model to assess the consistency of people's reports of marijuana use in a national survey of substance use. Using this method, they were able to identify poor items and adjust prevalence estimates of marijuana use.

A LATENT CLASS EXAMPLE: ADOLESCENT DEPRESSION

We illustrate the latent class model in this section by examining adolescent depression in data from The National Longitudinal Study of Adolescent Health (Add Health; Resnick et al., 1997). We might expect there to be an underlying latent variable made up of two mutually exclusive and exhaustive groups of individuals: those who are depressed and those who are not. An alternate theory might hypothesize that there are several different types or levels of depression. These two competing theories can be examined empirically by fitting several different latent class models to a data set.

The Add Health study was mandated by Congress to collect data for the purpose of measuring the effect of social context on the health and well-being of adolescents in the United States. The first wave of the sample included 11,796 students in grades 7 through 12 who were surveyed between April and December of 1995, and the second wave included the same individuals interviewed again between April and August of 1996. The sample used in the latent class analysis includes all 1,892 adolescents who were in 12th grade at Wave I, consisting of all adolescents in the oldest cohort of the core data set.

The prevalence of depression in this sample of high school seniors is explored by examining eight survey items from the Add Health study. The items, listed in Table 26.1, include four items related to sadness, two indicators of feeling disliked by others, and two items related to feelings of failing at life. These six-level items were recoded so that 1 represents never or rarely experiencing the symptom in the past week, and 2 represents experiencing the symptom sometimes, a lot, most of the time, or all of the time during the past week.

TABLE 26.1   Eight Items From the Add Health Feelings Scale: Percent of 12th-Grade Students Who Reported Symptom Sometimes, a Lot, Most, All of the Time During the Past Week

	Male (%)	Female (%)
Sad:		
You felt that you could not shake off the blues, even with help from your family and your friends.	25.7	35.1
You felt depressed.	36.2	47.0
You felt lonely.	35.6	44.7
You felt sad.	43.2	56.0
Disliked:		
People were unfriendly to you.	36.8	33.5
You felt that people disliked you.	34.7	28.1
Failure:		
You thought your life had been a failure.	15.4	16.2
You felt life was not worth living.	8.9	10.1

Note. All items were coded. 1 = never or rarely during the past week; 2 = sometimes, a lot, most, or all of the time during the past week.

Because latent class analysis is based on data in the form of a contingency table, it is important to have only a few levels for each variable. Extreme sparseness of cells can lead to problems in the estimation. As the number of levels within variables increases, so does the number of parameters in the model. A balance between retaining information in the original variables and collapsing categories must be struck, as identification can be difficult to attain when too many parameters are estimated.

The eight questionnaire items are observed indicators of the latent variable, depression. In our example, latent class analysis allows us to arrive at a model that we believe best represents the relationship between these eight items and the latent variable depression. We will estimate the proportion of individuals in a sample who are in each class of depression.

The Mathematical Model and Parameters Estimated

The LCA mathematical model is be presented here in terms of our empirical example. Suppose that there are eight categorical manifest indicators with response categories $i, j, k, l, m, n, o,$ and p, respectively, and there are $c = 1, \ldots, C$ latent classes. Let $y = \{i, j, k, l, m, n, o, p\}$ represent a response pattern, and let Y represent the entire array of response patterns. Each individual can respond *yes* or *no* to each of the eight indicators of depression listed in Table 26.1, so there are $2^8 = 256$ possible ways to respond to the eight questions. For example, an individual reporting no symptoms of depression in the past week would have the response pattern $\{1, 1, 1, 1, 1, 1, 1, 1\}$, and someone experiencing symptoms related to sadness but none related to being disliked or failure might have the response pattern $\{2, 2, 2, 2, 1, 1, 1, 1\}$.

The estimated proportion of a particular response pattern, $P(Y = y)$, is expressed as a function of the latent class probabilities (the γ parameters) and the conditional response probabilities (the ρ parameters). These ρ parameters express the relationship between the eight observed variables and the latent variable depression. The probability of a particular response pattern is:

$$P(Y = y) = \sum_{c=1}^{C} \gamma_c \rho_{i|c} \rho_{j|c} \rho_{k|c} \rho_{l|c} \rho_{m|c} \rho_{n|c} \rho_{o|c} \rho_{p|c} \quad (26.3)$$

where

- γ_c represents the probability of being in latent class c (e.g., the probability of being in a certain latent class of depression).

- $\rho_{i|c}$ represents the probability of response i to Item 1, conditional on membership in latent class c (e.g., the probability of responding *yes* to *Could not shake the blues* given membership in a certain latent class of depression).

TABLE 26.2   Goodness-of-Fit for Various Models

Number of Classes	Degrees of Freedom	G^2
2	238	885.1
3	229	567.0
4	220	351.2
5	211	268.6
6	202	237.3
7	193	206.3
8	184	187.8

- $\rho_{j|c}$ represents the probability of response j to Item 2, conditional on membership in latent class c (e.g., the probability of responding *yes* to *Felt depressed* given membership in a certain latent class of depression), and so on.

For our example, we first fit a two-class solution, which yielded a G^2 of 885.1 with 238 degrees of freedom. We then fit models with three classes, four classes, and so on, up to eight classes. Table 26.2 reports the resulting G^2s. The most parsimonious model with a G^2 value close to the degrees of freedom is the five-class solution (G^2 of 268.6 with 211 degrees of freedom), and thus we select this as our final model. In order to explore the presence of multiple modes, or local maxima, we ran the analysis 100 times using a different set of random start values for each. If all 100 solutions were identical, then we could be confident that the global maximum of the likelihood had in fact been identified. In other words, there would be little doubt that we did in fact find the proper solution for our five-class model. However, two slightly different modes were identified, both with reasonable parameter estimates. In order to select the better mode we examined the

distribution of these 100 runs. One solution had a G^2 of 268.6 and was reached 88 out of 100 times. A second solution, reached 12 out of 100 times, had a G^2 of 323.5. Because the first solution was clearly dominant in frequency and had a superior fit, this solution is reported as the final one. If the dominant solution had an inferior fit, we might have considered restricting the parameter estimation (e.g., imposing some sensible equality constraints on the conditional response probabilities). This more constrained model would then have been run with 100 different sets of start values, and the distribution of solutions would have been examined.

The Five-Class Solution

The results indicate that the observed data were best represented by five types, or levels, of depression. Table 26.3 contains the parameter estimates for the five-class solution. The matrix of conditional response probabilities shows the probability of responding *yes* to each of the eight items given class membership. (The probability of responding *no* to each item given class membership can be calculated by subtracting the probability of *yes* from 1.) Probabilities greater than .50 are marked in bold, indicating that individuals in that latent class are more likely to report that symptom than not. It is interesting to note that, although no restrictions were imposed on the model parameters, the four indicators of sadness tend to operate similarly, as do the two indicators of being disliked and the two indicators of failure. Based on the pattern of conditional response probabilities, the meaning of the five latent classes can be interpreted and appropriate class labels can be assigned. Individuals in Latent Class 1 are expected to have a

TABLE 26.3   Results for Grade 12 Unconstrained Latent Class Model

Panel A. ρ Parameters: Probability of *Yes*

	Sad				Disliked		Failure	
	Couldn't Shake Blues	Felt Depressed	Felt Lonely	Felt Sad	People Unfriendly	Disliked by People	Life was Failure	Life not Worth Living
Class 1	.04	.06	.12	.18	.13	.00	.02	.01
Class 2	**.63**	**.89**	**.59**	**.80**	.07	.12	.16	.07
Class 3	.07	.16	.29	.37	**.63**	**.68**	.13	.04
Class 4	**.59**	**.83**	**.80**	**.91**	**.81**	**.66**	.16	.05
Class 5	**.90**	**.98**	**.95**	**.98**	**.67**	**.85**	**.88**	**.73**

Panel B. Class Prevalence

Class	Label	Proportion
1	No depression	.41
2	Sad	.18
3	Disliked	.17
4	Sad + disliked	.15
5	Depression	.09

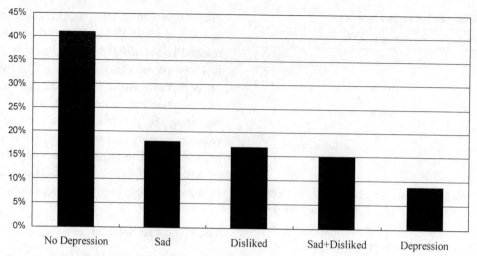

Figure 26.3   Overall prevalence of depression latent classes.

low probability of reporting any depression symptom, and thus Latent Class 1 is called *no depression*. Members of Latent Class 2 are likely to report *yes* to all sadness-related symptoms and *no* to the other symptoms, so we call Latent Class 2 *sad*. Similarly, Latent Class 3 is labeled *disliked* and Latent Class 4 is called *sad + disliked*. Latent Class 5 is associated with a high probability of reporting all eight depression symptoms, and is called *depression*.

Table 26.3 also reports the γ parameters, which represent the relative size of each of the five classes. Note that these parameters must sum to 1, as they represent the distribution of a discrete random variable. Figure 26.3 displays the prevalence of the five depression latent classes.

The no depression latent class has the highest prevalence, with 41% of the sample expected to be members of this class. We expect 18%, 17%, and 15%, respectively, to be in the sad, disliked, and sad + disliked classes. Only 9% are expected to experience the highest level of depression. The no depression class represents the largest segment of the population, the depression class represents the smallest segment, and half of the population is expected to fall somewhere in the three middle levels.

Examining the Effect of Gender

Now that a five-class model for depression has been established in this sample of adolescents, it may be useful to examine how the prevalence of each level of depression varies across different groups. For example, we might be interested in whether males or females experience higher levels of depression. This can be investigated by estimating the γ and ρ parameters for each group and comparing the probabilities of latent class membership. However, in order to make meaningful comparisons of the prevalence of latent classes, it may be helpful to impose some type of structure on the conditional response probabilities. One option is to impose measurement invariance across sex. For latent class models, this means applying constraints such that the conditional response probability matrix is the same for males and females. The unrestricted five-class model in which all parameters are freely estimated for both sexes, and an alternative model where measurement is constrained to be equal across sex, are nested and can be compared directly using a G^2 difference test. Such a test indicates whether it is reasonable to conclude that there is measurement invariance across groups. In our example, the model with all parameters estimated freely has a G^2 of 421.3 with 422 *df*, and the model that imposes measurement invariance across sex has a G^2 of 463.3 with 462 *df*. The difference test is not significant (G^2 of 42.0 with 40 *df*), indicating that males and females have the same probability of reporting each depression symptom given their level of depression. Thus, measurement invariance holds across sex, and so we constrain the ρ parameters to be equal for males and females.

Table 26.4 shows results for a latent class model of depression with sex as a grouping variable. The matrix of conditional response probabilities is very similar to that in Table 26.3. The latent class prevalences for males and females can now be compared. We can conduct an omnibus test for differences in the distribution of males and females' prevalence of depression by constraining all elements of the vector of γ parameters to be equal across sex, and comparing that to our present model. The G^2 difference test is highly significant ($G^2 = 80.6$ with 4 *df*), indicating that the prevalences of the five latent classes of depression differ substantially between males and females. Table 26.4 shows that the proportion of adolescents expected to be in the no depression latent class is similar for males and

TABLE 26.4 Results for Grade 12 Latent Class Model, Conditional Parameters Constrained Equal Across Sex

Panel A. ρ Parameters: Probability of *Yes*

	Sad				Disliked		Failure	
	Couldn't Shake Blues	Felt Depressed	Felt Lonely	Felt Sad	People Unfriendly	Disliked by People	Life was Failure	Life not Worth Living
Class 1	.04	.06	.13	.18	.15	.01	.02	.01
Class 2	**.62**	**.87**	**.59**	**.80**	.11	.10	.16	.08
Class 3	.09	.21	.30	.39	**.66**	**.78**	.14	.04
Class 4	**.61**	**.84**	**.82**	**.93**	**.78**	**.67**	.16	.04
Class 5	**.89**	**.98**	**.94**	**.97**	**.67**	**.85**	**.87**	**.73**

Panel B. Class Prevalence

Class	Label	Male Prevalence	Female Prevalence
1	No depression	.46	.41
2	Sad	.12	.24
3	Disliked	.22	.10
4	Sad + disliked	.12	.14
5	Depression	.08	.10

females (.46 and .41, respectively). The expected proportion in the highest level of depression is also similar for males and females (.08 and .10, respectively). However, gender differences appear in the middle levels of depression. Female adolescents are twice as likely to be in the sad latent class (.24 vs. .12), whereas male adolescents are twice as likely to be in the disliked latent class (.22 vs. .10). Figure 26.4 shows the gender differences in the prevalence of depression latent classes. A formal test of gender differences in specific γ parameters requires estimates of each parameter's standard error.

Although standard errors are not a byproduct of the EM algorithm, several methods for obtaining estimates of the standard errors have been proposed. One method involves a Bayesian approach for obtaining standard errors. In the section on recent developments in LCA appearing later in this chapter, this approach is used to compare the latent class prevalence of depression types in males and females. But first we turn our attention to latent class models for repeated measures.

EXTENSIONS OF LCA TO REPEATED MEASURES

Often in psychology we are interested in developmental processes—that is, how constructs change over time. Development is often characterized by increases or decreases in a

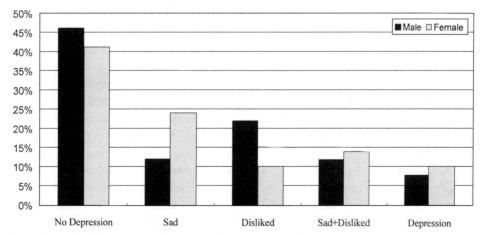

Figure 26.4 Sex differences in the prevalence of depression latent classes.

particular continuous variable over time. However, qualitative development can also be examined by modeling how individuals pass through qualitatively different stages over time. Examples of stage sequences are abundant in psychology. These include Piaget's (1973) stage model of cognitive development, Freud's (1961) stages of psychosocial development, Kohlberg's (1966) stage sequence of moral development, and Erikson's (1950) stages of ego identity. Following from our examination of adolescent depression, we might be interested in stability and change in depression throughout adolescence. In the following discussion we extend this previous latent class analysis by modeling transitions between different latent classes of depression over time.

Latent Markov Models

Latent Markov modeling is a framework for examining stability and change in a categorical latent variable measured by categorical variables repeatedly over time in the same sample of individuals (Langeheine, 1994; van de Pol & Langeheine, 1990). Latent Markov models assume that time is a discrete process, rather than a continuous one, and summarize change over time by estimating transitions from one time point to the next. Traditional Markov models involve a single indicator of class membership measured at multiple times, in which the conditional response probabilities are constrained to be equal over time in order to achieve identification. A multiple indicator Markov model measures class membership at each time using a set of two or more items. In this model the conditional response probabilities do not need to be constrained to be equal over time in order to achieve identification, although this constraint helps interpretability. The multiple indicator latent Markov model (Langeheine, 1994; Langeheine & van de Pol, 1994; Macready & Dayton, 1994) is identical to the latent transition analysis framework (Collins & Wugalter, 1992); this longitudinal approach is presented in the following discussion.

Latent Transition Analysis

Latent class theory has been extended to a longitudinal framework allowing modeling of change in a discrete latent variable. This framework, called latent transition analysis (LTA; Collins et al., 1997; Collins & Wugalter, 1992; Hyatt & Collins, 2000), provides a way of estimating and testing models of stage-sequential development in longitudinal data. In LTA, change is measured using multiple manifest indicators. This approach allows researchers to estimate the prevalence of stages (i.e., latent classes) and the incidence of transitions to different stages over time for multiple groups. In the following discussion, some applications of LTA in the behavioral sciences are briefly described. The LTA mathematical model and related issues are then presented by extending the empirical example on adolescent depression.

Previously we discussed the modeling of substance use onset and smoking cessation within the latent class framework. Because individuals' class membership in each of these sequences can change over time, it may be interesting to collect data at more than one wave and examine patterns of change between consecutive times. The transtheoretical model of behavior change presented earlier (see Figure 26.2) is, in this case, a sequence of four stages: precontemplation, contemplation, action, and maintenance. LTA has been used to test competing models of smoking behavior as individuals move from one stage to another (Martin et al., 1996; Velicer et al., 1996). The stage-sequential model of substance use onset has been modeled extensively using LTA. Collins et al. (1997) examined the relationship between heavy caffeine use and adolescent substance use. Other covariates of substance use onset have been explored using LTA, including pubertal timing (Hyatt & Collins, 1999), parental permissiveness (Hyatt & Collins, 2000), and exposure to adult substance use (Tracy, Collins, & Graham, 1997).

A similar application of LTA incorporated a *DSM-IV* diagnosis of alcohol abuse and dependence (AAD) at age 21 as the grouping variable, and modeled group differences in the stage sequence of alcohol use during elementary, middle, and high school. The stage sequence of drinking behaviors included the following four latent classes: nonuse, initiated only, initiated and currently using, and initiated and currently using with heavy episodic drinking. Different drinking patterns that emerged in middle and high school were related to individuals' subsequent AAD diagnosis (Guo, Collins, Hill, & Hawkins, 2000). Current alcohol use in middle school was related to an AAD diagnosis at age 21, whereas heavy episodic drinking in high school was related to AAD. This evidence suggests the need for differential intervention programs at various developmental periods throughout adolescence.

Children's drawing development from ages four through eight has been modeled as a stage-sequential developmental process with the following stages: scribbling or prestage, preschematic stage, schematic stage proper, and late schematic stage (Humphreys & Janson, 2000). These four stages were based on 12 items measuring features of the children's drawings at each of the five times, including *head, eyes* and *hair*. Development was hypothesized to be cumulative: That is, after skills are learned they are not lost. Cumulative models of development can be specified and tested in LTA by restricting the probability of movement between certain stages over time.

LTA has also been used to model change from year to year in the safety of sexual behaviors among injection drug users (Posner, Collins, Longshore, & Anglin, 1996). Four subscales were used to estimate the stage-sequence over two times: knowledge, denial of personal risk, self-protective behaviors, and sexual risk behavior. A six-class solution that allowed individuals to move to any stage over time was found to fit the data well. The six stages were labeled: high risk; knowledge only; safe sex only; sex risk; low risk, but denial; and low risk. It was found that individuals moved to a different stage over time quite often, indicating that sexual behavior prevention efforts should be ongoing and provided to all injection drug users regardless of the safety of their current sexual behaviors.

LTA can be used to aid both the design and evaluation of intervention programs. Competing models can be fit in order to describe development in processes upon which it might be possible to intervene. In addition, by incorporating a grouping variable, subgroups of the population that are at higher risk can be identified, providing useful information to researchers as they are designing interventions for prevention or treatment. For example, Collins et al. (1994) explored differences in substance use onset for Anglo, Latino, and Asian-American adolescents and discussed possible implications for designing an intervention. LTA also allows researchers to assess the effectiveness of interventions by incorporating treatment as a grouping variable. Because the outcome process is broken down into a stage sequence, we can identify differential effects of the intervention. The Adolescent Alcohol Prevention Trial (Hansen & Graham, 1991) was a school-based substance use intervention program. LTA was used to evaluate the effectiveness of a normative education curriculum. An overall program effect was detected, such that individuals who received the education were less likely to advance in substance use between seventh and eighth grade. More specifically, adolescents who received the education were more likely to stay in the no use stage in Grade 8 if they were in that stage in Grade 7, and less likely to begin advanced use during that time (Graham, Collins, Wugalter, Chung, & Hansen, 1991).

We present LTA by modeling change in depression from Grade 11 to Grade 12. Building on the previously described latent class example, we use the same eight items from the Add Health depression index, in this case measured at two times. The sample used in this longitudinal analysis includes all adolescents who were in 11th grade at Wave I and 12th grade at Wave II. The goal is to explore gender differences in the stability of depression over time. First an overall model is fit to the two waves of data for all adolescents, followed by a model incorporating the grouping variable sex.

The mathematical model is presented in terms of two times of measurement, with depression as our dynamic (changing) latent variable measured by eight items and sex as a grouping variable. There are eight discrete manifest indicators of depression with response categories i, j, k, l, m, n, o, and p respectively, which are measured at two times. The latent classes corresponding to the dynamic part of the model are called *latent statuses*. There are $a = 1, \ldots, S$ latent statuses at Time 1 and $b = 1, \ldots, S$ latent statuses at Time 2. Suppose also that there are $c = 1, \ldots, C$ latent classes measured by a manifest indicator with response categories $x = 1, \ldots, X$. In general, y refers to a response pattern (i.e., a cell of the contingency table made by cross-tabulating all items in the model). Let $y = \{x, i, j, k, l, m, n, o, p, i', j', k', l', m', n', o', p'\}$ represent a response pattern, a vector of possible responses to the latent class indicator and the eight latent status indicators at Time 1 and the same eight indicators at Time 2. In this example, the response pattern is a vector made up of the sex indicator, the eight depression indicators at Time 1, and the same eight indicators measured at Time 2. Let Y represent the complete array of response patterns. The estimated proportion of a particular response pattern, $P(Y = y)$, is expressed as

$$P(Y = y)$$
$$= \sum_{c=1}^{C} \sum_{p=1}^{S} \sum_{q=1}^{S} \gamma_c \rho_{x|c} \delta_{a|c} \rho_{i|a,c} \cdots \rho_{p|a,c} \tau_{b|a,c} \rho_{i'|b,c} \cdots \rho_{p'|b,c}$$

$$(26.4)$$

where

- γ_c represents the probability of being in latent class c (e.g., the expected proportion of females).

- $\rho_{x|c}$ represents the probability of response x to the latent class indicator, conditional on membership in latent class c (e.g., the probability of responding *female* to the indicator of sex, given membership in the female group).

- $\delta_{a|c}$ represents the probability of being in latent status a at Time 1 conditional on membership in latent class c (e.g., the probability of being in the depression latent status, given membership in the female group).

- $\rho_{i|a,c}$ represents the probability of response i to Item 1 at Time 1, conditional on membership in latent status a at Time 1 and membership in latent class c (e.g., the probability of responding *yes* to *could not shake the blues,* given membership in the female group and membership in the depression latent status); similarly, $\rho_{i'|b,c}$ represents the same quantity for Time 2.

- $\rho_{j|a,c}$ represents the probability of response j to Item 2 at Time 1, conditional on membership in latent status a at

Time 1 and membership in latent class c (e.g., the probability of responding *yes* to *felt depressed,* given membership in the female group and membership in the depression latent status); similarly, $\rho_{j'|b,c}$ represents the same quantity for Time 2, and so on.

- $\rho_{p|a,c}$ represents the probability of response p to Item 8 at Time 1, conditional on membership in latent status a at Time 1 and membership in latent class c (e.g., the probability of responding *yes* to *life not worth living,* given membership in the female group and membership in the depression latent status); similarly, $\rho_{p'|b,c}$ represents the same quantity for Time 2.

- $\tau_{b|a,c}$ represents the probability of membership in latent status b at Time 2, conditional on membership in latent status a at Time 1 and membership in latent class c (e.g., the probability of membership in the depression latent status in Grade 12, given membership in the female group and membership in the no depression latent status in Grade 11). The τ parameters are usually arranged in the form of a transition probability matrix.

Refer to Appendix B for a summary of the LTA mathematical model and its associated parameters. It is worth noting that the grouping variable can be treated as a discrete latent variable measured by several indicators. Here our grouping variable is sex, which is measured with a single indicator. With a single indicator there is no basis on which to estimate measurement error, so the relevant ρ parameters are fixed to 0 and 1. In general, there can be any number of manifest items and response categories, and the number of response categories can vary across items. As in LCA, LTA employs the EM algorithm. Issues of model selection and fit are identical to those in the latent class framework.

The use of parameter restrictions serves the same purpose as in a latent class framework. However, there are several reasons that these restrictions often play a larger role in LTA models. First, because complex models are often estimated in LTA, the number of parameters involved can be quite large. Imposing restrictions on the parameters can greatly aid in model identification. Second, as in all longitudinal models, it is important to consider the issue of measurement invariance over time. Measurement invariance over time can be explored by imposing constraints across the sets of ρ parameters, or conditional response probabilities, estimated at each time. Constraining these parameters to be equal across time ensures that the meaning of the latent statuses remains consistent across time. If the measurement is structurally identical at both times, then changes in the class membership over time can be attributed solely to development rather than development mixed with changes in the relations between the

TABLE 26.5 Latent Transition Model (Conditional Parameters Constrained Equal Across Time)

Panel A. Transition Probabilities From Grade 11 to Grade 12

| | Grade 12 | | | | |
Grade 11	No Depression	Sad	Disliked	Sad + Disliked	Depression
No depression	**.77**	.12	.09	.02	.01
Sad	.33	**.49**	.07	.07	.05
Disliked	.24	.08	**.46**	.16	.06
Sad + disliked	.01	.22	.28	**.40**	.10
Depression	.07	.22	.00	.13	**.58**

Panel B. Class Prevalence

Class	Label	Prevalence at Grade 11	Prevalence at Grade 12
1	No depression	.34	.40
2	Sad	.23	.22
3	Disliked	.20	.18
4	Sad + disliked	.13	.12
5	Depression	.09	.09

indicators and the latent variable. Third, parameter restrictions often play an important theoretical role in the τ matrix; restrictions can be imposed to test the nature of development over time. For example, models estimating the full τ matrix (implying that individuals can move around the stage sequence freely over time) can be compared to models that do not allow backsliding to stages earlier in a stage sequence.

Table 26.5 presents results from the first longitudinal analysis, where there is no grouping variable. This model was estimated twice, once with all ρ parameters estimated freely and once with ρ parameters constrained to be equal across time, representing measurement invariance over time. The G^2 difference test for these nested models is 47 with 40 df ($G^2 = 4,872$ with 65,431 df vs. $G^2 = 4,919$ with 65,471 df). This is nonsignificant, providing evidence that measurement invariance over time holds. Therefore, all subsequent findings reported are based on the constrained model. The matrix of transition probabilities provides information about stability in depression between Grades 11 and 12. Elements on the diagonal are bolded; these numbers represent the probability of membership in a particular depression latent status in Grade 12, conditional on membership in the same depression latent status in Grade 11. An interesting finding is that it is estimated that 77% of adolescents in the no depression latent status at Grade 11 were in that same latent status a year later. The probability of being in the same depression latent status at both grades is substantially lower for the other four groups. Table 26.5 also reports the depression latent status prevalence at each grade. The pattern appears to be similar in Grades 11 and 12, with a slightly higher proportion in the no depression latent status at Grade 12.

TABLE 26.6   Latent Transition Model by Sex (Conditional Parameters Constrained Equal Across Time and Sex)

Panel A. Transition Probabilities from Grade 11 to Grade 12 for Males and Females

Grade 11	No Depression	Sad	Disliked	Sad + Disliked	Depression
			Grade 12		
No depression	.71	.10	.16	.02	.01
	.82	**.14**	**.02**	**.02**	**.00**
Sad	.36	.39	.14	.07	.05
	.30	**.53**	**.05**	**.07**	**.05**
Disliked	.23	.04	.54	.15	.05
	.26	**.11**	**.38**	**.18**	**.06**
Sad + disliked	.02	.22	.41	.31	.04
	.00	**.21**	**.22**	**.43**	**.14**
Depression	.05	.13	.02	.09	.72
	.08	**.30**	**.00**	**.17**	**.46**

Note. Females are in **bold.**

Panel B. Class Prevalence for Males and Females

Class	Label	Prevalence at Grade 11	Prevalence at Grade 12
1	No depression	.39	.40
		.28	**.37**
2	Sad	.17	.15
		.29	**.27**
3	Disliked	.25	.26
		.18	**.12**
4	Sad + disliked	.10	.09
		.16	**.14**
5	Depression	.09	.09
		.10	**.09**

Note. Females are in **bold.**

The second longitudinal analysis incorporates sex as a grouping variable in order to examine gender differences in the prevalence of depression and the incidence of transitions over time in levels of depression. The ρ parameters were constrained to be equal across time and sex so that the latent statuses of depression are defined in the same way in Grades 11 and 12 for males and females. Table 26.6 shows the transition probabilities and latent status prevalences for males and females. The pattern of transition probabilities appears to be quite similar for males and females. For example, 71% of males in the no depression latent status Grade 11 are in this same latent status in Grade 12. Similarly, 82% of females experiencing no depression at Grade 11 are expected to have no depression at Grade 12. There does, however, appear to be an interesting but subtle gender difference in some of the transition probabilities. Notice that regardless of an individual's level of depression in Grade 11, males are more likely to transition to the disliked latent status in Grade 12 and females are more likely to transition to the sad latent status in Grade 12. For example, of individuals in the no depression latent status

in Grade 11, males are eight times more likely to be in the disliked latent status 1 year later (16% vs. 2%), and females are more likely to be in the sad latent status 1 year later (14% vs. 10%). Without estimates of the parameters' standard errors, we cannot assess the statistical significance of these differences. The Bayesian approach discussed in the next section can be applied to both latent class and latent transition models to obtain standard errors.

ADVANCED TOPICS IN LATENT CLASS MODELS

The final section of this chapter presents several advanced topics in latent class models. The purpose of this section is to give the reader an idea of how the latent class model can be extended to answer a wider range of research questions. Most of these extensions are relatively recent, and software is not currently available for everything discussed here. Existing software is pointed out as appropriate.

Bayesian Approach for Obtaining Standard Errors

Data augmentation is a Bayesian method that can be used to obtain estimates of standard errors of LCA and LTA parameters. With this approach, an individual's class membership is treated as missing data and imputed multiple times. By imputing multiple times, the uncertainty associated with latent class membership is taken into account. An estimate of the standard error is obtained for each parameter by combining the average variance within each imputation and variance between imputations (Rubin, 1987). Standard errors provide information about the variability of point estimates and enable the user to conduct hypothesis tests.

Data augmentation lends tremendous flexibility to hypothesis testing. This procedure yields standard errors for each parameter, allowing standard hypothesis tests of group differences. We know based on our G^2 difference test of sex differences in the γ parameters that the prevalence of the five depressive types is different for males and females. Standard errors from the parameter estimates can be used to compare formally the probability of membership in each type of depression for males and females. For example, based on Figure 26.4 it appears that females are more likely to be in the sad latent class, whereas males are more likely to be members of the disliked latent class. WinLTA (Collins & Wugalter, 1992; Hyatt & Collins, 2000) was used to conduct data augmentation. Based on these results, differences of proportions and relative risk ratios were calculated, along with their associated 95% confidence intervals (see Table 26.7), for each probability of class membership. As anticipated, two differences were

TABLE 26.7   Hypothesis Tests for Sex Differences in Levels of Depression at Grade 12

	Male Prevalence Based on DA	Female Prevalence Based on DA	Difference of Proportions (95% CI)	Relative Risk (95% CI)
No depression	.47	.42	−0.05 (−0.10, 0.00)	0.9 (0.8, 1.0)
Sad	.13	.25	0.13* (0.09, 0.17)	2.0* (1.6, 2.6)
Disliked	.22	.10	−0.12* (−0.16, −0.08)	0.5* (0.3, 0.6)
Sad + disliked	.11	.13	0.02 (−0.02, 0.07)	1.2 (0.8, 1.7)
Depression	.08	.09	0.01 (−0.02, 0.04)	1.2 (0.8, 1.6)

Note. *Difference is statistically significant at the .05 level.

found to be statistically significant: females are twice as likely to be in the sad latent class and half as likely to be in the disliked latent class. No other effects of gender were found.

In addition to conducting hypothesis tests, more complex tests involving multiple parameter estimates can be explored. For example, data augmentation can be applied to LTA to define a stability parameter that is the sum of all diagonal elements in the matrix of transition probabilities. Group differences in stability can then be examined. An example of this, as well as an explanation of how to calculate the difference of proportions, relative risks, and associated standard errors for combinations of LTA parameters, appears in Hyatt, Collins, and Schafer (1999). In this study WinLTA (Collins & Wugalter, 1992; Hyatt & Collins, 2000) was used to examine differences in the onset of substance use for females with early pubertal timing and females who do not experience early timing. It was found that early-developing females were less likely to be in the no substance use stage and more likely to be in the alcohol and cigarettes and alcohol, cigarettes, drunkenness, and marijuana stage in both seventh and eighth grades. Also, early-developing females were more likely to begin using substances between seventh and eighth grade. Although a group difference in the overall stability in substance use over time was found in the anticipated direction, this difference did not reach statistical significance.

Concomitant Variables

Often there are exogenous or concomitant variables that could be used to predict latent class membership. The terms *exogenous* and *concomitant predictors* have been used interchangeably in the literature. Both refer to the addition of unmodeled predictors to the latent class model. These concomitant variables have been used to predict all aspects of the latent class model: the latent class proportions (Dayton & Macready,

1988; Melton, Liang & Pulver, 1994; van der Heijden, Dessens, & Bockenholt, 1996), the transition probabilities in latent transition problems (Humphreys & Janson, 2000; Pfefferman, Skinner & Humphreys, 1998; Reboussin, Reboussin, Liang, & Anthony, 1998) and the conditional response probabilities (Pfefferman et al., 1998).

Concomitant predictors are added to latent class and latent transition models via logistic or multinomial logistic regression. Because these concomitant predictors are unmodeled, they can be discrete, continuous, or higher order terms, like powers or interactions. For example, consider our latent class model of depression. Perhaps it would be interesting to see whether alcohol use predicts membership in particular depression latent classes. With this model, it is possible to investigate questions like the following: *For a unit increase in alcohol consumption, how does the probability of membership in the depression latent class change?* The ability to include interactions makes the model quite attractive. For example, it might be reasonable to hypothesize that the effects of alcohol consumption on predicting level of depression could be different for males and females. Perhaps female alcohol-consuming adolescents are most likely to be members of one latent class, but male alcohol-consuming adolescents are most likely to be members of another latent class. The interaction becomes important if non–alcohol-consuming male and female adolescents are not likely to be in the same depression latent classes as their alcohol-consuming counterparts.

Concomitant predictors can also be brought into the measurement side of the latent class model—in other words, used to predict the conditional response probabilities in a latent class model. In a study of employment, Pfefferman et al. (1998) included variables thought to be related to the reporting of employment status, such as receiving unemployment compensation. Suppose the variable measuring whether unemployment compensation is received is dichotomous. Then using it as a concomitant predictor amounts to estimating the conditional response probabilities separately for people who do not receive unemployment compensation and for those who do receive unemployment compensation. It is important to note that this model would not be used to investigate whether those receiving unemployment compensation are more likely to be employed or not; rather, the model specifies that the probability of a particular response to the employment question, conditional on latent class membership, may differ between people receiving unemployment compensation and people not receiving unemployment compensation. One can think of this as a differential error rate for those receiving and those not receiving unemployment compensation.

In LTA models, concomitant predictors have been used to predict transitions among latent statuses. Reboussin et al.

(1998) used a latent transition model with concomitant predictors to model weapons-carrying behavior in a sample of children ranging in age from 8 to 11. These authors included many concomitant predictors, but for this discussion, we choose one, feeling safe alone in one's neighborhood. The model presented in Reboussin et al. (1998) examined transitions in weapons-carrying behavior—that is to say, given the former time point's weapons-carrying latent status, what weapons-carrying latent status is someone likely to be in now? The latent statuses in their analysis were no weapons carrying, stick for defense, and weapons carrying. The inclusion of a concomitant variable in predicting transitions in this model amounts to addressing the question *Given previous weapons carrying latent status membership and how safe one feels alone in one's neighborhood, what weapons carrying latent status are people likely to be in at the current occasion?* The authors found that boys were much less likely to move into the stick-carrying latent status from the no weapons latent status if they felt safe in their neighborhoods. If that concomitant predictor had not been included, the transition probability from the no weapons carrying latent status to the stick carrying latent status would have been an average over the different levels of feeling safe in one's neighborhood. This provides a much more nuanced view of the behavior under study. The program ℓem (Vermunt, 1993) fits models with covariates.

Additional Types of Indicators in the Latent Class Model

Various researchers have been working on the addition of ordinal and continuous indicators to the latent class model. An advantage of expanding the types of indicators that may be used is that more information may be brought into the analysis. Until recently, it has been necessary to categorize ordinal or quantitative variables in order to include them in the latent class model. For the purpose of estimation, the categorized indicator is treated as nominal level, regardless of the level of measurement of the original variable. This can result in a loss of information in the analysis, which in turn limits the conclusions that may be drawn.

Ordinal Indicators

Kim and Böckenholt (2000) presented the stage-sequential ordinal (SSO) model. The SSO model estimates stage-sequential development measured by one or more ordinal indicators. Measurement error in the ordinal data is estimated according to a graded-response model (Samejima, 1969), which assumes that there is an underlying continuous characteristic that is discretized to form an ordinal scale. The SSO

model can incorporate continuous covariates in the analysis using a multinomial logit model. Like LTA, this model assumes that change over time follows a first-order Markovian process, in which stage membership at one time is predicted by stage membership at the immediately prior time.

Kim and Böckenholt (2000) illustrate the SSO model with an analysis of attitudes toward alcohol use among a national sample of adolescents measured annually for 5 years. They find that a four-stage model, in which the stages represent levels of increasing acceptance of alcohol use, in combination with a restrictive transition probability matrix, fits the data well. The restrictions Kim and Böckenholt place on the τ matrix is that a single τ matrix describes the transitions over the entire 5-year period. The τ matrix is further restricted in that individuals only change by one latent status between assessments. That is, respondents become no more than one step more or less accepting of alcohol use between assessments. Also, by including covariates in the model, they showed gender differences in initial level of acceptance of alcohol use (males more accepting), and cohort differences. Cohort differences indicated that older respondents were more accepting of alcohol use and less likely to change their attitudes over the 5-year span. The authors demonstrated that a similar model also fits marijuana attitudes of the same respondents. Kim and Böckenholt (2000) describe how to use the program ℓem (Vermunt, 1993) to do these analyses.

Continuous Indicators

Interval- and ratio-level indicators have been added by modeling them as normally distributed conditional on latent class membership (Moustaki, 1996). In this extended model, categorical indicators are treated the same as they are in the basic latent class model, and continuous indicators are accommodated by regressing them on the latent class variable. As with the categorical indicators in the latent class model, the continuous indicators are assumed to be conditionally independent, given latent class membership. Just as the conditional response probabilities (ρ parameters) characterize the relation between the latent variable and the categorical indicators, means and residual variances of the continuous indicators characterize the relation between the continuous indicators and the latent class variable. If the mean levels of a continuous indicator are different across the latent classes and the within-class residual variance is small, then that item does a good job of discriminating among the classes.

Consider an example in which we have categorical depression items and a standard depression scale. By incorporating continuous indicators along with the categorical indicators, the depression scale would not require categorization. This has the benefit of retaining all available information in the scale. The results of this analysis for the categorical items might look similar to the latent class analysis presented earlier, but there would also be mean scale scores for each latent class. This could be useful for validation of the categorical measures against an established scale. Another purpose of such an analysis could be the investigation of types of depression and the examination of response patterns including scale means. The software program LatentGold (Vermunt & Magidson, in press) fits latent class models involving categorical indicators, continuous indicators, or both.

Random Effects Models

Random effects (or mixed) models are currently very popular in social science research. They provide a powerful way to accommodate clustered responses, which violate the standard data analysis assumption that observations are independently sampled. Much of the work in this domain has been in the area of regression modeling. In particular, Bryk and Raudenbush (1992) have described multilevel methods for modeling quantitative responses and Hedeker has addressed nonmetric responses (Hedeker & Gibbons, 1994; Hedeker & Mermelstein, 1998). There has also been some development of the incorporation of random effects in latent class and latent transition models (Humphreys, 1998; Qu, Tan, & Kutner, 1996).

By adding random effects to the latent class model, one is able to expand the assumption of conditional independence to include the situation in which item responses are conditionally independent given latent class membership and unmeasured, subject-specific random effects. These random effects account for any unmeasured factors that induce relations among item responses beyond those due to latent class membership. Two common situations that often employ random effects are repeated measures on the same person and a design with people nested within organizations (e.g., schools).

Consider the case of students nested within schools. The incorporation of random effects allows one to account for the fact that students in the same class tend to report more similarly than do students in different classrooms. Rather than measuring and modeling all the different factors that could be causing this observed similarity, random effects models account for this similarity automatically. Note that random effects do not normally constitute factors that are of substantive interest. If there were additional substantively interesting variables that accounted for within-class similarity, then these other factors should be measured and modeled explicitly. Random effects models are meant to provide a convenient way of handling violations of the standard assumption of the independence of respondents in a sample.

General Growth Mixture Models

Muthén (2001; Muthén & Shedden, 1999) has recently introduced a new, very general framework that incorporates both latent class models and latent growth curve models. Using this framework, called general growth mixture modeling (GGMM), it is possible to fit ordinary LCA and latent growth curve models. However, the most exciting part of this approach is the combination of the two models, which allows the user to explore interindividual differences in intra-individual development. This is done by identifying two or more latent classes, each of which is characterized by a different pattern of growth. For example, Muthén (2001) identified three qualitatively different trajectories of growth in heavy drinking over time in a sample of young adults from the National Longitudinal Study of Youth: a normative trajectory of moderate heavy drinking across ages 18 to 25, a second group with an increasing trend over time, and a third group involving a steep decline over time. Using this new framework, both predictors and consequences of latent class membership can be explored. The Mplus software (Muthén & Muthén, 2001) can be used to fit general growth mixture models.

Goodness-of-Fit Issues

As stated previously, standard missing data procedures are available for LCA and LTA that successfully adjust parameter estimates for MAR missingness. However, the G^2 statistic used to assess the fit of the resulting models is potentially misleading. This is because the G^2 reflects two components: deviations between the expected response pattern frequencies and the observed frequencies, and deviations from MCAR missingness. To the extent that missing data are not MCAR, the G^2 can be inflated, making model fit appear poorer than it really is. This happens even when MAR missingness has been successfully adjusted for in the parameter estimates. By separating the two contributions to the traditional G^2 statistic, lack of fit and departures from MCAR, we can clearly assess the fit of latent class models for incomplete data. The contribution due to departures from MCAR can be identified by fitting the saturated model to the variables in the model. By subtracting this value from the traditional G^2 value we can determine the fit of the latent class model after taking missing data into account (Little & Rubin, 1987). Note that when the effect of missing data on model fit is ignored because the G^2 value is inflated, in general researchers are more likely to reject models that actually provide adequate fit to the data. Both WinLTA (Collins & Wugalter, 1992; Hyatt & Collins, 2000) and Mplus (Muthén & Muthén, 2001) incorporate this adjustment to model fit for latent class models with incomplete data.

Even without missing data, there are some serious limitations associated with goodness-of-fit assessment in some LCA and almost all LTA models. The limitations fall in two areas. First, goodness-of-fit testing relies upon the idea that the distribution of the G^2 is approximated reasonably well by the chi-square distribution. However, when the ratio N/k becomes small, where N is the sample size and k is the number of cells in the contingency table, the distribution of the G^2 deviates more and more substantially from the chi-square. Unfortunately, under these circumstances the true distribution of the G^2 is not known, rendering it of limited utility for model selection. This applies to all contingency table models, and is particularly a problem in latent class models with large numbers of indicators. Second, the standard hypothesis testing approach using the G^2 difference test can be used to compare only nested models. However, many important research questions addressed using latent class methods call for comparing models that are not strictly nested. An alternative to the standard approach to goodness-of-fit testing is badly needed in order to overcome these two limitations.

Bayesian methods may provide the needed alternative. Rubin (1984; Rubin & Stern, 1994) describes a general procedure for model monitoring based on the posterior predictive check distribution of any test statistic. This is an empirical, simulation-based procedure in which the observed value of the test statistic is compared with its posterior predictive check distribution under the null model to determine whether the data are consistent with the null model. The p value indicates the probability of a result more extreme than the data under the posterior predictive check distribution of the test statistic. This is an appropriate method for comparing two models when no single parameter, but instead a set of parameters distinguishes them. For example, the posterior predictive check distribution can be used to test the validity of a five-class model versus a six-class model. The first step is to draw a set of parameter values from their joint posterior distribution using a Markov chain sampling approach, in particular a data augmentation algorithm. The second step is to create a data set the same size as the original using random draws from appropriate distributions with the chosen parameter values. The fit of the model to this imputed data set is assessed, and this process is repeated many times to obtain a distribution of the fit statistic. This is a very promising but complex approach, and widely available software for this procedure is not yet available. Hoijtink (1998; Hoijtink & Molenaar, 1997) presents several examples in which the fits of constrained latent class models are assessed by applying the posterior predictive check distribution to several goodness-of-fit statistics.

A closely related area in which more work is needed is statistical power for testing the fit of complex latent class and latent transition models. In order to assess the statistical power of any test involving the G^2, the distribution of the G^2 under the alternative hypothesis, called the noncentral distribution, is needed. As the central distribution of G^2 is unknown when the contingency table is sparse, it follows that the noncentral distribution is unknown as well. Of course, the usual factors that affect statistical power operate in this context—namely, sample size, choice of alpha, and effect size—which in model selection is the overall difference between the true model and the model under consideration. It is possible that the Bayesian posterior predictive check distribution approach to hypothesis testing discussed above will provide an avenue for assessing statistical power for latent class models.

Sample Size and Related Considerations

In addition to statistical power considerations, other sample size considerations come up in LCA and LTA. Sparseness can take a toll on parameter estimation. Several simulation studies (Collins et al., 1993; Collins & Tracy, 1997; Collins & Wugalter, 1992) have demonstrated that parameter estimation in LTA remains unbiased even in very sparse data tables. However, the standard errors of certain parameters can become unacceptably large. This is particularly true for the τ parameters, as these transition probabilities are conditioned on the latent class membership and latent status membership at Time 1, and thus often based on considerably smaller Ns than the other parameters. In addition, identification problems become more frequent as sparseness increases. This means that researchers who are faced with small samples currently are unlikely to be able to make use of LCA and LTA in their current forms. The problems with small samples are due to a lack of information. Naturally, small samples contain less information than do large samples. More work needs to be done in the area of latent class and latent transition models applied to small samples.

A Two-Sequence Latent Class Model

Previously in this chapter we discussed models using discrete or continuous exogenous variables to predict latent class membership. Flaherty and Collins (1999) have developed LTA models in which one stage sequence (e.g., substance use) can be used to predict another (e.g., depression). This two-sequence model can address a number of interesting research questions. Suppose we wish to examine initial level and changes in depression (e.g., as modeled in our example discussed previously) conditional on initial level and changes in substance use behavior. Some questions may pertain to a single time of measurement. For example, how are people in various depression latent statuses at one time of measurement distributed among substance use latent statuses (e.g., no use; tobacco only; alcohol only; tobacco and alcohol; and tobacco, alcohol, and marijuana)? Are tobacco users more likely to be in one depression latent status than another? Also, are tobacco users more likely to be in a particular depression latent status than alcohol or marijuana users? Other questions may pertain to change over time. With the two-sequence model, interesting and complex patterns of contingent change can be examined. For example, are people who change from no use to tobacco and alcohol, compared to those who remain in the no use latent status, more likely to transition from no depression to a particular depression latent status? Are people who remain in the alcohol only latent status more or less likely to remain in the no depression latent status, compared with those who advance from the alcohol only latent status to a more advanced level of substance use? Two-sequence models are currently an area of active inquiry, with software for general users expected in the future.

CONCLUSIONS

The usefulness of latent class models in psychological research will continue to grow as the model is extended. Already important steps have been taken to improve the utility of this method, including extensions to longitudinal data, improvements in the assessment of model fit, and the incorporation of continuous predictors of latent class membership. Additional work in areas such as estimation with small sample sizes, Bayesian methods, concomitant variables, and two-sequence models will further increase the power of latent class and related methods. LCA and LTA play an important role in understanding categorical latent constructs in psychology and their related processes of change over time.

APPENDIX A: THE LATENT CLASS MODEL AND ASSOCIATED PARAMETERS

$$P(Y = y) = \sum_{c=1}^{C} \gamma_c \rho_{i|c} \rho_{j|c} \rho_{k|c}$$

- γ_c represents the probability of being in latent class c.
- $\rho_{i|c}$ represents the probability of response i to Item 1, conditional on membership in latent class c.
- $\rho_{j|c}$ represents the probability of response j to Item 2, conditional on membership in latent class c.
- $\rho_{k|c}$ represents the probability of response k to Item 3, conditional on membership in latent class c.

APPENDIX B: THE LATENT TRANSITION MODEL AND ASSOCIATED PARAMETERS

$$P(Y = y)$$
$$= \sum_{c=1}^{C} \sum_{p=1}^{S} \sum_{q=1}^{S} \gamma_c \rho_{x|c} \delta_{a|c} \rho_{i|a,c} \cdots \rho_{p|a,c} \tau_{b|a,c} \rho_{i'|b,c} \cdots \rho_{p'|b,c}$$

- γ_c represents the probability of being in latent class c (e.g. the expected proportion of females).
- $\rho_{x|c}$ represents the probability of response x to the latent class indicator, conditional on membership in latent class c.
- $\delta_{a|c}$ represents the probability of being in latent status a at Time 1, conditional on membership in latent class c.
- $\rho_{i|a,c}$ represents the probability of response i to Item 1 at Time 1, conditional on membership in latent status a at Time 1 and membership in latent class c; similarly, $\rho_{i'|b,c}$ represents the same quantity for Time 2.
- $\rho_{j|a,c}$ represents the probability of response j to Item 2 at Time 1, conditional on membership in latent status a at Time 1 and membership in latent class c; similarly, $\rho_{j'|b,c}$ represents the same quantity for Time 2, and so on.
- $\rho_{p|a,c}$ represents the probability of response p to Item 8 at Time 1, conditional on membership in latent status a at Time 1 and membership in latent class c; similarly, $\rho_{p'|b,c}$ represents the same quantity for Time 2.
- $\tau_{b|a,c}$ represents the probability of membership in latent status b at Time 2, conditional on membership in latent status a at Time 1 and membership in latent class c.

REFERENCES

Aitkin, M., Anderson, D., & Hinde, J. (1981). *Journal of the Royal Statistical Society, Series A, 144,* 419–461.

Akaike, H. (1974). A new look at the statistical model identification. *IEEE Transactions on Automatic Control, 19,* 716–723.

Biemer, P. P., & Wiesen, C. (2002). Latent class analysis of embedded repeated measurements: An application to the National Household Survey on Drug Abuse. *Journal of the Royal Statistical Society, Series A, 165,* 97–119.

Bozdogan, H. (1987). Model-selection and Akaike's information criterion (AIC): The general theory and its analytical extensions. *Psychometrika, 52,* 345–370.

Bryk, A., & Raudenbush, S. W. (1992). *Hierarchical linear models: Applications and data analysis methods.* Newbury Park, CA: Sage.

Bulik, C. M., Sullivan, P. F., & Kendler, K. S. (2000). An empirical study of the classification of eating disorders. *American Journal of Psychiatry, 157,* 886–895.

Clogg, C. C., & Manning, W. D. (1996). Assessing reliability of categorical measurements using latent class models. In A. von Eye & C. C. Clogg (Eds.), *Categorical variables in developmental research* (pp. 169–182). San Diego, CA: Academic Press.

Collins, L. M. (2001). Reliability for static and dynamic categorical latent variables. In L. M. Collins & A. Sayer (Eds.), *New methods for the analysis of change* (pp. 273–288). Washington, DC: American Psychological Association.

Collins, L. M., Fidler, P. L., Wugalter, S. E., & Long, J. D. (1993). Goodness-of-fit testing for latent class models. *Multivariate Behavioral Research, 28,* 375–389.

Collins, L. M., Graham, J. W., Rousculp, S. S., Fidler, P. L., Pan, J., & Hansen, W. B. (1994). Latent transition analysis and how it can address prevention research questions. In L. M. Collins & L. A. Seitz (Eds.), *Advances in data analysis for prevention intervention research* (pp. 81–111). Rockville, MD: National Institute on Drug Abuse.

Collins, L. M., Graham, J. W., Rousculp, S. S., & Hansen, W. B. (1997). Heavy caffeine use and the beginning of the substance use onset process: An illustration of latent transition analysis. In K. J. Bryant & M. Windle (Eds.), *The science of prevention: Methodological advances from alcohol and substance abuse research* (pp. 79–99). Washington, DC: American Psychological Association.

Collins, L. M., Schafer, J. L., & Kam, C. (2001). A comparison of inclusive and restrictive missing-data strategies with ML and MI. *Psychological Methods, 6,* 330–351.

Collins, L. M., & Tracy, A. J. (1997). Estimation in complex latent transition models with extreme data sparseness. *Kwantitatieve Methoden, 55,* 57–71.

Collins, L. M., & Wugalter, S. E. (1992). Latent class models for stage-sequential dynamic latent variables. *Multivariate Behavioral Research, 27,* 131–157.

Dayton, C. M., & Macready, G. B. (1988). Concomitant-variable latent-class models. *Journal of the American Statistical Association, 83,* 173–178.

Dempster, A. P., Laird, N. M., & Rubin, D. B. (1977). Maximum likelihood estimation from incomplete data via the EM algorithm. *Journal of the Royal Statistical Society, Series B, 39,* 1–38.

Erikson, E. H. (1950). *Childhood and society.* New York: W. W. Norton.

Everitt, B. S. (1988). A monte carlo investigation of the likelihood ratio test for number of classes in latent class analysis. *Multivariate Behavioral Research, 23,* 531–538.

Evers, K. E., Harlow, L. L., Redding, C. A., & LaForge, R. G. (1998). Longitudinal changes in stages of change for condom use in women. *American Journal of Health Promotion, 13,* 19–25.

Flaherty, B. P. (in press). Assessing reliability of categorical substance use measures with latent class analysis. *Drug and Alcohol Dependence.*

Flaherty, B. P., & Collins, L. M. (1999). *Modeling transitions in two stage-sequences simultaneously* (Tech. Rep. No. 99-33). University Park, PA: The Methodology Center.

Freud, S. (1961). The Ego and the Id. *Standard Edition, 19,* 3–66.

Gebhardt, W. A., Dusseldorp, E., & Maes, S. (1999). Measuring transitions through stages of exercise: Application of latent transition analysis. *Perceptual and Motor Skills, 88,* 1097–1106.

Goodman, L. A. (1974). Exploratory latent structure analysis using both identifiable and unidentifiable models. *Biometrika, 61,* 215–231.

Graham, J. W., Collins, L. M., Wugalter, S. E., Chung, N. K., & Hansen, W. B. (1991). Modeling transitions in latent stage-sequential processes: A substance use prevention example. *Journal of Consulting and Clinical Psychology, 59,* 48–57.

Guo, J., Collins, L. M., Hill, K. G., & Hawkins, J. D. (2000). Developmental pathways to alcohol abuse and dependence in young adulthood. *Journal of Studies on Alcohol, 61,* 799–808.

Hansen, W. B., & Graham, J. W. (1991). Preventing alcohol, marijuana, and cigarette use among adolescents: Peer pressure resistance training versus establishing conservative norms. *Preventive Medicine, 20,* 414–430.

Hedeker, D., & Gibbons, R. D. (1994). A random-effects ordinal regression model for multilevel analysis. *Biometrics, 50,* 933–944.

Hedeker, D., & Mermelstein, R. J. (1998). A multilevel thresholds of change model for analysis of stages of change data. *Multivariate Behavioral Research, 33,* 427–455.

Hoijtink, H. (1998). Constrained latent class analysis using the gibbs sampler and posterior predictive *p*-values: Applications to educational testing. *Statistica Sinica, 8,* 691–711.

Hoijtink, H., & Molenaar, I. W. (1997). A multidimensional item response model: Constrained latent class analysis using the Gibbs sampler and posterior predictive checks. *Psychometrika, 62,* 171–189.

Humphreys, K. (1998). A latent markov chain with multivariate random effects. *Sociological Methods and Research, 26,* 269–299.

Humphreys, K., & Janson, H. (2000). Latent transition analysis with covariates, nonresponse, summary statistics and diagnostics: Modeling children's drawing development. *Multivariate Behavioral Research, 35,* 89–118.

Hyatt, S. L., & Collins, L. M. (1998). *Estimation in latent transition models with missing data* (Tech. Rep. No. 98-22). University Park, PA: Pennsylvania State University, The Methodology Center.

Hyatt, S. L., & Collins, L. M. (1999). *Pubertal timing and the onset of substance use: Detailed results based on data augmentation* (Tech. Rep. No. 99-35). University Park, PA: Pennsylvania State University, The Methodology Center.

Hyatt, S. L., & Collins. L. M. (2000). Using latent transition analysis to examine the relationship between parental permissiveness and the onset of substance use. In J. Rose, L. Chassin,

C. Presson, & S. J. Sherman (Eds.), *Multivariate applications in substance use research: New methods for new questions* (pp. 259–288). Hillsdale, NJ: Erlbaum.

Hyatt, S. L., Collins, L. M., & Schafer, J. L. (1999). *Using data augmentation to conduct hypothesis testing in LTA* (Tech. Rep. No. 99-34). University Park, PA: Pennsylvania State University, The Methodology Center.

Jöreskog, K., & Sörbom, D. (1996). Lisrel 8: User's reference guide [Computer program manual]. Chicago: Scientific Software International, Inc.

Kagan, J. (1989). Temperamental contributions to social behavior. *American Psychologist, 44,* 668–674.

Kandel, D. (1975). Stages in adolescent involvement in drug use. *Science, 190,* 912–914.

Kim, J., & Böckenholt, U. (2000). Modeling stage-sequential change in ordered categorical responses. *Psychological Methods, 5,* 380–400.

Kohlberg, L. (1966). Cognitive stages and preschool education. *Human Development, 9,* 5–17.

Kolb, R. R., & Dayton, C. M. (1996). Correcting for nonresponse in latent class analysis. *Multivariate Behavioral Research, 31,* 7–32.

Langeheine, R. (1994). Latent variables Markov models. In A. von Eye & C. C. Clogg (Eds.), *Latent variables analysis: Applications for developmental research* (pp. 373–395). Thousand Oaks, CA: Sage.

Langeheine, R. Pannekoek, J., & van de Pol, F. (1996). Bootstrapping goodness-of-fit measures in categorical data analysis. *Sociological Methods and Research, 24,* 492–516.

Langeheine, R., & van de Pol, F. (1994). Discrete-time mixed Markov latent class models. In A. Dale & R. Cavies (Eds.), *Analyzing social and political change: A casebook of methods* (pp. 170–197). London: Sage.

Lazarsfeld, P. F., & Henry, N. W. (1968). *Latent structure analysis.* Boston: Houghton Mifflin.

Lin, T. H., & Dayton, C. M. (1997). Model selection information criteria for non-nested latent class models. *Journal of Educational and Behavioral Statistics, 22,* 249–264.

Little, R. J. A., & Rubin, D. B. (1987). *Statistical analysis with missing data.* New York: Wiley.

Macready, G. B., & Dayton, C. M. (1994). Latent class models for longitudinal assessment of trait acquisition. In A. von Eye & C. C. Clogg (Eds.), *Latent variables analysis: Applications for developmental research* (pp. 245–273). Thousand Oaks, CA: Sage.

Martin, R. A., Velicer, W. F., & Fava, J. L. (1996). Latent transition analysis to the stages of change for smoking cessation. *Addictive Behaviors, 21,* 67–80.

Melton, B., Liang, K. Y., & Pulver, A. E. (1994). Extended latent class approach to the study of familial/sporadic forms of a disease: Its application to the study of the heterogeneity of schizophrenia. *Genetic Epidemiology, 11,* 311–327.

Moustaki, I. (1996). A latent trait and a latent class model for mixed observed variables. *British Journal of Mathematical and Statistical Psychology, 49,* 313–334.

Muthén, B. (2001). Second-generation structural equation modeling with a combination of categorical and continuous latent variables: New opportunities for latent class-latent growth modeling. In L. Collins & A. Sayer (Eds.), *New methods for the analysis of change* (pp. 291–322). Washington, DC: American Psychological Association.

Muthén, B., & Muthén, L. (2001). Mplus User's Guide [Computer program manual]. Los Angeles, CA: Muthén & Muthén.

Muthén, B., & Shedden, K. (1999). Finite mixture modeling with mixture outcomes using the EM algorithm. *Biometrics, 55,* 463–469.

Parker, G., Wilhelm, K., Mitchell, P., Roy, K., & Hadzi-Pavlovic, D. (1999). Subtyping depression: Testing algorithms and identification of a tiered model. *Journal of Nervous and Mental Disease, 187,* 610–617.

Pfeffermann, D., Skinner, C., & Humphreys, K. (1998). The estimation of gross flows in the presence of measurement error using auxiliary variables. *Journal of the Royal Statistical Society, Series A, 161,* 13–32.

Piaget, J. (1973). *The child and reality.* New York: Grossman.

Posner, S. F., Collins, L. M., Longshore, D., & Anglin, M. D. (1996). The acquisition and maintenance of safer sexual behaviors among injection drug users. *Substance Use and Misuse, 31,* 1995–2015.

Qu, Y., Tan, M., & Kutner, M. H. (1996). Random effects models in latent class analysis for evaluating accuracy of diagnostic tests. *Biometrics, 52,* 797–810.

Read, T. R. C., & Cressie, N. A. C. (1988). *Goodness-of-fit statistics for discrete multivariate data.* New York: Springer-Verlag.

Reboussin, B. A., Reboussin, D. M., Liang, K. Y., & Anthony, J. C. (1998). A latent transition approach for modeling progression of health-risk behavior. *Multivariate Behavioral Research, 33,* 457–478.

Resnick, M. D., Bearman, P. S., Blum, R. W., Bauman, K. E., Harris, K. M., Jones, J., Tabor, J., Beuhring, T., Sieving, R. E., Shew, M., Ireland, M., Bearinger, L. H., & Udry, J. R. (1997). Protecting adolescents from harm: Findings from the National Longitudinal Study of Adolescent Health. *Journal of the American Medical Association, 278,* 823–832.

Rindskopf, D. (1983). A general framework for using latent class analysis to test hierarchical and nonhierarchical learning models. *Psychometrika, 48,* 85–97.

Rubin, D. B. (1984). Bayesianly justifiable and relevant frequency calculations for the applied statistician. *Annals of Statistics, 12,* 1151–1172.

Rubin, D. B. (1987). *Multiple imputation for nonresponse in surveys.* New York: Wiley.

Rubin, D. B., & Stern, H. S. (1994). Testing in latent class models using a posterior predictive check distribution. In A. Von Eye &

C. C. Clogg (Eds.), *Latent variable analysis: Applications for developmental research* (pp. 420–438). Thousand Oaks, CA: Sage.

Samejima, F. (1969). Estimation of latent ability using a response pattern of graded scores. *Psychometrika Monograph, 17*(Suppl.), 100.

Schafer, J. L. (1997). *Analysis of incomplete multivariate data.* London: Chapman & Hall.

Schwarz, G. (1978). Estimating the dimension of a model. *Annals of Statistics, 6,* 461–464.

Spiel, C. (1994). Latent trait models for measuring change. In A. von Eye & C. C. Clogg (Eds.), *Latent variable analysis: Applications for developmental research* (pp. 274–293). Thousand Oaks, CA: Sage.

Stern, H. S., Arcus, D., Kagan, J., Rubin, D. B., & Snidman, N. (1995). Using mixture models in temperament research. *International Journal of Behavioral Development, 18,* 407–423.

Sullivan, P. F., Kessler, R. C., & Kendler, K. S. (1998). Latent class analysis of lifetime depressive symptoms in the national comorbidity survey. *American Journal of Psychiatry, 155,* 1398–1406.

Tracy, A. J., Collins, L. M., & Graham, J. W. (1997). *Exposure to adult substance use as a risk factor in adolescent substance use onset* (Tech. Rep. No. 97-13). University Park, PA: Pennsylvania State University, The Methodology Center.

van de Pol, F., & Langeheine, R. (1990). Mixed Markov latent class models. In C. C. Clogg (Ed.), *Sociological methodology* (pp. 213–247). Oxford, UK: Blackwell.

van der Heijden, Dessens, J., & Bockenholt, U. (1996). Estimating the concomitant-variable latent-class model with the EM algorithm. *Journal of Educational and Behavioral Statistics, 21,* 215–229.

Velicer, W. F., Martin, R. A., & Collins, L. M. (1996). Latent transition analysis for longitudinal data. *Addiction, 91,* S197–S209.

Vermunt, J. K. (1993). *ℓem: Log-linear and event history analysis with missing data using the EM algorithm* (Work Paper 93.09.015/7). Tilburg University. Tilburg, The Netherlands.

Vermunt, J. K., Langeheine, R., & Bockenholt, U. (1999). Discrete-time discrete-state latent Markov models with time-constant and time-varying covariates. *Journal of Educational and Behavioral Statistics, 24,* 179–207.

Vermunt, J. K., & Magidson, J. (in press.) Latent class cluster analysis. In J. A. Hagenaars & A. L. McCutcheon (Eds.), *Applied latent class analysis.* Cambridge, UK: Cambridge University Press.

Author Index

Subject Index

ISBN 0-471-66665-3